D1559827

A LETHAL OBSESSION

ROBERT S. WISTRICH

A LETHAL OBSESSION

Anti-Semitism from Antiquity to the Global Jihad

RANDOM HOUSE

NEW YORK

Copyright © 2010 by Robert S. Wistrich

Published in the United States by Random House, an imprint of
The Random House Publishing Group, a division of Random
House, Inc., New York.

RANDOM HOUSE and colophon are registered trademarks of
Random House, Inc.

LIBRARY OF CONGRESS CATALOGING-IN-PUBLICATION DATA
Wistrich, Robert S.
A lethal obsession : anti-Semitism from antiquity to the global
jihad / Robert S. Wistrich.
p. cm.
Includes bibliographical references and index.
ISBN 978-1-4000-6097-9 (alk. paper)
1. Antisemitism—Europe—History—20th century.   2. Anti-
semitism—Europe—History—21st century.   3. Antisemitism—
Arab countries—History—21st century.   I. Title.
DS146.E85W57 2009
305.892'4—dc22   2008054178

Printed in the United States of America on acid-free paper

www.atrandom.com

2 4 6 8 9 7 5 3 1

FIRST EDITION

Book design by Simon M. Sullivan

For Matan, Eden, Noia,
and the generations to come

Woe unto them that call evil good
and good evil;
that change darkness into light,
and light into darkness;
that change bitter into sweet,
and sweet into bitter.

Isaiah 5:20

Most devious is the heart;
It is perverse—who can fathom it?

Jeremiah 17:9

Even if all the festivals should be annulled,
Purim will never be annulled.

Midrash

Do not fear sudden terror
or the fury of the wicked,
when it comes.

Proverbs 3:25

CONTENTS

A LETHAL OBSESSION

The Return of Anti-Semitism

Future historians may well regard the past seven decades as a golden age of ideological politics. Millions have been slaughtered on the altar of false messianisms and their salvationist logic. In the totalitarian nightmare of the past seventy-five years, a special role has undoubtedly been played by the political religions of Nazism, Stalinism, and Islamism. It is certainly no coincidence that in all three cases, a remarkably similar anti-American and anti-Jewish demonology has been manipulated in the cause of destroying Judeo-Christian values, individual freedom, and liberal democracy. All three anti-Western ideologies have shared the same penchant for conspiracy theories of history, society, and civilization; they are equally characterized by a similarly closed system of belief, addiction to historical inevitability, and an unquenchable will to power. At their very heart we can find the oldest and darkest of ideological obsessions—that of anti-Semitism—for which nearly twenty years ago I coined the term "the longest hatred."

In the case of the Nazi movement, there is by now a consensus among most serious historians concerning the axial role of "eliminationist" anti-Semitism in the domestic and foreign policies of the Third Reich. However, much less attention has been given to the postwar aftermath. Hitlerism did not really die in April 1945 nor, unfortunately, was Auschwitz truly "liberated." In the mid-1980s, I had occasion to point out that the Nazi poison was by no means extinguished, having infiltrated the former Soviet Union and especially the Arab-Muslim world—where hard-core anti-Semitism systematically defaming Israel and the Jews was widely (and officially) propagated. These pages expose the intensity of the "culture of hatred" that currently permeates books, magazines, newspapers, sermons, videocassettes, the Internet, television, and radio in the Middle East on a scale unprecedented since the heyday of Nazi Germany. Indeed, the demonic images of Jews presently circulating in much of the Islamic world are sufficiently radical in tone and content to constitute a new warrant for genocide. They combine to devastating effect the blood libel of medieval Christian Europe with Nazi conspiracy theories about the Jewish drive for world domination and dehumanizing Islamic quotations about Jews as the "sons of apes and donkeys."

After the Iranian Revolution of 1979, the Koranic motifs sharply increased in importance, along with virulent anti-Americanism. In the Islamic demonology, both America and Israel are firmly bonded together as "Satanic forces" that threaten the core identity, values, and existence of Islam. Contemporary Islamist apostles of jihad have in recent years turned Israel and Jewry into their great surrogate in the holy war against America and the corrupt modern world. Uncle Sam, so to speak, has coalesced with Shylock into a terrifying specter of globalization ("Americanization") threatening to swamp the world of Islam, much as late-nineteenth-century European anti-Semites liked to depict "international Jewry" as the satanic engine of finance capitalism and supranational cosmopolitanism.

The Palestinian al-Aqsa intifada in the autumn of 2000, followed by the jihadi assault on the Twin Towers in New York and the Pentagon in Washington, D.C., on September 11, 2001, provided the initial triggers. An astonishing number of Muslims sought to place the blame for this mass murder on the Jews and the Mossad, Israel's intelligence service. Encouraged by the Islamists, they saw the fingerprints of an all-powerful Zionist lobby everywhere, spreading its tentacles and deadly lies, draining the lifeblood of Arabs and Muslims, gratuitously inciting the American war against Iraq, and pursuing their sinister plans for global conquest.[1]

Conspiracy theories of this kind have intoxicated millions of Arabs since 2000 through the impact of such popular television series as *Horseman Without a Horse* in Egypt and the gory depiction of the blood libel (Jews slaughtering Christian children in order to use their blood for Passover matzo) in *Al-Shattat* (The Diaspora), a Syrian-Hezbollah production first broadcast in Lebanon. The blood libel has also been a prominent part of the anti-Semitic propaganda regularly promoted by fundamentalist and oil-rich Saudi Arabia. This is the same soil from which Osama bin Laden and his al-Qaeda movement sprang—a major hotbed of jihadism and the primary bankroller of anti-Western hate speech. A no less anti-Semitic and anti-American outlook holds sway in more secular Arab societies such as Egypt, Syria, Iraq, and Jordan, not to mention Shiite Iran.

Such anti-Semitic and anti-Western bigotry cannot be adequately understood in terms of the Arab-Israeli conflict alone or the so-called question of Palestine. Certainly, the Palestinian cause has been periodically hijacked by radical Islamists and pan-Arabists in order to broaden their political support in the Muslim world. But the "Jewish question" in radical Islam (as with its Western Christian, Nazi, and Marxist predecessors) is not centered primarily on Palestine—at least not as a territorial or national issue amenable to rational bargaining. The mythical thinking that animates Islamist ideology is much closer in spirit to the Nazi model, with its fixation on destroying a secret Jewish power that strives for global hegemony.

Totalitarian anti-Semitism reached its genocidal apex with Hitler's ideology and a Nazi political praxis that, though it grew up on Christian soil, was ultimately determined to replace and supplant Christianity. National Socialism was racial politics carried out under the sign of the Apocalypse, in which the either-or struggle between the Aryan world and international Jewry stood at the heart of an armed global confrontation on an unprecedented scale. Anti-Semitism immediately after 1933 was transformed by the Nazis into a crucial lever in the restructuring not only of the new Germany but of the entire international order—initially as a weapon for undermining Hitler's domestic adversaries and then for subverting or neutralizing opposition to his policies abroad.

The war against the Jews was conceived by the Nazi leader—especially after 1938—as an apocalyptic *Vernichtungskrieg* (war of destruction) to establish the universal rule of National Socialism. The choice of target grew out of centuries of Christian teachings that had singled out the Jews as a deicidal people. Yet the top Nazi leaders were themselves totalitarian atheists who believed in the so-called natural laws of race and blood. Social Darwinist racism was not, however, the root of their anti-Semitism. It was rooted much more in an older eschatological political agenda—one in which the Jew was the satanic wellspring and dark side of history, driving mankind relentlessly into the abyss.

Much of this anti-Semitic worldview has infected the body politic of Islam during the past forty years. Its focus has become the "collective Jew" embodied in the State of Israel. Its geographic center of gravity has moved to the Middle East, but the tone and content of the rhetoric, along with the manifest will to exterminate the Jews, are virtually identical to German Nazism. The leadership of Iran does not even disguise its desire for a *judenfrei* (Jew-free) Middle East—a "world without Zionism," to adopt more politically correct language. Radical Islamists of every stripe openly proclaim at every opportunity that the eradication of Israel is a divine commandment, the will of God, and a necessary prologue to the liberation of mankind. In a manner reminiscent of the Nazis, they see themselves as engaged in a war of civilizations against terminal Western decadence (analogous to *jahiliya,* or pre-Islamic barbarism), equated with social chaos, sexual permissiveness, idolatry, and apostasy. All these evils are symbolized by perfidious "Jewish influence." As in Nazi anti-Semitism, this singular and sinister root of evil is held to be primarily responsible for Marxism, psychoanalysis, sociology, materialism, pornography, and the general destruction of morals. Islamofascism today builds on the same mythological figure of the satanic, ubiquitous, immoral, and all-powerful Jew that once haunted the European anti-Semitic imagination from Richard Wagner to Adolf Hitler. The principle of evil, according to this ideology, is not in ourselves; it comes from outside. It is the product of conspiracy and devilish forces whose incarnation is the mythical Jew. As far back as 1886, this delirious causality was succinctly expressed in words attributed to the pope of French anti-Semitism, Édouard Drumont, in his bestselling book *La France Juive:* "All comes from the Jew, all returns to the Jew."

Even the outwardly rationalistic Marxist-Leninist ideology of the Soviet Union was ravaged by this poison after the stunning Israeli victory in the 1967 Six-Day War. Zionism was now officially equated with racism, and a "chosen people" superiority complex. In the Leonid Brezhnev era of Soviet expansionism during the 1970s, anti-Semitism grew precipitously into a cardinal feature of the new Russian national Socialist doctrine. Jewish nationalism was systematically defamed as the incarnation of evil, as one of the darkest forces of world reaction and an ideology no less dangerous than Hitlerism and Aryan racism. It was declared to be bent on planetary domination, in conjunction with American imperialism and Freemasonry. Soviet publicists claimed that Zionists had seized control of the economy in the largest Western capitalist states. Their aims allegedly included the overthrow of the Communist systems in the USSR and Eastern Europe and the liquidation of national-liberation movements in the Third World. The goal of the Zionist bourgeoisie was proclaimed to be the enslavement of the

Arabs and other non-Western peoples, along the lines of South African apartheid. Moreover, the Soviet anti-Zionist demonology (whose traces can still be felt to this day on the Western Left and in parts of the Third World) compulsively twisted the grand sweep of Jewish history into a narrative of pure criminality, sadism, and immorality.

Far more intensively than the Nazis or the Arabs, it was Soviet propaganda hacks who began to brand the Hebrew Bible as a book of hatred, preaching genocide; it was they who reinvented Judaism as a teaching of racial exclusion designed to justify an expanded Israeli *Lebensraum* (living space). Such fantasies presented modern Israeli policies as the logical outcome of biblical Judaism. By the spring of 2002, they had metamorphosed into mainstream comment in western Europe among some of its most prominent intellectuals and artists. An April 21, 2002, article published in the widely read Madrid newspaper *El País,* written by Portuguese Nobel Prize laureate in literature José Saramago, perfectly illustrated the new fashion. Saramago's diatribe echoed the most hate-ridden rhetoric of Soviet propagandists thirty years earlier, decorated with a thin layer of unadulterated psychologizing of the crudest kind:

> Intoxicated mentally by the messianic dream of a Greater Israel which will finally achieve the expansionist dreams of the most radical Zionism; contaminated by the monstrous and rooted "certitude" that in this catastrophic and absurd world there exists a people chosen by God, and that, consequently, all the actions of an obsessive psychological and pathologically exclusivist racism are justified; educated and trained in the idea that any suffering that has been inflicted . . . on anyone else, especially the Palestinians will always be inferior to that which they themselves suffered in the Holocaust, the Jews endlessly scratch their own wound, to keep it bleeding, to make it incurable, and they show it to the world as if it were a banner. . . . Israel, in short, is a racist state by virtue of Judaism's monstrous doctrines—racist not just against the Palestinians, but against the entire world, which it seeks to manipulate and abuse.[2]

Saramago's anti-Semitic essay went on to suggest that Israel's struggle against its neighbors had "a unique and even metaphysical quality of genuine evil" (he had previously called the situation in the West Bank "a crime comparable to Auschwitz"), and that Palestinian suicide terrorism was the inevitable result. The Jews were triply guilty—of crimes against humanity and the Palestinian people; of implementing monstrous biblical doctrines that were based on chosenness and racist exclusion; at the same time, of allegedly exploiting the horrors of the Holocaust to make Gentiles "renounce the most elemental judgement" and turn them into a "docile echo" of Israel's will.[3] The perversity and falseness of Saramago's insinuations did not keep western European intellectuals from embracing them in recent years. Increasingly, in their eyes, the only "reasonable" solution to the Palestine conflict is the de-Zionization of Israel. Leftists like Saramago seem incapable of overcoming their long-standing resistance to an independent Jewish polity and its right to a collective Jewish life. Even classical liberals appear unwilling to embrace the idea of Israel existing as a free nation among other nations, or the right of Jews to fully identify with its goals without suffering stigmatization for perversely resisting mainstream opinion. Refusal to conform to the anti-Israeli witch hunt can easily engender charges of fostering a "kosher conspiracy." As British academic Shalom Lappin has observed, "Sneering chatter of a powerful international Jewish Lobby, once the stock in trade of fascist propaganda, has now become a staple of left-wing comment on Israel in the British and European press."[4]

•   •   •

No less oppressive is the growing respectability of anti-Semitic discourse on university campuses and among the educated elites. There is a return to the advocacy of economic and academic boycotts, as well as to more subtle forms of social ostracism directed against Jews who publicly support the State of Israel. True, in the West this has not yet led to discriminatory legislation, violent pogroms, or expulsion, let alone calls to mass murder. But such extreme rhetoric has long been mainstream in the Middle East. In the Arab-Muslim world, demonization of the Jews, calls to liquidate Israel, and Holocaust denial are three sides of the same triangle—an unholy trinity whose potential global implications far transcend the region or the fate of the Jewish state.

Anti-Semitism, it should be recalled, is much more than mere prejudice about or discrimination against Jews. While it has some common features with other human hatreds such as racism, homophobia, and misogyny, anti-Semitism is uniquely complex. Directed against Jews rather than "Semites" (a term describing any number of peoples of ancient Southwestern Asia and properly applicable only to languages, not the peoples themselves), the ideology of anti-Semitism has always treated the Jews—whether individually or collectively—as a despised "other." It is a worldview driven by hate and fear, which are themselves normative parts of mankind's historical experience and powerful emotions that continue to shape the formation of group identities. The hatred analyzed in this book is not, however, confined to historical legacies and individual or social psychology—nor to their varied expressions in religion, philosophy, literature, economics, or politics. At the heart of our holistic and global approach is the attempt to analyze and understand the evolution of a whole "culture of hatred" that has over centuries produced an almost unfathomable abyss of dehumanization of the Jews. To grasp the full measure of this hatred we must dig into the past to fully explore the bimillennial tradition of Jew hatred in the culture of the West, and recall that the preaching of hate and the teaching of anti-Jewish stereotypes were, for many centuries, an integral feature of Christianity. Today, the primary heirs of "eliminationist," apocalyptic, Nazi-style anti-Semitism are found among radical Muslims from the Near East and Asia, rather than among Europeans. Nevertheless, at no time did the anti-Semitic myths that defame Jews or attribute an extraordinary occult power to them disappear after 1945—whether in Russia, eastern Europe, or western Europe. "Anti-Zionism" in many cases provided the indispensable cover under which the prewar anti-Jewish amalgams could be resurrected. But the underlying vision of cursed, malevolent Jews, with their all-embracing control of the media and the international financial system, long preceded political Zionism and the establishment of Israel. Certainly, the existence of the Jewish state and an unresolved "Palestinian question" have served as a compelling catalyst, pretext, and alibi but hardly as the root cause of the deadly anti-Semitic fantasies that have returned to center stage.

A number of investigations of anti-Semitism conducted since 2005 in eleven European countries confirm the enduring power of long-standing Judeophobic myths. For example, according to an Anti-Defamation League–sponsored survey, 36 percent of all Europeans still believe that Jews have "too much power in business." The figure rises to 40 percent when it comes to Jewish influence in international financial markets. It would appear that one in two of all Europeans are convinced that Jews have dual loyalties—being more attached to Israel than their own countries of residence. As many as 45 percent of correspondents in the ADL surveys agreed that Jews "talk too much about the Holocaust." At the top of the anti-Semitic league table, according to these indices, are three predominantly Catholic countries—Hungary, Spain, and Poland—where the belief in Jewish economic power appears to be especially tenacious. One in two people in these nations accept classical anti-Jewish stereotypes. The least anti-Semitic countries in 2005 were in Protestant northern Europe, particularly the Netherlands, Great Britain, and Germany. On the other hand, a high percentage of the Dutch remain anti-Israel, and their prejudices against Jews, gays, and Muslims have grown, more recently, as part of a general trend toward xenophobia.[5] Barely half of the Dutch would vote for a Jewish prime minister today. In the Netherlands, there was a 64 percent rise in anti-Semitic incidents in 2006 over the previous year.

In the middle of the European league table, with almost one in three people accepting a range of traditional anti-Semitic myths, we find Austria and Italy, followed closely by Belgium and Switzerland. Among the Latin countries, Spain is strikingly more hostile to Jews than Italy; Austria is notably more anti-Jewish than Germany, particularly on issues related to Israel and Holocaust memory. Traditional Christian anti-Semitism—above all the deicidal myth claiming that the Jews killed Christ—remains strongest in Poland (39 percent), followed by Hungary (26 percent); it is weakest in France (14 percent) and Germany (13 percent). Nevertheless, one in five Europeans and Americans apparently believe this insidious libel. In a broader sense, traditional anti-Semitism seems to be making a comeback since 2005, according to various indications. This has not, for the most part, been a function of hostility toward the State of Israel. In 2007, for example, only one in four Europeans declared their view of Jews to be directly influenced by Israel's actions—with the highest figures coming from Spain and Austria (35 percent) and the lowest from France (15 percent). Among those respondents who do admit to such an influence, 58 percent say Israel has negatively shaped their view of Jews. Nevertheless, anti-Israel sentiment is blamed as the primary cause for anti-Jewish violence in only five out of the thirteen European countries surveyed.

The majority of Europeans (particularly in Poland, Hungary, Germany, and Austria) attribute attacks on Jews to anti-Jewish, rather than anti-Zionist, feelings. In France, 33 percent blame the violence of recent years on outright anti-Semitism and only 29 percent on hostility toward Israel. Indeed, attitudes toward the Jewish state in the European Union have improved slightly (31 percent were positive in 2007), especially in France and the Netherlands. On the other hand, anti-Zionism with an *anti-American* and *anti-Semitic* coloring (an important theme of this book) remains strong across Europe, with 45 percent agreeing that American Jews control U.S. policy in the Middle East. In Poland, Hungary, and Spain, this anti-Semitic cliché remains dominant among more than half of the general population, coinciding with the survey findings about "Jewish power." Similar views about the influence of Jews in the United States are widely held in Switzerland, Austria, and Belgium. Slightly more than a third of those polled in France, Germany, Italy, and Great Britain agreed with these opinions.[6]

Since 2005, there has also been a notable rise in anti-Semitic incidents around the world, especially in Australia, South Africa, Canada, Argentina, and Great Britain. The Community Security Trust (CST) recorded no fewer than 561 anti-Semitic incidents in the United Kingdom in 2007, the second highest figure since it began recording such cases in 1984. Though there were no so-called trigger events that year, the number of *violent* anti-Semitic assaults reached an all-time high. Moreover, the true figures are, in reality, much higher, since not all incidents are reported or counted unless there is clear-cut evidence of anti-Semitic motivation or content. The ethnic makeup of the perpetrators is particularly interesting. Of those who could be physically identified, it is estimated that 53 percent who engaged in anti-Semitic acts in the United Kingdom during 2007 were white, 27 percent were of Asian or Arab appearance, and 13 percent were black. The number of anti-Semitic incidents involving neo-Nazis or resulting from Far Right racist motivations remained stable, but there was a notable decline in overtly anti-Zionist actions that related directly to Israel or the Middle East.[7]

This trend continued in 2008 when a total of 541 anti-Semitic incidents was recorded—a slight fall of 4 percent from the previous year. In January 2009, following Israel's military offensive in Gaza, however, there were no less than 250 anti-Semitic incidents registered in Great Britain in four weeks. This was the highest total ever reported in a single month. Similarly, in France, Sweden, Denmark, and Holland, the numbers of assaults against Jews and arson attacks on Jewish congregations were growing. Assailants rammed a burning car into the gates of a synagogue in Toulouse, in southwest France; a Jew at the Auber RER railway station was savagely assaulted by twenty youths screaming "Palestine will kill the Jews"; burning rags were shoved through the mailbox of a Jewish home in Antwerp; thousands demonstrated against Israeli actions in Madrid, Amsterdam, Stockholm, Athens, and other European cities. In Denmark, two Israelis were shot and wounded at a shopping mall in Odense. In Helsingborg, Sweden, the congregation had to take shelter as windows were broken and burning cloths were thrown into the synagogue.[8] The costume often seems to be anti-Israel or anti-Zionist in these assaults, but beneath the surface, ancient myths, dark hatreds, and irrational fantasies continue to nourish anti-Semitism.

A few years ago, the British historian Paul Johnson neatly summed up the fundamental irrationality behind anti-Jewish hostility:

> Asked to explain why they hate Jews, anti-Semites contradict themselves. Jews are always showing off; they are hermetic and secretive. They will not assimilate; they assimilate only too well. They are too religious; they are too materialistic, and a threat to religion. They are uncultured; they have too much culture. They avoid manual work; they work too hard. They are miserly; they are ostentatious spenders. They are inveterate capitalists; they are born Communists. And so on. In all its myriad manifestations, the language of anti-Semitism through the ages is a dictionary of non-sequiturs and antonyms, a thesaurus of illogic and inconsistency.[9]

This insight is by no means new. Theodor Mommsen, perhaps the leading German liberal historian of the late nineteenth century, was equally struck and even driven to despair by the unshakable irrationality of the anti-Semites:

> Whatever I or anybody else could tell you are in the last analysis reasons, logical and ethical arguments which no anti-Semite will listen to. They listen only to their own envy and hatred, to the meanest instincts. Nothing else counts for them. They are deaf to reason, right, morals. One cannot influence them. What is there really to tell someone who follows the *Rektor* of all Germans? Such a man is hopeless. There is no protection against the mob, be it the mob of the streets or of the parlours. *Canaille* [mob] remains *canaille*. It is a horrible epidemic, like cholera—one can neither explain or cure it. One must patiently wait until the poison has consumed itself and lost its virulence.[10]

Mommsen wrote these words in 1893, following a disturbing rise in German popular anti-Semitism. Forty years later, an infinitely more powerful wave would bring the Nazis to power and sweep away the Jews of Europe with the force of a mighty tsunami. What is unusual for a classical liberal was Mommsen's conclusion that all appeals to reason and tolerance would prove impotent in holding back the mass appeal of anti-Semitic demagogy— a viewpoint shared by the Austrian founder of political Zionism, Theodor Herzl. European racist anti-Semitism was, after all, the driving force that had returned Herzl to the core of his Jewish identity—prompting him to write his epoch-making *Der Judenstaat* (*The Jewish State*) in 1895. It was a time of rising hostility to the Jews in France, Germany, Russia, and the multiethnic Austro-Hungarian Empire, especially in its capital city of Vienna. When Herzl called the first World Zionist Congress in Basel in 1897, Vienna was already in the hands of a talented, skillful anti-Semitic demagogue, Karl Lueger, who was *democratically* elected on a platform of Catholic social reform and fiercely anticapitalist Jew-baiting. Lueger was no ideological fanatic like Hitler. He did not abolish Jewish civic equality or openly threaten Vienna's Jews with expulsion. Despite Lueger's relative "moderation," however, Theodor Herzl foresaw with prophetic clarity the danger posed by the new populist anti-Semitism in France, Algeria, Germany, Austria, Hungary, Romania, and Russia. In his view, the coming disaster could be averted only by a mass exodus of Jews from Europe to Zion. Unfortunately, the warning was not heeded in time, and the results for European Jewry were truly disastrous.

· · ·

Most Zionists have regarded anti-Semitism as an *ineradicable* disease that cannot be corrected merely through education, reason, or enlightenment, let alone assimilation. Leaders of the movement, beginning with Leo Pinsker, Theodor Herzl, and Max Nordau, perceived Jew hatred to be a permanent structural feature of Diaspora Jewish life. Since Jews were a homeless people living everywhere as "guests" in the lands of the Gentiles, they would continue to incur the inevitable wrath and hostility reserved for the *alien*. In other words, anti-Semitism was seen through the Zionist prism as a radical species of generalized xenophobia whose resolution depended on *territorializing* the Jews. The Zionist therapy was to "normalize" the Jewish people by resettling them as productive citizens in their ancient homeland of Zion. The hope was that as a nation among the nations and as a state among states, Jews would no longer exist on the "sufferance of others." This was common ground in the Zionist movement between the liberal Chaim Weizmann, the socialist David Ben-Gurion, and the integral nationalist Vladimir Jabotinsky.

Though this theory was simplistic in many respects, it had at least one weighty argument in its favor. The history of anti-Semitism during the past two thousand years has been closely linked to the existence of the Diaspora and non-Jewish awareness of Jewish "difference," which already featured in the biblical story of Esther. It is worth remembering that anti-Semitism first appeared during the Hellenistic period inaugurated by the conquests associated with Alexander the Great (365–323 B.C.E.). In those years the Jews of the Diaspora came to constitute more than 10 percent of Hellenistic society as a whole, and in the Egyptian city of Alexandria (the major cultural center of Hellenism) they were at one stage no less than 40 percent of the population. The first recorded pogrom in history occurred in first-century Alexandria; the first Jewish apologetic works by thinkers of the caliber of Philo and Josephus emerged in response to the sharp hostility shown by Alexandrian anti-Semites such as Apion.

The traditional, premodern Jewish view of anti-Semitism regarded pagan (or Gentile) hatred as an inevitable reality that had to be endured with confidence in the power of God and pride in the values of Judaism. Had not God himself defeated the Egyptian Pharaoh's army that sought to destroy Israel on the edge of the Red Sea? Did not Jews annually recall the demise of the arch Jew-baiter Haman during the Purim festival and celebrate his failure to annihilate them? Did the rabbis ever doubt that Rome's victory over Judah would be only temporary? In the biblical vision, the great empires—Babylonian, Assyrian, Persian, Greek, Roman, or those of more modern conquerors—were hardly the true makers of history. Rulers were ultimately instruments of God. When Israel fell it was because God had temporarily engineered its demise as a punishment for backsliding from the path of righteousness. But Israel would be saved with the coming of the Messiah and the ensuing redemption of the world, and those nations that had persecuted the Jews would surely be punished by the hand of God, wreaking retribution through history.

The secular Zionist analysis eliminated God from this sequence while preserving some elements of the underlying structure. Thus, the *Galut* (exile) was still considered the necessary prelude to redemption. However, by the twentieth century, the Diaspora had become a very dangerous place for Jews, who appeared increasingly powerless in the face of growing persecution. Zionists of all persuasions agreed that only radical political action could remedy this pathology, which was endemic and would eternally remain so long as Israel did not return to its land, reclaim its independence, and fight for its freedom. Both socialist Zionism and its nationalist adversaries provided secular messianist reinterpretations of the Jewish tradition that emphasized organized collective action to acquire, modernize, and transform the land of Israel. For many Orthodox Jews, especially before the Shoah, this was heretical and even blasphemous doctrine. The secular Zionists proved, however, to be more prophetic when it came to anticipating the imminent catastrophe that would envelop European Jewry. More clearly than most of their Orthodox, liberal assimilationist, Reform, or Marxist opponents in the Jewish world, they understood that the ground was burning under the feet of European Jews, though they hardly imagined the scale of the coming slaughter.

Contrary to the Zionist prognosis, anti-Semitism did not dissolve or significantly diminish, let alone disappear, after the establishment of Israel in 1948. Instead, Israel itself would gradually emerge as the new "Jewish question." It was violently resisted by the Palestinians, kept at arm's length by the surrounding Arab world, and ostracized by the Communist bloc, especially after 1967. Though many still refuse to acknowledge the fact, the hostility that the Jewish state has faced ever since its creation was not at all comparable to the "normal" enmity between two national movements fighting over the same territory. Nor did it resemble a conventional confrontation between states that can readily bargain, negotiate, or rationally resolve their conflicts of interest. Israel's enemies have always disputed or rejected outright its very right to exist—something that is by definition not open to compromise. Nevertheless, there are many so-called critics of the Jewish state (including some Jewish and Israeli "post-" or anti-Zionists) who insist that Israel is primarily responsible for this state of affairs. They attribute the dramatic rise in global anti-Semitism, especially since 2000, to Israeli occupation of the territories acquired in the 1967 war. They point to oppressive treatment of the Palestinians and alleged crimes against humanity, atrocities, or systematic infringements of human rights to explain the widespread hatred of Israel. This explanation is doubtless attractive to those blinded to

Arab wrongs or who are unaware of the long history of anti-Semitism. Nevertheless, the question of Jewish "responsibility" for anti-Semitism must be posed rather than be simply rejected out of hand.

Bernard Lazare—author of the first serious history of anti-Semitism, which was written in French and completed in 1894 on the eve of the Dreyfus affair—did not flinch from dealing with this contentious issue. Observing that hostility to the Jews had been continuous from pagan antiquity until the modern era, Bernard Lazare boldly (if one-sidedly) argued that its general causes must reside "in Israel itself," in the "unsocial" character of the Jews, their special Torah laws, and Talmudic teaching. The Law of Moses, so he believed, had inculcated in the Jewish people an unshakable sense of pride and superiority. They felt themselves to be the "chosen people of God," the sole beneficiaries of the divine covenant. The decrees and commandments of the Mosaic Law were seen by Jews as being divinely inspired, eternal, good, and just. At the same time in the world of pagan antiquity, these laws (reinforced by Ezra and the scribes, the Pharisees and the Talmudists) tended to isolate Jews from the rest of humanity; they limited social intercourse with foreign peoples and prohibited the acceptance of their gods, laws, or customs. Hebrew monotheism also encouraged the feeling among their pagan neighbors that Jews were indeed arrogant and exclusivist, even seeking to dominate other nations.[11]

Lazare's treatment of the Haman story in the Book of Esther was illustrative of his general approach. The anti-Semites, he observed, were probably correct in taking this Purim story as "the beginning of anti-Semitism," since its author had put into the mouth of Haman (apocryphal persecutor of the Jews in the Persian Empire) accusations that would, at a later period, be repeated by Tacitus and many other Latin or Greek writers: "And Haman said unto the king Ahasuerus: there is a certain people scattered abroad and dispersed among the people in all the provinces of thy kingdom; and their laws are diverse from all people; neither keep they the king's laws: therefore it is not for the king's profit to suffer them" (Esther 3:8). Hence, Haman's call for the extermination of the Jews was based on the argument that they were the only people in the multiethnic empire who lived apart, followed their own laws, and refused to acknowledge the gods of other nations. Lazare might have added that at the core of biblical Judaism, as transmitted at Mount Sinai, was indeed the idea that the children of Israel "shall have no other gods before Me." Did not Jewish history begin with the patriarch

Abraham, who had broken the idols of his father, Terah, and de facto began the long war of the Jews against the pagan cults of kings, emperors, and the worship of "divine beings" on earth?

Bernard Lazare was convinced that the "revolutionary spirit of Judaism" had been a major factor in anti-Semitism through the ages. Abraham, Moses, Jesus, and Karl Marx were prime examples of Jewish iconoclasts who had smashed the idols of their time. The Jews, by creating an intensely demanding God of morality and justice whose stern monotheism brooked no toleration of alien deities, threatened the natural order. The prophetic vision of an abstract transcendent Godhead *above* nature, a deity without form or shape, who had nonetheless created the universe and would in the fullness of time redeem all mankind, was disconcerting, powerful, and mysterious to the pagan world. It was rendered especially irritating by the Jewish claim to be a "chosen people," a "kingdom of priests," and a ferment among the Gentiles. Anti-Semitism could best be seen as an instinctive response by the nations of the world to this provocation—to the uncanny challenge of an eternal people, whose refusal to assimilate defied all established historical patterns. Hatred of the Jews was often combined with fear, envy, and attempts to emulate their messianic vocation.

. . .

The French Catholic theologian Jacques Maritain, writing in 1939, further developed Lazare's insight, specifically linking the messianic Jewish role in history to the longevity of anti-Semitism:

> Israel . . . is to be found at the very heart of the world's structure, stimulating it, exasperating it, moving it. Like an alien body, like an activating ferment injected into the mass, it gives the world no peace, it bars slumber, it teaches the world to be discontented and restless, as long as the world has not God, it stimulates the movement of history. . . . It is the vocation of Israel which the world hates.[12]

The distinguished Catholic scholar Edward H. Flannery provided another pithy variation on this theme: "It was Judaism that brought the concept of a God-given universal moral law into the world"; willingly or not, "the Jew carries the burden of God in history [and] for this he has never been forgiven."[13] In the same vein, the non-Jewish social psychologist Ernest van den Haag observed that the Jews had "suffered from their own invention ever since; but they have never given it up, for it is, after all, what makes the Jews Jewish."[14] Such astonishing fidelity to a single, invisible, irrepresentable, and all-powerful deity (though accompanied by frequent relapses into idolatry) has extracted a high price in Jewish suffering. It necessarily involved the flat denial of all other gods. Indeed, these idols were *reduced to nothing* by the prophets of Israel—"they have mouths but cannot speak, eyes but cannot see, ears but cannot hear"—to quote the psalmist. The Caesars of Rome were not the first or the last to discover that the Jews were the only people in their empire who systematically refused to place imperial statues in their Jerusalem Temple. Two thousand years ago when a Jewish delegation came to see him, the megalomaniac emperor Caligula bitterly remonstrated with them: "So you are the enemies of the gods—the only people who refuse to recognize my divinity, and yet you worship a god whose name you dare not pronounce."[15]

Despite the ferocity of the Jewish revolts against Rome and the cruel repression carried out by the Roman military machine (according to some estimates, well over half a million Jews were killed during the revolt of 66–73 C.E. alone), ancient Romans never demonized Judaism as a faith. They did, however, see it as *subversive* of Roman hierarchical and warrior virtues. Judaism was also mocked as a superstition by many Latin writers and generally despised as misanthropic by Roman intellectuals. However, they stopped short of regarding Judaism as the epitome of cosmic, satanic evil. That would be a singular innovation of Christianity. To quote British historian Bernard Lewis, "demonization as distinct from common or garden-variety prejudice or hostility, began with the advent of Christianity and the special role assigned to the Jews in the crucifixion of Christ as related in the Gospels."[16]

From the fourth century C.E., under Constantine the Great, Christianity would be transformed into the official religion of the Latin West, claiming to possess the absolute divine truth. In the Gospel of John and the teachings of the church fathers, the Jewish rejection of Christ as Messiah and savior became an unforgivable error meriting an eternal curse. The synagogue itself would be repeatedly execrated as a temple of Satan.[17] Similarly, the church fathers institutionalized the belief that Jews were a "deicidal" people—debauched, depraved, and in the words of Saint John Chrysostom ("the Golden Mouthed")—"worse than wild beasts." From the time of the

Crusades, killing these so-called Christ killers would be transmuted into "an act of faith." The leader of the First Crusade, Godfrey of Bouillon, even promised in 1099 "to leave no single member of the Jewish race alive."[18] Worse still, from the twelfth century on, Jews in medieval Christian Europe were increasingly accused of ritual murder and desecration of the host. With the cult of the Cross firmly established, the Jews as a whole (or all individual Jews) gradually metamorphosed into a *demonic abstraction* more real than any of its individual components. It was not so much empirical Jews who were the issue (though "usury" often provided a helpful pretext), but rather the symbolic reference to the collective Jew as a *threat* and the deep anxieties that this evidently aroused. An obsessive focus on the Jewish menace was at the core of Christian anti-Semitism. Not only had the Jews killed Christ, not only were they blind to divinely revealed truth, but they were perceived as a dangerous source of *unbelief* in general.[19]

Attacking the Jews became an accepted way for Christians to affirm their faith and repudiate their own doubts. In so doing, they had to ignore the concrete reality of Jewish life, substituting in its place what the medievalist Gavin Langmuir once described as "fantasies, figments of the imagination, monsters which, although dressed syntactically in the clothes of real humans, have never been seen and are projections of mental processes unconnected with the real people of the outgroup."[20]

Christianity introduced a radically new element of "satanization," which not only postulated the inferiority of Judaism and the eternal punishment of Jews as the deserved consequence of their disbelief but insisted on their irrevocable damnation. Gruesome fantasies with no objective basis in fact, such as the ritual murder by Jews of Christian children at Easter in order to use their blood in the ceremonial Passover meal, were invented to reinforce the faith, to promote pilgrimages, or to intimidate the doubters. The first blood libel in Norwich (England) in 1144 helped to forge together a Christian collectivity by demonizing the Jews along with the Francophone heirs of the Norman Conquest. The blood libel that immortalized "Saint William" of Norwich (the young Christian victim at the heart of the medieval cult) also branded the Jews as bloodthirsty "others" who deserved to be killed.[21]

One can find echoes of such medieval delusions eight hundred years later, in Nazi anti-Semitism—secularized and transmuted into the image of the Jew as blood poisoner and bastardizer of the white Aryan peoples. At the sexual core of this projective persecution fantasy was the Hitlerian myth of the Jew as a diabolical seducer, a serial rapist of the German *Volk,* and a destroyer of all the higher civilizations. At a meta-historical level, Hitler's boundless Jew hatred represented an apocalyptic convergence of Christian anti-Judaism with anti-Christian *völkisch* (ethnic racist) nationalism. The demonological view of Jews and Judaism as a satanic force ultimately derived from Christian precedent. Yet the vitriolic Christophobia of the Nazi leadership remained solidly anchored in their loathing for the "Semitic" origins of Christianity.[22] Hitler was literally obsessed by the Jewish claim to be a "chosen people" and the need to negate it. "There cannot be two Chosen peoples," he told Hermann Rauschning. "We are God's people," he insisted, whereas the Jews were "the men of Satan." Like other apocalyptic anti-Semites intoxicated by conspiracy theories, Adolf Hitler envisaged "a struggle for world domination" that would be fought out between Germans and Jews. Everything else was façade or illusion: "Behind England stands Israel, and behind France, and behind the United States. Even when we have driven the Jew out of Germany, he remains our world enemy."

According to Rauschning, the Nazi leader perceived this metaphysical rivalry as nothing less than an "actual war of the gods." One god inevitably excluded the other. "Israel, the historical people of the spiritual God," Rauschning wrote, "cannot but be the irreconcilable enemy of the new, the German, Chosen People."[23] As unscrupulous vulgarizers of the nineteenth-century German philosopher Friedrich Nietzsche, the Nazis held Judeo-Christianity responsible for outdated conceptions of sin, conscience, and divine redemption. The Jews, in particular, were the mortal enemy of the Nazi creed, with its blind worship of power, hierarchy, blood, soil, and the natural order. In elevating the Jew into a mythical and abstract prototype of all those liberal, democratic, rationalist, and humanitarian values that the National Socialist revolution sought to sweep away, Hitler raised anti-Semitism to a new level of either-or totalitarian politics. The war against the Jews now became an existential issue of "victory or downfall" (*Sieg oder Untergang*), a vengeful, apocalyptic reckoning to determine the future of civilization. It was a bellicose call to the Last Judgment.[24] This was perhaps the single most dangerous legacy that Hitler would bequeath to the postwar world—the dark fantasy that by physically destroying the "satanic Jews," the road would finally be paved for the liberation of mankind. An SS indoctrination leaflet of 1936 expounding the "political faith" of Nazism summarized this special role of the Jew as the negative pole of its totalitarian creed: "It is the Jew and Judaized Europe with its incurable diseases such as weakening Christianity, corrupt Marxism, that are the contradiction per se; therefore the Jew is the main obstacle for the fulfillment [*Vollendung*] of our global and historical mission."[25]

Such redemptive anti-Semitism combined the claim to salvific power of the führer with a grotesque parody of Nietzsche's "revaluation of all values." Its apocalyptic assumptions were based on the presumed inevitability of the coming cosmic struggle between the forces of light and darkness (symbolized by the anti-German Jews), and on the need for radical ethnic cleansing, the unmasking of all social evils, and final deliverance from "parasitic" Jewish financial capitalism. To achieve salvation, the Germanic *Herrenvolk* (master race) would have to crush the "lower races" embodied by the Jew. Catastrophe, in the shape of a final armed conflagration, would necessarily precede ultimate redemption.[26] This redemptive ideology of anti-Semitism, evoked by such historians as Uriel Tal and Saul Friedländer, as well as by the present author, must be distinguished from banal, everyday, "normal" prejudice.[27] It cannot be understood without grasping the continuity as well as the dialectical interplay between traditional Christian and modern anti-Christian anti-Semitism. Christian Judeophobia, as we have already implied, was a necessary but insufficient cause for the Holocaust—whose finality and exterminatory drive radically transcended the theological hatred of its predecessors.[28]

• • •

The cataclysmic impact of the Nazi Final Solution prompted the founder of postwar French existentialist philosophy, Jean-Paul Sartre, to describe anti-Semitism in 1946 as a "criminal passion" rather than as a mere opinion. Sartre's striking portrait of the anti-Semite would, for several decades, exercise a great influence on liberal intellectuals in the West, especially in France. His writings contain passages that, even today, sound remarkably prescient, as if Sartre had uncannily anticipated the paranoid universe of radical Islamist anti-Semites sixty years later. One example was Sartre's cool observation that (in the mind of the anti-Semite) "the Jew is assimilated to the spirit of evil," to Satan himself—blamed for all that is bad in society (crises, wars, famines, upheavals, and revolts). The anti-Semite "localizes all the evil of the universe in the Jew." He imagines him constantly manipulating oppressive governments, or controlling international capitalism, "the imperialism of the trusts and munition makers"; but the Jew is also the hook-nosed agitator and demagogue, the piratical Bolshevik with a knife between his teeth, intent on seducing the workers. At bottom, Sartre regarded extremist anti-Semitism of the kind espoused in the 1930s by the French literary anarchist Louis-Ferdinand Céline as a form of Manicheanism—a dualistic worldview that best explained and thoroughly conditioned radical anti-Semitism. It was based on a relentless either-or struggle between the principles of good and evil.

> Between these two principles no reconciliation is conceivable; one of them must triumph and the other be annihilated. Look at Céline: his vision of the universe is catastrophic. The Jew is everywhere, the earth is lost, it is up to the Aryan not to compromise, never to make peace. Yet he must be on his guard: if he breathes, he has already lost his purity, for the very air that penetrates his bronchial tubes is contaminated. Does that not read like a Manichean?

Sartre shrewdly noted that the mania of Manichean anti-Semites from Drumont to Hitler was always directed toward *destruction*. Behind the bitterness of the anti-Semite, he detected a concealed optimism that "once Evil is eliminated" (as embodied in the Jew) then harmony would finally be reestablished in and of itself. For the anti-Semite "there is no question of building a new society, but only of purifying the one which exists." Since his mission was purely negative, the anti-Semite chose only passion and rage, avoiding instinctively any recourse to reason. He was incapable of a constructive plan of action, long-term enterprises, or the reform of a complex modern society. Sartre's portrait of the "holy" savagery behind anti-Semitism reads like a prologue to the first decade of the twenty-first century: "Knight-Errant of the Good, the anti-Semite is a holy man. The Jew is also holy in his manner—holy like the untouchables, like savages under the interdict of a taboo. Thus the conflict is raised to a religious plane, and the end of the combat can be nothing other than a holy destruction."[29]

The compelling image of the anti-Semite as a "holy destroyer" seeking to reconstitute a lost paradise was an original Sartrean touch. Jew haters were permanently enraged sadists fighting evil as "a pretext to avoid the anguished search for the Good." Their Manicheanism concealed a "deep-seated attraction toward Evil," even as the anti-Semites claimed to be unmasking its machinations. This explained the perverse taste for the ignoble and base in modern French anti-Semites such as Édouard Drumont. They felt an irresistible compulsion to glut themselves "to the point of obsession with the recital of obscene or criminal actions" that could only excite their jaded appetites. Sartre insisted that in anti-Semitic hatred there was "a profound sexual attraction towards Jews" mixed with the strong need of all racists to exercise power over the object of their hate. Anti-Semitism could build on this underlying sadism, nourished by awareness of the vulnerability of the individual Jew and provoked still further by his "inoffensive" nature: "But since Evil, to the anti-Semite, is incarnated in unarmed and harmless men, the latter never finds himself under the painful necessity of being heroic. It is *fun* to be an anti-Semite. One can beat and torture Jews without fear."

This acute observation brought Sartre to propose a definition of the anti-Semite that still seems as chillingly relevant today as it was six decades ago: "A destroyer in function, a sadist with a pure heart, the anti-Semite is, in the very depths of his heart, a criminal. What he wishes, what he prepares, is the *death* of the Jew."

There were some weak points in the Sartrean analysis. The French philosopher disconnected anti-Semitism from any link to Jewish or world history. The Jew, he wrote, "is one whom other men consider a Jew." In 1946, there was no distinct historical identity that Sartre could imagine beyond "the hostility and disdain of the societies which surround them [the Jews]." Hence, "the Jew only serves [the anti-Semite] as a pretext; elsewhere his counterpart will make use of the Negro or the man of yellow skin."[30] This was a shallow and misleading conclusion. Jews were not mere scapegoats of an arbitrary ethnic prejudice, victims of capitalism or objects of the base psychology of the anti-Semites. They were also actors in their own right. Many Sartrean insights came at the price of denying to the Jews the richness of their past, their culture, and their messianic energy. It was utopian (to say the least) to believe that the socialist revolution could eliminate the "Jewish question" through class struggle and assimilation. Moreover, it showed surprising ignorance tinged with prejudice to suggest that Jews did not have a real identity, as if they were mere phantoms or fictional creations of the anti-Semitic gaze.[31]

Sartre did not, however, deny that Jews could (and even should) opt for

a more authentic existence; he specifically related to Zionism and the creation of an independent Jewish nation as one such possibility. Moreover, in
contrast to many on the French Left, he did not adopt an anti-Zionist position after the Six-Day War. His partner, Simone de Beauvoir, was even
firmer in her defense of Israel against all efforts to delegitimize it as a
"settler-colonialist state." Moreover, toward the end of his life, Sartre (influenced by his personal secretary Benny Lévy) was increasingly attracted to
the messianic hope underlying Judaism as an ethics founded on "recognition of the Other," with a powerful universalistic message of fraternity. Nevertheless, in later years, Sartre felt no need to revise his phenomenological
analysis of anti-Semitism, written under the impact of the Nazi Holocaust.
Though sensitive to Jew-baiting, he never truly grasped its amazing resilience or its deep roots in European culture.

•   •   •

Even as Sartre's *Réflexions sur la Question Juive* was being published in 1946,
the myths and fantasies that had made the Holocaust possible had revived
with a vengeance in Poland. Despite the Nazi mass murder on Polish soil of
millions of European Jews, the surviving remnant of Polish Jews soon
found themselves held responsible for the postwar Sovietization of Poland.
Worse still, there were pogroms in Kraków (August 1945) and Kielce (July
1946). At least fifteen hundred Jews were murdered by Poles within two
years of the war's end.[32] My own parents, who had been repatriated to
Poland from the Soviet Union in the summer of 1946, experienced this anti-
Semitic atmosphere at firsthand. Like many other surviving Polish Jews,
they felt gripped by an intense fear, and within a year they left for France.
One reason for the seething anti-Jewish mood was the popular desire to acquire or hold on to Jewish property that had fallen into Polish hands under
the German occupation. The return of Jews from deportation to the USSR
aroused great anxiety in the local Polish population that they might seek to
reclaim their possessions. Indeed, the historian Jan Gross regards this factor
as crucial in explaining the lethal hatred for Jews in postwar Poland.

> Jews were perceived as a threat to the material status quo, security, and
> peaceful conscience of their Christian fellow citizens after the war be-
> cause they had been plundered and because what remained of Jewish
> property, as well as Jews' social roles, had been assumed by Polish neigh-

bors in tacit and often directly opportunistic complicity with Nazi-instigated institutional mass murder.[33]

There is no doubt that opportunistic motifs, material interests, and sheer greed played an important part in the postwar events in Poland, just as they had done during the Holocaust itself and throughout the long history of anti-Semitism. Nevertheless, there were deeper factors involved. The 1946 pogrom in Kielce began after rumors spread that Jews had kidnapped a Christian child with the intention of murdering him. Even prominent churchmen in Poland gave credence to this gross anti-Semitic lie. Moreover, both before and after the pogrom, the Polish primate August Cardinal Hlond categorically refused to publish a pastoral letter on the subject of ritual murder, anti-Semitism, or the mob killing of Jews in Kielce. These and other signs prompted the British ambassador in Poland to cable London in late August 1946: "I fear the Polish clergy are fundamentally anti-Semitic."[34]

Catholic clerics had figured prominently among those nurturing the post-1918 myth that the Jews were plotting to enslave postwar Poland to Soviet Communism. The legend of *żydokomuna* (Judeo-Communism) had indeed taken root in Poland (as in many other European countries) in the early 1920s. It had been vigorously propagandized after 1933 in the Third Reich and cynically exploited as a justification for the Nazi mass murder of Jews on Soviet soil during World War II. It would obtain a new lease of life after 1945. Polish suffering and the systematic massacre of Jews on Polish soil by the ferocious German enemy did nothing to eradicate the effect of twenty years of prewar anti-Semitic incitement in Poland. If anything, the ease with which Jews had been murdered by the Nazis (and the silent complicities it created) appears to have blunted compassion and unleashed the ugliest mob instincts in the postwar Polish population. Although Jews had accounted for no more than 20 percent of the small prewar Communist Party, the myth of *żydokomuna* became all-pervasive after 1945, along with the idea of an anti-Polish "Jewish conspiracy."[35] Such stereotypes continue to be extraordinarily tenacious. In January 2004, the popular weekly *Wprost* reported a nationwide survey in which 40 percent of Poles still believed the legend that their country was ruled by Jews.

Soon after 1945, such popular beliefs were already being utilized by the leader of the Polish Workers' Party (PPR), Władysław Gomułka, who complained to Stalin that there were too many Jews in responsible positions in

Poland. Ironically, some of the most prominent Jewish Communists fully identified with Poland, actively disliked Jews, and mistakenly thought they were joining an internationalist movement that was "ethnically blind"— only to discover that their comrades still considered them Jewish in spite of everything.[36] In March 1968, when there were barely fifty thousand Jews left in Poland (completely assimilated for the most part), those Communists of Jewish origin who still held positions in the party were subjected to a massive and public anti-Zionist witch hunt.[37] This was the ignominious end of a rich millennial history of Jews in Poland. Far from being a Jewish conspiracy, national Communism in postwar Poland turned out to be closer in spirit to National Socialism. Gomułka and his Communist henchmen finally fulfilled the dream of the prewar integral Polish nationalists and fascists in virtually "cleansing" Poland of its surviving Jewish remnant.[38]

· · ·

Joseph Stalin was the first ruler to give a decisive impulse from above to anti-Semitism in the postwar period.[39] We know that in the midst of the "Great Patriotic War," Stalin told the Polish general Władysław Anders that "Jews make poor soldiers," though their heroism in the Red Army was second to none, and (unlike Hitler) Stalin never dispensed with their military services. Though the Jews numbered only about three million inhabitants within the mighty USSR, they were in fourth place among the multitude of Soviet nationalities in the *absolute* number of medals awarded for bravery at the front. This fact was well-known to the Soviet dictator. Stalin was equally aware of the growing anti-Semitism in the USSR during the war. He had seen the requests from certain party officials that the Communist Party purge the arts and culture of "pernicious Jewish influences"—a chauvinist wave that had begun to infiltrate Soviet institutions and party organizations around 1942. By the late 1940s, this trend would become official Soviet policy, as if the dead führer in Berlin had handed on the anti-Jewish baton to his nemesis in the east.

The Soviet Communist Party first began to organize an unprecedented anti-Semitic campaign between 1948 and 1953, initiating a process of "investigative genealogy," which weeded out and purged unwanted Jewish personnel.[40] For the first time since the Bolshevik Revolution (and in flagrant contradiction to its self-declared ideology), the USSR started to persecute prominent Jewish members of the Soviet elite simply because they were ethnic Jews. The result was the rapid spread of anti-Semitic rumors, insults, leaflets, threats, and assaults culminating in the hysterical unmasking of murdering physicians—the so-called Doctors' Plot of 1953.[41] Stalin personally orchestrated these postwar anti-Semitic campaigns and purges under the banner of an assault on "rootless cosmopolitanism" and Jewish bourgeois nationalism. The apparent contradiction in attacking Jews both as national chauvinists and internationalists without roots did not in the least disturb Stalin's followers. Nor did Soviet support for Israel's foundation in 1948 prevent an anti-Semitic campaign against Zionism from being simultaneously carried out throughout the Soviet bloc.[42]

The political cartoons in the Soviet press and satirical magazines around 1952 recalled the obscene style of Nazi caricatures and were matched only by what was beginning to emerge from the Arab world. The original Jewish family names of prominent Communists were paraded in brackets in the Soviet press as if this were prima facie evidence of a crime. At the same time, during Stalin's last years, the latent Russian imperial and national-Bolshevik strands in Soviet Marxist-Leninist ideology encouraged the transformation of cosmopolitan Jews and "Zionists" into enemies of the Russian people.[43] These trends grew in intensity after 1967, transmitting a poisoned legacy to Eastern Europe, the postwar international Communist movement, and much of the Third World. Stalin and his heirs skillfully disguised their anti-Semitism under an anti-Zionist mask, especially for foreign consumption. The Communists also made sure after 1945 that the uniqueness of Jewish suffering under the Nazis (including the massacres perpetrated on Soviet soil) would never be made more widely known to the Soviet public.[44] The Jews simply disappeared from public representations of the war—both as victims and as soldiers—despite their great contribution to the war effort.

. . .

Postwar Soviet anti-Semitism is one of many examples that sharply contradict the myth that the Holocaust somehow neutralized the Judeophobic virus. In the Communist bloc, the Arab-Muslim world, and even in the West, anti-Semitism was never on the point of vanishing. Between 1944 and the establishment of Israel in 1948, it was still extremely active across the world, sometimes exploding in pogromistic violence, as in Eastern Europe or North Africa. Though the strictly racist and neo-Nazi manifestations had been somewhat attenuated, a new version of the "Jewish problem" would soon metastasize. At its heart was the notion that the recently founded State of Israel stood at the crossroads of a worldwide conspiracy already laid out in the notorious *Protocols of the Elders of Zion*.[45]

The *Protocols*, it is worth recalling, were fabricated by Russian anti-Semites in Paris working as agents of the Okhrana (the czarist secret police) between 1898 and 1903. The first full Russian edition, edited by an apocalyptic-minded Russian Orthodox mystic, Sergei Nilus, appeared in 1905.[46] They presented the Jews as instruments of the Antichrist engaged in a secret conspiracy to overthrow the existing political order and establish their own global rule. Later editions in Germany, like that of the proto-Nazi Theodor Fritsch (in 1922), took Zionism and the "Elders of Zion" to be one and the same thing. The *Protocols* were even said to be identical to the "secret" speech that Theodor Herzl had supposedly made to delegates at the World Zionist Congress in 1897.[47] The subsequent history of the *Protocols* showed that for anti-Semites, Zionism was a vital link in a broader Jewish-Masonic world conspiracy. Probably no other single text in the annals of anti-Semitism would have such a deadly effect as the *Protocols* in preparing the Holocaust or in inspiring hatred of the Jewish state after 1948. No doubt, its authors never imagined that their crass forgery would one day become a worldwide bestseller. The *Protocols* were widely disseminated in America in the 1920s by the famous automobile manufacturer Henry Ford. They profoundly influenced Adolf Hitler and the Nazi Party, as well as nationalist anti-Semites across the European continent, convinced that Jews were striving to destroy the nation-state and Christianity in order to establish their own world despotism. The spread of Communism after 1917 seemed to be living proof to many conservatives and fascists of the truth of the *Protocols*. Although Zionism was still far from being the primary target of the anti-Semites, it was already perceived in the 1920s as a major political arm of world Jewry and the more visible part of a shadowy Judaic "world-government" operating beneath the murky surface of events.

Stalin's demonology of Zionism after 1950 followed this mold and would become an integral part of Soviet propaganda during the Cold War. In the crusade against Wall Street capitalism and American imperialism, the Jews—already sixty years ago—were being assigned a special role.[48] Stalin's totalitarian anti-Semitic legacy would continue to influence Communist-controlled Eastern Europe for four decades after 1945. It affected not only

Poland, but Hungary, Romania, Czechoslovakia, and other Soviet satellites in the Eastern bloc. From the Rudolf Slánský show trial in Prague in 1952 (which led to the hanging of twelve leading Jewish Communists falsely accused of treason) to the aftermath of the Soviet invasion of Czechoslovakia in August 1968, neo-Stalinist and anti-Zionist anti-Semitism played an important role in Communist Eastern Europe.[49] Though there were fewer than twenty thousand Jews in Czechoslovakia in 1950, their prominence in the postwar Communist leadership provided enough cover for fabricated indictments against them as "Zionist spies," pro-imperialists, "counterrevolutionary agents," and subversive intriguers. As elsewhere in Eastern Europe, Stalinist anti-Semitism served to intimidate and discredit any efforts to liberalize the totalitarian system from within. Similarly, in the late 1980s, in the Soviet Union and Eastern Europe, anti-Semitism would be used as a weapon by opponents of President Mikhail Gorbachev's liberal Communist reforms.[50]

The collapse of the USSR accentuated this trend. In the chaos of post-communist Russia, after 1991, wild conspiracy theories about Judeo-Masonry flourished—along with a revival of Orthodox Christian Judeophobia, brazen Black Hundred proto-fascism, neo-Stalinist anti-Zionism, and fascist hooliganism. In the Russian parliament, anti-Semites such as the leader of the Russian Communist Party, Gennady Zyuganov, and former general Albert Makashov presented Jews as parasites and enemies of the Russian people. Makashov even called for them to be rounded up and "sent to the grave," a death threat that encountered remarkably little protest. Another influential Communist, Viktor Ilyukhin, openly attacked former president Boris Yeltsin's "Jewish entourage"—especially tycoons such as the highly influential Boris Berezovsky. The Liberal Democratic leader, Vladimir Zhirinovsky, was no less anti-Semitic. Pro-Nazi groupings such as Alexander Barkashov's Russian National Unity movement also began to expand. They espoused an extreme xenophobic program of "Russia for the Russians" and an openly fascist-style anti-Semitism.

At the same time, a significant part of the Russian intelligentsia relapsed into a traditional anti-Western, neo-Slavophile style of Jew hatred typical of the nationalist camp. Though they might despise the jackbooted skinheads and Blackshirts who waved swastika flags while marching through some of Russia's cities, their own metaphysical anti-Semitism was no less dangerous. In the early 1990s, such pathologies reflected a debilitated Russian society in

acute crisis—torn by Mafia corruption, xenophobia, economic disorientation, anomie, and a deep sense of national humiliation after the collapse of
the Soviet empire. This post-Soviet disorder enabled populist anti-
Semitism to rear its ugly head, while, at the same time, democratization had
clearly brought some real benefits to Jews. During Yeltsin's postcommunist
liberalization, Jewish communal structures and education revived under
the relatively benign gaze of the authorities. No fewer than one million ex-
Soviet Jews took advantage of the unexpected opening to freedom in order
to start a new life in Israel. Some of those who remained quickly reached the
top of the economic and political pyramid in postcommunist Russia. Apart
from the remarkable number of Jews among the multimillionaire oligarchs,
there were also high-profile politicians such as Yegor Gaidar, Anatoly
Chubais, Boris Nemtsov, Grigory Yavlinsky, and even Vladimir Zhirinovsky
(who had a Jewish father), not to mention half-Jewish prime ministers such
as Yevgeny Primakov and Sergei Kiriyenko. Not since the early years of Bolshevik rule had so many persons of Jewish origin been as politically prominent in Russia as they would be in the 1990s.

Today, anti-Semitism has become established as an integral part of nationalist ideology and is still very strong among the older generation of
Russian Communists who denounce the Zionization of existing power
structures. President Vladimir Putin's successor, Dmitry Medvedev, has
been attacked, for example, on nationalist websites for his allegedly Jewish
background and that of his wife—as well as for visiting the Moscow Jewish
community center. In 2007 there was a notable increase (as in western Europe) of neo-Nazi rhetoric with the first-ever official rally (on April 21)
honoring Hitler's memory in downtown Moscow. Despite such street manifestations, the number of known physical attacks on Jews did not increase
in Russia, though cemetery vandalism is on the rise. Anti-Semitic literature
is also widely available in bookstores, and the stereotypes on which it is
based periodically surface in the mass media. For example, a film on Leon
Trotsky, shown on federal TV channels in February 2007, was replete with
anti-Semitic myths, including that American Jewish bankers had financed
the Russian Bolshevik revolutionary. On the other hand, anti-Semitic candidates did not do particularly well in the December 2007 elections, though
there are at least ten parliamentarians in the State Duma (lower house of
the Federal Assembly) who hold such views. During 2007, the law enforce-
ment bodies—probably on "instructions from above"—became more ac-

tive in prosecuting those anti-Semites not considered to be sufficiently loyal to Vladimir Putin and the state authorities. Putin's own style of centralized authoritarian rule and Russia's stability under his presidency may indeed have contributed to containing the considerable anti-Semitic potential that still exists within the Russian Federation. In 2008 there were several attacks on synagogues in western Russia and more recently, with the spread of social unrest in the wake of falling oil prices and economic hardships, general xenophobia is resurgent once more.

In Ukraine, anti-Semitism in 2007, as in the past, accompanied the election campaigns, and there appeared to be a slight increase in the number of violent assaults on Jews. Particularly disturbing was the inability of the Ukrainian authorities to halt the flood of anti-Semitic propaganda coming out of MAUP (Interregional Academy of Personnel Management), Ukraine's largest private university. The publications of the MAUP Academy are intensely anti-Zionist and anti-Jewish, influencing large numbers of Ukraine students. The academy has organized conferences and round-tables, and established ties with racist anti-Semites in Russia, the Middle East, and the West. Its propagandists are particularly active in disseminating Ukrainian conservative-nationalist ideology while expanding their Arab connections. Among MAUP's partners and sponsors are the Libyan and Iranian embassies, representatives of the Palestinian Authority, and several nongovernmental Arab organizations.

Unlike western Europe, in postcommunist Russia and eastern Europe the tenacity of traditionalist and popular anti-Semitism was not sparked off by a mass influx of Arab Muslims or seriously influenced by events in Israel/Palestine. Once official Soviet-style anti-Zionist indoctrination disappeared in 1990, the old Jew hatred simply burst forth from the lower depths of Russian and Eastern European society as part of the "return to history" and the new freedom of speech throughout the former Communist bloc. Ancient religious and ethnic prejudices previously frozen by state repression reemerged with renewed energy, reflecting the general postcommunist search for new collective identities. The greatly reduced size of the Jewish population, especially in Eastern Europe, did not in the least diminish the power of classical anti-Jewish stereotypes. The trend was intensified by a widespread fear of globalization, the penetration of Western capitalism, and the impact of modernization.[51] There was also the difficult problem, especially in Eastern Europe and Ukraine, of coming to terms with wartime complicities related to the Nazi occupation. Together with the new economic hardships and political instability, these factors aggravated the postcommunist panic.

During the 1990s, there was a marked propensity to believe in the myth of the Jewish conspiracy in eastern Europe and to promote texts like the *Protocols of the Elders of Zion*. No less than 42 percent of Slovaks in 1992 believed that "Jews have too much power"—a strikingly high figure. Losers in the modernization process were especially likely to give credence to ridiculously inflated notions about Jewish global influence. They were encouraged by such popular demagogues as Corneliu Vadim Tudor in Romania, obsessed with the role of the Israeli Mossad and Jewish control of eastern European economies. Anti-Semitism also went hand in hand with "revisionist" views of the Holocaust, turning such wartime collaborators as the Hungarian regent Miklós Horthy de Nagybánya, Slovakia's clerical ruler Monsignor Josef Tiso, and Romanian dictator Marshal Ion Antonescu into heroes in "the struggle against Communism."[52] In 1990s Romania, it became increasingly fashionable to claim that Jewish Communists had destroyed Romanian culture. Similar arguments were made in Poland, Slovakia, Hungary, and the Baltic states, where an imaginary Jewish guilt for Communism was used to offset or repress local responsibilities for wartime crimes committed against Jews in those countries.

· · ·

The "Palestinian question" and Western liberal anti-Zionism have played little role in stimulating anti-Jewish feelings in Russia and eastern Europe since the early 1990s. The Middle East crises appeared irrelevant compared to fears of economic chaos, anxieties about privatization, and the growing ethno-nationalism that rapidly began to fill the postcommunist ideological vacuum after 1989.[53] It was this exclusivist nationalism that inflamed anti-Semitic reflexes even among the Communist oppositionists in Russia whose catchwords were often indistinguishable from those of the ultraconservatives or local fascists. In Austria and eastern Europe, the resurgent ethno-nationalism after 1990 produced an "anti-Semitism without Jews"—related more to the ghosts of the past than to the real problems of the present. There was no post-Shoah "Jewish question" of the kind that had indeed existed in east-central Europe between 1918 and 1939.[54] Except for Hungary, the Jews had almost disappeared, yet it seemed life could not go on without the *Judaeus ex machina.*

Something similar had happened in western Europe during the Middle Ages following the expulsion of Jews from England, France, and the German lands. Christian anti-Semitism did not vanish after these draconian measures any more than it disappeared in Spain after 1492. Indeed, it was to some extent aggravated even as it became more abstract. This Christian Jew hatred was a set of diabolical constructs or chimerical beliefs of a theological or ideological nature—implemented by the dominant groups within what had become a persecuting society. Once such symbolic myths as the blood libel had infiltrated the popular culture, the physical presence of real Jews was no longer necessary in order to generate anti-Semitism.

The history of the Holocaust itself illustrates the same point. As the last German Jews were being expelled from the soil of the Third Reich in late 1943, the apocalyptic anti-Semitism of the Nazi regime did not wane; on the contrary, it intensified.[55] This was a function of deliberate incitement that perfectly dovetailed with popular myths and a widely disseminated hallucinatory vision of the so-called Jewish peril threatening Germany and the rest of Aryan mankind.[56] Nazi military defeats toward the end of the war were interpreted in this ideological framework as living proof of Hitler's warnings that the Jews were determined to exterminate all Germans. In Joseph Goebbels's propaganda, the German people were always the *innocent victims* of a vast worldwide Jewish network of power. On the other hand, the "invisible Jew" was the international wire-puller behind Franklin D. Roosevelt, Winston Churchill, and Joseph Stalin, the plutocratic manipulator of the world's stock exchanges, the organizer of Freemasonry and other secret societies, and the underground architect of permanent revolutionary subversion.[57] Invisible Jews would prove to be equally indispensable in the postwar era. They would be marked as obstacles to such new totalitarian forces of evil as Soviet Communism and jihadi Islam, striving for world domination and projecting their despotic ambitions against the Jewish people.

• • •

When the renowned Greek composer Mikis Theodorakis, a few years ago, called "this small people" (the Jews) "the root of evil," he was spontaneously giving voice to the perennial power of anti-Semitic mythical thinking. His resentment at the scandal of Jewish particularity and the long-suppressed rage at its symbolic chosenness all too easily found their outlet in a relentlessly negative focus on the State of Israel. Even in such highly sophisticated societies as those of Great Britain and France, a similar strain of exasperation has begun to burst through the increasingly thin layer of postwar taboos. According to British journalist Petronella Wyatt, writing at the end of 2001, it was notable that "since September 11 anti-Semitism and its open expression has become respectable at London dinner tables."

"Well," Wyatt recalled being told by a liberal member of the House of Lords, "the Jews have been asking for it, and now, thank God, we can say what we think at last."[58] In recent years, the Jewish state has evidently provided a long-awaited opportunity for Britons to express widespread if previously repressed feelings of anger and even hatred.[59] This is less surprising when one observes how sections of the British media have so actively participated in singling out Israel for disproportionate criticism and contesting its legitimacy as a state. When some years ago the *New Statesman* used a well-established anti-Semitic iconography to illustrate its cover line "A Kosher Conspiracy?" (about the Jewish lobby in Great Britain), it clearly crossed a line.[60] When the European press began to publish innuendoes about Jews as warmongers and drop heavy hints about Jewish cabals and Israel's secret control of America, this also followed a classic Judeophobic mold. Even when presented in impeccably shiny anti-Zionist wrapping, such views all too often have reflected anti-Semitic bias—whether overt or covert.[61] Unfortunately, much of the European intelligentsia prefers to deny this fact, reducing anti-Semitism to a mere card played in bad faith by Israel and world Jewry. Since Jews are a priori deemed to be powerful, even addressing anti-Semitism as a serious problem tends to be seen as suspect in certain quarters or, worse still, as a Jewish invention.

• • •

The old-new anti-Semitism can itself be as inventive as it is repetitive. It often appears to imply that Jews are never victims but *always victimizers,* which may sound original to some but is clearly false. It generally avoids positions that smack of deliberate economic or political exclusion of Jews qua Jews from the national community or that echo the discourse of a discredited biological racism. On the other hand, depicting Zionism and the Jewish lobby as a world power is not considered racist or defamatory. There is no law against suggesting that Zionists deliberately provoke wars and revolutions, even though this is a classic anti-Semitic fabrication that has been widely propagated by Nazis, Communists, and Islamists.

Another favored formula of the "new" anti-Semites has been the apartheid analogy—originally pioneered by the Soviet Union and Third World nonaligned states in the 1970s. The big lie that Israel is an apartheid state has become firmly entrenched in recent years in many Western countries and has been turned into an integral part of the "boycott Israel" strategy. All the salient and obvious differences between white-controlled South Africa and the Jewish state are ignored by the purveyors of this patent falsehood. Apartheid South Africa enshrined and institutionalized racism in law; apartheid involved the enforced undemocratic domination of a white ruling minority over an oppressed disenfranchised black majority (constituting 90 percent of the population); it forbade and criminalized mixed marriages, practiced heavy censorship, and explicitly discriminated according to skin color. There has never been anything remotely comparable to this legally enforced separate development in Israeli society, its ethos, or its political culture. Yet the mendacious parallel is endlessly parroted not only by the dogmatic "antiracist" Left but by well-meaning though often ignorant liberals, Anglican priests such as Desmond Tutu, grossly partisan UN officials such as John Dugard, and a bevy of ideologically driven pro-Palestinian academics around the world.[62] By ripping apartheid out of its original South African context purely in order to stigmatize or delegitimize Zionism, the anti-Zionists (some of them Jews) have displayed a pitiful lack of historical insight, deplorable anti-Jewish bias, and a stunning intellectual dishonesty.[63]

In France, the boycott movement and the apartheid lie have been less central in anti-Zionist discourse than in Great Britain. The anti-Semitic tradition in France, as well as the shame of wartime collaboration in the German Final Solution, have gradually seared themselves into the collective consciousness. However, until President Jacques Chirac's official apology in 1995, the pretense was maintained that the Vichy regime had never enjoyed any legitimacy in France. Many Frenchmen clung to the myth that the wartime head of state, Philippe Pétain, sought to protect the Jews, despite the strict racial laws after 1940, the widespread institutional anti-Semitism, the daily vilification in the wartime media, and the crucial role of the French police and judicial system in the deportation of Jews to the death camps. In the 1950s, especially on the nationalist and Catholic Right, the Vichy legacy and political anti-Semitism still exerted a certain influence in France. On the other hand, French xenophobes also faced a more vigorous tradition of antiracism and anti-anti-Semitism than was present in most European countries at the time. By the 1970s, a number of Jews, such as Simone Veil began to play an important role in French politics. This was even more evident after 1981, under the left-wing Socialist president François Mitterrand. Among Mitterrand's leading ministers or closest advisers were Laurent Fabius, Robert Badinter, Jacques Attali, and Jack Lang, to name only the most prominent.[64] Twenty-five years later, for the first time in its history, France has a president of partly Jewish descent who has publicly expressed pride in his origins. Nevertheless Islamic and left-wing anti-Semitism remains a force on French soil.

During the closing decades of the twentieth century, the main force promoting anti-Semitism in France was, however, the radical right-wing National Front (FN), led by Jean-Marie Le Pen. For more than ten years, the FN could claim to be the largest racist and xenophobic movement in western or central Europe. Supported by about 15–20 percent of the electorate, it thrived on the demagogic exploitation of real social problems such as large-scale immigration (especially of North African Muslim Arabs), high unemployment, and the erosion of French national identity.[65] In FN literature, some classical themes of French anti-Semitism found their mouthpiece. Jews were the ultimate anti-France symbols for the FN, identified primarily by their wealth, international links, and role in the Socialist government of the 1980s. A "Judeo-cosmopolitan *médiocratie*" was deemed to control the mass media and high finance. A traditionalist Catholic theology espoused within the FN still presented the Jews as a God-rejected people. Integral Catholicism neatly merged with ethno-nationalist intolerance; anti-Semitic innuendoes; dislike of liberalism, pluralism, and dissent; and as a crass xenophobia directed against the influx of North African immigrants.[66] One significant new element in this witches' brew of hate was the National Front's implicit encouragement of Holocaust "revisionism." Le Pen himself went on record in the late 1980s as saying that the Holocaust was "just a detail in the history of World War II." Others, like French Holocaust denier Robert Faurisson—whose following was not restricted to the FN—went much further. In 1978, Faurisson categorically rejected the existence of the gas chambers and dismissed the Holocaust itself as a "historical lie" and a "gigantic political fraud" whose main beneficiary was the State of Israel.[67] It is worth noting that since the end of World War II, France has proved to be a world leader in spontaneously propagating Holocaust denial as an export article, despite vigorous government legislation to repress the phenomenon. Moreover, in no other country has Holocaust "revisionism" proved to be as attractive to the extreme Left.[68]

The radical intelligentsia in France and a number of other western European countries have been major intellectual spearheads of the "new" anti-Semitism since 2000. In the name of antifascism, antiracism, human rights, and slogans like "Never Again Auschwitz," French intellectuals have been prominent in the anti-American, anti-Israel, and anti-Zionist charge.[69] As "antiracists" they have tended to repudiate the "illegitimate" Zionist State of Israel with the same revulsion that they usually reserve for Le Pen and his acolytes.[70] However, while Zionist Jews have been sharply condemned for their alleged particularism, exclusivism, and national egoism, Palestinian nationalism and Islamism generally escapes such vitriolic criticism. Similarly, the role of Muslim fundamentalism as a factor in exacerbating the wave of anti-Jewish violence in France and Israel during the past eight years has been deliberately downplayed by the leftist intelligentsia. Instead, the French Left reinvented the old Jacobin-republican bogey of "communitarianism" (*le communautarisme*), implying that it was somehow unacceptable or even racist for Jews to display any bond of solidarity with Israel.[71] Whether in the name of abstract French universalism or multiculturalism, the result has been that communal Jews have increasingly found themselves outside the politically correct European intellectual consensus. Instead, their anti-Zionist critics have feverishly sought to transform Israel itself into the ultimate paradigm for racism.[72]

• • •

Anti-Jewish incidents in France, Great Britain, Germany, Holland, and many other European countries, as well as in Russia, Canada, Argentina, and Australia, have dramatically increased since 2000. The volume of such attacks in France has until recently been especially high, far outstripping racist acts directed at Muslim targets.[73] Moreover, many of the perpetrators have been Arab immigrants from the Maghreb—a point reluctantly conceded only in recent years by government officials and elite opinion. These assaults have included arson attacks; vandalism; face-to-face harassment in the streets, at bus stops, in coffee shops, and on public transport; they include bricks thrown through the windows of Jewish community centers and schools, swastika daubings on Jewish buildings and homes, the desecration of Jewish cemeteries, and the burning of synagogues. The graffiti sometimes calls for killing Jews. Hate mail and threatening telephone calls have, in crisis moments, reached epidemic proportions, especially when Israel has been in the news. Nevertheless, hatred for Israel more often appears to be the *result* of Jew hatred, rather than the reverse. The email texts, in particular, reflect visceral anti-Semitism along with such familiar themes as loathing for the Talmud, references to the mythical "Elders of Zion," denunciations of imaginary Jewish crimes against humanity, and delirious rants against the "Auschwitz lie." The theme of a Jewish conspiracy remains omnipresent and universal.

The full extent of anti-Semitic activity is notoriously difficult to quantify, especially across national boundaries. In this study I have included references to the results of diverse surveys and opinion polls regarding contemporary anti-Semitism, especially in Europe and North America. This data can be a useful barometer of attitudes and prejudices toward Jews in a given time and place. Nonetheless, the surveys have some serious drawbacks. The questions posed in many of the polls are outdated and likely to miss new forms of expression adopted by anti-Semites, especially in relation to Israel and Zionism. Moreover, without a clear concept of what constitutes anti-Semitism today and how that definition has become more fluid, one must doubt the value of inquiries that barely scratch the surface, let alone attempt to go deeper into the motivations, influences, or agendas that animate anti-Semitic opinions. Furthermore, such surveys rarely take into account the reluctance of many respondents today to be identified as anti-Semites. This is true, for example, in Germany, for reasons that are obviously connected with the Holocaust and its aftermath. According to official German surveys, the average level of German anti-Semitism has remained remarkably consistent since 1949. Anti-Semitic opinions appear to be shared by 15–20 percent within a total German population that today stands at about eighty-three million people. This is troubling enough, but the real figure is most certainly higher, given the strength of latent prejudices in a society where taboos concerning the Holocaust still inhibit the public expression of anti-Jewish feelings.[74] It is clearly not easy to assess the strength of such sentiments when they are repressed or involve deep ambivalences and resentments toward Germany's post-Auschwitz burden. Surveys have not yet found a way to capture such nuances or to effectively measure the cumulative effect of a tradition of hostility toward Jews existing in any given society or culture.

Much latent German anti-Semitism is explicitly connected to the public desire for closure on the Nazi past and the increasingly obsessive wish— heightened in recent years—to perceive Jews as "perpetrators" while turning Germans into victims. Israel may often be the pretext for such inversions, but it is not necessarily the major source of this syndrome. Its deeper roots lie in the power of age-old anti-Semitic stereotypes and the wish for release from oppressive though unavowed feelings of guilt and malaise. Otherwise, it would be difficult to comprehend the willingness of 68 percent of Germans to believe the myth that Israel has been relentlessly implementing a *Vernichtungskrieg* (war of extermination) against the Palestinians. The use of such a manifestly Nazi term suggests the compulsiveness of the projective mechanisms at work. To some extent, this is also true of the trend to focus so intensively on the fate of German civilians as victims of massive Allied wartime bombing and Red Army outrages in the eastern half of Germany at the end of the war. As with the mass expulsion of millions of Germans from Czechoslovakia, Romania, and Poland after 1945, these events did really happen, and they were certainly crimes against humanity. Open discussion of atrocities or crimes committed against German civilians is necessary, legitimate, and inevitable. What is disturbing and dangerous are the attempts to remove these facts from their Nazi and wartime context, or worse still, to equate them with the Holocaust.[75]

Motifs presenting Germans exclusively as victims have long been favorites of the neo-Nazi National Democratic Party (NPD), the nationalist conservative political party the Republikaner (REP), and the weekly newspaper *National-Zeitung*, affiliated with the German People's Union (DVU). These are the extremist mouthpieces of the German radical Right that invariably deny or relativize the Holocaust out of existence. Like their counterparts in Austria, Hungary, and eastern Europe, they have adopted an intensely anti-American, anti-globalist, and anti-Semitic discourse. Indeed, their "anti-imperialist" language is almost indistinguishable from that of the Far Left. After 2001, neo-Nazis attended public rallies with T-shirts proudly bearing portraits of Saddam Hussein and Osama bin Laden, while they denounced "Israel's state terrorism" and America's "neo-colonialist" atrocities. In the same vein, contemporary German neo-Nazi ideologues such as Horst Mahler (a radical left-wing anarchist in the 1970s) brazenly pronounce anathemas against Israel and East Coast American Jewish organizations for their "genocide" of the Palestinians. The neo-Nazis emphatically define the Palestinians as fellow victims (like the German people) who have been totally enslaved under "Judeo-American foreign rule."[76]

The ideological overlap between German right-wing extremists, Palestinian terrorists, and Islamofascists has become increasingly apparent during the past decade. It logically culminated in the invitations to neo-Nazis (and other so-called revisionists) by President Mahmond Ahmadinejad to participate in Iran's 2006 state-sponsored Holocaust denial conference held in Tehran. German and American Holocaust deniers, no less than their Iranian patrons, claim to be fighting the world-devouring "Zionist-occupied government" in Washington, D.C. This makes them firm allies of radical Muslim terror groups and conspiracy theorists around the world. Like the Far Left, the neo-Nazis pathetically try to deflect the well-grounded accusation of anti-Semitism by insisting that such charges are merely a Jewish invention to secure Israel's immunity from criticism or to obtain a free hand in massacring Palestinians. It is no accident that both the radical Muslims and the neo-Nazis so eagerly quote from such left-wing anti-imperialists as Noam Chomsky and Norman Finkelstein and use such venal Israel bashers as ultra-Orthodox "Rabbi" Moishe Arye Friedman from Vienna as Jewish alibis to cover up their own virulent racism.[77] Jewish self-accusation remains invaluable as a weapon to bolster the anti-Semitic claim that Israel has greedily *profited* from the Holocaust at German expense, or fraudulently monopolized the status of victimhood. This Shylock metaphor has unfortunately acquired renewed resonance since the late 1990s against the background of substantial restitution claims, the politicization of Holocaust memory, and an increasing focus on the purely material aspects of the Shoah.

In Austria, as in Germany, "secondary" anti-Semitism related to the mass murder of the Jews has for decades existed alongside the more traditional religious or modern racist manifestations of Judeophobia. The shadow of Nazism in Austrian postwar politics has been impossible to ignore. But it took massive international pressure after 1986, resulting from the Waldheim affair, to finally force the public issue of the Holocaust on a reluctant Austrian population and a highly evasive political establishment. The shock effect was all the greater, since Austrians (unlike Germans) had never been required by the Allies at the end of World War II to accept their coresponsibility for the Shoah. After 1945, popular opinion in the Alpine Republic remained steadfastly hostile to any notion of reparations. Austrian government officials were equally determined to avoid paying any meaningful financial compensation to the Jewish victims of Nazism.[78] The failure of de-Nazification (especially superficial in postwar Austria) and the rapid reintegration of Austrian ex-Nazis into the political process after 1949, reinforced these trends. Reluctance to deal with the implications of the Nazi past was closely tied to electoral expediency—with the dominant Conservative and Socialist parties in postwar Austria competing to win the support of the ex-Nazis. They could see no political benefit in confronting the prevailing collective amnesia in a country where wartime service in the Wehrmacht was still seen as a "patriotic duty," and war criminals were regularly acquitted by the courts.[79]

Despite the tenacity of postwar anti-Semitism, the Jewish-born Socialist leader Bruno Kreisky was elected federal chancellor of Austria in 1970, holding power for the next thirteen years until ill health finally obliged him to retire. Chancellor Kreisky has thus far been the only Jew ever to hold supreme office in a German-speaking nation. He achieved remarkable popularity, was respected as an international statesman, and introduced important reforms, yet ultimately his ascendancy barely affected the anti-Jewish feelings in the Austrian population. In the mid-1970s, at the height of his popularity, polls showed that one-third of all Austrians were unequivocally anti-Semitic, and this number did not decline during the next decade. A militant anti-Zionist, Kreisky was also the first European leader in the 1970s to make PLO leader Yasser Arafat *salonfähig,* or politically acceptable, in the West. Later, he would become disillusioned with what he privately called Arafat's "self-destructive activity" and the wave of Palestinian terror attacks on Jewish targets (between 1979 and 1982) in Vienna, Frankfurt, Paris, Brussels, and Rome. However, he chose not to make these criticisms public.[80] Even more difficult to fathom was Kreisky's willingness to court ex-Nazis. He nominated no less than four ministers with "brown" pasts in his first Socialist cabinet of 1970. At the same time, Kreisky deliberately vilified Austrian Nazi hunter Simon Wiesenthal as "a Jewish fascist," and after 1977 he would lash out at Israeli premier Menachem Begin in the most offensive terms.

After 1986, under the Conservative presidency of Kurt Waldheim (a Wehrmacht staff officer in the Balkans during the war) the anti-Semitic trend further increased. Waldheim, a former UN secretary-general, had shamelessly lied about his past. His exposure by the World Jewish Congress (WJC) merely exacerbated and reinforced long-standing Austrian resentment toward world Jewry and influential "East Coast circles," a popular code phrase for New York Jews who had succeeded in placing President Waldheim on the blacklist, thereby preventing his entry to the United States.[81] The Waldheim affair doubtless helped to feed the spectacular rise of populist politician Jörg Haider in the 1990s—a charismatic demagogue who turned his Freedom Party (FPÖ) into the most successful Far Right xenophobic movement in Europe. Having won 27 percent of the vote in the 1999 Austrian national elections, the FPÖ entered the government coalition a few months later. In recent years it has suffered a series of setbacks, though this decline does not necessarily signify a diminution of anti-Semitism or xenophobia in Austria. Indeed, in the summer of 2008 the Far Right achieved its best ever results in postwar Austria, winning close to a third of the national vote.

Haider's radical ethno-nationalism expressed the classic worldview of the populist Right, which is by no means dead in European politics.[82] However, since 2000 the "new" anti-Semitism in western Europe has tended to come from the traditional *victims* of the Far Right—the alienated, uprooted, marginalized, relatively poor immigrants (Arab, Turk, and African) who have settled in Europe over the past thirty years. For example, British polls revealed several years ago that 46 percent of Muslims in the United Kingdom thought Jews were in league with Freemasons to control the media (only 22 percent opposed this view); 53 percent agreed that Jews had "too much influence over the direction of UK foreign policy" (19 percent disagreed); and 37 percent ominously believed Anglo-Jews were "legitimate targets as part of the ongoing struggle for justice in the Middle East." According to the Pew Global Attitudes Project in 2006, 47 percent of British Muslims polled had an unfavorable attitude toward Jews, hostility far greater than that of the general public. In the same survey, 44 percent of German Muslims expressed a hostile view of Jews, against 22 percent of other Germans. French Muslims may be less blatantly prejudiced than their counterparts in Great Britain, but they are still notably more anti-Jewish (28 percent) than the nominally Catholic or secular French majority (13 percent). The Pew survey for 2006 also showed that 60 percent of Muslims in Spain manifested a negative view of Jews, compared to 39 percent of the general population.[83] Spain, it should be emphasized, has good reason to be regarded as one of the most anti-Semitic countries in Europe. In early 2009 three-quarters of all Spaniards evidently believed in the myth of Jewish financial power while also displaying strong anti-Israel prejudices.

Anti-Semitism "from below" has enjoyed remarkable indulgence from an important section of the European media for whom Judeophobia, when exhibited by so-called victims of racism, apparently does not exist.[84] The apologists claim that the "youth from the suburbs" do not have a structured ideology—that they are politically powerless and themselves objects of discrimination. This may well be true, but it hardly proves that they are immune from bigotry, racism, or fanaticism. It does, however, suggest that we are facing a novel phenomenon—an anti-Semitism of the excluded—strongly influenced by Islam, self-segregation, and the fashionable politics of ethno-religious identity.[85] It may be manifested in the everyday language of insult as a spontaneous form of group affirmation; it may express a desire for provocation; it might be no more than a social identity marker, but that does not cancel out its inverted racism. Moreover, in the immigrant milieu, the passage from word to act is likely to be less inhibited than in the majority population. Hence, Islamist anti-Semitism in such countries as France, Belgium, Sweden, and Great Britain tends to be more visceral and violent, recalling some features of black nationalist demagoguery in the United States.[86]

The French case has been particularly aggravated by the wide socioeconomic gap between two rival North African immigrant communities of Jews and Arabs—many of them originally from Algeria. The Algerian Jews arrived nearly three decades earlier and had been, for the most part, French citizens for many years. Their civic equality went back to the Crémieux decree of 1871—a major source of French settler anti-Semitism and Muslim Arab *ressentiment* for the next seventy years. Following Algerian independence in 1962, Jews arriving in France came as part of the "repatriated" European *pied noir* (black foot) population, not as *étrangers* (foreigners) as in the case of most Arabs. The social, economic, and cultural success of the North African Jewish minority in France since the 1960s has been a source of envy for many Arabs. The high level of acceptance of Maghrebian Jews in French society, it should be said, contrasts sharply with the growing suspicion toward Muslims felt by many ordinary French people. Hence, the Jew, as in a mirror reflection, has come to highlight for many underprivileged Muslims their own sense of powerlessness, economic failure, and illegitimacy within French society.[87] There is no easy exit from this complex mixture of social reality, a negative psychology of resentment, and the kind of fundamentalist identity politics that seeks to whip up Muslim rage. The Palestinian intifada that began in September 2000 provided the spark and an alluring mirage for French and other European Muslims of vicarious revenge against the more successful "Jewish other." By adopting the politically correct Palestinian cause and brandishing anti-Zionist or anti-American slogans, marginalized Muslims in the West could seemingly establish common ground with left-wing pacifists opposed to imperialist plots against Iraq, Palestine, and the Third World.[88] In the context of this make-believe political bond, a relatively new anti-Semitic myth (first forged in 1967) would be reinforced—that of the Jews as ferocious conquerors and pitiless racist oppressors of colonized Third World Arabs. From the late 1960s, the criminalization and demonization of Zionism began to gradually fuse together with more traditional images of the sinister Jewish lobby and its allies in America.

• • •

The problem of Islam in Europe has undoubtedly been aggravated by the extraordinary anti-Semitic hysteria that has seized the Arab Middle East during the past decade. In 2002, I sought to summarize what I still believe to be the dominant Arab media image of Jews, as follows:

> The Jews are portrayed in Arab cartoons as demons and murderers, as a hateful, loathsome people to be feared and avoided. They are invariably seen as the origin of all evil and corruption, authors of a dark, unrelenting conspiracy to infiltrate and destroy Muslim society in order to eventually take over the world. . . . Judaism . . . is presented as a sinister and immoral religion, based on cabals and blood rituals, while Zionists [are called] . . . racists or Nazis. The aim is not simply to morally delegitimize Israel as a Jewish State and a national entity in the Middle East but to dehumanize Judaism and the Jewish people as such.[89]

The levels of hostility toward Israel and the Jewish people in the contemporary Arab world are indeed shocking. Even the crudest inventions of Christian and Nazi anti-Semitism have been thoroughly internalized and Islam-icized.[90] These themes (pioneered during the European Middle Ages) include ritual murder; poisoning the wells; fictitious Talmudic quotations that supposedly permit Jews to rob, rape, and slaughter Gentiles; Masonic conspiracy theories; and the conviction that world Jewry is seeking to dominate the world. In this paranoid universe, there are no limits to the Jewish world plot against the Arabs, Islam, and humanity in general. Israel is the "little Satan" controlling America and the West—the source of all corruption. Behind the imperialist or Zionist enemy, there stands the eternal Jew whose depraved evil is "innate and genetic, going back to remote iniquity."[91]

Hitler repeatedly used this notion of innate evil and the belief that Jews are genocidal killers in the 1920s. He would obsessively insist that the "Jewish world enemy" was seeking the destruction of Germany. Hence, he felt justified to mass murder them first.[92] The Islamists, for their part, assert that Israel and world Jewry are determined to extinguish Islam, so they, too, must wipe them out. In the case of Iran and radical Islam, there is every reason *not* to dismiss these criminal threats as fantasies. Though some well-meaning liberals may be loath to take fanatics at their word, failure to do so today could have fatal consequences, as in the late 1930s.[93] By that time, Arab nationalists, the Muslim Brotherhood, and the Palestinian leader Haj Amin al-Husseini had already developed close links and even ideological affinities with the Nazis, which provided the seedbed for contemporary Islamo-fascism. The Muslim Brothers were committed to jihad from their very foundation in 1928, and have remained radically anti-Semitic in outlook for the past eighty years. Equally, the ideologies of Hezbollah and Hamas are viscerally anti-Jewish, embracing conspiracy theories derived from the *Protocols of the Elders of Zion* as well as the Koran.[94]

Many of the major themes in contemporary Arab anti-Semitism were anticipated in the writings of the Egyptian fundamentalist thinker and activist Sayyid Qutb (1906–66), whose own intellectual roots lay in the teachings of the Muslim Brotherhood. In the early 1950s, in a seminal essay titled *Our Struggle with the Jews,* Qutb presented the Middle East conflict as a cosmic and fateful war waged without relief from the time of Muhammad until the present day. As with all fundamentalist literature, the Prophet's "Jewish wars" in Medina and Khaibar were taken as *exemplary*—ending as they did in the expulsion or extermination of the Jewish tribes in seventh-century Arabia. The Koranic attitude toward the Jews and their religion that formed the core of Qutb's ideology was indeed harsh and (with a few exceptions) unremittingly hostile. The Koran deemed the Jews to be arrogant counterfeiters of God's truth, responsible for persecuting and killing the prophets.[95] They had turned into a grotesque caricature of their god-fearing ancestors, the Banu Israel (People of Israel) led by Moses. Indeed, they were alleged to have falsified their own Holy Scriptures to justify crude self-interest and shameless infidelities.[96] The Jews, by rejecting Muhammad and his followers (and conspiring with the Prophet's enemies) had definitively demonstrated their perfidious nature. Worse still, they were perceived as encouraging Muslims to apostatize from the sole true faith.

In order to understand Qutb and his fundamentalist followers, it is important to realize that in their eyes neither Jews nor Christians, though they were defined as Ahl al-Kitab (People of the Book), ever enjoyed equal status with Muslims. The followers of Muhammad, to this day, consider that they alone have received the final and perfect revelation of divine truth through the Koran. They generally accept that prophetic monotheism began with Abraham, but the patriarch is nonetheless regarded as the first Muslim or, in the words of the Koran, as "neither a Jew nor a Christian." The chain of the prophets mentioned in the Koran transmitted the "Islamic truth," not that of Judaism or Christianity, which have always remained imperfect, falsified, and even inauthentic versions of the original monotheism to which Islam alone was heir. However, Muhammad did not conduct a war with the Christians, nor did he clash with them as he did with the Jews of Medina. Henceforth, Jews (and polytheists) came to be seen as "the worst enemies of the Believers." This credo provided the irrevocable foundation for a continuing theological antipathy toward Judaism. Archetypes formed out of this early encounter thirteen hundred years ago have continued to shape Islamic self-identity until the present, deeply influencing negative perceptions of Jews and Judaism.[97] Many centuries ago, it would seem, the dark portrait of Jews as obdurate, disloyal, and moral enemies of Islam was already fixed as a religious dogma. There was a permanently deviant Jewish character whose wicked nature impelled them to malevolently conspire against true Muslim believers. A supreme example of this perfidy lay in Jewish attempts to poison the Prophet.[98] Contemporary fundamentalists see a direct line of continuity between such treacherous Jewish conduct toward the messenger of Allah and the present-day struggle over Palestine. Now, as then, the goal of the Jews is assumed to be the destruction of Islam. Their evil role did not end with Khaibar (the oasis in Arabia where Muhammad defeated them) but has continued until the present as an expression of an eternal Jewish propensity to do violence to others, especially Muslims.

Sayyid Qutb, the most influential Sunni fundamentalist theorist of the twentieth century, was certainly convinced of this evil predisposition and of the pivotal role of the Jews in Islam's civilizational crisis. His hatred of the United States and modern civilization was nourished by the years he spent in America between 1949 and 1951, which turned him against Western decadence and corruption. Imprisoned by Gamal Abdel Nasser three years after his return to Egypt, he was executed in 1966, though not before he had written several seminal works in prison that have remained an inspiration to Islamists around the world.[99] They had a direct influence on those who assassinated Egyptian president Anwar al-Sadat and an indirect one on Ayatollah Khomeini's Shiite revolution that triumphed in Iran in 1979.[100] Qutb gave new vigor to the Islamist doctrine that made the Jews and Zionism a supremely important indicator of the Muslim world's contemporary weakness, its failures, and its moral bankruptcy. For Qutb the lethargy and lost glory of the *umma* (the Muslim nation) had been graphically underscored by the depredations of Western imperialism and its science, technological superiority, and cultural invasiveness. The establishment of Israel (seen as part of the Western imperial project in the Islamic world) was an especially heavy blow to Muslim self-esteem. Israel exemplified the successful revolution of the *dhimmis* (protected peoples)—non-Muslim minorities who were beginning to break out of the institutional straitjacket of social and political discrimination to which they had been subjected for so long within the *dar al-Islam* (abode of Islam).[101]

It must be remembered that, well before 1948, with the rise of modern egalitarian ideas in the Middle East an entire hierarchical conception of the world began to crumble. In the old order, Muslims were always superior to non-Muslims within their own society as surely as men dominated women or ruled as masters over slaves. "In this specific realm of change," wrote Ronald Nettler, the Canadian-born Arabist, twenty years ago, "they [the Muslim authorities] could see signs of the general severity of Islam's breakdown; just as later the Jews' total emancipation from Muslim rule and their establishment of a Jewish State on Muslim lands would signal Islam's total collapse."[102]

The emancipation of Jews in Israel/Palestine from Muslim rule by 1948 was a theological-political problem of the first magnitude. It came to haunt Islamic fundamentalists precisely because of its *symbolic* importance. Muhammad's early victory over the Jews was traditionally seen as a prelude to Islam's impending world conquests and future ascendancy. However, repeated Muslim military defeats by Jews after 1948, the fact of Israel's political independence and its rule over a sizable Muslim population—not to mention the capture of East Jerusalem in 1967—seemed to signal the opposite trend. It was as if Islamic civilization itself was beginning to unravel.[103] The rapidly expanding anti-Jewish literature inspired by the Koran, the hadith, and other Islamic sources must be seen in this historical context. The harshness, hysteria, and apocalyptic tones built upon a systematic satanization of the Jews no less extreme than anything in medieval Christendom or in Nazi propaganda. None other than the rector of al-Azhar University in Cairo (under President Sadat) declared in 1974: "As for those who struggle against the Faithful [the Muslims], they struggle against the elimination of oppression and enmity. They struggle in the way of Satan. Allah commands the Muslims to fight the friends of Satan wherever they may be found. And among Satan's friends—indeed, his best friends in our age—are the Jews."[104]

Such statements are not marginal or unusual in the Arab-Muslim world, they are *mainstream*. They come out of the prestigious al-Azhar University in Cairo; from the government-controlled mosques in Saudi Arabia; from Shiite Iran, Alawite Syria, and Islamist political circles around the world. Such anti-Semitic demonization is commonplace, from the Palestinian Authority to Lebanon, Jordan, and Algeria. The images of Jewish perfidy and malevolence always rely on ancient Islamic stereotypes—the Jews were Muhammad's enemies, rejecters of Allah's truth, tormenters of his prophets, double-dealers, blasphemers, and conspirators against the one true faith.[105] These anti-Jewish archetypes are projected onto the State of Israel and Zionism far more often than is generally assumed. Manichean Islamic images of Jewish falsehood and satanic evil have become pervasive perceptions that shape Arab and Iranian thinking about the Middle East conflict.

Sayyid Qutb was one of the key thinkers to open the floodgates to this religious-based Judeophobia, intimately linked to jihad—the Muslim obligation of holy war against the infidel. Qutb also revived the theme of denouncing avowed Muslims as *kaffir* (unbelievers)—agents of the West, Zionism, and the Jews—when they acted against Islamic law, whether wittingly or unwittingly. Fundamentalists, ever since, have tended to see so-called secular Arab leaders as servants of the Jews (or even as crypto-Jews), especially if the rulers are pro-Western or display any proclivity toward normalizing relations with Israel. Leaders like Sadat who ostensibly went down this road were accused of heresy since, according to the fundamentalist perspective, the "liberating struggle of jihad" can never cease.[106] Anything else is a betrayal of Islam. Qutb's essay *Our Struggle with the Jews* (the title itself suggests a disturbing Islamic echo of *Mein Kampf,* or *My Struggle*) illustrates the point that the Jewish danger to Islam has never been greater, necessitating an all-out mobilization of the Muslim *umma* and its moral rearmament through a return to the pristine Islamic creed. In this seminal text (widely disseminated by the Saudis after 1970, as well as by the Muslim Brotherhood), Qutb insists that "the Jews will not be satisfied until this Religion [that is, Islam] has been destroyed." The Jews are taken as a metaphor and as a symbol of all the corruption and immorality resulting from Western domination; but, more important, they have been and will remain enemies of Islam, from the time of the Prophet until the End of Days. The mundane history of this world merely provides the living exemplars of an eternal truth that had already been revealed in the Koran.

Qutb unequivocally declared that the war with the Jews has not been extinguished for fourteen centuries, and that it still continues "until this moment, its blaze raging in all corners of the earth."[107] At its core was the "Jewish war against Islam," an attack on *al-'aqidah* (its creed) and on fundamental values inseparable from past greatness. According to Qutb, the struggle had to be redefined as a war of religion waged by Judaism (representing defective and corrupted truth) against the final and absolute truth of Allah. Contemporary events were the continuation of a "Jewish-pagan conspiracy" against Muhammad recorded in the Koran; as they had done in the distant past, the Jews still aimed to split the Muslim community through sectarian strife. Fundamentalists for the past fifty years have simply assumed the total enmity of Jews toward Islam, treating it as a permanent reality. Jews, they suggest, have always conspired to subvert and undermine the *umma*. Hence it was only natural that they should have introduced "anti-Islamic" Western ideas (including Communism) into the Middle East.[108] Liberalism, Darwinism, Marxism, psychoanalysis, and, of course, Zionism, have all been branded as "Jewish" toxins.

Except for its Islamic dress, this indictment is in many ways indistinguishable from Hitlerian anti-Semitism. Qutb explained, for example, that the Jews had always incited to civil disturbances, revolutions, and chaos, often using Islamic converts to weaken the faith. Judeo-Christian myths and modern pagan idolatry were among the weapons mobilized in the "Crusader-Zionist war" to destroy Islam. Jewish "subversion" was indeed a never-ending saga of *betrayal*. The "children of Israel" had met Islam's offer of kindness "with the ugliest plot and the most painful treachery, from the first day." In Muhammad's time they had already shown their natural ingratitude, misanthropy, isolationism, and jealousy at the new and definitive revelation of God's word. Hence they had "gathered all the polytheistic forces of the Arabian peninsula against Islam and the Muslims"; they were responsible for the Sunni-Shia schism; they were even behind Turkish leader Kemal Atatürk's abolition of the Muslim caliphate in 1924, seeking wherever possible to sabotage any and every sign of Islamic revival. Three Jewish thinkers—Karl Marx, Sigmund Freud, and Émile Durkheim (Qutb's Saudi editor added the atheist Jean-Paul Sartre as a fourth Jew)—had spearheaded the war on tradition and morality: "Behind the doctrine of atheistic materialism was a 'Jew'; behind the doctrine of animalistic sexuality was a Jew; and behind the destruction of the family and the shattering of sacred relationships in society, . . . was a Jew."[109] From the polytheists in Arabia to the "Hindu idol worshipers" of India, nothing could compare to the ferocity of "the war which the Jews launched against Islam" or "the viciousness of world Zionism which considers Marxism as a virtual branch of (its own activities)."[110] Qutb was nonetheless confident that the satanic subversion of the Jews against Allah's chosen people was doomed to failure as soon as the Muslims would return to the absolute truth of the Koran.

While basing himself predominantly on Islamic sources, Qutb—like other Muslim fundamentalists—borrowed extensively from European Christian traditions of anti-Semitism. In particular, he was influenced by the *Protocols of the Elders of Zion,* with its scenario of a Jewish plot to seize control of the Gentile world. This belief in the fantasies of the *Protocols* is not confined to Qutb and his fundamentalist believers. To this day it remains absolutely mainstream in the Muslim world. A telling illustration came in 1995, with the appearance of the Arabic translation of then Israeli foreign minister Shimon Peres's *The New Middle East* (an idyllic view of future Arab-Israeli peaceful cooperation). The Egyptian blurb justified its publication as follows: "It is precisely Shimon Peres who brings the decisive proof of their [the *Protocols*'] authenticity. His book confirms in so clear a way that it cannot be denied that the *Protocols* were true indeed. Peres's book is the last but one step in the execution of these dangerous designs."[111]

Thus, in Egypt, even the most dovelike visions of peace proposed by Israeli leaders were and are likely to be seen as part of the universal Jewish conspiracy. Especially common are the insidious tales that have filled the Egyptian and Arab media for many years, recounting how Israel sells hormonally altered fruit to kill Arab men's sperm and supplies aphrodisiac chewing gum to women in order to stimulate lust and destroy Muslim morality. Variations on such conspiracy theories in the Islamic world are literally without end. They dwarf in scale anything comparable coming out of the West. In this scurrilous literature, global Zionism and the Jews already hold the world by the throat—controlling its economy, media, and the key political levers of command. Globalization, liberalization, and the drive for democracy are seen as so many devious techniques to drive forward the accelerated modernization of the Middle East in order to serve the cause of Jewish and American domination. At the same time, globalization (in the eyes of its adversaries) further erodes Islamic values and threatens Arab national and cultural identity.

The Jew is often depicted in contemporary Arab discourse as a prime agent of capitalist globalization, controlling American policy. If, fifty years ago, the Jews and Zionism were synonymous with Communist world revolution, today it is so-called neoconservative Jews who are seen as manipulating democracy and secularism in order to bring down the pillars of Islam. At the same time, after 9/11, in order to deflect criticism of Saudi Arabia in the United States for having nurtured fundamentalist terror, Saudi spokesmen did not hesitate to resort to anti-Jewish motifs. As the Saudi minister of defense and aviation, Prince Sultan bin Abdul Aziz, put it in June 2002: "It is enough to see a number of Congressmen wearing a Jewish Yarmulke to explain the allegations against us."[112]

The equating of Jews and Israelis with Nazis is especially popular in the Arab world. The Saudi ambassador to Great Britain, Ghazi al-Qusaibi, in a July 2002 speech to an academic conference at London's University of Westminster called Israel's Operation Defensive Shield "far more severe than anything the Germans did when they occupied Europe in World War II." Literally thousands of such declarations appear in the mainstream Arab media with monotonous regularity. In July 2007, Ahmad Bahgat, a prominent journalist, wrote in the Egyptian government daily *Al-Ahram:* "Israel is acting in a way which we thought is not common anymore. This is the way of Nazism. . . . Israel has learned a lot from the Nazi method, and put the Palestinian people to the test. So far the test has succeeded." This is a relatively mild expression of the rampant Nazi-Zionist equation. Another Egyptian government daily, *Al-Gumhuriya,* never tires of informing its readers that the State of Israel was founded on a Nazi master race ideology while claiming that the Jews invented the Holocaust or use it continually for their material gain and benefit.[113]

The brazenness of this discourse is all the more remarkable given the extent of the real collaboration that existed during the Holocaust era between Nazi Germany and the Arab world. A key figure in this Arab-Nazi collaboration before 1945 was the grand mufti of Jerusalem, Haj Amin al-Husseini, the dominant personality in the Palestinian Arab nationalist movement under the British mandate. His Berlin-based broadcasts between 1941 and 1945 distributed an increasingly deadly message of anti-Semitism to the Arab world that has continued to wreak terrible havoc ever since. In a speech on November 2, 1943, Haj Amin not only stressed the ideological closeness among radical Islam, Arab nationalism, and National Socialism but also emphasized the fact that "most of all they [the Germans] have *definitively* solved the Jewish problem" (my emphasis). That same day, the mufti received a congratulatory telegram from the supreme SS leader Heinrich Himmler, on the occasion of the Balfour Declaration.[114] The telegram specifically reminded him that the Nazi Party had (in Himmler's own words) inscribed on its flag "the extermination of World Jewry" from the very beginning.[115] It was as if the German Nazi leadership through Himmler himself (the organizer of the Final Solution) was symbolically handing over the relay baton of genocidal anti-Semitism to the Arabs just as its own star began to wane.

· · ·

For the past forty years the Palestinians have turned the murder of Jews into a sacred cause under the sign of "national liberation." One striking feature of Palestinian anti-Jewish terrorism that is particularly horrifying and exceeds even Nazi methods was pointed out a few years ago by the historian Michael Oren: "For all the kudos discreetly given SS killers by the regime, Nazi Germany never publicly lionized them, they never plastered their pictures on the streets, or openly encouraged children to emulate them. That kind of adoration for mass murderers can only be found in abundance, among the Palestinians."[116]

Such behavior might seem incomprehensible until one realizes that every stratum of modern Arab society (as well as large chunks of the Muslim world) has been nourished for decades on the myth of Israel's criminality and illegitimacy. One can hardly exaggerate the toxic results of such conditioning. In the following chapters I examine the causes and effects of this culture of hatred in the contemporary Arab-Muslim world—consequences that are potentially no less genocidal than those produced by the rise of Nazism during the interwar period in Europe. My research reveals that paranoid and hysterical anti-Semitism has provided perhaps the deepest substratum underlying the ongoing Middle East crisis, yet it is barely evoked in the mainstream media and simply ignored in most scholarship that relates to the Middle East conflict.[117] The miserable failure to resolve the Palestinian problem is less surprising when one considers the implications of such blindness. Far from being a mere epiphenomenon or marginal offshoot of the Arab-Israeli conflict, this culture of hatred lies at the very core of the Middle East conflict. The terrible social, economic, and cultural regression experienced by much of the Muslim and Arab world is undoubtedly related to the abyss of irrational hatred into which it has been plunged by its blinkered and mediocre leaders.

Although Arab anti-Semitism is by no means a simple function of the conflict with Israel, it has, of course, been influenced by changes in the international and Middle Eastern political configuration. One of the more important shifts occurred after 1967 with the growth of an informal American-Israeli convergence of interests on a scale that had never previously existed. As a consequence, Israel increasingly became a surrogate target for those reluctant to take on the might of the United States but antagonistic to the presence of any Jewish state in the region.[118] Another unsurprising result of the de facto American-Israeli alliance has been a growing convergence in the demonization of both nations. Indeed, there are many striking parallels between contemporary anti-Americanism and anti-Israelism, despite the obvious differences in power, scale, and international influence of the two countries. In the minds of their adversaries, the United States and Israel have come to symbolize in recent years a whole cluster of threats—including globalization, neoliberal capitalist exploitation of the Third World, ethnic intolerance, Judeo-Christian fundamentalism, self-assertive arrogance, technological prowess, and a Rambo-like readiness for military intervention.[119] America, to quote Josef Joffe, publisher of the German newspaper *Die Zeit,* also represents "the great temptress who seduces our children into wolfing down fast food, watching Hollywood violence and buying navel-exposing slut wear. America, in short, is the steamroller of modernity that flattens tradition and leaves behind a few rich winners and many poor losers."[120]

Even worse, the "great temptress" claims to be called by God. Americans, no less than Jews, are perceived as having arrogated to themselves the idea of a "divine mission," while nurturing a self-righteous sense of their own "chosenness" and the belief that they live in "God's Own Country." Like the Jews, Yankees are widely stereotyped as inveterate money grubbers, relentlessly pursuing profits and Mammon while backed up by awesome military power. Such a combination of riches, power, and self-assertiveness is always likely to arouse envy, resentment, and considerable hostility. The transformation of little "David" into mighty "Goliath" has particularly affected Israel's image in the wider world since 1967.

Nevertheless, the themes of anti-Americanism and anti-Semitism long preceded the rise of the United States to superpower status, let alone Israel's Six-Day War conquests, or the settlement of the West Bank and Gaza. These events doubtless exacerbated the problem, but they did not create it. [121] The demonization of America and Israel was nothing new and ultimately reflected preexisting anti-Semitic and anti-Yankee clichés. The fusion of the two mythologies, as Joffe points out, encouraged an old-new version of conspiracy theory:

> Indeed, the United States is an anti-Semitic fantasy come true, *The Protocols of the Elders of Zion* in living color. Don't Jews, their first loyalty to Israel, control the Congress, the Pentagon, the banks, the universities, and the media? This time the conspirator is not "World Jewry," but Israel. Having captured the "hyperpower," Jews *qua* Israelis finally do rule the world. It is Israel as the *Über*-Jew, and America as its slave.[122]

Whether Super Jew really controls the United States or merely acts as its stooge, Israel is still seen by most Arabs as its "agent," "cat's paw," or even its clone. As journalist Polly Toynbee (granddaughter of the notoriously anti-Zionist British historian Arnold J. Toynbee) so delicately put it: "Ugly Israel is the Middle East representative of ugly America."[123] When Israel as the mythical Shylock-in-arms met with Uncle Sam and his Rambo offspring and they merged together into the bulky mass of Bush-Sharon, the conflation was designed to arouse the maximum moral and aesthetic revulsion. Even the briefest acquaintance with current visual forms of anti-Zionism graphically underlines this fact.

Much of the impact of anti-Semitism derives from its uncanny ability to adapt. In modern times, its practitioners have usually known how to link the "Jewish question" with much broader historic movements or processes such as secularization, capitalism, fascism, Communism, Islamic fundamentalism, globalization, and far-reaching cultural or political revolutions. For the anti-Semite, the Jew generally stands for all the disorienting transformations of modernity that he loathes and fears—a factor as true in the Arab world today as it was in late-nineteenth-century Europe and during the "golden age" of interwar fascism. Hence, a central feature of this book will be to explore the various mutations of the abstract and protean Jewish *symbol* where it connects with contemporary social or political crises. One such crisis has been the massive influx of Third World migrants from the ex-colonies to postwar Europe, which has brought with it the seeds of new conflict.[124] European multiculturalism has, thus far, vainly tried to defuse this potential explosion by acquiescing in the kind of "separate development" demanded by more radical Muslim leaders. Great Britain has gone furthest down this road, with the archbishop of Canterbury even prepared to give the sharia (Muslim law) a foothold in the United Kingdom. His colleague, the bishop of Oxford, John Pritchard, publicly supported the Muslim demand that the muezzin be heard throughout Great Britain's major cities—this at a time when Anglican Christianity is not only on the defensive but heading for the margins.

Defenders of multiculturalism seem curiously indifferent to the fact that their policies might actually be encouraging a form of cultural and social apartheid rather than integration. Recent events—especially in Great Britain—have shown that terrorism and anti-Semitism can thrive more easily in self-segregated Muslim enclaves. Not only that, but multicultural-

ism has, if anything, contributed to accelerating Europe's long-term transformation into "Eurabia," with all the resultant loss of a distinctive cultural
identity that that could entail. This outcome is unlikely, in the present international constellation, to benefit Jews, though the results of multiculturalism in Australia, Canada, and the United States have generally been more
positive.[125] In France, however, the multiculturalist cult of *métissage* (hy-
bridity) and the accompanying conceptions of "universal fraternity" have
once more highlighted the latent resentment toward any special Jewish connection with Israel. One consequence has been to heighten traditional
charges of tribalism, racism, and communitarianism made against Jews.[126]

The spread of multiculturalist and anti-globalist concepts in recent
decades has added a new dimension to trends that idealize Palestinian terrorist nationalism while execrating Israel. We already noted the genesis of
this tendency in the late 1960s when Communists and New Leftists adopted
Palestinian national liberation as a progressive cause. The Soviet Union, the
PLO, and the Arab states duly invented the unholy trinity of Zionism =
Racism = Nazism, thereby sowing the seeds of a new anti-Semitism.
The Soviets were the main architects of this delegitimizing strategy, but
sections of the Western left—partly influenced by their own Third World
romanticism—arrived at similar conclusions.[127] Jewish intellectuals antagonistic toward Zionism, from Hannah Arendt and Isaac Deutscher to
Maxime Rodinson and Noam Chomsky, played an important role in encouraging this process. Though not themselves anti-Semites, they helped to
poison the discourse about Israel and Zionism to the point where its pro-
imperialist and even racist image became permanently entrenched. In the
1970s, the leading Jewish anti-Zionist was probably the Socialist chancellor
of Austria, Bruno Kreisky. When it came to his own Jewish identity, the Nazi
Holocaust, or the State of Israel, Kreisky undoubtedly had a blind spot. In
many ways he was the emblematic *Grenzjude* (marginal Jew) aspiring to become the golden goy.[128] In large measure he succeeded, but the price was
high. His compulsive efforts to put the Nazi legacy behind him by encouraging Austrian collective amnesia boomeranged, and his repeated vilification of Israel as a police state and an apartheid society, not to mention his
insults about Jews being *ein mieses Volk* (a wretched people) hardly contributed to the struggle against anti-Semitism. As in many similar cases, a
narcissistic, self-obsessed loathing for Jewishness was wrapped up in a sugar-
coating of humanitarian ethics.

· · ·

Since the Enlightenment, secular leftist Jews have often sought to promote a universalist form of integration that would permit them to jettison their Jewishness as a relic of the medieval ghetto. They either denigrate the Jewish people as a marginal enclave in Western history or treat Zionism as an ugly, decaying branch of Western imperialism.[129] Another method, particularly favored by liberal or Reform Jews, has been to try to play off the "prophetic" tradition in Judaism as being antithetical to Jewish nationalism and the existence of a Jewish state. Since the establishment of Israel (and especially in more recent years), such objections have been given an exaggerated importance in the Western media. This overexposure sits uneasily together with the self-proclaimed halo of "heroic" dissidence assumed by some so-called progressive Jews toward Israel.[130] If this is dissent, it appears to be of the *deluxe* variety. Moreover, it has inflamed some of the ugliest stereotypes about Israel as a bloodthirsty racist state occupying stolen Palestinian land.[131] On the Far Left, such clichés often embrace a conspiracy view of Jewish history that accuses Zionists of manipulating the Holocaust and acting as direct accomplices of Nazism.[132] The Trotskyists have been among the worst offenders, even surpassing the neo-Stalinists in their outpourings of anti-Zionist bile that feeds anti-Semitic myths of Jewish power and perfidy. Jewish Trotskyists, in particular, have been prominent among those who turned Zionism into a symbol of the blackest "imperialist reaction," preventing the coming of the worldwide proletarian revolution. As in the case of early Christianity, the stubborn particularism of the Jews is held responsible for delays or obstruction in the advent of universal redemption.

The same radical Left that foams at the mouth at the very mention of Israel/Palestine has had little difficulty in closing its eyes to the religious and gender apartheid in Islam, the murderous crimes of such Communist leaders as Stalin, Mao, Kim Il Sung, and Pol Pot, not to mention the mass murders in Africa from Idi Amin's Uganda in the 1970s to Rwanda over a decade ago, and Sudan today. While real massacres are ignored, a huge propaganda effort continues to be invested globally in pillorying Israel as a perpetrator of genocide.[133] This far transcends the Left since it also involves the United Nations, the Arab states, the Muslim world, nongovernment organizations, and parts of the Western media who black out Israeli victims of suicide bombers, even as they rationalize Islamist and Palestinian terrorism. To the extent that anti-Semitism is even acknowledged as a problem, its intensity in the Muslim and Arab world is played down or completely ignored. The prevailing concept of anti-Semitism as the exclusive property of the fascist Right, a notion especially popular on the Far Left, seems permanently stuck in a seventy-year-old time warp. No less outdated is the liberal assumption that victims of racist discrimination (including Palestinians, North African Arabs, blacks, and other immigrants) can never be anti-Semitic. This is manifestly contradicted on a daily basis by the evidence of the streets. Hence, the silence on the Left over the popularity of *Mein Kampf* in Arab-owned bookshops of the Muslim diaspora, or the blind eye displayed in such quarters over the dissemination of the *Protocols* at such gatherings as the 2001 UN "antiracism" conference in Durban, South Africa, is less than surprising.[134] "Antiracist" anti-Semitism is obviously a painful topic for the Left.

. . .

It should go without saying that the contemporary flood of defamation with which we shall deal in this study has nothing in common with legitimate criticisms of Israel (or any other state) for its domestic and foreign policies. The focus of this book is not, however, to examine the rights and wrongs of Israeli government policies, let alone the virtues and vices of Israeli society—except insofar as misleading propositions on these matters have provoked an anti-Semitic discourse about "the Jews."[135] No fairminded person, let alone the author of this book, would contest the right of critics to argue that the long-term Israeli occupation of the West Bank and Gaza after 1967 might have been mistaken, counterproductive, or even corrupting in some of its aspects; nor is it anti-Zionist, let alone anti-Semitic, to criticize the building of settlements in the territories or to protest the treatment of Palestinians under military occupation.[136] Criticism of any government is a vital part of the normal cut and thrust of argument within any open, democratic society such as Israel, where such issues are often debated with fierce intensity. On the other hand, the notion that by analyzing and evoking anti-Semitism as a serious international issue, one is trying to silence debate over Israeli policies is simply not serious. That debate has been vehemently conducted for over three decades inside and outside Israel. Its repression would be and is a nonstarter. Moreover, if Jews really controlled the U.S. media or were determined to suppress all criticism of Israel, mediocre works like that of Stephen M. Walt and John J. Mearsheimer on the "Israel lobby" could never become bestsellers and would have sunk without a trace.[137]

This book does not assume that all forms of anti-Zionism are a priori anti-Semitic. There have been principled ideological reasons to oppose Israeli statehood that derived from a tradition of Jewish anti-Zionism that was devoid of any stain of anti-Semitism. For example, there were diverse anti-Zionist currents competing for the allegiance of Jews before the Shoah. They included the Bund (a Jewish proletarian movement especially strong in interwar Poland), classical Reform Judaism, Agudat Yisrael, nationalists, the ultra-Orthodox Haredim of eastern Europe, the Diaspora autonomists, and the liberal "assimilationist" representatives of Western Jewry. They all developed respectable and rational arguments (from their standpoints) against establishing a Jewish state.[138] None of these trends, movements, or ideologies could be accused of the group stigmatization of Jews that generally characterizes anti-Semitism.

It was hardly anti-Semitic for such modern German Jewish philosophers as Hermann Cohen and Franz Rosenzweig to reject the idea that a Jewish nation-state (or even territorial autonomy) was necessary for the survival of Judaism. They objected vigorously to the classical Zionist *shlilat ha-Galut* (negation of the Diaspora), and by the same token they tended to idealize the glories of exile compared to any return to mundane history. Unlike contemporary Jewish anti-Zionists, they did not deny the *national* distinctiveness of the Jewish people and of Judaism. On the contrary, philosophers like Franz Rosenzweig highlighted the "spiritual" and timeless *uniqueness* of Judaism, which they feared might be damaged by political Zionism. Other critics, like the pacifist Brit Shalom faction in Palestine, which included outstanding German-speaking intellectuals such as Martin Buber, Shmuel Hugo Bergmann, Hans Kohn, and Gershom Scholem, and the American Reform rabbi Judah Magnes (the president of the Hebrew University of Jerusalem) favored a binational solution to the Jewish-Arab problem in Palestine. They were sharply critical of mainstream Zionist policy without being specifically anti-Zionist, let alone hostile to Jews. Their philosophical or ethical objections to Zionism must be distinguished from the posturings of self-flagellating Jewish or Israeli "post-Zionist" intellectuals who have embraced a Palestinian narrative. Their bottom line is the dismantling or destruction of the thriving Jewish democratic polity of Israel—a profoundly reactionary idea masquerading as progress.

Contemporary anti-Zionism, whether espoused by Jews or non-Jews, is a very different creature from its pre-state forerunners. All too often it begins to slide into an "antiracist" racism and Holocaust relativism whose main purpose is to delegitimize or even to dehumanize Israel. A good example was British Trotskyist Jim Allen's anti-Zionist Holocaust drama from the mid-1980s, *Perdition,* which was recently restaged by the Scottish Palestine Solidarity Campaign (SPSC). This stricture is equally valid for virulently anti-Zionist Jewish leftists such as Norman Finkelstein who link their violent diatribes against Israel to a highly politicized assault on the use and abuse of the Holocaust. Though not himself a denier, Finkelstein's attack on the so-called Holocaust industry has been grist to the mill of neo-Nazis, anti-Zionists, and anti-Semites around the world. This is no accident. His polemics feed into a gushing torrent of Israel-baiting for which such "high-profile" Jews are like manna from heaven. Similarly, when Israeli post-Zionist academics such as Ilan Pappé mendaciously claim that their country is committing genocide in Gaza, the Zionism = Nazism equation entrenches itself still further.

Jewish anti-Zionist leftists have been especially active on American campuses in accusing Israel of "ethnic cleansing," denying its right to national self-determination and branding its social system as "worse than apartheid." Such views have even infiltrated august institutions like the British parliament. They are often voiced by members of the British Respect Party, led by left-wing MP George Galloway. Anti-Zionism is the glue that holds together this bizarre Islamo-Marxist alliance, which totally rejects Israel's existence in accordance with its more general anti-American and anti-globalist stance. Like the Trotskyists, the misnamed Respect Party has fully embraced the classic Soviet propaganda myth of Nazi-Zionist collaboration. It militantly advocates the boycott of Israel and openly favors the return of *all* Palestinian refugees to the Jewish state in order to dismantle it. Galloway is on record as repeatedly glorifying the "democratic" credentials of Hamas and Hezbollah. The primitive anti-Semitism and Holocaust denial of both of these Islamist terror organizations does not in the least inhibit members of the Respect Party.[139] After all, like so many other left-wing or Islamist groupings, Respect insists that the Jews are not a nation and must therefore disappear as a distinct entity.[140] As for Israel, its dissolution, by violent means if necessary, remains a major revolutionary objective.[141]

It is important to remember that the emergence of anti-Zionism as a distinctive left-wing mode of post-Auschwitz Judeophobia was already apparent more than thirty years ago.[142] By November 1975, with the UN Zionism = Racism resolution, Israel had been turned into the world's favorite whipping boy, the "collective Jew" to be harassed and, if possible, destroyed. This demand was openly articulated under the labels of "anti-imperialism" and "anti-racism" in the anti-Zionist literature of the 1970s, along with absolute negation of any Jewish right to national self-determination. Then, as now, the fact that Arabs outnumbered Israelis by forty to one in population and more than six hundred to one in territory was plainly irrelevant to those who turned apoplectic about the "expansionist" Israeli-Jewish reich—approximately the size of tiny Wales or the state of New Jersey! This orchestrated campaign was led behind the scenes by the then mighty Soviet propaganda apparatus, often coordinated with the radical Arab states, the PLO, and the Third World Nonaligned Movement, which remained influential at the United Nations until the mid-1980s.[143]

Almost immediately after the 1967 Six-Day War, "Zionism" would become a left-wing term of abuse, a propaganda tool for a multitude of Arab Israel-baiters, a form of hate speech inciting violence, intimidation, and terror.[144] This is what prompted the Franco-Italian artist Herbert Pagani to write in 1975:

> Now that the Jews have a homeland, anti-Semitism rises again from its ashes, or better, *our* ashes, and it is called anti-Zionism. Before it was applied to individuals, today it is applied to a nation. Israel is a ghetto, Jerusalem is Warsaw. We are\ no longer besieged by the Germans, but by the Arabs, whose crescent has often been disguised as a sickle to better fool the Left around the world. I, a left-wing Jew, do not care about a Left whose wish is to liberate all mankind at the expense of one minority, because I belong to that minority.[145]

In the past thirty years, this left-wing masquerade has become considerably more toxic, even when anti-Semitism comes nicely wrapped in the radiant and beatific glow of human rights.[146] This is a post-Holocaust Jew hatred with a good conscience because it claims to speak in the name of the

oppressed and the "damned of the earth"—a language also adopted by Ayatollah Khomeini at the very outset of the Iranian Revolution in 1979. It is
unavowed—an "anti-Semitism without anti-Semites"—impeccably "anti-
imperialist" yet fully mobilized, in the Iranian case, to wipe Israel off the
planet or to forcibly remove it elsewhere. As a consequence of this Islamofascist axis (backed by "Islamo-progressive" fellow travelers), the genocidal
perspective has been reopened after sixty years, aiming once more at the
radical uprooting of the Jewish people from its homeland. The focus of
the "new" anti-Semites is disproportionately centered on one tiny spot on
the world's surface—the State of Israel—as if that place were the source of
all discord, dissension, subversion, and terror in the world today. This negationist anti-Zionism that delegitimizes and dehumanizes Israel is not only
Manichean in the philosophical sense, but totalitarian in its political
essence, and *theological* in its insistence that Israel was "born in sin." Its demonological fantasies about the "wickedness" of Israeli Jews have become
obsessive, animated by the conspirational anti-Semitism embodied in the
Protocols of the Elders of Zion—currently so popular in the Arab world.[147]

•   •   •

Anti-Zionism has never been completely identical to anti-Semitism, but
some thirty years ago it began to fully crystallize as its offspring and heir. At
times it even seems like its Siamese twin. Today it exerts the same mesmeric,
hypnotic, and mysterious power as anti-Semitism did in the 1930s and
1940s—almost as if it were the most compelling political ideology left in an
increasingly disoriented and morally bankrupt world.[148] As the chief rabbi
of Great Britain, Sir Jonathan Sacks, pithily put it a few years ago: "German
fascism came and went. Soviet Communism came and went. Anti-
Semitism came and stayed."[149] The persistence of this sickness does not
mean that anti-Semitism has remained static or unchanging. Today its
dominant forms are political, ideological, and eschatological, rather than
being racial-biological or rooted in traditional Christian theology. Its focus
is on the State of Israel, which is relentlessly stigmatized while crocodile
tears are shed over the dead Holocaust "victims."[150] This mutation began
almost immediately after World War II, attaining new heights during the
heyday of the Soviet-Arab alliance between 1967 and 1982. Holocaust inversion (turning Jews into Nazis and mythologizing Palestinians as the real victims of genocide) greatly intensified during those years. A more popular

version of the same discourse has by now thoroughly infiltrated the West, reinforcing the overt or covert wish for the extinction of Israel.[151] Like its predecessors, this discourse is based on the assumption that the Jews are a "phantom people" who have no right to a state of their own. It turns the existence of Israel into a stain on mankind, an illegitimate and bastard creation. While the Muslim adversaries of the Jewish state prefer to use Islamic language (based on theocratic principles), more liberal anti-Zionists in the West often mask their hostility by a highly selective humanitarianism that sees only Palestinian victims as worthy of their compassion.[152] The Muslim fundamentalist version of this ideology is in many respects more honest and straightforward than that of its secularized equivalents. Islamists routinely describe the triplet Jews/Zionism/Israel as a "cancer" and call for the physical "eradication" of the Jewish state by violent means. This is an unmistakable return to the annihilationist Nazi language of the late 1930s and therefore potentially embarrassing to those who advocate the politics of appeasement. The long veil of silence drawn over the subject was recently ripped apart by the exploding hatred and rage in the West over Israel's Gaza incursion of January 2009.

Anti-Semitic expressions are, however, omnipresent in the repetitive litany of incitement and lies routinely told about Jews that fill the pages of state-controlled media in the Middle East. This literature is full of sinister tales about Israeli and Jewish plots to crush the Arabs, humiliate Muslims, and take over the world. The crudest conspiracy theories about the Jews dominate this discourse to an almost unimaginable degree. The vilest anti-Semitic slander enjoys total freedom of expression in societies that are fundamentally undemocratic and authoritarian, and normally exercise the strictest vigilance over any opinions that might be dangerous or undesirable for the regime. Evidently anti-Semitism and hatred of Israel do not fall into this taboo category. On the contrary, such opinions offer a welcome and probably invaluable relief for most Arab and Muslim regimes—a trustworthy method to redirect mass discontent away from their own failings.

In the Muslim Arab world of today, demonization of Jews has been completely divorced from any empirical or lived reality. After 1945, the nearly one million Jews still present in the Arab Middle East were gradually intimidated and expropriated, and in many cases had to flee for their lives. The expulsion or flights of these Jewish communities did not, however, reduce the hatred of Jews, which became more and more palpable. Since 1948, this underlying hostility has been systematically nourished by Arab regimes and (with even greater ferocity) by the Islamic movements. Six decades of incitement have provided a bedrock both for Holocaust denial and the scarcely concealed desire to perpetrate a new genocide. Though this inflammatory hatred has been shaped by significant medieval Christian motifs, these borrowings should not distract attention from the more ancient Islamic roots of the phenomenon or the *dhimmi* status of the Jews. Modern Arab or Muslim anti-Semitism, unlike its European models, is religious *and* political at the same time. The premise of the equality of non-Muslims with Muslims contravenes the core of its culture. Jewish auto-emancipation in the shape of Zionism and an independent Jewish polity in the land of the Bible is anathema because it offends fundamental discriminatory principles that remain normative in the "abode of Islam."[153]

The Arab and Muslim anti-Semitism analyzed in this book clearly has a different history, order of priorities, and background from that which was prevalent in Europe, despite the many convergences that have taken place during the past century. Without a doubt, the struggle against Israel has played a more central role in Arab narratives.[154] Anti-Semitism was, for example, massively encouraged by Middle Eastern governments after 1948 and has been enthusiastically spread by local Arab political and literary elites. The racial factor has perhaps been less evident than in Europe, but Arab racism is a reality that influences the systematic distortion of Jewish history and culture. Terms like "world Jewry" and "world Zionism" have been used interchangeably for decades in a pejorative manner. Jewish characteristics are uniformly vilified. The Jews of antiquity are anachronistically referred to by Muslim intellectuals, writers, and propagandists as "Zionists" to emphasize their negative traits. The imagined depravity of the Jews is grafted onto the negative perception of Israel and vice versa in a vicious circle of self-reinforcing and self-fulfilling prophecies. Jewish perfidy is not a by-product of Israeli actions or behavior but is presented as a *permanent* quality that has existed since the dawn of Islamic history—its contours and characteristics fixed by the Koran itself.

In recent decades, Middle Eastern anti-Semitism has become unmistakably "Islamicized" with all the fateful consequences of becoming integrated into a "holy war." The harsh anti-Judaism present in the Koran has facilitated this shift, enabling Islamists to claim that their hostility to the Jews has a firm anchorage in religious tradition. At the same time, the current Islamist construction of "the Jew" clearly resembles a mythical monster wholly detached from empirical reality—it is an unequivocal image of the *total enemy.* As in its most extreme European antecedents, the Jew has been turned into the incarnation of darkness and evil, a symbol of decay, the personification of corruption, and the sworn enemy of *umma.* This culture of anti-Jewish hatred permeates the public communication systems across the Muslim world from Algiers to Cairo and Damascus, from Khartoum to Tehran, from Gaza city to Karachi.[155]

The failed state of Pakistan, a country of 150 million inhabitants (98 percent Muslim) with no Jews, is an excellent example of Islamic preoccupation with Jewish iniquity. Here is the description of Michael Kamber, the *Village Voice* correspondent in Pakistan, reporting from a land "where anti-Semitism flows as easily as water." He wrote these lines in 2002, not long after the gruesome filmed beheading of the American Jewish journalist Daniel Pearl by al-Qaeda members in Karachi:

> In interviews I conducted while I was there, government officials would occasionally veer off into long diatribes about the Jews; fundamentalist religious leaders, who educate hundreds of thousands of children in the country's *madrassas,* spoke of little else. In Islamabad . . . an elderly mullah responsible for the education of hundreds of youngsters said, "To me [the bombing of the World Trade Center] seems the design of the Jewish lobby. The Jewish lobby wants to pit Islam against Christianity."[156]

In Pakistan, three-quarters of the populace are illiterate. The uneducated masses—lacking any contact with real Jews or the requisite tools for critical thinking—tend to follow the lead of the religious and political authorities. Blaming the Jews and America for all the world's evils (and the deficiencies of their own society) is not only normal but an essential element in their reality. Hence the ease with which conspiracy theories about the Zionist role in the 9/11 attacks could swiftly spread. The Lahore-based *Jihad Times* and other Pakistani media compulsively recycled the legend that around four thousand Israelis and Jews working in the World Trade Center had received a secret directive from the Mossad *not* to report for duty on September 11, 2001. Interviewed three days later, Major General Hamid Gul (former head of Pakistani intelligence) was no less convinced that there had been a conspiracy: "I tell you it was a coup [attempt] and I can't say for sure who was behind it, but it's the Israelis who are creating so much misery in the world. The Israelis don't want to see any power in Washington unless it's subservient to their interests and President Bush has not been subservient."[157]

A month later, according to Pakistani opinion polls, more than two-thirds of those surveyed agreed it was possible that Jews had been forewarned not to go to work on September 11. Millions of Pakistani Muslims evidently believed that world Zionism was behind the slaughter, that Jews controlled the media treatment of 9/11, and that they had dictated the "vilification" campaign against Muslims. Seven years later, at the end of November 2008, it was Pakistani jihadists who carried out a terrorist slaughter in India's financial capital, Mumbai—during which nearly two hundred innocent victims were murdered and three hundred persons wounded. The carnage was motivated by supremacist Islamist doctrine and driven by fundamentalist hatred for Hindus, Jews, Americans, British, and non-Muslims in general. Lashkar-e-Toiba, the group that planned the operation, is primarily concerned with liberating Indian Kashmir, though it shares al-Qaeda's goal of establishing a global Islamic caliphate. Yet, it deliberately chose to target a small group of Orthodox Jews in Chabad House, a tiny drop in the ocean of Mumbai's fifteen million inhabitants. Not only that, but the reports of the Indian medical investigation revealed that the Jewish victims were singled out for particularly brutal torture. The Western media reporting from Mumbai characteristically played down the ideological, Islamic, and anti-Semitic colouring of the attacks.

No less sobering is the fact that oil-rich Saudi Arabia, bursting with petrodollars and willing to spend billions to spread its fundamentalist Wahhabite version of Islam, has long been a major source and a leading exporter of the crudest anti-Semitism. An interesting light on such totalitarian indoctrination was provided by the Somali-born former Dutch MP Ayaan Hirsi Ali in an autobiographical piece for the *International Herald Tribune* published in December 2006.

> Growing up as a child in Saudi Arabia, I remember my teachers, my mom and our neighbors telling us practically on a daily basis that Jews were evil, the sworn enemies of Muslims whose only goal was to destroy Islam. We were never informed about the Holocaust. Later in Kenya, as a teenager, when Saudi and other Gulf philanthropy reached us in Africa, I remember that the building of mosques and donations to hospitals and

the poor went hand in hand with the cursing of Jews. Jews were said to be responsible for the deaths of babies, epidemics like AIDS, for the cause of wars. They were greedy and would do absolutely anything to kill us Muslims. And if we ever wanted to know peace and stability we would have to destroy them before they would wipe us out.[158]

Until very recently, it was comparatively rare for such revelations to appear in the Western press. More commonly, the Western media would treat a single skinhead attack on a synagogue or the desecration of a local Jewish cemetery in Europe as more newsworthy than the frenzied, paranoid Jew hatred of the Arab world. This may be a typically European reflex or a symptom of patronizing indifference to Arab views, but it often leads to a grave distortion of reality. One cause and consequence of this distortion is the ignorance in the West about the fanatical indoctrination in Palestinian society, manifested through political rallies, summer camps, the press, TV, the mosques, madrassas, and schools. This culture of hatred is directed against Jews, Christians, and the West as a whole, yet it is scarcely reported on in any depth. The jihadist indoctrination that engendered the suicide bombers in the first place and the escalating extremism that now plagues the Arab-Muslim world and has infected Islam's Western diaspora is treated as a sideshow. Yet, in Great Britain, for example, where there is no Israeli-style "occupation," an identical Islamist poisoning of young minds produced British-educated jihadis (many with family roots in Pakistan) ready to blow up their fellow British citizens in the name of a worldwide jihad. Violent Islamism has become the Frankenstein monster that today threatens not only the West but Asia, Africa, and millions of Muslims themselves, from Casablanca to Riyadh, from Islamabad to Baghdad, where the intra-Muslim Sunni-Shiite slaughter has already exacted a terrible toll. Indeed, the jihadists have thus far succeeded in killing far more Muslims than Jews or Christians. What begins with the Jews never ends with them.

· · ·

One of the many symptoms of the neglect of Muslim and Arab anti-Semitism can be seen in the relative thinness of scholarship on the subject. For example, there has been no lack of detailed studies of the *Protocols* in Europe, Russia, and the Americas, but its reception in the Arab world has barely been touched upon, even though the first translations into Arabic date from the mid-1920s.[159] Today, the *Protocols* reach an Arabic-speaking mass audience of hundreds of millions through popular television series, sermons, the press, and the Internet. Regrettably, Israel itself has done comparatively little to stem the tide of Arab and Muslim anti-Semitism over the years. Yehoshafat Harkabi, the first Israeli scholar to seriously investigate the topic in the mid-1960s, encountered considerable hostility, denial, and even protests within the Jewish state for fear that his research could provide an excuse for "hawkish" Israeli attitudes toward the Arabs. However, as Harkabi himself pointed out, Israel's extremists, no less than the moderates, "tried to paint the Arab position as more moderate than it was; Arab radicalism upset their argument that the Arabs, in the end, will accept Israel's conquests."[160] The dovish Israeli tendency to gloss over Arab-Muslim anti-Semitism has continued in some circles, despite the massive evidence of its ravages. This is not only intellectually dishonest, but it is also clouded by politically wishful thinking that offends the vital need to form a truthful picture of reality. Its only achievement is to encourage Israeli and Jewish self-deception while blocking the incentive for Arab self-criticism. Twenty years ago Harkabi himself posed a pertinent question: "How could the world be expected to be impressed or repelled by anti-Semitism if the Israeli public remained unimpressed? How could one expect the world press to deal with it or decry it if the Israeli press dealt with it only perfunctorily?"[161]

This syndrome has begun to change in recent years, accelerated by the Iranian threat, the second Palestinian intifada, the aggressiveness of Hezbollah, the rise of "Hamastan," and the return of al-Qaeda and the Taliban. The sheer viciousness of Muslim Jew hatred is a moral scandal that cannot forever be covered up by well-meaning liberals, cynical opportunists, or misguided Israelis. The Islamist strain of anti-Semitism is, after all, far more dominant than it was thirty years ago and inextricably tied to jihad; the link to anti-Americanism has also become much more pronounced. Iran's imminent nuclearization and Mahmond Ahmadinejad's threats against Israel have added a stark existential dimension exacerbated by Iranian Holocaust denial, growing Shiite messianism, and the export of a revolutionary form of Islamist-populist anti-Semitism. Moreover, the growth of a large Muslim diaspora in the West—influenced by Islamic fundamentalism and jihadism—has provided yet another dangerous ingredient to an already toxic phenomenon. Islamist Judeophobia, whether it fuses with Marxism, right-wing nationalist ideology, or medieval Christian dogmas, is liable to produce more and more combustible forms of hatred. At the same time, the virulence of the phenomenon also reflects growing levels of mass discontent, frustration, rage, and powerlessness within the Arab world that are all too easily channeled into anti-Jewish directions.

The content of the violent sermons in the mosques of Palestine, Egypt, Saudi Arabia, and Iran that slander Jews and Christians has barely changed over the past forty years. There is still the same satanization of the Jews as the evil "other," a race apart—depicted as diabolical conspirators and as a "cancerous tumor" imported by the West—which must be totally excised. There is still the same linkage of Jews with drugs, pornography, disease (AIDS is a more recent addition to the litany), and financial corruption. Apart from the amplification and more rapid dissemination of such libels, what is relatively new is the connection between anti-Jewish demonization and apocalyptic visions of an Islamic caliphate that will come to rule the entire world. In the contemporary Iranian version of the apocalypse, the emphasis is on the coming of *Emam-e Zamari* (the Lord of Time) or the Shiite "Messiah." The battle against the Jews has metamorphosed into an integral part of this eschatological perspective in the eyes of the present clerical and lay leadership in Iran, especially in the worldview of President Ahmadinejad. As the personification of evil, Jews have come to represent (as they did in the medieval legends of the Antichrist) the diabolical forces of corruption that must be vanquished in order to establish God's kingdom on earth. Since Jews are purportedly engaged in a global conspiracy to rule the world, this makes them a major target.[162] Moreover, Ayatollah Khomeini's successful revolution in 1979 subsequently gave a lease of new life to the messianic belief that Shiite Muslims under Iranian leadership were destined not only to implement the final reckoning with the Jews but also to conquer the world for Allah and Islam. This belief is a major motivating force behind President Ahmadinejad's apocalyptic politics.

Since 2000, Sunni Muslim fundamentalist clerics and politicians have also been pursuing a no less radical and murderous ideology of hate in which hallucinatory visions of jihad, anti-Semitism, and apocalypse intermingle. The Hamas Charter and its proclamations about implementing Allah's promise and annihilating the Jews are as genocidal in their implications as the rhetoric of the current Iranian leadership. This language of mass murder is shared by virtually all the Islamist political movements that seek to reshape the present world order, including al-Qaeda. For example, at the center of Osama bin Laden's universe is the radical nihilist teaching that the purpose of life is to seek death; that all the comforts of this world must be voluntarily surrendered in order to spread the faith through martyrdom and eternal battle against the *Kaffir*. Speaking of bin Laden's credo, the veteran Israeli commentator on Arab affairs Ehud Ya'ari observed: "A new form of Islamic fascism is spreading. It is a cult of death; an addiction to destruction and revenge; a whole culture that promises 'to paint the world (blood) red,' as one of the Bin Ladenist anthems that can be downloaded from the Internet goes, or 'to crush and kill,' in the words of another."[163]

This revolutionary nihilism, the joy in destruction for its own sake, and the pseudo-Nietzschean accents are indeed reminiscent of Nazism. There are other parallels, too. Like their twentieth-century totalitarian predecessors, the Bin Ladenists believe that they possess the absolute truth, immune to all refutation or criticism; they, too, loathe modernity and the West yet borrow its technology to better destroy it. Their utopia, like that of the Nazis and Communists, cannot be established without force and terror. No less than Hitler or Stalin, they fervently believe in the Jewish conspiracy and regard global American capitalism as their key enemy. One can, of course, also find differences. Unlike the secular religions of the twentieth century, political Islam has drawn its inspiration "from an apocalyptic vision rooted in religious radicalism." Al-Qaeda emerged in a global political culture "in which elements of Leftist anti-globalization discourse and reruns of fascist and Nazi visions of Jewish conspiracies merge with religious passions."[164]

Bin Laden's language, like that of Khomeini, Hassan Nasrallah, and Ahmadinejad, sometimes overlaps with Third World radicalism; yet, on matters relating to death, suicide, and rationality, the rhetoric seems closer to the Nazi worldview or to the fascist ethos than to the Communist tradition. The jihadi style of terrorism practiced by all the Islamist movements is consistent in their preference for apocalypse over all discussion and debate. It flows logically from their belief in *absolute* truths that not only provide ideological rationalizations but even set out a religious *obligation* to murder the innocent. This is terrorism *and* anti-Semitism with a "clean conscience." In the case of the Jewish state, such actions have the added halo of resisting the "intolerable"—namely any recognition of Israel's legitimate existence as a sovereign nation in the Middle East. As the hysterical response to the conflict in Gaza during January 2009 revealed, there are growing numbers of Westerners ready not only to appease the jihadists but even to chant "We are all Hamas now!"

Terrorist exultation over violence, death, and destruction has been a key feature of Islamofascism from the outset and is intimately connected to the "annihilationist" character of jihadi anti-Semitism. A similarly nihilist syndrome existed in European fascism from 1919 to the early 1940s, especially when it was driven by the myth of a global Jewish conspiracy. Moreover, as in the early 1940s, the United States is often presented in demonic terms as the spearhead of what Bin Laden has labeled the "Zionist-Crusader alliance." Jew hatred in the guise of conspiracy theory serves the Islamists as the cement for their all-out assault on Western liberalism, capitalism, modernity, secularism, and the very idea of female emancipation. Indeed, on the status of women, the attitudes of Islamic fundamentalists are in many ways far more reactionary and regressive than those of European fascists and Soviet Communists.[165] Since Muslims represent about one-fifth of the world's population, the impact of such misogyny is as worrying as the ominous record of Muslim bellicosity in recent decades.

Since the early 1980s, to quote the recently deceased political scientist Samuel Huntington, Muslims have been "far more involved in intergroup violence than the people of any other civilization." Whether one agrees with the "clash of civilizations" thesis is wholly irrelevant to the fact that wars between Muslims and non-Muslims, as well as conflicts within the Islamic world during the past two decades, have been far more numerous than those in any other civilization. The current worst case is the genocidal war being waged in the Sudan by an Arab Muslim fundamentalist regime (and the militias it supports) against the black peoples of the south (Christians, animists, and Muslims). This horror story has already resulted in hundreds of thousands of deaths. Then there are the huge number of dead on both sides produced by the intra-Muslim Iran-Iraq War of the 1980s. The casualties during eight years of this bloody conflict totally dwarfed the number of victims in *all* Arab-Israeli confrontations since 1948.

Referring to these and other examples, Huntington observed in the 1990s that "two-thirds to three-quarters of intercivilizational wars were between Muslims and non-Muslims." This is a stunning record of aggressiveness that speaks for itself, overshadowing by a wide margin the resort to violence by Western countries, led by the United States.[166] Muslims against Hindus in

Kashmir, India, and Pakistan; Russians versus Chechens, Armenians, and Turks; Muslims versus Christian Orthodox in the Balkans; Sinhalese against Tamils in Sri Lanka; and Arab Muslims against black Christians across Africa are only a few of the more obvious examples.[167] In examining the virulent anti-Semitism of the contemporary Muslim world, one cannot ignore this more general propensity to violence nor the radically dysfunctional nature of so many Muslim societies confronted with the cultural and political challenges of globalization. Islam has remained a religion of the sword, prizing military virtues, expanding primarily through conquest and holy war—from the deserts of Arabia outward to the rest of the Middle East, central and western Asia, the Balkans, and across the African continent. Except for Sufism, the concept of nonviolence has virtually no place in its doctrine or practice. To this day Muslims continue to draw a sharp line between *dar al-Islam* (the abode of Islam) where peace alone can reign under Muslim law and *dar al-harb* (the abode of war)—the realm of non-Muslims that have yet to be brought to the true faith—if necessary by the sword.

• • •

Islamic anti-Semitism is a particularly dangerous and revealing symptom of anti-Westernism and the turmoil in the Muslim world today. Israel and the Jewish people find themselves caught in a particularly exposed position in this clash between the West (led by America) and a dislocated Islamic civilization in search of its own identity. The revival of religion ("the revenge of God," as it has been called) as the basis for cultural identity and transnational commitment has been especially extreme within the Islamic world as a result of the delayed impact of economic modernization, political stagnation, and the absence of democratic social change. Israel's victories over the Arabs, its relative prosperity and Westernization, and its de facto American alliance have coincided with this cultural crisis, with a dramatic demographic explosion in the Muslim world and anguish over the destiny of Islam. The rage of fundamentalist Muslims has been further exacerbated by the threat that they feel from the advances made by secularization.[168] In this context, the militant Islamic revival might best be seen as simultaneously aggressive and defensive—aspiring to global rule yet full of paranoid anxieties about the possible extinction of Islam. The intolerant fury and drive to annihilate the Jewish or the infidel other thrives on such fears and relentless indoctrination toward sacrificial death, inspired by a messianic reading of Islam. The group psychology behind such hatred is not without its analogies to Nazism.

. . .

The annihilation of Israel as an Islamic "commandment" reflects not only anti-Semitism but the global missionary zeal of a revitalized Islamism and its insatiable desire for revenge against the West. The combination of such an ideology with the abundance of petrodollars, the prevalence of authoritarian regimes, illiteracy, underdevelopment, and a clear propensity to terrorism makes radical Islam a potentially deadly threat to world peace. Moreover, the totalitarian ideology of political Islam is no mere megalomaniac fantasy of marginalized fanatics.[169] Anti-Semitism and the destruction of Israel are integral to its broader aims and the agenda of global jihad. Moreover, the expectation that the Jewish state can be wiped out extends far beyond fundamentalist radicals and jihadi terrorists. This macabre message and design is firmly anchored in mainstream Islam. The contemporary manifestations of anti-Semitism, even when they originate in more "moderate" Cairo, Riyadh, Beirut, or Amman, are as venomous as anything that emanates from Tehran, Damascus, Gaza, or from the ideologues of al-Qaeda. When it comes to Muslim Jew hatred, the demonization is almost *universal*. Certainly there are distinctions to be made between Sunni and Shiite doctrines or between radicals and conservatives in contemporary Islam, but anti-Jewishness mostly forms part of the common ground. It is no less axiomatic for true believers than the doctrine of jihad and the need to subordinate non-Muslims to Muslims and women to men; no less "normal" than enmity toward the infidel West. Indeed, these assumptions are all part of the same interlocking system of discrimination and oppression allegedly sanctioned by Islam in the name of the Koran, the sharia, and the *dhimma*.

The millenarian jihad advocated by the Bin Ladenists (and other radical Islamists) that promotes a universal Islamic empire as its ultimate goal is by no means a marginal item existing only on the extremist fringe of Islam. There are millions of Muslims who share these utopian dreams. There is a whole army of clerics, scholars, intellectuals, and journalists who support the fundamentalist credo and disseminate anti-Semitic hate speech.[170] Those who believe in "apocalypse now" are especially likely to support the *eradication* of Judaism (as a mortal enemy of the one true faith) and the idea of Jews as the servants of Satan. In contrast to the transformation of Catholic attitudes toward Jewry during the past forty years or the changes in Protestant Christian millennial theology, which have moved in a far more philo-Semitic and philo-Zionist direction than ever before, the movement on the Islamist side has been exactly the reverse. Muslim monotheist triumphalism is unabashedly imperialist—eagerly determined to reestablish the humiliated, inferior status of premodern Islamic Jews and Christians as *dhimmis,* or protected people, subject to Muslim control. Each lost war with Israel since the *naqba* (catastrophe) of 1948 has further reinforced the obsession with restoring the honor, superior status, and lost glories of the Arab world.[171] The frustration engendered by repeated defeats at the hands of the despised *dhimmi* nation of Israel has turned to uncontrollable rage at the Jews, America, the West, and "secular" Arab rulers. The Jews, in particular, are perceived as Satan's agents in a cosmic drama, in which the world is (to paraphrase Shakespeare's *Hamlet*) radically "out of joint." This disorder can be put right only by a general slaughter of Jews, Christians, and "pagan" nonbelievers. Such a grim scenario cannot be disguised by platitudinous mantras about Islam as a "religion of peace"—propagated by the champions of political correctness in the West.

Apocalyptic anti-Semitism has grown dramatically since 2000 in the Muslim world. Hence it is a central theme in the concluding chapters of this book. At one time a major feature of medieval Christianity, it has been annexed by the Islamists and other Muslims convinced that the "evil Jews" are moving history forward to its climax. The Elders of Zion are allegedly preparing (with the help of the Freemasons and their other agents) new disasters for humanity. The lies and deceptions of this "hidden enemy" (World Jewry/Israel/the Zionists) know no bounds.[172] They have already subjugated the West as well as the Middle East through their financial power and satanic trickery. They represent a cultural and ideological menace as well as an economic and military challenge to the worldwide Islamic community— a dire threat to its whole value system. Moreover, since 1967 the Jews have also taken full control of Al-Quds (Jerusalem), the apocalyptic capital of Islam from which—according to some accounts—the Mahdi (or Muslim Messiah) will eventually rule. The Zionist "usurpation" of Al-Quds is particularly highlighted in Iranian propaganda, but it resonates no less strongly throughout the Sunni Arab world. The centrality of Jerusalem—*borrowed* from the Jewish and Christian traditions—has become more fundamental than ever before to contemporary Islamic messianic beliefs. Equally compelling is the notion of a *final battle* in which the Jews (envisioned as the Antichrist) will be defeated and wiped out. According to Muslim apocalyptic belief, the end of the world and universal human liberation cannot occur unless Israel is eradicated and replaced by an Islamic Palestine.[173]

As we have seen, it is highly significant that Islamic anti-Semitism has enthusiastically embraced the *Protocols* as the most authoritative road map for deciphering a world in chaos dominated by the Jews and their demonic activities. No exception is made for Judaism—"the very creed of Satan"—which is deemed to reflect the fundamentally corrupt and depraved nature of the Jewish people from antiquity to the present. Every plague under the sun is attributed by Islamic Judeophobes to the wicked machinations of the Jews and world Zionism. It is as if the Islamists had discovered how to distill together in a single poisonous witches' brew all the toxic ingredients bequeathed by the residues of pagan, Christian, nationalist, socialist, and Nazi anti-Semitism. Even the most paranoid anti-Semites in the West—except for the Nazis—would have had great difficulty in equaling the pathological levels of paranoid delusion, delirium, and raw hatred that echo from the ever-expanding corpus of writings and speeches consulted in researching this book. The roots and sources of these conspiracy theories can be found in Muslim traditions of anti-Judaism and have been continuously inflamed by the importation of Western anti-Semitic toxins during the past hundred years.

Holocaust denial is one of the more recent of these imports. The most notorious Muslim Holocaust denier today is President Mahmoud Ahmadinejad of Iran, who has repeatedly quoted Ayatollah Khomeini's demand that Israel should be "wiped out from the map."[174] In October 2005 he promised protesting Iranian students that they would "soon experience a world without the United States and Zionism"; he added that "anybody who recognizes Israel will burn in the fire of the Islamic nation's fury."[175] In December 2006, Ahmadinejad again predicted (to great applause) that the Zionist entity would be "wiped out," just as the Soviet Union had collapsed. These words were spoken while addressing delegates at the Iranian-sponsored Holocaust denial conference in Tehran. Several times during this speech, he referred to the Holocaust as a "myth" used to impose the State of Israel on the Arab world.[176] His words were strongly echoed by David

Duke, a rabid American anti-Semite and former Ku Klux Klan leader. Duke was one of sixty-seven "researchers" from around the world invited to this international conference organized by the Iranians in the name of "academic freedom."

Throughout 2007, Ahmadinejad continued in a similar vein, combining prophecies of imminent doom for the Jewish state with free-floating Holocaust denials. As precedents for Israel's demise, he pointed to the disappearance of the shah's regime in 1979, to the collapse of the Soviet Union after 1991, and to the fall of Saddam Hussein in 2003. Three sworn enemies of Iranian Shiite Islam had met their downfall in a succession of cataclysmic events within living memory. Why not Israel? From the ideological standpoint of the Iranian leadership, the vanishing of the Zionist regime, or its imminent collapse would hugely enhance Iranian power and prestige, while being presented to the non-Muslim world as a *liberation* for all mankind. It would not only "solve" the "Palestinian question" but also herald a new dawn for Islam. In February 2008, the Iranian president and other top leaders referred, yet again, to Israel's imminent destruction. Ahmadinejad even seemed to mimic Hitler's zoological anti-Semitism when he referred to the "Zionist entity" as a "filthy microbe."[177]

It is no accident that President Ahmadinejad has so assiduously denied the mass murder of European Jewry while constantly prophesying and seeking to expedite the ruin of the Jewish state. His evil words, wrapped in mystical visions of the end days, fall on fertile terrain in an Arab-Muslim world increasingly attuned in recent decades to fundamentalist intoxication, apocalyptic formulas, hatred of America and Israel, rage, frustration, and bellicose rhetoric. This should be particularly alarming to anyone familiar with the bimillennial history of anti-Semitism. Throughout their age-old sojourn in the Diaspora, Jews have long served as a reliable barometer for the sickness or health of various host societies. All too often the non-Jewish majority and their rulers have succumbed to the temptation of scapegoating a vulnerable minority that had no physical means of self-defense. For the poor and underprivileged, the Jew was an easy target for opprobrium as a result of usury and church teachings. In Christian (and then Muslim) theology, Jews and Judaism became the perennial symbol of secret powers and dark forces that could threaten the triumph of their dogmatic and universalist creeds. In the modern era, the Jew became Antichrist,

Satan, and master conspirator rolled into one—a primary obstacle to universal redemption. In its secularized, neo-pagan, and hyper-radical form, this credo would be incorporated by Nazism. The poisoned legacy has now been passed on to the warriors of the Muslim apocalypse. In the contemporary jihadi scenario the end of Jewry is irrevocably connected with the demise of America and the decline of the West.

ONE

From Deicide to Genocide

There has been no hatred in Western Christian civilization more persistent and enduring than that directed against the Jews. Though the form and timing that outbursts of anti-Jewish persecution have taken throughout the ages have varied, the basic patterns of prejudice have remained remarkably consistent.[1] Particularly striking is the deeply irrational and counterfactual character of most accusations that have been leveled against the Jewish people over the past two thousand years.[2] As noted in the introduction, the Jews were charged with deicide (the killing of Christ), with piercing holy communion wafers to make them bleed (desecration of the host), and with the ritual murder of Christian children at Easter; they have been held responsible for poisoning wells and for the Black Death during the Middle Ages; for practicing witchcraft, forging an alliance with the mythical Antichrist, and conspiring to destroy Christendom.[3] In modern times, new and no less sinister variations have been added to the theme of the "Jewish peril"—that Jews are striving for world domination by achieving control of the international financial system, by promoting revolutionary socialist ideologies, or through the alleged machinations of Zionism and the State of Israel. Modern anti-Semitism has thrived on irrational Manichean myths such as the Judeo-Masonic, the Judeo-Communist, or Zionist-American conspiracies, and the belief in an occult global Jewish power, embodied in the *Protocols of the Elders of Zion.*[4] The litany of stereotypes and accusations seems endless and has acquired a seemingly timeless quality, despite its lack of any empirical basis.

The persistence, longevity, and mythic power of such group hatred makes it an especially revealing barometer of the tensions and conflicts within European Christian culture where it was incubated. Moreover, the fact that anti-Semitism culminated in the Holocaust of World War II—the systematically planned mass murder of six million Jewish men, women, and children—is evidence of the extreme irrationality that has been one of its chief distinguishing features. The traumatic, cataclysmic nature of this event has sparked many attempts in the past sixty years to find theories and explanations that could illuminate anti-Semitism, racism, and the roots of murderous hatreds of the other in general.[5] Yet despite the many contributions from historians, political scientists, sociologists, psychologists, theologians, and researchers in other disciplines, an element of mystery remains. There are factors in anti-Semitism that both derive from and yet clearly transcend the hatred of the different and the alien that are so characteristic of religious bigotry and racism in general. There are a number of parallels between Jew hatred and the persecution of heretics, witches, homosexuals, Gypsies, blacks, and other minorities, yet the sacral, quasi-metaphysical quality of anti-Semitism is singularly absent in the other cases. Moreover, some of the more obvious factors in racist prejudices, such as the legacy of colonial oppression, slavery, or economic exploitation, have only a very limited value in understanding the specificity of Judeophobia.

The paranoid power of anti-Semitic myth cannot, in fact, be understood without reference to its religious sources and deeper roots in classical antiquity. Moreover, as pointed out in the introduction, it cannot be separated from widespread Gentile resentment provoked by the Jewish sense of being a "chosen people" with a unique vocation that has made them appear unable to assimilate in the eyes of surrounding cultures. In the Jewish self-understanding, the people of Israel (later the Jews) had been delivered by God from Egyptian bondage and granted a law of freedom (the Decalogue, or Ten Commandments), which laid the moral foundations of human civilization. Though upbraided by their own prophets for disregarding this law (the Torah) and later punished by centuries of exile, the Jews never lost confidence in their divine mission, which was simultaneously particular and universal. However, for the leading pagan cultures of antiquity— Egyptian, Greek, and Roman—the chosenness of the Jews appeared to be something incorrigibly exclusivist and separatist, and more like a stubborn, intolerant, and incomprehensible resistance to cultural assimilation.[6]

In seeking the origins of the modern virus of anti-Semitism, the historian cannot ignore this ancient clash of civilizations.[7] It contained many strands, from the animus of the Greco-Egyptian literati against Jews and Judaism in Alexandria to Roman brutality in suppressing Jewish revolts in the land of Israel and North Africa during the first centuries of the Common Era. Vulgar and intellectual anti-Semitism in the Hellenistic world could, moreover, always draw on the fact that no other nation in antiquity, apart from the Jews, so consistently refused to acknowledge the gods of its neighbors, partake in their sacrifices, and send gifts to their temples, let alone eat, drink, or intermarry with them.[8] As if to compound the insult, Jews claimed superiority over the "heathens" in the religious sphere (something Judaism involuntarily bequeathed to Christianity and Islam)—committed as it was to a transcendent monotheistic faith and a rational code of ethics.

The Seleucid ruler Antiochus Epiphanes was especially irritated by the Jewish refusal to bow to the norms of Greek culture. In 168 B.C.E., he imposed the worship of Zeus in the Jewish Temple of Jerusalem and forbade the practice of Judaism.[9] In Alexandria, in the three centuries before the Christian era, similar expressions of pagan anti-Semitism found a fertile soil among the populace and especially the Greco-Egyptian intelligentsia. For example, the Alexandrian Apion—taking his cue from the Egyptian priest Manetho—presented the Hebrews as a race of lepers cast out of Egypt in the days of Moses. Jewish civilization was depicted as sterile, and the Jews were derided as a superstitious godless people who were isolationists and filled with loathing for other gods. Once a year they allegedly kidnapped a Gentile Greek and fattened him up to be eaten by their deity in his Holy of Holies (an anticipation of the Christian ritual murder charge).

Not surprisingly, the first recorded pogrom of antiquity exploded in Alexandria in 38 C.E. at a time when Caligula was emperor in Rome.[10] The rival Greek community accused the Jews, who represented almost 40 percent of the city's population, of being unpatriotic and of manifesting dual loyalties when the Aramaic-speaking Judean king Herod Agrippa I visited Alexandria. Long-standing envy at the Jews' position of privilege, wealth, and power, whipped up by professional agitators and abetted by the studied inaction of the Roman governor Flaccus, resulted in mob passions running riot.[11] However, Flaccus did not respond to this violence by punishing the rioters. Instead, he stripped the Jews of their civic rights and herded them into a small quarter of the city—the first known ghetto in recorded history. Alexandria erupted again in 66 C.E., following news of the first Judean revolt against the Romans. When the mob seized three Jews in order to burn them alive, the whole Jewish community rose up to rescue them. The ensuing riot was ruthlessly crushed by the Roman governor, a Jewish apostate "whose troops reportedly killed 50,000 Jews."[12] Similar long-standing frictions between Jews and non-Jews existed in the land of Israel during this period—notably in Caesarea, Ashkelon, and Jerusalem.

The anti-Semitism of classical antiquity was a complex phenomenon that would later provide the bedrock on which early Christian hostility to Jews could develop. As we have noted, it was in part a response to Jewish religious and social particularism—the strangeness (to Gentile minds) of the Jewish way of life and thought as prescribed by the Torah. Jews were seen as foreigners, and they unquestionably had very distinct customs; more than that, they were a *monotheistic* minority somehow surviving in dispersion. Yet this minority enjoyed a privileged status under Roman rule—especially in Alexandria—something that especially exasperated the local Greek population.[13]

However, relations with the Romans, despite periodic and ultimately explosive tensions, would remain reasonably good until the great Judean revolt against Rome of 66–70 C.E. Judah Maccabee contracted an alliance with Rome, and King Herod's ambitious expansion of Jerusalem during the time of Christ would have been impossible without Roman imperial support. Moreover, the Romans had recognized the right of Jews to practice their special worship and observances. The Roman authorities appreciated that Jews were an important element in their domains (10 percent of the population in the reign of Augustus and 20 percent in the eastern half of the Empire)—not worth antagonizing. Despite the bitterness of the three Jewish revolts against Rome (66–70 C.E., 115–17 C.E., 132–35 C.E.), the Roman state did, for the most part, continue to protect Jews from local anti-Semitic mobs who felt driven to violence by hatred, envy, or greed of plunder.

Anti-Jewish prejudices were nonetheless increasingly apparent in Roman writings of the first century. Seneca, Juvenal, Cicero, the historian Tacitus, and other great names of Latin literature repeated some of the more scurrilous accusations made in the older Greek anti-Jewish literature. Many Romans shared the Hellenistic repugnance against Jewish exclusiveness— distaste for circumcision, the dietary laws, and the Sabbath (merely a day of idleness to the jaundiced eye); they not infrequently embraced the claim that Jews hated the gods of other peoples and hence the rest of mankind (*misanthropia*).[14] Moreover, as we have seen, the long-standing refusal of Jews to accept the imperial cult and deify the Roman rulers was an acute source of friction.[15]

First-century Roman intellectuals and writers were generally dismissive of Judaism as the ignorant "superstition" of an intolerant and culturally backward people. Tacitus, like Juvenal, dwelt on the perverse clannishness of the Jews: "But toward every other people they feel only hatred and enmity. They sit apart at meals, and they sleep apart, and although as a race they are prone to lust, they abstain from intercourse with foreign women; yet among themselves nothing is unlawful."[16]

But this pagan antipathy (which resurfaced during the eighteenth-century European Enlightenment) was also accompanied by anxiety at the spread of Judaism in Roman society, its penetration into the upper ranks of men and women in the senatorial class, and its growing influence on Roman youth. To patricians like Tacitus, Judaism—with its palpable disdain for the pagan gods and abduration of the imperial glory—was a threat to Rome's traditional manly virtues and military values; its growing appeal in Rome itself was taken as a symptom of corruption and decadence.

The potentially seditious aspects of Judaism (allied with proselytism), fused with the logic of Roman imperial repression, led to the quashing of three major Jewish revolts against Roman rulers. The murderous Roman assault against the Jews of Judea left its mark down the centuries on both Judaism and Christianity. Josephus and Tacitus put the number of Jewish dead in the war of 66–70 C.E. at around 600,000. Sixty years later, during the third "Jewish war," the Judean victims may have reached 850,000—a vast number considering the nonmechanized methods of warfare existing at the time.[17] Not only was the Second Temple destroyed (never to be rebuilt) and the Jews massacred, but many of the survivors were brought to Rome as pitiful prisoners. Roman losses in the Jewish wars were also heavy and would lead to spectacular punishment for the people who had caused them.

Emperor Hadrian, a zealous Hellenizer, sought in 130 C.E. to eradicate Judaism for good by erecting a pagan city, Aelia Capitolina, in place of Jerusalem. This highly provocative act may well have caused the Bar Kokhba uprising (132–35 C.E.).[18] Hadrian turned the site of Jerusalem into a miniature Rome, devoted to Roman religious rites and settled by Gentiles. The main cult of the Roman god Jupiter Capitolinus would dominate the new city, displacing once and for all (so Hadrian hoped) the cult of the Jews. The ensuing war was ruthlessly prosecuted. In the succinct words of Roman chronicler Dio Cassius, "Hadrian sent against them [the Jews] his best generals . . . to crush, exhaust and exterminate them." The new Jewish state, like the old, had been named "Israel," and its leader Simeon Bar Kokhba used many of the same rallying cries ("freedom," "redemption," "Jerusalem") as in the earlier Jewish rebellion.[19] However, as historian Martin Goodman has pointed out, "Israel" was definitely a significant appellation since the Roman state never used this name to refer to the Jews. Following the costly Roman victory in 135, Hadrian made sure the name of the whole province was changed from Judea to Syria Palestina—an ancient Greek designation referring not to the Jews but to their sworn enemies, the Philistines.[20] (This later became the origin of the term "Palestine" and the "Palestinians," adopted by the Arab conquerors.) Hadrian not only banned circumcision and other Jewish observances, he also issued ordinances absolutely forbidding the whole Jewish nation "from entering thenceforth even the district around Jerusalem, so that not even from a distance could it see its ancestral soil."[21] This collective punishment meant that in the eyes of Rome, the Jews had definitively ceased to exist as a nation in their own land.

The New Testament and Christian anti-Judaism would be incomprehensible without this context of the Roman war against the Jews. As James Carroll, author of *Constantine's Sword: The Church and the Jews,* has put it, to completely separate the two phenomena would amount to reading Anne Frank's *Diary of a Young Girl* without reference to the Holocaust.[22] It was the total defeat of the Jews in the second century C.E. that led to a parting of the ways between Judaism and Christianity. By 70 C.E. many, perhaps most, Christians already lived outside Judea, and the majority had not been born Jews. They had begun to come under the influence of Paul's novel doctrine: that adoption of the Torah by Gentile Christians would show a complete lack of faith in Jesus.[23] Moreover, Jewish Christians had to adapt after 70 C.E. to a triumphant Roman power knowing their own credibility depended not only on denying their Jewishness but on the negation of Judaism altogether. If they were to succeed in winning over converts in a Roman society where hostility to Jews had become the conventional wisdom, they had to move to the attack. This mental switch was relatively swift. As a result, Christians came to view the destruction of the Jewish Temple as a providential act and to believe that the resurrection of a Jewish state in Judea was both unthinkable and undesirable.

Demonization of the Jews began in earnest, however, only with the special role assigned to them in the dramatic crucifixion of Christ the Messiah as related in the Gospels.[24] The original polemics had grown out of a conflict among Jews, since Christianity had started out as a movement *within* Judaism. It was only the transformation of Jesus into a divine sacrificial figure—the center of a new religion claiming to supersede Judaism—that finally led to the split. In Paul's writings, the Jews are already condemned for murdering their own prophets sent by God (culminating in the death of Jesus); the "Pharisees," in particular, are given mythical status as divinely appointed enemies of Christ.[25] In Pauline theology, Jews are regarded as the slaves of a limited law overcome by a higher spirituality. Baptism symbolizes this new spiritual principle, in contrast to the external, and by now irrelevant, mark of circumcision. "Spiritual" man transcends "carnal" man just as the gathered-in Gentiles within the church transcend the old Mosaic Covenant.

In the Gospel of John, the hostile resonance of the term "the Jews," embodying everything that resists the light, is more explicit still, as is the portrayal of the malevolent Jewish authorities who seek the demise of Jesus. John insists that Jesus is crucified by the Jews under Jewish law (a totally improbable accusation), and his account establishes the core of the deicide charge—that the Jews murdered Christ, God's own essence and self-expression. The Jews willfully sought to kill Christ because they are not of God but of the Devil.[26] Thus, in the New Testament itself, we already have a theological form of diabolizing the Jews, which would later be greatly expanded by the church fathers.[27]

The Gospels, written after the defeat of the first Judean revolt against Rome, were to operate a fateful shift in attributing the responsibility for Jesus's crucifixion (a typical Roman punishment) to the Jews. The consequences of this religious myth were incalculable, for by killing the Son of God, the Jews would be deemed by Christendom to have become an *accursed* people, condemned to permanent exile and wandering. Henceforth, it was the Christian church that took on the mantle of the "new Israel" and became the sole recipient of the divine promises to Abraham. To quote the acerbic comment of the late Hyam Maccoby, prominent Jewish scholar: "All the blessings of the Old Testament were regarded as applying to the Christian Church, while all the curses were allotted exclusively to the Jews: a neat division."[28]

In the writings of Saint Augustine, the most important theologian of the early Latin church, this convenient division of labor becomes explicit. The Jews are now depicted as a wandering, homeless, and rejected people—

incurably "carnal," blind to spiritual meaning, perfidious, faithless, and apostate. Their crime is one of *cosmic* proportions. Saint Augustine even likens the Jewish people to Cain, the first criminal recorded in biblical history, who had murdered his own brother and merited death but instead had been condemned to wander unhappily ever after. The Torah is the mark of Cain granted to the "deicide people," who have misinterpreted their own scriptures and continue to live in blindness and error. They fully deserve to be eradicated for their crime, but Saint Augustine prefers that they be preserved as "witnesses" to Christian truth until the end of time, when they will finally turn to Christ at the Last Judgment.[29] This witness theory protected the Jews from mass murder but ensured their continued suffering and humiliation.

In Saint Augustine's *Contra Judaeos,* not only Cain but also Hagar, Ishmael, and Esau symbolize the Jews who have been rejected, while their contrasting pairs, Abel, Sarah, Isaac, and Jacob, prefigure the election of the church. Thus the biblical heroes of the Old Testament are detached from Jewish history and turned into a proof of the permanent and irrevocable reprobation of Israel. The blinded and dejected synagogue is left only with the empty vessel of the law, while the beautiful, triumphant Ecclesia—so strikingly depicted on medieval cathedrals—radiates nothing but truth and light.

Demonization of the Jews was even more palpable in the writings of Greek fathers of the church, such as Saint John Chrysostom, who told his flock in fourth-century Antioch that wherever Christ killers gather "the cross is ridiculed, God blasphemed, the father unacknowledged, the Son insulted, the grace of the Spirit rejected."

Indeed, Chrysostom justified the burning down of synagogues, asserting that they were "a temple of demons devoted to idolatrous cults, a criminal assembly of Jews, a place of meeting for the assassins of Christ . . . a gulf and abyss of perdition."[30] His angry diatribes reproached Jews with dissolute living, depravity, extravagance, and gluttony, as well as the supreme crime of deicide. His denunciations were echoed by Saint Jerome, who vilified the synagogue in almost identical terms: "If you call it a brothel, a den of vice, the Devil's refuge, Satan's fortress, a place to deprave the soul . . . you are still saying less than it deserves."[31]

The early church fathers were undoubtedly fearful of successful Jewish missionizing in places like Antioch, where there was a relatively large Jewish population. Their anti-Jewish invectives were in part designed to warn the Christian faithful against fraternization with the Jews; hence their strong advocacy of segregation and a strict ban on Jewish proselytism. By the fourth century, the theologians of the church had forged a grotesque Jewish stereotype completely divorced from the concrete Jews of everyday life— a demonic image that blended superhuman malevolence with total spiritual blindness. Their morbid fear of all sexuality (identified with lust, filth, and licentiousness), the hatred of women, and the downgrading of marriage to mere procreation were closely linked to this theological anti-Semitism. In the writings of the monkish, ascetic Saint Jerome, as well as of Saint Augustine and other Latin church fathers, virginity was the ultimate Christian ideal, while Judaism was reduced to the carnal baseness of a wicked world.[32] In this context, it seems significant that ascetic monks would so frequently be in the forefront of Jew-baiting in the succeeding centuries—during the Crusades, in medieval Spain, and in Reformation Germany.

A major transformation in Christian-Jewish relations came with the conversion of Constantine the Great in 312 C.E., which transformed Christianity into the official religion of the Roman Empire—a decision sealed by the First Council of Nicaea (325 C.E.). As its influence grew on Christian emperors, the church quickly changed into a persecuting institution, and those rights still enjoyed by Jews under pagan Roman emperors were increasingly eroded.[33] Indeed, the more that a continent-wide European identity based on Christian dogmas crystallized, the more marginalized Jews became in terms of their citizenship rights.[34] Jewish communities became heavily dependent on the benevolence of princes, bishops, and popes. Jews could under no circumstances exercise authority over Christians; proselytism became punishable by death; sexual relations with Christian women were forbidden; rabbinical jurisdiction was greatly restricted. In the eighth century in Visigothic Spain, Jews were victims of forced baptism but objects of deep suspicion as converts. They had to swear to renounce their obstinate "unbelief" and the deep-rooted "aberrations" of their forefathers, to repudiate all Jewish customs on pain of death, and to avoid all contact with their former coreligionists.[35]

A decisive turn for the worse would come with the first Crusade (1096), which led to massacres hitherto unprecedented in the history of Jewish-Christian relations. Between a quarter and a third of the Jewish population in Germany and northern France (about ten thousand people) were killed in the first six months of 1096, mainly as a result of mob actions reinforced by religious fanaticism. The Crusades exacerbated preexisting grassroots hostility to the Jews, embedding the notion of Christ killers more firmly in the popular consciousness. Theological scapegoating of Jews also hardened. The influential abbot of Cluny, Peter the Venerable, even suggested that Jews should finance the Crusades from their own money. To Louis VII (1120–80) he wrote that they should be punished severely for, more than the Muslims, they defiled Christianity and mercilessly exploited Christians. They were clearly beyond the pale.[36] Even the great medieval philosopher of the twelfth century Saint Thomas Aquinas affirmed that Jews should be held in "perpetual servitude" though not deprived of the right to life. Punishing the Jews for their "disbelief" by making them legal pariahs in European society was becoming irrevocably institutionalized.[37]

The Fourth Lateran Council (1215) further codified the segregation of Jews, requiring them to wear distinctive dress—a conical hat in the Germanic lands and a "Jew badge" in the Latin countries—that made them simultaneously more visible and vulnerable to attack. The new legislation sought to rigidly protect Christian society from "contamination" through living, eating, or engaging in sexual relations with Jews. Other canonical restrictions forbade Jews from entering churches, working on Sundays, or walking in the streets on holy days. Their synagogues had to remain lowly and miserable buildings. In addition to these social humiliations, the Talmud came under fierce attack in the thirteenth century (following its denunciation by a converted Jew, Nicholas Donin), as the repository of "blasphemy" against the Christian faith. The burning of the Talmud in Paris at the request of the church was one more sign of growing social and theological hostility to Jewry.[38] The image of mysterious Talmudic Jews, plotting and blaspheming against Christianity, would continue to be an integral part of the anti-Semitic armory and enjoy considerable popularity through to the present time.

Even more devastating in the long term was the fantasy of the blood libel, invented in Norwich, England, in 1144, following the murder of a twelve-year-old Christian boy just before Easter. The crime was attributed without any evidence to local English Jews. A few years later, a Jewish convert named Theobald claimed that "the Jews of Norwich bought a Christian child before Easter and tortured him with all the tortures our Lord was tortured." Ritual crucifixion of a Christian was (according to Theobald) expected to expedite the coming of the Jewish Messiah. Each year, he insisted, there was an international gathering of Jews in Spain to select a ritual victim against whom to avenge themselves on Jesus.[39] Thus the blood libel was linked over 850 years ago to the notion of an international Jewish conspiracy. William of Norwich would become Europe's child martyr in the wake of these fabrications, which would eventually spread across England and to the Continent. By 1255, when "Little Saint Hugh of Lincoln" became England's most famous child saint, the blood libel was firmly established.

One of the most notorious of all blood libels happened in the northern Italian town of Trent in 1475. Local Ashkenazi Jews were accused of having murdered a two-year-old Christian boy called Simon, whose body had been found in the Adige River. As often occurred in such instances, Jews were arrested, tried, and confessed under extreme torture. The criminal proceedings that followed had especially grave consequences because of the obsessive focus of the judges on ritual murder; the constant references to the killing of the Easter lamb and the smearing of doorposts during the paschal night in Egypt; and the clear insinuation that Jews murder children out of their supposed "hatred for the Christian faith"—a belief particularly strong in regions north of the Alps and within the German community of Trent.

Little Simon almost immediately became the object of a popular cult (the church officially recognized it only in 1582) and was turned into a martyr overnight.[40] The main promoters of his cult were above all the bishop-prince of Trent, Johannes von Hinderbach (a convinced "humanist" and promoter of education!) and a number of fervently anti-Semitic Franciscan preachers, such as Bernardino da Feltre. Through the Franciscan preaching, a vast number of tracts and treatises by jurists and humanists reached the wider public. The anti-Semitic propaganda also spread to areas far removed from Trent through woodcuts depicting the martyrdom of little Simon in graphic detail. Indeed, the first book to be printed in Trent was *The History of Simon of Trent* in 1475, written by Bishop Hinderbach's personal physician.[41]

A recent revisionist work in Italian, *Pasque di Sangue* (Bloody Passovers), by the Israeli historian Ariel Toaff—son of the former chief rabbi of Rome—tries to claim that a group of Ashkenazic fundamentalist Jews might actually have been guilty of the charges in the Trent affair. Incredible though it may seem, Toaff bases his groundless suppositions largely on testimonies extracted from the accused under cruel torture, after they broke down and gave the Inquisitors the "truth" they wanted to hear. He also relies heavily on the biased opinions of Jewish apostates, without any critical questioning of trial transcripts—something that profoundly shocked leading Italian scholars of the 1475 Trent ritual murder case, such as Anna Esposito and Diego Quaglioni.[42] Although Toaff ultimately recanted some of his views and revised the book, the initial edition of *Pasque de Sangue* reflects the author's essentially wholesale acceptance of the testimony of these baptized Jews in the Trent Affair who had been heavily involved in missionary work and anti-Jewish propaganda.[43] His sensationalist account cites anti-Christian feelings among Jews as a plausible motive without ever explaining why such murders should involve draining of the blood—with the huge risks involved in such criminal acts. After all, the blood libel was a matter of life and death to Jewish communities in the Christian world.[44] The murdered child would generally become a focus of pilgrimage, piety, and devotion—often provoking a new wave of persecution. Such hysteria was not driven by any Jewish obsession with blood (powdered or otherwise) but by the macabre assumption that "Jews constantly recrucify Christ in countless ways, of which this is the most horrible."[45] As the historian Ronnie Po-chia Hsia eloquently put it: "For the Jews of Trent, and for other communities throughout the ages, Passover was indeed bloody, but it was the blood of the Jews that bore witness to a violent fantasy born out of intolerance."[46]

The mythical Jew of the Christian Middle Ages was the product not only of blood libels, theological polemics, and anti-Semitic sermons, but also of mystery plays, fiction, and the visual arts.[47] The wickedness of the Jews was one of the central themes in the Oberammergau passion play in Bavaria, which enjoyed extraordinary popularity well into the twentieth century.[48] In the lower depths of Western culture, the kinship of the Jew with Satan was deeply embedded long before the modern era. The Jewish thirst for Christian blood, the infidel Jew, the mysterious Jew practicing black magic and deliberately spreading poison—these were stock clichés of popular literature and folk tales. The unspeakable crime of crucifying Jesus was attributed to *all* Jews collectively—and hence for medieval Europe there was no crime of which this enemy of mankind was potentially incapable.[49] He was a creature of a different order, not really human—at least not in the sense that Christians were. Most significant of all, he was constantly linked with the devil in medieval Christian writing, painting, and sculpture.

For the medieval Christian, Satan was a very real personage, the archenemy of mankind, who had been at war with the church from the very beginning of its mission. The devil embodied all the forces of heresy and revolt against God; he constantly tempted believers with doubt, and most important of all, he sought power over *this* world. From the twelfth century onward, he is an undeniably repulsive figure in Christian art, with an oversized head, bulging eyes, horns, a tail, and long, flamelike hair symbolizing the fires of hell. These frightening and grotesque images frequently appeared as symbols of Jews and Judaism. Moreover, in painting and sculpture, the devil was often represented as riding on the back of a Jew or of Synagoga—herself depicted as a blindfolded young woman, incapable of perceiving the true light of Christian faith.[50] There were many parallel characteristics attributed to the Jews and the devil. For example, both were depicted as arrogant, full of self-love, and masters of logic (the *ars diaboli*), seeking to ensnare believers with their perverse argumentation.[51]

Jews, like the devil, were frequently identified with the sin of unbridled lechery—a stereotype that echoed the fulminations of Saint John Chrysostom against the synagogue as a bordello and dwelling place for demons. The billy goat, the devil's favorite animal and a symbol of satanic lechery for the Middle Ages, was particularly associated with the Jew. The notorious image of the *Judensau* suckling her Jewish offspring in the presence of the devil was another familiar caricature of the Middle Ages. Here, as in other depictions, the association of Jews and the devil with dirt and excrement was commonplace.[52] No less potent was the belief in the so-called *foetor Judaicus*—a distinct and odious stench ascribed to the Jews—and supposedly a mark of the demonic Jew. While such ascriptions were common enough as stigmas designed to bolster the sense of superiority of one group against another in various cultures, in Christian Europe the "Jewish stench" was seen as punishment for the *unbelief* of the Jews and their crime against Jesus.[53]

The Jew devil with horns and tail was not only physically repulsive but also a mortal enemy of Christendom in the *spiritual* realm. Stricken with blindness and stubbornness by Satan after the crucifixion, the Jew had not only rejected the true doctrine but supposedly spared no effort to destroy Christian souls. Having made common cause with the devil, the Jews looked to the Antichrist as their long-awaited Messiah. The Antichrist (child of a union between the devil and a Jewish harlot) represented the sinister and truly satanic role of the Jews in world history. In this potent myth, Jews were perceived as the spearhead of the Antichrist's legions in the coming battle to annihilate Christendom. The apocalyptic threat represented by the Antichrist legend was to become one of the more terrifying themes of medieval anti-Semitism, and its influence would carry over into the late twentieth century and the beginning of the new millennium.[54]

At the theological level—as in such highly influential anti-Jewish tracts as Raymond Martini's *Pugio Dei* (The Dagger of Faith, written toward the end of the thirteenth century)—the Jewish pact with the devil is no less salient. It was used, for example, to explain why the Jews arrogantly rejected Jesus, why they respected the ritual commandments, and why they remained willfully blind to the truth of Christianity. The Jews, in effect, were assumed to believe in the revelation of Satan rather than God. Even their *kiddush hashem* (sanctification of the Holy Name) to forestall baptism was interpreted as a kind of martyrdom for the devil.[55] In a similar vein, the Spanish theologian Alonso de Espina, in his fifteenth-century polemic *Fortalitium Fidei*, suggested that when Jews preferred to be burned alive at the stake, they were behaving as "damned devil's martyrs."[56] Thus, in their greatest hour of distress, Jews were stigmatized as children of the devil, perversely invoking demons and giving them the honor due to God.

Spanish Catholicism was unique in the late Middle Ages for its adoption of the "purity of blood" idea and obsession with aristocratic linage.[57] In no other Christian society before the Nazi era had a set of racial values become so entrenched. The Catholic author of the *Fortalitium*, who presented Jews as the offspring of monsters (half human, half beast) and demons of unlimited wickedness, was, to quote renowned historian Benzion Netanyahu, "full of race-hatred and race bias that characterized the thinking, feeling, and attitudes of the anti-Marrano party of the time."[58] Espina's assault on the Judaizing of the conversos (converts) was typical of the "Old Christians" in fifteenth-century Spain and the mind-set of the Spanish Inquisition.[59] The aim of the Inquisition (in many ways an authentic expression of the popular will) was "to defame, degrade, segregate and ruin the whole group [of conversos] economically and socially, and finally eliminate it from Spanish life."[60]

Spanish Jewry had hitherto enjoyed a privileged position that had lasted until the late fourteenth century—they had excelled in commercial and intellectual pursuits and were showered with honors by royal benevolence. Spanish Jews even acted as ministers, councillors, and physicians to the kings of Castile and Aragon. Their success had aroused the envy of the nobility and populace, as well as the ire of the church, who saw the striking prominence of Spanish Jewry as an insult to the "true faith." The massacre of four thousand Jews in the Jewish quarter of Seville in 1391—incited by the demagogic preaching of Ferrant Martinez against Jewish wealth and "false doctrines," would permanently transform the situation of Spanish Jewry.[61] The carnage soon spread to other parts of Spain, and within three months almost fifty thousand Jews were dead and many more had been baptized. Some of these converts, like Pablo de Santa Maria (formerly Solomon Levi), who became a powerful bishop, did not hesitate to malign Judaism and advocate anti-Jewish legislation.[62]

The wave of baptisms continued in 1411–12 under the impact of the Dominican preacher Saint Vincent Ferrer and was soon followed by the setting up of the first compulsory Spanish ghettos. The converts began to penetrate the upper ranks of the Spanish universities, the judiciary, the professions, and even the highest rungs of the church. The resulting anti-converso feeling created a new type of anti-Semitism—one that held Jewish blood to be a hereditary taint that could not be eradicated by baptism. This was the origin of Spanish racism, the first of its kind in Europe to be specifically directed against the *mala sangre* (bad blood) of the Jews and to become fixated on the issue of *limpieza de sangre* (blood purity).[63] The prevalence of crypto-Judaism (the secret practice of Judaism while outwardly observing Christianity) exacerbated this racist hatred. The fanatical inquisitor general Tomás de Torquemada (himself a convert) became convinced that only by expelling *all* Jews from Spain could the phenomenon of crypto-Judaism be definitively stamped out. The fatal decree was issued by Ferdinand and Isabella, rulers of a newly united Spain, on January 2, 1492, shortly before the fall of Granada, the last stronghold of Muslim Spain. The pretext was provided by the hideous affair of the Holy Child of La Guardia, an Inquisition trial based on the mendacious blood libel and the medieval myth that Jews were planning to destroy Christians by means of magic and sorcery.[64] Anti-converso hysteria and the search for "hidden" Jews would continue to influence the antiliberal, antimodernist Spanish Right down to the twentieth century. In the 1930s, for example, the "prescience" of Los Reyes

Católicos (the Spanish monarchs), global standard-bearers of hard-line Catholicism, was still being glorified by the Falangist Right for having protected Spain against Jewish "plots."

Fifty years after the Jews' banishment from Spain, the German Protestant reformer Martin Luther would advocate a similar solution of expelling the Jews. His German-language tract of 1543, *Concerning the Jews and Their Lies,* depicted the Jews as poisoners, ritual murderers, usurers, devils incarnate, and parasites on Christian society. Luther openly called for setting synagogues on fire, breaking down Jewish homes, depriving Jews "of their prayerbooks and Talmuds"; he thundered from the pulpit that their rabbis "must be forbidden under pain of death to teach any more." Luther firmly advocated withdrawal of all passport and traveling privileges. The money-lending exploiters would also have to be sent into the fields to do hard labor in the sweat of their brows. Finally, Martin Luther appealed to the German princes and nobles to follow the examples of Spain and France—"let us drive them out of the country for all time."[65] "Mild mercy" would not be enough to assuage God's rage against the blaspheming, devilish Jews—who would be harder to convert than Satan itself. Indeed, Jews and Judaism, for the aging Luther, were nothing less than storm troops of the Antichrist, whose demise would bring about the end of time. Not surprisingly, at the Nuremberg trials of 1946, the Third Reich's arch-anti-Semite Julius Streicher was able to claim that he had invented nothing not previously asserted by the German founder of the Protestant Reformation.

Abraham a Sancta Clara, the populist seventeenth-century Viennese Catholic preacher, expressed sentiments similar to Luther's when he claimed, "After Satan Christians have no greater enemies than the Jews. . . . They pray many times each day that God may destroy us through pestilence, famine and war, aye, that all beings and creatures may rise up with them against the Christians."[66] Like Luther, Abraham a Sancta Clara believed that Jews had changed God into the devil and were themselves devils. Thus, at the intellectual heights of European Christendom, as in its lower depths, Jews ceased to be living human beings. They had been ineluctably transformed into a theological abstraction of diabolical perversity and malice.

The gruesome vision of ritual murder did not dissipate with the Reformation, the Counter-Reformation, or even the European Enlightenment. The scenario and the stereotypes would repeat themselves with stunning regularity well into the modern era. For example, a baby or young boy is allegedly killed by Jews, cut to pieces, eaten, and its blood is drunk during religious ceremonies, usually at Passover.[67] Toward the end of the nineteenth century, the leading French Catholic anti-Semite, Édouard Drumont, placed this legend of Jewish "ritual murder" (in which he fervently believed) against a mystical and pagan background, emphasizing the similarities with ancient barbaric practices. "In the ghetto it is not the God of Moses who is really worshipped, but the horrible Phoenician Moloch, who demands sacrifices of children and virgins."[68] In Austria-Hungary, there were no less than twelve ritual murder cases during the nineteenth century—the most notorious being in the Hungarian town of Tisza-Eszlar (1882) and the Hilsner case in Polná (Bohemia) in 1899. These blood libel affairs provided a major boost for the political activity of Hungarian, Austrian, and Czech anti-Semites.[69]

The Polná affair was especially revealing of the differences between medieval and modern accounts of Jewish ritual murder. Although the victim was a nineteen-year-old Catholic woman named Anezka Hruzová from a small Czech village near Polná, there was virtually no religious symbolism in the accounts of the murder that appeared in the Catholic press: no "signs of crucifixion" that had identified medieval blood libels as "Jewish"; no dwelling on the religious antagonism between Judaism and Christianity, no mocking of God, no martyrdom. As Hillel Kieval, a well-known historian of Czech Jewry, has observed, "What defines the Polná case as 'Jewish' can be reduced to blood and brutality, to the imagined 'butcher's cut' of kosher slaughtering. The Jews, themselves, finally, are not religious adversaries: they are Yids."[70]

In the descriptions of the accused, Leopold Hilsner (an unemployed Jewish vagrant) and his purported accomplices, the trial documents reflect current racial stereotypes of sinister, slightly deformed, unshaven dark strangers. We are treated to the specter of Galician or Russian Jews who exude an aura of menace and criminality. The medico-legal narrative of the trial added its own "scientific" authority to the vulgar anti-Jewish images inherited from the past. As in the medieval discourse, brutality and cruelty are assumed to be Jewish characteristics, and Jews, by definition, are beyond the pale of civilized humanity. But with the crucifixion and the redemptive message of Calvary removed, there is no longer a comprehensible motive for Jews to murder and collect the blood of their victims. What remains is a

tale of "grotesque violence and acts of animal slaughter" without any meaning beyond the racist assumptions about Jewish criminality.[71]

At the end of the nineteenth century there was an equally ominous shift
in the attitudes of the Vatican and the Catholic Church, which displayed a
growing readiness to identify Jews with horrendous acts of ritual murder.
Since the early 1880s the Jesuit periodical *La Civiltà Cattolica* (over which
the Vatican exercised direct control) began to publish analyses suggesting
that the Talmud commanded Jews to kill Christians (the Damascus affair of
1840 was specifically cited); that Jews needed Christian blood for both
Purim and Passover; and that they sucked this blood "out of principle, in
obedience to their law." A series of articles by the Jesuit priest Giuseppe
Oreglia focused on the Trent and Damascus cases (where Jews themselves
had "confessed" and criminal trials had determined their guilt) as clear
proof of Jewish ritual murder. At the same time, Oreglia went to great
lengths to deny that medieval popes (such as Innocent IV) had ever rejected
the blood libel. A similar view was taken by the Vatican daily *L'Osservatore
Romano* in the 1890s, which kept up a steady drumbeat maintaining that the
Jews were utterly depraved, as demonstrated by their continued torture and
murder of Christian children. Catholic papers with close links to the Vatican across Italy and Europe trumpeted the same tune. These proliferating
accounts of the bloodthirsty, "treacherous" Jews, commanded by the Talmud to slaughter Christian children, were part of an organized anti-Semitic
crusade in the fin de siècle Catholic press of Italy, France, Germany, and
Austria.[72] This journalistic campaign reinforced the older medieval image
of Jewish "vampires" crucifying their innocent prey in a demonic reenact-
ment of what their ancestors had done to Christ.

For example, *La Croix*—France's most popular Catholic newspaper at
the end of the nineteenth century—had an irresistible passion for the blood
libel and encouraged the notion that Jews were a separate and dangerous
race of parasites. The editors firmly believed that a Judeo-Masonic conspiracy was destroying the Christian foundations of the nation. Christian Democratic Congresses in Lyon in the mid-1890s openly called for an economic
boycott of Jews and their exclusion from the judiciary, the army, and politics. Neither Pope Leo XIII nor his secretary of state Mariano Rampolla objected to such rampant anti-Semitism, though they had their doubts about
militant Catholic involvement in the anti-Dreyfusard cause.[73] Such prudence did not, however, apply to *La Civiltà Cattolica,* which blamed the rise

of French anti-Semitism on the "detestable provocations of Judaism" and the Dreyfus affair on the treacherous character of the "deicidal people."

The Holy See was particularly sympathetic to Karl Lueger's highly successful Christian-social anti-Semitic movement in Vienna. Indeed, the Vatican was even ready to brave the disapproval of the Hapsburg authorities and repudiate the views of the ecclesiastical establishment in Austria in order to support Lueger's frontal assault on the "Judaic-liberal" domination of Vienna. The nuncio in Vienna, backed by Cardinal Rampolla in Rome, defended some of the worst anti-Semitic demagogues of the age. They included the Jesuit priest Stanisław Stojałowski in Galicia and Viennese Christian-social agitators like Ernst Schneider and Monsignor Josef Scheicher, whose openly racist rhetoric called for the extermination or expulsion of Jews. Moreover, the popes and their top officials, from the mid-nineteenth century onward, no longer condemned the blood libel as some of their more enlightened predecessors had done in earlier centuries. Indeed, from the Damascus blood libel in 1840 through to the Mendel Beilis case in Russia seventy years later, the Vatican remained either indifferent or hostile to Jewish pleas to condemn the ritual murder myth, while the Catholic press relentlessly spread this dangerous fabrication.[74]

Nevertheless, the Holy See officially disapproved of "racist" anti-Semitism as "unchristian," unlike "good" anti-Semitism—understood as the "natural" reaction of honest, hardworking Christians to "Jewish arrogance." Agitation that sought to "awaken" Christians to the defense of their faith and to rechristianize society and the state was praiseworthy. Only violent Jew-baiting was objectionable, although the churches sympathized with many ideological assumptions of the secular anti-Semites. Clerics were in the forefront of those who insisted that Jews were subversive, dangerous, and immoral, and engaged in a conspiracy to achieve world domination. The Catholic Church even agreed with much of the anti-Semitic *political* program of the 1930s in such countries as Poland, Austria, Hungary, and Slovakia. This included proposals to restrict Jewish occupational activities (especially in finance, commerce, and the free professions), to severely limit Jewish influence in public life, to socially and culturally segregate Jews, and to isolate them under special laws. Nothing better illustrates the outlook of the Vatican and the Catholic Church on the eve of the Holocaust than the following remarks by the primate of Poland, August Cardinal Hlond, in a pastoral letter issued in February 1936:

So long as Jews remain Jews, a Jewish problem exists and will continue to exist. . . . It is a fact that Jews are waging a war against the Catholic Church and that they are steeped in free-thinking, and constitute the vanguard of atheism, the Bolshevik movement, and revolutionary activity. It is a fact that Jews have a corruptive influence on morals and that their publishing houses are spreading pornography. It is true that Jews are perpetrating fraud, practicing usury, and dealing with prostitution. It is true that from a religious and ethical point of view, Jewish youth are having a negative influence on the Catholic youth in our schools.[75]

Cardinal Hłond did call on Poles to "honour and love Jews as human beings," even acknowledging that there were also "honest, just, kind and philanthropic" Jews; he also claimed that the church opposed "anti-Christian" racism and physical violence. But his slanderous assault on Jews, which included support for segregation and boycott, reflected a broad consensus in the European church leadership of the 1930s. The Catholic elites of that generation were thoroughly intoxicated by their vision of Jews as a mysterious, fearsome, and implacable enemy of the Church.

The powerful emotions released by this tradition of Christian anti-Semitism (even before it became a raging fever under the Nazis) reflected deep unconscious fears that have a profound symbolic significance. Historians have often overlooked this psychological dimension, preferring to deal with the more "objective" economic, social, and political factors on the surface. We cannot, however, afford to ignore unconscious factors if we wish to come closer to understanding the riddle of anti-Semitism. The Viennese founder of psychoanalysis, Sigmund Freud, himself a Jew who suffered acutely from anti-Semitism, left us some valuable hints concerning this enigma.[76] At one level, Freud regarded Judeophobia as the displacement of unresolved murderous urges of the sons against their fathers. According to Freud, the Christian religion, which had put the Son in place of the Father (but admitted complicity for his death), had more successfully absolved itself of guilt while projecting it onto the Jews. On the other hand, through the accusation that they were "murderers of God," Jews—who had refused to acknowledge the divinity of Jesus—found themselves cast into the role of parricides. Freud also thought that anti-Semitism might be a displaced form of *Christenhass* (Christophobia). Christians, who unconsciously resented the exacting demands of their own faith, especially its moral strictures and repression of instincts, could more easily direct these forbidden or unacknowledged feelings against Judaism—traditionally stigmatized as a lower form of revelation.[77]

Freud was equally aware of the powerful charge of sibling rivalry or jealousy of the Jews as the "chosen people" of God, the favored nation of God the Father. Freud did not elaborate on this point, but as I will show throughout this book, antagonism toward the claim of chosenness has been a constant theme in anti-Semitism through the ages. One testimony to its force lies in the usurpation of God's promises to the Jews by the Christian churches, as the heirs of ancient Israel, who claim to have superseded it in divine favor. In Islam, too, there is a doctrine of supersession (of both Judaism and Christianity) in which Muslims become the elect people of Allah. Moreover, in many modern nationalisms, the Judaic idea of chosenness has been adopted (often in a secularized and politicized form) and has led to fierce hostility against Jews and Judaism. As the most ancient repositories of chosenness, the Jews almost inevitably become a lightning rod for rival claims of election, whose psychological dynamics all too easily trigger boundless envy and an irrational hatred.

In his last work, *Moses and Monotheism* (1939), Freud hypothesized that anti-Semitism was "rooted in the remotest past ages," in "the unconscious of the peoples," and even in such customs as circumcision, which reinforced Jewish separateness while evoking dread, anxiety, and fear of castration. For Freud it was clear that this was one of the deeper roots of anti-Semitism "which appears with such elemental force and finds such irrational expression among the nations of the West."[78] In another context, commenting on the misogynist, self-hating Jewish philosopher Otto Weininger—whose book *Geschlecht und Charakter* (*Sex and Character*) caused a sensation when first published in Vienna in 1903—Freud somewhat simplistically argued that the common hatred of Jews and women derived from what he called the castration complex. "The castration complex is the deepest unconscious roots of antisemitism; for even in the nursery little boys hear that a Jew has something cut off his penis—a piece of his penis, they think—and this gives them a right to despise Jews. And there is no stronger unconscious root for the sense of superiority over women."[79]

Freud did not ignore other more mundane reasons for anti-Semitism.

He noted that Jews, as a comparatively small and physically powerless cultural group, had provided a perfect target for the instinct of aggression "in the form of hostility against intruders." Evoking with characteristic sarcasm the massacres of Jews in the Christian Middle Ages, he observed that "the Jewish people scattered everywhere, has rendered the most useful services to the civilizations of the countries that have been their hosts."[80] In terms of his own theory, the Jews embodied both the moral constraints of the superego and the forbidden lusts of the id (or libido). Freud had no doubt that much of the opposition to his new "science" of psychoanalysis was due to its emphasis on sexual instincts and drives. We might add that for anti-Semites this was yet another illustration of the old Christian stereotype of the "carnal," "lewd," and "materialistic" Jew, linked to sex, women, and lust. In Nazi mythology, it was reflected in the image of the debauched Jew represented as a predatory seducer, rapist, and contaminator of the "blood purity" of innocent Christian maidens. Adolf Hitler's morbid fantasy about the devilish Jew seeking to bastardize the whole Germanic race and poison its blood through sexual intercourse is an obvious case in point. In *Mein Kampf*, there is a chilling evocation of the black-haired young Jew lurking for hours, "satanic joy in his face, waiting for the unsuspecting girl whom he defiles with his blood and thereby robs from her people." For Hitler, this was an example of how the Jew "tries by every means to destroy the racial foundations of the peoples he plans to conquer. . . . So he tries systematically to lower the racial level by a continuous poisoning of individuals."[81]

From deicidal to genocidal anti-Semitism, there is a common fantasy about the Jew as a *persecutor* of Christians. This is the driving force of the blood libels that have persisted into the present—as it is of the nominally "secular" anti-Semitism of modernity. A good example can be found in *Der Stürmer*. The Nazi anti-Semitic paper, in a May 1934 special issue, revived the Damascus ritual murder legend to demonstrate the sadism, bloodthirstiness, and cruelty of the Jews—characteristics that were hallmarks of Nazism itself.

> Through this case, it became known that Jewry in its entirety knows about, and tolerates, ritual murder; that it protects the murderers when they are arrested; and that it spares no means or methods to free those awaiting punishment. Jewry demonstrated in the case of Father Thomas [the Capuchin friar killed in Damascus] that it is nothing else but a well-organized gang of murderers and criminals.[82]

The paper unmasked the Jews as "criminals, murderers and devils in human disguise." It insisted that ritual murder was as old as the Jewish race; that Jesus Christ, "the mighty preacher of Nazareth," had called Jews sons of the devil and murderers "from the beginning of time"; and quoted Martin Luther's denunciation of the bloodthirsty Jews "whose only aim is to murder and strangle gentiles." Julius Streicher, the violently anti-Semitic editor of *Der Stürmer*, placed enormous emphasis on this ritual murder campaign.

Streicher (who became *Gauleiter* of Nuremberg after 1933) prided himself on the fact that the *Stürmer* was the only newspaper in Weimar Germany that "openly and directly accuses the Jews of ritual murder." The special issue of 1934 quoted from various Talmudic references describing non-Jews as animals, who may be lied to, cheated, and robbed. For Streicher and other leading Nazi anti-Semites, "the history of the Jewish people is a series of mass murders and atrocities. It begins with Moses and ends with Trotsky and Zinoviev." The Jewish Bolsheviks (heirs to the ancient Purim mass murder carried out by Mordecai and Esther against Haman and his "75,800 antisemitic Persians") were supposedly responsible for the shooting, starving, and beating to death of thirty-five million non-Jewish Russians. This belief in a Jewish-Bolshevik genocide perpetrated in Soviet Russia was fervently held by Adolf Hitler and the Nazi leadership, but it also enjoyed great resonance in Europe and other parts of the world.[83]

Such fantasies were a testament to the unresolved and unacknowledged hatred, fear, and aggression buried deep in the recesses of European popular culture. All the negative qualities, dark drives, and crimes attributed to the Jews (and sometimes to other dissidents, outsiders, or marginalized groups) represented parts of their own selves that Europeans could not live with and therefore sought to expunge from their midst. The countless anti-Semitic persecutors who plundered Jewish property and burned and massacred Jews over the centuries always prepared the ground by first accusing their victims of the crimes they themselves intended to commit.

Demonizing others is not, of course, confined solely to Jews. An instructive parallel is provided by the persecution of witches. In the period between 1575 and 1700 (a time of social distress and upheaval), it is estimated that at least a million witches in Europe may have been burned at the stake.

Witches, like Jews, were ideal scapegoats for sexually repressed fanatics; they, too, were viewed as allies of the devil, and their defenders were branded as his agents.[84] It would appear that scapegoating and the projection of evil intentions and acts onto humans who have been demonized is therefore a universal human problem. It serves to exorcise unavowed guilt; to create boundaries between in- and out-groups; and to define social, religious, and national identities. Demonization is a classic technique for exclusion of the disruptive, defiling other. The other (who is generally assumed to share a different moral and social code) must take the blame and responsibility for everything that goes wrong in "normal" human society. Yet, as we have seen in the case of the Jews, the object of projection is ultimately a reflection of the self—the flawed and even wicked self that is out of control and unable to deal with its own repressed, sadistic impulses.

The demonization of the other as a means of "ethnic cleansing" has played an important role in many modern nationalisms that prey on ethnocentric group differences to solidify their own community against a common enemy. Ethnic-national belonging, defined by common blood and language, can easily become genocidal when the enemy other is assumed to be bent on one's destruction.[85] Always it is the other who is responsible. It is *they* who behave like beasts, *they* who understand only violence. This is the familiar litany of reproach in territorial and ethnic-national conflicts throughout modern times. The possibility of massacres becomes much greater once the enemy has been metaphorically dehumanized and made to appear beyond the pale of civilization. The more monstrous the image of physical deformity, moral depravity, and general backwardness, the easier it will be to rationalize mass killing. This link between the awesome power of stereotypes and genocidal activities has been particularly obvious in the twentieth century, thus far the bloodiest in the history of mankind.

In the evolution of *modern* anti-Jewish stereotypes, perhaps no single intellectual or artist played a greater role than Richard Wagner in rationalizing the transition from religious to racial anti-Semitism. His pamphlet *Das Judentum in der Musik* (1850) had already identified the "spirit of Judaism with that of modernity—understood not as progress but as decadence and artistic decline."[86] The most famous German composer of his time, who in 1848 had joined forces with his Russian anarchist friend Mikhail Bakunin on the barricades in Dresden, Wagner turned vehemently against liberalism, abstract rationalism, and Jewish emancipation after the defeat of the revolution. He came to see in Jewry the embodiment of the corrupt, money-making principle of the new bourgeois world he held responsible for modern artistic decay.[87] According to Wagner, the Jew, even when outwardly assimilated, remained wholly divorced from the *Volksgeist* (spirit of the race) without passion or soul, music or poetry—"the most heartless of all human beings"—alien and apathetic in the midst of a society he did not understand. The only conceivable redemption from this artistic barrenness lay in the *Untergang* (going under) of Jewry, its complete dissolution and disappearance. By the late 1870s, Wagner had himself become a theorist of blood purity, convinced that European civilization must be cleansed from the "spiritual pollution" of the Jews. In 1881 he wrote to his benefactor, the mad King Ludwig II of Bavaria: "I hold the Jewish race to be the born enemy of pure humanity and everything noble in it. It is certain that it is ruining us Germans and I am perhaps the last German who knows how to hold himself upright in the face of Judaism, which already rules everything."[88]

Wagner represents a crucial link between the Christian Judeophobic tradition and the "redemptive" anti-Semitism of Nazism. His vision looked toward the future transformation of European man and the salvation of humanity through the radical solution of the "Jewish question."[89] Wagner embraced (partly under the influence of the German philosopher Arthur Schopenhauer) the idea of an "Aryan Christianity" free from "narrow-hearted" Judaism—a religion he equated with egoism, Mammon, parasitism, and the bloodthirsty urge for domination.[90] In 1850, the composer contemptuously wrote: "The Jew has never had an art of his own, and therefore never led a life that was capable of sustaining art. We are bound to describe the period of Judaism in modern music as one of total uncreativity and degenerate antiprogressiveness."[91] Wagner's hatred of Jews had a murderous edge that was later resurrected in the ideology and practice of the Third Reich: "Society's body is dead," he proclaimed, "and the Jews lodge in it like a swarm of insects corrupting it."[92] The ghastly metaphor of Jews as insects corrupting the social organism and the libelous assertion that "Judaism is the evil conscience of our modern civilization" are only a few among the many ominous notions that Richard Wagner bequeathed to his passionate Austrian disciple, Adolf Hitler.[93]

In Linz as a seventeen-year-old adolescent, the young Hitler had already enthusiastically identified with Wagner's music, whose emotionality had a totally hypnotic effect upon him. His dream of becoming a hero, a leader, and a messianic redeemer of the German people principally derived from operas such as Wagner's *Rienzi,* which became more real to him than the real world itself.[94] Wagner's theater of intoxication and his romantic German nationalism, racial obsessions, and extreme anti-Semitism were decisive influences on Hitler, just as they had been on a whole generation of *völkisch* anti-Semites, such as Houston S. Chamberlain, in the Wilhelminian era.[95] While dictating *Mein Kampf* in the Landsberg prison in 1923, Hitler typically would listen to excerpts of Wagnerian operas, including Siegfried's funeral march from the *Ring of the Nibelungs* and the prelude to *Parsifal.*[96] Writing from prison, he prophetically announced that Bayreuth (Wagner's self-created shrine) was "on the line of march to Berlin"; indeed it was the place where "first the Master and then Chamberlain forged the spiritual sword with which we fight today."[97]

Hitler was absolutely serious when he insisted that "whoever wants to understand National Socialism must know Wagner."[98] Nor was it an exaggeration for him to declare, "For me Wagner is a god, his music is my religion. I go to his operas as others go to church."[99] But his racist anti-Semitic ideology was no less Wagnerian. There were the images of maggots "in a rotting body, often dazzled by a sudden light—a kike"; passages in Hitler's speeches stigmatizing money lending as an evil monopolized by the Jews; and the remorseless obsession with the *Volk* and the Aryan race as the sole creative element of mankind.[100] All these metaphors fused together in one overpowering paranoid vision that linked the salvation of Germany with the destruction of the Jews. As Hitler put it without equivocation in *Mein Kampf:* "The Jews are fighting unremittingly for the domination of the whole world. The only way to get rid of the hand that has us by the throat is by the sword. The only force that can stand up against this worldwide enslavement is the concerted resistance of a powerful national passion. This cannot happen without bloodletting."[101]

• • •

The road from deicide to genocide was not always linear and smooth, nor was it predetermined by an inexorable fate. But myths about the all-powerful "Semites," and fantasies of the Jew as Antichrist, agent of Satan, reincarnation of Judas, corrupter of morals, or the modern representative of the cursed deicidal people, were amazingly tenacious.[102] Without such a bedrock of chimerical beliefs, neither a stupendous fabrication like the *Protocols of the Elders of Zion* nor the whole structure of twentieth-century totalitarian politics could have ultimately emerged. This deadly legacy of medieval Christianity mixed with and transformed by modern secular post-Christian ideologies like nationalism, socialism, and racism created an *eliminationist* anti-Semitic platform with real genocidal potential. Under propitious circumstances of mass unemployment, alarming political instability, a deep sense of national humiliation, and a paranoid fear of Communism—such as operated in the last years of the Weimar Republic—this exterminationist ideology could mobilize millions of ordinary Germans and many Europeans outside the borders of Germany. The culture of hatred became profoundly entrenched and seemingly invincible during the Nazi era. After 1933, Hitler's regime was able to proclaim morning, noon, and night the inferiority and harmfulness of Jewry, using all the means of mass communication at its disposal, without a single voice in favor of the Jews being publicly raised inside Germany. Political scientist Daniel Goldhagen succinctly summarized anti-Semitism in the Third Reich thus: "Genocide was immanent in the conversation of German society. It was immanent in its language and emotion. It was immanent in the structure of cognition. And it was immanent in the society's proto-genocidal practice of the 1930s."[103]

An acute observer from within the Warsaw ghetto, Chaim Kaplan, describing the "gigantic catastrophe" about to descend on Polish Jewry in early 1940, emphasized "the depth of hatred" that now seemed to possess the German soldiers and was about to turn them into genocidal killers.[104] "This is not just hatred whose source is in a party platform, and which was invented for political purposes. It is a hatred of emotion, whose source is some psychopathic malady. . . . The [German] masses have absorbed their masters' teachings in a concrete, corporeal form. The Jew is filthy, the Jew is a swindler and an evildoer; the Jew is the enemy of Germany who undermines its existence. . . . The Jew is Satan, who sows dissension between one nation and another, arousing them to bloodshed in order to profit from their destruction."[105]

German Nazism succeeded in inculcating this extreme anti-Semitic mythology into the hearts of millions of Europeans, linking it to a conspiracy theory about the hidden, imaginary power of the Jews.[106] The otherness of the Jews, which had already existed two thousand years earlier in Alexandria, Rome, and Persia, had provoked real hostility and periodic violence. It did not, however, transform Jewry into the ultimate incarnation of darkness and death. It was Christian demonology that laid the foundations during the Middle Ages for the most frighteningly irrational myths, such as ritual murder, well poisoning, satanic conspiracies, and the specter of the Antichrist. But even Christianity still left open the escape hatch of conversion to the "true faith." In the modern racist worldview, this option disappeared even as the image of the satanic Jew was radicalized, becoming an apocalyptic, visceral threat to the existence of Germany, its living space, and its "purity of blood." The otherness of the Jews had metamorphosed into an absolute, so that they now stood completely beyond the pale of humanity. This ineradicable otherness was something indefinable, amorphous, and infinitely fluid. Jews were deemed capable of endless adaptation even as they maintained their own unchanging "racial" character.[107] At the same time, they were also perceived by the Nazis as a *subhuman* threat—dehumanized as microbes, vermin, a cancer in the bloodstream of Aryan humanity—execrated as the "racial tuberculosis of the peoples." This was the language of pest control, the medicalized vocabulary of Nazi pseudoscience.[108] It was a Final Solution directed against the Jewish Satan that would be carried out with Zyklon-B gas on an assembly-line basis. Hitler's relentless war against the phantom Jewish *Weltfeind* (world enemy), which had its more distant origins in the age-old Christian demonization of the Jews, had mutated by 1939 into a lethal backlash against the Christian substance that originally incubated it.[109] But the "redemptive" and apocalyptic anti-Semitism that lay at the core of Hitler's program would survive even the monstrous genocide it had set in motion.

TWO

Between Marx and Stalin

Modern European anti-Semitism was profoundly shaped by the upheavals of the Industrial Revolution, incipient secularization, democratization, and the challenges posed by Jewish emancipation. From its beginnings as an organized movement in the late 1870s it contained radical as well as conservative elements. Alongside the dominant cultural matrix of late-nineteenth-century nationalism, *völkisch* racism, and imperialism, there was also a populist *social* dimension that combined plebeian radicalism with antiestablishment protest.[1] The Catholic social movements of France, Germany, and Austria-Hungary in the 1890s—despite their pronounced conservative coloring—skillfully utilized a popular form of anticapitalism in seeking to restore the declining fortunes of the Christian church. This was as true of the Protestant court-preacher Adolf Stoecker in Germany as it was of L'Union Nationale (led by Abbé Garnier) in France or the most successful of the anti-Semitic Christian populist movements—that of Karl Lueger in imperial Austria. In predominantly Catholic countries like France, Austria, Poland, Hungary, and Slovakia, believing Catholics provided much of the leadership, ideology, and mass support for anti-Semitism. They received behind-the-scenes encouragement from the Vatican, even though these movements sometimes bypassed the establishment hierarchy.[2] Christian-social parties usually appealed to the urban lower middle classes (who felt threatened by Jewish economic competition), the peasantry, the declining aristocracy, and the lower clergy. They could draw on centuries of clerical Judeophobia, medieval superstitions, blood libels, and the still tenacious theological and popular odium attributed to the deicidal people.[3] Leading theoreticians such as La Tour de Pin in France and Karl von Vogelsang in Austria reconstructed an idealized vision of a corporatist society of estates that would prohibit usury and restore the guilds and the organic harmony of the medieval Christian social order. Anti-Semitism was part of their critique of laissez-faire capitalist society—execrated as materialist, egoist, atomistic, and driven by a corrupt individualism. Their anti-Semitic appeal to small businessmen, tradesmen, craftsmen, and shopkeepers was based on the premise that Jews were the driving force of modern capitalist exploitation and the liberal political oligarchies that held sway in central Europe between 1860 and 1880.

There was also a modern positivist strand of anti-Semitism—pseudoscientific and anticlerical—that drew sustenance from the general backlash against liberal political culture. This racist brand of anti-Semitism, often inspired by socialists such as Eugen Dühring or atheists such as Wilhelm Marr (who first coined the term *Antisemitismus*), had its origins on the German Left.[4] An influential contemporary German publicist in this tradition was Otto Glagau, who in 1874 specifically identified the "Jewish Question" with the "social question" in his pamphleteering works about the stock-exchange swindles of the era. In Glagau's denunciations of the cash nexus, the "bourse-wolves," and the iniquities of "Manchester liberalism," the identification of Jewish merchants and bankers with *Homo capitalisticus* is palpable. This position was inextricably linked to his view of Jews as a racially distinct tribe, essentially parasitical in nature.

Marxian socialists usually denied any common ground with religious or racial anti-Semites. They emphasized their commitment to emancipation in the broadest sense and opposed any attempt to deprive Jews of their civil rights.[5] This was particularly true of such luminaries as Friedrich Engels and August Bebel—the leading figures of German Social Democracy in the 1880s—who condemned anti-Semitism as a deviation from the class struggle and a movement of the decaying *Mittelstand* (lower middle class), openly despising it as the "socialism of fools." Communists, Trotskyists, and New Leftists would subsequently criticize anti-Semitism as a reactionary weapon of the exploiting classes. The Marxist worldview encouraged belief in the immunity of the working classes to anti-Semitism and other forms of racism.[6] The somewhat naïve assumption was that socialists would oppose any credo setting forth "the primacy of the national and the integral over the universal."[7] Closer investigation demonstrates, however, that anti-Jewish resentments were widespread among many rank-and-file socialists. In popular working-class literature, in caricatures, feuilletons, anecdotes, verses, short stories, and serial novels, traditional anti-Semitic stereotypes and modes of thought within the dominant bourgeois culture flourished unchecked.[8] Conventional prejudices against Jews remained unaffected by the official opposition of the European Socialists to political anti-Semitism.[9] Indeed, anti-Jewish vocabulary, images, and associations were often entrenched at the highest echelons of the labor leadership. Such attitudes can be found in Karl Marx's early writings on the "Jewish question" and in the work of French utopian Socialists such as Charles Fourier and Pierre-Joseph Proudhon, whose antipathy to commercialism and Jewish *haute banque* (high finance) was closely linked.[10]

For example, Proudhon (one of the founders of modern anarchism) had no difficulty in combining Enlightenment rationalism with traditional Christian loathing of the "deicidal race." Following Voltaire, he blamed Judaism for Christian intolerance and fanaticism. In the 1850s, Proudhon even embraced the Aryan myth (popularized in France by Joseph-Arthur Comte de Gobineau and Joseph-Ernest Renan)—claiming that monotheism was not Jewish but "a creation of the Indo-Germanic spirit." Proudhon's visceral diatribes against Jews and Judaism went hand in hand with his hatred of *la féodalité financière* (financial feudalism). Like his contemporaries Alphonse Toussenel, Pierre Leroux, and Louis-Auguste Blanqui, he saw in the Jews the incarnation of the banking system, the mercantile capitalist spirit, and the new industrial feudalism.

This *antijuif* socialist tradition still remained potent after the Dreyfus affair, especially among the anarcho-syndicalist intellectuals like Georges Sorel. It was a connecting thread between the Sorelian Left and the integral Nationalists of Action Française around 1910. The extreme Left and the Nationalist Right found common ground in their hatred of Jewish finance, Jewish intellectualism, liberal democracy, and bourgeois parliamentarianism.[11] The French Right partially succeeded at this time in infiltrating the working classes with national-socialist, xenophobic, and anti-Semitic ideas that helped to create the seedbed of interwar French fascism.[12] The protectionist slogans of "France for the French," invented by such fin de siècle anti-Semitic thinkers as Édouard Drumont and Maurice Barrès, combined with racist thinking, succeeded in moments of national crisis to transcend the Left-Right schism in French society.

Marxism itself was not immune to such archaic patterns of prejudice and the internalization of anti-Jewish stereotypes drawn from the Christian legacy.[13] Even the young Marx—founder of modern Communism—

reflected in his 1844 essay on the "Jewish question" the medieval linkage of Jewry with Mammon.[14]

> Let us not seek the secret of the Jew in his religion, but let us seek the secret of his religion in the real Jew. What is the profane basis of Judaism? *Practical* need, *self-interest*. What is the worldly cult of the Jew? *Huckstering*. What is his worldly god? *Money*. Very well: then in emancipating itself from *huckstering* and *money*, and thus from real and practical Judaism, our age would emancipate itself.
>
> An organization of society which would abolish the preconditions and thus the very possibility of huckstering, would make the Jews impossible. . . . In the final analysis, the *emancipation* of the Jews is the emancipation of mankind from *Judaism*.[15]

For Marx, "money has become a world power" through the Jews, whose commercial spirit had attained its highest development in North American Protestant Christianity. Mocking both Judaism and bourgeois Christianity, Marx insisted: "The god of the Jews has been secularized and has become the god of this world. The bill of exchange is the real god of the Jew."[16]

When Marx declared that "the emancipation of the Jews is the *emancipation of mankind from Judaism*," he provided generations of Marxists with a powerful myth that fixed the Jew as a symbol of material self-interest, social alienation, and predatory capitalism.[17]

Though the 1844 essay was never developed in systematic fashion, there are many harsh anti-Jewish remarks that appear in the Marx-Engels correspondence. Both Marx and his closest collaborator, Friedrich Engels, liked to refer to their Socialist rival Ferdinand Lassalle (himself a self-hating Jew) as "Baron Itzig," "Jüdel Braun," or "Ephraim Gescheit"—all derogatory, anti-Semitic epithets widely used in Germany at that time. Moses Hess, a close associate of Marx and Lassalle in the German labor movement, acerbically noted in 1862 "that in every personal controversy they [the party comrades] make use of this [anti-Semitic] 'hep' weapon, which in Germany seldom fails to have its effect."[18]

Left-wing anti-Semitism naturally focused on Jewish financiers. For example, Marx did not spare Jewish bankers such as Königswarter, Raphael, Stern, Rothschild, Mendelssohn, Bleichröder, and Fould for cooperating in raising loans for the Russian government to finance the Crimean War. Crude generalizations about Jews and Jesuits were par for the course: "Thus we find every tyrant backed by a Jew, as is every Pope by a Jesuit. In truth, the cravings of oppressors would be hopeless, and the practicability of war out of the question, if there were not an army of Jesuits to smother thought and a handful of Jews to ransack pockets." Marx lashed out at the "loan-mongering Jews" of Europe, engaged in "gambling and jobbing of securities," emphasizing their powerful networks. The following passage almost sounds like an anti-Jewish version of Christian liberation theology avant la lettre:

> The fact that 1855 years ago Christ drove the Jewish money-changers out of the temple, and that the money-changers of our age enlisted on the side of tyranny happen again chiefly to be Jews, is perhaps no more than a historical coincidence. The loan-mongering Jews of Europe do only on a larger and more obnoxious scale what many others do on one smaller and less significant. But it is only because the Jews are so strong that it is timely and expedient to expose and stigmatise their organization.[19]

Marx's fiercest opponent in the French labor movement, Pierre-Joseph Proudhon, was considerably more vitriolic. In Proudhon's notebooks of 1847 he propounds a chillingly violent "final solution" of the "Jewish question":

> Jews—Write an article against this race which poisons everything, by meddling everywhere without ever joining itself to another people— Demand their expulsion from France, with the exception of individuals married to Frenchwomen—Abolish the synagogues; don't admit them to any kind of unemployment; pursue finally the abolition of this cult.
>
> It is not for nothing that the Christians call them deicides. The Jew is the enemy of the human race. One must send this race back to Asia or exterminate it.
>
> H. Heine, A. Weil, and others are nothing but secret spies; Rothschild, Crémieux, Marx, Fould—malignant beings, bilious, envious, acrid, etc., etc., who hate us. By fire or fusion, or by expulsion, the Jews must disappear.[20]

Proudhon's revolutionary libertarian socialism was not only compatible with unadulterated racism but it also branded "Semites" (meaning Jews) as the embodiment of a universal cosmic evil:

The Jew is by temperament an anti-producer, neither a farmer, nor an industrialist, nor even a true merchant. He is an intermediary, always fraudulent and parasitic, who operates in trade as in philosophy, by means of falsification, counterfeiting and horse-trading. He knows but the rise and fall of prices, the risks of transportation, the incertitudes of crops, the hazards of demand and supply. His policy in economics has always been entirely negative, entirely usurious. It is the evil principle, Satan, Ahriman incarnated in the race of Shem, which has already been twice exterminated by the Greeks and by the Romans, the first time at Tyre, the second time at Carthage.[21]

The Russian revolutionary Mikhail Bakunin was no less racist and anti-Semitic in his worldview. The founder of Russian anarchism described the Jews as "an exploiting sect, a bloodsucking people, a unique devouring parasite, tightly and intimately organized . . . cutting across all the differences in political opinion."[22] In a passage dating from the end of 1871, Bakunin asserted that Marx and the Rothschilds were linked by secret sympathies, an early example of the classic "Jewish conspiracy" thesis so effectively used by National Socialist propaganda during the 1930s. Here is Bakunin's anarchist version of the Jewish world conspiracy:

This may seem strange. What can there be in common between communism and high finance? The communism of Marx wants a mighty centralization by the State, and where this exists there must nowadays inevitably be a Central State bank, and where such a bank exists, the parasitical Jewish nation, which speculates on the labour of the people, will always find a means to sustain itself.[23]

Bakunin's malevolent anti-Semitism was shared by many Russian populists who defended the pogroms of 1881 in Russia as a rising of the masses against the czar, the nobility, and the Jewish usurers. For instance, the Ukrainian revolutionary Yantsin regarded Jews as an undifferentiated mass of "exploiters," dismissing their incipient radicalization: "the weight of their [the Jews'] exploitation is great and their harmfulness unlimited. . . . If we find it possible to preach revolution, and only revolution against the nobles, how can we defend the Jews? . . . We cannot have any faith in the laughable Yiddish International nor in the sympathies of the Yids for the Revolution."[24]

The racist prejudices of Russian and Ukrainian social revolutionaries were sometimes shared by Jews who had rebelled against their traditional Jewish heritage, felt alienated from the Jewish collectivity, and had adopted Russian culture. Vladimir Iokhelson spoke of his own indifference to all things Jewish and the willingness of his comrades to refer to Jews as *zhidy* (kikes) as a result of

> our estrangement from the culture of the Russian Jews and . . . our nega-
> tive assessment of their religious and bourgeois leaders. Regarding the
> Jewish lower classes we thought that the liberation of the whole of Russia
> would bring along the liberation of all nations living there. . . . One has
> to admit that Russian literature has instilled in us a view that Jewry was
> not a nation but a parasite class.[25]

On August 30, 1881, the executive committee of the revolutionary terror-ist organization Narodnaya Volya (The People's Will) issued a proclamation to the Ukrainian people that vindicated the pogroms as an authentically popular, anticapitalist movement.

> The damned police beat you, the landowners devour you, the kikes, the
> dirty Judases, rob you. People in the Ukraine suffer most of all from the
> kikes. Who has seized the land, the woodlands, the taverns? The kikes.
> Whom does the peasant beg with tears in his eyes to let him near his own
> land? The kikes. Wherever you look, whatever you touch, everywhere the
> kikes. The kike curses the peasant, cheats him, drinks his blood. The kike
> makes life unbearable.[26]

The pogroms caused a part of the Jewish socialist intelligentsia in Russia to realize for the first time that the majority of Russian society, including the radical elements, "considered all Jews—a pious Jewish worker, a petit bourgeois, a moneylender, an assimilated lawyer, a socialist prepared for prison or deportation—as kikes, harmful to Russia, whom Russia should get rid of by any and all means."[27]

On the other hand, populist revolutionists such as the Yiddishist Chaim Zhitlovsky rejected all philo-Semitism with contempt as a way of "justifying Jewish merchantry" and a "parasitic" way of life:

Wherever I turned my eyes to ordinary, day-to-day Jewish life, I saw only one thing, that which the antisemites were agitating about: the injurious effect of Jewish merchantry on Russian peasantry. No matter how I felt, from a socialist point of view, I had to pass a death sentence not only on individual Jews but on the entire *Jewish* existence of individual Jews.[28]

This ethnic death wish would continue to characterize generations of Jewish revolutionists who have looked to socialism to bring an end to Jewish tradition, the Jewish people, Jewish identity, and Jewish heritage.

The Jewish founder of the German Social Democratic Party, Ferdinand Lassalle, a passionate Hegelian in his youth, was a good example of this syndrome. His poisoned barbs against the Jewish intelligentsia, the so-called Press Jews, and the liberal bourgeoisie undoubtedly influenced some of his followers.[29] Thus, one of his successors as head of the General German Workers' Association (ADAV), Wilhelm Hasenclever, wrote in the *Neuer Social-Demokrat* in 1872: "Only in Lassalle's organization, only in the *Allgemeiner Deutscher Arbeiter-Verein* [ADAV] can workers find the fulfillment of their aspirations, where all other organizations, spawned by the overheated imagination of arrogant Jew-boys and other mischief-makers, are falling apart."[30]

Wilhelm Hasselmann, another leading Lassallean agitator, went still further in the demagogic use of anti-Semitism, distinguishing between Judaism as a "religious sect" and Jewry as a tribe of "worldly jobbers." Sarcastically he asserted that "we shall never object to the paring of the flesh in the Judaic rite of circumcision, while strenuously opposing the Jewish habit of the paring of ducats." In election speeches Hasselmann encouraged farmers to believe that the Jew was responsible for their economic plight. In his journalistic articles he quoted Marx, Lassalle, and Heinrich Heine (all radical Jews) to prove "that the Jews are the embodiment of egoism and that for centuries past they have been burrowing, haggling and deceiving."[31]

Hasselmann's rhetoric was no less extreme than Proudhon's or Bakunin's. He asserted that it was necessary not only to *exterminate* the Jewish "press bandits," but to "lead the Jews altogether, with a few exceptions, not through, but into, the Red Sea."

"Egoism must be exterminated," he wrote, "and for those who will not renounce it, death by drowning would only mean liberation from the bondage of devilish egoism."[32] Although no Marxist, Hasselmann enjoyed quoting and putting his own gloss on Marx's invectives against Jews: "All other clear-headed Socialists look upon the Jewish tribe as the nucleus of bourgeois society and as the enemy of the workers' causes, bound to perish when the hour has come for the emancipation of the proletariat."[33]

In his article on "the Jewish tribe," published on November 6, 1872, Hasselmann crossed an already thin line into outright racism. He denounced the "naked selfishness" of the Jews as a "congenital defect of that tribe," which had "a pernicious effect on all nations and all states."

"The Jewish Tribe," Hasselmann insisted, "is exploitation of the workers personified"—it is "*the* enemy of the proletariat." This brand of left-wing anti-Semitism preceded by several years the racist rants of writers such as Wilhelm Marr, Otto Glagau, and the ex-socialist Eugen Dühring. They all shared an undisguised hostility to the stock exchange and "Manchester liberalism," which was frequently equated with *Judentum* (Jewry). The new anti-Semites of the 1870s used this rhetoric to appeal to embittered artisans and small businessmen adversely hit by the stock-market crash of 1873 in Berlin and Vienna. The "socialism of fools" contained a strong tinge of anticapitalist and racist *ressentiment* directed at the prominence of Jews in banking, the stock exchange, and the liberal press.

• • •

Across the Rhine, racist anticapitalism found a receptive audience among the followers of the revolutionary insurrectionist and militant atheist Louis-Auguste Blanqui. He was one of the first to popularize doctrines originally invented in France in the 1850s by Count Joseph-Arthur Gobineau and Joseph-Ernest Renan. Blanqui himself was an Enlightenment Judeophobe in the eighteenth-century rationalist tradition of Voltaire and Baron d'Holbach. His primary target was the Catholic Church. Indeed, he loathed Christianity as the most ferocious of the "terrible monotheistic sects" whose function was to reduce the people to a mass of docile beasts in the hands of clerics, capitalists, and aristocrats. The watchword of Blanqui and his radical followers, *Ni Dieu, Ni Maître* (Neither God, nor Master), expressed the central role they assigned to their assault on the foundations of Judeo-Christian monotheism. Blanqui and his chief lieutenant Gustave Tridon, who wrote his seminal *Du Molochisme juif* in 1868 (it was first published in 1884), had soaked up the hatred of "Semitism," already fashionable by the end of the second Napoleonic empire. Tridon presented "Semites" as the "evil genius of the world" who worshipped a perverse, sadistic God and practiced cannibalism, ritual murder, and human sacrifice. Jewish "Moloch-worship" with its insatiable bloodlusts (a prevalent myth in the 1840s with the German Young Hegelians) was supposedly the root of Christian sacrifice, which in turn inspired the bloodsucking greed of modern capitalism. Tridon, like Blanqui and Proudhon, regarded Jews as a nation of rapacious "swindlers" and "Shylocks." He insisted that the origins of modern exploitation went back to the Bible and the divine covenant, through which Israel had been given "universal domination" over the nations. For Tridon, Jews were the archetypal "Semites" (the "shadow in the picture of civilization")—who, as the French scholar Joseph-Ernest Renan had already proved, were inferior to Aryans in culture and creativity. It was, therefore, the task of revolutionary socialists "to fight the Semitic spirit and ideas" in the name of the "Indo-Aryan race."[34]

The racist fantasies of the Blanquists were much appreciated by the future pope of French anti-Semitism, Édouard Drumont, author of the bestselling *La France Juive,* first published in 1886. "Of all the revolutionaries," he wrote in *La Fin d'un Monde* (1889), "only the Blanquists have had the courage to refer to the Aryan race and to proclaim that race's superiority." Hence, it was no surprise to discover that during the Dreyfus affair, the Nationalist wing of the Blanquist party adopted an extreme anti-Dreyfusard and anti-Semitic position, libeling French Jews as "Prussians from within," agents of the German enemy across the Rhine and servants of an international capitalist conspiracy against the working class.

The mainstream socialist theoretical journal, *La Revue Socialiste,* edited by Benoît Malon, also adopted an anti-Semitic line in the 1880s. Malon had been influenced by Proudhon and Bakunin in his earlier years before coming under the spell of Drumont. In 1887 he began to publish a series of articles entitled "Aryans and Semites," authored by the Blanquist revolutionary Albert Regnard. It was claimed that capitalism was mainly a "Jewish creation" whereas socialism "is a Franco-German creation, Aryan in the fullest sense of the term."[35] Regnard borrowed freely from Gobineau, Renan, and other theorists of race. For him, "Aryan" was a term embracing the Greco-Roman, Indian, and Iranian civilizations, deemed vastly superior to the nomadic, sterile, materialistic "Semitic" race. Regnard's "scholarly and superb study" breathed "the spirit of genuine Aryanism," according to Malon—and was extravagantly praised for complementing the research of Édouard Drumont. Malon also threw open the columns of *La Revue Socialiste* to Auguste Chirac, a socialist anti-Semite whose sweeping attacks on the *féodalité financière* focused on Jewish international financiers engaged in shady deals that were allegedly ruining France.[36]

By the early 1890s "the socialism of fools" had developed into an embryonic National Socialism combining chauvinism, protectionism, populism, and calls for the expropriation of Jewish fortunes in France. In his *Le Testament d'un antisémite* (1890), Drumont predicted that the day would come when "a man of the people," "a Socialist leader" independent of the "synagogue," would take up his anti-Jewish campaign and rally the *déclassés*—the oppressed, disinherited, and uprooted of all classes—around the nationalist, socialist, and anti-Semitic banner. The Boulangist deputy Maurice Barrès gradually adopted a similar stance in the 1890s. So, too, did other French anti-Semitic leaders like the Marquis de Morès and Jules Guérin, who embellished their populist demagogy with "socialist" rhetoric designed to attract the workers. It was Guérin, for example, who coined the telling phrase: "The more distant one is from the Jews, the closer one is to the people." Guérin defined anti-Semitism as "a precise and formal claim of national labour against Jewish speculation." Anti-Semitic socialists such as Guérin, just like the socialist anti-Semites who preceded them, regarded the Jew as the embodiment of capital and as the enemy of the worker. During the Dreyfus affair, this rhetoric escalated into open attacks on republican Dreyfusard socialists such as Jean Jaurès, accused of being a mercenary of Rothschild and the capitalistic "Jewish system." Since the liberal French Republic was supposedly dominated by Jews, Protestants, Freemasons, and cosmopolitan bankers, only anti-Semitic socialists could be true "liberators."

The intellectual origins of French fascism can be discovered in this ideological hybrid fusing nationalism with socialism as a battering ram against the radical "Republican synthesis" that was being consolidated after 1905. Syndicalist intellectuals like Georges Sorel, Édouard Berth, and Robert Louzon greeted the rehabilitation of Captain Alfred Dreyfus as a victory of "the Jewish party" over its Catholic rivals. Some trade unionists, such as Emile Janvion and Emile Pataud, even claimed that the Jews, through their "control of high finance and freemasonry," had successfully infiltrated and seized control of the labor movement. Together they sponsored a mass meeting in Paris in April 1911, which was advertised as "a great anti-Jewish and anti-Masonic demonstration."[37]

Similar trends emerged in the late Victorian era in Great Britain. During the nineteenth century, the British Empire had emerged as a bastion of liberalism, much admired by most Continental Jews. But the marked increase in Jewish immigrants, mainly from Russia and Poland, fleeing persecution and arriving in England after 1880 placed a new strain on traditions of asylum and religious toleration. Political agitators fulminated against "destitute aliens" (read: Russian Jews), claiming that they were driving British workmen out of the labor market, lowering the moral tone of their neighborhoods, reducing wages, and encouraging nihilist violence.[38] Trade-union leaders rode the mounting wave of "anti-alienism," calling for the drastic restriction of foreign immigration. Virtually all the big British unions, from the dockers to the miners, engineers, carpenters, shoemakers, and tailors, favored these controls. In 1892, the Trades Union Congress (TUC) responded by adopting a resolution calling for government legislation to stop the entry of pauper aliens. At the same time, the socialist press denounced sweated trades, the inroads of cheap labor, and the clannish outlook of the Jewish immigrants. The future Fabian socialist Beatrice Webb, who surveyed the Jews of Whitechapel in the late 1880s, particularly singled out their lack of class solidarity and professional ethics. In her view they were solely concerned with preserving themselves and their families, motivated by the love of profit and unmoved by any moral considerations. The Jewish immigrant, according to Beatrice Webb, "seems to justify by his existence those strange assumptions which figure in the political economy of Ricardo—an always enlightened selfishness, seeking employment or profit with an absolute mobility of body and mind."[39]

When it came to Judeophobe prejudices, the British left-wing intelligentsia was no more immune than the xenophobic working class. In this respect, it could build on such indigenous English radicals as William Cobbett and some of the Chartist propaganda from the first half of the nineteenth century. There was also a significant strand of anticapitalist anti-Semitism in British socialist circles directed at the rich Jews of Hampstead, Bayswater, and the West End, especially those prominent in international finance.[40] The outbreak of the Boer War in 1899, perhaps the most controversial conflict in British imperial history, enhanced this trend. The growing antiwar movement exploited the Jewish origins of prominent financiers in South Africa in order to influence public opinion against the war and to discredit the Conservative government. "Jewish finance" came to represent everything shady and disreputable about the South African war in the eyes of the British Left. Jewish entrepreneurs such as Barney Barnato, the Hamburg-born Alfred Beit, Lionel Phillips, George and Leopold Albu, and others with banking or business connections who had become millionaires through the discovery of diamonds and gold in South Africa symbolized a nouveau riche class of cosmopolitan "foreign" financiers. Many journalists blamed them for the imperialist machinations that had drawn Great Britain into the unpopular South African war.

By seizing on the Jewish factor (most of the "Jewish" magnates had only marginal ties with Judaism), the radical Left clearly hoped to discredit British imperialism per se. The newspaper of the Social Democratic Federation (SDF), *Justice,* edited by Henry Hyndman, led a particularly malicious campaign against the "capitalist Jew." Jewish financiers were pilloried as the soul of a sinister "Gold international," locked in mortal conflict with the socialist "Red international." Hyndman and his followers repeatedly identified Judaism with the corrupt domination of money in late-nineteenth-century Britain and Europe. They openly sympathized with the anti-Jewish campaign that had begun to develop in France during the Panama Canal scandal. In 1893 Hyndman described Jewish newspaper magnates in Great Britain as "poisoners of the wells of public information" and protested that "capitalist Jews of the baser sort are already influential in both our political parties."[41]

The nexus between "international" Jewry and late-nineteenth-century imperialism, especially in Egypt and South Africa, was a constant theme of many British radicals. In a vitriolic article entitled "Imperialist Judaism in South Africa," Hyndman charged that Beit, Barnato, and their fellow Jews were planning "an Anglo-Hebraic Empire stretching from Egypt to Cape Colony and from Beira to Sierra Leone."[42] Hyndman, Harry Quelch, and other British Marxists openly blamed the outbreak of the South African war on the "Jew-jingo" gang and the "Jew press," which had supposedly manipulated the British public into supporting "piratical imperialism in the Transvaal and elsewhere." The Jewish financiers represented "that gold international which today dominates the Government and jingo press of all countries." *Justice* did not hesitate to characterize the South African war as the "Jew war in the Transvaal" engineered by a "Jew clique" around Joseph Chamberlain and Arthur Balfour, a war in which it was "us common Englishmen [who] shall have to pay . . . in blood."[43] The parallels with the more recent British military involvement in Iraq and suggestions of a "kosher conspiracy," or a secret Jewish cabal, behind former Prime Minister Tony Blair seem rather striking.

The blatant Judeophobia of Hyndman and his socialist colleagues aroused some criticism in the columns of *Justice,* especially among Jewish members of the SDF. In a letter to the editor on October 21, 1899, Theodore Rothstein wrote: "In Hyndman and in you [Harry Quelch] the Socialist movement of this country has two leaders ready—in theory, at least—to go hand in hand with Lueger [leader of the Austrian anti-Semites], Stoecker, Drumont and others. . . . [*Justice* is] preaching from its pulpit rank anti-Semitism. Is it not a strange and sad spectacle?"

Rothstein pointedly asked how Jewish socialists could combat Zionism in the face of such prejudice. How could they expect that Jew hatred would eventually disappear under socialism, given the hostile political line that *Justice* had taken on "the subject of Jew-capitalism"? How could Jews trust their class comrades when they were collectively branded as accomplices in an "imperialist Jewish plot" to seize the gold-rich Boer lands? What made matters worse was the realization that this anti-Semitism had infiltrated the work of distinguished economists and radical liberals such as John Hobson, whose seminal study *The War in South Africa: Its Causes and Effects* had been published in 1900. Prominent Labour leaders, such as Keir Hardie and John Burns, contributed to envenoming the debate. According to Hardie, it was a fact that "modern imperialism is really run by half a dozen financial houses, many of them Jewish, to whom politics is a counter in the game of buying and selling securities."[44]

The stop-the-war movement in 1900 tended to embrace the conspiratorial view that the British government was in the hands of a small clique of Jewish capitalists, liberal imperialists, and "foreign financiers." The press campaign even escalated into blatantly racist attacks on Jews as "bloodsuckers" and corrupt vampires preying on their innocent victims. John Burns, MP for Battersea, considered by some to be an outstanding leader of the British Labour movement, fully subscribed to the myth of a Jewish conspiracy. In a speech in the House of Commons on February 6, 1900, he announced:

> Wherever we go in this matter we find the same thing. Wherever we examine, there is the financial Jew, operating, directing, inspiring the agonies that have led to this war. They were supreme at the South African

Committee in 1897. I thought I had landed myself in a synagogue when I went to hear the trial of the Johannesburg prisoners before the Chief Justice. . . . The trail of the financial serpent is over this war from beginning to end.[45]

Burns's public rhetoric against the war was not much different from the anti-Semitic socialism rampant in France during the Panama scandal. His diaries reveal that he regarded all Jews, rich and poor, capitalist and proletarian, native and alien, with the same hatred and contempt. The allegations of a Jewish plot spread by Burns and often found in the pamphlet literature put out by the antiwar leagues were also accepted by the trade-union elite. In September 1900, the TUC adopted a resolution condemning the war as designed "to secure the gold fields of South Africa for cosmopolitan Jews most of whom had no patriotism and no country."[46]

Although it may seem surprising at first sight, the British Left around 1900 was more hostile to Jewry than their counterparts in Russia. Russian Marxism had made considerable strides since the pogroms of 1881 in shedding Judeophobic strands in its revolutionary outlook. Populism was losing ground, and the beginnings of industrialization had created an urban working class more open to Western social democratic principles. The revolutionary movement had also been swelled by Jewish Marxists, driven into its arms by persecution, oppression, and the desire to achieve civic equality. A powerful Jewish labor movement, the Bund, had been established in 1897 in the Pale of Settlement, which helped to bring into being the Russian Social Democratic Labor Party (RSDRP). The Bund vigorously opposed both anti-Semitism and Zionism, which did not prevent it from being accused of "national separatism" by the founder of Russian Marxism, Georgy Plekhanov.[47] Plekhanov sharply rejected the Bund's demands for "cultural-national" autonomy on behalf of the more than five million Jews in the Russian Empire. According to Lenin, writing in 1900, Plekhanov not only despised the Bund but indulged in anti-Semitic aspersions against it:

He declared straight out that this is not a Social Democratic organization, but simply an organization of exploitation—to exploit the Russians. He felt that our goal is to kick the Bund out of the Party, that the Jews are all chauvinists and nationalists, that a Russian [*ruskaia*] party must be Russian and not "give itself into captivity to the tribe of Gad," etc.[48]

Lenin's own polemics against the Bund were also extremely harsh, though devoid of such prejudices. In 1903 he wrote that "the idea of a separate Jewish people is politically reactionary and scientifically untenable." The only "progressive" solution to the "Jewish question" was complete assimilation on the French or American model. In his struggle against the Bund, Lenin insisted that "Jewish national culture is the slogan of the rabbis and the bourgeoisie, the slogan of our enemies." It was a throwback to the ghetto and contrary to the revolutionary "internationalism" that Jews had brought to the Social Democratic Labor movement. Lenin was, of course, the founder (since 1903) of the Bolshevik faction within the RSDRP, and his attacks against the Bund would later achieve canonical status. However, there was a significant difference of emphasis between Lenin's position and that of Joseph Stalin, whose *Marxism and the National Question* (1913) also dealt extensively with the Bund and the "Jewish question." Though this work was much influenced by Lenin, it highlighted only the negative sides of Jewish culture, castigating the desire of the Bund to "isolate" itself from everything non-Jewish as a *nationalist betrayal* of Marxism. The demand of Jewish workers to have Jewish hospitals and schools and an autonomous Yiddish culture was branded as wholly divisive. The Jews could not legitimately demand national rights since they were (in Stalin's opinion) a nebulous, amorphous entity, lacking all the fundamental attributes of nationality—a common language, unified territory, a shared economic life, or any genuine community of culture rooted in the land. Many years later, Stalin would throw off his Marxist-Leninist straitjacket and openly label the Jews as "rootless cosmopolitans." But in 1913 he could still claim to be within an orthodox Marxist consensus.

The young Stalin, himself of Georgian origins, was by no means insensitive to ethnic differences. At the same time, he was far from immune to traditional prejudices against Jews, Muslims from Caucasia, Armenians, or Germans. By 1907 he was already unfavorably struck by the high percentage of Jews in the rival Menshevik wing of the RSDRP (led by a former Bundist, Julius Martov), which espoused a Westernized, parliamentary system of government for the multinational empire. In a report to his Bolshevik comrades in Baku, Stalin made a casual remark that uncannily heralded the policy he would implement forty years later as the supreme autocrat of the Soviet Union: "One of the Bolsheviks . . . jestingly remarked that the Mensheviks were a Jewish faction while the Bolsheviks were *truly Russian* [my emphasis] and hence it would not be amiss for us Bolsheviks to instigate a pogrom in the party."[49]

As an "Old Bolshevik," Stalin was the heir of a Marxist-Leninist ideology whose class basis was the very antithesis of counterrevolutionary pogroms or Nazi-style anti-Semitism. But creeping totalitarian rule would gradually blur the distinction. Already in his successful political campaign against Leon Trotsky in the late 1920s under the slogan of "Socialism in One Country," Stalin knew how to appeal to ancient Russian reflexes of national messianism tinged with anti-Semitism.[50] Between 1928 and 1933 his policies also significantly contributed to the Nazi rise to power. Under his instructions, the German Communist Party (KPD) became a passive and at times even an active auxiliary of Hitler's assault on the Weimar Republic. The German Communists concentrated their main fire against the Social Democrats, whom they described as representing "Fascism in its currently most dangerous form."[51] This Stalinist strategy of the Comintern, which consistently minimized the Nazi danger, claimed that fascism itself already ruled under the Catholic chancellor Heinrich Brüning. Such blindness, as Leon Trotsky had presciently argued, helped to ensure the victory of Hitler in Germany.[52] The same trend continued after 1933. For the Stalinists, Hitler was a mere tool of the German industrialists and the Reichswehr (army).[53] This grossly mistaken assessment encouraged a trivialization of the danger that Nazism might represent to the USSR. From the beginning of Nazi rule, Stalin clearly hoped for an accommodation with the Third Reich. At the Seventeenth Party Congress of 1934, he explained: "Of course, we are far from enthusiastic about the fascist regime in Germany. But fascism is beside the point, if only because fascism in Italy, for example, has not kept the USSR from establishing the best of relations with that country."[54]

The show trials and terrible purges of 1936–38 can be seen inter alia as his way of signaling to Hitler that he was ready to do business.[55] The fictitious charges in these trials against the Trotskyist and Bukharinist opposition (to the effect that they had secretly negotiated a deal with the Nazis) were an uncanny anticipation of what Stalin himself would do within two years. The defendants in the Moscow show trials included leading antifascist Communists, many of them Jews—which was duly noted in Rome and Berlin. Benito Mussolini, writing in *Popolo d'Italia* (March 15, 1938) on the Bukharin trial, even wondered aloud if Stalin had not secretly become a fascist.[56]

Hitler, too, had been impressed by the great purges, seeing them as a sign that Stalin was determined to liquidate the Jewish intelligentsia. He was not entirely mistaken, though the Soviet dictator proved to be far more pragmatic than his German counterpart. When Stalin removed Maksim Litvinov (born Meir Wallach) as his foreign policy commissar in May 1939, he was indeed preparing the ground for his rapprochement with Hitler. Stalin would continue to scrupulously adhere to the Nazi-Soviet pact until Hitler's invasion of the USSR in June 1941. But he kept his anti-Jewish prejudices in check for most of the war years.[57] Stalin knew perfectly well that the Jews fought heroically in the Red Army after the German invasion and that he needed their services.[58] Hence he encouraged the creation of the Jewish Anti-Fascist Committee (JAC) to tap American wealth at a time when the Soviet Union was in mortal danger of military collapse. A degree of latitude was even allowed for the stimulation of Soviet Jewish national feelings. Contacts with Jews in America and Great Britain were encouraged in order to obtain vital financial support and political goodwill for the USSR.[59] Soviet policy toward the Jewish community in Palestine, the Yishuv, also showed signs of positive change in the war period, foreshadowing the shift toward Soviet support for a Jewish state in 1947.

Nonetheless, the Soviet government during the war years remained virtually silent about Nazi policy to single out Jews for destruction in German-occupied areas of the USSR. Though they claimed that Nazi terror was equally directed at the entire Soviet population, the authorities knew this was not the case and that anti-Semitism had spread widely among different Soviet nationalities and in the Red Army, actively encouraged by Nazi propaganda. But Stalin had no interest in revealing this information. Immediately after the end of the war, a bitter campaign against "nationalist deviations" was instigated, and in 1946 Jewish writers were already being severely criticized for "harping" on the theme of the Holocaust. In early 1949, Stalin adapted a leading theme of Nazi anti-Semitism—the accusation of rootless cosmopolitanism—for use against the assimilated Russian Jewish intelligentsia. The "cosmopolites" were assailed in the Soviet press as persons without backbone or identity, worshipping everything foreign and behaving like "passportless wanderers." They were accused of defaming Soviet culture and the heroic Russian people, of lacking loyalty to their socialist fatherland, and of kowtowing toward Western imperialism. The Jewish names of the offenders were prominently displayed in an effort to incite popular sentiment against them.[60]

Soviet anti-Semitism in Stalin's last years found its lowest common denominator in the desire to promote Russian national culture by removing Soviet citizens of Jewish nationality from all positions of influence in the arts and sciences, as well as state political institutions. Anti-Jewish purges among artists and intellectuals had already begun during the war years. At the same time, there was concern about growing national self-consciousness awakened during World War II among Ukrainians, Kazakhs, and Caucasus peoples, as well as Jews, which might threaten the cohesion of the Red Empire. Hence, the JAC became an obvious target for the Soviet leadership once its wartime mission had been accomplished. The fact that the JAC had written to Foreign Minister Vyacheslav Molotov and Stalin in 1944 suggesting the establishment of a Jewish autonomous republic in the Crimea ultimately sealed the death warrant of several of its leaders.[61] The idea of a "Crimean Palestine" designed to normalize the situation of Soviet Jewry after the Holocaust and to replace the palpable failure of the Birobidzhan experiment (in the Soviet Far East) did not at all appeal to Stalin. On the contrary, it suggested that JAC leaders now thought of themselves as a political force, capable of expressing Jewish hopes and national interests—something inadmissible in the socialist fatherland. It would not be long before a Soviet investigative commission would accuse the committee of abandoning the fight against Western (especially Zionist) propaganda and of being an "ideological captive" of Jewish nationalism.

In 1946 the JAC was increasingly seen as an instrument of international Jewish organizations, the Zionist movement, and American imperialism.[62] Its foreign links became a pretext for Soviet security services to see the "hand of Washington" everywhere and an American-Zionist plot behind all of its contacts and activities. Stalin's paranoia, reinforced by mass arrests, intimidation, and relentless torture, built up the "evidence" to show that JAC leader Solomon Mikhoels (the onetime head of the Moscow State Yiddish Theater) was the ringleader of a deadly conspiracy against the Soviet leader.[63] Ironically, in 1947 Stalin was actively supporting the formation of a Jewish state in Palestine to gain a foothold in the Middle East and drive a wedge between Great Britain and America.[64] This coincidence was one of the factors that led Stalin to prefer the secret assassination of Mikhoels rather than an open trial. The Soviet leader managed to conceal his hatred of Mikhoels (and Soviet Jewry) by granting him a state funeral, even as he encouraged his own Ministry of State Security to fabricate a large-scale case about an American-Zionist espionage center in the USSR. At the same time, Stalin had to reckon with the growing sense of solidarity displayed by Soviet Jewry toward the newly founded State of Israel—the unheard-of fact that Soviet Jews were ready to fight "when the blood of our brothers and sisters is being shed" by "Arab fascist gangs with the support of Anglo-American imperialism."[65] The arrival in September 1948 of Israel's first ambassador to the USSR, Golda Meir, and the very public Jewish enthusiasm that she aroused, was a serious shock for Stalin. This event would be the beginning of Soviet Jews' postwar struggle for national survival, one that was intensified by Stalin's anti-Semitism and that of his heirs.

A mark of the shift in Soviet Jewish consciousness was the highly critical response by many Soviet Jews to Ilya Ehrenberg's essay in *Pravda* in favor of assimilation and against Zionism. An internationally famous writer, Ehrenberg (who was close to Stalin) regarded "Jewish solidarity" as a lie engendered solely by renewed anti-Semitism and German fascist barbarism. He also insisted that there was as little in common between Tunisian and American Jews as there was between red-haired and snub-nosed persons who happened to be victimized one fine day by a madman.[66]

The manifest failure of such assimilationist arguments (long favored by Marxists) encouraged Stalin to accelerate the destruction of the JAC, and what was left of Jewish culture in the USSR, by violent repressive methods. By 1949, alongside the literary campaign to ferret out "rootless cosmopolitans," there was another, more brutal, offensive to uproot the international Zionist plot. The Stalinist leadership declared war against the Zionist "fifth column," arresting writers and intellectuals, closing down such Yiddish publications as *Der Emes* and *Einigkeit,* as well as Jewish theaters and all cultural activity in the Jewish Autonomous Oblast of Birobidzhan. Between 1949 and 1953, the inquisitional spirit reigned supreme as Stalin's henchmen carried out anti-Jewish purges, accompanied by an intense popular eruption of anti-Semitism, which had been building ever since the war. The two-pronged campaign against "bourgeois nationalists" and "cosmopolites" now aimed to annihilate Jewish culture and its propagators. Under the impact of the Cold War, totalitarian paranoia, internal power struggles, Stalin's diseased mind, and the widespread belief in an omnipresent American-Zionist threat, past restraints were thrown to the winds.[67] The regime now defined all Jews as potential agents of the West, engaged in separatist and other subversive activities against the Soviet state. It simultaneously persecuted those who were devoted to the Jewish nation and its traditions as well as those who only wanted to dissolve their national identity into a universal humanity.

The escalation of the anti-Jewish purges ultimately led to the notorious Doctors' Plot—in which nine physicians (six of them Jews) were falsely accused of being "Zionist" spies as well as American agents.[68] This affair, which first attracted worldwide attention in January 1953, was not only directed against Jewish doctors but aimed to undermine the Ministry of State Security (which Stalin no longer trusted) and to prepare for war against the ultimate enemy, America. It was America that allegedly stood behind the Jewish saboteur-doctors and had infiltrated Soviet intelligence.[69] In such matters, the Soviet state, like Hitler's Germany, did not hesitate to use its own updated version of the *Protocols* to create an inverted, fictional world through the unlimited, arbitrary nature of its totalitarian power. The result was the thorough eradication of Jews from important positions in journalism, opera, and fine arts; pedagogical colleges and university faculties of humanities, social sciences, philosophy, history, economics, physics, and chemistry; not to mention from their scandalous "domination" of management and industry.[70] In the uppermost party elite, the purge was less intense, only because there were so few Jews left.

The Doctors' Plot also created an unprecedented anti-Semitic pressure from below, an ugly mood of demagogy, defamation, and Russian national chauvinism. The propaganda goal was to show the world that there had been a global plot by Western intelligence services to disable Soviet leaders by medical terrorism, a conspiracy in which nationalistically minded Jews had penetrated a vital sphere of Soviet society, and were being used as "doctor-poisoners" by the Anglo-American imperialists to eliminate Stalin and his entourage.[71] Such "hidden enemies" of the people were "foul spies and murderers, disguised as doctors, who have sold themselves to the slave-owner cannibals from the USA and England."[72]

In these circumstances certain Jews close to the Kremlin decided to sign a collective declaration of loyalty to the socialist fatherland to be published in *Pravda*. They included *Pravda* staff members David Zaslavskii and Yacov Khavinson, the historian Isaak Mints, the philosopher Mark Mitin, the well-known novelist Vasily Grossman, and General David Dragunsky. Others, such as Ilya Ehrenberg (who wrote anxiously to Stalin on February 3, 1953), questioned the wisdom of the declaration, which might provoke counter-productive international measures.[73] The writers of the open letter, which was never published, clearly sought to distance themselves from the Jewish doctors. They also vehemently denied the "unity" and "common interests" of Jews as proclaimed by Zionists and the State of Israel—"a kingdom of exploiters of the common people, a kingdom of profit for a small bunch of rich people."[74] The ruling clique of Israel represented only "Jewish millionaires connected with the monopolists of the USA." The Jewish state, they insisted, was nothing but "a bridgehead for US aggression against the Soviet Union and all peace-loving peoples."[75] The Israelis were playing with fire and increasing "the tension in the world situation, created by American-English warmongers." They were turning Israel "into the homeland of America"; source of the most horrible capitalist exploitation, "the most unbridled racism" and anti-Semitism. Imperialist America was not the "friend" of the Jews but the supporter of fascist gangs around the world. It was only the Soviet Union and primarily the Russian people, "with its selfless, heroic struggle," that had saved humanity from the yoke of Hitlerism—and the Jews—"from complete destruction and humiliation."[76]

The same open letter, signed by Jewish Stalinists, sharply denounced the monstrous crimes of the "killer-doctors," an espionage gang supposedly controlled by the international Zionist group "the Joint" and American intelligence. (The American Joint Distribution Committee was in reality an *anti-Zionist* philanthropic organization.) The criminal doctors ("the majority consisted of Jewish bourgeois nationalists") were depicted as having been recruited by the Joint.[77] These "patriotic" Soviet anti-Zionist Jews were, in their own way, helping Stalin to prepare his "Final Solution" of the Jewish question in the Soviet Union; the "voluntary" deportation en masse of the bulk of Soviet Jewry to Kazakhstan and Siberia. At a time when meetings at factories and offices ("almost all openly antisemitic") across the country called for the "criminal doctors" to suffer a terrible fate, such deportations would be presented as necessary to *protect* the Soviet Jews.[78] Stalin died less than two months later (on Purim), before he could implement the ultimate bloody climax to his career in the land that claimed to have fulfilled Marx's vision of history.

THREE

The Soviet War Against Zion

I t has been said of Joseph Stalin that he was "an anti-Semite by most definitions," but until 1945 this was more of a Russian mannerism than a dangerous obsession. Even before World War I he was suspicious of the "mystical," intangible aspect of Jewish Diaspora existence, which had persisted without a homeland or territory for so many centuries.[1] Moreover, as a Bolshevik who became a Great Russian chauvinist after rejecting his own Georgian origins, Stalin always distrusted cosmopolitan Jewish intellectuals such as Leon Trotsky, Lev Kamenev, and Grigory Zinoviev, against whom he waged his ideological war in the 1920s.[2] Never a biological anti-Semite like Hitler and careful to preserve an outward veneer of Marxist internationalism, Stalin did retain a number of Jews in his closest entourage, such as the commissars Lazar Kaganovich and Lev Mekhlis and the novelist Ilya Ehrenberg. But deep down, the Soviet leader loathed any people such as the Jews, who appeared to have mixed loyalties and transnational connections, especially with the United States.[3] The paranoia and vulgar prejudice that characterized Stalin's outlook publicly came out at the Yalta Conference when he informed President Franklin D. Roosevelt that Jews were all "middlemen, profiteers and parasites."[4] It was a revealing prelude to the seething, pathological anti-Semitism that would be a feature of the last years of his rule. Ever since the 1930s, Stalin, like Hitler, had come to see the world in conspirational terms, ruthlessly purging those he defined as "enemies of the people" or as a threat to the Soviet fatherland.[5] By then, Leon Trotsky was already convinced that anti-Semitism was part of Stalin's campaign to discredit the Left opposition as a Jewish machination.[6] A decade later, Jew hatred had been fully integrated into Stalin's totalitarian mind-set.

Stalin's so-called anti-cosmopolitan campaign of 1948 formally initiated a witch hunt against Jews that would last for five years and had some astonishing resemblances to the Hitlerian model. Stalinist propagandists began to brand Jews as "parasites" and unassimilable aliens who were allegedly eroding or denigrating Russian national culture. Loyal Communists in the USSR were arrested and in some cases shot on false charges of "Jewish bourgeois nationalism," when they were not being arbitrarily denounced for the opposite crime of "rootless cosmopolitanism." This Nazification of Communist ideology in the late 1940s was all the more insidious for being covered up in Marxist-Leninist jargon and by an official propaganda apparatus that vehemently denied the existence of anti-Semitism in the Soviet Union. Moreover, at the height of the Cold War between East and West, Stalinist anti-Semitism was able to hide behind a climate of extremely widespread paranoia about imperialist intrigues, fears of neofascist "revanchism," and general hysteria relating to espionage and national security secrets. Furthermore, the Communists (with the Soviet Union marching at their head) cleverly utilized the prestige they had acquired as major architects of Hitler's military defeat to attack and discredit the anti-Semitism of their adversaries, even while appropriating some of the ugliest features of the National Socialist system.

• • •

It was during World War II, when seventy million Soviet citizens had first found themselves under Nazi rule, that the anti-Semitic poison began to enter deep into the multiethnic bloodstream of the USSR. Popular rumors about Jews shirking military service were rampant despite the extraordinarily heroic fighting spirit revealed by Jewish soldiers in the Red Army. In the summer of 1942 some high-placed Communist officials made secret proposals to cleanse Soviet art and culture from "Jewish domination," on purely ethnic or racial grounds. Stalin's own encouragement of "Russification" and his increasing glorification of Russian nationalism during the war also brought in its wake xenophobic, anti-Western, and anti-Semitic currents of thought that would fully crystallize only after 1945.[7] However, use of the term "cosmopolitan" as a code word for "Jew" permitted the Stalinist regime to more effectively maintain its pretense of nondiscrimination against minorities in general and Jews in particular.

The anti-Zionist campaign fulfilled a similar function, masking Russian imperial Communism and the state-inspired anti-Semitism of the late Stalinist period. For Stalin, unlike Hitler, stood at the head of a multinational state and a global Communist movement that was obliged to pay lip service to Marxist internationalism even as it consolidated its totalitarian control over Eastern Europe. The proletarian-Communist ideology was indeed a necessary instrument for extending the Soviet empire (under Russian hegemony) and preserving Stalinist "anti-imperialist," revolutionary credentials in the West as well as in nonaligned countries. These facts placed certain constraints on the blatant public use of anti-Semitism. However, since the early 1920s, the Soviet leadership had no problems terrorizing "enemies of the people" and earmarking "class traitors" and mercenary "agents of imperialism" for elimination. Jews after 1945 were well suited for assuming this scapegoat role, given their ties with coreligionists in the West and in the new State of Israel, not to mention their vulnerability to a well-entrenched popular anti-Semitism from below, related in part to ethnic competition for scarce resources.

In 1952, Stalin undertook a major effort to extend anti-Semitism beyond the borders of the Soviet Union and cement his control over the subordinated nations of Eastern Europe. Czechoslovakia, with its prewar democratic system, its Western orientation, and popular-based Communist Party (with a strongly internationalist prewar tradition) was an obvious target for his hostility. Stalin's suspicion of it was even greater since Czechoslovakia had sent desperately needed arms to Israel for its self-defense in 1948. This fraternal assistance turned into the basis for an indictment once Soviet-Israeli relations began to deteriorate after 1950. The case against the Jewish-born Rudolf Slánský, general secretary of the Czechoslovak Communist Party, and thirteen other leading party and state functionaries that began on November 20, 1952, was clearly an anti-Semitic show trial. No fewer than eleven of the fourteen defendants were of Jewish origin, a point the Czech prosecutors constantly stressed. Moreover, the Israeli connection featured prominently in the indictment as part of the so-called Trotskyite-Titoist-Zionist conspiracy to overthrow the socialist order in Czechoslovakia.[8]

The racist tone of the proceedings was the direct result of orders transmitted to the Czech security organs by Soviet "advisers." It was certainly no accident that Major Smola, a passionate admirer of Hitler, had been put in charge of the Slánský case. Artur London, the deputy foreign minister, was interrogated by this rabid anti-Semite and recalled in his memoir *L'Aveu*: "Major Smola took me by the throat and in a voice shaking with hatred he shouted, 'You and your dirty race, we shall exterminate it. Not everything

Hitler did was right; but he exterminated the Jews and that was a good thing. Far too many of them managed to avoid the gas chamber but we shall finish where he left off.' "[9]

Another victim of the Slánský purge also noted how similar the Soviet security advisers and the Gestapo were in their behavior, "both by their marked antisemitism and by their methods of interrogation."[10] The chief Russian adviser was particularly eager to demonstrate the "dangers inherent in the world Zionist movement" and persuaded Klement Gottwald, the non-Jewish head of the Czech Communist Party and government, to establish a special anti-Zionist department in the Ministry of Home Security. At the time of the Slánský trial, the Czech Communist press, following Soviet instructions, began to publicly identify Zionism with fascism and American imperialism. *Rudé Právo* declared on November 24, 1952, that "the Zionist organizations with which Slánský was associated were nothing but Fascist shock troops. It is, moreover, self-evident that any bourgeois nationalism, including of course its Jewish variant, must inevitably produce fascism."

Such Stalinist incitement soon led to a revival of virulent anti-Semitism in Czechoslovakia, with remarks like "Hitler ought to have finished them all off" becoming increasingly common. The Czech Communist apparatus encouraged this mood, spreading views that were redolent of Hitler's propaganda, down through every level of "public opinion" to the man in the street. Klement Gottwald gave his official blessing to this intoxication of the masses at the Czech Communist Party Conference of December 1952. Turning the truth on its head, he accused Zionists of exploiting non-Jewish sympathy for their sufferings under Nazism to penetrate and subvert the labor movement and Communist parties.

> The Zionist organizations and their American masters were thus able to exploit shamelessly the sufferings Hitler and the other Fascists inflicted on the Jews. It could almost be said that they were quite willing to make capital out of Auschwitz and Maidanek. Normally, former bankers, industrialists, estate owners or Kulaks would hardly have been accepted into a Communist party, let alone allowed to rise to leading positions.[11]

Gottwald embraced the official Moscow-inspired version that Jewish leaders of the Czech party were bourgeois traitors to the working masses who had been brought up in "a spirit of Jewish nationalism." In reality

Slánský and other leading Communists of Jewish origin had been militantly anti-Zionist since their teens and were thoroughly estranged from their origins.

From 1946 on, Stalin pursued his Cold War strategy with the utmost cynicism, using loyal Jewish Communists as strategic pawns in order to consolidate the deeply unpopular Communist regimes in Poland, Hungary, and Romania.[12] He did not hesitate to take advantage of their services in the Sovietization of recalcitrant nations. He knew that the pro-Muscovite Jews in the top ranks of the new postwar Stalinist governments in Eastern Europe could always be sacrificed to popular wrath. When Stalin decided, therefore, on large-scale purges in Eastern Europe, in order to accelerate the process of satellitism, it was not difficult to divert anti-Communist rage against the Jews. This was a useful way of satisfying Eastern European nationalism while opening the door for careerist ambitions among the younger generation of home-grown Communists at the expense of an unpopular minority. The removal of Jews from key positions in the Communist Party hierarchy under the cover of the struggle against Zionism would be virtually complete in the Soviet Union, Romania, and Czechoslovakia by the time of Stalin's death.[13]

The Romanian case was especially intriguing. It involved the rise and fall of Ana Pauker (the first female foreign minister in the world), who from 1947 to 1952 had sanctioned the unrestricted emigration of two hundred thousand Romanian Jews to Israel, while remaining firmly committed to revolutionary internationalism and Communist rule in east-central Europe. Pauker had played her part in ruthlessly converting Romania into a Soviet-bloc people's democracy.[14] A true believer, she saw in Communism the best road to admission into a traditionally nationalist and anti-Semitic peasant society. Though her husband (a thoroughly assimilated Romanian Jewish Communist) had been shot in Moscow in 1938, Ana Pauker survived the terror regimes of Romanian fascism, German Nazism, and postwar Stalinism; this, despite her opposition to the ruthless collectivization of the Romanian peasantry and her efforts to protect those internationalist comrades who had been charged by the Stalinist regime as Western spies. From 1951, however, she had to answer to equally serious accusations—initiated by Stalin himself—that she was a right-wing and a left-wing "deviationist," a fractionalist, an American agent, a bourgeois nationalist, and a Zionist.[15] To this day Ana Paucker unjustifiably remains a bête noire for Romanian anti-Communists eager to demonize her as a symbol for all the evils of the Communist system.

In Poland, it was not until 1968 that the "dejudaisation" of Communism would be fully complete. The surviving Jews in Poland after 1945 had, for the most part, been convinced Communists. They provided an indispensable reservoir of cadres for helping to impose Stalinism on a highly resistant population in the most inflammable of Moscow's satellites. Though Poland had been spared the postwar show trials that occurred in Hungary, Bulgaria, and Czechoslovakia, the repercussions of the infamous Doctors' Plot soon revealed to the Polish Stalinists the utility of the new anti-Zionist conspiracy theories forged in Moscow. In January 1953 the theoretical review of the Polish Communist Party published an article vilifying Zionists for collaborating with the Hitlerites in the extermination of Jews during World War II. Among their other crimes, they were accused of concealing the truth of the Holocaust from the Jewish masses on the orders of the U.S. State Department.[16] American imperialist circles, it was said, wished to delay the opening of a second front in Europe during the war. They had paralyzed mass movements of resistance on the Continent that might have pressed the Western Allies to act more speedily. At the same time, Israel's prime minister, David Ben-Gurion, was accused in late 1952 of unleashing (with American connivance) a "real campaign of extermination of the Arab population living in the State of Israel." The Communists deemed this "genocidal" policy to be identical to that of the Hitlerites. Ben-Gurion and Nahum Goldmann (head of the World Jewish Congress) were alleged to be in collusion with Federal chancellor Konrad Adenauer in order "to revive Hitlerism in West Germany." This tissue of lies constituted the core myth of Nazi-Zionist collaboration that appeared in the Polish Stalinist media at the end of 1952, many decades before it became politically correct in the West.

Political anti-Semitism did not disappear with the de-Stalinization that led to the Polish revolt of October 1956. On the contrary, Communists of Jewish origin who had been denounced in the USSR in 1949 as pro-Western "cosmopolites" were now accused in Poland of pro-Stalinism. Anti-Soviet riots, like the one in Poznań, sometimes degenerated into anti-Semitic demonstrations. Following the return to power of the "national" Communist Władysław Gomułka, everything was done to stimulate a physical exodus of the remnant of Polish Jewry.[17] The role of Soviet political and police agents in encouraging the purge of Jewish Stalinists in 1956 was central.[18]

Indeed, it was part of Nikita Khrushchev's pseudo-"liberal" de-Stalinization policy to spread the idea that Jews were responsible for all the crimes of Stalinism in Poland, a myth widely believed by Poles. Within four years Jews had been systematically removed from the civilian and military security apparatus as well as from high positions in the state and party administration. This was a Polish as much as a Soviet initiative.[19]

In the early 1960s, Gomułka gave orders to strictly survey senior officials of Jewish origin, and a full card index for Polish Jews was prepared with Soviet blessing. By 1963 a Polish Politburo plan for the complete purge of Jews from all positions of influence was operationally ready.[20] A younger generation of careerists, who resented Russian domination and the influence of the "Communist Jews" who returned to Poland from the USSR after 1945, looked to the former partisan leader General Mieczysław Moczar (minister of the interior) and his ultra-nationalist brand of Polish Communism to advance their interests. The power struggle between the Gomułka and Moczar cliques, both of whom were anti-Semitic in varying degrees, provided the backdrop to the so-called anti-Zionist crusade of 1967–68. As a result of this witch hunt, Poland was made virtually *judenrein* (free of Jews).[21]

The campaign was ostensibly sparked by the Six-Day War of June 1967 and the student unrest in Polish universities in March 1968, following the banning of a nineteenth-century patriotic drama, *Dziady,* by Poland's national poet Adam Mickiewicz. The regime blamed the internal unrest on a conspiracy between liberal Marxist "revisionists," Zionists living in Poland, the Israelis, West German revanchists, and American imperialists. The aim of these diverse forces was allegedly to separate Poland from the Soviet Union and to restore Western-style bourgeois democracy. A book by Tadeusz Walichnowski, *Israel a NRF* (Israel and the German Federal Republic), published in Warsaw in 1967, tried to substantiate the conspiracy thesis. Shortly after its publication, Gomułka accused Polish Jews in June 1967 of being a fifth column of Israel and the Western imperialists. The Communist regime had revived the myth of the Jew as an enemy of Poland under the mask of its anti-Zionist campaign.[22]

In a transparently demagogic address of March 19, 1968, Gomułka now divided Polish Jews into "cosmopolitans" who were neither Jews nor Poles but served Israel, and those who saw themselves as loyal Poles. For the first time in the history of Communism, Jews qua Jews were *openly* made the scapegoats for the failures of the regime. Gomułka went out of his way to emphasize that even the most loyal Polish Jews could not expect to hold any post of national responsibility. Once the signal had been given from the top, the anti-Zionist purge soon swept through all layers of Polish society. The official Communist Party newspaper blamed the Zionists on June 16, 1968, for instigating the students' riots; it demanded the removal of persons of "Jewish origin" from the universities, from the government, party, and security organizations on the grounds of their "inner cosmopolitanism." It especially deplored their "privileged" positions and condemned their (imaginary links with) Zionism.

The theoretical reflection of this witch hunt came in an article by the head of the Cultural Section of the Polish Communist Central Committee, Andrzej Werblan, published in June 1968. Werblan solemnly inscribed the anti-Semitic principle of the *numerus clausus* into Marxist theory. In the past, Werblan claimed, the "ethnic composition" of the Polish Communist Party had "not been correctly balanced." The disproportionate number of Jewish militants in the postwar party had led to the sins of "sectarianism" and "dogmatism." Similarly, in the period before 1939 it had produced an excessively "cosmopolitan" interpretation of internationalism associated with the legacy of Jewish revolutionists such as Rosa Luxemburg. Both Stalinism and its antitheses (Trotskyism/Luxemburgism) were equated with a Jewish ethnic background. According to Werblan, no society would be willing to tolerate "an excessive representation of a national minority in the leading councils of the nation, particularly in departments concerned with national defence, security, propaganda and diplomacy. . . . Every society rejects such privileges with disgust."[23] Jewish cadres were not only incapable of correctly harmonizing Polish national interests with internationalism for ethnic reasons, they were assumed to be inherently prone to the deviationist sins of "revisionism" and Zionism. For the less sophisticated, a speech on April 11, 1968, by Communist Party first secretary in the Gdansk region Stanislaw Kociolek made the same point in more vulgar language. Kociolek, a strong supporter of Gomułka, presented the anti-Zionist crusade as a way of "throwing off the humpback of the nationalist [i.e., Jewish] misrepresentation of internationalism, and of the nationalist defence of group interests. . . . There can be no philosophy of humility towards any *Herrenvolk* thrown up by history."[24]

By 1968, Polish Jews had been redefined as a *Herrenvolk* in the new Communist dispensation. This Stalinist purge was supposedly about Poles de-

fending their national honor against "alien" domination. In using this vocabulary, leading Polish Communists were effectively returning to the prewar rhetoric of the anti-Semitic fascists with their rallying cry of "Jews to
Palestine!" They were imitating the language of Roman Dmowski's National Democrats before 1939, who had demanded the "transfer" of Polish
Jewry abroad. But thirty years later there were barely thirty thousand Jews
(0.1 percent of the population) who had survived the Holocaust and remained in Poland. In contrast to prewar Poland with its three million Jews,
there was no "objective" minority problem in 1968. An inner-party power
struggle had been masked by the demagogic use of anti-Zionist anti-
Semitism, now an integral part of the nationalist Communism espoused by
General Moczar and his "partisans." The Moczarites favored eradicating all
trends toward liberalization, dissent, and social democracy, while advocating an eastward, pro-Moscow orientation for Polish policy.

The veteran Gomułka played the same ethno-nationalist card in order to
hold on to power in a context where anti-Zionist hysteria offered the best
diversion from his own failures.[25] There was also strong pressure from the
Soviet Union and Polish internal security organizations to stage show trials
of Jews in 1968 (which was resisted by Gomułka) and to "Aryanize" the Polish Army, a measure that was duly carried out.[26] In the state-controlled
mass media, the myth of the Zionist/Jew as an enemy of Poland, a threat to
the party, and polluter of the national culture still held sway.

Anti-Semitic anti-Zionism in Poland (as in Czechoslovakia after the Soviet invasion of August 1968) proved a useful tool in *re-Stalinizing* a system
in which too many liberal-democratic cracks had begun to appear. The
crushing of the intelligentsia and all manifestations of dissent in both countries was the immediate result of this neo-Stalinist war on Zionism and a
good measure of its demoralizing effect. Here, too, the Communist rulers of
Poland and Czechoslovakia, under Soviet prodding, had evidently taken a
leaf out of Hitler's book. They well understood that governmental anti-
Zionism could serve as a powerful deterrent against free criticism, intellectual independence, aspirations for greater personal freedom, and a more
representative popular democracy. By raising the specter of the abstract, demonic Jew in his Zionist incarnation, supposedly responsible for subverting
the socialist system, the neo-Stalinist leaders could more easily repress the
legitimate aspirations of their own people and hold on to power. In Hungary, on the other hand, the Stalinist system had been run by Jews before

1956, but it now gave way to a more liberal "goulash" Communism that avoided the anti-Zionist witch hunts of Poland and Czechoslovakia.[27] At the same time, the ultranationalist Communism practiced in President Nicolae Ceausescu's Romania fused a semi-independent foreign policy (that maintained diplomatic relations with Israel) with a corrupt and intolerant authoritarian dictatorship that tolerated no dissent. Under Ceausescu, although Romanian nationalism was rampant, anti-Semitism remained muted while the supreme leader sought to mediate between Israel and the Arabs.[28]

In the Soviet Union itself, postwar anti-Semitic policy continued, though at a lower level of intensity following Khrushchev's bold de-Stalinization program.[29] It received a new dimension with the increasing orientation of Soviet foreign policy toward anti-Western Arab nationalism and Third World liberation movements—a change that began in the mid-1950s.[30] The menacing warning of Soviet premier Nikolay Bulganin to the Israeli government during the Sinai campaign (November 5, 1956), that the "very existence of Israel as a state was in jeopardy," signaled the definitive end of a brief post-1948 honeymoon in Russian-Israeli relations.[31] That rapprochement had been intended to drive the British out of Palestine and perhaps to establish a pro-Soviet satellite in the Middle East. It boomeranged partly because of Stalin's paranoia and his fear that Soviet Jewry might have become too enthusiastic about the foundation of Israel. But after Stalin's death, the closer Moscow drew to "progressive" allies in the Arab world, the more Israel found itself shunned as a reactionary puppet of Western imperialism.[32] At the same time, domestic anti-Semitic propaganda continued unabated. Under Khrushchev it tended to be focused on Jewish "economic crimes" and the vilification of Judaism as part of a sweeping atheist campaign against religion. True, a proto-Nazi work such as Trofim Kichko's *Judaism Without Embellishment* (1963), which alleged the existence of a universal Jewish conspiracy involving Judaism, Jewish bankers, Zionism, and Western capitalism, was still something of an anomaly. Even the hard-line French Communist daily *L'Humanité* felt obliged to condemn the vile caricatures in Kichko's opus, and the book was withdrawn from circulation a year later.[33] But within a decade, Kichko would be back in favor.

The Six-Day War transformed the periodic but isolated diatribes into a long and intensive anti-Semitic campaign without parallel in the history of the Soviet Union.[34] After 1967, the USSR began to flood the world with a constant flow of anti-Zionist propaganda whose intensity far exceeded its earlier broadsides against the ideological heresies of Trotskyism, Titoism, or Maoism. Only the Nazis in their twelve years of power had ever succeeded in producing such a sustained flow of fabricated libels as an instrument of their domestic and foreign policy. This post-Stalin Soviet offensive did not admittedly aim at the expropriation, expulsion, or extermination of Soviet Jewry. But under the guise of anti-Zionism, the rulers in the Kremlin could continue Stalin's legacy, expressing more openly a primitive anti-Semitism officially proscribed by Marxist-Leninist ideology.[35] The Great Russian chauvinism popularized by Stalin gradually began to reconnect with the older xenophobic traditions of late czarism.[36] The USSR was gradually being transformed under Brezhnev into a cross between Russian state fascism and National Socialism. The hollow shell of official Marxist-Leninist verbiage was being filled with old-new prejudices whose sources went as far back as the counterrevolutionary pogroms of 1905.[37]

The Communist crusade to delegitimize Israel began on the morrow of Israel's lightning victory over Moscow's Arab allies. This crushing defeat of three Arab states was a severe blow to Soviet prestige as an anti-American superpower and to the reputation of its armaments. Soviet diplomatic representatives and domestic media in the USSR immediately accused the Israelis of "behaving like Nazis." On July 5, 1967, Communist Party general secretary Leonid Brezhnev, speaking to graduates of the military academies gathered at the Kremlin, bluntly stated that "in their atrocities it seems they [the Israelis] want to copy the crimes of the Hitler invaders."[38] From this point it became almost obligatory to slander the State of Israel and its Jewish inhabitants as imitators of the Nazis, ardent advocates of "racism," "barbarians," "pirates," "vandals," and "practitioners of genocide." All the clichés, images, and trigger words like *Blitzkrieg, Herrenvolk, Gauleiter,* concentration camps, and SS executioners would be mobilized on a massive scale for the benefit of foreign as well as Soviet domestic audiences.

The Nazi metaphor linked to the charge of Zionist racism assumed a central place in the Soviet effort to defame Israel, Zionism, and the Jewish people. Yuri Ivanov, one of the "Jewish experts" at the higher levels of the party apparatus, insisted that Jewish nationalism was no less racialist than Nazism. In his *Beware! Zionism!* (1969), he maintained that Zionist "superiority" was confined solely to the cunning use of corruption, media control, and news distortion on a global scale to achieve its pernicious ends. Zionists were the sworn enemies of the Soviet Union and the Communist movement. Ivanov "enriched" Soviet Marxism with a "dazzling" new insight into Zionism: It was now defined as "the ideology, the ramified system of organization and the political practice of the big Jewish bourgeoisie that has merged with the monopolistic circles of the USA and other imperialist powers. Its basic content is militant chauvinism and anti-communism.[39]

Ivanov was one of a new breed of anti-Zionist publicists, which included Yevgeny Yevseyev (author of *Fascism Under the Blue Star*), Vladimir Bolshakov, Vladimir Begun, Dmitri Zhukov, and Lev Korneyev, who would adapt Marxist-Leninist ideology to official requirements. In their narrative, Zionism resembled a great invisible power whose octopus-like tentacles extend into every sphere of politics, finance, religion, and the communications media in capitalist countries. It was an international Mafia, controlled by big Jewish bankers and financiers, who had a vast intelligence service at its disposal. The villainy of the big Jewish bourgeoisie and Zionism had no equal in history. The Zionists themselves were, however, by no means only Jews. According to Yevgeny Yevseyev, writing in *Komsomolskaya Pravda* (October 4, 1967), they numbered as many as twenty to twenty-five million people in the United States alone, where they owned most of the news agencies (80 percent) and much of the industry (43 percent), and exerted a decisive influence over banking, law, journalism, and the professions. Such writing, in the best anti-Semitic tradition, combined wholly spurious statistics with a truly stunning and servile mediocrity. In these diatribes, the classic Nazi fantasy of a Western world controlled and manipulated by Jewish high finance resurfaced as if there had never been a Holocaust, let alone a life-and-death struggle of the Soviet Union against German fascism.

Zionism in the official Soviet dispensation was merely a cover for the Jewish bourgeoisie "to enhance its position in the economy of the largest capitalist states . . . and in the capitalist system as a whole."[40] According to Vladimir Kiselev, writing in 1977, the ultimate objective of Jewish capital was to exploit its special kinship relations to achieve world domination through control of the international banking system. This was plainly an old-new version of the *Protocols of the Elders of Zion,* revived in pseudo-Leninist disguise. Another Soviet journalist, the prolific Lev Korneyev, added his own gloss. He believed that the American Jewish capitalists were well on their way to achieving their sinister aim, since the military-industrial monopolies in the United States were to a large degree already "controlled or belong to the big pro-Zionist bourgeoisie."[41] Many of the oil companies allegedly fell into this category. So, too, did McDonnell Douglas and Lockheed Aircraft, "controlled" by Lazard Frères & Co., a finance empire "founded . . . by bankers of Jewish origin."[42] Although such major financial institutions as the Rockefeller Chase Manhattan Bank were hardly Jewish, in Soviet propaganda they would invariably be described as "crypto-Zionist." In this way, Korneyev and his ilk could maintain that Zionism "controls and directly owns 158 of the 165 largest death corporations in the West." The main point was to identify Jews as controlling the "war-mongering" industrial-military complex.[43] Beyond the substitution of the word "Zionist" for "Jew," there was little to differentiate this fifth-rate Communist hack literature from earlier Nazi or fascist productions.

Soviet versions of the *Protocols* dwelt on the "superprofits" of the big Jewish bourgeoisie whose real aim was to bring about a supergovernment under its own control. Israel was seen as an important connecting link in this vast design of the Rothschilds, Rockefellers, Lehmanns, and Lazard Frères. But the key role belonged to the "Zionist Corporation," understood as a complex network of interlocking parts with tentacles in every single area of business, politics, the media, culture, and religion. The metaphysical concept that drove this well-oiled machine and cemented the "cosmopolitan Mafia" was the Judaic concept of the *chosen people*.[44] This distinguishing mark of Judaism was presented by Soviet publicists as the ideological-religious mask for expanding Jewish power and its desire for world domination. Particularly striking was the Communist attempt to present Jewish chosenness as a racist doctrine of *anti-goyism* (hatred of Gentiles) obligating Jews to ruthlessly exploit, humiliate, and kill all non-Jews who refused to submit to their dictates. This was a blatantly anti-Semitic fabrication drawing on the long tradition of anti-Talmudic vilification in Christian Europe.

In his *Judaism and Zionism* (1968) Trofim Kichko had denounced with special vehemence the "chauvinistic idea of the God-chosenness [*bogoizbrannost*] of the Jewish people, the propaganda of messianism and the idea of ruling over the peoples of the world."[45] This "dogma," according to Kichko and other anti-Zionist ideologues, had been the justification for Israeli "criminality," responsible for the "extermination" of Palestinian Arabs and "hatred towards other peoples." Vladimir Begun's *Creeping Counterrevolution* (1974) developed this Soviet hate propaganda in classical anti-Judaic

language. Describing the Bible as "an unsurpassed textbook of bloodthirstiness, hypocrisy, treason, perfidy and moral degeneracy," Begun wrote that
Zionist "gangsterism," too, had "its ideological roots in the scrolls of the
'holy' Torah and the precepts of the Talmud."[46] Judaic messianism was
nothing but "a specific version of ultra-imperialism, an international trust
of capitalists exploiting the world."[47] Such Soviet propaganda had a considerable resonance in the Arab world, especially among more secular client-
states such as Syria.

Soviet anti-Semites such as Vladimir Begun worked to revise the traditional Marxist-Leninist interpretation of Judeophobia as a reactionary tool
of the ruling classes. In their new interpretation, the prerevolutionary Jew-
baiting of Polish, Ukrainian, and Byelorussian peasants and the czarist
pogroms of 1881 and 1905 were metamorphosed into a populist class struggle against merciless Jewish usurers. Dmitri Zhukov, reviewing Begun's
work in the mass circulation *Ogonyok,* fully supported the proposition that
anti-Semitism was a spontaneous reaction of the oppressed classes to "barbarous exploitation by the Jewish bourgeoisie."[48] Thus, the Black Hundred
pogromshchiki of the early twentieth century found themselves rehabilitated
seventy years later as precocious heralds of a Russian (national) socialist
order.

Communist bigotry found a resounding echo in the United Nations at a
Security Council session on September 25, 1971. Soviet ambassador Yakov
Malik replied to the Israeli representative's remarks about Soviet anti-
Semitism with a vicious diatribe against the "chosen people" and "long-
nosed" Jews.

Don't stick your long nose into our Soviet garden. History shows that
those who have stuck their noses into our garden have usually lost
them. . . . The Fascists considered that the ideal was the Aryan with his
blue eyes and blond hair. I do not know what the external signs are with
the Zionists; but their racist theory is the same that the Fascists advocated
towards all peoples. . . . The chosen people: is that not racism? What is
the difference between Zionism and Fascism, if the essence of its ideology
is racism, hatred towards other peoples? The chosen people. The people
elected by God. Where in the second half of the twentieth century does
not hear anyone advocating this criminal absurd theory of the superiority of one race and one people over others? Try to justify that from the

rostrum of the United Nations. Try to prove that you are the chosen people, and the others are nobodies. . . .

I must only regret that some political leaders—including those in the city [New York] in which we find ourselves—under the influence and pressure of the Zionists, because of mercantile and electoral considerations, follow on the leash of the Zionists and support them by every means.[49]

The USSR publicly encouraged such equations of Zionism with anti-Semitism, fascism, and Nazism at the United Nations. Indeed, as early as 1965, the Soviets had formally proposed that Zionism be linked to colonialism, racism, and other imperialist evils. They rejected the proposal by the United States and Brazil that anti-Semitism be condemned as part of the UN General Assembly's initial draft convention to eliminate all forms of racial discrimination. A further escalation occurred in March 1967 at the UN Commission on Human Rights in Geneva. The Soviet delegate did not shrink from attacking his American counterpart (Morris Abram) for "obeying the orders of the Zionists and the Jews of America" and allegedly "serving two masters."[50] These anti-Semitic aspersions of dual loyalty against American Jews were made at a time when the USSR was deliberately inciting both Egypt and Syria against Israel. In 1967 the Soviet Union and the Communist bloc (except for Romania and Cuba) broke off diplomatic relations with the Jewish state, lining up unreservedly with Israel's enemies. Between 1967 and 1973, the USSR greatly intensified its domestic and foreign propaganda against Zionism, which rose to new heights of vituperation.

One symptom of this anti-Jewish escalation was the reproduction in 1972 in the Soviet Embassy journal in Paris, *URSS*, of extracts from a 1906 pamphlet issued by the pogromist czarist organization Soyuz Russkii Narod (Union of the Russian People): The one change in the text was, of course, to substitute the word "Zionist" for "Jew." The original brochure had been called *The Jewish Question, or The Impossibility of Granting Rights to Russian Jews.* The Soviet Embassy article, entitled "The School of Obscurantism," consisted of various fabricated quotations from czarist and other anti-Semitic sources designed to prove that Zionism was based on a goy-hating Judaic religion that claimed divine sanction to massacre Gentiles.[51] On April 24, 1973, a Paris court found the French publisher of *URSS* (the Communist deputy mayor of Nanterre) guilty of public slander and incitement to racial discrimination, hatred, and violence. During the trial a Catholic witness, Rev. Braun, aptly commented: "Unfortunately the text we are studying today is reminiscent of the worst fabricated theories of *Der Stürmer* and other sheets distributed by the Nazi propaganda. It stupefied me, for in it I found the identical falsifications which have been exploited in all antisemitic publications, whether recent or old."[52]

The anti-Semitic propaganda contained in the *URSS* journal was no anomaly. It fused the made-in-Russia tradition of the *Protocols* with Nazi and Communist influences to substantiate the fantasy of a well-organized Jewish drive for world supremacy.[53] An imaginary national conflict between Russians and Jews was being fabricated and transformed into a confrontation between cosmic forces of good and evil that assumed an apocalyptic significance.[54] The age-old suspicion of Jews as a *malevolent* power anchored in *muzhik* (peasant) popular traditions, in Russian Orthodoxy as well as in the state bureaucracy, was reactivated on an unprecedented scale to do battle with the forces of "international Zionism." Once more, as in czarist Russia, the destructive power of "international Jewry" could be highlighted—this time as a force responsible for subversion within the USSR, including the encouragement of liberalism, Freemasonry, and intellectual dissent.

The Brezhnev years also saw the emergence of such fanatical anti-Semites as Valery Emelianov, an Arabist lecturer from the Oriental Institute of the Russian Academy of Sciences in Moscow, who would later become a Pamyat propagandist. In a memorandum of January 10, 1977, submitted to the Communist Party of the Soviet Union (CPSU) Central Committee, Emelianov claimed that the United States was in the hands of a "Zionist-Masonic" government, led by President Jimmy Carter. The U.S. president was supposedly under the thumb of the B'nai B'rith "gestapo," a philanthropic organization said to be engaged in worldwide espionage rather than antidefamation work. In lectures given during this period to Soviet audiences, Emelianov liked to warn of a deadly Zionist-Masonic (*zhidomasontsvo*) plot aiming to achieve world mastery by the year 2000.[55] This obsession with a vast network of secret (Jewish Masonic lodges) aiming at penetrating party, government, and ideological institutes was yet another link to the anti-Semitic worldview of the *Protocols of the Elders of Zion* and the Nazi leadership. According to Emelianov, the "Zionists penetrate into the goy's midst through the Masons." Every Mason is "an active informer of the Zionists." After the mid-1970s the theme of the Zionist-Masonic conspiracy, hitherto restricted to the fringes, began to appear much more widely in official Soviet publications. Since the fall of Communism, this classic anti-Jewish theory of the Jewish-Masonic plot has continued to flourish in Russian neo-Slavophile, neo-pagan, and Orthodox Christian-nationalist circles.

For Soviet-era anti-Semites like Emelianov, Freemasonry provided the vital fifth column of Gentile support in a world where Jews were decidedly short on manpower.[56] The Masons were paving the way for Zionism (which already dominated the Western economy) to achieve global hegemony. "The Zionists base themselves on the Judaic-Masonic pyramid, controlling 80 per cent of the economy in the capitalist countries and 90–95 per cent of the information media," Emelianov wrote.[57] Hence, the apocalyptic war against "the Zionist-Masonic danger" threatening the Soviet Union required a "merciless struggle." Emelianov even suggested deportation of Jews to remote areas of the Soviet Union in the event of a war with the West. He argued that the mass emigration of Soviet Jews to Israel should have removed the last Russian illusions about their true loyalties: "They have emigrated from Socialism to Fascism under the blue star of David. Is this not a threatening warning of the possibility of an even greater mass betrayal . . . if a new military situation arises?"[58]

Emelianov recommended the creation of a worldwide anti-Zionist and anti-Masonic front to expose the "crimes" of Judaism and to unmask the Western campaign for human rights and other fronts used by American capitalist interests. Freemasonry was nothing but a "screen for the 'chosen ones' "—the representatives of finance capital who sought unrestricted mastery in the "free world."[59]

Emelianov's last work, *De-Zionization*, published in 1980 by the Palestine Free Press in Paris, revealed a strong neo-pagan influence. The Christianization of Russia, he argued, had been part of "an international Zionist plot." It was the deep cause of all Russian disasters. Judeo-Christianity had undermined the Slav race ("the backbone of the Aryans")—the "greatest creative force" in antiquity.[60] Christianity was nothing but a Jewish secret weapon for weakening the *Slav* master race, according to this Russian reconstruction of the Aryan myth. Jews were an anti-Aryan "criminal genotype of a hybrid character," the result of crossbreeding "in the criminal world of the black, yellow and white races."[61] Emelianov's semi-delirious ravings (reminiscent of Nazi pamphleteering) did not prevent him from achieving a certain following as the Soviet system began to disintegrate from within.

Russian fascism had already emerged as a significant intellectual trend by the 1970s.[62] In the armed forces, anti-Semitic beliefs were indeed widespread, with the "imperialist" Western world perceived as being ruled by Zionists. In army circles, as on the "New Right," within the nationalist core of the Communist Party (and in dissident fascist groups centered around the samizdat publication *Veche*), hatred of the West, Great Russian nationalism, and Nazified anti-Semitism were fusing together in an unholy trinity. The ex-naval officer Ivan Shevtsov's two very popular anti-Semitic novels, published in 1970 (and compulsory reading in the armed forces), *In the Name of the Father and the Son* and *Love and Hate,* enjoyed official Politburo backing. They provided an insight into the flavor of this Soviet mutation in the direction of National Socialism. In the first novel, world Jewry, led by Zionists, has already obtained control of American imperialism and is busy secretly infiltrating the life cells of all the countries in the world, "undermining from within all that is strong, healthy and patriotic." Agents of Zionism like "Judas Trotsky" and his followers are shown to be part of the same subversive strategy that eventually will lead to the noxious penetration of liberal ideas, modernist art, and pornography from the West into the Soviet Union.[63]

In Shevtsov's second novel, the Jewish villain Nahum Hotzer is depicted as a sadistic pervert, drug peddler, and murderer who kills his own mother for money and dismembers the body of a beautiful Aryan teenager, after first seducing her and turning her into a dope addict. Other characteristics in this popular novel include treacherous Jewish scientists ready to sell Soviet nuclear weapon secrets to the United States and a Russian hero murdered by Jewish colleagues for wishing to reveal that Albert Einstein had plagiarized the theory of relativity. Shevtsov's "aesthetic" division of humanity into racially pure, blue-eyed, fair-haired Russians and diabolical dark-haired Jews is one more indication of how deeply the Nazi anti-Semitic poison had infiltrated the political culture of Soviet Communism. Russian television programs like *Skupshchki dush* (Traders of Souls), first shown on January 22, 1977, which branded persecuted Jewish activists as "soldiers of Zionism within the Soviet Union," provided particularly graphic examples of the new genre. Such films and novels denigrated Jews as congenital traitors, deliberately appealing to the basest instincts of the population and actively sowing hatred of Soviet Jews.[64]

Pseudo-historical works that depicted all the activities of Jews in Russian and Soviet history as dangerously subversive offered a more academic version of the same poison. But throughout the Soviet media, the message of Zionist ideological subversion, of Jews as a fifth column, and of international Jewry as a vast intelligence-gathering apparatus threatening the socialist fatherland, were widely popularized. Zionism was consistently depicted as the "enemy of the Soviet people," seeking to overthrow Soviet power.[65] There were times when the struggle against the "Zionist enemy" seemed to be placed on a par with the war of survival waged by the Soviet Union against Nazi Germany between 1941 and 1945.

This mountain of vilification against Israel and Zionism was a testimony to the mythical power with which it was credited. Zionist influence and omnipotence was deemed to have a cosmic dimension, truly satanic in character. Diabolical talents were attributed to the Zionist movement as it perfidiously moved to achieve domination over all other peoples and nations in keeping with the biblical concept of the "chosen people." At least until Mikhail Gorbachev's ascent in 1985, such propaganda relentlessly focused on the idea of Jewish chosenness and global hegemony as the master plan of Zionist devils in human form.[66]

The roots of Zionist Satanism, according to such anti-Semitic writings, lay in the Jewish religion and its racist postulates. Valery Skurlatov, for example, categorically asserted that "the racist concept of Judaism had served as a prototype of European racism."[67] According to Skurlatov—one of the leading neo-pagan nationalists during the Soviet era—the preservation "of the purity of their blood was proclaimed as the most sacred obligation of Jewry" while "the despised goyim were useful only as 'speaking tools' or slaves."[68] The ultimate aim of Zionist doctrine, as in the case of Nazism, was "to realize world domination."[69] At the same time, in the shorter term, it served to justify Israeli aggression throughout the Middle East and the repression of Arabs in the Jewish state.[70] According to Radio Moscow, "Everyone who believes in Zionism admits that a non-Jew in the Jewish State is a sub-human."[71] This was typical of the Goebbels-like incitement that characterized the Soviet media.

As part of its massive disinformation offensive directed at Africa, Radio Moscow told its listeners on October 4, 1967:

It is known that the ruling circles of Tel Aviv justify their aggressive policy by the policy of the "chosen people"—which in plain words means
racism. It would seem that a people who suffered from Hitler's Nazi theory should hate racism, but the leaders of Israel have adopted racism, this
extremely reactionary ideology of imperialism as their own. The theory
of the Israelites being the chosen people is now being energetically
spread. . . . It is well known that the Israeli extremists despise the people
of Africa . . . consider them to be second-class people.[72]

The goal of Communist indoctrination aimed at the Third World was to
build support for Soviet foreign policy in Africa and Asia, which included
the isolation of Israel. The constant visual and verbal comparisons in the Soviet media between Israel and South Africa were especially important for
Moscow's campaign to win influence in black Africa. Thus, according to
Radio Peace and Progress in a broadcast on October 15, 1975, it was monopoly circles representing Zionist organizations who "invest their capital in the
economy of the South African Republic and together with the local businessmen, control various branches of industry and agriculture."[73] The
South African Zionists, it was alleged, were "highly interested in preserving
the regime of exploitation in the South of the continent."[74] The South
African diamond billionaire Harry Oppenheimer was a special target of
this "new" Soviet-style anti-Semitism exported to the Third World. The
Moscow-based *Asia and Africa Today* described Oppenheimer (a Jewish
convert to Anglicanism) as the uncrowned king of South Africa, "a secret patron of the Zionist community in South Africa."[75] Repeatedly, the point was
made that behind the Pretoria–Tel Aviv nexus lay the interests of the "rich
120,000 strong Jewish community of South Africa, which has amassed huge
capital by exploiting the native population."[76] The "pious" among them
have assumed "the key positions in economy and trade and obtain great
profits from the system of racial inequality that reigns in that country."[77]

Emphasizing the South African connection became an integral part of
Soviet efforts to portray Zionism as a Trojan horse for Western imperialism
and racism in the Third World.[78] Israel, it was claimed, existed in order to
ensure the subversion of the Afro-Asian and Arab liberation movements. It
was an integral part of the neocolonialist ambitions of world imperialism
and a cover for American infiltration into Africa, though it had also developed its own plans for exploiting the continent's natural resources.[79] Natu-

rally, only the most corrupt methods were employed by the money-grabbing Zionists. Thus Israelis in Africa were reviled by Moscow for "selling untested and unproven vaccines . . . having the effect not so much of curing the patient's ailments as of emptying his pockets."[80] Far from being altruistic experts, Israeli technicians and advisers were depicted as permanently engaged in subversive activities against African countries. In propaganda directed to the Third World, Israelis would usually be shown as deliberately sowing dissension between Africans and Arabs in line with a broader imperialist conspiracy.[81]

Russian and Arab efforts to persuade more and more African states to break off relations with Israel finally bore fruit at the end of 1973. The Soviets intensified their campaign against the "close military cooperation" between Pretoria and Tel Aviv in these years. According to Moscow, both countries pursued identical "racist policies" and had a common ideological outlook. Both Israel and South Africa (unlike the USSR) favored territorial expansionism and had fought against Third World national-liberation movements, and they were jointly developing nuclear and chemical weapons. The constant twinning of apartheid and Zionism by Communist propagandists proved to be one of their more effective methods for infiltrating and influencing Third World, and especially African opinion.

The ferocity with which the Soviet Union pursued its campaign of abuse against Zionism was undoubtedly aggravated by the sympathy the Israeli victory of 1967 had aroused among Soviet Jews. For the first time, Zionism came to be seen as a comparable problem to that of other nationalist movements the Soviets (like their czarist predecessors) had consistently repressed. Anti-Zionism provided a valuable ideological instrument for containing what the Soviet government now saw as a serious competitor for the loyalties of its "Jewish nationality." The campaign against the Zionists was also a means for discouraging national liberation movements among the other subject peoples of the USSR.[82] The anti-Semitic component in this "black" propaganda was clearly devised to sow suspicion and division abroad. In Eastern Europe, as we have seen, Zionist conspirators were blamed for dissident trends in Poland and Czechoslovakia. In America and Europe, Jews who opposed Soviet policies were defamed as Zionist agents, while in the Third World (above all in Africa), with its sensitivity to issues involving Western imperialism, race, and color, Zionism was damned as part of a diabolical neo-colonialist plot. Soviet propaganda would therefore leave no stone unturned in its efforts to artificially transform Zionism into a "racial problem."[83] Moreover, in its broadcasts to the Muslim world, Radio Moscow was particularly extreme, entertaining its listeners with invented horror stories about Arabs being used as human targets by Israeli soldiers, Arab women being raped, and lurid accounts of atrocities against Palestinians, the destruction of whole villages, and the arrests and torture of innocent civilians—all of these actions being presented as a normal part of "the theory and practice of Zionism."[84]

This was the backdrop to the November 10, 1975, vote on UN General Assembly Resolution 3379 (72 in favor, 35 against, and 32 abstentions) that determined that "Zionism is a form of racism and racial discrimination." The vote was widely perceived as being a victory for Soviet strategy against the West, while at the same time demonstrating Arab oil power and the great voting strength of Third World countries in the United Nations (including many Muslim nations).[85] At the same time, virtually all Western countries strongly opposed the resolution, with U.S. ambassador Daniel P. Moynihan adopting a particularly outspoken attitude in condemning Soviet and Arab libels against Zionism.[86] Among the more eloquent journalistic responses was that of British literary critic Goronwy Rees, who noted that the UN resolution was passed on the thirty-seventh anniversary of the horrifying Nazi pogrom known as "Crystal Night":

> There were ghosts haunting the Third Committee that day; the ghosts of Hitler and Goebbels . . . grinning with delight to hear, not only Israel, but Jews denounced in language which would have provoked hysterical applause at any Nuremberg rally. . . . And there were other ghosts also at the debate; the ghosts of the 6,000,000 dead in Dachau and Sachsenhausen and other extermination camps, listening to the same voices which had cheered and jeered and abused them as they made their way to the gas chambers. For the fundamental thesis advanced by the supporters of the resolution, and approved by the majority of the Third Committee, was that to be a Jew, and to be proud of it, and to be determined to preserve the right to be a Jew, is to be an enemy of the human race.[87]

Writing in the "Observer" column of the *International Herald Tribune*, Russell Baker also evoked the Nazi specter and the Soviet embrace of Hitlerism:

Hitler must have had a good laugh down in hell last week when the United Nations General Assembly formally endorsed antisemitism by a large majority. After thirty years in odious repute the old dictator's theory of what made the world go wrong has finally been declared the collective wisdom of the higher-minded nations of the planet. The sweet irony of it, of course, was that the Soviet Union was right out in front. . . . The last time Russia embraced Hitler was in the non-aggression pact on the eve of World War II. By signing it, Stalin gave the Nazis the security they needed to march into Poland, a march that eventually led to the deaths of 20 million Russians. . . . The Soviet government has been so helplessly mired in political cynicism for so long that one has to come to take it for granted. . . . But rehabilitating Hitlerism—surely there were some things they wouldn't do. There weren't.[88]

Such moral indignation had some weight in the West at the end of 1975, but its impact was questionable in the longer term. Once Zionism was officially declared by the United Nations to be a synonym for racism, the Soviet Union and its Arab allies (each with their separate and distinct agendas) could remorselessly escalate their efforts to blacken Israel's reputation. On the other hand, the collapse of the USSR, the dissolution of the Communist bloc, and the repeal of the UN "Zionism-Racism" resolution in 1991 were decisive blows exposing the "Tower of Babel" of falsifications and lies on which the USSR had built its foreign policy. In the 1990s one million Soviet Jews came to Israel once Gorbachev had opened the gates—a resounding victory over Soviet totalitarianism.[89]

Yet there was a darker side to the neo-Stalinist legacy that survived the death of Soviet Communism. One symptom of this poisonous heritage was the apartheid analogy with Zionism, which constituted an integral part of Soviet "anti-imperialist" policy. It was a totalitarian fiction that would be eagerly adopted by much of the Western New Left starting in the late 1960s, despite its tainted origins. The Trotskyists, for all their uncompromising anti-Stalinism, became the most enthusiastic propagators of this Soviet falsification and avid purveyors of the "Zionist-racist" mythology. The Trotskyite Left (with Jews prominent in their ranks) not only systematically slandered Israel as a racist state but also unabashedly mobilized the Holocaust in the service of their anti-Zionist dogmas. Like the Soviet "revisionists," they did not so much deny the Holocaust but rather accused the

Zionists of collaborating with the Nazis in implementing it—a no less horrendous and baseless charge—which enabled them to reinforce the fabrication that Zionism had always been intrinsically racist and evil.[90] Soviet
disinformation further bequeathed to the Western Left (including its more
liberal wings) an utterly spurious portrayal of Zionism as the outgrowth of
Judaic chosenness. The racist hubris of self-definition as a "chosen people,"
called by God to rule over colonized peoples, was mendaciously attributed
in the USSR both to Jewish theology and Zionist ideology. These fictions
provided employment for a whole army of propagandist hacks. In the
1970s, the PLO as well as Arab governments joined forces with the USSR
and its Communist allies to spread these noxious lies about Zionism as a
dangerous twin brother of "racism," "imperialism," and "militarism" and a
spearhead of world reaction.[91]

The apartheid libel concerning Israel has probably been one of the Soviet
Union's most toxic legacies to the West, the United Nations, and the Arab-
Muslim world. It transformed Zionism (and by implication Jews and Judaism) into an inhuman ideology and the foundation of a state policy that
supposedly divides the world into Jews (a "chosen people") and goyim (inferior beings designated to be slaves). The "God-chosen Jews" have in effect
followed in the footsteps of Nazi Germany and South Africa. This Soviet
anti-Semitic fabrication, intended from the outset to delegitimize, isolate,
and reduce Israel to pariah status, has proven remarkably successful in the
international arena during the past forty years. It also provided, among
other things, a basis for recent academic and trade boycott resolutions in
the United Kingdom, Canada, and Norway; for continuing UN-sponsored
conferences and meetings like the notorious Durban anti-Semitic spectacle
of 2001, which—under the umbrella of "anti-racism"—openly fostered hatred of Jews.[92] Equally, it has contributed to envenoming the Israeli-
Palestinian conflict at every conceivable level.

In apartheid South Africa, it needs to be said, 90 percent of the black
population was disenfranchised and lacked fundamental civil rights—a situation of minority rule with some parallels in the Arab world but certainly
none in Israel.[93] Apartheid was a form of draconian discrimination enshrined in harsh race laws that were strictly applied—including the banning of sexual relations between whites and nonwhites. Nothing remotely
similar has ever existed in Israel. Nor is there any analogy between the
poverty-stricken Bantustans reserved as separate "homelands" for blacks

under apartheid and Israel's temporary control of Palestinian areas for security reasons pending negotiations to resolve the conflict. Foolish statements by former U.S. president Jimmy Carter, by certain UN officials, and some Arab spokesmen deliberately ignore the huge differences in history, context, and democratic ethos between Israel and apartheid South Africa.[94] They strengthen the feeling that the term "apartheid" is simply being utilized (as it was in Soviet propaganda) in a purely pejorative and abusive sense in order to defame the Jewish state.

"Apartheid," in its original South African setting, literally meant the keeping apart of the races (sexually, socially, politically) by a long list of legal prohibitions: They included separate housing, separate areas governed by pass laws, separate bus seats, whites-only beaches and benches—all of which would be unconstitutional in Israel.[95] Hence, the South African system, in total contrast to Israeli democracy, was built not on equality but on racial hierarchy and purity. Equally absurd is the designation "apartheid wall" for Israel's security fence. The barrier was not put there to separate the so-called Jewish race from Arabs, but to stop Palestinian suicide bombers from infiltrating Israel within the green line in order to murder Israeli civilians. This had nothing whatsoever to do with apartheid. Like other absurd analogies that pillory Israel as a racist or Nazi state, the myth of Zionist apartheid is yet another dark legacy of neo-Stalinist anti-Semitism bequeathed to a confused and disoriented Western world.

FOUR

Beat the Jews, Save Russia!

In the annals of anti-Semitic demonology there is no document quite as deadly as the made-in-Russia fabrication called the *Protocols of the Elders of Zion*, a text concocted between 1899 and 1902 at the behest of Piotr Ratchkovsky, head of the Paris Okhrana (czarist secret police) as a propaganda weapon to be used against the forces of liberalization and modernization within the autocratic Russian Empire.[1] Its main author was probably Matthieu Golovinsky, a Russian journalist and police agent living in the French capital at the end of the nineteenth century. He had plagiarized whole sections from the text of a forgotten French dissident writer, Maurice Joly, who had published in 1864 a satirical critique of Emperor Napoleon III's authoritarian rule entitled *Dialogues aux Enfers entre Machiavel et Montesquieu* (*Dialogues in Hell Between Machiavelli and Montesquieu*). Joly was long deceased and his work had nothing to do with Jews or anti-Semitism. But Golovinsky and his team of forgers transformed Joly's liberal tract into a purportedly "Jewish" document that laid out the diabolical project of world Jewry, or the "learned Elders of Zion," to achieve world conquest. The document, so it was alleged, contained the secret protocols of the first World Zionist Congress held in Basel (1897) under the direction of Theodor Herzl. At the time none of the forgers could envisage that this Russian fabrication would one day assume such great importance for anti-Semites around the world.[2] Nor could they imagine that the *Protocols* would eventually circulate in millions of copies in so many languages, from Germany to Argentina, from Turkey to Pakistan and Japan, to its current bestseller status in the Arab world.

For the forgers this was probably just one more anti-Semitic fantasy that might perhaps be useful in inflaming the sick minds of bigots and fanatics in order to block the progress of liberalism and revolutionary agitation in czarist Russia. Joly's text provided a general vocabulary and literary framework, but the *Protocols* also drew on German anti-Semites such as Hermann Goedsche (author under an English pseudonym of the 1869 novel *Biarritz*), who had visualized mysterious bearded representatives of the twelve tribes of Israel conspiring in an ancient cemetery in Prague to implement plans that would make Jews the rulers of the world. In addition, Golovinsky and his fellow forgers were doubtlessly influenced by anti-Semitic theories in fin de siècle France about the "Jewish syndicate"—an international conspiracy of Jewish bankers supposedly seeking to destroy the French nation at a time when the Dreyfus affair was still raging in Paris. Above all, there was czarist Russia itself, the fountainhead of global anti-Semitism in 1900; the classic land of violent pogroms against Jews and of prominent Slavophiles, Russian Orthodox priests, and nationalist intellectuals convinced that Jews were sworn enemies of Holy Russia, its autocratic rulers and peasant masses. There was no other country at the beginning of the twentieth century so receptive to the myth of a Jewish world conspiracy aiming to destroy the Christian faith and the hierarchical pillars of a backward autocracy. Nowhere else was the "Jewish question" mixed up so intimately with the crisis of liberal modernization, devious plotting, secret police intrigues, and a mystical belief in occult satanic forces.

Before World War I, czarist Russia was unique in Europe in its openly practiced discrimination against Jews, its conversionist pressures, and its forced assimilation (Russification) of other minorities. The five million Jews of the empire were second-class citizens parked together in a vast ghetto known as the Pale of Settlement. They could not live or work where and how they wished; they could not take Christian (or Russian) first names. In many ways they were morally "untouchables." As Lenin wrote in 1914 (only three years before the Bolshevik Revolution that he inspired and instigated): "No other nationality in Russia is so oppressed and persecuted as the Jews." Like other socialists (and indeed most Jews), he was convinced that the czarist regime and the secret police deliberately instigated the pogroms and anti-Semitism as a matter of state policy. Certainly, the pogromistic Soyuz Ruskii Narod, an ultra-chauvinist and proto-fascist organization founded in October 1905, was subsidized by the czarist government. The authorities encouraged and even sponsored anti-Semitic propaganda, and never opposed the violent activities of the monarchist *chernaia sotnia* (Black Hundred) detachments who terrorized Jews during the revolution and counterrevolution of 1905–6.

It was no accident that the *Protocols* were first published in Russia in their complete form in 1905, though a truncated version, propagated by the publisher Pavel Krushevan (a militant Bessarabian anti-Semite who helped instigate the Kishinev pogrom) had appeared two years earlier.[3] The first publisher of the document as a book was the Russian Orthodox mystic Sergei Nilus, who included it as an appendix to his prophetic work of 1905, *The Great in the Small and the Antichrist Considered as an Imminent Political Possibility: Notes of an Orthodox Believer.*[4] Nilus, a follower of the Russian religious thinker Vladimir Solovyev, interpreted the *Protocols* in Manichean terms as a cosmic struggle between satanic forces of darkness (led by Jews as agents of the Antichrist) and divine forces of light embodied in the Russian Orthodox Church. Nilus's edited version of the *Protocols,* revised and enlarged after the Bolshevik Revolution, would eventually become a significant force in world history and even "a warrant for genocide."[5] Already during the Russian civil war (1918–20), especially in the Ukraine, as many as sixty thousand Jews were massacred by White "counterrevolutionaries" who had systematically used the *Protocols* to incite massive pogroms.[6] Their political goal was to discredit Bolshevism, portraying it as a sinister Jewish conspiracy to seize power by destroying the landowning elites, the Romanov dynasty, Orthodox Christianity, and Russian national traditions.[7]

The Russian-inspired myth of Judeo-Bolshevism would be eagerly adopted by conservatives, monarchists, and nationalists in the early days of the Weimar Republic, especially by the young Nazi movement, which (under the influence of the *Protocols*) soon learned to identify Jews with Bolsheviks. National Socialism was in certain respects an international synthesis of the post-1918 German and Russian radical Right ideologies. The influence of anti-Semitic and nationalist White émigrés from Russia, Ukraine, and the Baltic region on Hitler, his mentor Dietrich Eckart, and the early Nazi Party (NSDAP) was indeed considerable.[8] The Baltic German architect Alfred Rosenberg, who had studied in Moscow, is a case in point. By 1921 he was already the chief ideologue of the NSDAP. Hitler very much admired another Baltic German from Riga, Max Scheubner-Richter (shot dead in the 1923 Munich putsch). There were also other White Russian émigrés, such as Fedor Vinberg and Piotr Shabelskii-Bork, who transferred the *Protocols* from Ukraine to Germany. Rosenberg and the White Russian émigrés played an important role in convincing Hitler and Eckart around 1919 to greatly intensify both their anti-Semitism and their anticommunism. The religiously inspired apocalyptic dimensions of Russian thought would merge by the early 1920s with *völkisch* notions of German racial and spiritual superiority. The *Protocols* in particular were planted on fertile soil after the humiliating German surrender of November 9, 1918; the Munich Soviet Republic of that year; the abortive Spartacus revolt in Berlin in January 1919; followed by Béla Kun's Hungarian Revolution carried out—under a predominantly "Jewish" leadership. It was these events, as interpreted by Russian émigrés through the prism of the *Protocols*, that helped to turn Hitler into a fully fledged anti-Semite and a sworn anticommunist in postwar Munich. In his *Mein Kampf* (1924), the same anti-Jewish conspiracy theories that were bread and butter for the Russian White émigrés are omnipresent.

Hitler identified profoundly with the *Protocols*, explicitly referring to them as a major influence on his thinking. They demonstrated "in an incomparable manner" that "the whole existence of the Jewish people is based on a continual lie." The text consciously revealed what many Jews thought and did, "perhaps unconsciously." The document had, in his view, definitively exposed the "inner logic" and "final aims" of the Jewish nation. Moreover, like the Russian authors of the *Protocols*, Hitler passionately believed in the virtues of inequality, hierarchy, and the subordination of inferiors to superiors. In fighting the Jews, he, too, claimed to be "acting according to the purposes of the almighty Creator." Like his Russian models, he was "fighting the Lord's battle!" in resisting the Jew; he was even acting as a messianic apostle of light in order to foil a demonic conspiracy. Moreover, like the first German editors of the *Protocols*, who insisted that the Jews had instigated World War I, Hitler made sure to "prophetically" blame world Jewry (in advance) for the outbreak of World War II. In the *Protocols* scenario, Jews are, of course, "warmongers" by definition, since violence, chaos, and disaster are the chosen means to further their dark goals. In 1933 Hitler told his Nazi colleague Hermann Rauschning (then president of the Danzig Senate) that he had very carefully read the *Protocols*, which both appalled and fascinated him. He had learned enormously from this document, which guided him "down to the last detail" when it came to techniques of subversion, intrigue, disguise, and political organization. "The stealthiness of the enemy, and his ubiquity. I saw at once that we must copy it—in our own way, of course. . . . It is in truth the critical battle for the fate of the world."[9] For the Nazi führer, the *Protocols* were literally a handbook for defeating the Jews (and all his other enemies) by using their weapons.

Since the 1920s, the *Protocols* have permitted anti-Semites around the world to reach a wider international audience, even in societies such as Japan, where there were literally no Jews. White Russian officers first exposed Japan to the *Protocols* in 1920 during the Russian civil war.[10] They would influence Japanese decision makers and ideologists until the end of the war in the Pacific in 1945. Forty years later, in the mid-1980s, there was a new wave of fascination with the *Protocols*. Dozens of books based on the idea of a ruthless, shadowy cabal plotting to subvert Japan and rule the world were published, some of them even selling millions of copies.[11] This highly profitable "literary" anti-Semitism reflected both the traditional anticommunist paranoia (from before 1945) and the increasingly intense (though sublimated) anti-Americanism that was linked to economic competition. The leading *Protocols* author in postwar Japan has been a Christian Protestant fundamentalist, Uno Masami, who successfully mixed anti-Jewish conspiracy theory with Japanese xenophobia and ethnic nationalism. Uno had previously published a number of works of Christian prophecy based on the Old Testament and visions of Armageddon. "Jews" in this kind of eschatology often become detached, free-floating signifiers for predictions about mass destruction, visions of the end, megalomaniac fantasies, identity crises, and salvationist politics. For example, Shoko Asahara, national leader of the extremist Japanese sect Aum Shinrikyo, which carried out the sarin gas attack on the Tokyo subway in 1995, combined all of these eschatological motifs in his attempt to implement a predetermined doomsday scenario. To this apocalypticism we should add the complex symbolic role that Jews have played during the twentieth century in the Japanese discourse on nationalism, identity, and modernization.[12]

. . .

The potent destructiveness of the *Protocols* initially drew on a long tradition of fear and awe toward the Jews in Russia and Christian Europe, which regarded them as supernaturally powerful, despite their small numbers. They were said to personify all the forces of modernity, secularism, the rule of law, democracy, and the capitalist market that potentially threatened the stability of established monarchies, aristocracies, and their religious underpinnings.[13] This destabilizing role was sweepingly attributed to Judaism per se and its "secret" allies (Freemasons, liberals, and socialists). Such paranoid thinking was likely to appeal to those who felt they were helpless victims of vast uncontrollable forces; who resented a rapidly changing industrialized world; or who desperately sought to escape from the uncertainty, burdens, and challenges of individual freedom.

Ironically, one of the great symbols of America's industrialization, the millionaire automobile manufacturer Henry Ford, embraced the *Protocols* in 1920 and did much to spread them around the world. According to Ford, the Jews controlled high finance, sponsored world revolution, and had already seized power in Germany, France, England, and Soviet Russia. Their power was now threatening the United States.[14] In Great Britain, too, the *Protocols* flourished for a time, until they were finally exposed by *Times* correspondent Philip Graves in 1921. But the image of the Jew on the British radical Right (much influenced by the *Protocols*) did not fundamentally change.[15] There were those in the British elite, such as Baron Sydenham, who genuinely believed that Jewish Bolshevism and Zionism posed a great threat to the British Empire and Christian civilization. A popular Catholic writer of that era, Nesta Webster, also identified "Jewish power," Bolshevism, Freemasonry, and descendants of the early nineteenth-century Illuminati with a frighteningly destructive plot to ruin Christian civilization. In her book *World Revolution* (published in 1921) Webster lamented the dissolution of patriotism and Christian virtue by international socialism, while "one race alone, a race that since time immemorial has cherished the dream of world power, is not only allowed but encouraged to consolidate itself . . . and to fulfill all its national aspirations at the expense of other races."[16]

But Judeophobic conspiracy theories were nonetheless weaker in Great Britain than in Russia or Eastern Europe. The intense belief in the Antichrist and a Jewish-Bolshevik onslaught of anti-Christian forces, which animated Sergei Nilus, never struck deep roots in the Anglo-Saxon democracies. But it has been strongly revived in contemporary postcommunist Russia. For instance, in 1993, the publishing house of the famous Holy Trinity–St. Sergius Lavra (home of the Moscow Theological Academy) published a book containing excerpts from Nilus's writings and from the *Proto-cols*. It became an instant bestseller, prompting repeated editions.[17] The core theme was "Russia before the Second Coming"; at center stage was Satan, the Antichrist, and various demons with their allies on Earth—above all the Jews. Nilus's books and the *Protocols* are still being published today with the benediction of local Orthodox Church authorities. Efforts since 2001 to persuade the state attorney's office to initiate legal proceedings against such circles for incitement to anti-Jewish hatred have failed. Nor is there any legal recourse against so-called "patriotic" works of those like the economist and historian Oleg Platonov who specialize in unmasking the "secret powers" of the Masons, the Jews, and their "Zionist protocols."[18]

More subtle versions of the *Protocols'* worldview are also reproduced in the work of Russia's most popular and best-known painter, Ilya Glazunov ("the king of kitsch")—a militant nationalist, anti-Semite, and passionate dabbler in conspiracy theories. Glazunov's huge canvas of 1990, *Grand Ex-periment,* contains a collage of prominent figures from twentieth-century Russian history. One can find in this work many prominent "Jewish" Com-munists, including Leon Trotsky, Grigory Zinoviev, Lev Kamenev, Yakov Sverdlov, Moisei Uritsky, Karl Radek, Rosa Luxemburg, Béla Kun, and Lazar Kaganovich. The Jewish assassin of the czar is also on display, drinking blood-red liquid from a cup. Nearby there are his victims: Nicholas II and his family, their heads surrounded by haloes. Underneath is a serpent cov-ered with five-pointed stars, his head pierced with a lance by Saint George (patron saint of Moscow). This is almost certainly the "Symbolic Serpent" of the *Protocols*—starting out from Jerusalem at the time of King Solomon, gradually moving over centuries through the major European capitals, and finally returning to Zion, three thousand years later. In other words, the world has been encircled and is now ruled from Zion. At the center of the large, red pentagram (a so-called cabalistic symbol of evil in anti-Semitic circles), directly in the middle, is another small star—"the Seal of the An-tichrist" borrowed from the apocalyptic work by Sergei Nilus containing the *Protocols*.[19] German historian Michael Hagemeister tersely interprets the painter's symbolism: "Marx and the—mostly Jewish—Bolsheviks are depicted as agents of the 'Judeo-masonic conspiracy' as described in the *Protocols,* and their victim is none other than Holy Russia."[20]

At the heart of Glazunov's vision and that of the Russian *Protocols* stands a radical division of the cosmos between good and evil, light and darkness,

Christ and Antichrist—very close to the traditional Russian Orthodox eschatology.[21] But this dualistic demonology was no less congenial to German National Socialism; and in a different way it was also present in the Stalinist theory of the "two camps," which presupposed that socialist redemption would supplant the morally bankrupt world of rotting capitalism. Rootless cosmopolitan Jews, along with Zionists, were assigned the classical role of Antichrist by late Stalinism, and they have once more had their contracts renewed in the contemporary postcommunist aftermath. In each phase (precommunist, Bolshevik, and postcommunist), both the Jews and Zionism have represented a "cosmic evil" and a mortal enemy, locked in a final struggle with the forces of light—whether they are embodied by Holy Russia or Soviet power.[22] In each case, the Judaic concept of the "chosen people" has been closely linked to a central theme of the *Protocols*—the alleged Jewish striving for global domination—and intimately related to the agents of *zhidomasontsvo* (Judeo-Masonry), who are assigned a special role in the diabolical conspiracy against Mother Russia.[23] No less characteristic is the continual linkage of Jews with money power, high finance, and hidden control of the global capitalist system.[24]

The failure of President Mikhail Gorbachev's policies of perestroika (restructuring) and glasnost (openness) after 1985 would prove to be a mixed blessing for the two million Jews then still living in the territory of the USSR—mainly in Russia, Ukraine, and Belarus.[25] On the one hand, the gates of the "socialist paradise" were opened for an unprecedented mass exodus of Soviet Jewry in the 1990s; no less than a million Russian-speaking Jews settled in Israel. As the old Marxist-Leninist ideology crumbled after 1989 (the sclerosis had set in long before), new liberal ideas dramatically improved opportunities for Jews to prosper and enjoy a sense of equality with other citizens. But there was also a striking increase in Great Russian xenophobia alongside the centrifugal nationalisms on the periphery of the Soviet Union—in the Baltic republics, Ukraine, Moldavia, Armenia, Azerbaijan, Kazakhstan, and Georgia. These "secessionist" nationalisms, interacting with ethnic Russian resentments, undermined the already fragile liberalization and reforms of the Gorbachev years. Economic decline also escalated existing social and interethnic conflicts as the Communist system entered its terminal crisis. In this tense atmosphere, Russian anti-Semitism began to revive and reconnect with precommunist national traditions and *Protocols*-inspired conspiracy theories.

In Russia, Pamyat (Memory) and other Russian nationalist groups, which had first surfaced during the Gorbachev period, became more open and direct in their use of anti-Semitic propaganda. They repeatedly affirmed that Zionists were responsible for Russia's disintegration as a great power and to blame for its military and economic failures and the loss of internal cohesion. A Zionist plot lay behind the disaster of Chernobyl; the social blight of alcoholism; the plague of crime, drugs, and pornography; and the infiltration of Western-style popular music.[26] Not only that, but Jews were now damned as being responsible for the historic "catastrophe" of the 1917 Bolshevik Revolution, the horrors of the Soviet Gulag, and the "genocide" of the Russian people during the dark years of Soviet terror. This "old-new" anti-Semitism suddenly raising its head in the Russian Republic was by no means a marginal protest phenomenon. Pamyat's leader, Dmitri Vasiliev, boasted in 1989 that his movement had twenty thousand members in Moscow alone and many more in other major Russian cities. For several years his followers controlled the Moscow section of the All-Russian Society for the Protection of Historical and Cultural Monuments, the Russian Republic Culture Fund, and a number of environmentalist movements.[27] The organization had many sympathizers in the Russian Writers' Union, including one of its presidents, Yuri Bondarev, and a number of respected popular novelists, including Valentin Rasputin, Victor Astafiev, and Vasily Belov, whose widely read books disseminated some ugly anti-Jewish stereotypes.

Vasiliev, a born showman and actor-photographer who died in 2003, attributed the destruction of national monuments in Moscow during the Soviet era primarily to Jewish architects, acting together with the Masonic enemies of Mother Russia. In its heyday, most Pamyat meetings would typically open with the ringing of church bells and the playing of patriotic marches. Speeches would harp on Russia's social and moral decline. Western rock music was, for example, singled out as a vicious form of Satanism—a vile product of "American-Zionist anti-culture" that was poisoning the soul of Russian youth.[28] Pamyat was supported in the late 1980s by powerful conservative forces inside the Communist Party hierarchy and the KGB, who were clearly interested in using anti-Semitism as a weapon against Gorbachev's policy of liberalization and perestroika. At the same time, there was also a backlash against such nationalist propaganda—reflected in some sharply condemnatory articles that appeared in the party press and important Soviet journals.[29] Critics pointed to analogies between the notoriously anti-Semitic Union of the Russian People created in the late czarist period and contemporary ultraright demagogy attacking the "Zionist-Masonic" plot in Russia.[30] By 1991 Pamyat had begun to lose ground to rival factions, movements, and ideologues of the New Right.[31]

But anti-Semitism remained the glue that held all these chauvinist and xenophobic organizations together—providing a vehicle for their bitterness at Communism and their frustration with the spiritual crisis of a collapsing Soviet society, and offering an outlet for anti-Western paranoia.[32] Additional intellectual credibility came in the writings of the renowned mathematician Igor Shafarevich, whose *Russophobia* (1989), with its apocalyptic anti-Western, anti-socialist, and anti-Jewish gospel, caused a considerable stir among the Russian intelligentsia.[33] The so-called Russophobes that Shafarevich denounced were those émigrés, dissidents, and Jews who had allegedly denigrated Russian history and mocked the backwardness of Russian culture. Shafarevich proclaimed that Jews in particular had molded Russophobic literature, driven by their own "nationalist sentiments" and a visceral hatred of everything Russian. The diabolical aim of this *maly narod* (little [Jewish] nation) was to destroy "the religious and national foundations of our life," to subvert Russian destiny, "resulting in a new and terminal catastrophe, after which probably nothing will be left of our people."[34]

Shafarevich's preoccupations found a strong echo in several prominent conservative publications, such as *Nash Sovremennik* (Our Contemporary), *Molodaya Gvardiya* (Young Guard), *Moskva*, *Sovetskaya Rossiya*, and *Nedelya*, which then enjoyed a combined circulation of around 1.5 million copies. The resulting debate over anti-Semitism was interpreted in these circles as further proof of the power of the Jewish lobby in Russia and its negative impact on domestic and international politics. Jewish "cosmopolitanism" was particularly attacked for being the antithesis of *pochvennichestvo* (rootedness in one's native soil). According to such nationalist critics as Vladimir Bondarenko and Stanislav Kunyayev, Jewish culture was inherently rootless and had been aesthetically impoverished by two millennia of exile; Jews were divorced from nature and remained "alien" to the "blood and soil" values of the nation; their "genetic memory" and "national traits" were totally different from those of Russians.[35] It is not difficult to detect in this literature some obvious parallels with German *völkisch* anti-Semitism of the Weimar period; one can find the same illiberalism, a similarly dark apocalyptic mood and obsession with cultural decadence, and a special aversion for omnipotent and ubiquitous Jews—symbolizing everything that was abhorrently Western, modernist, corrupt, cosmopolitan, and above all non-Russian.[36]

The nationalist ideology of post-Soviet Russia as it crystallized in the 1990s increasingly focused on Jews as a malevolent agent throughout most of Russian history—from the time of the Khazar kingdom in the Middle Ages until the present. In Russian chauvinist historiography, in science fiction and belles lettres, it was as if there had been a continuous negative development in the eighth century from the wars between "Jewish" Khazaria (whose ruling elite had adopted Judaism) and the Slavs, followed by the ravages of the Bolshevik Revolution and then the traumatic fall of the Soviet empire—one single malignant Judeo-Khazar conspiracy against the Russian nation.[37] The objective of "the enemy" was not simply to corrupt Russia but to pave the way for Jewish world supremacy. This far-reaching conspiracy theory was eagerly embraced by some high-ranking Russian Orthodox Church dignitaries, such as the Metropolitan Ioann, who had long believed in the veracity of the *Protocols of the Elders of Zion*. It was no less congenial to the neo-pagan wing of postcommunist Russian nationalism, which regarded Judeo-Christianity in racist terms as a historic disaster for Aryan Russia. They enthusiastically adopted the myth of a cosmic struggle between Russians and Jews to redeem the world.[38] The Russian neo-pagans and the Orthodox believers had adopted a very different philosophy of life, yet their positions on the "Jewish question" were not so different. Indeed, postcommunist anti-Semitism has proved to be very eclectic—blending currents from nineteenth-century Slavophilism, Orthodox Christianity, Black Hundred monarchism, proto-fascism, Russian nationalism, Aryan mythology, neo-Nazism, and neo-Stalinist "anti-Zionism."[39]

This post-Soviet anti-Semitism cannot be dismissed as a passing intellectual fad or opportunist mobilization of thuggish alienated youths. It found an initial political synthesis in the meteoric ascent after 1991 of Vladimir Zhirinovsky (leader of the misnamed Liberal Democratic Party), who garnered more than six million votes in the presidential elections of that year. Zhirinovsky called for a new imperial policy but focused his appeal on the defense of Russians in non-Russian republics, on promises to slash vodka prices, and a vague program of get-rich-quick privatization.[40] His Russian ultranationalism was designed to blend the Blackshirted skinheads and the intellectuals, the underclass in the cities and disaffected groups in the remote countryside, disillusioned Communists and Orthodox believers. Though half Jewish himself, Zhirinovsky did not hesitate to use anti-Semitic and anti-Zionist slogans in his political propaganda.[41] Zionism in particular was demonized as an evil force striving for economic supremacy and world domination, which had already achieved major influence over the American, French, and British governments and controlled many international organizations. As part of his project for a countervailing anti-American and anti-Zionist international alliance, Zhirinovsky set about forging links with such like-minded authoritarian populist leaders as Gerhard Frey in Germany, Jean-Marie Le Pen, and the Iraqi tyrant Saddam Hussein.

In the December 1993 parliamentary elections, Zhirinovsky's Liberal Democrats (LD) took 23 percent of the popular vote, becoming the second largest party in the lower house—an unprecedented breakthrough for a semi-fascistic party in Russia.[42] Although mistakenly dismissed by many as a charlatan and a buffoon, the Russian populist leader (subsequently deputy speaker of the national parliament) has proven over the years to have a remarkably durable appeal, based on Great Russian chauvinism and xenophobia, as well as his television skills and rabble-rousing showmanship. In the early 1990s, during Yegor Gaidar's liberal reforms, Zhirinovsky was able to exploit popular discontent with Russia's ailing economy, demanding a harsh crackdown on crime and a more effective foreign policy. He repeatedly spoke of restoring Russia's imperial frontier of 1900, of a military thrust to the south to eliminate "communist, Turkic, and Islamic threats," and the need for a strong centralized state based on one dominant nationality (Russian), sharing one culture and language.[43] Using highly ethnocentric rhetoric about defending "the white race," he openly favored an ethnically pure state within Russia and challenged the dominant cosmopolitan "new world order" represented abroad by the Untied States. It was in this context that Zhirinovsky strongly supported Saddam Hussein, even suggesting that Russia and Iraq should unite against "the American-Israeli plot" to dominate the world. Like other Russian ultranationalists, he now began to attack Israel more frequently, accusing it inter alia of seeking "to create a second Jewish State on Russian territory."[44] For good measure he held Jews to be entirely responsible for anti-Semitism and for all the major domestic problems inside the ex-USSR. In a conciliatory interview in June

2006, during a visit to Israel (in which he vehemently denied that he was an anti-Semite), Zhirinovsky even unfavorably related former prime minister Gaidar's privatization program to his Jewishness, adding: "Look at all the oligarchs—Gusinsky, Berezovsky Gaydamak, Khodorkovsky, Nevzlin—they are all Jews. . . . They were poor people who suddenly became billionaires. How do you think they did that? They robbed and stole the money of the Russian people."[45]

But how extensive is the primitive Russian anti-Semitism to which Zhirinovsky and others brazenly sought to appeal? Public opinion polling, which began to blossom only after 1989, does, at least, give researchers a glimpse into the feelings and stereotypes harbored by Russians. The initial surveys showed that Jews had a consistently more negative profile than many other nations (secretive, cunning, miserly, power loving), yet there was no massive hostility toward them.[46] A comparative poll in 1992 revealed that 26 percent of Russians held anti-Semitic views—less than in Poland (34 percent) but slightly higher than Germany (24 percent), Ukraine (22 percent), or France (15 percent).[47] On the other hand, there were and still are far more newspapers and periodicals with anti-Semitic content easily accessible in Russia than in any European country.[48] Moreover, one should not forget that the fear of mass anti-Jewish violence (along with the economic crisis) were major factors in the huge emigration of Jews from the ex-USSR in the 1990s, especially toward Israel. A particularly troublesome finding was the fact that 18 percent of Muscovites agreed in 1993 that a global Zionist conspiracy against Russia really did exist, with another 24 percent undecided.[49] This was a remarkably high figure for affirming belief in such a *hard-core* anti-Semitic myth. Another significant indicator was that between one-third and two-thirds of those surveyed in ten ex-Soviet republics opposed intermarriage with Jews. Seventy percent believed Jews avoid physical work. The same percentage thought Jews were mercenary. Two-thirds of the citizens of the ex-USSR were frankly reluctant to see a Jew as president of their republic, and 52 percent did not want to have one as their boss at work.[50]

Interestingly, although Russia, Ukraine, and Belarus no longer had a semi-official politics of anti-Jewish discrimination after 1991, a quarter of the former Soviet Jews questioned still believed state policy to be the main locus of anti-Semitism; another quarter saw the threat coming mainly from ultranationalist organizations and 10 percent from the anti-Semitic press. But the largest single group of Jewish respondents (40 percent) regarded hostility from ordinary people as the biggest danger facing them. Naturally this has varied in different republics. In the early 1990s, various surveys suggested that the most negative attitudes toward Jews were not in Russia and Ukraine (where anti-Semitism has traditionally been the strongest) but in Belarus and the Muslim republics of Uzbekistan, Azerbaijan, and Kazakhstan. The impact of decades of Soviet anti-Zionist brainwashing, as well as a natural sympathy for Arab nations in certain Islamic regions of central Asia, no doubt played their part. So, too, did interethnic tensions and the weakness of democratic values. In Uzbekistan, for example, 76 percent did not like the idea of a Jewish president, 68 percent opposed intermarriage for a female relative, 45 percent were against synagogues in their city, 30 percent astonishingly thought that Jews "must answer for killing Christ" (in a predominantly Muslim republic!), and 26 percent agreed that all Jews should be deported to the Far East.[51] Fortunately, the number of Jews in Uzbekistan remains very small compared to Russia and the Ukraine, while Kazakhstan has emerged as a relatively constructive force in Muslim-Jewish dialogue.

In the Russian heartland, anti-Semitism has generally tended to rise in response to cyclic spiritual, economic, and political crises—which ventilate suppressed and bottled-up hatreds that have traditionally been turned against the Jews. In the mid-1990s, during the economic chaos of the Yeltsin years, an anti-liberal, "red-brown" (Communist-nationalist) alliance was formed in which anti-Semitism played a significant role. For example, the leader of the Russian Communist Party, Gennady Zyuganov (who won 24 percent of the vote in the 1999 parliamentary elections), has often used anti-Semitic allusions in his political discourse, defending both the obscurantist views of Metropolitan Ioann of Saint Petersburg and the anti-Jewish vituperations of the young Karl Marx.[52] The Communists' mouthpiece, *Sovetskaya Rossiya* (with a circulation of about three hundred thousand copies) has been consistently anti-Semitic, sometimes even printing quotes from the *Protocols* and other equally virulent anti-Jewish literature.[53] The Stalinist anti-Jewish code word of "rootless cosmopolitans" is also back as part of contemporary Russian Communist discourse. Indeed, by the mid-1990s, the Communists (with their half a million members, they were still the largest and best organized party in the country) were openly propagating Russian chauvinism and anti-Semitism. They continually harped on Jewish control of Yeltsin's government, the business world, and the media and on the Jewish role in the regime's "predatory privatization," while stressing the close links of Jews with Western imperialism, their loyalty to Israel, and alleged hostility toward Russia.[54]

At their Fifth Congress in 1998 the Russian Federation Communists specifically referred to Russians "being forced out from essential spheres of the State."[55] As if to illustrate his point, in the spring of that year Zyuganov blocked the appointment of the half-Jewish Sergei Kiriyenko as prime minister, partly because of his Jewish roots; for Zyuganov, the fact that ethnic Russians made up 85 percent of the population, but the government was "dominated" by minorities, was intolerable. In a similar spirit, a letter by thirteen Communist parliamentary deputies in October 1998 spoke of popular disgust at "the anti-Russian invasion," the infiltration of the executive and the mass communications media by members of a "non-indigenous nationality": "individuals with dual citizenship," who had unfairly enriched themselves at the people's expense.[56] These barely veiled anti-Semitic euphemisms were directed primarily at the Russian-Jewish business elite, especially such "oligarch" millionaires as Boris Berezovsky and Vladimir Gusinsky.

In early October 1998, hard-line Communist State Duma member and retired general Albert Makashov brought the resentment against Jews in powerful state and business positions to the boiling point for the first time. In a television interview he bluntly stated that "it is time to expel all the yids from Russia"—repeating this piece of racist incitement at mass rallies in Moscow and Samara. In an article that same month, Makashov declared that the "yid reformers" and bankers had brought Russia to its knees by "usury, deceit, corruption, and thievery"; they had destroyed industry, agriculture, the army, the navy, and the Russian nuclear deterrent; they "drink the blood of the indigenous peoples of the State"; they had taken over the mass media, and they already owned 60 percent of Russia's capital.[57] His solution was to restore "proportional representation" for each nationality, a new kind of *numerus clausus*.

General Makashov's virulent anti-Semitism was not well received by most Muscovites or by the mainstream media. Initially, the Communist leader Zyuganov tried to ignore the unenthusiastic public response, claiming that the uproar had been fabricated by his opponents "to distract attention from the fact that people are hungry and unemployed in freezing buildings." While eventually conceding that Makashov might have overstepped a red line, Zyuganov promptly resurrected the old Stalinist canard that "Zionism is a blood relative of fascism." According to Zyuganov, the only difference between the two ideologies was that Hitlerian Nazism had attempted "to subjugate the world openly," whereas the Zionists "acted in secret and employed the hand of others."

Significantly, the Communist-dominated Duma (lower house of the Federal Assembly) did not censure General Makashov for his repulsive "expel the yids" insults. Indeed, they defended him at the time as a patriot, with Zyuganov even suggesting that his reaction was only "natural," given that Yeltsin had surrounded himself with Jewish cabinet members and thereby humiliated ethnic Russians.[58] In the same tone, *Sovetskaya Rossiya* blamed the spontaneous eruption of anti-Semitism on the "domination of individuals of Jewish nationality in the Russian mass media, their Zionist propaganda being explicitly hostile towards the Russian people."[59]

The Communist and nationalist backlash against "the oligarchs" came at a time of prominent Jewish participation in politics and a rapidly worsening economic situation. By the end of 1998 about a third of all Russians believed that it was necessary "to keep track of and limit the number of Jews holding senior posts" while two-thirds thought it undesirable to have a Jew as president of Russia. Opposition was smaller to Jews filling the positions of foreign minister or head of the treasury, for which there were several precedents. Interestingly enough, there was no marked rise in popular anti-Semitic attitudes, despite the provocative behavior of some of the more outspoken oligarchs, such as Boris Berezovsky, who had imprudently boasted that he (along with six other top businessmen—all of them Jews, with one exception) controlled 50 percent of the Russian economy—mainly in oil, gas, metals, and the media. Berezovsky's controversial personality and influence in Yeltsin's Kremlin—which at times appeared to be enormous—made him seem the personification of the "Jewish Mafia." Moreover, Yeltsin could not have been reelected in 1996 without the millions of dollars and the control exercised in his favor by Berezovsky and the other oligarchs.[60] Their prominence and that of other Jews like Anatoly Chubais and Yegor Gaidar at the head of the post-Soviet privatization program (or of Grigory Yavlinsky as leader of the liberal Yabloko bloc in the Russian Federal Assembly) have naturally been a gift to the ultranationalists while underlining Jewish economic and political success in postcommunist Russia.[61]

What is extraordinary is that twice at pivotal moments in modern Russian history, Jews should have entered the ruling elite in significant numbers—first as revolutionary Communists between 1917 and 1930, and then as bankers in the "liberal" postcommunist transition since 1989. The potential in such circumstances for intensified anti-Semitism has obviously been very considerable. This has been especially true for the past eighteen years, since Russian anti-Semites have traditionally equated Jews with Western influences and identified them with an *alien* capitalist spirit. Indeed, of the forty-eight extremist groups who formed the hard-line opposition to Yeltsin's regime, no fewer than forty regularly exploited anti-Semitism.

Some, like Alexander Barshakov's Russian National Unity (RNE) with about twenty thousand members at its peak, openly used Nazi symbolism and ideology. The RNE was born as a splinter group from Pamyat in October 1990. Within a few years it became the biggest pro-Nazi group in Russia, replete with "Hail Russia" salutes, swastika emblems, and black uniforms.[62] The RNE ingenuously claims that its black shirts are not an imitation of the SS but are linked to the robes of medieval warrior monks. In 1999–2000 the movement split into several organizations, but its ideology of a corporate ethnically pure Russian nationalist state remains unchanged. Its leaders compare contemporary Russia with Weimar Germany on the eve of Hitler's rise to power, branding liberalism, democracy, internationalism, "Zionist globalism," and the Jews as their chief enemies. The movement's key publication *Russkii Poriadok* (Russian Order) fuses together National Socialism, racism ("Russia for the Russians"), Orthodox Christianity, and a violent anti-Semitism that explicitly calls for driving the Jews from Russia.

Astonishingly, there are many other groups in this country, which did so much to defeat fascism in World War II, who today unabashedly espouse Hitlerian ideology; use graffiti with the traditional Nazi swastika; exhibit the *Totenkopf* (skull and bones) emblems, Gothic script, and runic symbols; and highlight the number eighteen (for Adolf Hitler). The skinhead image (as in the West) includes Nazi tattoos and greetings. Some of these groups, including the ultraradical Russian Orthodox National Socialist Movement, trace the swastika back to Christian symbolism. They see Hitler as a "Christ-loving leader" and Orthodoxy as "religious-racial doctrine" and call for a "Russian intifada" to destroy the "international yids." Others, such as the Slavyansky Soyuz (Slavic Union) led by Dmitry Demushkin, also openly identify with Adolf Hitler and his SS troops. Defining themselves as a quasi-mystical Russian National Socialist movement (engaged in an eschatological battle against "international humanism and its agents—Jews and Zionists"), they gather under a banner featuring a white swastika against a red background. The Partiya Svobody (Party of Freedom), based in St. Petersburg, is yet another small group that regards Hitler as a political genius, *Mein Kampf* as an "eternal book," and nonwhite races as *Untermenschen* (sub-humanity). All of these organizations favor the deportation of "hostile alien elements," the forced isolation of "all degenerates and perverts," and a self-conscious apartheid policy. The Opritchnina Fellowship in the Name of Saint Mikhail Volotsky has been particularly active in the past decade in calling for a "Russian Orthodox Hitler," forerunner of the returning Messiah, allegedly anticipated by the prophet Daniel. They, too, see the swastika as fully compatible with the cross, a sacred symbol of righteous hatred toward the modern world. In the future uprising, it goes without saying, the synagogues will all be set on fire as a herald of the coming Russian Nazi apocalypse.

The neo-pagans have their own websites and obsessions with Russian racial theory, and they deny the Holocaust. Along with other Russian "revisionists," they rely a great deal on Western negationist "experts," such as Roger Garaudy and Jürgen Graf, and quote from Oleg Platonov, Igor Shafarevich, and the Russian-Israeli anti-Semite Israel Shamir (now apparently a Swedish citizen and "Orthodox believer") whose multiple identities are almost impossible to disentangle. Then there are the National Bolsheviks (NBP) with about seven thousand adherents, hounded by the authorities and more leftist in recent years than Nazi oriented; and the overtly racist People's National Party, which has sought to mobilize skinheads against the "Jewish occupation of Russia," the Gypsies, and the darker-skinned peoples of Caucasia—Chechens, Azeris, Armenians, and others. Almost every month racial attacks take place against Asians and Jews—many of them fueled by the neo-Nazi ideology. The songs of Valery Poryvayev expressing "the right to fascism" give one a glimpse of the darker side of this hate-filled Russia. Here is an extract from a typical lyric:

> All of us are ready to become fascists
> If the right for glory is taken away
> And the light of dream is dissipated
> The people have their last right

The right to fascism
Two poisonous rascals will be destroyed
Twins: democracy and Zionism
Force of freedom and joy of revenge—
Our right to fascism.[63]

Although the Russian Far Right is notoriously fractious and splintered, on April 20, 2002 (Hitler's birthday) there was a joint demonstration in front of the Israeli Embassy protesting the Jews' siege of the Church of the Nativity in Bethlehem. The "zhids" (yids) were universally cursed during this rally as "Satan's children," "God's enemies," and "visible demons."[64] The Russian Orthodox element was very prominent in this demonstration just as it has become a fundamental component of post-Soviet anti-Semitism.[65] This is partly because, in contrast to Catholicism and Protestantism in the West, there has been no revision of Eastern Christian theological doctrines toward the Jews. For instance, there is very little Russian awareness of the Holocaust or of Christian responsibility for the history of anti-Semitism, and no retraction of the deicide charge. The Eastern Orthodox Church, especially in Russia, adheres strictly to dogma, remains conservative, and is traditionally subservient to political authority. Moreover, in the postcommunist era, the powerful fundamentalist wing of Orthodoxy has been thoroughly marked by currents of Russian nationalism, xenophobia, antimodernism, and anti-Semitism.[66]

Although there are some liberal reformist currents within the Russian church that repudiate the outlook of the zealots, they have to fight an uphill struggle against the traditional Orthodox view of Jews as Christ haters and dangerous agents of the Antichrist. The Metropolitan Ioann of Saint Petersburg (the highest religious authority) emphasized throughout the 1990s that "the whole brunt of the hatred of this nation of deicides logically and inevitably was concentrated against the nation that carried God within itself." The Jewish "spiritual essence" was far more incompatible with Orthodoxy (so he believed) than that of other sects or religions: No other challenge could be compared "with the religious war that Judaism has been waging stubbornly and uninterruptedly against the Church of Christ for two thousand years."[67] This was much more than mere theological disagreement. Even converted Jews (such as the liberal priest Rev. Alexander Men, who was assassinated in September 1990) were perceived as racially antithetical to the dominant faith and as a fifth column within the church. The "Christianized" Jews who entered the church, according to spokesman Deacon Andrei Kuraev, were organically incapable of grasping the totality of its heritage or shaking off their own inbred national religiosity.[68] The underground dissident Orthodox churches are, if anything, even more anti-Semitic in their either/or insistence on the total antithesis between Holy Russia and "anti-Christian Talmudism." They repeat the traditional blood libel as if it were fact (the execution of Tsar Nicholas II and his family being seen as a Jewish "ritual murder") and exclusively blame the Jews for the destruction of churches and the killing of priests under Soviet rule.

It is true that the contemporary Russian state does not rely on Orthodoxy as a major ideological pillar or on anti-Semitism as a nation-consolidating factor. (The phobia against Chechens and Caucasus peoples is another matter, however.) For the moment this somewhat marginalizes anti-Jewish currents but is hardly a guarantee for the future in the event of a serious economic decline. Extreme anti-Semitism remains central within the Orthodox patriotic and radical nationalist press, where Jews are regularly described as carriers of Communism, Satanism, the new world order, and international cabals designed to destroy Russia and "enslave the nations." In the Far Right *Chernaia Sotnia* magazine, one can read the following kind of typically anti-Semitic delirium:

> The Communists are people who accept dogmas of the imported Satanic ideology created by the Satanist Marx, representing the international cabal ... implemented by a gang of dangerous international criminals in our land, led by the supreme bloodthirsty pogromist and agent of world Zionism—Satan in human form—the syphilitic Ulyanov-Blank [Lenin].[69]

At the turn of the twenty-first century there were more than two hundred Russian nationalist publishers issuing such newspapers as *Zavtra, Duel, Russkii Poriadok,* and *Era Rosii,* as well as many magazines, books, and leaflets, that contain extremely toxic anti-Jewish propaganda; the total circulation of these publications exceeded several million copies and had no equivalent anywhere else in Europe. In addition, there are dozens of blatantly xenophobic and anti-Semitic Internet sites that openly propagate their witches' brew of hate. Classics like the *Protocols* are constantly being revamped in order to unmask the "Jewish plot to subjugate Russia" and establish a secret "world government."[70] All the tragedies that have befallen the Russian people in recent decades are ascribed to *zhidy* (Jews)—from famine and chemical warfare to intentional destruction of the ozone layer and the environment—not to mention moral degeneration, pornography, drugs, and huge economic inequalities. "Jewish rule" in Russia from Gorbachev to the present (as in the early Bolshevik era) is seen not only as satanic but even as genocidal.[71] This is an anti-Semitism that blends the czarist Russian tradition and dogmatic Stalinist myths about the criminal character of Zionism with borrowings from European racist and Nazi sources. The Russian neo-pagans, for example, who call for a modernized "Aryan awareness," reject the Jewish origins of Christianity and declare war on "Zionist globalism."[72] They see the contemporary period of reform in Russia merely as a transition stage in the ancient and eternal struggle between heroic Aryans and cunning Semites, who used Christianity as a destructive tool to erase Russia's true soul.[73]

Russian ultranationalists and fascists have developed an extensive vocabulary of hate over the past twenty years. Among the most familiar epithets, apart from *zhidy* and *sionisty* (Zionists), are *yudy* (Judases), *trotskisty* (Trotskyites), *kosmopolity* (cosmopolitans), and *degeneraty* (degenerates). Since the late 1980s, terms such as *sionomasontsvo* (Zionist-Masonry), *Siononatsisty* (Zionist Nazis), *Sionofashizm* (Zionist fascism), and *evreiskiifashizm* (Jewish fascism) have become commonplace. The anti-Semites have taken over much of their imagery and invective from Soviet anti-Zionist rhetoric, even while presenting the seventy years of "Jewish" Communist rule as a genocide of the Russian people. The Bolsheviks were rebranded as "Red Zionists" or "Jewish Nazis"—part of an *antigoiskii* (anti-Gentile) plot whose driving force was the "Elders of Zion." But postcommunist "democracy" and neoliberalism is seen as no less devastating. It is supposedly aimed at the total robbery and enslavement of ordinary Russians by means of privatization—theft on a massive scale practiced by foreigners, Jewish oligarchs, and their political allies. The liberal-Jewish-Masonic "plot" was all about transforming Aryan Russians into the poorest and most exploited of all peoples, following the collapse of Soviet Communism.

The reluctance of the authorities to open criminal cases against most of the Russian extremists, let alone prosecute them, has been unfortunate. The official response under Yeltsin and President Putin remained ambiguous at both the federal and local levels. Nonenforcement of the law against evident manifestations of anti-Semitism has continued for years, despite the fact that state legislation bans incitement to ethnic and religious animosity. Not even one hate-crime case in the year 2000 saw its way through the Russian courts. The approximately three to four hundred thousand Jews living on Russian Federation territory have therefore remained vulnerable to popular anti-Semitism and its uses in the political arena.

The Russian State Duma has played a particularly negative role in this regard. In December 1998 the Communist deputy, Viktor Ilyukhin (head of the State Duma's Security Committee) brazenly asserted in a parliamentary session that Jews were committing genocide against the Russian people. Complaining that there were too many Jews in Yeltsin's inner circle, he specifically called for ethnic quotas in government positions. Incredibly enough, he was supported by Oleg Mironov, Russia's human rights commissioner, who evidently regarded anti-Semitism as an integral part of the "Russian idea"—namely that ethnic Russians should have a "special status." This was entirely legitimate "in a country where the majority of the population is Russian."[74]

Against such ultranationalist definitions of human rights, the fate of those such as Duma member Galina Starovoitova (who fought hard for political pluralism, developing a more liberal Russian democracy, and outlawing anti-Semitism) has been a grim one. Starovoitova, a leading human rights advocate and adviser to President Yeltsin on nationality issues, was assassinated in November 1998. Yeltsin himself was shocked and did speak out belatedly about the growing threat from the ultranationalists, anti-Semites, and neo-Nazi movements. But the fundamental weakness of Russia's democratic ethos has nonetheless allowed all-too-crude manifestations of ethnic hatred and violence to go unchecked.

Following Putin's accession to the presidency in 2000, the domestic picture became somewhat mixed.[75] Since Gorbachev, anti-Semitism has been no longer state sponsored, but radically anti-Semitic politicians still have influence and are active within the Duma. The viciousness of anti-Semitic propaganda has not abated, nor have the periodic acts of violence against Jews and other minorities. Vladimir Putin, though no anti-Semite, rose to power in 2000 on a wave of nationalistic fervor (with racist overtones) related to the war in Chechnya. If people of Caucasian background are now public enemy number one, anti-Semitism is in no way diminished, since these forms of racist xenophobia tend to be complementary rather than mutually exclusive.[76] Moreover, anti-Semitic publications continue to be hawked openly at kiosks in Moscow and other cities, including Russian editions of *Mein Kampf,* the *Protocols,* and Holocaust denial literature. The newspaper *Duel* featured a major article in 2001 stating that "the Holocaust of Russians, organized by the Jewish Soviet power after the October Revolution" was *the* mass murder of the twentieth century, while the Nazi Holocaust was dismissed as "a vile lie."[77] Publications like *Za Rus!* (For Russia!) rant in Nazi-like language against Russian Aryan women having interracial sexual relations. A book by Yuri Kozenkov, *Will Putin Save Russia?* declares that "Jewish racism and discrimination against the Russian people have become intolerable"; the author predicts that the twenty-first century will be the era witnessing "purification from the filth of the Zionists' leprosy, greed, impudence, meanness and sadism."[78]

Despite Russia's veneer of stability and the economic consolidation during the Putin presidency (2000–2008), the wide availability of such hate literature from Kaliningrad in the west to Vladivostok in the east is real cause for concern. True, the government did pass a tough anti-extremism law and shut down two anti-Semitic newspapers in August 2002. But to this day police rarely apprehend the perpetrators of violent anti-Semitic acts, which have steadily risen in the past five years.[79] Between January and April 2007 there were 172 anti-Semitic and racially motivated attacks, resulting in twenty-three fatalities. In the winter of 2006, a Moscow-based monitoring center recorded a 30 percent increase in such attacks over the previous year.[80] They included a greater number of cemetery desecrations, assaults on passers-by presumed to be Jews, and cyber attacks on Jewish Internet sites. In its 2005 report the Moscow Bureau for Human Rights had noted that there were about fifty thousand skinheads in Russia (the highest number in the world); that members of neo-Nazi groups frequently targeted synagogues with small-scale bombings; and that Russian society was infested with various racist phobias and national hatreds that caused at least thirty murders on ethnic grounds during 2004–5.[81] A survey from that year also showed that more than 42 percent of Russians wanted "to limit the influence of Jews in government bodies, politics, business jurisdiction, the educational system and show business."

Although Putin publicly condemned the fascist version of the nationalist ideology and in principle supported legal action against anti-Semitism, such statements have found little resonance with local officials, unconcerned with Russia's international image. As Gasan Mirzoyev (president of the Russian Guild of Defense Lawyers) observed in 2005, efforts to implement the Russian Criminal Code against ethnic hatred have generally met with great difficulties, because "certain individuals in Russian society and the Russian government are still affected by antisemitism." He strongly disputed the position of high-ranking officials and the Prosecutor General's Office that "the problem of anti-Semitism was fabricated and is artificial."[82] Equally, he dismissed the tendency of local authorities to treat the issue as one of "hooliganism" rather than a real threat to the structure of Russia's multiethnic state and its underdeveloped civic society.

The Moscow Bureau of Human Rights has also noted in recent years that the amount of hate speech in the Russian mass media (including its more respectable outlets) has significantly increased.[83] Moreover, nationalist rhetoric and the "ethnic" factor are widely used politically, especially in the state Duma and local elections. Members of the Rodina (Motherland) and the Edinaya Rossiya (United Russia) factions in the Russian parliament freely engage in xenophobic incitement that heightens ethnic fears, anxiety, and distrust toward other nations within the Russian majority. In the case of Jews, this popular sentiment is present in parts of the bureaucracy, the security services, and the army, where Jews have long been perceived with suspicion as protégés of the United States and linked to the predatory capitalistic stripping of Russia's national assets. No doubt this fact played some background role in President Putin's putsch against the Russian Jewish oligarchs, including multibillionaire Mikhail Khodorkovsky (arrested in October 2003, charged, and then imprisoned), and the dismantling of Khodorkovsky's Yukos oil empire. Like most of the other oligarchs, Khodorkovsky made the mistake of trying to translate his huge wealth into political dissent, by supporting two libertarian parties opposed to Putin's authoritarian methods.[84] For Putin himself to strike out against Jewish entrepreneurs—seen at the grass roots as ruthless plunderers of the state's wealth—only increased his popularity with voters.

There were, however, no consciously anti-Semitic motives behind Putin's campaign against the oligarchs, in contrast to the deliberate moves made by twenty Duma lawmakers to ban all organized Jewish groups in Russia. In January 2005 the anti-Semitic legislators sent a letter asking the prosecutor general Vladimir Ustinov to prohibit "all religious and ethnic Jewish organizations as extremist." They argued that the teachings of Judaism and Jewish behavior were responsible for anti-Semitism, not the justified opposition to them by "Russian patriots."[85] The signatories included six Communist deputies, members of Zhirinovsky's Liberal Democrats, and deputies of the Rodina faction. In essence, the lawmakers suggested that "the typical Jewish qualities and actions" that provoked non-Jewish antagonism had been prescribed by Judaism for two millennia.[86] These negative traits were rooted in the Talmud and the Shulkhan Arukh (Jewish law code). They had produced contemporary "Jewish fascism" and generated ethnic disharmony in Russia. The Duma rejected these bigoted claims by a 306–58 majority, but the incident led Putin to acknowledge in a ceremony at Auschwitz on January 27, 2005, that to his shame anti-Semitism and xenophobia had indeed returned to Russia. Among its manifestations was a stabbing rampage against Moscow synagogue-goers (ten of them were injured by a local skinhead) as well as the Duma petition to outlaw Judaism.[87]

In June 2005, Russian Jews were stunned when the state prosecutor announced that he was going to investigate claims that the Russian translation of an abridged code of the Shulkhan Arukh from the nineteenth century contained racist incitement against Gentiles. After Jewish and international protests, Russian prosecution officials eventually concluded there was no reason to open a criminal investigation.[88] Against the background of rising anti-Semitic attacks, such probes into the Jewish religion (following another appeal to the prosecutor by five hundred public figures) only intensified Russian Jewish uneasiness. Many of the signatories had come from the Narodno-Patriotichesky Soiuz Rodina (People's Patriotic Union Motherland), which between 2004 and 2006 had obtained 10 to 20 percent of the votes in regional elections.

Today, there are probably no more than 250,000 officially recognized Jews left in Russia (some believe, however, that the true number may be two or three times as high), nearly 70 percent of whom live in Moscow and St. Petersburg. They have developed many active communal programs, thriving educational institutions, growing philanthropic networks, and good relations with the Russian authorities and the State of Israel. Nevertheless, they live in a society with a corrupt and dysfunctional criminal justice system, unable to deal effectively with such legal issues as hate crimes and hate speech.[89] Moreover, although anti-Semitism is not the main ethnic phobia in contemporary Russian society, Jews still have to face widespread everyday prejudice in addition to the rowdy ultranationalists, violent skinheads, hooligans, reactionary Orthodox priests, Russian neo-Nazis, Communists, and demagogic chauvinist politicians in the Duma.[90]

Worse still, Russia has remained a leading producer of intellectual anti-Semitism in the postcommunist era—a major source for the return of the ominous Judeo-Bolshevik legend. Even a great dissident writer like the late Alexander Solzhenitsyn was unable to shake off this long-standing obsession with the "overrepresentation" of Jews in the Soviet apparatus of repression until the late 1940s.[91] In his vast panoramic account of Russia's Jewish history, *200 Years Together,* Solzhenitsyn evidently determined to nail down a special Jewish responsibility in creating the terrorist Soviet state "insensitive to the Russian people and disconnected from Russian history."[92] He seemed excessively eager to blame Jewish provocations for the czarist pogroms; to disproportionately single out Jewish officers in the Soviet secret police; and to overemphasize the "isolationism" of the Jews, their so-called economic parasitism, ontological otherness, and revolutionary subversion, without providing any historically accurate context. These are the standard clichés of Russian conservative "patriots," neo-Slavophiles, and Orthodox nationalists, and are not made more palatable by Solzhenitsyn's undisputed literary talent. Moreover, Solzhenitsyn's insistence on seeing Russians and Jews as engaged in a "dualistic struggle," presented as a zero-sum game, only sharpened his polarizing vision, which generally reflects the imperial czarist version of events. Once he had arrived at 1917 (the "original sin" of modern Russian history), Solzhenitsyn compulsively began to hunt down the racial origins of his carefully selected Communist villains—especially those with Jewish-sounding names.

As in earlier writings, such as *Lenin in Zurich,* it is evident that for Solzhenitsyn, Russian Communism was an *alien* project, a catastrophic import of foreign manufacture whose organizers and instigators were predominantly Jews.[93] Ultimately for the Russian Nobel Prize laureate, the study of the past two hundred years can only conclude that the "Jewish essence" remains irredeemably foreign to the Russian soil and soul, while Jewish materialism stands fundamentally opposed to Slavic spirituality and idealism—a binary opposition present in virtually all European cultural anti-Semitism. Sociologically, too, the Jews are alien outsiders. They are peddlers portrayed as petty traders, usurers, or tavern keepers (engaged in "unproductive occupations") while the Russians (as hardworking peasants rooted in the land) are their productive antithesis. These stereotypes blend effortlessly into others that Solzhenitsyn exploited almost at will—about Jewish "clannishness," disloyalty to Russia (including desertion in wartime), ideological ferocity, arrogance, and tribal solidarity. It is indeed sobering to see that even when Solzhenitsyn claimed to be completely objective and nondogmatic, his ideological stance pushed him into perpetuating some of the most primitive Russian myths about Jews: perceptions that have their roots in endemic anticommunism, traditional Slavophile values, and the anti-Western core of Russian Orthodoxy.

Solzhenitsyn was, of course, a moderate in comparison with those Russian artists, intellectuals, priests, and politicians who still perceive World Jewry as the main enemy of Russia and Orthodoxy. The radical Orthodox nationalists are convinced that not only Jewry but the entire West and the new world order are servants of the Antichrist. They also have a notion of imminent Armageddon, reinforced by the al-Aqsa intifada in the Holy Land, the events of 9/11, the Chechen wars, and the growth of Islamic militancy inside Russia itself. This, in turn, is connected with the Muslim demographic explosion and the massive Russian population deficit. But an understandable fear of Muslim aggressiveness does not lead Orthodox nationalists to drop their guard concerning the Jews. As one writer in the *Russkii Vestnik* (Russian Herald) put it: "Dark forces, specifically the followers of Talmudic Judaism, try to produce a clash between Orthodoxy and Islam. . . . Therefore, to achieve their aims, the Talmudists use Wahhabism—a remake of Islam, a current that adapted Islam for its aggressive goals."[94]

In this paranoid conspiracy scenario, it is the Jews who are (vainly) seeking to manipulate Islamism as part of their plan to undermine Russia and Orthodox Christianity. Andrei Moskvin, writing in the same newspaper after 9/11, suggested a more apocalyptic interpretation: The terrorist attacks were needed to provoke a Middle East war in which the two mosques on the Temple Mount would be destroyed, the Jewish Temple would be rebuilt, and the Antichrist could begin his reign—a necessary prelude for ultimate salvation.[95] At the same time, on the Far Right there is a growing Islamophobia related to Muslim terrorism and the expansion of militant Islam inside Russia. Thus Islam in the past six years has begun to feature as one of the enemies utilized by the Antichrist, without any clear conclusion being drawn about Russia's role in the "clash of civilizations." But from the ideological perspective, Muslims are still some distance from being perceived by anti-Semitic nationalists as a threat to Russia comparable to that of the Jews or the liberal West.

Russians do, of course, follow events in the Middle East, but they are not much influenced by the "Palestinian question," Western-style political correctness, European "colonial guilt," or radical anti-globalism, which is still a relatively weak force. There are virtually no calls by Russians to boycott Israel, and many sympathize more with the Israelis—confronted by jihadi terrorism—than with the Palestinians. Moreover, in contrast to Western Europe, there are almost no *Arab* Muslims in Russia; the fifteen million Muslims are primarily ethnically Turkic or northern Caucasian peoples, such as the Tatars, Chechens, Bashkirs, Karachais, and Dagestanis. Except for the Chechen fighters (who are indeed part of the global jihad), there is little desire on the part of most Muslims or ethnic Russians to be drawn into the Middle East conflict, let alone into the war of civilizations. On the other hand, Islamic fundamentalism in the ex-USSR does constitute a danger to security. Some of the Islamist organizations, financed from Saudi Arabia, are engaged in terror, and their activity has been banned.[96] There is some spillover effect in central Asia (especially in Uzbekistan and Tajikistan) of Taliban influences from Afghanistan. Chechen rebel leaders have called for war against worldwide Zionism and incorporated some of the anti-Semitism of their Arab mentors into their own propaganda. Moreover, despite their reciprocal hostility, Islamic fundamentalists and Russian neo-Nazis do agree on many issues relating to Jews and the State of Israel.

Muslim anti-Semitism in the Russian Federation, as elsewhere, draws on Koranic and religious sources, feelings of pan-Islamic solidarity (the sense of belonging to the global Muslim community), and anti-Zionist ideology. Between 1996 and 1999, Chechnya became a prime example of such Muslim "anti-Semitism without Jews," with fundamentalist militants claiming that their people were the victims of a world Zionist plot. The Chechen separatists distributed literature to journalists about the *zhidomasontsvo* (Jewish-Masonic conspiracy) identical with that published by Pamyat and similar groups in Moscow. The militants presented Chechnya as a major front in the global war between Zionism and Islam, no different from Palestine or Lebanon. When Islamists invaded Dagestan in the summer of 1999, they announced that the ultimate goal of the war was to liberate Jerusalem. According to their reasoning, the Zionists had instigated the Chechen wars in order to subjugate the worldwide Muslim nation—the last major obstacle to their scheme of global conquest! Since the fundamentalists preach that Judaism seeks to foment wars and stands behind *all* the enemies of Allah (including Freemasonry and Communism), Jews are obviously responsible for any contemporary conflict in which Islam is involved. According to the Wahhabite teachings, which have spread to the Northern Caucasus and the former Soviet Central Asian republics, Jews are also intent on undermining Islam's "moral and spiritual values"; they do this through seeking to spread modern Western democratic values, which are essentially Jewish. As with Russian Orthodox anti-Semites, the Islamists view the struggle against the Jews as a battle against the West, democracy, and Satan himself.[97]

Aggressive propaganda against the State of Israel is organically linked to this dogmatic anti-Semitism driven by conspiracy theories. The war to liberate Jerusalem from the infidel has some resonance with the Muslim masses, and support for Palestine is an axiom for virtually all Russian Islamic leaders. By stressing anti-Zionism and the Palestinian cause, it is easier for fundamentalists to find a common language with Communists, National Bolsheviks, and even the latently "Islamophobe" Orthodox nationalists. Such links between Russian and Islamic radicals do exist (based on anti-Westernism and anti-Semitism) but are unlikely to expand as long as major internal problems, such as the Chechen conflict, persist. But the growing anti-Semitic trend among a broad segment of Russian Muslims is already a fact, aggravated by the terrorist assault on the United States in September 2001 and the Western response.[98] Many Russian Muslims believe that the West declared war on Islam after 9/11, urged on and manipulated by a global Zionist conspiracy. It is Israel and its supporters who are, therefore, responsible for inciting Christians against Muslims and using the war on terror to justify the repression of the Palestinians. Such conspiracy theories concerning world Zionism are now as fashionable on Russian Muslim Internet sites as they are in Europe or the Middle East. They bring new life to the paranoid visions of the Russian secret police forgers who originally fabricated the *Protocols of the Elders of Zion*.

FIVE

The Postcommunist Trauma

The collapse of the Soviet empire, which began to unfold in 1989, was a cataclysmic event, even though (with the exception of Romania) it took place relatively peacefully. The USSR—the most potent military force on the continent of Europe since 1945—simply disintegrated, thereby ending the Cold War. So, too, the stranglehold of Communist ideology and the endemic fear induced by semi-totalitarian regimes in the hearts of their subjects began to wither away. While the old order crumbled, however, what replaced it was hardly a brave new world. New rules of the game had to be invented in eastern Europe, faced as it was with acute poverty, chaos, political backwardness, moral confusion, and the dizzying but also potentially self-destructive consequences of personal freedom. Exclusivist, integral nationalisms suddenly emerged out of the deep freeze in which they had been left to fester during the era of Soviet hegemony. In 1990, "*les vieux démons*" (the old demons) of anti-Semitism and interethnic hatreds seemed to be alive and well, dancing on the grave of the Communist despotisms that were being freshly buried.

The palpable revival of anti-Semitism in eastern Europe puzzled most observers at the time. For in many respects this was an "antisemitism without Jews."[1] On the eve of the Holocaust, there had been 3.2 million Jews in Poland alone—the second largest Jewish community in the world; by 1990 there was only the pale shadow of some 10,000 Jews still left to maintain the shattered legacy. In 1939 there had been approximately 850,000 Jews in Greater Romania. Today, the 8,000 survivors represent less than 0.1 percent of the population, yet the anti-Semitic discourse in Romanian nationalist circles has remained pervasive. In the postcommunist transition, similar phenomena have existed elsewhere in eastern Europe, in the Balkans, and in the Baltic states, regions that only sixty years earlier contained 80 percent of Europe's

Jewish population and one-half of world Jewry. Only Hungary and Ukraine, with their estimated 100,000 Jews each, formed limited and partial exceptions to the nearly total decimation of these great communities wrought by Hitler's Holocaust. Yet despite the small number of survivors, postcommunist anti-Semitism is still a factor in public life.

In the Hungarian elections of March 1990, for example, the Alliance of Free Democrats (a party generally favored by Hungarian Jews) was targeted in an unmistakably anti-Semitic way by supporters of the victorious Hungarian Democratic Forum.[2] The Forum's vice president and one of its leading spokesmen at the time, the talented playwright István Csurka, scathingly referred to the Jews as a "dwarfish minority" who had made the whole of Hungarian society accept "that their truth is the only truth." The populist Forum called on the public to vote for "true Hungarians," and Stars of David were daubed on some posters of the Social Democratic Party, in which Jews were known to play an important role.

In Hungary, the link between Jews and the Left went back to the ill-fated and short-lived Bolshevik Revolution of 1919 led by Béla Kun, in which Jewish involvement had been especially heavy. This had encouraged bloody pogroms directed against Communists and Jews, increasingly regarded by the traditional elites and ordinary Hungarians as identical. This collective trauma was repeated again after 1945 when a small clique of Hungarian "Muscovite Jews," rallying around the ultra-Stalinist Mátyás Rákosi, succeeded in hanging on to the reins of power until the 1956 popular rising in Budapest to overthrow Soviet rule. This naturally revived the myth of Judeo-Bolshevism, which in Hungary, at least, had some partial validity.[3] After the fall of Communism in 1990, István Csurka openly blamed these same "Jewish" Stalinists for having destroyed the self-esteem of the Hungarian people. He contemptuously dismissed the liberal Hungarian president Árpád Göncz for being a puppet in the hands of "Jews, Bolsheviks and world bankers."[4] As editor in chief of the influential *Magyar Fórum*, Csurka called for restoring power to the "ethnic Magyars" and the "Christian" middle class. At the same time, the playwright constantly emphasized "the holy concept of the people," in opposition to the Jews, Communists, and liberals who had dominated Hungarian politics since 1945. Csurka's rhetoric was highly nationalist and irredentist in its appeal to the Hungarian minorities in Transylvania, Slovakia, and Yugoslavia. It also attracted all those Magyars who felt their advance had been blocked by Communist rule, including those in the less educated and more conservative rural Hungary—always suspicious of urban, cosmopolitan Budapest, with its Jews, liberals, and Marxist intelligentsia.[5]

But how representative was such ethno-nationalist anti-Semitism of the general Hungarian population? In a broad study first published in 1999, sociologist András Kovács came to some interesting conclusions. His examination revealed that 25 percent of Hungarians were clearly anti-Semitic, while 32 percent accepted some of the key economic stereotypes formed about Jews over the centuries. Anti-Semitism was more frequent among residents of Budapest. It was generally related to xenophobia, especially among older and less educated groups. If such prejudices still appeared weaker than in Poland, Slovakia, or Austria in 1991, Hungary had closed the gap by the end of the decade. Jews were generally seen as "materialistic" (78 percent), "pushy" (66 percent), "cunning" (63 percent), and "rapacious" (62 percent). Fifty-three percent of adult Hungarians thought it would be better if the Jews' role in national affairs reflected their proportion (less than 1 percent) in the population; 35 percent agreed that fewer Jews should be politicians, journalists, and bankers; 41 percent stated that when doing business with a Jew, "one cannot be too careful."[6]

A further survey in 2002 did not produce any dramatic changes. True, there were more Hungarians who thought that Jewish influence in the media and culture to be excessive (34 percent) or that the liberal parties represented Jewish interests (24 percent). On the other hand, fewer respondents believed that Jews were the chief beneficiaries of Hungary's democratization (22 percent). It would appear from this study that xenophobia and conservatism are far more significant as correlating factors with anti-Semitism than either social or economic status.[7] In 2002, as in 1995, one in four of all Hungarians could be classified as anti-Semites. Yet Holocaust denial in Hungary remained an extremely marginal phenomenon. Only 2 percent of Hungarians thought it possible that the Holocaust never happened—a low figure even by comparison with western Europe.

An ADL survey of six European countries (including Hungary) published in July 2007 provides a comparative dimension to the broader picture. Fifty percent of all Hungarians polled in May–June 2007 believed Jews were more loyal to Israel than their native land (close to the European average); 60 percent felt Jews had "too much power in the business world" and in international finance—the highest percentage in Europe—except for

Spain.[8] Fifty-eight percent of Hungarians also considered that Jews spoke too much about the Holocaust—again, this was the highest percent among the European countries in the survey. Twenty-six percent held Jews responsible for the death of Christ—this, too, was higher than the European average but lower than the Polish figures (39 percent). Overall, one in two Hungarians were susceptible to *classical* anti-Semitic stereotypes. This is likely to rise still further as Hungary is battered by the global economic crisis and rising unemployment. More than most Europeans, Hungarians have long held the belief that Jews exercise great influence in commerce, banking, and industry. This was certainly true in pre-Holocaust Hungary and has survived into the present, with Jews generally belonging to the prosperous, highly assimilated bourgeoisie, while voting on the left.[9] Hence, center-right governments in Hungary, like that of Viktor Orbán (swept from power in 2002), have usually been less receptive to Jewish concerns. Not accidentally, it was the Orbán government that established the "House of Terror" museum in Budapest, highlighting Hungarian suffering under Communism while downplaying the mass murder of Hungarian Jews during the Holocaust.[10] In Hungary, as in Romania, Slovakia, Croatia, and Poland, the "history cleansers" have been hard at work in recent years sanitizing the dark wartime past and blaming Jews for bringing Communist tyranny to their lands. In this nationalist narrative, the "Red Holocaust," supposedly masterminded by Jews, has supplanted and repressed the evils of the Final Solution.[11] Not surprisingly, neo-Nazi and fascist skinhead groups have found this to be a congenial soil in which to sow the seeds of hate.

Postcommunist anti-Semitic discourse in Hungary, as elsewhere, has often focused its attack on liberal Jews as the promoters of globalization, the new world order, and an Americanized capitalist modernity in east-central Europe. One prime target has been the multimillionaire Hungarian-American-Jewish philanthropist George Soros, who did indeed finance programs in the region designed to advance such goals. Also targeted were the "Jewish liberals" around President Bill Clinton in the late 1990s, including Secretary of State Madeleine Albright, Defense Secretary William Cohen, and National Security Adviser Sandy Berger. Csurka's right-wing Party of Hungarian Justice and Life (MIÉP), which won just over 5 percent of the vote in the 1998 national elections, frequently indulged in illiberal and even paranoid rhetoric against the "Jewish conspiracy," linking Budapest with New York and Tel Aviv. His supporters are firmly convinced that there is a U.S.-Israeli-Jewish axis of evil. Csurka himself responded to the Durban antiracism conference and the attacks on the World Trade Center in September 2001 by identifying with "the downtrodden of the Third World," denouncing America, and condemning the "exploitation and purposeful genocide in Palestine."[12] In *Magyar Fórum*, there were many spiteful articles in this vein, many of them written by an ex-Israeli Jew named Jozsef Herring.

· · ·

Anti-Semitism in postcommunist Romania has been even more intense and popular than in Hungary. Its roots go back to medieval Christian myths and the power of Romanian folkloric legends. In the nineteenth century, Jews came to be regarded as exploiters and "parasites" in the only European land (outside czarist Russia) that had *not* emancipated its Jews before 1914, still treating them as invaders imposed on the nation by foreign powers.[13] Jews were considered by the mass of Romanians as dangerous and subversive agents of modernity, and as antinational—an alien, enemy population.[14] Academicians, writers, and artists such as the nineteenth-century "national poet" Mihai Eminescu and the joint founders of Romania's first explicitly anti-Semitic political party in 1910—the renowned historian Nicolae Iorga and the law professor A. C. Cuza—gave anti-Semitism a certain intellectual respectability. In 1927 the Legion of the Archangel Michael was founded (its adherents known as "legionnaires")—committed to an antidemocratic authoritarian order, which crudely mixed Italian fascist ideology and Nazi racist slogans. At its core was an intensely *populist* Romanian nationalism, which blended nativism, Christian Orthodox mysticism, and a quasi-metaphysical anti-Semitism shared by such charismatic academics as Nae Ionescu and great scholars such as Mircea Eliade. This movement evolved into the so-called Iron Guard, whose leader Corneliu Codreanu was Romania's most notorious Jew-baiting demagogue until his execution ("while trying to escape") in 1937.[15]

In the critical decade of the 1930s, the Romanian intellectual elite and millions of their compatriots held Jews responsible for everything considered as alien, morally perverted, or culturally decadent. They were depicted as the antithesis of the nation's popular values, rooted in the peasantry—symbolizing all the sinful, immoral, materialist, and hybrid characteristics of capitalist modernity. In a December 1935 parliamentary speech delivered as leader of the National Christian Party, the aging poet Octavian Goga crudely attacked the Jews for thinking "that they can direct our soul, the ethereal impulse of our thought; they imagine that any moral manifestation of ours is their patrimony and grasp it with their filthy hands; they have transformed their printing presses, quite simply, into a tool for the ruination of Romanian society."[16]

In 1937, as prime minister, Goga would initiate anti-Semitic decrees that deprived tens of thousands of Romanian Jews of their citizenship and other rights. In January 1941, during their brief reign of terror, the Iron Guard exhibited a much more brutal and bloody anti-Semitism, hanging the corpses of Jews from the Bucharest ghetto on hooks under a sign that said "Kosher Meat." Under Marshal Ion Antonescu's dictatorship, a policy of expropriation, deportation, and finally mass murder was set in motion and accepted by a majority of the country's political, cultural, and religious elites. Between 280,000 and 380,000 Romanian and Ukrainian Jews were murdered during the Holocaust by the Antonescu regime in Romania and the territories under its control.[17] Nonetheless, until the summer of 2002, numerous streets and squares were still named after Romania's wartime dictator. His statues were even prominently displayed in public places.

Antonescu's supporters deliberately ignored the horrible crimes committed under his direct command, mendaciously presenting him as a "protector" and savior of Jews. After 1990, on radio and TV stations, as well as in the press and the Romanian Academy, both the denial of Romanian responsibility for Jewish deaths during the Shoah and the downplaying of the numbers of those killed were commonplace.[18] From the floor of the Senate, in the nationalist opposition weekly *Romania Mare* (Greater Romania), edited by Corneliu Vadim Tudor, and in the general media, the populists shamelessly minimized and mocked the Holocaust, quoting Roger Garaudy, Norman Finkelstein, and various Western "deniers" while calling on Romanian Jews to erect statues to Antonescu as a mark of their gratitude. Professor Gheorghe Buzatu, a respected historian affiliated to *Romania Mare*, a vice president of the Senate, and a leading figure in promulgating the cult of Antonescu as martyr and hero, provided additional intellectual reinforcement for the Holocaust deniers. He focused primarily on the "millions of victims throughout the world" who had been murdered by the Communists.

Anti-Semites in the Romanian parliament (as in the press) began to spread the myth of Judeo-Communism with impunity. Even a totally assimilated, self-denying, and patriotic Jew like ex–prime minister Petre Roman (the last practicing Jew in his family was his paternal grandfather) became the frequent target of nationalist anti-Semites for "disguising" his true identity. Ultranationalists claimed that as a Jew he was deaf to "the call of the people," a call that only ethnic Romanians could hear.[19] Graffiti on Bucharest walls read, "Roman isn't Romanian." Silviu Brucan, another highly assimilated Jew, éminence grise and theorist of the "ex-Communist" National Salvation Front, was accused by political opponents of "organizing the genocide of the Romanian people" (along with other Jewish Communists) during the postwar years.[20] *Romania Mare*, with a peak circulation of about six hundred thousand in the early 1990s (it has fallen since then), regularly featured anti-Semitic articles in this spirit. In April 1991, its editor claimed that too many Jews held key positions in Romania (at the time only eighteen thousand Jews still remained in the country): "The heads of TV and radio are all Jews, and in parliament it rains Jews by the bucket. It's not their fault—domination has been their style since the dawn of time—but can't they let us breathe a little, instead of trampling on us as they have been doing since 1947."[21]

As *Romania Mare* so delicately formulated the problem in February 1991, the "Eskimos" [Jews] who had brought Communism to Romania had also "nailed it into our bones and flesh until they crucified us."[22] The ferociously anti-Semitic and nationalist editor in chief of *Europa*, Iulian Neacsu, even suggested that Jews in postcommunist Romania were gradually turning the country into a colony of Tel Aviv.[23] In May 1991, an interview in *Europa* with ex–naval captain Nicolae Radu further elaborated on this theme, alleging that the Mossad and the CIA had organized the overthrow of Ceausescu. Their diabolical plan was to turn Romanians into "cesspit cleaners, dog catchers, refuse collectors and porters, serving individuals who are foreign to the nation and the country."[24] Radu even called on the army to act forcefully against the tiny Jewish population of Romania. President Ion Iliescu's response was rather hesitant, even though he condemned "such racist displays" as damaging to Romania's image abroad.

The extreme nationalists of the Greater Romania Party (GRP) had been ardent champions of Antonescu's rehabilitation from the outset and fervent admirers of Ceausescu's "national communism." The party's leader, Cor-

neliu Vadim Tudor, made his name as a poet, an able journalist, a demagogue, and a hagiographer of Ceausescu. He has combined unrestrained
verbal anti-Semitism with ultra-chauvinist propaganda against Romania's
1.7 million Hungarian minority and constant incitement against the large
Gypsy population (over 2 million). "Jewish accusations" regarding the
Holocaust are a special target—perceived as attempts to blackmail impoverished Romania and squeeze it dry.[25] Repeatedly, the *Romania Mare*
warned against "selling out to the kikes," globalization, the satanic character
of Marxism, and "Zionist exploitation" of the Holocaust.

For much of the Romanian radical Right, the "Red Holocaust" (of the
Communists) is the only one that actually took place. The "so-called Holocaust committed by *Romanians* against Jews" never happened at all. That
fictional Holocaust was a Zionist invention. At the first GRP press conference in 1993, the then forty-four-year-old Tudor emphasized that world Zionism was indeed the greatest single danger facing Romania. Zionists were
to blame for all foreign criticism of Romania's treatment of Hungarians, for
difficulties with the United States, and for other national misfortunes.
Tudor did not forget Israel's "terroristic" treatment of the Palestinians—the
victims of a real "ethnic cleansing." Zionism was a totalitarian "religious ultranationalism" virtually identical to German National Socialism. It was
"crucifying" the Palestinians, just as the Jews had killed Christ and had tried
to crucify the Romanian people. Indeed, according to *Romania Mare*, it was
no accident that President Ceausescu was executed on Christmas Day—
something no Christian people would have done of its own free will.[26] In
effect, his death was characterized as a ritual murder of the kind "prescribed" by the Talmud, the Torah, and other Jewish "racist" works. Ceausescu had allegedly been sacrificed because of his patriotic opposition to the
new world order, engineered by Bush, Gorbachev, and a broad-based
Jewish-Masonic conspiracy. Such extremist rhetoric is less common in
Poland, Hungary, and the Czech Republic.

Postcommunist anti-Semitism in Romania, whether radical or conservative, has been based to a great extent on prewar stereotypes about Jews that
had been superficially adapted to a post-Shoah world in which Israel and
Zionism have assumed special importance. Romanian-style Holocaust denial, for example, has heavily relied on the theories of Western anti-Zionist
intellectuals such as the French convert to Islam Roger Garaudy. Indeed,
Romania is probably the only European country in which Garaudy's "revi-

sionist" theses have been treated by the intellectuals with truly reverential respect.[27] The Romanian afterword to the translation of Garaudy's book claimed, for example, that France had been "groaning for more than fifty years under Zionist occupation." His French accusers were "exactly the same people who created a worldwide business by selling the bones of their grandparents." No less disconcerting have been the tendentious and self-exculpatory parallels drawn between the Holocaust and the Soviet Gulag, between fascism and Communism. Certainly these comparisons are also frequent in the Baltic states, Poland, Hungary, and Russia, along with the attribution of responsibility for Communist terror to Jews. But such apologetics are particularly widespread among Romanian intellectuals.

In the autumn of 2000, Romania's Far Right leader Corneliu Vadim Tudor won 33 percent of the vote in the second round of the presidential elections. In November 2002, his Greater Romania Party became the principal opposition party in Parliament. Although it attracted far less attention in the West, Tudor's presidential score was even better than that of Austrian populist Jörg Haider only a year earlier. It was also the highest percentage of the vote ever obtained in postwar Europe by an unequivocally anti-Semitic proto-fascist politician. During his campaign, Tudor denounced Israeli and Jewish businessmen in contemporary Romania, as well as former Jewish Communists, while denying that Jews had suffered any wartime Holocaust in Romania. That same year, Paul Goma, a famous Romanian dissident living in Paris, furiously attacked Jews for being "executioners" of non-Jewish communities in the Diaspora and Palestine.[28] Goma's subsequent book, *The Red Week,* published in 2004, even accused Jews of having provoked anti-Semitism during the Holocaust! Goma whitewashed the Antonescu regime while pouring out all his bile against Jewish Communists ("these unpunished executioners") for crimes that had "blooded the entire 20th century."[29]

When he opposed Ceausescu in the 1980s, Goma was much admired as "the Romanian Solzhenitsyn." The "Red week" of his recent book referred to events in Bessarabia between June 28 and July 3, 1940, when the area had passed under Soviet control, and Jews were accused of committing heinous "crimes" against the local Romanian population. In these and other writings Goma also denounced the Zionist state and the sins "of the bloodthirsty [Jewish] people," while blasting so-called denigrators of Romania, including former president Iliescu. He also vociferously opposed the decision of the

Romanian government to appoint a thirty-member Historical Commission (headed by Elie Wiesel) to examine the Romanian chapter of the Holocaust. In response to the commission's final report (printed in July 2005) he demanded an investigation of the "Bolshevik terror in Romania, which had been supported with enthusiasm by the Jews during fifty years."[30] Goma's stance was backed by Far Right nationalist circles and a not inconsiderable number of Romanian intellectuals.

Such a phenomenon testifies to the persistence of a powerful anti-Semitic mythology in Romania, in which the Jews are the supreme evil, and their "Judeo-Masonic conspiracy" aims to Judaize or destroy Orthodox Christianity, to transform Romania into an Israeli and/or American colony, and ultimately to dominate the world.[31] In Romania, it is not only paranoid literary hacks who are attracted by these verbal toxins, but professional journalists, well-known artists, politicians, university professors, and former Securitate officers. There are also young intellectuals with a more Western cultural training able to combine their nationalism with a newly minted Orthodox Christian fundamentalism. Among such true believers there is a remarkable willingness to imagine that the chaos in Romania and the world at large is "conducted diabolically by the Zionist movement." In their bizarre scenario taken straight out of the *Protocols of the Elders of Zion,* Europe is already on track to be "Judaized" and dominated by a Jewish world government.

At the beginning of the twenty-first century, the idea of a Judeo-Masonic conspiracy feeds primarily on fears of a dismembered Romania, anxieties about predatory Great Powers, globalization, cultural standardization, and the hidden forces (especially world Zionism) that allegedly manipulate Romania, the United States, the European Union, the papacy, and international financial institutions.[32] Before 1989, according to this logic, Romania had been enslaved by Judeo-Masonic Communists; since the fall of Ceausescu, it has been in the hands of the CIA, the Mossad, and world Zionism. In either case the anti-Semites always emphasized the *criminal* nature of the Jews. Jews were a deicidal people with a demonic character, forever seeking to corrupt and dominate the Gentiles. Masters of ruse, deception, intrigue, manipulation, and violence—whether in establishing or overthrowing Communist rule—they hold the key to the Romanian past, present, and future.

Despite the presence of such a powerful and paranoid Right and the resonant traditions of literary-intellectual anti-Semitism, Romania is not at present a land where the Jewish community lives in immediate physical danger. For several decades its remaining Jews have enjoyed a unique position as the only minority to be recognized, both as an ethnic group and as a state-sanctioned religion.[33] There is even a notable interest in knowing and understanding Jewish culture. Moreover, the Romanian government, after some initial hesitation, has shifted its position on the Holocaust, desirous to maintain good relations with the United States, Israel, and the European Union—to which it was finally admitted in 2007.[34] As former president Iliescu admitted some years ago (after making a major faux pas), "the recovery of memory" was part of Romania's "new status as a democratic country" and as a "dignified member of the Euro-Atlantic community."[35]

Such declarations are not divorced from Romania's broader strategy of courting international respectability. Similar considerations doubtless explained Vadim Tudor's unconvincing repudiation of anti-Semitism in 2003, when he decided to take members of his Greater Romania Party to Auschwitz. Tudor even hired an Israeli adviser and personally sponsored the erection of a statue of Yitzhak Rabin in Transylvania. In the November 2004 presidential elections a relatively philo-Semitic Tudor won only 12 percent of the vote, down by nearly a third from his results four years earlier. Since then, he has returned to the more familiar chords of anti-Semitism, anti-Zionism, and Holocaust denial with his standing somewhat improved. It should be noted that Tudor's typically Romanian form of Holocaust negation did not argue that the mass murders never happened. Its main point was to deny any participation of Romanians in their perpetration. As historian and political activist Michael Shafir has shrewdly observed, nowhere else in postcommunist east-central Europe "is selective negationism so blatant as in Romania."[36] In other words, the mass killings occurred but they happened *elsewhere* and, besides, Romanians were not involved!

· · ·

Since 1945, in ex-Yugoslavia (whether during or after Communist rule) there have generally been far fewer manifestations of popular anti-Semitism than in other east European or Balkan countries.[37] During the civil war of the early 1990s the tiny population of five to six thousand Jews (evenly split between Serbia, Croatia, and Bosnia-Herzegovina) was not targeted by any of the warring parties, despite the existence of extreme nationalist movements, such as the Serbian People's Party and the Croatian Party of [Historical] Rights, led at the beginning of the twentieth century by a converted Jew, Josip Frank. Nevertheless, the first president of the newly independent Croatia, Franjo Tudjman, was widely regarded outside his own country as a "historical revisionist" and an anti-Semite. During the 1991 election campaign he had allegedly stated, "Thank God, my wife is neither a Serb nor a Jew."[38] In his 1989 book, appropriately entitled *Wanderings of Historical Truth*, Tudjman grossly minimized the number of Jews and Serbs killed at the hands of the pro-Nazi Croatian fascist regime (Ustasha) headed by Ante Pavelić.[39] Worse still, Tudjman claimed that Jews had themselves participated in liquidating Gypsies at the notorious Jasenovac concentration camp, and that they even initiated the mass murder of Serbs, Gypsies, partisans, and Communists. Tudjman quoted, without any critical examination, the prejudiced comments of inmates who referred to the "craftiness" and "underhandedness" of the Jews, their alleged superiority complex (as a chosen people), and their religious commandment "to exterminate others and take their place."[40] For good measure, the Croatian president, citing Israeli professor Yeshayahu Leibowitz, labeled Israel a "Judeo-Nazi" State.[41] Only in February 1994 did Tudjman finally issue an apology for these and other statements in his earlier writings that have generally been considered as anti-Semitic.[42]

In Slovakia and Croatia, the only modern experience of independence before the 1990s happened during World War II, when both countries were clerical fascist states allied to Nazi Germany. The rehabilitation of wartime collaborationist leaders, following the collapse of Communism, was seen by many Croats, Slovaks, Romanians, and others as a way to reconnect to this tradition and reinforce their national aspirations.[43] The pro-Nazi Roman Catholic priest Josef Tiso (president of the wartime Slovak state) had been directly responsible for the deportation of more than eighty thousand Jews to their deaths in Poland after 1942. Fifty years later, on January 1, 1993, after a "velvet divorce" from the Czech Republic, Slovakia became fully independent. The desire to rehabilitate Tiso (like Antonescu, he had been executed by the Communists after the war) was, by then, closely entwined with the Slovakian nationalist drive for state sovereignty.[44] It was also linked to anti-Semitism, which had, from the beginning, accompanied modern Slovak nationalism. This did not deter many nationalist Slovak exiles (returning from abroad after 1989), who dedicated themselves to honoring the

memory of Tiso as a national hero and martyr who had fallen victim to perfidious Communist executioners. Their efforts were countered by diametrically opposed attempts to admit Slovak complicity in the Holocaust for the
first time, and to commemorate the tragedy of the murdered Jews. Surveys
in 1993 showed that a plurality of Slovaks did, in fact, accept that the Tiso-
era politicians had some responsibility for the extermination of the Jews. At
the same time, the numbers of Slovaks who preferred to let the memory of
the Holocaust fade had risen to around 40 percent.[45]

By the mid-1990s there were no more than 5,000 Jews left in Slovakia
(down from around 150,000 before World War II) in a society where tense
relations still existed with Czechs, the Hungarian national minority, Gypsies, and Third World immigrants. As in Poland, about one-third of the
adult population had negative attitudes toward the Jews, higher than in
Hungary (25 percent) or the Czech Republic (14 percent). They generally
belonged to the economically insecure lower middle class, who feared liberal capitalism and modernization. In 1991 no less than 42 percent of Slovak
respondents thought Jews had too much influence on economic and political affairs, compared to only 12 percent of Czechs. No less than a quarter of
Slovaks thought Jews were behind the upheavals of November 1989, leading
to the downfall of the Communist regime. Slovak anti-Semites tended to be
antiliberal, against radical reform, pessimistic about openings to western
Europe, skeptical about parliamentary democracy, and intolerant of foreigners.[46] They often found political expression in such groups as the Slovak National Party (SNS), among neo-populists organized in the Slovak
Christian Democratic Movement (SKDH), the Slovak People's Party (SL'S),
and the Party of National Unity. This neo-populist propaganda during the
1990s may well have had some influence on the anti-Jewish bias in Slovak
public opinion.[47]

Neo-populist ideology in Slovakia emphasized Jewish ambitions for
world domination (the *Protocols* scenario), the nefarious role of Freemasonry and Zionist machinations, and tenaciously defended Tiso's
wartime record—an endeavor in which they enjoyed the full support of the
Catholic Church hierarchy.[48] Indeed, the church in postcommunist Slovakia seemed to ally itself with populism both as a movement and as an ideology. The Slovak Lutherans, on the other hand, took a much more critical
position with regard to Tiso, the wartime Slovak state, and the mass murder
of the Jews.[49] Unlike the Slovak Catholic Church (which still regards Tiso as

an "innocent brother in faith") or the radical nationalist Right, they seem more sensitive to the anti-Jewish implications of the Tiso cult. To this day, the charge of Jewish responsibility for Tiso's execution in 1947 is one of the more malicious sources for anti-Semitic incitement in Slovakia. [50]

Slovakia's entry into the European Union (EU) in May 2004 transformed its status without bringing to an end neo-populist efforts to rehabilitate the Tiso regime. The Catholic defense of his legacy has, if anything, hardened as have trends toward whitewashing his deeds. The Catholic author Stanislav Májek, in a fairly recent pro-Tiso book, even hinted that Jews were not only "among the most avid Magyarizers" but also responsible for the poverty of the Slovak people before 1939. On the other hand, according to the Pew Global Attitudes Project in spring 2007, 31 percent of Slovaks identified with the Jewish state, and only 17 percent sympathized with the Palestinians. This was far more than in Ukraine (15 percent pro-Israel, 11 percent pro-Palestinian) or Poland, where 13 percent supported the Palestinians and a mere 9 percent identified with Israel. In the forty-seven-nation survey, Slovakia appeared remarkably pro-Israel in comparison to western Europe—with the exception of Germany. Only the Czech Republic (with 37 percent in favor of Israel and just 14 percent supportive of the Palestinians) scored higher across Europe when it came to support for the Jewish state.

•   •   •

Czech opposition to anti-Semitism and anti-Zionism has been particularly noticeable ever since the fall of Communism in 1989. It was led by liberal president Václav Havel, himself the target of vitriolic attacks by extremist groups in his own country and in Slovakia. Before the breakup of Czechoslovakia, Havel was physically assaulted in mid-March 1991 at a rally in Bratislava during which thousands of Slovak separatists had chanted anti-Czech and anti-Semitic slogans.[51] His principled support for both the Jews and Israel was reminiscent of the prewar Czechoslovak president Thomas Masaryk and of the "Prague Spring" in 1968, when Czech writers had been virtually alone in raising their voices against the anti-Israel hate campaign instigated by Moscow throughout Eastern Europe. The sheer mendacity of official anti-Zionist propaganda in Communist Czechoslovakia in the 1970s and early 1980s (most of it blatantly anti-Semitic in tone) might in part explain the Czech public's backlash under postcommunism. Although Czech xenophobia existed and briefly found political expression in the ranks of the Republican Party (which in 1992 won 6 percent of the popular vote and gained fourteen seats in the Czech parliament), it did not threaten Jews.[52] In comparison with Romania, Hungary, and Slovakia, the neo-populists remained politically isolated and uninterested in the "Jewish question." As in other east-central European countries, anti-Gypsy feeling was, however, much more visceral.

It is noteworthy that throughout the 2006 Israel-Hezbollah war, the Czech Republic was one of the few places in Europe where the Jewish community did not feel pressured by an "anti-Israeli" atmosphere; the government and media were generally supportive, despite the growing threats from neo-Nazis.[53] Indeed, Jewish communal leaders reported that Czech media coverage of the conflict was reasonably fair and balanced—in contrast to coverage in many other countries of the European Union.[54] During the Gaza conflict in January 2009, the Czechs held the presidency of the European Union and once again took a notably positive attitude on Israel's right to self-defense.

Poland provides a sharp contrast to the Czech Republic in several respects, not least the matter of anti-Semitism. For example, in May 2006, the Israeli ambassador to Poland, David Peleg, felt obliged to convey his dismay over the inclusion of the ultranationalist and anti-Semitic League of Polish Families Party (PFL) in the new Polish government. The then thirty-five-year-old leader of this staunchly Catholic nationalist party, Roman Giertych (grandson of a leading Polish anti-Semite in the 1930s), was appointed education minister and deputy prime minister.[55] His party's youth wing had already become notorious for its Nazi salutes and for chanting Nazi slogans. Not long after the PFL's entry into the government, Poland's chief rabbi, Michael Schudrich, had been attacked in an anti-Semitic incident on a Warsaw street by a young man shouting, "Poland for the Poles."[56] The assault shocked Poland's tiny Jewish community and was firmly condemned by the Polish prime minister. But there is no doubt that such assaults became more likely in the climate shaped by an old-fashioned government pandering to nationalist, ultraconservative, reactionary Catholic and anti-Semitic prejudices.

In contemporary Poland there is a remarkable range of extreme Right weeklies, such as *Głos, Nasza Polska, Myśl Polska;* fortnightlies such as *Tylko Polska* and *Najjaśniejszej Rzeczpospolitej;* monthlies such as *Szczerbiec;* and more mainstream newspapers such as the daily *Nasz Dziennik* and the weekly *Tygodnik Solidarność*. Virtually all of them combine a nationalist discourse, fundamentalist Catholicism, racist comments about Gypsies, and diatribes against Jews as past and present enemies of Poland and Christendom.[57] Most of these publications can be bought at regular newsstands or kiosks and have never been prosecuted, let alone banned, for incitement. In the early 1990s *Tygodnik Solidarność* had a circulation of 200,000, though its sales have dropped since then. *Nasz Dziennik* claims, on the other hand, to sell 150,000 copies daily, and is closely connected to the vastly influential Radio Maryja radio station, with an audience of at least two million Poles. (The station misleadingly boasts that it has five million listeners.) Both the daily and the radio, though not officially connected with the Catholic Church, enjoy the support of a not insignificant group of influential bishops and mold the opinions of a considerable segment of the Polish public.[58]

Radio Maryja is the enfant terrible of Polish broadcasting. On March 27, 2006, one of the station's top broadcasters, Stanisław Michalkiewicz, accused the Jews of "trying to force our government to pay extortion money disguised as compensation payments" for property lost during and after World War II. He referred to the restitution efforts of American Jewish groups as "Holocaust business," maintaining that they were seeking to humiliate Poland internationally. The station's founder and director, Rev. Tadeusz Rydzyk—a priest from the Redemptorist order and a media mogul in his own right—did eventually make a public apology under pressure from Catholic authorities within and outside Poland. But Radio Maryja has been promoting vitriolic anti-Semitic propaganda of this kind ever since the early 1990s, including outright Holocaust denial. This fits well with its homophobia, xenophobia, anti-Europeanism, and support for the government campaign to identify all those who were linked with Communism in the past. It became a mainstream medium for the government after the Law and Justice Party (a rightist formation with a Catholic agenda) won the 2005 elections. The station can influence the careers of political leaders— hence all the main right-wing politicians are eager to be interviewed and supported by its listeners. Recent interviewees include Poland's president, Lech Kaczyński; his identical twin brother, outgoing prime minister Jarosław Kaczyński; and most of the governing elite.[59] Nevertheless, its intense political involvement irritated the Vatican, which sought to curb its extremism, without publicly raising the specific issue of anti-Semitism.[60]

In July 2007 a new scandal developed after Rydzyk was caught declaring on a tape recording that Jews were insatiably greedy and determined to extract huge sums of money from the Polish state. He crudely attacked the Polish president, calling him a swindler and a liar who had bowed to pressure from the international Jewish lobby to compensate Jews for their losses during the Holocaust: "You know it's about giving $65 billion to the Jews. They will come to you and say 'give me your coat. Take off your pants, give your shoes.'"[61] For good measure he also lashed out at the president's wife, calling her a witch and saying she should be "put down" for supporting the termination of pregnancies in the case of rape victims. Reverend Rydzyk unconvincingly suggested that the tapes had been doctored in order to discredit him and damage the media empire he had built up.[62] Despite pressure from abroad, neither Lech nor Jarosław Kaczyński condemned the priest, well aware that his support could be worth more than a million votes in the upcoming elections.[63] At the same time, the Rome-based Redemptorists—the missionary order to which he belongs—came out strongly in support of Rydzyk in a statement published in *Nasz Dziennik.*

There was some sharp opposition to Rydzyk's remarks coming from former prime minister Tadeusz Mazowiecki, ex–Foreign Minister Wladyslaw Bartoszewski, and more than seven hundred Poles who signed an open letter of protest. "As Polish Catholics, laymen and clergy, we express our moral protest against the worsening statements of the director of Radio Maryja," the letter noted. "It hurts us that the contemptible and antisemitic statements come from a representative of our church."[64] American Jewish organizations also deplored the ugly outburst of Judeophobia, demanding that the Polish government speak out against Rydzyk. Leaders of the Anti-Defamation League (ADL) cited their recent poll of anti-Semitic attitudes in Poland, which found that 45 percent of respondents believed in most of the classic anti-Semitic stereotypes, and 39 percent still held the Jews responsible for the death of Christ—the highest percentage anywhere in Europe.[65] Marvin Hier, dean of the Simon Wiesenthal Center in Los Angeles, went furthest—calling Rydzyk "a sort of a Goebbels with a collar"—and wrote to the pope to protest such incitement to bigotry and hatred.[66] Unfortunately, it turned out that Pope Benedict XVI had received the anti-Semitic priest on August 5, 2007, at Castel Gandolfo with a warm handshake, thereby appearing to give him the ultimate legitimacy. Whatever actually transpired between them, for most Jewish leaders this was a severe blow to Pope Benedict's image and to Jewish-Christian relations.[67]

Since then, the pope's credibility has been much more severely damaged by his revoking the excommunication of schismatic, fundamentalist bishops, including the British-born Holocaust denier and anti-Semite Richard Williamson. These and other blunders have cast a cloud over the postwar progress made in advancing Catholic-Jewish dialogue.

The Rydzyk affair in Poland was only the most recent in a series of anti-Semitic scandals connected with its nationalistic Catholic-based right-wing politicians. In February 2007, a well-known Polish Euro MP, Maciej Gier-tych (father of Poland's then education minister) and a prominent figure in the League of Polish Families Party, published a thirty-two-page booklet, *Civilizations at War in Europe,* replete with anti-Semitically tinged remarks. In the text, Giertych presented the philosophy of a 1930s Polish historian, Feliks Koneczny, as a guide for his own party, for contemporary Poland, and for a more traditionalist Christian Europe. In this treatise, Jews are essentially treated as a parasitical group, migrating from poor to rich lands, always forming a separate community wherever they settle; they use the Torah, Talmud, and rabbinical sources to justify endless legalistic casuistry and a hypocritical ethic. The bottom line is that the Jews' Torah-based civilization will always be incompatible with the Latin Catholic core of Polish values and European civilization.[68] Euro MPs were particularly embarrassed to discover that the logo of the European Parliament appeared over this implicitly racist publication, financed out of its funds. In his booklet, Giertych, a professor of biology at the Polish Academy of Sciences, wrote as follows about the Jews: "It is a civilization of programmed separateness, of programmed differentiation from the surrounding communities. . . . By their own will, they prefer to live a separate life, in apartheid from the surrounding communities."[69] At the same time he described Jews as a "tragic community," because they had not recognized Christ; Jews had gradually developed "a biological separateness," based on their collective consciousness of being the chosen people. Unlike Christians, their messianism derived from belief in a *tribal* God.[70]

In 1990 Giertych had been the editor of the monthly *Slowo Narodowy* (The National Word) and a close adviser of Josef Cardinal Glemp, then primate of Poland. He was a particularly enthusiastic disciple of Roman Dmowski, the leader of the anti-Semitic prewar Endecja (National Democratic Party) and clearly saw himself as the heir of this legacy. Like Cardinal Glemp and the prewar Endeks, he believed in the quasi-automatic identification of *Polak-katolik* (The Pole is a Catholic), regarded anti-Semitism as a legitimate form of self-defense, and defined it as a natural response to "Jewish anti-Polonism." Again, like Cardinal Glemp, Maciej Giertych had long blamed the Western media (and the "Jewish press" in particular) for artificially whipping up a "nonexistent antisemitism in Poland." There was, in his view, a concerted campaign by Jews with "a great influence in the world's media" directed against Poland in order to whitewash German war crimes.[71] *Slowo Narodowy,* it is worth noting, attacked not only international Jewry and the German menace, but also Communism, "cosmopolitanism," and Western materialism as values fundamentally alien to Catholic Poland.

Ethno-nationalists in Poland are frequently Judeophobic, markedly Catholic, opposed to the influx of foreign capital into Poland, anti-European, and above all anticommunist.[72] Since 1990 they have included the right-wing Christian National Union (CNU, with about six thousand members), the now extinct Polish National Community–Polish National Party of Boleslaw Tejkowski (which had four thousand members in 1992), and the equally defunct populist, anti-Semitic Party X of Stanisław Tymiński. There is also the Pax association with its own publishing house and press, under whose patronage anti-Semitic literature has for years been hawked in the streets of large Polish cities. The *Protocols of the Elders of Zion* was, until recently, sold unhindered at the entrance of the University of Warsaw and in the nearby Church of the Holy Cross. Tejkowski (a former Communist official and chairman of the Polish National Community) gave the *Protocols* conspiracy theory a new twist in the early 1990s by ranting against the "Judaization of the Catholic Church," or "the priests of Jewish nationality" in the Polish episcopate and the Vatican. In a 1991 leaflet Tejkowski vigorously protested that the authority of Christianity was being exploited in order "to subordinate Poles to the Jews." Members of his party invariably described the powerful Solidarity trade union as "Judeo-Solidarity" and the first postcommunist government of Tadeusz Mazowiecki as a Judeo-Masonic conspiracy.[73] According to its publications, Poland was living in the sinister shadow of "the Jewish church" or "Satan's Synagogue." The litany of names of Polish priests, politicians, journalists, artists, and scientists branded as Jews or labeled as a fifth column seeking to destroy Poland was seemingly endless. Tejkowski's paranoid followers even suspected the former pope, John Paul II, of being a "secret Jew."

The anti-Semitic hysteria about so-called hidden Jews has periodically flourished during Polish presidential and national elections. When Mazowiecki (who was not Jewish) ran against Lech Walesa for the presidency in 1990, he was constantly interpellated about his alleged Jewishness. Eventually the bishop of Plock had to trace the candidate's family history back to the fifteenth century in order to end the public debate about his genealogy and remove fears that, as a "crypto-Jew," he might be soft on Communism. This racist perspective reappeared six years later when Alexander Kwasniewski (also not Jewish) challenged Walesa and had to face similar allegations. Such preoccupations with "invisible Jews" recall the Marrano obsession in medieval Spain and have antecedents in Polish anti-Semitism at the beginning of the twentieth century when one of its pioneers, the prolific literary critic Teodor Jeske-Choinski, published lists containing names of "Jewish" Frankist converts to Christianity from a century before. This witch hunt for imaginary Jews continued throughout the interwar period and helped inspire the genealogical passions of Polish Communist officials in the late 1960s, searching in every dark corner for a Zionist fifth column.[74]

The victor in the Polish elections of 1990, Lech Walesa, did not hesitate to exploit the vocal anti-Semitism against "hidden Jews" that his populist supporters had whipped up during the electoral campaign.[75] Walesa, sensing the frustration of an electorate embittered by economic mismanagement, poverty, and soured promises of democracy, played the anti-Semitic card by suggesting that the time had come for "real Poles" (like himself) to govern. He repeated that he could not understand why his former advisers (Jewish intellectuals such as Adam Michnik and Bronisław Gieremek) hid behind Gentile names. It was such behavior, he slyly hinted, that created anti-Jewish feeling in Poland. In reality, it was, of course, Walesa's campaign that proved that anti-Semitism was alive and well in a country that for decades had been *judenrein*.

Postcommunist anti-Semitism in Poland has powerful Catholic roots. Cardinal Glemp greatly inflamed national passions on August 26, 1989, in his speech at Częstochowa during the controversy over the Carmelite nuns in Auschwitz, when he said: "My dear Jews, do not speak to us from the position of a nation raised above all others and do not present us with conditions that are impossible to fulfill. . . . Your power lies in the mass media which is at your disposal throughout many countries. Do not let this power serve to disseminate anti-Polonism."[76] The rising mood of anti-Jewish incitement was felt everywhere in Poland after this speech—heightened by the economic crisis, the crumbling of Communist power, and the persistent Polish perception of Jews as crafty and malevolent aliens with powerful international connections. At the same time, the Polish Church's Commission for Dialogue with Jews and Judaism did issue an important pastoral letter in December 1990 that sharply condemned anti-Semitism and the past injustices done to Jews, and expressed genuine sorrow over the sufferings they had endured on Polish soil. Walesa, too, eventually expressed contrition on a visit to Israel in late May 1991 (the first ever by a Polish leader) when he addressed the Knesset—asking "forgiveness" for Poland's history of anti-Semitism.[77]

But during the past decade it has become evident that many Polish Catholics continue to believe that Jews are a sinister influence behind world events and remain endemically hostile to Poland. This closed worldview with its ethno-nationalist exclusivism—traditionalist, ultraconservative, and backward looking—is all too frequently riddled with anti-Semitism.[78] One of its prime representatives has been Rev. Henryk Jankowski, the legendary chaplain of the original Solidarity movement, notorious for his anti-Semitic speeches and actions, who in late 2004 was finally dismissed from his position of vicar of Saint Brigida Church in Gdansk.[79] (Jankowski had for many years been the personal confessor and close confidant of Lech Walesa.) In April 1995 the traditional Easter decoration of Jesus's grave in Saint Brigida Church included a display of the Star of David, equating it with Nazi and Communist symbols—something that failed to elicit any response from Cardinal Glemp, the Polish primate.[80] At the time, Jankowski told his listeners that they should "no longer tolerate governments made up of people who have not declared whether they come from Moscow or from Israel." In his "clarification" Jankowski unconvincingly pretended that he was drawing attention to Jewish misdeeds in banking and finance.[81]

In August 1997 Jankowski again used a Catholic Mass to proclaim that members of the Jewish minority "could not be tolerated in the Polish government"; two months later, when Jewish-born Bronisław Gieremek was appointed foreign minister, the priest warned ethnic Poles that Jews wanted to take over the government. Attempts to prosecute him for inciting interethnic hatred failed. The years between 1995 and 1997, when Jankowski's anti-Jewish statements peaked, also saw a constant flurry of anti-Semitic broadcasts by Radio Maryja. Apart from harping on Kwasniewski's allegedly Jewish mother, or Hungarian-American entrepreneur George Soros as an "enemy of Poland" and various Polish politicians as "lackeys of the Jews," the station also focused attention on Jews as a cultural and spiritual threat.[82] Glemp's objection, as in the case of Jankowski, was not to the anti-Semitic libels of Radio Maryja but rather to the overly political content of the broadcasts.

Public condemnation by other clergymen was also very limited. Only the philo-Semitic Jesuit priest Stanisław Musiał (formerly secretary of the Polish Episcopacy Commission for Dialogue with Judaism) provided an unequivocal rejection of this Judeophobic hysteria and forthrightly criticized the feeble reaction of high church officials.[83] He would do so, once again, during the Jedwabne debate in 2001, sharply condemning Glemp's accusations that Jews had severely harmed Poland through their prominent role in postwar Communism.

As in Hungary and Romania, the Polish obsession with *żydokomuna* (Judeo-Communism) would resurface with a vengeance after 1989.[84] Some of the accusations concerned alleged Jewish collaboration with the Red Army in eastern Poland between 1939 and 1941. More central was the charge that Jewish Communists had seized control of Poland after 1944–45, committing grave crimes against the Polish nation. But this myth could never have obtained such a grip on the non-Jewish imagination without well-anchored preexisting beliefs in a Jewish conspiracy, a demonic Jewish power, and the imagined desire of Jewry to dominate the Gentile Christian world.[85] In relation to Judeo-Communism, such tenacious and stereotypical perceptions still persist today (in a more sophisticated form) among some prominent Polish historians. They claim that Jews were indeed disproportionately conspicuous in the Communist administration after 1944 and predominant in the secret police.[86] This interpretation reflects the view of the early postwar years that the long feared "Judaization of Poland" was about to be realized under Soviet Communism. In this context, Jews were seen not merely as the intellectual creators of Communism but as the faithful executors of a deadly Soviet threat. Individuals such as Hilary Minc, Jakub Berman, and Roman Zambrowski (who had all survived the war in the USSR) did hold important Polish governmental positions or top party posts after 1948. This unprecedented fact was perceived by many ethnic Poles and anticommunist Catholics as a traumatic reversal of the "natural order" of things—nothing less than a national catastrophe. The Communist Jews were damned as enemies not only because of their ethnic origin but also because they were "servants" of the USSR—a hostile and oppressive foreign power.[87] People in these circles even blamed Jewish Communists for the civil war in Poland between 1944 and 1947. A myth was born that the ruling Polish Workers' Party (PPR) essentially acted as a "Jewish party," run by Jews with the purpose of oppressing ethnic Poles.[88] Twenty years later, in 1968, it would emerge that the PPR was in fact an "ethnonationalist" Polish Communist Party regime endorsing anti-Semitic slogans that called for a Poland "free of Jews."

The Polish myth of *żydokomuna* rose from the ashes once more in 2001 with the revelations in Jan Gross's short book *Neighbours,* which reported how virtually all of the Jews in the small Polish town of Jedwabne had been horrifically massacred by ethnic Poles in July 1941. The stark exposure of the Jedwabne massacre to the full light of day provoked much soul-searching in Poland and punctured the myth that Polish hands were relatively clean of mass killing during World War II. The flattering self-image of Poles as a nation of ardent patriots—all of them brave underground fighters and knights in shining armor—proved to be rather misleading when it came to the "Jewish question." This was recognized by the Polish president Alexander Kwasniewski, by the more self-critical Catholic intelligentsia, and much of the Left in Poland, but it was fiercely contested by Catholic nationalists, ultrarightists, anti-Semites, and some prominent historians, including Professor Tomasz Strzembosz. They saw Jedwabne and similar massacres as being German rather than Polish in inspiration (despite powerful evidence to the contrary), downplaying the events by referring to the Jewish population's supposed collaboration with the Soviet authorities between 1939 and 1941 in eastern Poland.[89]

Cardinal Glemp shared this view, regarding Jedwabne as no more than a "local tragedy," not requiring any Polish national remorse. He even suggested that Jews owed Poles an apology for their wartime behavior! In a subsequent statement, the Polish primate tried to "contextualize" the massacre by comparing it to the bloodshed "among neighbours in Palestine" or in the Balkans. Other Polish priests, including Jedwabne's own Rev. Edward Orlowski, also relativized the crime as much as possible. Like most of the nationalists, they continued to uncritically defend the heroic image of Poles as selfless patriotic martyrs and to accuse Jews of Polonophobia.[90] The idea that Poles were not just the victims of Nazi brutality but could on occasion act as willing accomplices of the German murderers was wholly unacceptable on the Polish Right.

The insignificant physical presence of Jews in contemporary Poland stands in the sharpest possible contrast to their symbolic weight. Even after the Jews emigrated or were murdered or expelled, they have remained fixed not only in the anti-Semitic imagination but also in the language, national memory, and collective consciousness of many Poles. In its extreme form this obsession goes well beyond the old prewar slogan "The Jews Are Our Enemy"; instead, every enemy can potentially become a "Jew," irrespective of his genealogy or subjective identity.[91] This fits well with the widespread proclivity for believing in conspiracy theories about international Jewry, world Zionism, Judeo-Masonry, and Judeo-Bolshevism.

According to the Polish sociologist Ireneusz Krzeminski, the indicators of overt "modern" anti-Semitism rose sharply from 17 percent to 27 percent in Poland between 1992 and 2002. Traditional anti-Semitism has also been strong among Catholic believers and rural dwellers. In the industrial centers of Poland, secular anti-Semites tend to be concentrated among the poorer strata, those opposed to integration in Europe or hostile to foreigners in general. Today, unlike a decade earlier, Jews are perceived as being more harmful to Poland than Germans, Russians, Ukrainians, or Gypsies. Fears concerning the return of Jewish property have grown; so, too, have the number of Poles who believe that they suffered no less than the Jews during World War II. On the other hand, Polish scholars and intellectuals have advanced a more balanced understanding of the Holocaust in recent years. Their interest in preserving its memory has also coincided with a resurgence of Polish curiosity about the history of Polish Jewry, its culture and heritage.[92]

However, Polish attitudes toward Israel are less favorable than in the Czech Republic, Slovakia, or Hungary. During the Israel-Hezbollah war, there were those who attacked the biblical "eye for an eye" approach of Israel. Some even evoked Hamas and the PLO in the same breath as the battle of the Polish Home Army against the Nazis. The historian Tomasz Strzembosz roundly condemned Israel's retaliations against terrorist attacks, using shallow comparisons with the Third Reich—for which he was sharply reproached in some quarters.[93] Among his critics there were those who deplored the political correctness so fashionable in western Europe, which idealizes terrorists as freedom fighters. Many Polish commentators well remember the decades-long Soviet backing for Yasser Arafat and the PLO, not a point that endeared the average Pole to the Palestinian cause.[94] Moreover, unlike western Europeans, Poles have no colonial guilt complex—least of all toward Arabs. On the contrary, they suffered from a very different colonialism—that of Soviet Communism—with its ideological hatred of Israel and unconditional support for the Arab world. Not unnaturally, this encouraged many Poles to adopt a more positive attitude toward the Jewish state as an enemy of the USSR.

A note of sympathy for Israel and Zionism is not new in Polish history. It was there in the 1930s, though sometimes tainted by anti-Semitism, and again in 1967, when many Poles—despite the official Communist propaganda—were privately pleased that "our Jews trounced *their* [Soviet-supported] Arabs." In April 2002, Marek Król, the editor in chief of Poland's most popular weekly newsmagazine, *Wprost,* declared his feelings of shame and anger in observing western European hostility toward Israel.[95] The magazine front cover with the headline "Europe Terrorizes Israel" was backed up by a lead story excoriating the EU as a "Union of Hypocrites." There was a translation into Polish of Italian journalist Oriana Fallaci's fierce assault on western European appeasement of Muslim anti-Semitism, an interview with the Israeli ambassador to Poland, and graphic pictures of Israeli victims of Palestinian suicide bombings. Król declared himself appalled at EU threats to suspend economic agreements with Israel, as well as upset at its cowardice and refusal to do anything to help the Jewish state: "In the face of such hypocrisy, I can only say: I am an Israeli. I am with the nation that, condemned to extermination in cultured Europe, performed a miracle—it built a democratic state in a sea of Arab totalitarianism."[96]

During the 2006 Lebanon War, however, there were no such resounding declarations of solidarity. The media coverage was, however, reasonably objective, with the television channels and main Polish dailies giving space to the Israeli side of the conflict. Moreover, when the UN Secretariat and the European Union agreed to host a lead-up conference likely to become a replication of the anti-Israel masquerade in Durban in 2001, it was Poland that most vociferously condemned this move in August 2007. In April 2008, the new Polish prime minister Donald Tusk even went out of his way to condemn anti-Semitism, emphasizing the very good relations between Poland and Israel. Yet, despite such Polish government support, ordinary Poles seemed to have little sympathy with Israel's predicament. An ADL survey in 2006 revealed a negative image of Israel in public opinion as well as a relatively high level of anti-Semitism. Fifty-nine percent of Poles thought Jews were more loyal to Israel than Poland; over half of all Poles felt that Jews had too much power in business and international finance; 58 percent complained that they talked too much about what happened to them in the Holocaust. Only in Hungary and Spain were comparable or worse results recorded.

The level of anti-Semitism is also rising in Ukraine, scene of some of the bloodiest massacres in modern Jewish history. Approximately 900,000 Jews (60 percent of Ukrainian Jewry) were murdered on the territory of Ukraine during World War II. A taboo subject during the Soviet period, the tragedy of the Holocaust is now widely recognized, and the government is supportive of memorial projects, regarding the subject as integral to Ukrainian history. At the turn of the twenty-first century, according to some estimates, there were as many as 225,000 Jews in an independent Ukraine of 46 million people, though other assessments put the figure closer to half that number. As in Russia, government-sponsored anti-Semitism has disappeared, though extreme nationalist parties and sects freely propagate hatred against Jews. There is less ethnic violence than in Russia, and Christian Orthodox fundamentalists are not particularly active in the field of anti-Semitic propaganda. The Ukrainian political elite and intelligentsia, mindful of its relations with the United States, treats Jews with some cautious sympathy. President Yuschenko has generally presented Jewish sufferings in the Holocaust in the framework of his call for a multicultural and more tolerant society. But it was only one of the many ills that befell the Ukrainian people alongside Stalinist terror, deportation, and the "Great Famine" under the Soviet regime in 1932–33. Moreover, the question of Ukrainian collaboration with the Nazis in killing Jews is carefully avoided. There are some even darker spots on the horizon. Anti-Semitic articles periodically appear in Kiev and in such newspapers as *Silski Visti* (Rural News), with a daily circulation of 800,000. They often blame Jews, especially Lazar Kaganovich, for Communism, Stalin's repression, and the great famine. Nationalistic and Judeophobic sentiments are most frequently encountered in western Ukraine, and anti-Semites from that region have been among the strongest supporters of the reform-oriented Ukrainian leader Victor Yushchenko.[97] Moreover, since 2005 there has been a disturbing increase in violent attacks on Ukrainian Jews. The response of the authorities has generally been unsatisfactory. The tendency, as in contemporary Russia, is to dismiss such incidents as mere "hooliganism."[98]

According to Ireneusz Krzeminski's research team, in 2002, one-fifth of the Ukrainian population shared anti-Jewish attitudes of the modern variety. Around 17 percent could be classified as traditional anti-Semites—with especially high figures (about one-third of the population) in the western Ukraine—results that resemble the Polish pattern. Greek Catholicism appeared to fuel such feelings more than did other denominations. Among the youth, there has been a growing disposition to identify with traditional anti-Jewish stereotypes and prejudices, possibly as part of a return to religious beliefs.[99] Since the survey of 2002, the situation has clearly deteriorated. In December 2006 the results of a poll by the Kiev International Institute of Sociology revealed that 36 percent of the respondents (a shockingly high figure) did not want Jews as citizens of Ukraine. Among eighteen- to twenty-year-olds, the survey found that no less than 45 percent shared this view, a higher rate than among the older respondents. Also in 2006, the numbers of beatings and verbal assaults on Ukrainian Jews had increased sharply, even though the neo-Nazi movement is much weaker in Ukraine than in Germany or Russia.[100] Anti-Semitic attacks are rarely reported in the Ukrainian media, which appears far more indifferent to this phenomenon than its counterparts in Poland and Russia. Police officials and ministers are also in denial, even when violent assaults on Jews, desecrations of Jewish graves, and graffiti on Jewish communal buildings are unmistakably motivated by anti-Semitism. This official unresponsiveness coincides with a general laxity in regard to anti-Semitic statements made in public in the Ukrainian parliament, where such literature as the *Protocols* could until a few years ago be openly bought and sold.

However, the primary source of anti-Jewish agitation in Ukraine today is the Interregional Academy of Personnel Management (MAUP). Founded in 1989, it is the largest nonstate higher education establishment in Ukraine, with about fifty thousand students dispersed at its various campuses, the largest located in Kiev. Its graduates include many leading politicians, diplomats, businessmen, military leaders, and educators. Thus it is a *mainstream* institution in Ukraine, playing an important role in the broader society. Accredited by the Ministry of Education and recognized by UNESCO as a high-level educational institution, it has established many centers in the cities of neighboring countries. One of its academic periodicals, the weekly

Personal Plus, has regularly published anti-Semitic essays inciting ethnic hatred against Jews and seeking to outlaw Jewish organizations in the country. In September 2005 it ran a series of articles against the Shulhan Aruch; in November 2005 it put out a collection of articles demanding a halt to "the criminal activity of organized Judaism"; in December 2005 its publishing house translated a Holocaust denial book by the Swiss negationist Jürgen Graf, which was then sold at its campuses and MAUP kiosks in Kiev. Also in 2005, it organized a symposium in Kiev entitled "Zionism—The Great Threat to Contemporary Civilization" and another called "The Jewish-Bolshevik Takeover of 1917 as a Precondition for the Red Terror and Ukrainian Starvation."[101]

The president of MAUP, Georgy Tschokin (a leader of the anti-Semitic Ukrainian Conservative Party), has been a major driving force in promoting this virulent anti-Semitism. In a letter to UN Secretary-General Kofi Annan at the end of November 2005, he denounced the so-called Judeo-Nazis responsible for the Bolshevik Revolution and subsequent wars, starvation, and repression that had caused the deaths of more than fifty million people. Not surprisingly, American white supremacist David Duke is a welcome lecturer at MAUP, which also maintains close contacts with Saudi Arabia, Libya, and Iran.

Under the cover of academic respectability, Tschokin has spread a message of undisguised nationalistic anti-Semitism, even accusing Jews and their supporters of seeking to bring about another world war. He presents the criminal ideology of "Judeo-liberalism," masquerading under the banner of "humanism" and "democratic values," as an assault on authentic faith, tradition, and patriotism. The Jews, he insists, have already achieved control of finance, industry, the media, the state bureaucracy, and the Ukrainian parliament. [102]

Tschokin's worldview recalls that of the *Protocols* in many respects. Jewry is depicted as an extensive, tentacular network of secret societies seeking to concentrate all financial, media, and political power in its hands. Liberal and Communist utopias were merely Jewish instruments used to dissolve existing nation-states and prepare the rule of the chosen people. Bolshevism was nothing but a Jewish totalitarian ethnocracy, which had provoked the Russian civil war (1918–20), the starvation of the Ukrainian people in the 1930s, and all of its subsequent tragedies.[103] MAUP has, of course, tried to camouflage this virulent anti-Semitism under the cover of the "struggle against Zionism." However, this has not stopped it from reviving charges that Jews commit ritual murder (shades of the 1911 Beilis blood-libel case in Kiev); or from vilifying the Talmud and actively promoting Holocaust denial. When President Yushchenko belatedly urged Ukrainians to combat anti-Semitism and xenophobia on December 5, 2005, the MAUP website immediately accused him of being a stooge of Zionists. After the July 7, 2005, terrorist attack in London, Tschokin's party newspaper typically claimed that it was part of a Zionist plot to take over the world.[104]

MAUP may be responsible for as much as three-quarters of Ukraine's anti-Semitic pamphlets, publications, and other literature. Directly and indirectly, it has certainly contributed to an atmosphere in which synagogue vandalism, personal assaults, and virulent anti-Semitic public discourse have shaken the security of Ukraine's Jewish community.[105] On November 22, 2005, Tschokin issued the following revealing statement of solidarity with Iranian president Mahmoud Ahmadinejad's threat to wipe out Israel:

> We'd like to remind [you] that the Living God Jesus Christ said to Jews two thousand years ago: "Your father is a devil!" [that] Zionism in 1975 was acknowledged by [the] General Assembly of the UN as the form of racism and race discrimination that, in the opinion of the absolute majority of modern Europeans, is the biggest threat to modern civilization. Israel is the artificially created State (classic totalitarian type) which appeared on the political Earth map only in 1948, thanks to [the] good will of [the] UN. . . . Their end is known, and only God's True [*sic*] will rescue all of us.[106]

Since those apocalyptic remarks were made, countries like Ukraine have found themselves on the verge of bankruptcy. Partly this has been due to the world economic crisis and partly to the improvidence of foreign banks but also to their own endemic corruption, perpetual quarreling among the political elites, and weak leadership. The euphoria that had initially greeted Ukraine's independence in 1991 and then the pro-Western "Orange Revolution" of 2004 has begun to turn sour. The nationalist virus may well revive, as it did in the Balkans during the 1990s or more recently in Hungary, Slovakia, and Austria, where two far Right parties received almost 30 percent of the vote thanks to their xenophobic rhetoric. Anti-Semitism is part of the DNA of the populist nationalisms in east-central Europe, whatever the size of their Jewish communities. Every crisis of liberal capitalism, democratic institutions, and national identity tends to bring it to the surface, especially when times are hard. With budget cuts and deficits, with less foreign investments or credit and fewer jobs, the age-old temptation to look for "hidden forces" will likely grow and with it the search for the mythical "Jew" on whom to project all the blame.

This projection of guilt has already happened in Lithuania, where more than two hundred thousand Jews were murdered during the Holocaust, almost 95 percent of the pre-1939 Jewish population. These atrocities were largely committed by local Lithuanians, but they have remained almost wholly unpunished. On the other hand, Lithuanian prosecutors have shown remarkable zeal in interrogating and pursuing those elderly Jewish Holocaust survivors who had joined Soviet-backed partisan groups fighting Hitler during the Second World War. Thus a small number of Jewish Communists, active in the resistance, have been turned into war criminals complicit in the Soviet "genocide" of Lithuanians. This brazen distortion of history has managed to simultaneously defame Jews and deliberately obfuscate the Nazi Holocaust. [107]

SIX

Nazi Shadows over Austria

The immediate aftermath of the Holocaust was a decisive period in shaping the troubled postwar relations between Austrians and Jews. The deportations and mass murder of Austrian Jewry during World War II destroyed one of the wealthiest, most vibrant, and most culturally creative Jewish communities on the European continent. By 1945, only a tiny remnant survived of the great Jewish community numbering 2.25 million that once inhabited the Austro-Hungarian Empire. In 1910 there had been 175,000 Jews living in the multicultural imperial capital of Vienna—the driving force of economic and cultural life in the city. Their brilliant galaxy of talent helped shape the contours of twentieth-century culture.[1] The Jewish presence was also heavily felt in the free professions. Most city lawyers and doctors were Jews, a predominance that would continue until the *Anschluss* in 1938. Jews stood out in journalism (especially the liberal and socialist press) and were disproportionately represented in commerce, banking, and entrepreneurial capitalism.[2] This prominence was not fundamentally changed by the anti-Semitic Christian Social administration of the city of Vienna after 1897.[3] Anti-Semitism in Vienna was indeed stronger than in any other central or western European capital, but the populist mayor, Karl Lueger, was astute enough to realize that Jews were an indispensable element in the life of the metropolis.[4]

Following the collapse of the multinational empire in 1918 and the postwar peace treaties, Austria (like Hungary) suffered a massive loss of territory, population, and national self-confidence. The Jewish community was reduced to a tenth of its former size and overwhelmingly concentrated in Vienna. In 1923 the Jewish population peaked at 201,513 (10.8 percent of the total population), which made Vienna the third largest Jewish city in Europe—after Warsaw and Budapest. Ethnic prejudice was exacerbated by a massive influx of Galician Jewish refugees during World War I and in the early 1920s, as well as by the loss of empire, the postwar inflation, high unemployment, and the endemic status anxiety of the Viennese *kleine Mann* (little man). Anti-Semitism could be found in virtually all social classes, age groups, and political parties[5]—especially in the ruling Catholic, conservative Christian Social Party and the more virulently racist Grossdeutsche Volkpartei (Greater German People's Party), which favored union with Germany.[6] Its strongest constituency was German nationalist university students who, by the late 1920s, had emerged as the avant-garde of the growing Nazi movement in Austria. The "inviolable territory" of the universities (where police could not enter) transformed them into "Brown Houses" with open season on Jewish students, well before the *Anschluss*.[7] In the Austrian countryside, too, anti-Semitism was strong—fueled by time-honored religious prejudice, hidebound provincialism, and resentment against "Red Vienna" (usually identified with Jews), as well as by German nationalist propaganda.[8]

With the *Anschluss* of March 1938, the annihilation of Austrian Jewry began in earnest as the accumulated social and political discontent of the indigenous population exploded with elemental force. As the historian Gerhard Botz put it: "The attacks consisted mostly of symbolic acts and historic rituals aimed at the destruction of a sense of identity—humiliations, abuse and arrests—but there were also physical attacks, beatings, murders and also robberies on a mass scale. It was as if medieval pogroms had reappeared in modern dress."[9] The pogrom-like atmosphere was accompanied by a swift, large-scale Aryanization of Jewish property (the ruthless expropriation of Viennese Jews), including well-known Jewish businesses and big department stores.[10] Nearly seventy thousand Jewish dwellings were seized. This doubled as a way to alleviate the housing shortage in Vienna and to reward citizens and party comrades who had served the aims of the Nazi movement.[11] The enforced exodus of Jews proceeded apace and by November 1939 126,445 Jews had "emigrated" from Austria to the United Kingdom, the United States, Shanghai, Palestine, and other destinations—altogether about two-thirds of Austrian Jewry. The brutality of Viennese anti-Semitism, which accelerated this mass exodus, was more visceral than anything hitherto seen in Nazi Germany.[12] During the war years, the remaining third of Austrian Jewry would be deported to death camps in

Poland, where approximately 65,000 Jews would be gassed or murdered by other methods.

At the end of 1945 there were approximately four thousand members of the *Israelitische Kultusgemeinde* (Jewish religious community) still alive. They scratched out a living in a hungry and despondent Austria under four-power Allied occupation. At that time the Red Army still controlled Vienna and the eastern half of the country, with the Soviet troops leaving only in 1945 after the signing of the Austrian State Treaty. The British Labour MP Richard Crossman, who visited Austria in February 1946 as a member of the Anglo-American Committee of Inquiry into Palestine, described the Jewish communal leaders he met as "shrill and pathetic, self-assertive and broken"; he noted their conviction that there was no more future for Jews in Austria and that immigration to Palestine was the only solution for European Jewry. They told him that anti-Semitism (despite the Holocaust) was as strong as ever; hence they advised against encouraging any Jews to return to their Austrian homeland.[13]

In 1945, as had already happened after World War I, the divisions in Austria between *Ostjuden* (Eastern Jews) and Westernized Jews continued, though the differences were perhaps less acute than similar divisions in Germany.[14] The Eastern European Jews, four-fifths of them from Poland (the rest from Hungary, Romania, and the Czech lands), crossed the Austrian border after 1945 to flee pogroms, impoverishment, and the imminent Communist takeover in their respective countries. The displaced persons (DP) camps in Austria (as in Germany) soon turned into recruiting grounds for smuggling Jews illegally into what was still the British mandate of Palestine. The American zone of occupation in Austria was more favorable for this activity than the DP camps under British jurisdiction for obvious reasons. The problem of these Jewish DPs played a significant role in reviving postwar Austrian anti-Semitism. It blurred any latent Austrian sense of guilt for the Holocaust by focusing attention on the special accommodation and better rations (at a time of food shortages) that some Jews were receiving in the American zone.[15] Rumors swiftly spread that Jews engaged in *Schleichhandel* (black market activities) and were responsible for the increase in venereal disease.[16] Even the Socialist newspaper, the *Arbeiter-Zeitung*, deplored the influx of "hordes of illicit foreign traders and desperadoes," the "unwelcome guests" and "wretched, unemployed and overly excitable Jews whose presence inevitably promote antisemitic whisperings."[17]

There were growing calls to expel the foreigners, "parasites," and *Volksschädlinge* (a Nazi term for antisocial elements harmful to the nation) from the Tirol and Vorarlberg. In these Alpine areas the Jews, in fact, represented only about 1 percent of the sixty-five thousand DPs after the war. Between 1945 and 1948, they never averaged more than 10 percent of the six hundred thousand displaced persons at any time, but their numbers were invariably exaggerated. American surveys taken in 1947–48 of public opinion in Vienna, Salzburg, and Linz show, however, how much the local population blamed Jews for food, housing, and other problems, still believing that they had received their just deserts under the Nazis. About 40 percent of the population in all three cities thought the "Jewish character" was responsible for anti-Semitism; 43 percent of Salzburgers, 34 percent of the Viennese, and 47 percent of the Linzers were convinced that Jews had it too good in the DP camps and that they were *Nutzniesser* (profiteers) living at the expense of the indigenous population. Austrian responses were similar to those recorded in Germany—especially in Bavaria, Hesse, and Baden-Württemberg, where anti-Semitic sentiments in 1947 were also running high.[18] Rabbi Philip Bernstein, Jewish adviser to the U.S. military government in Germany, commented in May 1947 that if the Americans were to withdraw, there would be a pogrom.

The resentment against foreign Jews in German-speaking Europe was particularly strong in rural areas. The local population in Bavaria (where 93 percent of the Jewish population were DPs) and in Alpine regions of Austria could not fathom why they should host eastern European Jews for whom the American military government provided special treatment. In the Salzburg region there were about fourteen thousand Jewish refugees— an unprecedentedly high figure for an area where there were fewer than three hundred Jewish inhabitants in the prewar era. Salzburg had long been a hotbed of pan-German racism and anti-Semitism, dating back to the late nineteenth century. This *deutschnational* tradition further sharpened the backlash against the Jewish DPs.[19] Nevertheless, postwar anti-Semitism in Austria and Germany remained less lethal than in neighboring Poland, Hungary, Czechoslovakia, or Romania. There were anti-Semitic incidents but no pogroms like that in the Polish town of Kielce in July 1946.

In contrast to Germany, Austria was never required by the Western Allies to examine its own Holocaust legacy. Germans knew that their behavior toward the Jews was seen as a test of their maturity and democratic credentials in the West. They experienced direct pressure from Washington and from American Jewish organizations, making clear the link that existed between German-Jewish relations and the moral legitimacy of Germany in the postwar world. A degree of philo-Semitism would therefore be required if Germany were to regain its political sovereignty. This factor played its part in the positive German decision on *Wiedergutmachung* (reparations) to Israel and world Jewry. A combination of political prudence, moral scruples, and a healthy respect for Jewish influence in America would mark German chancellor Konrad Adenauer's attitude on these issues. It was also significant that the chairman of the German Social Democratic Party (SPD), Kurt Schumacher, had demanded the payment of restitution to the Jews as early as 1946, repeatedly referring in speeches and interviews to Nazi guilt toward the Jews.[20] Without the principled support of the Socialist opposition for *Wiedergutmachung*, Dr. Adenauer could never have pushed through the historic legislation in 1952 against serious resistance in his own Christian-Democratic Party and from a majority of the German population. None of these considerations operated in postwar Austria.

Nevertheless, although Austrian politicians did not have to prove their democratic credentials by developing special relations with the Jews or Israel, they were aware that public displays of anti-Jewish prejudice might be damaging.[21] It was no accident that the socialist mayor of Vienna, Theodor Körner, chose in February 1947 to dismiss "the fairy-tale of antisemitism" in his city, calling it "totally alien to the Viennese." Sharply criticizing unfriendly reports in the foreign (especially the American) press, he misleadingly stated that "Vienna had never witnessed antisemitic outrages of the kind found in other countries . . . for the Viennese is a cosmopolitan and thus from the word go not an anti-Semite."[22] In a letter to the World Jewish Congress in April 1947 Körner confidently claimed that the Austrian Socialists would remain the best guarantee against the revival of anti-Semitism in the future. Körner forgot, however, to mention that the post-1945 Socialist leadership carefully avoided inviting veteran Austro-Marxist Jews in the emigration to return to Austria.

The conservative Austrian chancellor Leopold Figl no less vehemently denied that Austrians were anti-Semitic. His views on the subject seemed wholly divorced from reality. In June 1947 he naïvely suggested that sympathy with persecuted Jews had eradicated anti-Semitism in Austria. "I don't think this question will ever acquire even the slightest significance," he said. Figl, who had spent several years in a concentration camp, evidently believed that since *all* Austrians had suffered, there were no grounds for any differentiation on the basis of race or religion. The law should be applied "even-handedly for everyone who returns from the camps and prisons." In one of the very rare public statements ever made by a politician in welcoming back Jewish returnees to Austria, he proclaimed that the Jews were "Austrians like all of us," with the same right to be reinstated to their former rights as all the others. The problem with this universalist egalitarianism was that it rejected even minimal affirmative action for the unique suffering inflicted upon Austrian Jews.[23] Figl depicted any special consideration for Jews as "racism in reverse"—an argument frequently used in Austria to resist Jewish demands for moral and material restitution after 1945.

It is a fact that postwar Austrian politicians rarely, if ever, sought to counteract the anti-Semitic opinions of the population. Until the 1990s, there were few who saw fit to express remorse about the fate of the Jews or to confront unpalatable facts about the Austrian role in the Holocaust.[24] Significantly, when prominent Christian Social politician Leopold Kunschak made anti-Semitic statements against the acceptance of Polish-Jewish refugees in Austria, it did not terminate or affect his career. In a speech on April 16, 1946, Kunschak declared, "The Polish Jews should not come to Austria; we Austrians don't need the others either! . . . Austrian industry should not fall into Jewish hands."[25] Kunschak had been a radical Catholic populist and militant anti-Semite since 1918, if not earlier. He had also been interned for seven years in a concentration camp as a Catholic anti-Nazi. Indeed, he was one of the founders of the Second Republic in 1945 and was even elected president of its National Assembly. Chancellor Figl excused his bigotry by saying that Kunschak was an "economic," not a racial anti-Semite, as if this distinction made his remarks more acceptable.

If official Austria showed little willingness to combat the anti-Semitism of the man in the street after 1945, there was even less desire to encourage the Jews to return, let alone to pay restitution for Nazi crimes. The Austrian authorities often obstructed the repatriation of Austrian Jews from abroad, refusing them the status accorded to political victims of the Nazis. Moreover, they generally resisted Jewish claims to restore to their original owners property, homes, and businesses that had been Aryanized. Survivors often found themselves greeted with indifference, hostility, and bureaucratic ob-tuseness.[26] By contrast, great efforts were made to integrate former Nazis, the bulk of whom were amnestied in 1948 and henceforth represented hun-dreds of thousands of potential voters for the major political parties. Mem-bers of the Austrian Socialist Party (SPÖ), like the conservatives of the Austrian People's Party (ÖVP), were undoubtedly corrupted by this elec-toralism, renouncing moral principle in their bid for ex-Nazi votes, which represented at least 15 percent of the electorate.

The SPÖ had moved to the right after 1945, decisively breaking with its prewar Austro-Marxist legacy. The dominant figures at the top were the party chairman, Adolf Schärf; the interior minister, Oskar Helmer; and the president of the republic, Karl Renner. Helmer was the most influential of all the Socialist ministers when it came to the "Jewish question." He blamed the "Jewish" party leadership under Otto Bauer for the fiasco of the abortive February 1934 workers' rising and the collapse of democracy in the First Re-public. According to Helmer, the SPÖ before 1934 had been *jüdisch belastet* (burdened by Jews). They had been far too numerous in the party leader-ship.[27] Holding such views, it is not surprising that Helmer felt free to make racist remarks whenever it seemed expedient. In a cabinet meeting on No-vember 9, 1948, he once again said that Jews had too much influence in business and finance. Moreover, they engaged in dishonest practices and were allergic to manual labor. Though there were only a few thousand native-born Jews left in Austria after the Holocaust, he considered them omnipresent: "Everywhere I can see only Jewish expansion, among the doc-tors and in commerce—especially in Vienna."[28] He pointedly commented that the Jews, too, would have "to earn their living like everyone else in Aus-tria." This was indeed a widely held view. For good measure, Helmer added that since the British began fighting the Jews, the "atrocities of the Jews in the Palestine war have had an effect"—which could help the Austrian gov-ernment to further procrastinate in negotiations over restitution. The Jews, Helmer concluded, would eventually understand, once they "realise that a lot of people are opposed to them."[29]

Karl Renner, the first postwar Socialist chancellor and one of the greatest theorists of prewar Austro-Marxism, was another who seemed to display more empathy for ex-Nazis than for the Jewish victims of the Holocaust. Renner warned his cabinet colleagues not to apply sanctions against those who had simply followed orders, with no idea that they were supporting a

war of aggression. In a speech before officials of the new Austrian administration on April 30, 1945, he expressed the hope that the Nazis "can all go
peacefully back to their normal life and that they will be able to carry on
quietly in their jobs."[30] It was not right, he believed, to confiscate their
property. At the same time, with the help of a vague, generalized definition
of "victims," he was able to play down Jewish persecution, and he explicitly
opposed making a special law for the Jews. This would, he argued, discrim-
inate against the Socialists whose property and assets as a political party had
been confiscated by the clerico-fascist state in 1934. Renner's comparison
implied that the prewar repression of the labor movement by "Austro-
fascism" should be put on the same level as the mass murder of Jews by the
Nazis. It also suggested that those who had been persecuted for political
reasons deserved priority over those who had *merely* suffered for racial reasons.[31] Socialist policy was dictated above all by the desire to weaken their
Conservative rivals through winning over anticlerical pro-Nazis in the Austrian middle class. To this end, Oskar Helmer contributed to establishing a
third party in 1949, the Verband der Unabhängigen (VdU, the League of Independents), which represented ex-Nazis, German nationalists, and some
liberal malcontents.[32] Its top officials had, for the most part, been members
of the NSDAP. A few of them had even served short prison sentences after
1945.

The chairman of this new political group, Dr. Herbert Kraus, immediately called for compensation for his fellow Nazis, the abolition of de-
Nazification laws, and the rapid integration of the *ehemaligen* (former
members of the NSDAP) into Austrian society.[33] Kraus vigorously defended the rights of the Aryanizers, of fallen and wounded Wehrmacht soldiers, and members of the SS who had "heroically" defended Austria in an
allegedly defensive war. The VdU even stigmatized the postwar de-
Nazification law as comparable to Nazi terror and injustice between 1938
and 1945.[34] Allied internment camps were depicted as if they were identical
to German concentration camps. In the March 1949 elections the VdU won
fifteen seats in the Austrian parliament and, shortly after, pension rights for
ex-Nazi civil servants were restored.

Between 1945 and 1966, the Second Republic was governed by a grand
coalition of the conservatives (ÖVP) and the Socialists (SPÖ), which discouraged any challenge to the cozy consensus that claimed Austria had been
the first victim of the Nazis. There was, on the contrary, a common interest

in repressing the history of anti-Semitism in Austria, the story of massive wartime collaboration, and the unique fate of the Jews, whose continuing presence as DPs, survivors, or returning refugees remained an obvious embarrassment. If returning Wehrmacht soldiers and *Heimkehrer* (home comers) from the Soviet Union in the 1950s were treated almost as martyrs, Jews who survived the Holocaust were expected to be very discreet. As British historian Robert Knight shrewdly observed, Jews were too subversive for the new Austria because they were "rivals" who had "a better claim to victimhood, and [were] furthermore victims of the non-Jewish Austrian population itself."[35]

Regular acquittals at war crimes trials, and the hostile atmosphere in which they were conducted, were one of the more negative results of the Austrian political and educational failure to fight Jew hatred without compromise.[36] Moreover, the prosecutions of war criminals were seriously handicapped by a lack of resources, public indifference, and the rapid reintegration of former Nazis into the judicial system. Hence, the single-minded pursuit of Nazi war criminals by an individual survivor such as Simon Wiesenthal, working in isolation out of a small office in Vienna, was bound to arouse intense antagonism in Austria. Wiesenthal reminded postwar Austrians of everything they wanted to forget.[37]

This was the unpromising context in which Austria would in 1970 elect for the first time a Jew and a Socialist to head its government. Bruno Kreisky, leader of the Austrian Social Democrats, continued to hold the position of federal chancellor for the next thirteen years, until his retirement in 1983. During that period he achieved considerable popularity and exerted a remarkable degree of influence over Austria's domestic and foreign affairs. Yet Kreisky's career—first as chairman of the SPÖ in February 1967 and then as chancellor—surprised many people, including himself. He had returned to Austria only in 1951 after thirteen long years in Swedish exile. He had married into a highly assimilated and wealthy Swedish-Jewish family and developed close ties to the Scandinavian labor movements. During the war he had been active on behalf of Austrian prisoners of war in Soviet captivity. On the other hand, he appears to have been totally detached from the terrible fate visited on the Jews of Europe in those years, despite losing many of his own relatives during the Holocaust.

Kreisky's personal biography explains, to a certain degree, his reticence and deep ambivalence on the "Jewish question."[38] His own family belonged to the *grossbürgerlich* (upper bourgeois) milieu in Vienna, where he had been born in 1911. From the age of sixteen he had been a militant in the Socialist movement, strongly influenced by his Austro-Marxist mentor Otto Bauer. He had spent time in the prisons of the Christian Social corporate state, which had crushed the Socialist workers' uprising in 1934.[39] He had been arrested again by the Gestapo in 1938 but was released thanks to the intervention of a young Austrian Nazi he had previously befriended in prison.[40] For the young Kreisky, his interaction with Nazis imprisoned by the clerico-fascist regime in Austria between 1934 and 1938 convinced him that Nazis could be educationally recuperated—they were essentially misguided proletarians and lower-middle-class patriots who had been driven by unemployment into the arms of the National Socialists. This was an important factor in his soft attitude toward ex-Nazis after he became Austrian chancellor.

In addition to maintaining his strange silence concerning the Holocaust, Kreisky grossly underplayed the role of anti-Semitism in the 1930s. He tended to accept superficial Marxist explanations that depicted anti-Semitism as a tool of the ruling classes against the labor movement or as a temporary excrescence of decaying capitalism. In his memoirs, he insisted that he had never been discriminated against as a Jew and that his forced emigration from Austria had nothing to do with his Jewish origins.[41] He dismissed the idea of treating anti-Semitism as a "special phenomenon," just as he vehemently rejected any notion about the Jews as a distinct "nationality"—something he condemned as "inverted racism." Jews should, in his opinion, be treated solely as a religious group—like Catholics or Protestants—without any reference to Israel or the Holocaust.[42]

Kreisky's evident wish to negate his own Jewishness did not pass unnoticed in Far Right circles that swiftly detected a *deutschnational* emphasis in his public comments. In February 1967 the neo-Nazi leader in Austria, Norbert Burger, affirmed that he had no objections to Kreisky, whom he considered a "German" belonging neither to the "Mosaic religious community" nor to the Zionist movement.[43] This vote of confidence by the extremist Right appeared to be vindicated when Kreisky appointed no fewer than four ex-Nazis—out of eleven ministers—to his first cabinet.[44] Since 1945, nothing like this had occurred in Austria or elsewhere in Europe. The shock galvanized Nazi hunter Simon Wiesenthal into action. His investigations revealed that Kreisky's minister of agriculture, Hans Öllinger, had once been an SS lieutenant. Öllinger resigned, but Kreisky angrily argued that everyone had the right to make political mistakes in their youth.[45] The only thing that mattered was whether a former member of the NSDAP had committed a criminal act or not. The minister of the interior, Otto Rösch (acquitted in 1947 on insufficient evidence for past Nazi activity) was defended on similar lines, along with Josef Moser and Erwin Frühbauer, the other former Nazis in his cabinet. Kreisky's Socialists were evidently angling for the support of the Freedom Party (FPÖ), heir of the League of Independents, which though small in size (it enjoyed about 6 percent of the vote in 1970) held the narrow balance between the two leading parties. Neither Socialists nor conservatives wished to alienate former supporters of Hitler. However, no previous Austrian chancellor had gone so far as Kreisky in signaling to the FPÖ that its leaders might be *persona grata* in a new Austrian government. It was this escalation that prompted Simon Wiesenthal to act.[46]

Wiesenthal's disclosures upset Socialist political strategy, leading to ominous warnings that his War Crimes Documentation Center might be investigated and closed down. For this purpose Kreisky himself was willing to use deliberately leaked material from the Communist bloc branding Wiesenthal as an agent of Mossad, the CIA, and British Intelligence. Rumors alleging that Wiesenthal had been a Nazi collaborator during the war were spread, in order to bring his name into disrepute.[47] Chancellor Kreisky took an active part in this anti-Wiesenthal campaign. He told a Dutch socialist newspaper, *Vrij Nederland,* that Wiesenthal was a "Jewish Fascist," sarcastically adding that "one finds reactionaries also amongst us Jews, as well as thieves, murderers and prostitutes."[48] Wiesenthal responded, calling Kreisky a Jewish "renegade" and pointing out that Austria was the only country in Europe that still had former Nazis in its government, twenty-five years after the war. He deplored the fact that Kreisky was reinforcing Austrian reluctance to deal with the Nazi past, helping to trivialize the Holocaust, and in effect encouraging national fantasies of innocence.[49] In the new atmosphere, it seemed as if former Nazi Party members were guiltless, but those who investigated them could be slandered with impunity.

However, once the *Kronen Zeitung* and other mass circulation tabloids lined up on Kreisky's side, Wiesenthal's persistence appeared increasingly quixotic. He faced widespread indifference, not to say open public hostility.[50] Simon Wiesenthal's long struggle against Austrian historical amnesia appeared to have run aground. A neo-Nazi paper gleefully concluded that

Kreisky's principle was *Wer ein Nazi ist, bestimmt die SPÖ!* (The Socialist Party of Austria decides who is a Nazi!).[51] Matters climaxed in October 1975 with the spectacular Socialist victory at the polls. This was a personal triumph for Bruno Kreisky, who now stood at the pinnacle of his political career. However, just before election day, Wiesenthal produced evidence that the FPÖ leader (and potential ally of Kreisky) Friedrich Peter had been involved as a tank commander on the Russian front in the First SS Infantry Brigade. This unit was responsible for the murder of 10,513 innocent men, women, and children, mainly Jews. Peter did acknowledge membership in the Waffen-SS unit but denied involvement in any shootings, "illegal acts," or war crimes.[52]

After the election, Kreisky promptly accused Wiesenthal of using "political Mafia" methods "to bring me down" and denounced what he called Zionist interference in Austria's internal affairs. Zionism, he believed, asked Jews outside Israel "to be bound by a special commitment . . . to work for it as though they were Israeli citizens." For the benefit of Arab or pro-Palestinian media, he added that "there is nothing which binds me to Israel or to what is called the Jewish 'people' or to Zionism."[53] To his Jewish critics he stressed that "the fact of being a Jew is without meaning," while angrily denying that he was a "Jewish anti-Semite like Marx." In an interview with an Israeli journalist he lashed out at Wiesenthal's background (he was a Polish Jew) and at his investigative methods, insisting that "*Der Mann muss verschwinden*" (the man must disappear). Kreisky's parting salvo, intended as a witticism, was headlined in the popular German weekly *Der Spiegel:* "*Wenn die Juden ein Volk sind, so ist es ein mieses Volk*" (If the Jews are a people, then they are a repulsive people).[54] Such vilification of Wiesenthal and of the Jews as a group did not apparently damage Kreisky's popularity at home, though it was adversely commented upon in the German and some of the European press.[55] The *Widerstandsbewegung* (Austrian antifascist resistance) protested vigorously, as did the Communist *Volksstimme.* The Jewish community was sufficiently stung by Kreisky's hostile remarks to indicate its disquiet, though it was still reluctant to go public with its concerns. The SPÖ, though disturbed by the escalation, rallied around its leader.[56]

Kreisky's most vocal support came, ironically enough, from neo-Nazis in Germany and Austria. They could scarcely contain their delight that a Jewish chancellor wished to neutralize their most feared adversary. By the end of 1975 Kreisky had become an honorary Aryan in their eyes, whose outbursts against "boundless Zionist intolerance" were grist to the mill of the extreme Right.[57] The neo-Nazis enthusiastically recorded Kreisky's professions of loyalty to German Austria and information about his ancestors, who had been German-speaking teachers, doctors, officials, and even deputies in the Austrian imperial parliament. A typical headline trumpeted the good tidings: "Kreisky wants a reconciliation with the former Nazis."[58] Right-wing Austrians sympathetic to National Socialism could heave a collective sigh of relief. The time had come to bury once and for all the file on the Nazi past.

Kreisky's undisguised hostility toward the new Israeli prime minister, Menachem Begin, was not disconnected from his general aversion to anything that recalled the Holocaust—a subject that literally obsessed Begin. Added to this was the fact that Kreisky, an upper-middle-class Viennese descended from assimilated Czech-German ancestors, was distinctly allergic to Polish shtetl Jews like Begin or Simon Wiesenthal. Ideological anti-Zionism and distaste for the *Ostjuden* fused in Kreisky's defamatory references to Begin as a "criminal terrorist" and "little Polish lawyer or whatever he is."[59] For the Austrian chancellor, Menachem Begin embodied the "warped mentality" of Eastern European Jews "alienated from normal ways of thinking." The Israeli leader's integral nationalism was misleadingly presented as a "blood and soil" ideology, a "mysterious racism in reverse." In the late 1970s Kreisky would further inflame matters by his compulsive comparisons of Israel to South Africa. Long before former U.S. president Jimmy Carter made it fashionable to do so, he blasted the "Bantustans" on the West Bank as a form of apartheid.[60] When Jews protested at such analogies, Kreisky escalated the deepening sense of mutual alienation by claiming that Israel was a fascist police state.

The Austrian chancellor did not hesitate to brand Simon Wiesenthal as part of the Zionist "conspiracy" against him, launched because Kreisky had not fulfilled his task "in the service of Israel."[61] In 1986, at the height of the Waldheim affair, Wiesenthal publicly responded to Kreisky's angry denunciations of the World Jewish Congress: "If Bruno Kreisky were chancellor today, Waldheim would be the joint candidate of both big parties. And Kreisky would defend Waldheim against the World Jewish Congress and the Jews with all his power."[62] This internal Jewish war was unsparing. It is not surprising, therefore, that Kreisky found himself accused in certain circles of Jewish self-hatred. The Hungarian-Israeli satirist Ephraim Kishon mockingly observed in *Der Spiegel* magazine: "Our big brother has decided he's got a hump, and therefore he hates all humpbacks." It was all too evident to Israelis like Kishon that Kreisky was "'a first class antisemite,' going around like an angry bull with his own private red flag."[63]

The adulation with which Bruno Kreisky was received by Arab public opinion as well as the applause he received from neo-Nazi sources, provides some ammunition for the charge of self-hatred. Though a convinced antifascist, Kreisky seemed a shade too eager to denigrate Jewry whenever possible and to morally discredit Zionism. During the Simon Wiesenthal–Friedrich Peter affair he acted as if the Holocaust was a mere side issue and his prime duty was to exculpate Austrians from the burdens of their recent past. The fact that a Jewish chancellor was providing them with absolution from terrible sins, and with an alibi for ignoring the Nazi legacy, was doubtless reassuring to many of his fellow citizens and ultimately increased Kreisky's popularity.[64] Thus the first and only Jewish statesman ever to rule a German-speaking country provided little comfort for Israel or for the Jewish people, despite his undeniable political skills and international prestige.

The Waldheim affair began in 1986, three years after Kreisky's retirement from politics. It had a distinctly international dimension, involving a former secretary-general of the United Nations who was now the official candidate of the Conservative Party for the Austrian presidency and had been unexpectedly accused of concealing his Nazi past. The affair was exacerbated by Waldheim's determination to indulge in a smoke screen of denial, inexplicable amnesia, and patriotic bluster. He claimed to speak in the name of Austria against a campaign directed from abroad "to discredit" the nation as a whole.[65] If the Wiesenthal-Kreisky-Peter case had largely been a domestic Austrian scandal, the Waldheim affair pitted "little Austria" against most of Western public opinion and the main international Jewish organizations, especially the World Jewish Congress (WJC).[66]

The "interference" of the WJC in Austria's internal affairs was indeed what prompted many Austrians, including Bruno Kreisky, to react with special vehemence.[67] Kreisky even accused the new Israeli prime minister, Yitzhak Shamir, "of seeking to mobilize the West against Waldheim" and trying to falsely paint Austria as an anti-Semitic state.[68] But the Waldheim story went far beyond conflicts between individual Jews or Jewish organizations. Indeed, it perfectly encapsulated the postwar Austrian inability to confront the moral implications and meaning of the Nazi Holocaust. The Waldheim affair also provoked a stream of discourse about Jews that had been officially taboo since 1945, thereby opening up a new space for fantasies about the "international Jewish conspiracy" against Austria.[69] Anti-Semitic attitudes from pre-Nazi Austria and the period of the Third Reich could now be expressed much more brazenly than before, with the mass circulation press (the *Kronen Zeitung* and *Die Presse*) reinforcing and often shaping entrenched popular prejudices.[70] The time-honored idea that the Jew was at the root of any given problem (the *Judaeus ex machina*) could once more be revived, this time to serve the conservative politics of the Waldheim campaign.[71] Such a resurgence of anti-Semitism doubtless served to justify Austria's conduct in the Nazi era, and reflected the latent popular fear of "Jewish revenge." During the Waldheim affair, older stereotypes of Jewish world power, negative Christian images about vengeful Jews, and the tendency to hold Jews themselves responsible for anti-Semitism became part of the "we-they" confrontation pitting a "pacific" Austria against an "aggressive" international Jewry.[72] The effects could be seen in the survey conducted by the Gallup Institute of Austrians in the summer of 1991 showing that substantial portions of the Austrian population had strongly negative perceptions of Jews and believed it was time to put the Holocaust aside.[73] Waldheim clearly drew part of his support from such attitudes, which were no less widespread in Germany.

The Waldheim affair had originally begun with revelations about the candidate's "brown past" in the left-wing weekly Austrian magazine *Profil*. The story quickly spread to the Western press. The allegations that Waldheim had been a war criminal, involved in savage reprisals against Yugoslav partisans in the Balkans and in the deportation of Greek Jews from Thessaloníki, were never actually proven, and Waldheim was eventually elected president. But much previously unknown evidence surfaced that demonstrated beyond a doubt that Waldheim had systematically lied about his past in the Third Reich and that he knew far more than he cared to divulge about atrocities against partisans and Jews. Some of his supporters, however, chose to treat the evidence against Waldheim as a "Jewish inspired" libel. The abrasive secretary-general of the Austrian People's Party, Michael Graff, openly accused the WJC of indulging in hate-filled attacks and deliberate defamation.[74] The campaign against Waldheim, he stated, was provoking "feelings that we don't want to have."[75] Other spokesmen of the ÖVP, including Foreign Minister Alois Mock, branded the WJC as a "mafia of slanderers," and dishonorable people who were driven solely by hatred and blind rage.[76] They were particularly incensed by the interview with WJC leaders Israel Singer and Elan Steinberg, in which Austrians were warned that if they elected a former Nazi as president they would experience six difficult years.[77] This was perceived by many as a collective threat against *all* Austrians.

When Michael Graff in a TV interview responded to charges from the Jewish community that he was pandering to anti-Semitic prejudice, he sarcastically suggested that to show Israel Singer on television "would really accentuate antisemitism in Austria."[78] Graff surpassed the crudity of this remark in another interview with the French weekly *L'Express* in November 1987, in which he said, "As long as it is not proven that he [Waldheim] single-handedly strangled six Jews, then there is no problem."[79] Similarly offensive remarks became part of the Conservative campaign against the WJC and "Jewish circles on the East Coast." American Jews were principally blamed for the heavy criticism of Austria that culminated in President Waldheim being placed on the "watch list" of undesirable aliens by the U.S. Justice Department in 1987. For his part, the new Austrian president insisted on presenting himself as the *persecuted victim* of those seeking to indict his generation, which had only done its duty as "decent men who faced a terrible fate."[80] Waldheim was unable to rise above the level of such sentimental clichés whenever he evoked World War II and the *Pflichterfüllung* (sense of patriotic duty) with which his fellow Austrians had defended their country. His arrogant dismissal of the investigation into his past and the evasive lies he provided about his own biography contrasted all too unfavorably with the moving remarks made in 1985 by the West German president Richard von Weizsäcker, who fully accepted German responsibility for Nazi crimes.[81] When Waldheim finally managed to condemn anti-Semitism and evoke the Holocaust, it was only *after* his election and sounded unconvincing.[82]

The Waldheim affair was a painful experience for Austrian Jews, revealing unsuspected levels of anti-Semitism and undermining certain illusions about the degree of their acceptance in Austrian society.[83] The communal leadership remained exceedingly cautious, fearing to make any statements that could exacerbate the nationalistic, xenophobic, and anti-Jewish atmosphere. Moreover, the aggressive policy of the New York–based WJC placed Austrian Jews in a particularly difficult situation. On the one hand, they felt their own position had been endangered and exposed by this high-profile international campaign led from America. If they sided openly with the WJC they might be stamped as "betrayers of the fatherland" and directly targeted. Even with the low profile they actually adopted, there was a notable rise in hate mail and threatening telephone calls, warnings, and physical abuse directed at members of the *Kultusgemeinde* (the official Jewish community). Increasingly under siege, the *Kultusgemeinde* saw its interests being ignored both by the Austrian government and by the WJC. Indeed, at a meeting of the European Jewish Congress in the summer of 1986, *Kultusgemeinde* president Paul Grosz complained about "outsiders" who were misguidedly telling Austrian Jews how to fight anti-Semitism.[84] He criticized both the political use of anti-Jewish prejudice by the ÖVP and the exaggerated generalizations from abroad that had stereotyped Austria in blanket fashion as an anti-Semitic country.[85]

The local communal leadership in Vienna officially proclaimed the restoration of Austria's prestige as its prime goal—a formula that disguised more than it revealed.[86] Simon Wiesenthal, for his part, engaged in a bruising war of words with both the World Jewish Congress and Bruno Kreisky, and was less diplomatic. He warned that exaggerated personal accusations against President Waldheim would only increase anti-Semitism in Austria. In the next few years, Wiesenthal's own image would be steadily transformed. By the mid-1990s, the "Nazi hunter" had become a much respected elder statesman, honored and even popular in many circles—something inconceivable during the Kreisky era.

Although the Waldheim affair was a traumatic event for many Austrian Jews, very few left the country. There were those who felt encouraged by the anti-Waldheim sentiment found among some Austrian intellectuals, a section of the youth, and the more educated elites.[87] Moreover, in the wake of the affair, more self-conscious and self-confident Jewish voices began to emerge in Austria (as they did in Germany), suggesting that an era of resignation might be finally drawing to a close.[88] The federal government and municipal authorities began to support Jewish museums, synagogues, research projects, and scholarly conferences on Jewish topics. A serious educational effort was undertaken in the 1990s to counteract anti-Semitism and increase knowledge about the Holocaust.[89] Above all, a younger generation of Austrian politicians and intellectuals appeared in the 1990s, willing to revise older myths about Austrian identity and to acknowledge the horrors of the past. In 1991 the Conservative deputy chancellor Erhard Busek admitted the need to recognize historic injustices toward the Jews committed by Austrians.

In July 1991 Socialist federal chancellor Franz Vranitsky publicly accepted Austrian coresponsibility for what had happened during the Third Reich.[90] On a subsequent visit to Israel in 1994, Vranitsky solemnly repeated in the name of the Austrian nation the acknowledgment of its *Mitschuld* (complicity) in the Holocaust. In the same spirit, Austria's leaders, after much delay, finally created an official commission of inquiry to look into the issue of Jewish property in Austria confiscated during World War II. The failure of the Austrian authorities to return property and artworks to survivors of the Holocaust or their descendants had done much to sour relations between Austria and the Jews.[91] During the past decade this has changed, reflecting not only a generational shift in European consciousness but also the impact of pluralist values on Austrian society—its greater openness and awareness of the lessons of the Holocaust.

Paradoxically, this new awakening owed a lot to the dramatic impact of Jörg Haider's populist politics in Austria during the past twenty years.[92] Born in 1950 in Upper Austria, son of a former Nazi storm trooper and a mother who belonged to the NSDAP's League of German Girls, Haider always expressed loyalty to his family background and was strongly influenced by the pan-German milieu from which he stemmed.[93] Elected to Parliament in 1979, the young lawyer became FPÖ leader seven years later at a time when party fortunes were at their lowest ebb—down to 5 percent of the national vote. The progression under Haider's authoritarian charismatic leadership would be spectacular, culminating in the FPÖ joining the right-wing coalition led by conservative Wolfgang Schüssel in February 2000 and becoming a party of government.

In 1990 the FPÖ had already garnered 16.5 percent of the vote; in the 1994 national elections, it got 22.6 percent—jumping from 13 to 42 seats in the 183-seat Austrian Parliament. This success made it the strongest Far Right party in any European democracy. Under Jörg Haider, the FPÖ was more *völkisch* than liberal.[94] A significant part of his appeal derived from the anti-foreigner message, the relentless anti-corruption campaign, and clever manipulation of public resentment at the SPÖ/Conservative monopoly of

Austrian politics for almost fifty years.[95] The FPÖ's anti-European stance also paid off in the 1997 elections to the European Parliament where it scored 28 percent of the vote. In local provincial elections, Haider's party achieved equally spectacular results. It had emerged by the mid-1990s as the strongest single party in the provinces of Salzburg and Carinthia. Haider had already been elected as governor of Carinthia in 1989—a position he would continue to hold despite his steep national decline. True, he was forced to resign over comments made in a July 1991 debate in the Carinthian parliament, after he praised "the orderly employment policy carried out in the Third Reich." But he was reelected two years later and continued to dominate local politics in this conservative southern province bordering Yugoslavia and Italy. In 1999 Haider won the Carinthian elections in a landslide victory; in 2005, 42 percent of voters in Carinthia reelected him as governor.

Haider's extreme right-wing populism reached its first peak of success in the general elections of October 1999 when the FPÖ finished second with a stunning 27 percent of the national vote.[96] Its entrance into the Austrian coalition government headed by the Conservative ÖVP led to an international outcry, spearheaded by EU governments who officially sanctioned Austria. They were joined by many Jewish and non-Jewish organizations around the world.[97] Israel's ambassador was pointedly recalled from Vienna. Haider, under pressure, resigned as head of the FPÖ and did not personally enter the new right-wing government, though he still controlled party policy behind the scenes. But support for the FPÖ fell dramatically, to 10 percent, in the November 2002 elections, as a result of internal intrigues and machinations. The telegenic, perennially boyish Haider seemed destined for an irreversible national slide.[98] Splitting off from the FPÖ and forming his own Alliance for the Future of Austria, he gained a bare 4 percent of the vote (and only seven parliamentary seats) in the October 2006 elections.[99] "Haiderism" without Haider did, however, regain some lost ground. The Freedom Party, running on an anti-Islamic and anti-immigration platform, received 11 percent of the vote in 2006, thereby depriving the Conservatives of first place. These results indicated that radical right-wing xenophobia was still a force in Austria and that the FPÖ preserved a hard kernel of racist ethnocentrism.[100]

The question of Haider's anti-Semitism and its pervasiveness within the FPÖ was a complex one. The pan-German heritage of a party stemming from the League of Independents had traditionally been linked to the Nazi concepts of *Anschluss* (union with Germany), *Volksgemeinschaft* (people's community), *Heimat* (homeland), and the exclusion of Jews.[101] At the same time, authoritarian nationalism has coexisted uneasily with a pro-Western liberal strand within the FPÖ ever since the 1960s. Haider's internal party *putsch* of 1986 greatly weakened the moderates. At the heart of his program was a deliberate xenophobia aiming to expel foreigners as the best cure for the country's unemployment problems. Moreover, in 1986 Haider had gained international attention during the controversy over Walter Reder, a notorious Austrian ex-SS major involved in the mass killings of Italian civilians in 1944. Freed by Italy from a life sentence, he was greeted in Austria with full military honors by a leading FPÖ politician, Friedhelm Frischenschlager, then serving as defense minister in a Socialist-led coalition government. Haider approved this action (which unleashed an international scandal), provocatively declaring: "Walter Reder was a soldier like hundreds of thousands of others. He performed his duty as demanded by the soldier's oath. . . . All our fathers could have met the same fate."[102]

Haider was equally unrepentant about his support for Nazi employment policy in the 1930s. Similarly, in May 1992, he came out strongly against government criticism of gatherings by "respectable" war veterans (of the Waffen-SS). In September 1995, Haider himself publicly addressed a reunion of Waffen-SS veterans, insisting that the reason why some people opposed them was "simply that in this world there are decent people who have character and who have stuck to their beliefs through the strongest headwinds and who have remained true to their convictions until today."[103]

Defending his speech after an amateur video of it had been broadcast on German TV in December 1996, Haider stated that the Waffen-SS was a part of the Wehrmacht "and hence it deserves all the honor and respect of the army in public life." The FPÖ leader added that though he rejected Nazism, he stood by the wartime generation and fought "against the way it is disparaged." This defense of the Waffen-SS went hand in hand with repeated calls to amnesty Nazi war criminals, to ridicule notions of Austrian collective responsibility for the "brown past," and to relativize the Nazi mass murders of Jews, Gypsies, and Slavs. Hence it was not surprising that the FPÖ was the only major Austrian political party absent in May 1995 from the ceremonies marking the fiftieth anniversary of the liberation of Mauthausen death camp. Shortly before, Haider had referred to Mauthausen as a

Straflager (punishment camp), as if its inmates were ordinary criminals who had simply broken the law.[104] Such trivialization of the Holocaust was disturbingly reminiscent of the German "revisionists" who consistently denied the uniqueness of the Shoah. Like them, Haider periodically equated Hitler with Stalin and Winston Churchill in order to relativize Nazi crimes. Haider and FPÖ representatives have frequently asserted that the Western Allies, in bombing Dresden, behaved no better than the Germans in World War II; or that the post-1945 expulsion of Germans from the Sudetenland was on a par with the mass murder of the Jews.[105] In March 2001, during the Vienna elections, Haider demanded financial compensation for refugees from the Sudetenland and for Austrian POWs who had suffered at Allied or Soviet hands. Restitution should be equivalent to that which had been agreed for the Jews.

During the 1990s Haider did occasionally attempt to improve his international image by making symbolic gestures toward Jews. In 1996 he appointed the Viennese Jewish journalist Peter Sichrovsky as a leading FPÖ candidate for the European Parliament elections, but this move failed to alleviate charges of anti-Semitism and right-wing extremism. Sichrovsky was elected in October 1996 and even served for a time as party general secretary. During his years with the FPÖ, he acted as Haider's "court Jew," providing him with an alibi against accusations of racism.[106] Sichrovsky performed his assigned task, launching stinging broadsides against "the professional Jews of the World Jewish Congress" and greedy New York lawyers for manipulating Holocaust survivors and trying to extort money from Austria. Whenever the party boss had a "Jewish problem," Sichrovsky was always there with an explanation, until he, too, became disillusioned and broke relations with Haider in 2002.

Before 2000 Haider rarely used the word "Jew" in any context, preferring euphemisms such as "East Coast circles" (which had become fashionable during the Waldheim affair), or making coded references to "minorities." In the 2001 local elections in Vienna, he dropped the mask, attacking Stanley Greenberg, the American campaign adviser of the Social Democratic mayor, in anti-Semitically tinged language. At the end of February 2001, Haider became even more explicit in his references to Ariel Muzicant, leader of Austria's Jewish community. He openly wondered how someone with the name "Ariel" (a popular detergent brand) "could catch so much filth."[107] Though the Vienna public prosecutor did not think such demagoguery constituted anti-Semitism, the Muzicant affair undoubtedly helped to revive some classic anti-Jewish stereotypes.[108] The image of "dirty Jews" and "tricky Jews" engaged in monkey business at the expense of honest citizens has long been a staple element in Austrian and European anti-Semitism which it is all too easy to revive.[109]

As Haider's fortunes declined, his sympathy for the Arabs emerged more openly. During successive visits to Iraq in 2002 he expressed solidarity with and the sympathy of the FPÖ for the Iraqi dictator Saddam Hussein; so, too, did another leading FPÖ politician, Ewald Stadler, who openly blamed 9/11 on America's Zionist policies.[110] In November 2001 Haider had visited the Middle East, where he was warmly received as an "enemy of Israel." He was especially popular in Libya, due to his close friendship with Mu'ammar Qadaffi's son.[111] Borrowing a motif from the Left, in 2002 Haider sharply condemned the Israeli Army's "war crimes" in the West Bank and rationalized Palestinian suicide bombings as legitimate resistance.[112] In the FPÖ press during 2002, Israel was frequently accused of "state terrorism" against the Palestinians, of creating "concentration camps" and becoming a *Tätervolk* (nation of perpetrators); as well as being a "racist state" that carried out policies based on its self-proclaimed chosenness. In their anti-Zionist propaganda, which was barely distinguishable from that of the Far Left, FPÖ publications claimed that Israel indulged in "ethnic cleansing."[113]

During the Lebanon War of July 2006, Haider once again vilified Ariel Muzikant, this time as a "Zionist provocateur." Following the death of an Austrian peacekeeper during an Israeli aerial attack, one of Haider's Styrian lieutenants lashed out at Muzicant and other Jewish leaders in Vienna and Graz, demanding their public condemnation of this "cruel and cowardly murder."[114] An FPÖ local councillor from Neunkirchen also blasted Muzicant—for criticizing Austrian trade links with Iran. The FPÖ councillor urged a full boycott of Israeli goods in retaliation for criminal Zionist actions. In an open letter to local Palestinians, the councillor deplored the fact that "the mass murderers with the Jewish star shall always remain unpunished."[115] Not surprisingly in such a hostile climate, the Austrian Jewish community has experienced a sharp increase in anti-Semitic acts and threatening letters.[116]

Nevertheless, defaming Jews still lacks the electoral appeal of the much more broadly based anti-foreigner sentiment, rampant for several decades in Austria. In the early 1990s its main targets had been refugees, asylum seekers, and immigrants from the Balkans, the Slavic East, and the under-developed southern hemisphere. Today, the prime source of anxiety is once more a flood of immigrants from the East and the Third World. There are also growing fears of Muslim terrorism, and the demographic/cultural threat posed by Europe's gradual Islamicization. The FPÖ's electoral revival is connected to this resurgent pan-European focus on immigration and a growing popular awareness that Islam has been penetrating Europe and threatening to erode already fragile Christian values and insecure national identities. This theme has set a new agenda for all of Austria's political parties. But it is the FPÖ that most stridently embraced it.[117] As a party built on xenophobic protectionism, the rejection of foreigners, and suspicion of the European Union, both Islamophobia and anti-Semitism come more naturally to its supporters.

Haider's unexpected death in an automobile accident in the summer of 2008 happened shortly after the spectacular performance of the xenophobic Far Right in the Austrian national elections. The FPÖ, led by the ultra-nationalist Heinz-Christian Strache, gained 18 percent, and Haider's more "liberal" Alliance for the Future won 10 percent of the votes cast. Their combined vote gave the populist Right the support of almost a third of the Austrian electorate. It was the best electoral performance ever by a postwar radical Right movement in Austria or western Europe, made potentially more ominous by the looming economic crisis.[118] It was a belated triumph for Haider's legacy and ability to break the mold of Austria's postwar politics. However, like Kreisky and Waldheim before him, Haider did not encourage his compatriots to face the implications of the Nazi past more honestly. On the contrary, Haiderism simply flaunted its anti-establishment populism, combining it with a chauvinist discourse, *Fremdenfeindlichkeit* (hostility to foreigners), anti-Semitism, and a "revisionist" attitude to the Nazi legacy.

SEVEN

German Guilt, Jewish Angst

I n 1879 the Berlin historian Heinrich von Treitschke coined the notorious declaration *"Die Juden sind Unser Unglück"* (The Jews are our misfortune)—which would later become a catchphrase during the Nazi era. The new political concept of anti-Semitism (as opposed to Jew hatred) had been invented in that very same year by an obscure German journalist, Wilhelm Marr. During the next twenty years, more than five hundred anti-Semitic publications would appear in the newly unified Second German Empire. There were crude productions such as Theodor Fritsch's racist *Handbuch der Judenfrage* (Handbook on the Jewish Question), which went through repeated editions; and pseudo-philosophical bestsellers such as Houston S. Chamberlain's *Foundations of the 19th Century*—the magnum opus of an expatriate Englishman (although written in German) that appeared in 1900. Chamberlain's glorification of the Teutonic race and so-called Aryan virtues bewitched the German emperor Wilhelm II as well as the young Adolf Hitler. Although anti-Semitism before 1914 was politically stronger in Russia, Austria, and Romania, it was only in Germany that Jew hatred found itself elevated to the rarefied heights of a *Weltanschauung* (worldview). German intellectuals, artists, and professors lent scientific respectability to noisy and vulgar mob agitation.

German anti-Semitism, in comparison with that of other Western nations, was especially marked among the ruling elites—the aristocratic Prussian landowners (Junkers), military officers, civil servants, and academics—though it subsequently proved to be a powerful tool for the mobilization of the *Mittelstand* (lower middle classes).[1] It had also been solidly entrenched among Lutheran Protestants ever since the Reformation, receiving renewed reinforcement at the end of the 1870s from the Christian Social Party of the Protestant court preacher Adolf Stoecker. Ever since the

1819 anti-Semitic riots in Germany, university students had shown their receptivity to counter-emancipatory and illiberal agitation that adamantly opposed civil equality for Jews. In Germany, the fusion of romanticism and organicist nationalism, with its emphasis on concepts of "blood and soil," as well as the unique individuality of the German "soul," was particularly deadly; after 1815, the ethnic nationalists called for the removal of all things "alien" (and non-Christian) from the German lands. The Heidelberg professor Jakob Friedrich Fries, in a particularly malevolent 1816 essay on the danger represented by the Jews to "the well-being and character of the Germans," called for the extirpation of Judaism, and unabashedly justified the hatred of the masses for Jewry. Three years later, the so-called Hep-Hep movement (a Latin acronym for *Hierosolyma est perdita*—"Jerusalem is destroyed") swept the German lands. These disturbances were part of the stormy debate over Jewish emancipation, in which nationalistic students (organized in *Burschenschaften* or fraternities) took an active part. The riots occurred at a time of acute social unrest and in a climate of increasingly racist nationalism that had arisen in the wake of the German "war of liberation" against Napoleon.[2]

Opposition to Jewish emancipation in Germany was closely related to the fact that it had first been implemented at the beginning of the nineteenth century by the French armies under Napoleon and could therefore be seen as an alien imposition. German romantic nationalism therefore tended to stigmatize the Jews as pro-French and anti-national, and as a negative cosmopolitan influence on the emerging but still insecure German national identity. Soon after Germany had belatedly achieved its national unity in 1870–71, such charges assumed new importance, especially as the stock-exchange crash in Berlin began to erode the influence of economic and political liberalism in central Europe. The rapid industrialization of Germany resulted in a crisis that adversely affected many artisans, craftsmen, shopkeepers, small businessmen, and peasants in the countryside.[3] They began to mobilize in anti-Semitic political groupings dedicated to the struggle against "exploitative Jewish capital," "Jewish liberalism," and the "mercantile spirit"—which Germans linked to industrial England and to *das Judentum* (Jewry) in general. The aristocratic landowners (who favored protectionist tariffs) and the upper middle classes—eager to weaken their Jewish competitors—placed themselves at the head of the anti-Semitic movement, which found its most powerful echo in the German Conservative Party (DKP). In December 1892 its Tivoli program was already formally and unequivocally anti-Semitic.[4]

At the same time, *Mittelstand* movements from below, such as Dr. Otto Böckel's Anti-Semitic People's Party, succeeded in the 1890s in winning considerable peasant support. Böckel campaigned for a program that combined anticapitalist social legislation with "the repeal by legal means, of Jewish emancipation, [and] the placing of Jews under an Aliens' Law."[5] Such populist movements led by such demagogues as Böckel, Hermann Ahlwardt, and the propagandist Theodor Fritsch were invariably antiliberal, antimodernist, and antisocialist; they were also *völkisch* (ethnic racist) in character, adopting the concept of race as an *immutable* quality or "essence" that determined that Jews could never become Germans.

The issue of race provided a certain coherence to the diverging and sometimes contradictory strands of anti-Semitism that existed in pre-Nazi Germany—conservative, liberal, *völkisch*, socialist, Christian (Protestant or Catholic), and anti-Christian; it enabled the development of an all-embracing discourse on the innately dangerous, malevolent, parasitic, and perverse characteristics attributed to Jews—accusations that were latently genocidal in their implications. When the anti-Semitic agitator Hermann Ahlwardt spoke in 1895 in the imperial parliament about a coming race war between Teutons and "Semites" and insisted on the need to "exterminate" parasitical Jewry, he was expressing the growing power of the *völkisch* myth. *Deutschtum* (Germandom) and *Judentum* in central Europe were being posited by anti-Semites as irreconcilable racial antitheses whose fateful struggle would determine the future not only of Germany and Europe but of human civilization. Implicit in this vision was a secularized and *racialized* vision of the medieval Christian view of the Jews as agents of the devil, which had achieved a special resonance in Germany. As political scientist Daniel Goldhagen pithily put it, the "symbolic power and metaphorical implications of the new master concept of race gave antisemitism an explosive new charge."[6] In the racist dispensation, even baptism to Christianity was no longer sufficient to wipe away the ineradicable ancestral, hereditary taint of Jewishness.

German anti-Semites from Wilhelm Marr and Eugen Dühring to Theodor Fritsch, Paul de Lagarde, and Houston S. Chamberlain had by 1900 developed a worldview in which the Jews endangered the core values of German morality and culture. Though, for the most part, the racist anti-

Semites did not yet speak of physical extermination, the implication was unmistakable that German society must be *entjudet* (de-Jewified)— altogether cleansed of "Jewish influence," if it were ever to be redeemed. Similar ideas were rampant in Austria, Romania, and France, while in czarist Russia the Jews were subject to pogroms without yet enjoying the benefits of civic equality. But nowhere else, outside of Germany and Austria, did *völkisch* anti-Semitism penetrate so deeply into citizens' associations, cultural societies, middle-class economic associations, agricultural interest groups, gymnastics clubs, student fraternities, and artisanal guilds.[7] Powerful extra-parliamentary organizations such as the Bund der Landwirte (Farmers Union), the Deutschnationale Handlungsgehilfenverband (German National Association of Commercial Employees), and the Alldeutscher Verband (Pan-German League) also joined in the policy of making their associations *judenrein* (free of Jews), long before the advent of Nazism. Even the German Catholics and Social Democrats, though less corrupted by anti-Semitism (Otto von Bismarck declared them "enemies of the Reich" in the 1870s), were by no means immune to a milder form of the disease.[8]

At the outbreak of the World War I, there was already something obsessive about the way in which "hard" and "soft" anti-Semites had come to identify Jews with everything that was wrong in German society. There was, moreover, an increasingly ominous insistence on defining the Jews not only as "alien" but as poisonous and demonic threats to the health and morality of the Germanic *Volk*. In the 1880s the German philosopher Friedrich Nietzsche (despite his own ambivalences) had poured contempt on his anti-Semitic countrymen, calling them *Schlechtweggekommene*—life's losers, born misfits, bungled, botched, and envious creatures, eaten up with neurotic *ressentiment*.[9] By 1918, at the end of four years of uninterrupted battlefield carnage, such critical verdicts had been left behind by events and an unprecedented sharpening of the so-called *Judenfrage* (Jewish question). In 1916, despite their ardent patriotism and bravery on the battlefield, German Jews had already been subjected to a humiliating census by the Prussian authorities to assess their contribution to the national war effort.

The military defeat of Germany would greatly exacerbate not only the utterly false charges that Jews had shirked military service but feed the legend (much encouraged on the conservative Right) that Jewish traitors and pacifists had stabbed the fatherland in the back.[10] In late 1918, with the crumbling of the Hohenzollern monarchy, the abdication of the emperor, the growing threat of Communist revolution, the humiliation of the Versailles Treaty, and the prospect of huge reparations payments to the Western Allies, anti-Semitism suddenly found an extraordinarily fertile terrain. Although the half million Jews in Germany constituted less than 1 percent of the general population and had little political influence, they nonetheless provided the ideal scapegoat for Germans in a time of acute national insecurity and economic chaos. Jews were visible enough in publishing, journalism, the arts, science, the free professions, trade, and commerce, and as pioneers of the new department stores and private banks, to give a superficial plausibility to the anti-Semitic slogan that Weimar was a *Judenrepublik* (Jew republic).

Anti-Semitism became especially rabid among the declining middle classes who had lost their savings during the catastrophic inflation of 1923; and among doctors, lawyers, small businessmen, artisans, shopkeepers, and academics fearful of Jewish competition in the more open and egalitarian Weimar democracy.[11] In the upper classes and military leadership (stung by a lost war) it remained as virulent as ever. The role of Jewish radicals in the abortive German Revolutions of 1918–19 intensified upper-class and bourgeois hatred of Jews as a dangerous ferment of subversive revolt—a fear that went back at least seventy years to the 1848 "springtime of peoples." In the course of the German counterrevolution in 1919, such prominent "Jewish" revolutionaries as Rosa Luxemburg, Gustav Landauer, Kurt Eisner, Eugen Leviné, and the independent socialist leader Hugo Haase were brutally assassinated. This wave of political killings culminated in 1922 in the premeditated murder of Germany's first and (to this day) only Jewish foreign minister, Walther Rathenau. A Prussian patriot and wealthy industrialist who had virtually saved the German economy during World War I through his organizational skills, the intellectually versatile Rathenau was totally assimilated and by no means free of Jewish self-hatred. His assassins—young right-wing nationalist fanatics—evidently believed that Rathenau was also a "Jewish Bolshevik" and one of the "Elders of Zion" plotting to destroy Germany.[12]

The pogrom-like mood of the early Weimar Republic was especially alarming since virtually every social group or institution—including the military, the bureaucracy, the judiciary, the political parties, the churches, and the universities—was thoroughly infected by racist anti-Semitism. Student organizations and bodies throughout the country were easily infiltrated by *völkisch* and anti-Semitic trends, resulting in so-called Aryan paragraphs that excluded Jews or restricted Jewish rights at the universities. In 1920 the famous German sociologist Max Weber commented in a letter to a colleague that "the academic atmosphere has become extremely reactionary, and in addition radically antisemitic."[13] A decade later, the student organizations had indeed been taken over by the Nazis. The National Socialist German Students' League had successfully won the support of the majority of students in Germany and Austria even before Hitler had put an end to the Weimar Republic. Albert Einstein, who returned to Germany from Switzerland in 1914, was stunned by the endemic and ubiquitous nature of anti-Semitism at the German universities, which continually expanded in the 1920s, turning him into a lifelong Zionist. In a letter of March 19, 1921, to Fritz Haber he explained his joy at the prospect of a Hebrew University in Jerusalem "after seeing on numerous occasions how treacherously and uncharitably one deals here [in Germany] with splendid young Jews and seeks to deny them opportunities for education."

In an article for the *Jüdische Rundschau* three months later, Einstein referred to the plight of young Jewish students (especially from eastern Europe) living in "anti-Semitic surroundings [which] prevented them from pursuing regular studies." Einstein returned to this theme once more in 1929 in a letter to Willy Hellpach, defending the imperative necessity for Zionism as a way for Jews to bear "the hatred and the humiliations" endured throughout the Diaspora. There could be no Jewish dignity, self-sufficiency, productive work, or authentic union with humanity unless there was a Jewish homeland in Palestine to liberate and "revive the soul of the Jewish people."[14] Again, it was his German experiences that pushed him to Zionist conclusions: "I saw worthy Jews basely caricatured, and the sight made my heart bleed. I saw how schools, comic papers, and innumerable other forces of the Gentile majority undermine the confidence even of the best of my fellow-Jews, and felt this could not be allowed to continue."

Einstein, as a pacifist, an internationalist, a German Jew, and the world-famous discoverer of the relativity theory was himself a prime target of the anti-Semites, the *völkisch* Right, and the Nazis. Prominent German Nobel Prize–winning physicists Johannes Stark and Philipp Lenard scathingly attacked what they called Einstein's "Jewish physics" and the so-called relativity-Jews who were undermining German science. Nationalist students interrupted Einstein's lectures, and there were even threats on his life. In 1933, after the Nazis came to power, he was almost immediately deprived of his professorship in Berlin and membership of the Prussian Academy of Sciences. His books were among those burned publicly on May 10, 1933, as manifestations of the "un-German spirit." Einstein left for America but continued to warn the world against the Nazi "war of annihilation against my defenseless fellow Jews." He regarded Nazi anti-Semitism somewhat simplistically as the classic method of an unscrupulous power-crazy group "to place the German people in a state of complete bondage." At the heart of the assault on the Jews was the fear engendered by their "intellectual independence," critical spirit, and "insistence on popular enlightenment of the masses." Einstein's scathing view of Hitler (written in 1935) presented him as a cynical and paranoid demagogue driven by "bitter hatred of everything foreign and, in particular, his loathing of a defenseless minority, the German Jews." Hitler, he wrote, had built his whole career on hatred and on deceiving people with "romantic, pseudo-patriotic phrasemongering," mobilizing "the human flotsam on the streets and in the taverns" with promises of glorious future triumphs. What ultimately made Hitler possible was the legacy of centuries in which Germans had been trained to slavish submission. "He shrewdly exploited for his own purposes the centuries-old German taste for drill, command, blind obedience and cruelty. Thus he became the *Fuehrer*."[15]

. . .

German university professors themselves often encouraged or collaborated in propagating the Hitler cult. Germany's most distinguished philosopher, Martin Heidegger (who had joined the Nazi Party on May 1, 1933), was in full sympathy with "blood and soil" National Socialist doctrines well before Hitler's seizure of power. Politically, by 1930 he regarded Nazi dictatorship as the only salvation from Communism, accepting that this would mean the elimination of political opponents. Metaphysically, his embrace of the Nazified meanings given to concepts like *Schicksal* (destiny), *Macht* (power), and *Opfer* (sacrifice) placed him firmly in the *völkisch* camp. In the late 1920s he began to explicitly write in private correspondence about the *wachsende Verjudung* (growing Jewification) of German spiritual life. Like the Nazis, Heidegger did not simply resent and oppose the increasing number of Jewish professors and teachers at German universities but also the universalist liberal-democratic and neo-Kantian values that they generally advocated. For Heidegger, these rationalist values lacked any deep roots in the German soil, belonging rather to the artificial, inauthentic productions of urban Western civilization. By 1933, the philosopher had become a fully fledged National Socialist, a *völkisch* fundamentalist, and an advocate of the *Volksgemeinschaft* (homogeneous racial community) and of excluding Jews from the universities of the German Reich. Far from opposing the new Nazi anti-Semitic legislation, Heidegger as rector of Fribourg University enthusiastically approved it and supported the academic struggle against the "Judeo-Marxist decomposition" of the German people.[16] Indeed, Heidegger was a hard-line admirer and eulogist of Adolf Hitler during the early years of the regime, proclaiming the central importance of authority, racial strength, work, struggle, the "purification of society," and the cult of the dead—even celebrating the Germanic *Sendung* (mission) of National Socialism.[17] Significantly, after 1945, Heidegger never renounced the core of these Nazi beliefs, nor his *völkisch* anti-Semitism, which was expressed inter alia by a stunning and callous indifference to the Holocaust.[18]

Heidegger, like millions of other Germans without his philosophical training, had been seduced by the Austrian-born Adolf Hitler, a humble soldier in the trenches who after his demobilization in 1919 would turn the "Jewish question" into the central thrust of his passionate tirades in the beer cellars of Munich.[19] His National Socialist Party (NSDAP) in its twenty-five-point party program of 1920 called for the exclusion of Jews from membership in German society and its institutions. Only those of German blood could be part of the nation; Jews, on the other hand, would never be *Volksgenossen* (national comrades). Like other right-wing groups, the Nazis were also committed to combating what they called the "Jewish materialist spirit." What differentiated Hitler's rhetoric from that of his predecessors and rivals was not the party program but rather his terrifyingly murderous and apocalyptic language about the Jews, and his absolute insistence that only through the "assembled and concentrated might of a national passion" could the "Jewish question" be resolved.[20] Hitler made it clear that the process would be very bloody, a zero-sum game in which either the Jews would be destroyed or Germany itself would go under. In *Mein Kampf* he looked back on World War I, chillingly remarking that millions of "real Germans" would have been spared if only "twelve or fifteen thousands of these Hebrew corrupters of the people had been held under poison gas."[21] For the

Nazi leader, the Jews represented evil on a cosmic scale. They negated "the aristocratic principle of Nature," "the eternal privilege of power and strength," and the vital importance of personality, nationality, and race— values without which the earth would descend into complete chaos. "If, with the help of the Marxist creed, the Jew is victorious over the other peoples of the world, his crown will be the funeral-wreath of humanity and this planet will, as it did thousands of years ago, move through the ether devoid of men."[22]

Hitler's nationalist oratory, along with the Great Depression, skillful propaganda, organized street violence, and fear of a Communist revolution, helped convince more than thirteen million Germans to turn the NSDAP into the largest political party of the Weimar Republic in July 1932. The Nazis won 37.4 percent of the vote and 230 seats in the Reichstag in democratic elections. Their incendiary anti-Jewish rhetoric evidently did not deter voters. By January 30, 1933, Hitler was chancellor, and within a matter of months Nazi anti-Semitism became state doctrine—a central feature of the ruling ideology in what was to become the most powerful nation in Europe. The whole apparatus of an increasingly totalitarian German state was now devoted to creating a hallucinatory demonic image of the Jews in order to justify their isolation, segregation, defamation, persecution, and eventual expulsion. In April 1933 the entire German nation was organized to collectively *boycott* the Jews—who were still German citizens. An avalanche of legal measures followed in the next six years, intended to purify the German state and society from the "Jewish peril."[23] Jews were excluded from the civil service, the army, the judiciary, the universities, the free professions, and the arts and sciences—irrespective of their contributions, achievements, political beliefs, or individual commitment to the fatherland.

All over Germany, at the entrance to villages, restaurants, hotels, and inns, racist signs appeared, proclaiming "Jews Are Not Wanted Here." The judiciary (far from upholding any notion of justice and fair play) displayed a persecutory, anti-Semitic ardor that was particularly glaring. The medical profession was no better, greeting the Nuremberg Race Laws of September 1935, which officially segregated Jews (while stripping them of citizenship), with undisguised satisfaction. These measures were by no means imposed on an unwilling German populace. On the contrary, the new racial legislation, which also forbade sexual relations between Germans and Jews, was well received. Moreover, the steady barrage of anti-Semitic propaganda and laws led the mass of Germans to unquestioningly accept the transformation of Jews into social pariahs, as if it were something normal and inevitable. By the time of the "Crystal Night" nationwide pogrom of November 9–10, 1938 (an unprecedented orgy of anti-Jewish violence), the German public was either numbed or, in certain cases, willing to participate in the brutalities. The storefront glass of about seventy-five hundred businesses and other properties owned by Jews were shattered; more than four hundred synagogues burned across Germany. Approximately one hundred Jews were murdered, and many more were injured; thirty thousand Jews were packed off to concentration camps, where they would suffer unspeakable indignities.

Kristallnacht (Crystal Night), as it was euphemistically called, failed to arouse any public German protests, not even from the churches. The Nazi conception of the Jews as a race apart had already been burned into the German national consciousness and political culture, along with the notion that popular justice was well served by the expropriation of Jewish wealth and property. Ordinary Germans, as Daniel Goldhagen has pointed out, were not merely passive pawns or terrorized victims of their government in this process of uprooting the Jews of Germany. The majority appeared to accept the "eliminationist" program being applied to German (and then European) Jewry as the eradication of an "alien body" that was continuously presented as the root of all evil.[24] Hence, there was little opposition to Hitler's consistently proclaimed goal throughout the 1930s of making Germany *judenrein*. However, as *Kristallnacht* made plain, the Nazis did not only want to "cleanse" Germany of Judaism, they also wished to spill Jewish blood. Two weeks after Crystal Night, the SS newspaper *Das Schwarze Korps* published a terrifyingly violent article explaining that the German people could not tolerate hundreds of thousands of impoverished Jews—"a breeding ground for Bolshevism . . . and politically criminal subhuman elements." The only remaining choice must be to "exterminate the Jewish underworld" by fire and sword. "The result," according to the SS publication, "would be the actual and final end of Jewry in Germany, its absolute annihilation."[25]

This genocidal prophecy, less than a year before the outbreak of World War II, perfectly reflected the demonological racist anti-Semitism of the Nazi leadership and their will to exterminate the Jews in order to inaugurate a new Aryan millennium and achieve global hegemony for Germany. What was striking in this megalomaniac Nazi ideology was its either-or politics of

Sieg oder Untergang (victory or destruction). An apocalyptic vision became fused with a fortress mentality, political paranoia, and a racialized perception of the Jew as a "world enemy" and a vampiric "counter-race." The Jew became the incarnation of the democratic leveling that threatened to corrode the "blood purity" and strength of the Germanic race. With their destructive critical minds, Jews were the absolute other, the source of all *Zersetzung* (decomposition) in modern society—the carriers of a spiritual plague and the source of all cultural decay. They had poisoned German society like deadly germs, bacilli, and microbes that attack the organism in order to destroy it. According to Julius Streicher, editor of the semi-pornographic *Der Stürmer,* the Jews represented a sexual and biological peril of the first order to German womanhood and to the future of the race. A single act of sexual intercourse with a Jew would permanently poison the blood of German women, who "would henceforth transmit hereditary Jewish characteristics even to children conceived by German fathers."[26] This sexual satanization of the Jews owed much to medieval Christian demonology, but it radicalized Jewish otherness still further, to the point of complete dehumanization. It provided yet another signpost on the road to mass murder by suggesting that racial miscegenation was a deadly Jewish plot to pollute and uproot the German people. The Jews, as Heinrich Himmler bluntly declared in 1938, "want to destroy us"; they were the real aggressors who wished to extinguish the German *Volk* and the Aryan race as a whole.[27] Supposedly this had been their satanic goal during World War I.

Hitler had totally convinced himself and his followers that the Nazi war against the Jews (including the act of genocide) was an act of Germany's self-defense to prevent its total demise. This view was fully shared by Joseph Goebbels, who in the 1920s had already concluded: "Either the Jew annihilates us or we neutralize him. No other issue can be imagined." Goebbels, like Hitler, frequently expressed himself in apocalyptic language, using slogans like *Endkampf* (final struggle), *Endsieg* (final victory), and *Endlösung* (Final Solution)—with their quasi-religious connotations of the Last Judgment—to evoke either total redemption or looming catastrophe.[28] Hitler, in using this same terminology, self-consciously presented himself as a prophet as well as a German *Realpolitiker,* warning in January 1939 that if the Jews ever initiated a world war, they would be completely exterminated.[29] In his fevered mind, war, genocide, and the Jews were inextricably linked in a single apocalyptic perspective.[30]

Hitler's final decision for the total extermination of European Jewry was not, however, undertaken until late 1941 (between October and December) as the Red Army counterattacked and the United States entered the war. Only at that point did his self-fulfilling 1939 prophecy of a world war come fully into play, with Germany now facing extremely powerful enemies, in both the east and the west. On December 12, 1941, the führer addressed his innermost circle of *Gauleiter* and *Reichsleiter,* men almost as fanatical in their outlook as himself when it came to the "Jewish question."[31] The day before he had told the Reichstag that Germany was declaring war on the United States, while thanking Providence that he had been chosen to lead this historic confrontation that would determine the fate of the world for the next millennium. Pouring out his bile against President Franklin Roosevelt, he made it clear that the American leader had been driven

> by the circle of Jews surrounding him, who, with Old Testament-like fanaticism, believe that the United States can be the instrument for preparing another Purim for the European nations that are becoming increasingly anti-Semitic. It was the Jew, in his full satanic vileness, who rallied around this man [Roosevelt] but to whom this man also reached out.[32]

Goebbels recorded Hitler's secret speech to his closest intimates the following day in his diaries. He noted that "Führer is determined to wipe the slate clean." He had prophesied to the Jews in 1939 "that if they once again brought about a world war they would be annihilated." These were not mere words, Hitler had stressed on December 12, 1941.

> The world war is here, the extermination of the Jews must be its necessary consequence. . . . We are not here to have compassion for the Jews, but to have compassion for our German people. As the German people has once again sacrificed some 160,000 dead in the eastern campaign, those responsible for this bloody conflict will have to pay for it with their lives.[33]

Hitler would return to this prophecy of annihilation again and again in wartime speeches, intended to rouse the German people against the international conspiracy of Wall Street capitalism, English plutocracy, and Judeo-Bolshevism. As the Allied bombing campaign against German cities intensified, Hitler presented the massive civilian casualties as proof of the Jewish will to destroy Germany through the deployment of Anglo-American aerial power.

On September 30, 1942, in the Berlin Sportpalast, Hitler once more reminded an enthusiastic overflow audience that "it will not be the Aryan peoples, but rather Jewry, that will be exterminated," to long applause. He prophesied to the assembled Nazi faithful that as "the wirepullers of the lunatic in the White House dragged one people after another into the war," anti-Semitism would rise to a new crescendo, seizing hold of one state after another. "Each will emerge from it [the world war] one day as an anti-Semitic state." With equal vehemence, he repeated how the German Jews had "once laughed about my prophecies," and now he grimly added: "I can promise only one thing. They will stop laughing everywhere."[34] There is little doubt that his Berlin audience understood what Hitler meant when he promised *Ausrottung* (extermination) and hinted at mass murder on a huge scale. The fact is that his German listeners vociferously applauded whenever their führer vowed to destroy those who had once laughed at him.

Hitler's last political testament was dictated on April 29, 1945, in his Berlin bunker as the Red Army was closing on the Reich Chancellery. Addressing the German people for the last time, he denied that he had ever wanted the war in 1939; on the contrary, it was "exclusively willed and triggered by the international statesmen, who were either of Jewish descent or worked for Jewish interests." Equally, he emphasized that nobody had been left in any doubt "that if the peoples of Europe were treated again as bundles of stocks belonging to the international conspiracy of money and finance, then the culprit for this murderous struggle would have to pay."[35]

Hitler did not simply deny any responsibility for the outbreak of war in 1939. In effect he laid all blame for the destruction of Jewry solely on the victims. The Jews were not only guilty for their own deaths, but for the murder of "hundreds of thousands of [Aryan] women and children," who were being "burnt and bombed to death in the cities." As Nazi propaganda had constantly stressed, it was the Jews who stood behind the massive Anglo-American bombings of Germany, just as world Jewry had incited all the atrocities committed by the devilish Bolshevik enemy. Hitler proudly admitted that he had made the Jews pay for their culpability "albeit by 'more humane' methods" (presumably the gas chambers!). He once more prophesied a (postwar) retribution: "From the ruins of our cities and our monuments hatred will arise against the people that bears the responsibility in the end, the one to whom we have to thank for all of this: international Jewry and its acolytes!"

Hitler's final exhortation was to commit the leadership of the nation and the German people to "the strictest keeping of the race laws and the merciless struggle against the universal prisoner of all peoples, international Jewry."[36]

Fortunately, Hitler was grossly mistaken in his 1945 prophecy that postwar Germans would readily embrace his paranoid fantasies concerning the international Jewish conspiracy. To a certain extent, the utter destruction Hitler brought upon his countrymen inoculated postwar Germany against any temptation to indulge in a repeat performance. On the other hand, the dead führer could have drawn comfort from the unexpected ways in which the Nazi anti-Semitic legacy found many eager disciples, imitators, and potential heirs in the Middle East, from Gamal Abdel Nasser in Egypt through Saddam Hussein in Iraq, the PLO's Yasser Arafat, and Mahmoud Ahmadinejad in present-day Tehran. The toxic seeds Hitler's Germany planted during the 1930s have come to ominous fruition seventy years later in the Muslim and Arab world.

The de-Nazification of Germany itself was far from a smooth and straightforward success story. Nor did anti-Semitism simply vanish into thin air. A relatively high number of Germans in the immediate postwar era maintained strong prejudices against Jews, according to polls taken in 1947. No less than three-quarters of all Germans considered Jews to belong to a different race, and more than one-third felt it would be better if there were no Jews at all in Germany.[37] One-third stubbornly insisted that anti-Semitism was caused by Jewish behavior. But the conservative Christian Democratic Union (CDU) chancellor Konrad Adenauer, who largely determined West German policy until 1963, insisted on the need to pay reparations to Israel and Jewish Holocaust survivors—voluntary payments for past wrongs that have amounted to more than $55 billion over the past sixty years. In Communist East Germany, however, there was no question of reparations. The purportedly antifascist German Democratic Republic (GDR) marginalized the whole subject of anti-Semitism and the Holocaust until the late 1980s. From the beginning the regime decried Zionism as a form of "racial exclusiveness," chauvinism, and bourgeois ideology—as did most Communist states and movements. In 1965, as its relations with Egypt and other Arab nations developed, the GDR's condemnation of tiny Israel as an "imperialist power" increased.[38] So, too, did such myths as the world-wide Jewish conspiracy. Of all the Soviet bloc newspapers, the official East German Communist government and party newspaper *Neues Deutschland* was the harshest in its anti-Israel tone on the eve of the Six-Day War. In May 1967 it smeared Israel as a tool of American global strategy, labeling it a "warmongering state" that threatened its neighbors and the entire Socialist camp. The East Germans unconditionally supported Nasser's Egypt, keeping silent about his calls to eradicate Israel. At the same time as they expressed their full solidarity with Israel's enemies, the Communist state authorities in Berlin pompously boasted that they had "eradicated Fascism and militarism, the twin brothers of antisemitism, root and branch."[39]

In West Germany a pro-Israel mood was, by contrast, widely shared across the political spectrum on the eve of the 1967 war.[40] Protest marches, demonstrations of solidarity, and press reports reflected a broad public sympathy for the Jewish state. Israel's preventive strike against its threatening Arab neighbors was generally seen as a lifesaving act of self-defense. The mass-circulation *Bild-Zeitung*, owned by Axel Springer—a passionately pro-Israel German entrepreneur—regarded the 1967 war essentially as a battle for Western freedom against Communist totalitarianism. But the unconditional defense of Israel's right to exist was also seen as an *ethical* imperative—a litmus test for many Germans of Springer's generation.[41] The parallels between Nasser's declared aim to wipe out the Jewish state and Hitler's calls to genocide after 1939 seemed all too evident to Springer and the popular boulevard press.[42] Moreover, there was an undisguised admiration for Israeli patriotism and the Spartan soldierly virtues of its citizens. The German term blitzkrieg, much used in World War II, was now revived as a *positive* description of Israel's unprecedentedly swift victory. Many Germans hailed Moshe Dayan as one of the great commanders in history and the Jews in Israel as a model of courage.[43]

In addition to respecting its socially progressive features and its politically dominant labor movement, the German Social Democrats and the liberal press also demonstrated considerable empathy for Israel's military actions in 1967.[44] The center-left *Frankfurter Rundschau* stressed that the Arab world and the PLO represented a real threat of annihilation.[45] There was also some sharp criticism of the refusal by Arab states to financially assist or integrate Palestinian refugees in their own countries, instead of permanently misusing them as a propaganda weapon against Israel. Nevertheless, neutrality rather than sympathy remained the dominant characteristic of German establishment policy when it came to the diplomatic aspects of the Arab-Israel conflict.[46]

But the cool distance of the highly influential left-liberal magazine *Der Spiegel* toward the Jewish state was a significant indication of potential clouds on the horizon. Within weeks of the 1967 war's conclusion, the Hamburg weekly had slammed Israel's "occupation" of Arab lands, while ignoring Prime Minister Levi Eshkol's offer of exchanging *all* the territories in return for genuine security and peace.[47] *Spiegel*'s long-serving editor, Rudolf Augstein, lost no time in comparing the "expansionism" of the small Jewish state with that of militarist Prussia and the Second German Reich. Indeed, during the next forty years, the magazine would frequently caricature Israel as a brutal, expansionist, and warlike state, while from time to time denigrating Judaism as a religious tradition.[48] On the other hand, it was equally relentless in its exposure of Nazi war criminals, right-wing anti-Semitism, and nationalist undercurrents in German public life.

When it came to the Middle East, however, *Der Spiegel* and most of the German media increasingly downplayed Arab anti-Semitism and ideological hostility toward Israel after the Six-Day War.[49] There was little reference to the violent and genocidal nature of Arab rejectionism and jihad, in contrast to the recent extensive coverage in the conservative *Frankfurter Allgemeine Zeitung* and most other leading German newspapers of racist prejudices against Muslims, Arabs, and foreigners in general.[50] In reporting on Israel, much of the prevailing consensus has portrayed its settlements as illegal, criminal, and the source of all problems in the Middle East.[51] Jews, not Arabs, are largely held responsible not only for the conflict but also for any anti-Semitic fallout in the Middle East.[52] In recent years the trend has been to minimize Palestinian violence and focus instead on the shadow of terror running through Israel's own history. The late Rudolf Augstein, for example, liked to make absurd comparisons between al-Qaeda's terrorism and the Jewish underground organizations in Palestine fighting the British Empire after 1945—as if the Irgun or Lehi had ambitions to impose fundamentalist Judaism or a worldwide Jewish caliphate on the rest of the world.[53]

Der Spiegel's delegitimizing of Israel, Judaism, and Jewish history has, at times, been perfidious. In April 2002 it attributed the roots of the entire Middle East tragedy to the bloody ferocity of Yahweh and the ancient Israelite tribes. The Hebrew Bible was presented as an unending tale of zealotry and fanaticism, from which the Crusaders, jihadists, and modern Zionists had all taken their cue.[54] The suicide bombers of today were supposedly following in the footsteps of Samson and the Zealots of Masada.[55] Arabs under the contemporary Israeli "jackboot" were compared to Jews at the time of Jesus, persecuted by the ruthless *Imperium Romanum. Der Spiegel* even called the biblical exodus from Egypt the "first *Pessach* mass murder," regarding it as analogous to the terrorist slaughter of Jews at a Passover seder in Netanya that provoked Operation Defensive Shield. Such insipid and totally distorted images of Jewish history have a long pedigree in the history of German and European anti-Semitism. They have been endlessly recycled in recent years, inundating the public with pejorative references to "Jewish arrogance," "chosenness," "fanaticism," "bloodthirstiness," and "vengefulness" stretching from biblical times to the present. This "liberation" of the (anti-Jewish) world from the straitjacket of Auschwitz and collective guilt reflects the hubris of an uncritical and sweeping antifascism, preoccupied with turning Jews into bloody perpetrators and Germans into innocent lambs.[56]

This attitudinal shift in West Germany had already begun in the mid-1970s. One indication of the change was the highly controversial play *Garbage, the City and Death,* written by the radical filmmaker Rainer Werner Fassbinder. It would eventually be banned from public performance in 1985 after vehement Jewish protests.[57] Fassbinder's central character was an anonymous rich Jew in Frankfurt—depicted as a ruthless property speculator, swindler, bloodsucker, and friend of the German establishment. This character was loosely based on the late Ignatz Bubis, a Holocaust survivor, property tycoon, and the future leader of German Jewry. The Shylockian protagonist is ugly, lascivious, sexually potent, greedy, and bent on revenge against the Germans. Whatever the filmmaker's intentions, the "rich Jew" recalls the ignoble obscenities of Julius Streicher's Nazi rag, *Der Stürmer.* His mere presence is shown to upset ordinary Germans. As long as he is there, they can never be themselves. Fassbinder places in the mouth of a resentful old Nazi, Hans von Glück, the obscenely anti-Semitic lines:

He sucks us dry, the Jew. He drinks our blood and puts us in the wrong, because he's a Jew and we have to bear the guilt. And the Jew bears the blame, because he makes us guilty simply by his being here. If he had only remained where he came from or if only they had gassed him. . . . But they forgot to gas him. That is no joke, thus it thinks in me (*so denkt es in mir*). I rub my hands together when I picture how the breath goes out of him in the gas chamber.[58]

These dark, brooding thoughts offer us a glimpse into the deeper wellsprings of postwar German anti-Semitism. They echo the astute remark of the Israeli psychiatrist Zvi Rex that "the Germans will never forgive the Jews for Auschwitz." The left-wing Fassbinder claimed to be different—an antifascist intent on countering the "hypocritical" philo-Semitism that was being "instrumentalized" in order to whitewash the sins of West German capitalism. But his cold, calculating, and "vengeful" Jew derives more inspiration from the Shylock myth in Western Christian culture than from a neo-Marxist critique of the system. The newly appointed principal of the Frankfurt Theater, Günther Rühle (who attempted to restage the play in October 1985) only made matters worse by insisting that the "normalization" of the German past demanded blunt criticism of Jews. *Die Schonzeit ist vorbei* (The no-hunting season is over), he informed protesters—as if only stereotypical depictions of "rich Jews" could release Germans from feelings of personal and collective "abnormality," guilt, or suffocation.[59]

• • •

Since the late 1960s, the German radical Left had become increasingly obsessed with Zionism. In an open letter to his leftist comrades published in 1980, the German journalist Henryk Broder (himself of Polish-Jewish background) challenged their preconceptions and what he saw as the phony "good conscience" of the postwar West German generation.[60] He described their anti-Zionism as "nothing more than a left-wing version of antisemitism"—the same logic, methodology, and vocabulary, only with the word "Jew" replaced by "Zionist." Israel, he trenchantly observed, was "the Super-Jew," judged by entirely different standards from other non-Jewish states. According to the German antifascist mantra, "the only thing which Jews had learned from their own persecution was how to persecute others"; or more explicitly, "Israelis are doing to the Arabs just what the Nazis did to the Jews." Broder dismissed these "despicable equations" as a form of diversionary tactics employed by Germans to avoid any real confrontation with their forebears' past. If the guilt could be projected on the Jewish victims of their own parents, they would be in the clear. ("At last you can look them in the face, because you now know where the Nazis, who were never here [in Germany], really are.") But the escapist alibi that Zionists were the true Nazis ("We have nothing against the Jews, only against the Zionists") did not free Broder's German "comrades" from their compulsive need for resurrecting the classical scapegoat.

> Today, your Jew is the State of Israel; just as your parents believed that they would be much better off without the Jews, so you believe there would be no strife in the Middle East without Israel. There isn't a single Arab state which is not involved in an incessant quarrel with at least one other [Arab] country. . . . But for you, Israel is the only warmonger in the area.[61]

In 1980, the radical Left was already looking the other way when it came to "Marxist" and Islamist genocides, such as those of Pol Pot in Cambodia, the "war crimes" of the Soviet Union in Afghanistan, the clampdown in Communist China, and executions of homosexuals in Iran. Third World tyrants such as Qadaffi and Khomeini were hailed as "anti-imperialist," but Israeli prime minister Begin was a "terrorist"—despite signing a peace treaty with Egypt. So, why the obsession only with Palestine? "The fact that it is Jews who are oppressing the Palestinians," Broder wrote. "That's it. That's the mechanism which gets you going. Were it not for that, you wouldn't give the Palestinians a thought. For you, they are no more than a pretty alibi to carry out your anti-Semitic designs."[62] An indirect example was provided in 1984 when Brigitte Heinrich, a German Green Party Euro MP, explained why she felt a "special responsibility" for the Palestinian victims of Israeli occupation: "The genocide of the Jews created the psychological prerequisites for setting up Israel as an internationally recognized state. The expulsion of the Palestinians is therefore indirectly the result of the Nazi persecution of the Jews."[63] Brigitte Heinrich was reflecting a contemporary trend (legitimized several years earlier by the German Social Democratic chancellor Helmut Schmidt) that transferred identification away from the Jews as victims of Germany to the Palestinians as the *Opfer der Opfer* (victims of the victims). Heinrich insisted that precisely as a member of the post-1945 German generation who had accepted moral guilt for Nazi crimes, she could not keep silent when "the Israeli occupying forces are torturing prisoners, committing night attacks on villages and murdering women and children." But here is Micha Brumlik's assessment of these "universalist" moral arguments: "The sole relic of Germany's past that is considered fit to attack is the State of Israel. In her [Heinrich's] imagination the descendants of the murdered Jews become one with the murderers and in a context outside of time and space the Jews are once again guilty of their own fate."[64]

In the mid-1980s, West German conservatives under Chancellor Helmut Kohl strove mightily to "normalize," "historicize," or "relativize" the Nazi era. The so-called *Historikerstreit* (battle of the historians) of twenty years ago revolved around these issues, complicated by a debate about the weakness of German national identity and the place of Auschwitz in German history.[65] Prominent conservative historians like Andreas Hillgruber displayed far more personal empathy for the suffering of German civilians (especially raped women) at the hands of the Red Army in 1944–45 than for the mass murder of the Jews. The well-known philosopher of history Ernst Nolte (a pupil of Martin Heidegger), provoked a storm when he insisted that Auschwitz was "above all a reaction born from anxiety about the annihilating occurrences of the Russian Revolution." He suggested that the Stalinist Gulag was the "original," and "the so-called annihilation of the Jews during the Third Reich" merely a distorted copy.[66] Nazi Germany before 1939, according to the "revisionist" Nolte, might have been "considered as a constitutional and liberal idyll" in comparison with the mass purges and collectivization in the Soviet Union. He subsequently came to half-embrace Holocaust denial in his repeated relativization of the cold-blooded murders inflicted upon European Jews.

In September 1990, a book by the prominent German film director Hans Jürgen Syberberg provided a somewhat perverse sequel to Nolte's highly speculative ruminations and the ensuing "battle of the historians." Syberberg declared that "we are living in the Jewish epoch of cultural history"— dominated by a "Jewish interpretation of the world." Fortunately, he added, this was now coming to a close. Syberberg viewed the "paralysis of post-1945 German culture" as deriving from an "ill-fated alliance of Jewish and leftist aesthetics." The disciples of Marx and Freud had established an intellectual ascendancy in Germany as part of the policy of the occupation authorities and through the return of such Jewish-Marxist professors as Theodor Adorno, Max Horkheimer, Ernst Bloch, and others. The huge cultural influence of the Weimar intellectuals and the Frankfurt School (Walter Benjamin, Siegfried Kracauer, Leo Löwenthal, Erich Fromm, and Herbert Marcuse) had for decades stultified any possibility of a German national discourse about art, culture, and history. According to Syberberg, "whoever went along with the Jews, like with the leftists, could enjoy professional success." What the Jewish intellectuals wanted was not love, understanding, or affection. "They wanted only one thing: power." But the process of German reunification offered hope of a new dawn, the crumbling of philo-Semitic barriers, and the final liberation from Jewish domination.

Writing after the fall of the Berlin wall, Syberberg clearly saw a link between forgetting Auschwitz, reclaiming a lost German identity, and creating an art of rediscovered "inner authenticity." In particular, he stressed that "the path does not go left or right, through the Auschwitz of the merchants and the Sunday speeches of our educators." Syberberg's hope was that "a reunification of land and continent" would finally remove the Germans from "external constraint" and "the destructive pathologies deriving from a lost identity."[67] Syberberg's romantic nationalism, mixed with a dose of German cultural anti-Semitism (whose sources went back to Richard Wagner), was by no means unique. It was driven by the widely held but repressed conviction among many Germans that only a "healthy national spirit" could put an end to the guilt for Auschwitz. The reunification of Germany after 1991 offered a golden opportunity to free German patriotism from the shackles of the past. But the immediate result merely released many of the demons from Germany's bloodstained racist and anti-Semitic past.[68]

For example, in October 1991, neo-Nazis and skinheads in the Saxon town of Hoyerswerda besieged 230 foreigners whose hostel they subjected to a six-day barrage of stones and Molotov cocktails. During 1992, there were more than twenty-five hundred xenophobic attacks, causing seventeen deaths, injuring six hundred, and severely damaging many refugee shelters. The most murderous incidents were directed against Turkish guestworkers who had lived in Germany for more than a generation and had contributed much to its "economic miracle." The violence was equally vicious toward Third World asylum seekers, Gypsies, and refugees from the east on a scale that had not been seen since 1945. No less than 367 Jewish cemeteries were vandalized between October 1990 and the summer of 1992—more even than on the eve of the Nazi seizure of power in 1933. In 1993, there were seventy-two violent attacks against Jews, while a growing number of Holocaust sites and local synagogues were targeted.

During the past fifteen years, racist anti-Semitism and neo-Nazi activity have been particularly evident in eastern Germany, where the National Democratic Party made some electoral gains in recent years in the state legislatures of Saxony (winning 9 percent of the vote) and in Brandenburg-Anhalt. In February 2005, extremists exploited the sixtieth anniversary of the Allied bombing raids on Dresden to portray Germany as the "war victim," while totally ignoring Nazi atrocities. The marchers carried balloons saying: "Allied bomb terror—then as now. Hiroshima, Nagasaki, Dresden, and today Baghdad. No forgiveness, no forgetting."[69]

According to the Federal Office for the Protection of the Constitution (BfV) there are today about fifty thousand members of Far Right political groups in Germany, split among more than 140 organizations, with the National Democratic Party (NPD) as the most prominent and active among them. These groups have embraced an ideology of German *völkisch* socialism mixed with anti-globalization rhetoric and vehemently anti-Semitic and/or anti-Zionist slogans ("Israelis are building concentration camps," and so forth). The number of German Far Right websites has more than tripled in recent years, as has the production of skinhead racist rock music with its incitement to hatred against Turks, Gypsies, Jews, and other minorities. This proliferation may help to explain why there were more than one thousand anti-Semitic acts in June–July 2006—many of them due to the Lebanon War and others to a more general climate of xenophobia in which calls for the massive repatriation of foreigners became more common.

There has always been a close connection between the rise in *Fremdenfeindlichkeit* (xenophobia) and revivals of anti-Semitism in German history. Developments since the fall of Soviet Communism and German reunification nearly twenty years ago have once again confirmed this truth.[70] The problem does not lie in the numbers or influence of the neo-Nazis. They are still isolated and totally outside the political mainstream, confronted by successive German governments (including that of Angela Merkel) that are firmly committed to liberal parliamentary democracy and the rule of law. There is no hint of any nostalgia for the Third Reich, no German desire to revive the militarist past. Nonetheless, radical Right rhetoric, even on the "Jewish question," has surreptitiously made increasing inroads into the German media and mainstream discourse. It was, for example, the Far Right that always insisted on the gravity of Allied war crimes against Germany, and that consistently railed at world Jewry and portrayed Israel as an "aggressor" state (with Germans and Palestinians as their innocent victims)—long before this became more politically correct. Likewise, ever since 1945 (in direct continuity with Nazi propaganda), it was the ultranationalist Right that attacked the "Zionist world conspiracy" and American domination of West Germany, along with the tyranny of Soviet Communism. For more than fifty years, the German ultranationalist Right enthusiastically embraced Palestinian and Arab claims against Israel. Today, a more sophisticated and softer version of this discourse can be heard among conservatives, liberals, and leftists. It is significant, for example, that the mainstream German media was little different from neo-Nazi publications in its condemnation of Israel's "total war" against the Palestinians after 2000 and its "Old Testamentarian" methods, scathingly portrayed as "an eye for an eye, a tooth for a tooth."[71] This much misunderstood biblical metaphor (which relates to compensation, not revenge) was a leitmotif in Hitler's wartime speeches—one that he used (by implication) to justify the mass murder of Jews. Today, these concepts have returned and are sometimes used in mainstream political discourse against the Jewish state.

During an interview in February 2002, Karl Lamers (a prominent CDU parliamentarian) bluntly described Israel as a "foreign body" in the Middle East, an aggressive and "artificial" state whose policies served to "discredit" the West.[72] Germany, he pontificated, must face its historic responsibility for Israel's establishment, which had resulted in millions of Palestinians living in refugee camps. This was something Germans could no longer be silent about. Lamers deplored the fact that Israel was neither a model nor a source of hope for its neighbors—a strangely unreal demand not made of any other state. He added, for good measure, that the record of the Jewish state reflected badly on Europe. Two months later, he was already considering sanctions against Israel.[73]

Another leading conservative politician, former minister of labor Norbert Blum, was even more explicit, informing the German public that he did not regard the actions of the Israeli military as self-defense against terrorism. The Jewish state was conducting a blind, vengeful *Vernichtungskrieg* (war of destruction)—a term that Hitler had very specifically applied to his own genocidal war in the east to exterminate Jews, Communists, partisans, and enemies of the Reich. Blum accused Israel of deliberately ignoring international law and human rights while instrumentalizing anti-Semitism and using it as a "moral cudgel" to silence freedom of thought and justified criticism.[74] He also spoke about the need for Jews to finally have their own piece of land, as if there was no legitimate and established State of Israel already in existence. These remarks constituted a crass example of delegitimization of Israel's right to existence as an independent state in the Middle East.

In April 2002, the German media became especially vociferous in maintaining that Israel was violating civilized rules of combat, ethical norms, and human rights. It reported that Israelis were carrying out "coldblooded executions" in Jenin as if these were actual facts. The *Frankfurter Rundschau* wrote hyperbolically about a Palestinian variant of "ground zero" being provoked by Israeli hands.[75] The conservative *Frankfurter Allgemeine Zeitung* (*FAZ*) sharply reproved Israel's policy as a form of "State terrorism." It recalled that former Israeli prime ministers Menachem Begin and Yitzhak Shamir had once been "terrorists," and that in the Middle East (as elsewhere) negotiations with former terrorists were perfectly normal.[76] Such a relativization of terror provided implicit justification for Palestinian suicide bombing, ignored the suffering of ordinary Israelis, and showed a curiously perverse disregard for the obligation of any state (including Israel) to defend its own citizens.

The German media was not alone in expressing indignation and rage at Israeli actions. Some Muslims, too, have reacted vehemently. There are at least thirty thousand persons in Germany linked to Islamist fundamentalist organizations, such as the Turkish Milli Görüs, whose ideology is anti-Western and anti-Semitic. In the courtyard of the Mevlana Mosque (affiliated to this Islamist movement) in the immigrant neighborhood of Kreuzberg in Berlin, anti-Semitic literature and videos have been freely sold at local book fairs. For example, the Turkish Islamist newspaper *Vakit*, with its promotion of Holocaust denial *and* praise for Hitler, was widely available until a recent ban.[77] Such literature openly disseminates popular Turkish anti-Semitic conspiracy theories relating to the "Dönme"—descendants of the false Messiah Sabbatai Zevi, who converted to Islam more than three centuries ago. Turkish anti-Semites claim that these converts destroyed the

Ottoman caliphate and were plotting to subvert the Muslim faith.[78] Books about the Zionist bid for world domination, religious texts identifying Jews as the "sons of apes and pigs," and Henry Ford's 1920s anti-Semitic classic *The International Jew* have also been for sale. The Islamist literature (in Turkish, Iranian, and Arab variations) invariably accuses Jews of falsifying their own Scriptures, murdering the prophets, breaking contracts, and seeking world rule. They are defined as prime enemies of the "community of the oppressed." Indeed, some Muslim youths in Berlin use the term "Jew" primarily as a swearword. Many of them glorify the 9/11 terrorists and the Palestinian suicide bombers in Israel. Others reject any discussion in school of topics like the Holocaust.[79]

Not surprisingly in this growing climate of hate, anti-Semitic graffiti have proliferated in immigrant neighborhoods, as have violent attacks on Jews carried out by Muslims. Ironically, the perpetrators themselves are often objects of stigmatization by a substantial part of mainstream German society that rejects their permanent presence on German soil. Muslims in Germany, largely of Turkish origin, cling closely to their ethno-religious identity, identifying much more with their homeland than with Germany. They live in a parallel society, largely indifferent to German history, to issues of German national identity, or to the "secondary anti-Semitism" whose origins lie in German guilt projections deriving from the Holocaust.[80] Their own anti-Jewish prejudices have independent roots in Islamist ideology, revolving around questions of collective Muslim identity and the larger issue of their cultural self-definition in the non-Muslim lands. But with regard to Israel, there is undoubtedly some convergence. In 2004, no less than 68 percent of the German population agreed with the shocking and totally false statement, "Israel is carrying out a war of extermination [*Vernichtungskrieg*] against the Palestinians."[81]

Germans today are no different from many other Europeans in believing that Jews are "too powerful," especially in business, finance, and the media. In November 2003, an amazing 65 percent of Germans branded the Jewish state as the greatest single threat to world peace.[82] There is ample reason to think that the media reports on Israel have also influenced general attitudes toward Jews in a negative manner, without necessarily being the main cause of this response.[83] The head of Frankfurt Jewry, Salomon Korn, gave thoughtful expression in May 2002 to the growing sense of communal isolation and insecurity this wall of hostility has provoked. He maintained that

Jews in postwar Germany had enjoyed relative immunity only so long as they were perceived as *victims*. Their presence served as a reminder to Germans of everything that had been wrong in their past and still needed correction. The Jew symbolically represented "the darker sides of German history and of their own family history."[84] But this admonitory function produced a tremendous burden of unwanted tension, guilt, and anxiety from which the mass of Germans have long wished to escape. Aggressive criticism of Israel finally enabled many Germans to off-load their inability to deal with the mountain of unresolved guilt. Korn observed: "The Israelis are ultimately transformed into 'Nazis,' the Palestinians into persecuted and murdered 'Jews.' In the repeatedly cited picture of the 'beer-bellied Sharon' (was Helmut Kohl ever described in this way?), the stereotype of the ugly 'Stürmer-Jew' finds its current Israeli-Jewish rebirth."[85]

In truth, this transformation had, embryonically at least, taken place at least twenty to thirty years earlier, especially on the German radical Left. But only now did German Jews find themselves being held collectively liable *as a community* for Israeli actions, enabling anti-Semitism to "legitimately" unburden itself.

The burdensome question of German guilt and its exoneration became more acute following the remarks by the prominent writer Martin Walser on receiving a prestigious peace prize at the Frankfurt Book Fair on October 11, 1998.[86] In that speech, Walser attacked the abuse of the Holocaust in German public discourse, calling it a "means of intimidation," and deploring the "constant presentation of our disgrace" (Auschwitz) with its paralyzing effect on contemporary German culture.[87] Many cultivated Germans widely applauded this outburst, which echoed statements by Hans Jürgen Syberberg nearly ten years earlier. It led Ignatz Bubis, by now the leader of German Jewry, to accuse Walser of indulging in *geistige Brandstiftung* (mental arson).[88] But as the British weekly *The Economist* accurately observed, Walser "spoke for vast numbers of his countrymen." His call for a "normal" national identity was very much in line with Chancellor Gerard Schröder's position. Bubis, on the other hand, was rather isolated in his alarm at the "spreading intellectual nationalism" in Germany, to which Walser had given voice. Bubis soon found himself attacked by the German media for losing his self-control and encouraging unjustified suspicion of Walser's motives.[89] The aggressive reactions to Bubis's warning were the forerunners of ever harsher criticisms that would be directed against the Zentralrat (the

Central Council of Jews in Germany) for trying to "dictate" opinions on controversial German national issues. German Jews were increasingly accused of striving to impose censorship when it came to deciding whether critics of Israel ought to be dubbed anti-Semitic. Indeed, communal leaders Bubis, Paul Spiegel, and Michel Friedman were all charged at various times after 2000 with attempting to "silence" the German media by using the *Antisemitismusvorwurf* (antisemitism reproach).[90]

Walser's outlook on the "Jewish question" was curiously reminiscent of mainstream *völkisch* concepts in vogue since the late nineteenth century. His unsympathetic depiction of Jews implied that they were foreign to the wellsprings of German national consciousness. Walser's nostalgia for a tribal, pre-Christian past exuded a "neo-pagan" animus toward biblical monotheism, a Nietzschean loathing for Judeo-Christian morality, and a romantic aversion to abstract Enlightenment universalism. Like Syberberg before him, he played with Wagnerian anti-Semitic clichés, contrasting an *ureigen* (original) depth and creativity anchored in the genius of the German language with superficial Jewish rationalism, the "Judaic" will to dominate, and the lack of any organic tradition, or "feeling," for Germanic myth. Like Syberberg, Walser suggested that Germans had fallen victim to a "Jewish-Western" neo-Enlightenment imposed primarily by the United States after 1945. This version of modernity had stripped German culture of its content, neutralized healthy natural instincts, and imposed a false guilt-ridden morality—the source of a permanently "bad conscience." Walser saw his mission as helping to "liberate" Germans from their "Auschwitz complex," from Jewish angst, and the false ideal of universal redemption. The German soul had to be freed from the incubus of the death camps and an "alien" Jewish memory that had been imposed from the outside.

Walser's nationalist rhetoric fell on fertile soil because he was able to identify the post-unification German patriotic mood and the strong public desire for acceptance as a "normal people."[91] His outspoken attack on "the instrumentalization of our shame for contemporary purposes" undoubtedly struck a nerve: "Auschwitz must not be used as a threatening routine, as an always available means to intimidate or a moral drumstick or even just as an act of duty."

The standing ovation that greeted this 1998 speech was an indication that he had spoken for many Germans.[92] A survey that same year had revealed that no less than 63 percent of the population wanted closure on constant references to anti-Jewish persecution under the Nazis; another 50 percent believed that Jews had opportunistically used the Holocaust for their material advantage at German expense.[93] Walser made such deep resentments more *salonfähig* (respectable), especially with his complaint that constant evocation of the Nazi past disturbed his *Seelenfrieden* (peace of mind).

Walser's subsequent bestselling novel *Tod eines Kritikers* (Death of a Critic), published in 2002, sharpened the controversy still further. This novel could best be described as a metaphorical assassination of Germany's leading literary critic, Marcel Reich-Ranicki, himself a Holocaust survivor of Polish-Jewish origin—who responded by calling it "a really blatant anti-semitic outburst."[94] It is a fictional portrait heavily laden with Judeophobic clichés. Many reviewers felt that the central protagonist in the novel was a monster of vulgarity, corruption, and lecherousness—"a pure figure of hate."[95] This character, called Ehrl-König, is endowed with an insatiable lust for power, an obsession with his own sexual potency, and an irrepressible urge to dominate German culture. Jews are implicitly seen in the novel as cultural parasites and sterile imitators rather than creators, as persecutors rather than victims.[96] The resonances from the era of the Third Reich are all too apparent.

The Walser affair, replete with the author's own self-serving rhetoric of victimization, exposed a nationalist mood that found an overt political expression in the anti-Semitic utterances of the flamboyant, media-obsessed deputy chairman of the liberal Free Democratic Party (FDP), Jürgen Möllemann. Until his mysterious suicide in June 2003, Möllemann had attempted to smash whatever was left of German taboos concerning Israel and the Jews.[97] He evidently hoped to duplicate Jörg Haider's electoral successes in Austria by manipulation of the media, shock tactics, and a calculated dose of populist anti-Semitism. Möllemann was FDP chairman in North Rhine–Westphalia and had for thirty years stood at the head of German-Arab society. He had developed very lucrative business ties with the Arab world, which were doubtless helped by his credentials as a virulent critic of Israel. This critique escalated after 2001 into a vehement personal campaign against Ariel Sharon's "state terror" and public endorsement of Palestinian suicide bombers sent to murder civilians inside Israel. Möllemann made it clear that in similar circumstances, he, too, would have taken up arms to resist the Zionist enemy.[98] His intemperate remarks were strongly challenged by lawyer Michel Friedman—at the time vice chairman of the Central

Council of Jews in Germany, a CDU politician, and a provocative television talk-show host whose abrasive style had made him numerous enemies. Möllemann responded by conceding that although anti-Semites did indeed exist in Germany, "hardly anyone makes them more popular than Mr. Sharon and, in Germany, Friedman, with his intolerant and malicious manner."[99]

Michel Friedman was undoubtedly the favorite Jewish target of Möllemann and the FDP—in part, at least, because of his pugnacious opposition to racism and anti-Semitism. Friedman's personality, which was considered sarcastic, arrogant, and obnoxious by many of his adversaries, also aroused antagonism. The German media liked to characterize him as the "Great Inquisitor" (for his TV talk-show grilling of guests) and to deride his "foreignness," which grated on viewers. Some commentators even called his political interviews "sadistic executions" with a public dissection of the corpse thrown in for good measure; others implied that his Jewishness was completely antithetical to the German identity and character. The widespread resentment toward Friedman played on the image of a cheeky, upstart Jew exploiting German guilt for self-aggrandizement.[100] In articles, interviews, and commentaries about him before his fall from grace in a sex-and-drugs scandal, Friedman was repeatedly portrayed as a rootless outsider and an aggressive manipulator profiting from his Jewish background for personal gain. His manner, tone, and militancy about anti-Semitism were deemed inimical to German-Jewish rapprochement.[101] Some German critics even accused Friedman of harboring "hatred for Germany," in the light of his constant reminders of the Nazi past. Hence, Möllemann's highly personalized assault on Friedman fell on fertile soil in broad strata of the German population, happy to see the downfall of an uncongenial Jewish parvenu.

Jürgen Möllemann's high-flying ambitions, hubris, and obsession with publicity encouraged him in the belief that by injecting the "Jewish question" into the public debate, he could become a big-time player. He had shown himself to be adept at blaming the Jews for anti-Semitism and then indignantly complaining that he himself was being victimized by those he attacked.[102] He managed to unleash a new scandal by defending the Syrian-born Jamal Karsli (a former member of the Greens), whom he had encouraged to join the FDP despite his blatantly anti-Semitic remarks.[103] Karsli not only raged against the "Nazi tactics" of the Israeli army and the iniquities of the "Zionist lobby" but obviously believed in the existence of a "world Jewish conspiracy." He told the right-wing *Junge Freiheit* that Zionists had "the major part of the media power in the world, and can easily ruin even the most influential individual."[104]

The FDP party chairman Guido Westerwelle did not protest at this turn of events. He supported both Möllemann and Karsli, protesting that it was wrong to brand Israel's so-called critics as anti-Semites.[105] Indeed, Westerwelle initially seemed enthusiastic about Möllemann's demagogic tactics. He had no objection to the idea of transforming the FDP from a small though highly respectable liberal party (which had been a regular coalition partner in most postwar German governments) into a third force, comparable to Jörg Haider's populist Freedom Party in Austria. Möllemann's hostile stance against Israel and his attempts to appeal to new German Muslim voters through anti-Jewish allusions were part of what was called "Project 18." The aim was to win at least 18 percent of the vote in the national elections of September 2002, which would double the FDP's representation. The cynical appeal to anti-Semitism was part of a more far-reaching project that singularly failed to increase the liberal vote.[106]

Möllemann's attempt to transform the FDP into a populist German form of "Haiderism" unraveled in part because of a closing of ranks by the political establishment and media against such strident demagogy. Chancellor Schröder spoke out against the party and expressed concern that the high-profile debate on anti-Semitism might damage the image of Germany abroad.[107] Chairman Westerwelle felt constrained by mounting public pressure to (belatedly) distance himself from Möllemann. But Möllemann's efforts to make a lower-middle-class anti-Semitism politically *salonfähig* in Germany backfired, even though many Germans agreed with his harshly anti-Israel standpoint. Shortly before the national elections, Möllemann published a leaflet that was massively distributed in his constituency singling out Ariel Sharon and Michel Friedman as the "enemies of peace." The content of this propaganda did him no harm with his electors, but the affair helped to bring about his demise. On June 5, 2003, Möllemann parachuted to his death just as prosecutors were about to raid his premises during an investigation into his campaign financing.

The Möllemann affair was a disturbing reminder to German Jews of the stubborn reality of anti-Semitism and the visible chill in public attitudes toward Israel that had taken place since 2001. Perhaps the only prominent

German politician to respond adequately to growing Jewish anxieties was Foreign Minister Joschka Fischer. This was noteworthy, since in his youth, the colorful leader of the Green Party had been a typical anti-Zionist of the New Left stripe. In the controversy over Möllemann, the foreign minister deplored the lack of a spontaneous national outcry against the liberal politician's defense of Palestinian terrorist attacks. Though Fischer affirmed the right of Germans to criticize Israel, he also insisted that this should be exercised "only on the firm basis of indelible solidarity."[108] According to Fischer, attempts to deal with unresolved problems of German identity by projecting them against the Jewish state could "only end in the abyss of antisemitism." His reassuring message to German Jews was that they were not alone. Anti-Semitism was a threat not only to the Jewish community but to German democracy as a whole.[109] This was far from being a shared sentiment in German society, but it was symbolically important that such comments had been made at the highest official level.

The darker side of the German coin remains, however, the powerful desire to lift the burden of the Shoah and create a tabula rasa around the question of German guilt. This syndrome almost certainly explains the extraordinary popularity in Germany of Norman Finkelstein's *Die Holocaust-Industrie,* with its thesis that American Jewish organizations deliberately and illegitimately sought to enrich themselves at German expense. The book went straight to the top of the bestsellers list. Sixty-five percent of Germans basically agreed with Finkelstein's accusations, and only 15 percent thought his thesis was false. Among twenty- to twenty-nine-year-olds, no less than 80 percent were in favor and only 17 percent disagreed with Finkelstein's assertions. This was an appalling result, as the weekly *Der Spiegel* readily conceded.[110]

Finkelstein focused much of his critique on the "moral blackmail" allegedly practiced by organized American Jewry in exploiting the Holocaust to deflect criticism from Israel and their own "morally indefensible policies." His indictment called for closure on all reparation claims. This message was music to the ears of millions of ordinary Germans weary of hearing about Auschwitz. Only a maverick American Jew (himself the son of Holocaust survivors) could have provided such respectable cover for what millions of Germans had long believed—that Israel and organized Jewry capitalized on the Holocaust for their own financial benefit.[111] A study by the University of Bielefeld in 2002 confirmed that 70 percent of Germans held this latently anti-Semitic view and strongly resented being reminded of Nazi crimes.[112] Another survey at the end of 2002 confirmed that 20 to 30 percent of all Germans held generally anti-Semitic attitudes, suggesting that neither Holocaust education nor media "enlightenment" had much affected popular attitudes.[113]

This failure is not surprising when one observes how a growing number of intellectuals and politicians have sought to blur the relations between contemporary Jews, Germans, and the Third Reich. In an article in the Hamburg paper *Die Zeit,* one Social Democratic politician, Freimut Duve, maintained that the real historic tragedy was that Israel itself had become infected with the central Nazi *völkisch* idea of the homogeneous ethnic state. The German "contribution to peace" must therefore consist of helping Israel to overcome this *racist legacy* of the German past![114] Franziska Augstein (daughter of Rudolf, the deceased editor of *Der Spiegel*) also linked Israel's policies to *der deutschen Hitlerei* (Nazism) in a blatantly distorted manner.[115] In her view, it was historic predestination and a "horrible example of philosophical dialectics" that the Israeli nation ("legitimized as victims" by German crimes) *had to* carry out a policy of expelling Palestinians. Israeli "criminality" in this scenario becomes a fatal prolongation of the Holocaust—which she totally divorced from decades of Arab rejectionism, Islamist anti-Semitism, and Palestinian terror. In the same article, European Jews were presented as aliens, having no more right to the Holy Land than the Crusaders. The author compared Israel to Weimar Germany, as if there were an imminent danger of a new Nazism springing from its internal politics. Augstein even presented "criticism of Israel" as if it was a taboo in Germany, when the opposite had been true for many years. Zionism itself was caricatured as the myth of a four-thousand-year-old Jewish presence in Palestine that only existed in the minds of "war criminals" like Ariel Sharon. The circle was closed by the familiar transfiguration of suicide bombers into "victims of the victims" (that is, of the Jews).[116] The bombers, as in so much Western discourse, were assumed to be acting out of pure "desperation" rather than in accord with their own jihadist ideology or any consistent strategy.[117] They were presented as totally innocent victims deserving only compassion. Israel, on the other hand, was accused of betraying its own moral standards—relying solely (like America) on military solutions and brute strength. Such a sweepingly one-sided account of the conflict could only feed the growing hostility toward Jews, whatever one might think of the individual criticisms.

A revealing example of the growing anti-Semitic mood in Germany was the scandal that developed in October 2003 following remarks by Martin Hohmann, then a fifty-five-year-old member of the Christian Democrat parliamentary group and ex-mayor of Neuhof. He told his party constituents rather bluntly that Germany had atoned enough for the Holocaust. Hohmann had apparently spoken in a similar vein at political gatherings in the past. He had also strongly protested at the "preference" given by the authorities to foreigners over native Germans. But this time Hohmann went further, pouring scorn on the notion that Germans were a *Tätervolk* (guilty people) because of the Holocaust.[118] He insisted that in any case the same accusation would apply to Jews because of their nefarious role in Russia's Bolshevik Revolution. According to Hohmann's logic, Jews were the source of global evil because individuals of Jewish origin, such as Leon Trotsky, had been key figures in the early years of the Red Terror in the Soviet Union. Since millions had been killed in this first phase of Communist revolution, one had to ask about "the 'guilt' of the Jews."[119] Hohmann did not, of course, evoke the responsibility of the Georgian people for Stalin's murder of an infinitely greater number of victims in the former Soviet Union, since this would have immediately exposed the hollowness of his argument.

In a television interview, the CDU deputy extended his point by suggesting that "the Jewish people's history also has dark stains." In meetings with fellow conservative lawmakers in Berlin, he refused to retract "the tenor and the spirit of his speech." But Angela Merkel, the Christian Democratic leader, publicly castigated his remarks as anti-Semitic and "under no circumstances tolerable," which led to his expulsion from the parliamentary caucus. Nevertheless, despite the unequivocal reprimand of Hohmann by conservative party leaders and by the SPD-led ruling coalition, German public opinion clearly disagreed with the political establishment. CDU critics of Hohmann received abusive and even threatening phone calls. The flood of faxes and emails protesting efforts to seek the deputy's expulsion ran nine out of ten in favor of the controversial parliamentarian.[120] The Hohmann affair was further aggravated by a glowing letter of praise he received from Brigadier General Reinhard Günzel, commander of Germany's elite special forces. Günzel expressed admiration for "an excellent speech, of courage, truth and clarity, which one seldom hears or reads in our country." He added that "you can be certain that you clearly speak for the majority of our people." German defense minister Peter Struck swiftly dismissed Günzel for these laudatory remarks, which he called not only "unacceptable" but damaging to Germany's military reputation. The rapidity of the official reaction did much to contain the damage surrounding what the late Paul Spiegel (then the leader of German Jewry) called "the worst case of antisemitism that I have experienced in the last decade."[121]

Hohmann's speech was no spontaneous aberration or momentary rhetorical exaggeration. In its reliance on the myth of Judeo-Bolshevism it echoed the classic anti-Semitic worldview of the radical Right. One of Hohmann's most important sources was the American automobile manufacturer Henry Ford, whose anti-Semitic tract *The International Jew* had deeply influenced Adolf Hitler.[122] The essential premise of these conspiracy theories was that the Jews were bent on achieving global domination. To achieve their aims, they had invented world Communism and international revolution with a view to destroy Christian civilization. The relatively high level of participation of individual Jews in the Communist revolutions of 1918–20 (especially in Bolshevik Russia, Germany, and Hungary) was grist to Hohmann's mill. The Catholic conservative deputy provided lists of Russian Jews in the Bolshevik Politburo, the secret police, and the revolutionary committees. He told his listeners that Jews had carried out the murder of the Russian czar, and that they accounted for 60 percent of the Marxist leadership in Austria, as well as most of the top revolutionary cadres in the short-lived Soviet republic in Bavaria. The climax came with his charge of genocide, based on wholly spurious assumptions and statistics: for example, that "Communist Jews" before 1924 had eliminated 1.7 million innocent victims in the USSR—including 815,000 peasants and 355,000 intellectuals! Hohmann not only accepted the anti-Semitic equation of "Jew" and "Bolshevik" but tried to establish a false symmetry between "Jewish Communists" and Nazis as *Täter*, or perpetrators of mass murder.[123] Perhaps without realizing it, he was himself echoing one of the central myths of National Socialism.

There is no doubt that since 2001 German Jewry has had to live in a state of growing anxiety and apprehension.[124] This nervousness was in part fueled by the large number of aggressively anti-Semitic emails, letters, and phone calls sent to the Central Council of Jews and other Jewish communities in Germany, especially since April 2002. Indeed, in 2002 the number of anti-Semitic crimes rose to 1,629—the highest recorded number in the history of the Federal Republic. In the wake of the Hohmann affair, a poll by *Die Zeit* revealed that no less than 40 percent of west Germans (and 28 percent in the former East Germany) supported Hohmann's statements. Research by Professor Wolfgang Findte, head of the Communications Psychology Department at the Friedrich Schiller University of Jena, demonstrated that almost 50 percent of Germans did not feel any sense of responsibility to Jews as a result of the Holocaust; more than 60 percent were extremely critical of Israel, and approximately one-third of all Germans held anti-Semitic views. Moreover, there appeared to be a significant correlation between anti-Jewish opinions and the insistence on closure with regard to the Holocaust—which was notably higher among right-wing voters. So, too, there was also a growing correspondence between hostility toward Israel and anti-Semitism. No less than 80 percent of Germans agreed that Israelis were occupiers who "have no business being in Palestine";[125] 57 percent of those surveyed believed that "Israelis treat the Palestinians the way the Nazis treated the Jews"—tribute to the prevailing ignorance, stupidity, and bad faith. No doubt the overwhelming desire to be free of any residual guilt about Jews also played its part in such obsessive comparisons.

A Forsa Institute opinion poll commissioned by the German magazine *Der Stern* following the IDF operation in Gaza (January 2009) confirmed that 49 percent of Germans regarded Israel as "aggressive" and 59 percent believed it ruthlessly pursued its interests. No less than 60 percent rejected any "special relationship" with Israel because of the Holocaust—a figure reaching 70 percent among younger Germans. The poll found that 13 percent of the respondents fundamentally rejected Israel's right to exist.[126] During the Gaza confrontation of early 2009, some of the demonstrations in Germany even had the character of a lynch mob with protestors screaming slogans like "Death to Israel." One such demonstration organized by an Islamist group in Duisberg produced a singular response by police officials. Rather than restraining the crowd, the authorities broke down the door of a city apartment in which a student had the temerity to hang two Israeli flags and confiscated them. A week later, Germany's neo-Nazi NPD (National Democrats) announced they would hold a solemn vigil in the center of Berlin to "stop the Israeli holocaust in the Gaza Strip." It announced on its Berlin website that the NPD's efforts "to defend ourselves against foreign rule" were parallel to the Palestinian struggle against Israeli domination. Echoing a widely held belief among the German public, the NPD branded the Gaza campaign a "war of extermination."[127]

The neo-Nazi NPD had performed reasonably well in the elections to the state parliament of Saxony in 2008, as well as in Mecklenburg-Western Pomerania two years earlier. It was also represented in a number of local city councils in Berlin districts. Since the Second Lebanon War of 2006, it should be observed, the neo-Nazis had found ever more common ground with the Islamists. Indeed, some Germans of Palestinian origin openly declared that they intended to vote for the neo-Nazi party in the next election. Hatred of Israel and latent anti-Semitism also provided an important link between the German Left Party (with fifty-four deputies, currently the fourth largest party in the German Parliament) and the pro-Hamas Islamists. In the anti-Israel demonstrations of January 2009 throughout Germany, in which some protestors implicitly called for the murder of Jews and Israelis, members of the Left Party were to be found alongside their Palestinian and Islamist allies—who have in recent years shown a growing proclivity for violence.

The German government has publicly warned against such trends. Foreign Minister Frank-Walter Steinmeier remarked in March 2008: "We will not allow the Islamists' viewpoint to be carried into a society that has a special responsibility toward the State of Israel and its right to exist. This poisons the social climate and undermines the foundations on which our society exists."[128] German chancellor Angela Merkel has been even more forthright in defense of Israel's right to self-defense, in praise of the rebirth of German Jewry (there are now around 130,000 Jews living on German soil), and in demanding zero tolerance for anti-Semitism in Germany. In sharp contrast to the mood of German popular opinion, Merkel has repeatedly insisted on Germany's "special responsibility" toward Israel. Indeed, she has pursued a policy of close scientific, economic, diplomatic, and military cooperation with the Jewish state. On the other hand, as Iran's leading trade partner in the European Union, Germany has done relatively little to clamp down on its own companies dealing with the Iranians. Despite Merkel's pronouncements and her behind-the-scenes efforts in speaking to the business sector in Germany, there has not been a significant reduction in German financial investment in Iran. German leaders did, it is true, strongly condemn Mahmoud Ahmadinejad's Holocaust deniers' conference of December 2006 in Teheran as a "shamefully aggressive and ideologically inspired act." They even publicly acknowledged Germany's moral obligation toward Israel "to protect its existence." But in practice, Germany has been very hesitant in applying European trade sanctions against the Iranian regime despite the existential threat that it poses to Israel and to Europe itself.[129]

Germany, to be sure, has more memorials and museums commemorating the death camps than any other nation in Europe. The Shoah has been extensively examined in the education system, though there is some evidence of growing "Holocaust fatigue" and a boomerang effect in which excessive focus on the subject can foment more anti-Semitism. As Holocaust survivor Jean Améry shrewdly observed forty years ago, "Antisemitism, which is contained in anti-Zionism as the thunderstorm is part of the cloud, is again respectable."[130] Already in 1969, Améry discerned that Jews were no longer regarded as victims but as oppressors of the Palestinians. Since then, most of the taboos in postwar Germany against publicly expressing anti-Jewish prejudices have been broken. Anti-Semitic stereotypes have been revived, often linked to anti-Americanism and antipathy toward Israel. No less significantly, the desire for "normalization" and Holocaust exoneration has found new channels of expression.

Today, more than a third of all Germans believe their countrymen were victims of World War II, just like the Jews. Since the turn of the new millennium, the dominant trend is to extend discussions on victimhood to include the perpetrators, and to create a new cult of victimhood in which patriotic Germans are once again center stage.[131] Such reinterpretations of history have the additional advantage of reconciling Germans with one another, while expressing their opposition to threatening others, such as the United States and Israel. For instance, Jörg Friedrich's bestselling books about the wartime Allied bombings of Germany (depicting them as utterly inhuman and futile) have focused on the Germans exclusively as victims of a brutal air war. There is no mention of a German war of aggression, no hint of the forcible occupation of the European Continent; there are no persecutions, murders, or expropriations of Jews in these books. The SA, the SS, and the death camps have disappeared down the proverbial memory hole. There is no eastern front and no Holocaust. The ruins, the ashes, the burned bodies belong solely to German civilians much as Hitler hoped that they would in his last political testament of April 1945. There is not a word in Friedrich's work about the 1.5 million Jewish children murdered by the Germans. Winston Churchill, on the other hand, is damned by the author as "the greatest child-slaughterer of all time."[132] Adolf Hitler, had he survived the war, would surely be rubbing his hands with unmitigated glee.

The Allied bombing of German cities during World War II did, of course, bring death, disfigurement, terror, and a tragic loss of life and property to innumerable civilians. But these bombing campaigns, even if retrospectively judged to be excessive, never had the deliberate killing of civilians as their primary strategic aim. Hence Friedrich's inflated use of Holocaust terminology (describing German bomb shelters as being equivalent to "gas chambers" or the destruction of German libraries as "the greatest book-burning of all time") ultimately relativizes and falsifies the broader historical picture. It also misrepresents the position of German civilians. Unlike Europe's Jews, they were not simply helpless and abandoned victims but an integral part of the country's total war effort. Until the end of 1944 they knew their own government still commanded massive military and strategic capabilities. Indeed, their loyalty to the führer was maintained to the bitter end.

Cultural and political hostility toward Jews in contemporary Germany is noticeably more palpable since the post-1989 reunification and the forging of a new German national consciousness. Despite the positive attitude of Chancellor Merkel toward Israel and German Jewish concerns, her commitment is not reflected in public opinion. Indeed, German anti-Semitism, which never truly vanished during the postwar era, has reemerged through a self-exculpatory discourse about the Holocaust and the desire to be freed of its burden. It is also linked to resentment against some admittedly questionable American and Israeli policies that may adversely affect German interests.[133] However, the prominent role of German business and industry in building up Iran's nuclear potential while ignoring President Ahmadinejad's brazen threats to wipe out the Jewish state is a deeply troubling symptom of greed and moral indifference.[134] No less shocking, though in a different way, is the transformation by the German Left of Jews into "perpetrators" and of their worst enemies into "victims." The murdered Jews of Europe are constantly commemorated in Germany as a paradigm for antiracist education.[135] But the living Jews of Israel are all too often scandalously "Nazified" as a paradigm of contemporary inhumanity.

EIGHT

Frenchmen, Arabs, and Jews

The French Revolution of 1789 was the cataclysmic event that inaugurated the emancipation of Jewry on the European continent. For many Jews it seemed like a new dawn—the passage from darkness to light, from servitude to freedom.[1] The revolution, with its secular trinity—*Liberté, Egalité, Fraternité*—would be celebrated a century later by the French rabbinate as "our modern Passover."[2] Franco-Judaism rapidly learned how to adapt itself to the republican credo of liberal universalism. French Jews became "Israélites de France," accepting an essentially French identity and ideals while retaining their distinctive communal organization and philanthropic structures. In the new context of an open society and full equality before the law, Jewish national sentiment would have only a modest appeal in France before 1945. The liberal Catholic author Anatole Leroy-Beaulieu pointedly observed in the mid-1890s that French Jews were not in search of a new homeland. They had found their *patrie* by the rivers of the West, and in his opinion they were not at all desirous of changing it for "the deserted banks of the Jordan."[3]

Among the few Jewish intellectuals in fin de siècle France who did embrace the new creed of Zionism, those like the revolutionary anarchist Bernard Lazare, who sharply questioned the dominant ideology of assimilation, were very much the exception.[4] For the majority of French Jews before the Holocaust the worship of *patrie* and religion was directed toward Paris and not Jerusalem as their final destination. If anything, the rise of integral nationalism in France during the 1890s further strengthened this tendency. Faced with an exclusivist French nationalism that damned them as a "state within a state," the Jews of France reaffirmed their commitment to the universal principles of reason, progress, and humanity—ideals solidly anchored in the French liberal tradition.[5] They knew that since 1789 the republic, "one and indivisible," had left no public space open for the expressions of Jewish politics or ethnic particularism. Cultural and political pluralism were firmly discouraged by the state, in the name of Jacobin centralism and full assimilation. Moreover, republican Jews instinctively feared that any expression of sympathy for Zionism or Jewish national autonomy might strengthen anti-Semitic assertions about their "dual allegiance," identifying them as *étrangers* (foreigners) in their adopted fatherland.[6] At a time when the streets of Paris and other French cities reverberated with denunciations of Alfred Dreyfus as a "Jewish traitor," this argument had a powerful resonance with many French Jews that would continue to echo through the first half of the twentieth century. Nevertheless, late-nineteenth-century anti-Semitism was seen by most Jews in France as less chronic than its counterparts in Germany, Austria, and Russia; in the words of the renowned sociologist Émile Durkheim, it was supposedly nothing more than an "acute crisis triggered by a temporary set of circumstances." Durkheim, a secular Alsatian Jew and Sorbonne professor, regarded the paroxysm of hate that had swept France during the Dreyfus affair as an offshoot of the humiliating defeat in the Franco-Prussian War, passing economic difficulties, moral distress, and the perennial human need for a scapegoat. Anti-Semitism was a pathology that, in France at least, could be cured, a "superficial consequence and symptom of the state of social malaise."[7]

Modern French anti-Semitism from the time of Édouard Drumont in the mid-1880s until the Holocaust, was, however, a much more formidable force than this simplistic diagnosis suggested. It sharply contrasted the noble heritage of Catholic France with the "corruption" of the "Jewish-Masonic Republic" established in 1871; it attacked the intellectual foundations of Enlightenment rationalism and the universalistic political tradition of the 1789 revolution, which had permitted what Drumont called "the Jewish conquest of France." The nationalist revival in France after 1900 added a powerful racist charge to the prevailing anti-Semitic imagery—demonizing Jews as "microbes," vermin, and "sources of putrefaction" that had invaded and were now busy destroying a rapidly decomposing French social organism.[8] The monarchist and ultranationalist Action Française and its royalist student organization, the Camelots du Roi, had a popular anti-Semitic theme song, which began with the following words:

Now that the Jew has taken everything,
has picked Paris clean,
he says to France: "You're ours now."
Obey! On your knees!
No, no, France is on the move.
She sees red. No, no, enough of treason . . .
Shut up, insolent Jew!
Here comes the king, and ahead of him
marches our entire race.
Jew in your place! Our king is leading us!
Yes, France for the French[9]

Street-fighting anti-Semitism of this kind was perceived by such nationalist leaders as Charles Maurras, Maurice Barrès, and Leon Daudet as the most revolutionary, populist, and subversive force in their political arsenal—the weapon that had the most attraction for the plebeian masses. It brought Maurras's movement close to insurrectional fascism by combining a visceral race consciousness with integral French nationalism, quasi-socialist appeals to the working class, and violent anti-republican rhetoric. Henri Vaugeois, writing in 1900, made it clear that the two passions (plebiscitary and anti-Semitic) that had reappeared in France "are undoubtedly the only revolutionary forces that nationalism can at present set against the parliamentarism that delivers us up to the foreigners."[10] Hence, anti-Semitism was more than simply xenophobia or Jew hatred, it was a *political* concept used by internal nationalists and sections of the revolutionary anti-Republican syndicalist Left to try to smash the basis of liberal democracy. The new Right quickly saw its expediency and potential ability to integrate all social classes into a more unified nationalist camp. In Maurras's striking words: "Everything seems impossible or terribly difficult without the providential appearance of antisemitism. It enables everything to be arranged, smoothed over, and simplified. If one were not an anti-Semite through patriotism, one would become one through a simple sense of opportunity."[11]

In the 1930s, the growing ferocity of French anti-Semitism was exacerbated by the coming to power of the Popular Front government of 1936, headed by Léon Blum—a socialist and a Jew.[12] The various fascist leagues and the Action Française now identified Jews with the threat of Bolshevism,

French cultural decadence, the inundation of the country by foreigners, demographic decline, and growing anxieties over racial "pollution." There was also the imminent specter of possible armed conflict with Nazi Germany, with Jews being presented as dangerous "warmongers" seeking to push France into a confrontation with Hitler. By 1938 pacifism on both the left and the right, had emerged as an important source of anti-Semitism.[13]

Following the military defeat of France in June 1940, the collaborationist Vichy government under Marshal Philippe Pétain greatly reinforced France's rich anti-Semitic tradition—nourished by Catholic, socialist, racist, and nationalist sources. The *Statut des Juifs* and other draconian measures of French anti-Semitic legislation totally eliminated all "Jewish influence" in public life; they also swiftly led to the complete "Aryanization" (dispossession) of Jewish property and to the deportation of eighty thousand Jews to their deaths in the east—an unprecedented crime that could not have been effectively implemented without the full cooperation of the French police. Indeed, nowhere in western Europe did the Nazis receive such substantial collaboration from the local administration.[14] Moreover, the French government also initiated the "national revolution" under Pétain, abolishing the emancipation decree of 1791 and establishing concentration camps on French soil that held thousands of Jews, some of whom died of starvation and disease even before they could board the death trains. It was French bureaucrats who prepared the detailed race censuses and stamped identity cards with the word "*Juif*"; French gendarmes who rounded up the Jews—the old, the sick, and the mothers and children, as well as the young and able-bodied men—to be later sent to Poland. Under Vichy the anti-Semitic media was given free rein to indulge in the most ignoble, hysterical slander and stigmatization of the persecuted Jewish population.

After the Allied liberation, the "Jewish question" was partly suppressed in postwar France but hardly disappeared. The philosopher Jean-Paul Sartre noted in his *Réflexions sur la Question Juive* (1946) the silence and malaise of his compatriots concerning the Jews at the end of the war: "Now all France rejoices and fraternizes in the streets. . . . Do we say anything about the Jews? Do we give a thought to those who died in the gas chambers at Lublin? Not a word. Not a line in the newspapers. That is because we must not irritate the anti-Semites."[15] But the uneasy silence did not apply to the neofascist and populist Right, nor did it disarm anti-Jewish prejudices in the

1950s. Prime Minister Pierre Mendès-France, who began the process of withdrawal from the French colonial empire was, for example, presented by the radical Right and the rising Poujadist movement as a servile lackey of cosmopolitan Jewish capitalism.[16] Indeed, since the late 1930s he had been pilloried and would be covered with anti-Semitic slurs throughout his political career, including "Mendès Jerusalem," "Mendès Palestine," and "Mendès Anti-France."[17]

Ironically, the mid-1950s inaugurated a decade of unprecedented Franco-Israeli cordiality and a strategic alliance forged by the bloody seven-year-long Algerian war and the rise of Arab nationalism and its new champion Gamal Abdel Nasser. The French Socialist prime minister Guy Mollet saw Israel not only as a buffer against rising Arab ambitions for independence in North Africa but also as a staunch ally of the West against Soviet expansion throughout the Middle East. Paris allowed Israel carte blanche in the purchase of French weaponry, including its most advanced aircraft; it cooperated very closely with Israel in a top-secret program of nuclear research that enabled the Jewish state to develop the ultimate deterrent, which was vital to its defense. The Suez War of 1956 consolidated Franco-Israeli military and commercial ties that developed apace for the next seven years. After 1956, admiration for "brave little Israel" was something of a defining mood in government circles and public opinion; it was also shared by many of France's most respected cultural figures.[18]

The accession of Charles de Gaulle to power in May 1958 did not initially change that climate. De Gaulle was undoubtedly impressed by Israel's growth and progress. French armaments manufacturers constituted a formidable industrial lobby in favor of the Israeli connection; Israeli pilots and officers shared in specialized French military training programs; and aeronautical engineers from Israel were seconded to French aircraft plants.

Nevertheless, once De Gaulle completed the French withdrawal from Algeria in 1962, the focus of his policy changed completely. During the next three years, France restored relations with the Arab world. The reticent and rather hostile attitude of the Quai d'Orsay (French Ministry of Foreign Affairs) and its diplomats toward Israel, still present even in the early postwar period, found a renewed scope and impetus.[19] This was especially true after Israel had refused to accept General De Gaulle's cold-blooded warning not to strike first in June 1967, even though it was threatened with extinction by three neighboring Arab states. On November 27, 1967, five days after the UN

Security Council issued Resolution 242, putting paid to his hopes for an immediate Israeli withdrawal and a four-power Middle East conference (including France), a frustrated De Gaulle called what would become the most notorious press conference of his political career. While perfunctorily acknowledging Jewish energy and courage in building Israel, he now asserted that after 1956 "we watched the emergence of a State of Israel that was warlike [*guerrier*] and set on expansion," one that was only seeking a new pretext for war. Only five months after the end of the Six-Day War, De Gaulle had already concluded that Israel was "organizing an occupation which can only be accompanied by oppression, repression, and expulsion." It was not only the vindictive tone of such statements, instantly transforming Israel into an "aggressor" and "oppressor" that astonished many observers at the time; it was De Gaulle's insistence on characterizing "the Jewish people" in terminology that recalled the language of Drumont and Maurras.

> Some even feared that the Jews, hitherto scattered but remaining what they had always been, that is an elite people, self-assured and domineering [*un people d'élite, sûr de lui-même et dominateur*] might, once they were reunited in the city of their former grandeur, turn the very moving hopes of 1900 years into a burning ambition of conquest.[20]

De Gaulle then referred to the rising and falling waves of *malveillance* (ill feeling) that Jews "aroused in certain countries and at certain times"; to the "immense capital of interest and even sympathy" that their plight and their biblical legacy had inspired in Christendom; to the satisfaction that France and many other countries had felt over the establishment of Israel—"while at the same time wanting them to reach a peaceful modus vivendi with their neighbors through a little modesty."[21]

De Gaulle's "sermon to the Hebrews" profoundly shocked most Jews in France. Its alarming images relating to Jewish expansionism, arrogance, chosenness, and power—presented as national characteristics of a bimillennial history—threatened to reawaken the old demons of anti-Semitism. After the chief rabbi of France, Jacob Kaplan, solemnly protested, he was duly invited to the Elysée Palace and told by the president that his words about "an elite people" were intended as a compliment! In reality, however, De Gaulle's carefully chosen language was a serious delegitimization of the Jewish state; it implied that the Jews were responsible for anti-Semitism and that they had been inherently "domineering" from antiquity until the present.[22] Not only that, but De Gaulle had also invoked the "vast assistance in money, influence and propaganda which the Israelis received from the Jewish milieux of America and Europe." Here, too, he was echoing some of the best-known clichés of anti-Semitism, especially the myth of excessive Jewish wealth and control of the media.[23] There was, of course, no reference to the centuries of pogroms and massacres that Jews (despite their "power") had been unable to prevent; and no hint that Christendom (especially the Catholic Church) had the slightest hand in any of these persecutions.

The French president essentially blamed Israel for the Six-Day War, in which it opportunistically "seized the objectives it wished to obtain"—a travesty of the events actually leading up to the war. This was the first time that a leading postwar Western head of state had so openly linked a clear condemnation of Israel with a stereotypical image of the Jewish people as a whole.[24] Raymond Aron, a distinguished political thinker and onetime admirer of De Gaulle, was one of many Jewish observers who was stung by the presidential press conference. He observed that state anti-Semitism had all of a sudden become *salonfähig* in France, providing a green light to Jew haters "to use the same language as before the great massacre."[25] Aron also expressed disappointment at the silence of such famous writers as François Mauriac and André Malraux, symbols of French conscience and intimates of De Gaulle, from whom he had expected at least a word of protest. Instead, other Gaullists began to complain of the preponderance of Jews in the radio and press; to deplore Israeli and Jewish "propaganda" against De Gaulle's pro-Arab Middle East policy; and to hint at dual allegiances. One Gaullist author openly wrote in *Le Monde* about the "invisible domination" of Israel—"a pure colonial fact; the metropolis of an omnipresent and imperceptible empire that uses the Old Testament for less than religious purposes."[26] The former Vichy commissioner for Jewish affairs, the extreme rightist Xavier Vallat, although in sympathy with Israel, immediately identified himself with the spirit of De Gaulle's remarks about the Jewish sense of "racial" superiority. Arab leaders, too, were delighted with the general's biting comments—especially relishing his condemnation of Israel's "expansionist" policy. On the other hand, former French foreign minister, the socialist Christian Pineau, bluntly declared that he had "always known De Gaulle to be an anti-Semite and an ardent disciple of Charles Maurras."[27]

De Gaulle's hatred for the British and especially the Americans was, however, even more evident than his new-found aversion toward Israel, a country toward which he had initially been well-disposed. His mid-1960s conviction that the Jewish state was drawing closer to Washington and was therefore becoming an obstacle to French Middle Eastern ambitions profoundly irritated him. Ever since the end of the Franco-Algerian war in 1962, De Gaulle had been seeking Great Power status for France by mustering the Third World behind his leadership and adopting a firm anti-American posture. The irony was that his abandonment of the Franco-Israeli alliance (which had been maintained for more than a decade) definitively pushed the Israelis into the arms of the United States.[28]

By 1967 De Gaulle had adopted the long-standing view of the Quai d'Orsay that France was indeed a "Muslim power." From Napoleon's 1798 conquest of Egypt, through the French colonization of Algeria after 1830 to the domination of the Maghreb for the next 120 years, there was, historically speaking, some basis to this claim. Furthermore, the Quai d'Orsay certainly preferred Arabs to Jews when it came to questions of French imperial interests in North Africa or the Levant. In 1840, the French government strongly defended its anti-Semitic consul in Damascus who had accused local Jews of being implicated in ritual murder. The polished diplomats of the Quai d'Orsay themselves regularly displayed Catholic and aristocratic prejudice toward Jews. They regarded Zionism above all as a tool of German intrigue and (subsequently) of British imperialist machinations. Throughout the interwar period, the French Foreign Ministry generally looked at the Zionist project with the utmost hostility and distrust, characterizing it as detrimental to French colonial interests. Many of the dispatches and memoranda from French Middle East diplomats were riddled with obnoxious comments or aspersions on the Jewish religion or the intransigent character and unsavory national characteristics of the Jews. Most of the diplomats would certainly have agreed with France's leading Orientalist scholar, Louis Massignon, who wrote in 1934 that only a "Franco-Islamic bloc" could save the Holy Land from the ravages of "cosmopolitan Jewish bankers" and Anglo-Saxon imperialists. For Massignon and the French Arabists who advised the Quai d'Orsay, the Jewish national home in Palestine was a dangerous "imposture" that undermined French control in North Africa, Lebanon, and Syria. Jewry was not really a nation at all, and Israel's creation was deemed a political catastrophe. These views were also shared by the first French consul general in Israel, who depicted the Jews in his dispatches as being "racist through and through," fanatical, imbued with a sense of their own chosenness, and "the ancestral traits of a completely Oriental cast of mind."[29] Naturally enough, the Franco-Israeli honeymoon during the Algerian war and the aftermath of Nasser's nationalization of the Suez Canal had been a painful thorn in the flesh of the Quai d'Orsay, which persistently pursued its Arabophile bent. After 1969, it was finally free to push ahead with the full approval of De Gaulle's successors, Georges Pompidou and Giscard d'Estaing.[30]

Under Georges Pompidou, France's pro-Arab orientation further intensified, partly driven by commercial considerations and growing dependence on North African and Middle Eastern oil. The embargo on all military equipment to Israel (initiated by De Gaulle in 1967) continued, as did periodic Gaullist aspersions on Israeli "interference" in French political affairs and anger at Jewish lobbying. Pompidou was outraged when American Jews staged demonstrations against his policies (including the controversial sale of Mirage aircraft to Libya) during his visit to the United States. He also disparagingly referred to Israel on several occasions as a "bridgehead of Western imperialism" in the Middle East, mischievously suggesting that Israelis were a "foreign body" in the region, intruders imbued with a "racialist" philosophy.[31] Following the combined Arab attack on Yom Kippur against Israel in October 1973 the French foreign minister, Michel Jobert, callously dismissed any suggestion that the Arabs had engaged in aggression.[32] The French reward was exemption from the 1973 Arab oil embargo.

This official policy did not change under Giscard d'Estaing, as France embraced the oil-rich Gulf states and became the leading European advocate of Yasser Arafat's PLO. Furthermore, d'Estaing's government, led by Jacques Chirac, sold the Iraqi regime a nuclear reactor capable of producing weapons-grade fuel, and aggressively courted the Arab states while displaying a chilly hostility toward Israel's interests and Jewish sensitivities. This was glaringly exposed in the reaction of Prime Minster Raymond Barre to the bombing of the liberal rue Copernic synagogue on October 3, 1980. The bomb was timed to kill a maximum number of worshippers emerging from the synagogue service—the first time such an event had occurred in a western democracy since the Holocaust.[33] Three of the four passersby killed were not Jewish. Prime Minister Barre inexplicably expressed regret that the terrorists "intended to kill Jews, but wound up killing innocent Frenchmen instead"—a comment that sounded unpleasantly racist. As one journalist in *Libération* put it on October 6, 1980: "Those passing in the streets were French and innocent, those praying in the synagogue were strangers and guilty."

President Giscard d'Estaing also displayed cold insensitivity to the Jewish victims of this act of Palestinian terror. Giscard took five days to even respond to Copernic, greatly underplaying the danger of anti-Semitism and offensively warning Jews not to retaliate. Many French Jews saw in Giscard's unfriendly posture a symptom of governmental laxity toward terrorism, indifference to anti-Semitism, and obtuseness regarding the domestic consequences of its anti-Israel policy.[34] A survey of October 11, 1980, confirmed that 55 percent of all French people believed anti-Semitism to be widespread. Though open, unrestrained expressions of such sentiment were generally frowned upon, it remained by no means negligible as a current of opinion. Significant numbers of those surveyed regarded Jews as a closed group that had successfully infiltrated French society and effectively seized control of the banks and media.[35] Prime Minister Barre's crass insensitivity has to be seen in this light.

Nearly three decades later, Barre's "innocent Frenchmen" gaffe took on a more sinister coloring following his remarks during a March 1, 2007, interview with the state-run radio station France Culture. Barre stated that "opposing the deportation of Jews from France was not a matter of major national interest." During this interview the former prime minister claimed that French Jewry had turned Vichy collaborator Maurice Papon ("a courageous civil servant"), whom Barre had chosen in 1978 as his budget minister, into a "scapegoat." Papon, who had died only a month earlier, was responsible for confiscating Jewish assets and for the deportation of sixteen hundred Jews as a high official in the pro-Nazi wartime Vichy government. By praising Papon and minimizing his guilt, Barre was implicitly playing down French responsibility during the Holocaust. The ex-premier also retrospectively attacked the "Jewish lobby" in France for deliberately distorting his statement after the Copernic bomb attack of 1980 and of mounting "disgraceful operations": "The campaign undertaken by the Jewish lobby with the strongest links on the Left came from the fact that we were in an electoral climate." If that were not enough, Barre also defended National Front (FN) deputy leader Bruno Gollnisch's record as a municipal councilor in Lyon, dismissing as irrelevant his Holocaust "revisionism."[36] The Council of French Jewish Institutions (CRIF), the mainstream representative body of French Jewry, declared it was "scandalized" by Barre's comments. The renowned film maker Claude Lanzmann went much further, openly calling Barre an anti-Semite whose attitude to the "Jewish lobby" was little different from that of the propagators of the *Protocols*. His remarks about Copernic were equally appalling because, once more, they clearly made a distinction between terrorists targeting "guilty Jews" (understandable) and "innocent" French people who had nothing to do with the Arab-Israeli conflict. Pierre Weill, like Lanzmann, saw in Barre's remarks the demonstration that archetypal prejudices against Jews were still alive and that anti-Semitism had merely become "an opinion like others" that should not weigh in the wider scheme of things.

The atmosphere in France had initially improved after François Mitterrand's election to the presidency in May 1981, which was euphorically greeted in large parts of the Jewish community. An admirer of Léon Blum and Mendès-France, the Socialist Mitterrand appointed a number of influential Jewish advisers, such as Jacques Attali, and included Socialists of Jewish origin such as Justice Minister Robert Badinter and Minister of Culture Jack Lang in his cabinet. On the other hand, his first foreign minister, Claude Cheysson, was hardly a friend of Israel, any more than some of his successors, such as the pro-Syrian Roland Dumas. Though Mitterrand considered himself a supporter of Israel and in 1982 was the first French head of state to pay an official visit to the country, he also rescued Yasser Arafat from the Israelis when he was besieged in Beirut.[37] Mitterrand assiduously promoted the Palestinian cause and persuaded Arafat to formally (and deceptively) accept Israel's existence in May 1989. Under Mitterrand's presidency, much of the French Left began to systematically stigmatize Israel as a fascist state.[38] Not only that, but Mitterrand (who in the late 1930s had been a nationalist anti-Semite and then a Vichy official) cynically opened the door to the National Front's increase in mandates by tampering with the electoral system—in order to divide his adversaries on the French Right.

By the 1980s the radical Right in France was far removed from the "pro-Zionism" of its early years. At the time of the Dreyfus affair, anti-Semites like Édouard Drumont, Jules Soury, Urbain Gohier, and others had enthusiastically unfolded the formula: "France for the French! Palestine for the Jews."[39] In the 1930s, too, some racists saw Zionism as a valuable justification for excluding Jews from integration into the French nation. Even during the Vichy period, the anti-Semitic French fascist and collaborationist Pierre Drieu La Rochelle emphasized his respect for the Zionists and his hopes for a Jewish return to the ancient biblical homeland in Palestine. In the post-1948 era, there were many more such declarations from the Far Right in favor of Israel as a "nationalist warrior state" rooted in the soil. Xavier Vallat and the fanatical wartime anti-Semite Lucien Rebatêt both strongly supported the Jewish state immediately after the June 1967 war; Vallat, despite his anti-Semitism, even embraced "the cause of Israel" as being "the cause of Westerners" in general.[40] Many followers of Maurras in the wake of 1967 regarded Israel more positively as "the complete opposite" of the international Jewish *haute banque.* Nevertheless, this enthusiasm proved to be short-lived.

The anti-Semitic backlash against Israel within the Far Right could draw on a powerful strand of Catholic anti-Zionism in France, which had always fought against the axis of "Jewish Anglo-Saxon" imperialist domination. Influenced by the *Protocols,* some reactionary and fascist anti-Semites denounced Zionism as a branch of the Jewish world conspiracy and supported Palestinian Arab resistance to it throughout the British mandatory period. Radical rightists such as Charles Saint-Prot continued this trend in the 1980s, waxing lyrical over the "great desert warrior" Saddam Hussein, who bravely stood up to sinister "cosmopolitan powers" epitomized by Israel and Anglo-Saxon capitalism.[41] The struggle of Arab nationalists against these dark forces was supposedly identical to that of the radical Right in defense of France's Catholic identity. The common enemy was "the lobby" and the threat of encroaching American-Jewish materialism. Such racist anti-Semites as Pierre Sidos revealingly gloated over Saddam Hussein as the Iraqi heir of Nebuchadnezzar, king of Babylon, who had destroyed the first Jewish state in antiquity; *National Hebdo,* a leading FN publication, rejoiced that Jews now felt intimidated by the threats of an "ethnic Assyrian" from "the race of empire builders."[42]

The Far Right FN leader Jean-Marie Le Pen was even blunter about Israel, describing it in 1990 as an "artificial State created for the oil interests of America and Great Britain"—a terminology identical to that of the Third Worldist Left. He and his supporters vocally condemned the so-called Jewish war and the imperialist United States because of its unconditional support for "Israel's sordidly mercenary policy."[43] In the suceeding years FN militants could be heard simultaneously chanting slogans such as "France for the French," "Zionists-racists," and "Bush-assassin."[44] During the Second Persian Gulf War, Le Pen himself, like the Far Left, was vitriolic about the "barbarism" of the Anglo-Saxons in Iraq and of Israel in the Palestinian areas.

Le Pen's anti-Semitism was by no means a new phenomenon. A member of the French National Assembly since 1956, the young Breton deputy was a nationalist ex-paratrooper who had initially been part of Pierre Poujade's populist protest movement. Ever since his political rise in the early 1980s, Le Pen adopted a rabid xenophobic tone, often using racist stereotypes in his campaigns against North African immigration to France.[45] But his populist language also identified Jews with wealth, and anti-Semitism with "ordinary folk" in the classic tradition of the French radical Right. The FN daily, *Présent*, regularly attacked Jews in the Socialist government of the early 1980s, including Robert Badinter, Jack Lang, the Communist transport minister Charles Fiterman, and the head of the CGT (the largest French union) Henri Krasucki—who were caricatured as cosmopolitan nomads, outcasts, and vagabonds. FN publicists viciously labeled the popular former minister of health, Simone Veil (an Auschwitz survivor), as "the abortionist," the perpetrator of the most "abominable" crime imaginable in Catholic France—and one laden with faint echoes of the deicide libel in the Middle Ages. For the past quarter of a century the FN built its chauvinist appeal on the rising challenge to French national identity posed by the multicultural society. FN supporters felt threatened by an uncontrollable North African immigration as well as the triple specter of Euro-federalism, American cultural imperialism, and excessive "Jewish" influence. Le Pen's movement could draw sustenance from the persistence of a quasi-fascist ideology dressed up as nationalism, which had deeply marked French culture for almost a century.[46]

But did Le Pen's relative success involve a return to the fascist spirit of the 1930s? At first glance, in the 1980s, nothing resembled the hysterical anti-Semitism rampant in the mass circulation French press only fifty years earlier. The murderous language that was publicly licensed throughout the Vichy era had been outlawed and placed morally beyond the pale. The debate over the demons of French anti-Semitism would, however, revive with a vengeance during the summer of 1990—following the macabre desecration of a Jewish cemetery in the southern French town of Carpentras. Then, as now, comparisons were made with the 1930s and the rise of French, Italian, and German fascism. Reassuring declarations were issued (including by the leaders of French Jewry) to the effect that "France was not an anti-Jewish country," even if it had rather a lot of anti-Semites.[47] In fact, some three hundred thousand people attended a huge protest demonstration against anti-Semitism and fascism in May 1990, including President François Mitterrand. During that same month, no fewer than 175 anti-Jewish incidents occurred (more than reported in any single month for the previous ten years). Throughout France, there were 372 known instances of anti-Semitism in 1990—with a particularly large number of cemetery desecrations in the weeks after Carpentras. There were also charges of cynical manipulation made against the Left, for using Carpentras as a political weapon to discredit the FN. The left-wing sociologist Paul Yonnet (who partly agreed with this assessment) even blamed the French Jews themselves for self-ghettoization "in a way that is racist towards non-Jews: they do not accept exogamous marriages, keep their schools for their own children." According to Yonnet, the publicity around Carpentras was highly suspect, and he criticized the media for the exaggeration surrounding "the real, but soft, antisemitism of Le Pen and the people who surround him."[48]

Though most of the French public was genuinely shocked by Carpentras, 35 percent agreed that "people should be able to openly express hostile attitudes to Jews" while 56 percent opposed this statement. A majority accepted that the FN was an anti-Semitic party, but 57 percent also felt it was "natural" that Le Pen take part in televised debates. Polls taken before and after Carpentras showed about 20 percent of the population agreeing that Jews wielded too much power in France.[49] (No less than 88 percent of participants at the FN congress of April 1990 held this anti-Semitic position!) It was also in 1990 that Le Pen repeated his repulsive remark, first made in 1987, that the gas chambers were a "mere detail [*un point de detail*] in the history of the Second World War."[50] In 1990 the FN once again began to renew its onslaught on "Jewish power": It evoked the preponderance of Jews in the French media and the transformation of anti-Semitism into a legal offense rather than a legitimate opinion. The FN also deplored the local influence of Franco-Jewish representative institutions such as CRIF and international "lobbies" such as B'nai B'rith. It was apparent from its well-produced journals *National Hebdo, Le Choc,* and *Présent* that "Judeo-Masonry was still up to its old tricks," that international Jewish capital controlled the French media, and that world pornography was "in the hands of the Jews."[51]

By the time of the 1992 regional elections, the FN was able to win 14 percent of the vote, thereby demonstrating an impressive progression since its extremely modest score of 0.35 percent in the first round of the 1981 parliamentary elections. The FN now had 239 regional councillors, along with a solidly implanted and structured organization across France. Within its ranks there was a complex ideological mix of integral Catholicism, "new Right" neo-paganism, militant populism, and (more conventionally) defecting conservative voters who deplored the French government's inability to control immigration or protect ordinary people from violence.[52]

For the past twenty-five years the radical Right has continued to represent between 12 and 20 percent of the French electorate, focusing electoral campaigns mainly against Arabs, Africans, and Third World immigration. The six million Muslims in France (from the standpoint of electoral expediency) represented a more visible fifth column and more obvious target for indigenous racist attack than six hundred thousand French Jews. Living in virtual ghettos, les Maghrébins (North African Arabs) could be more readily identified and linked to endemic social problems of law and order, drugs, prostitution, AIDS, urban decay—and especially unemployment.[53] Their challenge to the French ethnie (ethnic group) also appeared more palpable, augmented as it was by alarm at growing Islamicization in France and the threat of Muslim terrorism. Nevertheless, Jews, too, in the coded discourse of the French radical Right, clearly belong to l'étranger—the cosmopolitan, internationalist, and subversive forces of anti-France; they are still accused of controlling the mass media and the financial system, in addition to wielding excessive power in international and domestic French affairs.

Significantly, during the past decade, contacts between the FN and Muslim extremists in underprivileged urban suburbs have increased. At street demonstrations in Paris against the war in Iraq, for example, North African Arabs shouted "Death to the Jews, death to Israel." With Far Right militants they share the same mix of anti-Americanism; opposition to globalization; and hostility to French Jewry, Israel, and the war in Iraq.[54] On the radical Right, within the pro-Palestinian Left, and among such French Muslim leaders as Maurice Latrèche, anti-Semitic rants about Israel's "warmongering" role, the "Jewish lobby," and the "Judeo-Nazi Ariel Sharon" offered a mobilizing cause.

Anti-Semitism had also achieved something of a revival in the liberal center and on the left since the late 1970s, especially with the decline of French public support for Israel. *Le Monde,* the most prestigious French newspaper, has over several decades permitted a number of offensive articles that either hinted at or openly accused French Jews of dual loyalties.[55] A nasty example of this tendency was pointed out in 1981 by Simone de Beauvoir and Olivier Todd (then editor of *L'Express*) when *Le Monde* published an explicitly anti-Semitic contribution on its front page, only a few months after the rue Copernic bombing.[56] This piece was not an isolated case, especially during the First Lebanon War of 1982. Day after day there were mendacious reports about the imaginary Israeli "genocide" in southern Lebanon and fabricated atrocities splashed over the front pages of *Le Monde,* the leftist *Libération,* the hard-line Communist paper *L'Humanité,* and the Left-Catholic weekly *Témoignage Chrétien.*[57] In the early 1980s *Le Monde* provided a forum for French Holocaust denier Robert Faurisson to spout his poisonous witches' brew that exploited the fashionable wave of anti-Zionist rhetoric to call into question Hitler's genocide. The term "Zionists" had by then virtually become a synonym for monsters, killers, executioners, and even Hitlerites.[58] The supposedly critical French media was proving to be as susceptible to Orwellian Newspeak as their counterparts in the USSR and other authoritarian dictatorships. Even the moderate, pacifist, antitotalitarian Left seemed imprisoned in the myth that Israel was the only state in the world that had ever infringed international law.[59] This hostile atmosphere prompted the eminent French-Jewish philosopher Vladimir Jankélévitch (himself a man of the Left) to sharply condemn *Le Monde* for what he called its "sophistry," "bad faith," and responsibility for reawakening "the old demons" of anti-Semitism.

These charges appeared to be borne out by a full-page advertisement in the paper that appeared in March 1983, signed by Rev. Michel Lelong, a Catholic priest; Rev. Etienne Mathiot; and the ex-Marxist convert to Islam, Roger Garaudy. It seemed as though this disgraceful production had come straight out of the *Protocols of the Elders of Zion.* Under the pompous heading "The Meaning of the Israeli Aggression," it hysterically denounced "the extraordinary hegemony of the Zionist lobby over the world-wide media," summarily accused the Jewish state of racism, identified Judaism with tribalism, and implicitly called into doubt the 1965 Vatican declaration on relations with the Jews. None of the anti-Semitic slanders in the ad evoked any critical response from the Christian churches in France.[60] For its part, the vehemently anti-clerical Communist daily *L'Humanité* gratuitously evoked King Herod's "massacre of the innocents" (as recorded in the New Testament), calling it mild in comparison with the "murderous and genocidal operations launched by Israel." President Mitterrand, caught up in this witch-hunting mood in early July 1982, malevolently compared the Israeli bombardment of Beirut with the wartime Nazi mass murder of French civilians at Oradour-sur-Glane.[61]

During the 1980s, anti-Semitism itself began to be manipulated in the service of left-wing "antiracist" causes that equated the suffering of new Arab immigrants from French societal discrimination with the memory of the Vichy anti-Jewish persecutions. The slogans of SOS Racisme (affiliated with the French Socialist Party) marketed this totally misleading analogy between wartime eliminationist French anti-Semitism, which led to forced deportation and mass murder, and anti-Arab xenophobia in the 1980s and 1990s.[62] Arabs were even *encouraged* to compare themselves to Jews, thereby merely stimulating envy of Jewish success in achieving social integration, prosperity, and cultural and political influence. Anti-Semitism was reduced to the status of a metaphor, or mere subcategory of racism, losing its concreteness and specificity; the Shoah, too, was instrumentalized and ultimately turned against the Jews. At the same time, the expression of Jewish collective existence (especially in Zionism) was increasingly treated as something suspect and potentially racist.

Instead of being recognized as a real community, Jews were perversely being turned into symbols of desirable *victimhood*, providing they were sufficiently de-Judaized and dissociated from Israel. On the other hand, when the Jewish community or Israel itself evoked the Shoah, they were accused of taking part in "identity politics," and attacked for cynically exploiting misfortune for Israeli financial or political goals. Such reactions acted like a hall of distorting mirrors. In a highly caricatural manner these reactions reflected real changes in Jewish communal and political behavior that began with the massive immigration of Sephardic Jews from North Africa to France in the 1960s. The strong revival of ethnic and religious consciousness among the new Sephardi arrivals had indeed created a much larger, more vibrant, and ethnically conscious presence in France. This was a Jewish community determined to express itself with complete freedom and far less ready to absorb anti-Semitic insults than its Ashkenazi predecessors.[63]

"Communitarianism," in the sense of redefining French Jews (or any other minority, for that matter) as a community *apart*, has in recent years become one of the great catchphrases and accusatory reproaches in contemporary French discourse. In France, this notion has traditionally had a highly pejorative connotation of retreat into the closed "tribal circle," reflecting a narrow religious or ethnic identity—one that flies in the face of the republican state and its Enlightenment legacy. Yet, for a time in the 1990s it seemed that many different groups in French society were, in fact, keen to reemphasize *le droit à la difference*—to rediscover their communal roots—and a muted multiculturalism slowly began to make some headway in French political culture. Since 2001 the growing wave of anti-Semitic attacks has regrettably become a pretext for those seeking to condemn so-called excesses of Jewish (or Muslim) communal self-affirmation, or wishing to blame "inter-communal tensions," rather than Muslim aggression, for the dramatic rise in assaults on the Jewish community.[64]

"Communitarianism" has become *the* stigmatizing label. It is widely used as an insidious arm of intellectual intimidation, serving to politically delegitimize as "anti-republican" any coherent communal responses to the threats French Jewry must confront. Yet, in reality, most French Jews (like their American coreligionists) are far more individualist than communitarian. They are in favor of equal opportunity, rather than multiculturalism or the right to be different; they are supportive of the individual pact between the citizen and the state, rather than favoring a fragmented decentralized republic of ethnic communities. Hence, the charge of *communitarisme* is not only spurious but intellectually dishonest and politically motivated. What the anti-communitarians (many of them Jewish themselves) appear so upset about is the strong identification of French Jews with Israel. The mere fact of French Jews defending the existence of Israel as a Jewish state is seen as exclusivist, tribal, and even racist—an act deemed to be partisan and ethnically motivated. Behind such grossly misleading propositions that treat Zionism, pro-Israel sentiment, and *communautarisme* as synonymous, there lies a more insidious criminalization of Israel and a particularly sinister marginalization of French Jews as a community.[65] No less harmful has been the Manichean conceptual world of progressive antiracism, with its uncritical glorification of hybridized identities and cultures. For those who are hooked on the miracle-working properties of *métissage* (mixing, cross-breeding), the continued existence of Israel and the Jews is, at best, a dangerous anachronism.[66]

Since 2000, French Jews have increasingly felt that their current and future position in France is threatened and the republican pact imperiled. The injection of ethno-religious identity politics into the French electoral arena has contributed to this anxiety. In 2001, Pascal Boniface, director of the Institute for International and Strategic Relations in Paris, drafted a report for the French Socialist Party leadership that in effect advocated a change in Socialist strategy in order to win over French voters of Muslim background. Boniface argued that French Jewry, by linking its struggle against anti-Semitism with an "all-out defense of Sharon's Israel," had provoked public irritation and "isolated itself at a national level." It was time for the Socialists to pay serious attention to "the community of Arab and/or Muslim descent," which was already becoming more organized—"and in France at any rate it will soon yield enormous influence." This domestic political reality required a new Socialist policy that no longer sought a "balance between the Israeli government and the Palestinians" but instead took into account "electoral efficacy"—meaning the party should essentially adopt the views of French Muslims on the Middle East conflict.[67]

Boniface rejected any suggestion that this might imply complicity with anti-Semitism, instead accusing those who raised the issue of engaging in "intellectual terrorism." His book, *Est-il Permis de Critiquer Israël?* (Is it Permissible to Criticize Israel?) with its clearly provocative title, insisted that French Jews were no longer victims of discrimination; according to Boniface, they suffered far less from racist attacks than Arabs. This was, in fact, wholly untrue. Boniface also asserted—no less dishonestly—that Jews had twisted every criticism of Ariel Sharon's policy in the territories into an expression of anti-Semitism. Furthermore, he charged that Jews had deliberately encouraged an alarmist view of France by falsely comparing it to Europe in the late 1930s. Predictably enough, he dismissed the writings of French authors (especially Jews) who pointed out that there had been a rise in anti-Semitism in France.[68] By the same token he eagerly seized on misleading comments about the Shoah by nonspecialists such as Esther Benbassa—who had stridently attacked so-called communitarian Jewish intellectuals and Jewish leaders for serving Israeli interests by focusing on anti-Semitism as a problem.[69]

Boniface's strictures, given their intellectual mediocrity, would not be of much importance were it not for the rapid growth in the number of Muslims in France (predominantly from North Africa). Today they number between six and eight million people—more than 10 percent of the entire French population, a fact that has markedly changed the religious, cultural, and political geography of France. Mainly living in bleak and overcrowded *banlieues* (urban suburbs) that are seedbeds of violence, trapped in low-paid, unskilled jobs (with an unemployment rate more than twice the national average), these *Maghrébins* have brought with them a strong element of Islamic anti-Semitism and fundamentalism.[70] Such organizations as the Party of French Muslims have, for example, complained bitterly about so-called Jewish privileges in France. When protesting the ban on Islamic head scarves in French public schools, party leader Mohamed Latrêche accused former president Chirac of "doing everything" for Jews and "nothing for Muslims" and even attacked the newspaper *Le Monde* for being a "Zionist-controlled" daily![71]

Confusion and distrust in France have been exacerbated by the ghosts of the Algerian war fifty years ago and unresolved issues from that colonial past that continue to haunt the present. The Francophobia still present among part of the Maghrebi immigrant wave has readily spilled over into Judeophobic resentment. Blatant anti-Semitism is by no means representative of the French Muslim leadership as a whole, but it did not prevent Latrêche from achieving a high profile as a radical Muslim leader "of the suburbs." Based in Alsace, he demagogically played on Muslim resentments concerning the Middle East and their stigmatization and relative poverty in the ghettos. Latrêche questions the very existence of anti-Semitism, and maintains that, if it exists, then it is merely a "Zionist tool" (like the Holocaust) that has illegitimately usurped the central place that by right belongs to anti-Arab racism. The quibbling over words cannot, however, disguise the fact that at various demonstrations organized by Latrêche's movement in Paris and Strasbourg, the chilling cry of *Mort aux Juifs* (Death to the Jews) has been heard.[72]

Since September 2000, there have been many such anti-Israeli and anti-American meetings organized throughout France, often accompanied by anti-Jewish words or deeds.[73] In early October 2000, in the center of Lille, graffiti equating the swastika with the star of David filled the walls; in Nice there were bomb threats; and in Paris Molotov cocktails were thrown at a synagogue in the nineteenth arrondissement. The Muslim youth from the suburbs, which tend to identify with Islam more than with the republic, were not only responding to images of the Israeli-Palestinian conflict on their television screens. They clearly regard the Jews of France as a rich and powerful lobby and as part of an establishment that excludes them. Hence, it is no accident that the largest group of people implicated as known perpetrators of anti-Semitic acts in recent years are marginalized Muslims. They have been primarily responsible for the fires, bombs, graffiti, insults, and physical attacks against Jews on a scale not seen in France since the end of the World War II. It is essential to realize that such acts are *not* directed primarily at Israeli institutions but at *Jewish* targets—synagogues, Jewish community centers, Jewish schools, and individual Jews. Nevertheless, hostility to Israel and Ariel Sharon's policies often provides a cover, alibi, or pretext for perpetrating *anti-Jewish* violence.[74]

On October 7, 2000, the escalation had begun with a bomb directed at the Aubervilliers synagogue and an attack on the La Duchère synagogue in Lyon. In Paris, Arabs tried to force their way into several Jewish restaurants. The first wave of anti-Semitic attacks in France from the autumn of 2000 exceeded *all other acts of racist violence in France* by a margin of four to one. According to the Commission Nationale Consultative des Droits de l'Homme (CNCDH), there were 116 *serious anti-Jewish acts of violence* in 2000—virtually all of them occurring in the last four months of the year, compared to only thirty directed during the entire year toward *all* other groups. During the previous three years there had been just thirteen gravely anti-Semitic acts of violence (three in 1997, one in 1998, and nine in 1999); even during the First Persian Gulf War (1991), an earlier peak in the graph, there were no more than twenty-four such incidents. But a tremendous leap took place in 2000. Anti-Semitic verbal *threats* also reached a record high of 603, compared to only 119 of a more general racist and xenophobic nature, far outstripping similar acts against Arabs. Of *violent* anti-Jewish attacks, only two were identified as coming from the Far Right, exposing yet another cherished myth about contemporary sources of French anti-Semitism.[75] In October 2004, when the non-Jewish writer and physician Jean-Christophe Rufin presented his officially commissioned report to the French Ministry of the Interior, he cautiously noted some of these shifts and the link between social marginalization, radical Islam, and the spread of anti-Semitic violence in France. He also mentioned the troubling turmoil provoked in French schools by mounting anti-Semitic harassment.[76]

Nowhere, indeed, was the climate of physical and verbal violence more graphically revealed than in the lycées and schools of the Fifth Republic. An incident in a large Parisian secondary school in March 2002 involving twin sisters provides a small glimpse into what was happening almost daily across the country: For forty minutes the teenage girls had to endure a revolting torrent of insults ("Jew bitches," "Yids," "You're a slut as well as a Jew") and physical violence from a group of twelve students as their faces and clothes were coated with apple and cheese—because "Jews stink." Finally, the girls were ordered to kneel down and beg "forgiveness for being Jewish."[77] By early 2001 such anti-Semitic slurs had become so commonplace that they were being hurled by North African students at other pupils, teachers, and administrative personnel who were not even Jewish. In June 2001, in a suburb of Grenoble, a non-Jewish history teacher was abused and physically threatened as a *sale Juif* (dirty Jew) by his fifth-year students. In November 2001, in Villepinte (a northern suburb of Paris), a North African student shouted "*Mort aux Juifs*" (Death to the Jews) when a teacher passed by. Two months earlier, in Épinay-sur-Seine, a school principal was assaulted by parents who heaped anti-Semitic abuse on her, even threatening her with death. In February 2002, in Le Pré-Saint-Gervais, a Jewish youngster was viciously assaulted by a group of young Maghrebis, who held a knife to his cheek while flinging the usual racist insults at him. On May 21, 2002, two thirteen-year-old Jewish religious girls in a Paris suburb were beaten up by six Maghrebi girls. A month later, also in Paris, Jewish schoolchildren found themselves assaulted by twenty adolescents (mostly of Maghrebi origin). They were continuously insulted as "dirty Yids" and then severely beaten. For the most part such facts went unreported in the French press, and the perpetrators were rarely punished.[78]

The Maghrebi culture of hatred drew sustenance from the Nazi legacy. On November 28, 2002, in a Beaumarchais de Meaux secondary school, a young Jew was beaten up by a North African Arab schoolmate, apparently inspired by a history lesson about the mass murder of the Jews. At the Turgot School in Paris, nearly a month later, a Jewish student heard her Maghrebi classmate (who had just insulted her during a lesson) brazenly tell the teacher: "Hitler should have finished his work and exterminated you." On January 15, 2003, a terrified Jewish student at the Arago School in Paris was surrounded by some thirty young *Maghrébins* shouting "*sale Jude*" (dirty Jew), using the German word for Jew! On May 22, 2003, a Jewish public school teacher in the eighteenth arrondissement of Paris found, on the table of a Muslim student, graffiti describing her as a *sale Juive* (dirty

Jewess) with the macabre racist message: "We will burn you all, you arse-holes!" In another incident, a plastic arts teacher of Jewish origin in a fifth-year class of Maghrebi students was first subjected to an obscene torrent of abuse ("Fuck the Jews!" "Fuck Israel!" "Hitler was right, they should all be gassed!," and so on), and then, at the end of the lesson, pelted with paper pellets, erasers, pens, and anything else her students could lay their hands on, as she crouched behind her desk for protection.

Such violence seems, if anything, to be fed by history lessons about the Holocaust. A third-year student from Algeria in a Lyon suburb told his French teacher, "We like history at the moment because we're doing Hitler and he killed off many Jews. So we like him." A second student, in order to ram the message home, then shouted out "Death to the Jews!" Similarly, a French teacher and writer invited to a secondary school in the south of France recounted the following experience: "During a discussion of one of my novels about the Holocaust, a student asked me: 'What is your ethnic origin?' I answered: 'Jewish.' I then heard him say in a low voice: 'Bring on the guns!' " Even more revealingly, after a lesson on the Holocaust in a Parisian suburban school, a young Maghrebi shouted: "*Hitler aurait fait un bon musulman*" (Hitler would have made a good Muslim).[79] On February 27, 2003, a student in a working-class area of Paris heard this cry: "Jews, we will screw you, we will massacre you, you Yids [*youpins*], we will massacre you all!" In Lille, two months later, a young Jewish girl on her way to school was caught by a gang of four young Maghrebis, who yelled out as they slapped her, "Hitler did not finish what he began, but we will finish his work, and you will end up in the ovens."

Ever since the teaching of the Holocaust was first instituted in French schools in the early 1990s, there have been reports by teachers of Muslim students making obnoxious anti-Semitic remarks during history lessons. What were once merely isolated incidents, however, now assumed epidemic proportions, repeated week after week. The problem was not the lack of information or of exposure to the Nazi genocide. In early 2004 a Muslim teenager in the Val de Loire (central France), after visiting a Holocaust exhibit, wrote, "This is what we feel: 'the poor wretches,' especially [in] the crematoria, it's hot in there! Great, you couldn't escape. As for me, I'm doing well. Thank God! [*Alhamdulillah*]."[80] These and other similar comments suggest that far too many Maghrebi Muslim teenagers think of the Holocaust as nothing but the merited misfortune of the Jews; for some it is evidently a matter to rejoice over or something they dream of emulating. As the French historian Georges Bensoussan has aptly pointed out, Holocaust education has hardly stemmed the post-2000 wave of anti-Semitism in France: "It is [precisely] in the twenty year period which has seen a marked improvement in the teaching of the Holocaust in French schools, that anti-semitism has flourished as never before, adopting an outspoken virulence the likes of which have not been known in France since the Occupation and the Vichy regime."[81]

Learning about the Holocaust clearly does not prevent young Muslims from embracing a militant ethno-religious identity built on hatred of the West, France, and the Jews. This Islamist identity is derived in large measure from their cultures of origin, including a Koran-based hostility and contempt for Jews that, at best, regards them as *dhimmis* (protected persons) fated to be eternally subordinate to the rule of Islam. Jewish wealth and success in France, compared to their own marginal position in French society, is, therefore, all the more galling for the Maghrebis. But the victim status of Jews as a result of the Holocaust is doubly infuriating to a significant number of French Muslims, especially those who have been exposed to Salafist and radical preachers. They are as little inclined to listen empathetically to the story of Jewish persecution in Europe as they are interested in visiting churches and synagogues or hearing about the Crusades.

French universities, too, are by no means immune to the demonization of Israel, expressions of anti-Semitism, or anti-Western hatred. Thus, at the University of Paris X in Nanterre, the climate of verbal violence (anti-Semitic insults, threats, and sometimes blows) was palpable soon after the turn of the millennium. Radical pro-Palestinian propaganda and the stigmatization of Zionism are no less common at many other universities, as well, as they are among the intellectual, cultural, and media elites in general. After September 11, 2001, this trend was further reinforced by a rampant anti-Americanism. Among Muslim students, slogans such as "Death to the Jews" and "Death to the USA" soon began to proliferate alongside graffiti in the suburbs that read "Long live bin Laden!" The myth of a Jewish world conspiracy was also reinforced by the widespread belief among Arabs in France that Jews stood behind the 9/11 assault, just as they supposedly controlled the world media.[82] Hostility to the French state, the rejection of all authority, anti-Semitism, racist insults, offensive graffiti, and a heightened climate of aggression were all part of the general exultation felt by many young Muslims at news of the al-Qaeda attack on New York and Washington. In the face of these proliferating incidents, the academic and school authorities, like the French government, preferred to adopt a low profile and play down the violence. When it came to the "Palestinian question" and radical Islam, many teachers themselves wished to avoid trouble, and some even justified the militant attitudes of their Maghrebi pupils. Not surprisingly, then, the resistance to Islamic anti-Semitism was barely noticeable.[83]

Throughout 2001, denial of the existence of anti-Semitism in France was rampant. An early 2002 Sofres public poll of young people (fifteen to twenty-four years old) in France showed, however, that 35 percent of the Maghrebis considered Jews to have too much economic power, compared to 22 percent of all respondents. Thirty-eight percent of the young Maghrebis agreed that "Jews have too much influence in the media," compared to 21 percent in the general population. With regard to political clout, the difference was less striking, but when it came to "living with a Jew," three times as many Muslim Arabs rejected the idea, as compared to non-Muslims in France.[84] Georges Bensoussan has argued that this anti-Semitism is a function of the "traditional anti-Judaism in the Maghreb," quoting Magyd Cherfi, the lead singer of the Toulouse group Zebda, in January 2002, who admitted: "When I was young, we didn't like Jews. My parents were anti-Semitic, as people are in the Maghreb. The word 'Jew' in Berber is an insult. It was nothing to do with Palestine, or with politics, that's just how it was."[85]

This culture of hatred is indeed still virulent in Algeria and other parts of the Maghreb, where a *Protocols* vision of history is rife. According to Cherfi, anti-Semitic hatred in the Maghreb (especially Algeria) went back to the colonial situation and the perception of local Algerian Jews as having "succeeded," as being white and culturally French. Following their immigration to France, French Arabs like himself discovered a vicarious identity through the "Palestinian question." Suddenly they were "heroes" without doing anything.

There are causes, within the far Left milieu, which make you untouchable. . . . Palestine, Arabs in France [*les beurs*], they sometimes create unanimity. I am more pro-Palestinian now than I used to be, consciously, like an adult who has developed political thinking. They tell us about antisemitic incidents connected to the Intifada. I don't believe it. The Arabs

in France who attack Jews are uprooted but they do understand that antisemitism attracts the media. They are looking for the biggest transgression and that is it. But these attacks are not political or conscious. The
urban youth don't [even] know Palestine![86]

Cherfi added that Jewish leftists (and the French Left in general) "were
more radical than the *beurs*" and "more pro-Palestinian than the Arabs," as
if they felt personally responsible for the Middle East problem. Indeed, the
mobilization on behalf of the "martyred" Palestinians (in the Christian
rather than Islamic sense) on the French Left—among Third Worldists,
anti-globalists, Greens, neo-Communists, and new Leftists—has not
stopped for four decades. Equally, it has been accompanied throughout
(and more viscerally since 2000) by a seemingly endless stigmatization of
Israel and the Jewish community. The constant use of epithets such as
"racist," "fascist," "imperialist," or similar amalgams relating to Israel can
only incite toward hatred of Jews as Jews.[87] This anti-Jewish antiracism ultimately implies the destruction of the Israeli state, society, and culture—at
the very least an act of *politicide*—suggesting that Jews have no right to national self-determination as a people in their own land.

In France, the cult of the Shoah combined with Third Worldist anticolonialism has accentuated this trend since the 1970s. By sheer force of repetition, Israel has been turned into the incarnation of an almost
metaphysical injustice and evil. Significantly, the antiracist forces in France
have refused to see the struggle against anti-Semitism as a central part of
their own ideology, but instead they have gradually transformed opposition
to the Jewish state into a core theme of their so-called anti-fascism.[88]
Driven by the French intellectual mania for polarizing abstractions, extremist rhetoric, and an absolutist morality, the theoretical constructions of
the antiracist left have become more and more detached from reality with
the passage of time. The postwar impregnation of the French intelligentsia
by Marxism (Stalinist, Trotskyite, Althusserian), *gauchisme* (a semi-
anarchist leftism), existentialism, structuralism, postmodernism, and other
highly intellectualized ideologies, has only *aggravated* this tendency. Not
surprisingly, then, it was in France that a more intellectually coherent if perverse form of Holocaust denial emerged, in the Left as well as the Far Right,
closely connected to anti-Zionism.[89]

Pierre-André Taguieff, the leading French chronicler of these trends, pointed out in 2001 that the anti-Jewish amalgams that have proliferated in France since the turn of the millennium have encountered remarkably little resistance from the country's political and media elites. There were no great mass demonstrations protesting against racism and anti-Semitism, as had been the case after the Carpentras cemetery desecration in 1990;[90] no flamboyant public expressions of solidarity with the Jewish community of France; no nationwide mobilization. Yet the scale of the violent incidents, the burning of synagogues, and the level of insult were far greater after 2000 than they had been ten years earlier. This absence of response itself testified to a state of disorientation, confusion, and cumulative intoxication of minds that the anti-Zionist mythology had created, especially among the intellectuals. Israelophobia was the common banner uniting the militant Left, the Islamists, Franco-Palestinian organizations, the anti-globalists, and myriad antiracist groups.[91]

A sign of the times were statements by the notorious Venezuelan left-wing terrorist Carlos the Jackal (Illich Ramirez Sanchez), who nearly thirty years earlier had secretly converted to Islam in order to better implement his dream of world revolution. Carlos, speaking from his Paris prison, gave an interview in November 2001 praising the convergence of right-wing and left-wing extremism with radical Islam in order to battle "Yankee imperialism and Zionism," both of them qualified as "enemies of humanity." For Carlos, the jihad to liberate Palestine and the Holy Places (including Mecca and Jerusalem), as well as to bring down the American "hyper-power," was now redefined as a *sacred* cause demanding "heroic sacrifices" on the scale of 9/11. Submission to Allah's kingdom and the espousal of the pure Communist ideal had become identical for the imprisoned Carlos. Bin Laden was his model of the mujahid (holy warrior) struggling for universal liberation, which naturally required the eradication of Israel.[92] The anti-Semitic slogans chanted in antiwar demonstrations in the heart of Paris could be seen as anticipatory signs of the "Islamo-progressive" apocalypse still to come.[93]

The passions provoked by left-wing solidarity with the Palestinians and the rising Islamist wave seemed to have inexorably pushed anti-Israel sentiment into an unadulterated hatred of Americans and Jews.[94] Predictably enough, pro-Palestinian Trotskyist revolutionaries such as Daniel Bensaïd (himself a North African Sephardic Jew) blamed this state of affairs entirely on Jewish communal leaders. The "pyromaniac firemen" of French Jewry

had combined Judaism and Zionism to the point where any political struggle against Israeli occupation was liable to become Judeophobic. This claim
was, however, pure sophistry. Bensaïd, like many leftist French intellectuals,
was a priori convinced that Israel was a theocratic-ethnic state. He declared
that anti-Semitism was being exaggerated and that Arabs in France (as in
Palestine) remained the wholly innocent victims of the Middle East conflict. In reality, as a fellow socialist, Jacques Julliard, pointed out, such delusions were part of the betrayal by the French Left of its own secular,
antiracist principles.[95]

The blindness of many French intellectuals to the visceral reality of anti-
Semitism flowed in part, at least, from a profound distaste for anything
smacking of "judeocentrism" or "communitarization," and a politically correct compulsion to always insist on the priority of the *general* struggle
against racism, xenophobia, or Islamophobia.[96] It also reflected a disturbing
indifference within the wider French society to verbal or physical attacks on
Jews qua Jews. Conventional wisdom preferred to classify anti-Semitic violence as a manifestation of class war by poor people against rich bourgeois,
or as a regrettable symptom of urban anomie. This was, for example, the
simplistic view of the late Jean-Marie Cardinal Lustiger—the Jewish-born
archbishop of Paris.[97] Lustiger did at least react to the violence, however inadequate his analysis may have seemed. Within the French Catholic milieu,
the response was generally disappointing—ranging from deafening silence
to evasiveness and passivity. The question of Israel and Palestine had created a deep malaise. As the French socialist Euro-MP François Zimeray, observed: "I see how the Middle East events revived old anti-Semitic myths.
Every month, from session to session, Israel is judged, Israel is accused, Israel is sanctioned. Since Vatican II, it is no longer possible to say the Jews
killed Jesus, but it is possible to portray Israel and the Jews as the people
who . . . kill children in Bethlehem."[98]

Rev. Patrick Desbois, secretary of the Episcopal Committee for Relations
with Jewry, one of the rare Catholic voices to speak out openly about the
subject, added his own personal gloss:

> The new credo of anti-Semitism is that Jews are, first of all, crucifying the
> poor rather than Jesus, and second, that they are taking the land. Whereas
> a century ago Jews were accused of trying to take over countries like
> France and Poland, today they are accused of trying to control the Pales-

tinians' land. The percentage of anti-Semites in Europe is now the same as right after World War II.[99]

The anti-Semitic wave of the past seven years brought to an end the golden age of postwar French Jewry—a community unique in Europe both for having doubled its Jewish population since 1945 and for achieving a cultural revival of impressive dimensions. The destruction by arson of the synagogue of Villepinte in northeast Paris on October 3, 2000, was the first such occurrence since the Middle Ages, if we exclude one such case in Nazi-occupied Strasbourg. It might be taken as a symbolic turning point and the beginning of a new era. Over the next ten days, four more synagogues would burn across the Greater Paris region, while there were at least another twenty such attempts at arson directed against Jewish buildings, homes, businesses, and other synagogues. Throughout October 2000 there were further incidents of vandalism, desecration, and anti-Jewish violence (from stone throwing to personal assaults), especially in mixed neighborhoods with Jewish and Muslim residents. Among the victims of such attacks was a rabbi in Créteil, a young Jew in Belleville, female synagogue worshippers in Lyon, Orthodox pupils in the thirteenth arrondissement of Paris, and young Jewish children in Lille. Graffiti reading "*À mort les juifs*" (Death to the Jews), "*Les Juifs au four*" (Jews to the oven), and "*Les Juifs sont des meurtriers*" (Jews are murderers) became commonplace across the country, along with such inscriptions as "*Vive la Palestine*" and "*Vive les Arabes*," sometimes accompanied by swastikas.[100] Further peaks of anti-Jewish violence occurred after the 9/11 terrorist attack on the United States and during Passover 2002 with the Israeli military Operation Defensive Shield in the Palestinian territories. Unfortunately the racist perpetrators were not tracked down vigorously, and the French judges frequently handed down derisory sentences for those who were actually brought to court.

In February 2002, the head of CRIF, Roger Cukierman, sent a searing open letter to President Chirac about French official passivity and the politics of denial—a protest that was published in *Le Monde*:

The leaders of the country like to play down anti-Jewish acts. They prefer to see these as ordinary violence. We are deluged with statistics designed to show that an attack against a synagogue is an act of violence and not

anti-Semitism. Some Jews who have lost touch with reality like to buttress their personal status by turning a deaf ear and a blind eye to danger,
in order to curry favor with the public consensus. . . . Judicial authorities
don't like to mete out strong punishment for acts of anti-Jewish violence,
even when the perpetrators are caught red-handed: . . . Why this laxness?
Because this violence, perpetrated by only one side, is linked to the conflict in the Middle East. Because too often Jew and Israeli mean the same
thing. . . . Because the Muslim population is all-important. . . . Once
again, we are the scapegoat. . . . It's a part we are no longer prepared to
play.[101]

President Chirac was not amused. He was still smarting from undiplomatic comments by an Israeli deputy minister, Michael Melchior, in January 2002, that France was the "most anti-Semitic country in Europe."[102] He
now warned French Jews that any effort "to give too strong an echo to anti-
Semitic incidents could only rebound against the Jewish community."[103]
This was a strangely discordant note for Chirac, since as mayor of Paris, he
had shown considerable sensitivity to Jewish concerns. In July 1995 he had
been the first head of state to accept French co-responsibility for the extermination of the Jews, putting an end to Mitterrand's earlier evasiveness
over the place of Vichy in the history of France. In March 1997 he had welcomed Jewish leaders to the Elysée Palace to express "the gratitude of our
nation for all that the Jewish community has contributed and is contribut-
ing to it." Chirac deliberately highlighted the "successful commitment" of
Jews "to serving France and the Republic while adhering to their own values
and faith"—praising the community's strong republican identification.[104]
He recalled his own insistence on formally acknowledging the responsibility of the French state "in the arrest, deportation, and death of thousands
upon thousands of Jews." It was also Chirac who had formally dedicated the
new Musée d'Art et d'Histoire du Judaïsme in the Marais quarter of Paris—
the largest such museum of Jewish history and art in Europe—one financed
by the French state and the city of Paris.[105]

Four months later Chirac found himself unexpectedly facing Jean-Marie
Le Pen (who had beaten Socialist prime minister Lionel Jospin) in the second round of the presidential elections. Chirac won barely 20 percent of the
vote in the presidential first-round elections. Le Pen had obtained 17 percent of the national vote in that opening round on a program of combating

criminality, establishing law and order, and opposing accelerated European integration, while sharply denouncing uncontrolled immigration. The anti-Semitism traditionally linked to his movement had little, if anything, to do with the burning of synagogues and violence against Jewish institutions during the previous eighteen months. Le Pen did, however, benefit from the political indifference of the electorate, the endemic divisions on the left, and the general sense of insecurity widespread among French voters, which left them vulnerable to his xenophobic appeals. In Provence, Le Pen did especially well: high rates of crime and unemployment, a large population of brown-skinned immigrants, *pieds noirs* (white European settlers who had fled Algeria forty years earlier), and unruly *beur* (Muslims of North African descent) youngsters played into his hands.[106] In the city of Marseille (France's second largest city), where one in four residents are Muslim, Le Pen finished first with 23 percent of the vote against 18 percent for the incumbent President Chirac. His toughness on crime explained this success, as much as local factors and fervent nationalism. He even attracted a small group of French Jews into his ranks. Le Pen sought to woo Jewish voters by condemning anti-Semitism and expressing understanding for Israel's crackdown on the West Bank. Two years later, he appointed a Sephardic Jewish woman, Sonia Arrouas, as his running mate in the Provence-Alpes–Côte d'Azur regional elections. Her campaign letter argued that only Le Pen "can put an end to the authorities' incompetence in the face of anti-Semitic aggression."[107] Le Pen's daughter Marine even claimed that Jews were beginning to perceive the FN differently: "They understand that the real danger for them lies in the [Arab] immigration. The Jews are being forced to take the aggression and racism of the immigrants twice—once for being French, and again for being Jews."[108]

In a debate in January 2008 with the Swiss Islamist ideologue Tariq Ramadan, Marine Le Pen insisted that if immigration continued unchecked, Europe would soon turn into an "Islamic Republic" while the French cultural and historic identity would be extinguished. At the same time she appeared to repudiate the blunt hostility to Jews and Muslims that had characterized her father's political positions.

Nevertheless, neither anti-Semitism nor Holocaust denial has disappeared from the FN's repertoire. For example, in September 2004, the party's second in command, Bruno Gollnisch, a professor at the University of Lyon and FN regional councilor of Rhône-Alpes for many years, questioned yet again the outcome of the Nuremberg trials and the number of Holocaust victims. In the past Gollnisch had supported Le Pen's dismissal of the gas chambers as a "point of detail" in the history of World War II, also praising negationists Robert Faurisson and Bernard Notin—both of them academics from his own University of Lyon. He had attacked the Klaus Barbie trial as a *procès spectacle* (show trial) in 1987 and for two decades had opposed all legislation restricting the freedom of expression of Holocaust deniers. For Gollnisch and an important part of the FN, the right to Holocaust negation had become a battle for freedom of speech against obscurantism, intolerance, and repressive legal practices.[109]

Though condemned by the more liberal-minded Marine Le Pen for having "opened old wounds" and seeming to confirm that the FN is indeed an anti-Semitic movement, Gollnisch nonetheless retained the confidence of his party. Evidently, Jean-Marie Le Pen also agreed with his deputy more than with his daughter, since in an interview with the anti-Semitic weekly *Rivarol* on January 7, 2005, the FN leader was quoted as saying: "In France, at least, the German occupation was not particularly inhumane, even if there were a few blunders, which is inevitable in a country of 550,000 square kilometers."[110]

Naturally, Le Pen had nothing to say about the eighty thousand Jews deported from France (including twelve thousand children), many of them to Auschwitz, who presumably did not count at all. This obscene declaration confirmed Le Pen's repellent indifference to Nazi barbarity, to the Holocaust victims, and to historical truth. Not surprisingly, then, during the presidential elections of 2007, the FN leader publicly deplored Chirac's recognition (twelve years earlier) of French responsibility for the deportation of the Jews. According to Le Pen, this had been a scandalous concession that unjustifiably tainted the French national image.[111]

Despite their extremism, many of Le Pen's ideas on immigration and law and order had become much more acceptable by 2006, influencing political discourse. Nicolas Sarkozy, then interior minister, zeroed in, for example, on the problem of polygamous African families and the need for tighter immigration controls and for expelling illegal immigrants. It was evident that far more than the 4.6 million French voters who supported Le Pen for the presidency in 2002 agreed with the FN's trademark themes—no less than 63 percent concurring that there were too many immigrants in France. Another poll in 2006 showed that one in three French people unabashedly considered themselves "racist."[112] It is worth noting that Sarkozy's campaign for the presidency adopted similar language to Le Pen on certain issues, inter alia calling those who rioted across France in November 2005 *la racaille* (thugs) and vowing to purge crime-ridden housing projects. This strategy paid off handsomely for Sarkozy in the April 2007 presidential elections. Le Pen finished in fourth place with 3,835,000 votes (10 percent)—1,000,000 fewer than in 2002. The FN leader also paid the price of overpolishing his image as a republican democrat, even flirting with Muslim immigrants at the expense of his hard-core white working-class electorate. His forty-year-old daughter Marine has continued this policy, provoking the resignation of hard-line campaigners like the pampheleteer Alain Soral and before him Jacques Bompard and the Catholic traditionalist leader Bernard Antony.[113]

Le Pen's tactical blunder during the elections was ably exploited by Sarkozy—who held high the tricolor, promised to strengthen French national identity and limit immigration, and denounced the fetishists of "human rights" who blithely ignored questions of personal security. In effect, Le Pen was outpenned and outgunned by the inheritor of the Gaullist mantle, himself a child of an immigrant family of Hungarian, Greek, and Jewish background. Perhaps the biggest irony in Le Pen's decline was the ardent support that this Islamophobe demagogue received from anti-Semitic Muslim circles. Radio Islam, for example, issued an appeal to the Muslims of France to vote for Le Pen because he was an ardent French patriot, an ally of the Arab world, and an enemy of the Zionist Jews who "held power in France," along with their Socialist and Freemason allies.[114]

After Sarkozy's electoral victory and his appointment of Socialist Bernard Kouchner as foreign minister, radical Islamist sources poured out their vitriolic anti-Semitic bile without restraint. They painted the new French president as the purest product of a Judeo-Masonic sect from Thessaloníki with a maternal grandfather who had been a "fanatical Zionist." Vilified as a cynical opportunist and a "racist Talmudic Jew" who totally supported the Zionist "butchers," Nicolas Sarkozy was the incarnation of Satan. Alongside France's first "Jewish president," Kouchner, too, was execrated as a "bellicose Jew" who had supported the invasion of Iraq, backed George W. Bush, and favored the illegal Jewish occupation of Palestine along with the "extermination" of all Arab resistance. According to the Islamist websites, the half-Jewish Kouchner had only been installed to head the Quai d'Orsay as a result of relentless Israeli pressure and the intervention of the Jewish lobby in France. The muckraking journalist Pierre Péan added his own vitriolic indictments in 2009, presenting Kouchner as the representative of "Anglo-Saxon cosmopolitanism," neocon adventurism, liberal capitalism, and a counterfeit *droits-de-l'hommisme* (the ideology of human rights). Kouchner, like Sarkozy, had sold out French interests to his Atlanticist proclivities and exploited his African connections for personal profit. He was the pro-American, pro-Israeli embodiment of "Anti-France."[115]

This discourse is today found on the Far Right, the radical Left, and among the Islamists. France, as the largest Muslim state of the European Union, is especially exposed to such influences, often linked with the Muslim Brotherhood and other branches of fundamentalist Islam. In its Algerian variant (the Islamic Salvation Front), the Islamists have combined anti-French xenophobia with anti-Zionism, anti-Semitism, and a visceral rejection of the kind of hybridized "modernity" associated with the West.[116] Since Algerian and other Maghrebi Muslims see France as a key crossroads for international Zionism (from which it supposedly threatens the world of Islam), the war of cultures that has unfolded on its soil is particularly intense. For the Algerian Islamists, "the Jews are everywhere hatching their plots"—hence the only possible relationship with them is one of jihad, which must bring down the core institutions of the republic. The Jews (together with Freemasons) are deemed to be behind liberal democracy and "secularism" (the dominant religion of the French Republic)—hence they are marked as the biggest current threat to authentic, hard-core Islam.[117] In this worldview the call to jihad is frequently connected with the presumed existence of a global conspiracy in which Jewry controls the banking structures and financial system of the West.[118] The Jews are often portrayed as part of a monstrous imperialist or Crusader plot against Islam, in which the State of Israel plays a central role. The Algerian-born, Syrian-trained, Strasbourg imam Mohamed Latrêche, who founded the Parti Musulman de France, is a good example of this Islamic demonization of Jews. In Paris and Strasbourg he has held several rallies in which representatives of Hamas and Hezbollah also participated, calling for the boycott of all Jewish-owned enterprises and those believed to be "under Jewish control."[119]

Nevertheless, the percentage of Muslims identifying with fundamentalism is much lower in France than in Great Britain. Far more French Muslims regard their French identity as *primary* than do their counterparts in Germany, Spain, or the United Kingdom. A relatively low percentage (28 percent) see any conflict between being devout Muslims and living in a modern society, and a majority believe that democracy can work in Muslim countries. On the other hand, nearly half of French Muslims (46 percent) refused to admit that Arabs carried out the 9/11 attacks, while as many as one-third thought that violence against civilian targets could be justified in certain circumstances.[120] The anti-Israeli obsession remains widespread, especially on the Islamic websites that relentlessly Nazify the Jewish state while presenting Muslims worldwide as victims of multiple Holocausts at the hands of the "secular, racist, and anti-Islamic West." Classic themes of Holocaust denial are also omnipresent, along with conspiracy theories about the role of the Israeli Mossad in the 9/11 massacre and a seemingly unrestrained contempt for America. No less typical for such Islamic sites as Quibla.com or Stcom.net is the ongoing denial of anti-Semitism in France. The sites consider such attacks an invention and attribute them to Zionist machinations and a deliberate Jewish disinformation campaign. The main objective of the Zionists, they maintain, is to create a diversion in France from Israeli repression of the Palestinians and to discredit French Muslims, per se. Additional goals are to silence all criticism of Israel and encourage the *aliyah* (immigration) of French Jews to the Zionist state. Not surprisingly, therefore, the Islamist websites have been thoroughly impregnated with a *Protocols of Zion* vision of the world, reinforced by a Manichean representation of the Middle East conflict as a battle between the Zio-Nazi "Goliath" and the Palestinian "David." Third Worldist Islamism fuses with an ideologically driven Judeophobia focused on the "Palestinian question."[121]

Muslim anti-Semitism in France has been strongly affected over the past nine years by the spillover effect of foreign conflicts as well as by the relationship between the various communities on French soil. Decolonization, the mass migration of Jews and Arabs from the Maghreb to France, and the politicization of ethnic identities have steadily exacerbated tensions since 1967, despite repeated attempts at interfaith dialogue. The conciliatory efforts of moderates, including the Algerian-born rector of the Paris Mosque, Dalil Boubakeur, have been handicapped not only by external factors but by internal challenges to the very notion that Muslims must adapt themselves to French values or show unconditional loyalty to the French state. The truth is that growing numbers of the present-day radicalized generation tend to identify with the transnational Islam of the Tabligh and the Muslim Brotherhood—a *political* Islam that is often virulently anti-Western and anti-Semitic.

Moreover, though French Muslims tend to see Westerners more positively than their coreligionists elsewhere in Europe, they increasingly suffer from the negative effects of discrimination and high unemployment. Their integration is no less undermined by their own aloofness from mainstream society and increasing religious assertiveness. The demographic transformation (from one hundred thousand Muslims in France in 1945 to eight million today) allied to poverty, violence, and crime make this issue a ticking time bomb.[122] Hence, French Jews, outnumbered ten to one by the growing Muslim population, naturally regard the nonintegration of the newcomers as a special danger. The growth of the Salafi movement in French Islam (financed by Saudi Arabia)—with its self-segregation and strict adherence to the sharia—is particularly worrying, given its religious hostility to both Jews and Christians. There is no doubt that Salafist imams and populist agitators in the suburbs of French cities continue to preach an Islamist form of Judeophobia and contempt for Christianity as part of their anti-Western fundamentalist propaganda.[123]

A more commercially oriented, if no less virulent form of prejudice is represented by Tawfik Mathlouthi, the owner of Radio Méditerranée—a station that broadcasts to about six hundred thousand listeners a day, mainly French people of Arab descent. On Radio Méditerranée, the word "Israel" is never pronounced, only delegitimizing references to "the Zionist entity." According to Mathlouthi, the term "Israel" historically represents divine prophecy and is therefore inappropriate for "Zionist people who are terrorists and criminals," and have "no legal right to exist."[124] Mathlouthi made a fortune by founding Mecca Cola as part of his boycott of American and Israeli products. He claimed the soft-drink manufacturer sold more than 165 million gallons of the cola in the first year of production. Mecca Cola's protest slogan, "*Ne buvez pas idiot, buvez engagé*" (Stop drinking stupidly, drink with commitment), was presented as a soft form of anti-American struggle and commercial opposition to the "Jewish lobby."[125] For Mathlouthi, all French politicians from the Right and Left (especially the Socialists) were in the clutches of the Zionist lobby, which supposedly explained French preoccupation with anti-Semitism rather than Islamophobia.

Much more sophisticated than Mathlouthi is the forty-five-year-old Swiss-born Arab Islamic philosopher Tariq Ramadan—the maternal grandson of Hassan al-Banna, supreme guide and founder of the Muslim Brotherhood in Egypt. Tariq's father, Said Ramadan (al-Banna's son-in-law and favorite disciple), had established the Muslim Brotherhood's network in Europe during the 1950s with the help of Saudi money and patronage.[126] Tariq has continued their missionary impulse, authoring twenty books and a constant stream of articles and audiotapes, in order to spread the Islamist message, while also taking to TV and the Web. Outwardly, he preached obedience to the laws of the European society in which Muslims found themselves, even declaring that Islam was "completely compatible with the separation of Church and State." Though he resided in Geneva, Tariq Ramadan's shadow has fallen heavily across the French intellectual and political landscape. For some he was the "Muslim Luther," advocating the reform of Islam. It was this misleading reputation that led to his invitation to Notre Dame University and the subsequent revocation of his visa request to the United States because of suspected links with Islamic terrorism.[127] However, despite his claims to encourage rationalism, he clearly belonged to the Salafi stream of revolutionary fundamentalism associated with Hassan al-Banna, Sayyid Qutb, and Abu al-A'la-Mawdudi, all of whom had strongly opposed Western individualism and liberal reformism as the antithesis of Islam. As the Egyptian journalist Adel Guindy noted in October 2005, Tariq Ramadan's ideas were perfectly consistent with those of the Muslim Brotherhood, even if his Islamism had a Western dress.

The key to understanding Ramadan is to decode his doublespeak— a prudent strategy based on the dissimulating Arabic principle of *taqiyya* (hiding one's true belief out of fear it will be repressed). In the context of France and other Western democracies, doublespeak is intended to secretly advance long-term goals without arousing undue suspicions. Thus, the Union of Islamic Organizations of France could publicly denounce suicide bombings while its fatwa council simultaneously legitimized them. Ramadan, too, could deplore the 9/11 attacks but cast doubt on the fact that Arabs carried them out; he could condemn terror but support *muqawama* (resistance), which in practice was the same thing. He could seem to criticize Palestinian terrorist killings of Israeli civilians but then suggest that they had no other choice.[128] Jihad was, by implication, acceptable as "legitimate" defense in struggles against oppression—whether in Iraq, Palestine, or Chechnya.[129] Ramadan's position on integration was equally ambiguous, appearing to give equal weight to the terms "French" and "Muslim," but in effect saying that Muslims could respect secular laws only "if they do not contradict any Islamic principle." The ultimate goal was to create "an alternative Islamic European culture that is clean of all non-Islamic influences"—not to accept the Western separation of religion and politics. In Ramadan's worldview there is no place for the modernization of Islam, but only for the Islamicization of modernity.

Ramadan is generally more attractive to educated but confused young Muslims in France, rather than to the urban poor in the suburbs or the older first generation of immigrants. His discourse, appealing to the desire for respectability and dignity, relies on a traditionalist approach to Islam, open to universal values but sharply rejecting Western materialism and global capitalism. What links him to the anti-globalists is precisely his hostility to neoliberal economics, as embodied in the International Monetary Fund and the World Bank.[130] Ramadan's "Islamic socialism" undoubtedly facilitated his patronage by neo-Communist, Trotskyist, and Third Worldist circles in France, beginning with his friend the left-wing editor in chief of *Le Monde Diplomatique*, Alain Gresh—himself an Egyptian Jew by origin.[131]

Ramadan's mastery of doublespeak extends to anti-Semitism. In December 2001 he published a laudable article in *Le Monde* taking to task Muslim preachers who allowed themselves to be carried away by anti-Semitic hate speech. He also criticized those misled youths who had engaged in violent acts against Jewish institutions. Ramadan qualified anti-Semitism as "unacceptable and indefensible," contrary to Islam and to the teachings of the Prophet. He called for respect toward Judaism, honoring the memory of the Holocaust, and recognizing the spiritual tie between Jews and Muslims. He strongly opposed the sense of victimization felt by many marginalized Muslims.[132] At the same time, Ramadan attacked Ariel Sharon and those Jews (religious and secular) who remained silent in the face of unjust Israeli policies. In April 2002, Ramadan was also among the fifty-seven Muslim, Christian, and Jewish signatories to a petition "to stop the fighting"—an appeal that regretted the fact that "the Israeli-Palestinian war has awakened criminal tendencies in France that endanger human lives and places of worship, including Jewish synagogues."

Ramadan's article and his subsequent position in an interview with Israeli daily newspaper *Haaretz* seemed on the surface to be rational and even enlightened. Leaders and imams, he repeated, had a responsibility to educate Muslims against anti-Semitism, whatever the feelings of anger and frustration among Muslim youth resulting from their economic distress or bitterness toward Israel. He insisted that it was perfectly possible to be against Israeli policy in Palestine and (as a matter of conscience and ethics) to "evince special sensitivity to the Holocaust." But it was categorically not admissible to exploit this tragedy to justify oppressive actions "which many define as State terror against the Palestinian people." A frank and serious dialogue between Jews and Muslims was indeed urgent but "the self-criticism must be mutual." Questioned about his well-known admiration for his grandfather Hassan al-Banna (who had been murdered by Egyptian government agents in 1949), Ramadan misleadingly called him a "reformist." Aware that al-Banna had totally rejected Israel, Ramadan cautiously hinted that his own opinions were more appropriate to a "different era and a different historical context."[133]

However, in September 2003, the Islamist Internet site Oumma.com posted a text by Ramadan that had previously been turned down by Le Monde and Libération entitled "Critique of the [new] communitarist intellectuals." In this highly polemical attack, Tariq Ramadan singled out a number of "French Jewish intellectuals" including Pierre-André Taguieff, Bernard-Henri Lévy, André Glucksmann, Alain Finkielkraut, Bernard Kouchner, and Alexandre Adler, for acting as knee-jerk defenders of Israel. They had thereby "relativized the defense of universal principles of equality and justice." If these would-be cosmopolitan Jews had, at one time, seemed to be "universalist intellectuals," they were now exposed as being no more than servile apologists for Ariel Sharon.

Ramadan's assertions were, in fact, grossly inaccurate. Taguieff, the first target on Ramadan's list, was not even a Jew, though he was France's preeminent scholar of anti-Semitism. A secular republican historian of ideas, he considered militant Islam to be a serious danger to French democratic values. Former health minister Bernard Kouchner, a socialist, and the ex-Maoist philosopher André Glucksmann had been very active in trying to stop the mass killings in Rwanda and the massacres of Muslims in Bosnia and Chechnya; they had never been remotely involved in Jewish communal affairs, nor were they even known as defenders of Israel, though they had been supportive of the American invasion of Iraq—something that Bernard-Henri Lévy had, in fact, opposed, contrary to Ramadan's claims.

Glucksmann was brief though trenchant in his reply to Ramadan, writing: "What is surprising is not that Mr. Ramadan is anti-Semitic, but that he dares to proclaim it openly." Alain Finkielkraut pointed out that if Ramadan's hit list of "Jewish intellectuals" had been published by Le Pen, there would have been a universal explosion of outrage.[134] Instead, the grandson of Hassan al-Banna had become a celebrity, invited to the popular TV talk show of Thierry Ardisson, *Tout le monde en parle.* Not only that, but the anti-globalist European Social Forum in November 2003 publicly hailed Ramadan as a precious Islamist ally, despite his communitarist insistence that the movement accept Muslim specificity. Ramadan's attack on French Jewish intellectuals and his blaming of the Iraq War on Paul Wolfowitz (a "notorious Zionist") and other neocon, "pro-Likud" American Jews was hardly a problem for most of his anti-globalist friends. Their unconditional pro-Palestinian positions, reinforced by radical anti-Americanism, anti-Zionism, and a transparent desire to win over young Muslims, made them only too willing to ignore the anti-Semitic implications of Ramadan's remarks. Bernard-Henri Lévy deplored this uncritical "libertarian" reflex. He observed that Ramadan had crudely attacked his book on the assassination of Daniel Pearl in Karachi, as if it were part of a pro-Sharon plot to discredit Pakistan and an attempt to justify an Indian-Israeli alliance. Such absurd conspiracy theories were all too reminiscent of the *Protocols of the Elders of Zion.*[135]

Ramadan's assault on those he considered as Zionist intellectuals in France was consistent with his deep personal and ideological roots in the anti-Semitic Muslim Brotherhood. As a theologian and as a preacher he owed much of his teaching to the Muslim Brothers—an elitist, fundamentalist organization born in Egypt that had subsequently spawned every important Sunni Islamist group of the past eighty years, from al-Qaeda to Hamas. The Muslim Brotherhood had been anti-Western, anti-secular, anticommunist, and anti-Semitic ever since the late 1920s. A kind of Islamic cross between Opus Dei and the Bolshevik Party, the Egyptian core of the Brotherhood had been heavily involved in the war for Palestine before 1948, in the political struggle against British imperialism, and in ideological opposition to the "materialist atheism" of the Soviet Union. Tariq Ramadan (following his father and grandfather) is the lineal and ideological heir of this tradition, even when adopting as cover a gentler, more "modern" and quasi-socialist language to defend his Muslim identity politics.

Ramadan's attitude toward the Jewish state is ultimately an updated, more sophisticated version of the Muslim Brotherhood ideology, which presupposes that Israel will disappear to be replaced by a single state—nominally respecting the equality of all its citizens but Islamic in its essence.[136] Like that of the most influential spiritual authority in the contemporary Muslim Brotherhood, Youssef al-Qaradawi, Ramadan's position does not oppose or exclude terrorist violence against the Israeli occupation.[137] It is worth noting that in a March 2003 sermon in Qatar (widely circulated on Francophone Islamist websites), Qaradawi had called the American-led war against Saddam Hussein a Zionist plot: "Look for the role of Israel and Zionism behind the recent events [the destruction of Iraq] and you will see their invisible hand intervening in a great number of these affairs." The anti-Semitic concept of a so-called Jewish war in Iraq (reminiscent of fascist and pro-Nazi propaganda in the late 1930s) has indeed become common ground for Islamists, pacifists, and anti-globalists in France—as it had been elsewhere in Western Europe—ever since the great antiwar demonstrations of 2002.

Ramadan's influence on Muslim youth in France could not have happened without the self-imposed *dhimmitude* of Europe—a posture of cringing anticipatory appeasement when confronted by Islamist self-assertion. It presupposed a debilitating and one-sided belief in multicultural diversity that eroded any prospect of robustly defending Western values and the foundations of a coherent national identity. Self-abasement and post-colonial guilt only encouraged more and more aggressive responses. For example, Muslim organizations and the League of the Rights of Man took the French novelist Michel Houellebecq to court for calling Islam a "stupid" and "dangerous" religion. Like the Italian author Oriana Fallaci before him, Houellebecq won his case, but the intimidatory effect was palpable. The director of the satirical journal *Charlie Hebdo,* Philippe Val, was also subjected to a court case and personal harassment for reproducing some of the Danish caricatures of the Prophet Muhammad.[138]

Even more chilling was the scandal involving the article of well-known French philosopher Robert Redeker—a member of the editorial board of *Les Temps Modernes,* which had been founded by Jean-Paul Sartre. The piece was entitled "In the Face of Islamist Intimidation, What Must the Free World Do?" and it had been published as an op-ed in *Le Figaro* in September 2006. Redeker described the Koran as "a book of extraordinary violence." The Prophet Muhammad appeared in its pages as a polygamist, a warlord, a looter, and a leader who had ordered the massacre of Jewish tribes. Redeker plausibly considered that in comparison with Jesus, who was "a master of love," the Prophet of Islam was *un maître de haine* (a master of hatred). He deplored the fact that Islam was trying to impose its rules on Europe, "demanding that swimming pools adopt special hours for women only and forbidding caricatures of Muhammad." As with Communism in the past, Europe now found itself under "ideological surveillance," and even Pope Benedict XVI had been subjected to serious intimidation for making an indirect criticism of Islam.[139] Following this expression of a perfectly legitimate and widely held opinion, Redeker was subject to a battery of emails and postings on Islamist websites, threatening him and his family with death; as a result he was forced to leave his home, give up his teaching position, and go into hiding.

For some on the Far Left (especially the Trotskyists), the Redeker affair reduced itself to an effort by "reactionary politicians" to create a mood of hysteria around Islamofascism. The Communist mayor of Saint-Orens-de-Gameville (where Redeker had taught high school) focused his anger not on the outrageous death threats but on the trivial fact that the philosopher had listed his affiliation at the end of the article. Worse still, the two largest French teachers' unions (both of them socialist) ostentatiously emphasized their disagreement with Redeker's views, while the leading human rights organizations condemned his "irresponsible statements." In the media, prominent figures, including Jean-Pierre Elkabbach, called on Redeker to apologize; *Le Monde* thought his remarks about Muhammad were "blasphemous" and his piece "misleading and insulting." True, a small group of intellectuals (including the same "Jewish" trinity denounced by Ramadan— namely Lévy, Finkielkraut, and Glucksmann) protested against this new form of totalitarianism in the name of France's "most fundamental liberties." Prime Minister Dominique de Villepin declared that a fatwa directed against any French intellectual was unacceptable, and Interior Minister Sarkozy described "those threatening the philosophy teacher" as being "in contempt of the rules of democracy and the Republic." The Far Right leader Philippe de Villiers, who had previously warned against the Islamicization of France, was also supportive. Nevertheless, much of the French establishment and media offered only tepid responses, obviously fearing to touch the hot potatoes of Islam, race, and religion.[140]

The Redeker affair occurred exactly one year after riots and protests in French cities had rocked the republic. Once again, the violence came from the ghettos—bleak housing estates that encircle French cities—places with excessive crime rates and sky-high unemployment of around 40 percent in the so-called sensitive urban zones. These ghettos are predominantly inhabited by the French-born children of Muslim immigrants, often marooned between two cultures. In October 2005 it was as if France had been hit by an uncontrollable burning rage—a social turmoil first projected against the Jews, and then five years later against French society and the state itself. The unrest that began in one suburb northeast of Paris soon spread around its periphery, and then to cities across the country. Within less than a fortnight more than six thousand vehicles had been set alight in nearly three hundred towns, more than fifteen hundred people were arrested, and three people died. The perpetrators of violence were mostly poor, jobless, angry, and of Maghrebi or West African origin. Neither the ban on the Muslim head scarf in state schools in 2004 nor the expulsion of radical imams and efforts at tougher policing had made much of a dent in containing the malaise that produced the riots. Neglect of the deprived suburbs, which permitted the emergence of a soft form of neighborhood terror, combined with the socioeconomic alienation of the population deriving from mass unemployment, bad housing, poor schools, and inadequate transport had all taken their toll. Above all, the homegrown but completely unassimilated insurrectionists felt no stake in France and its future, no link to its mainstream culture, no respect for state authority. In the no-go suburbs, even *before* the riots, no less than nine thousand police cars had been stoned by youths in the first eight months of 2005 alone.[141]

The riots demonstrated once more the fragility of the "French model of integration," the failures of republican social policy, and the lack of a coherent political vision in dealing with the marginalized populations in the urban ghettos.[142] Interior Minister Sarkozy, evoking the public sense of insecurity, called the rioters "scum," earning points on the Right and sharp criticism on the Left, without offering any clear solution beyond more police repression and use of emergency decrees.[143] The acute sense of exclusion, the lack of social mobility, and a feeling of political powerlessness within the immigrant population—which had been feeding Islamic radicalism, extremism, and anti-Semitism for nearly a decade—had now boomeranged against France itself, despite four decades of pro-Arab foreign policy. The republic was paying the price for its elitist arrogance, its lack of social solidarity and integrative community-based policies. The riots exposed the collapse of any consensual national project or unifying social bond, let alone commonly shared ideals. Bernard-Henri Lévy described the riots as an "unprecedented meltdown of despair and barbarism" that had replaced any politically focused protest.[144] The violence seemed to confirm an old truth about the relationship between anti-Semitism and the broader social and political crises that periodically engulf whole nations, societies, and civilizations. As long as French Jews stood alone in the front line exposed to a mini intifada, the mirage persisted that events in France were mere offshoots of the Middle East conflict. There was no general mobilization of public opinion or resolute response to anti-Semitism. But as the events of November 2005 revealed, what begins with the Jews never ends with them.

NINE

Liberté, Egalité, Antisémitisme

I n an interview with *Le Figaro* published on November 15, 2005, the philosopher Alain Finkielkraut called the urban riots sweeping through French cities at the time *un gigantesque pogrom antirépublicain* (a gigantic antirepublican pogrom). He did not mean to suggest that they were anti-Jewish in character but rather to indicate their elemental destructive dynamics as an explosion of immigrant hatred (totally illegitimate in his eyes) toward France as a country. Two days later, in an unguarded interview with the Israeli daily *Haaretz,* the normally media-savvy intellectual explicitly rejected any notion that the riots might also have been a social protest against discrimination, exclusion, and high levels of unemployment: "The problem is that most of these youths are blacks or Arabs, with a Muslim identity. Look, in France there are also other immigrants whose situation is difficult—Chinese, Vietnamese, Portuguese—and they're not taking part in the riots. Therefore, it is clear that this is a revolt with an ethno-religious character.[1]

Recalling the soccer match between Algeria and France in 2001, he pointed out that the young French citizens of Algerian descent booed the multiethnic French team ("black-white-Arab") throughout the match. In his view the riots were an expression of "hatred for the West, deemed guilty of all crimes," and of loathing for France as "a former colonial power" and as a European country with a "Judeo-Christian tradition." This Francophobia had been internalized and had penetrated into the French education system along with a political correctness that sacrificed and distorted the meaning of words. Finkielkraut believed that a combination of Islamic radicalization, identity politics, the constant blaming of others, and the spreading multiculturalist mind-set was fragmenting the French identity. This was also a threat to French Jews, since "life will become impossible for Jews in

France when Francophobia triumphs." Comparing the "understanding" response in France to the riots with reactions fifteen years earlier against white neo-Nazi youths on the rampage in Rostock, Germany, he added: "When an Arab torches a school, it's a rebellion. When a white guy does it, it's fascism. I'm 'color blind.' Evil is evil, no matter what color it is. And this evil, for the Jew that I am, is completely intolerable."[2]

Finkielkraut subsequently apologized in the face of a flood of indignation and accusations that he was a "racist," a "colonialist," or a "neoreactionary" apologist for French chauvinism. However, though more extreme than most, his contempt for *les bobos* (the bourgeois-bohemian Left) was shared by a number of other intellectuals—some of them Jewish—who also deplored the dominant anti-Americanism and intellectual capitulation in the face of Islamist totalitarianism sweeping France. Some, including writer Pascal Bruckner, had preceded him in warning of the dangers of antiwhite racism that carried with it a total repudiation of the French or Western colonial past, as well as the seeds of the "new" anti-Semitism. Daniel Lindenberg and others slammed Finkielkraut's views on colonialism and slavery—comparing him with black stand-up artist Dieudonné M'bala M'bala, who had caused an uproar with his anti-Semitic statements.[3]

Finkielkraut's views on anti-Semitism *were* contentious. He argued that it was being fueled by a humanitarian backlash conducted as a crusade by the paragons of anti-Nazism against all wars, nationalisms, power politics, and neocolonialism. This neo-humanist anti-Semitism was angry with Israel for flouting its "religion of humanity" and post-nationalist credo, and for relying on aggressive force where necessary to protect its national security. In France this backlash had nothing to do with nostalgia for Vichy or a discredited fascist ideology. On the contrary, it was obsessed by the Holocaust trauma. The "new" anti-Semitism in France totally repudiated integral nationalism and was driven by an "antiracist exuberance" that rejected the core values of French republican identity. The pillorying of French Jewry, viscerally tied to hatred for Israel as a nation-state, was a part of the broader trend to "detribalize, Europeanize, and cosmopolitanize" the French inheritance. Hence, this was no return of traditional French anti-Semitism (associated with the *petits blancs,* or small whites, of the old France) but rather a new wave of Muslim-Arab violence received with understanding by leftist anti-chauvinists of the new millennium.[4]

Among Finkielkraut's bitterest opponents were a number of so-called progressive Jews whose whole worldviews and identities were threatened by such propositions. Many in this milieu believed that Israel's policies of "apartheid and ethnocracy"—its alleged brutalities and humiliation of the Palestinians—were the true cause of Muslim reactions in France and had endangered the status of French Jews. There were some prestigious Jewish names among the critics and accusers, such as former health minister and cancer specialist Leon Schwartzenberg and Holocaust survivor Stephane Hessel (a former ambassador to the United Nations in Geneva). There were also pro-Palestinian and anti-Zionist militants, including the former president of Doctors Without Borders Rony Brauman (born into an Eastern European Zionist family), who had become a relentless opponent of Israel as a "colonialist" state. Brauman was one of those French Jewish intellectuals who had most vehemently denounced the "blackmail of anti-Semitism," denying that it had any real resonance or ideological motivation, or even that it represented a serious danger in France. French-Jewish solidarity with Israel was one of the main reasons for the existence of this supposedly fictive anti-Semitism. In other words, the fact that most Israelis and some French Jews insisted on the identity of Judaism and Zionism had created the problem. The whole debate over anti-Semitism was nothing but a Zionist conspiracy, a form of rhetorical intimidation to cover up the Israeli occupation and repression of the Palestinian people.[5] The Trotskyist Michel Warschawski was particularly vitriolic about Israeli "occupiers" fraudulently turning themselves into victims of Palestinian terror. For relentless Jewish vilifiers of Israel, such as Warschawski, any charge of anti-Semitism that did not come from the radical Right was automatically dismissed by such critics as Israeli propaganda. Similarly, pro-Israel declarations by French Jewish leaders were treated with contempt as an attempt to silence dissent, especially if anti-Semitism was invoked.[6]

· · ·

Jewish left-wing intellectuals have been noticeably active in signing petitions "as Jews" in *Le Monde* from the outset of the second Palestinian intifada—though some of them in the past had rarely, if ever, proclaimed their origins. Now, all of a sudden, Jewishness had become a marketable asset if its purpose was to blame Israel for the explosion of Palestinian hatred.[7] Jewish leaders were even held responsible for Muslim attacks on their communal institutions, as if this was an interethnic conflict with equal guilt on both sides. (Yet there has not been *a single instance* of Jews attacking Muslim or Arab targets in France—whether individual or institutional— during the past eight years.) Among the most acerbic accusers has been the Israeli filmmaker Eyal Sivan (today living in France), for whom both Israel and the French Jewish leadership were entirely to blame for any anti-Semitism that exists. Sivan publicly branded French Jews as "accomplices" of a "murderous colonial situation that has prevailed in Israel-Palestine for more than 50 years." In his fevered imagination, Israel's colonial policies were apparently preventing the coexistence of Jews and Arabs in France, and the identification of French Jewry with the Jewish state had naturally exposed its communal centers and synagogues to assault. Worse still, Zionist leaders, by brandishing the "specter of anti-Semitism," were deliberately encouraging panic and alarm in the hope of encouraging French *aliyah* to Israel.[8] Like Rony Brauman, Dominique Vidal, and the Trotskyist Daniel Bensaïd, Sivan not only trivialized anti-Semitism but also accused Jewish communal leaders of being "pyromaniacs," deliberately engaged in a persecutory campaign to disqualify all criticism of Israel instead of seeking harmonious relations with the Muslims in France.

In the eyes of these Jewish anti-Zionists, communal Jews were themselves *guilty* of "inventing" anti-Semitism or "inflating" it out of all proportion, while the real, Muslim perpetrators were completely innocent. As journalist and author Maurice Szafran pointed out, this perverse form of blaming the victim was a particularly ugly exercise in political demonization.[9] It was a peculiarly visible and prevalent affliction among Jewish intellectual anti-Zionists of the leftist persuasion. A classic example was the sociologist Edgar Morin, writing in *Le Monde,* who defined the Israeli-Palestinian conflict as "the cancer not only of the Middle East, but of relations between Islam and the West, whose metastases have very rapidly spread all over the globe."[10] His coauthored article led to a court case in which he was found guilty of racist incitement.[11] But it was not only Jews who indulged in such language. One of Morin's collaborators, the left-wing atheist and feminist Danièle Sallenave (author of *dieu.com*), had, in 1998, written a bestselling travelogue on "occupied Palestine" suffused with an almost palpable revulsion for Jews, Judaism, and the people of Israel; the religious Jews, in particular, were described as if they were fake, inauthentic aliens in the land—a kind of cancerous tissue that was wiping away the

Palestinian landscape and its indigenous inhabitants. Not surprisingly, Sallenave was a signatory against the French head-scarf legislation of January 2005, which had been attacked by some of the more radical French feminists as a "reactionary offensive . . . that stinks to high heaven of colonialism." At the same time, Sallenave and other left-wing feminists rejected all the accusations of anti-Semitism directed at Maghrebian or African immigrant youth. Equally dismissive were Jewish academicians Esther Benbassa and Jean-Christophe Attias, who wrote as if anti-Semitism was merely a fantasy or psychological disturbance of Jews suffering from mental sclerosis or from being frozen in their identity as *victims*. In what must rank as one of the more bizarre comments made during the post-2000 explosion of anti-Jewish violence, these two authors concluded: "In constantly returning to antisemitism and relentlessly condemning every speech that is not entirely standard, in tirelessly tracking down the smallest indices of hatred, rejection or mere indifference, one undoubtedly creates a community of fantasied suffering."[12]

If anything, the truth was exactly the opposite. It was the stunning obliviousness to anti-Semitism and the conceited complacency of the French elites (including many Jews) that caught the eye. Even as the synagogues were burning across the country, some narcissistic pundits in their misplaced arrogance were pouring scorn on the idea that there was any problem at all. Instead, they were insisting that the Jews of France were in a psychotic state and "playing with fire" by even talking about anti-Semitism! Benbassa and others not only ridiculed the entire subject of "Jewish suffering" but also identity politics as such and the anxiety expressed about the future of French Jewry as a whole; they also mocked those French politicians who believed in the "totally imaginary" existence of a Jewish vote.[13] Benbassa and Attias were not alone in their barbs against any hint of Jewish "victimization" or singularization. Alfred Grosser, a French academic of German-Jewish origin, wrote an article in *L'Express* adamantly denying the reality or severity of the anti-Jewish violence, repeating the wholly inaccurate mantra that racist acts and insults affected Arabs in France far more than Jews.[14]

Dominique Vidal, adjunct editor of *Le Monde Diplomatique,* is another prominent Jewish author and journalist who has been assiduous in spreading such legends.[15] A neo-Communist and anti-Zionist militant heavily engaged in anti-globalist and pro-Palestinian propaganda, Vidal published many articles trashing the idea that there is any significant anti-Semitism in France. His specialty has been to denounce those who fight against mythical anti-Semitism for serving the interests of some ill-defined Jewish/Zionist "extreme Right." On the other hand, he presents anti-Zionist activists such as Pascal Boniface, Daniel Mermet, and many others of their ilk as "martyrs," or victims of Israeli machinations in France. A master of turning statistics about anti-Jewish violence into the opposite of what they actually say and then burying them under the general rubric of "racism," Vidal has regularly repeated the canard that campaigning against anti-Semitism in France was a political maneuver carried out by fanatical "Sharonists" imbued with racist concepts.[16] Writing in September 2006, Vidal distorted the figures of the CNCDH (French National Commission on Human Rights), pretending that racism in France was primarily anti-Muslim and anti-black. Not only did he downplay anti-Semitism, but he even complained about double standards *in favor of Jews;* at the same time, all the Arab-Israeli wars since 1948 were blamed on Israel's "aggression" since its birth. Israel's policies, he reminded readers of *Le Monde Diplomatique,* were much worse than the laws of the Old Testament—they amounted to "ten eyes for one eye." In his account of the Middle East one gained the impression that Arabs were unblemished lambs and the Jews voracious wolves, whose main joy in life was to flout international law.[17] Evidently, it was inconceivable to Vidal and his friends that in France, Arabs were by no means without guilt, and Jews were both law-abiding citizens and victims of their aggression!

The French Commission on Human Rights observed in its 2000 annual report that there had been 116 incidents of anti-Semitic violence, as compared to only 9 in 1999 and just 1 in 1998—a staggering leap in hostility toward Jews whose significance was deliberately ignored by the anti-Semitism deniers. All except 5 of these incidents in 2000 happened in the last few months of the year, after the second Palestinian intifada had broken out. A similar rise occurred across western Europe and the United States, but it was much more marked in France. In October 2000, one-third of all incidents worldwide and a half of all acts of arson occurred on French soil. In 2001 (until mid-November) there were 26 violent incidents and 115 threats or acts of intimidation—most of them occurring in the months after 9/11. These figures are far from exhaustive—most of the less serious acts of aggression were not recorded at all. The perpetrators were essentially Muslims (euphemistically described as originating from "*les milieux issus de l'immigration*").[18] But the official response was a stubborn refusal to admit that "victims of racism" could also be racists themselves, and an omnipresent fear of pouring oil on the flames. Even those who understood the gravity of the events constantly repeated that France as a country was not anti-Semitic and stressed without evidence that there was no *political* consciousness behind the hatred, as if this were a consolation. A former head of the French Jewish community, Théo Klein, even went out of his way to *minimize* the anti-Semitic events, stressing their unorganized character; burning synagogues suddenly became a footnote to the problem of urban anomie totally disconnected from social, political, or racist Jew hatred.[19] For Klein and other observers like him, anything less than rampant Nazi-style pogroms did not count as anti-Semitism.

The stark fact remained that in 1996 there had been just 1 act of anti-Semitic violence, and six years later there were 193; that in 2002, 80 percent of *all* racist violence in France targeted Jews; that in the same year there were 725 anti-Semitic acts (including threats of violence)—a record for France. This was eight times more than in 1992. Since Jews were a mere 1 percent of the overall population and ten times less numerous than Muslims in France, these figures were astounding. April 2002 was the worst month, with 118 recorded cases of anti-Semitic aggression, clearly linked with Operation Defensive Shield in Israel. At the same time, political scientist Nonna Mayer claimed in 2002 that anti-Semitism in France was declining and opposition to it was growing.[20] Although an extensive survey in April 2002 indicated that only 10 percent of the French population strongly disliked the Jews, as many as 29 percent of the French sympathized with the Palestinians compared to only 10 percent with Israel.[21]

The standard surveys were not geared to examining the "new" anti-Semitism. Verbal aggression, hate speeches, and violent acts against Jews in France were in practice increasingly focused on Israel/Palestine, at times to the point of resembling a low-level intifada.[22] In the case of the North African Arab perpetrators it appeared as if many of them even considered attacks on French Jews as revenge for Israel's policies toward the Palestinians. On the other hand, the defamatory graffiti messages in Jewish neighborhoods were unmistakably anti-Semitic as well as anti-Israel. They included such slogans as "Dirty Jews!" "Jews to the gas chamber," "Jews! Prepare for an intifada in France," and "Death to the Jews." The chief editor of *L'Express* weekly, Denis Jeambar, observed that the attacks were also directed against French society, but "they strike Jews because [they] are well-established, wealthy, integrated in the society and, in particular, because they support Israel and its policies."

The CNDC's 2002 report indicated that 60 percent of all racist violence in France was aimed at Jews and only 24 percent at the *Maghrébin* community. When it came to threats, no less than 74 percent of the incidents recorded were against Jews.[23] One of the more traumatic acts of violence was the setting on fire of the Or Aviv synagogue in Marseille, which was totally destroyed. France's second largest and most ethnically diverse city had already experienced the setting alight of the Gan Pardes school in September 2001, an epidemic of anti-Jewish graffiti, and the defacing of Jewish cemeteries. The city was the political base of Le Pen's National Front, and approximately one-quarter of its population (about 200,000) were of North African Arab origin. Its Jewish community (80,000) is the third largest in the European Union. After the Or Aviv assault, however, there was notably less violence than in Paris, Lyon, Strasbourg, and other urban centers, despite its de facto tolerance of communitarianism and cultural separatism.

This relative calm could in part be attributed to the unique geography and sociology of a city with its own distinct sense of space—an agglomeration of small neighborhoods that form a complete fabric. Unlike other French cities with their menacing suburban slums, in Marseille the *banlieue* was in the city itself. The immigrant quarters were evenly distributed throughout the city; young people (regardless of ethnicity) congregated in the same parts of town. Moreover, the police presence was greatly intensified to repress anti-Semitic crimes as soon as the Chirac government gave the green light. Permanent contacts between the ethnic-religious communities and the police also helped, as did the more leisurely, open nature of a cosmopolitan southern port city with its sun, beaches, and long experience in absorbing new immigrants. The mayor of Marseille, Jean-Claude Gaudin (a convinced Zionist and philo-Semite), also contributed to the different atmosphere in Marseille that helped to keep the extremists at bay.[24]

But in the spring of 2002 there was no sign of calm across France. On the contrary, anti-Semitic aggression reached a new peak. On March 31, 2002, a shotgun was fired into a kosher butcher shop in Toulouse. A Jewish couple was assaulted in a small village along the Rhône. In Lyon, on the same day, around twenty masked assailants forced the city's synagogue door, entered with two stolen vehicles, and set them on fire. In April 2002, several members of the Maccabi football team were physically assaulted on the outskirts of Paris; later that month, a bus driving pupils and teachers from a Jewish school in Paris was stoned. In Montpellier and Strasbourg, as well as in the capital, synagogues were attacked with Molotov cocktails.

During 2003, there were 588 anti-Semitic acts in France—82 percent of *all* the racist incidents in the country, with a surge following the start of the Iraq War. The overall number of violent acts against Jews, including physical attacks, grew to 223 (compared to 185 in 2002), with a sharp rise in aggressive manifestations of hatred and anti-Semitism in the schools—overwhelmingly involving young Muslim pupils from the Maghreb.[25] For the first six months of 2004, the Justice Ministry in France reported no fewer than 180 acts of anti-Semitism, a substantial increase over the previous year. These figures prompted Israeli prime minister Ariel Sharon to call on France's 650,000 Jews to immigrate to Israel without delay—remarks that provoked a furious response from President Chirac and sharp criticism from many French Jews. Any suggestion of interference from Israel immediately raised the specter of "dual loyalties" in France.[26]

Despite the best efforts of the French authorities to crack down, the number of reported anti-Semitic incidents continued to soar, with cases of violence rising by 113 percent in 2006. Eighty percent of these cases were unsolved, and the reasons for them remain unclear. Documented acts carried out by persons of Arab or Muslim origin were five times as high as those known to have been committed by members of the extreme Right. [27]

Among the worst of the anti-Semitic incidents in 2004 were the arson attack in Toulon against a Jewish community center on March 2; the anti-Jewish assault by Arab youths on the son of a local rabbi in Boulogne-Billancourt (May 28); and the stabbing of a young religious Jew by a man screaming "*Allahu akbar*" (God is great) in the Seine-Saint-Denis district on June 4. Jewish graves were daubed with swastikas in Saverne, Alsace, on July 28, and in the de la Mouche cemetery in Lyon on August 9.[28] On August 13, 2004, anti-Semitic graffiti, including signs saying "Death to the Jews," were found on a wall by Notre Dame Cathedral in Paris. In the suburbs of Garges-lès-Gonesse, Muslim youngsters ran riot outside the local synagogue gates, throwing rocks at worshippers. Subsequently, an iron wall had to be built and closed-circuit security cameras installed for protection. Neither warnings from the government about stiff sentences against perpetrators of anti-Semitic crimes (which in 2004 represented 75 percent of all racist offenses in France) nor tentative efforts at social and civic mobilization had any material effect. The interior minister at the time, Dominique de Villepin, went out of his way to deny "that religion is a source of hatred and divisiveness in our country," but the cold facts belied his smooth reassurances.[29]

According to the CNCDH's report for 2004, racist, and especially anti-Semitic, attacks had nearly doubled in 2004, reaching their highest level in a decade. Of the 1,565 recorded threats and violent attacks (up from 833 in 2003), 970 were directed against Jews, with most of the known attackers coming from a Muslim Arab background. The assaults or threats against Muslims (595 in number) were mostly committed by Far Right supporters. The anti-Semitic attacks were also more violent than in the past and more concentrated in schools than previously. The report added that "anti-Semitism is becoming established in a continuous and lasting manner," undermining the assumption that it was always directly linked to international events.[30] The Parisian region had the largest number of anti-Semitic incidents (551 altogether, or 42 percent of the total), followed by the Rhône-Alpes, Provence-Alpes-Côte-d'Azur, and Alsace, where the number of cemetery profanations was particularly high. According to the sociologist Michel Wieviorka, the tenacious traditional rural "anti-Semitism without Jews" of Alsace was closer to that of Poland and Austria than to other regions of France.[31] What struck him about contemporary French anti-Semitism was its ever-changing blend of old and new, local and globalized elements that echoed not only the Israel-Palestine conflict but the cultural fragmentation of France and the crisis of its republican model of integration. The mushrooming "ghettoization" and "ethnicization of certain suburbs and *quartiers populaires*" [popular neighborhoods], demonstrated the inability of republican institutions to integrate the newcomers. Despite acknowledging this crisis, elite opinion was still extremely reluctant to accept that "victims of colonialism" could themselves fall into the racist trap or become anti-Semitic.[32]

The riots in France in late 2005, though primarily directed against French society rather than the Jews, exposed some of the deeper structural problems and fissures related to the nonintegration of so many Muslims and blacks. The torching of more than ten thousand cars, kindergartens, shops, schools, and libraries predominantly by Maghrebian immigrants and West African Muslims revealed a shocking level of alienation, as well as anti-French and antiwhite racism.[33] This syndrome had taken on increasingly criminal dimensions in the *quartiers difficiles* (difficult neighborhoods), though some so-called experts tried to rationalize the violence as opposition to the "racist police state."[34] Jews, for the most part, remained largely untargeted, though two synagogues were attacked with Molotov cocktails. This time, France as a whole was experiencing what the Jewish community had stoically lived through for the previous five years.

The riots also drew attention to questions concerning Afro-Caribbean, black African, and Maghrebi identity in France. The debate that began to rage after 2000 over the public commemoration and recognition of slavery brought to the surface some resentment toward the Jewish community that had been granted financial compensation for its sufferings during the Shoah, albeit belatedly. Although it had taken fifty years, Jews successfully lobbied the French state to finally recognize that it had some responsibility for the genocide in World War II. Blacks were now seeking official recognition and compensation for the role of the French state in the Atlantic slave trade and for its categorization as a "crime against humanity," a goal that was eventually achieved on May 10, 2001.[35] Six years later to the day, in the presence of President-elect Nicolas Sarkozy, a memorial ceremony dedicated to the victims of France's slave trade was finally held in the Luxemburg Gardens in Paris on May 10, 2007. In these efforts at recognition, black activists modeled themselves on the Jewish community. Nevertheless, some in the black community have objected to recognition of the Holocaust, developing a distinctive brand of leftist ideology coupled with a strong anti-Zionism and elements of anti-Semitism.[36]

Since 2003, there have been two black supremacist movements in France (the Tribu Ka and the Parti Kémite) reminiscent of Black Power and of Louis Farrakhan's anti-Semitic Nation of Islam movement in the United States. Both have tried to spread an ideology based on the total separation of black people in the West from their white compatriots. Anti-Semitism has been a part of this shift in black consciousness, no doubt confined to a small but violent and generally Muslim minority in the deprived *banlieues*. Since the second intifada began in 2000, the descendants of black Africans in France have not only identified with the Palestinians but began to see Jews as an obstacle to their own advancement in French society; the path from envy to *ressentiment* to hatred has proven to be rather short. For many

black militants the Jews symbolically represent the power of capital, financial success, social acceptance, and cunning political manipulation. Adopting the model of black American extremists, black Africans in France have
distributed polemical literature highlighting the role of Jews in *la traite né-
grière* (the slave trade).[37]

The most prominent symbol of the new black consciousness was the hu-
morist Dieudonné M'bala M'bala, known simply as Dieudonné (God provides), who had been active in politics since 1997. One of France's most
popular comedians, he had even planned to run for the presidency on an
anarchist and an "anti-Zionist" ticket. (He dropped out in October 2006.)
In early 2002, the thirty-five-year-old Dieudonné, the charismatic and popular hero of the Parisian suburban slums, singled out the patriarch Abraham as the "inventor of racism," dismissing with contempt the whole
concept of a "chosen people" as a scam, mocking the Jews as "a sect and a
fraud." For good measure he also took aim at "apartheid in Israel." This was
evidently intended to be the opening shot in Dieudonné's candidacy for the
French presidency.[38] Then, on December 1, 2003, in a live skit on the
show *You Can't Please Everyone* on the state-run France 3 TV channel, the
stand-up comedian appeared, clad in army fatigues, a hood, a black ski
mask, a large ultra-Orthodox hat and fake sidelocks mimicking Hasidic
Jews, shouting "Heil Israel!" with his arm raised in a stiff Nazi-style salute.
Mockingly, he urged young Muslims from the suburbs to "join the axis of
good [*l'axe du bien*], the American-Zionist axis! . . . The only one that offers you happiness, and the only one to give you a chance of living a little
longer."[39] The Jewish talk-show host, Marc-Olivier Fogiel, was speechless
and incapable of responding. Far from expressing regret, the rebellious
Dieudonné (born to an African father from Cameroon and brought up by
his Breton Catholic mother) repeated this sketch several times in the succeeding months at the very moment when anti-Semitic acts of aggression
were becoming rampant in France. It was as if he sensed the new resonance
of anti-Semitism across the political spectrum and sought to instrumental-
ize it in order to more viscerally connect with his public. Such a deliberate
provocation, equating Orthodox Jews with Nazis onstage, would earn him
the title of the "black Le Pen" in a part of the media, thereby confirming in
his own eyes the occult power of the "Jewish lobby."[40]

Dieudonné's paranoia was further reinforced when promoters canceled
a number of his shows, including one at the world-famous Olympia

Theatre in Paris. Dieudonné then gave an interview to the *Journal du Dimanche,* France's leading Sunday newspaper, in which he accused Jewish leaders of "building empires on trade in Blacks and slavery." They had then turned, he said, "to banking or the entertainment business and now to terror activities." The Jews, he crudely stated, "had France by the balls." In Dieudonné's view, CRIF was nothing but a "Mafia organization." At the same time, the comedian insisted that though he was anti-Israel (because the Jewish state had given "complete support for the apartheid regime in South Africa"), he rejected anti-Semitism.

Ironically enough, before 1997, Dieudonné had achieved great success in a duo with a childhood friend, the Jewish comedian Elie Semoun, especially with their joint skit "Cohen and Bokassa," in which both artists cast racist aspersions on one another. In a kind of French multicultural version of Laurel and Hardy they had relentlessly parodied the problems of the *banlieues*—the delinquents, the police, neo-Nazis, social workers, and intellectuals commenting on the decadence of French society. Seven years after they had definitively parted, Semoun published an open letter in *Libération* on February 23, 2005, pointedly reproaching his former friend for his incendiary language.

Dieudonné did not retract but on the contrary escalated his diatribes against Jewish control of the French media. His target was "Jewish power," as well as the "lobby of Israeli extremists" who had supposedly fomented the war in Iraq and daily practiced their lies and dissimulation.[41] The core problem, as he saw it, was that a band of swindlers, hysterical chauvinists, and paranoid warmongers (the Zionists) were cynically using the dogmas of Judaism—especially the myth of *le people élu* (the chosen people) against the rest of humanity. The Jews did not suffer from racism at all, he maintained; they were themselves racists: white people who despised blacks and Arabs.[42] If they had been persecuted in European history, that was merely a "settling of accounts between whites," a part of white history. Thus, in justifying his anti-Semitism, Dieudonné presented himself as an antiracist champion of the black minority in France, with more than a tinge of Malcolm X and American Black Power demagogy in his rhetoric. This was the basis of his electoral campaign in Sarcelles against his prominent Socialist opponent Dominique Strauss-Kahn (himself Jewish). It was also reflected in his aggressive counterattacks directed at CRIF, the LICRA (the International League Against Racism and Anti-Semitism), and the Union of Jewish

Students in France (UEJF)—whom he caricatured as "fascists" and "Jewish religious fundamentalists." Dieudonné's bigotry was equally visible in his barbs against the French Socialists (a "Zionist party"); Malek Boutih, head of SOS Racisme ("an Arab lackey"); and *Le Monde* ("a paper which systematically defends Zionist positions").[43] But the idiom of this prejudice was "antiracist," a hatred for "Jewish racism" and for Israel as an "apartheid" state and a form of Nazism.

The "antiracist" Dieudonné likes to assume the posture of a martyr. Thus, he was allegedly the victim of a "media lynch mob," orchestrated by French Zionists.[44] Speaking to *24 Hours* on December 10, 2004, he evoked the "Zionist domination" of France and twice expressed his hope and wish that "the Arabs [would] possess the atomic bomb."[45] He alleged that the Israeli Mossad was after him; that "pseudo-philosophers" such as Bernard-Henri Lévy had supported, with their personal fortune, the "monstrous political lie" of Zionism in order to legitimize fifty years of Israel's colonialist and fascist policies; and that the exploitation of the Shoah to this end was nothing but "an enormous fraud." As a black descendant of slaves, he insisted that his "people suffered more than any other. I reject the idea that my children should learn [that there is] a hierarchy of crimes against the nations with the Shoah as the ultimate ignominy." He expressed outrage that Bernard-Henri Lévy had branded his utterances as anti-Semitic, alleging that Lévy sought to destroy him financially and morally by instigating a boycott of his theatrical performances.

From the stage of his Main d'Or theater, Dieudonné lampooned Lévy, a leading public figure in France, heir to a huge family fortune made in the African timber trade, and perhaps his fiercest critic. "Every time Bernard Lévy writes about me, it's 'Dieudonné, bastard!' 'Anti-Semite!' 'Anti-Semite!' As soon as anything annoys him—'Anti-Semite!' It's a great system, really!" Swatting an imaginary mosquito on his cheek, the comedian shouted, to hysterical laughter, "Anti-Semite!" Along with Alain Finkielkraut and other "Islamophobe and Negrophobe" Zionist intellectuals, Lévy was branded as head of a clique of Jewish mafiosi and racists who incited others to hatred in order to silence criticism. Despite the extremism of such utterances, the comedian continued to insist that he was no anti-Semite.

The so-called cult of the Shoah was another favorite target. At a press conference in Algiers in February 2005, Dieudonné bitterly complained that while funds were readily available for films about the Holocaust, he could not obtain funding for a film about the slave trade. On a previous occasion he told a journalist that he had torn the pages on the Shoah out of his son's school textbook because they did not mention slavery. Now, for good measure, he also described the recent national commemoration (on January 27) of the liberation of the Auschwitz death camp as "pornographic," and libeled CRIF as a "band of criminals." The prime minister Jean-Pierre Raffarin, so Dieudonné claimed, had been forced to "lick the ass" of the leading French Jewish organization—"a Mafia that runs the Republic." A few days later, at a press conference in Paris, Dieudonné scandalously declared that Zionism was "the AIDS of Judaism."[46]

The Paris courts, until very recently, dismissed virtually all of the different legal complaints against the comedian for "racial slurs," although in one case he was fined five thousand euros for his statements about Jews being "slave traders" who supported Sharon's "terrorism" with their profits.[47] On September 11, 2007, he was, however, fined the equivalent of just over nine thousand dollars, by another Paris court for complicity in slandering a group of persons on the grounds of race and religion. Dieudonné, in response to one of the earlier court cases, had asserted that "the Jewish lobby detests the Blacks! Given that the blacks symbolize suffering in the collective unconscious, the Jewish lobby cannot stand it, because that's their business."[48] Mostly, such remarks went unpunished. Even the justice minister Dominique Perben's complaint about the comedian's "racial defamation" against Jews was not accepted by a Paris tribunal. The relative laxity of the legal system encouraged continual escalations from Dieudonné, a practiced provocateur, polemicist, politician, and media personality. He has generally known how to play his cards within the gray zone between anti-Zionism and anti-Semitism, social commentary, legitimate criticism of religious beliefs, and open incitement to hatred. Dieudonné consistently told journalists, for example, that he identified with the French Enlightenment and had no problem with individual Jews, though he totally rejected the idea of the chosen people. He also skillfully mastered the art of posing as the authentic descendant of slaves and the antiracist representative of black Africans and les antillais (Afro-Caribbean) population—though neither of his parents had any known family history as slaves. Indeed, there was probably more chance that their ancestors had been slavers rather than victims of this abominable traffic. However, by claiming to speak for his black compatriots, Dieudonné could pretend that the Jewish emphasis on the Holocaust had prevented the world from showing empathy for the history of slavery and black suffering.

For Dieudonné it has become an axiom that the Zionists (a synonym for Jewish power) are the true masters of the world. Hence, he remarked that it was only natural for the Gaullist leader Nicolas Sarkozy (a "Zionist puppet") to obtain the blessing of the Israelis and New York Jews before becoming president of the French Republic.[49] "Jewish power," in his eyes, had been built on the successful monopolization of human suffering through the Holocaust narrative. This was a cunning maneuver by the Jews to silence discussion over Jewish "racist crimes" in the past and present—and especially suppressing the true story of black slavery. The charismatic stand-up comedian insisted that the alleged role of Jews in the slave trade was exceptionally cruel and "genocidal"—a particularly vile anti-Semitic lie also spread by Nation of Islam advocates in the United States. He totally ignored the much bigger part in slavery played by Arabs, by Africans themselves, and, of course, by white Europeans since the sixteenth century. Dieudonné has also remained stunningly silent over the real genocide being carried out *today* by an Arab fundamentalist government in Khartoum—massacring hundreds of thousands of his own "black brothers"—whether animist, Christian, or Muslim.[50]

Dieudonné's intimate entourage reveals much about his politics. There is the ardent pro-Palestinian activist and a cofounder of the Green Party, Ginette Skandrani, from Alsace. This notorious anti-Semite and Holocaust denier coedited *Le Manifeste judéo-nazi d'Ariel Sharon*—a peculiarly vicious and totally fabricated anti-Zionist document. There is also Israel Shamir, an Israeli convert to Christianity who is very close to the anti-Semitic Russian extreme Right and a well-known enthusiast of the *Protocols*. Shamir supported Le Pen's electoral campaign in 2002. Most influential is probably the ex-Communist sociologist and *libre penseur* (freethinker) Alain Soral, a former adviser to Le Pen and a very radical anti-Zionist imbued with hatred of Jews, especially of such intellectuals as Lévy and Finkielkraut. Soral reinforced Dieudonné's belief that "the Zionists control the Socialist and Gaullist parties." He proudly describes himself as a "freethinker" in the Voltairean tradition, fighting for French democracy, national independence, and freedom "to speak the truth," including about the

Holocaust and Jewish machinations to dominate the world. An admirer of Dieudonné, he advised Le Pen to recruit the black comedian in order to break the FN's image as a racist party.

No less revealing was the positive meeting between Dieudonné and the anti-Zionist rabbis of Neturei Karta—including David Weiss from New York. The same rabbis who had glorified Arafat and would later embrace President Ahmadinejad of Iran assured the black comedian that Israel would soon collapse, since it was founded on "usurpation, blasphemy, and lies." The Zionists, they intoned, had manipulated the "Holocaust Industry" as they had exploited anti-Semitism, because their whole political project "depended on the spilling of Jewish blood."[51] This libelous accusation (which proves that Hasidic Jews can also be driven by pathological self-hatred) was, of course, music to the black comic's ears.

Anti-Zionist Hasidim were not Dieudonné's only supporters of Jewish origin. The initiator of the Euro-Palestine list in the June 2004 European elections, Olivia Zemor, was another enthusiast. As the president of the pro-Palestinian Coordination of Appeals for a Just Peace in the Middle East, she is a particularly militant Jewish anti-Zionist journalist and advocate of the unimpeded return of *all* Palestinian refugees to Israel. Zemor was initially impressed by Dieudonné's political potential. He had passed the 5 percent threshold in twelve out of forty communes of the Seine-Saint-Denis region in an earlier election. At La Courneuve he had received 7 percent of the vote, and 8.6 percent at Trappes—a fairly respectable performance. But Dieudonné's growing anti-Semitism proved too much even for the radical anti-Zionist Zemor, and their relationship collapsed in October 2004.[52]

Dieudonné also found himself in conflict with some prominent black voices, including Harlem Désir (former head of the human rights organization SOS Racisme), who opposed his explicit anti-Semitism. This posture of relative moderation had earned Désir the unflattering epithet of "bounty"— black outside and white on the inside—just like the soft chocolate bar. His successors, Malek Boutih and Dominique Sopo, were also suspect for their rejection of the antiwhite, anti-Semitic, and communitarianist currents within the antiracist camp. They had deplored the reality of an emerging anti-Semitism in the *quartiers difficiles* that sought refuge in a race-conscious identity politics and in vocal opposition to globalization. They drew the line at cheap demagogy based on sowing hatred. The ugly competition between blacks and Jews over victimhood, suffering, slavery, and the Shoah was disastrous in their eyes. On May 16, 2004, SOS Racisme organized a demonstration of twenty thousand people against anti-Semitism—a mixture of *black-blanc-beur* (black-white-Arab) protesters; such actions prompted Dieudonné to cynically comment: "This is not SOS Racism but SOS Zionism. SOS Racism has never been interested in the black cause."[53]

By the beginning of 2004 Dieudonné had become increasingly intoxicated with the theory of a Zionist conspiracy. He was already far removed from his first political crusade in 1997 against the National Front in Dreux (where its candidate Marie-France Stirbois would win 36 percent of the vote). His youthful antiracism had given way to the cheap manipulation of anti-Semitic clichés. Black youths in France were being told that Jews had caused all their misfortunes. Since Dieudonné performed before packed houses across France, was still a media star, and had become a symbol of black success, this preaching of hatred had an impact. Invited by talk-show host Thierry Ardisson to his very popular TV show on December 11, 2004, the comedian suggested that there should be a serious investigation into the claims of Al-Manar (the Hezbollah TV channel) that Israel "invented AIDS" to contaminate the black population in Africa.[54] Such appearances suggested that Dieudonné hoped to mobilize alienated blacks and Arabs together around a platform of anti-Jewish incitement. Anti-Semitism might be an effective way for him to create a negative unity and defiant identity within a splintered black community of immigrants from West Africa and the Caribbean. By contrast, he had little to say concerning Europe, capitalism, social security, the fight against unemployment, and other major social issues—the traditional rallying cries of the Left and the Greens, with whom he had once enjoyed close relations.

On December 29, 2004, Dieudonné enjoyed an artistic "triumph" with his Paris show *Mes excuses* (My Apologies), which opened at the Main d'Or. It was anything but what its title suggested. The anti-Jewish tonalities (enthusiastically applauded by spectators from all walks of life) made it one of the most anti-Semitic gatherings held in France during the past sixty years. The opening was certainly dramatic. The curtain rose on an obscure, smoky landscape with a choir mournfully chanting in the background, as Dieudonné staggered onto the stage, dressed in black and almost invisible. "I'm sorry, I'm sorry!" he cried. "I'm sorry, O Chosen People. Forgive the beast that I am, the offenses that I have caused, but I have no soul. My words are but meaningless grunts. They make no sense, I submit to your greatness,

O chosen People!" Then, pulling himself upright, with one fist aloft, he screamed: "Fuck your ass, O master!" However hilarious, or even "cool," the audience (including many middle-class French white people) may have found such sketches, it is hard to see them as the expression of that universal humanistic vision that the comedian has claimed to uphold. On the contrary, such a demagogic style is a clever but unmistakable incitement to derision and contempt for Jews. There were a few voices of protest, including that of the Socialist deputy Julien Dray (himself a Jew) and Patrick Klugman, vice president of SOS Racisme. But not until Bernard-Henri Lévy's article "Dieudonné, fils de Le Pen" in *Le Point* was the public silence effectively broken. Lévy acerbically observed that if the same anti-Semitic and homophobic remarks had been made by Le Pen or one of his followers in the heart of Paris, inside a prestigious hall and before a mass audience, all hell would have broken loose in the media. Instead there was only an embarrassed silence. Jean-Marie Le Pen, he concluded, had two biological daughters, but Dieudonné's performance proved that the FN leader now had a *spiritual* son.

It was perhaps fitting that 2005 proved to be the year of rapprochement and solidarity between Dieudonné and the FN. The comedian had already drawn a parallel in February 2004, when speaking positively of Le Pen as a "veteran of Algeria" who had attracted public support precisely because of the opposition of the media and the Zionists, who "were losing their power." On March 6, 2004, returning from Martinique (where he was assaulted at the airport by demonstrators whom he accused of being Zionist agents), Dieudonné promptly identified himself with the FN's deputy leader, Bruno Gollnisch, who had just been suspended from the University of Lyon for Holocaust denial. For Dieudonné this had turned Le Pen's right-hand man into yet another presumed victim of the all-powerful "Jewish lobby." On November 11, 2006, the comedian paid a visit to the FN convention, hypocritically declaring that he was in favor of everything that might calm "communitarianism" in France. Le Pen welcomed the unexpected support. Then, on December 18, 2006, an imposing group of FN leaders, including Gollnisch and Le Pen's wife, Jany, attended the Zenith Theatre in Paris to watch Dieudonné's act, in response to his public invitation. The performance mocked Roger Cukierman, the president of CRIF, demanded "freedom of speech" for the French Holocaust denier Robert Faurisson, and attacked the *hiérarchisation victimaire* (grading of victims).[55] Among those present and close to the comedian was Thierry Meyssan, the bestselling author of *L'effroyable imposture*—another "freethinker" whose book had accused the U.S. military-industrial complex and the Mossad of organizing 9/11. Meyssan was himself taxed with anti-Semitism by some of his former associates.

On November 21, 2006, Le Pen admitted to journalists that he found Dieudonné's anti-Semitism to be "funny" and perfectly legitimate as a motif in his comic performances. He reminded one surprised journalist that "the people who mock Jews the most are Jews themselves."[56] But there was nothing particularly amusing about Dieudonné's reciprocal praise for the FN's presumed openness and diversity ("there are people of all religions, all colors") compared to the exclusive monolithism of CRIF. Dieudonné, like Gollnisch, continuously complained of being persecuted for his political opinions, particularly by the "Jewish lobby." Like the FN, he and his supporters enjoyed posing as "victims of the system," scapegoats "lynched by the media," harassed for their nasty little remarks about Holocaust commemoration as a form of *"pornographie mémorielle."* Such provocations were all too reminiscent of the techniques of Le Pen and his denigration of the Shoah as a *"point de détail de l'histoire."*[57] It was a particularly manipulative way to achieve maximum shock impact, to be politically center stage, and to claim victimization by the mysterious "lobby." Le Pen and Dieudonné relied on a similar coded language of insinuation to achieve their effects—appealing to free speech and the sovereign right to break taboos, especially when it came to the "hidden" power of the Jews. Dieudonné's remarks were, however, less inhibited and, far more anti-Zionist and violent in their anti-Semitism than those of Le Pen. This antagonism had its roots in Dieudonné's leftist "antiracist" outlook, in his insecure identity as a person of "mixed race," in black *ressentiment* against Jews, and the overheated post-2000 anti-Semitic climate in France.[58] The virulence of his hallucinations about Jews monopolizing the slave trade and castrating black males also owed something to the malevolent influence of the Nation of Islam movement centered in the United States.

At the end of May 2006, the self-styled militia of the Ka Tribe (Tribu Ka), a black separatist group originally connected to Dieudonné, stormed the Marais (the old Jewish quarter of Paris), terrorizing the local residents, shopkeepers, and Sunday strollers. They marched into the rue des Rosiers, according to some accounts, armed with baseball bats, sticks, and knives.

After twenty minutes of stomping and shouting insults against Jews and "Zionist extremists," they left; a couple of weeks earlier, the Ka militia had stormed a gym in the ninth arrondissement looking for Jewish Defense League "strongmen"; failing to find them, they terrorized some non-Jewish kids on the premises who were learning an Israeli martial art. Their intellectual leader was the twenty-one-year-old Kémi Seba, a French-born college-educated student of Haitian and Ivory Coast background—who preached a radical version of *negritude,* the ideology of blackness pioneered by poet Aimé Césaire. Seba had absorbed the extremist teachings of Malcolm X, the Black Panthers, the Nation of Islam, and Frantz Fanon's revolutionary Third Worldism from the early 1960s. He developed the esoteric mythology of Ka, built around worship of the Egyptian god Aton, along with the cult of noble warriors and perfect mothers. The sect advocated dispensing with words such as "blacks," "Africans," or "Antilleans," which they said were inventions of the white man, and replacing them with the term "*kémites*"—the true chosen people destined to rule the world. The leader, or *Fara* (pharaoh), demanded of his followers a total separation from the *leucodermes* (whites) or anyone deemed to be less than 100 percent pure black. Indeed, the Ka Tribe excluded nonblacks from its meetings. Though having a soft spot for Islamism, Seba rejected all the monotheist religions, especially Judaism. According to some reports, he even praised Hitler's ideas on race at some of his meetings. The Ka website specialized in attacks on "Sarkozy the Jew," before it was eventually taken down by the interior minister. The site typically proclaimed that "Jews presently governed the world and even the West" as well as their own Jewish state, but true superiority belonged to the black race, which, it was said, had created all of the highest values of civilization. This did not prevent white racists from sympathizing with its identity politics and anti-Semitism.[59]

The extremist black groups could not compete with Dieudonné's iconic status. But they did find a certain echo in the deprived suburbs, playing on the prevailing sense of victimization and the demand to receive reparations for the crimes of slavery and colonialism. The promotion of an Afrocentric ideology, antiwhite racism, and calls for self-segregation within the black community stood, of course, in sharp opposition to more mainstream efforts at the integration of *La France noire.*[60] Kémi Seba's virulently anti-Western speech at a black rally where Dieudonné also spoke on October 15, 2005, attacked "the integration of our people" as a disaster. Seba singled out (to great applause) the "négrophobe" TV producer Marc-Olivier Fogiel ("white, homosexual, and Jewish") who had allegedly evoked the "smell of blacks" in reaction to Dieudonné's TV sketch mocking Nazi-like Orthodox Jewish settlers. On October 26, 2007, Kémi Seba was finally charged with racial defamation with the prosecution calling for a ten-thousand-euro fine, five months in prison, and loss of civic rights for five years.[61] On April 7, 2008, he was condemned to six months' imprisonment for denying crimes against humanity and incitement to hatred.

The alarming spread of anti-Jewish feelings in France's black community was demonstrated by a number of violent incidents. In the Parisian suburb of Sarcelles (where 20 percent of the population are Jews, and an even larger percentage are black), no less than three successive anti-Semitic assaults took place in two days during early March 2006. On March 3, the seventeen-year-old son of the local rabbi was attacked near the synagogue by two black men, and suffered a broken nose. The same afternoon, an eighteen-year-old Jew was set upon by four blacks and an Arab, who insulted him and then stole his cell phone. The following night four black teenagers assaulted and verbally abused a twenty-eight-year-old religious Jew wearing a yarmulke, dislocating his shoulder. There were also anti-Semitic incidents in Lyon and the nearby suburb of Villeurbanne. A survey at the time confirmed that two-thirds of the French were now convinced that anti-Semitism was rising in their country. Following meetings with the families and local officials, Interior Minister Sarkozy promptly announced the deployment of police reinforcements after the attacks in Sarcelles, an area where, it is worth noting, young Arab immigrants and blacks had indulged in several days of rioting during October 2005.[62]

Some French politicians, such as Julien Dray (a spokesman for the Socialist Party, a Jew, and an expert in urban security), considered "the Dieudonné effect" a major factor in the rise of black anti-Jewish violence, especially among blacks of Muslim background. This was especially evident after the brutal torture and murder of a twenty-three-year-old Parisian mobile phone salesman, Ilan Halimi, in February 2006. Dray asked whether the comic did not bear "part of the moral responsibility" for Halimi's kidnapping and torture at the hands of Les Barbares (a gang called "the Barbarians") led by twenty-six-year-old Youssuf Fofana, an African Muslim from the Ivory Coast.

Dray was referring to the cumulative effects of Dieudonné's incitement against Jews—the impact of his live theatrical spectacles, his DVDs, and his website—on many black and Muslim immigrants, as well as their French-born children. On December 15, 2005, at a performance in Paris, the black comedian had listed the names of certain well-known Jewish artists and philosophers whom he particularly disliked, encouraging the audience to boo. He also proclaimed his support for the Hezbollah Al-Manar satellite TV, banned in France for its anti-Semitic programming. It was no surprise, then, that in February 2007, Dieudonné spent a "resistance weekend" in Tehran, where he expressed his approval of Iran's nuclear program as well as his opposition to the so-called American-Zionist conspiracy. By the end of 2006, Dieudonné did acknowledge that Halimi's killing was a racist act, but denied that any of his own anti-Semitic provocations represented an incitement to murder.[63]

The Tribu Ka responded very differently, however, to Fofana's capture. It threatened to kill Jews in retaliation, warning Minister Sarkozy of dire consequences should anyone so much as touch a hair on the gang leader's head. A French judge nonetheless charged Fofana for the premeditated murder of Halimi, with the aggravating circumstance that it was racially motivated. The Halimi murder stunned the whole of France—not only the Jewish community. The victim of indescribable cruelties, Ilan Halimi died in agony, found in the street near a suburban train station south of Paris, naked and handcuffed. He had sustained horrific injuries and burns over 80 percent of his gagged and battered body, after being held prisoner and tortured for twenty-one days by his captors. The whole gory episode seemed like an anti-Semitic rewrite of the sadistic hooliganism evoked many years earlier in Stanley Kubrick's prophetic film *A Clockwork Orange*. The gang, according to Interior Minister Sarkozy, had links with Salafist Muslim groups and with supporters of the Palestinian cause, though its leader has denied any ideological, political, or ethnic motivations. It was reported that gang members had several times proffered openly anti-Semitic insults to Ilan's father during the negotiations for his release; that they had previously sought out Jewish targets; and that the kidnappers imagined all Jews to be wealthy.

The Halimi family certainly believed that anti-Semitism was an important element in the case. Ilan's uncle noted the racist content of what had been said on the phone to the family. He added: "When we said we didn't have five hundred thousand euros to give them they told us to go to the synagogue and get it."[64] Nicolas Sarkozy, for his part, considered the kidnapping to have been planned "out of sordid, villainous motives" and with the conviction that Jews have money or would pay up out of a feeling of communal solidarity. Prime Minister Dominique de Villepin, guest of honor at the CRIF annual dinner, promised full disclosure, underlining the "absolute priority of the struggle against anti-Semitism," which represented the "negation of the republican spirit."[65] Nevertheless, there were the usual minimizers among the Jews themselves, including Théo Klein (the former head of CRIF), who believed the amalgam of Jews with money had nothing whatsoever to do with anti-Semitism. Once again, he seemed to assume that Jew hatred existed only if it came from the Far Right or involved a calculated, deliberate, and organized political struggle as in the 1930s. No less absurd was Esther Benbassa's argument that labeling the crime as anti-Semitic would aggravate relations between Jews and Arabs in France.

The young French Muslim writer Morad al-Hattab swiftly exposed the hollowness of such claims. He deplored the failure to halt anti-Jewish (and anti-Zionist) hatred in French society, as well as efforts to relativize or minimize the act of savagery that was behind Halimi's murder.[66] Trivializing references to "hooligans," "barbarians," "idle youth," and a "zero degree of thought" were euphemisms for those still in denial or engaged in articulating politically correct platitudes. It was misguided to believe that silence could prevent a further escalation of hatred or to act as if anti-Semitism had no past, present, or future. French society, since 2000, had abandoned the reality principle in dealing with its own sickness. It was especially dishonest to blame the Jewish community for its "emotional reactions" whenever it was physically or verbally attacked.[67]

The sheer barbarity of the Halimi murder did briefly shock the French media and public. It even led somewhat to a belated and grudging recognition that anti-Semitism was probably the main catalyst for such exceptional violence. As the left-wing *Libération* pertinently observed: "The whole nature of this affair—the combination of gangland criminality with exceptional sadism and a brute anti-Semitic instinct that equates Jews and money—gives it an extraordinary character that inspires both revulsion and dread."[68]

Nevertheless, after the massive riots in the suburbs, the temptation to play down anti-Semitism as a possible mobilizing force cementing urban violence was still evident.[69] This obtuseness characterized the position of the police investigators and the public prosecutor, despite evidence that clearly showed that four of the six victims previously targeted by the Barbarians gang had been Jewish.[70] They included Jérôme Clement, director of the Arte TV channel, and the anti-Zionist militant Rony Brauman. (Brauman, predictably enough, dismissed any connection to his Jewish origin.) Yet the gang had sent an audiocassette of Halimi to a rabbi the family did not even know; and they had very specifically told Ilan's father to "ask each Jew for one thousand euros." Apparently, only Jewish leftist intellectuals in France could be blind enough to believe that the relentless physical cruelty perpetrated against Ilan Halimi was unrelated to his Jewishness.

Following the Halimi murder the feelings of insecurity within the French Jewish community were exacerbated.[71] This was not only because of anti-Semitism but also because of shock at the indifference of residents in the suburb of Bagneux. Halimi had been interrogated, kept naked, bound, hooded, and subjected to the most gruesome torments for three weeks without any neighbors noticing or caring about what might be happening. Then there was the lack of urgency and the incompetence of the French police, who from the outset ignored the ethnic and possible religious dimension of the crime. No less disappointing was the lack of any appropriate Israeli reaction. The story was never front-page material in the Israeli press, television, or radio. The Israeli Embassy in Paris took ten days to publicly express condolences to the Halimi family after his death; no Israeli official flew to Paris for his funeral, and no government minister or spokesman even condemned his murder. This was all the more astonishing since Halimi had been intending to make his *aliyah* to Israel.[72]

At the same time, however, the highest echelons of the French government, led by President Chirac and Premier De Villepin, did go out of their way to show public solidarity with French Jewry—attending memorial services for Halimi at the Great Synagogue of Paris.[73] The grisly attack had come at a time when there was a deceptive lull in anti-Semitic aggression, sparking exaggerated claims from some French officials that they had the situation fully under control. The Halimi murder was a reminder of how difficult and politically controversial this struggle was proving to be, despite appearances. The Socialist Party (PS) supported the government's firm position, but some antiracist organizations, including the Movement Against Racism and for Friendship Among the Peoples (MRAP) and the League of the Rights of Man (LDH), continued to marginalize the anti-Semitic factor and objected to transforming "an isolated fact into a problem of society."[74] The FN, for its part, considered the murder to be "a consequence of forty years of uncontrolled immigration and irresponsible policy toward up-rooted populations." It was swiftly excluded from the large demonstration planned for February 26, 2006, in homage to Ilan Halimi. The participation of Philippe de Villiers's Far Right MPF (Movement for France), which had also blamed immigration and Islamicization for most of France's ills, led to further ugly recriminations from the Left and various antiracist organizations.[75]

Participants in the main demonstration in Paris included Nicolas Sarkozy; Socialist ex-premier Lionel Jospin; the president of the National Assembly Jean-Louis Debré; the mayor of Paris; the first secretary of the PS, François Hollande; Cardinal Lustiger; François Bayrou; Dominique Sopo, president of SOS Racisme; and many other prominent French personalities. According to the police there were thirty-three thousand participants, but SOS Racisme estimated the numbers at eighty thousand while CRIF proposed a far higher (and clearly exaggerated) figure of two hundred thousand demonstrators. Roger Cukierman, president of CRIF, declared himself pleased with the level of internal Jewish mobilization and the solidarity shown by the French political, religious, and professional elites. Others, like Samuel Blumenfeld, writing in *Le Monde* a year later, drew a less sanguine picture. Ultimately, he concluded, the wider French public had remained passive during the Halimi affair, despite the organized demonstrations in some French cities. The Jews had largely been left to their own devices.[76]

The young French author Émilie Frèche came to even harsher conclusions. She emphasized the inhuman indifference, egoistic complicity, and lack of social solidarity shown by the inhabitants of the Bagneux neighborhood where Halimi had been tortured.[77] Equally shocking was the primitive anti-Semitism of Fofana who said, "*J'ai choisi un Juif, parce que les Juifs sont riches*" (I chose a Jew because Jews are rich), even as he denied any prejudice against Jews. This contradiction, so characteristic of the age, revealed an important difference between France in the early twenty-first century and the Vichy years. Nobody could claim that there were anti-Jewish laws or deportations in 2007. But there had been plenty of cemeteries desecrated, Jewish schools and synagogues burned down, and rabbis assaulted during the previous seven years. The Holocaust was being inverted, Israel Nazified, and anti-Semitism itself trivialized in the name of antiracism or the Palestinian cause.[78] What kind of progress, one could ask, did this represent after sixty years? Had one culture of hatred merely replaced another? The discourse of today might appear less structured or ideological; it was perhaps more instinctual than intellectual, but the destructive potential was still intact. As *The Economist* pithily observed: "The murder seemed to some a grotesque fusion of many of France's current troubles: violence, immigration, the *banlieues,* nihilism, racism, anti-Semitism." The appallingly inhuman acts perpetrated by a gang of French-educated youths of both immigrant and white French descent (including some Islamist extremists) did, if only for a brief moment, take the country aback.[79] It was all too clearly "a crime of the times," a kind of magnifying glass unveiling the rotten state of French society. But there is, as yet, little sign that the message has been taken to heart.

The Halimi tragedy had been preceded two years earlier by the murder of another twenty-three-year-old Paris-born Sephardic Jew—this time by his Muslim neighbor—in an act no less chilling for its sadism yet virtually ignored by the French media and government. Even the Jewish community maintained a remarkably low profile over the case of Sebastien Sellam, whose parents had left Morocco for France in 1956. Their son was a highly successful DJ on the Paris nightclub scene. He was horrifically stabbed to death by a former friend, Adel Boumedienne, who had come to hold Jews responsible for all the troubles facing Muslims. Boumedienne had convinced himself that all Jews were rich "because they were stealing money from the French."[80] This change did not occur in a vacuum. According to Sebastien's mother, soon after the beginning of the second intifada, there had been a noticeable transformation for the worse in attitudes among her Muslim neighbors: "I saw hatred in their eyes, as if I and my two sons killed the Palestinians. 'What do you want me to do' I told them, 'It's not me.' But for them, it's the same. The Jews of France and the Jews of Israel."

Not long afterward, she found her mezuzah pulled out of the doorpost and a huge swastika painted on the wall in the hallway, with the words *"Mort aux Juifs"* in big letters above it. In that building there were ten Jewish and twenty Muslim families, all from North Africa. But while most North African Jews have successfully integrated into French schools and society, the Maghrebi Arabs discovered that many whites considered their culture alien and their Frenchness conditional. They were discriminated against in housing and jobs, and mostly unable to emulate Jewish success.

Thus social envy joined latent Muslim hatred of Jews, the Israel-Palestine confrontation, and growing Islamic radicalism as factors aggravating anti-Semitism.

The personal story of Adel and Sebastien—as the Israeli journalist Daniel Ben-Simon summed it up—was "a microcosm of the lives of their respective communities."[81] Sebastien continued his schooling while Adel dropped out; the Jewish teenager was popular with girls and embarked on a financially successful career; Adel, on the other hand, became introverted, took to drugs, and felt he was a social failure. Individual jealousy and collective Jew hatred became inextricably entwined. Driven by an unstoppable maniacal loathing, Adel fell on Sebastien in the underground parking lot of a modest building in the 10th district, armed with a kitchen knife and fork, stabbing him in the head and neck till his face was slashed beyond recognition. A few minutes later he told his mother that he had murdered Sebastien. "Maman, I killed my Jew," he declared. "I did what God commanded me. I had to do it." The prime motive seemed unmistakably anti-Semitic, and the killing had apparently been planned for a long time. Yet doctors swiftly decided that Adel was insane and committed him to an institution. Thus he was never tried in court for his horrific crime. Nor was any Jewish institution willing to take up the case, perhaps for political reasons and out of fear of confrontation with the Muslim community. Thus a case that could potentially have shaken France out of its lethargy was effectively silenced by the police, and establishment, with the connivance of the leaders of French Jewry.[82]

The French Jewish leadership, despite its failure in this instance, was by no means passive in its appeals to the French government in recent years to deal more firmly with anti-Semitic assaults.[83] CRIF's executive director, Haim Musicant, had strongly complained to the authorities in March 2002 that eighteen synagogues had been burned in France in the two previous years—something absolutely unprecedented on French soil since 1945.[84] The CRIF also robustly opposed the Jospin-Védrine government's misleading claims that there had merely been an increase in vandalism but not in anti-Semitism since 2000. French Jews were frankly taken aback by President Chirac's astonishing statement in early 2002 that "France is not anti-Semitic neither historically nor currently," a fiction supported at the time by Israeli foreign minister Shimon Peres. By April 2002, however, President Chirac felt obliged to change direction and significantly increase government security measures in order to protect Jewish institutions. He now described the mounting tally of anti-Semitic acts of violence as "completely unimaginable, unpardonable, unspeakable."[85] At the same time, ambiguous declarations by various political leaders (including Socialist premier Lionel Jospin) multiplied to the effect that France must not become a battleground where Jews and Muslims reenacted the bloody violence of the Middle East. What they ignored was the crucial fact that *not a single act of Jewish violence against Muslims on French soil was (or would be) recorded,* despite the massive scale of the provocations since 2000. In other words, there was no symmetry at all in the behavior of Jews and Muslims despite the misleading insinuations to the contrary, some of them spread by anti-Zionist Jews.

Ordinary Jews were particularly stunned and angry that senior French government officials, while belatedly stressing the inadmissibility of anti-Semitic violence, continued to imply that Israel's "aggression" against the Palestinians was its cause. French Jews began to see the national melting pot and its sanctified republican shell dissolving before their very eyes. Indeed, in 2002, they felt increasingly abandoned by the republican state. The pro-Palestinian bias of the media and its perceived incitement against Israel reinforced this sense of acute anxiety and isolation. Between Le Pen's success at the ballot box in the 2002 national elections, the "new" left-wing anti-Semitism, and the mini insurrection of the *beurs,* the Jews of France had every reason to feel squeezed in a knuckle sandwich. Nazi and Islamist graffiti of every description surrounded them: *Nique ta mere les Juifs* (F——— your mother, Jews) had become so common that it appeared as *NTM les juifs;* "In Paris as in Gaza—Intifada!" was another popular hit, alongside old standbys "Death to the Jews" and "Hitler was right." Yet the political class and the world's largest antiracist establishment seemed to have been struck by a collective epidemic of glaucoma in the left eye. They were looking at the wrong target, desperate to dissolve the rising anti-Jewish tide into an anonymous and amorphous wave of right-wing racism or delinquency; as if all the anti-Semitic thugs through the ages—from the medieval Crusaders to the peasants of czarist Russia and the criminal anti-Semites in Nazi-occupied Europe—had not been "delinquents" at some elementary level of violent behavior. Using the label of "delinquency" to drain the term "anti-Semitism" of any meaning was decidedly unhelpful.

After the 2002 presidential elections the government began to respond more vigorously. The new prime minister, Jean-Pierre Raffarin, declared in

July 2002 that "to attack the Jewish community is to attack France and the values of our Republic which can allow no place for antisemitism, racism and xenophobia."[86] Interior Minister Sarkozy told a delegation from CRIF that he would categorically *not* tolerate any anti-Jewish violence. A new law initiated by Gaullist deputy Pierre Lellouche significantly augmented the penalties for racist and anti-Semitic acts, putting some teeth into these statements of intent.[87] Articles began to appear in the French media deploring the official fear of actually identifying the principal perpetrators of anti-Semitic assaults and criticizing misguided efforts to reduce their importance.[88] Growing dissension and a lively debate concerning anti-Semitism and Israel began to emerge on the right and the left, among the intellectuals and leading journalists as well as within the Jewish community. While most left-wing doctrinaires continued to blame Israel and its "unconditional" supporters in France, there were others who charged these same anti-Zionist intellectuals with stoking the fires of anti-Semitism.[89] However, the facts on the ground indicated that the deeper causes of the violence and unrest were little affected by these intellectual debates.[90] For the younger Muslim and black members of the immigrant community, their reflexive hostility to Israel (encouraged by extensive and one-sided French TV coverage) and a vicarious identification with "oppressed Palestinians" reinforced their growing sense of exclusion and failure in France. Although traditional anti-Semitism (Catholic and racist) was clearly in retreat, resentment toward Sharon's Israel and a diffuse suspicion of "Jewish power" (34 percent of French citizens thought it was too great in 2000) remained high.

In January 2003, Roger Cukierman lashed out at a CRIF dinner (in the presence of Prime Minister Raffarin) at the "new brown-green-red alliance" that, he argued, threatened Israel and French Jewry. The pro-Palestinian leftists, environmentalists, and the Far Right were nourishing a growing anti-Israel phalanx.[91] He pointed out that Jews were on the front line in the defense of republican values but expressed disappointment that the judicial system had failed to punish racist attacks more severely or maintain the authority of the state.

The most forceful of the government ministers in pursuing this endeavor was Sarkozy. At a Franco-Israeli friendship rally in June 2003, he described the Jewish state as "a great democracy, that deserved to be saluted and respected." He also condemned the burning of the Israeli flag in street

demonstrations in France as an intolerable form of "incitement to racial hatred." Sarkozy added that anti-Semitism was "the affair of the Republic," of
the "national community." Hence if a Jew was "insulted as a Jew," that was
not merely a problem for the Jewish community but for the French as a
whole. President Chirac, in November 2003, following the act of arson directed at a Jewish private school in Gagny (Seine-Saint-Denis), was no less
unequivocal, declaring that "the French Republic cannot tolerate any anti-
Semitic act." Chirac and Raffarin promised stern repression and prosecution of such actions as well as preventive measures in the schools. The
French president now qualified anti-Semitic violence as an assault on "the
fundamental rights of each citizen, the right to the respect of his beliefs and
convictions." He added that "when a Jew is attacked in France, it must be
understood that this is an attack on France itself."[92] In October 2003, Chirac
also expressed his displeasure at the Malaysian premier's comments to the
Islamic World Conference about the Jews "ruling the world by proxy," even
though at the EU summit shortly before this announcement, he had tried to
block a statement against the speech.[93]

French Jewish leaders felt somewhat reassured by Chirac's strong message regarding measures against anti-Semitism in France, including within
the educational system. Nevertheless, when it came to the Muslim perpetrators of anti-Semitic acts, French policy still remained ambiguous. On the
one hand, it adopted a hard line toward Islamic militancy on French soil,
swiftly expelling preachers who fomented anti-Western sentiment in their
sermons.[94] Yet officials who were quick to condemn any expression of Far
Right Jew-baiting were usually silent about explicitly naming the Islamist
variety. The tripling of attacks on Jews since the start of 2004 indicated the
gravity of the problem, despite the more robust governmental response.
The denial syndrome was especially blatant among the intellectuals. Among
the minimizers was Jean Daniel, an Algerian Jew by origin and editor of the
influential left-wing weekly *Le Nouvel Observateur*. Though this publication carried some important analyses of the topic, Daniel himself smugly
dismissed the concerns of French and American Jews over anti-Semitism in
France as a "kind of allergic reaction."

Then there was the sociologist Freddy Raphaël, writing in *Le Monde,*
who blasted the invitation of Israeli prime minister Ariel Sharon to French
Jews to leave their French homeland because of rampant anti-Semitism.
Raphaël distorted the fact that this call for "desertion" had fallen on the an-

niversary of the Vel' d'Hiv deportation of French Jews under Vichy into a form of negationism (Holocaust denial). Raphaël, himself an Alsatian Jew, accused Sharon of denying the specificity of Franco-Judaism and of rejecting the egalitarian model of a democratic citizen-nation and the republican contract between the Jews and France. Sharon had supposedly tried to imprison France in "an anti-Semitic essence" while attributing an inherent racism to the Muslim community. The former Israeli premier had, of course, done no such thing. A farmer and soldier totally remote from such philosophical or historical abstractions, Sharon was a perfect punching bag for Jewish anti-Zionists whether in France, in Israel, or in the western world as a whole. In the same jaundiced spirit, Raphaël blamed Zionism for supposedly building the house of Israel on "nonrecognition of the other," on the violation of Palestinian rights, and on the refusal to admit equal Arab dignity. This was simply one more example of the endless mix of half-truths and self-righteous falsehoods about Israel that *Le Monde* had been assiduously promoting for decades.[95] Over a period of forty years anti-Zionism in France, as elsewhere in western Europe, had become the favored alibi or the weapon of choice for posturing liberals, compassionate reformers, humanist freethinkers, and "journalists of integrity" to self-righteously vent their prejudices.

An instructive case was that of Alain Ménargues, who was appointed in June 2004 as adjunct director-general of Radio France Internationale (RFI). He would resign a few months later (in October), after publicly characterizing Israel as a "racist state." Author of a depressingly mediocre book about "Sharon's Wall," he told the Catholic Far Right Radio Courtoisie on October 12, 2004, that "the key" to understanding contemporary Israel was "the separation of pure and impure" in the Book of Leviticus. It was the Jews, according to this historical novice, who had supposedly established the world's first ghetto (in sixteenth-century Venice)—a legacy they were continuing in Palestine today. Ménargues regarded Israel as uniquely "racist" precisely because it was a *Jewish* state, in which nationality was based on religion. He also asserted that his resignation had been forced by the pressure of "communitarist Jews," because he dared to boldly criticize Israel, Zionism, and the Torah's doctrine of "racial separation."

None of these pretentious claims (while widely believed in certain circles) were true, any more than his obsession with Jewish chosenness—a favorite theme of anti-Semites through the ages. In virtually all his interviews,

Ménargues nonetheless referred to the biblical concept of a "chosen people" as if it were a modern *Zionist* doctrine (the opposite is generally the case) or a Nazi-like racist ideology. In reality, mainstream Zionist ideology, which sought to *normalize* the Jewish condition, rejected the "chosenness" motif, especially in its original religious meaning. It was, moreover, absurd to present Sharon's wall as a racist attempt to exclude the dangerously "impure Palestinian goys." The security barrier had nothing to do with keeping out Gentiles. The dominant stereotype in these ramblings was totally detached from empirical reality and unequivocally anti-Semitic.[96] The support that Ménargues received from Holocaust deniers Serge Thion, Roger Garaudy, Israel Shamir, and others was therefore perfectly logical. No less revealing were the declarations of sympathy from anti-globalists, Islamists, Arab journalists, pro-Palestinian leftists, Dieudonné admirers, and other assorted believers in the great "Zionist conspiracy" against free thought.

The case of Alain Ménargues was only one among many revealing symptoms that exposed the ease with which anti-Zionism in France has crossed the line into anti-Semitism. The promoters of inflammatory anti-Israel language invariably did at least one of the following: They questioned the legitimacy of Judaism, of Jewish nationalism, and of a Jewish state, but not that of any other state or ideology. They labeled any collective desire to be Jewish as *racist* but never criticized the desire of France to be French, Pakistan to be Muslim, or Saudi Arabia to be Arab. At the same time, they demonized Israel, expressing a wholly disproportionate and obsessive concern with its shortcomings. They protested at the sufferings of Palestinians, while ignoring far worse examples of conflict and catastrophe. Real genocides such as Rwanda or Darfur provoked little excitement among anti-Zionists who vibrated at every Palestinian death but in practice prolonged the violence through their rejection of compromise. They preferred to focus on "the sins of Israel," as if Jews were uniquely responsible for the conflict and had always acted with demonic, Nazi-like intensity to oppress, exclude, and ultimately destroy the people they "dispossessed." Such "critics of Israel" (whether in France or the Middle East) have generally excelled in the fabrication of empty slogans. Their credo can be readily summarized as follows: Israel equals apartheid; Jews equal money; Judaism equals racism. Once these catchphrases have been fully internalized, all thought ceases.

French foreign policy, while persistently pro-Arab, anti-American, and anti-Israeli for the past forty years, could not, of course, embrace such a totally Manichean paradigm. Despite the near equivalent of a state funeral that France abjectly offered to Yasser Arafat; despite the Gallic flirt with Saddam Hussein, the more understandable courting of the Gulf states, and an endemic bias against Zionism, the French establishment is well aware that Israel remains a vibrant democracy. Moreover, even acute tensions with Israel did not prevent most French leaders from demanding, in President Chirac's words, "the greatest vigilance in the prevention, the greatest firmness in the pursuit, the greatest severity and swiftness in punishing antisemitic acts."

Both Chirac and Sarkozy (since attaining the presidency) have been insistent that anti-Semitism is a *French* problem, concerning the entire nation; that Jewish places of worship and schools required extra security; that civics courses in French schools must educate children in the virtues of dialogue, tolerance, and respect for others. After 2003 France adopted, both in theory and practice, a tougher policy than in any other European state with regard to its judicial arsenal and defense of republican values against anti-Semitism and racism. There was a distinct shift in attitudes and a growing concern at the elite level. For example, in November 2003 the education minister Luc Ferry admitted to Parliament that France was facing "a new form of anti-Semitism" ever since the Middle East conflict had entered French schools. This was "no longer an anti-Semitism of the extreme Right," he said, but one of "Islamic origin."[97] In the same month, Mideast expert Gilles Kepel (who in the past had wrongly claimed that Islamism was a spent force) told *Libération* that youths who watched Arab satellite television in France felt "they should identify with those shown as victims, the Palestinians, and fight with them by beating up their Jewish classmates."[98] A survey toward the end of 2005 confirmed that anti-Jewish prejudices were undoubtedly much higher among Muslims than the rest of the population: 46 percent of religious Muslims had such sentiments, while only 28 percent were without them. Among nonpracticing Muslims, 30 percent were found to be anti-Semitic—still twice the national average.[99]

One consequence of the anti-Semitic crisis was that in 2001 the number of French Jews who left to settle in Israel (2,556) was double the number in the previous year and the highest figure since the 1967 Middle East war. In the summer of 2003, one-third of *all* French Jews were reported to be considering emigration; another poll in December that year suggested that nearly half (46 percent) were ready to go—some were considering the

United States and Canada, but the majority were seriously contemplating possible *aliyah* to Israel.[100] Relations between France and Israel became strained over this question following Premier Sharon's reiterated call in July 2004 for French Jews to immigrate "immediately" to Israel to escape *l'antisémitisme déchaîné* (the unhinged anti-Semitism) that threatened their future. President Chirac had responded petulantly at the time, even barring Sharon from visiting France. But in July 2005, on the eve of Israel's withdrawal from Gaza, Chirac changed his attitude after the Israeli prime minister explained his remarks and praised France's fight against anti-Semitism as a "model for other European countries." In fact, a record number of French Jews did move to Israel in 2005. Moreover, the previous year at least one hundred thousand French Jews had visited Israel as tourists, most of them Sephardim whose parents had originally come to France from North Africa and had been successfully integrated. But among French Jewish fifteen- to eighteen-year-olds, polled in early 2005, three-quarters said they did not see a future for themselves in France; one-half admitted that they had suffered from some form of anti-Semitism in the previous five years. The rise of Muslim extremism had obviously created a sense of diminishing confidence in France and Europe, and in their own prospects. A report from the French Interior Ministry in December 2004 showed that there had been an increase of 70 percent in racist violence in that year, reflected above all in anti-Semitic acts and threats.[101]

The massive investment of French Jews in buying up apartments and other real estate in Israel can hardly be disconnected from this growth of anti-Semitism and personal insecurity in France. The rate of *aliyah* continued to rise in 2006, with increasing acceptance of this trend even among French Jewish organizations who had been embarrassed by Sharon's call for mass *aliyah* only two years earlier. The realities on the ground in France could not be wished away. Despite the serious efforts of the French government, hundreds of violent anti-Semitic incidents continue each year. The rowdy Muslim youth in the suburbs of Paris and other cities torched nearly twenty thousand cars in the winter 2005 riots; their alienation, violence, and rising numbers have created a "new reality" for Jews. Here is the testimony of David Edri, the proprietor of a pastry shop in Sarcelles (who had immigrated to France from Morocco in the early 1960s): "We were never liked here, but now our schools and shops and even the synagogues are under attack. The Jews in Sarcelles are walking a thin line and so we are thinking of leaving."

Here is another representative comment by sixty-year-old Yosef Ben-Zion, a recent *oleh* (immigrant) to Israel. Born in postwar Tunisia, he left for France in 1960 at the age of fourteen, settling in the Parisian suburb of Noisy-le-Sec, which is now largely Muslim: "I started to feel that there was a real problem about 10 years ago. I started hearing Muslim youth say '*sale Juif*' as I was on my way to the synagogue. They used to throw rocks over the wall into the synagogue garden, and the police did nothing about it." His wife added that well before the riots and the car torchings, Muslim firebrands "would start preaching in the street—'Beware of the modern ways, beware of the influence of the Jews.' "[102] Although the older generation of Jews and Arabs had coexisted reasonably well in the 1960s after immigrating to France, the second generation of Muslim youth had no common history of living with Jews, were poorly integrated in France, and were easily susceptible to anti-French and anti-Semitic incitement.

The acute malaise of French Jewry has been steadily growing since 2000, expressed among other signs in the rising number of pupils registering in private Jewish schools.[103] In the eyes of many Jewish parents this was the most obvious way to escape the violence, intimidation, harassment, and racism against their children in French schools. More surprisingly, perhaps, one in three French Jews were ready to send their children to private Catholic schools—a reflection not only of the general crisis in the public school system but of rising levels of intermarriage.[104] But the schools of the republic are only one battleground. The simmering tensions and need to physically defend the Jewish community have also led to the establishment of special patrols made up of muscular young Jews in more sensitive neighborhoods. The patrols were spontaneously created in order to offset the seeming powerlessness of the French state and mainstream organizations to stem the tide of racism, anti-Semitism, and lawlessness. In the wake of Ilan Halimi's savage murder, the calls for self-defense greatly increased, even troubling the CRIF leadership who were evidently out of touch with sentiment on the "Jewish street."[105]

For younger Jewish activists, it is frustrating to observe the French government's fear that overenergetic police action might only provoke further riots in the suburbs. At the same time the toxic concentration of social ills in the *banlieues* continue to fester. There is crime, gang terror, illegal immigration, family breakdown, and, above all, unemployment, all of which feeds a culture of hatred that has been channeled into anti-Jewish directions and into hostility toward the state. Inequality is rampant at the level of job discrimination, incomes, and housing. Moreover, the political establishment barely reflects the multiethnic character of French society. There is not a single member of Parliament from a nonwhite immigrant background representing mainland France. There are hardly any nonwhite mayors and only two prefects.[106] Jews, on the other hand, have done well in all those domains where the disaffected Muslim youth have failed to make any progress. This has greatly strengthened envy, resentment, and hostility toward the more established and integrated Jewish minority. When one adds the spread of radical Islam and the Palestinian tinderbox to these sociological realities, the result is a highly combustible mixture of elements.

What has most worried French Jews is the seeming "normalization" of nihilistic hatred and of the anti-Semitic acts that have accompanied it, despite the firm declarations of Chirac, Raffarin, and Sarkozy. The envelope of solidarity that once protected the Jews has eroded. Phillipe Elyakim, the senior editor of a well-known French economic journal, made the following comment: "There is something insane about the ease with which people in France call you 'dirty Jew,' as though they wanted to say 'idiot' or something. You hear anti-Semitic remarks and you feel like raising heaven and earth and telling the French what has happened to you?"

Elyakim's father had survived the Shoah as a boy in Thessaloníki and came to France after the war. His son grew up as a totally assimilated Frenchman who had not experienced any personal anti-Semitism until his thirteen-year-old son returned from school, deeply upset that one of his classmates had called him a *sale Juif*.[107] Such classic experiences have today become commonplace and so, indeed, has the state of siege felt by Jews in the poorer urban neighborhoods with a relatively large concentration of militant Muslims. There are areas where Jewish schools and synagogues have to be guarded as though they were military sites. Wearing a yarmulke in public in some parts of Paris or other cities is almost an invitation to be harassed or aggressed. As the principal of one school in a Muslim-populated area noted: "There isn't a student in the school who has been spared an anti-Semitic incident. When they go home, they encounter curses and imprecations for being Jewish."

The journalist Daniel Ben-Simon observed that of the older students in one school he visited in December 2003, nearly all saw their future in Israel and not in France. Their experiences had reinforced their pride in Jewish identity, their sense of solidarity, and a feeling that even in France they would "always remain Jews in the eyes of others."[108] It would appear that the golden age of French Jewry, which reached its peak in the 1990s, has clearly gone, only to be replaced by an atmosphere of vulnerability, threats, and volatile anti-Semitism. Despite feverish efforts to relativize the problem or to find a positive gloss in the number of anti-Semitic incidents recorded in France, the cold and somewhat surprising fact remains that Judeophobia has proven itself more tenacious than Islamophobia, or any other racist prejudice in France. No other group has been subjected to the same level of violence against individuals or institutions as the Jewish community.[109] However unpleasant this may be to acknowledge, denial is the worst of all possible options.

Though *le vieil antisémitisme classique* (traditional prejudice against Jews) has indeed declined, the real level of *threat* has dramatically increased—something implicitly recognized by 70 percent of the French population.[110] With regard to anti-Semitic acts on French territory, the statistics provided by CRIF for 2006 leave little room for comfort. There was a general increase of 24 percent in anti-Semitic incidents compared to the previous year, with a rise in physical assaults of 45 percent (112 cases) and of 71 percent in the level of insults.[111] Though there were fewer overall anti-Jewish incidents than in 2003 and 2004, this was still the third worst result since statistics began to be recorded. Moreover, an ADL survey in 2006 showed that twice as many French people sympathized with the Palestinians than did with Israel (only in Spain was the margin higher); and that nearly 40 percent thought American Jews control U.S. Middle East policy (similar results were recorded in Germany and Italy). On the other hand, there were some healthier signals. No more than a quarter of the French people believed Jews had too much power in business and finance; a majority still considered Israel an open and democratic society; and the number of those who had a favorable view of the Jewish state had increased since 2005 from 26 percent to a more respectable 40 percent. Moreover, under former prime minister Raffarin, the French government had put in place a whole battery of measures to fight anti-Semitism, including guarding Jewish establishments, instructing prosecutors to severely punish anti-Semitic acts, and even publishing a book to educate students on the subject.[112]

Nevertheless the Israel-Hezbollah war of 2006 once again increased the level of anti-Semitic incidents in France, as elsewhere in western Europe. During the months of July and August 2006, there were sixty-one such acts—an increase of 79 percent over the previous year. During anti-Israel demonstrations in various French cities there were again placards visible with slogans reading "Death to the Jews—Death to Israel" as well as Stars of David emblazoned with swastikas. Though the French press was relatively moderate in its coverage, President Chirac nonetheless characterized the Israeli military response as "completely disproportionate" on Bastille Day, July 14, 2006; Le Pen predictably went further and accused Israel of being the sole aggressor; and the Socialist candidate for the presidency, Ségolène Royal, called on Europe to pressure the United States to change its Middle East policy. Only the candidate of the conservative Union for a Popular Movement (UMP) party, Sarkozy, emphatically insisted that Hezbollah was the aggressor and that "Israel must and has the right to defend itself."[113]

Official French policy during the Second Lebanon War in 2006 was, however, far less supportive of Israel. During a visit to Beirut French foreign minister Philipe Douste-Blazy made the mind-boggling remark that "Iran constitutes a stabilizing force in the Middle East and it should be taken into account and included in any arrangement for restoring quiet to the region."[114]

On the domestic front, recurrent anti-Semitic violence has continued to drive those Jews who are wealthy enough to flee away from the northern suburbs of the capital to quieter neighborhoods in eastern Paris. The Sarcelles community of about ten thousand Jews has lost approximately 20 percent of its population over the past decade, and according to Sammy Gozlan, president of the Seine-Saint-Denis Council of Jewish communities, at least sixteen thousand Jews moved out of the suburbs between 2001 and 2008. The Jewish community of Villepinte in a northern working-class suburb of Paris graphically illustrates this unprecedented trend. In just three years, since 2005, roughly half of the Jewish families in Villepinte left the district as a result of anti-Semitic harassment. Its forty-year-old synagogue (torched in 1991 and 2001) faces closure. The community president told a reporter in April 2008 that a whole history was being erased—a stark example of what was happening to Jewish life throughout the Seine-Saint-Denis region. Maurice Fellous, head of the Jewish community in Noisy-le-Sec, another northern Paris suburb, commented to the same reporter,

Devorah Lauter: "By the next generation there will be practically no more Jews in the northern Paris periphery." Roughly two-thirds of the mostly Sephardic Jews in these close-knit communities have already left. Moreover in places like Noisy-Le-Sec, nearly 40 percent of Jewish families with children of school age have removed them since 2000 from public schools and enrolled them in Jewish institutions. This shift to Jewish schools has been taken in order to spare the children insults and taunts like "Dirty Jew!" As one North African Jew put it, recalling the flight of his own family from the Magheb to France in the 1960s: "They chased us in Algeria and they followed us here."[115]

This flight from the suburbs is gradually turning French Jewry into a semi-ghettoized community, fearful for its future. To underline the point, in March 2008 a young Sephardic Jew, Matthieu Roumi, was tortured and beaten by the same gang, Barbarians, who had kidnapped and murdered Ilan Halimi two years earlier. The six perpetrators, mostly in their twenties, consisted of Muslims, Africans, and two Portuguese immigrants who expressed their admiration for Youssouf Fofana, the imprisoned leader of the Barbarians, as they scrawled the words "Dirty Jew" on their victim's forehead.[116] At the end of June 2008 a brutal mob assaulted another Jewish teenager, seventeen-year-old Rudy Haddad, on his way to synagogue, in Paris's nineteenth arrondissement, further underlining the fragility of Jewish existence in certain districts of the French capital. More than fifteen young blacks, armed with iron blocks, attacked Haddad, who was wearing a *kippa* (Jewish skullcap). He had to be placed in intensive care and remained in a coma for some time. The press attaché of the district's Socialist mayor hastened to tell reporters on July 3, 2008, that this was not primarily an anti-Jewish attack![117] Most of the French press, like the police and local officials, also trivialized the incident as if it were merely a dispute between Jewish and black gangs, part of a pattern of interethnic violence. Journalists postulated the existence of imaginary "Jewish gangs" beating up Muslims, taunting imams, or stealing motor scooters—all without any real evidence. They misleadingly portrayed Rudy (a member of the local Lubavitch sect) as a "tough guy" with a police record who had been looking for trouble. This was pure invention.

The fact that Rudy's assailants had bashed his skull, broken his ribs, and screamed *sale juif* as they jumped on his battered body was evidently not enough to qualify as anti-Semitic.[118] Moreover, Jewish teenagers from the poor multiethnic neighborhood confirmed to reporters that they were frequently harassed and insulted in the metro or on the street by African and Arab youths. One fifteen-year-old Sephardic girl called Emilie, describing the atmosphere around the main park in the area, stated: "I dream of being able to walk down the street without being called a dirty Jew."[119] On Bastille Day that same year (July 14, 2008) it was Muslim and black gangs who burned some six hundred cars in the suburbs, attacking police with baseball bats and firecrackers.[120]

The savage beating of Rudy Haddad provoked a sharp reaction from President Sarkozy, who was traveling to Israel for a state visit. On the day of the assault he expressed his "profound indignation" and "total determination to combat all forms of racism and anti-Semitism." With the accession of Nicolas Sarkozy to the French presidency, the tone had slightly changed with regard to anti-Semitism but not the core of the problem.[121] However, the anti-Israel orientation of French foreign policy was more visibly modified. During an official visit to the United States shortly before his election, Sarkozy told the American Jewish Committee: "In France some call me Sarkozy the American. I am proud of it. I am an action person, I do as I say and I try to be pragmatic. I share many of the American values."

It was no accident that his election was greeted with general satisfaction in the United States, even in the French-bashing tabloids.[122] This sentiment was unmistakably vindicated when the new French president told his own ambassadors in early September 2007, "I am among those who believe that the friendship between the United States and France is as important today as it has been over the course of the past two centuries."[123]

French policy over Iran, with its calls for sanctions to punish its pursuit of nuclear weapons, was one clear demonstration of the greater alignment with the United States. Soon after meeting with President Bush in August 2007, Sarkozy warned that the world risks "a catastrophic alternative: an Iranian bomb, or the bombing of Iran" if diplomacy and sanctions fail. This message was reinforced by his foreign minister Bernard Kouchner in September 2007. Kouchner also made it plain to his own diplomats that "permanent anti-Americanism" is "a tradition we are working to overcome."[124] France, which had once spearheaded European antagonism toward the U.S. invasion of Iraq, now seemed to be taking the lead in making a case for tough action against Iran.

In contrast to Chirac, who believed in building up Europe as a counterweight to America, Sarkozy and Kouchner appear as "Atlanticists," unsympathetic to the idea of forging a European identity in opposition to the United States.[125] Not only that, but the current French president understands that the French in general (who are avid consumers of American popular culture) are far less anti-American than the leftist intellectuals, the academics, or the political elites. Hence, the Atlanticist shift is not a wholly unpopular move, though it represents a clear rupture with the past direction of French foreign policy since President Charles de Gaulle pulled France out of NATO's military command in 1966—a move that has now been reversed.

No less striking is the contrast between Chirac's coolness and Sarkozy's more positive attitude toward the Jewish state. The new president has unequivocally reaffirmed on many occasions the right of Israel to live within secure, recognized, and defensible borders. Repeatedly he has said that Israel's security is "not negotiable." While favoring the establishment of a Palestinian state, he has made this conditional on its unambiguous recognition of Israel and readiness to clamp down on terror. During Israeli prime minister Ehud Olmert's visit to Paris in October 2007, the shift of tone was already evident. President Sarkozy reemphasized his commitment to the security of Israel, emphasising that the Palestinians could not demand an independent state for themselves *and* insist on the "right of return" of their refugees to the Jewish state. On the Iranian nuclear program, French and Israeli positions, according to Olmert, were "identical."[126] Sarkozy also went beyond conventional diplomatic language, calling Israel's establishment "a miracle" that "may have been the most significant event of the twentieth century." Israel was not only a state that had gathered together the scattered remnants of the Jewish people, but it had "introduced diversity and democracy to the Middle East."[127] As if to reinforce these words, the first foreign leader to be officially invited by Sarkozy to Paris was Israel's president, Shimon Peres.[128]

Sarkozy's determination to warm up Franco-Israeli relations did not imply any abandonment of France's traditional friendship with the Muslim world, despite his tougher position on Syrian machinations in Lebanon and Iranian nuclear weapons. Indeed, Sarkozy caused controversy in France itself by the speed with which he welcomed a "reformed" Muammar al-Qaddafi to Paris and closed a significant armaments deal with the Libyan dictator despite his lamentable human rights record. Nor did his openness to the Maghreb prevent anti-Semitic remarks by the Algerian minister for ex-combatants, Mohammed Abbès, in late November 2007—shortly before Sarkozy's state visit to the former French colony. Abbès, himself a veteran of the bloody war of independence in the 1950s against France, told the nation's largest daily newspaper, *El Khabar*: "I do not believe that the relations between France and Algeria are founded on the principle of equality. . . . You know the origins of the President of France and you know who are the parties that brought him to power." The Algerian minister added that the real architect of Sarkozy's rise to the presidency had been the "Jewish lobby," which determines all the key decisions in France.[129] Similar libels could be found on websites of the Islamists, and of the extreme Right and Left, denouncing Sarkozy as a "Zionist agent" of America and Israel—a satanic symbol of international Jewry.

Sarkozy is, in fact, the first French *president* to be partly Jewish and, notwithstanding the political risk, he has chosen to proudly affirm his origins. True, there were Jewish prime ministers before him, including Léon Blum and Mendès-France (who were also friends of Israel), but they did not enjoy the same power. They did not symbolize the French nation and republican state authority in the way that the presidential system created by De Gaulle has permitted to its contemporary incumbents. Sarkozy's maternal grandfather, Aron Mallah, was, in fact, a Sephardi Jew from Thessaloníki who immigrated to France, converted to Catholicism, and married Adèle Bouvier, a French Christian girl. He changed his name to Benedict and integrated fully into French society, but he also remained close to his Jewish family, origins, and cultural roots. Under Vichy's race laws he was in danger of deportation, and therefore hid himself and his family in the Corrèze region of western France. No fewer than fifty-seven members of the Mallah family were murdered by the Nazis, mostly those who stayed in Thessaloníki but also some who moved to France. In 1950, Sarkozy's mother, Andrée Mallah, married the descendant of a prominent Hungarian aristocratic family. The marriage ended in divorce and, partly as a result, the young Sarkozy grew up with his maternal grandfather and was very conscious of his Jewish roots.

For French Jews, the rise of Nicolas Sarkozy to the presidency has provided a first glimpse of light at the end of an increasingly dark tunnel after seven years of intimidation, threats, and a growing sense of abandonment. Today, the French public is less pro-Palestinian in its attitudes to the Middle

East and more aware of the dangers of Islamic terrorism. A survey conducted in May 2009 indicated that Iran's arming and funding of terrorists was considered by 79 percent of respondents as the main obstacle to peace, followed by the Palestinian shooting of rockets into Israel (75 percent). Israeli incursions into Gaza came in third, with the Arab refusal to accept Israel's right to exist close behind. Two-thirds of French respondents also pointed to the continuing "teaching of hate" in Palestinian schools as a major problem. To be sure, the French still view the Palestinians more favorably than Israel, but they hold Hamas leaders primarily responsible for Gaza's humanitarian plight. A clear majority of the French (69 percent) also admitted that anti-Semitism was an issue in their country against only 8 percent who denied it. Indeed, 41 percent of those surveyed even considered hostility to Jews to be "a very big problem."[130] The French also had few illusions about Iran, with three-quarters convinced that its leadership was developing nuclear weapons and a similar number believing that this would be a threat to France. These findings, while less than flattering for Israel, reveal a nuanced and complex perception of the Middle East conflict with a profound distrust of Iranian intentions.

TEN

Britain's Old-New Judeophobes

On January 13, 2005, the London *Sun* published a photograph of Prince Harry, third in line to the British throne, dressed in Nazi regalia at a birthday party. Expressions of dismay came from many quarters, including from MP Michael Howard, the first nonbaptized Jew to lead the Conservative Party, and the heads of many Anglo-Jewish communal organizations, who widely expected a full-throated public apology. They were disappointed. The prince, a twenty-year-old raised in the reserve of royalty and acutely aware of the resonance of public symbols in the media, chose the most limited of apologies—a brief statement read by his spokesman, declaring only that "Prince Harry has apologized for any offense or embarrassment he has caused. He realizes it was a poor choice of costume."[1] No mention of the Holocaust, nor even any indication of whether his apology was directed at Jews, or—equally plausibly—at the memory of fallen British servicemen.

Moreover, when Jewish leaders called upon the prince to make a more sincere effort, such as a public appearance explicitly acknowledging his insensitivity, they were swiftly drowned out by British elites saying that the poor fellow ought to be left alone. "I don't think he needs to make a public apology," said Lord Falconer, who held the title of lord chancellor, one of the senior positions in the House of Lords, and was a close adviser to then prime minister Tony Blair. "I think already he must understand what has happened and I think that should be the end of it." According to one poll, more than half of British adults aged eighteen to twenty-four "could see no problem with the outfit."[2]

Taken in isolation, one could find reasons to ignore both the incident itself and the general reluctance of the British establishment to condemn it. Yet it came at a time when anti-Semitism has emerged as a serious problem in Britain, turning in just a few years from a public nuisance into something of a crisis.[3] According to the annual report of the Community Security Trust (CST), which tracks anti-Semitic incidents in Britain, 2006 was the worst year of anti-Semitic violence, vandalism, and harassment since the group began keeping statistics in 1984. There were 594 anti-Semitic incidents reported to the CST, a rise of 31 percent from the 2005 figure of 455 incidents. This statistic was 12 percent higher than the previous record of 532 cases recorded in 2004. During the thirty-four days of fighting in Lebanon during the summer of 2006, the CST recorded 134 anti-Semitic incidents in the United Kingdom—more than the previous highest monthly total of 105 incidents during the thirty-one days of October 2000. However, Israel's more recent military operation in Gaza in early 2009 produced 250 anti-Semitic incidents *in a single month* (nearly ten a day)—eight times more than during the same period a year earlier. There were attacks on synagogues, including arsons and many physical assaults. In Golders Green, two men punched and kicked a Jew to the ground, shouting, "This is for Gaza."[4]

Yet Britain is unusual not simply in the frequency and severity of anti-Semitic incidents. While many European countries have come to associate anti-Semitism with the forces of the extreme Right, the radical Left, or the increasingly vocal Muslim minorities, in Britain anti-Semitic sentiment is also a part of mainstream discourse, continually resurfacing among the academic, political, and media elites. Indeed, while a great deal of attention has been focused on anti-Semitism across western Europe in the past eight years, and especially in France, in some ways British anti-Semitism (often masquerading under the banner of anti-Zionism) is more prevalent, and enjoys unusual tolerance in public life. While the French state, for example, marshaled its resources to fight anti-Semitic words and actions, with greater or lesser success, in Great Britain the response was far less decisive. A significant change only came about with the report of the All-Party Parliamentary Inquiry into Antisemitism in September 2006 (an important document in itself).

There are many possible explanations for the surprising quarter that anti-Semitism in Britain currently enjoys. Whereas the efforts to combat anti-Semitism in France and Germany have been intimately connected with the memory of the Holocaust that took place on their soil, Britain has never had to undergo a similar kind of soul-searching. At the same time, London has become a world center for Muslim anti-Semitism and the demonization of Jews and Israel that accompanies it.[5] As Melanie Phillips, the *Daily Mail* columnist, wrote in September 2003: "It is not an exaggeration to say that in Britain at present it is open season on both Israel and the Jews. . . . I no longer feel comfortable in my own country because of the poison that has welled up toward . . . the Jews."[6]

In a country such as Britain, with its proud history of tolerance, moderation, and multiculturalism, this is indeed a damning indictment. Unless there is a major shift in attitudes, the United Kingdom risks becoming the country where anti-Semitism has free rein, and where Jews feel the most troubled in all of Europe.

To understand the special nature of British anti-Semitism, and the degree of legitimacy it presently enjoys in the public discourse, it is important to recognize its deeper roots in British history. While it is true that, unlike Germany, France, Russia, and Poland, Britain was not a major stronghold of anti-Semitism in the modern era, its democratic tradition has nonetheless been far more ambivalent toward Jews than is often assumed.[7] Not only that, but in the more distant past Britain was the first European state to expel its Jewish population altogether.

Medieval English anti-Semitism was both innovative and lethal before the removal of the Jews in 1290. The British historian and lawyer Anthony Julius has noted that the anti-Jewish measures that preceded this expulsion encompassed torture, expropriation, and murder, and established the horrific precedent of the blood libel for the rest of medieval Christendom. It was in Norwich in 1144 that the ritual murder charge first appeared, accusing the Jews of using the blood of Christian children for their Passover matzoth. Predatory rulers, an unruly and violent populace, and a hostile Catholic Church combined to make Jewish lives in medieval England "often intolerable, and finally impossible."[8] Britain in the years between 1144 and 1290 was in effect a *persecuting* society, replete with "massacres, forced conversions, and a zealotry in enforcing discriminatory Church laws against the Jews unmatched in the rest of Europe."[9]

The forcible ejection of Jews from England did not bring to an end the resonances of a murderous, triumphalist Christian anti-Semitism—one that was immortalized in ballad and song, drama, fiction, and poetry. In the late thirteenth century, the ballad "Sir Hugh, or The Jew's Daughter" commemorated a notorious blood libel. Geoffrey Chaucer's "Prioress's Tale" (in his canonical *Canterbury Tales*), Christopher Marlowe's super-

Machiavellian *The Jew of Malta,* and William Shakespeare's more subtle *The Merchant of Venice* (to name only some of the best-known cases) established a formidable literary tradition of anti-Semitism in which Jews and Judaism were portrayed in negative and often sinister terms. These hostile images were thoroughly honed in the 350 years that the Jewish presence altogether disappeared from English soil.[10]

The readmittance of Jews in the 1650s did not fundamentally change the prevailing stereotypes, though they were somewhat modified by the vain hope that Jews would be ripe for conversion to Protestant Christianity. A century later, in the mid-1750s, the savage popular outcry against the proposal to naturalize foreign-born Jews without their adopting Anglicanism indicated just how limited the break with the past had really been. The full repertoire of medieval anti-Semitism (condemning Jews as Christ killers, bloodthirsty usurers, thieves, and spreaders of disease) came back into play in the context of English party politics and popular agitation. It should be said that this anti-Jewish paroxysm had little to do with the relatively small Anglo-Jewish community that numbered about twenty-five thousand—mainly Sephardic and primarily concentrated in commerce or in the city of London as merchants, stockbrokers, and bankers.[11]

However, in Victorian England, the more violent strand of anti-Semitism had begun to ebb away as the British Empire arrived at its apogee. Nineteenth-century Britain was transformed into the manufacturing hub of the industrial world and the global market. The formal emancipation of the Jews in 1858, the election of a converted Jew, the exotic and unconventional Benjamin Disraeli, as prime minister, and the rise of veritable aristocratic dynasties among the Anglo-Jewish elite pointed to the emergence of a more liberal dispensation. With its free-trade gospel, Victorian England valued entrepreneurial initiative and self-help very highly. No less important, religious tolerance had gradually become enshrined in Britain, along with parliamentary democracy and political pluralism. A philo-Semitic tradition of Protestantism, which not only revered the biblical Hebrews but also felt some affinity for modern-day Jews, helped to attenuate past hostility. Moreover, commercial capitalism, having come earlier to England (and without any major Jewish input) was not as intense a source of conflict between Jews and Christians as it would be in France or Germany. Wealthy Jews were, for example, almost as legitimate in Britain (or America, for that matter) as wealthy Gentiles.

Nevertheless, there was an anticapitalist populist undercurrent in British political discourse, epitomized by William Cobbett, the radical MP for Oldham and the celebrated author of *Rural Rides*. Cobbett's strident rhetoric was especially directed at Scotsmen, Quakers, and Jews—considered by him to have a special talent for making money without working. Moreover, they were bearers of those rational modernizing and urban values that threatened the yeoman rural England that he so ardently defended. Cobbett fiercely attacked the prospect of Jewish political emancipation in the 1830s, evoking Jews with special virulence as the "descendants of the murderers of Jesus Christ," and as willing tools of the oppressors throughout history; they had, he believed, a natural propensity to bribe and corrupt others. Not for nothing did the great British liberal historian (and parliamentary opponent of Cobbett) Thomas Babington Macaulay describe him as a "reasoning bigot" who justified the persecution of Jews by libeling them as "a mean race, a sordid race, and money-getting race . . . averse to all honorable callings."[12] Cobbett's radical anti-plutocratic anti-Semitism subsequently found echoes in the Chartist movement of his time and then in the anti–Boer War agitation of the British Left around 1900. Indeed, it might even be seen as a distant precursor of the anti-Zionist agitation on the British Left after 1967.

A new factor in British anti-Semitism was the rapid growth of the Jewish population of Great Britain from a modest 35,000 in 1850 to 243,000 in 1910. It reached a prewar peak of 350,000 in 1939. The largest single wave of immigration (from czarist Russia) came in the two decades before World War I, creating a xenophobic backlash reflected in the Aliens Bill of 1905. The "alien invasion" of Jews from the Russian Pale of Settlement prompted some British ideologues such as Arnold White to invoke the specter of "rule by foreign Jews" in a secret conspiracy with the British aristocracy. White's xenophobic anti-Semitism did not, however, prevent him from visiting Russia on behalf of Jewish groups to investigate czarist persecution and from proposing alternative solutions to the "Jewish question," including America and Palestine. The same was true of the Conservative MP for Stepney, Sir William Evans-Gordon. A leading progenitor of the Aliens Act, Evans-Gordon was an avowed anti-Semite but one who was sensitive to Jewish suffering in Russia and sympathetic to Zionism. Such voices (like those in the trade unions) opposed unrestricted immigration to Britain mainly because it was liable to depress wages and increase social tensions.

These arguments had the support of the established Anglo-Jewish leadership and of Zionists convinced that further Jewish immigration to Britain would only aggravate anti-Semitism. The future Zionist leader Chaim Weizmann suggested in his memoirs (perhaps too generously) that Evans-Gordon was solely driven by English patriotism rather than anti-Jewish prejudice. The Conservative MP believed that the great industrial centers of England had reached saturation point. Weizmann agreed, cryptically observing that Evans-Gordon was "ready to encourage settlement of Jews almost anywhere in the British Empire, but failed to see why the ghettos of London or Leeds or Whitechapel should be made into branches of the ghettos of Warsaw and Pinsk."[13]

Anti-Semitism in late Victorian and Edwardian England was essentially driven by such protectionist sentiment, though it was not devoid of sympathy for persecuted Jewish refugees. At the same time, racism was certainly present in Britain, often directed against the Irish, Germans, Italians, Chinese, blacks, and others. Racial stereotypes, with their degrading assumptions about the ineradicable difference between Anglo-Saxons and "Semites" or "Orientals," and the moral inferiority of Jews, added a new dimension of pseudo-rationality to old prejudices. The "rich Jew anti-Semitism" of the Left bizarrely cohabited with conservative claims that Jews were all radical subversives, secret plotters, and clannish and dishonest knaves unwilling to assimilate.[14] Even Arthur James Balfour, Conservative prime minister in 1905 (and future author of the famous 1917 declaration that bears his name) was concerned, during the debate over the Aliens Act, that Jews, despite their patriotism and abilities, "remained a people apart, and not merely held a religion differing from the vast majority of their fellow-countrymen."[15] Before World War I (and for the next thirty years), Balfour's Conservative Party would be hostile to "alien" immigration, regarding Jewish "slums" (with the vice and crime they entailed) as a "threat to the Anglo-Saxon race."[16] Conservatives were in the forefront of those who speculated about a Jewish fifth column loyal primarily to international Jewry or to Germany rather than to Great Britain. During the military conflict with imperial Germany, this campaign against dual loyalties led to attacks on prominent German-born Jews such as Sir Ernest Cassel and Sir Edgar Speyer and calls for their removal as privy councillors. Similarly, the October 1917 Bolshevik Revolution in Russia increased resentment toward the far less assimilated eastern European Jews in Britain.[17] There were even some violent outbursts against Jews in the East End and Leeds, driven by the refusal of most Russian Jews to volunteer for military service at a time when the hated czarist regime in Russia was Britain's wartime ally.

In October 1917, at a critical moment during the war against Germany, the issue of Zionism was very high on imperial Britain's foreign policy agenda. The positive Zionist attitude toward the British Empire helped to give their advocacy a newfound legitimacy, and they were seen by influential British Gentiles as supportive of the Allied war effort. This stood in sharp contrast to the poor image of those Jews suspected of being pacifists, revolutionaries, pro-German, or cosmopolitan representatives of high finance.[18] In December 1917, at the very time that the Jewish-born Leon Trotsky, the Bolshevik commissar for foreign affairs, was preparing Russia's exit from World War I, British troops captured Jerusalem. This conquest came only a month after Lord Balfour had promised Palestine as a national home for the Jews. The Foreign Office and British establishment circles—convinced that Jews exercised an almost magical influence on international events—now looked to Zionism to pull their chestnuts out of the fire.

Ironically enough, the most formidable opponent of the Balfour Declaration within the British cabinet was the new secretary of state for India, Edwin Montagu—a prominent Jewish anti-Zionist who favored total assimilation into British society. In a memorandum of 1917 entitled "The Anti-Semitism of the Present Government," Montagu somewhat hysterically declared that the policy of His Majesty's government on Palestine was "anti-Semitic in result and will prove a rallying ground for Anti-Semites in every country in the world." Montagu insisted that Zionism was a "mischievous political creed," untenable by any patriotic British citizen. He even declared himself ready to *disenfranchise* every Zionist and to ban the Zionist organization as inimical to the British national interest. Montagu gloomily predicted that if the Jews were granted a national home in Palestine, it would become "the world's ghetto." At a meeting of the war cabinet on October 4, 1917, he went further still, suggesting that the civil rights of Jewish Britons like himself would be seriously damaged by the proposed declaration. His own ability to negotiate with the peoples of India (including millions of Muslims) on behalf of the British government might be gravely impaired if it was implied that his real home was in Palestine—an anxiety that proved to have no foundation whatsoever.

In a personal letter to British prime minister David Lloyd George shortly after this cabinet meeting, Montagu complained that "every anti-Semitic organisation and newspaper will ask what right a Jewish Englishman, with the status at best of a naturalised foreigner, has to take a foremost part in the government of the British Empire."[19] When news of the Balfour Declaration reached him in India, Montagu wrote in his diary on November 11, 1917: "The Government has dealt an irreparable blow at Jewish Britons and they have endeavoured to set up a people which does not exist; they have alarmed unnecessarily the whole Moslem world; and insofar as they are successful they will have a Germanised Palestine on the flank of Egypt."[20]

The protests of Montagu and other leading British Jews did, in fact, delay and modify the final text of the Balfour Declaration. As James Malcolm (a strong Gentile supporter of Zionism) recalled in 1944, the war cabinet was "very apprehensive because from the point of view of wealth and influence, the anti-Zionist Jews greatly outweighed the few Zionist leaders who were in London."[21]

The backlash from leaders of the Anglo-Jewish "Cousinhood" was not slow in coming. On November 14, 1917, the newly established League of British Jews (including some of the wealthiest and most prestigious families in Anglo-Jewry) began to organize Jewish opposition to Zionism, proclaiming its determination to resist the allegation that their coreligionists constituted a separate political nationality.[22] Though it represented only a narrow elite of British Jews, the League had considerable influence. But the League soon had to confront a different kind of anti-Zionist onslaught, led by British newspapers such as the anti-Jewish *Morning Post,* the *Daily Mail,* and *The Times.* Editorials and articles in the press did not hesitate to impugn the so-called dual loyalties of British Jews or to demand the removal of leading Jewish officials in Palestine, including the recently appointed high commissioner, Herbert Samuel.[23] The *Daily Express* openly suggested that anyone who defended Zionism was indeed unpatriotic and un-British. Lord Beaverbrook even called the Zionists "the most dangerous foe of the patriotic British Jew."[24] The *Sunday Express* ostentatiously contrasted patriotic English Jews with the wicked, anti-British Zionists. Somewhat unctuously it declared: "No one knows better than the anti-Zionist Jews how much the Zionists have done to stir up anti-Semitic prejudices by their hysterical advocacy of the Palestine Administration."[25] The anti-Zionist campaign in British conservative circles was heavily tainted by anti-Semitism. This posed an awkward dilemma for the League of British Jews, who had no desire to be associated with such hostile forces. In April 1919, ten Anglo-Jewish dignitaries linked to the League felt obliged to publicly deny any similarity between Judaism and Bolshevism at the same time as they condemned Jewish nationalism. By 1922, when Zionism itself had become the object of relentlessly *anti-Semitic* attacks, the League began to mute its own propaganda.

The ultraconservative *Morning Post* and its editor H. A. Gwynne had seen a Jewish "hidden hand" behind Bolshevism, Lloyd George's policies in Ireland, the Paris Peace Conference, the emerging League of Nations (a "conspiracy" of American Jewry), and Marxist-inspired attempts to wreck the British Empire.[26] The paper insisted that the "secret rulers of Jewry" controlled the destiny of the world and the diplomacy of the nations and were clandestinely allied either to Germany or Communist Russia—archenemies of the British Empire.

Lord Sydenham of Combe was one of a number of prominent British peers who agreed that it was impossible to disentangle nefarious German and Judaic conspiracies. A former army officer and colonial governor of Victoria (Australia), and of Bombay, he fully believed in a global Jewish plot to undermine Great Britain. In an article of November 1921 in the *Fortnightly Review,* Sydenham blamed the Jews for the fact that "the British Empire is now being subjected to attack wherever it is thought to be most vulnerable, and notably in India, Ireland, Egypt and Palestine." He added that the "strenuous efforts directed from Moscow to promote World Revolution" were not of Slavic but Jewish origin. The League of Nations, he told a distinguished Australian correspondent, Sir James Barrett, "is a Jewish invention directed principally against our Empire."[27]

While Winston Churchill shared Lord Sydenham's repugnance for Bolshevism as a worldwide "conspiracy for the overthrow of civilization," he sharply rejected the idea of any connection between Zionism and the "international Jews." On the contrary, in February 1920, Churchill explained that there was a *split* in the soul of Jewry, whom he called "the most formidable and the most remarkable race which has ever appeared in the world." The Zionists were the "good Jews," in his eyes, constructive patriots seeking to build the Jewish national home, which Churchill passionately supported. The Bolshevik Jews from Marx to Trotsky and Béla Kun were, on the other hand, their complete antithesis—sinister terrorists fanning the flames of unrest and rebellion around the globe. These Jewish revolutionaries had now "gripped the Russian people by the hair of their heads and have become the undisputed masters of that enormous empire."[28] The popularity of the *Protocols of the Elders of Zion* in Britain during the early 1920s (it was translated for *The Morning Post* by the paper's Russian correspondent, Victor Marsden, in 1919) was directly related to such assumptions about "Judeo-Bolshevism" within the British establishment. Fortunately, they did not take deeper root in interwar Britain after Philip Graves, Istanbul correspondent for *The Times,* exposed the *Protocols* as a fraud in August 1921.[29]

On the other hand, literary anti-Semitism continued to flourish in interwar Britain. There was an abundance of "cultural anti-Semites" including Hilaire Belloc and G. K. Chesterton, both Anglo-Catholics preoccupied with the intellectual, economic, and political power of the Jews in the Western world. The French-born Belloc was much influenced by the venomous anti-Semitism of Édouard Drumont's *La Libre Parole,* and the ultranationalist Action Française across the English Channel. His own anti-Jewish polemics were often strident and obsessive, though he (rather comically) denied being an anti-Semite. Belloc called for recognition of the "Jewish nation" while insisting on the exclusion of Jews from any influence in Britain.[30] Complex, bizarre, and convoluted to the end, he blamed the 1939 German invasion of Poland on "Jewish bankers who had allowed Prussia to re-arm," and on Oxford dons.[31]

An antithetical left-liberal version of English intellectual anti-Semitism (also with roots in the Edwardian era) was that of the supposedly cosmopolitan, progressive writer H. G. Wells. Before 1914 Wells was already convinced that Jewish *difference* must be eliminated—along with that of other "inferior races"—by total assimilation into "mankind." Wells, along with a number of other Edwardian writers, disliked the allegedly "Jewish" traits of vulgarity and materialism, hoping that in the twentieth century, "irrational" Jewish particularism would completely disappear. By contrast, Jewish internationalism fitted well into his utopian idealist framework, and at times he related to Diaspora Jews as a possible foregleam of his vision of a coming "world-state." From his early science fiction of the 1890s to the late novels of the 1940s, there are more than a few decadent, reactionary, and selfish Jewish characters in Wells's writing, embodying the "Semitic plutocracy" of a decaying British social order. In his bestselling *Outline of History* (1920), written for the common man, Wells characteristically presented Judaism as a "curious combination of theological breadth and an intense racial patriotism." He had always identified with the "universalist" prophetic strand and despised the Jewish particularists as bigoted, "exclusivist," "Pharisaic," and "racist." H. G. Wells managed to uneasily combine respect for internationalists of Jewish origin with loathing for "Hebraic tribalism" and a clear tendency to hold Jews responsible for anti-Semitism. By the late 1930s, he foresaw the "systematic attempt to exterminate" European Jewry, but absurdly enough he attributed it to the failure of German Jewry to assimilate! In the same spirit, he explained away the rise of interwar English anti-Semitism as an understandable reaction to the inability of local Jews to fully integrate into British culture.[32]

The position of the celebrated Anglo-American poet T. S. Eliot was much closer to that of Hilaire Belloc. He, too, had imbibed French Judeophobic influences through his pre-1914 familiarity with Charles Maurras's Action Française. The anti-Semitic poems Eliot published in a 1920 collection entitled *Ara Vos Prec* included lines such as those in "Burbank with a Baedeker: Bleistein with a Cigar" and "Sweeney Among the Nightingales" that were partly written in reaction against the evils of a self-indulgent romantic individualism, execrated by the classicist Maurrasian school. Since 1910 Eliot had absorbed their critique of feminine emotionalism and liberal intellectual decadence. For the young Eliot cultural dissolution was associated with women and Jews. The lines spoken by Gerontion creepily evoke the linkage of Jews, alienness, and sexual corruption:

> My house is a decayed house,
> and the jew squats on the window sill, the owner,
> Spawned in some estaminet of Antwerp,
> Blistered in Brussels, patched and peeled in London.

Eliot's Venetian poem in the same collection was no less anti-Semitic in its imagery:

> A lustreless protrusive eye
> 　　Stares from the protozoic slime
> At a perspective of Canaletto.
> 　　The smoky candle end of time
> Declines. On the Rialto once
> 　　The rats are underneath the piles.

The jew is underneath the lot.
Money in furs. The boatman smiles,

A number of characters in these poems have somewhat unpleasant-sounding Jewish names. In the "Sweeney" lyric, for example, we learn about a Jewish woman (probably a prostitute):

Rachel *née* Rabinovitch
Tears at the grapes with murderous paws.

There is Sir Ferdinand Klein and Bleistein himself (who also features as a decaying corpse with "dead jew's eyes" in a deleted section from Eliot's *The Waste Land*)—a symbol of the "Jewish" cosmopolitanism that Eliot heartily detested, despite his own sense of rootlessness. For Eliot, the preeminent poet of his generation in the English-speaking world, the Jew was evidently a negative symbol of the unsettling features of modernity—destructive of harmonious order and security. He was the undesirable outsider in the rigidly hierarchical, Christian society to which Eliot nostalgically wished to return after his conversion to Anglo-Catholicism in the 1920s. A classicist in literature and a royalist in his politics, with a theocratic vision for contemporary society, Eliot wrote in his *After Strange Gods* (1934) that "reasons of race and religion combine to make any large number of free-thinking Jews undesirable." They could be only an irritant in a racially homogeneous Christian order, founded on organic principles, which repudiated free-thinking secularism as abhorrent.[33]

Eliot's anti-Semitism in the 1930s was influenced not only by the reactionary royalist politics of Frenchmen such as Charles Maurras but also by the homegrown Social Credit movement of the autodidact Major C. H. Douglas, who warned that Great Britain's economy was being craftily manipulated by a worldwide Jewish conspiracy. Douglas regarded Jews as the major protagonists of collectivism in all its forms (not only of the socialist kind but also in "big business"). Moreover, Jews were the bearers of an unparalleled "race consciousness." Douglas was convinced that the plan and methods of enslavement outlined in the *Protocols of the Elders of Zion* were actually "reflected in the facts of everyday experience." His belief in the "Jewish peril" echoed through all his books, with a special emphasis on "the existence of great secret [Jewish] organizations bent on the acquisition of world-empire." In 1938, Douglas fiercely lashed out against the unbearable "parasitism" of the Jewish race and their (supposed) control of the global financial system: "It is Trade, with its Black Magic of Finance, Salesmanship and Advertising, which is the Jewish National Home."[34] The Bank of England, he added, ruled the country "and the Jews rule the Bank of England. . . . The problem of the Jews themselves is one which will require a solution, and it ought to be solved." It is a remarkable fact that despite such vitriolic anti-Semitism, Major Douglas's Social Credit schemes enjoyed considerable support, not only from T. S. Eliot but also from other well-known members of the English literary intelligentsia in the 1930s.

This was the same decisive decade in which Sir Oswald Mosley and his British Union of Fascists (BUF) first introduced a new motif into British political discourse: the claim that warmongering Jews were trying to drag Great Britain into a futile and unnecessary confrontation with Nazi Germany. After 1934 Mosley had discarded the sound advice of his diplomat friend Sir Harold Nicolson that the English were "always impressed by propagandists who take their boots off before they start kicking below the belt." Instead, he chose the path of unrestrained fascist demagogy associated with Hitler and Mussolini, combining it with a pseudo-pacifist rant and an open appeal to anti-Semitic feeling, especially in London's East End.[35] The BUF had a very limited impact, compared to the barbaric persecution in Nazi Germany and the severe anti-Jewish legislation of the late 1930s in Romania and Hungary. Nevertheless, anti-Semitic residues of British fascism did carry through into World War II. For example, between 1939 and 1945 the British government was continuously preoccupied with not being seen to fight a "Jews' war"; there was an often hysterical fear of fifth columns and "enemy aliens," not to mention the paranoid linkage of Jews with black marketeering, spying, and subversive activities.[36]

This nasty undercurrent of anti-Semitism during the war years was also a factor in Britain's refusal to undertake any serious rescue effort to save European Jewry during the Holocaust. The British government's intransigent policy in blocking Jewish immigration to Palestine after 1939 (thereby breaking solemn commitments under the mandate), while driven mainly by cold realpolitik and imperial strategy, was not altogether free of anti-Semitic sentiments.[37] Such feelings had been present from the beginning of the mandate among military, colonial, and Foreign Office personnel. Many, including E. T. Richmond of the Palestine secretariat, believed that the mandate was "iniquitous," a sustained aggression against the Arabs in favor of an "alien and dangerous" Jewish invader. Some, such as the British civic adviser in Jerusalem, C. R. Ashbee, expressed an undisguised anti-Semitic loathing for the squalor, foulness, lying, and "arrogant obscurantism" of the Jews.[38] Others, such as the sophisticated governor of Jerusalem, Sir Ronald Storrs, loftily objected to the idea that "Arab soil" should be treated as an "involuntary dumping ground for people unacceptable elsewhere."[39] Other British administrators in the Middle East, including Sir Harold MacMichael and Sir Edward Grigg, unabashedly compared Zionism with Nazism, even as the Jews were being mass murdered by the Germans across Europe. In March 1945, Lord Gort, high commissioner for Palestine, wrote to the colonial secretary in London that "the establishment of any Jewish State in Palestine in the immediate future will almost inevitably mean the rebirth of National Socialism in some guise." He felt that Britain should not agree too quickly "to any solution which might perpetuate in the Middle East the Fascist ideals we have sought so hard to eradicate."[40] He was referring to the Zionists and not to the Arab nationalists who in some cases had actively collaborated with Hitler.

One of the rare examples of a pro-Zionist British officer in Palestine, the highly unconventional Captain Orde Wingate, noted in a letter of January 1937 that British officials "hate the Jew and like the Arab, who although he shoots at them, toadies to them and flatters their sense of importance."[41] Bartley Crum, an American Catholic lawyer and member of the 1946 Anglo-American Committee of Inquiry into Palestine, was stunned to discover the extent of anti-Semitism in the British military after the war. For example, in the British zone of Austria, a red-faced British officer told him how much he hated "the Jew-bastards" and wished "they'd all be burned to death."[42]

Such attitudes were even reflected on occasion at the highest levels of the British government. The first U.S. ambassador to Israel, James G. McDonald, passing through London, recorded in his diary on August 3, 1948: "Facing Bevin across his broad table, I had to tell myself that this was not Hitler seated before me but His Majesty's Principal Secretary of State for Foreign Affairs. . . . His bitterness at [American president] Mr. Truman was almost pathological: it found its match only in his other scapegoats—the Jews, the Israelis, the Israeli Government."[43]

Thus, sixty years ago, anti-Americanism, anti-Zionism, and anti-

Semitism were already intertwined in the mind of a former trade union official, now presiding over the declining British Empire. Richard Crossman, the young Labour MP who was close to Ernest Bevin at the time, concluded that by 1947 British policy in Palestine was largely motivated by "one man's determination to teach the Jews a lesson."[44] The refusal of Palestinian Jewry to conform to British plans for them had pushed Bevin into "overt anti-Semitism." The British foreign secretary became convinced that "the Jews were organizing a world conspiracy against poor old Britain," in which they [the Zionist Jews], together with the Soviet Union, would seek to bring down the British Empire.[45] A no less venomous, if more banal and petty-minded, anti-Semitism was expressed in 1947 by Lieutenant General Evelyn Barker, the commander of British forces in Palestine. He determined that the British army would henceforth avoid any fraternization with Palestinian Jews and "punish the Jews in the manner this race dislikes as much as any, by hitting them in the pocket, which will demonstrate our disgust for them."[46]

The Palestine troubles reached a new climax in July and August 1947. For the first time anti-Jewish riots erupted in postwar Britain, following the hanging of two British sergeants by the Irgun (a militant Zionist organization) in Palestine in revenge for the execution of an Irgun member by the British. On August 1, 1947, mobs of youths rampaged through Jewish districts in Liverpool, Manchester, Glasgow, East London, and other cities. Jewish property was looted, synagogues attacked, and cemeteries desecrated. Postwar diaries for this period indicate a remarkably bitter, vengeful, and hostile attitude in England toward British Jews, which was assiduously exploited by fascist agitators.[47] Moreover, by the time of the unprovoked assault of five Arab states on Israel in May 1948 in order to strangle it at birth, British policy was widely perceived in the outside world as hostile to the Israelis and seeking to abort the rebirth of the Jewish nation. *The Manchester Guardian,* still mildly sympathetic to Zionism in those days, called on Bevin not to compromise Britain's reputation by his complicity in efforts to destroy the fledgling Jewish state. Its editor specifically reproached Britain's foreign secretary for his obstinate determination to provide "British gold and British officers" to the Arab side in the Palestine war.[48]

At the heart of the Arab military campaign against Zion was Sir John Bagot Glubb, British commander of the Jordanian Arab Legion, who undoubtedly believed that the creation of Israel was a dreadful injustice to the

Arab Palestinians. A conservative Englishman who had devoted himself to the cause of the desert Arabs, Glubb was also an unabashed anti-Semite persuaded that the "unlikable character" of the Jews was the prime cause of anti-Semitism. Glubb held that Russian and Eastern European Jews were really Khazar Turks with no connection at all to the Promised Land; that the Jews were by nature an aggressive and stiff-necked people; and that their vengeful mentality had been "passed down without a break from generation to generation."[49] Since biblical times, Jews had supposedly been imbued with "the idea of a superior race" whose blood must not be contaminated "by inter-mixture with others." They had not only invented the idea of chosenness and the "master race" theory, but their behavior toward Arabs was an example of pure Hitlerite politics. The Jews, according to Glubb's skewed vision of history, were also to blame for the habit of religious persecution and massacres in the history of Christendom.[50]

Glubb invariably depicted Zionist Jews as arrogant, intolerant, and enjoying complete control of world public opinion, especially in America.[51] In Palestine they had conducted themselves like ruthless military conquerors hell-bent on achieving domination of the entire Middle East. In July 1946, in a memorandum to the British government, Glubb wrote that the "new Jews" in Palestine had a mentality that fused the ancient Hebrew tradition (full of narrow hate) with "a layer of up-to-date Eastern European fanaticism." Worst of all, they had copied Nazi techniques—embracing "the theories of race, blood and soil, the terrorism of the gunman, the inculcation of hate into the young, and the youth movements." The young Jew of Palestine, Glubb concluded, was "as hard, as narrow, as fanatical, and as bitter as the Hitler youth on whom he is modeled."[52] Like other leading British officials and military personnel in the Middle East, Glubb was prone to caricature, and defamed Zionism as a form of "Jewish Nazism." This would prove to be a libel with a great future ahead of it.

Another prominent British exponent of the Nazi-Zionist theory in the 1950s was the world-renowned historian Arnold J. Toynbee. His monumental *Study in History* indicted the Jewish Zionists in Palestine as "disciples of the Nazis." Indeed, they were much worse than their teachers because they had *knowingly* chosen "to imitate some of the evil deeds that the Nazis had committed against the Jews."[53] Hence Toynbee, though professing some perfunctory shock at the extent of the German "apostasy" from the West, concluded that the "Nazi Gentiles' fall from grace was less tragic than the

Zionist Jews'."[54] The immediate reaction of the Zionists to the "worst atrocities ever suffered by the Jews or any other human beings" had been to let themselves become "persecutors" taking revenge on the Arabs and inflicting upon them similar "wrongs and sufferings."[55] Toynbee was half a century ahead of his time in spewing out these grossly misleading assertions.

Toynbee was both influenced and felt reinforced in his views by the anti-Zionist Jewish Fellowship, founded in 1944, which (like the now-defunct League of British Jews) included some of the most illustrious Anglo-Jewish names and a number of Conservative MPs of Jewish origin. One of them was Colonel Louis Gluckstein, a particularly vociferous opponent of Zionism and a member of the board of deputies. He told members of the Anglo-American Committee in 1946 to discard all the evidence of Jewish concentration camp survivors, because they were not "mentally or physically fit to form a judgment."[56] Like Fellowship chairman Basil Henriques, he suggested not only that some of the survivors were psychologically unhinged but that Zionism itself was a mental delusion brought about by Nazism and the Holocaust.[57] Gluckstein bizarrely warned the committee that "to believe that this [Jewish suffering] is a justification for Jewish separatism and Jewish nationalism seems to me the adoption of the Hitler doctrine." Julian Franklyn, the secretary of the Jewish Fellowship, went further still. He argued that the Zionists had taken their cue from the Germanic philosophy of race, blood, and iron, thereby becoming the heirs of Nazism.[58]

The Nazi-Zionist analogy would fall on very fertile soil in Britain after 1945, when its soldiers were busy repressing the Jewish armed revolt in Palestine. The parallel was eagerly taken up not only by Glubb Pasha and Arnold Toynbee but also by Sir Edward Grigg (Lord Altrincham) and the chairman of the Committee for Arab Affairs in Britain, Sir Edward Spears. Spears, in particular (who was suspected of having Jewish blood), hammered away at the idea that Zionist policy in Palestine had adopted the Nazi doctrine of *Lebensraum* (living space). Zionist Jews, he indignantly insisted, were posing as the "master race" and committed to the totalitarian indoctrination of Jewish youth.[59]

Thus many decades before it became a fashionable left-wing mantra, the Nazi-Zionist equation was already a favorite weapon of the pro-Arab British elites. Totally ignoring the Arab resolve (in contradiction to international law and UN decisions) to strangle the infant State of Israel in 1948, they suggested that Jews, in a bloodthirsty and unprovoked frenzy, had gratuitously murdered or expelled peaceful, law-abiding Arabs. This was a mockery of the facts. The only event that even remotely could be construed in such a light was the assault on the Arab village of Deir Yassin by the Irgun on April 9, 1948—an action deplored by the mainstream Jewish leadership. Even today the truth about this incident is contested. But it was ranked by Arnold Toynbee on a par with Nazi crimes. Yet, similar or far worse Arab atrocities both before and during the 1948 war over Palestine were invariably disregarded or ignored.[60]

At the end of the World War II, for prominent Arabists and Foreign Office mandarins such as Sir Harold Beeley, it went without saying that Zionism was a disaster for British interests to be repudiated as an artificial nationalism. On the other hand, Toynbee and his friends approved Arab aspirations as natural, organic, and morally irreproachable. Significantly enough, the "post-national" Toynbee (he had once been a Zionist), like many British intellectuals after him, proved to be tone-deaf when it came to proto-fascist Arab nationalism and anti-Semitism, which stood in the most flagrant contradiction to their self-proclaimed liberal principles.

The continuities in arguments between the Toynbee generation and today are striking, even though the schooling, outlook, politics, and identity of the protagonists is obviously different. From the mid-1940s onward, members of the British establishment (colonial administrators, military officers, former ambassadors to the Middle East, Conservative MPs, missionaries, and Arabists) were especially prominent in promoting the Arab cause. Today, it is left-wing militants, anti-globalists, "peace activists," Islamists, and some prominent Anglicans who set the tone. But in all these cases, the demonization of Zionism and the uncritical embrace of the Palestinians is the lowest common denominator. The older British anti-Zionist organizations were, however, more elitist and less successful than the present-day Palestine Solidarity Campaign (PSC) in reaching the broader British public and organizing boycott and disinvestment campaigns against Israel. Then, as now, the anti-Zionists denied any anti-Semitism, but there is ample evidence to show that this claim was false.

Rory Miller, a lecturer at King's College, London, quotes from the private correspondence in 1946 of two well-known members of the Committee for Arab Affairs (CAA), Rev. Professor Alfred Guillaume (then the leading academic theologian in Britain) and MP Henry Longhurst. Both men were in contact with the chairman of CAA, Sir Edward Spears. Professor Guillaume categorically opposed opening up England, let alone Palestine, to any Jewish immigration after the Holocaust: "Everywhere one hears complaints about their behavior, their control of industry and finance and their increasing weight in the universities. I am not anti-Jewish myself, but I confess I do not want to see this country [England] dominated by Jews." Longhurst concurred, worrying that there was "a serious chance of our national stock being affected" if Jews were to be let into the British Isles.[61] The hypocritical denial of racism in advocating such actions is striking. Thus long before the 1967 Israeli conquest of the West Bank and Gaza, such advocates vehemently delegitimized Zionism with a crass anti-Semitism that denied its own existence.

After 1967 the pro-Arab lobby reorganized under the flag of the Council for Arab-British Understanding (CAABU), among whose founders were the intensely pro-Arab journalist Michael Adams and the Labour MP Christopher (later Lord) Mayhew. The lobby began to use increasingly sophisticated propaganda techniques to win over trade unionists, students, politicians, and youth in general to the Palestinian cause.[62] Mayhew, in particular, was extremely active. He had become convinced in the early 1950s that Bevin was right about Palestine. Mayhew believed that Zionism was indeed "racialist" and, in his view, permanently wedded to terror and violence. More important, Mayhew was extraordinarily persistent in his denunciations of the "Zionist lobby," especially in the British Labour Party.[63] In his distorted view of history, three-quarters of a million Palestinian Arabs (an exaggerated figure) had been callously dispossessed solely because of illegitimate Jewish and Zionist pressures, bordering on blackmail, inside British politics. According to Mayhew, Israel was a new South Africa—a racist apartheid state—but the British Labour Party, under excessive Jewish influence, had refused to recognize this obvious fact. It was no accident that in the 1970s Mayhew and other pro-Palestinian Labour MPs such as Andrew Faulds would consistently charge British Jews (and especially Jewish MPs) of having dual loyalties— an accusation historically tainted by anti-Semitism. It was also characteristic that Mayhew's closest associate, Michael Adams, would claim that the British press was under Zionist control.[64] Forty years ago, Adams (an avowedly pro-Arab lobbyist) was already insistently pressing the point that the "Jewish lobby" sought to silence legitimate criticism of Israel by mendacious accusations of anti-Semitism.

The Adams-Mayhew line began to find a certain echo on both the right and the left of British politics in the 1970s. Dr. Israel Shahak and other self-hating Israeli anti-Zionists were already being lavishly praised in pro-Arab quarters and invoked to assert that Israel was an institutionally *racist* society, systematically discriminating against all non-Jews, and undergoing a relentless process of Nazification. Shahak and his Gentile admirers also accused Zionists of having a vested interest in promoting anti-Semitism and of deliberately instrumentalizing it to justify the persecution of Palestinians.[65] In the mid-1970s such stereotypes underpinned the "campus war" that led to the banning of some Jewish societies at British universities for supporting Israel.

At the heart of this campaign was the New Left brand of anti-Zionism—initially an offshoot of revolutionary Marxist efforts to root themselves in black and Asian immigrant populations. A typical article in the *Socialist Leader* in October 1970 castigated Zionism as a form of "religious fascism" seeking to create a racial state. At the same time, the anti-Zionists denied that Jews were a nation with any claim to their ancestral homeland or to collective self-determination.[66] This was the period when the British New Left (partly influenced by Soviet and Third Worldist propaganda) began to systematically depict Israel as a "colonialist settler state."[67] It was also the era that produced Jim Allen's tawdry play *Perdition*—a Trotskyite dramatization of the Nazi-Zionist collaboration myth using the controversial Kastner case and the wartime extermination of Hungarian Jewry as a backdrop and a bill of indictment. Not only was *Perdition* tainted by a wide range of anti-Jewish images but it reeked of conspiracy mongering wrapped up in pseudo-Marxist phraseology. Allen divided the world into "good Jews" (assimilated, leftist, anti-Zionist) and nationalistic "bad Jews" who were, of course, guilty of double-dealing, betrayal, and unfathomable cruelty.[68]

Since 1967, anti-Semitism has in effect reentered leftist discourse not only through its obsessive focus on the sins of Israel but in its ideologically driven singling out of Jews, Judaism, and Zionism as dire impediments to revolutionary progress. Jewish nationalism, for example, was (and is still) seen as a wholly *illegitimate* movement that must be forcibly overthrown by supporting the "eliminationist" politics of Palestinian liberation. In 1982, the Trotskyite Socialist Workers Party (SWP) in Great Britain produced, for example, a booklet in this spirit, entitled *Israel: A Racist State*. It unambiguously asserted: "There will be no peace in the Middle East, while the State of Israel continues to exist."[69]

Some Marxist Jews have been prominent in Britain (as in France) in advocating these views. But the British Left has rarely, if ever, made such arguments about the existence of any other states in the Middle East or in other parts of the world. This discriminatory attitude is de facto anti-Semitic, as is the insistence that Jews alone constitute a chimerical, artificial, phantom people whose distinct national existence and ethnic identity must be rejected *on principle.*[70] No less prejudicial is the use of highly abusive language about Zionism, traditionally applied only to Nazi crimes against the Jews. In this sort of inquisitorial argument, international Marxists in Great Britain (as elsewhere) have insisted that Zionist Jews could only be *perpetrators* and never victims; or else that they had always collaborated with fascists, Nazis, and anti-Semites. Tony Greenstein, a left-wing British Jew, has propagated this ridiculous thesis ad nauseam for a quarter of a century. He even managed to suggest that the Zionists had provided the Nazis with an "alibi" for the Holocaust.[71] Equally, they were guilty of supporting the radical Right throughout contemporary Europe. Such libels were all the more macabre since the National Front magazine, *Sussex Front,* went out of its way to praise Greenstein's anti-Zionist diatribes in January 1983, calling them "a seminal work, as important in its own way as Richard Harwood's *Did Six Million Really Die?*" a work of Holocaust Denial.[72]

By 1980, Britain's radical Left had become explicitly or implicitly anti-Semitic in its demonization of Jews, its equation of Zionism with racism or Nazism, and its malevolent undermining of any moral basis for Israel's existence.[73] This was glaringly evident during the Far Left's verbal onslaught in the summer of 1982 against "Zionist racism and terror" in Lebanon. Significantly, perhaps, this propaganda campaign was indistinguishable (except for the Marxist jargon) from the British National Front's enthusiastic embrace of Palestinian national self-determination. The National Front hated Menachem Begin and presented Israel's history as one long litany of criminal atrocities. The British Far Right also hammered away at the façade of Israeli "democracy," quoting Dr. Israel Shahak and the Israeli Communist Felicia Langer as crown witnesses for the prosecution.

The Trotskyist Left, not to be outdone by the National Front, ranted against "the Zionist and British imperialists" engaging in so-called wars of extermination against oppressed peoples. Israeli premier Begin was slammed for "turning Lebanon into a mass graveyard" with the help of his paymasters in Washington. *The News Line* called this "final solution" of the Palestinian problem "horribly reminiscent of recent history." The Zionist blitzkrieg had been embedded "in the very history of Zionism," which was "a racist, fascist ideology" whose leaders had in the past shamefully collaborated with Nazi Germany. The establishment of Israel had been an affront to Jewish culture and history as well as a disaster for the Palestinians; it was therefore the duty of all true Marxists to totally smash this state and the "terrorist gangsters" who ruled it. *The News Line,* a publication of the Workers Revolutionary Party (WRP), passionately embraced the Palestinian cause and used Holocaust terminology to describe virtually every action of the Israeli army in southern Lebanon. Horror gas weapons ("which were once used against the Jewish people by the Nazis"), so it headlined, were about to turn west Beirut into "a gas chamber for the PLO and its supporters."[74] There were lurid (and wholly fictive) descriptions of Israeli concentration camps set up to torture Palestinian POWs.[75] The WRP organized demonstrations with Palestinian and Libyan support against "the Nazi-style barbarism of Zionism and imperialism" (the unholy trinity of Reagan, Thatcher, and Begin) in the name of the world working class.[76]

Rising left-wing Labour politicians such as Ken Livingstone agreed with the Trotskyist WRP that the 1982 Lebanon War had to be seen in the framework of "the international struggle against capitalism"; he, too, unreservedly supported the PLO and complained bitterly about "powerful [Jewish] influences in the press and the media." Livingstone denounced the British Labour Party leadership for their silence over Lebanon when "Israel slaughters thousands and seizes half a nation," blaming this abstention on their cowardly "fear of Zionist pressure."[77] He was equally willing to believe that a BBC television exposure of extensive Libyan funding for the WRP was a "Zionist plot."

Indeed, the British Trotskyists in April 1983 were publicly insisting that the "world Jewish conspiracy" extended from Jews in Margaret Thatcher's Conservative government to the newly appointed "Zionist" BBC chairman Stuart Young and the "so-called Left of the Labour Party." This convoluted racist logic prompted the more levelheaded Socialist journalist Sean Matgamna to write that "WRP-style anti-Zionism is the anti-imperialism of idiots ... indistinguishable from antisemitism." Matgamna astutely diagnosed the *Protocols* imagery in Trotskyite efforts to stigmatize all Zionist

Jews as "the international janissaries of imperialism" and to substitute secret "conspirators" or subterranean "agents" for the international class
struggle as a driving force of world history. He attacked the Trotskyist leader
Gerry Healy and other international Socialists in Great Britain for indulging in paranoid obsessions that pitted Jews "against all the rest,"
"putting Zionism and anti-Zionism at the centre of world politics." It was a
hysterical form of left-wing anti-Semitism to pretend that Zionists were the
main enemy everywhere, a worldview worthy of Hitler and Stalin.
Matgamna sharply rejected efforts by the Third Worldist left in Britain to
stigmatize all Zionists ("the vast majority of Jews") as racists and drive
them out of the Labour movement. As he perceptively noted, "there is simply no way that this sort of anti-Zionism can avoid shading over—despite
the best 'anti-racist' intentions—into antisemitism."[78]

There is little doubt that the 1982 Lebanon War ignited a furnace of hatred toward Israel across the British cultural and political spectrum. Both
the so-called quality press and the tabloids grossly exaggerated Lebanese
and Palestinian casualties and perniciously indulged in misplaced Holocaust imagery. Anglo-Jewry as a community came under intense scrutiny
and attack for its presumed responsibility in not condemning Israel. *The
Times* even referred disparagingly to British Jews as "expatriates." In 1982
more than fifty student campuses were hit by an organized and concerted
anti-Israel campaign. In April 1983, several trade unions passed conference
resolutions attacking Israel and threatening it with a boycott. Then, as now,
Israeli anti-Zionists such as Haim Breeshith (an expatriate Israeli Trotskyist), were extremely active in encouraging such hostile moves. Moreover,
with Ken Livingstone's election as the leader of the Greater London Council (GLC), his anti-Zionist tirades acquired an added legitimacy, reinforced
by the council's financial support for an anti-Arab-racism conference in
London. It turned out that the conference organizers considered the principal cause of anti-Arab racism in London to be Zionism. Hence the main
thrust of the antiracist conference was to attack Israel and its allegedly sinister influence.[79] Livingstone's *Labour Herald* also published highly offensive material suggesting that Zionists had betrayed the Jews during the
Holocaust in order to achieve their own "devious" political ends. Their inhuman, "greedy," and hypocritical ideology was focused solely on stealing
Palestine away from the Arabs, rather than saving the Jews of Europe.[80] Indeed, by 1983, some British Trotskyites had openly embraced left-wing

Holocaust "revisionism" of the scurrilous kind espoused by the American-Jewish author Lenni Brenner—full of underlying contempt for Jews in general and poisoned by the theory of Zionist-Nazi congruence. The Trotskyites eagerly embraced a left-wing version of the conspiracy myth, which during the last twenty-five years has steadily moved into the mainstream of British and American political discourse, especially among academics.

The contemporary soft-porn version of this myth is that American Jews control the United States and through America strive to dominate the Middle East and world politics.[81] The more politically correct adaptation of this thesis is that the "Israel lobby" has pushed Washington into conducting a foreign policy that is not only against the American national interest but has gravely aggravated terrorism, hostility, and hatred toward the Western world, especially in the Middle East.[82] In Britain, this idea of a Jewish conspiracy, or "cabal," controlling U.S. policy is particularly rife, with no less than 34 percent of those surveyed in the United Kingdom in 2007 agreeing with the statement. It is a viewpoint constantly trumpeted by the U.K. Muslim media, by such pro-Palestinian journalists as Robert Fisk and John Pilger, by the Liberal democrat Baroness Jenny Tonge, and by the Scottish-born Labour MP Tam Dalyell, who in May 2003 proclaimed to the world that Prime Minister Tony Blair was "unduly influenced by a cabal of Jewish advisers."[83]

British leftists have been especially obsessed with promoting this theme of Jewish political influence in Washington and London. Hence the recurring attacks on individuals such as Lord Levy, a wealthy British Jew whom Tony Blair used for many years as his personal envoy to the Middle East. The insinuations about Levy have come from Far Left MPs such as George Galloway (a fervent apologist for Saddam Hussein before the tyrant's demise), but also from conservatives, liberals, and even moderate Labour MPs. They evidently shared the suspicion that New Labour and American foreign policy was being shaped by a "dangerous" Jewish lobby.[84] The liberal-left *Guardian* even published a painfully shallow article by former South African archbishop Desmond Tutu, comparing the "all-powerful" Jewish lobby with murderous dictators like Hitler, Stalin, Mussolini, Pinochet, and Idi Amin as a force for evil in the contemporary world.[85] Such comments reflect a troubling change in attitudes toward Israel, the Middle East, and Jewish communities in the Western world.

Unfortunately there are whole swathes of educated opinion in the media, British politics, and academia that have bought heavily into this demonization of Israel and America. They tend to lionize the Palestinians, the Third World, and almost anyone who claims to be a victim of capitalism, Zionism, and the West. Such simplistic thinking has even infiltrated the churches, the free professions, and the civil service, as well as middle-of-the-road public opinion in the shires. The growing strategic nexus between Europe and the Arabs has provided a political basis for "blaming the Jews" when it comes to the Middle East impasse.[86]

The pervasive influence of the BBC has been a major factor in this gradual transformation, which became more palpable after 9/11. The BBC, while reluctant to confront the jihadist motivations of militant Islam, had no such reticence in misrepresenting Israel as being driven by vengeful feelings toward Palestinians. In its current-affairs programs, the dominant BBC image of a ruthless, implacable Ariel Sharon (embodying Israel) was regularly juxtaposed with that of a benign Yasser Arafat—amiable and "paternalistic"—unrecognizable as the godfather of postwar terrorist hijacking. Palestinian spokespeople received respectful treatment on British television while official Israelis could expect to be handled far more harshly.[87] This lack of impartiality extended to vocabulary, with the BBC gently referring to Hamas and Islamic Jihad terrorists as "militants" or "radicals."[88] The bogey word "terror" was almost never used, even during the massive Palestinian assaults on civilians (including women and children) in Israeli streets, buses, cafés, restaurants, pizzerias, and discothèques. In tune with this stance, BBC broadcasts rarely focused on the human suffering of Israelis. While repeatedly suggesting that Israeli reprisals were grossly "disproportionate," no context was provided to tell the viewer whether these actions might have been carefully selected military retaliations. On the contrary, the impression was fostered of Israel being a peculiarly vicious militaristic state, constantly overreacting and unleashing irrational and deadly attacks without the slightest justification against innocent Palestinians.[89] This was more than mere sympathy for the underdog. Israeli soldiers were presented as faceless, ruthless, and brutal killers—a dehumanized image that has continued until the present.

The same pattern of bias was revealed when the BBC quoted verbatim from Palestinian allegations about the use of poison gases and depleted uranium by Israel but queried the authenticity of any hard evidence presented in its defense. In the same mold, months after a UN investigation concluded that there was no massacre in Jenin, BBC anchors and its website were still insinuating that there were doubts about what had really happened.[90] A similarly compulsive need to stain the good name of the Jewish state was evident in the screening of "Israel's Secret Weapon" on *BBC Correspondent*—a program hosted by journalist Olenka Frenkiel. The purported aim was to explore Israel's nonconventional capabilities, but the result was a travesty of journalism. Its transparent goal was "to paint Israel as the Middle East's real rogue regime, and Ariel Sharon as a Jewish Saddam Hussein."[91]

The harshness toward Israel contrasted sharply with the soft approach the BBC took toward Arab nationalists, Palestinians, and Muslim fundamentalists. Before the terror assault spread to Great Britain itself in 2005, the BBC treated radical Islam, à la Hamas, as if it were nonviolent, a "cross between the Good Samaritans and the Girl Guides."[92] As in British TV discussions of the prospects of the road map to a two-state solution, there was barely a hint that Palestinian "activists" (to use the fashionable Newspeak) could have been responsible for the stalemate in the peace process.[93] Such fudging of the terrorist nature of the Hamas, Islamic Jihad, Fatah, and various Islamist anti-Israel organizations extended, of course, to their anti-Semitic politics and the systematic incitement to hatred in the Arab school system. This pattern has not just been a matter of residual prejudices among individual editors and reporters, though they enjoy a remarkable degree of license when it comes to the Jewish state. According to Media Tenor, a neutral Bonn-based media research group that conducted an independent study of the BBC's Israel coverage in 2002, the result was 85 percent negative, 15 percent neutral, and zero percent positive.[94] In other words, the BBC could not find a single good word to say about Israel! In this context it becomes clearer why terrorist acts perpetrated against innocent Israeli civilians—unlike those against any other nation on earth—were not counted as terrorism but implicitly seen as politically legitimate.[95] While the BBC had no difficulty in describing massacres in Manhattan, Bali, Tunisia, Saudi Arabia, Morocco, Turkey, and Russia as terrorist attacks, it suddenly became terror-blind when teenagers in Tel Aviv, religious worshippers in Netanya, schoolchildren on buses, or kids at a pizza bar in Jerusalem were unceremoniously murdered by Palestinians. Such double standards have greatly nourished the vilification of the State of Israel, wittingly or unwittingly feeding acts of anti-Semitism and violence against Israelis and Jews world-wide.

BBC coverage of the Middle East doubtless reflects a widespread antipathy toward Israel in contemporary Britain and inside the organization itself. Moreover, the BBC tends to recruit people who have the same liberal-left viewpoint that it is so eager to propagate. For the new generation of broadcasters, who were either born or came of age after 1967, Israel has indeed always been seen as an "occupying power," culpable and responsible for Palestinian suffering by its very existence. BBC journalists either tend to view the Jewish state as an anachronism at best or as based on a criminal conspiracy at worst. Typical of the latter approach was a June 2001 *Panorama* documentary presented by Fergal Keane that portrayed Ariel Sharon as the mass murderer of Palestinians at the Sabra and Shatila refugee camps and guilty of terrible "crimes against humanity," while ignoring the Lebanese Christian Phalangist perpetrators.[96]

In the British media for the last quarter of a century there has been an unrelenting fixation on Israel's "iron fist"—the spectacle of Israeli tanks and F-15s taking up the cudgels against "defenseless" Palestinians or Lebanese. This is the almost routine message of the television news, which invariably tends to ignore or play down threats to Israel's existence. Such selective reporting can easily make Israel's liberal democracy—like that of America—seem more "terrorist" than totalitarian regimes such as those in Iran, Iraq (under Saddam), or North Korea. It provides the necessary backdrop for presenting Israel as the ultimate rogue state. The intellectuals can then provide the philosophical and moral basis for placing the Jewish state beyond the pale. Thus, British academics such as Professor Ted Honderich have had no difficulty in asserting that Palestinian suicide bombers are practicing "terrorism for humanity" and "have a moral right to their terrorism" against Israel.[97] For "thinkers" like Honderich, suicide bombing is not merely legitimate "resistance" but can be perceived as an admirable humanitarian act.

Naturally it helps the British media whenever Jews can be harnessed to the cause of Israel bashing. Over the years, the former Labour foreign secretary and MP for Manchester, Sir Gerald Kaufman, has willingly assumed this role in the media and in the House of Commons. His all-too-predictable TV retrospective *The End of an Affair* (screened by the BBC in a gesture of stunning insensitivity on Rosh Hashanah in 2002) was a wearisome hatchet job on contemporary Israel, with not even the remotest glimmer of empathy for the country's dilemmas. Kaufman has continued his vitriolic campaign against the Jewish state in the House of Commons over the last seven years, periodically urging the British government to impose an arms embargo on Israel.[98]

Channel 4 did manage to hire a more presentable, though prickly, Jewish anti-Zionist in the shape of Professor Jacqueline Rose to provide the commentary in a nasty little documentary that blasted both America and Israel. Even by BBC standards it contained an overdose of malignant abuse.[99] The message about Palestine was one of a peaceful land wickedly stolen from its serene Arab owners and consolidated by the force and fanaticism of violent Zionist settlers. The Israelis were generally depicted as brutal and sectarian invaders determined to drive the Arabs out at any price. Their appalling behavior had been made possible only by Britain's inexcusable "betrayal" of the Palestinians and then by ruthless American imperialism. Israel, according to this malevolent script, received everything from America, which got nothing back in return. Moreover, the "sinister" power of the Christian fundamentalist and Jewish lobbies in America came off in this BBC documentary as not only frightening but catastrophic for the Palestinians and the cause of world peace.

In the autumn of 2002, only two hours after the end of Yom Kippur, Carlton TV gave free rein to a grossly distorted documentary by the left-wing crusading journalist John Pilger.[100] He introduced the Middle Eastern conflict to viewers by boldly stating that the stateless, humiliated Palestinians "have risen against Israel's huge machine." Some of the Palestinian "militants" may have used "desperate means," but "the routine terror is perpetrated by the army of occupation." Naturally, Pilger did not mention such trifles as Arab rejection of the UN partition plan in 1947 (intended to create a Palestinian state alongside Israel), or Gamal Abdul Nasser's encirclement of Israel and the tripartite Arab alliance to extinguish it in 1967. Viewers were simply told that "the Palestinians fled their homes" as Israel "greedily occupied" their territories without any provocation or justifiable cause. The 1993 Oslo Accords were then dismissed as a "classic colonial fix" that offered the Arabs only the "autonomy of a prisoner of war camp." Naturally, Pilger glossed over Ehud Barak's offer in 2000 to return virtually all of the West Bank to the Palestinians and even to divide Jerusalem. More ominously, he totally ignored the culture of hatred that produced the ghastly suicide bombings in the first place. In the telling words of Stephen Pollard, this documentary was a "massacre of the truth."[101]

British media coverage did not improve during the 2006 Lebanon War. While the plight of the Lebanese was reported in the most graphic detail, almost all of Israel's actions were termed "disproportionate"; the suffering of three hundred thousand Israeli refugees, driven from their homes by Hezbollah terror attacks, was not considered particularly newsworthy. TV studio discussions with invited guests were predictably monopolized by individuals known for their hostility toward Israel. Much of the public discussion, led by the media, seemed to assume that Israel was engaged upon a willful mission of indiscriminate destruction, without rhyme or reason. A "From Our Own Correspondent" piece by BBC reporter Nick Thorpe on Radio 4 even claimed that "every day Israel seizes more Palestinian land"— though this was less than a year after the total Israeli pullout from Gaza, which had resulted in nothing but further Qassam rocket attacks directed at the Jewish state. According to Thorpe, the Palestinian Qassams "mostly needle the Israelis, like pinpricks in the ankles of a giant, taunting him to stamp back with his big, US-issue army boots. The Katyushas [fired by Hezbollah] are like poisoned arrows. They drive him mad."[102]

Apart from the gross partiality revealed by these and other flippant statements, it is impossible not to feel the contemptuous hatred oozing from the description itself. But this bias has been present throughout the past seven years, reaching its first climax over events in Jenin in April 2002.

The Jenin affair was a perfect microcosm of Israel-baiting in the British and international media. Israeli soldiers entered the booby-trapped alleys of Jenin refugee camp (in the north of the West Bank) on April 9, 2002, demolishing houses but also suffering considerable casualties. The action was taken after a Palestinian suicide bomber had killed more than twenty Israeli civilians celebrating the traditional Passover meal in Netanya on March 29. The grossly inflated claims of three thousand Palestinian dead were quickly hailed by many British journalists as proof of a major atrocity, without any attempt at serious verification. The highly emotive tone of the reporting, with its endlessly mushrooming tales of mass murders, common graves, summary executions, and "war crimes," was breathtaking.[103] A. N. Wilson, a leading columnist of the London *Evening Standard,* informed his readers with arrogant certitude that "we are talking here of massacre, and a cover-up of genocide."[104] The same writer six months earlier had asserted that Israel was an artificial state and should never have been created. Now he falsely accused it of "the poisoning of water supplies," an echo of hoary medieval anti-Semitic myths. *The Guardian* also lost its compass, comparing Israel's incursion into Jenin to al-Qaeda's murderous 9/11 attack on New York. The Israeli action, it said, was "every bit as repellent in its particulars, no less distressing, and every bit as man-made." *The Guardian* added a particularly lurid touch when it proclaimed that "Jenin already has that aura of infamy that attaches to a crime of especial notoriety."[105]

The Times's correspondent in Jenin was no less carried away in her judgment. After a decade of reporting from Bosnia, Chechnya, Sierra Leone, and Kosovo, Janine di Giovanni wrote that rarely had anyone seen "such deliberate destruction, such disrespect for human life."[106] It should be stated for the record that in the 1990s, about 250,000 people were killed in Bosnia and at least 100,000 in Chechnya. The documented death toll in Jenin (on both sides) was 79 persons, the majority of which were combatants.

Equally divorced from reality was Phil Reeves, the Jerusalem correspondent of *The Independent,* who spoke of "killing fields" (a clear echo of Pol Pot's Cambodia), quoting without any verification Palestinian claims of "mass murder" and wholesale "executions." Reeves's dispatch began with a hugely misleading statement: "A monstrous war crime that Israel has tried to cover up for a fortnight has finally been exposed."[107] There was not even the barest acknowledgment of the high price Israel had paid (the loss of twenty-three soldiers, compared to fifty-six Palestinians) in the door-to-door fighting in Jenin, or the fact that it did *not* adopt the ruthless air strafing tactics that the British and Americans had used in Afghanistan. Yet, speaking in the House of Commons about this fictitious "massacre," the Jewish Labour MP Sir Gerald Kaufman once again slammed Sharon as a "war criminal" and denounced the "barbarism" of the Israeli army as "staining the Star of David with blood." A Welsh Labour MP, Anne Clwyd, drew the logical conclusion and called on all European states to withdraw their ambassadors from Israel. Some Conservatives joined this ugly chorus. The veteran British journalist Tom Gross pointedly summed up the general pattern of reporting and political comment in March 2003 as follows: "The systematic building up of a false picture of Israel as aggressor and deliberate killer of babies and children, is helping to clip away at Israel's legitimacy. How can ordinary people elsewhere not end up hating such a country?"[108] A rare dissenting voice protesting this twisted cacophony of lies about Israeli "genocide" was Britain's bestselling tabloid newspaper, *The Sun*. Its ed-itorial, sensing the ugly mood, felt it necessary to remind Britons that Jews did not "run the world," that Judaism was not evil, and that Israelis had no reason to trust Great Britain and every reason to vigorously defend them-selves against existential threats.[109]

The "quality" press has little patience with such claims. In Britain, as else-where, it pretends that Zionists equate any opposition to the Israeli govern-ment with anti-Semitism. This remarkably tendentious charge is usually made with a high degree of moral indignation.[110] *The Guardian, The Inde-pendent,* and (at times) *The Economist* insist that those who criticize *them* confuse anti-Semitism and "anti-Sharonism."[111] Journalists such as Robert Fisk, Seumas Milne, Peter Beaumont, and William Dalrymple go further, suggesting that allegations of anti-Semitism are nothing but reprehensible Israeli or Jewish attempts "to muzzle justified criticism of a thoroughly bru-tal occupation."[112]

An alternative strategy has been to imply that anti-Semitism is in any case marginal, an *exaggerated* threat, the fault of the Far Right, or else an understandable if perhaps misguided response to Israeli policy.[113] As jour-nalist Mick Hume already pointed out in 2002, such arguments are evasive, irrelevant, and reflect the fact that much "criticism" of Israel is little more than an ersatz anti-imperialism, a sanctimonious moral posturing, or ex-pressions of a latent self-hatred of Westerners when confronting their own history and culture. Israel has become the emblem of everything that ill-assorted groups of Islamic fundamentalists, European neo-Nazis, and left-wing anti-globalists hate about contemporary capitalism. The British Left, in particular, in turning on Israel, succumbed to an "anti-imperialism of fools" that equated Western civilization with genocide and condemned any defense of it as "Eurocentric" or even racist. It grossly inflated Israel's real power and the centrality of the Palestinian cause, descending into a morass of "conspiratorial anti-capitalist-speak that we might call globaldegook," when it was not busy resurrecting a cliché-ridden and mindless anti-Americanism. The prevailing anti-Israeli barbs, according to Hume, were a form of infantile leftism: "no more progressive when aimed against Israel as a symbol of the West than when they are directed against GM crops and the literature of Dead White Males."[114]

More common among British intellectuals since 2000 has been the con-trary view that creating a Jewish state was a truly historic mistake. The real problem with Israel, according to A. N. Wilson, was "its very existence."[115] Wilson, a literary critic and born-again Anglican, maliciously claimed that the world had botched it in 1948 by agreeing to recognize the "State of Israel"—the quotation marks already implying an act of moral delegitimization. In an op-ed article for the mass-circulation London *Evening Standard* in February 2003 he escalated his virulently anti-Israel invective. He warmly recommended to his readers a despicable book entitled *The Israeli Holocaust Against the Palestinians*, even using items from it to blast Israel's record as a nation. As it happened, of the two American authors whom he quoted (Brigadier-General James J. David and Michael A. Hoffman II) in order to support his so-called "facts," both had connections with Holocaust-denial circles in the United States, and one—Hoffman—was also linked to U.S. white supremacist circles. Hoffman had previously authored a sympathetic biography of the neo-Nazi Holocaust denier Ernst Zündel. His public website was overwhelmingly dedicated to anti-Israeli and anti-Jewish polemics. While such tainted sources do not turn A. N. Wilson into an anti-Semite, the similarity in language between his own column and that of the white supremacist anti-Semites he quoted was disturbing, to say the least.[116]

Another article in the *Evening Standard* in June 2002 by conservative art critic Brian Sewell was no less insipid. First came the familiar anti-Judaic aspersions against "Old Testament fanaticism." This contrasted sharply with the idyllic picture of an "ancient race" of peace-loving, "noble" Arabs overrun by "greedy alien immigrants from Moscow and New York"—anti-Semitic images, well entrenched in pro-Arab literature on Palestine. To rub the point in, Sewell decried Israeli-style "genocide" as far more terrible than Nazism. In this twisted vision of history, the Palestinians under Israel "have suffered far worse and far longer" than the Jews under Hitler.[117] Such inversions of historical truth have become commonplace in contemporary Great Britain and much of western Europe.

Another right-winger, the former editor of *The Daily Telegraph*, Sir Max Hastings (who had once been a friend of Israel), while not quite so reckless in his indictment, repeated all the standard half-truths of the Israel bashers as if they were universally established axioms. He bitterly castigated Israel's "ruthless exploitation" of "the Holocaust card" as a ploy to deflect international criticism; any reference to "self-hating Jews" was dismissed without further ado as shameful and cruel. Hastings sympathetically quoted a prominent but unnamed postwar German leader who felt unable (because of his nationality) to vent his true feelings "about the wickedness of what is being done in Israel's name."[118] Hastings also gave implicit credence to the old canard about the dual allegiances of British Jews and an excessive Jewish influence on the media, even using loaded terms such as "moral blackmail" to characterize this phenomenon. Insistently denying that he was anti-Jewish, Hastings blamed the rise in "genuine antisemitism" *wholly* on the Israeli government and the "recklessness" of unnamed pro-Israel lobbyists.

There were some honorable exceptions to this chorus. Columnist Julie Burchill trenchantly pointed out that anti-Americanism and anti-Semitism had turned into the only forms of prejudice that still united both Left and Right. Expressing her disgust at the "slime of hypocritical hatred" and the *danse macabre* of resurgent Judeophobia in Britain, Burchill added: "Make no mistake, the Jews are not hated because of Israel; they are hated for their very modernity, mobility, lust for life and love of knowledge. Their most basic toast, "L'chaim!" (To Life!), is a red rag to those who fetishise death because they have failed to take any joy from their life on earth."[119]

Burchill did not swallow the mainstream British media pretense that "anti-Zionism is entirely different from antisemitism."[120] In a spunky op-ed piece on November 29, 2003, she explained why she was leaving *The Guardian* newspaper for the more hospitable pastures of *The Times*. It was specifically the treatment of Israel that had angered her during the previous year. "As a non-Jew," Burchill had noticed "a quite striking bias against the State of Israel . . . which, for all its faults, is the only country in that barren region that you or I, or any feminist, atheist, homosexual or trade unionist, could bear to live under." Toward the end of her farewell to *Guardian* readers, Burchill lashed out at fellow journalist Richard Ingrams for demanding that Jews declare their "racial origins" when writing about the Middle East.[121] Ingrams had confessed to his readers: "I have developed a habit when confronted by letters to the editor to look at the signature to see if the writer has a Jewish name. If so, I tend not to read it."[122] This attitude reflected the time-honored caricatures of Jews as always sticking together, looking out for one another irrespective of the rights or wrongs of any issue, and having a uniform view of Israel. The British Press Complaints Commission dismissed any objection to such views. One wonders, though, how the council would have reacted if a similar complaint had been lodged regarding the ethnic stereotyping of blacks or Muslims.

Ingrams and others like him belong to a school of British journalism that seems to be implying that the act of *complaining* about anti-Semitism is the main *cause* of it. Thus Deborah Orr, writing in *The Independent*, targeted pro-Israel journalist Barbara Amiel, ridiculing her for the sin of seeing "anti-Semitism at every party she attends in London." In Orr's view, Israel was indeed "a shitty little country" and disliking those that support it was perfectly legitimate. The problem lay entirely with the "paranoid" critics who protested at every criticism of Israel: "If the likes of Ms. Amiel continue to insist that everyone with a word to say against Israel is an anti-Semite, she is going to find one day that the world is once more divided neatly between anti-Semites and Jews."[123] In other words, those who saw a connection between anti-Zionism and anti-Semitism were themselves guilty of creating hostility to Jews. This has undoubtedly been one of the historic discoveries of Western journalism during the past decade.

The indignation of so many British journalists, artists, writers, intellectuals, and academics at being described as "anti-Semitic" is at one level reassuring. It means that this accusation is not viewed with equanimity or as a compliment. On the other hand, the vehement denials often generate more heat than light. Responding to an inquiry from *The Independent* about the relative justice of the Israeli or Palestinian cause, Philip Hensher completely dismissed all reference to the Holocaust or anti-Semitism as a "cynical and opportunistic manipulation of history" by Israel and its supporters.[124] Author and critic Marina Warner willfully reduced anti-Semitism to anti-Sharonism, thereby trivializing the whole subject. The poet Tom Paulin caustically remarked that only a Primo Levi (the British literati's favorite Holocaust survivor) could adequately describe Israeli "atrocities"; and a Jamaican British respondent, Benjamin Zephaniah, bluntly labeled the Israeli occupation a "genocide." Louis de Bernières added that Israel was using "Nazi" tactics, while expressing mild regret at Palestinian terrorism and Muslim fanaticism. A number of other British writers offered their own form of psychobabble, suggesting that the "brutality" of Israeli behavior reflected the *abused child* syndrome. It was evidently the result of having been "educated" by the Nazis.

Such repellent fantasies and gross exaggerations have assumed epidemic proportions in recent years. Thus the respected British professional journal *Architectural Review* could run an article in May 2002 that tried to parallel Israeli actions in Ramallah to the Holocaust. The author was a British architect called Tom Kay, who coyly described himself as a Jew only "if questioned by an antisemite." According to his highly charged account, in the spring of 2002, young Israeli soldiers had deliberately destroyed the Palestinian town of Ramallah. On finding hundreds of spectacles in piles on the floor of an eye-testing room damaged in the fighting, Kay could think of nothing but the Auschwitz museum in southern Poland.[125] The only missing element in the description was the claim that the Israelis were actually gassing Palestinians.

As the physical and verbal attacks on Jews have escalated in Britain, a deep vein of anti-Jewish prejudice has been reopened.[126] The poison has been flowing out, with the "criminalization of Israel," conspiracy theories about the Jewish lobby, and a deep loathing for America emerging among the leitmotifs. As Melanie Phillips has pointed out, there are still some "good" Jews—those who pronounce anathemas or sign petitions against Israel as an "apartheid State," or who fiercely deny that anti-Semitism is resurgent and unconditionally embrace the cause of Palestine. But then there are the "bad" Jews (the majority) who identify with the Jewish people, defend Israel's right to self-defense, criticize the Palestinians, and expose the threat of radical Islam.[127] These "bad Jews" are the ones who do not turn the other cheek, who fight back when attacked, who display a modicum of Jewish pride, who insist on the right of Jews to an independent national identity and state.

Robust self-assertiveness has not usually been the style of Anglo-Jewry in the face of past or present British anti-Semitism. The Anglo-Jewish leadership has usually preferred not to rock the boat, to work quietly behind the scenes rather than publicly mobilize or organize opinion against anti-Semitism, hatred of Israel, or the academic boycott.[128] This has led it, at times, to seriously underplay the scale of anti-Semitism in contemporary Britain. However, there are honorable exceptions, such as Britain's chief rabbi, Sir Jonathan Sacks, who are aware that increasing numbers of educated Britons question the right of Israel to exist—something that impacts profoundly on Jewish identity. This makes intelligent and sensitive Jews feel that once more an "invisible ghetto" of hostility surrounds them—not so different from that which existed in Europe a century ago. "Suddenly it doesn't feel safe to be a Jew again" is how the talented Anglo-Jewish writer Howard Jacobson put it a few years ago. Israel may only be the pretext, but it has brought up to the surface "the sediment of hate and irrationality waiting at the bottom of society."[129] Even *The Guardian* acknowledged in November 2003 that a new anti-Semitism was "on the march across the globe, making the Jewish community in the UK . . . unsettled, uncomfortable and fearful."[130] After the usual denial that criticism of Israel could ever resemble anti-Semitism, the paper admitted that the liberal Left "which in an earlier era vigilantly sought to protect Jews from prejudice and bigotry" had shown little active concern for the growth of anti-Semitism. Its editorial conceded that some Jewish peace activists had, in early 2003, been beaten up by fellow demonstrators during an antiwar march in Paris. "There were less dramatic confrontations in London's million-strong protest march but something similar happened." The editorialist deplored the fact that "it did not matter to the attackers that Jewish writers and activists have been vocal against the Iraq war. Nor did the attackers care that many criticize the current Israeli government's policies towards the Palestinians. Their victims were targets just because they are Jews."[131]

Nor has the more traditional racist anti-Semitism completely disappeared from Great Britain, though since 1945 it is no longer the force that it used to be. True a movement such as the British National Party (BNP), which is primarily anti-Asian, anti-Muslim, and Europhobe, has enjoyed some local gains in recent years, but it is hardly a major threat to Anglo-Jewry. Its leader, Cambridge-educated Nick Griffin, is clearly anti-Semitic and has openly flirted with Holocaust denial in the past, but he is not in the same league as some of his European counterparts.[132] The "anti-Zionism" of the British Far Right also lacks the sophistication and public resonance of its left-wing rivals in Great Britain. The BNP, for obvious reasons, cannot stigmatize Israel as a Nazi state with the same conviction as a leftist radical like George Galloway, who unabashedly declared in January 2009 to a crowd of Londoners: "Today the Palestinian people in Gaza are the new Warsaw ghetto, and those who are murdering them are the equivalent of those who murdered the Jews in Warsaw in 1943."[133] It is this kind of vehement rhetoric, branding Israel as the epitome of evil, that could (in certain circumstances) incite a crowd to torch a synagogue or communal center.

The perpetrators of violence are often British Muslims from Asia, systematically whipped up to hate the "Zionist" enemy. Organizations like the Muslim Association of Britain (MAB) have for years sought to equate Zionism with Nazism. Among the MAB senior spokesmen is the Palestinian Dr. Azzam Tamimi, who publicly supports suicide bombings, martyrdom for Islam, and the dissolution of Israel. For him Israelis are the new Nazis and Palestinians have been their main victims. This was also the position of Sheikh Omar Bakri, the most incendiary of Britain's Muslim preachers until he fled to Beirut following the London terrorist bombings of June 2005. Bakri, and many like him, accused Jews of exploiting and manipulating the Holocaust to achieve "hegemony" over Muslims. Like the MCB (Muslim Council of Britain) he advocated boycotting Holocaust Memorial Day in favor of a more universal "Genocide Day" that would highlight the Palestinian tragedy.

British Muslims have been supported in such efforts by militant groups like the Scottish Palestine Solidarity campaign, which constantly regurgitates the old libel that Zionists collaborated with the Nazis in implementing the Holocaust.[134] Both the Far Left and militant Muslims in Britain regard such an inversion of Holocaust discourse as a powerful weapon in undermining the moral legitimacy of Israel.[135] The Islamists, however, are by far the most focused on the desirability of direct action against the Jews. In Britain they have found an ideal environment for freely distributing their hate propaganda, including Hamas publications like the monthly *Filastin al-Muslima* (Muslim Palestine), which spread the doctrines of radical Islam, spew out Jew hatred, and incite to terrorist acts under the mask of "resistance." The same hate message (especially against Jews) is being spread by Saudi-trained imams in Britain's mosques. Indeed, there is a wide variety of Islamic organization in Britain that are violently anti-Israel, outspokenly anti-Zionist, and tend to be anti-Jewish. They include the MAB (which is partly infiltrated by the Muslim Brotherhood), the British Muslim Initiative, the Federation of Student Islamic Societies, the General Union of Palestinian Students (GUPS), the openly anti-Semitic *Hizb-ut-Tahrir* (HUT), and various front organization for Hamas, Hezbollah, and Iran. Arab and Muslim students influenced by this broad spectrum of support and strongly backed by the Far Left have been in the forefront of harassing Jewish students on British campuses and organizing boycotts. Certainly, not all the acts of violence against Jews emanate from Muslims. Nevertheless, in recent years a large number of such attacks have been committed by Muslims against west European Jewry as a whole.

ELEVEN

The Red-Green Axis

In September 2006 an all-party parliamentary committee of the House of Commons concluded that anti-Semitism had indeed become an acute problem in British society.[1] Their findings corresponded with a growing sense of siege within the Anglo-Jewish community, despite its economic success, professional achievements, and sociocultural integration. The figures for anti-Semitic incidents were depressingly high, including 112 *violent* assaults recorded in 2006—the largest number ever registered by the Community Security Trust (CST) and a 37 percent rise over the previous year.[2] Police statistics revealed that Jews were four times as likely to be attacked in the United Kingdom because of their religion than Muslims.[3] Moreover, Israel's conflict with Hezbollah led to a new wave of anti-Semitic attacks in the summer of 2006, spread out across the British Isles, with Muslims noticeably overrepresented among the perpetrators.[4] There were several attacks in Golders Green and other areas of North London with a large Jewish population. The owner of a café-restaurant in the Golders Green Road, Ruth Cohen, was physically threatened by two young men: "They said they were going to kill me and called me a 'dirty Jew,' a 'stinking Jew.' One of them had a knife. A colleague came out. They started punching him and throwing chairs."[5]

This pattern continued in 2007 with 547 anti-Semitic incidents recorded by the CST, escalating still further at the beginning of 2009.[6] Though extremely difficult to measure, the negative portrayal of Israel in the British media has almost certainly contributed to an atmosphere in which local anti-Jewish hostility can only increase.[7] No less than 30 percent of the known attackers involved in anti-Semitic acts in 2006 were Asian Muslims, from the Indian subcontinent. A smaller percentage among the known perpetrators were Arabs or blacks. Whites were still the largest group of perpetrators (47 percent) by a diminishing margin.[8] In 2005 two events acted as specific triggers for Far Right though anti-Semitic incidents—the sensational pictures of Prince Harry wearing a Nazi uniform and the angry remarks of London mayor Ken Livingstone gratuitously accusing a Jewish journalist, Oliver Finegold, of acting like a concentration camp guard.[9]

Livingstone's relations with the Jewish community had been strained for more than two decades, despite his antiracist record and known opposition to fascist anti-Semitism. However, London's mayor refused to apologize for his slur against Finegold, criticizing the reporter's employer, the *Evening Standard* (part of the *Daily Mail* group) for its history of supporting anti-Semitism and fascism in the 1930s. Shortly thereafter, he published a harsh piece in *The Guardian,* claiming that Ariel Sharon "is a war criminal who should be in prison, not in office"; adding for good measure that "Israel's expansion has included ethnic cleansing."[10] At the same time Livingstone reiterated his view that the Holocaust was the "worst crime of the 20th century." He warmly acknowledged the great contributions of Jews to human civilization and to the city of London, and he duly emphasized his commitment to police action against anti-Semitic violence. But without any evidence, the mayor also accused the Israeli government of wholly distorting the question of racial and religious discrimination in Western society. He insisted that "the great bulk of racist attacks in Europe today are on black people, Asians and Muslims." Predictably, Livingstone also resurrected the left-wing canard that Israeli governments had attempted for the last two decades "to portray anyone who forcefully criticizes the policies of Israel as antisemitic." The mayor strikingly ignored any reference to the fact that the Jewish community had suffered a 41 percent escalation in anti-Semitic incidents during 2004, much of it in London and under his own stewardship. All appeals to him for contrition and for an apology to Finegold were also ignored—a mayoral position that was backed by fully three-quarters of all Londoners. Thus, far from seeking to combat the rising flames of anti-Semitism, the mayor appeared to be resolutely fanning it with his crass provocation. As a *Jerusalem Post* editorial put it in March 2005: "Livingstone demonizes, applies double standards and delegitimizes Israel. Indeed he portrays Israel as 'a threat to us all.' "[11]

As if determined to compound his troubles, Livingstone then publicly insulted two Jewish property developers—David and Simon Reuben—whom he declared to be obstructing progress and overcharging in the preparatory work on the 2012 Olympic Games site in East London. The mayor told them to "go back to Iran and try their luck with the Ayatollahs"—this at a time when Iranian president Mahmoud Ahmadinejad was loudly calling for the annihilation of Israel. The fact that the Reuben brothers were born in India of Iraqi extraction and had lived in the United Kingdom for more than forty years made the mayor's call for their return to Iran seem even more glib and offensive.[12] The politically correct chief administrator of a "great, multicultural city" had descended to the level of a common fascist street thug.

Livingstone's loutish behavior in the Finegold affair led to an initial one-month suspension from office.[13] He followed up by accusing the Board of Deputies of British Jews of using "McCarthyite" tactics to silence him, and then posing as the common man's martyr in the cause of democracy.[14] Repeatedly, "Red Ken"—the people's friend—claimed that he was being targeted by a Zionist witch hunt. This posturing for the media did nothing to damage his popularity with Londoners. It was also perfectly in tune with the Marxist revolutionary credo that he had adopted since the 1970s, which continually sought to demonize Israel as a pariah state.[15]

Instead of promoting communal harmony between Jews and Muslims, Livingstone polarized tensions during his eight years in office. The problem was not solely his defense of the Palestinian suicide bombers, whose actions he conveniently blamed on Israel. It was also his embrace of Islamists in such organizations as the Muslim Association of Britain (MAB). Moreover, by sucking up to the Egyptian-born fundamentalist cleric Sheikh Youssef al-Qaradawi, the mayor of London not only dismayed Anglo-Jewry but also deeply disappointed his rainbow coalition of gays, feminists, Sikhs, Hindus, and secularists. To quote *The Economist*: "Mr. Qaradawi, whom Mr. Livingstone lauds at the 'leader of a great world religion,' supports the murder of Israeli children by Palestinian terrorists, praises female genital mutilation and thinks that homosexuals deserve to die."[16]

The mayor vigorously argued that Qaradawi was a liberal "progressive figure" and a "moderate." He turned a deaf ear to gay protests that the sheikh openly supported the right of Islamic theocracies to murder homosexual citizens using various barbaric methods. Livingstone also disregarded the fact that Qaradawi's sermons had called for the destruction of "the American and British aggressors" as well as the Zionists, and his fervent belief that "Islam will return to Europe as a Conqueror." The sheikh had admittedly softened the pill by maintaining that this conquest would be achieved through "preaching and ideology rather than by the sword," but his intentions could hardly be termed pacific. After all, this was the same cleric who repeatedly proclaimed that "every man has the right to become a human bomb," especially if engaged in "martyrdom" operations inside Israel. In a sermon on October 18, 2002, Qaradawi had called on Muslims to "destroy the aggressive Jews"; and on his Al-Jazeera show of May 15, 2004, he demonized Judaism as "the number one propagator of violence"—blaming the propagation of brutal deeds on American mass culture and "Torah" Judaism, as if these two antithetical worldviews were bound together into some kind of malevolent conspiracy. Yet this was the very same Kuwait-based sheikh whom the Socialist mayor of London had invited in mid-2004 to preach a sermon at Regents Park Mosque—a wretched example of red carpet left-wing sycophancy toward "clerical" Islamofascism.[17]

Livingstone also ignored the sheikh's very publicly expressed desire to die a "virtuous death" for Allah as a jihad warrior, repeated once more at a solidarity conference in Qatar on February 17, 2005.[18] During the conference a film about Qaradawi's life was shown, in which Livingstone praised his teaching, calling his ideology "utterly remote from extremism" and attacking "the unbridled distortions" spread about his work by Israeli sources such as the Middle East Media Research Institute (MEMRI). Not surprisingly, such positions were much appreciated by British Muslim leaders including the secretary-general of the Muslim Council of Great Britain (MCB), Sir Iqbal Sacranie. During the Feingold affair, Sacranie had publicly declared that he was "proud" to stand by the mayor. This was the same Iqbal Sacranie who nearly twenty years earlier had vilified Salman Rushdie's book *The Satanic Verses,* suggesting that execution was perhaps "a bit too easy" as a punishment for the apostate British Muslim author. Yet Sacranie was nonetheless rewarded with a knighthood by Her Majesty's government.[19]

Livingstone's closest rival on the Far Left in pandering to the Muslim vote has been former Scottish Labourite MP George Galloway, who today represents the antiwar Respect Party in Parliament—a strange blend of Marxist and Islamist politics. A longtime apologist for Saddam Hussein and a supporter of the Palestinian cause ever since the early 1980s, Galloway was previously the architect of the Stop the War Coalition (StWC), jointly organized by the Trotskyite Socialist Workers Party (SWP) and the Muslim Association of Britain (MAB). Virulent anti-Americanism and anti-Zionism have become his trademarks.[20] Galloway has repeatedly stated his determination to "make reparation to the Palestinian people for the crimes of Balfour"—the Scottish aristocrat who became British foreign secretary and in 1917 promised to create a Jewish national home in Palestine. In the spring of 2005 Galloway found himself pitted against Labour MP Oona King, a black half-Jewish woman, in a highly charged electoral contest in London's Bethnal Green district, the second largest Muslim constituency in Great Britain. After youths threw eggs at King as she honored East End Jews killed in Nazi bombing raids, one young Muslim told the *Daily Telegraph:* "We all hate her. She comes here with her Jewish friends who are killing our people and then they come to our backyards."[21]

King, herself a militant anti-Zionist, lost by 823 votes. After the campaign the incitement continued. The following month, on May 21, 2005, a major rally was held in Trafalgar Square, with a crowd waving Palestinian flags and anti-Israel banners despite the heavy rain. Speakers included Palestinian representatives and local Muslim leaders, but most notable was the presence of left-wing non-Muslim public figures. Jeremy Corbyn, a backbench Labour MP, called for the British government to "cease all trade with Israel," while Tony Benn, a former Labour MP and veteran leftist of the British political scene, called George W. Bush and Ariel Sharon the "two most dangerous men in the world." Paul Mackney, president of the country's second largest union of teachers, called for the widespread boycott of Israel by British academia, while Andrew Birgin of the StWC demanded the dismantling of the Jewish state. "The South African apartheid state never inflicted the sort of repression that Israel is inflicting on the Palestinians," he said to cries of "*Allahu akbar!*" from the audience. "When there is real democracy, there will be no more Israel."[22]

The rally's most prominent speaker, however, was the ubiquitous George Galloway, fresh from his election victory over Oona King. Galloway used the rally as an opportunity to announce an international boycott of Israel. "We will join them," he said, referring to the Palestinians, "by boycotting Israel. By boycotting Israeli goods. By picketing the stores that are selling Israeli goods." To cheers and applause, Galloway added, "It's about time that the British government made some reparations for the Balfour Declaration."[23]

Given the legitimacy that such rhetoric enjoys in Great Britain today, the emergence of efforts among the intellectual elites to convert their rhetoric of hate into action—principally through the boycotting of Israeli products and people—comes as no surprise. It is this powerful trend that has, more than anything else, turned the public atmosphere in Britain into among the most uncomfortable for Jews in all of Europe. First came the much-publicized Mona Baker affair, which involved her removal of two Israeli colleagues from the board of a scientific publication. Baker claimed to have been inspired by the boycott initiative of two Jewish academics, Steven Rose and his wife, Hilary. Supporters of the petition included the Association of Union Teachers (AUT), the National Association of Teachers in Further and Higher Education (NATFHE), and more than seven hundred academics. Matters escalated when Andrew Wilkie, a professor of pathology at Oxford University, flatly rejected the application of an Israeli student simply because of his nationality. On June 23, 2003, Wilkie told the student that he had "a huge problem with the way that Israelis take the moral high ground from their appalling treatment in the Holocaust, and then inflict gross human rights abuses on the Palestinians."[24] Oxford University promptly slapped him with two months of unpaid leave.

Matters only worsened in April 2005. The AUT, which had some forty thousand members at the time, voted by sizable majorities to impose a boycott on two Israeli universities, Bar-Ilan University and the University of Haifa, in solidarity with the Palestinian cause. According to the AUT secretary general, this ban would "take the form described in the Palestinian call for academic boycott of Israeli institutions." The rushed vote was held on Passover eve, preventing most Jewish members from taking part, and opponents of the motions were denied right of reply due to "lack of time." Just before the vote, speakers addressing the AUT's executive union meeting declared Israel a "colonial apartheid state, more insidious than South Africa," and called for the "removal of this regime." While some British institutions, such as Oxford, considered action to override the ban, in general it was international pressure, rather than repercussions within British society, that made this nasty boycott a matter of serious controversy and ultimately led to its reversal a month later.[25]

Boycotts against Jews arouse painful associations. Attempts to remove Israeli products from Selfridges, Harrods, Tesco, Marks & Spencer, and other British chain stores, under the slogan "Isolate the Racist Zionist State," have been both a symbol and a rallying point for the resurgence of anti-Semitism in Britain.[26] Demonstrators gather to collect money and signatures, sell pamphlets comparing Ariel Sharon to Adolf Hitler, and shout slogans at passersby. One woman, Carol Gould, offered a telling example of her own experience of a demonstration outside Marks & Spencer on Oxford Street, London, in November 2003. Gould described how the Moroccan conductor of her double-decker bus harangued his passengers about "all Marks & Spencer money that goes to the 'Zionist murderers.' "[27] Once outside the store, she encountered "an hysterical crowd of hate-filled people," in which Britons outnumbered those of Middle Eastern origin. One woman in religious Muslim attire screamed, "You Jews destroyed my country, Iraq." Some non-Muslims shouted, "You people invented terrorism in Palestine!"; "Israel is expanding every day and will soon own the whole Middle East!"; "Israel is slaughtering thousands of Palestinians every day!"[28] An elegantly dressed English businessman told Gould: "I love and revere the suicide bombers. Every time I hear of a suicide bomb going off I wish it had been eighty or ninety Jews instead of a pitiful handful."[29]

The persistent efforts in recent years by some British lecturers to achieve an academic boycott of all Israeli universities, while less violent in tone than such street incidents, has been unmistakably discriminatory in content. It was the Jews, not Muslims or Christians, who were the sole target of the boycott against Israel. The boycotters were uninterested in universities in North Korea, Zimbabwe, or Sudan, whose governments had been accused with good reason of perpetrating genocide against their own citizens. Militant left-wing organizers of the boycott such as Sue Blackwell from Birmingham University draped themselves in Palestinian flags and posted messages on their websites that said, "Victory to the academic intifada!," indulging in their own brand of political prejudice, wrapped up in jargon-ridden verbiage. *The Times*, like several university heads and even some anti-Israel newspapers, was shocked by the sheer brazenness of the boycott resolutions. It deplored this "mockery of academic freedom"—blinkered, ill-timed, and "perverse"—which "can quickly become an excuse for anti-Semitism."[30] The academic boycott movement, while supposedly defending Palestinian human rights, was by no means universally welcomed by all Palestinians, either, with the president of Al-Quds University in Jerusalem, Sari Nusseibeh, deploring the move as completely counterproductive.

In May 2006, NATFHE, Britain's largest teachers union, renewed the boycott call in protest against "Israeli apartheid policies."[31] NATFHE's boycott motion passed, it is worth noting, despite Israel's unilateral withdrawal from Gaza and the resulting electoral victory of Hamas, a movement explicitly committed to extinguishing the Jewish state. Yet the anti-Israeli hysteria, far from being assuaged in British academia, appeared to be reinforced.[32] Britain's National Union of Journalists, with about forty thousand members, followed suit in April 2007, urging the British government to impose sanctions and a boycott of Israeli goods along the lines of past trade union struggles against apartheid South Africa.[33] This decision, damaging to the whole notion of journalistic integrity and objectivity, took place slightly more than a month after the pro-Palestinian BBC journalist Alan Johnston was kidnapped by a local Gazan Islamist group. Naturally, there was no call for a boycott of the Palestinian fundamentalists. But there was an epidemic of calls from English writers, musicians, and artists to institute a *cultural* boycott of Israel in view of its systematic flouting of Palestinian rights and UN resolutions, and its repressive policies. This was succeeded by yet another debate on the academic boycott by the newly formed University and College Union (UCU).[34] Driven forward by the Far Left, the success of the motions exhibited the extent to which anti-Semitic discrimination, infringement of academic freedom, and delusional forms of militant activism had taken over the minds of the boycotters, further poisoning the atmosphere in British universities.

The passage of two boycott resolutions by the UCU on May 30, 2007, prompted a cogent response from academic lawyers Anthony Julius and Alan Dershowitz. They observed that the boycotters had aligned themselves with three increasingly powerful anti-Semitic forces—Hamas, Hezbollah, and Iran—which actively desire Israel's destruction. The boycott had mendaciously defined Israel as a country with an "entrenched system of racial discrimination" and made exchanges with its universities virtually conditional on the disappearance of the Jewish state. Moreover, the boycott implicitly continued the tradition of hostile rejectionist measures adopted against Jews in medieval Christendom, Hitler's German Reich, and the Arab League. It was also predicated on the continual defamation of Jews and the Jewish state as a pure "aggressor," not entitled to self-determination, whose foundations were based on an ideology (Zionism) that was uniquely pernicious. At the heart of this and every other boycott lay the principle of *exclusion*: "Jews and/or the Jewish State are to be excluded from public life, from the community of nations, because they are dangerous and malign."[35]

As Julius and Dershowitz pointed out, in the case of an academic boycott this meant also exclusion from the principle of the universality of science and learning.

The UCU boycott was undoubtedly a stain on British academia and, by extension, on British society itself. Its moral blindness and anti-Semitic nature were exposed by the crass singling out of Israel, irrespective of the personal motivations of the advocates. Even the *Financial Times* (strongly opposed to Israeli policy in the territories) denounced the academic boycott as intrinsically absurd. Israeli academics, it pointed out, had "an honourable record of opposing the occupation." Moreover, boycotts were an obstacle to peace and would only strengthen the Israeli political Right. Furthermore, "double standards" were obviously at work, since Russian academics were not being targeted over Chechnya, Chinese lecturers over Tibet, or Indian scholars over Kashmir.[36]

Most of the British and American press shared this viewpoint. Thomas Friedman of *The New York Times* was particularly scathing, unequivocally calling the boycott an act of "rank anti-Semitism."[37] *The Economist,* with cool detachment, deplored the lack of subtlety and differentiation in the resolutions, noting that "more than 2,000 American scholars, including several Nobel Prize winners, have pledged to stay away from any event from which Israelis are excluded."[38] The magazine also made the fundamental point that "Israel's universities enjoy far greater academic freedom than any other in the Middle East. Why, in these circumstances, should Israeli academics be shunned while those from the other side are welcomed?"[39]

The boycott movement nonetheless continued, as UNISON, Britain's largest labor union (with 1.6 million members), voted at the end of June 2007 to impose sanctions on Israeli companies, boycott manufactured products, cut ties with businesses, and end investments in Israeli pension funds.[40] The UCU academic boycott was scrapped as "unlawful" by the end of September 2007, but the five-year campaign did not stop by itself. It took a vigorous counteroffensive by Israeli, American, and independent groups, including eleven thousand academics who signed a petition organized by Scholars for Peace in the Middle East (SPME). A month earlier, in August 2007, nearly three hundred American universities and college presidents declared in a *New York Times* ad that they would not work with institutions that were boycotting Israeli academics. There were also robust protests by prominent individuals, among them no less than thirty-three Nobel Prize winners. Tony Blair, while still British prime minister, condemned the boycott, as did Liberal Democrats and the Conservative Party leader David Cameron.[41] But the focus of protest in Great Britain related more to fear of the damage it would do to academic freedom and to the image of British academia. Despite the criticism of the hard Left that led the boycott, its sheer obstinacy and determination should not be underestimated. The pro-Palestinian, anti-Israel (and implicitly anti-Jewish) campaign lost a battle, but it will continue the campus war.[42]

For British leftists, since the 1970s "Zionism" has primarily been a code word for the "forces of reaction" in general. Jews, in their minds, are linked to aristocratic privilege, capitalist money power, and, often, a vengeful biblical morality. For many leftists of this hue, the decade of Tony Blair's New Labour rule was literally a nightmare come true. Blairism meant not only subservience to U.S. foreign policy and to Zionist "cabals" but also a sharp turn to the right—the Thatcherite wolf of neoconservatism having been resurrected in a pseudo-socialist sheep's clothing. The drive to boycott Israel did, however, produce some heated discussion on the British Left. Critics daring to suggest that the boycott might be an anti-Semitic move were liable to be insulted as "apologists for Israeli oppression."[43] The radical instigators were set on denying the moral legitimacy of any form of Jewish national self-determination in the Middle East.[44] The much-touted presence of Jews in their ranks did not change the truth that anyone supporting *active discrimination* against Israel had moved himself into the anti-Semitic camp. The fact that some pampered "progressives" of the Jewish faith pretended that their criticism was being "silenced" by an Israeli diktat (even as *they* sought to totally isolate the Jewish state) was so patently false as to be laughable.

For several decades now, the so-called progressives have had every prestigious public forum in the West available to them, hardly justifying their claims to heroic dissident status.[45] Not only that, but it has been a part of the respectable liberal bon ton, especially since 2000 (in Britain as in America and western Europe) to delegitimize Israel as a colonialist anachronism and to advocate its dismantlement or forced conversion into a "binational state." While the boycotters (both Jewish and Gentile) may well believe that Israel's treatment of the Palestinians is scandalous and morally indefensible, their rage all too often seems highly selective and even hypocritical. In the case of Jewish progressives there is a curiously nasty edge of self-flagellating, narcissistic indignation barely hidden under the high-flying banner of human rights. They barely seem aware that their portrayal of democratic, law-abiding Israel as a serial human rights abuser (while compulsively ignoring the systematic and brutal violation of fundamental liberties by Arab governments throughout the Middle East) is a classic example of patronizing double standards. The narrow, exclusive obsession with the "sins of Israel," while turning a blind eye to the nuclearization of Iran, to global terrorism, the Hamas-Fatah civil war, the mayhem in Iraq, the evils of jihad, the Syrian-sponsored murders in Lebanon, and the ongoing genocide in Darfur involves a level of hidebound parochialism that perhaps only radical Jewish intellectuals are still capable of attaining.[46]

The vilification of Israel is not in itself definitive proof of anti-Semitism.[47] But neither does it demonstrate the opposite—least of all when just one small country is so deliberately selected for unreasoning hatred and abuse.[48] Radical British leftists who seventy years ago could still stand shoulder to shoulder with East End Jews against Mosley's Blackshirts are now themselves in the *vanguard* of anti-Semitism. It is no accident that the pro-Hezbollah groupies of George Galloway's misnamed Respect Party have made common cause with the Islamofascists in their struggle against America and the global "neocon Zionist conspiracy." Labour MP John Mann, who instigated the British All-Party Parliamentary Inquiry into Antisemitism, recently declared himself appalled at the way "many on the [British] Left have become almost casually and routinely anti-Semitic." He told the journalist Richard Littlejohn that there had been a resurgence of *Protocols*-style anti-Semitism in Labour circles based on the idea that Jews run the world.[49] His parliamentary committee concluded in September 2006 that in Britain "violence, desecration and intimidation directed towards Jews is on the rise. Jews have become more anxious and more vulnerable to attack than at any time for a generation or longer."[50] The chairman of the committee, centrist Labour MP Denis MacShane, who presented the report to Prime Minister Tony Blair, saw it as ringing the alarm bells for Great Britain. British Jews, he noted, felt compelled "to raise millions to provide private security for their weddings and community events"; Jewish students felt intimidated on campus by Islamists and Far Left Israel bashers; schoolboys were jostled on public transport and rabbis had been punched or knifed.[51] Most worrisome to MacShane and his parliamentary colleagues (all of them non-Jews) was the mood and tone of the anti-Jewish discourse in Britain whenever Jews are talked about—whether in the media, at universities, among the liberal elites, or at London dinner parties: "To express any support for Israel or any feeling for the right of a Jewish state to exist produces denunciation, even contempt."[52]

A perfect example of this extreme contempt is Tom Paulin, the Irish poet and professor of English literature at Oxford University, praised by some as a "writer of conscience."[53] On February 18, 2001, Paulin's poem "Killed in the Crossfire" was published in *The Observer*. Its ten lines oozed with hatred of what he called the "Zionist SS" and led to a subsequent controversy over his invitation to guest lecture at Harvard University.[54] Chosen as poem of the week by *The Guardian*, Paulin's effort read as follows:

> We are read this inert
> This lying phrase
> Like comfort food
> As another little Palestinian boy
> In trainers jeans and a white tee-shirt
> Is gunned down by the Zionist SS
> Whose initials we should
> —but we don't—dumb goys
> Clock in that weasel word
> Crossfire

Winston Pickett, director of the European Institute for the Study of Contemporary Antisemitism, has pointed out that the term "dumb goys" also occurred in *Mein Kampf* (1924), where Adolf Hitler wrote: "While the Zionists try to make the rest of the world believe that the national consciousness of the Jew finds its satisfaction in the creation of a Palestinian state, the Jews again slyly dupe the dumb Goyim."[55]

For the anti-imperialist Paulin the "dumb goys" evidently represent the easily duped British public unable to see through the real intentions of Nazi Zionism. For Hitler, it was Gentiles in general who were being taken in by an "international world swindle." Some months later Paulin told the Egyptian *Al-Ahram Weekly,* "I never believed Israel had the right to exist at all"— a sentiment he shared with the Nazi leader, whom he maliciously accused Israel of trying to emulate. As for those he described as "Brooklyn-born" Jewish settlers, Paulin was chillingly precise: "I think they should be shot dead. I think they are Nazis, racists. I feel nothing but hatred for them."[56]

Such "antiracist" hate speech is unusually frank and it was further compounded by Paulin's visceral contempt for those he ridiculed as "Hampstead liberal Zionists": "They use this card of anti-Semitism. They fill newspapers with hate letters. They are useless people."[57] Paulin's remarks passed with barely a ripple of criticism from the "antiracist" Left, many of whom were probably only too eager to see Israel painted in diabolical colors. Paulin continued to teach at Oxford and to regularly appear on the BBC2 arts program *Newsnight Review*. His barbs at Prime Minister Blair for presiding over a "Zionist government" and his artistic empathy with Palestinian suicide bombers were, after all, not unpopular views in Britain. His transmutation of Jews into Nazis and of Israeli soldiers into child murderers was already pervasive in contemporary British society and culture. It is also worth noting that Paulin's imagery reconnected with a much older discourse of English medieval and modern literary anti-Semitism in which perfidious Jews seem predestined to kill Gentile children.[58] Above all, however, Paulin was incensed by what he called Jewish manipulation of the "a-s" (anti-Semitism) card: "their game / . . . the ones who play the a-s card— / of death threats the mail talking touch / the usual cynical Goebbels stuff."[59]

Paulin was not the only British artist to exploit dark associations of Jews with propaganda, dissimulation, cruelty, and blood libels. When *The Independent* published an insidious cartoon by Dave Brown on its op-ed page showing Israeli prime minister Ariel Sharon in the act of devouring the head of a Palestinian baby, it seemed that the medieval blood libel had indeed returned in a new form.[60] Sharon, nearly naked, is shown wearing a Likud fig leaf. In the background Apache helicopters fire missiles and blare, "Vote Likud." This cartoon would not have looked out of place in *Der Stürmer*.[61] Nevertheless, the Press Complaints Committee in the United Kingdom dismissed all protests. Worse still, the caricature was subsequently awarded first prize in the British Political Cartoon Society's annual competition for 2003.[62] The newspaper's editor Simon Kelner (who is himself Jewish) unconvincingly argued that there was no anti-Semitic or even anti-Israel intent in the cartoon, though it was obvious that the bloodthirsty Sharon in the caricature personified Israel as the "State of the Jews." Moreover, the publication of this vile cartoon on Britain's national Holocaust Memorial Day insidiously suggested that the Jewish state (born out of the debris of the Shoah) was now executing its own genocidal bloodlust against the Palestinian people.

No less shocking was the anti-Semitic imagery featured on the front cover of the *New Statesman* weekly in mid-January 2002. It showed a very small, horizontally placed Union Jack, pierced by a large, vertically positioned Star of David shining with a strangely golden luster. Below it, in prominent black letters, were the rather ominous words "A Kosher Conspiracy?" The prostrate British flag was being stabbed by a dagger-shaped symbol of the Jewish people, and the use of the word "kosher" only heightened the ethnic-religious (anti-Semitic) connotations. No less unpleasant was the implication that Anglo-Jews used their money power against British national interests.[63]

The repellent *New Statesman* caricature prompted the general secretary of the Labour Party, David Triesman (himself from a Jewish Communist family) to sharply protest the use of an iconography so redolent of Nazi anti-Semitism.[64] The editor of the journal, Peter Wilby, responded at some length nearly a month later.[65] He apologized for "unwittingly" having given the impression that there was a Jewish conspiracy against Great Britain. But the editor very much doubted "whether a single person was provoked into hatred of Jews by our cover." Peter Wilby went on to unconvincingly assert that "racism against white people is of no consequence" and to suggest that Jews were probably "safer than most minorities," which was manifestly not the case. Wilby seemed to imply that Jews had achieved security and hence were less entitled to antiracist protection. Moreover, he studiously ignored the implicit and explicit echoes of anti-Semitism in two of the articles he had published in January 2002. John Pilger's polemic attacked Lord Levy's roles in helping to fund the Labour Party and as British "special envoy" to the Middle East, suggesting that his Jewish background would prevent him from negotiating impartially with Palestinians. Dennis Sewell's "Kosher conspiracy" piece flirted more craftily with the notion of a nefarious Zionist lobby in British politics, simultaneously countenancing, minimizing, and then feeding such fantasies. Behind these apparent contradictions lay a barely disguised mockery of incompetent Zionist Jews unable to effectively organize their would-be cabal.[66]

This view of Zionist "incompetence" was clearly not shared by veteran Labour MP Tam Dalyell. A much respected and well-bred legislator, the seventy-year-old "Father of the House" managed to combine cultivated aristocratic disdain with his own left-wing conspiracy theories about the Jews. According to Dalyell, Blair's Middle East policy was indeed being run by a "Jewish cabal" that included not only the ubiquitous Lord Levy but also Foreign Secretary Jack Straw and the man whom the British press loved to call the "Prince of Darkness," New Labour spin doctor, Peter Mandelson. In May 2003, fearing that Blair might follow the Iraq adventure by joining with President Bush in armed assaults on Syria and Iran, Dalyell said the time was ripe for "candor." He appeared to be convinced that hawkish "Jewish neocons" in Washington had apparently taken over Blair's thinking. As *The Economist* dryly noted, apart from being fuzzy and nasty, Dalyell's remarks about the "cabal" were remarkably inaccurate: "Two of the three men he mentioned, Peter Mandelson and Jack Straw, are not, by their own description, actually Jewish. Their partially Jewish ancestry would make them so only under Nazi-style race laws."[67]

Indeed, Jack Straw, with just one Jewish grandfather, could have qualified, at best, as a "*Mischling* second degree" in the Third Reich. Straw had never previously been outed as a Jew, nor was he even known as a particular friend of Israel.

Dalyell's anti-Semitic comments would probably have finished his career in America, but in Britain (with a few notable exceptions) his outburst was lightly shrugged off as a minor misdemeanor or eccentricity. His militant opposition to the Iraq War and to Blair's foreign policy had in any case endeared him to the anti-American wing of the Labour Party. They certainly identified with his negative characterization of leading Jewish hard-liners in the Bush administration, including Deputy Defense Secretary Paul Wolfowitz, Pentagon adviser Richard Perle, and White House spokesman Ari Fleischer. Dalyell's concern that Blair's Britain was "being led up the garden path on a Likudnik-Sharon agenda" probably struck a positive chord.[68]

Some of these concerns also found an echo on the anti-American Tory Right. Among Dalyell's strongest defenders was the conservative columnist Andrew Alexander, who wrote in the right-wing *Daily Mail* that Britons were entitled "to be alarmed" by the Jewish hawks in top positions in Washington. Together with the Christian fundamentalists, they had formed "a dangerous combination" of special concern to Britons. Alexander seemed to accept as fact that an American "Jewish clique" stood behind the invasion of Iraq. This adventurous war was really "about helping Israel and in particular premier Ariel Sharon."[69] Such was also the position taken in the United States by Virginia congressman Jim Moran (though he was very much the exception), who publicly proclaimed that there would have been no Iraq War without "the strong support of the Jewish community." The truth was, in fact, quite different. No other ethnic group in America opposed the Iraq War more strongly than the Jews.

Prime Minister Tony Blair's own commitment to the war against Saddam Hussein and on global terror, his strong defense of Israel's right to security, and his intimate relationship with wealthy Jews such as Lord Levy were factors that may have accelerated his political demise after a full decade in power. From March 2003 onward Blair faced a minirevolt on the anti-American and anti-Zionist Left of his own party, which never forgave his ultimate sin of loyalty to George W. Bush. The Left regarded Blair as being in thrall not merely to the arrogant, unilateralist "warmongers" in Washington but also to the "racist military junta" of Tel Aviv—seen in leftist circles (and by a majority of Britons) as more dangerous to world peace than Saddam's Iraq. Blair did indeed identify with the United States more than any other British prime minister since Winston Churchill. In a speech to the joint session of the U.S. Congress in July 2003 he attacked anti-Americanism, Islamist terrorism, and the "vile propaganda used to indoctrinate [Palestinian and Arab] children not just against Israel but against Jews." At the same time he reaffirmed his faith in the values of the West and of the United States.[70] Blair's strained relations with unreconstructed leftists such as Ken Livingstone were primarily related to domestic issues, but their diametrically opposed views on America and Israel were also an aggravating factor.[71] The British premier's backing of Israel during the 2006 war in Lebanon was the last straw for many in his own party.

Blair made no secret of his appreciation for the communitarian values of Diaspora Jews, their emphasis on education, their sense of tradition, and their ability to integrate into the larger society. His successor, Gordon Brown, son of a Church of Scotland Presbyterian minister (who had himself been an ardent Christian Zionist), undoubtedly shares Blair's positive view of the Jewish people and its social ethic rooted in community, mutual obligation, and hard work.[72] No less of an Atlanticist than Blair and his new counterparts Nicolas Sarkozy in France and German chancellor Angela Merkel, Brown's stewardship signified an important pro-American shift at the helm of western Europe. Moreover, Brown certainly does *not* identify with the old Left's anti-Israel and sometimes anti-Semitic malevolence, any more than he does with the loathing of America, the overly obsessive fixation on Palestine, or the politics of appeasement toward militant Islam.

Radical leftist anti-Semitism in Great Britain has been closely connected with this deep antagonism to America, a smoldering resentment at the success of Western liberal democracy, ambivalence toward the existence of nation-states, and a neurotic frustration fueled by years of unfulfilled revolutionary illusions. With this kind of worldview Leftists are almost predestined to find in the State of Israel the perfect scapegoat. After all, Israel remains pro-American, an oasis of democracy in a desert of tyranny, intensely patriotic, and long ago outgrew the socialist collectivism of its early years. It boasts a thriving high-tech economy, despite having lived for nearly sixty years under conditions of nearly permanent siege. What marks it out in the region is its impartial judiciary, quality medical care, free press, and vibrant civil society.

For the political culture of the British Left, built as it is on envy, resentment, and a cult of patronizing Third World "victims" of the West, this is reason enough to hate Israel. The fact of its Jewishness may in certain cases transform ignorant contempt into outright hostility.[73] This socialist culture of resentment can also translate into a thinly disguised antipathy toward British Jews. Anglo-Jewry is too well established, professionally successful, and positively orientated to free-market capitalism to be considered a client group. The radical Left does, however, maintain its soft spot for Third World liberation struggles against "racist oppressors," even when they produce such tyrants and systematic violators of human rights as Idi Amin, Robert Mugabe, Saddam Hussein, Chairman Mao, Pol Pot, Fidel Castro, Gamal Abdul Nasser, and Yasser Arafat. The extraordinary indulgence shown to Palestinian and Islamist terrorists as romantic martyrs for a just cause often conceals an unavowed fascistic hankering on the Left for the concept of "total war" for victory or death. Bin Laden, like Arafat before him, becomes the contemporary Arab reincarnation of Che Guevara for armchair "apostles" of revolutionary violence in the West.

The Marxist-Islamist axis achieved its first mass expression on February 15, 2003, during what was perhaps the largest political demonstration held in postwar England: one that took place under the slogan "Don't Attack Iraq—Freedom for Palestine." Nearly a million people marched through the streets of London. The demonstration had been coordinated by the SWP and the MAB. The MAB banners significantly read "Palestine from the Sea to the River"—reflecting the position of an organization that has supported the anti-Semitic Hamas, publicly justifies suicide bombers, and retains close ties to the Muslim Brotherhood.[74] The Islamists may sharply disagree with their Trotskyist and Far Left allies about feminism, homosexuality, religion, secularism, and the validity of socialist ideals, but they share a common anti-Western, anti-globalist, and anti-Zionist agenda.[75] Radical Islamists in Britain are not, of course, interested in the traditional class struggle of the proletariat. But like the Far Left, they hate America, revel in the myth of a Jewish world conspiracy, and are determined to eliminate Israel. Palestine is *the* issue where their cooperation with the Left is most harmonious.

In Britain, as in France, the anti-globalist Left and the Islamic fundamentalists also share a common rejection of liberal modernity and the entire Enlightenment project. Yet, ironically, both want to *globalize* the Middle East conflict, demanding "humanitarian" intervention by the wicked Western imperialists, if only to "stop Israel," while at the same time threatening it with UN and EU sanctions.[76] The interventionist militancy of the Islamists and anti-globalists is partly based on a ludicrously inflated image of Israel as a superpower able to determine the foreign policy of the United States and the West. The websites of the anti-globalists in Britain, as elsewhere, are often soaked in the most vulgar anti-Americanism drawing on *Protocols*-inspired anti-Semitic conspiracy theories, mixed with insipid slogans about Israel as a Nazi state and a totally idealized view of the Palestinians.[77] Nowhere is the morbid emotionalism and self-indulgence of a victim-centered culture more palpable than in the pro-Palestinian partisanship of the International Solidarity Movement.

In the pro-Palestinian narrative of liberals and Marxists remarkably little attention is paid to the crazed ideology, the poisoned culture of martyrdom, or the violently anti-Semitic hatred emanating from much of contemporary Islamism. Instead, terrorism and Islamist suicide attacks are explained away as a product of social conditions and the general misery induced by Israel's policies. Such facile assumptions led the British prime minister's wife, Cherie Blair, to unguardedly remark at a charitable event in London in June 2002 that young Palestinians "feel they have got no hope but to blow themselves up."[78] The comment was particularly offensive coming as it did only hours after a Hamas suicide bomber blew up a bus packed full of Israelis, including schoolchildren—killing nineteen and maiming many more. *The Daily Telegraph* ironically chided Blair, reminding her that the martyrs lived on "hope" rather than "despair": first, the hope they would go to heaven if they murdered Jews; second, the hope they would destroy Israel; and third, the hope that their families would receive a $25,000 reward from the Iraqi and Saudi governments.[79] Even more extreme was Jenny Tonge, a physician and the Liberal Democrat spokesperson for children's affairs, who was sacked from her position when she, too, expressed sympathy for suicide terrorism as a response to Palestinian "humiliation" and the "provocations" of the Israeli occupying power. At a pro-Palestinian rally in the British parliament, Dr. Tonge explained: "I think that if I had to live in that situation—and I say that advisedly—I might just consider becoming one [a suicide bomber] myself."[80]

Such comments betrayed remarkable political naïveté about the techniques used to brainwash Palestinian children. They would soon spill over into overt anti-Semitism during a speech Tonge made about the "pro-Israel Lobby." In September 2006, Baroness Tonge, addressing a meeting of the Palestinian Solidarity Campaign, declared that "the pro-Israeli Lobby has got its grips on the western world, its financial grips"—even having squeezed the Liberal Democratic Party into its clutches. Two months later, in November 2006, she would quote the John J. Mearsheimer and Stephen M. Walt "research" on the Israel lobby in the United States, to bolster her jaundiced views. She was, however, strongly censured by the Liberal Democrat leader for the "clear anti-Semitic connotations" of her remarks.[81]

Although the leadership of the main political parties in Great Britain has *not* been hostile to Israel, popular and elite opinion is a different matter. Britons as a whole have been more sympathetic to the Palestinians since 2000 by a factor of two to one.[82] The pro-Palestinian attitude was noticeably stronger among Liberal Democrats and Labour voters than with Conservatives, and more frequently encountered among men than among women. (By comparison, American polls have shown popular support for Israel outrunning that for the Palestinians by nearly four to one.) This anti-Israeli British climate of opinion has inevitably made life for Anglo-Jews that much more testing than in the past, especially for those Jews (the majority) who affirm Israel's right to self-defense.[83] It is not only the anti-Semitic canards that are profoundly shocking but also the implicit endorsement or indifference toward terrorism against Israeli civilians, which (as we have seen) is considered legitimate in the reporting and commentary of so much of the British media.

In May 2005, another side of this coin was revealed—the active desire to turn pro-Palestinian militants into saints and martyrs. A new British play, called *My Name Is Rachel Corrie,* glorified the young American activist who was killed in the Gaza Strip in 2003 while attempting to prevent a bulldozer from destroying a home that had been used to supply Palestinian terror networks. Rather than challenging the obvious bias of the play or its moral perspectives, theater critics chose to compare it to dramatizations of the lives of Anne Frank and the most famous Italian witness to the Holocaust, Primo Levi, who had been deported to Auschwitz in 1944 but survived to write about his experiences. The staging of Caryl Churchill's short play *Seven Jewish Children* in early 2009 at London's Royal Court Theatre added a new twist to the anti-Jewish agenda in the name of "solidarity with Palestine." Most British Jews regarded the play as an anti-Semitic propaganda. The author Howard Jacobson called it "wantonly inflammatory" and a "hate-filled little chamber-piece."[84]

However, the most troubling development for British Jewry has been the emergence of the United Kingdom as a major world center of political Islam with its myriad channels of anti-Semitic, anti-Israel, and anti-American political propaganda. Through its Arabic newspapers, magazine, and publishing houses, not to mention its flourishing network of bookshops, mosques, and community centers, radical Islam has taken full advantage of what British democracy has to offer to promote its *anti-Western* goals, reaping the benefits of London's significance as a hub of global finance, electronic media, and mass communications technology.[85] The effect of this with regard to anti-Semitism and virulent anti-Zionism has in some respects been more severe than elsewhere in Europe. Although the Muslim population of the United Kingdom (about 2.5 million) is only a third of that of France, the growing influence of British Muslims has given the most inflammatory of ideas a greater legitimacy in Britain's political and cultural discourse than they enjoy in most of western Europe.

Much of this Islamist energy has in recent years been directed at mobilizing Muslims to fight against Israel and America. The impassioned calls of Sheikh Omar bin Bakri Muhammad (until 2006 a leading Muslim cleric in London) to celebrate the September 11, 2001, attacks as a "towering day in history," and to recruit Muslim youth for holy war in Afghanistan, Iraq, and Palestine, struck an emotional chord in the Muslim ghettos.[86] This is less surprising when one recalls that 40 percent of British Muslims surveyed in a *Sunday Times* poll not long after 9/11 believed Osama bin Laden was "justified" in his war against America. They even supported those of their core-ligionists from Britain who volunteered to fight with the Taliban against the Western allies.[87] At the same time, Islamists such as Anjem Choudary, the spokesman of the al-Muhajiroun ("the Exiles"), regarded Britain and the West as mere pawns controlled by the Zionists. Sheikh Bakri himself warned Jews in Great Britain after 9/11 to avoid any support for Israel lest they "become targets for Muslims." Al-Muhajiroun combined calls for "the black flag of Islam to fly over Downing Street" with demands for the liberation of Palestine and the jihadist demand to "de-Judaize the West."[88] When the group was belatedly outlawed, it simply reorganized itself under another name.

The highly inflammable cocktail embracing Palestine, jihad, the dream of a worldwide caliphate, Koranic indoctrination, and classical Judeophobia was exposed by the London Old Bailey trial of Sheikh Abdallah al-Faisal in February 2003. The cleric, a Jamaican convert to Islam educated in Saudi Arabia, was found guilty of inciting to murder and racial hatred on the basis of his lectures and videocassettes—some of them on sale at specialty bookshops in Great Britain—and sentenced to nine years in prison. Overwhelming evidence was produced at the trial to demonstrate his encouragement for a violent jihad to kill nonbelievers. Particular venom was reserved by the sheikh for the "filthy Jews."[89] In a spine-chilling speech that seemed to anticipate the May 2003 suicide mission of two young British Muslims to Tel Aviv, el-Faisal ranted: "People with British passports, if you fly into Israel it is easy. . . . Fly into Israel and do whatever you can. If you die, you are up in Paradise. How do you fight a Jew? You kill a Jew."[90]

This kind of extreme Muslim Judeophobia is a fairly recent phenomenon in Britain. It is best seen as a direct extension of the global jihad from the Middle East to the *dar al-kufr* (abode of the infidels). Unfortunately, little attention was paid to the jihadis until the terrorist attacks on London's transport system in July 2005. The British authorities then discovered to their horror that the suicide bombers were not foreigners radicalized by Middle Eastern oppression but mainly homegrown Anglo-Pakistanis from good families who not only repudiated British values but also rejected the elementary codes of common humanity.[91] Their leader, Mohammed Sidique Khan, left behind a chilling and almost surreal video in which (kaffiyeh-atttired and speaking in a broad Yorkshire accent) he blamed the London bombings on British "atrocities" against *his* people, the Muslim *umma* (nation). Even more alarming for the British security services were the surveys showing that perhaps as many as two hundred thousand British Muslims could see some justification for megaterror attacks in the West, while around four thousand had received terrorist training in the al-Qaeda camps of Afghanistan and Pakistan.[92]

According to a *Guardian* poll in March 2004, about 13 percent of all British Muslims unequivocally approved of the al-Qaeda assault on New York. Moreover, the reservoir of sympathy for Islamist causes among ordinary British Muslims is, of course, much higher. About one in five expressed understanding for the motives behind the London bombings of July 7, 2005. Some British Muslim leaders, too, have been uncommonly aggressive, with their implicit threats of blackmail if the alleged (but largely fictive) "demonization" of Muslims in Britain persists. Thus the secretary-general, Muhammad Abdul Bari, warned that if the United Kingdom treated Muslims as if they were all terrorists (the opposite is in fact the case), "then Britain will have to deal with 2 million terrorists—700,000 of them in London."[93] Since Britain's abandonment of support for Israel is one of the key demands of such demagogic leaders, this is a source of obvious concern for the Anglo-Jewish community, especially since "anti-Semitism is a fixture of even the most mainstream Muslim organizations" in the United Kingdom.[94] Such Muslim animus has had a cumulative effect on growing numbers of middle-class educated whites in Britain who almost reflexively blame Israel for provoking Islamist terrorism; this, in turn, places additional pressure on British Jews to repudiate Israel or else to lose their liberal (and British) credentials.[95]

It is a fact that anti-Semitism and anti-Westernism have found increasing grassroots support in the Muslim diaspora among radicalized youth, for whom Osama bin Laden remains a hero and an icon.[96] This has been particularly true in Britain. For example, in September 2002 around one thousand British Muslims gathered under police protection at Finsbury Park Mosque in North London to glorify the first anniversary of the 9/11 Manhattan massacre. The Egyptian-born Abu Hamza, who presided over the mosque, had successfully turned it into a magnet for young Muslims embracing jihadist Islam, terror, and armed struggle in places ranging from Afghanistan, Chechnya, and Kashmir to Palestine.[97] It was in this mosque that the so-called shoe bomber, Richard Reid (a British convert to Islam)— who narrowly failed to blow up a transatlantic flight in December 2001 and was later sentenced to life imprisonment—had gravitated; it was also at Finsbury Park Mosque that Zacarias Moussaoui, the French-Moroccan Muslim arrested in America as the twentieth 9/11 hijacker, received his indoctrination into radical Islamism. The fundamentalist message at such mosques routinely transmitted the call to young Muslims to take up arms against Jews, Hindus, and other "infidels."

Abu Hamza preached this kind of incendiary propaganda, undisturbed by the British authorities for many years. Only in early 2003 was he belatedly stripped of his British citizenship under a new nationality act and banned from preaching at Finsbury Park Mosque. Predictably, he denounced the ban as yet "another example of the oppression of Islam" provoked by any criticism of America and Israel; at an extremist rally in Trafalgar Square he pointedly dismissed the 9/11 mass murder as an "American-Zionist plot to blame the Muslim world." He then provoked a more general revulsion in Britain by describing the *Columbia* space shuttle disaster on February 1, 2003 (in which eight astronauts, including an Israeli, Colonel Ilan Ramon, died), as "an act of God." The Almighty, according to Abu Hamza, had punished the "trinity of evil" (represented by the Americans, Jews, and Hindus) on board the shuttle.[98] His Supporters of Sharia movement, along with al-Muhajiroun and other Islamist groupings such as Hizb-ut Tahrir (the Islamic Liberation Party), not only regularly attacked the "Jewish-controlled media" in Britain for its alleged bias against Muslims and its justification of "Zionist crimes" but obsessively promoted the apocalyptic *hadith* that the "final hour will not come until the Muslims kill the Jews."[99] In other words, an Islamic anti-Jewish massacre would be a central part of the Last Judgment. This did not stop left-wing Labour MP Clare Short (a bitter critic of Tony Blair) from hosting a "love-in" with Hizb ut-Tahrir in the British parliament in 2006. More recently, in September 2007, Short achieved a new record in anti-Zionist absurdity by claiming that no progress was possible on climate change treaties because Israel "undermines the international community's reaction to global warming." It is mind-boggling that no matter how ludicrous the proposition, the Red-Green Axis will still blame Israel. For the radical Islamists this is not merely theoretical but often leads to deadly consequences.

Among the Muslims converted to religious extremism at Finsbury Park Mosque were two young Anglo-Pakistani suicide bombers, Asif Mohammed Hanif from West London and Omar Khan Sharif from Derby.

Both of them had also been markedly influenced by the al-Muhajiroun group led by Sheikh Bakri—the "spiritual guide" who later lauded their actions as "freedom fighters" seeking to liberate Palestine. In May 2003, the twenty-one-year-old Hanif blew himself up at Mike's Place, a bar on the Tel Aviv beachfront, killing three innocent bystanders. Nothing in his Westernized education and respectable upbringing seemed to have predestined him to become a *shahid* (Islamic martyr); that is, until his sudden turn to living a devout Muslim life and the influence of a study course in Arabic in Damascus, which probably radicalized his views on Palestine.[100]

The case of Ahmed Omar Sheikh, a young Anglo-Pakistani terrorist and a London School of Economics student, heavily implicated in the gruesome beheading of American Jewish journalist Daniel Pearl in Karachi in February 2002, was analogous in certain respects. Omar Sheikh, too, was as much a child of British culture as of radical Islam, from a well-educated middle-class immigrant family.[101] Once he metamorphosed into a Muslim militant—radicalized by the Bosnian massacres in Europe, by his spell in the Afghan training camps of al-Qaeda, and by his return to Pakistan—the door was wide open to the culture of martyrdom, terrorism, and an anti-Semitic hatred that fused the rants of *Mein Kampf* with appropriate Koranic verses.

The profiles and statements of the 9/11 and the 7/7 bombers in New York and London, as well as those terrorists who have struck inside Israel, reveal that "martyrdom" killings are a strategic *choice*. They are perceived by their perpetrators as an exalted act of *religious self-sacrifice*. They have little if anything to do with economic deprivation or social despair. Similarly, the anti-Semitism manifested by global jihadis and their British offshoots is at best a secondary outgrowth of Israeli treatment of Palestinians or American support for the Jewish state (though these are useful triggers to whip up hysteria and increase recruitment figures). Rather, hatred of the Jews and Israel often lies at the heart of rabid Islamist hostility to the West. For Jews are perceived as de facto controlling Western society (including Britain) and acting as a satanic force engaged in a "conspiracy to destroy Islam and rule the world."[102] The battle with Israel is understood by virtually all Islamists as a metaphysical struggle between good and evil, no less than as a geopolitical or territorial issue, something that the empirical British mind has great difficulty in being able to fathom.[103]

The British authorities were, for example, astonishingly slow to act against the Egyptian exile Abu Hamza (born Mustafa Kamel Mustafa), even after a raid on his mosque in January 2003 had discovered an arsenal including chemical warfare protection units, blank-firing pistols, stun guns, false passports, knives, and radio equipment. He was finally detained in Belmarsh prison in May 2004 but only after the Americans had demanded his extradition as one of the world's most-wanted terrorists. Eventually he was charged and found guilty of "incitement to racial hatred" and soliciting murder, resulting in a sentence of seven years in prison. In his fire-and-brimstone sermons, he had for many years railed against the vices of Western society (sexual immorality, drugs, alcoholism), called for blood sacrifice in the name of Allah, and justified killing the *kaffir* (unbelievers) "even if there is no reason for it."[104] The court was told that the forty-seven-year-old cleric had declared in some of his sermons that "Hitler was sent into the world" to cleanse it of Jews, who were blasphemers and "dirty traitors"; they were presented as the "sons of monkeys" who had managed by stealth to seize "control of the West." At the end of the trial it emerged that more than a quarter of young British Muslims (eighteen- to twenty-four-year-olds) agreed with the views of this insidious hate preacher.[105]

Hamza's closest rival in the bigotry stakes was the previously mentioned Syrian-born cleric Sheikh Omar bin Bakri Mohammed, head of the al-Muhajiroun, who for two decades preached jihad in Britain. Though a fanatical opponent of the British and American governments, his immediate aim was to encourage the overthrow of the "apostate" regimes in the Arab Middle East.[106] Bakri was the founder of Hizb ut-Tahrir in Britain, and a fund-raiser for Hamas, Hezbollah, and Islamic Jihad who shared Osama bin Laden's fundamentalist worldview. Incredibly enough, Bakri had been left free by the British government, despite his declaration in 1991 that Prime Minister John Major was a legitimate target for assassination during the First Persian Gulf War. Bakri even lived off British welfare-state handouts for many years while claiming that he scrupulously observed a "covenant of peace" with the U.K. authorities. Presumably the deal was that his group would discourage attacks on British targets in return for political asylum. But this did not prevent Bakri from recruiting Muslim volunteers who later fought against British troops in Afghanistan, or from sending them to Jordan, Lebanon, and other areas of conflict.[107] In July 1999 Bakri called on Osama bin Laden to act against the West in the name of the "*Ummah* of Jihad . . . chosen by Allah to rule the world" and to restore *al-*

Khilafah (the caliphate).[108] With regard to the United States, he advised bin Laden (three years before 9/11) to "bring down their airlines," to "occupy their embassies," and to "force the closure of their banks."[109] But nobody in the West was listening.

Bakri's hatred of Jews was well attested, and undoubtedly poisoned the minds of many young and easily impressionable British Muslims. Calls to "kill the Jews" were frequently posted on al-Muhajiroun websites along with dismissal of the Holocaust as a political tool used by Zionists "in order to justify their hegemony over Muslims in Palestine." Far worse crimes had supposedly been committed in Palestine, Chechnya, and Kashmir.[110] Not only that, but Bakri unabashedly told the BBC in 2000 that Israel was "a cancer in the heart of the Muslim world" that had to be excused and removed.[111] This could only be achieved through violent jihad and the restoration of the caliphate—an Islamic revolution that had to begin in London. Only after the flag of Islam was flying over Downing Street and the Elysée Palace, could Muslims, Christians, and Jews live peacefully under an Islamic authority.[112] The Islamic state would then be established over the entire world, enabling synagogues and churches to flourish under sharia law.[113]

As a recent insider account by onetime radical Islamist Ed Husain crisply puts it: "While the British State fed Omar he sowed the seeds of terror in British Muslim minds."[114] Under Bakri's leadership in the 1990s, Hizb leaflets had openly proclaimed the urgent need for an Islamic state in Britain. The Hizb also distributed homophobic and anti-Jewish literature, swore by the jihad, and preached a policy of noncooperation with *kaffir* legislation. Bakri's activities in the United Kingdom were not stopped until new antiterrorist legislation convinced him that he should leave for Beirut in October 2005. But he left behind many disciples. In an interview with the London daily *Asharq Al-Awsat* published on July 7, 2006, Bakri warned Muslim youth "not to assimilate into the pagan [*jahiliya*] British society" and to "distance themselves from infidels and polytheists." He declared "Londonistan" to be "Heretistan," or *dar al-kufr* [the abode of heresy], but prophesied that it would one day become "Islamastan," or *dar al-Islam* (the abode of Islam). He still looked forward confidently to seeing the banner proclaiming "There is no God but Allah" flying over Big Ben and the British parliament.[115] Bakri, along with the Palestinian Sheikh Abou Qutada, Abu Hamza, and Anjem Choudary, was adept at spreading the jihadi mission of

Islam in Britain, preaching the "war of civilizations" against a confused and disoriented Judeo-Christian West. The Islamists skillfully exploited the theme of Palestinian liberation as a revolutionary prelude to the aims of global jihad—as a mobilization strategy for rallying alienated British Muslims in search of an identity. The more secular Muslims still focused on "illegal" Jewish settlements, the "apartheid wall," and Israeli colonialist "racism." This provided some common ground with the British Left and even with some liberal "progressive" Jews.[116] But the Islamists were much more fixated on issues such as Jewish control of Islamic holy places and the cultural war against the West.

Radical Islam in recent years has even attracted some neo-Nazi converts, including David Myatt (founder of the hard-line British National Socialist Movement and a former leader of Combat 18), who duly changed his name to Abdul Aziz ibn Myatt. Although at one time staunchly opposed to nonwhite immigration into Britain and an ideologically convinced racist, Myatt now embraced the pure, authentic form of jihadi Islam as "the only force that is capable of fighting and destroying the dishonor, the arrogance, the materialism of the West." In an Internet essay published in 2006 explaining his conversion, Myatt denounced the idolatry of the West, for which nothing is sacred "except perhaps Zionists, Zionism, the hoax of the so-called Holocaust, and the idols which the West and its lackeys worship, or pretend to worship, such as democracy."[117] Myatt, described by the antifascist *Searchlight* magazine in July 2000 as "the most ideologically-driven Nazi in Britain, preaching race war and terrorism," now firmly believed that the jihadists best incarnated the warrior values of honor and loyalty that he had once propagated. Jihadi Islam exuded strength, unity, and faith in the face of capitalist decadence; it offered a rock-hard identity and a revolutionary alternative to the declining Jewish-bourgeois "civilization" of the West.[118]

For British Muslims, as opposed to radicalized converts, there is the added appeal of identifying with a global *umma* (peoplehood), as defined by 'Azzam al-Tamimi, the leading intellectual spokesman of Hamas in Britain.[119] In November 2006 Tamimi told a Muslim conference in Manchester that "we are Muslims in Europe and European Muslims," with an identity based on the Islamic sharia and a transnational *umma*.[120] Tamimi, who was born in Hebron, has never recognized Israel's right to exist, calling it "a racist and fascist state" that would disappear the same way as the Crusaders did many centuries ago. Defending suicide bombers as sublime martyrs for a "holy cause," he lauded their love of death, the ultimate guarantee of victory—since it "exceeded the Israelis' love for a life of security, safety and comfort."[121] This struggle of martyrs was a religious not a nationalist duty, an "act of worship" to be rewarded by Allah, against which Israel had no defense. The Zionist project was in any case doomed, and the only purpose of negotiations with Israel was to "dismantle and eliminate" its existence. Jews who so wished could then live under Islamic "protection" in accord with well-known Koranic precepts.[122] As an advocate of the Hamas ideology that territorial compromise was impossible and the peace process an "aberration," Tamimi has invariably emphasized that the only acceptable solution is liberation through armed struggle of "the entire land of Palestine."[123] However, like President Ahmadinejad, he has no objection to the expelled Jews being given half of Austria, part of Germany, or perhaps even a corner of their own in the United States.

Tamimi represents the more articulate British or European face of Palestinian Islamist extremism. He skillfully avoids overt anti-Semitism even as he insists on the inevitable victory of Islam and the destruction of Israel. What he shares with the majority of British Muslims (80 percent of whom are from the Indian subcontinent) is an insistence on the absolute primacy of Muslim identity over any identification with the United Kingdom. No less than 81 percent of British Muslims do indeed regard themselves first and foremost as Muslims, only 7 percent as being above all British. This is a uniquely lopsided result for western Europe.[124] However, this does not mean that British Muslims (as a community) support suicide bombing. Moreover, they *are* concerned about the rise of Islamic extremism—with which the British Muslim majority does not publicly identify. Nevertheless, a significant hard-core minority (about 15 percent) supports the fundamentalists.[125]

The Islamists, it must be said, are extremely active and effective in utilizing the fiery rhetoric of jihad to win over disaffected young Muslims. They provide a growing library of militant books and videos that feed the jihadi fever and contain vile expressions of anti-Semitism reminiscent of the ravings of Nazi propaganda. Bookshops in London, Leicester, and Birmingham, for example, contain incendiary material about the Jewish conspiracy, martyrdom operations, and jihad.[126] The journalist Suhayl Saadi was struck by the prevalence of apocalyptic jihadi texts, including classic works of Muslim fundamentalism such as those of Maulana Maududi (founder of the Indo-Pakistani movement Jamaat-e-Islami) and the anti-Semitic Sayyid Qutb, alongside cheap hate books that exhort young Muslims to "become time bombs." Ever since the 1980s when the deadly cocktail of Islamofascism, anticolonialism, and a puritanical Wahhabism (financed by Saudi Arabia) first hijacked the efforts of the Salafi reformist movement to "purify" Islam, this literature has become abundant. As Saadi puts it: "The driving force of 'third-generation' jihadism today is simply the will to power. Its publications justify political statements by quoting the Koran or Hadith (sayings of the Prophet) but the tone is of supremacist rage." As global populist resentment against the West plunges growing numbers of young Muslims into the hallucinatory cyberworld of Islamism, anti-Semitic myths have proliferated almost beyond belief. For example, a passage from *The Ideological Attack* reads: "The Jews strive their utmost to corrupt the beliefs, morals and manners of Muslims." In *The Islamic Ruling on the Peace Process,* one can find a similar pearl of enlightenment: "The Jews have ever been moving across the earth to create troubles."[127]

The receptivity to jihad, terrorism, anti-Westernism, and anti-Semitism appears strongest among a militant minority of outwardly assimilated but inwardly "born-again" Muslims. Their adolescent revolt and search for a new identity has nourished a backlash against both Western secularism and the more conservative Islamic culture of their parents.[128] But the fiercest reaction against the West (often accompanied by extreme anti-Semitism) not unexpectedly comes from converts imbued with a burning neophyte zeal to prove their Muslim credentials. A good example is Ahmad Thomson of the Association of Muslim Lawyers, who openly accused Jews of controlling Europe and America, of pushing Tony Blair into the Iraq War, and of manufacturing the "big lie" of the Holocaust. Almost as virulent is Ibrahim Hewitt, who insists that it was Palestinians who have suffered the real genocide at Israel's hands.[129]

The passive and unhelpful role of Muslim leaders in the United Kingdom has seriously aggravated the problem of radical Islam. Symptomatic of the leadership's grievance politics has been the MCB's boycott of Holocaust Memorial Day since 2003. Its then secretary-general Sir Iqbal Sacranie (a so-called moderate) reasoned that Muslims were unable to join in the memorial ceremony "because in its present form it excludes and ignores other ongoing genocide and human rights abuses around the world, notably in the Occupied Palestinian Territories." Other Muslim leaders insisted that

Holocaust Memorial Day sounded "too exclusive to many young Muslims," suggesting "that the lives of [some people] are to be remembered more than others." Muslims, it was claimed, felt aggrieved at this "double standard" and the (imaginary) implication that "their lives are not equally valuable to those lost in the Holocaust time."[130] Indeed, according to Sacranie, criticism of the Muslim boycott in the British press was itself proof that they were being subjected to what he darkly referred to as the "Israel test."[131]

Such negative attitudes are mirrored at the grass roots. As in France, Muslim pupils sometimes vehemently react to classroom lessons about the Holocaust. The result has been that a number of schools in Britain have dropped the subject from their history lessons to avoid "offending" Muslim pupils. They evidently fear "upsetting students whose beliefs include Holocaust denial," according to a recent government-funded study that confirmed the alarming extent of anti-Semitic sentiment among British Muslim pupils.[132]

The British government regards the MCB as a reliable mainstream voice of the local Muslim community. Yet its known support for Hamas suicide bombers has never been hidden. The MCB even regards the Hamas "freedom fighters" as comparable to Nelson Mandela or the great Indian guru of nonviolence, Mahatma Gandhi. Sacranie also referred admiringly to the assassinated Hamas founder, Sheikh Ahmed Yassin—a firm advocate of terror—as "the renowned Islamic scholar." In addition, he warmly praised Sheikh Qaradawi (another advocate of suicide bombings in Israel) and has repeatedly accused Israel of the "ethnic cleansing of Palestine."[133] The MCB's public affairs officer, Inayat Bunglawala, another presumed moderate, has also been an admirer of Hamas, lauding it as an authentically Muslim movement. He has at various times praised Osama bin Laden, defended extreme Wahhabite clerics in Saudi Arabia, and expressed support for the extremely violent Islamic Salvation Front in Algeria. In the past Bunglawala scathingly referred to the British media as being Zionist controlled, and attacked the Jews for considering themselves as "God's chosen people." He considered Jews racists who acted as if they could do "whatever the hell they like." The "blessed prophet Jesus" had called Jews the "children of the Devil."[134] This was the same "moderate Muslim" who would subsequently be selected as convener of the British government's task force against Muslim extremism.

An investigation by The Times, published in September 2007, exposed equally disconcerting information about the scale of the Islamist problem.[135] It revealed that almost half of Britain's mosques were under the control of a hard-line ultraconservative Islamic sect called the Deobandi, whose roots lay in British-ruled India, where the movement had founded its first madrassa in 1867. The Deobandis expanded to Pakistan, where there are today an estimated thirteen thousand seminaries, eighty-five hundred of which are Deobandi. It was they who supplied the cadres of the Taliban leadership that eventually won control of post-Soviet Afghanistan. Furthermore, the isolationist Deobandis have always opposed any integration with the *kaffir* (the non-Muslim majority) as a dire threat to the pure faith. Their leading preacher in Britain, the thirty-six-year-old Sheikh Riyadh ul-Haq, frequently expresses in his sermons a deep loathing of Western society and of the "evil influence" on his fellow believers of non-Muslim British neighbors; he evidently shares bin Laden's conviction that America and its British ally are seeking to destroy Islam.

According to the Deobandis, Muslims must not walk in the footsteps of Jews and Christians. Their food, clothing, the cut of beards, and their whole way of life must emphasize *separateness* from the non-Muslims in the *kaffir* West.[136] The imperialist West is demonized as being engaged in a continuous genocidal mission—to humiliate, murder, or rape Muslim peoples and conquer their lands. Israelis are, of course, a part of this sinister conspiracy, and it is therefore a sacred mission for Muslims to shed their blood and to die for Allah—especially to liberate the sacred al-Aqsa Mosque in Jerusalem. Such appeals contain an unmistakably *apocalyptic* edge, for Muslims are deemed to be already living in a time of darkness "before the day of reckoning."[137] Jews, whether in Jerusalem, London, Birmingham, or New York, were clearly marked as an integral part of the oppressive West. "They [the Jews] have monopolised everything: the Holocaust, God, money, interest, usury, the world economy, the media, political institutions . . . they monopolised tyranny and oppression as well. And injustice."[138]

Haq's Deobandi movement, with its teaching of contempt for Jews, Christians, and Hindus, runs around 600 out of Britain's 1,350 mosques. They include 59 out of the 75 mosques in the five northern English towns of Blackburn, Bolton, Preston, Oldham, and Burnley. The Deobandis also control 17 of Britain's 26 Islamic seminaries, producing 80 percent of its homegrown Muslim clerics. These seminaries outlaw soccer ("a cancer that has infected our youth"), as well as art, television, and chess. Many of its graduates apparently regard popular music as particularly dangerous—a way in which Jews have spread "the Satanic web" to corrupt young Muslims. Haq, who runs an Islamic academy with branches in Leicester and Birmingham, is a central voice in the spread of this hate-consumed radical Puritanism—today even more extreme in Britain than in its Pakistani cradle of origin. As *The Times* pointed out, the Deobandi message is not the unrepresentative extremism of a fringe, but a serious threat to Britain's civil society, as well as to moderate Muslims. One of the July 2005 London bombers, Shehzad Tanweer, studied at the Deobandi seminary in Dewsbury, while Mohammed Sidique Khan, the leader of the 7/7 terror plot, was a regular worshipper at the adjoining mosque.

Muslim anti-Semitism in Britain cannot, as we have seen, be divorced from the effects of such extremist separatism, Koranic indoctrination, Islamic suprematism, jihadi fever, and incitement over Palestine—some of it (perhaps unwittingly) encouraged by the British media. The impact of al-Qaeda and bin Laden's Islamofascist message has certainly exacerbated matters, but its roots lay much deeper in the anti-Western jihadist ideology that has infiltrated Britain since the early 1990s—feeding off Muslim paranoia and persecution complexes. In Britain, the hatred of Jews was a natural corollary of the "war of civilizations"—directed primarily against America and the West as part of the struggle for Islam's worldwide hegemony.[139] "Londonistan" became the communications nerve center in the West for preparing this global jihad and a uniquely favorable terrain for the radicalization of British Muslims.[140] The siren-call of Islamophobia, constantly exaggerated by British Muslim leaders and journalists, further inflamed the atmosphere.

The British Left eagerly participated in this charade by bolstering the victim mentality and the Muslim sense of oppression by Western imperialism, "Zionist occupation," the war in Iraq, and racism in Europe itself.[141] This made it easier to attribute the alienation of Muslims to British foreign policy, especially Tony Blair's support for America and Israel. The Left (with a few honorable exceptions) blacked out Muslim bigotry and anti-Semitism as if it did not exist. Yet surveys have demonstrated that a staggering 46 percent of British Muslims believe Anglo-Jews are "in league with Freemasons to control the media and politics"; more than half of those surveyed think that British Jews have "too much influence over the direction of foreign policy."[142] This is full-blown anti-Semitism, hardly explicable by the usual mantras or platitudes about Iraq and Palestine. Yet when Muslims themselves have admitted the growth of Islamic anti-Semitism, they fall back (like leftist apologists) on half-truths and clichés. Fuad Nadhi has insisted that Muslim hostility is a natural outgrowth of Israeli violence; that if Jews only returned to their *dhimmi* status, they could then enjoy true spiritual elevation and be granted security by Muslims. This extended hand of friendship comes, however, with a health warning attached. If Jews do not agree to dismantling the Jewish state they can expect to be targeted by Muslims.[143] This intimidatory tone is not only characteristic of fundamentalists; it has seeped into British public discourse. This is the poisoned fruit of a decade of laxity and irresponsibility, but for a while it was confined mainly to Jews. While Muslims were spewing out their anti-Semitic poison, the British authorities and media mostly remained silent.[144]

Those who broke the taboo of silence or offered a mild rebuke about Muslim behavior were and still are liable to be attacked as racist. When former Foreign Office minister Denis MacShane, speaking to his Rotherham constituency, plainly stated that the Muslim community in Britain needed to choose between supporting terrorism and "the democratic rule of law," the remark aroused widespread Muslim rage and a storm of protest.[145] The secretary-general of the MCB said his community was "shocked and dismayed." Having been made to apologize to the MCB, MacShane was then shamefully stripped of his ministerial position.[146] How deeply the pathology of appeasement sunk its roots into the Labour government would be revealed shortly before the 2005 general election when another minister, Mike O'Brien, seemed to be (not so subtly) appealing to Muslim prejudices against Israel and the Jews. Ignoring Arab and Muslim terror, he wrote that there could be no peace unless Israel conceded all the land it occupied on the West Bank and Gaza—thereby effectively blaming it for the conflict. He then turned on the Conservative Party leader Michael Howard (himself a Jew), pointedly asking: "Will his foreign policy aim to help Palestine? Will he promote legislation to protect you [the Muslims] from religious hatred and discrimination? Will he give you the choice of sending your children to a faith school? Will he stand up for the right of Muslim women to wear the hijab?"[147]

Such electoral appeals were, however, moderate compared to the Red-Green Axis implemented by former Labour MP George Galloway. In creating his new political party, Respect, he aimed from the outset at mobilizing Muslim support in the wake of the Iraq War. This deliberately *sectarian* approach, which pandered to extremist religiosity while indulging in anti-Western (and anti-Israel) incitement, was a new phenomenon in Britain. Admittedly, it was no surprise, since Galloway had embraced essentially every Muslim "hero" of recent decades. He had even gone to Damascus to encourage the Arab masses to rise up against the West. But Galloway's party was the first in Europe to consciously try to fuse the Far Left and radical Islamism. Yet these moves did not discredit Galloway with most of his left-wing Socialist friends. Though by no means universally respected, the British public regarded him at worst as "a minor irritant or pantomime villain."[148]

The combination of a multiculturalist liberal-left intelligentsia, the fear of being charged with Islamophobia, a stifling political conformity, and a dominant victim-oriented culture has severely muted the critique of militant Islam in Great Britain.[149] It has, moreover, discouraged moderate or secular Muslims from challenging the Islamofascists, the fundamentalists, and the anti-integrationists. The Islamists insist on full communal autonomy, official recognition of sharia law, imposition of the *niqab* (face veil) or burka, and such illegal practices as female genital mutilation. The supine British establishment and media, terrified of offending Islam, have helped to bring about this "lethal culture of grievance" among British Muslims. By their soft response, they have, in effect, increased Muslim attraction toward militancy and violence. Symptomatic of this paralysis was the stupefied and ostrich-like reaction of the deputy assistant commissioner of the Metropolitan Police to discovering the identity of the four suicide bombers in London's 7/7 slaughter: "As far as I am concerned, Islam and terrorism are two words that do not go together."[150]

In the mainstream British media there is still a palpable reluctance to recognize that Islamists want to destroy the West, impose sharia law, and reestablish the medieval caliphate throughout the world. Radical Islamist interpretations of theological texts are virtually ignored as a source of terrorism, let alone as a threat to the West. Many Britons turn a blind eye to the proven potential of the anti-Western jihad. The religious fanaticism that ultimately drives the holy war is subordinated to secondary geopolitical and economic factors that almost always predominate in Western eyes. In such a constellation of denial, it is less than surprising that America, Britain, and the leaders of Israel (not Iran or al-Qaeda) are seen as being responsible for global terror.

Despite this gloomy picture, there have been a few small rays of light. Anglo-Jewry has developed a positive relationship with British government agencies, reinforced by the initiative of the All-Party Parliamentary Group, which initiated the investigation of anti-Semitism in Great Britain during recent years. Cooperation with the police, the Crown Prosecution Service, and the Inter-Departmental Working Group on Anti-Semitism has led to a more cohesive effort to monitor racist activity against Jews, including on university campuses.[151] The London Conference on Combating Anti-Semitism in February 2009, organized by British Labour MP John Mann, managed to extract a firm commitment by the assembled parliamentarians to a comprehensive program of anti-anti-Semitic legislative action. Unfortunately, such positive steps will not easily stem the current tide of radical anti-Zionist feeling, of Islamic extremism, and the deliberate targeting of Jews. In May 2008 alone there was a flurry of anti-Semitic graffiti (forty incidents in three days) directed at London's ultra-Orthodox community. At the end of December 2008, the British media backlash against Israel produced a new and bigger wave of anti-Semitism. Its ostensible rationale was indignation at Israeli aerial attacks on "defenseless" Palestinian refugees in Gaza. There was little reference to the unprovoked firing of more than six hundred rockets into Israeli territory during the previous six years by the Gazans. This was treated as a minor pinprick. Equally little attention was given to Hamas's genocidal intentions toward the Jewish state and its criminal use of its own civilians as human shields. Instead Israel was accused of deliberately slaughtering Palestinians. The result was a sharp rise in malevolent anti-Jewish comment. The Anglo-Jewish community was obliged (yet again) to step up its already intense security measures in order to protect synagogues, communal centers, and Jewish schools. On British university campuses there was a revival of student demands to disinvest from companies involved in any business with Israel and to boycott Israeli education institutions.[152]

At the beginning of March 2009, this protest wave culminated in a sharp verbal attack on Britain's Science Museum, accused of promoting Israeli universities and their research achievements, which had allegedly aided in the military assault on Gaza. More than four hundred British academics (including forty professors) were among the signatories of a petition calling for the canceling of workshops for English schoolchildren that would highlight Israel's scientific advances. Among the protestors was a Nobel Peace Laureate Mairead Maguire from Belfast who chose to characterize Israel's siege of Gaza as a crime against humanity. Other signatories of the petition included the Labour MP Dr. Ian Gibson (a former chairman of the House of Commons Science Select Committee), who insisted that science could not be separated from politics, especially in the Middle East. The London *Times* severely criticized such a "vindictive" and "arbitrary" campaign, which it saw as a further extension of the "iniquitous academic boycott" and a symptom of British intellectual impoverishment. The *Times* concluded that anti-Israel sentiment among the highly educated in Britain was, in its sheer animus and malignancy, a "model of anti-intellectualism."[153]

Perhaps coincidentally, the relentless delegitimization of Israel, rampant in English academia, occurred on the eve of "Israel apartheid week" and the publication in a prominent British medical journal of new libels against the Jewish state. Thus, according to the *Lancet,* Israel had illegally executed thirty-five thousand Egyptian PDWs in the 1967 war. Moreover, it was currently using unconventional weapons in Gaza, allegedly murdering Palestinian women, children, and old people in cold blood. These and other claims were pure historical invention. They do, however, reflect the obsessive demonization that has now become the opium of many academics, intellectuals, and even members of the British political elite. As John Mann, the blunt-speaking Labour parliamentarian and a former trade-union official from Yorkshire, pertinently observed in February 2009, there was a "deliberate and calculated confusion of anti-Israel sentiments with antisemitism." Invoking his own experience as an MP in the Palace of Westminster, he added: "As a non-Jew I hear things that people would not say if they perceived I was Jewish. I have witnessed shocking disgraceful and outrageous anti-Semitism in Parliament, including statements from those who are meant to be bastions against racism. One of the things I've challenged is the perception that Jews are rich and therefore 'good for donations.' Other antisemitism has been more abrupt and upfront—and completely cross-party."[154]

TWELVE

Welcome to Eurabia

A nti-Semitism at the beginning of the twenty-first century has been undergoing a significant mutation. It is no longer primarily ethnic, *völkisch,* or racist in character, as it was just over six decades ago in Europe. Though xenophobic forms of radical populism and ultranationalism are still closely linked with anti-Semitism, they have found other, more electorally profitable, targets, such as foreign immigrants (especially Muslims), guest workers, Arabs, Africans, Gypsies, and Balkan refugees, upon whom to expend their wrath. There are other considerations, too, that have weakened right-wing nationalist anti-Semitism in many countries of the European Union. In contrast to Russia and eastern Europe, the dominant ethos of most Western countries today is officially post-national, multicultural, and pluralist. It claims to look beyond outdated nineteenth-century concepts of the territorial nation-state, and the sanctity of national sovereignty and a homogeneous cultural community.[1] This supranational evolution should logically have suited the Jews of Europe down to the letter. Indeed, until the turn of the millennium they had never seemed so prosperous, so accepted, and so well integrated into the economy, culture, and politics of their respective countries.

Yet the resurgence of anti-Semitism since 2000 throughout the European Union is undeniable. One aggravating factor has been anti-Americanism and the view of the European Union as an alternative bloc to the United States, offering a more egalitarian, civilized, and pacific model of society. Many Europeans link Israel's uncouth "militarism" and largely mythological "religious extremism" to the United States. The European obsession with the American Jewish lobby is one aspect of this blend of politics and prejudice that has led to the United States and Israel—to quote the German philosopher Peter Sloterdijk—becoming the world's sole existing "rogue states." The banners at European peace rallies a few years ago obscenely proclaimed "Hitler Had Two Sons: Bush and Sharon." Europe's rivalry with the United States, "pacifism," and anti-globalization protests have undoubtedly fed anti-Zionist and anti-Semitic sentiment. Extensive business interests in the Arab world have also made Europeans extremely reluctant to recognize certain unpalatable facts; one such reality is that the mass migration of more than twenty million Muslims to the European Union in recent decades has encouraged the import of virulent Middle Eastern anti-Semitism into Europe.

In "Eurabian" conventional wisdom even to discuss Islamic terrorism and anti-Semitism is to risk accusations of racism. However, to consistently single out Israel, accusing it of waging a "war of annihilation" against Palestinians, is perfectly normal. Hence the European Monitoring Centre for Racism and Xenophobia in Vienna felt obliged in 2003 to repudiate a report—commissioned under its own auspices—that confirmed that anti-Semitic violence in Europe was rising, much of it perpetrated by Muslim immigrants.[2] Such news was profoundly unwelcome at a time when Brussels insisted on pouring enormous, unaccountable subsidies into the Palestinian territories, and when every public reference to anti-Semitism had to be balanced by a parallel condemnation of Islamophobia.

Even in seemingly tolerant multiconfessional societies such as Germany, where there are today more than three million Muslims, there is a serious problem. For example, the Turkish fundamentalist Milli Görüs—one of the most influential organizations of political Islam in Europe—is viscerally anti-Western, anti-Semitic, and opposed to integration. At the same time, Europe itself, with its demographic shrinkage and vulnerability to Islamic terrorism, is increasingly afraid of its own shadow. Close to 10 percent of its population come from Islamic areas in North Africa, the Middle East, sub-Saharan Africa, Pakistan, and Bangladesh. A far higher percentage of Europeans under twenty-five are Muslims—suggesting an uncertain future in such countries as France, Belgium, Spain, the Netherlands, Germany, Sweden, and Britain. Henryk Broder's recent book *Hurra, Wir kapitulieren!* (Hurrah, We're Capitulating!) captures the general atmosphere of fear, cowardice, denial, and defeatism that has accompanied these changes. There is no more stomach for *resistance* to Islamicization, and every aggressive Muslim act is followed by calls for dialogue, appeasement, and even outright surrender—in Germany as in most of western Europe.[3]

The eruption of radical Islam in Europe after 2000 has certainly affected the future prospects of its vulnerable Jewish communities. The late Italian journalist Oriana Fallaci exclaimed back in April 2002:

> I find it shameful that in France, the France of "liberty, equality, fraternity," synagogues are torched, Jews are terrorized, and their cemeteries profaned . . . that in Holland and Germany and Denmark youngsters show off the kaffiyah like the vanguard of Mussolini displayed the stick and Fascist emblem . . . that in almost every European university, Palestinian students take over and nurture anti-Semitism.[4]

Fallaci was viciously attacked in the spring of 2002 for her courage in denouncing the silence of the European media about anti-Semitism. The Italian Green Party issued statements against her "extremism," as did former prime minister Giulio Andreotti. Italy's Communist newspaper, *Liberazione,* ran a highly personal attack on her by one of its directors with the headline in English: "Fuck You Fallaci." In Britain's *Guardian* newspaper, she was reproached by columnist Rana Kabbani for "anti-Muslim hysteria" and her "equally hysterical fervor for Jews."

So-called antiracist groups in France, including the League of the Rights of Man (LDH), the International League Against Racism and Antisemitism (LICRA), and the left-wing Movement Against Racism and for Friendship Among the Peoples (MRAP) all vilified her book against Islamic terrorism, *The Rage and the Pride.* The woman who had been Italy's best-known radical journalist during the Cold War, and a symbol of antifascism, found herself sued in court and execrated by liberals for daring to expose Islamist totalitarianism and the cowardly response of Europe's intellectuals, including their complicity in whitewashing anti-Semitism. On the left, Oriana Fallaci was transformed into a symbol of fascist fanaticism, nationalism, and xenophobia. Her exposure of "the [anti-Semitic] scoundrels with the turban or kaffiyah . . . who today praise the massacres in Jerusalem, Haifa, Netanya and Tel Aviv," was received with outrage.

The anti-Semitic virus was, however, present in the cultural baggage of many Muslim immigrants and Palestinian students well before their arrival in Europe. It had been heightened by the encounter with the West, by fundamentalist preaching in the mosques, and by the explosion of Islamic websites from Stockholm to Madrid.[5] Moreover, the "new" anti-Semitism has been embraced by broad sectors of the anti-globalist movement, which, like the Islamists, fervently believe in the existence of an American-Zionist conspiracy to dominate the world. As we have seen, the western European Left and radical Muslims may be light-years apart when it comes to secularism, socialism, feminism, and homosexuality. But the "Islamo-progressives" loathe Western values of capitalism, democracy, and individual freedom and strongly oppose the use of American military power abroad (especially in the Middle East). The "Red-Green" alliance detests Israel with special vehemence as an agent or stooge of American imperialism. Indeed they firmly believe that Jews control the domestic and foreign agenda of the United States. Today, this belief is held by one-third of those polled in America and Europe, revealing how much such myths have become mainstream.[6]

The strange alliance between the radical Left and the hard-line Islamists in western Europe took on a new lease during the European elections of June 2004, especially in France and Britain. The radical Left alliance of Revolutionary Communists and Lutte Ouvrière (Workers' Struggle) groups turned to Islamic militants to help it secure seats in Parliament. According to Arlette Laguillère, the Trotskyite passionara of the working class, "the struggle for Palestine" was now an integral element in the "global proletarian revolution." Wiping Israel off the map had become part of the fight to overthrow the global economic system and American power. Muslim immigrants were supposed to become the new underclass who could help to realize the old dream of destroying world capitalism. In Britain, the Marxist-Islamic alliance was born out of the antiwar coalition created to prevent the attack on Saddam Hussein's regime in Iraq.[7] More than half of its steering committee came from the hard Left, and its chairman Andrew Murray was a leader of the British Communist Party and formerly an employee of the Novosti Russian News and Information Agency. Cochair was Mohammad Aslam Ijaz of the London Council of Mosques. For both the extreme Left and the Islamists it goes without saying that Israel is a racist, imperialist, and apartheid state that has no moral or historical legitimacy.

Similar assumptions have been embraced by many liberal Europeans and much of the mainstream media. In January 2004, for example, Dave Brown's repulsive caricature for *The Independent,* showing Ariel Sharon crunching Palestinian babies, won the Political Cartoon of the Year award in Great Britain.[8] The secular left-wing *Libération* in France, not to be outdone, evoked memories of the deicidal charge to communicate its anti-

Israeli message. A Christmas cartoon showed Ariel Sharon nailing a cross for Yasser Arafat while an Israeli tank parks nearby; the caption read: "*Pas de Noël pour Arafat*" (No Christmas for Arafat)—"but you are welcome for Easter."[9] Such messages were a telling reminder of the staying power of archaic Christian imagery over "secular" minds. The Shylock image of a cruel, mean, rapacious, bloodthirsty, and vengeful Jew has returned to European public discourse.

Christian theological images have also been mobilized in the service of the anti-Zionist cause.[10] The crucifixions of Jesus Christ and of Yasser Arafat by deicidal Israelis/Jews readily merged into a bizarre and timeless blur of suffering. Poor, downtrodden Palestinians mutate into tortured sacrificial lambs slaughtered by the ancient Christ-killing people.[11] A de-Judaized Jesus has been transmuted into the first Palestinian martyr, reviving the replacement theology that the Christian churches in the West repudiated in recent decades. Some Protestants, especially Anglicans, seem curiously receptive to this travesty of Christian history. The Catholic Church, which has come a long way since Vatican II in the mid-1960s, appears more resistant and insistent on the need to positively acknowledge the Jewish roots of Christianity. The Holy See has at times exaggerated the distinction between Christian anti-Judaism and modern secular anti-Semitism (thereby attempting to diminish its indirect responsibility for the Shoah), but it has also denounced various manifestations of hatred, persecution, and anti-Semitism during the past four decades.[12] The present pope, on his visit to the synagogue in Cologne in August 2005, did not, for example, ignore disturbing signs of a rising anti-Semitism and xenophobia in Europe.[13] After justified criticism of his speech at Auschwitz-Birkenau at the end of May 2006 (which had subsumed Jewish victims of the Shoah among the Polish fatalities and seemed to "Christianize" the Shoah), the pontiff corrected his remarks and condemned racial hatred with greater vigor.

It is also noteworthy that Pope Benedict XVI has been more forthright than his predecessor, John Paul II, in condemning terrorism. He told representatives of the Cologne Muslim community, for example, that such acts were perverse and cruel, showing "contempt for the sacred right to life" and undermining the foundations of civil society.[14] In January 2006, the pope repeated these warnings in a New Year's address at the Vatican to all the diplomatic representatives, castigating such criminal activity as all the more deplorable "when it hides behind religion, thereby bringing the pure truth of God down to the level of the terrorists' own blindness and moral perversion."[15] At the same time, during the 2006 Lebanon War, the pope appeared to place Israeli retaliation and Hezbollah terrorism on the same moral plane. Indeed, the Vatican's traditional anti-Israel policy has not dramatically changed. What is new is the pope's strong stand against religious justifications for violence (clearly directed at militant Islam), which he expressed once again on September 12, 2006, in a controversial lecture at the University of Regensburg in Germany. Many Muslims were outraged, but the pope stuck to his guns, though expressing regret that he had been misunderstood. Benedict XVI caused another storm in late January 2009 after a British-born bishop from the traditionalist St. Pius X society (which he had rehabilitated) made public statements denying the Holocaust. The insensitivity and slowness of the Vatican to respond caused consternation among Jews, also angering large numbers of Catholics, especially in Germany. The German chancellor Angela Merkel even requested a clarification from the pope, whose personal credibility was undermined alongside the general damage done to Catholic-Jewish relations. Benedict XVI nonetheless visited the Holy Land in May 2009, on a mission of peace. The results were mixed. He affirmed Israel's state sovereignty and the Palestinian's right to a homeland, condemned anti-Semitism, yet failed to apologise for the Holocaust.[16]

The pope did, however, avoid the partisanship of the secular liberal press, which seven years earlier had gratuitously blamed Israel for the siege of the Church of the Nativity in Bethlehem. Part of the French press at the time had echoed the symbolism of "the massacre of the Innocents" by King Herod, a theme graphically depicted in the New Testament and in Western art.[17] The enduring image of the siege in Bethlehem was *not* the sacrilegious invasion of a major Christian holy place by armed Palestinians but the photo of one intrusive Israeli tank guarding the entrance to Manger Square. The stereotype of a Jewish state hostile to Christianity was thereby reinforced in the Western psyche.[18]

Subliminal perceptions of Israel and the Jews as Christ killers even found expression in a liberal Italian daily like *La Stampa*, on April 3, 2002, with a cartoon showing the infant Jesus besieged in Bethlehem. An Israeli tank points its gun at the baby Christ, who cries out: "Are they coming to kill me again?" This ironic reference to the deicide myth underlined both the ambivalence and resilience of the Christ-denying image in the recesses of the European imagination.[19] Motifs of a similar nature also appeared in the Easter 2002 issue of the Swedish newspaper *Aftonbladet*. Its editorial page fiercely condemned Israel's policy toward the Palestinians under the banner heading: "The Crucifixion of Arafat."[20] The liberal Swedish *Expressen*, not to be outdone, identified Israel's military actions with Old Testament tribalism, deploring its acts of war for exemplifying the primitive biblical teaching of "an eye for an eye, a tooth for a tooth."[21] The British *Guardian* newspaper also invoked the "obdurate," Old Testament policy of Israel, singling out the (un-Christian) "unforgivingness of Jews" and the biblical vengefulness of the Jewish state.[22] The viscerally anti-Israel Robert Fisk, writing in *The Independent*, played off the Old and New Testaments in order to expose Judaic intransigence: "The rabbi's dad had taught him [the settler] about an eye for an eye—or 20 homes for one stone in this case—whereas my dad had taught me about turning the other cheek. Judaism and Christianity had collided. So was it any surprise that Judaism and Islam were colliding." The same journalist had a long track record in vilifying Israel as a cruel, warmongering state.[23]

The Anglican *Church Times* was no less vitriolic in disparaging Israel's "inhumanity," deploring Palestinian suffering and the unjust behavior of the Jews in the Holy Land.[24] It published articles (especially at Christmas time and Easter) juxtaposing classical Christian virtues of peace, hope, and goodwill with their supposed absence in Israel.[25] The *Church Times* chose to mark Holocaust Memorial Day in Britain with an extraordinary article by Rev. Richard Spencer describing what was happening in Ramallah as a "suffering and deprivation that I could only imagine in Auschwitz."[26] By February 2006, the Anglican General Synod was overwhelmingly backing a call from the Episcopal Church in Jerusalem and the Middle East to disinvest from any "companies profiting from the illegal occupation of Palestinian territories."[27] The Anglican Church thereby lent its moral weight to the boycott of Israel. Influential Anglican writers and preachers like Rev. Stephen Sizer even returned de facto to a pre–Vatican II theological position by effectively denying any validity to Judaism and treating Israel as morally *illegitimate* and intrinsically racist. Their works espoused an anti-Jewish theology that effectively delegitimized Israel's existence, presenting Palestinian Christians as "the true Israel," oppressed by a malevolent "occupation" government of theologically "cursed" Jews.[28]

Anti-Semitic clichés about the deicidal, bloodthirsty Jews, wrapped up in cool anticolonialist terminology, have not been confined to English, Swedish, and German Protestants. France's most popular Catholic priest, Abbé Pierre, coined the malevolent catchphrase that "the Jews, once victims, have become executioners" during the first Palestinian intifada. Throughout the 1990s he would repeat this ugly canard, insisting that the Jews *invented* genocide; that the Old Testament God was relentlessly legalistic, tribal, and punitive; and that Zionism remains a uniquely murderous example of the ravages inflicted by capitalist globalization upon the "wretched of the earth."[29] Abbé Pierre's grassroots Catholic populist version of "liberation theology" doubtless facilitated his readiness to defend the anti-Semitic theories of his close friend Roger Garaudy—a lapsed French Catholic intellectual, ex-Stalinist, and convert to Islam. Garaudy's conviction by a Paris court for promoting Holocaust denial would turn him into a culture hero in the Arab world.[30]

Nor was the libel of Zionist Nazism confined to Protestant and Catholic countries in Europe. A classic illustration of the genre can be found in the April 7, 2002, caricature in *Ethnos,* a major center-left pro-government Greek newspaper. It shows two Israeli soldiers in the disputed territories: One says to the other: "Don't feel guilty, my brother! We were not in Auschwitz and Dachau to suffer but to learn."[31] The Nazi-like soldiers, with the Star of David on their helmets, are shown ruthlessly slaughtering Palestinians with knives. The case of Greece is particularly instructive since there are barely 5,000 Jews living there among 10.5 million Greeks—overwhelmingly Orthodox Christian by faith. In contrast to priests in western Europe, Greek Orthodox priests continue to include anti-Jewish references in their Good Friday prayers with the consequence that religious prejudices against the so-called Christ killers remain potent. For many years, the Orthodox Church even insisted that religious affiliation must be included on Greek identity cards. When the Greek government was obliged by the European Union to remove such references, it was vilified in religious circles for "bowing to Jewish pressure."

Equally striking has been the paranoid vision of Zionism as a Jewish plot for world domination, embraced by populist elements within most Greek political parties. In the 1980s, the Greek Social Democratic Party (PASOK) was perhaps the most strident labor movement in Europe in its use of anti-Semitic and anti-Zionist rhetoric.[32] After 2000 there was a sharp rise in anti-Semitic activity in Greece, linked to the strengthening of anti-Israel sentiments and anti-Americanism. The plethora of viciously anti-Israeli editorials, cartoons, articles, and letters to the editor published in the press doubtless contributed to the epidemic of desecrations of Jewish cemeteries and Holocaust memorials in the spring of 2002. Reports concerning the anti-Semitism of the Greek media during the past decade indicate a pattern of impugning the loyalty and identity of Greek citizens of Jewish ancestry. Disgust and outrage have been directed at "the [Israeli] descendants of Holocaust victims copying their victimizers," and at Greek Jews for not expressing revulsion at the "Hitlerist Sharon" and his heirs. Some texts referring to Greek Jews hold them responsible for Israel's actions, or in extreme cases for most of the world's evils.

Italy, too, has not been free of offensively anti-Semitic messages. True, its present government under Signor Berlusconi, is probably the most pro-Israel in Italian history. But the fascist Far Right and the heirs of the Italian Communists continue to portray Israel as a warmongering, arrogant, and racist state with a pronounced sense of divine chosenness; this message has also spread among a number of liberal and leftist intellectuals in Italy.[33] Islamic groups, especially during the 2006 Lebanon War and the recent Gaza conflict have hammered away at similar themes. Nevertheless, in contrast to many other European states, there has been *no* overall increase in *violence* against Jews, which remained at a relatively low level.[34] Anti-Semitism and anti-Israel feeling tended to be expressed mainly in written and verbal forms, for example, with graffiti reading "Israel Is a Killer" spontaneously appearing in moments of crisis on synagogue walls or Jewish communal buildings. Nevertheless, even in Italy, the awareness of Jewish difference and suspicion toward Italian Jews and Israel has remained high over the past eight years.

A poll conducted in 2001 by the *Corriere della Sera* newspaper showed a sharp increase in hostility toward Jews. At that time, 75 percent of Italians considered Jews to be different in mentality and lifestyle; 44 percent felt that Jews should stop presenting themselves as Holocaust victims. Sixty-two percent were convinced that Jews had a special attitude to money; 23 percent said "Jews are unpleasant and do not evoke trust," compared to only 14 percent who said that in 2000. Most Italian commentators related this change to the outbreak of the second intifada. A 2003 survey of Italian teenagers conducted by Professor Enzo Campelli at the University of Rome said that more than one-third of respondents agreed that "financial power is largely in the hands of Jews," and more than 20 percent thought that they cannot be trusted, they feel superior to others, and they are too attached to money.[35] An ADL poll in 2006 was even more sobering: 33 percent of Italians believed Jews have "too much power in the business world" and 55 percent thought they were "more loyal to Israel" than to Italy. These results reveal the tenacity of anti-Jewish economic stereotypes and of the dual loyalty canard, despite the fact that since 2001 Silvio Berlusconi has shown greater comprehension of Israel's dilemmas than any other government in western Europe.

Anti-Semitism camouflaged as anti-Zionism remains a continuing concern in Italy. Influential liberal intellectuals such as Sergio Romano, a former ambassador to Moscow, have written vitriolic tracts against Jews, Judaism, and the Jewish state. Romano contemptuously described the Jewish religion as "angry, archaic, and psychologically impenetrable to any form of tolerance and coexistence." He accused Israel of using the "evocation of the genocide and the denunciation of anti-Semitism" as a political instrument and justification for murderous reprisals against Arabs. He did not hesitate to attach the most pejorative epithets to the Jewish state, describing Israel as "the Superman [*Übermensch*] of the Near East" and as a "domineering" Nazi-like imperialist entity.[36] He also called into question the solidarity of Italian Jews with Israel and their right even to be considered as real Italians.[37] A similar objection came from another well-known columnist, Barbara Spinelli, who complained that Italian Jews, by supporting Israel, had made their loyalty to Italy seem suspect.[38] Writing in *La Stampa* in October 2001, the partly Jewish Spinelli venomously attacked the religion of Moses and its sacred texts for inflicting suffering on the Palestinians. At the same time she dismissed any claim of historic Jewish rights to the land of Israel.[39] She presented Judaism as a dogmatic faith immune to philosophical or theological doubt, insisting that Jewry owed an acknowledgment of guilt to Palestinians and to Islam in general. The journalist even demanded "a solemn mea culpa" from Israel and the Diaspora, and ordered them to publicly dissociate the Jewish faith from colonialism, fascism, Nazism, and racial superiority. Hers was by no means an isolated view. A part of the Italian press constantly made distorted comparisons between Israel and the fascist era in order to discredit the Jewish state. A disturbing number of Italians (and other Europeans) were ready to lend credence to those false analogies.[40]

The widespread European perception of Jewish dual loyalties was confirmed by an ADL poll in July 2007 that studied anti-Semitic attitudes in Austria, Belgium, the Netherlands, Switzerland, the United Kingdom, and Hungary.[41] Across these six countries, 49.7 percent of respondents stated that it was "probably true" that Jews were more loyal to Israel than their native countries—a considerable increase over the 38 percent who had believed this proposition two years earlier. In Austria and Belgium 54 percent of those polled agreed that Jews have divided loyalties, compared to 44 percent in Switzerland. Thirty-four and one-half percent of those surveyed thought that Jews have too much financial and business clout—a significant rise from the 26.7 percent recorded in 2005. Such anti-Semitic clichés (which were once the preserve of the extreme Right), along with a strong antipathy to Israel, have been increasingly legitimized in much of the European Union since 2000. They have been reflected in parliamentary debates, television shows, street demonstrations, and the dinner parties of Europe's chattering classes. Israel's withdrawal in 2005 from the Gaza Strip failed to make a dent in this negative image. On the contrary, the media and public opinion were, if anything, more hostile than before. And during the ugly little midsummer war in Lebanon of July and August 2006, Israelis were once again the "bad guys" accused of unleashing "disproportionate" use of military force.[42] The Gaza war in 2008 further heightened this perception.

Nationalist-populist movements in Austria, Switzerland, France, Italy, Belgium, and the Netherlands also cannot be ignored. Before his assassination in 2002, the Dutch populist Pim Fortuyn successfully tapped into a strong vein of anti-immigrant and anti-Muslim sentiment. He won more than a third of the votes in the municipal elections of Rotterdam, the second largest city in the Netherlands. No less than 40 percent of the population in Rotterdam were foreigners (mostly Moroccans and Turks). There was a high crime rate, which combined with uncontrolled immigration, the "alienness" of the predominantly Muslim newcomers, and a crisis of Dutch national identity to accentuate the appeal of the volatile, shaven-headed ex-professor of sociology.[43] Fortuyn's death was followed two and a half years later by the macabre killing of filmmaker Theo van Gogh. This murder, perpetrated by a radical Dutch Muslim (who was also anti-Semitic), exposed the growing racial and religious tension in the Netherlands. More recently, Geert Wilders (a right-wing Dutch MP and head of the Freedom Party) has been facing prosecution in Amsterdam for inciting to racial hatred on the basis of a seventeen-minute film *Fitna,* which sharply attacks the Koran. Regarded by many as an "Islamophobe," he has nonetheless touched a popular chord with his focus on radical Islam.

The small Dutch Jewish community (thirty to forty thousand) finds itself caught in an awkward position, given that a disproportionate number of the perpetrators of anti-Semitic acts and threats have been Moroccan immigrants. Muslim violence exists alongside the more traditional Christian, racist, and anti-Israel variations of anti-Semitism. In 2004, there were 326 reported incidents in the Netherlands, compared to 532 in the United Kingdom—a country with ten times as many Jews. In France there were close to 1,000 anti-Semitic acts that year, but the Jewish population was twenty times the size of Dutch Jewry. In other words, in the Netherlands, the incidence of reported anti-Semitism is unusually high.[44] Yet the quantitative evidence is contradictory. ADL surveys of European attitudes toward Jews in 2007 show that Dutch hard-core anti-Semites (around 9 percent) were *less* numerous than in most European countries. Dutch "tolerance," on the other hand, is hardly evident in the soccer stadiums, where chants like "Hamas, Hamas, Jews to the gas" have been commonplace. Moreover, in November 2003, it turned out that the Netherlands had the *highest* percentage of respondents in the European Union who considered Israel to be the number one danger to world peace. No less than 74 percent of the Dutch people supported this extraordinary idea.[45] In other words, when it came to anti-Israel sentiment, the Dutch (once considered loyal friends of the Jewish state) outclassed even the Germans, Austrians, British, and French. This, then, was the Dutch paradox: near the top of the anti-Israel league and low in the anti-Semitic table. However, when it comes to telling the truth about Muslim anti-Semitism, the Netherlands scores poorly. The case of Professor Pieter van der Horst, a scholar in early Christian and Jewish studies (who broke the taboo of speaking about Nazi influence on anti-Semitism in Arab countries) illustrates the point. Utrecht University refused to publish his farewell lecture on this topic in its academic series for fear of provoking controversy.[46]

Belgian opinion has been especially hostile in recent years toward the Jewish state. The Belgian media have, for example, long been ready to draw grossly misleading parallels between Israeli army actions in the territories and the Holocaust. One prominent Catholic journalist, Simon-Pierre Nothomb (writing in *Le Soir*), painted a particularly twisted picture of the occupied territories as if they were extended concentration camps, comparing them to the nightmarish history of the Warsaw ghetto. He appeared unaware that *half a million* defenseless Jews from Warsaw had been sent to their deaths in the Treblinka gas chambers, while the total casualties on *both* sides of the second intifada came to a mere three thousand people.[47] Nothomb and other Belgian journalists nonetheless described the Palestinians as being imprisoned and strangled in the viselike grip of a ruthless Israel, determined to "liquidate" their resistance, as if this were a replay of the German mass murder. In fact, during the past seven years of Israeli-Palestinian confrontation, there were fewer general fatalities than on an average *day* during the Holocaust.[48]

A long article by Francis Martens, president of the Association of Practicing Psycho-Analysts in Belgium, in *La Libre Bélgique* in April 2002 summed up the accusatory style and extraordinary obfuscations of so much "informed" opinion in western Europe. For Martens, Israel exists only thanks to Hitler, the "bad European conscience," and the electoral weight of American Jewry. It had been "born in sin" in 1948 and was a democracy in name only. For decades it had systematically trampled on Palestinian rights while Europe remained silent. Martens mocked the "myth" of a "small people" who had made the desert bloom, the "uniqueness" of the Holocaust (the dark face of "chosenness"), the Jewish attachment to Jerusalem, and the "use" of anti-Semitism to bolster Israeli identity. Jews in Israel had learned nothing from history—they actively supported apartheid South Africa and they had continually invented sadistic racist practices of their own. The "Hebrew State," according to this prominent psychoanalyst, had "become the top producer in the world of anti-semitism," practicing torture, destruction, and assassination in the name of its imaginary "struggle against terror."[49] Martens did not so much as hint that tiny Israel might actually be threatened by any of its neighbors—whether by Iran, Syria, radical Islamists, the suicide bombers, the Palestinian rejectionists, or a wider Muslim Arab world that, for the most part, still denied its right to exist. But such one-sidedness has become all too typical of "enlightened" opinion in western Europe.

The effects of such intellectual and journalistic bias have inevitably been destructive. There has been a notable rise in Internet hatred, anti-Zionist articles in the press, and in graffiti daubed on Jewish-owned homes. There was the vandalizing of the Jewish Holocaust Memorial in Brussels, and a palpable increase in insults against easily identifiable Jews on the street. In Belgium, moreover, there are only forty thousand Jews, outnumbered ten to one by Muslim immigrants. In August 2006 a large anti-Israel demonstration in Belgium was garlanded with Hezbollah flags. The participants were mainly of North African Arab origin. This rapidly growing population has been a prime source of aggression in recent years against individual Jews, Jewish property, and synagogues. Significantly, it was in Antwerp in 2000 that the Arab European League (AEL) was created, a group widely known for its militant anti-Zionism. According to its leader Dyab Abou Jahjah (a Lebanese-born Shiite Muslim and former Hezbollah guerrilla), since "Antwerp is the bastion of Zionism . . . this city has to become the Mecca of the pro-Palestinian movement." At an AEL demonstration on April 3, 2002, participants shouted "Death to the Jews," and young Muslims descended on the Jewish quarter of Antwerp and smashed shop windows belonging to diamond merchants.[50] In July 2006 Jahjah left Belgium to fight Israel in Lebanon. At the same time he remained committed to the goal of mobilizing European Muslims against the Zionists.

At the end of 2008 anti-Semitic violence returned to Belgium in the course of several pro-Hamas rallies. In Brussels city center a protest march led to clashes between the police and local Muslims. The Beth Hillel synagogue in the city was set on fire, shop windows were smashed, and cars wrecked. Belgian Jews were subjected to constant threats, and on January 3, 2009, the home of a Jewish family in Antwerp, where twelve children were asleep, was set on fire at night—an act of attempted murder. The house was damaged, but fortunately there were no fatalities. That same day, Muslims gathered in Antwerp's city center, some of them with firearms and Molotov cocktails, intending to attack Jewish targets. Three days earlier, the AEL had organized a demonstration where leaflets were handed out in predominantly Muslim areas of the city, blaming the Jews for the Gaza war. Several hundred masked Muslims gathered close to the heaviest Jewish populated area in Antwerp chanting slogans like "Jews out!" and "Hamas! Hezbollah!," destroying shops and cars. The police had to forcibly prevent the protesters from invading the Jewish diamond district near Antwerp's city center.

Death threats were also made at the time against Jewish schools, synagogues, and prominent individuals.

Anti-Semitism is not, of course, confined to Islamist groups alone. The Far Right Vlaams Belang, the strongest party in the city of Antwerp and the surrounding province, has in the past had links with neofascist and anti-Semitic groups. Among its founders were former members of the Flemish SS, neo-Nazis, and Holocaust deniers. Its aim remains the establishment of an independent Flanders and forced "repatriation" of non-European immigrants. Its xenophobic leader Filip Dewinter has nevertheless been relatively friendly toward Israel. He has decried attacks on Jewish targets, leading some Orthodox Jews in Antwerp to look more favorably on the Vlaams Belang as Muslim extremism has grown.

Caught between the Far Right and fear of Muslim violence, Belgian Jews have found little joy on the radical anti-globalist Left, which is militantly anti-Israel and anti-American. The Francophone Socialist Party (SP), while somewhat more congenial, has become increasingly hostile to Israel, even choosing at one point to co-opt a fanatical anti-Zionist to the Senate.[51] This is less surprising when one realizes that a significant number of the SP municipal councillors in Brussels are of Muslim North African background. Electoral politics has undoubtedly contributed to the less-than-friendly Socialist stance on Israel, especially in French-speaking Belgium. At the turn of the new millennium, some Belgian politicians tried to cover up this opportunism with a high-minded humanitarian ethics. But Belgium is poorly placed to preach to Israel about the merits of pluralism, multiculturalism, post-nationalism, and the place of morality in politics.

Anti-Israel rhetoric may make some Belgians feel better about their own appalling legacy of colonial oppression in Africa. For others it may offer a relatively painless platform for liberal posturing in the name of human rights.[52] The Palestinian cause has, for example, served as a new civic religion for many self-styled progressives and compassionate "humanitarians" who scarcely shed a tear for the victims of the Rwandan genocide only a decade earlier. Evidently this new religion, like its predecessors, requires a Manichean struggle between good and evil. Ariel Sharon was perfect for the role of the devil incarnate, while Yasser Arafat was incongruously given the part of a Christlike angel. Palestinian suicide bombers were duly turned into saints and martyrs in this ghoulish mockery of a Christian morality play. This supposedly progressive division of labor simply assumed that Palestinians must always be right and Israelis always wrong; that the Holocaust and the Palestinian *naqba* (catastrophe) of 1948 are somehow morally equivalent; and that the Jewish state has been solely responsible for all the violence in the Middle East.[53]

Belgium is a fragile and divided bilingual state in danger of collapse. But when it comes to pillorying Israel, Flemish-speaking and Francophone Belgium are not so far apart. They share the same borrowing of vocabulary, images, and analogies from the Shoah, as evidenced in the nasty satirical poem "The Free-Thinker" by a certain Rodolphus, which appeared in 2002 in the very popular Flemish *P-Magazine*. The lyrics contain all the core themes of the new Judeophobia, from revulsion against the Jewish religion and the implacable Sharon, to familiar accusations of "Jewish racism"—all in the name of human rights. The poem concludes by rejoicing that Europe was slowly but surely liberating itself from the exaggerated "penitence" inflicted on it after World War II.

> At bottom it's bizarre that it took so long
> for the world to comprehend
> that one genocide does not justify another
> yet another monument, museum or memorial
> erected under the pressure of the industrialists
> of the Holocaust
> will not make any difference.
> To dance on the graves of the ancestors
> is in any case indecent.[54]

The poet naturally denies that he is an anti-Semite; instead, he accuses Israel of "squeezing" the anti-Semitism it attributed to others, down to the last drop of blood, in order to cover up its own crimes. This claim, as we have seen, has become almost a signature tune of the "new" anti-Semitism, highlighting yet again the deeply ingrained stereotype of the mercenary, cynical, and bloodsucking Jews.

The verbal war against the Jewish state extends to prominent politicians in the supposedly "neutral" state of Norway.[55] In January 2006 Finance Minister Kristin Halvorsen, chairman of the Socialist Left Party, actively encouraged a consumer boycott of Israel also favored and approved by her party, which has consistently presented Israeli Jews as brutal, insensitive, and warlike.[56] Gerd-Liv Valla, chairman of the Federation of Labour Unions, also supported a boycott of Israeli goods, as did Gry Larsen, leader of the Labour Youth Organization and political adviser to the Norwegian foreign minister.[57] Moreover, Deputy Foreign Minister Raymond Johansen was the first Western high official to visit Hamas leaders in March 2007.[58]

Norwegian leftist organizations have indeed been at the forefront of boycott attempts against Israel, though most of their initiatives have failed. Journalists in the mainstream media have also helped to encourage a conducive atmosphere for such hostile actions with their prejudiced portrayal of Israel's actions. This has led to a notable increase in anti-Semitic incitement and the harassment of the tiny Jewish community. Hostile visual depictions of Jews in Norwegian newspapers and weeklies (sometimes recalling the most repulsive caricatures from the Nazi era) have exacerbated the problem. The left-wing caricaturist Finn Graff is a prime offender. His 2006 cartoon of Israel's prime minister, Ehud Olmert, portrayed him in Nazi uniform and jackboots as the commandant of a death camp holding his sniper gun and laughing while an Arab victim he had deliberately shot in the head, bled to death.[59] Such images are only the tip of the iceberg when it comes to anti-Semitic stereotypes in a Norwegian society so often (misleadingly) presented as a model of tolerance—peaceful, prosperous, democratic, altruistic, and incorruptible.

Similar phenomena abound in Sweden, a country with only fifteen thousand Jews where the moralistic hectoring of Israel is a standard feature of much of the political and media elite. Several times during her term in office, former Swedish foreign minister Laila Freivalds liked to compare the behavior of Israelis toward the Palestinians with that of the Nazis toward the Jews. On a visit to Yad Vashem in June 2004, she lectured her Israeli hosts on the need to accept this kind of "criticism" while she herself remained notably silent about the Arab hostility toward Jews in the suburbs of major towns in her own country.[60] Swedish society, the media, and the government doubtless maintain such discretion out of a misguided fear of stimulating racism in general and Islamophobia in particular.

Writing on this topic in October 2003, history professor Sverker Oredsson, together with Swedish researcher Dr. Mikael Tossavainen, noted that many Muslim students in Sweden were extremely anti-Semitic. They frequently labeled the Holocaust as "Zionist propaganda," expressed undisguised admiration for Hitler, and regretted that he had not killed more Jews. Such students absorbed their anti-Semitism from the Koran, Muslim fundamentalist culture, and their own countries of origin, via satellite TV and the Internet. They were also influenced by the media reports about the Middle East coming from Swedish sources. Tossavainen, author of a detailed report on Swedish schools, confirmed the spread of Muslim anti-Semitic propaganda in Stockholm, Göteborg, and Malmö—much of it pillaging the *Protocols* and using false quotations from the Bible and Talmud. Equally widespread were allegations of a Jewish world conspiracy to enslave the Palestinians, humiliate the Arab nation, and subvert Islam itself. The results of such propaganda have, not surprisingly, been a sharp increase in harassment, threats and attacks by Arabs and Muslims against Jews in Swedish society.

Rather than addressing the alarming spread of such crude Jew hatred, Swedish politicians, intellectuals, and artists have endlessly focused on Israel's alleged misdeeds and continued to espouse a universalistic form of "Holocaust education" that completely ignores the rise of radical Islam. Yet a poll in March 2006, carried out by a Swedish government-sponsored body, pointedly concluded that 39 percent of Muslims in the country displayed "systematic" anti-Semitic attitudes. One of the study's authors, Henrik Bachner, noted that the immigrants were clearly influenced by anti-Jewish trends in the Arab world. More than a quarter of all Swedes partly or completely agreed with the idea that "Israel's treatment of the Palestinians is reminiscent of Nazi treatment of the Jews." A similar number accepted the tendentious myth that "Israel's politics is based on Old Testament vengefulness," that is, an eye for an eye—a favorite cliché of the Swedish press. Twenty-six percent of all Swedes also agreed that "Jews have a decisive influence over the world economy" and nearly one in five believed "the Jews are directing U.S. foreign policy." Forty-six percent had "no opinion" as to whether Israel was involved in the 9/11 attacks on the United States. Close to 40 percent of all Swedes were somewhat prejudiced with regard to Jews.[61] Swedish prime minister Göran Persson called the study "surprising and terrifying," especially the fact that one in four Swedes were against the election of a Jewish premier.[62] Yet there was nothing surprising in these results. Earlier surveys had shown that more than 80 percent of Swedes disliked Israel. Decades of distorted coverage of the Middle East were hardly likely to produce a different result.

Religious background has proven to be a crucial variable in recent surveys that show that Muslims are far more likely to hold anti-Semitic opinions than the Swedish population in general. Segregation, social alienation, and the impact of radical Islamist propaganda via TV broadcasts, the Internet, or other media are additional factors along with the daily fallout from the Israeli-Palestinian conflict. In today's globalized and technological world, the accessibility of Islamist propaganda to the largely segregated immigrant population has been especially pernicious. It is all the more effective in cities like Malmö where more than a quarter of the population is Muslim and 40 percent of the inhabitants are foreign-born. It is important to realize that in Sweden (as elsewhere in Scandinavia) many of the Muslim organizations openly engage in anti-Semitic activities. In some of the mosques there has been incitement to kill Jews across the world in the name of Allah. According to Swedish Radio News (SRN), a leading Stockholm mosque was even selling cassettes calling for a murderous *jihad* against the Jews. However, the Swedish Ministry of Justice discouraged any serious investigation of the mosque despite its brazen incitement in referring to Jews as "brothers of apes and pigs."

The ministry considered that such statements "should be judged differently—and therefore be regarded as permissible—because they were used by one side in an ongoing and far-reaching conflict where calls to arms and insults are part of the everyday climate in the rhetoric that surrounds the conflict."[63] In effect the Swedish chancellor of justice, Goran Lambertz, was treating genocidal anti-Semitism as if it were acceptable as part of the Israeli-Palestinian conflict, even though he admitted that the cassettes made highly degrading and dehumanizing statements about Jews. The minister was also reducing Swedish Jews and Muslims to mere extensions of Israel and its Arab adversaries in the Middle East. Behind the legal formalism and the usual sophistry about free speech also lay electoral considerations in a Swedish society where half a million Muslims heavily outnumbered Jews by more than twenty-five to one. In the September 2006 elections, Swedish Social Democrats and left-wing groups were clearly looking for Muslim votes with the assistance of radical Islamic groups and their clerical leaders. Turning a deaf ear to the protests of Swedish Jews was evidently a small price to pay in return.

Similarly, in its foreign policy under the Social Democratic prime minister Goran Persson, Sweden preferred to embrace authoritarian Middle

Eastern dictatorships rather than a fellow democracy such as Israel. This tradition had been firmly established as far back as 1969 by then Swedish prime minister Olot Palme, a left-wing socialist who was probably the first Western statesman to brand Israel as a Nazi state. His hatred of Israel (and America) was legendary. The legacy was continued after his assassination, by other Swedish leading Social Democrats (who also became foreign ministers) like Sten Andersson, Anna Lindh, and Laila Freiwalds. The persistence of such hostility under Persson was, at first sight, more suprising since he had inspired and organized the 2000 Stockholm conference on Holocaust education. Persson was well aware of Sweden's highly problematic record of collaboration with Nazi Germany in the 1940s, genuinely troubled by Holocaust denial, and worried by a resurgence of neo-Nazism in his own country. But he did precious little to stem the tide of left-wing anti-Zionism in his own party or to improve Sweden's abysmal record in investigating or prosecuting its own suspected Holocaust perpetrators.[64] Under his stewardship, Sweden was proactive in condemning Israel at the UN Commission of Human Rights and in falsely accusing it of mass killings in its territories. In 2006 it pulled out of a NATO air force exercise because of Israeli participation. At the same time, Sweden was the first European democracy to invite senior members of Hamas to visit the country.

During the Sweden-Israel Davis cup tennis match (March 6–8, 2009), deliberately whipped up anti-Israeli hatred exploded in Malmö. The city council's sports committee had already decided that the match would be played without spectators and held behind closed doors, for fear of disturbances. This decision, in itself a capitulation to mob violence, did not prevent hundreds of rock-throwing pro-Palestinian activists (mainly Muslims and Swedish leftists) from seeking to storm the closed arena. Hundreds of riot police were required to push back the mob. Earlier they had been addressed by Sweden's Left Party leader Lars Ohly, who told the crowd that the EU and the rest of the world should "boycott the racist regime in Israel." A little over a month earlier, the vice-chair of the Social Democratic Women's organization in southern Sweden, Ingalill Bjartén, had branded Israel an apartheid state and angrily compared Gaza to the Warsaw ghetto. Such mindless comparisons have unfortunately become commonplace across western Europe in recent years.

In March 2007, a BBC poll showed negative perceptions of Israel in Germany (77 percent), France (66 percent), and the United Kingdom (65 percent)—a shockingly high level of antipathy toward the Jewish state in the three leading countries of the European Union.[65] In Britain in the spring of 2007, a mere 16 percent identified with Israel, compared with 29 percent who supported the Palestinians. In France the results were similar. Germany was the one western European country in the Pew Global Attitudes Project survey that still had a pro-Israel majority. During the thirty-three days of the Lebanon War in 2006, there was, nevertheless, a rash of anti-Jewish acts in Germany, and a new peak for anti-Semitic incidents in Great Britain. In France during this same period, there were 61 attacks, compared to 34 such cases noted in the previous year. Altogether in 2006, there were 360 reported episodes of anti-Semitism in France, up considerably from the previous year's figures. In March 2007, the Council of French Jewish Institutions (CRIF) revealed that during the past twelve months there had been a jump of 71 percent in verbal attacks and a rise of 45 percent in physical assaults on Jews over 2005. The French government's eagerness to claim a decrease was therefore misplaced. French Jews remain the target of anti-Semitic violence, primarily by Muslims. But, as elsewhere in western Europe, the flames had also been fanned by the universities, intellectuals, the media, some politicians, and the European Union itself.

France had, however, become significantly less hostile toward Israel than Spain and was more nuanced than Britain and Sweden. According to the Pew Global Attitudes Project, Spain remained the most anti-American and anti-Israel country in western Europe. With regard to the Israel-Palestine conflict, a mere 9 percent of Spaniards supported the Jewish state while more than 30 percent expressed pro-Palestinian attitudes.[66] In 2007, the results were not much different. The establishment of diplomatic relations with Israel in 1986 evidently did not alter traditional Spanish attitudes. Spain was by now officially pluralist, tolerant and multicultural in outlook. It emphasized coexistence, conciliation, and a greater interest in Spain's historical roots. But attitudes were still heavily influenced by neutralism, pacifism, dislike of America, and powerful anti-Semitic stereotypes.[67] In Spain, the prejudice that simultaneously presents Israel as a "vassal" of the United States and as *the* driving force of American foreign policy (especially of the war in Iraq) appears to be deeply entrenched.[68] It is reinforced by a striking ignorance about Israel and a lack of any direct experience with Jews, compared with many other European countries. Anti-Muslim sentiments were also rampant, exacerbated by a growing immigration from Morocco and awareness of the terrorist threat from the radical Islamists who had wreaked such havoc in Madrid in 2006.

The Spanish Right (which in the 1930s was blatantly anti-Communist, anti-Masonic, and anti-Semitic) is today notably more sympathetic than the Left toward Israel. It is sharply critical of the Socialist prime minister of Spain, José Luis Rodríguez Zapatero, who has been one of Israel's fiercest critics inside the European Union. At a rally on July 19, 2006, Zapatero was photographed wearing a kaffiyeh at a time when Hezbollah was firing rockets at Israel. He had sharply attacked Israel's policy of using "abusive force" and the U.S. invasion of Iraq for producing only "fanaticism and instability." The conservative Popular Party responded by calling Zapatero's views on Israel the product of "anti-Semitism, anti-Zionism, and Israelophobia."[69] Several months later, Juan José Laborda, a veteran Spanish Socialist senator, repeated these same charges, noting that anti-Semitism was strongly rooted in Spanish history, from the expulsion of Jews in 1492 to the pro-Arab Franco dictatorship (1939–75), and the "infantile anti-Americanism" of contemporary Spain.[70] These sentiments were stirred up again by the Second Lebanon War, in which Israel was blamed for the confrontation, with some of the commentaries containing an unmistakable anti-Semitic slant.

Prime Minister Zapatero himself contributed to the ugly climate by referring to the Israeli-Palestinian conflict as a cancer that metastasized and has spread into all the other Middle Eastern conflicts. He left the impression that Israel rather than Islamist terror (which he never condemns) is the cancer in question—anti-Semitic imagery all too familiar from the Nazi era. A year earlier, 2005, at a dinner party in the Spanish equivalent of the White House, Zapatero concluded yet another anti-Zionist tirade by expressing understanding that "someone might justify the Holocaust." Such rhetoric fits in well with Zapatero's loathing for capitalist globalization on the American model—an animus often linked on the Spanish Far Right and Left with "Jewish influence." Indeed, a *majority* of Spaniards appear to believe that "Jews have too much power in international markets." This is all the more striking since today there are no more than twelve thousand Spanish Jews (0.05 percent) out of a total population of forty-two million. Yet anti-Semitism is notably stronger in Spain than in France, whose Jewish population is fifty times larger.

Judeophobia still retains a certain hold in grassroots popular folklore and even influences some of Spain's leading intellectuals.[71] Indeed, in an ADL study of 2002, Spaniards appeared to be the most prejudiced of all Europeans in their stereotypical beliefs about Jews dominating global finance (71 percent agreed with this proposition), the media, and American politics.[72] Seventy-two percent of Spaniards further agreed that Jews were more loyal to Israel than to their own country. Fifty-seven percent believed that Jews dwelt too much on the Holocaust (in other European countries the average was 49 percent); a third of all Spaniards considered that Jews cared only about themselves and used dubious means to achieve what they wanted. Overall 34 percent of Spaniards could be seen as anti-Semitic, a higher figure than for Germany, France, or Italy. Five years later, in 2007, these figures had barely changed, and only Poland appears to rival Spain when it comes to deep-rooted classically anti-Semitic stereotypes. Yet in both countries today, the Jewish communities are totally insignificant in size, making them—along with the Asian states of Pakistan, Malaysia, and Japan—prime examples of "anti-Semitism without Jews." The difference, of course, is that in the past both Poland and Spain had been large and thriving centers of Jewish life that left a permanent mark on Jewish history, as well as on the cultures in which they had once flourished.

Contemporary Spanish media have, with a few exceptions, adopted an anti-Israel line that not infrequently demonizes Jews. A cartoon in *La Razón* on June 9, 2001, showed two Israeli policemen beating a Palestinian, while one says to the other, "There's no time for me to reflect on the Holocaust."[73] The May 24, 2001, issue of the leftist *El País* depicted an Orthodox Jew carrying an Israeli flag and rifle in his right hand while reading from a Bible in his left hand. He says, "We are the chosen people for the manufacture of weapons." The same paper had, only one day earlier, illustrated Israel's prime minister, with a small figure flying in his direction, holding the caption "Clio, the muse of history, placing the moustache of Hitler on Sharon." On April 21, 2001, the Catholic *El Mundo* one-sidedly blamed Israel for rejecting "the proposal of Arafat to work together, for an end to violence"— naturally omitting any reference to Palestinian terrorism. A particularly ugly cartoon in the June 4, 2001, issue of *Cambio* pictured Sharon with a yarmulke and a swastika inside the Star of David on his chest, announcing, "From bad can come good. At least, Hitler taught me to invade a country and exterminate every living vermin." These and other examples suggest that many Spanish journalists believe it is legitimate to Nazify Israel and fail to see any anti-Jewish prejudice in such caricatures.[74] In practice, however, most Spaniards do not appear to distinguish between Israel and the Jews, regarding them as one entity.[75] Not only that, but those Spanish cartoonists who are venomously anti-Israel do not hesitate to draw on traditional stereotypes and stigmatizations of Jews, whether from religious paintings and popular drawings during the Inquisition period or from the Franco era of clericofascism.[76]

Spanish journalist Javier Nart, a frequent contributor to radio and TV, not only vilified Israel as if it were the main problem in the modern world but openly referred to Ariel Sharon as "an animal, a criminal."[77] One leading journalist, Enrique Curiel, writing in La Razón in April 2003, explicitly qualified Israel as the source of all unrest in the Middle East and throughout the world. According to his account, Barak, Sharon, and Bush had deliberately provoked the Palestinian intifada through Sharon's visit to the Temple Mount; similarly, it was the Jewish state that was to blame for the Iraq War.[78] Spanish academic Gema Martín Muñoz, writing in El País, went even further, claiming that Sharon's plan had always been the "final solution of the Palestinian question."[79]

Demonization of Israel and its leaders was not uncommon in the mainstream Spanish media, including its main TV channels. The "criminality of Israel," so it seems, was not even a topic that required empirical proof. For example, the April 2002 events in Jenin were spoken of, almost axiomatically, as "ethnic cleansing" by Israel or, worse still, as a "Holocaust." In this context, the bland remark of a leading Spanish diplomat, Javier Solana, head of foreign affairs in the European Union, made on June 26, 2003, that "there is no anti-Semitism in Europe," is all the more striking.[80] It testifies above all to a mind-numbing lack of Spanish and European awareness about the nature, strength, and underlying persistence of anti-Jewish prejudice, especially where Israel is involved. In the Spanish case it often appears as if only Americans and Jews commit "massacres" and acts of "state terror," while their Muslim adversaries are all paragons of virtue. Pilar Rahola, a left-wing Spanish journalist who has courageously exposed these double standards, observed in May 2003: "The Jewish victims in Israel also end up . . . as their own killers. There are no Jewish victims, just as there are no Palestinian executioners. . . . Arab terrorism becomes comprehensible and even acceptable."[81]

Rahola had been shocked by data from 2002, published by the Gallup

Organization, concerning anti-Jewish sentiment in Spain. A disturbingly high percentage of Spaniards favored the demise of Israel; only 12 percent would accept having Jewish neighbors; 69 percent believed Jews were too powerful, and 55 percent attributed "dark intentions" to them. Relating to these findings, Rahola observed with alarm that her native Catalonia and the Basque country showed the highest levels of Judeophobia. But the same situation existed "to a greater or lesser extent across the length and breadth of Europe." What was especially distressing to her as a non-Jewish member of the Spanish parliament from the Catalan Republican Left party, was the anti-Semitic flavor of much leftist rhetoric hiding behind severe "criticism" of Israel's policies. In an interview in October 2002, Rahola noted that the Spanish Left had reduced Israel to one wholly misleading image: "a country that occupies territories and whose vocation is to make life miserable for the poor Palestinians. The history of the Holy Land is being reinvented. Everything takes place as if there were instructions: Never recall the faults and errors of the Palestinians, never recall their alliances with dangerous countries such as [Saddam's] Iraq."[82]

Spain has undoubtedly been among the pacesetters when it comes to contemporary left-wing anti-Semitism in Europe. Gaspar Llamazares, leader of the Izquierda Unida (United Left) movement, declared in April 2003 that his party was fed up with hearing about the six million Jews killed in the Holocaust and would no longer participate in any homage to their memory. Even more offensive were the remarks of the Portuguese Nobel Prize laureate for literature, José Saramago, writing in *El País*. He told his readers that Israelis were motivated by the "monstrous and rooted 'certitude,' " that they are "chosen by God"; that they were in the grip of an "obsessive psychological and pathologically exclusivist racism," which they had rationalized by evoking their suffering during the Holocaust. Saramago, a veteran Communist by conviction, had notoriously compared the situation in Ramallah to Auschwitz on a previous visit to the occupied territories. Once more, he repeated that Israelis were committing crimes "comparable to Auschwitz" while endlessly scratching their own wounds to show them off to the world "as if it were a banner." Pilar Rahola's scathing comment on this outburst seems wholly apposite: "When did José Saramago ever feel any sympathy for the Jews? He is the old uncritical Communist, corroded by dogmas and countersigns, and so blind that he has loved dictators and assassins who murdered in the name of liberty."[83]

Saramago's outburst was typical of the hard-line Communist Left's loathing for Israel. A very different approach was that of the conservative politician Ana Palacio, appointed as Spain's first female foreign minister in 2002, who warned against the anti-Semitism and anti-Americanism rampant in contemporary Europe.

There have been attacks on Jewish cemeteries and synagogues in France and Spain. In 2002 the Star of David was displayed together with a swastika on the Web page of the Barcelona City Council. Also in Barcelona, a plaque in honour of Holocaust victims was vandalized. To raise money for a "human rights" program, the mayor of a small village in northern Spain sold T-shirts showing Israeli prime minister Ariel Sharon as a dragon, eating the corpses of Palestinian children, while President Bush smiled approvingly. Another T-shirt on sale shows the American flag as a roll of toilet paper with the words "use me" written underneath.[84]

Ana Palacio, like Pilar Rahola, lucidly exposed the signs of this dramatic return of anti-Semitism in Europe, particularly evident in her own homeland. Seven years later, in January 2009, one hundred thousand Spaniards marched through Madrid carrying banners like "SOS Gaza" above a red-stained hand and mock bloodstained bodies of children. Speakers compared Gaza to a concentration camp with Israel as its guardian.

Some of the more chilling aspects of this contemporary anti-Semitic resurgence were anticipated in the interview given by the renowned Greek artist Mikis Theodorakis to *Haaretz Magazine* on August 27, 2004. The composer of the *Zorba the Greek* sound track and a hero of the "progressive" Left in Europe, Theodorakis ranted on about the fanatical and domineering traits of the Jews, their control of Wall Street, the banks, the mass media, and the world of music. He repeatedly compared Israel to Nazi Germany, suggesting that Prime Minister Sharon was currently leading the Jews "to the root of evil," just as "Hitler led the Germans."[85] Like so many other left-wing European intellectuals and artists, the Greek composer declared that he was flabbergasted that "the Jewish people, who have been victims of Nazism, can support such a fascist policy." At the same time he called himself an antiracist, a fighter against anti-Semitism, and a friend of Israel who supported its right to exist. Theodorakis vehemently denied that there was any anti-Semitism in Europe—this was merely "a sick reaction" of Jews who wanted to avoid self-criticism and to deny the grim reality of Israeli fascism.[86] Yet his interview literally reeked of the very evil that he claimed to oppose.

According to Theodorakis, the Jews were cunning sadomasochists, cynically exploiting past victimization, yet enjoying unlimited support from the United States and dominating the global capitalist system. They had clearly manipulated President Bush, provoked the war in Iraq, and (together with the Americans) engineered 9/11. The Jews were de facto in control of the sole great superpower. But there was also a deeper layer in Theodorakis's anti-Semitism, evident when he spoke of the Jewish rejection of Jesus's message of love. He recalled his Greek Orthodox grandmother's warnings not to go to the Jewish quarter at Easter because Jews drank the blood of Christian children. Later, as a Communist he felt that Jews were "fanatics" convinced of their own chosenness and superiority. Their arrogance and aggressiveness, he still believed, stemmed from their monotheistic religion. Judaism was a judgmental faith that had implanted the notion of sin in European culture. Jewish feelings of superiority were not only a product of the Bible. They were also the outcome of the battle for survival, reinforced by outstanding Jewish success in the arts, the sciences, and music. Nonetheless, he was bitter that Jews had boycotted his own work after he had written the Palestinian national anthem. Theodorakis's statements neatly assemble together many salient strands of the old and "new" Judeophobia. They are all the more striking coming from an artistic icon of the European Left embodying its so-called enlightened aspirations, cosmopolitanism, and belief in progress. This is another illuminating expression of anti-Semitism with a "good conscience," part of the old-new secular religion of humanity.[87] The repressive nature of Hebrew monotheism, chosenness, the blood libel, Jewish media control, economic and cultural domination of America, fanaticism, and "Zionist racism" are all are thrown together into the pan-European anti-Semitic melting pot.

It would be more accurate to speak of a reinvention of European anti-Semitism after 1989, rather than of a new phenomenon.[88] In reality, "the longest hatred" had never disappeared from the Old Continent. Its revival was made easier by the fall of Communism and the gradual erosion of guilt and shame over the Holocaust. Israel, with its Jewish assertiveness, was certainly another factor that reactivated it, especially following the mobilization of the Western New Left for the Palestinian cause after 1967. The drift of Europe away from the United States and its ever closer links with the Arab world, along with old-new "pacifist" currents, have also played their part. Above all, the traditional distrust of Jewish "otherness"—particularly in the form of an independent Jewish national identity—remains very much alive.

Europe's Muslims constitute the one truly novel feature in the Judeo-phobe explosion visible during the past eight years in such countries as France, Belgium, the Netherlands, Sweden, and Great Britain.[89] In a city like Amsterdam, the perpetrators of anti-Jewish acts are virtually all of Muslim origin;[90] in Berlin, Antwerp, Brussels, Stockholm, Paris, and London, Muslim attacks have heightened the Jewish sense of physical *insecurity,* along with thoughts of immigration to Israel. By the end of 2006, assaults on Jewish communities in Europe had reached unprecedented levels, though continental elites (and some Jews themselves) continued to downplay the facts. Enamored by their multiculturalist ideology and self-induced fear of Islamophobia, many European governments still seem paralyzed by the Islamist specter. This pusillanimity will hardly deter the Islamists or prominent preachers like Sheikh Youssef al-Qaradawi, who only a few years ago solemnly promised his followers that Islam would conquer Europe "by preaching and ideology."[91] Other imams gleefully point out Europe's declining birth rate.[92] A critical question for the Jews of western and central Europe must therefore be whether Islam will be Europeanized or Europe will be be Islamicized.[93]

A few courageous Arab and Muslim voices have spoken out vigorously in Europe against this danger of Islamicization. One of the more vocal critics of the fundamentalist sickness has been the Tunisian-born Abdelwahab Meddeb, who teaches comparative literature at the University of Paris X in Nanterre. Meddeb has deplored the infiltration of a puritanical, life-hating, and misogynist Wahhabi Islam into contemporary Muslim thought. In his recent writings, xenophobia and anti-Semitism are among the most serious symptoms of the growing Islamic malady. Muslim preachers and secular editorialists alike, he contends, tend to blame all the shortcomings of Muslim society on "the evil and malignant foreigners," and especially on the Jews or Israel "whose success is a source of vexation [for Muslims] in the light of their own failure, which they are unable to acknowledge." Meddeb notes with mounting concern that the wound inflicted by Israel has metamorphosed into "a putrid infection"; theological debate has become confused with Arab policy, "which is itself permeated with racist perversion." Meddeb added that even the outwardly more measured, official voices of Islam, such as the Al-Azhar Sheikh Tantawi, had embraced an irrational anti-Semitism "imported from the West," sometimes without even realizing what they were doing.[94] He observed that Arabs had superimposed this European anti-Semitism (based on the fictitious *Protocols* theory of a world Jewish conspiracy) onto their own Islamic anti-Judaism, which went back to the days of the Prophet.

Currently Arabs directed their unbridled hatred "against imaginary Jews—nurtured by TV footage showing ferocious [Israeli] military power cold-bloodedly killing their unarmed [Palestinian] brothers." Arab anti-Semitism, he wrote, was aimed against "Jews who have renewed their sovereignty in Israel," but it was divorced from any true knowledge of Jews and Jewish culture. It had erased both the memory of "once-friendly coexistence between Jews and Arabs," and pretended that the "inferior legal status of People of the Book" (Jews and Christians) under Islam is some kind of idyllic solution.[95] The result was a repulsive caricature. Meddeb attacked the tacit approval of Mahmoud Ahmadinejad's Holocaust denial by the current spiritual guide of the Egyptian Muslim Brotherhood. This aberration was itself contradicted by the memoirs of the much admired pro-Nazi collaborator, Haj Amin al-Husseini, the Palestinian mufti of Jerusalem under the British mandate.[96] Far from denying the Holocaust, al-Husseini had confirmed it with some satisfaction, and on this point at least his testimony was reliable.

Meddeb condemned European multiculturalism for having misguidedly legitimized Islamism. Indeed, it had promoted its spread with disastrous results in such liberal societies as the Netherlands.[97] Great Britain, he perceptively remarked, was "now paying the price of its incomprehensible tolerance towards these sowers of dissension, trouble, and apocalyptic [doom]." Britain's democratic tradition was being systematically abused by extremist Muslims determined to undermine "other people's right to live."[98] Meddeb looked to France and the Maghreb as having a special role to play as a counterweight in the worldwide cultural battle against the Islamists.[99] But this struggle could succeed only if Muslims were prepared to accept strong criticism and even to de-Islamize their Arab identity.

These are still minority voices insufficiently heard in the resounding cacophony of polemics surrounding the "clash of civilizations" and the threat of global terror.[100] Europe's old-new anti-Semitism, too, stands suspended on the edge of this abyss, potentially affected by every crisis in the Middle East and beyond. This has placed many Jewish communities in acutely embarrassing and often difficult situations. As German-Jewish leader Charlotte Knoblauch told *Der Spiegel* in August 2006, the Israel-Hezbollah war had seriously aggravated anti-Semitism in Germany:

> We are currently organizing a fundraising concert, for example, and even there we get negative, antisemitic mail. No distinctions are made. We're sucked into the current Middle East conflict one hundred per cent, as Jewish citizens in Germany. And those politicians who latch onto this hostile mood with carefully prepared statements are of course doing better than ever.[101]

Emanuele Ottolenghi, director of the American Jewish Committee's Transatlantic Institute in Brussels, has observed that Europeans in general have come to see Israel "as the embodiment of the demons of their own past." The European Union was supposed to have transcended war, nationalism, and conflict, but Israel repeatedly reminds it of darker forces and darker days.[102] This is not a welcome memory for a continent peculiarly vulnerable to the totalitarian threat of jihadi Islam, having allowed itself to be infiltrated with alarming ease by those claiming to have been politically persecuted.[103] Moreover, western Europe has barely begun to deal seriously at the level of ideas with the existential threat that Islamism now poses to human rights, to its democratic values, to its own cultural identity, and to the future of its minorities. For Muslims, Jews, and Christians, as well as the secular majority in the European Union, the challenge is not ultimately one of race or ethnicity.[104] It is about ideology, identity, and the very possibility of democratic pluralism; it is about the need to transcend a black-and-white image of Palestinians as victims and Israelis as aggressors; and it entails awareness that anti-Semitism is a Trojan horse within its gates that will remain the lowest common denominator of European culture as long as tolerance for intolerance remains its distorted and self-defeating liberal credo.

THIRTEEN

Bigotry at the United Nations

A bba Eban became Israel's first permanent representative to the
United Nations in 1949. Nearly fifty years later in an interview he
gave to the Israeli National Archives, Eban recalled how grim the
situation of the Jewish people had seemed at the end of World War II. Not
only did the fearful anguish provoked by the scale of the Holocaust lie heavily on Jewish minds, but Palestine was being assailed by mounting regional
violence.

> The victorious powers, the three of them—the United States, Britain and
> the Soviet Union—showed no intention whatever, at first, of recognizing
> the Jews of Palestine as a political reality. There wasn't a single ray of light
> on the horizon. The Jewish representatives of the United Nations confer-
> ence at San Francisco were humiliatingly seated in some distant balcony,
> looking down at the 50 member nations, none of which had made any-
> thing like the sacrifices demanded of the Jewish people by its own mar-
> tyrdom.[1]

Yet within four years an unprecedentedly speedy, abrupt, and providential
transformation had taken place in Jewish national fortunes. Israel was established; it had won its war of survival against the odds and was recognized by the United Nations.

One of the biggest surprises in the dramatic upheaval was the positive
role briefly played by the Soviet Union, despite its traditional anti-Zionist
outlook. Even before the spring of 1947, the Soviets were helping Jewish survivors of the Holocaust in Eastern Europe reach Germany and Austria—
knowing full well that they intended to make their homes in Palestine.[2] In
May 1947, Soviet deputy foreign minister Andrei Gromyko unexpectedly

declared qualified Russian support for the establishment of two independent states in Palestine, one Arab and one Jewish.[3] In October 1947, the Soviets went further, actively supporting partition and working in tandem with American representatives for its implementation under the UN aegis.[4] On November 29, 1947, the USSR voted *for* partition, despite the onset of the Cold War and the beginning of Stalin's secret anti-Semitic campaign to destroy Jewish culture inside the Soviet Union. Before and during the 1948 Jewish war of independence the Russians helped to provide crucial military aid (sent from Czechoslovakia) to the fledgling Jewish state, at a time when Britain was assisting the Arabs and the United States had imposed an arms embargo detrimental to Israel. The USSR's unmitigated support of Israel in the international arena continued until May 1949. Indeed, except for the brief severance of diplomatic ties in February 1953, Stalin opted to maintain outwardly normal and even friendly relations with Israel, despite the domestic anti-Zionist and anti-Semitic offensive that was raging within the USSR.

The Soviet delegate at the UN, Gromyko, in an emotional speech to the General Assembly on November 26, 1947, explicitly referred to the torments inflicted upon the Jews in Europe during the Holocaust as a justification for Israeli statehood. He further emphasized the *historic* connection of the Jewish people to Palestine.

> The representatives of the Arab States claim that the partition of Palestine would be an historic injustice. But this view of the case is unacceptable, if only because, after all, the Jewish people had been closely linked with Palestine for a considerable period in history. Apart from that, we must not overlook . . . the position in which the Jewish people found themselves as a result of the recent world war . . . it may not be remiss to remind my listeners again that, as a result of the war which was unleashed by Hitlerite Germany, the Jews, as a people, have suffered more than any people.[5]

Gromyko was referring here to "the Jewish people" (or the "Jews as a people"), not merely to the Jewish community in Palestine. In other words, he was implicitly accepting a cardinal Zionist principle, despite the reams of Marxist-Leninist-Stalinist verbiage denying the existence of any Jewish nation. Once Soviet leaders had determined that a binational Arab-Jewish state in Palestine was not feasible, Gromyko's ardor in extolling the decision to set up a Jewish state was impressive:

> The solution of the Palestine problem based on a partition of Palestine into two separate states will be of profound historic significance, because this decision will meet the legitimate demands of the Jewish people, hundreds of thousands of who, as you know, are still without a country, without homes, having found temporary shelter only in special camps in some western European countries.[6]

When the Arab armies invaded Palestine in May 1948 in order to throttle at birth the Jewish "national liberation movement" (Gromyko's terminology), the USSR and the rest of the Soviet bloc had no hesitation in condemning this "outrageous" violation of UN legality. As Abba Eban would later wittily comment: "Truth does not change simply because those who proclaim it become tired of their own veracity."[7] Or to put it another way, if Israel's existence was "the original sin," then the Soviet Union was as complicit in it as anyone else.

The United States was the first country to recognize Israel de facto on May 14, 1948, although President Truman had to overrule the State Department, the Pentagon, key cabinet members such as Secretary of State George Marshall and Defense Secretary James Forrestal, the oil lobby, and virtually the entire U.S. intelligence community to do it.[8] The USSR recognized Israel de jure, only four days later. For a brief historic moment, under the UN umbrella, the world's two superpowers were in full agreement. It seemed as if, diplomatically speaking, the Messiah had returned to the Promised Land. But such an idyllic state of affairs did not survive the ravages of the Cold War, which would later paralyze the United Nations. Nor could it revive that fleeting interlude between 1947 and 1949, when a battered postwar world was temporarily willing to regard Jewish refugees from the Holocaust in terms beyond those of narrow *Realpolitik*.[9] The UN Special Committee on Palestine (UNSCOP), established on May 15, 1947, definitely took the Holocaust into account in its majority report, which favored partition. The representative of Uruguay emphasized that the "Palestinian question" was directly linked with "the problem of [Jewish] immigration," which, in turn, derived from the Nazi mass murder and the danger of "fresh outbursts of persecution and violence."[10]

The debate over Israel's admission to the UN in 1949 revealed that many countries were influenced by their awareness of the Holocaust. The French representative observed that "the thoughts of many were turned to those who had suffered persecution throughout the long years under the yoke of the totalitarian regimes." The Polish delegate fully supported Israeli statehood, recalling the common suffering of Poles and Jews under Nazi occupation and the racial anti-Semitism of "reactionary elements predominant in Poland's pre-war government circles."[11] Israel was finally admitted to the UN on a vote of 33 to 12, with 12 abstentions. The positive votes came mainly from Europe and the Western Hemisphere, plus Australia, New Zealand, Liberia, and the Philippines. The negative votes were from African and Asian members, overwhelmingly Arab or Islamic. At that time, of course, the UN was still dominated by Western states, where parliamentary democracy was the prime tool of political action; the Communist bloc backed the creation of Israel; and Latin America was consistently supportive of the Jewish state at the United Nations.

In the 1960s, however, there was a dramatic change in the composition of the United Nations and its dominant philosophy. The African nations had reached independence and, with their division into more than forty states, acquired a wholly disproportionate numerical weight in the UN system. Central and South America nominally enjoyed twenty-three times more power than the United States, which under UN rules had only one vote. Similarly, the twenty-plus Arab states, with a total population only one-tenth of India or China, were far more influential in the eccentric arithmetic of the United Nations. In the 1970s, the combined voting power of almost fifty Muslim countries, the (still intact) thirteen states of the Communist bloc, and the Third World "solidarity" ensured crushing majorities against Israel at the United Nations. The immediate effect was a gradual liberation from whatever restraints had previously existed on UN rhetoric and resolutions. Neither deliberation nor objectivity was required in order to ensure a majority vote against the solitary Jewish state. An appeal to material or political interests would often suffice. The "morality" and the ideological rationalizations would come later.[12]

At the same time, Israeli rule over the "occupied" territories after 1967 facilitated the shift against the Jewish state and in favor of the Palestinian cause. Moreover, following the 1973 Yom Kippur War, acceptance of the "inalienable" Palestinian right to national self-determination found a growing echo among western European states (led by France) as well as from Russia, China, the Arabs, East European Communist countries, and nonaligned nations. In 1974 the UN General Assembly recognized the PLO as the representative of the Palestinian people, and on November 13, 1974, its leader, Yasser Arafat, addressed the UN General Assembly in person, bearing "an olive-branch and a freedom-fighter's gun."[13] Arafat's speech was a vicious attack on Israel as "the most fanatic, discriminatory and closed of nations." It accused the "Zionist racists and colonialists" of usurping Palestinian lands and committing "murderous acts of terrorism" against Arabs. Arafat even devoted a paragraph to explaining "the unity of Zionism and anti-semitism" in a Soviet-style discourse about their common "retrograde and reactionary" tenets. When Zionists called on Diaspora Jews to alienate themselves from the nations of which they were a part and to solve the Jewish problem by "immigrating to and forcibly settling the land of another people," then this—according to Yasser Arafat—was identical to anti-Semitic positions.[14]

Arafat's 1974 speech and the special UN observer status subsequently accorded to the PLO were symptomatic of the emergence of the "Palestinian question" as a major international issue. Henceforth it was permanently on the UN agenda, and by the end of the 1970s, many European Community nations and Latin American states were moving toward a more pro-Palestinian position. Alongside these developments, it was proving virtually impossible to obtain any condemnation of anti-Semitism in UN forums. For example, General Assembly resolutions in 1960 in response to a worldwide outbreak of swastika daubings omitted mention of anti-Semitism. The UN General Assembly's Third Committee could not adopt a resolution in 1965 to include anti-Semitism as part of the Convention on Racial Discrimination. The Arab states did, however, enthusiastically support a Soviet counterproposal to condemn Zionism, Nazism, and neo-Nazism, in that order. Arab spokesmen argued that to single out anti-Semitism was a crude attempt by Israel to use "blackmail" against them or anyone who sympathized with their cause.[15] Zionists would be the only beneficiaries. The Zionist motive (according to the Russians) was to heighten indignation over the treatment of Soviet Jewry.

In the Arab narrative, Zionists deliberately used anti-Semitism to encourage mass immigration to the Jewish state. The Afro-Asian bloc, for its part, was generally indifferent to religious or political discrimination in which color was not involved; thus anti-Semitism was seen by most Afro-Asians as an undesirable diversion from issues of colonialism and racial matters, in particular apartheid.[16] Neither anti-Semitism nor the Holocaust was, after all, a part of the Afro-Asian experience. Moreover, it was expedient for the Nonaligned Movement of some 120 countries (which now dominated UN votes and General Assembly resolutions) to go along with Arab anti-Israel moves when they might secure useful economic benefits. At a minimum, such backing was expected to guarantee Arab reciprocity when it came to their own anticolonial and antiapartheid agendas.

By the 1960s, the USSR had also moved far away from its earlier support for the Jewish state. Speaking in the UN Security Council on June 9, 1967, the Soviet ambassador described Israel's assault on the Syrian Golan Heights as walking "in the bloody footsteps of Hitler's executioners."[17] Soviet premier Aleksei Kosygin, speaking at the Fifth Emergency Special Session of the General Assembly, evoked the specter of Israeli gauleiters in the newly occupied territories.[18] Foreign Minister Gromyko (fully recuperated from his pro-Israeli exertions of twenty years earlier) accused "the propagandists from Tel Aviv" of singing melodies from Goebbels's song sheets. The Soviets now made common cause with the strengthened Arab bloc at the United Nations, encouraging them to equate Israel's treatment of Palestinian Arabs with South African apartheid at every opportunity—a move guaranteed to ensure black African support. As a result, after the 1973 Yom Kippur War, only three out of forty-two African states still maintained diplomatic relations with Israel.

In the summer of 1975, the link of Zionism to racism and apartheid was being vigorously promoted by the Soviet-Arab coalition in all international forums. In July 1975, the World Conference of the International Women's Year in Mexico City specifically called for the elimination of various racist evils, including Zionism. A conference ostensibly devoted to the equality of women and their contribution to development and peace was unceremoniously hijacked in order to stamp "Zionism" as a term of opprobrium on a par with neocolonialism, alien domination, and apartheid. Part of the Mexico resolution stated:

> Recognizing that women of the entire world, whatever differences exist between them, share the painful experience of receiving or having received unequal treatment, and that as their awareness of this phenome-

non increases they will become natural allies in the struggle against any form of oppression, such as is practiced under colonialism, neocolonialism, Zionism, racial discrimination and apartheid ...[19]

This resolution was the work of the so-called Group of 77, which embraced the developing countries in the Third World. It was presented as a breakthrough in the economic and political aspect of the women's struggle by lining up Zionism with apartheid as a malignant force.[20] As American ambassador Barbara White pointed out, there was no attempt even to negotiate over the terms, which "we felt could be interpreted as saying that Israel should not exist."[21] Despite the protests of the United States, West Germany, and the United Kingdom over the superfluous condemnation of Zionism, it was nonetheless retained by a roll call vote of 59 to 19 with 25 abstentions.[22] Thus the 1975 launching of the United Nations Decade for Women rapidly descended into a morass of Third World political grievances, crude anti-Zionist propaganda, and chauvinist cant in which "the word *woman* was scarcely mentioned."[23] The delegates from different countries (especially the Arab states) were, in effect, promoting their national interests rather than women's rights.

At the July 1980 World Conference of the United Nations Decade for Women in Copenhagen, the trend toward politicization continued more vigorously with women from Third World and Arab countries (where the female condition screamed out for reform) leading the charge against Zionism and America.[24] In this august UN setting, Jewish feminists heard truly chilling comments, such as "The only good Jew is a dead Jew" and "The only way to rid the world of Zionism is to kill all the Jews." One eyewitness overheard other delegates saying that the American women's movement had a bad name because its most prominent founding figures, Gloria Steinem, Betty Friedan, and Bella Abzug, were all Jewish. The feminist activist Sonia Johnson described the anti-Semitism at the Copenhagen conference as "overt, wild, and irrational." Barbara Leslie, a nongovernmental organization (NGO) observer from the International Council of Jewish Women, recalled an American black woman being enthusiastically applauded by women of all colors for insisting that Zionism was racism. The psychologist and feminist author Phyllis Chesler recorded the savage response when one Jewish woman mentioned that her husband had been shot without trial in Iraq and that she had to escape to Israel with her children. The place went wild: "Cuba si! Yankee no! PLO! PLO!" they shouted. "Israel kills babies and women. Israel must die."[25]

Chesler later described this particular world conference as "a pogrom of nonstop words and ideas, an exercise in total intimidation." She recalled that there had been bands of thirty to fifty Russian-trained Arab women, headed by PLO representatives, roving the hallways. "They had been trained to interrupt each and every panel and to take them over with propaganda against America and Israel. . . . They did not pretend to be feminists or to be concerned with women." She also noted that the "progressive" Scandinavian women automatically supported the PLO and espoused "the most profound disgust and hatred for all things American, Jewish, and Zionist— and in the most aggressive manner."[26] For these Left feminists, pro-Palestinianism, anti-Americanism, and anti-Zionism were part of a uniform, politically correct universal language from which no deviations could be tolerated.

Chesler began to discover after 1980 that among many Christian feminists (both white and people of color) Israel was perceived as a negative symbol of patriarchy, capitalism, and religious misogyny; that Jews were generally regarded as rich, powerful, reactionary, and racist; and "Zionism" was held "responsible for racism in America today." Such blatant anti-Semitism on the feminist Left extended from open resentment at "pushy Jews who had taken over the feminist and lesbian movements" to a widespread loathing for Israel as an "apartheid" state. Equally, after 2001, Chesler observed that these same feminists, while extremely sensitive to Palestinian suffering, had failed even once to condemn terrorist assaults on Jewish civilians in Israel or Europe, let alone criticize the long history of Palestinian airplane hijacking and suicide bombing. Nor did Christian feminist academics and militants in the West provide much (if any) support for that small minority of dissident women in the Muslim world, who bravely spoke out against Islamic fundamentalism, the systematic repression of their own sisters from Saudi Arabia to Pakistan, and the endemic misogyny in Muslim culture. This shocking silence has extended to some American Jewish militants who romanticize or justify fundamentalist terrorism, and on occasion have even outdone Christian feminists in their antireligious and anti-Zionist rhetoric. Indeed, in this milieu to raise the question of Islamic gender apartheid will lead to accusations of being a colonialist, racist crusader. To even discuss gender segregation, female genital mutilation, and honor killings is to divert attention from the only issue that supposedly matters—that of the Israeli occupation.

At Copenhagen in 1980, the UN Decade for Women had been turned into a crude means not only for attacking Zionism but also for denigrating any Jewish women who dared to protest against this incitement. Moreover, as in Mexico City five years before, it appeared that the same Third World nations who practiced sexism were more likely to be anti-Semitic or else particularly zealous in bashing Zionism.[27] But the fallout from the new UN agenda was also felt in supposedly sophisticated countries such as Britain. For example, the British women's rights magazine *Spare Rib* adopted a highly discriminatory anti-Zionist position, making it virtually impossible for any Jewish feminist to identify with her own cultural background. Anti-Zionism, as one Jewish feminist remarked, had become "nothing more than a smokescreen for antisemitism."[28] In response to Israel's 1982 invasion of Lebanon, *Spare Rib* totally embraced pro-Palestinian propaganda in the name of antiracist feminism.[29] It portrayed the extremely rare massacres of Palestinians in Deir Yassin (1948) and at Sabra and Shatila (1982) as a *consistent* and *permanent* feature of Zionist history,[30] and said that the Lebanon War was rooted in the Zionist *nature* of Israel. The Israeli Labor Party was attacked for being fully complicit in Menachem Begin's "fascistic," militaristic methods.[31] Zionist ideology was blamed for the "institutionalized racism" in Israel, for the separation between Jew and Gentile, and for the "apartheid" nature of the whole society.[32] All the familiar libels could be found in this left-wing feminist discourse, which has continued until the present time. Then, as now, many feminists perceive Zionism as inherently repressive, segregationist, racist, and patriarchal—a blood brother of fascism and Nazism.[33] British feminists in the spring of 1983 even swallowed the outright lie that Palestinian schoolgirls had been gassed by the Israel Defense Forces (IDF) and that Zionism deliberately endangered the health and safety of women.[34] Such fabrications suggest that anti-Zionism had become the unacknowledged racism of the international feminist movement, much as it had steadily corrupted various branches of the United Nations ever since the mid-1970s.[35]

The anti-Zionist declaration in Mexico City at the World Conference of the International Women's Year had soon been followed by an even harsher condemnation at the Summit of the Organization of African Unity (OAU) held in Kampala, Uganda, from July 28 to August 1, 1975. The resolutions adopted by African heads of state denounced "the common imperialist origin" of "the racist regime in occupied Palestine and the racist regime in Zimbabwe and South Africa." They called for all OAU member states to take measures that might eventually deprive Israel of membership in the United Nations. They also labeled Zionism as "a danger to world peace."[36] The Conference of Nonaligned Countries, which met in Lima, Peru, toward the end of August 1975, adopted a similar resolution. It, too, condemned Zionism "as a threat to world peace and security," calling upon all countries to oppose "this racist and imperialist ideology."[37] In a direct line of lineal descent from the 1973 Nonaligned Conference in Algiers, Zionism was being organically linked in every international forum to such evils as South African apartheid and "settler-colonialism" in Rhodesia, Angola, and Mozambique.

The stage was now prepared for action at the UN General Assembly's Thirtieth Session. The Soviet-Arab coalition presented a draft resolution confirming Zionism as "a form of racism and racial discrimination," based on the earlier resolutions that had been agreed to in 1975 in Mexico, Uganda, and Peru. On November 10, 1975, the General Assembly finally adopted Resolution 3379 with 72 votes in favor, including all the Arab and Islamic countries and the Soviet bloc, as well as various Afro-Asian states, China, Brazil, Cuba, India, and Yugoslavia. All the Western nations, except for Greece and Portugal, were among the thirty-five countries that voted against the resolution. So, too, did many Latin American states and five African countries. The usually solid African bloc provided no less than 14 out of the 32 abstentions.[38]

The Soviet Union undoubtedly played a major behind-the-scenes role in bringing the United Nations to condemn an "ism" for the first time in its history. Zionism was the first postwar idea or ideology, as opposed to government action or policy, ever subjected to such sweeping international damnation. This decision smacked of something more akin to a doctrinal inquisition than a political debate—which may explain some of the revulsion expressed in much of the international media at the time.[39] In his speech before the General Assembly, the Israeli ambassador to the United Nations, Chaim Herzog, noted the symbolism of the Zionism = Racism resolution having being passed on a day when, thirty-seven years earlier, Nazi storm troopers had unleashed the nationwide "Crystal Night" pogrom.

Editorials across Western Europe and North America deplored the bigotry, fanaticism, and brazen anti-Semitism behind the UN resolution. *The New York Times* headlined "Shame of the UN," recognizing that by this act, the United Nations was "challenging the very right of existence of Israel," a member state it had helped to bring into being. A number of American papers proposed that the United States withdraw from the United Nations, controlled as it was by godless dictatorships, tyrannies, and anti-American regimes. Many saw the resolution as a definitive statement of UN moral bankruptcy. There were numerous attacks on the falsehood and absurdity of tainting Zionism with "racial bias," and sharp comments on the obscenity and hypocrisy of "police regimes," including the USSR, Poland, East Germany, Albania, China, Cuba, Syria, Libya, Saudi Arabia, and Uganda, determining the meaning of such concepts as democracy, Zionism, racism, and religious tolerance. Numerous editorialists concluded that the resolution was itself a demonstration of UN support *for* racism, rather than expressing opposition to it.

The sense that November 10, 1975, was a black day for the United Nations seemed widespread. Indeed, many felt it to be intolerable that only thirty years after the end of World War II, the organization founded to prevent crimes such as the Holocaust was turning the charge of racism against the Jewish people. Moreover, the United Nations appeared to be denying Jews equal rights and "lawful sovereignty within the community of nations." The discriminatory principle that traditionally characterized anti-Semitism had simply been transferred from the realm of individual rights to the domain of collective identity.[40]

A leading black American voice in the fight against such discrimination in the United Nations was Bayard Rustin, who called it "an act of gigantic hypocrisy." He observed that the UN resolution was stripping terms such as "racism" of any real substance, obscuring their roots and true nature, in order to use them as a political weapon. For the Soviet Union it was yet another excuse to persecute Jews. In the Middle East, none of the Arab or Muslim nations promoting the "horrible resolution" came to the table with clean hands.

Kurds in Iran, Copts in Egypt, Jews in Syria have all suffered the most terrible and brutal persecution. The Constitution of Jordan forbids Jews from becoming citizens, while Arabs sit in the Israeli parliament and Arabic is an official language. The Soviet Union has practiced systematic discrimination against Jews and forcibly uprooted entire peoples. With the aid of the Soviet Union and the Arab countries, Sudan carried on a near-genocidal war against non-Muslim blacks in which perhaps 500,000 were killed.

These remarks were published thirty years before Darfur.

Rustin also quoted Martin Luther King's observation "When people criticize Zionists they mean Jews." It was a way to emphasize that the "antiracist" attacks on Israel in the United Nations were themselves anti-Semitic and intended to justify future Arab efforts to destroy the Jewish state. Having experienced four hundred years of slavery, segregation, and discrimination, Rustin argued that blacks in America could not stand idly by and watch this organized incitement to anti-Semitism, "one of the oldest and most virulent racisms the world has ever known."

Another Afro-American denunciation of "Third World racism at the UN" came from the pen of Eldridge Cleaver, then still serving time in a prison cell in California. One of America's best-known black radical leaders, Cleaver had lived for several years with Arabs in Algeria. He described them as being "among the most racist people on earth." No one knew this better than the "black Africans living along the edges of the Sahara" who were subjected to "a hypocritical form of slavery" and constant abuse. Cleaver deplored the feebleness of the "guilt-ridden" Western democracies in swallowing "every half-baked argument" emanating from the General Assembly. The United Nations, he suggested, was no longer a forum for morally upright anticolonial leaders such as Gandhi but rather a refuge for "hired killers like Idi Amin Dada, the hatchet man of Uganda." It was an ideal playground for Communist tyrants, theocratic Arab dictatorships, and the Third World enemies of democracy. As for Zionism, it was "the Jewish survival doctrine," a life raft for a nation that had not only suffered intensely from persecution but has "done more than any other people in history to expose and condemn racism."[41]

More than thirty years later, it is sobering to witness the extent to which the Soviet-Arab view of Zionism derided by Cleaver has deeply penetrated into the liberal, open societies of northern and western Europe, and the degree to which UN notions of Zionist racism and colonialism (still repudiated by most of the liberal enlightened world in 1975) have become solidly anchored in mainstream public consciousness. What *The Daily Telegraph* could dismiss three decades ago as "a ghoulish inversion of morality, truth and justice" by the United Nations is part of today's conventional wisdom. In retrospect, one could argue that the Arab-Soviet-PLO effort to place Israel "beyond the pale" has in part succeeded. The "abomination of anti-Semitism" (as U.S. ambassador to the United Nations Daniel Patrick Moynihan called it in 1975) was indeed given "the appearance of international sanction."[42] Moynihan lucidly anticipated that institutionalized anti-Zionism at the United Nations would be a powerful weapon against the liberal Western democracies. He foresaw that the coalition of forces behind the UN resolution would continue to exploit anti-Semitism as a battering ram for their totalitarian and illiberal agendas. As one farsighted British writer had noted in 1976: "Today, the authentic voice of anti-Semitism, strengthened and invigorated by the riches and hatred of the oil-producing nations, is once again respectable; it has become *salonfähig* and speaks in the best society, and nowhere more blatantly or stridently than in the General Assembly of the United Nations."[43]

Bernard Lewis, the distinguished historian of the Middle East, observed in 1976 that the primary Arab purpose in cosponsoring the anti-Zionist resolution had been to delegitimize the State of Israel—a goal for which anti-Semitism was a most useful auxiliary. The condemnation of Israel's founding ideology was intended as a kind of "incantatory prefiguration of the expulsion of Israel from the United Nations" and the ultimate dismantling of the Zionist state.[44] Arab efforts to claim that this aim had no connection to anti-Semitism were rightly dismissed by Lewis as nonsense. Indeed, experience would rapidly demonstrate that the United Nations, by giving anti-Zionism a solid legal basis, was substantially helping to demonize Israel and the Jewish people.[45] The ramifications soon began to permeate the whole network of UN institutions in its many departments and specialized agencies. For example, on the same day Resolution 3379 was adopted, the General Assembly decided to establish the "Committee on the Inalienable Rights of the Palestinian People." With a large budget at its disposal and acting as an integral part of the United Nations, it has for more than thirty years done everything in its power to establish a Palestinian state in place of Israel. Similarly, other UN departments have been able for decades to distribute UN documents in millions of copies around the world, which inter alia include innumerable anti-Zionist and/or anti-Semitic resolutions and protocols. This propaganda material—along with the mandatory proposition that "Zionism is racism"—found its way into many universities, schools, libraries, textbooks, and churches, and was widely distributed to NGOs.

Professor Yoram Dinstein pointed out at a 1986 international legal conference on "Anti-Zionism at the UN" that the Zionist-racism resolution went far beyond disputes over transitory policies of the Israeli government. It also transcended mere opposition to Zionist ideology, seeking to sap any principled foundation for Israel's sovereign existence. The resolution had been turned into hatred of Jews per se (that is, anti-Semitism) once Israel was blamed not only for real transgressions but also for imaginary sins. Moreover, it was intolerable that Israel could be condemned for actions not perceived as deplorable when committed by other nations.[46] Such blatant double standards had become characteristic of the UN General Assembly, transforming Israel into the epitome of a wicked state or (to borrow the words of Professor Irwin Cotler) "an anti-human rights metaphor."[47] Moreover, anti-Zionism was beginning to permeate a large section of the UN Secretariat in ways that affected its fundamental integrity and impartiality. Worse still, the United Nations had been turned into a political arena for the continuation of the war against Israel by other means.[48] The United Nations had inadvertently exposed the slippery slope leading from anti-Israelism through anti-Zionism to anti-Semitism. As soon as those who sought Israel's demise would encounter resistance, anything Jewish automatically became suspect in their eyes.[49]

Such paranoia was regularly reflected in the anti-Semitic statements heard in the 1970s from the rostrum of the General Assembly, especially by Arab delegates. The permanent representative of Saudi Arabia, Jamil Baroody, made countless speeches; their obsessive, anti-Zionist, and anti-Jewish chords did not in the least diminish his influence or impact.[50] One of his favorite themes was the veracity of the *Protocols of the Elders of Zion*. Baroody would also spend hours at the United Nations accusing the Jewish people of causing World Wars I and II, as well as all the problems of the Middle East.[51] For him, Jews were really Khazars from southern Russia who had to be expelled from the region. But it was left to another Saudi representative, in Geneva, to tell a UN seminar in 1984 that, according to the Talmud, Jews who did *not* drink the blood of Gentiles each year would be "damned for eternity."[52] A year later, in the UN General Assembly, the Kuwaiti representative brought this blood libel more up to date, maintaining that the Zionists had developed an "unquenchable thirst for Arab blood."[53] No less popular at the United Nations was the anti-Semitic theme of Jewish cabals and conspiracies, as developed by such Arab speakers as the Jordanian ambassador, Hazem Nuseibeh. He told the Security Council in 1979 that "every day a Mr. Rothschild meets with a cabal in London behind closed doors, to decide on fixing the price of gold. A flash is sent out to agents around the world to observe. . . . How can the billions of struggling human beings . . . compete with such awesome powers?"[54]

Nuseibeh's most sparkling contribution to the Middle East debate came, however, on December 15, 1980, when he accused the "representative of the Zionist entity" of harboring a "deep-seated hatred of the Arab world" because Muslims had successfully liberated themselves from the Jewish cabal. Once again, Lord Rothschild was invoked as an example of how Jews cleverly manipulate the rest of humanity by "controlling the money and wealth of the world." Nuseibeh did not forget to target South African tycoon Harry Oppenheimer, "who holds 15 million blacks in bondage to exploit and monopolise the diamonds, the uranium and other precious resources which rightfully belong to the struggling African people of South Africa and Namibia. It is a well-known fact that the Zionists are the richest people in the world and control much of its destiny."[55]

In the same debate, he had extensive support from Ambassador Falilou Kane from Senegal (chairman of the PLO-dominated Palestinian Committee of the General Assembly), who insisted that all the major news organizations in the United States were "dominated by Jews."[56] The American representative did not bother to protest. But *The New York Times* expressed its disgust with diplomats who resorted to ugly forms of anti-Semitism, observing: "The members of the UN seem ready to tolerate the most explicit racism provided only that it comes in an anti-Israel context." Equally indignant was Florida congressman William Lehman, who deplored "the new anti-Semitism" institutionalized at UN forums, which were obsessed with "isolating Israel at every juncture." He quoted from a 1981 essay by Harris O. Schoenberg that described anti-Semitism as "spreading like a political cancer through the body politic of the United Nations."[57] Arab rejectionism of Israel had amplified and transmitted "hate messages which defame the Jewish people." The UN Secretariat had become a place in which it was difficult for young Jews to find a job—where the State of Israel had fewer than one-third of the staff positions to which it was entitled.

In analyzing outbursts like that of Hazem Nuseibeh, Schoenberg noted that Jordan was considered a "moderate" country in UN terms. Nevertheless, it still forbade citizenship by law to Jews. Anti-Semitism was a part of its cultural life and the official school curriculum. The *Protocols of the Elders of Zion* were frequently a key text. Prominent American performing artists who were Jewish had even found themselves banned in Jordan. As elsewhere in the Arab world, religious radio programs openly called for jihad against "these impure, accursed and treacherous Jews." In conclusion, Schoenberg emphasized that all UN efforts to fight racism and sexism had been totally perverted by its anti-Semitic resolution of November 10, 1975. Most sobering of all, the following characterization of UN anti-Zionist propaganda by Schoenberg could be applied today without the need for any significant changes.

> The new anti-Semitism asserts that the Jewish people is imaginary, that it has never existed, that it does not now exist, that it never had connections with the Holy Land, that the Holocaust never happened and that the Jewish people, accordingly, has no rights accorded to other peoples. These views are reflected in the publications of the UN Special Unit which services the Palestinian Committee and of the UN Economic Commission for Western Asia, which seats the PLO as a member-state but not a real state such as Israel.[58]

By the early 1980s the glass palace on the west bank of the East River in New York City that housed the United Nations had acquired a richly deserved reputation as a major center of world anti-Semitism.[59] Located in the heart of the largest Jewish city on earth (where two million Jews lived), its treatment of Israel was already a source of great bitterness. New York's undiplomatic mayor Edward Koch bluntly called the UN "a body without conscience or morality," best compared with a cesspool.[60] Whatever hopes were once invested in it as a symbol of peace, brotherhood, and cooperation had been dramatically eroded by its double standards, its cold-blooded efforts to vilify or delegitimize Israel, and its complicity with international terrorism.[61] In 1982, the levels of stigmatization and demonization of Israel reached new depths of depravity. The Syrian delegate, Mr. Khaddam, told the General Assembly that the sufferings of humanity were "a result of the plots of world Zionism to establish a racist empire starting in Palestine and extending to other parts of the world, defined by Zionist doctrine as being from the Nile to the Euphrates."[62]

No country in antiquity or in the modern world had "a record as dark as Israel's." Khaddam's Syrian colleague in the Special Political Committee even called the Zionist usurpers "enemies of mankind," compulsively driven by hatred of all humanity. The UN Iraqi delegate, not to be outdone, insisted that Zionism was based on "the purity of the Jewish race . . . terrorism, repression, treachery and expansion," exactly like Nazism.[63] A similar theme was taken up by Mr. Farah from Djibouti, who ranted on about Zionist neo-Nazis espousing Nazi concepts of institutionalized terror, "racial superiority," and mass killing. This, in turn, was echoed by the Cuban delegate and by the Libyan speaker, Ali Treiki, who, on December 8, 1983, descended into the vilest anti-Semitic abuse. He accused "Jewish Zionists in the United States" of exploiting and attempting through vice and immorality "to destroy Americans."[64] Al-Hadawy, speaking on behalf of Saddam's Iraq, focused explicitly on "absolute Jewish domination of finance, the mass media and various sectors of public opinion." He explained that the influential Jewish lobby in the United States had achieved decisive control of the White House, the American Congress, and the Department of State.[65] For his part, the PLO delegate, Abdel Rahman, centered his remarks on the harmful Jewish role in crime, prostitution, and drug taking.

For several decades, UN delegates (especially those representing Israel) have been treated to a sickening litany of anti-Semitic abuse at the General Assembly, in the UN Human Rights Commission, and sometimes even in the Security Council. Over time, Zionism has become synonymous with racism, crime, aggression, bloody massacres, and Nazi-style extermination. Many of the slurs have spilled over into general denigration of Jews, Judaism, and the Jewish people.[66] In 1985, the Syrian delegate to the Security Council declared that Israel as a nation had no religion or human values, only a myth of being "God's chosen people" and a falsified history to back it up.[67] Other Arab delegates elaborated on similar themes. They also consistently used the term "Judaization" to describe nonreligious measures taken by Israel in Jerusalem or the territories. The intent and consequence was evident: to cause religious antipathy. Even official UN documents investigating Israeli human rights practices write prejudicially about Israeli plans to Judaize the West Bank, whether the subject relates to building highways or confiscating land.[68]

Distinctions among Israelis, Zionists, and Jews have been consistently blurred for the past thirty years or more, both within the United Nations and without; hate-filled idioms predominate in all three areas among the Arab/Muslim states and the PLO.[69] As Yehuda Blum, Israel's former ambassador to the United Nations, observed in 1984, "anti-Zionist" and "anti-Israel" slogans were all too often used by closet anti-Semites to disguise their true intentions.[70] Statements ostensibly directed at "the Zionist entity" were, in practice, bound to promote hatred, violence, and discrimination against Jews. This fact alone made them unreservedly anti-Semitic, whatever disclaimers a particular orator may have offered.

Such declarations went far beyond the requirements of normal group conflict, including the hostilities and prejudices that usually accompany political confrontations. Arab, Muslim, and Third World anti-Zionists of the type that were rampant at the UN in the mid-1980s clearly belonged in this category.[71] Such fictive anti-Zionism involved a deliberate misuse of language and destruction of rational discourse.[72] It drew on UN General Assembly Resolution 3379 in order to turn Zionism into a "crime against humanity" and an ultimate symbol of illegitimacy. Unfortunately, with the exception of occasional intercessions on Israel's behalf from Canada, Britain, and a few other Western states, only the United States consistently condemned such incitement to hatred within the United Nations.

The Zionism = Racism strategy of the Soviet-Arab coalition worked by promoting its agenda through many UN-sponsored educational, political, and other agencies. It could count on Third World ignorance about anti-Semitism and the Holocaust, the frequent confusion of Zionist ideology with Israeli policies in the territories, the post-1973 fear of antagonizing oil-rich Arab states, and the remarkably inflated profile of the "Palestinian question." Within the UN system itself, equal voting power irrespective of size, population, wealth, power, or regime type had for years guaranteed that life would be difficult for Israel and far from easy for the United States and Western democracies in general. But Zionism = Racism, with its built-in irrationality and double standards, was the ultimate "big lie."[73] It could only happen in an institution where the tyranny of the majority had already subverted the rule of law in any meaningful sense of the word. When the General Assembly established a Special Committee to Investigate Israeli Practices Affecting the Human Rights of the Population of Occupied Territories, its aim was clearly *political*, not humanitarian. As with the UN Commission on Human Rights, the outcome would prove to be grossly disproportionate in terms of the time, energy, and resources wasted on condemning Israel, while ignoring virtually all major atrocities and massive examples of human rights violations worldwide, from Rwanda to Darfur.

In November 1975 Israel fell victim to a global confrontation between Third World countries (led by a Soviet-Arab bloc) and the Western-dominated status quo represented by the United States. The split was especially sharp in the Middle East, following the Yom Kippur War and the Arab oil embargo of 1973. However, following the passage of the Zionism = Racism resolution, the United Nations lost a great deal of credibility in public opinion in the United States and in many other Western countries.[74] In the United States, the UN resolution was widely regarded as a grave abuse of the one-nation, one-vote principle in order to delegitimize a sovereign, democratic member of the United Nations. As a result, harsh criticism of the United Nations became acceptable, and even fashionable, in the United States.

During the past thirty years, the countless UN resolutions condemning Israel or Zionism have turned the topic into a kind of ritualistic incantation whose long-term significance it is tempting to dismiss altogether. But this would be a serious mistake. It would be equally wrong to underestimate the international respectability the United Nations granted to Middle Eastern terrorist organizations such as the PLO after 1974.[75] The PLO-dominated UN committees that were created after 1975 gave a huge boost to the public relations campaign of the Palestinians and their international diplomacy. Political credentials at the United Nations transformed the PLO into a legitimate national liberation movement without its having to renounce terrorism. Annual propaganda events such as Palestinian Solidarity Day (under UN auspices), which erase Israel from the map of "Palestine," have further encouraged the message that violence pays. Moreover, the UN Relief and Works Agency (UNRWA), which still funds the refugee camps for Palestinians, has, in effect, perpetuated their status as a homeless people for sixty years—a unique case in the postwar world. The wealth of the oil-rich Gulf states, rather than being channeled to rehabilitate the refugees, has been consistently misused to stoke the fire of Palestinian anger against Israel. The camps, by fostering the myth of the "return" (linked to the jihad for reconquering *all* of Palestine), have only reinforced terrorism and the Arab fantasy of eliminating the Jewish state.

For more than three decades the United Nations has provided a world stage for the global dissemination of a viciously anti-Zionist and anti-Jewish propaganda. Western states have generally failed to neutralize this plague promptly or vigorously enough. Thus, ill-informed citizens, especially in Third World countries (where UN resolutions always enjoyed great prestige), have been easily deceived. The obscene denigration of the Jewish people has become enshrined in many UN documents, bringing the demonization of Israel an unknown degree of respectability. The general opprobrium attached to racism and apartheid has been gradually transferred to Zionism, which has increased the power of the anti-Israel forces at the UN, cemented relations between its Arab and African blocs, and (incidentally) driven a wedge between black and Jewish communities in the United States.[76]

It took sixteen years of intense political and diplomatic struggle to repeal the infamous Zionism = Racism resolution. The campaign proceeded in fits and starts, and did not initially gain any enthusiastic support from top Israeli politicians. Indeed, twenty years ago it seemed as if the issue of repealing Zionism = Racism was higher on the policy agenda of the United States than it was for Israel. It was the U.S. assistant secretary of state for international organizations, Alan Keyes, who insisted in 1986: "Of all the UN wars, that [which is] waged against Israel has been in many ways the most persistent, insidious and offensive . . . [and has] embodied a shameless double standard, reflecting an unbridled hatred that leaves no room for fair judgment or a search for equitable solutions."[77]

Five years later, the U.S.-led victory in the First Persian Gulf War opened a new window of opportunity. For the first time the Zionism = Racism issue was addressed directly by a U.S. president, George H. W. Bush. In a firm statement of September 23, 1991, to the UN General Assembly, the elder Bush explained:

> Zionism is not a policy, it is the idea that led to the creation of a home for the Jewish people, to the State of Israel. And to equate Zionism with the intolerable sin of racism is to twist history and forget the terrible plight of the Jews in World War II and indeed, throughout history. To equate Zionism with racism is to reject Israel itself, a member of good standing of the United Nations. This body cannot claim to seek peace and at the same time challenge Israel's right to exist. By repealing this resolution uncon-

ditionally, the United Nations will enhance its credibility and the cause of peace.[78]

The next day, the new Soviet foreign minister, Boris Pankin, in his address to the assembly, dramatically followed suit, calling on the United Nations to "once and for all leave behind the legacy of the ice age, like the obnoxious resolution equating Zionism with racism." The Chinese foreign minister also made it plain that his government believed the wording of the 1975 UN resolution was a gross distortion of the truth and a slander against the Jewish people. Clearly, the world had changed greatly since 1975. The Soviet empire had unraveled, China was well advanced on the road to capitalist modernization, there were growing splits in the Muslim and Arab world, and the power of the Third World had virtually dissolved. Above all, the United States had achieved a dominant influence as the sole remaining superpower. Only the Arab states, led by an intransigent Egypt (despite its peace treaty with Israel), stubbornly resisted any change. They were supported by eight non–Arab/Muslim countries—among them Cuba, North Korea, Sri Lanka, and Vietnam. The revocation of Resolution 3379 was finally achieved on December 16, 1991, passing by a decisive vote of 111 to 25, with 13 abstentions.[79]

Nevertheless, the optimistic belief that this was a historic watershed in the United Nations' relationship to Israel, the Jews, and anti-Semitism has proven to be premature. Although the Cold War is over, the United Nations is far from having abandoned its penchant for sterile rhetoric, gross inversions of historical truth, and reckless slander against the Jewish state. Between the repeal of the Zionism = Racism resolution in December 1991 and the 2001 UN World Conference Against Racism, Racial Discrimination, Xenophobia, and Related Intolerance, Israel did not suddenly cease to be Everyman's favorite international pariah. Nor did the "Palestinian problem" (inflamed by the first intifada between 1988 and 1992) fade away as a result of the Oslo peace process. On the contrary, ritual indictments and condemnations of Israel at the United Nations continued as if the Zionism = Racism resolution had never been repealed and there were no dialogue between Israelis and Palestinians. In the new world order, the cause of Palestine became virtually synonymous for many with human rights itself, and Israel was increasingly vilified as *the* systematic violator of international law.[80]

The UN conference in Durban at the end of August 2001 brought such trends to a new peak. At this major international gathering, ostensibly devoted to the fight against racism, Israel was singled out "as a sort of modern-day geopolitical Anti-Christ." A flood of anti-Semitic slanders mixed with political criticism of Israel, Iranian-inspired conspiracy theories, Trotskyist anti-Zionism, and hecklers chanting "Jew, Jew, Jew" under the banner of human rights, filled the streets and characterized the sessions. Recalling the Durban masquerade, Canadian MP Irwin Cotler observed:

> Durban became the tipping point for the coalescence of a new, virulent, globalizing anti-Jewishness reminiscent of the atmospherics that pervaded Europe in the 1930s. In its lethal form, this animus finds expression as state-sanctioned genocidal anti-Semitism, such as that embraced by Mahmoud Ahmadinejad's Iran, and its terrorist proxies, Hamas and Hezbollah.[81]

One of the flyers distributed at Durban had a picture of Adolf Hitler with a question below: "What would have happened if I had won? The Good things. There would have been no Israel and no Palestinian's [sic] bloodshed. The Rest is your guess." Along with such obscene flyers, the anti-Semitic *Protocols of the Elders of Zion* were freely handed out, together with mountains of Islamic, Arab, leftist, and anti-globalist propaganda relating to Israel as a racist, theocratic, and apartheid state. The NGO Forum in Durban was especially virulent in its relativizing references to genocide, holocausts (with a small "h"), and the "ethnocide" against Palestinians supposedly carried out by Israel.[82] If that were not enough, the United Nations made Durban the centerpiece of its future "antiracism" agenda—thereby allowing follow-up resolutions to become a further forum for denouncing the Jewish state.[83]

There are those who draw hope from the more recent UN willingness to institute an annual Holocaust remembrance event—this, after a prolonged sixty-year bout of amnesia concerning the mass murder of Europe's Jews. But this is small change indeed, as long as the United Nations continues to foment rather than condemn the contemporary crime of "Zionicide"—or the attempted genocide directed against Israeli Jews. As human rights scholar Anne Bayefsky has explained:

Instead of championing Jewish self-determination, the UN leads the global movement to undermine it. UN conferences, web sites and publications regularly include comparisons of Israeli to Nazi Germany or apartheid South Africa. Israel is a second-class citizen at the UN, as the only country not fully admitted to any one of the UN's five strategic regional groups.[84]

Not only is there a long-standing institutional discrimination within the United Nations, but a third of all critical resolutions passed by its Human Rights Commission during the past forty years have been directed exclusively at Israel. By way of comparison, there has not been a single resolution even mentioning the massive violations of human rights in China, Russia, North Korea, Cuba, Saudi Arabia, Syria, or Zimbabwe. In the month of December 2005 alone, the General Assembly adopted nineteen resolutions critical of human rights in Israel and only twelve for all the other 190 UN states combined. At the same time, the UN General Assembly defeated a resolution condemning the horrors committed in Darfur, Sudan, by a Muslim Arab regime, which had already created two million displaced refugees and more than two hundred thousand dead in the preceding three years.[85] The tyrannical, automatic majorities of the Nonaligned Movement, which once again shaped such disgraceful outcomes, have produced mockery of human rights. Most of the members of this so-called nonaligned club are authoritarian, anti-Western regimes that habitually repress their own citizens. Naturally, it suits them to make Israel their universal scapegoat for worldwide human rights violations.

The deplorable combination of discrimination, delegitimation, and double standards at the United Nations (including in its newly created Human Rights Council) has, in recent decades, been a lethal source of globalized anti-Semitism. The ancient plague proliferates under the mask of criticizing the Jewish state while covering up the crimes of a long list of dictators and despots.[86] At the same time, the bias and venom against Israel is structurally built into the propaganda apparatus of the Division for Palestinian Rights in the UN Secretariat.[87] The UN-financed group flies the UN flag and operates globally to encourage divestment and academic boycott campaigns against Israel. This propaganda apparatus systematically condemns any Israeli defensive measures against terrorist suicide bombings, beginning with the security fence.[88] At the same time, UN human rights commissioners will invariably turn a blind eye to Hamas and Hezbollah violence and to the intimidation and killing of Israeli civilians, and ignores anti-Semitic incitement by Muslims.

In the UN General Assembly and the international human rights community, antiracism has never seriously included the struggle against anti-Semitism. On the contrary, the United Nations has been far more concerned with greatly inflated charges of "Israeli racism" against Arabs and with isolating Israel as an "apartheid state."[89] The "South African strategy" of equating Zionism and apartheid, which has been in place for well over thirty years, is gathering ever greater momentum, especially among fundamentalist Muslims, leftists, liberals, human rights activists, NGOs, and within the UN system as a whole.[90] In this context, the deification of the Palestinian cause becomes inextricably tied to the demonization of Israel. The UN special rapporteur for the Human Rights Commission, John Dugard—a white South African law professor—could scarcely contain his admiration for the "new determination, daring, and success" of the Palestinian suicide bombers in spawning "terror in the Israeli heartland." The one-sided mandate of the special rapporteur, it needs to be said, was solely established to investigate *Israeli* violations of international law. Human rights violations by Palestinians *against* Jews cannot, indeed, be addressed at all in the UN framework. Unlike Arabs, when Israelis or Jews fall victim to Palestinian terror, for example, they are never designated by their ethnic or national identity.[91]

The palpably misleading UN-promoted claim that occupation of Palestinian land is the root cause of the Arab-Israeli conflict has by now become an undisputed dogma and is even blamed for fueling global anti-Semitism. In the United Nations and in much of Europe today, the so-called occupation is responsible for Arab poverty, lack of democracy, denial of equal rights for women, and acts of gratuitous terrorism around the world. It is enough to pronounce the word "occupation" and all critical thinking stops. Since the Israeli "occupation" (even after the withdrawal from Gaza) has become a synonym in UN rhetoric for "Nazi-Israeli apartheid," to dismantle it by terrorist violence or economic boycott can easily be interpreted as a *moral* imperative.[92] So, too, the hostility toward those Jews who identify with Israel comes to be seen by its perpetrators and even by onlookers as a laudable act.

The seemingly endless repetition of the apartheid libel over the past three decades has proven to be a particularly effective tactic in defaming Israel. Standing behind this fiction one can find not only an extensive UN apparatus and vast swathes of "progressive" opinion (among them *Jewish* liberals, leftists, and professional Palestinian propagandists) but also a broad network of NGOs, including respectable organizations such as Human Rights Watch, Amnesty International and Christian Aid.[93] Their unrelenting campaign against Israel's security barrier to protect its citizens from suicide bombers is a major example of how contemporary political doublespeak continues to dominate international discourse on the Middle East.

On December 8, 2003, the security fence became the object of a UN General Assembly resolution requesting an advisory opinion from the International Court of Justice (ICJ) in The Hague. This Palestinian and Arab tactic was combined with an extensive worldwide propaganda campaign.[94] The Palestinian Authority's permanent observer at the United Nations, Nasser al-Kidwa, presented the security wall as an Israeli attempt to entrench the occupation and annex large areas of Palestinian land. He expressed the hope that a ruling against the fence would pave the way for international sanctions against Israel, similar to those taken against South Africa.[95] The ICJ ignored the reasons why Israel built the fence (Palestinian terror) and effectively handed the Palestinian Authority and its supporters in the UN General Assembly a significant propaganda victory. Even the Europeans voted with the 150 countries in favor of the draft resolution demanding Israel comply with the ICJ ruling. Apart from Israel itself, only the United States, Australia, and three tiny Pacific islands opposed the resolution. Once again the power of the automatic majority against Israel in the UN General Assembly had been demonstrated. In his public statements hailing the outcome, al-Kidwa termed the fence the "apartheid wall" and Israel an "outlaw" state for not complying with the UN demands or the World Court.[96] The Arab strategy to isolate Israel as a pariah state and undermine its international legitimacy found its strongest support—as in the past—within the UN General Assembly; this time, however, it was reinforced by world public opinion and the international legal courts.

The stigma of Israel as an apartheid state is much more entrenched than it was thirty years ago, despite the fact that Israeli laws have always guaranteed equal citizenship to its Arab minority. The accusers never explain why

the Jewish state is more racist than Pakistan or Saudi Arabia (which officially call themselves "Islamic" states) or than nations that have recognized
the special position of Catholicism and any other established Christian
churches in their domain. Nor did Israel ever develop an ideology or practice about the right of a "white minority" to dominate its "nonwhite inferiors." Yet, in 2002, the highly respected Anglican churchman Archbishop
Desmond Tutu chose to blur all rational distinctions and place "apartheid
Israel" on the moral level of Adolf Hitler, Joseph Stalin, General Pinochet,
Slobodan Milošević, and Idi Amin.[97]

Former U.S. president Jimmy Carter is another prominent celebrity who
has systematically abused the term "apartheid" in the context of Israel and
Palestine. In his recent book *Peace Not Apartheid,* Carter's visceral dislike
for Israelis (secular and religious) is all pervasive. For a would-be mediator
who consistently whitewashed the practices of such outstanding human
rights abusers as Kim Il Sung, Nicolae Ceausescu, Hafez al-Assad, Saddam
Hussein, and the present-day Saudi rulers, his indignation at Israel's violation of Palestinian national rights seems remarkably disproportionate. He
naturally avoids any serious reference to Arab rejectionism, Israeli security
problems, Palestinian terrorist violence (in Carter's historical account
Arafat emerges as a "Christian" pacifist), or Hamas-like jihadism. In
Carter's biased perception of the Middle East conflict, peace is totally dependent on Israel's compliance with "international law." His rancor extends
beyond Israel to American Jews, whom he has accused of seeking to suppress views like his own, despite the very extensive publicity his own book
attracted. Carter has been no less vociferous in lashing out at Israel's antiterrorist barrier as an "imprisonment wall" and a prime example of the segregationist, apartheid Israeli society that he believes has emerged in the
Holy Land.[98]

The reality is that South African apartheid never had anything in common with Israeli democratic structures, with the ethos of Israeli society, or
with its fundamental values. In an apartheid Israel, Muslim Arab voters and
legislators could never influence the outcome of elections as they have often
done in the past. The country's literary prize would never have gone to an
Arab. Road signs throughout Israel would not be indicated in Arabic as well
as in Hebrew and English. Nor would the Jewish state open its universities
to Arab students, let alone permit viscerally anti-Israeli human rights organizations to operate freely within its borders. In an apartheid state, there

would never be articles galore in the Israeli press about the Zionist project being a failure—some of them written by Arabs as well as Jews. A so-called Zio-Nazi or apartheid state would hardly bother to translate hostile Palestinian authors, such as the late Edward Said, into Hebrew.[99] Nor would such a Nazified state permit its supreme court to consistently defend the human rights of Israeli Arabs and Palestinians against army interventions or considerations of national security. Yet the intellectual shallowness and mendacity of the apartheid comparison has in no way limited or prevented its broad acceptance. Indeed, the Zionism = Apartheid equation has turned into a kind of litmus test for defining individual membership in the so-called progressive camp.[100]

Though it dates back to the 1970s, the hyperbolic rhetoric about "apartheid Israel" is mainstream today, not confined to Jimmy Carter, Desmond Tutu, liberal opinion in the West, the UN, and the NGOs that revel in such high-flown stigmatization of the Jewish state. Jewish and Israeli anti-Zionists as well are often in the forefront of this discourse, organizing or promoting "Israel Apartheid Week" in foreign capitals in order to denigrate their nation and country. At a conference in London of the School for Oriental and African Studies (SOAS) in December 2004, one Israeli *yored* (emigrant), Haim Breeshith, emphasized to his British audience that Israeli apartheid was much worse than the South African model since it had "expelled and committed genocide against its native population."[101] Similar sentiments have been repeated ad nauseam by Israeli pacifists and leftists, including the late Tanya Reinhardt, Ilan Pappé, Uri Davis, and others. This is also the position of South Africa's most prominent Jewish cabinet minister, Ronnie Kasrils, who has never lost an opportunity to execrate Israel's "fascist-style brutality" against the Palestinians. In a message to the organizers of "Israeli Apartheid Week" in London, Kasrils (a longtime Communist and a member of the African National Congress for the last twenty years) bluntly attacked the UN Partition Plan of 1947. In his perception it "set in motion the monstrous Zionist plot to violently dispossess the Palestinian people of their land and rights, and their dispersal through serial ethnic cleansing that has continued in one form or another to this day."[102] Kasrils's demonization of Zionism as a "monstrous plot" is precisely the kind of invention that was pioneered in the United Nations more than thirty years ago and has become such a popular mantra in our time. Zionism equals racism, equals colonialism, equals occupation, equals dispossession. No empirical proofs, rational demonstrations, or impartial historical evidence are ever required in order to validate such self-evident axioms or "progressive" self-reinforcing tautologies. Its main claim to truth lies in its compulsive repetition; its primary goal remains the stigmatization and dismantlement of Israel.

The ideological foundations for this assault were laid in the United Nations during the mid-1970s under the cover of "Palestinian rights" and anti-Zionism. The Jewish state was verbally crucified as a "poisoner of the international wells," a repository of global vice and crime.[103] This "new" discourse has been the contemporary analogue of classical and theological anti-Semitism.[104] It has decried Israel as a warmongering rogue state that does not morally deserve to exist. Under the self-righteous mask of antiracism, anti-apartheid, and UN protection, a thoroughly corrupted language of defamation seeks to belatedly abort the creation of Israel just over sixty years ago.

Nothing illustrates this betrayal more clearly than the buildup to the Durban II conference held in Geneva April 20–24, 2009. Like its notorious predecessor, eight years earlier, its planning was hijacked early on by the Islamic states and NGOs whose primary goal has been to single out and demonize Israel as an apartheid state and perpetrator of genocide against the Palestinians.[105] In truth, a conference whose organizing committee has been chaired by Libya (with Iran, Pakistan, and Cuba as vice-chairs), Durban II could hardly provide an appropriate forum for any serious progress on human rights. Despite this, the United States under George Bush and then the new Obama administration took a surprisingly long time to follow the lead of Canada and Israel, finally pulling out of this ignominious farce. Already in October 2008, an eighty-eight-page Durban II draft declaration set the stage—accusing the United States, Israel, Western Europe, and other liberal democracies of racist attitudes and policies against Islam. Naturally there was not a word devoted to the hundreds of thousands of innocent victims murdered on racist grounds in Sudan, or the atrocities inflicted in the Congo and Kenya. At the same time, while singling out Israel as an enemy of humanity, the draft resolution pushed to criminalize defamations of religion—a proposal made by Muslim nations and ratified by the UN Human Rights Council in March 2009.

Another symptom of UN perverseness has been the anti-Israel venom spewed by General Assembly president Miguel d'Escoto Brockmann. An ordained Catholic priest from Nicaragua, the leftist Brockmann has demanded international sanctions against Israel, whom he accuses of "crucifying" the Palestinians. His repellent remarks branding Israel as an apartheid state were made on November 24, 2008, during an event marking the 1947 UN General Assembly partition resolution for Palestine. They represented a gross abuse of his position as a supposedly impartial symbol of the United Nations. Brockmann had previously (in September 2008) embraced Holocaust-denying Iranian president Mahmoud Ahmadinejad, after the latter's UN speech unabashedly echoed conspiracy theories of Jewish world domination. Such a degeneration of the UN (which had acted as Israel's midwife in 1947) reveals the shocking extent to which it has betrayed its core principles and mission.

FOURTEEN

The Anti-Zionist Masquerade

On October 11, 1982, the Soviet Communist Party newspaper *Pravda* featured a political cartoon in which Israel's prime minister was shown carrying a sword marked "Blitzkrieg," while at his feet appeared the word "genocide" and a pile of skull bones to illustrate the point. Behind him stood a grinning Hitler in full uniform, hand outstretched in a *Sieg Heil* salute, while a sign on the right-hand side of the cartoon read, "Concentration camp for Arabs." On the left an Israeli steamroller, replete with the American dollar sign, was shown executing "scorched earth tactics." A caption below read: "The aggressor from the Nazi learns. Rivers of blood flow in his path. But the Fascist bands of Zionists will not escape the people's court!" Similar caricatures, emphasizing the "genocidal" policies of the Israeli "expansionists," wreaking havoc on innocent Palestinian Arabs and Lebanese civilians, would flood the Soviet press after the Israeli invasion of Lebanon in June 1982.

In a message to Yasser Arafat, Soviet president and Communist Party leader Leonid Brezhnev commented that "this is the same genocide against Palestinians that the Nazis committed against other people during World War II."[1] Soviet media continued to embellish the same theme, exploiting the massacre carried out at the refugee camps of Sabra and Shatila, which was with deliberate falsehood attributed to the Israeli army. (The direct responsibility lay with the Christian Phalangist militia.) The ideological offensive against "Israeli fascism" was carried out with relentless fervor, even by Soviet standards, while never forgetting to stress direct American complicity in the war at every level. Nevertheless, the central issue, as one Tass political commentator coolly observed, "is not the simple coincidence of ideological aims and political methods of militant Zionists and Fascism—

but the fact that in Israel the Zionist and Fascist regime has gained a foothold and shown its true face, in essence placing itself outside the world community."[2]

The Soviet government newspaper was equally categorical. According to *Izvestia*, the crimes of the Nazi barbarians were not merely being repeated, but "the Fascist clique headed by Begin and those like him are trying to surpass them."[3] Soviet media did not hesitate to compare Israeli "atrocities" in Lebanon with crimes committed by the Germans at Babi Yar on the outskirts of Kiev in September 1941. At the same time, Zionists were accused of collaborating with the Nazis to massacre Soviet civilians. An article in the leading Soviet trade union newspaper, *Trud*, even asserted that although one of the branches of fascism had been cut off in 1945, "another, having found conditions favorable, blossomed and bore horrible fruit in the environment of the Zionist elite of Israel."[4] Such examples, perpetually twinning the Nazi swastika and the Star of David as symbols of genocidal fascism, underlined the visceral hostility behind Moscow's policy toward Israel and Soviet Jewry in the early 1980s.

Anti-Zionism had, of course, long been a constant of Communist ideology. Since the last years of Stalin's rule, age-old Judeophobic canards had been channeled into Soviet propaganda against Israel, Jews, and Jewish institutions.[5] But the orchestrated campaign that unfolded in 1982, and the unexpected resonance it found in the West, eroded the already flimsy distinctions between anti-Zionism and anti-Semitism inherited from the past. Indeed, Stalin had initiated the crucial shift in terminology in the late 1940s when he sought to mask his campaign against Soviet Jews.[6] It was out of the question in a Marxist-Leninist state to attack Jews as a racial or ethnic group. But this objection emphatically did not apply to so-called Zionists or to the ideology of Zionism, understood as a transnational conspiracy to take over the world.[7]

Anti-Zionism seemed immune to criticism precisely because it could be dissociated from hatred of a particular nation or minority group. It had originally defined itself in opposition to the idea of creating a *Jewish state* in Palestine. Before 1948, anti-Zionism had been especially widespread in the Jewish world—among assimilationists, Orthodox Jews, Reform Jews, Bundists, and liberals, as well as Communists.[8] Stalin himself, like other Marxists in the USSR and beyond, had always been anti-Zionist in theory, though in 1947–48, he acted as godfather to the Jewish state for reasons of Soviet *Realpolitik*. But "anti-Zionism" assumed new dimensions once it became associated with a vast, global conspiratorial theory.[9]

By the early 1950s the concept of "international Zionism" had come to assume all those demonic characteristics formerly attributed by radical anti-Semites to the mythical forces of "world Jewry."[10] This conspiratorial vision of Zionism, shared by Arab nationalists, fundamentalist Muslims, neo-Nazis, Communists, and Third World ideologues, assumed the existence of a dangerous, shadowy international conglomerate with its political headquarters in New York and Tel Aviv. The terminology of this post-1945 anti-Jewishness would no longer be predominantly Christian, fascist, or racist but neo-Marxist, Islamic, or anti-globalist. Nonetheless, there were similarities and continuities between the old anti-Semitism and the new anti-Zionism.[11]

The transformation of contemporary anti-Zionism into an engine of war against the Jews became manifest soon after the end of World War II. There was an urgent need for useful euphemisms and labels that could deflect unwelcome charges of racial bias.[12] The Nazi genocide had given anti-Semitism a bad name, at least in official government policy. But there were no laws against defaming Zionists. They could be presented as agents of a noxious creed and servants of a pernicious system, rather than as Jews in the national or religious meaning of the term. As a prominent Soviet publicist put it in 1971: "A person who adopts the Zionist faith automatically becomes an agent of the international Zionist concern and consequently an enemy of the Soviet people."[13]

Neo-Stalinist anti-Zionism was built on the myth fabricated by the czarist secret police around 1900 in the *Protocols of the Elders of Zion*.[14] It viewed Zionism not as an attempt to achieve Jewish national liberation through territorial concentration in a Jewish state, but rather as the adjunct of a mysterious international Mafia—a "Jewish world-enemy"—with a vast intelligence system and unlimited financial resources at its disposal.[15] This slogan, with its Nazi roots, was far removed from the Marxist critique of "petty-bourgeois" Zionism espoused by Lenin and the generation of Bolshevik revolutionary internationalists who had founded the Soviet Union. In *Mein Kampf*, Adolf Hitler had already laid the foundations for this *Protocols* version of anti-Zionism. He made it clear that the creation of a Palestinian Jewish state was nothing but a façade. The Jewish international financiers simply needed a "central organization" to facilitate their plans for world domination.[16]

Adolf Hitler, Alfred Rosenberg, and other Nazi ideologues, far from supporting the establishment of a Jewish state in Palestine (as postwar Soviet and Arab propaganda pretended), adamantly opposed this proposal. Such a state was consistently perceived as part of an international Jewish conspiracy. At best it would be "a haven for convicted scoundrels and a university for budding crooks," as Hitler so crudely put it in 1924; more dangerously, as German foreign minister Konstantin von Neurath explained in June 1937, an independent Jewish state would serve as a political base for *das Weltjudentum* (world Jewry), just as Moscow did for Communists or the Vatican for Catholics. It was one thing for the Nazis to use Palestine as a convenient dumping ground for unwanted German Jews between 1933 and 1938; it was quite another to support the goal of a Jewish state that could economically dominate the Middle East and would politically oppose National Socialism.[17]

Between 1938 and 1945, Nazi propagandists and research institutions began to produce an array of works in which anti-Zionism and anti-Semitism fully converged under the banner of the global Jewish conspiracy. In these writings and broadcasts, British (and later American) policy in the Middle East was derided as a tool of world Jewry's financial power. The British upper stratum, its aristocratic elites, and Churchill himself allegedly acted as a fifth column for international Jewish interests. The "English war" against the Nazi Reich and the Arabs was in reality a "Jewish war" based on common capitalist motives and a messianic desire to dominate the world. Once the United States entered the war, similar accusations were directed at the Roosevelt administration, unmasking the Jewish machinations that supposedly controlled American Middle East policy. As Nazi links with Islamic and Arab nationalist circles grew, support for the Palestinian Arabs also intensified. Nazi literature emphasized their "freedom struggle" against "British betrayal," the "Atlantic swindle," and insatiable Jewish greed. Zionism, as the quintessential expression of this materialistic "Jewish essence," was transformed into a deadly enemy of both Germans and Arabs. Thus opposition to a Zionist state and full support for Arab nationalist aspirations became a national security issue for Nazi Germany in its global struggle against Britain, America, Communism, and the *Weltfeind* (Jewish world-enemy).

The Nazis did not, therefore, oppose the Zionist movement out of genuine sympathy for the idea of Palestinian Arab national self-determination. They attacked Zionism as the epitome of the Judaic will to power, as a "Jewish imperialism" whose true goal was to destroy the state structures of the Aryan world. Zionism sought global *empire* under the benign cover of recognition for an independent Jewish Palestine. Stalinists and Arab propagandists of the 1950s usurped this Nazi paradigm while shedding its racial terminology. The taint was no longer hereditary. Its deeper roots lay in the Bible and in the *doctrine* of Zionism, redefined as "criminal" in its essence and roots.

For the Nazis, "Jewish Bolshevism" had always been a crucial link in the vast international Jewish conspiracy connecting Moscow with Wall Street and the City of London. For Stalin, however, the world Zionist cabal was primarily seen as a conspiracy to subvert the Soviet Union and the Socialist camp.[18] In both mythologies, the Jewish state was merely the mask for achieving global domination through a complex network of international financiers and capitalist monopolies.[19] More important, "Zionists" became a code word for spies, saboteurs, assassins, and beastly agents of "American warmongers" who sought to destroy the Communist system from within. In the Cold War climate of the early 1950s, Jewish nationalism had turned from an ideological deviation into the capital crime of treason against the Soviet fatherland and the socialist state.[20] The anti-Zionist campaigns in Czechoslovakia after the crushing of dissent in August 1968, the mass expulsions of Jews from Poland in the same year, and the attack on the "Zionist revisionist" elements in the Polish trade union Solidarity in 1981 followed a familiar pattern orchestrated by Moscow.[21] In each case anti-Zionism was cynically exploited as a tool to crush dissent and repress trends toward liberalization, democratization, and greater freedom in Eastern Europe.[22]

The political expediency of anti-Zionism was also apparent in Soviet foreign policy. Starting in the mid-1950s it proved to be an effective means of penetrating the Middle East, the Muslim world, and the Afro-Asian bloc. Nazi Germany had successfully exploited anti-Semitism as a weapon in its foreign policy during the 1930s. Anti-Zionism would be no less useful thirty years later in promoting Soviet arms sales to the Arab enemies of Israel. Moreover, it proved easy enough to fuse anti-Zionism with other pillars of Soviet ideology, such as anti-Americanism, anticapitalism, "antiracialism" and antifascism. During the 1960s, for example, before West Germany initiated its *Ostpolitik* (Eastern Policy), anti-Zionism conveniently fitted in to the Soviet political offensive against West German "revanchism." In the 1970s the focus shifted to the so-called Tel Aviv–Pretoria Axis (slyly evoking memories of the Nazi-Fascist "Pact of Steel") portraying Zionism as a Trojan horse of imperialism and racism in the Third World.[23] The main function of Israel in international affairs was to further American exploitation of Africa and consolidate "neo-colonialist" rule over the oil-rich Middle East.[24]

In the West, too, anti-Zionism had become a more potent force by the mid-1970s, encouraged by commercial and military-industrial interests, not to mention the politics of appeasement. The rise of Arab financial and diplomatic muscle power after the 1973 oil crisis accelerated the shift in Western (especially European) perceptions of the Arab-Israeli conflict, first toward an evenhanded, then a highly critical, view of Israel, which veered at times toward open hostility.[25] The First Lebanon War, and especially the carnage in Beirut during the summer of 1982, was flashed night after night across the world's television screens and reinforced the antagonism to Israel, leading even former friends to question the premises of Zionism itself. Ugly stereotypes of the "Israeli-Zionist militarists," long the stock-in-trade of Communist and Arab propaganda, began to penetrate the mainstream politics of the Western world. At one time, such images had been the preserve of sectarian extremist groups of the Far Right or the Far Left— neo-Nazi, Trotskyist, or Maoist. However, by the mid-1970s, liberals, social democrats, and conservative pro-Arab circles began to jump on the anti-Zionist bandwagon, lending a new respectability to what had once seemed confined to the language of Soviet Newspeak. As Israel-baiting began to proliferate in the summer of 1982, previously suppressed anti-Jewish feelings in the West boiled to the surface. These toxic sentiments, exacerbated by a powerful wave of anti-Americanism, have become visible for all to see in recent years.[26]

One of the first European commentators to appreciate the significance of the new trend was the former editor of the London *Observer,* Conor Cruise O'Brien, whose experience in Irish politics and at the United Nations may have sharpened his eye for the intellectual dishonesty behind the anti-Zionist masquerade. Quoting from letters to *The Guardian,* O'Brien noted that an increasing number of people in Great Britain these days "like to say 'Israel' and 'Hitler' in one breath and convey to others their conviction that the two are in some way the same thing."[27] But this new refrain was not confined to Britons. "Incident by incident, atrocity by atrocity, Americans are coming to see the Israeli government as pounding the Star of David into a swastika," wrote U.S. journalist Nicholas von Hoffman in June 1982 in a conservative London weekly, as he compared Lebanon with Lidice.[28] The implications went far beyond the right to criticize specific Israeli policies, with which (then as now) anti-Zionism is so often confused. Israel's friends and Jews in general were made to feel complicit with "Hitlerian" policies unless they would unequivocally denounce Zionism. They were guilty by association in the "attempted genocide of the Palestinian people"; hence "the day will come when an increasing number of non-Jews in Europe and America say that perhaps Hitler had a point," to quote one letter to the editor mentioned by O'Brien.[29]

Similar examples could be cited from the influential French daily Le Monde, which had excelled in pillorying Israel behind a high-minded mask of mandarin objectivity and schoolmasterly rectitude. Always the master of subtle insinuation, Le Monde was among the pioneers in Western highbrow journalism of the technique of turning public revulsion against anti-Semitism and Nazism into a stick with which to beat Israel.[30] Indeed, the paper was a leading proponent of the idea that Zionists in their prejudices, passions, and behavior were simply a new version of the old anti-Semitic European Right and even of the Nazis.[31] During the First Lebanon War in 1982, the French daily was full of rabid outpourings against "le fascisme, aujourd'hui aux couleurs d'Israel" (fascism in contemporary Israeli colors) and vitriolic calumnies against Israel as the inventor of a new anti-Semitism— "a racism directed against the sons of Shem," meaning the Palestinian Arabs.[32]

While crowning Palestinian Arab terrorism with the martyr's wreath of "resistance" against Nazi-Zionist occupation, Le Monde did not shrink from drawing a parallel between the Israeli destruction of Kuneitra on the Golan Heights and the burning of the village of Oradour-sur-Glane in central France, whose population had been massacred by the SS in 1944. Almost as virulent in its anti-Israelism and anti-Americanism as the Communist daily L'Humanité, but intellectually far more sophisticated and prestigious, Le Monde, like much of the Western news media, positively gloated over the erosion of Israel's image during the Lebanon War, blasting the "vocation suicidaire" (suicidal mission) of the Begin government and the "Nazi war crimes" perpetrated by the Israeli army. *Le Monde* did not demonstrate a similar compassion for human suffering when it came to inter-Arab conflicts such as the Iran-Iraq War (one million dead on both sides) or the Syrian leadership's cold-blooded massacre in 1982 of twenty thousand "enemies" of the regime in the city of Hama—mostly civilians of the majority Sunni Muslim Arab population. Nor was there much criticism of the Syrian occupation of Lebanon, let alone concern for the survival of the Lebanese Christian Maronites, during the Syrian bombardment of east Beirut and Zahle.

Such examples of double standards are legion. There have always been those ready to interpret this as a sign that the Western world expects higher standards from Jews. But was this really the case—then or now? Were the Western news media truly interested in the "morality" of Judaism, or in the Jewish conscience, except where it could be turned against Israel? Those voices who continually queried the *ethical* justification for Israel's existence never questioned the raison d'être of repressive Iranian, Syrian, or Sudanese regimes in terms of the morality of Islam. Britain's right to exist was not challenged in the light of the jingoist Falklands War, conducted in the summer of 1982, or measured against Christian pacifist principles; the Soviet Union's right to exist was not put under a microscope in the name of Marxist humanism because of "colonialist barbarities" perpetrated in Muslim Afghanistan during the 1980s. Rabid anti-Americanism does not generally lead its proponents to deny the right of the United States to its national independence. Despite its oppressive occupation of Tibet, nobody has denied that China is a legitimate nation.

On the political level, much of the concern with Jewish conscience seems, therefore, more like an attempt to play the Diaspora off against Israel or to delegitimize Zionism within its natural constituency. To hold *only* Israel to standards of absolute moral purity, to negate Zionism in the name of a timeless Judaism, or to compare the Jewish state with apartheid South Africa, is plainly perverse. So, too, is the attempt to stigmatize the Jewish national renaissance as a kind of original sin against God. Even worse is the obsession with feverishly turning Jews into Romans/Nazis while Arabs/Palestinians become the reincarnation of Diasporic Jews.[33] This has been a significant development in the history of post-Holocaust anti-Zionism.

The brief immunity that Israeli and Diaspora Jews enjoyed from European anti-Semitism after World War II was only superficially about guilt feelings. More important was the unconscious *Christianization* of the Jew as a model of sacrifice and a collective expression of Christ's suffering at Calvary. The prevailing postwar antifascist consensus helped consecrate this Christian image of the Jew as the paradigmatic victim. But the *Christological* image of the crucified Jewish people and of the Nazis as a metaphor of the eternal essence of evil has boomeranged against Jews with a vengeance. Europe mourns and commemorates the dead Jews of Auschwitz; it is much less enthused by those who fight for their lives in the land of Israel. They have been endlessly execrated for "crucifying" the Palestinian people in the Holy Land.

For many European Christians, the empowerment of relatively prosperous, powerful Jews in the post-1948 era as a politically independent, technologically advanced, and self-assertive power in the land of Jesus seems difficult to digest. This is especially true for those Christians whose vision of Zion has remained purely spiritual, ethereal, and disembodied. For them, Israel betrayed its mission from the moment it abandoned its role as model victim or exemplary sacrifice. Only a poor, powerless, disinherited "nation" such as the Palestinian Arabs could be permitted to collectively represent the vision of the Christian savior. This leftist-oriented form of "liberation theology" evidently appeals to many Catholics in Europe and Latin America; and it has been enthusiastically embraced by Palestinian Arab Christians as well as many Anglicans today.[34] Such views revive the anti-Semitism of traditional Christian replacement theology, negating the legitimacy of an independent Jewish *political* existence in Zion.

Anti-Zionism in the West draws on a latent Christian resentment that the Jew is no longer subordinate but has become master of his fate. To quote Charles de Gaulle's notorious sermon to the "Hebrews" of November 1967, Jews are an "elitist, self-assertive and dominant people."[35] For the Communists, on the other hand, Zionism is forever tainted with the "colonialist" stigma. Thus the Marxist historian Isaac Deutscher, in July 1967, vilified the Israelis as arrogant militarists, colonial occupiers, and oppressors of the Palestine Arabs.[36] No less revealing were the Third Worldist myths that swiftly emerged after the Six-Day War, especially among the younger generation of radicals involved in the student revolt of 1968. Their heroes came from the Third World—leaders of national-liberation movements with a Communist revolutionary halo, such as Mao Tse-tung, Ho Chi Minh, Che

Guevara, and Fidel Castro. Romantic Third Worldism led the student radicals to an instinctive identification with the Palestinians rather than with Israel.[37] This generation of New Left student activists (many of whose leaders in America and France were themselves Jewish) concentrated their fire on American imperialism and Western consumerist materialism, though they were often critical of the Soviet system as well.[38] Their image of Israel as a self-confident, coldly efficient power conflicted with their desire for solidarity with victims of oppression. The overwhelming Israeli military triumph of 1967 irredeemably damned it in the eyes of a whole generation of militants intoxicated by their identification with the vanquished.

For a Western postwar generation that had embraced Third World national liberation ideology, crimes against humanity were exclusively the preserve of colonialist aggressors. Palestinians were embraced as a poor, nonwhite, stateless people of refugees fighting for their homeland—paragons of resistance enjoying the halo of absolute victims. In defeating them, Israel had assumed the mantle of a conquering *Herrenvolk* (master race).[39] The New Left argumentation was scarcely different from official Communist rhetoric. Trotskyists were particularly vitriolic in their loathing for Israel as a racist, Nazi state whose destruction was an indispensable prerequisite for socialist revolution in the Middle East. Jewish radicals, especially conspicuous in Western Trotskyism, were often in the forefront of these denunciations. For the past forty years they and other radical Jews have exploited their ethnic origins to deflect charges of anti-Semitism whenever the Left negates Israel's right to exist.[40] Liberal Jewish progressives in Britain and America have joined the fray in recent years, pouring their scorn on Israel as an anachronism that should be replaced by a binational state.[41] Their espousal of universal human rights above ethnic loyalties invariably leads to blaming Israel exclusively for Palestinian suffering and questioning or denying its moral legitimacy.

Since the 1970s, solidarity with the PLO has inexorably led a section of the radical Left to equate the struggle against racism and anti-Semitism with the destruction of Israel as a progressive goal. In West Germany (where Jewish involvement with the Left was less extensive than in France or the United States), anti-Zionism produced some particularly macabre actions. For example, a leaflet signed by the anarcho-communist Black Rats in November 1969 justified the bombing of the *Gemeindehaus* (communal hall) of West Berlin's Jewish congregation on the anniversary of the *Kristallnacht* pogrom, while mocking German feelings of guilt.[42] The brochure declared that the time had come to stop doing penance for the gassing of Jews in World War II. It called for "pitiless combat" against "the combination of Fascism and Israeli Zionism."[43]

The Berlin trial in December 1972 of Horst Mahler (at that time an anarchist lawyer involved in the Baader-Meinhof terrorist movement) exposed the underlying anti-Semitism in such radical antifascism. In court Mahler read a polemical declaration of the Red Army Faction (RAF), justifying the murder of Israeli athletes at the Munich Olympic Games by Palestinian terrorists. The action was "anti-fascist . . . because it was in the memory of the 1936 Olympics." It was allegedly a blow against the strategy of imperialism and West Germany's law-and-order state. "Israel weeps crocodile tears. It has burned up its sportsmen like the Nazis did the Jews—incendiary material for the imperialist extermination policy."[44] Perhaps not surprisingly, Horst Mahler is today one of Germany's leading anti-Semites and an ideologue of the racist National Democratic Party.

Ulrike Meinhof, who gave evidence for Mahler, insisted that unless the German people were pronounced "not guilty" of fascism, they could not be mobilized for the revolution. The German Left and the Communists had failed to explain Auschwitz properly to the masses.[45] Anti-Semitism was simply anticapitalism—it expressed the unconscious longing of the people for Communism. Their justified hatred of finance capital and of the banks had been diverted by the Nazis against the Jews. "Auschwitz means that six million Jews were murdered and carted on to the rubbish dumps of Europe for being that which was maintained of them—'Money-Jews' " (*Geldjuden*).[46] Hence, the mass murder of these *Geldjuden* was not an act of racism but of class hatred. The German people must be pronounced "not guilty" of genocide and mobilized in the future for their apocalyptic mission of destroying global capitalism.

Like many leftists before and since, Ulrike Meinhof felt compelled to express her historical sense of identity with the Jews of the Warsaw ghetto. Her terrorist group, so she claimed, was suffering from treatment at the hands of the West German authorities similar to that which Jews experienced under the Third Reich.[47] The meaning of such "antifascist" fantasies would soon be revealed in the Entebbe hijacking saga. A member of Ulrike Meinhof's gang, Wilfried Böse, was involved in the June 27, 1976, hijacking of an Air France airbus flying from Tel Aviv to Paris. He and his comrades forced the plane to land at Entebbe in Idi Amin's Uganda as part of a terrorist operation masterminded by the notorious Venezuelan revolutionary Carlos the Jackal. Böse and his colleagues separated the Jewish passengers from the non-Jews, who were quickly released. It turned out, however, that some of the Entebbe hostages were survivors of Nazi concentration camps. One of the captives even showed Böse the ID number indelibly branded on his arm and told his captor that he could see no difference between the new postwar German generation and the Nazis. Once again, Jews were being *selected* by Germans to die, even though the Baader-Meinhof group claimed that they were *internationalists* fighting for world revolution.[48] The main difference between 1936 and 1976, as the spectacular Entebbe rescue of the hostages by Israeli paratroops soon revealed, was the presence of a highly trained Israeli army and its capacity to take bold action to rescue Jews in distress.

The New Left in Germany, as elsewhere, has been assiduous ever since the 1970s in its efforts to transform Palestinians, Third World migrants, guest workers, homosexuals, students, feminists, and other so-called oppressed groups into "the Jews of today." In the suspended limbo of their historical false consciousness, radical German leftists evidently believed they were overcoming the Nazi past, even as they began to repeat it in a new form.[49] Israel, it turned out, was judged by altogether different standards from other states. It alone was the living reincarnation of what the Third Reich had once represented—namely, racism in action.[50] In 1981 the German Jewish journalist Henryk Broder tellingly described the diversionary techniques underlying this historical and psychological campaign of self-delusion, in which Zionism emerged as a kind of bogeyman for explaining away the world's evils.[51] For his former comrades on the German Left it had become a matter of sacred principle that "the Jewish State must not be."[52] Indeed, during the past four decades, the destruction of Zionism has become a cardinal point in the ideological politics of the radical Left across the Western world.[53] They reject in theory and practice any concept of Jewish historical continuity, Jewish ethnic identity, or a living religious tradition, let alone the right of Jewish national self-determination in the land of Abraham, Joshua, and David. Alone among the nations of the world, Israel is singled out by the anti-Zionist Left (and growing numbers of liberals) as an *organic* obstacle to peace and progress. In the name of antiracism and their own subjective revolutionary utopias, the radicals negated any national framework for collective Jewish existence. Thus they could arrive at the chilling formula that parodies ancient Rome's drive to wipe out its Carthaginian rival: *Israel delenda est!* The Jewish state, having come to represent the principle of absolute injustice in its very essence and existence, *deserves* to be destroyed.[54]

Nevertheless, the anti-Zionist mythology of the *gauchistes* (leftists) has a different political goal from that of classical anti-Semitism. It does not seek to undermine the civic equality of Jews in bourgeois society. European anti-Zionists of the radical persuasion have no plans to confiscate Jewish property, expel Jews from the country, or to physically extirpate the biological roots of Jewry.[55] Their anti-Zionism aims at dismantling Israel—today the homeland of nearly five and a half million Jews.[56] In the event of a successful Arab or Iranian assault on Israel, those Jews who might physically survive the cataclysm would inevitably be turned into homeless wanderers or miserable refugees. They would again become totally dependent on the mercy of the nations, as they had been during the Holocaust, with the direst of consequences. In that crucial respect, anti-Zionism is no less genocidal than its anti-Jewish forerunners.

This did not prevent the renowned Norwegian author of *Sophie's World*, Jostein Gaarder, from embracing such a perspective during the Second Lebanon War of July and August 2006. Claiming to speak for his country's liberal conscience, he wrote in *Aftenposten*: "Israel is history. We no longer recognize the State of Israel. There is no way back. The State of Israel has raped the world's recognition and will get no peace until it lays down its weapons. The State of Israel in its current form is history."[57] Gaarder had a "new" gospel of statelessness and powerlessness to propose to Jews in place of the old conceit of "God's chosen people," which he considered arrogant and racist. Israel's "chosenness" had become a "license to kill," a mandate for "apartheid," "ethnic cleansing," the willful murder of children, and the systematic violation of international law. Enlightened Europe could no longer tolerate such "crimes against humanity." Indeed, according to Gaarder and other so-called intellectuals, contemporary Israel represented the apex and culmination of all postwar atrocities. It was a perfect amalgam of the apartheid regime in South Africa, the Taliban theocracy in Afghanistan, Saddam Hussein's tyranny in Iraq, and Serbian ethnic cleansing. In Gaarder's words, the State of Israel was built on apartheid, occupation, and a "license to kill" based on stone tablets and burning bushes.

Gaarder's conclusion was a macabre prophecy. Israelis would once more become a refugee people begging for the compassion of the world. Only then would they merit any sympathy: "Peace and right of passage for the fleeing civilians who no longer have a state that can protect them! Don't shoot at the refugees! Don't aim at them! They are as vulnerable as snails without their houses now, vulnerable like the slow-moving caravans of Palestinian and Lebanese refugees, defenseless as the women, children, and elderly in Qana, Gaza, and Sabra and Shatila. Give the Israeli refugees shelter, give them milk and honey!"[58] Such cynical compassion for Jews seemed conditional on the destruction of the Zionist state.[59] It did not extend to Israeli victims of Palestinian terror but could be taken to justify Israel's demise as an a priori moral objective.[60] Yet the liberal Left for the past thirty years has nonetheless insisted that it does not oppose Jews, only "Zionists."

Double standards in judging Israel and Zionism have been a prime source of its delegitimization.[61] This malady has been combined with a wholly uncritical attitude toward Palestinian terror organizations, extolled by Western progressives ever since the 1970s for their heroic resistance to Israeli imperialism. Yet Palestinian bomb attacks during the early 1980s in Paris, London, Rome, Milan, Antwerp, Brussels, Berlin, and Vienna against Jewish targets were anything but anti-imperialist or antifascist acts. They were, on the contrary, a deliberate extension of the anti-Zionist crusade to Diasporic Jewish communities. In the 1990s the expanding Muslim holy war against the Jewish state continued to pursue this PLO tactic of striking at the vulnerable Diasporic hinterland. A good example was the 1994 destruction of the Argentine Jewish community building in Buenos Aires, the largest single *anti-Semitic* bombing attack since World War II. Almost certainly planned in Tehran by the highest Iranian government officials and carried out by Hezbollah operatives with local complicity in Argentina, these assaults once more underscored the intertwining of Israeli and Jewish fate.[62] For today's Islamic anti-Semites, *all* Jews are irrevocably part of the Zionist fifth column and hence potential targets for annihilation.

The PLO terrorist war against Israel that began about forty years ago opened the door to this strategy. Its sinister possibilities were revealed in bombings such as those in Paris against the synagogue on rue Copernic in October 1980 and the machine-gun attack on the Goldenberg restaurant on rue des Rosiers on August 9, 1982. The Middle East connection to these odious crimes was soon apparent, along with their swift rationalization as blows struck by the Palestinian resistance against world imperialism and its

Zionist agents. Since Jews were now depicted as the real Nazis, it was surely as natural and moral to kill them as it would have been praiseworthy to assassinate Hitler and his henchmen. The rational conclusion of this rewriting of modern Jewish history as the Israeli Final Solution of the "Palestinian problem" was to glorify in advance any terrorist attacks on Israelis and Jews as resistance to Nazism.[63] Through such a perverse chain of reasoning, the Jewish tragedy of yesterday became the a priori justification for Arab retribution in the present and a herald of the future apocalypse.

The writing was already on the wall a quarter of a century ago. At the time of the 1982 Lebanon War I dissected the "new anti-Semitism" in the following terms:

> In the eyes of the world David has now become Goliath, the oppressed Jew has become the oppressor of Palestinians, the paradigmatic victims of history have become ruthless victors. As a result, contemporary anti-Semitism centers on the theme of Jewish arrogance, and hatred of Israel expresses itself in the name of the "wretched of the earth," the humble, the suffering and the vanquished. But the new anti-Semitism is still sufficiently embarrassed by the term *Jew*, with its emotive historical associations of Holocaust and mass murder, to avoid its use where possible.[64]

As I wrote these lines in *Partisan Review,* it struck me that anti-Zionism had induced "a self-satisfied innocence among those enemies of Israel, who claim only to be against imperialism, racism, oppression." I made it clear that "the only beneficiaries of this vicious campaign can be the enemies of the West—the Soviet Union, the Islamic fundamentalists, and the radical forces of the Arab and Third Worlds."[65] The libel of Zionist Nazism, so carefully orchestrated by the Communist rulers in the Soviet Union, had spread with surprisingly little resistance to the West, where it was nourished by the images of nightly Israeli bombing raids over Lebanon, the excessive flexing of Israeli military muscle, and the unpopular actions of the Begin-Sharon government. Unfortunately, successive Israeli governments have learned little from that experience, whether in the field of actual policy or public relations.

An infernal dialectic was set in motion that has proved difficult to reverse. The memory of the Shoah, relentlessly politicized and abused on all sides, was one casualty of the violent polemics following the First Lebanon War, as I wrote in 1983:

> From the standpoint of Israel's enemies and of anti-Semites everywhere, the mass murder of European Jewry and the backlash of sympathy it created after 1945 has always constituted an intense irritant to their objectives, conferring a maddening immunity from criticism. . . . For Israel's own leaders it provided, if not the *raison d'être* of the Jewish State, at least a major argument in favour of Zionism and a source of support (much of it admittedly guilt-ridden) from Western Christians. . . . Never again [Israelis believed] must the Jewish people be defenceless, never again must they rely solely on the goodwill or "toleration" of non-Jews, never again should Jews take lightly the verbal rhetoric of anti-Semitism—the avowed intent to destroy them as a nation.[66]

This attitude reflected the changed perception of many Israelis, who before 1967 had taken little interest in anti-Semitism, regarding even the visceral hostility of the Arab states as a legitimate expression of national conflict. Soviet anti-Semitism, too, had been largely downplayed, especially by the Israeli Left, for many years. But the new anti-Israel climate on student campuses in America and elsewhere in the Western world; the hostile speech of November 1967 by French president Charles de Gaulle about "domineering Jews"; the breaking of diplomatic ties with Israel by the USSR, Eastern Europe, and African and Asian states after the Six-Day War: These were all baffling, disturbing, and even shocking experiences. They were reinforced by the anguish of the 1973 Yom Kippur War and the infamous 1975 UN Resolution 3379 perceived as a deliberate effort to undermine Israel's historical legitimacy.

The international response to the 1982 Christian Phalangist massacre of Palestinians at Sabra and Shatila reinforced this feeling.[67] The fact that Lebanese Maronite militias were the actual culprits had not prevented a new wave of anti-Semitism all over the world. In Mediterranean countries such as Greece and Italy, the 1982 war in Lebanon wrought havoc. The anti-Jewish campaign in Greece received a green light from the Socialist government of Andreas Papandreou, whose vicious pronouncements on the Nazi war crimes of the Israeli army went far beyond the needs of his Arab clients.

In Italy, shortly before Yasser Arafat was granted a hero's welcome by the government, no fewer than two hundred thousand trade unionists passed before the Holocaust memorial of a Rome synagogue uttering cries of "Death to the Jews" and "Jews to the ovens." They even deposited a mock coffin at the foot of the memorial. In Paris, Brussels, Vienna, and other European capitals, synagogues became the targets of Palestinian anti-Jewish terror.[68]

Alongside Holocaust inversion, the summer of 1982 also witnessed a return to classic anti-Semitic stereotypes and beliefs that had temporarily disappeared from the public sphere. Thus, in purportedly enlightened Sweden, there was a revival of Christian theological constructs that starkly contrasted Jewish vengefulness, cruelty, malevolence, and refusal to forgive with idyllic Christian virtues of humanitarian love and compassion.[69] Israeli behavior was equated with Old Testamentarian wrath and bloodthirstiness. It was presented as the *genocidal* antithesis of New Testament pacifism and universal fraternity. The Social Democrat *Aftonbladet* more bluntly stated that in Lebanon Israel had reverted to biblical "extermination." Israeli oppression of Palestinians reminded the paper's editorialist of "the persecution of the Jews in Europe."[70] Another Swedish Social Democratic daily commented in June 1982 that genocide was being perpetrated in Lebanon under the shadow of the [Israeli] swastika in Beirut: "Children are being murdered because the Jewish people were persecuted for hundreds of years by the Christians of Europe. Human beings are of no import. Only chosen peoples matter."[71] Writing in the Socialist daily *Arbetarbladet,* yet another enlightened Swedish moralist blamed Israel's "brutal" policy toward civilians squarely on the Old Testament. "Anything alive should be killed. The enemies of the Jews must be exterminated. These are second-rate people for whom Jehovah has no compassion."[72]

Swedish Social Democrats appeared extraordinarily eager to relate Zionist "atrocities" to the ideology of the "chosen people." In the new witch hunt against Israel, motifs of biblical chosenness fused with allegations of Jewish racism and an apparently irrepressible Zionist thirst for global domination. In Sweden, as in other parts of northern Europe, the compulsive transformation of yesterday's Holocaust Jews into today's Nazis was clearly becoming the rage.[73] Even then, it was apparent that no other conflict in the world (irrespective of casualty figures) came anywhere close to inspiring such a flood of Holocaustal imagery.[74] In the new demonology of Israel as a Nazi state, the victims of the 1930s had been definitively metamorphosed into the perpetrators of the 1980s. Only this time, yesterday's bystanders decided not to remain silent. One of the pioneers in the West of this new militancy was Olaf Palme, head of the Social Democratic Party and Swedish prime minister for many years before his assassination in 1983.[75] Unfortunately, his humanism tended to be highly selective—some victims (especially Palestinians) being much more equal than others.

In Great Britain, too, fictionalizing the Holocaust and demonizing Zionism as a form of Nazism became fashionable during the 1982 Lebanon War.[76] Roald Dahl, the bestselling children's author (and himself of Scandinavian origin) was especially vitriolic in his collective stigmatization of the Jewish people. His verdict was implacable: "Never before in the history of mankind has a race of people switched so rapidly from being much pitied victims to barbarous murderers." According to Dahl, Prime Minister Begin and Defense Minister Sharon were "almost exact carbon copies in miniature of Mr. Hitler and Mr. Goering." They were equally shortsighted "and no less bloodthirsty." It was tragic "that now, only thirty-seven years later, Begin and Sharon . . . should themselves be qualifying for the same treatment."[77] Dahl suggested that the time had come for "the Jews of the world to follow the example of the Germans and become anti-Israeli." But it was more likely, he intimated, that "Israel, like [Nazi] Germany, would be brought to her knees before she learns how to behave in this world."[78] For good measure, Dahl added a peculiarly malevolent gloss, claiming that Jews had acted like "cowards" in World War II and "even a stinker like Hitler didn't just pick on them for no reason."[79]

Dahl's outbursts were by no means exceptional at the time. There were those in Britain who (like their Swedish counterparts) could not resist seeking the roots of Israeli "genocidal" behavior in biblical sources such as the Book of Joshua, or who intimated that the Israeli bombardment of Beirut in the summer of 1982 was alien to Christian ethics. Even the normally sober *Economist* indulged in such tendentious judgments.[80] In tune with this, "Zeitgeist," a poem by Peter Reading in the prestigious *Times Literary Supplement*, referred in especially ugly language to Israeli soldiers in Lebanon as "Old Testament shitters" whose thick hatred was "in the genes."[81] The BBC and other respectable news media flaunted no less offensive parallels. On the Far Right, the vogue of anti-Zionism had similar results. Some members of the British National Front openly called for the destruction of Israel and unconditional solidarity with the Palestinian people. Vitriolic National Front pamphlets such as *Israel: The Hate State* combined denial of the Nazi Holocaust with grotesque hyperbole about the Zionists perpetrating the liquidation of the Palestinians—"a horribly real Arab Holocaust" in Lebanon.[82] The *Caribbean Times* (financially assisted by Colonel Qaddafi) provided a slightly different ethnic and political gloss, portraying the Arabs of besieged Beirut as a reincarnation of Auschwitz Jews. Just as the Nazis sought to exterminate Jews, so "the Israelis have not made any bones about their determination to exterminate the Palestinian fighters."[83]

For the radical British Left, the First Lebanon War not only exacerbated its increasingly endemic anti-Zionism but cast a long shadow of anti-Jewish feeling. Unsuspecting readers of the progressive press would never have realized that Israel enjoyed a free parliament, a free press, democratic opposition, strong trade unions, and a fiercely independent judiciary—scarcely attributes of any fascist or Nazi state. Local militants were hardly encouraged to grasp the huge gulf between besieged Beirut in 1982 and the Warsaw ghetto of 1942. There were no Arabs in Lebanon, the West Bank, or Gaza who were wearing the yellow star; no Palestinians who were condemned to forced labor by the Israelis; no slow death by ghettoization; no mass murder by mobile firing squads in the occupied territories or assembly-line death camps with gas chambers.[84] Far from being abandoned by the civilized world like European Jews during the Holocaust, Palestinians—then as now—enjoyed unprecedented media coverage. Their leaders were lionized and given red-carpet treatment in the capitals of the world. His Holiness, Pope Jean Paul II, warmly greeted Yasser Arafat in the Vatican after his highly publicized exit from Beirut, in stark contrast to the deafening silence of his papal predecessor Pius XII and the stony imperviousness of the wartime Allies while European Jewry was being annihilated forty years earlier.[85]

But the vast differences between World War II and the Israeli-Palestinian conflict did not stop sections of the British Left from pursuing their obsession with imaginary genocide. Thus the renowned actress Vanessa Redgrave, one of the leaders of the Trotskyist Workers Revolutionary Party (WRP), told a Hyde Park rally in July 1982 that the Israeli invasion of Lebanon included the "most barbarous and ferocious acts committed since the days of the Nazi terror." The mind-set of the Reagan administration in

America was described as "the mentality of the Auschwitz torturers, the thinking and policies of Auschwitz and Dachau."[86] Redgrave promised her British audience that the Palestine Revolution would surely "triumph over the Nazi-style barbarism of Zionism and imperialism."[87] The organ of the WRP, *Labour Review,* published equally inflammatory statements against "Israel's genocidal strikes" and Begin's "Nazi-like" doctrines of "superior and inferior races."[88] The *Socialist Review,* for its part, engaged in attacks on the racist ideology of Zionism, as if it were a clone of *Pravda* and *Izvestia.*[89]

The Trotskyists—some of them, like Tony Cliff, of Jewish origin—did not hesitate to blacken Zionism as a particularly evil form of fascism that was seeking to implement the Final Solution of the "Palestinian question."[90] Israel was falsely accused of employing "horrendous gas weapons . . . once used against the Jewish people by the Nazis"; of turning West Beirut into "a gas chamber for the PLO"; of herding Lebanese civilians into concentration camps; and of deliberately trying to murder four million Palestinians.[91] The Israeli bombing of Beirut was presented as equivalent to General Jürgen Stroop's destruction of the Warsaw ghetto.[92] British Labour MP Ernie Ross, chairman of the Emergency Committee Against the War in Lebanon, made similarly wild charges against Prime Minister Begin. His colleague, Ted Knight, Lambeth Labour leader and editor of the *Labour Herald,* added that Israel was a "bandit capitalist state," created on stolen land as a stooge of American imperialism. Knight demanded an international inquiry into Israel's war crimes in Lebanon at a London rally "condemning genocide."[93] Knight's close comrade-in-arms Ken Livingstone, then head of the Greater London Council, was equally unrestrained in his indignation, deploring the exterminationist policy supposedly practiced by Israel. *Labour Herald,* which Livingstone coedited with Knight, carried a sinister and repulsive cartoon in June 1982 featuring a bespectacled, Jewish-looking Menachem Begin dressed in Nazi jackboots and uniform, replete with Death's Head insignia and a Star of David armband. His right arm is raised in a *Sieg Heil* salute over a mountain of skull bones. Begin stands impassively, left hand on hip in a conqueror's pose, while a bleeding Lebanon lies sprawled at his feet. The headline, in Gothic script, reads, "The Final Solution." The caption sarcastically exposes the American-Jewish-Zionist conspiracy: "Shalom? Who needs Shalom with Reagan behind you?"[94] This caricature, drenched in the "new anti-Semitism," was even more obnoxious than the efforts of *Pravda*'s hack propagandists.

Twenty-five years later, American commentators appear no less prone than their Soviet or European forerunners to fall for the perverse Nazi analogy. For example, a University of California professor, Richard Falk, currently the UN investigator on human rights in the West Bank and Gaza, declared in early February 2009 that Israel's actions in the Gaza Strip evoked "the worst kind of international memories of the Warsaw Ghetto." Falk, who is himself Jewish, was clearly referring to the deliberate starvation and murder of Warsaw's Jews by Nazi Germany after 1942. Falk made similar allegations at a "Gaza and Human Rights" symposium held at the University of California, Los Angeles (UCLA). He baldly asserted that both America and Israel continue to practice "genocidal geopolitics." A number of the speakers at the same symposium, in early February 2009, also libeled Israeli soldiers as "war criminals." This campaign of delegitimization and demonization against Israel, while less prevalent than in Western Europe, did not spare the United States. Typical of the genre was the syndicated cartoon by Pat Oliphant, a prizewinning cartoonist, which was published in newspapers across the United States on March 25, 2009. It featured a jack-booted Israeli in uniform marching in goose step, swinging a sharply edged sword in his right arm, and pushing a large Star of David on a wheel with his left hand. The star is fanged and shown to be pursuing a tiny (Palestinian) woman carrying a child labeled "Gaza." The result is a repulsive "Nazification" of Israeli soldiers as being heartless, sadistic aggressors who rely on nothing but brute force to smash the helpless inhabitants of Gaza.[95]

FIFTEEN

Jews Against Zion

Jews throughout their long history of exile and subordination have continually faced the problem of being a small minority dependent on the goodwill and toleration of their successive masters. Their precarious situation at the periphery of non-Jewish societies has extracted a heavy price—including the desire of some sections within the Jewish minority to definitively throw off the markers of their otherness.[1] In markedly anti-Semitic environments, the greater the sense of stigma and inferiority attached to Jewishness, the more it has been likely to prompt intense efforts to deny, reject, or escape from Jewish origins. Self-hatred in such cases is the product of aggression turned inward against the self—the "enemy within"—and outward toward the Jewish group whose difficult history had produced a special sense of vulnerability. In the past, such self-hatred often led to identification with the aggressor. This happened in Christian Spain after the anti-Jewish massacres of 1391. Not only did mass conversion take place, creating the converso problem and culminating in the wholesale expulsion of nonbaptized Jews in 1492, but apostates such as Solomon ha-Levi, who became Pablo de Santa Maria—bishop of Burgos—even justified the persecutions and conversions as being providential. Conversos in Spain frequently took the lead in deriding the perfidy of Jewish contemporaries, calling for their degradation or social segregation, as well as using biblical, rabbinical, and other writings against them.[2]

In later centuries, converts and their secular heirs have also been prominent in efforts to expose the supposed crimes and sins of the Jewish people. Self-loathing Jews have not hesitated to ascribe to other Jews (or, more fashionably, to the State of Israel) the source of their own and the world's afflictions.[3] Rarely, however, have such efforts to throw off the religious, tribal, cultural, or racial taint of Jewish origins been crowned by more than a transient success, though the damage caused is often considerable. A Jew who embraces the worldview of the anti-Semites and transfers his loyalties to the seemingly stronger group may thereby confess his sin, and submit to the numerical superiority of the majority,[4] but this act of conformity is not guaranteed to heighten trust. Instead, it tends to reinforce the dominant prejudices rather than challenge them. Conversos were hunted down and persecuted by the Inquisition—in search of "crypto-Jews"—as late as the nineteenth century; hyperassimilated German Jews who despised the Ost-juden (their East European coreligionists) were later sent with them to the gas chambers. The fervent internationalism of Communist Jews did not provide much protection against the purges of the Stalinist Gulags.

Self-hatred was already rampant among assimilated Jewish intellectuals in central Europe at the end of the nineteenth century. The playwright and novelist Arthur Schnitzler was an acute observer of this psychopathology in fin de siècle Vienna.[5] In his memoirs he recalled a popular slogan from his own university days: "Anti-Semitism did not succeed until the Jews began to sponsor it."[6] Schnitzler noted the groveling servility and cowardice of Jewish renegades who sought to curry favor with the clerical and nationalist anti-Semites by aping their crudest prejudices.[7] Heinrich Bermann, the skeptical anti-Zionist hero of his novel Der Weg ins Freie (Road into the Open), had become an expert in navigating "enemy territory" (the Gentile world); but he was constantly mortified by the shame and embarrassment that his Jewish coreligionists' behavior provoked in him:

> I will not deny that I am particularly sensitive to the faults of the Jews. Probably the only reason is that I, like all others—we Jews, I mean—have been systematically educated up to this sensitiveness. We have been egged on from our youth to look upon Jewish peculiarities as particularly grotesque or repulsive, though we have not done so with regard to the equally grotesque and repulsive peculiarities of other people.[8]

A good example of this syndrome was the young Viennese philosopher Otto Weininger, who committed suicide in 1903 at the age of twenty-three, shortly after publication of his book Geschlecht und Charakter (Sex and Character). This convoluted pseudoscientific tirade against women and Jews would come to exert a strangely mesmeric influence over many leading European artists and intellectuals.[9] In the 1920s, Weininger would become popular reading for Italian Fascists and very useful to the Nazis for his "Jewish self-revelation." They could certainly exploit stereotypes about so-called Jewish materialism, soullessness, and immorality that came from "a decent Jew" who (to quote Hitler) took his life once he realized that Jewry was a parasite living "from the destruction of other peoples."[10]

Weininger's anti-Zionism derived logically from his internalized anti-Semitism. He was obsessed with Jews as rootless chameleons, divorced from any idea of chivalry, heroism, or virility; spineless, effeminate, lacking ego, soul, or any concept of value—attributes they supposedly shared with women. Self-loathing merged into Weininger's apocalyptic claim to be the messianic, Christlike redeemer of a corrupt world, the herald of a Salvationist ethic. In 1903, he explicitly rejected the possibility that Jews could ever build a state of their own. Zionism would never succeed in overcoming the corrupt "ghetto Judaism" from which it had sprung.

This was also a constant refrain of Karl Kraus, Vienna's foremost satirist, who spent thirty years of his life waging a relentless war against the "corrupting" influence of capitalist Jewry. An anti-Jewish Jew who secretly converted to Catholicism at the age of twenty-four, Kraus reviled the rapacious "Semites" who dominated the stock exchange and the liberal press, agitated for female emancipation, founded psychoanalysis, and, worst of all, preached Zionism—against which Kraus wrote a particularly vitriolic pamphlet.[11] Kraus's neurotic self-hatred came out in poisonous diatribes against the "oriental" ghetto mentality that expressed itself in ineradicable *Mauscheln* (Yiddishisms), unappealing gestures, and lack of aesthetic form.[12] His anti-Zionist fervor was part of a broader demand for the radical purging of all visible Jewish characteristics as the royal road to redemption.

These were not isolated cases. Jewish anti-Semitism and hostility to Zionism were commonplace among the intellectuals who founded the Austrian Social Democratic Party after 1889. No less than Weininger or Kraus, they were afflicted by a powerful urge to escape their Jewish roots. The party leader, Victor Adler, had converted to Protestantism at the age of twenty-six. Always embarrassed at finding "too many Jews in my soup" (as he sarcastically told Socialist delegates at a party congress in 1898), Adler took every opportunity to denigrate Judaism, Jewry, and the emerging Zionist movement. Other Jewish leaders of the Austrian labor movement, such as Friedrich Adler, Otto Bauer, Robert Danneberg, Wilhelm Ellenbogen, and

Julius Deutsch, similarly despised the "uncivilized *Ostjuden*" from Galicia, singled out "Jewish capitalists" for opprobrium, ridiculed Zionism, and often trivialized the dangers of anti-Semitism. This was also the political line of Friedrich Austerlitz, editor of the Socialist *Arbeiter-Zeitung*—another converted Jew and vehement anti-Zionist.[13]

From the Austro-Marxists through to the Stalinists, from the New Leftists of the 1960s to contemporary pro-Palestinian Jews, there is a remarkably persistent lineage of Jewish anti-Zionists engaged in castigating communal particularism and the existence of Israel. Beginning with the "convert" Karl Marx, this tradition (unparalleled in any other ethnic group) has compulsively reproduced all the hostile stereotypes of medieval Christian culture that piled up through the centuries and updated them in modern secular form. Aware that others still regarded them as Jews, their self-conscious universalism has often seemed like a convoluted attempt to prove that they were really non-Jews. A classic illustration of this syndrome was the indignant reply in 1917 by the international Marxist revolutionary Rosa Luxemburg, to a close friend's lament about the Russian pogroms: "Why do you come to me with your special Jewish sorrows? I feel just as sorry for the wretched Indian victims of Putamayo [Colombia], the negroes in Africa. . . . I cannot find a special corner in my heart for the ghetto."[14]

Revolutionary Marxist Jews such as Rosa Luxemburg, Leon Trotsky, and Karl Radek always denied the existence of any "special Jewish sorrows," because they insisted on regarding any distinctive Jewish identity as a reactionary relic of the past. It was as if the Socialist Messiah could not come unless every other oppressed group in the world *except the Jews* was first liberated; as if Communist Jews had to feverishly block out the needs of their own people in order to prove their internationalist credentials; or as if execrating Zionism as a "petty-bourgeois" utopia for long enough could actually make it vanish. Such incantations merely disguised the extraordinarily selective form of humanism practiced by anti-Jewish and anti-Zionist Jews. Their sense of solidarity, or even humanity, disappeared as soon as their fellow Jews entered the picture. Bernard Lazare had already observed the psychological mechanisms of this affliction during the Dreyfus affair: "It is not enough for them [the French Jews] to reject any solidarity with their foreign-born brethren; they also have to go charging them with all the evil which their [own] cowardice engenders . . . like all emancipated Jews everywhere they have also of their own volition broken all ties of solidarity."[15]

A good example of this neurosis was Walter Rathenau, the only Jew ever to reach the lofty position of German foreign minister. In 1897, Rathenau had used a pen name to write a notorious article deploring the "foreignness" of the impoverished *Ostjuden* and the vulgarity of the Jewish nouveaux riches.[16] In this embarrassing diatribe, he vilified his fellow Jews as an unprepossessing "alien tribe" of nomads parked on the sandy plains of Prussia. Rathenau, of course, dismissed Zionism as a parochial irrelevance. But his love for blond Nordic Germans did not prevent these same "Siegfried types" from slandering him as a *Judensau* (Jewish sow) and applauding his political assassination in 1922 as a blow struck against a dangerous "Jew-Bolshevik" *and* "Elder of Zion."[17] His killers were young, blue-eyed *völkisch* fanatics convinced that the ultrapatriotic Rathenau had betrayed the German fatherland.

Another tragic victim of self-hatred was the German-Jewish writer Theodor Lessing, a vocal pacifist, feminist, and socialist, who, before World War I, had already turned to Zionism as a possible therapy for his affliction. This did not, however, prevent his being assassinated by Nazi thugs in August 1933. Lessing's book, *Der jüdische Selbsthass* (The Jewish Self-Hatred)— a strange mixture of masochism, questionable racial stereotypes, and pseudo-philosophical diagnosis—was a monument to the troubled and tormented history of German-speaking marginal Jews.[18] In his earlier years Lessing had been a prime example of the social disease he now sought to exorcise. In 1909 he had caricatured Galician Jews, following a visit to the Austro-Polish province, in a particularly repulsive manner that had thrilled the German anti-Semites.[19] Lessing was well aware of his own crippling pathology:

> Am I myself not the fruit of people and conditions which I hate and want to destroy? Am I not handicapped, inferior, ill-bred, botched? . . . Since I had childishly absorbed all the patriotic and religious prejudices of the [German] school, and there was nothing to counter balance them at home, I became convinced that being Jewish was something evil.[20]

A very different form of self-hatred was exhibited in the so-called Canaanite ideology of the 1940s, which spread among a section of sabra youth in Palestine who sought to cut off the umbilical cord with Judaism and Zionism. Although its vision of a united Hebrew or Semitic Middle

East had little political impact, the influence of Canaanism on Israeli artists and intellectuals was considerable.[21] The movement aimed for a purely *secular* Israel purged of any religious trappings, "de-Zionized," and willing to sever all links with the Jewish Diaspora. Its ideological leader, the poet Yonatan Ratosh, in his outspoken 1944 tract *The Opening Discourse*, not only branded Judaism as a "sickness" but also referred to Zionism itself as a "leprosy" infecting wide areas of the new Hebrew nation then emerging in Palestine. His neo-pagan philosophy was thoroughly imbued with Jewish anti-Semitism, containing observations that would not have been out of place in *Mein Kampf*. Ratosh was merciless in his portrayal of the Zionist Jews in Palestine; first they had cut off their sidelocks, then they "learned to mouth the Hebrew language" and declaim empty nationalist slogans: "But let us look with open eyes. He is the same Jew, the eternal Jew of the eternal Diaspora. In France he pretends to be a Frenchman, in Germany a German. Here he plays his game in Hebrew. . . . He is the enemy within who eats up all the best parts."[22] Ratosh gave a certain credence to the *Protocols of the Elders of Zion*, at least where Palestine was concerned. For this was *the* place where the danger was greatest: "where world Jewry does seek to gain control, and which world Jewry wants to subjugate to the concept, spirit, and inner needs of the Jewish world, the world of the Diaspora."[23]

Yaacov Shavit, professor of Jewish history at Tel Aviv University, has described this proclamation as "one of the most self-hating, anti-Semitic texts ever written in Hebrew in Palestine." More shocking still, it was composed at the very moment when the mass murder of six million Jews was reaching its climax in Europe.[24] Fully aware of these tragic events (which merely aggravated his callous contempt), Ratosh continued to focus on the "ancient Jewish poison" that was seeping into the blood and soul of the "new Hebrews." His program called for an absolute divorce between nativist "Hebrews" (good) and foreign "Jews" (bad); it insisted on *cleansing* Palestine from the plague of Zionism and Jewish history ("a foreign history for us") and expunging the burden of religious symbols inherited from the past. In its broader vision of the Near East, Canaanite ideology was both chauvinist and imperialistic in its ambitions for a sweeping Hebrew hegemony. In their nativist narcissism (drawing on romantic Hebraism and neo-pagan myths) the Canaanites were not so different from the German *völkisch* model of nationalism.

One of Ratosh's first disciples was Uri Avnery (born in Germany as

Joseph-Helmut Ostermann), who in the 1940s preached "a new resurrection of the Hebrew race in the great land of Ever."[25] An admirer of Hitler in his early teens, he became a firm believer in an armed "Hebrew Revolution" to be carried out along totalitarian nationalist lines. In the early 1950s, Avnery moved toward a "pan-Semitic" vision of the Middle East in which the "Hebrew national movement" would help to purify the Arab world of its reactionary social elements. Only after the Suez War of 1956 did Avnery begin his long march toward the Israeli "peace camp," culminating in his enthusiastic embrace of Yasser Arafat's PLO.[26]

But even in the Zionist mainstream, the anti-Jewish animus was apparent in the early years of the state. Both Labor Zionism and "revisionist" nationalism (of which the Canaanites were a "heretical" offshoot) were vulnerable to the malady of Jewish self-hatred. Implicit in all the secular Zionist ideologies was the notion that the customs, attitudes, and business practices of *Galut* Jews were thoroughly reprehensible; that Jewish life in exile was immoral and degrading; and that "assimilation" to Gentile culture was a sign of spiritual weakness—and even a danger to non-Jewish society.

Some Labor Zionists openly sympathized with the anti-Semitic critique of Judaism and with the dominant stereotype of Jewish parasitism that was widespread among socialists in general. They wrote as if all Diaspora Jews were allergic to physical exertion, had been corrupted by middleman occupations, or else lived like *luftmenschen*, without any roots on the land. As Zionists, they blamed the *Galut* for having turned the Jew into an eternal alien, thereby producing anti-Semitism, whose objective causes were grounded in the structural abnormality of Diasporic existence.[27] A good Labor Zionist would therefore have to kill the Jew in himself if he took this ideology seriously. On the other hand, the positive side of Socialist Zionism was its honest attempt to overcome the distortions of life in the *Galut* by creating a productive nation of farmers and workers on the soil of Zion.[28]

The Israeli scholar Yehezkel Kaufman argued forty years ago that this outlook represented a Zionist mirror image of anti-Semitism, since it attributed national misfortunes solely to Jewish vices, failings, and unattractive characteristics. Kaufman observed that Jews, no less than Gentiles, were prone to *fabricating charges* against their own people, "singling out certain faults as 'typically Jewish,' and denying to the Jews the right to behave like any other people."[29] Whether Zionist or anti-Zionist in motivation, such a propensity accepted (at least in part) the validity of the complaints and harsh accusations made against Jews by the anti-Semites. There were indeed some Zionist self-haters who related to Diaspora Jews as if they were all dishonest money lenders, peddlers, parasites, endemic separatists, and reactionary exclusivists. Others, who sought to normalize Jewry at any price, dwelt on the self-inflicted cultural backwardness provoked by an "obscurantist" religion.[30] According to Kaufman (writing in 1968), "the vocabulary of abuse contained in Hebrew literature (in which Jews can speak to one another without fear or exaggeration) is paralleled only in overtly anti-Semitic literature of the worst kind."[31] Kaufman's essay sharply attacked the proposition that Jewish self-hatred could be a constructive path to salvation. Zionism should not try to capitalize on such negative feelings, he wrote. There was nothing worse than to accept "the false image of a people burdened with a sense of their sin."[32]

Zionism obviously had its inner demons to contend with. So, too, does the progressive anti-Zionist Jewish intelligentsia in Israel and the Diaspora. The Israeli novelist Aharon Appelfeld shrewdly observed in 1988 that anti-Semitism directed at oneself was "an original Jewish creation."[33] This is equally true of the prewar bourgeois revulsion at "caftan Jews," the Israeli contempt for Jewish victims who did not "fight back" during the Holocaust, and recent anti-Zionist self-flagellation that blames Israel exclusively for Arab rejectionism. In Israel, the left-wing version of this malady began in the 1960s with the theses of the small Matzpen group (Israeli Socialist Organization), most of whose members eventually emigrated abroad. Their utopian goal of a single nonsectarian socialist federation in the Middle East included from the outset the demand to "de-Zionize" Israel and abolish the 1950 Law of the Return for Jews. Matzpen aimed at "deconstructing" Israeli history as one uninterrupted colonialist conspiracy against oppressed "native" Palestinians.[34] After the Six-Day War, the group briefly became more vocal before fading into permanent obscurity. Nevertheless, it was ahead of its time and less stricken by infantile prejudices than some of its pretentious successors.

Jewish Trotskyists in the Diaspora have proved especially tenacious and unyielding in their anti-Zionist polemics. One of the movement's first icons, martyred at the age of twenty-six, was the Belgian Trotskyist Abram Léon, who wrote a remarkable sketch of the "Jewish question" in 1940, under the harsh conditions of Nazi occupation. Léon impatiently dismissed Zionism as irrelevant to the spiraling tragedy of European Jewry under global capitalism.[35] It was no more than a "petty-bourgeois utopia," a mere "ideological excrescence" and diversion from the great cause of proletarian revolution, which alone could provide salvation for the Jewish masses.[36] Zionism was thereby downgraded to the status of a fleeting product of "capitalist decay" in the imperialist era. Even if the British or Americans would actually create "some kind of abortive Jewish state," the situation of world Jewry would remain unchanged.[37] Clearly Léon had little idea of the scale of Nazi plans to exterminate the Jews. Shortly after writing these lines, he would himself disappear into the Auschwitz inferno.

Like so many other Jewish Marxists before and since, Léon genuinely believed that international socialism would do away with any persisting anti-Semitic relics of history. No specialized therapy such as Zionism was therefore required. This view was partly shared by the late Maxime Rodinson, a well-known Arabist and ex-member of the French Communist Party, who prefaced Léon's book. Rodinson was more realistic about anti-Semitism but hostile to Israelis as "a foreign people [who] had come and imposed itself on a native population," the Arabs, as part of a broader European-American movement of expansion in the nineteenth and twentieth centuries.[38] In Rodinson's account of the Middle East conflict, there was no Jewish historical specificity, only the perverse will of Zionist Jews to create a separate civilization. They were to blame for all the problems in Palestine. As for the Arabs, they had every reason to reject "foreign domination" and the Zionist "colonialist" fait accompli that had emerged in 1948.[39] It is striking that Rodinson never once felt the need to mention the Holocaust in his 1967 "history" of the Arab-Israel conflict. Nor did he see fit to evoke the liberation struggle of Palestinian Jewry against British imperialism in the 1940s—except indirectly through some casually pejorative references to Jewish terrorism.

Marxist critics such as Rodinson and the Belgian Trotskyist Nathan Weinstock (a follower of Léon) indulged in a clear double standard.[40] Whenever Arabs fought the British, that was anticolonialism; when Jews rose up against British policy in Palestine, that was terrorism. As with standard Communist analyses of the "Jewish question," Arab nationalism was always progressive while Zionism invariably epitomized imperialist reaction.[41] Rodinson learned this lesson in the days of late Stalinism, when he had glorified Soviet policy toward Jews to the point of defending and justifying the notorious Doctors' Plot.[42] He would continue such Manichean practices in later years but was sophisticated enough to blur them with the mask of detached scholarly rigor.[43] But the personal animus in his writings on Jewish issues can hardly be divorced from questions of personal identity. Rodinson considered himself to be culturally French, but he regarded all forms of nationalism as a "mental illness."[44] He admitted that as a de-Judaized Jew, he found Zionism repulsive, especially its claim to represent *him*. At the same time, he evoked a sense of obligation toward the Arabs whom Zionism had allegedly "robbed of a homeland." Nevertheless, he distanced himself from Arab anti-Semitism and counseled the Palestinians to display greater political realism in their attitudes toward Israel.[45]

Rodinson liked to define himself as a "non-Jewish Jew"—a category he had borrowed from the Polish-born historian and Jewish Marxist Isaac Deutscher. In the 1950s Deutscher had invented this term for revolutionary Jews such as Spinoza, Freud, Marx, and Trotsky, who had lived on the "borderlines" of various national cultures, "transcending" Jewry and creating new horizons for the future. Their universal *Weltanschauung* led them to reject Judaism as far too "narrow" and parochial.[46] Deutscher unmistakably identified with these Jewish heretics, admiring their dynamic concept of social reality, their relativist perspectives, and their action-oriented ethics. In his view they had correctly grasped that all nation-states (including Israel) were anachronisms. The Jewish tragedy was to have embraced national sovereignty at the very moment when it was becoming "a factor of disunity and disintegration."

This is certainly an issue worth debating. But Deutscher's response to the 1967 Six-Day War revealed that his Marxist explanations disguised a much less attractive layer of anti-Israel and anti-Jewish prejudice. Ignoring the concrete Arab preparations and threats to extinguish the Jewish state, Deutscher mercilessly lashed out at the Israelis, calling them "the Prussians of the Middle East." They were, he claimed, imbued with the same Prussian "absolute confidence of their arms, chauvinistic arrogance and contempt for other peoples."[47] Everywhere he looked, Isaac Deutscher could see nothing but a "frenzy of belligerence, arrogance and fanaticism," the obnoxious conjuring up of "biblical myths and all the ancient religious-national symbols of Jewish history."[48] Israel was not merely execrable in his eyes as a Western anticommunist outpost in the Middle East blocking Arab national aspirations; it had become a bastion of "racial-Talmudic exclusiveness and superiority." Indeed, Deutscher could scarcely contain his disgust at the medieval scenes of Hasidim "jumping with joy at the Wailing Wall."[49] The fact that most of these pious Jews did not even recognize Israel as a legitimate state scarcely interested him.

Isaac Deutscher typically invoked his Jewish origins only to better trash Israeli leaders' "over-exploitation" of Auschwitz and Treblinka. His own explanation of the Holocaust was, however, dismally superficial—rehashing empty and worn-out Marxist clichés about the Jews' role in the money economy, the mass unemployment of the 1930s, and the anticapitalist frustrations of the *Lumpenproletariat*. Nazi Jew-baiting, he asserted, had attracted millions of Europeans only "because the image of the Jew as the alien and vicious 'blood-sucker' was to all too many people still an actuality."[50] Israel, however, was blindly replicating the role that had always marked the Jews out as scapegoats in the past: "Yet they now appear in the Middle East once again in the invidious role of agents . . . of powerful Western vested interests and as protégés of neo-colonialism. This is how the Arab world sees them, not without reason."[51]

No less acidic though less politically blinkered than Deutscher in his assessment of the Zionist enterprise was that quintessential Jewish cosmopolitan intellectual, George Steiner, who has served as professor of comparative literature at Cambridge, Oxford, and Geneva. Steiner's animus toward Zionism does not derive from Trotskyite Marxism, self-hatred, or the denial of Jewish singularity in history. Its roots lie in a humanist interpretation of the moral "mission" much vaunted in central European Jewish circles before 1933. The true vocation of the Jews, he says, was to act as the cultural ferment of humanity rather than to establish a territorial state based on cannon and bayonets—hence his cult of the "wandering Jew," his self-conscious glorification of the exile, his cult of perpetual otherness, and the "text" as the true homeland of the People of the Book. Nationalism, with its propensity for tribal and ethnic fantasies, was by contrast the true nightmare of the twentieth century. The Zionists, by establishing a Jewish nation-state armed to the teeth in the heart of the Middle East, had betrayed the sublime history of Judaism in the name of mere normalcy and an obsession with physical security. In other words, they had estranged Jews from their authentic universalist calling and falsified their historic role. Following the German-Jewish philosophical tradition of Hermann Cohen and Franz Rosenzweig, Steiner condemned Zionism for returning the Jews to history and to the corrupting influence of power politics. Yet Steiner's vision also reflected to an uncanny degree some long-standing Christian archetypes of exiled Jews (deprived of land and sovereignty)—doomed by their obduracy to restlessly wander the earth.[52]

Steiner's 1981 novella, *The Portage to San Cristobal of A.H.*, went several steps further, coming close to classic anti-Semitic apologetics. Steiner implied that the Nazi concept of the *Herrenvolk* (master race) had ancient roots in the biblical sources. In a hypnotic and demonic speech that he put into the mouth of a fictional ninety-year-old Adolf Hitler (captured by Israelis in the South American jungle), Steiner offers a justification for genocide in the name of the Book of Joshua. His imaginary Hitler insists that he learned everything about racial separatism, the millennial Reich, the Promised Land, and chosenness from the biblical Israelites. The führer also declares his admiration for Theodor Herzl's *Der Judenstaat* but remonstrates with his Israeli captors that it was his [Hitler's] actions alone that had "made of the long vacuous daydream of Zion a reality." Thus the State of Israel owed Adolf Hitler a profound debt of gratitude, just as the führer himself had learned so much from Moses and the racist visions of the Old Testament. This closing speech of Hitler remains unanswered in the play. As one who in 1982 attended the public performance of this play in London, I can testify that Hitler's concluding rant was received with remarkably enthusiastic applause. Steiner's deeply misleading amalgam of Judaism, Zionism, and Nazism fell on especially fertile soil at the time of the 1982 Lebanon War.[53] Never had the accusation that Israel was disfiguring Judaism and deforming "the position of the Jewish people in history" seemed so appealing. Indeed, there was no dearth of Diaspora and Israeli Jews eager to adapt to this new Zeitgeist under the banner of dissent from Israel's hard-line policies. The same dissenters had little if nothing to say about the barbaric methods of Palestinian terror.

In this climate, even such marginal figures as the Israeli Communist lawyer Felicia Langer, who represented Palestinian terrorists in Israeli courts, and the anti-Zionist Hebrew University professor Israel Shahak could be paraded as Israeli witnesses for the prosecution against their own country. Since those modest beginnings, the stream has turned into a flood. Western and Arab media regularly solicit vitriolic anti-Israeli comments from the secularized heirs of the conversos or from pampered progressives of the Jewish faith. Whether it be *The New York Times, The Guardian, Le Monde, El País,* the BBC, or National Public Radio, every prestigious platform has been open for decades to Jewish anti-Zionists in Western democracies who aspire to the status of heroic dissidents. In many cases their Jewish identity is so skin-deep that it scarcely extends beyond their willingness to denigrate Israel.[54] Yet the flimsiest evidence of a "Jewish conscience"—usually revealed by an appropriate tirade against Israel—may entitle its bearer to be crowned with glory.

Student radicals of the late 1960s were among the earliest contenders for the prophetic halo. They tended to identify with blacks in the United States, with Cubans or Vietnamese, with the indigenous Indians of the Americas, and the global struggle for national liberation. They happily saw themselves as the avant-garde of Western youth fighting against middle-class hypocrisy (including the embourgeoisement of their own parents), mindless consumerism, and Western materialism.[55] A few of them, such as the leader of the anarchist wing of the American hippie movement, Jerry Rubin, admitted to being torn about their Jewishness: "I know it made me feel like a minority or outsider in Amerika from my birth and helped me become a revolutionary."[56] On the other hand, Judaism meant nothing to Rubin because "Jews have become landlords, businessmen and prosecutors in Amerika." Some of these prosecutors and judges had indeed tried the cases of student revolutionaries in 1968. According to Rubin, they were establishment Jews, "so American" that they had forgotten they would always be considered Jewish, however much "power and security" they acquired in "Amerika"![57] Like others of the 1968 generation, Rubin spelt America with a "k" to Germanicize and Nazify it—in itself a revealing fashion that would return after 2000.

The confused and alienated sense of Jewishness among such 1960s American radicals as Jerry Rubin, Abbie Hoffman, and Mark Rudd is revealing. Their language at times mimics that of the Black Power movement but is usually devoid of any Jewish content or ethnic demands. Often hailing from permissive and affluent families, most Jewish New Leftists went to elite American colleges. Nonetheless, they regarded the U.S. government as fascist. They remained scornful of the consumer society and deeply estranged from their own roots. Neither anti-Semitism nor the Holocaust exercised any obvious influence on their outlook nor does it explain their disproportionate involvement in American protest movements. They were "Jewish radicals" without any Jewish identity or commitment.

The French case was different from that of the United States. Though Jews were important in the American New Left, the relative scale of the Jewish presence in the May 1968 student revolt in France was much greater. Of the most prominent student leaders in France, three out of four (Daniel Cohn-Bendit, Alain Krivine, and Alain Geismar) were Jews; close to 60 percent of the central figures in the 1968 student rising can be identified as Jewish; and a who's who of 1968 veterans indicates at least 55 Jewish family names out of the 153 persons who are listed.[58] One of the key groups in the May 1968 events was the Trotskyist Ligue Communiste Révolutionnaire (Revolutionary Communist League, LCR). Only one out of twelve of its politburo members in the founding years was *not* Jewish. Ten were French Jews from an eastern or central European background; the eleventh member was Daniel Ben-Saïd, a French Jew of North African descent, which gave rise to the following anti-Semitic joke: "Question. Why don't they speak Yiddish in the politburo of the LCR? Answer. Because of Ben-Saïd."[59]

Even the French Maoists of La Gauche Prolétarienne (The Proletarian Left) were led by two maverick Jews—Alain Geismar and the Egyptian-born *apatride* Pierre Victor (Benny Lévy). Lévy would subsequently serve as Sartre's personal secretary through the 1970s before immigrating to Israel, where he became an idiosyncratic Orthodox rabbi and philosopher until his premature death in 2003.[60] But in the 1960s and '70s most of the so-called New Leftists were at best "existential" or "involuntary" Jews—defined (in the classic Sartrian sense) by the anti-Semitic other. On the other hand, in France both the Holocaust and wartime resistance to fascism loomed much larger in their self-consciousness and family histories than it did with their American Jewish counterparts. This fact may have somewhat diluted elements of self-hatred and hostility in their underlying attitudes toward Israel and the French Jewish establishment.

As children of the war and of Holocaust survivors, not all of the French Jewish activists were willing to erase the memory of the death camps, German occupation, and the French collaboration. For example, the militant anarchist Pierre Goldman profoundly identified with his parents' generation of Polish-Jewish antifascist fighters who had dreamed of socialism and international fraternity.[61] For him they represented a heroic model of how to be Jewish. Goldman would write about these underground fighters: "No one was more Jewish than these new Hasmoneans, these new Maccabees, sons of the People of the Book, who bore weapons in order to write the holy history of the Jewish rebellion."

Goldman, who had been born in Lyon in 1944, embraced his family's radical political tradition while still in high school and then as a communist student at the Sorbonne. As a true militant, he preferred to join Latin American revolutionaries in Venezuela rather than play-act in the May 1968 Paris student uprising. In the early 1970s he wrote his autobiographical memoir of "a Polish Jew born in France," while serving a life sentence for armed robbery and murder. Goldman described himself as a total outsider, "a man without a country, with no homeland other than this absolute exile, this Jewish exile in the Diaspora." At the end of 1976, Goldman was released on parole after a second trial had acquitted him of murder charges. He continued to maintain close links with the French Trotskyists, but in contrast to many of his comrades on the extreme Left, he insisted on Israel's right to exist. In an interview a few weeks before he was murdered in September 1979 by a French neo-Nazi group called Honneur de La Police, Pierre Goldman summed up his tortured sense of Jewish identity as follows: "To be Jewish is to convey the past. And why is this so important? Because of Anti-Semitism. Because of the hatred. The only answer to the question of what it means to be a Jew is Auschwitz. The Holocaust has renewed Jewish identity for centuries."[62]

Others, such as Daniel Cohn-Bendit, the redheaded German-Jewish icon of May 1968, reinvented a diffuse cosmopolitan identity for themselves ("neither French nor German, Jewish or non-Jewish"). Cohn-Bendit's brief sympathy for the socialist kibbutzim before the Six-Day War was quickly extinguished after a visit to Israel in the spring of 1970. Under the influence of Israeli "comrades" from Matzpen, he ceased to regard the Jewish state as a small embattled country threatened by Arab belligerency. Instead, he embraced the cliché of Israel as a racist, elitist state and colonialist occupier.[63] Radio Cairo was not impressed by the change. It reported that "the Zionist agent Cohn-Bendit has arrived in Tel-Aviv. Thus is exposed the true face of the one who already in France had supported the Zionist organizations."[64]

Though still a revolutionary anarchist, Cohn-Bendit had become somewhat more circumspect by 1978, admitting that he had "enormous difficulties" in dialogue with the Palestinians because they considered him to be an "opportunist Jew." Maoist leader Alain Geismar also underwent a shift in attitude during the 1970s. In 1972, he was quoted by *Le Monde* as a pro-Palestinian radical who execrated the Zionists as the "new Nazis."[65] Six years later he had been thoroughly disillusioned by the indiscriminate terrorism, political ineptness, murderous practices, and anti-Semitism of the PLO.[66]

In Britain, too, so-called dissident Jews played a part in the increasingly "pathological anti-Zionism" of the radical Left. Some pamphleteers, such as Tony Greenstein, focused on recycling the image of Zionism as an ideological "Siamese twin" of anti-Semitism.[67] Others, who proclaimed themselves in agreement with the American Jewish Trotskyite Lenni Brenner (much quoted in British Left circles), expounded on the prewar "collaboration" between Zionists and Nazis. The point was, of course, to demonstrate the unique iniquities of the Jewish national movement.[68] What was labeled as Zionism in this stunningly repetitive discourse was almost always pure fabrication. Thirty years ago, Israel had already become the contemporary version of *Blut und Boden* ideology, the living reincarnation of the Third Reich. In the predictable Trotskyite mythology of such authors as Lenni Brenner, Zionism metamorphosed one stage further, into the *cause* of the Nazi mass murder.[69] The Zionists and world Jewry, by refusing to mobilize the working classes against capitalism, had made themselves complicit in the victory of Nazism and were therefore responsible for sacrificing millions of Jews and Gentiles on the altar of their cruel nationalism.

In the early 1980s Trotskyites found themselves with some unlikely bedfellows—neo-Stalinists in Moscow, Iranian anti-Semites and Haredim such as Rebbe Moshe Schonfeld—who accused Israel of being a state criminally established "on the blood of Europe's Jews." One could sum up the new political and theological consensus as follows: No Zionism, no Holocaust. Not surprisingly, when the Irish working-class Trotskyite Jim Allen wrote his two-act play *Perdition* in the mid-1980s to expose "the most abiding myth of modern history, the Holocaust," most of the leftist intellectuals who leapt to his defense were Jewish.[70] In Allen's play (loosely based on the Rudolf Kastner trial of the 1950s in Israel), a whole array of Jewish anti-Zionist witnesses pillory the racialist "ghetto state" of Israel: a nation that "commits outrageous crimes and then silences its critics by invoking the Holocaust."[71] Twenty years later, such insidious libels would become a staple diet for the chattering classes in Britain and western Europe.

One enthusiastic defender of *Perdition* was the American anarchist intellectual Noam Chomsky. Among his specialties has been the compilation of endless lists of American and Israeli massacres, war crimes, and acts of state terrorism. Needless to say, Chomsky invariably sanitizes or ignores atrocities inflicted on innocent civilians by Palestinian or Muslim terrorists.[72] In his inverted view of reality, for decades Palestinians have been bastions of moderation faced by a ruthless power-hungry Israel, which (with full American backing) has terrorized the entire Middle East. In Chomsky's warped judgment Israeli "apartheid" is far worse than that of South Africa in the 1960s. As for the leaders of the United States, they are simply genocidal war criminals, guilty of relentless brutality and violence against millions of innocent people around the globe. In the Chomskian worldview, Islamic terrorism is, at most, a minor irritant. But if necessary, it can always be defended as legitimate resistance against the world's greatest terror state (America) and its Israeli proxy.[73]

Chomsky had originally supported a binational socialist state of Arabs and Jews in 1948, only to gradually give up on this utopian idea. But he did consistently oppose the "warrior state" of Israel, stigmatized for its dangerous "Samson complex," and its presumed readiness to destroy everything around it in the name of a divine right to "living space."[74] Chomsky is not shy about bringing the Nazi analogy into play, seeing "similarities in planning, policies, and thinking" between Hitler's actions and those of Israel and the United States. This parallel was once again manifest during his highly publicized visit in May 2006 to Hezbollah headquarters in Lebanon. Chomsky warmly praised Hezbollah's resistance and described the Palestinian Hamas as more reasonable than Israel. He insisted that the 1973 U.S.-backed overthrow of Salvador Allende's Chilean Marxist regime had been far worse a crime than 9/11. Chomsky's Lebanese interviewer eventually asked him about charges that he was a self-hating Jew and an anti-Semite. His modest reply was to compare himself with the legendary Old Testament prophet Elijah:

> Well, actually, that notion has its origins in the Bible, and I'm happy to accept the criticism. The origins in the Bible are King Ahab, who was the epitome of evil in the Bible, and he condemned the prophet Elijah for being a hater of Israel . . . because he was criticizing the acts of the evil king, and the king, like totalitarians throughout history, identified the state—himself—with the people, the country, and the culture. So if you

criticize state policy, you are a hater of Israel or a hater of America . . . so yes, I am delighted to be in that company.[75]

One has to doubt, though, if Elijah the prophet would ever have stooped to the level of offering support to Holocaust denier Robert Faurisson and defending his credentials, as Chomsky did. It was not as if the French literature professor was engaged in serious historical research.[76] Chomsky had not read Faurisson's despicable book, for which an essay by him was used as a preface. Apparently without studying the evidence, he asserted that there was no proof of Faurisson's anti-Semitism. Yet anyone familiar with the relevant text would have known that, contrary to Chomsky's claims, Faurisson was no "apolitical liberal" but a slippery anti-Semitic bigot whose vicious anti-Zionism appealed equally to both Left and Right.[77] More than twenty-five years ago, Chomsky's position on the Faurisson Affair was effectively demolished by another French intellectual, the late Pierre Vidal-Naquet, himself an outspoken left-wing Jewish anti-Zionist.[78]

Chomsky informed *Le Monde* on January 19, 1981, that he was personally "agnostic" about the Nazi massacres. He did not want people "to have religious or dogmatic positions about the existence of the Holocaust." This, too, was grist to the mill of many Holocaust deniers and neo-Nazis, who eagerly promote Chomsky's books and speeches condemning American and Israeli imperialism on their websites. They understand that Chomsky's backing for Faurisson and such left-wing libertarian Holocaust deniers as Pierre Guillaume has considerably bolstered the "revisionist" cause. In 1991 Chomsky even asserted that anyone claiming Jews had been singled out by Hitler for total annihilation was engaged in a form of "pro-Nazi apologetics"! At the same time, the MIT guru has been perfectly happy to quote from the scurrilous diatribes of deceased Jerusalem chemistry professor Israel Shahak, whose special talent was to adapt innumerable anti-Talmudic slanders contained in the classical anti-Semitic literature. Shahak provided these libels with the "authentic" stamp of Israeli anti-Zionist "scholarship."[79] In fact, his writings presented Judaism (including the works of such sages as Maimonides) as a rabidly racist credo of *anti-Gentile hatred*. For Shahak (the Israeli pinup boy of Palestinian anti-Zionism), Judaic monotheism was the true source of the world's problems.

From Israel Shahak, one can pick up pearls of wisdom such as the insight that Jews worship Satan on a daily basis and that their religion is totalitarian. Contemporary Israel, we are told, is *the* terrorist state, far more racist than Nazi Germany. No wonder that the Hebrew University professor was hailed by Palestinian intellectual Edward Said as a courageous "dissident." Chomsky, too, obviously admired Shahak, embracing his "discoveries" with genuine enthusiasm, as did a motley crew of neo-Nazi cranks, Holocaust deniers, and Islamist groups throughout the world. Given this track record no one can accuse Chomsky of inconsistency, when he chose to whitewash the malevolently anti-Semitic remarks made by former Malaysian premier Mohammed Mahathir in 2005 at an international conference of Islamic states.[80]

Chomsky's brashest disciple, Norman G. Finkelstein, though lacking his mentor's superstar status, has surpassed him in sheer vituperative rant.[81] The son of Holocaust survivors, Finkelstein achieved his worldwide notoriety with his bestselling assault on *The Holocaust Industry*.[82] This fierce polemic set out a ruthless indictment of Jewish America's alleged manipulation of the Holocaust in order to defend Israel. Finkelstein lambasted the "outright extortion racket" operated by big international Jewish organizations to wrest huge sums of money from Germany, Swiss banks, and other targets—ostensibly for victims of the Holocaust.[83] He also accused American Jewish leaders of silencing criticism of Israeli atrocities by their constant accusations of anti-Semitism.[84]

In recent years Finkelstein has become the go-to Jewish icon for Islamists, neo-Nazis, Holocaust deniers, and deluded leftists determined to believe that demonic Israel is the source of all their woes. Even cruder than Chomsky, Finkelstein does not see Jews as a people at all. They have no right to a historic homeland in Israel, to self-defense, or to the implementation of a law of return to preserve their group identity.[85] He considers the Jewish state wholly *illegitimate,* merely parroting anti-Semitic arguments "to justify Jew-hatred."[86] Finkelstein's surreal vision of Israel highlights the image of Jewish colonialist parasites exploiting Arab labor and foreign subventions.[87] Like other anti-Zionist Jews, Finkelstein is adept at completely ignoring Arab efforts to liquidate Israel, while grossly inflating any and every Israeli threat to its neighbors. Such polemics are conducted in the kind of demagogic street-fighting style much relished by college student audiences in America. In the gospel according to Saint Finkelstein, Palestine has always been exclusively Arab. Anything that contradicts this canonical asser-

tion becomes a Zionist fabrication, myth, or fairy tale. It goes without saying that in this topsy-turvy world, all Israelis are invariably sadistic oppressors; Gentiles who support Israel are "mindless dupes" of the mighty
Zionist propaganda apparatus; and charges of anti-Semitism are either
cheap blackmail by Israel or a means to deflect attention from its "permanent" aggression.[88]

An odor of unmitigated self-loathing mixed with contempt for Jewish
history, religion, and politics ineluctably emerges from such attacks. Their
shamelessness is all too apparent in an interview Finkelstein gave to
Lebanese TV in late June 2006, in which he reduced the Holocaust to a mere
political ploy "to immunize Israel from criticism." He insisted that there has
been "a gross inflation of Holocaust survivors"; asserted that "the Holocaust industry" was cynically set up to "blackmail Europe"; and concluded
that the very existence of the U.S. Holocaust Museum was a monumental
act of "pure hypocrisy."[89] According to Finkelstein, the notion of "unique
entitlement" fostered by the Shoah has served as a permanent alibi to justify
Israeli oppression, as if the Jewish state were any kind of guarantee against
outbreaks of homicidal anti-Semitism.[90] He asserts that the same sense of
"entitlement" produced the money-grubbing restitution pressure that
merely aggravated anti-Semitism in Germany, Switzerland, Austria, and
eastern Europe. The Holocaust and restitution were crude ideological instruments to help Israel and American Jews claim their phony victim
status—one that conveniently fitted into postmodern identity politics and
the general culture of victimization. From this radical perspective, the
Holocaust becomes the flip side of "their [American Jewry's] worldly success: it served to validate Jewish chosenness."[91] The so-called Holocaust industry was nothing but a self-serving power game—made possible after
Israel's spectacular military victory in 1967 and its emergence as an important American strategic asset.[92] As muckraking polemics or macabre stand-
up comedy, this is hot stuff. Scholarship it is not.

Finkelstein's heartfelt compassion goes out to all those who have been
ripped off by the Holocaust industry. They include millions of "exploited"
Germans, as well as the poor Palestinians. Such dramatic assertions naturally
rocketed Finkelstein to the top of the German bestseller lists (reflecting a
long-standing gut feeling among many ordinary Germans); it guaranteed
him two full pages plus an editorial in Le Monde, and a serialization of the

book in Great Britain, though not in the United States. Polish and Russian anti-Semites, Islamist bigots, and neo-Nazis such as Ernst Zundel and David Irving have all hailed their Jewish ally as a star witness able to validate their own Holocaust denial ravings. In Poland, Finkelstein caused a major stir with his vitriolic review of Jan Gross's *Neighbours* (about the 1941 massacre of Jews in Jedwabne by their Polish neighbors). With withering contempt he dismissed this short book as a typical product of the Holocaust industry.[93] The Jedwabne massacre, so it appeared, was part of a scandalous scheme by the U.S. authorities and East Coast American Jews to bankrupt poor Poland by bludgeoning it into paying Holocaust compensation. This was a position more extreme than that initially adopted by Polish nationalist Jew-baiters. Coming straight from a child of Holocaust survivors, the good tidings could only be music to anti-Semitic ears.

Not too many Jewish academics can compete with such electrifying fire and brimstone. An exception is Canadian professor Michael Neumann of Trent University. On June 4, 2002, Neumann's "What Is Anti-Semitism?" appeared in the American political newsletter *Counterpunch*, edited by veteran Israelophobes Alexander Cockburn and Jeffrey St. Clair. Neumann proposed that no intelligent person should take anti-Semitism seriously, given the definitional inflation it has undergone. If anti-Zionism was indeed anti-Semitism, then Jew hatred must become a *universal* "moral obligation," since Israel was indeed "a racial state" based on a hideously supremacist ideology, ruthless persecution, and the continuous dispossession of Palestinians. For Professor Neumann, it was evidently apparent that Israelis and Jews in general were complicit in crimes against humanity, more so than the German people during the Nazi era. Hence it was perfectly reasonable to despise and hate them. The real scandal for Neumann was not indifference to anti-Semitism but the *importance* assigned to it. The Jewish state was allegedly conducting a "race war" against the Palestinians, which had already resulted in several thousand fatalities and massive property damage suffered by Arabs. In comparison, anti-Semitism was a wholly trivial affair—at most, a mild irritant or a benign form of verbal recrimination. To even raise the issue was racist. Moreover, if the price of supporting the Palestinians was "vicious, racist anti-Semitism, or the destruction of the State of Israel, I still don't care. . . . To regard any shedding of Jewish blood as a world-shattering calamity . . . is racism, pure and simple."[94]

These twisted reflections, which ooze with Jewish self-contempt and to-tally false accusations of an Israeli race war against Palestinians, make Chomsky and Finkelstein sound almost moderate.

A more sophisticated form of anti-Zionist distortion is exhibited by Anglo-Jewish academic Jacqueline Rose. In her book *The Question of Zion*, Rose, a professor of English literature at the University of London, has trou-ble finding words sufficiently trenchant to adequately communicate the diseased and demonic nature of Zionism.[95] Thus she successively describes the movement as "bloody," "defiled," "deadly," "cursed," "corrupt," "cruel," "blind," "fanatical," and responsible for the ruin of Judaism's moral her-itage, which it has comprehensively betrayed.[96] Virtually no contemporary platitude about the Jewish state is left unmentioned; even the nasty innu-endo that the Israeli army deliberately kills Palestinian children finds its niche. An innocent reader might have great difficulty in imagining that Is-rael is an open and thriving democracy within an Arab world still in thrall to cultural backwardness, illiteracy, tyranny, and religious fanaticism. On the contrary, Rose makes it transparently clear that Israel is very bad news for Diaspora Jews—threatening their safety, peace of mind, and sanity. She presents Zionism as an extremely dangerous messianic delusion, "a form of collective insanity,"[97] of an ideology that bears within itself the "seeds of ca-tastrophe" and untold suffering for the Palestinians. Naturally, such invec-tive would not be complete without the obligatory equation between Zionism and German anti-Semitism. There is even an "original" assertion that Herzl and Hitler listened to Wagner's music on the same evening in Paris—presumably around May 1895—inspiring the Zionist leader "to write *Der Judenstaat*, and Hitler [to compose] *Mein Kampf*."[98] Since, on that date (the only one that fits Herzl) Adolf Hitler had just celebrated his *sixth* birthday, the reader can better appreciate the level of historical accuracy un-derlying Jacqueline Rose's statements.

The systematic denigration and disparagement of Israel underlying Jew-ish anti-Zionism challenges not merely its policies but also its essence, le-gitimacy, and right to any *independent* future. Such reprobation is intended to justify the dissolution of the Israeli state and its replacement (in the best-case scenario) by an integrated binational state of Jews and Arabs.[99] Apart from the massive bloodshed such a utopian solution would inevitably en-tail, this would once again expose Jews to the exilic sense of powerlessness from which Israel delivered them. But for many progressive Jews in Britain and America, power and the responsibility it brings are precisely what they cannot accept. Their moral absolutism demands that Israel be ostracized and brought to its knees. Two namesakes of Jacqueline Rose—Hilary and Steven Rose—who launched the British academic boycott of Israeli institutions in 2002, invoked as their inspiration the earlier campaigns of the 1980s against South African apartheid.[100] Other Jews have been in the forefront of disinvestment campaigns, calling for sanctions against the Jewish state. Some have also ostentatiously renounced their right of return to Israel even though they were neither asked to do so nor ever intended to implement this right.[101] Their fierce polemical language and vilification of Israel has an overwrought quality of anger, bitterness, and militancy that has little in common with rational criticism. While claiming to speak in the name of Jewish ethics, they appear to have internalized some of the most aggressive anti-Semitic stereotypes and projected them outward against Israel.

The role of growing numbers of expatriate Israelis and Diaspora Jews in hatefests of incitement has been escalating. Among the most extravagantly publicized culprits is the historian Ilan Pappé, formerly of the University of Haifa, who helped to spearhead the British effort to boycott Israeli universities.[102] For Pappé, ethnic cleansing began in the 1948 war. It was a long-premeditated crime ruthlessly implemented and then systematically denied.[103] Indeed, for Pappé and many of the other so-called New Historians, the story of the Zionist enterprise in Palestine is nothing but a tale of occupation, expulsion, discrimination, and racism perpetrated by alien Jewish invaders.[104] The Palestinians are the permanent victims, the Zionists forever "brutal colonizers" in this totally partisan narrative. Hence it is no surprise to discover that Pappé has exhibited warm feelings for Hamas and Hezbollah, while favoring the acquisition of nuclear weapons by Iran.[105] In that context, his decision to leave Israel for Britain is certainly a logical career move.

An active member in the Hadash Party, Pappé typically took a more radical stand than the official Israeli Communist position of advocating "two states for two peoples." He called instead for the replacement of Israel by a unitary Palestinian state. Pappé was also one of the supervisors at Haifa University of a scandalous master's thesis by a left-wing student, Teddy Katz, which apparently fabricated the massacre of Arabs by Palmach veterans at

Tantura in May 1948. The only practical result of such charlatan research was to encourage Arabs from the area to engage in violent riots in September 2000.[106]

There are, unfortunately, many other Israeli academics who deliberately and systematically undermine the legitimacy of the Jewish state.[107] At Ben-Gurion University, for example, political scientist Neve Gordon sings the praises of Norman Finkelstein; and psychology professor Dan Bar-On advocates international tribunals to conduct war-crimes trials of Israeli military personnel.[108] Sociologist Uri Ram, also at Ben-Gurion, at one point asserted that Jews had no more right to Palestine than did the British in India; while geographer Oren Yiftachel has classified efforts to persuade Israeli Jews to move to the Galilee as "pure racism." Tel Aviv University has its own anti-Zionists, including Yoav Peled and the late Tanya Reinhart, an intransigent advocate of the foreign boycott against Israeli universities. Reinhart liked to present Israel's government as consisting of a behind-the-scenes secret military junta, driven by unparalleled sadism and cruelty and always ready to slaughter Palestinians.[109] Naturally, such hallucinations have been enthusiastically welcomed by anti-Zionists and anti-Semites throughout the world. They confirm the prejudices of enlightened liberal humanists in post-nationalist Europe and America, who are more than willing to accredit any lurid tale about Israel's dastardly racist deeds.[110] Israeli testimonies of this sort further reinforced the moral outrage of "progressive" Diaspora Jews such as the late British playwright and Nobel Prize laureate Harold Pinter. The British author normally eschewed any reference to his own Jewishness like the plague, but he was only too eager to invoke his shame as a Jew when reviling Israel as "the central factor in world unrest."[111]

"Progressive" Jews who have so swiftly issued their certificates of divorce from the Jewish state seem strikingly indifferent to the many *Israeli* civilian victims of savage Palestinian atrocities. It is as if the numbing of any residual Jewish or Israeli sympathies is felt to be a requirement for entry into the club of universalist loyalties and fashionable multiculturalism. As U.S. author Anne Roiphe points out, the various Jewish groups in the West who support the Palestinian cause as if it were synonymous with peace or social justice generally show through their deeds that "they have empathy for all victims of violence, greed and abuse—except for the Jews. They cry for Palestinian children, and turn their heads away from the Jewish dead. They love all mankind, except for their own people, the Jews."[112]

Their moral self-validation is evidently linked to an exaggerated cult of the Palestinian "other"—glorified as a victim of their fellow Jews. One example among many would be the French Jewish sociologist Edgar Morin, who coauthored what was subsequently condemned by a French court as an anti-Semitic article in *Le Monde* in June 2002. Morin not only accused Jews in Israel of a cancerous racism and Nazi-like oppression of Arabs but claimed that the insidious "Zionist ghetto" was deliberately ghettoizing the Palestinians behind its "apartheid wall."[113] Yet, even to criticize such transparent defamation of Israel is often greeted by anti-Zionist Jews as a form of moral blackmail.[114]

Delegitimization of the Zionist state as the embodiment of an almost metaphysical evil is also to be found in Israeli universities.[115] Still more widespread is the demonization of particular sectors of Israeli society. Prominent Israeli writers and artists have not been immune from the temptation of branding Gush Emunim settlers as "criminals against humanity," or as "pogromists and murderers, that burst forth from some dark corner of Judaism," to quote Amos Oz.[116] To this one might add the diatribes of the avant-garde sculptor Yigal Tumarkin, a recipient of the Israel Prize, against the caftan Jews. Some years ago he told a local Tel Aviv newspaper, "When I see the *Haredim*, I understand the Nazis."[117]

But no prominent Israeli in recent years has been as extreme as Avraham Burg, former Labor Party Knesset member, speaker of Israel's parliament (1999–2003), and onetime chairman of the Jewish Agency for Israel. In a widely publicized article that appeared in September 2003, Burg prophesied the imminent demise of the Zionist enterprise. He announced that it was floundering in a morass of oppression, corruption, injustice, and callousness. Israelis faced a stark choice between either "Jewish racism" (meaning continuation of the settlements) or democracy; complete withdrawal to the 1967 borders or the end of Israel. The suicide bombers, so he claimed, existed only because of the hunger, discrimination, and humiliation that Palestinians had experienced at Israel's hands.[118] In a subsequent interview in the winter of 2003 with *Haaretz,* Burg deplored the type of Zionism that had transformed Judaism "into the worship of trees and stones," turning God into a "Moloch" and Israeli children into "human sacrifices." The ultranationalist Zionism of the settlers represented a "cancerous process," a racist virus that was devouring Israel and destroying the remnants of its moral conscience. According to Burg, Israeli society was becoming blind and obtuse to the "horrific reality" it had created. Israel had begun to resemble its worst enemies. The former Speaker of the Knesset emphasized his complete indifference to any anti-Semitic fallout from his criticisms. ("If Israel-haters used me, that's fine as far as I am concerned.") Naturally, he blamed Islamic terrorism solely and exclusively on the "occupation."[119] What was most striking in his diatribe was the extent to which Burg had embraced the Palestinian narrative, totally disregarding any Arab responsibility for the conflict. Ignoring Israeli suffering and the Jewish right to national self-determination in Israel was the unsurprising corollary of such narcissistic, self-righteous dogmatism.

In an interview with *Haaretz* in June 2007, Burg continued to savage Israel as an insular, brutal, confrontational, and imperialist state, lacking even a glimmer of spiritual inspiration. He now declared that the very definition of Israel as a Jewish state was "explosive" and the "key to its end." The Law of the Return would have to be abolished—it was "the mirror image of Hitler." The Jewish Agency, which he had once headed, should be dismantled. Burg also declared that Israelis had become psychic cripples, gripped by dread and fear because of Hitler's Holocaust.[120] The Israeli concern over Hamas was mere paranoia. From his newly minted anti-Zionist standpoint, Israel was a traumatized, militaristic, and racist society, already standing on the abyss of National Socialism. A xenophobic hatred of Arabs had become mainstream. Burg even speculated that an Israeli parliament would eventually pass legislation forbidding sexual relations between Jews and Arabs.

By contrast, Burg glorified the European Union as an amazing "biblical utopia," "completely Jewish" in the best cosmopolitan sense of the term— the living antithesis of Israel's chauvinism, provincialism, and cultural sterility.[121] He proudly declared himself to be a European and a citizen of the world, having ostentatiously taken out a French passport and voted in the French presidential elections against Nicolas Sarkozy![122] To a cynic, Burg's provocations might seem to be no more than a cheap gimmick to sell his latest book; to his admirers a sign of his prophetic gifts; to the average Israeli yet another mark of the degeneration of the political elite. Whatever the truth of the matter, Burg's unbalanced outbursts against his fellow countrymen contributed yet another drop of poison to the increasingly fashionable defamation of Jews.

Some former Israelis like Avi Shlaim, a professor of international relations at Oxford University, have been no less venomous in their language.

Writing in the *Guardian* newspaper in early 2009, Shlaim seemed inclined to agree with the viciously anti-Israel opinions of Sir John Troutbeck, a top British Middle East official in 1948. In an internal communication to Foreign Secretary Bevin sixty years ago, Troutbeck had thoroughly deplored the creation of Israel—a "gangster state" headed by "an utterly unscrupulous predictably set of leaders" whose emergence he misleadingly blamed on America. To the libel of a "gangster state," Shlaim added his own jaundiced accusations of colonial exploitation, illegal settlement, and a "uniquely cruel" military occupation. Barely acknowledging that Israel had withdrawn from Gaza, he accused its leaders of demonizing Hamas, while managing to present the terrorist organization cum government of Gaza as if they were vegetarian pacifists and moderates confronted by a "heavily armed merciless and overbearing Israeli Goliath."[123]

Avi Shlaim, Tony Judt, Avraham Burg, and other anti-Israel Jews continue to rationalize terrorism, trivialize anti-Semitism, and demonize Israel in a shameful manner. The rhetoric may be high-flown ("justice," "humanity," and "Jewish ethics") but the emotional reality beneath the surface seems spiteful and splenetic. The Israel-baiters, even when reclaiming their Jewishness, appear to be obsessed with delegitimizing their "parochial," "tribalist," and "anachronistic" coreligionists. They exhibit a curious sadomasochistic delight in proclaiming Israel to be an irredeemably polluted society, close to collapse.[124] They have reversed the old patriotic dictum "My fatherland, right or wrong"; replacing it with the equally absurd axiom, "My country, always wrong," except, of course, when it happens to follow their own ideological prescriptions.

In the past Jewish self-hatred has generally been associated with the insecurities and lack of self-confidence produced by Jewish minority status. Historically it might be seen as a tragic side effect of exile, which repeatedly exposed Jews to harsh Gentile persecution and periodic massacre, especially after the Crusades. Radical Enlightenment and modern emancipation added a new dimension. Jews were freed from their legal disabilities, but their entry into non-Jewish society led to a greatly reinforced *internalization* of anti-Semitic stereotypes. Emancipated Jews became increasingly obsessed with their negative self-image and driven by an obsessive desire to be accepted by Gentiles. The rise of modern racial and political anti-Semitism intensified this neurosis still further, producing more and more pathological manifestations of self-hatred. Zionism added a powerful additional layer of radical self-criticism from within a national perspective. Though often destructive, such criticism was at least motivated by the desire to improve and reshape Jews into independent actors within history, able to determine their own fate.

As a result of the Zionist project, the "new Hebrews" would eventually mutate into Israelis with roots in their own land. They became masters of a self-sustaining state, a productive society, and a powerful army able to defend itself against external aggression. Contemporary Israeli and Jewish self-hatred nonetheless casts a shadow over this nation-building optimism of the founding fathers. The self-haters have shown that they can match and often surpass the most anti-Semitic Gentiles in their demonization of the Jewish state. There are even times when non-Jewish anti-Semitism seems to be no more than a pale, shoddy, and second-rate imitation of the authentic product—whether "Made in Israel" or fabricated in the Diaspora. The danger emanating from such masochistic, self-flagellating, and destructive postures is not negligible. Self-hating Jews, whatever their motives for betraying their own people and negating its history, have throughout the ages provided invaluable ammunition for the anti-Semites. That still remains the bottom line today.

SIXTEEN

Shylock Meets Uncle Sam

A nti-Americanism might be defined as an excessive distaste, aversion, or hostility toward American society, politics, and culture. In its reflexive disparagement of everything American, it resembles racism, sexism, and anti-Semitism.[1] For example, those who represent the United States as being synonymous with everything crassly materialistic, exploitative, crude, and bullying about global capitalism are engaged in something more than mere criticism. Similarly, the cultural animus that loathes the hollowness of the mass entertainment industry, the shallow philistinism of American middle-class values, and the hypocritical piety of some forms of Christian fundamentalism becomes anti-American once it attributes general characteristics of modernity, predominantly or exclusively, to the United States. This form of "bourgeoisophobia" has many structural similarities with modern secular anti-Semitism.[2]

In some ways such postwar anti-Americanism is indeed the most socially respectable form of anti-Semitism today, since it is untainted by the Holocaust. Those in Europe who vehemently attacked America's reaction to Arab terrorism after 9/11, for example, have often used latently anti-Semitic topoi—emphasizing the vengeful, bloodthirsty, and biblical character of the response.[3]

Warmongering, blind arrogance, and hubris seem to have become almost immanent attributes of America and Israel according to the new conventional wisdom—made more ominous by their apocalyptic flavor.[4] Both nations are said to exemplify military adventurism, arbitrariness, and a domineering will to humiliate other peoples in their neighborhood or beyond—Muslims and Arabs in particular.

Street demonstrations in 2003 against George W. Bush in London, Paris, Madrid, Rome, Brussels, and other European cities invariably depicted the

U.S. president as a reckless Texas cowboy, a warmonger, terrorist, assassin, or born-again Crusader. His image, like that of then Israeli prime minister Ariel Sharon, was thoroughly demonized through the use of a full array of Nazi-era references with swastikas to adorn his visage.[5] This Nazi imagery (in which Sharon had a starring role as the incarnation of the "ugly Israeli") undoubtedly exuded anti-American and anti-Semitic hostility. In such a poisoned atmosphere Jews could be smeared with impunity as Zionist pigs and Americans as rapacious thugs.[6] Conspiracy theories, suicide bombings, and terrorist attacks represent the violent face of this nihilistic rage. Condescending cultural critiques are its smoother, more cynical, and erudite European mask.

In 1935 Martin Heidegger, the influential proto-Nazi philosopher, described America as a demonic invasive force appropriating the soul of Europe and sapping it of strength, spirit, and creativity. Germany and Europe, he argued, would be doomed unless they successfully overcame the Anglo-Saxon world of "Americanism" with its inauthenticity, sameness, and indifference to real culture. Heidegger insisted that from a metaphysical standpoint, America was like Bolshevik Russia: "the same dreary technological frenzy and the same unrestricted organization of the average man."[7] But its soulless efficiency made it potentially more dangerous than its Communist rivals, since it reduced "being" itself to a mere commodity, an ersatz object, a uniform and standardized article of exchange. Postwar Marxist Heideggerians such as Jean-Paul Sartre and Herbert Marcuse would extend this philosophical anti-Westernism into a general assault on homogenized, administered capitalism and the one-dimensional world of American mass consumerism.

The postwar French philosopher Jean Baudrillard echoed this dark view of America as a cultural "desert," an "antiutopia of unreason," heralding the death of Western civilization. Like many of his countrymen he felt galled by the stifling power of the almighty dollar and threatened by a society deemed to be culturally inferior—"an artificial universe" of endless freeways, Safeways, Hollywood movies, TV soap operas, Disneyland, Microsoft, McDonald's and Coca-Cola. America was a world "completely rotten with wealth, power, senility, indifference, Puritanism and mental hygiene, poverty and waste, technological futility and aimless violence."[8] The jihadi assault on the United States of September 11, 2001, could only be regarded as cathartic by European intellectuals such as Baudrillard, a profound purging of the soul—one shared by a remarkable number of European artists, journalists, scholars, and commentators.

For example, German composer Karlheinz Stockhausen called the terrorist attack on the Twin Towers "the greatest work of art imaginable for the whole cosmos."[9] Italian Nobel Prize winner Dario Fo regarded it as "the legitimate daughter of the culture of violence, hunger and inhumane exploitation." Some fundamentalists saw it as a righteous act against the sinful city of New York—the multicultural Babylon of modernity. Others rejoiced in the shattering of the World Trade Center as a blow against the Tower of Babel of capitalist decadence.[10] It was regarded as payback time for American imperialist hubris. Conspiracy theories about the active role of the Israeli Mossad or the CIA in orchestrating the 9/11 massacre also abounded. Invariably, it was America and Israel who were in the dock, not the jihadists who had carried out the bloody deed. It was the "Crusader-Zionists" who were setting the world aflame with their greedy, technically advanced, gun-toting capitalism.

Josef Joffe, editor of *Die Zeit,* has noted a number of conceptual similarities between such anti-Americanism and the old-new anti-Semitism. First comes the *stereotypization*—general statements projecting negative attributes on the target group as a whole. This is usually followed by *denigration*—aspersions concerning the moral inferiority of the perpetrators and their irreducibly evil nature. *Demonization* is never far behind. These motifs are then connected together as part of a sinister Jewish conspiracy to dominate the world. The element of *obsession* takes over once the belief that America and Israel are at the root of planetary troubles becomes transformed into an idée fixe—not amenable to any empirical falsification.[11] Joffe offers tone and selectivity as further criteria for distinguishing between reasonable criticism of specific policy decisions and rabid delegitimation of Jews or Americans as Rambo-like warmongers seeking to consummate an imperialist dream of manifest destiny. Double standards are also apparent in the selective rage that singles out the United States and Israel for vituperation, while turning a blind eye to *real genocide* in Darfur, China's oppression of Tibet, or Russia's dirty war in Chechnya, to cite only a few examples. As Joffe points out, such "selective condemnation is a convenient way to hide bigotry from oneself and others."[12]

America and Israel have been routinely paired in recent years as rogue states overrunning weaker nations, trampling on indigenous cultures, and ignoring international law. The results of this disinformation have been toxic. In February 2003, for example, 57 percent of Germans thought the United States was a *nation of warmongers*, and only 6 percent thought it was interested in peace. Such prejudicial judgments reflect a phobic view of the United States as extremely aggressive and spiritually inferior, as ubiquitous and socially retrograde. Worst of all, America becomes synonymous with a wolfish capitalism rooted in its "divine mission"—a Calvinistic sense of chosenness and election originally absorbed from Old Testament Jews. Indeed, since the early nineteenth century, critics as well as admirers often labeled America as the most Jewish nation in the Christian world—with only Great Britain in its imperial heyday rivaling it for that title. This historic association renders the stereotypical anti-Semitic twinning of America and Israel even more tempting. The United States, as Joffe ironically observed, was like "an anti-Semitic fantasy come true, the *Protocols of the Elders of Zion* in living color." Only this time Israel, and not World Jewry, was *Über-Jew,* and America its lackey.[13] In its more extreme form this is the theory that Washington, D.C., is the center of ZOG (Zionist Occupied Government) with Israel and the Jewish lobby pulling the proverbial purse strings. Behind Uncle Sam stands Uncle Shylock with a hotline to Jerusalem.

A more widespread and popular notion is that a cabal of Jewish officials secretly engineered the Second Persian Gulf War in 2003. Attention abroad was especially focused on a small group of Jews holding high positions in the Pentagon (Paul Wolfowitz, Douglas Feith, and Elliott Abrams), working with another circle of Jewish intellectuals including Charles Krauthammer, William Kristol, Robert Kagan, and the unclassifiable Richard Perle. They were depicted as neoconservative architects of the Iraqi adventure. These hard-liners were presumed to be followers of a long-forgotten German Jewish philosopher named Leo Strauss, or else parodied as "inverted Trotskyists" who had somehow metamorphosed into hawkish neocons. More important, they were overwhelmingly Jewish. Hence their aim of democratizing the Middle East was interpreted by some more malevolent critics as primarily an attempt to weaken Israel's Arab neighbors. America's "super-hawks" (as the BBC sardonically branded them) must have had a hidden Zionist agenda, which they then successfully sold to the Gentile Republicans President Bush, Vice President Cheney, Donald Rumsfeld, and Condoleezza Rice. Thus they had cleverly managed to hijack American foreign policy in the service of Ariel Sharon.[14] As a result of their advocacy, so it was claimed, America had essentially done Israel's bidding in Iraq. This baseless theory even found some support in the United States. But in Europe and especially in the Middle East, millions believed it.[15] Ayatollah Khomeini's designation of America in 1979 as the "Great Satan" clearly extended far beyond Iran or the Sunni Muslim world, achieving a newfound global resonance with the United States depicted as a mere puppet of the "Little Satan," Israel.[16]

In its 2005 Global Opinion Survey of anti-American trends in 2005, the Pew Research Center confirmed that "anti-Americanism is deeper and broader now than at any time in modern history." The center pointed out that there had been "a global hardening of attitudes" that transcended the undoubted animus toward President Bush's foreign policies. There was real fear and resentment of the unrivaled power that the United States had amassed since the end of the Cold War. There was also intense dislike of its alleged unilateralism and accusations that it had deliberately widened the global gulf between rich and poor. Many nations around the world were deeply suspicious of U.S. motives in international security affairs, especially after the Iraq War. A majority of those polled thought that the American-led war on terror was more about controlling Middle Eastern oil and seeking world domination than a necessary act of self-defense or motivated by a sincere desire to spread democracy to the Arab world.

Between 1999 and 2004 the U.S. favorable rating in Britain had fallen from 83 percent to 58 percent. In Germany it declined from 78 percent to 38 percent, in France from 62 percent to 37 percent, while in Spain it had descended from 50 percent to a new low of 14 percent in March 2003. Positive ratings had also declined in Brazil from 56 percent to 34 percent; in Indonesia they had plummeted from 75 percent to 15 percent; in relatively pro-American Morocco from 77 percent to 27 percent; and in Turkey they were down from 52 percent to 30 percent (with a rock-bottom 12 percent recorded in early 2003). Russia was a rare exception to this general trend. Anti-American feeling was further strengthened by the Iraq War, with the majority opinion worldwide (except for Britain, Australia, Israel, Russia, and some African nations) believing that America had greatly exaggerated the terrorist threat. The jihadist attacks of 9/11, despite an initial short-lived outpouring of sympathy, hardly improved the U.S. global image. A poll in 2002 showed that in the Middle East, 81 percent considered U.S. policy to have provoked the attacks. Many Muslims even feared the U.S. could be a serious military threat to their own countries. This was affirmed once again in June 2006 by clear majorities: 80 percent in Indonesia, 71 percent in Pakistan, 67 percent in Jordan, 65 percent in Turkey, and 59 percent in Lebanon shared this anxiety. If that were not enough, a Eurobarometer survey in October 2003 showed that no less than 53 percent of all Europeans regarded the United States as *the* major threat to international security. This placed America on a par with Iran, though still behind Israel (59 percent). However, four European countries (Finland, Sweden, Greece, and Spain) singled out the United States as *the greatest threat* to world peace—a sobering reflection on deteriorating relations between America and Europe.

In his testimony before the U.S. House of Representatives on March 14, 2007, Andrew Kohut, president of the Pew Research Center, emphasized that anti-Americanism had become increasingly entrenched worldwide, with a steady worsening in Europe over the past three years. In China, India, Russia, and Japan opinions of the United States were significantly more favorable in 2006 than in France (39 percent), Germany (37 percent), or Spain (23 percent). In Turkey and Jordan positive attitudes had fallen below 15 percent. The global slide extended to Latin America and Asia, while still remaining virulent in the Muslim world.[17] Such negative opinions had spilled over into attitudes toward Americans as such. Excessive religiosity in the United States was another sore point for many. In secular France (61 percent) and the Netherlands (57 percent), the United States as a country was considered far too religious; pluralities in Britain and Germany (39 percent) also held this view. But it was emphatically *not* shared in Russia (27 percent) or Poland (a mere 6 percent agreed) where Christian religious values were much more firmly entrenched.

Similarly, in Muslim countries, Americans are not considered all that religious, and it is their perceived bias toward Israel that remains an especially bitter point. But surveys in 2006 revealed that a particularly high number of Muslims (including 56 percent of Moroccans and 49 percent of Jordanians) felt that suicide attacks against Americans and other Westerners in Iraq were justifiable. No less shocking, 38 percent of Pakistanis and 24 percent of the Jordanians polled in 2006 had confidence in America's most outspoken enemy, Osama bin Laden, doing the right thing in world affairs![18] Another alarming signal was the pervasive anti-Americanism in Turkey. By 2006, favorable views of the United States in this important NATO ally had collapsed to a mere 9 percent. In July 2007, the Turks tied with the Palestinians for the lowest percentage of citizens (2 percent) who thought that U.S. Middle East policy is fair. Turkey also had the highest number of respondents (81 percent) who disliked American ideas about democracy.[19]

Latin America also continues to be a hotbed of Yankee-phobia.[20] Polls in recent years indicate that more than 60 percent of Latin Americans strongly object to U.S. foreign policy and believe that it only increases the poverty gap. While many Latin Americans enjoy U.S. popular culture such as movies, music, and TV, they also viscerally oppose the spread of North American ideas and customs to their own countries (73 percent in Argentina and Bolivia). Popular antagonism to American-style neoliberalism remains a powerful force south of the Rio Grande, reinforced by Marxist, nationalist, and Third Worldist currents of opinion. The endemic economic inequalities in Latin American society, latent racial resentments, and several centuries spent in the shadow of the northern giant have ensured that sympathy for the gringos remains limited.[21] In Brazil, for example, 80 percent of the population opposed any U.S. retaliation for 9/11. As elsewhere in Latin America, there was a widespread feeling that, finally, the United States might have received a taste of its own medicine.

The intellectuals, as in the past, were especially vocal in joining the global anti-American chorus. No doubt this may have compensated some of them for their frustrated sense of being on the periphery of world events. Traditionally oriented to Europe, the educated elites of Latin America usually share the negative or ambivalent feelings toward the United States of their cultural role models in Paris or Madrid. The intelligentsia is also strongly influenced by the dominant anticapitalist ideology in Latin America, driven by a populist grievance culture and residues of Third Worldist Marxism.[22] It identifies with the general sentiment of victimization by Yankee imperialism rampant from Mexico to Argentina, and with resentment at the material gap between north and south. It also appreciates the need to solidify national identities against a common enemy. To a large extent it has been anti-Americanism that turned leaders like Che Guevara, Fidel Castro, martyred Chilean Marxist president Salvador Allende (killed in 1973 by General Pinochet's forces), the Sandinistas, and now Hugo Chávez into popular heroes and secular saints.

This anti-American mythology, as in Europe, is most vocal today under the anti-globalist flag or the human rights banner. The Argentine leftist Adolfo Pérez Esquivel, who won the Nobel Peace Prize in 1980, spoke for many Latin American intellectuals when he described President Bush as "a criminal against humanity" for unleashing the 2003 war against Iraq. Bush, he declared, was "threatening to free all the evils of the apocalyptic beast, seeking destruction and death."[23]

Similar comments were made during the run-up to the Iraq War in the left-wing Nicaraguan newspaper *El Nuevo Diario*. Leading local polemicist Fredy Quezada portrayed President Bush as the moral equivalent of Osama bin Laden.[24] Such lurid comments continued the legacy of the Sandinista National Liberation Front, which ruled Nicaragua between 1979 and 1990. Massively supported by Castro's Cuba, Nicaragua had been an international magnet for opposition to U.S. imperialism in the 1980s—a kind of Latin David fighting the rich, white northern Goliath. The Sandinista national anthem included such poetic lines as "The Yankee is the enemy of humanity." Under its leader, Daniel Ortega, the state and party apparatus constantly filled the airwaves, newspapers, and mass rallies with anti-American slogans; radical groups from around the world, including the PLO, set up shop in Managua—transforming it into a mecca of Third World nationalism. Since the beginning of the twenty-first century, anti-Americanism has returned in full force. On March 22, 2003, Daniel Ortega described the Bush administration's policies as "a continuation of the politics of death" that "different U.S. administrations have carried out in the most diverse regions of the world."[25] Once he was reinstalled as president of Nicaragua, Ortega, like Hugo Chávez, swiftly affirmed his heartfelt solidarity with such archenemies of the United States as Iran's president Mahmoud Ahmadinejad. Iran's embassy in Nicaragua today is the headquarters of a continually expanding Iranian presence in Central America.

No Latin American state has, of course, been as consistently anti-American as Fidel Castro's Cuba, going back to the early 1960s. After the failed Bay of Pigs invasion by Cuban exiles and the U.S. trade embargo, Castro escalated his anti-Yankee rhetoric. He reinvented Cuba as a major strategic enemy of the United States and vanguard of Third World progressive forces seeking to liberate the planet from U.S. influence. This was also the message of the Argentine-born Che Guevara (Castro's comrade-in-arms) to the Havana Tricontinental Conference in 1968: "Our hopes for victory [are] the total destruction of imperialism by eliminating its firmest bulwark: the oppression exercised by the United States of America. This means a long war."[26]

The Cuban Revolution, it is worth recalling, was much admired in American radical circles, especially by Communists and their fellow travelers, who felt at war with their own society. Ever since the early 1920s, American Communists had looked to the Soviet Union as the fatherland of the working class. Even after the disintegration of the Soviet bloc, the demise of Maoism, the disappearance of Eurocommunism, and the collapse of Third World socialisms, the old dogmas remain in place, above all a visceral anti-Americanism. Such prejudices are still surprisingly pervasive in American academia, in the arts, and among some of the more extreme feminists, multiculturalists, and anarchists.[27] Peace movements, too, in the United States and around the world have remained pervasively anti-American ever since the "ban the bomb" marches and the 1960s protests against the Vietnam War. However, contemporary Western peace activists currently tend to demonstrate their solidarity with the Third World more by focusing on Iraq and Palestine.[28] In comparison with the Vietnam War era, anti-Zionist and anti-Semitic elements in the increasingly stale anti-American repertoire have become far more visible.[29]

The antiwar Left in North America, though disproportionately Jewish in its intellectual leadership, has been involved for some time in a marriage of convenience with Islamic radicals openly at war with the West.[30] No individual has been more influential in articulating the common anti-American line than Noam Chomsky, who for decades consistently defended Marxist and nationalist dictatorships from Vietnam, Cambodia, Cuba, and Nicaragua to Saddam's Iraq, providing they were in conflict with the United States.[31] In Chomsky's strange inversion of history, even Pearl Harbor, like 9/11, was ultimately attributable to American aggression. Indeed, Chomsky reduces the history of the United States to a long and extraordinarily repetitive catalog of atrocities, massacres, and genocides. Hence it is no surprise that he told an MIT audience on October 18, 2001, that America was planning a "silent genocide" against the people of Afghanistan.

Such distorted views have unfortunately proliferated through American universities. They are echoed in many antiwar demonstrations across the United States and in educational curricula, which tend to portray white America as having been genocidal from birth. In this alternative history, America's efforts in ending slavery, liberating millions of people around the globe from totalitarian tyranny, creating spectacular wealth, spreading democracy, spearheading technological innovation, and promoting individual liberties are literally obliterated. All that remains from the wreckage is a totally skewed myth of America's intrinsically racist imperialism, designed to show that the United States can never do right.[32] Structurally, this narrative is remarkably similar to anti-Zionist distortions of Israel's past, present, and likely future.

What is most striking in both cases is the systematic denigration that exploits hostile stereotypes, turning them into dogmas impregnable to rational discourse. Thus for rabid haters of America such as the Nobel Prize–winning British playwright Harold Pinter, the enormity and sheer viciousness of U.S. crimes precluded any possibility of redemption. In his 2005 Stockholm acceptance speech, Pinter made it clear that even seemingly benign American actions were, in reality, malign: "You have to hand it to America. It has exercised a quite clinical manipulation of power worldwide while masquerading as a force for universal good."[33] Three years earlier in Turin, he insisted that the most powerful nation the world has ever known was "waging war against the rest of the world": "The U.S. administration is now a bloodthirsty wild animal. Bombs are its only vocabulary."

Pinter's views are not untypical of intellectuals and artists in Britain, long considered America's closest ally in the Old World.[34] Indeed, for many on the British Left, aggressive, unilateralist America is *the* major obstacle to world peace. One Labour minister, Michael Meacher, publicly suggested in 2003 that Bush's global war on terror was an all-too-transparent device to reach "the U.S. goal of world hegemony"—a widely held belief in Great Britain.[35] British opposition to the Iraq War in Parliament and on the streets reflected an endemic and ingrained distrust of American motives. The prevalence of such attitudes largely explains the huge success of left-wing American filmmaker and writer Michael Moore in Britain and other western European countries. Moore's acidic satire of George Bush and corporate America has fallen on the fertile soil of popular anti-Americanism, which in Britain had long despised the Yanks as brash, pushy, loud, uncouth, materialistic, arrogant, and oversexed.

Israel and Jews in general have often been perceived in similarly stereotypical terms by the British. Beyond that, American support for Israel has become a significant source of British tension with the United States. Most often, the blame for America's "pro-Zionist" policy is placed on the shoulders of the organized American Jewish community. In 2003, Labour MP Tom Dalyell told *Vanity Fair* magazine that there was "far too much Jewish influence in the United States."[36] He particularly singled out Tony Blair's excessive reliance on Jewish advisers such as Lord Levy, his special envoy to the Middle East at the time: "I believe his influence has been very important on the Prime Minister and has led to what I see as this awful war and the sack of Baghdad."[37] Such theories about the Jewish cabal are hardly new, but they actively feed anti-American and anti-Semitic sentiments. British journalist Daniel Johnson succinctly commented on the parallel: "Both rely on fantasies about power and influence, discerning hidden patterns, concocting atrocity stories, gliding over inconvenient disconfirming facts."[38]

The increasing entwinement of these two hatreds—nurtured by similar fears, resentments, and jealousies—is indeed unmistakable. On the one hand, there is envy of America and Israel as remarkable success stories— each within their own very different scale of possibilities and ambition. At another level, there is also an unconscious fear of the rootlessness that Diaspora Jews and Americans embody as highly mobile people—assumed to be the inveterate enemies of hierarchy and tradition. This backlash is especially intense in Islamist literature, which constantly warns against secularism, materialism, and the threat of a global culture "controlled by Hollywood Jews and a borderless world of finance controlled by Wall Street Jews."[39] Israel is seen by Arabs as *the* carrier of American modernity, as well as its Middle Eastern geopolitical spearhead. Many Muslims tend to regard Americanism and Zionism as the embodiment of a global, transnational, and cosmopolitan world that remains alien to them. At the same time, America and Israel are also perceived as colonizing nations, saturated by the Holy Scriptures and imbued with a strong sense of providential mission. Hence the challenge to Islam is all the more keenly felt.

America and Israel, unlike European states, are both self-made national creations, constructed out of populations drawn from many diverse cultures around the globe that had fled persecution and were in search of a new Zion.[40] The fact that the colonization of their respective promised lands also involved violent clashes with indigenous populations is not at all peculiar to North America or to Israel. It applies equally to the history of the British Isles, Europe, Russia, Asia, Africa, Latin America, Canada, Australia, and New Zealand. The main difference remains that the Jews in Palestine were returning home to their divinely promised homeland—an unprecedented adventure with which a biblically oriented Christian America can feel special empathy. Arabs are understandably less enthusiastic.

For radical Islamists, it is a cultural axiom to vilify the crusaders (led by America) and the Zionists as twin brothers—an amalgam eagerly repeated by such fiercely anti-American British MPs as George Galloway and the extreme-right French politician Jean-Marie Le Pen. But these extremes reflect a much broader mainstream in European public opinion that reflexively sides with the Palestinians as victims of a conflict that would supposedly not exist without the power of the Jewish lobby and its stranglehold over America. Such theories have now infiltrated the American academic establishment following the controversy aroused by two American professors, John Mearsheimer and Stephen Walt, who insisted that the so-called Israel lobby completely controls U.S. Middle East policy.[41] The lobby stands accused in this narrative of stifling any real debate about Israel within American politics, in the media, or on college campuses. At the core of the lobby are American Jews acting in accordance with their own narrow loyalties while supposedly damaging U.S. national security. According to Mearsheimer and Walt, the Bush administration was merely a pawn of these alien forces acting against American national interests. Thus the old anti-Semitic charge of Jewish dual loyalties has been subliminally revived, even in the United States.[42]

The suspicion of Jewish disloyalty was always especially potent in the German-speaking lands. In nineteenth-century Germany the stereotype of Jews as egoistic and unscrupulous stock-exchange speculators made tremendous headway—often linked to Anglophobia and anti-Americanism.[43] Industrial England and North America duplicated for many Germans (and other Europeans) the original sin of coarse materialism and worship of the golden calf, which they attributed to tribal Judaism.[44] This was particularly true of the conservative elites of semi-feudal Europe. The distrust of Americanism was so pervasive that a German historical catalog in 1906 equated it with *Verjudung* (Judaization). Forty years later, the link still held. The critical Marxist Max Horkheimer (who would soon return to his German homeland from the United States) observed that wherever one found anti-Americanism, "anti-Semitism is also present."[45] German resentment was directed not only against the American victors in World War II but "once again [at] the Jews, who supposedly rule America."[46]

In the twentieth century German anti-Americanism was strongly influenced by the decisive contribution of the United States to Germany's defeats in two world wars. But even during the Weimar Republic, when a modernist version of Americanization briefly held sway in Germany, the anti-American syndrome was still present—with a special distaste being reserved for the role of American big business in pulling the strings behind international politics.[47] In Berlin, the post-1918 Anglo-Saxon new world order (guaranteed by the League of Nations) was regarded by many as an attempt to permanently enslave Germany—already weighed down by Allied war reparations. Much more than in France or Britain, anti-Americanism was openly linked in Weimar Germany to anti-Semitism, portraying the United States as a bastion of global Jewish power—a *Judenstaat* (Jews' state) in its own right. It was widely assumed on the German nationalist Right that Jews were behind the Versailles diktat, President Wilson's Fourteen Points, the usurious Allied war loans, and efforts to subjugate the German economy.[48] Wilson's chief financial adviser, Bernard Baruch, received a starring role in this anti-Semitic literature, matched only by Roosevelt's Jewish secretary of finance in World War II, Henry Morgenthau.[49]

For both left and right-wing Germans the rapacity of Wall Street came to symbolize the world threat of *Amerikanismus* (Americanism) driven forward by Jewish speculators bent on establishing the global domination of their race. In 1923, the Communist newspaper *Die Rote Fahne* attacked the Weimar Republic as a "vassal state" of the United States, controlled by Jewish capital. The half-Jewish German Communist leader Ruth Fischer indulged in nakedly anti-Semitic appeals: "Beat down the Jewish capitalists; hang them from the lampposts; trample them down."[50] On the radical Right, the predilection for conspiracy theories was still more visceral, linking capitalism, financial corruption, modernity, and democracy with Jews and the United States. Some authors, such as Otto Bonhard in his 1928 polemic *Jüdische Weltherrschaft?* (Jewish World Domination?), insisted on defining Americanism as a masked form of Jewish imperialism. Others, including Alexander Graf Brockdorff, anticipated the demise of American civilization in 1929, since its "decadent" democracy was at the mercy of the Jews.[51] Jazz, for example, was dismissed as a particularly hysterical symptom of Negro-Jewish degeneracy—a socially acceptable form of barbarism, disguising America's shallowness and inner emptiness.[52] In the Third Reich, the term "Americanism" as a metaphor was equally negative—a synonym for what was considered rootless, international, abstract, and mercenary.[53] As the ultimate product of the corrosive *Judengeist* (Jewish spirit) the United States was predestined to become a sworn enemy of the Nazis.

However, before World War II, the Nazis did everything in their power to prevent America from becoming actively involved in European affairs. Hence on January 21, 1939, Propaganda Minister Joseph Goebbels penned a typically cunning article against American global interventionism that has some remarkably contemporary resonances. He began by observing that "the role of an international policeman fitted America remarkably badly"; moreover, American intervention was "economically ruinous," obliging the American people to pay far too great a price for "the follies of its government in seeking to maintain freedom and democratic institutions around the world." According to Goebbels:

> Nothing contradicts the character of the American people as much as the arrogant, unmotivated and dangerous intervention into things which are not its business . . . the destructive consequences of a policy of intervention. The hectic armament, inspired by the Jews, accounts for about half of economic activity and creates a mentality of hostility against the outside world. It has led the country to the belief that democracy should be exported and thus to plans for world domination.[54]

This text could just as easily have been written by certain liberal, leftist, or pacifist critics of the United States nearly seven decades later. Right-wing populists such as Patrick J. Buchanan could have signed on as easily as Gore Vidal and Noam Chomsky.

America's entry into the war in December 1941 greatly intensified Nazi hatred of the "world criminal Roosevelt" and his Jewish henchmen. It prompted Hitler to lash out against the "satanic perfidy" of the U.S. president for having widened the European conflict into World War II at the behest of his "Jewish circle"—all of them "motivated by Old Testament greed."[55] Hitler would subsequently electrify his enthusiastic listeners at the Berlin Sportpalast on September 30, 1942, with the promise that Jewry was going to be exterminated as a result of the actions of the "wire pullers in the White House." These Jews around Roosevelt had "dragged one people after another into the war"—from which each nation would eventually emerge as a fully fledged "anti-Semitic State."[56]

The continued resonance of anti-Americanism in Germany after 1945 demonstrates some striking continuities with the anti-imperialism of the

Nazis and their self-proclaimed opposition to the Judaized Western plutoc-racies.[57] In the early 1950s, the idea still held sway, especially in conservative and nationalist circles, that the Jews controlled America. A prime example of this myth was the so-called Morgenthau Plan (linked to Roosevelt's treasury minister Henry Morgenthau, Jr.) with its images of a deindustrial-ized postwar Germany reduced to one huge potato field. Hostility to Anglo-American imperialist power politics reinforced this stereotypical portrait of vengeful all-powerful American Jews determined to permanently cripple German economic capacity.[58] In East Germany, official Soviet-style anti-Americanism adopted a slightly different emphasis, indulging in latently nationalist attacks on U.S. monopoly capital's determination to "divide and dismember Germany." Anti-Semitic motifs, as elsewhere among the East European Communist regimes during Stalin's last years, also began to surface—linking Zionist conspiracies with American imperialist machina-tions.[59]

By the 1960s, German New Left opposition to the "dirty war" in Vietnam would add yet another dimension to entrenched anti-Americanism. To the postwar generation, the United States now appeared as the prime contem-porary example of the horrors of fascism.[60] Nazi metaphors of evil were ea-gerly projected against America with such student slogans as "USA-SA-SS" sweeping through the Federal Republic. The German radical Left raged against America as the enemy of the Third World, branding it as a global Moloch bent on repeating the atrocities of the Third Reich. In the early 1980s the Green Party staged its own war-crimes tribunal in Nuremberg during the Pershing and cruise missile-deployment debates, attacking the wickedness of American nuclear strategy in central Europe.[61] German New Leftists even suggested that America had taken over Nazi plans for world domination using instruments such as the Bretton Woods monetary system and nuclear blackmail. Like Nazi Germany, expansionist America was al-legedly willing to eliminate social revolution by techniques that included brainwashing, torture, and physical annihilation. In the German peace movement during the 1970s and 1980s, it was common to hear that America was world enemy number one. There was a strong suspicion that it had pro-grammed a partitioned Germany as the anticipated battleground for Ar-mageddon. If necessary, the United States would be willing to have the German people destroyed in order to preserve its own global dominance.

Indeed, by the mid-1980s, the notion that Germany was nothing but an American colony had gained considerable currency, well beyond the Communists, the New Left, the Greens, and the neo-Nazis.

The 1991 Persian Gulf War, following the end of four decades of Cold War confrontation, augmented the strength and resilience of German anti-Americanism. Green politicians such as Alfred Mechtersheimer railed against the successful Americanization of the entire world, made possible by West European passivity and the lack of any independent German political identity. He bitterly attacked George H. W. Bush's "new world order" and America's insatiable greed for oil.[62] The bloody war against Saddam's Iraq was simply the logical culmination of past massacres in American history. Since 1945, the United States had left behind only hecatombs of victims throughout the Third World.

The Second Persian Gulf War would spark an even stronger wave of German anti-Americanism, casting the United States as the villain responsible for all contemporary injustices. Ironically, the invasion of Iraq happened at a historical moment of renewed German public interest in the British and American firebombing of their cities during World War II. Jörg Friedrich and other authors helped to nourish this mood by writing bestsellers in 2003 comparing the Allied aerial war to "exterminate" German cities with the Final Solution of European Jewry. In this new vocabulary, German air-raid shelters for the civilian population were now termed "crematoria" and Anglo-American bomber groups retrospectively mutated into *Einsatzgruppen*—named after those special Nazi units sent to liquidate Jews on the Russian front after June 1941. American bombing of Iraqi civilians unconsciously merged with the memory of the many German civilian victims who had died in the Allied air attacks during World War II.[63] The younger German generation had little inclination to enthusiastically recall the American liberation of West Germany in 1945. In fact, by 2003 no less than 61 percent of Germans under thirty regarded the American president as more dangerous than Saddam Hussein. Certainly, this has changed with the accession of Barack Obama, though the deeper roots of anti-Americanism remain intact.

Many Germans simply refused to believe that Americans in the Bush era could ever be victims. In 2002, the theory of the neocon cabal was especially popular.[64] Rudolf Scharping, a Social Democratic leader and former defense minister in Gerhard Schröder's cabinet, told a meeting in Berlin on August 27, 2002, that the "overly powerful Jewish lobby" in America had encouraged George W. Bush to go to war.[65] (Ironically, no other ethnic group in the United States had been as *opposed* to the war as American Jewry!) Even as Scharping spoke, party leader Schröder was exploiting pacifist anti-Americanism in order to be reelected as German chancellor in September 2002. In the same month, his justice minister compared George W. Bush to Adolf Hitler.[66] Admittedly, similar sentiments could be heard in Belgium and Holland. But by so openly embracing defamatory anti-American epithets, French and German politicians seemed to be signaling that this was now a key building block to a new European identity.

Even in central and eastern European countries, whose historical memories of Soviet domination had made them instinctively pro-American, attitudes toward the United States were mostly ambivalent, though not as hostile as in Germany. There were exceptions, such as Romania (where George W. Bush was enthusiastically greeted), but the public in most of the states that were once part of the Austro-Hungarian empire remained tepid. In Slovenia, Croatia, Slovakia, and the Czech Republic, German influence was growing faster than that of the United States, with the regional press often dismissing Bush as a lightweight. Two-thirds of all Czechs opposed participation in the invasion of Iraq. Although Poland sent troops, most Poles (in this most militantly pro-American of all eastern European states) remained lukewarm. Antiwar sentiment was above all massive in Turkey (87 percent), France (82 percent), and Germany (81 percent), indicating a growing wish for independence from U.S. foreign policy among such nominally close American allies.[67]

French anti-Americanism was no less intense than anywhere else in Europe. This hostility has existed despite the fact that French soldiers had been American allies in achieving U.S. independence from Great Britain, as well as in two successive world wars. Starting in the 1920s prominent French commentators began deploring the voracity of America's "financial imperialism."[68] A left-wing French MP, writing in 1927, fished in murky anti-Semitic waters when he announced that "Uncle Shylock and American imperialism look so strangely alike as to appear to be one and the same person."[69] Another indication of the age was the trendsetting book *Le Cancer Américain,* published in 1931. According to a growing French consensus, the United States was conquering the world with gold bars and bank credits.[70] Before 1939 American hegemony seemed a matter of economics and technology, rather than brute military power.

After 1945, however, the gulf in wealth *and* military strength between France and the United States could only exacerbate tensions. General Charles de Gaulle, who never forgave his wartime slights at President Roosevelt's hands, would establish an independent French policy based on anti-Americanism, a greater orientation toward the Third World, and the consolidation of a Franco-German axis in Europe.[71] The powerful French Communist Party was no less anti-American than De Gaulle, accusing U.S. monopoly capitalism of practicing cultural and economic imperialism. Communist, Gaullist, and Catholic critics of America had no problem defending protectionist positions in a vain effort to stem the invasion of Hollywood B movies, cheap American novels, book digests, comics, chewing gum, Coca-Cola, and McDonald's.[72] Jean-Paul Sartre and other leading intellectuals no less vainly sought to cut off any dialogue with America for fear of cultural asphyxiation.[73]

Since the early 1980s, French anti-Americanism and anti-Semitism have also been influenced by a number of new factors—the growing impact of globalization, the rise of Le Pen's racist National Front, the massive Muslim immigration to France, and two new presidents (François Mitterrand and Jacques Chirac) who were no less suspicious of American intentions than their Gaullist predecessors. As in Germany, the First Persian Gulf War brought these currents clearly to the surface.[74] The anarchist editor of *L'Idiot International*, Jean-Édern Hallier, and some of his collaborators, such as the left-wing lawyer Jacques Vergès, give a populist color to these prejudices. They systematically stigmatized the United States and Israel in a scatological language reminiscent of the anti-Semitic French writer of the 1930s, Louis-Ferdinand Céline.[75] In writing about George H. W. Bush, Hallier left nothing to the imagination: "L'Américaca, that of caca cola. Its Cartesian motto: I shit, therefore I am. When Bush speaks, he shits. He never stops bombing us—or should I say shitting on us."[76]

America represented a "conceptual Hiroshima" in its innermost essence, exposed by Operation Desert Storm—the 1991 Iraq War. This was supposedly an "American-Zionist war" (Israel did not, in fact, take part) to establish a new world order—"the war of cosmopolitanism against the nations."[77] Hallier's Judeophobia fused with a boundless hatred of America, contempt for Mammon, and a paranoid belief in conspiracies organized under the anti-Zionist banner.

Look at the Zionist domination in America. This is the herald of its coming collapse. The Roman Empire fell because of yesterday's Zionists, the trouser merchants of the Capitol—the Christians around the Jew Jesus. The Austro-Hungarian Empire crumbled because of today's Zionists—the trouser merchants of Vienna who bought their aristocratic titles selling felt-hats to the Emperor Franz Joseph.[78]

Hallier tried to turn around the inevitable charges of racism by attacking the "abominable Jewish hatred" of non-Jews, their will to power, and the alleged suppression of free thought when it came to the Holocaust. In language close to that of Le Pen, he execrated the "gestapo of the unconscious" that had led to legislation against Holocaust denial in France. In his mind, Judaism was identical to Nazism and the "victims of yesterday had become today's executioners."[79] This Nazification of the Jews and of America (accused of carrying out a genocide in Iraq) was by no means confined to a few anarchist outsiders such as Hallier, to leftist Holocaust deniers, or to neo-fascist demagogues in France.[80] They became an integral part of street politics in France and the rest of western Europe.

These themes began to reach a peak during the neo-pacifist wave of mass demonstrations in February–March 2003. Slogans such as "Busharon assassin," the "Jewish war," and "Down with the American-Zionist aggression" accompanied the gathering rhythm of anti-Semitic violence on French soil. The Célinian rhetoric of the 1930s now returned in the guise of demonizing Zionism, criminalizing Israel and vilifying a bellicose America. The war criminal Bush was dubbed the "lackey of Sharon"; the Jews of the Pentagon were accused of occupying Iraq, just like their soul mates in Jerusalem had seized Palestine. Behind all these sinister plots stood the classic conspiracy myth of world domination, which, under Zionist auspices, was finally becoming operational.[81]

In France, as in Germany, Italy, and Britain, the enemy was now war itself—personified by the material greed of America and the cupidity of the Jews. In this context, the fascist dictator Saddam Hussein could be transformed into a hero of peace, for whom at least one-third of all French people were rooting in 2002–3. This was also the official policy of the French Foreign Ministry, which by supporting Saddam Hussein (and Yasser Arafat) had secretly hoped for decades to lever itself into a position of mastery in the Middle East at the expense of the United States and Israel. This strategy, pursued with obstinate persistence by former president Jacques Chirac, was bound to fail, since France lacked the resources to supplant the United States, to dismantle Israel, or to create a state of Palestine.[82] But the obsessive anti-Americanism and anti-Zionist bias that accompanied this effort contributed to creating a poisoned public debate in Europe. As conservative American columnist George F. Will pointed out in 2003, for many Europeans America had now become what Jews were for centuries: "From medieval times until 1945 Jews were often considered the embodiment of sinister forces, the focus of discontents, the all-purpose explanation of disappointments. Now America is all those things."[83]

Scandinavia was no better than France. Immediately after 9/11, the Swedish paper *Aftonbladet* blasted the United States "as the greatest mass murderer of our time"; warned that the United States was planning its own holy war against Muslims, which could only create "a disaster of biblical proportions here in Europe"; and falsely accused it of demonizing Islam. High-profile Norwegian intellectuals, academics, and peace scholars such as Johan Galtung kept up a relentless barrage of anti-American calumnies following the U.S. invasion of Afghanistan to overthrow the Taliban. There were increasingly frequent anti-Semitic insinuations about Bush as the puppet of a pro-Israel Jewish cabal seeking to destroy Islam. In Scandinavia and most of the western European media, the Guantánamo Bay detention center and Abu Ghraib prison soon *became the war on terror*—as if to underscore the point that the United States was the planet's evil empire and its most dangerous troublemaker.[84] Spouting anti-American vitriol along with anti-Zionism had emerged as the crucial litmus test for those holding progressive opinions—a new lingua franca for enlightened Europeans.

In an article published in *The New York Times* in February 2002, the novelist Salman Rushdie suggested that European anti-Americanism was "an altogether more petulant phenomenon than its Islamic counterpart and far more personalized." For example, he found the diatribes of Londoners against American patriotism, obesity, emotionality, and self-centeredness more offensive than the aversion of Muslim countries to America's power, arrogance, and success.[85] This observation ignores, however, the extraordinary intensity of the loathing currently exhibited in the Muslim world toward the United States. Osama bin Laden, in an interview with Al-Jazeera in December 1998, had already revealed the depths of his very personal hatred: "Every Muslim, the minute he can start differentiating, carries hate towards Americans, Jews, and Christians; this is part of our ideology. Ever since I can recall I felt at war with the Americans and had feelings of animosity and hate toward them."[86]

Such feelings are common among Islamists of every stripe. Immediately after 9/11, the Palestinian Hamas, for example, issued a vitriolic "Open Letter to America" rejoicing that Allah had given the United States "the cup of humiliation" from which to drink deep.

> America, Oh sword of oppression, arrogance and sin. Do you remember how the blacks lived under your wing? . . . Have you asked yourself about your actions against your "original" inhabitants, the Indians, the Apaches? Your white feet crushed them and then used their name, Apache, for a helicopter bearing death, demolition, and destruction for anyone who dared to whisper in his own ear that he has rights.[87]

From the minarets and mosques of the Palestinian Authority (PA) and in al-Aqsa sermons, Muslim sheikhs have called on Allah to destroy the American "crusaders" and the "infidels" for years, repeatedly branding Bush as "the enemy of God." Sheikh Ikremah Sabri (former mufti of Jerusalem) echoed the familiar mantra of the Palestinian street to the effect that "the Zionist lobby had pushed the United States in the direction of the war." Hamas leader Sheikh Abdel Aziz al-Rantisi (later assassinated by Israel) justified suicide bombers against U.S. and British troops in Iraq by calling America "the head of the snake" and the driving force behind Zionism. Sheikh Ibrahim Mudeiris from Gaza City, in a February 2003 sermon broadcast on Palestinian Authority TV, pilloried America as "the foremost enemy of the Muslim nation" and of the Palestinians.[88]

In Islamist and pan-Arab anti-Americanism, the United States is indubitably the embodiment of all evil, a nation that knows only the language of force. It is the Dajjal, the deceiver of early Islamic apocalyptic texts, the demonic organizer of a crusader holy alliance against the true faith of Islam; a synonym for the empire of oppression, tyranny, arrogance, bullying, and deceit.[89] Hence it was par for the course when the Egyptian-based journal of the Muslim Brotherhood, *Afaq Arabiya,* made it clear that 9/11 was divine retribution for American moral corruption and Judaization: "The Americans thought they could not be defeated. . . . They preferred the apes [the Jews] to human beings, treating human beings from outside the U.S. cheaply, supporting homosexuals and usury. They have forgotten that in this universe there is a God whose punishment no one escapes."[90]

Muslim rejoicing over the Manhattan disaster was fully shared by liberal, pan-Arab, and Nasserist Egyptian columnists, who continually stressed the iniquity of American backing for Israel. At the same time, they also emphasized that the United States had received its just deserts for "sucking the blood of peoples," for its colonialism, "malignant idiocy," and "sick ideology."[91] An exhilarating blow had been struck in New York against "the mythological symbol of arrogant American power" and "Jewish racist totalitarianism." One pan-Arab journalist writing in *Al-Usbu* enthusiastically described the 9/11 inferno as "incandescent hell," poeticizing about the destruction of the towers (symbols of the American regime) as "the most beautiful and precious moments of my life."[92] The blow against New York and the Pentagon, as a symbol of American military might, had provided deep emotional satisfaction to millions of downtrodden and humiliated Arabs. Indeed, another Egyptian columnist, Mahmoud Abd al-Mun'im Murad of the government-sponsored daily *Al-Akhbar*, was sufficiently carried away to predict that "the age of the American collapse has begun." Neither the United States nor "its spoiled offspring Israel" would escape punishment, any more than Adolf Hitler or Mussolini did.

Arab anti-Americanism has long thrived on the assumption that the West is engaged in a crusade against Muslims, intent on crushing both them and their faith.[93] Jews and Americans are often depicted as the twin agents in this destructive process, to whom no quarter can be given. Such libels, endlessly repeated in government statements, television, radio, the press, sermons, and schools, have produced an emotional vertigo that ultimately plays into the hands of the Islamists. For example, Saudi Arabia's state-run media continues to subsidize the most virulent anti-Semitic hatred, including poetry that equates Jews with apes and calls for their extermination.[94] For decades, Saudi money has also been funneled into madrassas around the world that disseminate radical anti-Americanism, even as the U.S. alliance with the desert kingdom (Saudi oil for U.S. protection) is portrayed on both sides as a pillar of Western foreign policy. Yet, without the petroleum-rich Wahhabite Puritanism of the Saudis, there would probably have been no al-Qaeda or 9/11; furthermore, militant Islam would not have spread across the world, including to Muslim communities in America, without massive Saudi cash infusions.[95]

Osama bin Laden and his followers were originally heroes of the Saudi people and government, as long as they fought against the Soviets in Afghanistan. Even today his jihad against America (as the fountainhead of heresy, tyranny, and aggression) is greatly admired among the Muslim masses. For Saudi dissidents, he still remains a glorious model, as the scholar Muhammad al-Khasif explains: "If Che Guevara was a model for the fighters in the world, and a beautiful symbol of the struggle against American imperialism in South America, then Osama bin Laden is the same symbol for the Muslims."[96]

The spokesmen of the global jihad, in explaining why they fight America, often used familiar anti-imperialist rhetoric, blaming the United States for all the oppression, injustice, and disasters that have befallen Muslims in Iraq, Afghanistan, Somalia, Palestine, and other centers of conflict.[97] They blacken American behavior as genocidal ever since the "extermination" of the native Indians. Comparing it with the barbarism of the Roman Empire and the Crusaders, they always emphasize the hidden machinations of the Zionists as a major driving force of this diabolical policy.[98] The American empire is moribund, like Pharaoh, since its godless credo is based on the annihilation of Muslims, according to one prominent Egyptian filmmaker.[99] President Bush's methods not only resembled those of Hitler but the Guantánamo Bay detention camp was identical to Auschwitz, according to a former Egyptian minister of war, Amin Huweidi, writing in *Al-Ahali* in February 2003.[100] But America is not merely more expansionist than the Nazis, it is also reviled as the source of a totally dysfunctional secular modernity, crippled by materialism, pornography, drug dependency, and high divorce rates. Such emotive outpourings provide the core of the anti-American hatred raging through the state-run Arab media.

From Gamal Abdel Nasser in the 1950s to Osama bin Laden fifty years later, Arab political, religious, and ideological leaders have never stopped venting their bile against the United States, Zionism, and the Jews. The demonization of America has indeed become normal mainstream discourse in the Middle East. For example, the leader of the Muslim Brotherhood,

Muhammad Mahdi Othman 'Akef, in an interview in 2004 to the Egyptian weekly *Al-Arabi,* declared: "We have no relations with the U.S. It is a Satan that abuses the region, lacking all morality and law."[101]

America's purportedly satanic activities have included treachery, lying, and gratuitous murder—something "generically ingrained in American culture," according to a Syrian-born columnist Husnu Mahali, writing in late 2004 in the Turkish Islamic daily *Yeni Şafak.*[102]

Preachers in the Palestinian Authority have been no less vitriolic. They have likened American actions in Iraq to the deeds of the Mongols and accused "the infidel and arrogant United States" of seeking to draw Muslims away from the Holy Koran. Like so many other clerics, the Gazan preacher Hayyan al-Idris dismissed American claims to be fighting for democracy. They had simply invaded the Middle East to steal its treasures and murder its people.[103] In the wake of their bloody conquest of Iraq came the economic invasion of the Jews—"a cancer spreading in the body of the Arab nation and the Islamic nation."[104] Even a "moderate" Palestinian like Arafat's former national security adviser, Colonel Jibril Rajoub did not hesitate to vilify the U.S. government as a "right-wing, fascist administration controlled by the Zionist Right."[105] President Bush, as a leading PA newspaper delicately put it, was the "Führer of the globalization era" (a phrase coined by Fidel Castro), with a far more frightening array of weapons of mass destruction than any of his predecessors. If Bush were not checked he would "return the world to the Stone Age."[106]

Anti-Americanism—contrary to a well-entrenched prejudice—is not merely a function of U.S. foreign policy and the alleged misdeeds of Americans, though these may at times exacerbate the intensity of the phenomenon. In practice the United States has done more than any power to try to resolve the Arab-Israeli conflict. It intervened to save Afghanistan from the Soviets; Kuwait and Saudi Arabia from Saddam Hussein; and Bosnian Muslims from a possible genocide in the Balkans. But despite its frequent support for Muslims against non-Muslims, anti-American sentiment has not diminished. Nor are Europeans today grateful to America for having liberated the continent three times—from German imperial ambitions in 1917, from Nazism, and from Soviet Communism. They are even less willing to wholeheartedly support any American confrontation with Iran, radical Islam, and jihadi terrorism.

The current appeasement policy of the Obama administration may well suit them better, though it will not solve any core issues. Anti-Americanism, like anti-Semitism, is organically resistant to empirical argument and rational discourse. Like all forms of hate-mongering, it inflates the power of the target group, demonizes its motivations, and holds it responsible for virtually all social evils.[107] Anti-Americanism, no less than anti-Semitism, focuses discontent against a common enemy in order to explain away internal failures; to mobilize public anger against malignant, "alien forces"; and to artificially reinforce national or religious unity. But as with other noxious demonologies that masquerade as rational critiques or even as full-blown ideologies, anti-Americanism and anti-Semitism are basically irrational at the core. The fears, fantasies, and hatreds from which they are fabricated are based more on myth than on any serious confrontation with reality.

SEVENTEEN

Multiculturalism and Its Discontents

n 1991, the Oxford philosopher Isaiah Berlin gave an interview on the gathering storm of nationalism just as the Soviet Union began to unravel. At the time, open ethnic warfare was already raging in Yugoslavia, which would eventually lead to its demise as a multinational state. Despite the rebirth of nationalisms following the fall of the Soviet empire, "the sage of Oxford"—like most people in the West—could not help but rejoice at the crumbling of the Berlin wall and the Communist Tower of Babel. "The Tower of Babel," as Isaiah Berlin laconically observed, "was meant to be unitary in character; a single great building, reaching to the skies, with one language for everybody. The Lord didn't like it. There is, I have been told, an excellent Hebrew prayer, to be uttered when seeing a monster. 'Blessed be the Lord our God, who introduced variety among thy creatures.'"[1] But what if multiculturalism, in the name of diversity and variety, is itself in the process of producing a monster?

In the story of Babel we have a powerful warning against empire builders, imperialists, totalitarian rulers, civilizing missions, Utopian ideologues, and jihadi fundamentalists who dogmatically seek to impose a single regime of homogeneity and sameness upon a plural world. After Babel, humanity—according to the biblical account—was divided into a multiplicity of cultures, languages, peoples, and civilizations. There is no longer a universal language, no one truth about the human condition that is valid for all times and places. In the Hebraic understanding, it is the *fact of difference* that henceforth defines the human condition. Does that make the creator of the universe a "multiculturalist"? Does it mean that contemporary Jews must necessarily favor cultural and political pluralism? Clearly that would be an oversimplification. But within the Jewish tradition—as part of its perennial tension between the particular and the universal—there is an unusual sensitivity to questions of identity, the dignity of human beings, the primacy of freedom, opposition to coercion, respect for difference, and the rights of the stranger. "To love the stranger" (the one who is not like us) is a command that appears no less than thirty-six times in the Hebrew Bible. In normative terms this is surely the humanist core of the Judaic message.[2]

We could make a good case that Jews were the first *global* people, the first to wrestle with the reality of worldwide dispersion, maintaining their identity as a nation despite being scattered across the face of the earth. Not only that, but in many respects Jews in the Diaspora were themselves a multicultural and polyglot people, able to adapt and survive tremendous adversity for nearly two millennia without the support of a state, a territorial homeland, or a political center. This extraordinary anomaly in the annals of history is clearly not unrelated to the longevity and near-ubiquity of anti-Semitism.

Ever since the French Revolution, when Jews first entered political modernity, they have been obliged to choose between their collective identity as a people and assimilation in return for full rights as individuals.[3] This dilemma raises the question of what are contemporary society's limits of tolerance and willingness to accommodate diversity? It suggests something imperial in the normative universalism of Europe and its cultural mission. As part of the emancipation contract, what the modern European state gave with one hand to its individual Jewish citizens (equality before the law) it took away with the other ("to the Jews as Jews nothing," in the words of the aristocratic deputy Stanislas de Clermont-Tonnerre at the French National Assembly debate in 1789).[4] Ever since, official France has looked upon cultural and religious diversity with suspicion—as an affront to its rigid republican ethos of secularism.

Yet there have been multinational, multiethnic, multicultural states in Europe, such as the Hapsburg Empire in the late nineteenth century, that appeared to offer a promising alternative to the Jews—the possibility of cultural autonomy *and* ethnic diversity, as well as civic equality. Though this never became official policy, even the Catholic Hapsburg rulers gradually came to regard the cosmopolitan, multilingual, and transnational Jews as a *staatserhaltend* (state-conserving) element in their extremely heterogeneous *Nationalitätenstaat* (multinational state). Unlike the pan-Germans or the Czech, Magyar, Slovak, Romanian, Italian, and Serb nationalists, Jews did not want to break up the Danubian monarchy.

At the turn of the twentieth century thinkers as diverse as Simon Dub-now, Nathan Birnbaum, and the Austro-Marxist Karl Renner (as well as the Jewish Bundists in the Russian Empire) thought the future of Jewish mi-norities was best assured in polyglot empires such as Austria, providing they were truly federalized and decentralized along democratic lines.[5] The hope was that central Europe could become a kind of Switzerland writ large. These illusions were dashed by the shots that murdered Franz Ferdinand, heir to the Hapsburg throne, in Sarajevo (the multicultural capital of Bosnia-Herzegovina) in July 1914. This assassination triggered World War I and would permanently unhinge central and eastern Europe, eventually opening the road to the victory of Nazism and quasi-fascist dictatorships.

One of the most important fin de siècle prophets of National Socialism was an expatriate Englishman, Houston S. Chamberlain—then living in Vienna—who in 1900 published a bestselling study *Die Grundlagen der neunzehnten Jahrhunderts* (*The Foundations of the Nineteenth Century*). This massive work, written in German, was an uncompromising assault on the *Völkerchaos* (national chaos), the "racial mishmash," and cultural de-generation of modern urban civilization—whose materialist egoism was primarily laid at the door of the Jews.[6] It would become a bible of modern racist anti-Semitism. Most of what we recognize as "multiculturalist" axioms—pluralism, the benefits of ethnic and cultural diversity, the contri-bution of peoples of color, the right to difference, the celebration of mar-ginal voices, gender history, and oppressed minorities—was anathema to Chamberlain, as it has been to white supremacists and anti-Semitic racists ever since. To this day, neofascists see the Jews as the destroyers par excel-lence of aristocracy, arch-subverters of hierarchy, authority, classical order, and Christian morality, and as the prime source of multicultural and mul-tiracial infection.[7]

The horror of miscegenation was best exemplified by Adolf Hitler's undisguised contempt for the multiethnic Hapsburg Empire (an "impossi-ble state") and his loathing for the *Rassenkonglomerat* (conglomerate of races), whose hybrid nature doomed it to destruction. In recalling his early years in Vienna, Hitler's imagery in *Mein Kampf* provides a racist parody of the Hebrew Bible. Austria is a *Völkerbabylon* (a Babylon of nationalities);[8] the Reichsrat (imperial parliament) is a "linguistic Babel" of chaos, confu-sion, and noncommunication; the accents he hears on the Vienna streets and in the Prater public park grate on his ears like a babble of tongues—

living proof of the *Blutschande* (the "original sin" of race mixing). Turn-of-the-century Vienna ("this ancient site of German culture") had been irredeemably corroded by the "poison of foreign nations growing away at the body of our nationality."[9] In *Mein Kampf*, Hitler records how totally sickened he felt "by the whole mixture of Czechs, Poles, Hungarians, Ukrainians, Serbs and Croats, and everywhere the eternal mushroom [*Spaltpiltz*] of humanity—Jews and more Jews."[10] For the future founder and leader of German National Socialism, this traumatic encounter with languages and races in Vienna became the seedbed of his murderous anti-Semitism. In its place he would construct a new Germanic Tower of Babel that would become totally *judenrein*—forever cleansed of Jews.

North America provides a striking contrast to central Europe. In many respects the cradle of democratic pluralism and multiculturalism, the United States has thus far been significantly less tainted by political anti-Semitism. It was no accident that the Nazis described American society in the 1930s as a thoroughly Judaized, negrified racial hodgepodge—a rubbish heap of social debris from Europe that had washed up on American shores. According to Goebbels, the great ethnic melting pot was not a real nation but a rootless civilization inspired "by the most vulgar commercialism"; a land of millionaires, mafiosi, beauty queens, stupid records, and irredeemably bad taste, ruled by a "Jew-ridden plutocracy."[11] President Roosevelt—as we have seen—was consistently branded a *Judenknecht* (servant of the Jews) in wartime National Socialist propaganda. Genocidal Jew hatred effortlessly blended with loathing for America and its multicultural mosaic.[12]

There are more than a few echoes of this anti-Semitic anti-Americanism in contemporary Europe, the Third World, and the Middle East. Some of the Islamist suicide bombers who attacked the Twin Towers of Manhattan on 9/11, for example, truly believed that they were striking at the evil heart of world capitalism and global finance, headed by Jewish Wall Street. The World Trade Center and Jewish New York symbolized for them the "anonymous powers" of globalized and plutocratic America. The jihadi warriors evidently thought that they had delivered a blow against the headquarters of Jewish-crusader civilization—the godless spearhead of those dark occult forces supposedly out to destroy Islam and erode the cultural identity of all true Muslim believers.[13] The al-Qaeda bombers were destroying the modern Tower of Babel, with New York as the whore of Babylon and themselves cast in the role of Allah's messengers and avengers of Islam against American imperial arrogance.

In an article published in *Partisan Review* in early December 2001, I wrote the following passage:

> The cataclysm of the Manhattan massacre is in fact far more than just another example of international terrorism. The symbolism of the burning towers announced a new kind of world-wide jihad. It was a dramatic fanfare for the Islamic fascism of the 21st century, whose perpetrators are bent on total confrontation, on the either/or politics of victory or death.[14]

It is important to recall that the politics of either/or toward the Jews and the West was a Nazi trademark—like the *Protocols*-inspired all-embracing theory of a world Jewish conspiracy—much as it has now become a standard feature of Islamofascism.[15] Some of the parallels are striking. Hitler's architect Albert Speer recalled in 1947 that toward the end of the war, Hitler "pictured for himself and for us the destruction of New York in a hurricane of fire." In a kind of delirium, the Nazi führer would describe to his acolytes visions of skyscrapers being turned into "gigantic burning torches, collapsing upon one another, the glow of the exploding city illuminating the dark sky."[16] Osama bin Laden's disciples would finally translate this Wagnerian-Hitlerian *Götterdämmerung* (*Twilight of the Gods*) into murderous reality over half a century later. Not surprisingly the massive assault on Judaized New York also electrified contemporary neo-Nazis, who hailed it as a stinging defeat for ZOG (the Zionist Occupied Government)—a favorite name for the U.S. federal government in extreme right circles. In Europe, there was also a degree of admiration for bin Laden's exploit—especially on the radical Left, among Muslims, and the anti-American intelligentsia. They, too, viewed 9/11 as an assault on the HQ of world capitalism and globalization. Observing this perverse Schadenfreude on the German Left, the American scholar Andrei Markovits commented:

> The aversion arises also because the United States—and, again, especially New York—represents the greatest social experiment on earth. We have an existing multicultural society which enemies of the United States reject.

Citizens from 82 countries and United States citizens of every conceivable religion, ethnicity, and skin color died in the World Trade Center. Anywhere else this would have been unthinkable, yet this kind of multiculturalism has become a part of everyday life in New York, and perhaps in Los Angeles, over the last 10 to 15 years. Potential success in constructing a truly multicultural society is as much of a red flag for the enemies of America as is its leadership in the process of globalized capitalism.[17]

Old World loathing of America has, of course, many other causes beyond hostile and condescending attitudes toward its multiculturalism—not least, resentment at the sheer magnitude of global American power. But, as we have seen, it is also an outlook that displays some striking similarities to anti-Zionism and anti-Semitism in its imperviousness to logic, facts, or even enlightened self-interest.[18] The animus is especially noticeable in European universities and mainstream media, where it has become axiomatic to suggest that Jews and the Israel lobby control America; where "neocon" has become a euphemism for "Jew"; and a soft version of the Zionist-crusader conspiracy holds Israel responsible for Islamist terrorism.

The cumulative influence of Muslim and Arab immigration to Europe, as well as the Euro-Arab dialogue, with its concomitant anti-Israel and anti-American reflexes, has been an additional factor in creating this hostility. It plays a role in the emergence of an Israelophobic culture full of disinformation, hatred of America, and vicious comments about Jews, partly driven by fear of Islamist terror.[19] This is all the more troubling given the extraordinary reluctance, especially by liberals, to recognize the dangerous aspects in the jihadi challenge to Israel and the West. Today this resurgent Islam, powerfully reinforced by the European Left and the kind of anti-Zionist rhetoric institutionalized for decades in the United Nations, represents the main threat to the security of Europe's Jews and Christians.

Jews in western Europe are particularly vulnerable since they number slightly more than a million in the face of approximately twenty-five million Muslims on the Old Continent, who are made more confident by their growing demographic strength. In the foreseeable future cities like Rotterdam, Antwerp, Marseille, Malmö, Bradford, and Leicester may even have a Muslim immigrant majority.[20] The low European birthrate (the continental average is a mere 1.37 children per woman) and continued Muslim immigration gives, therefore, some credence to Libyan president Qaddafi's hope that "Allah will grant Islam victory in Europe—without swords, without guns, without conquests."[21] Muslim radicalism may lack the centralized military power of the Nazi state in the 1930s, but it exhibits a similar dynamism and mobilizing potential that makes it possible to imagine the creeping transformation of Europe into Eurabia. This is the context in which the debate over Islamophobia has to be seen—one that has been obscured by multiculturalist dogmas discouraging immigrants from any serious efforts at integration.

The contemporary politics of appeasement cannot, however, be understood without reference to deeply rooted images of the Jew as an alien, nomadic, rootless, protean, highly mobile, and threatening outsider in the European imagination.[22] In the 1930s such anti-Semitic stereotypes assumed a predominantly ethnic, *völkisch,* and racial-biological character. Sixty years later this anti-Semitism has *mutated* rather than disappeared. In its place, there is a progressive consensus that formally renounces all dreams of empire, while simultaneously repudiating nationalism, xenophobia, and racism.[23] But it turns out that there is a catch. Many bien-pensant Europeans, who vehemently disapprove of nationalism and anti-Semitism, compassionately honor dead Holocaust victims, and abhor Nazism, also loathe Israel as a racist, apartheid country; a warmongering rogue state; and a new incarnation of the Third Reich.

Anti-Israel vilification frequently derives from an exaggerated antiracist exuberance in which the Palestinians and Muslims in general are depicted as *absolute victims* (whatever atrocities they may commit) and Americans or Israelis are irresponsibly stereotyped as their criminal oppressors—the supreme ethnic cleansers of our time. Indeed, contemporary demonization of Israel all too often takes place *in the name of human rights,* as part of the fight against racism and fascism.[24] Ken Livingstone, the populist mayor of London (one of Europe's greatest multicultural cities), exhibited this perverse syndrome to perfection.

Significantly, at the end of November 2006, Livingstone boycotted a conference in London on race relations marking thirty years of anti-discrimination legislation. The drafters of the 1976 Race Relations Act had banned racial discrimination and established the Commission for Racial Equality (CRE) to enforce the law. At that time the main concern was the unchecked black immigration from British Commonwealth countries and widespread white prejudice against Afro-Caribbeans. The 1981 riots in twenty-nine of Britain's inner cities exposed the seriousness of the problem. Though issues of higher criminality, poor school performance among blacks, job competition, fears of miscegenation, and white racism still exist, the Afro-Caribbean population in Britain has, on the whole, become part of mainstream British life. This is not the case with some Asians (especially Pakistanis and Bangladeshis) who have opted for separateness. An aggressive Muslim fundamentalism has made strong inroads among them, leading to an accompanying threat of homegrown terrorism. These negative trends prompted Trevor Phillips, the head of CRE (and himself of Afro-Caribbean descent), to sharply condemn Islamist violence and the related outbreak of anti-Semitism. He also warned that Britain was in danger of "sleepwalking into segregation." Phillips aroused Livingstone's particular ire by stressing that multiculturalism was not just about color—that a narrow-minded identity politics had to be fought, along with separateness in culture and religion among many Asian immigrants.[25]

These and other examples suggest that the concept of multiculturalism (which many liberals, leftists, and Western Jews continue to vigorously support) may have turned into a Trojan horse, enabling Islamic fundamentalists to establish a prime international hub in western Europe to promote global jihad. For example, such notorious preachers of hatred as Abu Hamza al-Masri and Sheikh Abdallah al-Faisal (both of them finally behind bars for "racial incitement") openly recruited mujahideen in Britain to battle the infidels in Afghanistan, Kashmir, Chechnya, Iraq, and Palestine. They helped to spread the vilest anti-Semitism, anti-Americanism, and hatred of Hindus. They were greatly helped by excessively liberal immigration laws, by the benign tolerance of the British government, police, and intelligence services (which only began to change after 2003); and above all by the extraordinary complacency of British elites in confronting the holy war waged by the Islamists against the Western world.[26]

An important factor in this politics of appeasement has been the iron-clad orthodoxy of contemporary multiculturalism and moral relativism, which holds that it is a racist act to condemn any minority belief or value system.[27] The British elites (like much of the western European establishment) refuse to accept that there is a global religious war that drives today's terrorism in the name of Allah and the right to Islamic conquest. The postcolonial, multiculturalist mind-set of the West is literally obsessed by the fear of stigmatizing all Muslims but singularly fails to see that it is the latter who are the most numerous victims of the worldwide jihad. At a deeper level, as in the Netherlands, Scandinavia, and Germany, the political class and the intellectuals in Britain have been hollowing out national identity and values to the point that those who uphold them can be shamelessly vilified as racists. The logical result of this value erosion is that there can be no majority culture at all. Worse still, the nation-state (invariably rooted in a *particular* history, language, legal system, cultural tradition, and religious heritage) is not only delegitimized but seen as the cause of all the world's ills. This value vacuum has opened the door to the radical Islamists to intensively recruit among alienated young Muslims and significantly spread their untruths about America and Israel—a discourse already rampant in the mainstream British media. As Melanie Phillips explains:

> If there is no longer an overarching culture, there is nothing into which minorities can integrate. Many young Muslims, stranded between the backward Asian village culture of their parents and the drug, alcohol and sex-saturated decadence that passes for western civilization, are filled with disgust and self-disgust—and are thus vulnerable to the predatory jihadis, recruiting in youth clubs, in prisons and on campus, who promise them self-respect and a purpose to life based on holy war.[28]

Multiculturalism, by reversing long-accepted notions of truth and falsehood, victim and victimizer, has aggravated this moral paralysis, playing into the hands of the Muslim victim culture. As many Muslims genuinely believe themselves to be under attack by the West (especially from America and Israel) and threatened by a gigantic conspiracy, terrorism can all too easily be rationalized as a legitimate act of "self-defense." Since minorities cannot by definition (in the multiculturalist dispensation) be held responsible for vile acts such as suicide bombings, it must be the fault of those who are now the targets of their vengeance.[29] Thus the satanization of Jews and Christians serves to avoid any individual or group accountability from Muslims for their own actions.

In Parliament, the media, academia, the churches (especially the Anglican Church), and among intellectuals and public opinion makers, every conceivable excuse has been found to explain away acts of Islamist terrorism.[30] In this one-sided discourse, interfaith dialogue (especially between Christians and Muslims) has tended to blur rather than clarify the issues.

True, more recently, there has been some questioning of multiculturalism in Britain, especially in the wake of the July 2005 terrorist atrocities on and under the streets of London. There has also emerged a growing realization at the highest political level of the need to assert the core values of identity, integration, and cohesion more strongly.[31] In October 2006, the leader of the House of Commons, Jack Straw, publicly revealed that he had asked veiled Muslim women in his Blackburn constituency to show their faces when they came to see him. The head scarf had suddenly become an issue in multicultural Britain—not only because of terrorism and fundamentalism but as a symptom of concern as to whether a formerly easygoing approach toward integrating ethnic communities is still working.[32] A number of commentators have pertinently observed, for example, that multicultural policies are an obstacle to the formal learning of English. They prevent integration, heighten intercommunal tensions, and reinforce the ghettoization of Asian Muslims into separate enclaves with high unemployment and increased social alienation.[33] After the July 7, 2005, bombings in London, broadcaster Kenan Malik wrote that "Britishness had come to be defined simply as a toleration of difference," with no political or moral center. This was a consequence of the multiculturalist ideology that had accentuated social fragmentation in an increasingly "tribal Britain." Among British Asians a siege mentality had emerged that "makes the Muslim communities more inward-looking and more open to religious extremism."[34]

During recent years, the Anglican Church in Britain has been especially receptive to Muslim concerns and sensitivities in the framework of multiculturalism and multifaith initiatives. At the theological level, Anglicanism—while gradually uprooting itself from its Judaic heritage—has begun to stress—in the words of Margeret Brearley—"the shared journey of Christians and Muslims."[35] Anglican clergy have been especially keen to distance Islamist terrorism from any association with the Muslim religion.[36] At the same time, Anglican anti-Zionism has become very influential, constantly vilifying Israel for its so-called intransigence and arrogance. The Reverend Stephen Sizer has fiercely denounced Christian Zionism and questioned the validity of Jewish nationhood, while accusing Israel of racial segregation, apartheid, and ethnic cleansing.[37] Like many other Anglicans, he has come to embrace Palestinian liberation theology, especially of the kind espoused during the first Palestinian intifada by Rev. Naim Ateek, canon of St. George's Anglican Cathedral in Jerusalem, where he founded the Sabeel Ecumenical Liberation Theology Center.[38] This institution has revived the traditional Christian teaching of contempt for Jews and Judaism, blending it with an extreme anti-Israel agenda.

The anti-Zionist obsession has led not only Anglicans but a large part of the secular European elite to ignore the real problems posed by demographic decline, the erosion of their own cultural patrimony, and the sapping of national identity. Despite some doubts, a fuzzy multiculturalism still prevails in Brussels and other European capitals, based on the unfounded premise that people only have to do their own thing and all will be well. Totalitarian Islam (especially the opposing brands promoted by Shiite Iran or Wahhabi Saudi Arabia) has made a mockery of this liberal approach. They sponsor imams all over Europe whose main goal has been to prevent Muslims from integrating into Western society. These imams encourage an exclusivist identity politics in Muslim faith schools, which serve as enclaves or parallel societies where youngsters are taught to despise and reject Western values. The fundamentalists seek the Islamicization of Europe, not the Europeanization of Islam. This entails spreading the virulent Islamist anti-Semitism that has taken root in the Middle East, injecting it into the mainstream Muslim diaspora in Europe. In order to protect themselves from criticism, the imams have sought to confuse racism with Islamophobia, while covering up their own anti-Semitism as resistance to Israeli oppression. According to the uncensored findings of the EU's unit to monitor all forms of racism, anti-Semitic incidents between 2001 and 2005 increased in Germany from 1,424 to 1,628; in France from 219 to 504; and in Britain from 310 to 455, and then to 594 in 2006. A large percentage of the perpetrators, it is now acknowledged, have been Muslims.

In 2001, Raphael Israeli pointed out that these new immigrants to Western countries "for the most part carry with them the anti-Semitic luggage which they had absorbed by education in their mother-countries and cultures."[39] The renewed encounter with Jews in the host countries offered them the perfect target against which to vent their fury toward Israel and Jewry, in alliance with the anti-Zionist Left and the anti-Semitic radical Right. Firebomb attacks against synagogues; assault on religious worshippers, community centers, schools, and anyone of Jewish appearance; graffiti; threatening phone calls; and Islamist anti-Semitic preaching: All have increased enormously since the onset of the new millennium. In France, there were 320 *violent* anti-Jewish incidents in 2001; in April 2002, there were no less than 400 such acts, necessitating large police reinforcements at Jewish sites.[40] In the United Kingdom the 2006 figures were the highest since such statistics began to be recorded in the early 1980s. The same trend has been observable in the Netherlands and Germany. Just over sixty years after the yellow star was officially instituted in Nazi-controlled Europe, authorities from France to Belgium and Sweden instruct Jews to hide any sign of their Jewishness in the public space in order to avoid intimidation or physical assault.[41]

Instead of directly confronting Muslim anti-Semitism and the concerted Islamist effort to brainwash Muslim children in the mosques, schools, and charity organizations, European political elites have mostly left the imams free to incite to violence and hatred.[42] They have also encouraged the myth of Islamophobia—of an anti-Muslim racism that supposedly resembles yesterday's anti-Semitism and might even produce the next Holocaust. Thus Muslims are misleadingly transmuted into Europe's new Jews even as their more radical cohorts harass and threaten the much smaller Jewish communities of the Old Continent.[43] The Muslim grievance industry in Europe builds on this sense of victimhood to promote its own Islamist political program, which is ultimately aimed at subverting Europe itself. There are, however, a few bright spots. The French minister of justice, Rachida Dati, speaking in Israel on September 21, 2008, emphasized that anti-Semitism was not only a form of discrimination but a criminal offense. It offended against fundamental principles of equality, dignity, and humanity. At the same time, while affirming the aspirations of Palestinians to justice, she insisted that Israel was a "great democracy" with the full right to live in peace "within secure and recognized borders."[44]

European Jews have once more become canaries in the mine. This time they are caught in the crossfire of Europe's contemporary culture wars over the place of Islam in the body politic. In France (with six million Muslims and six hundred thousand Jews in a general population of about sixty million) the issue has been especially bitter and controversial. Initially, there was a virtual blackout in the French media when it came to accurately reporting the violent assaults by radicalized young Muslims on Jewish individuals or institutions. Former President Chirac, high officials, the media, and French left-wing intellectuals stubbornly refused to admit that anti-Semitism had revived as a real force on French soil, spearheaded predominantly by North African Arab Muslims. In 2003, for example, no major

French newspaper even carried the story of the homicide of young French-Jewish disc jockey Sebastien Sellan, whose Algerian Muslim murderer triumphantly cried: "I have killed my Jew. I will go to heaven." Furthermore, the jihadist dimension of the February 2006 macabre torture and killing of twenty-three-year-old Sephardi Jew Ilan Halimi was initially downplayed by the French government, media, and police.[45] After some hesitation, however, they admitted that primitive anti-Semitism ("Jews equal money") did play a role in the affair.

Almost every country in postwar western Europe has, by now, had its own close encounters with radical Islamists. The Dutch case is especially instructive. For many years the Dutch prided themselves on being a model of European multiculturalism, religious tolerance, and respect for diversity. Two recent political murders shattered this idyllic image. First, the populist leader Pim Fortuyn was killed by a Dutch animal rights activist on May 6, 2002—the first such political slaying in the democratic Netherlands since the seventeenth century. Then, on November 2, 2004, the iconoclastic Dutch documentary filmmaker Theo van Gogh was brutally stabbed, shot, and beheaded in broad daylight on a street in Amsterdam by a young Dutch Moroccan jihadist, Mohammed Bouyeri.[46] Both Fortuyn and van Gogh were sharp critics of Islam and its religious fundamentalist intolerance. The murders heightened the Dutch backlash against a poorly integrated Muslim immigration (mainly from Turkey and Morocco), reinforced public demands to crack down on religious extremism, and demonstrated the need to strengthen a very much eroded sense of national identity.[47]

The multiethnic nature of the relatively tolerant postwar Dutch society, and the coexistence within it of distinct cultures, has not been the result of government planning but rather of the piecemeal immigration of foreign workers, decolonization, and the granting of political asylum to refugees from the Third World. Until the sensational murder of 2004 it was still politically correct to assume that the meeting between different ethnicities and cultures could only enrich Dutch society. But in recent years, such negative effects as high crime rates, violence, and intimidation by the *allochtones* (immigrants) have come much more to the foreground; so, too, have the calls (especially from the Right) for asserting a *Leitkultur* (a leading culture)—meaning that of Dutch civilization. At the same time, a general consensus has emerged across the spectrum that the sharia is fundamentally incompatible with the Dutch constitution. Nevertheless, on the Dutch

Left (as elsewhere in Europe) the possibility of racism or anti-Semitism among minorities is generally denied. This was one reason for the tension between Dutch progressives and the secular Muslim female dissident Ayaan Hirsi Ali—a liberal Somali-born parliamentarian driven from the Netherlands by constant death threats. She had authored the script of *Submission*, a short movie that led to van Gogh's murder.[48]

Hirsi Ali had been proclaimed the next target for assassination by Bouyeri, since she had dared to expose the abuse of women in the Muslim world and called for a rigorous self-examination by Muslims of their own faith. Her status as a heretic was made clear in the open letter found on van Gogh's body—a text written in Muslim religious style and containing many anti-Semitic remarks. Bouyeri's letter damned her as a willing tool of "Zionists and crusaders," a "soldier of evil" who would be destroyed, along with the United States, Europe, and Holland. Her so-called masters, of course, were the Jewish "cabal" that ruled the Netherlands—including Amsterdam mayor Job Cohen, a secular Jewish progressive who had tried hard to find common ground with the Muslim communities. Bouyeri's undisguised hatred for this kind of Dutch multiculturalist utopia and its "decadent" tolerance with regard to gays, drugs, and prostitution fused with loathing of the West in general and crass anti-Semitism.[49]

The very small post-1945 Dutch Jewish community was not the real object of Bouyeri's violent hatred. Highly assimilated, they had long been the target of neo-Nazi and racist abuse, and of verbal violence in soccer stadiums, and were accustomed over the years to the rampant anti-Israel media bias in the Netherlands.[50] In November 2003, a Eurobarometer poll even showed that the Netherlands had the *highest* percentage of respondents in Europe who considered Israel the number one threat to world peace. No less than 74 percent of the Dutch held this view, compared to 59 percent of western Europeans.[51] It was symbolically significant in this context that Gretta Duisenberg, wife of the Dutch former head of the European Central Bank, publicly fought to secure "six million signatures" (shades of the Holocaust) for presentation at pro-Palestinian rallies in the Netherlands. The number of anti-Semitic incidents in the Netherlands is unusually high in proportion to the tiny size of the Jewish population. A substantial number of the perpetrators are youngsters of Moroccan ancestry—a fact consistently downplayed by the Dutch media and politicians.[52] The explosive mixture of self-righteous moralism, bloody-minded illiberalism, the cult of death, revolutionary fervor, and visions of world salvation of this Islamist element has turned the enlightenment dream of Dutch multiculturalism on its head.[53]

Multiculturalism is clearly fading away in the polyglot, cosmopolitan Netherlands, where an unfavorable view of Muslims is currently higher than anywhere else in Europe. Over half of the Dutch regard Islam negatively and 63 percent believe it to be a religion incompatible with modern European society.[54] The Moroccan Muslims, who represent only 2 percent of the Dutch population, are estimated to be responsible for 40 percent of all the violent anti-Semitic incidents that occurred between 2002 and 2005.[55] This Moroccan immigrant population has certainly boosted the forces demonizing the Jews and Israel in the Netherlands and undoubtedly intimidated the local Jewish community. Jews wearing a yarmulke in public are likely to be subjected to verbal and at times physical abuse on the street. Muslims do not generally face such pressures, but attitudes toward Islam are hardening in the Netherlands and elsewhere across Europe.

For example, a growing hostility to Islam is becoming ever more pronounced in German public opinion. The Allensbach Institute for Public Opinion Research conducted a survey of ordinary Germans in May 2006 whose results were unequivocal. Eighty-three percent of Germans associated Islam with fanaticism; 70 percent with intolerance; 62 percent with backwardness; 60 percent held it to be "undemocratic." An overwhelming 91 percent of Germans agreed that Islam discriminates against women. Three-fifths of all Germans were convinced that the *Kampf der Kulturen* (the clash of civilizations) is a reality, and an even higher number are convinced that it can only worsen.[56]

Western European opinion may not continue to accept multiculturalism much longer, mainly out of fear of Muslim radicals and the danger of a creeping Islamicization of Europe. Yet Europe's elites—who are often out of touch with these popular trends—behave as if they were determined to avoid anything that could ruffle Muslim sensitivities. The quality media, for example, frequently censor themselves in reporting on crimes committed by Muslims. In Malmö, Sweden's third largest city, both the government and media ignored the rapes, robberies, school burnings, honor killings, and anti-Semitic incitement among local Muslims, blaming such problems on Swedish racism.[57] Then there was the Danish cartoons affair, which prompted an international furor, with dozens killed by rioting Muslims in

Europe, Africa, and Asia. To quote one critical commentator: "The Danes were suddenly the most hated people on earth, with their embassies under attack, their flag being burned, and their consciousness being raised by lectures on religious tolerance from Iran, Saudi Arabia, and other beacons of enlightenment."[58] Yet the EU foreign minister Javier Solana, in a remarkable act of cringing appeasement, immediately departed on a tour of Arab nations, assuring them he shared the "anguish" of Muslims offended by the cartoons. One might see in this European reaction a clear case of multiculturalist political accommodation run riot.

In the Scandinavian countries, as in the Netherlands and Belgium, the writing has been on the wall for some time. Twenty-five million Nordics concentrated in Sweden, Denmark, Norway, and Finland are facing a wave of immigration that is fundamentally transforming identities once based on a shared history and complete ethnic homogeneity. In the 1950s, a British report could still confirm that "no alien stock" had touched Scandinavia. That Nordic idyll has changed radically. To quote a recent British commentator, Adam Roberts:

> The streets of Stockholm or Copenhagen today are full of brown-skinned, black-haired immigrants from all over Asia, Europe, Latin America and Africa. Oslo has its "Little Karachi," and in one part of Malmö in southern Sweden immigrants make up 90% of the population. In Sweden as a whole, one in four people is foreign-born or of foreign parentage. In Denmark and Norway the inflow of foreigners has also increased, spawning anti-immigrant political parties and strict new laws to keep incomers out.[59]

Sweden's current influx nearly matches the peak of pre-1914 mass immigration to the United States.[60] Urban, cosmopolitan, welcoming to refugees, and providing the unparalleled security of its welfare-state benefits, it is not surprising that Sweden has acted as a magnet for Third World immigrants. Though about 15 percent of the population are very strongly against immigration, there have thus far been no equivalents in Sweden to the extremist Danish People's Party (which holds more than twenty seats in Parliament) or the populist, anti-immigrant Progress Party of Norway.[61] But the surging immigration has had unpleasant consequences—especially for Sweden's eighteen thousand Jews, confronted by a Muslim population that may already be higher than six hundred thousand. There have been many cases of harassment (including of Jewish minors and elderly Holocaust survivors) by Arabs and Muslims in schools and on streets and subways. Despite the bold initiatives of then–Swedish prime minister Göran Persson to deepen Holocaust education (as a way of defending human rights and democracy), the anti-Jewish climate in Sweden has steadily intensified. The perpetrators have mainly been from the Middle East and North Africa.[62] Whether they operate in the city suburbs, on Swedish websites, or in Swedish schools, they can feel relatively secure in the knowledge that representatives of the Swedish Left and the Green Party almost always deny the existence of such harassment, frequently justify Palestinian terrorism, and persist in their tendency to denigrate Israel.

Sweden's tolerant civilized elites, and especially its powerful Social Democratic Party, have long been characterized by a self-righteous antipathy toward Israel—mainly due to the country's Third World orientation, anti-Americanism, pro-Palestinian obsessions, the cult of the United Nations, and general humanitarian posturing.[63] The Swedish establishment is no less committed to multiculturalism than it is to anti-Israelism, despite the provocative behavior of many of the new immigrants and their unabashed aggressiveness toward the Jewish minority. Denial and the appeasement of undisguised *intolerance* reign supreme. This extends even toward those who openly preach contempt for democracy, secularism, female equality (a much cherished value in Scandinavia), extreme homophobia, and other illiberal values. If that were not enough, in Sweden, Norway, Denmark, Holland, France, and Belgium, local Muslim leaders have not hesitated to claim their neighborhoods as Islamic territory under Muslim legal jurisdiction.[64] In Norway the response to such challenges, according to American journalist Bruce Bawer, has been "grotesque condescension" and a view of the whole business "as a morality play, with Muslims in the role of needy victims and Norwegians as heroic benefactors."[65]

As of September 2001, no less than 65 percent of rapes in Norway were committed by "non-Western immigrants" (essentially a euphemism for Muslims), but according to the conventional academic wisdom it was Norwegian women who needed to take their share of responsibility. Bawer even quotes a female professor of social anthropology at the University of Oslo, Unni Wikan, who insisted that "Norwegian women must realize that we live in a multicultural society and adapt to it."[66] Evidently, Muslim men in Europe did not need to adjust their view that it is women who are always to blame for rape.[67] To suggest otherwise would be to go against the new mantra that all cultures are equal; that everyone has the right to maintain the most oppressive practices (genital mutilation, coerced marriages, multiple wives, honor killings) in the name of group minority rights, cultural specificity, and the right to be different.[68] This syndrome partly explains how in Norway, Denmark, and Sweden there is such leniency toward the expression of anti-Semitic attitudes, especially if they seem related to the Middle East conflict.[69] In the contemporary world of Eurabia, the golden rule remains never to criticize Arab governments or Muslim immigrants, to indulge in hypocritical and inflated public praise for Islamic culture; and to encourage massive funding for the utterly corrupt, violent, and anarchic Palestinian Authority, while engaging in periodic calumnies against Israel. Anti-American and anti-Semitic attitudes are the virtually inevitable corollary to this compulsive deference in the face of the most reactionary prejudices. What passes for interfaith dialogue in practice whitewashes Muslim anti-Semitism, along with jihadist ideology, terrorist practices, death threats to apostates, and the ugly persecution of homosexuals.[70] Beyond these grave misdemeanors, contemporary multiculturalism conceals a sustained effort to undermine the Judeo-Christian foundations of the West, which would leave Islam resplendent as the dominant pillar of modern European civilization.[71] Militant Islam can and does exploit the relative openness of the West to the "other" while preserving the exclusiveness of its own doctrine, which dissuades Muslims from accepting the influence of infidel cultures.

The refusal of some Jews in Europe to keep silent about Muslim persecution and acts of aggression against Jewish communities goes against the prevailing conventional wisdom.[72] For example, the standard European assumption in cases where Muslims harass Jewish children or adults is that while such acts may be deplorable, they are rooted in an understandable anger at Israel.[73] Increasingly common, too, is the claim that Jews have brought anti-Semitism upon themselves, especially in more recent times. This is the argument of a former Norwegian prime minister, Kåre Willoch, for whom contemporary European anti-Semitism is solely the consequence of Israel's 1967 conquests of previously Arab lands. In Norway, as in much of Europe, this highly simplistic view of the subject is considered a mark of great insight and corresponds to what most journalists want to hear.[74] It can rely for corroboration on post-Zionist Jews in Israeli academia for whom, it would seem, the whole world revolves around the Palestinians.

Canada provides an interesting point of comparison with the Netherlands and Scandinavia, since it is one of the world's foremost multicultural democracies in its determination to protect vulnerable minorities.[75] As in Australia, since the late 1960s, multiculturalism (in the sense of recognizing ethnic minority rights) has gradually replaced the reality of a whites-only British-dominated dominion guided by a policy of cultural assimilation. In both Canada and Australia, this shift was positive for the Jews in so far as it weakened narrow-minded nationalism with a racist tinge and Christian religious and xenophobic prejudice, and relieved the pressure of cultural homogeneity.[76] The existence of government funding also made it easier for Jews and other ethnic minorities to maintain the communal infrastructure for a distinctive identity and culture.

During the Holocaust years, Canada had the worst record of any Western nation when it came to admitting Jews fleeing from persecution. Only in the early 1960s, as Jews began to acquire significant professional, financial, and political clout, did this change. The 1967 Canadian immigration law finally brought down the barriers of race, religion, and descent. Two years later ethnic diversity was accepted as the basis of Canadian identity, and in 1971, under Prime Minister Pierre Trudeau (who had been an anti-Semite in his adolescent years), multiculturalism became federal government policy. Indeed, in 1988, it was even turned into *the* official defining characteristic of Canadian society.[77] By then, 40 percent of the Canadian population were no longer of British or French heritage, and in Toronto and Vancouver, a similar percentage were foreign-born. Cultural pluralism was emerging as the true reflection of Canadian society. Undoubtedly, for most Jews these developments were welcome, leading at last to their full equality. Having acutely suffered from Canada's former racist, exclusionary policy on immigration, Jews could only rejoice at the new mosaic with its pluralist worldview, concern for minorities, and abhorrence of hate speech.[78]

Yet the solid achievements of Canadian multiculturalism at the turn of the twenty-first century have not prevented a significant wave of anti-Semitism from affecting the 370,000 Jews of Canada (1.1 percent of the total population). No longer expressed through immigration quotas, restrictive land covenants, or discrimination in employment, such prejudice has been increasingly influenced by international, especially Middle Eastern, contexts. As elsewhere during the post-2000 worldwide increase in anti-Semitic attacks, the Arabic intonation of "Death to the Jews" has been heard on the streets of Canadian cities.[79] On campuses such as Concordia University in Montreal, anti-Israel protests and pro-Palestinian agitation have made use of Judeophobic themes.[80] Since 2001 radical leftist student organizations on campus have led the charge in issuing inflammatory statements and seeking to silence pro-Israel voices. At the same time, a spate of attacks has taken place against synagogues, Jewish cemeteries, properties, private homes, and individuals—especially between March and July 2004. There was an increase of 100 percent in anti-Semitic incidents over the previous year. On April 5, 2004, arson destroyed the library of United Talmud Torahs elementary school in Montreal. The oldest Jewish cemetery in the city was attacked just over three weeks later; Nazi symbols, including the words "Heil Hitler" and swastikas, were sprayed on the tombstones. This was part of a threefold increase in cemetery desecrations. The targeting of Jewish private property also rose dramatically (by 60 percent) compared to 2003. On March 21, 2004, for example, thirteen Jewish homes in the Toronto suburb of Vaughn were defaced with anti-Semitic graffiti. Racist messages and swastikas were daubed on front and garage doors and motor vehicles. The previous week there had been a similar defacement in the Toronto suburb of Thornhill.

In 2006, 935 anti-Semitic incidents were recorded—an overall increase of 12.8 percent from the previous year, and an all-time high for Canada.[81] This reflects a troubling upward movement that seriously belies the polite façade of Canadian multiculturalism.[82] Since 1997 there has indeed been a fourfold increase in recorded anti-Semitic acts in Canada. The number of attacks on Jews has jumped fifteen times as compared to 1982. In the Greater Toronto region, Jews were targeted in 29 percent of *all* cases, followed by blacks (27 percent) and Muslims in just 8 percent of the recorded incidents. The single most documented group among the perpetrators has been persons of Arab origin.[83] The year 2006 also produced Canada's first homegrown jihadi terrorists, who planned to blow up the headquarters of the national intelligence services as part of their war against the West. Some of the Canadian cultural and intellectual elites—like their European counterparts—were quick to find excuses for the terrorists in the name of preserving multicultural harmony and antiracism.[84] On the other hand, the current Canadian government led by Premier Stephen Harper has been exceptionally supportive of

Israel—even more than British New Labour governments under Tony Blair and Gordon Brown. But, as in Britain, academia remains outspokenly anti-American, anti-Zionist, and pro-Palestinian. It remains stubbornly unwilling to recognize the existential danger represented by radical Islam.

In the United States, ethnic conflict has traditionally been much more intense than in Canada. Multiculturalism in the late 1960s was part of a radical project of auto-emancipation for oppressed groups, freeing themselves from marginality, affirming ethnic identity, and asserting their submerged narratives against the white, Anglo-Saxon Protestant (WASP) establishment. This revolt of the '60s gave a powerful boost to ethnic pluralism, underprivileged minorities, and the cause of cultural diversity in general. At the same time, there were obvious strains and tensions between American Jews and Afro-Americans.

In 1967, Stokely Carmichael, a leader of the Student Nonviolent Coordination Committee (SNCC), denounced "kosher fascism" and "white" Israel's oppression of the "colored" Palestinians. As "prime minister" of the Black Panthers, he helped to popularize the concept of "Black Power" and to spread a vitriolic anti-Zionism.[85] Adopting the name Kwame Ture, he took advantage of every opportunity to vilify the Jewish state for the following three decades. At Columbia University in 1985 he began to use what later became his trademark inflammatory slogan: "The only good Zionist is a dead Zionist." At the University of Minnesota Law School in February 1990, he proclaimed that "Zionism must be destroyed" and echoed Louis Farrakhan's ugly description of Judaism as a "gutter religion." At Princeton University, in the same year, Kwame Ture accused Zionism of "controlling all the banks, businesses and financial institutions in our community, selling us rotten meat at the corner store, dry rotted clothes and charging high rent for slum buildings."[86]

As the black-Jewish civil rights alliance began to unravel in the late 1960s, it was accompanied by violently anti-Jewish rhetoric.[87] In the 1970s African Americans became especially embittered that Jewish organizations seemed so lukewarm toward affirmative action and firmly opposed to fixed quotas in higher education and employment. The Jews, as they saw it, had achieved access to white America and were now trying to close the door on their former allies. The Allan Bakke reverse discrimination case of 1978 roused blacks against Jews, as did the Andrew Young affair in 1979 and the demagogic forays of Rev. Jesse Jackson in the early 1980s, campaigning as the first black presidential candidate. Jackson was a genuinely charismatic African American preacher who, at the time, branded Zionism as a "poisonous weed," and contemptuously upbraided American Jews' "persecution complex." Above all, there was the Nation of Islam (NOI) and its firebrand leader Louis Farrakhan—the organizer of the Million Man March on Washington, D.C., in 1995. Farrakhan was antiwhite and antihomosexual as well as anti-Semitic. A brilliant orator, he publicly praised Hitler, openly flirted with the Libyan dictator Qaddafi, and blamed Jews for the Holocaust.[88]

Farrakhan, like his assassinated predecessor Malcolm X, had initially been under the spell of NOI founder Elijah Muhammad's millennialist teachings: a doctrine of racial redemption for the American blacks through total liberation from the "white devils." Crude anti-Semitism was part of the Nation of Islam from the outset, mixed at times with awareness of Jews as possible role models for successful emancipation from servitude. The predominant image remained, however, that the Jew was the most ruthless and demonic of the whites, smarter and shrewder—the epitome of the wily, back-stabbing exploiter.[89] In the black nationalist canon (tinged with biblical Christian fundamentalism and inverted racism) the Jew was a secular Antichrist. In the black Muslim variant, Jews were the most calculating and conniving enemies of black people.[90] They were also different from the "blue-eyed devils" and other so-called European-Americans because they were perceived as conspiring against blacks in a more sweeping, predatory, and indiscriminate manner. In the ghettos, they were the owners, the slumlord merchants, the parasitical shopkeepers, the creditors, and the canny businessmen who sapped the lifeblood of the Negroes.[91] Farrakhan himself told a huge audience in Madison Square Garden on October 7, 1985:

> The germ of murder is already sewed into the hearts of Jews in this country. . . . The Jews talk about "Never again." Well, I am your last chance, too, Jews. Listen, Jews, this little Black boy is your last chance because the Scriptures charge [you] with killing the prophets of God. But if you rise up to try to kill me, then Allah promises that he will bring on this generation the blood of the righteous. All of you will be killed outright.[92]

Farrakhan's left-wing nationalist appeal to many young, middle-aged, and upwardly mobile black professionals in America was scarcely diminished by his anti-Semitism. The former singer-songwriter, college dropout, and convert to Islam has held high the black Muslim standard for nearly forty years—blending it with Third Worldism, Black Panther rhetoric, and sympathy for the Palestinian cause. A large interest-free loan from Qaddafi undoubtedly encouraged this orientation and a sense of fellowship with Third World radicals.[93] At the same time, white racist groups have shown a certain attraction toward Farrakhan's anti-Semitic demagogy and paranoid populism. In the mid-1980s Farrakhan would rant against "the strong Jewish lobby which controls the United States" and represented "the great danger to America's future." His message was one that could appeal to white neofascists, neo-Nazis, and Holocaust deniers. He was openly preaching that the survival of America depended on defeating and destroying the Jews.[94]

Farrakhan's visceral anti-Semitism had its deepest roots in the desire to supplant the Jews and assert African American black Muslims as God's *new* chosen people. Appealing to Koranic sources he often claimed that the Jews were the fathers of a false religion who had stolen the identity of the true elect.[95] Fully aware that blacks completely lack Jewish rootedness in an ancient culture, history, and religion, he sought to redirect and channel their natal alienation against the Jews; to mobilize their feelings of inferiority, envy, and antiwhite resentments into a new sense of empowerment as upstanding black men under Allah's guiding hand. On February 25, 1996, Farrakhan gave a Savior's Day Speech in Chicago in which he said:

> Remember that I have warned that Allah will punish you. You are wicked deceivers of the American people. You have sucked their blood. You are not real Jews. . . . You are the synagogue of Satan, you have wrapped your tentacles around the US government, and you are deceiving and sending this nation to hell. But I warn you in the name of Allah, you would be wise to leave me alone. But if you choose to crucify me, know that Allah will crucify you.[96]

Throughout the 1990s, Farrakhan's chief spokesman, Khalid Muhammad, would make similarly incendiary statements. So, too, did Leonard Jeffries, a tenured professor at City University of New York and chair of its African American Studies Department. On July 20, 1991, Jeffries asserted that rich Jews had organized and controlled the colonial slave trade; that Russian Jewry (in league with the Mafia) had designed "a financial system for the destruction of black people"; and that Jewish Hollywood had conspired to paint African Americans in a consistently demeaning light. Such virulent bigotry would become a feature of radical black campus activities in the 1990s, relying on a rhetoric that depicted Jews as prime tormentors of the black race and architects of slavery.[97] In August 1991, rioting blacks in Crown Heights, Brooklyn, turned on local Hasidic Jews in what has been called "the first organized anti-Semitic riot in American history."[98] Henry Gates, Jr., then chairman of the African and African American Studies Department at Harvard and a rare dissenting voice, observed that this was an orchestrated anti-Semitism from the top down, "promoted by leaders who affect to be speaking for a larger resentment."[99] As a reward for his honesty, he received death threats from fellow African Americans and virtually no public support from other black leaders.

Beyond such outbursts of violent anti-Semitism, and a growing Jewish suspicion of blacks, there were other issues at work. If America was a Jewish Eden—a release from bondage—it seemed more like a house of oppression to many blacks. African Americans had always regarded themselves as the definitive other in American society and as the major victims of white racism. Jews, in their eyes, had white-skin privilege. It seemed obvious that they had been absorbed into the great American melting pot by the mid-1960s. Moreover, anti-Semitism was scarcely a major issue for black Americans. Race, not religion or nationality, was unmistakably the great dividing line for blacks. White racism against "the Negro" was the *only* oppression that really counted.[100] Jews, on the other hand, were deemed to be rich, successful, and powerful. Were they not already part of the dominant white establishment? How, then, could they claim to be a vulnerable minority? After all, had they not achieved a federally funded U.S. Holocaust Memorial Museum next to the National Mall in Washington, D.C.? Where was the equivalent monument to slavery or to the genocide of the American Indians? These were and still remain sources of resentment that trouble parts of American society, along with the current debate over legal and illegal Hispanic immigration and the terrorist threat posed by Muslim radicals to the United States.[101] An ADL survey for 2007 showed that 32 percent of black Americans still hold strong anti-Semitic beliefs, three times higher than the average among white Americans. Moreover, although the United States is much more of a multicultural society than ever before, 15 percent of Americans (nearly thirty-five million people) continue to embrace enduring anti-Semitic stereotypes.

Hence, for many American Jews, contemporary multiculturalism is a distinct source of unease that arouses ambiguous sentiments. Despite being a widely accepted part of white America, Jews often regard themselves as outsider/insiders, enjoying an anomalous status, and occupying a kind of liminal zone. Though close to the centers of American power, Jews in their overall size remain a relatively small minority (5.3 million); they are unquestionably American but determined to maintain a strong ethnic identity; they are simultaneously powerful *and* vulnerable; they believe in equal opportunity for individuals, but not for ethnic groups. Most American Jews can hardly feel comfortable with the nonwhite minorities' exclusive emphasis on race and ethnicity. Like other whites, they are instinctively distrustful of a multicultural identity politics based on grievance, resentment, complaint, and demand for reparation, especially at a time when visible and open discrimination against Jews in America has greatly diminished. Moreover, the prevailing politics of ethnic identity, which reifies difference to the exclusion of all else and essentializes race as a fixed quality, has too many disturbing resemblances to biological racism and anti-Semitism.[102]

The politics of ethnic identity ultimately denies what most American Jews still regard as genuinely equal opportunities to succeed in the United States. It was their own experience that convinced Jews in America that anti-Semitic exclusion, social restrictions, and discrimination in housing and employment (of the kind that undoubtedly existed between 1880 and 1950) could be overcome. Why should the same not be true for other immigrant groups? In that respect, much contemporary multicultural rhetoric—especially coming from the Left—seems counterproductive, impervious to integration, and even anti-American.[103] Moreover, it is strikingly unsympathetic to Jewish interests and usually refuses to seriously address anti-Semitism. It has erased the traditional Jewish status of being considered as victims, outsiders, or members of an oppressed group. Indeed, Jews are barely visible anymore in the larger multiculturalist narrative of racism and exclusion.[104] Their place has been taken by Native Americans, African Americans, Hispanics, and others.[105]

It is not only Jewish Americans who have begun to question the initial promise of multiculturalism and to see it more as part of the problem rather than its solution. There are a growing number of voices in America concerned at the fracturing of American identity, the watering down of English-language requirements, and the signs of tribalization and resegregation in American life. The classic American motto *E Pluribus Unum* (Out of Many, One) seems less reassuring in an age where assimilation to shared values appears to have been weakened while ethnic particularism and cultural relativism are increasingly dominant. Furthermore, say the pessimists, this is a very different America, in which 85 percent of the new immigrants are from Asia, the Caribbean, and Latin America.[106] Some of the critics now regard multiculturalism as a Trojan horse in American culture. By promoting a politics of race, ethnicity, and cultural separateness, it has not only sapped Judeo-Christian values and what is left of the melting-pot ideology but ultimately it can only reignite prejudice and discrimination.[107] If the *Pluribus* (the Many) succeed in drowning the *Unum* (the One) in the name of cultural diversity, bilingualism, and moral relativism, American democracy with its emphasis on individual freedom will be irredeemably eroded.

Multiculturalism, by promoting this agenda and focusing primarily on oppressed racial or other minorities, acts as a divisive ideology, highlighting only the flaws and negative features in American culture. Anxiety about its effects has been further intensified with the rise of a militant Islam whose hatred of the West is driven, among other factors, by a struggle of cultures. Its premise is the Muslim conquest of America from within, its decisive victory over Christianity, and the application of Islamic law to the United States to redeem it from decadence and corruption.[108] In their campaigns to convert Americans to Islam, Muslim radicals focus their attack on capitalist consumerism, secularism, immorality, and close relations with Israel. They systematically disparage America and the West in favor of Islamic civilization; they make bigoted statements against Jews and Christians; they claim to be victims of bias, and at the same time exploit the democratic pluralism of American society to bring about its demise.[109] For locally based Islamists, striking at American Jews is absolutely central to their strategy—equivalent to cutting off the head of the snake in their battle with Israel.[110] Although the four million Muslims in America are far less numerous than their coreligionists in Europe (twenty to twenty-five million), they are still a major source of verbal incitement against Jews. Their anti-Semitism is indeed more virulent than anything that exists among American Christians today. Hence the crucial importance for America in general, and Jews in particular, to strengthen the still weak, divided, and intimidated voices of moderation that undoubtedly exist within the Muslim community in the United States.

It remains an open question whether Jews in America can achieve a new relationship with Muslims, blacks, or Latinos under the banner of multiculturalism or pluralism, a term first coined by the American Jewish sociologist Horace Kallen in 1924.[111] Despite the seriousness of black anti-Semitism and the unraveling of the traditional civil rights alliance, Jews and blacks still have common bonds and mutual interests that transcend the antagonisms or conflicts whipped up by extremists. With regard to Latinos (the fastest growing ethnic minority in the United States) there is still much to be researched and done. The high levels of anti-Semitism reflected in some recent surveys of foreign-born Hispanics in the United States (44 percent) may partly reflect the conservative background of Latin American Catholicism and the sociopolitical prejudices originally formed on that continent. Among Latinos, traditional stereotypes of Jews as Christ killers are, for example, stronger than the average level existing in North America today. At the same time, some caution seems advisable in accepting the results of such surveys, which often lack depth and historical perspective.

The socio-demographic and economic profile of Jews and Latinos is also very different; Jews are the best educated and highest-earning income ethnic group in the United States, while Hispanics are fourth from the bottom in income and tied for second lowest on education.[112] In attitudes and values relating to religion, civil liberties, abortion rights, upbringing of children, euthanasia, unions, and financial outlooks, the gap is large between the two communities, though not as great as with Jews and blacks or Jews and Asians. Though Hispanics appear twice as anti-Semitic as other Americans on many indicators in the problematic ADL surveys (35 percent, compared to 17 percent for Americans as a whole in 2002), prejudice is much weaker among the American-born.[113] For 2007 the surveys showed that 29 percent of foreign-born Hispanics harbored anti-Jewish prejudices, learned in the homes, schools, communities, and churches of different Latin American countries. But only 15 percent of those born in the United States showed the same propensity.

When it comes to Islamic attitudes toward Jews in America, even basic empirical research is lacking, but the viciousness of the bias, calumny, and anti-Semitic conspiracy mongering in radical Muslim circles is "of a sort that has otherwise all but disappeared from American discourse."[114] Myths of Jewish world domination and talk of bloody battles with the Jews are rampant in parts of the American Muslim community, recycled at fundamentalist conventions, in the mosques, and before Arab Muslim youth associations. This is the language of jihad on American soil, intended to spread hatred, intimidate opponents, and attract new believers. It is, of course, a mockery of the original multiculturalist ideal, which unwittingly serves its purposes by permitting the toleration of fanatical intolerance and paralyzing legitimate criticism of an exclusivist racism in reverse.[115]

• • •

Perhaps the most interesting and ambivalent case of current multiculturalism and its discontents is that of Australia, a country that has actively fostered the diverse ethnic cultures of the many groups that have migrated to its shores since 1945. Before World War II, Australia was still a mono-culture with a deliberate policy of maintaining its population as 90 percent Anglo-Celtic. Anti-Asian prejudice was rampant, and only a very limited number of Jews were admitted under the "White Australia" policy during the most intense years of Nazi persecution after 1933. However, by 1945 the Australian government's desperate need to increase its population led to an opening of the doors to an accelerated non-British European migration program. Asians and blacks were still excluded from this policy until 1972 when the Labour government led by Gough Whitlam replaced the traditional posture of "whites only" (and assimilation to Australian culture) with multiculturalism. Five years earlier, in an anticipatory move, Aborigines had, for the first time, been recognized as Australian citizens.

Since the 1970s, multiculturalism has consistently affirmed the promotion of cultural diversity in an Australian society that has dramatically changed its ethnic composition during the past thirty-five years. The 2001 census indicated that nearly a quarter of all Australians had been born overseas, that no less than two hundred languages were spoken, and that a wide variety of religions already existed in the country.[116] The Jewish community, like other ethnic/religious minorities, would soon benefit from government funding to support its religious needs, its culture, and its identity. Hence it is not surprising that most Australian Jews by the late 1980s had come to support multiculturalism, though there were still some Jews who clung to the earlier liberal Anglocentric or melting-pot philosophy.[117] On the whole, Australian Jewry has succeeded in preserving a cohesive community structure and maintaining a strong sense of Jewish identity, which is helped by one of the lowest intermarriage rates in the Western world.

Since 1990, there has, nonetheless, been a rise in anti-Semitic incidents in Australia, coming mainly from extreme right-wing groups, left-wing anti-Zionists, and the more militant members of the Muslim community. In 1996, at a time when violent anti-Semitism was showing a general world-wide decline, it had nevertheless increased by 12 percent in Australia.[118] One factor may have been the emergence of Pauline Hanson's independent One Nation Party, with its populist xenophobic message of hostility toward Australian multiculturalism—especially the proliferation of nonwhite and non-Christian immigrants. Holocaust denial was another growing motif, vigorously promoted by the veteran Christian-identity racist Eric Butler (founder of the Australian League of Rights), by neo-Nazis, by so-called liberals such as John Bennett (head of the Australian Civil Liberties Union), and by the German-Australian "revisionist" Frederick Töben. The endless media debates over the refusal of an entry visa to Australia for the British Holocaust denier David Irving regrettably gave a higher profile to the negationists than would otherwise have been the case.[119] Anti-Zionism and Middle Eastern issues have taken an increasingly significant place in the activities of the deniers. They featured prominently in the verbal attacks of the Australian Islamic/Arab community against Israel, especially after the eruption of the al-Aqsa intifada in October 2000. During 2000–2001, the impact of the uprising contributed to an unprecedented level of anti-Semitic activity in Australia. The rate of attacks was running at 60 percent above average and was ten times higher than the previous record year. The trend continued in 2002–3, with more than five hundred reports of anti-Jewish violence, vandalism, harassment, and intimidation.[120]

In its 2008 report the Executive Council of Australian Jewry (ECAJ) recorded 652 anti-Semitic incidents—the highest number ever in any one year since close monitoring began, and twice the annual average.[121] The increase in such extremism shows no relation to individual behavior or communal attitudes to political matters or events in Israel, but it does appear to be linked to hostile media comment. On a global scale, Australia now ranks alongside the United Kingdom, France, Canada, and Russia as countries that have witnessed the most substantial rise in documented anti-Jewish violence in recent years. This is especially troubling in a society that has prided itself on its pluralism and multiculturalism—where Jews have been particularly well integrated since 1945. It is also worth noting that about two-thirds of the attacks on Jews appear to have come from extreme right or neo-Nazi groups, which are numerous and rather diverse in Australia; the remaining third of the anti-Semitic perpetrators seem to be evenly split between the Far Left and a number of Arab-Muslim groups.

Although white racism still remains the dominant strand in the attacks, the most salient "new" element in this anti-Semitic resurgence (as in western Europe) has been the emergence of militant Islam. In 1945 there had been virtually no Muslims in Australia, less even than the 32,000 Jews, who themselves represented only 0.4 percent of the general population. Today, there are around 320,000 Muslims and 120,000 Jews—both communities concentrated mainly in Sydney and Melbourne. Nearly half of Australian Muslims are under twenty-four years of age, in contrast to the largely aging Jewish community. The poor English skills of many Muslim immigrants, their lack of qualifications, the internally imposed restrictions on Muslim women, and the resulting low income levels have exacerbated the difficulties of social integration. Since the events of September 11, 2001, and the Bali bombings of 2002 (in which eighty-eight Australians were murdered and many more injured by Islamic extremists), suspicion toward the Muslim minority has greatly increased. Highly publicized incidents of gang rape involving Muslim youth have added more fuel to the fire.[122] So, too, did the statements of the Australian-born radical Muslim cleric Sheikh Feiz Mohammed, who blamed Australian white rape victims for their provocative way of dressing.[123]

Sheikh Feiz Mohammed, now living in Lebanon, is one of a number of Islamic preachers whose anti-Semitic rhetoric in Australia proved to be extremely harmful. In one DVD widely distributed among Muslims in Australia, Feiz Mohammed (a former leader of the Global Islamic Youth Centre in Sydney) blasted "the most extreme racial pride of the Jews," warning that "their time will come like every other evil persons' time will come." *The Sydney Morning Herald* reported on January 19, 2007, that, while lecturing, "Sheikh Feiz makes pig-like snorting noises when he refers to Jews." No less incendiary is the controversial mufti of Australia, Sheikh Taj al-Din al-Hilali (based at the Lakemba Mosque in Sydney), who, in addition to denying the Holocaust, has accused Jews of causing all wars, economic crises, treason, and sexual deviancy. The sheikh considered 9/11 to have been "God's work against oppressors"; he contemptuously branded Australians as inveterate liars and excused convicted gang rapists on the grounds that women who do not wear the *hijab* (Muslim headdress) are like uncovered meat.[124] Such reckless and repulsive statements have posed a serious challenge to the tolerance level of multicultural Australian society as a whole. Militant Islamists clearly reject the secular pluralist foundations of Australia's multiethnic democracy. They have deepened the already palpable sense of alienation between the white majority and the Muslim minority.

The December 2005 riots at the Sydney beachside suburb of Cronulla involving white racists, Christian religious extremists, and Lebanese Muslim youth highlighted the extent of the crisis.[125] In contrast to the postwar integration of Jews, Italians, Greeks, Balts, Chinese and Lebanese Christians into white Australian society, that of the Arab Muslim community has proven far more difficult. On the one hand, Arabs themselves have suffered racism and discrimination in Australia; on the other hand, unlike earlier waves of immigrants, a significant minority have opposed the core values of Western freedom and democracy. The anti-Semitic conspiracy theories and jihadist ideology promoted by the radical Islamists is a prime indication of their total opposition to multiculturalist democracy, while at the same time they cynically exploit its freedom of speech and its often misplaced tolerance for extremist incitement.

Australia, like Britain, is facing new challenges. It, too, has its fair share of white left-wing anti-Zionist fundamentalists who ethnically stereotype all Israelis and their Jewish sympathizers, support the academic boycott of Israel, and enthusiastically back the Palestinian jihad.[126] Though seemingly far removed from the Islamists, their quasi-Marxist language is not so different in its total delegitimization of the Jewish state, in its dabbling in crude conspiracy theory, and in its rabid anti-Americanism and perverse efforts to Nazify the Jewish state. Prominent Australian intellectuals such as Bob Ellis and the Labor MP Julia Irwin have been among those indulging in extreme language about Israel and the Jewish lobby in Australia. Moreover, as in western Europe and North America, there is no shortage of Jewish liberals and Marxists willing to advertise their own religious or cultural background, solely in order to execrate the Jewish people.[127] Their diatribes against Zionism are often as vitriolic as the demagogy typical of some members of the right-wing nationalist Australia First Party (AFP) and its Sydney branch president, Jim Saleam. For the AFP, visceral hatred of "Zionism" (a code word for Jews) goes hand in hand with the total rejection of Asian immigration and multiculturalism.[128] For the radical Left, on the other hand, anti-Zionism is more of an auxiliary of anti-Americanism and opposition to globalization than a reaction to Australia's multiculturalism experiment, which it generally defends.

The Australian government (notably pro-Israel) and mainstream political parties have been particularly vigorous both in defending the legacy of multicultural tolerance for ethno-religious difference and in unequivocally condemning anti-Semitism. The Australian parliament responded to the marked rise in anti-Jewish assaults in 2003 by passing resolutions that enjoyed strong support from across the political spectrum.[129] Winding up a Senate debate on March 22, 2004, Senator Julian McGauran, the National Party whip, pointed out that Australia was "one of the great multicultural societies in the world," housing more than one hundred nationalities in a broadly harmonious and tolerant society.

> Nevertheless, regrettably, like all countries, we have had to fight back strong elements of anti-Semitism and violent reaction against Jewish institutions. In politics we are only too aware of the fluctuating influence of the extreme Right and Left political groups—mad and racist groups such as the LaRouche society, the League of Rights, the Citizens Electoral Council. Now there is a new element with the extreme Islamic fundamentalists. All these groups are organized and resourced against the Jewish race.[130]

Multiculturalism raised hopes for creating a common public space that might overcome racial hubris, xenophobia, tribalism, and anti-Semitism. In Anglo-Saxon democracies such as the United States, Canada, and Australia, this effort—with its encouragement of cultural diversity, respect for the other, and acceptance of difference—has, to a degree, succeeded. But it may well become one of the first casualties of a resurgent militant Islam, whose war of civilizations, fanatical exclusivism, and religious bigotry are fundamentally incompatible with Western democratic values. Not for the first time in their history, the Jews and Israel may find themselves caught in the crossfire.

EIGHTEEN

The Globalization of Anti-Semitism

Each new stage in the history of anti-Semitism has been able to build on a prior legacy of negative stereotypes, adapting them to a novel domestic and international context.[1] In recent decades, for example, Israel has become the Jew of the nations on a planetary scale.[2] Both anti-Zionism and anti-Semitism have been *globalized* in an era where technology creates unprecedented opportunities for instant and continuous access to information. The Internet has eliminated older distinctions between center and periphery, mainstream and fringe opinion. Cyberspace is, in many ways, the fulfillment of every bigot's dream. True believers no longer need to attend mass rallies where they can scream "*Sieg Heil!*" or "*Allahu akbar!*" The "new" Judeophobes can take the age-old anti-Semitic narrative, link it to highly inflammatory images of real conflict (Iraq, Palestine, Lebanon), and spread a toxic message of fanaticism and Jew hatred that can reach millions of people at the click of a mouse.

Anti-Semitism is probably the most adaptable of all group hatreds, exuding a protean quality that seems to guarantee longevity. Its current focus on the bloodthirsty, expansionist settler-Jew sucking the blood of the poor Palestinians reflects, in a twisted fashion, some of the darker sides of the Arab-Israeli conflict. According to Daniel Goldhagen, such prejudice, available in many variations, appeals to all those "who dislike international influences, globalization or the United States. It is relentlessly international in its focus on Israel at the center of the most conflict-ridden region today, and on the United States as the world's omnipresent power."[3]

"Globalization" has become the new code word for American cultural and economic imperialism. Used pejoratively, it generally implies neocolonialism, homogenization, the destruction of cultural diversity, an erosion of state sovereignty, and the dissolution of traditional identities.[4] It has been unsettling both for advanced industrial societies and developing Third World states, impacting on such giants as post-Communist Russia, post-Maoist China, and post-Gaullist France. When the former French foreign minister Hubert Védrine wrote a book on globalization some years ago, he attacked the United States as a unilateralist "hyperpower," deploring the "uniformity" its mass culture has allegedly imposed on the rest of the world.[5] Such sentiments are widespread in Europe among those who regard globalization as a real threat to their social conditions, culture, and way of life. For example, among left-wing French intellectuals, anti-globalism has helped to fill the ideological vacuum left by the collapse of Marxism and the erosion of Third World myths.

In Germany, too, the backlash against a neoliberal capitalist world order often defines America and the Jews as its negative pole—the personification of everything antithetical to organic growth and cultural authenticity.[6] Leftist anti-globalists in France such as José Bové fulminate against a world dominated by the almighty dollar, greedy multinational companies, and sinister banking interests.[7] In recent years this animus against globalized capitalism has become increasingly linked to a mythical perception of contemporary Israel as the incarnation of evil.[8] For some anti-globalist intellectuals, including Dominique Vidal (himself Jewish), adjunct editor of the monthly *Le Monde Diplomatique,* Israel is not only guilty of "crimes against humanity" but was "born in sin"—since it "expelled" another people (the Palestinians) from the Holy Land.[9] Hence America (the patron) and Israel (the beneficiary) are the true authors of the terrorist scourge that afflicts the contemporary world.[10] American and European neo-Nazis, Aryan supremacists, Ku Klux Klan offshoots, and radical Islamists bent on promoting terrorism and a culture of hate have picked up on similar themes.[11] The Internet has offered new scope for the cross-fertilization of Far Right and radical Left ideologues, blending anti-globalization, anti-Zionism, and anti-Semitism with hatred for America. Major anti-Semitic themes such as the *Protocols of the Elders of Zion,* blood libels, Holocaust denial, and 9/11 conspiracy theories are part of this cyberspace world, which is difficult to control, monitor, or combat.

The Islamic extremists have been particularly adept at exploiting the new technologies. Indeed, without the Internet it is doubtful if there would be any al-Qaeda, once their physical base in Afghanistan was almost destroyed. Certainly, 9/11 itself would have been impossible without the Internet network that enabled the Islamists to bypass Western intelligence agencies, not to mention repressive Arab and Muslim regimes from the Atlantic to the Indian Ocean. Having failed to overthrow the "near enemy" (apostate Muslim rulers and infidels) in Algeria, Egypt, Chechnya, and Kashmir, the Islamic radicals opted for a more flexible, high-tech form of building terrorist communications. September 11, 2001, was the spectacular coup chosen to galvanize the Muslim masses by unexpectedly striking at the faraway enemy (America), followed by a long series of terrorist bombings in Europe and the Middle East. The hijackers of 9/11 were themselves sophisticated fanatics generally blending a Western education with bigoted and narrow interpretations of Koranic verses that belonged to the world of seventh-century Arabia. Mohammed Atta, the Egyptian-born, German-educated leader of the 9/11 hijackers, was a perfect exemplar of this schizophrenia: a "Westernized" Muslim anti-Westerner, a misogynist, and an anti-Semite, he had written his master's thesis in Hamburg on multicultural cohabitation between Muslims and Christians in the Syrian city of Aleppo. The outbreak of Arafat's second intifada gave him and his fellow al-Qaeda conspirators the chance to ride on the back of the anti-Israel cause in attacking their American targets. Though al-Qaeda has failed thus far to fulfill any of its long-term goals, it has certainly succeeded in turning terrorism into a central issue on the world agenda and in increasing recruitment for the cause of jihad. Anti-Semitism, too, has thrived with the spread and proliferation of Islamist, neo-Nazi, and anti-globalist websites that can potentially reach a worldwide audience.

The Internet has no borders. It allows insignificant local players such as American neo-Nazi Gary Lauck (who served time in a German jail for several years) to supply otherwise illegal hate propaganda from his U.S.-based website to many unsuspecting Germans. A former Klan head, Don Black, working out of Florida, built a racist and anti-Semitic website called *Stormfront* to considerable effect.[12] The Moroccan anti-Semite Ahmed Rami, based in Stockholm (where he set up Radio Islam in the 1980s), achieved a worldwide reach with his incendiary website. The late William Pierce, head of the National Alliance and author of the infamous *Turner Diaries*, also thought globally and strategically about how to attract young people through the Internet to his anti-Semitic conspiracy theories. One method was to buy up music websites, such as Resistance Records, to bring in substantial revenue and potential new recruits. Thanks to the Internet, Pierce and other white racists managed to reach a transnational audience in Arabic and other Middle Eastern languages, despite their Aryan myths and anti-immigrant domestic agenda.[13]

Formerly head of the Louisiana Ku Klux Klan and then a member of his local state legislature, David Duke is an excellent example of "globalized" anti-globalism on the Far Right. His international connections led him to collaboration with fellow anti-Zionists from Russia, Ukraine, Germany, and Austria. Paranoid hatred of Jews is the main cement that binds American and European fanatics together with the Islamists. They all share a common belief that Jews/Zionists are at the root of the world's problems. For true believers like Pierce and Duke, the Jewish conspiracy is primarily aimed at destroying the white race through immigration and miscegenation. "Jewish racial supremacists" who have managed to seize control of U.S. foreign policy are seen as the real enemy.[14] It was the Jews who had turned the Third World and the Arab Middle East into an "economic colony" of the new world order—a code word for the irresistible Zionist drive toward global hegemony.[15]

For American white supremacists, Jews and their allies (international capitalists and deranged liberals) are key movers behind the globalization process.[16] Similar charges have been made by Horst Mahler, the prominent German neo-Nazi ideologue and former anarchist who predicted in 2001 that globalism will sink down upon itself, like the towers of Manhattan, under a thousand dagger strikes from Islamic fundamentalists. This collapse will finally also signal to the [various] peoples in the metropolises to revolt. Globalization, according to the radical Right, has long been a concealed weapon of the Jews to exterminate national cultures in the name of modernism and enlightenment. Mahler believes that the Jewish plutocracy totally controls the mass media and global finance. They are the wire-pullers who have masterminded the U.S. war against global terrorism since September 11, 2001. East Coast circles and worshippers of Yahweh ("the cult of world power of the chosen people") are the clandestine manipulators of American imperialism. It is they who initiated the irresistible globalization that is destroying the rest of the world's economies, cultures, and independent nations.[17] Hence unconditional solidarity with Islamist terror attacks against the United States to shake off the "Jewish yoke" of liberal democracy is an obligation for right-wing extremists and Islamists alike. America, Israel, and the evil spirit of globalization are their common enemies.

A virtually identical message has been diffused in America and Europe by the Swiss-born Islamofascist financier Achmed Huber, who converted to Islam in 1962. An ally of Mahler and long active in Islamist organizations, Huber is said to have financially assisted Osama bin Laden. In his younger days he was strongly influenced by the pro-Nazi mufti of Jerusalem, Haj Amin al-Husseini, and the Muslim Brotherhood.[18] Another mentor was the notorious Johann von Leers, a virulently anti-Semitic Nazi polemicist who found refuge after 1950 in Juan Péron's Argentina, where he edited the Nazi monthly *Der Weg;* he then transferred to Cairo, where he served in the Egyptian Information Department and collaborated with his old friend, Haj Amin.[19]

Globalization has many adversaries around the world—some on the right and others on the left. Anti-globalism, too, is heterogeneous—attracting environmentalists, anarchists, Communists, and populists no less than ultranationalists and neo-Nazis. Indeed, it has potential appeal to millions of nonpolitical people who instinctively fear the threat of outside forces to their traditional communities and lifestyles. For them, the free movement of ideas, people, and money; the disappearance of frontiers; and the erosion of fixed ideas about country, religion, and ethnic identity are unnerving rather than exhilarating experiences. It is no accident that Far Right movements in Europe such as Jörg Haider's Freedom Party, Jean-Marie Le Pen's National Front, and their counterparts in Italy, Belgium, and Switzerland strongly oppose the economic consequences of globalization. In Russia and eastern Europe, the ultranationalists and the communists have fiercely attacked the ravages of the neoliberal order, which they often identify with Zionism and Jews. In the Muslim world, globalization tends to be viewed as an American-Zionist plot to subjugate Islamic peoples to Western domination.

Anti-globalization on the left has no explicitly anti-Semitic ideological agenda. Nevertheless, in their battle against the World Trade Organization (WTO), the International Monetary Fund (IMF), and the World Bank, many leftist anti-globalists do rely on conspiracy myths, including the idea that 9/11 was a pawn of "corporate globalization." Those who are anti-Semitically inclined tend to focus on the prominence of American Jews like Alan Greenspan, Paul Wolfowitz, Robert Rubin, Lawrence Summers, and James Wolfensohn in key global financial institutions. They are likely to display a special animus against Israel and world Zionism as driving forces of a new Middle East controlled by American finance capital. There is a wide-spread use, especially noticeable among Islamists, of imagery that paints Jewry as a dangerously mobile, rootless, abstract, and transnational Mafia feeding off the capitalist economy.[20] Islamist apostles of jihad have found in Israel and the Jews the great surrogate for their holy war against America. Uncle Sam, so to speak, fuses with Shylock into a fictitious though terrifying specter of globalization that threatens to swamp the world of Islam.

French farmers' leader José Bové has been no less vocal than the Islamists in his anti-Americanism, anti-Zionism, and assaults on such symbols of corporate capitalism as the McDonald's restaurant chain. For Bové, like many other pro-Palestinian advocates in Europe, Israel is the world's last colonialist state, imposing "an apartheid system on the occupied territories and the [Israeli] Arab population." This exploitative system was invented by the Western powers nearly a century ago to serve as a capitalist enclave in the heart of the developing world. Its task was "to integrate the Middle East into globalized production circuits, through the exploitation of cheap Palestinian labor."[21] But the conspiracy also extends to contemporary France. Bové claimed several years ago that Israeli intelligence deliberately orchestrated the wave of anti-Semitic violence in France to distract attention from their own country's repressive actions in the Palestinian territories.

It is no accident that there have been a number of assaults by anti-globalization activists on Jews carrying Israeli flags (even those with peace banners) at rallies held in Milan, Paris, London, and Berlin. Here is *Foreign Policy* senior editor Mark Strauss's description of the 2003 World Social Forum in Porto Alegre in Brazil: "Marchers among the 20,000 activists from 120 countries carried signs reading NAZIS, YANKEES, AND JEWS: NO MORE CHOSEN PEOPLES! Some wore T-shirts with the Star of David twisted into Nazi swastikas. Members of Palestinian organizations pilloried Jews as the 'true fundamentalists who control United States capitalism."[22]

Anti-globalist demonstrators at the 2003 World Economic Forum in Davos brandished similar slogans. One of them wore the mask of former U.S. defense secretary Donald Rumsfeld together with a huge Star of David, while being driven forward by a cudgel-brandishing likeness of Ariel Sharon, followed by an outsized golden calf.[23] Was this simply loathing of the U.S. government, George Bush, and Ariel Sharon—a feature of so many worldwide protests against the Iraq War and events in Palestine during 2002 and 2003? Or did it not imply that America was in the hands of Israel and Mammon-worshipping Jews—the mercenary avant-garde of capitalist globalization?[24]

The Israeli invasion of the West Bank in April 2002 undoubtedly revived the energies of many activists from Italy, France, Britain, and other European countries who rallied to a besieged Yasser Arafat, holed up in his Ramallah offices. Veterans of anti-globalization protests in Spain, Italy, and Sweden also trekked to the West Bank to serve as human shields for the PLO leader, confronting Israeli tanks in the war zone. Many would have agreed with the Vatican's official newspaper, *L'Osservatore Romano,* which during Easter 2002 accused Israel of launching an "extermination" of Palestinians in the Holy Land. An Italian Green Party leader, Paolo Cento, said as much in denouncing "the Nazi policies of Sharon," even while denying that anti-globalist rhetoric had any connection with anti-Semitism. But the movement's multinational and multilingual website, Indymedia.org, tells a different story. Its sites in Spain, Italy, and Belgium regularly refer to "Zionazis," and for many of the anti-globalist militants, it is an axiom that Israel has no right to exist.

For some anti-globalists, the world has revolved around absurdly simplistic equations such as neoliberal capitalism = fascism = USA = Israel = imperialism. To this left-wing infantilism, one should add the bizarre "antifascist" Holocaust denial that considers reference to Nazi crimes as a diversion from the class struggle or a deliberate attempt to whitewash Western colonialist atrocities.[25] Even more commonplace is the big lie, widely diffused on the left, the right, and among the Islamists, that Israel itself is a reincarnation of the Third Reich or perhaps an even more deadly version of it. In this anti-Semitic scenario America is a mere puppet in the hands of a Jewish neocon cabal that engineered the invasion of Iraq to defend Israel, while disregarding American national interests.

The conspiracy theories espoused by anti-globalists reveal a common hatred of America and Israel as powerful oppressors and warmongering rogue states imbued with a dangerously self-righteous sense of divine mission.[26] The United States is damned for advancing economic globalization and devouring local industries and jobs in dependent Third World countries. It is attacked for promoting rampant modernity and *cultural* globalism in its own image. With its export of popular music, blue jeans, junk food, celluloid violence, and sensationalist mass media, America is accused of destroying any sense of tradition or national identity.[27] Such subversion was the classic function of Jews in modern society, according to right-wing anti-Semitic perceptions. On the Far Left, anti-Americanism and antipathy to Jews became increasingly linked to the Palestinian cause since the late 1960s.[28] Anti-imperialism was not only a Marxist ideological commitment but also a repudiation of the colonial legacy and the Holocaust by a new postwar generation. Europe, to quote Alain Finkielkraut, embraced the credo of "Never again": "Never again power politics. Never again empire. Never again war-mongering. Never again nationalism. Never again Auschwitz."[29]

The antiracist exuberance of the 1968 generation tended to reduce the world to a Manichean schema in which the former victims of colonialism could never be in the wrong. Israel's sins against the Palestinians became the ultimate heresy against the new religion of humanity.[30] Israel was the ethnic cleanser par excellence—seeking to permanently exclude the [Palestinian] other. By the late 1960s, the spokespeople of the New Left generation were constantly repeating that Western wealth had been built on Third World exploitation; that Nazism had simply mutated after 1945, finding a new home in Western industrial societies; and that *internal* resistance to imperialism required solidarity with Mao Tse-tung, Ho Chi-Minh, Che Guevara, and Fidel Castro. The *anarchisants* (left-wing libertarians) were particularly prone to mistake Third World fantasies for political reality.[31] This was the context in which Palestinians were lionized as the definitive example of *colonisés* (colonized people) under the proto-Nazi jackboot of Israel. Such an inverted world made it seem natural to the future German foreign minister Joschka Fischer to attend a PLO convention in Algiers in 1969 and enabled his colleague Hans-Joachim Klein to sign on with a good conscience to join a PLO terrorist group.[32]

The Palestinian murder of Israeli athletes at the 1972 Olympic Games in Munich, the selection of Jewish passengers during the Entebbe hijacking in 1976, and the deliberately planned execution of prominent Diaspora Jews did admittedly prompt some of the saner heads in the German and French New Left to draw back from the *either-or* philosophy of Middle Eastern terrorism.[33] But the Third Worldist orientation (with its accompanying PLO sympathies) was clearly on the ascent by the late 1970s. It successfully penetrated many Social Democratic labor parties in western and central Europe. Even those who were skeptical about Third World Marxism, its endemic hostility to the West, and the romantic cult of guerrilla violence began to see the PLO as an authentic national liberation movement.[34]

·   ·   ·

The first major power to recognize the PLO was Communist China in 1965. In its revolutionary Maoist phase the country had serious pretensions to Third World leadership. Since the Bandung Conference of 1955, China had gradually come to see Israel as a "lackey of American imperialism"— though it never challenged its right to statehood. Mao Tse-tung, in receiving the PLO delegation in Beijing in March 1965, described both Israel and Taiwan as "bases of imperialism in Asia," telling his Arab visitors: "You are the front gate of the great continent [Asia], and we are the rear. . . . Asia is the biggest continent in the world, and the West wants to continue exploiting it. The Arab battle against the West is the battle against Israel. So boycott Europe and America, O Arabs!"[35] China promised arms, military training, and volunteers to help the Arabs regain Palestine. Indeed, after the crushing Israeli victory in the 1967 war, Radio Peking assured its Arab listeners that "700 million Chinese and the revolutionary peoples of the whole world" supported Arab unity.

Nevertheless, in practice, China did not support maximalist Palestinian aims or deny Israel's right to exist. There were no attempts to imitate Soviet-style anti-Semitism. China's rapprochement with the United States in the 1970s and its adoption of a capitalist road to modernization a decade later opened the way to establishing diplomatic relations with Israel in 1992. Since that time there have been extensive scientific, technological, economic, and military contacts between the two nations, though the Chinese still tend to sympathize more with the Palestinians than with Israelis. This is no longer the case with India. According to the Pew Global Attitudes Project, in a spring 2007 survey, 30 percent of Indians favored Israel, compared to 20 percent support for the Palestinians.

Indian-Israeli relations today are fueled by a common geopolitical interest to contain Islamic fundamentalism, combat jihadi terrorism, and improve border security. After the fall of Soviet Communism, India began to move closer to the United States and abandoned its earlier nonaligned foreign policy. The October 1991 peace conference in Madrid (to which most Arab countries sent senior delegations) encouraged India to put aside the objections of Israel's regional enemies to its ties with Jerusalem.[36] Upgrading relations with Israel was indeed part of a larger, post–Cold War global phenomenon among developing nations. In the 1990s they recognized the growing importance of the Jewish state as a technologically advanced country enjoying a very close relationship with Washington. India, as well as China, eastern Europe, and the central Asian (ex-Soviet) republics—especially Kazakhstan—understood the positive benefits of cooperation with Israel. In the Indian case, the presence of a large Muslim population—perceived as a potential fifth column in its ongoing conflict with a nuclearized Pakistan—was another serious concern that it shared with Israel, whose own Arab Muslim citizens represented 20 percent of its population.

Initially, however, the relations between India and Israel had been tense, despite the fact that both countries had obtained their independence from Great Britain in the first wave of post–World War II decolonization during 1947–48. Pressure from the Arab bloc helped maintain this estrangement, though India did officially recognize Israel and establish consular relations with it in September 1950.[37] But well before Israeli independence, the spiritual godfathers of Indian nationalism, beginning with Mahatma Gandhi, had adopted unequivocally anti-Zionist positions. Gandhi, for example, though by no means indifferent to Jewish suffering, was adamant in regarding Palestine as belonging to the Arabs. Writing in 1938, at the height of Nazi anti-Jewish persecution, he counseled "passive non-violent resistance" as the best policy for Jews facing Hitler. Not even distinguished philosophers, pacifists, and cultural Zionists such as Martin Buber and Judah Magnes could shake Gandhi from this entrenched position or modify his disapproval of Zionism.[38] Another leading Indian nationalist, Jawaharlal Nehru (later one of the great figures of the Nonaligned Movement), strongly supported Palestinian Arab national self-determination in the 1930s. Nehru, too, sympathized with the Jewish plight but condemned Zionism for "collaborating" with British imperialism. He feared that a Jewish state would turn Arabs into a minority in Palestine—which eventually happened after the 1948 war.[39] India's representative at the UN debates on the partition of Palestine presented Israel as an alien political entity created in western Asia against the wish of its peoples. During the following decade, India was in some respects even cooler than China toward Israel.

In the 1940s and '50s, the Jewish state was generally perceived in Asia as a Western phenomenon, foreign to its culture and society. Except for Palestine itself, there were barely more than ten thousand Jews living in the most heavily populated continent on the globe. Among the Muslim nations in Asia, only Iran under the shah (with its eighty thousand Jews) would develop close economic and security links with Israel. Secular Burma, too, was another exception to the rule. Governed by a democratic Socialist party in the 1950s, it enjoyed warm relations, doctrinal affinities, and commercial links with the Jewish state. Later, Turkey, Japan, Singapore, Hong Kong, and Thailand established strategic, cultural, and economic relations with Israel of mutual benefit. These were all countries with significant levels of secularization, modernization, and westernization. On the other hand, in emphatically Muslim states such as Pakistan, Israel was damned root and branch from the outset. Over the years, Pakistan's enmity toward Zionism spilled over into an anti-Semitism without Jews, driven by Wahhabite Sunni fanaticism, Saudi money, solidarity with the Arabs, and an extraordinary receptivity to conspiracy theories. Notwithstanding President Pervez Musharraf's overtures to Israel to act as a mediator in the Middle East conflict, Pakistani society has been deeply infiltrated by radical Islam, and Koranic-style anti-Semitism is still rampant. In spring 2007, according to the Pews project, 76 percent of Pakistanis sympathized with the Palestinians and only 2 percent with Israel.

The first postwar generation of nonaligned anticolonialist leaders (virtually all of them nationalist and socialist) were, for the most part, anti-Israel as part of their animus against Western imperialism. Charismatic figures such as Indian prime minister Jawaharlal Nehru; Yugoslavia's "heretical" Communist head of state, Josip Broz Tito; Ahmed Ben Bella from Algeria; Egyptian president Gamal Abdel Nasser; the Indonesian general Sukarno; and the Ghanaian leader Kwame Nkrumah set the tone for Third World solidarity.[40] One of the most important factors in drawing these and other Third World nations into the Arab orbit was the influence of Gamal Abdul Nasser. In 1956 his nationalization of the Suez Canal electrified the Arab world, and his militant anti-Western stand impressed leaders of the Afro-Asian bloc. As a career officer who fought in the lost war of 1948 against Israel, Nasser dreamed of revenge for this humiliation. Like Juan Péron in Argentina, he had initially been inspired by the German Nazi model of nationalism. By the 1960s, however, he moved closer to a pro-Moscow brand of nonalignment. Nasser saw Israel as a dangerous rival and a partner of Western imperialism, bent on weakening Egypt and dividing the Arabs.[41] He had no compunction about reaching out to anti-Semitic organizations as part of his counterstrategy to undermine and eliminate Israel. He established links with British Nazis and with the Tacuara, a virulently anti-Semitic movement in Argentina. Arab publications, especially in South America, began to incite against Israel and local Jewish communities. In black Africa and Asia, where anti-Semitism had only shallow roots, Egyptian propaganda nonetheless tried to arouse it. Thus Pope John XXIII's campaign to lift the charge of deicide from the Jewish people in 1962 led Egypt and the Arab world to try to prevent moves toward Catholic-Jewish reconciliation at all costs.

Egyptian anti-Semitism in Nasser's time was much influenced by the Nazis who had been given refuge in the country, especially after 1953. Some worked in the secret services and others in the design and building of rockets, but many were also specialists in anti-Semitic propaganda. They included Louis Heiden, formerly of the Reich Security Main Office, who under the name of Louis al-Hadj translated *Mein Kampf* into Arabic. The journalist Franz Buensche continued his former career by disseminating anti-Jewish and Holocaust denial publications in Egypt and other Arab countries. Especially important was the Nazi propagandist Johann von Leers, who had praised Islam in 1936 for successfully eliminating the "Jewish threat" in Arabia. He renewed his anti-Semitic crusade after 1955 in Nasserist Egypt. Von Leers became a political adviser and propagandist for the regime, even adopting a Muslim name, Omar Amin. His many contributions to the anti-Zionist cause included promoting the *Protocols* in Arabic, reviving the blood libel, cultivating neo-Nazis and encouraging Holocaust deniers around the world. He also organized anti-Semitic radio broadcasts in various languages.[42]

Nasser's own anti-Semitism expressed itself in various ways. He was, for example, an unequivocal Holocaust denier who confidently told the editor of Germany's leading neo-Nazi newspaper: "No one, not even the simplest of men, takes seriously the lie about six million Jews who were murdered."[43] The Egyptian dictator was a fervent admirer of the *Protocols of the Elders of Zion*, which he warmly recommended to a visiting Indian journalist, R. K. Karanjia, in 1958: "It is very important that you should read it. I will give you a copy. It proves beyond the shadow of a doubt that three hundred Zionists, each of whom knows all the others, govern the fate of the European Continent . . . and that they elect their successors from their entourage."[44]

• • •

The president's brother Shawqi Abdel Nasser would edit the *Protocols* in 1968 with an enthusiastic preface that called on Arabs everywhere to read them several times and propagate their message far and wide. No other document so clearly exposed the satanic program of the Zionist Jews, he said.[45] This was no isolated example. The Egyptian government used and quoted from the *Protocols* in Arabic and other languages for export purposes. They were disseminated in Africa at the beginning of 1965 by the Egyptian Information Department in an English-language pamphlet entitled *Israel, the Enemy of Africa*. Nasser's personal representative, in a lecture published by the Egyptian Armed Forces Supreme Command, observed that the *Protocols* were an "outstanding Zionist work" of political planning—a blueprint to achieve "Jewish domination" of the world through "the corruption of virtue, economic profiteering, the dissemination of vice, the destruction of religion and, finally, the use of murder."[46]

Israel was consistently pilloried in the Egyptian media both as a bridgehead of Western imperialism—the external enemy—and as an agent of domestic subversion. Egypt, under Nasser and his successor Anwar al-Sadat, had particularly emphasized the theme of Israel as a Trojan horse of neocolonialism thwarting pan-Arab aspirations and Third World national-liberation movements. Hence, the final goal of "annihilating the Zionist entity" was a vital part of the pan-Arab anti-imperialist struggle. The liquidation of Israel was presented as the rectification of a major "historic injustice." As one commentator on Radio Cairo chillingly put it on April 20, 1963: "Israel is the cancer, the malignant wound, in the body of Arabism, for which there is no cure but eradication . . . the liquidation of Israel and the restoration of the plundered Palestine Arab land are at the head of our national objectives."[47]

In the early 1960s Israel was able to counter this exterminationist propaganda with a modicum of success. It invested considerable efforts in cultivating relations with black African countries. Public and private Israeli companies in Africa worked on constructing housing projects, developing water resources, paving roads, and building airports. There was extensive technical cooperation in education, agriculture, industry, engineering, and in the military sphere. This was especially true in Kenya, Zaire, Gabon, Nigeria, Tanzania, Liberia, and Ghana, where commercial ties had expanded rapidly.[48] In 1957, Ghana, led by its national hero, President Kwame Nkrumah, had been the first newly independent African nation to initiate diplomatic relations with Israel. Twenty-seven other independent states in post-colonial Africa soon established similarly warm ties. Technical aid was a relatively altruistic and pragmatic way for Israel to act as a "light unto the nations" and display its skills as an innovative, developing country.[49] But from the outset, Arab states were determined to use their economic influence to undermine Israel and pushed for the right of return of the Palestinian refugees. At the 1961 Casablanca Conference, Nkrumah felt obliged to sign a Nasser-sponsored resolution that singled out Israel as "the pillar of imperialism in Africa."[50]

Predominantly Christian Uganda offers a particularly stark example of how easily Israel's close relations with a black African state could be overturned. Israel had trained the Ugandan military and developed its agriculture. But in 1971 a military coup brought a Ugandan Muslim, General Idi Amin, to power. Amin had earlier received his paratrooper's wings in Israel, and at first he continued the close military cooperation with the Jewish state. However, Israel's refusal to accede to his extravagant demands for money and arms, as well as strong Arab pressures from Egyptian president Sadat and Libyan leader Colonel Qaddafi, led to a shift and the closure of the Israeli Embassy in April 1972.[51] Saudi and Libyan financial aid no doubt contributed their share to a sudden flurry of anti-Semitic statements from the Ugandan leader.

Amin told a BBC correspondent in 1972 that Jews were the cause of war and most human suffering, that they had murdered Jesus, and that they controlled America and other countries through their money.[52] The Ugandan media inaugurated an anti-Israeli campaign, riddled with crude anti-Semitism. At the same time, Amin expropriated and expelled Ugandan Asians on August 4, 1972, justifying his measures inter alia by calling the Asian immigrants "brown Jews."[53] In the same month, Amin applauded the Munich massacre of Israeli Olympic athletes by Palestinian terrorists. He announced that Germany was the most appropriate venue for these killings, precisely because this was where Hitler had burned six million Jews. In a telegram to UN secretary-general Kurt Waldheim, Amin declared: "It [the Holocaust] happened because Hitler and all of the German people knew that the Israelis are not a people who work for humanity and because of that they burned them with gas on the soil of Germany."[54] The Ugandan dictator's justification of the Holocaust shocked many African leaders but was consistent with his own practices. His genocidal talents were given ample scope in the 1970s at the expense of his own people. Black Africans (mainly Christians) were murdered on Amin's orders in the hundreds of thousands, until a Tanzanian military invasion overthrew his tyrannical rule in April 1979. Today, Uganda is one of the most pro-Israel countries in black Africa—38 percent sympathizing with the Jewish state and only 19 percent favoring the Palestinians.

One of the most anti-Israel countries on the African continent over the past forty-five years has been Algeria, whose liberation struggle against France made it a symbol of Third Worldism in the 1960s. A key figure in that anticolonial war was Ahmed Ben Bella, for a time president of the newly independent Algeria. During an interview with a prominent French journal in the summer of 1982, Ben Bella insisted that the Arab world would never tolerate a Jewish state in its midst in any configuration. To recognize Israel, he emphasized, would be synonymous with "a sterilization, a loss of identity that no self-respecting Arab could accept." Israel was a "foreign body in the region," "a real cancer implanted in the Arab world."[55] Even a nuclear war was worth risking in order to destroy Israel, since the mere fact of its existence was the ultimate symptom of Arab weakness and "non-being." Ben Bella's worldview fused Pan-Arabism, Islam, and Third World ideology with a strong dose of anti-Semitic anti-Zionism. He bluntly told his French interviewer: "The Western press is almost totally dominated by Jews and Zionists . . . in the French government, there is a powerful Zionist lobby. I am personally very worried by this."[56]

Neither Ben Bella's Third Worldist extremism nor Idi Amin's paranoia were typical of black African states, despite the rupture of relations with Israel after the 1973 Yom Kippur War. But they were indications of a trend that would be reinforced by Israel's growing ties with the apartheid regime in South Africa, and the effects of the UN "Zionism-Racism" vote of November 1975.[57] The new stigma of Israel as a white racist state collaborating militarily with Pretoria began to seriously undermine the religiously rooted sympathy that many African Christians felt for Jews as the People of the Book, organically linked to the land of Zion and generally supportive of other racially oppressed groups.[58] The erosion was palpable in remarks by Nigeria's ambassador to the UN, Alhaji Yusuf Maitama-Sule (then chair of the UN Special Committee Against Apartheid), who declared in April 1982 that both Pretoria and Tel Aviv were outlaw regimes, relying on their military establishments and external imperialist support. He accused them of acting as "gendarmes" of the Western powers in Africa and the Middle East.[59] This distorted view almost exactly mirrored that of the PLO, the Arab media, and Soviet publications—which grossly exaggerated the security links and *common* ideology of racism that supposedly animated both countries.[60]

Moderate African leaders could not, however, ignore the South African issue or Israel's invasion of Lebanon in the summer of 1982. In a July 1982 communication to the UN Security Council Tanzanian president Julius Nyerere deplored "the death and destruction launched from Israel," the "arrogant disregard of international law," and the flagrant disregard of Lebanon's sovereignty.[61] Nevertheless, he and other black African leaders insisted on Israel's right to exist as an independent state, while supporting the same right for the Palestinians. Most African leaders, while increasingly critical of Israel, did not support Arab efforts to ban it from UNESCO, the World Health Organization, or the International Labor organization. There was, moreover, a growing tension with Arab leaders. Many African states were irritated by efforts to spread Islam or undermine their own societies. They were deeply disappointed by the broken promises of economic aid from oil-rich Gulf states, and increasingly angered by the relentless Arab pressure to dictate their policies toward Israel.[62]

Support for Israel in black Africa today remains high in most non-Muslim countries. The spring 2007 Pew Global Attitudes Project survey of forty-seven countries showed that in the Ivory Coast, 61 percent of those polled supported Israel and only 16 percent identified with the Palestinians. In Ethiopia the rate was 37 percent as opposed to 25 percent for the Palestinians. Similar results were obtained for Ghana, Kenya, and present-day Uganda. (For comparison, in Britain 29 percent favored the Palestinians and only 16 percent Israel.) One explanation may be that in many African countries the attitude toward Hamas and radical Islam is extremely negative. Africans have not forgotten the Arab slave trade and in recent years they have observed the genocide perpetrated by Sudanese Arabs against black Muslims and Christians in Darfur and southern Sudan. In addition, non-Muslim African leaders cannot fail to be concerned by the threat of jihad and Muslim expansion within their own countries.

At the same time, however, Third Worldist pan-Arab leaders such as Colonel Qaddafi have not been without influence on attitudes toward Israel and Zionism in Africa and Latin America. Interestingly enough, Qaddafi's conspiratorial view of Israel's activities in Africa (which relied on familiar anti-Semitic stereotypes) has almost exactly mirrored his own subversive techniques. The Zionists' "hidden objective," according to the Libyan dictator, was to "prepare militarists within the African armies" for future coups that would place their countries in the grip of Israel. Economic infiltration and exploitation was no less fundamental: "The Jewish organization cannot live except in banks and in economic activities, some of which are covert. They want to infiltrate African activities, African markets, African concerns and African companies . . . to serve Zionism."[63]

Along with Yasser Arafat, Qaddafi was one of the staunchest supporters of the African National Congress (ANC) and its leader Nelson Mandela during the long years of his imprisonment. This was not forgotten in the 1990s when Mandela (once in power) established ambassadorial relations with the still nonexistent state of Palestine—a source of some anxiety for South Africa's 120,000-strong Jewish community. Indeed, Mandela has praised an unseemly crew of dictators over the years, including the tyrant of Zimbabwe, Robert Mugabe, kept afloat by South Africa despite committing a silent genocide against his own people. Unfortunately, the ANC long ago departed from its self-proclaimed principles of human rights and political freedom. Its current friendliness with Iran, Hamas, Hezbollah, and Sudan is a testimony to its abandonment of human rights advocacy and the higher moral ground. Indeed, the ANC has become increasingly mired in the appeasement of Third World totalitarianism, as a result of its outdated anti-imperialist solidarities.

However, it was white Afrikaner nationalists (whose leadership had been openly pro-Nazi in the 1930s) that were initially the main source of anti-Semitism in South Africa. In 1948, the Nationalist Party came to power and established an apartheid regime. At that time, anti-Semitism was still very much an acceptable part of mainstream South African politics—something that changed only in the early 1960s, when the white regime became more concerned about oppressing the blacks than with excluding Jews.[64] At that time, the South African Jewish community represented the largest and most influential concentration of Jews living on the African continent. Like other whites, it benefited from apartheid and the community did not officially oppose the white minority regime. Indeed, starting in the mid-1960s individual Jews would become increasingly prominent in cultural, economic, and public life. Despite the upheavals during the transition from apartheid to a functioning multiracial democracy, this trend has continued to some extent. Politically aware Jews, it should be remembered, were always disproportionately represented in the antiapartheid struggle—far more than their counterparts in the rest of the white community. In his autobiography Nelson Mandela himself observed that Jews tended "to be more broad-minded than most whites on issues of race and politics, perhaps because they themselves have historically been victims of prejudice."[65]

This fact did not pass unnoticed among black Africans and may well have contributed something to maintaining relatively harmonious relations with Jews.[66] But this has not been the case with the eight hundred thousand Muslims in South Africa, who are increasingly influenced by inflammatory anti-Semitic preaching in the mosques. More than a decade ago a local Muslim leader, Faried Esack, pointed out that many South African Muslims despised Jews as "schemers, betrayers, exploiters and usurpers." They regarded Zionism as racist and rejected the idea of the chosen people as deeply condescending.[67] Such anti-Semitic clichés have been reinforced by the spread of the *Protocols,* a steady stream of anti-Zionist articles printed in the local Islamist press, and calls for mobilization for the Palestinian cause. Yasser Arafat's visit to Johannesburg in 1994 and his incendiary jihadist speech in the local mosque envenomed this atmosphere, as did the rise of People Against Gangsterism and Drugs (PAGAD)—an Islamist movement that has openly flaunted its links to Hamas and Hezbollah.[68] Against this background of radical Islam, it is not surprising that in 2006, South Africa registered a record number of anti-Semitic incidents since detailed records began to be kept twenty years ago. Four times as many incidents were reported than in 2005. The Jewish Board of Deputies observed that strong anti-Israel sentiment in the mainstream South African media and NGO culture had fueled the hostile climate.[69]

• • •

The Jews of Latin America, who number close to half a million, are much more diverse than their coreligionists in South Africa. Many have become part of the prosperous middle class and are professionally successful, though higher elective office and positions in the military, judiciary, and foreign service are far more difficult to attain. Like other Diaspora Jewish communities, they face problems related to mixed marriages, demographic decline, assimilation, and anti-Semitism. Their vigorous support for Israel has also, at times, provoked charges of dual loyalty in a continent that for centuries was culturally monolithic (the legacy of Iberian Catholicism) and non-pluralistic.[70] However, this phenomenon has been changing for the better in recent decades. The transition from military dictatorships to stable democracies has, on the whole, benefited the bulk of Latin American Jewry, concentrated in the so-called Cono Sur (Argentina, Uruguay, Chile, Brazil) and further to the north, in Mexico—where the great majority of Jews belong to the affluent classes.[71]

Relations with Israel in these and other South American countries have generally been normal and sometimes even cordial. The Latin Americans were, for example, the very last Third World grouping to come out in support of the Palestinian cause.[72] Only at the thirty-fifth UN General Assembly Session in 1980 did a pro-Palestinian position begin to emerge among the Latin American states, which owed much to the cumulative influence of the Nonaligned Movement on its politics. Even then, support for Palestinians was not seen as incompatible with maintaining good relations with Israel. Even today, public opinion in most Latin American nations—except for Cuba, Argentina, Mexico, and Nicaragua—is moderately sympathetic to Israel.

The United Nations could never have partitioned Palestine in 1947 without the agreement of almost all twenty Latin American states. They were undoubtedly influenced by Zionist pioneering achievements, the indescribable Jewish suffering during the Holocaust, and sympathy for the underdog, as well as to the position of the United States. It is worth recalling that much of the popular support for Israel came from radical parties, labor leaders, Communists, and intellectuals. Only on the issue of Jerusalem did Latin America, in accordance with its strong Catholic tradition, adopt a position opposed to Israel and close to that of the Vatican.[73]

After the 1973 Yom Kippur War, the pro-Israel policies of many Latin American states were gradually modified by the rise to prominence of the PLO, the centrality of the oil factor, the growing weight of Third World global solidarity, and increasing concern about Israel's occupation of the territories.[74] UN resolutions condemning Israeli annexation of East Jerusalem in August 1980 received particularly strong support from the Latin Americans. Third World–oriented Mexico and oil-importing Brazil, along with radical Marxist states Cuba, Guyana, and Nicaragua, were the most pro-PLO and anti-Israel. None of the last three countries had diplomatic relations with Israel by the end of the 1970s. Cuban leader Fidel Castro had dramatically broken off relations with Israel at the Nonaligned Movement summit in Algiers in September 1973. In November 1975, Cuba, Mexico, Brazil, Grenada, and Guyana backed the UN resolution equating Zionism with racism. Yet, despite these trends, antagonism toward Israel was weaker than in Asia or Africa. In the Brazilian case (more than in any other Latin American country) the question of oil supplies and exports to the Arab world was the critical factor. Argentina, before and during its brutal military dictatorship of 1976–83, also became more responsive to Palestinian national aspirations while maintaining an equidistance between Arabs and Jews. This evenhandedness would become characteristic of many Latin American countries in the coming decades

Anti-Semitism in Latin America has much deeper roots than in Africa or Asia. In modern times it has tended to be linked with a monolithic, xenophobic, and Catholic-oriented nationalism, particularly in Argentina, which still has the largest concentration of Jews on the South American continent.[75] In the early 1960s, during a brief democratic interregnum, physical attacks on Argentine Jews had accelerated. Right-wing Peronist congressmen accused Jews of dual loyalty, while neo-Nazis claimed that all Jews were simultaneously communists and Zionists. The anti-Zionist offensive in Argentina (and other countries on the continent) was encouraged by both the ultranationalist Right and representatives of the Arab League. Moreover, under the neo-Peronist regime in the early 1970s, Argentine Jews had to fight against a widely disseminated conspiracy theory known as the "Andinía plot," which claimed that Zionists were planning to annex mineral-rich Patagonia and establish a Jewish state in the remote southern province.[76] From the pro-Arab side, the Peronist minister of social welfare, José López Rega (a notorious anti-Semite and admirer of Colonel Qaddafi), actively pushed to remove Jews from positions of public influence.[77]

The military coup that brought down the neo-Peronists in 1976 was especially traumatic for Jewish and non-Jewish militants accused of Communist activities.[78] Thousands were tortured and killed in secret prisons or were thrown alive from airplanes into the ocean. The prominent left-wing journalist and publisher Jacobo Timmerman was tortured for hours with electrodes for having printed the names of kidnapping victims. He observed that some of the torture chambers contained portraits of Adolf Hitler; he and other prisoners had to listen to constant chants of "Jew! Jew!"

from his captors. There is little doubt that Jewish opponents of the military regime were subjected to special treatment, or that a Nazi-like anti-Semitism existed in sections of the Argentine armed forces and police.[79] After 1945 Argentina had served as a safe haven for Nazi war criminals Adolf Eichmann and Erich Priebke, and for notorious German Nazi propagandists Johann von Leers and Wilfred van Oven, who had been Goebbels's press secretary. There was a whole network of neo-Nazi newspapers, journals, and publications that glorified the Third Reich. Argentina became a haven for conservative-authoritarian ideologies, fascism, biopolitics, anti-Communism, the distrust of democracy, and overtly racist anti-Semitism.[80] Though the exiles' dream of a neofascist "third force" never fully materialized, their radical nationalist ideology had sufficiently strong local roots to leave an impact upon Argentina's society and culture. Its echo was felt in the various authoritarian regimes that preceded democratization in 1983.[81] Even today, the residues have not altogether disappeared, despite the dominance of left-wing governments across the Latin American continent.

In the 1970s, a greater orientation toward the nonaligned camp of Argentina, Brazil, and Mexico brought with it manifestations of a leftist and Third World anti-Zionist anti-Semitism. A Brazilian sociologist, Amilcar Alencastre, alleged in 1972 that Zionism was a vital instrument and auxiliary force in the global strategy of world imperialism, which had deliberately sought to divide Latin American countries from the Arabs, Asians, and Africans. He claimed that as a key "agent" of colonialist forces on three continents, Zionism was the sworn enemy of the Third World.[82] Israel's special relationship with the United States and its "exclusivist" character had turned it into a pivotal factor in Western penetration of developing countries. The Jewish state was "an oasis implanted in the midst of the misery of the Third World," intended to serve as a favored Western model for "inferior countries."[83] Alencastre stressed the close relationship between Israel, Portugal (then fighting to preserve its African colonies), South Africa, and Rhodesia, as well as its common interests with the United States, West Germany, and the shah's Iran. He maintained that Zionism as an ideology of the chosen people was more racist and colonialist than that of its Western allies in systematically expelling the "natives." Furthermore, its domestic influence in the United States, Argentina, and the rest of Latin America was unique. Zionists controlled the U.S. media; their penetration of the Argentine press, radio, TV, film, education, finance, unions, and political parties was astounding; and they were supposedly responsible for much of the vice, immorality, sensationalism, and commercial corruption across the Latin American continent.[84] Such Arab-sponsored libels, relying on hackneyed anti-Semitic and Third World rhetoric, continue to find an echo among extreme Right and Far Left organizations. To this one should add the anti-Zionist propaganda of the Communist parties in Latin America, which for several decades took their cue from Moscow. Trotskyist groups, as elsewhere, have been no less vociferous in calling for the dissolution of the Jewish state while insisting that they oppose anti-Semitism.

The most violent action against Jews in Latin America was nonetheless initiated by outside forces—Iran and Hezbollah—though they clearly required local help. The 1992 bombings that destroyed the Israeli Embassy in Buenos Aires and the Jewish community center (AMIA) only two years later have never been completely clarified. But it was surely no accident that this Islamist assault on Israel and the Jews took place in a country whose police and security services were notoriously riddled with corruption, proto-Nazism, and anti-Semitic sentiment. Argentina recently experienced another escalation of anti-Jewish attacks, despite its economic stabilization and the further consolidation of its democratic system. In 2006, according to DAIA (the main Jewish communal agency), a record number of 586 anti-Semitic acts in Argentina were recorded, as compared to 373 the previous year—a rise of 57 percent.[85] To a certain extent this corresponded with a growing climate of social violence and the persistence of discriminatory attitudes against new immigrants, the handicapped, and other marginal groups. The specific context, however, was the 2006 Lebanon War, which provoked an outpouring of graffiti and slogans in the streets of Buenos Aires, including "Death to the State of Israel," "Death to the Dirty Jews," "Let's kill the Jews," and "Jews are fascists." The catchphrase "*lobby judeo-norteamericano*" (Jewish–North American lobby) has become more frequent in the mass media. Radical left groups (as in Europe) have openly displayed Hezbollah flags at demonstrations and defended Iranian president Ahmadinejad. Their anti-Zionist Judeophobia involves a systematic banalization of the Shoah.[86]

An indication of this trend was the implantation of a Hezbollah branch in Argentina. It mixes radical right- and left-wing anti-Zionist elements on its website, while maintaining very close relations with the local Arab Shiite community and the Iranian regime. Hezbollah Argentina extensively uses

622 A LETHAL OBSESSION

anti-Semitic material, some of it derived from Shiite websites, from Ahmad Rami's incendiary Sweden-based Radio Islam, or from the anti-Jewish and anti-American writings of the Argentine sociologist Norberto Rafael Ceresole, a former Peronist who died in 2003.[87] Ceresole attributed the suicide bombings at the Israeli Embassy and AMIA in the 1990s to "Jewish terrorism."[88] He developed intimate links with both Iran and Hezbollah, and he considered Iran after the Khomeinist revolution to be "the center of resistance to Jewish aggression" and the only state capable of destroying Israel.[89] In his view (shared by the Argentine Hezbollah) the struggle against the Jewish state must include the Third World as well as the Middle East.[90]

The left-wing Argentine "patriots" (Movimiento Patriótico Revolucionario, MPR) who are linked to the Lebanese Hezbollah and the Islamic Association of Argentina (ASAI) are no less anti-globalist, anti-Zionist, and pro-Palestinian than the anti-Semitic Rightists.[91] Consisting mainly of converts to Shiism, ASAI cooperates closely with the Iranian Embassy, and its militants carry Khomeini posters at every anti-Israel demonstration. On August 20, 2006, the ASAI website published a revealing interview with Hassan Nasrallah, secretary-general of the Lebanese Hezbollah, in which he emphasized the moral support that he had received from Latin American socialists, especially President Chávez of Venezuela. Nasrallah saluted "the leaders and people of Latin America" for their "heroic resistance to the American bandits." This support, he claimed (with some exaggeration) had led the Lebanese people "to embrace Chávez and Ernesto Ché Guevara."

Nasrallah remarked that on the streets of Beirut the pictures of Chávez, Che, and Iranian leader Ali Khamenei could be found harmoniously intermingled.[92] Virulent anti-Israel and anti-American incitement lay at the heart of this Hezbollah-sponsored agitation in Latin America, which has skillfully manipulated Marxist, anti-globalist, and neo-Nazi concepts to serve Islamist purposes. Thus it is no surprise to find the openly fascist organization Partido Nuevo Triunfo, which regularly pours out its bile against the existence of "the self-proclaimed 'State of Israel,' " expressing its unequivocal solidarity with Hezbollah and the Palestinians. Argentine politicians of Arab descent such as Jorge Abib, provincial senator of Cordoba Province, have indeed been playing with fire. On July 29, 2006, Abib informed listeners on a local radio program that "the Jews put the bomb in the AMIA. What Hitler did was a good thing. . . . What Israel is doing is much worse than what Hitler did."[93]

A comparison with Fidel Castro's so-called Communist paradise in the Caribbean is instructive in this regard. Unlike Argentina, Cuba did not have a historical tradition of institutionalized prejudice against Jews. Anti-Semitism was, nonetheless, present on the eve of World War II, when the Jewish population peaked at around thirteen thousand. Sephardic Jews arrived in Cuba from the Ottoman Balkans before 1914. In the early 1920s some seven thousand Ashkenazic Jews fled from eastern Europe to the Caribbean island, mostly in the hope of facilitating their entry into the United States. Their presence sparked a growing anti-Semitic backlash, an imported malady brought to Cuba by Falangist Spanish exiles and pro-Nazi agents. The nationalistic revolution of 1933 in Cuba gave a new boost to xenophobia, reinforced by the economic slump of the Great Depression.[94] It was followed six years later by the largest anti-Semitic demonstration in Cuba's history (about forty thousand protestors), organized by local fascists and encouraged by the opposition leader, the previously deposed president Ramón Grau San Martín.[95] The May 1939 anti-Semitic rally happened just as the ill-fated SS *St. Louis,* carrying a thousand German-Jewish refugees to the New World, was refused landing rights in Havana. The tragic "Voyage of the Damned" back to Europe was a direct consequence of the anti-Semitic agitation in Cuba that peaked on the eve of the Holocaust.[96] Few of the ship's passengers survived, once they were forced to return to Europe.

Cuba's new authoritarian leader Fulgencio Batista did eventually suppress the local Nazis and fascists in late 1939, partly under American pressure.[97] However, in November 1947, Cuba was the only country in the Western Hemisphere to vote against the UN partition of Palestine.[98] Two years later this anomaly was corrected. Interestingly enough, the guerrilla leader Fidel Castro, who overthrew Batista and seized power in 1959, initially continued to maintain diplomatic relations with Israel, despite the 1967 Six-Day War. In 1969 he told a prominent left-wing journalist that although he strongly condemned Israel, he did not question its right to exist. Indeed, Castro was very critical of Arab propaganda in the late 1960s, commenting that true revolutionaries would never threaten a whole country with extermination.[99] He insisted that the United States was the real instigator of the war. Israeli officials were therefore surprised when in September 1973 at the Fourth Summit Conference of Nonaligned Nations in Algiers, Castro suddenly announced that he would indeed sever his diplomatic ties with the Jewish state.

Some observers have regarded this act as a transparent attempt by Castro to placate the Arabs (especially Qadaffi) and embrace the dominant sentiments of the nonaligned bloc assembled in Algiers. It was certainly a symptom of Castro's increasing dependence on economic assistance from the Soviet Union. Anti-Israel articles began to appear almost daily in the Cuban press. At the same time, any appearance of persecuting Jews inside Cuba was carefully avoided. Zionism, however, was continuously attacked as a "diabolical" and ultrachauvinist, racist ideology, based on the myth of the chosen people. After 1973, Cuba would become a major backer of resolutions labeling Zionism as racism, even supporting moves to expel Israel from the United Nations. For the past thirty-five years the Castro regime has indeed persisted in fostering the Third World big lie equating Zionism with racism—as if it remains forever frozen in a time warp.

When it comes to anti-Zionist rhetoric, Castro's most ardent disciple, the Venezuelan president Huge Chávez, long ago surpassed his mentor. Venezuela's prosperous upper-middle-class Jewish community (numbering about twenty thousand) now lives under heavy security and faces an increasingly tense environment. During the summer of 2006 streets in Caracas were decorated with numerous graffiti and signs such as "Judios go Home," "*Judios Asesinos*" (Jewish Murderers), "The US and Israel want to destroy Venezuela," and "Out with the CIA and Mossad." The large August 2006 demonstrations of *Chavistas* (Chávez supporters) in favor of Hezbollah, as well as the constant incitement against Israel in the media as a "genocidal" state, further aggravated the anxieties of local Jews—a thousand of whom left the country that year.[100] This state-supported propaganda may not necessarily reflect the real views of the Venezuelan people on the Israeli-Palestinian conflict, but it does create a climate of fear and intimidation against the upwardly mobile and hitherto prosperous if dwindling Jewish community. Until the end of the 1990s there had been virtually no signs of a serious anti-Semitic malaise in Venezuela. But since Chávez came to power the gap between the government and the Jewish community has dramatically grown, partly driven by fear of the loss of private property, of constitutional rights, and individual freedoms.

Hugo Chávez, a former military commander who heads the world's third largest petroleum producer, is largely responsible for this deteriorating situation. He has pursued a relentlessly anti-American policy, branding former U.S. president George W. Bush as the great Satan at the United

Nations—a terminology more usually associated with his allies in Tehran. Furthermore, Chávez built up a million-person-strong militia, thereby encouraging a siege mentality in the population, in which Israel and the American Jewish lobby are depicted as collaborating with the government of the United States to bring him down.[101]

The undisguised ambition behind Chávez's so-called Bolivarian revolution (named after the nineteenth-century liberator of Latin America, Simon Bolivar) has been to forge an axis of anti-American socialist regimes across the continent. His ideology has been based on an incoherent though heady mix of Jesus, Marx, Lenin, Castro, left-wing nationalism, and the authoritarian *caudillo* (leader) tradition of Latin America.[102] Government-inspired anti-Semitism has become a noticeable component of this potentially explosive cocktail. In the official press, members of the Jewish community of Venezuela were vilified during the 2006 war in Lebanon for "defending these mass murderers [the Nazis who govern in Israel], defending this genocide, defending this final solution that Israel wants to apply to the Arabs." Efraim Lapscher, the head of the Caracas Jewish community, was referred to in the weekly *Los Papeles de Mandinga* as if he were an SS *Obergruppenführer* "who applies the imbecile recipe of accusing of anti-Semitism anyone who does not applaud this genocide."[103]

Alberto Nolia, writing in the same newspaper in September 2006, further blackened the good reputation of Jewish community leaders, calling them a "criminal mafia" for daring to criticize President Ahmadinejad's visit to Venezuela.[104] In the same month the influential Marxist journalist Basem Tajeldine enthusiastically defended the Iranian leader, explaining in *Diario Vea* that the Holocaust had been perpetrated in order to wipe out lower-class anti-Zionist Jews who believed in assimilation. "The ideological affinity and collaboration between German Zionism and Nazism," he affirmed, was undeniable. Tajeldine concluded that "Zionist Nazis" was the most appropriate term by which to define "the capitalist Jewish elite of Israel responsible for the present Holocaust of the Arab people." Writing in May 2008, Tajeldine again presented Zionism as the ideology of an advanced European bourgeoisie that had grown out of the alienated, intimidatory logic of the Jewish religion. [105]

In the summer of 2006, cartoons in government-linked newspapers continuously recycled stark images of Israeli "Nazis" crucifying Lebanese and Palestinians. Their message was echoed by columnists such as "Marciano," writing in the pro-government daily *Vea,* who compared Gaza to the Warsaw ghetto.[106] "Marciano" turned out to be the nom de plume of Venezuela's foreign minister and vice president at the time, José Vicente Rangel. Adolf Hitler even appeared in one of these caricatures as an innocent babe in the arms of his "father," Israeli prime minister Ehud Olmert! Anti-Semitism oozed from the July 2006 newsletter of *Docencia Participativa* (Participatory Faculty)—distributed for free by the Ministry of Education—which bore the front cover text "Stop the Massacre. For the love of God. For the love of Allah. Assassin Jews! Apocalyptic Beasts!"[107] The same newsletter, one month later, featured a graphic for an article on the Second Lebanon War, showing a hideous Jew wearing a yarmulke. He was busy crushing a bleeding globe with his hands, as a Magen David hung suspended over his head. The front cover image displayed a swastika in the middle of a much larger Star of David and a headline "Nazis XX century. Jews XXI Century. Nuremberg." The cover story read: "The massacre of the Middle East. Children, women and elderly people destroyed by the bloody Jewish massacre [*la mascara sangrienta judia*]. . . . Judge the criminals of humanity."[108]

Such texts and graphics frequently appeared in government-affiliated media and educational institutes. National Assembly declarations by Venezuelan politicians and official government statements have attacked Israel's actions in Lebanon as "genocide" and slandered Israelis as "enemies of the world."[109] On July 22, 2006, Enrique Franco, minister for the environment in Carabobo state, spoke in a similar vein about Zionist "extermination policy," accusing the Israeli ambassador of plotting against the Bolivarian Republic in order to prevent Venezuela's election to the UN Security Council. Sarina Cascone, secretary of education and sports in the same region, execrated Israel, the Jews, and America for their "malicious alliance," based on treachery, greed, and the lust for power. She alleged that obnoxious Jewish cultural characteristics had existed "since the genesis of the Jewish people," and suggested that they had carried through to the present.[110] In the legislature of the state of Miranda on August 8, 2006, the president of the chamber (a member of Chávez's party) went further still, repeatedly insulting a Jewish opposition legislator and telling him that the Holocaust was a justified retaliation for Jewish guilt in the murder of Jesus. Anti-imperialism, class struggle, charges of deicide, and ethnic hatred merged in a paranoid assault on the so-called Zionist conspiracy against Venezuela.

In July 2006, *Diario Vea* struck another old-new chord of anti-Semitism. It carried an article vilifying Zionists as a "destructive sect of radical Jews" who had imbued the Jewish community with hatred against the rest of humanity. The paper warned that the Israeli "genocide" in Lebanon was creating a wave of global revulsion and sowing the seeds of a further Holocaust against the Jews.[111] Writing in early September 2006 in *El Diario de Caracas,* the journalist Tarek Muci Nasir (a pseudonym) was even more explicit, expressing a manifestly racist form of anti-Semitism. He asserted that the "Jewish race" could only maintain its unity by constantly provoking wars and genocide. He added for good measure that Venezuelan Jewish and Zionist associations, unions, and federations

> conspire . . . to seize our finances, industries, commerce, construction, even infiltrating public positions and politics. Possibly it will again be necessary to expel them from the country, like other nations have done before; this is the reason why the Jews are always in a continuous stateless exodus and thus in the year 1948 they invaded Palestine, guided by Albion [England].[112]

Anti-Semites in the government-sponsored media have continued to attack the "local Jewish mafia" and Jewish communities in Venezuela as a "Zionist enclave" pursuing a criminal policy of subversion against Chávez on behalf of the United States and international imperialism. Indeed, in this wild rhetoric, words like "terrorists," "assassins," and "criminals" have been inseparable from any mention of Israel or Zionism.

President Chávez himself set the tone by demonizing Israel at every opportunity, comparing its actions to those of the Nazis and accusing the Jewish state of perpetrating a "new Holocaust."[113] On August 25, 2006, during a visit to China, he referred to Israel as being even worse than Hitler, proposing that its leaders "should be judged by an international tribunal." A month earlier on a tour of the Middle East, he continually compared Israeli "fascist aggression" in Lebanon to Hitler's murder of the Jews. Invariably, he stressed that behind the "Israeli terror" stood the "hawkish brains of the Pentagon" and the evil American empire.[114] In an interview with Al-

Jazeera, first aired on August 4, 2006, Chávez was especially strident in evoking "the satanic imperialistic face of the U.S." and comparing America to "Count Dracula—always in search of petrol and blood." Lauding Jesus Christ as a socialist and identifying with the Christian promise of the kingdom of heaven, the Venezuelan leader branded the U.S. empire as "the number one enemy in the way of peace and justice." Speaking as a believing Catholic, Chávez prophesied that either the American fascist elite would be destroyed or the world itself would be annihilated. The Arab peoples were essential allies in the effort to forge a multipolar world that could bring down the dangerous beast called American imperialism. In that context, the Venezuelan president proudly termed himself "a Nasserist, ever since I was a young soldier."[115] His ties with the Arab world have been an essential part of Chávez's effort to become a global player as well as a regional leader.

On his visit to Damascus in the summer of 2006, Chávez again spoke of the need to "build a new world" in the twenty-first century that would "dig the grave of North American imperialism." His virulently anti-Israel and anti-American statements, and loudly proclaimed solidarity with Syria, were naturally hailed with enthusiasm by its state-controlled media. At the press conference with President Bashar al-Assad, Chávez stated: "What is Israel? We all know how Israel was born. It is an annex of the North American empire in the Middle East. Israel is the cause of conflict in the region. This [territory] 6,000 years ago was [inhabited by] the Canaanites and the Philistines, these lands belong to the Palestinians."

This was poor history and even weaker logic. But it served the Commandante's purpose of stigmatizing Israel's control of the Golan Heights as a "theft perpetrated against the entire world" and of ranting once more against Israel's "Nazi crimes" in Lebanon and Palestine.[116] Similarly, at a joint press conference with President Ahmadinejad in Tehran, first aired on July 30, 2006, compulsive Israel-bashing and the need to end "the rule of [American] hegemony" were once again central: "My brother Ahmadinejad informed me about the horrors of Israeli bombs against shelters where women and children are hiding. This is a cowardly attitude. . . . They want war because they have the devil inside them. . . . A force will emerge from the brave people that will put an end to the empire and to its people."[117]

Chávez's anti-Americanism and hostility toward Israel assured him iconic status among the Hezbollah fighters and their followers in Lebanon.

They were naturally enthused by his denunciation of Israeli actions against Lebanon, and fired up by his claims of a "new Holocaust" and his public support for Iran's nuclear program. At the Nonaligned Movement summit held in Cuba (before Ahmadinejad's visit to Caracas), Iran and Venezuela worked to direct the wave of anti-American feeling into support for Iran's right to nuclear power. Not surprisingly, since September 2006 fears of physical attacks have grown among Venezuelan Jews, especially as the government neither acted against the proliferating anti-Semitic graffiti nor rebuked the media when it defamed Israel or Jewry. The Jewish community has also been concerned about the inroads of Islamism into Venezuela, and the strong sympathy local Hezbollah groups express for Chávez's Bolivarian revolution and the anticapitalist populism they both share. This link and affinity are likely to nourish further anti-Semitism and local recruitment to terrorist activities financed from the Middle East.

Chávez had been introduced to the Muslim world by one of his most important mentors, the Argentinean social scientist, anti-Semite, and Holocaust denier Norberto Rafael Ceresole. By the mid-1990s Ceresole had gravitated from the Left toward an idiosyncratic ideological synthesis of communism, fascism, and radical Islam. Arriving in Venezuela in 1994, he became a close political adviser of Chávez, who had just been pardoned by the president for his failed coup attempt two years earlier. A year later Ceresole was exiled from Venezuela for his links with Islamic terrorists. But he returned in 1998, writing an enthusiastic and revealing book about the Chávez revolution called *Caudillo, Ejercito, Pueblo: la Venezuela del Comandante Chávez* (*Leader, Army, People: The Venezuela of Commandante Chávez*). Nazi and Communist symbols are mixed together in Ceresole's work. The first chapter, "The Jewish Question and the State of Israel," blames Zionism and world Jewry for the author's earlier exile. Ceresole insisted that he was no anti-Semite but nonetheless declared himself an admirer of known Holocaust deniers Robert Faurisson and Roger Garaudy. Indeed, in his book on the Chávez revolution, Ceresole proudly defined himself as part of the "new revisionism" that unmasks the "myth" of the Holocaust as a propaganda tool used by Israel and the Jews to financially blackmail Germany, Europe, and America. This myth had been cynically exploited to justify the dispossession of "Arab Palestine" and to promote a messianic-monotheistic creed of American-Zionist global domination. Significantly, Ceresole became a strong advocate of a Latin American alliance with Iran and Arab nationalism against the United States and the "Jewish financial mafia"—a strategy that Chávez appears to have embraced.

Ceresole evidently helped to shape Chávez's turn toward radical Islam, Iran, and Hezbollah as political allies in the war to overthrow U.S. imperialism. The anti-Semitic component in Chávez's messianic socialism has strengthened his embrace of a Third World nationalism adapted to the Latin American *caudillo* tradition. Fragments of radical populism, nationalism, Marxist economics, anti-Americanism, anti-globalism, political Islam, and Christian liberation theology are all part of the eclectic mishmash that forms Chávez's ideology. The "Christ killers" blend with the image of rapacious capitalists who have taken possession of the world's riches—its gold, silver, minerals, oil, and productive lands—a vocabulary much favored by Chávez. Old and new stereotypes come together with malignant conspiracy theories and anti-American politics to remold a Latin version of National Socialism to fit the twenty-first century. Scapegoating Israel has enabled Venezuela's leader to cement his strategic axis with Iran and a number of Arab states, while bolstering his aspiration to be the chief opponent of the United States in the Western Hemisphere.

Since early 2009 the result of this policy has been highly damaging to Venezuela's Jewish community. On January 31, 2009, intruders broke into the Tiferet Israel Sephardic synagogue in Caracas. They desecrated the Torah scrolls, damaged the building, and left graffiti calling on the Jews to get out of Venezuela.[118] A systematic media campaign against Israel as a racist "genocidal" state and against the "Jewish-Zionist bourgeoisie" in Venezuela undoubtedly contributed to the atmosphere of intimidation and fear that produced such violence.[119] It was greatly reinforced by the willingness of prominent parliamentarians and even government ministers to join in hysterical and frenzied accusations against the State of Israel. Already on January 6, 2009, Chávez himself publicly charged Israel with inflicting a "holocaust" against the Palestinians in Gaza. This was followed shortly afterward by the expulsion of the Israeli ambassador from Caracas, plunging relations to a new nadir and casting a dark shadow over the future of Venezuela's Jewish community.[120]

NINETEEN

Lying About the Holocaust

I n 1971 the French philosopher Vladimir Jankélévitch foresaw the emergence of an increasingly ominous connection between Israel, anti-Semitism, and Holocaust denial. He remarked on the extraordinary shadow the mass murder of European Jewry had cast over the events of World War II and modernity as a whole—a kind of invisible cloud of remorse. This was the "shameful secret" behind the European "good conscience"—the hidden anxiety of so many Europeans at their belated realization of the enormity of the crime in which they were so deeply implicated. How, then, could one be freed from such a terrible incubus? Jankélévitch suggested that anti-Zionism was likely to provide the providential and unexpected opportunity for much-needed relief, for it offered the freedom, the right, and perhaps even the duty to be anti-Semitic in the name of democracy. Anti-Zionism would become the new justifiable and democratized anti-Semitism of the future, finally placed within the reach of Mr. and Mrs. Everyman.[1] And what if the Jews themselves became Nazis? Why, that would be just perfect. One would no longer have to feel sorry for them—after all, they would have deserved their fate. What better alibi could there be for forgetting the unspeakable crime or diluting European responsibilities and thinking about happier things?

Such observations come more naturally nearly forty years later and may even seem self-evident. Some of the "new" Judeophobia in Europe and the West might be seen psychologically as a kind of overcompensation or rechanneling of latent and often unavowed guilty feelings about the Jews. In fact, by branding Israel as a Nazi state, two birds can be killed with one stone. One may point the finger at erstwhile victims who are no better than we, Europeans (in fact, they are worse, since they did not learn from their history); and one is finally free to express in politically correct anti-Zionist language those sentiments that have not been entirely respectable among educated people since 1945—namely dislike of Jews. The Star of David is thereby amalgamated into the swastika, victims mutate into perpetrators, and Jews or others who defend the "Nazi" State of Israel can expect to be vilified as racists, fascists, and ethnic cleansers. Palestine becomes the new measuring rod in discussing the Shoah, which is linked in a highly tendentious manner with the Palestinian *naqba* (catastrophe) of 1948.[2]

For several decades now, the Shoah has ceased to be a taboo topic. On the contrary, it is at the heart of contemporary Western consciousness—a subject of constant interdisciplinary research and media interest—integral to the culture, pedagogy, and politics of Europe at the dawn of the twenty-first century.[3] Yet this preoccupation has some perverse side effects. The most obvious is straightforward Holocaust denial—the surrealist claim that there was no extermination of the Jews, that there were no gas chambers, that the Jews and/or Zionists (with some help from the Western Allies or the Communists) simply invented the hoax of the century. If the classical anti-Semites traditionally screamed "Death to the Jews," the Holocaust deniers added something new: "the Jews did not die."[4] They have thereby committed a *double* assassination. To quote Swedish journalist Per Ahlmark: "First the antisemites take Jewish lives; a few decades later they take their deaths from them too."[5]

Holocaust denial in its most visceral sense is precisely this sickening effort of contemporary Jew haters to destroy memory. Beyond that, by accusing Jews and/or Zionists of inventing the Shoah to extract billions of dollars and blackmail Germany or the West, the deniers add a peculiarly vile conspiracy theory to the arsenal of millennial anti-Semitism and transform the victims into superlatively cunning, fraudulent, and despicable perpetrators. One of the main purposes of this perversion has been "to clear Nazism from its criminal stigma and rehabilitate anti-Semitism."[6] Hence this type of denial is frequently an expression of neo-Nazi, Far Right, and so-called revisionist politics in Europe, North America, and other parts of the world. Canadian jurist and professor Irwin Cotler summed up the anti-Semitic nature of their agenda: "The Holocaust denial movement whitewashes the crimes of the Nazis, as it excoriates the crimes of the Jews. It not only holds that the Holocaust was a hoax, but maligns the Jew for fabricating the hoax."[7]

Since 1945, France has been the main intellectual laboratory for Holocaust denial, sometimes termed "negationism" or, to sound more respectable, "revisionism." The first active "revisionist" in France was the literary critic Maurice Bardèche, an expert on Honoré de Balzac and Stendhal who had taught French literature at the Sorbonne. After 1942 he continued to teach at the University of Lille and wrote for the intensely anti-Semitic weekly *Je suis partout* (I Am Everywhere) during the Nazi occupation of France.[8] Its fascist editor, the youthful Robert Brasillach (Bardèche's brother-in-law), was executed by De Gaulle in 1945 for collaboration with the enemy. Bardèche, however, blamed "the Jews [who] . . . demanded the execution of this righteous man." They were, he said, falsifiers of history, manipulators, and criminal perpetrators. Three years later, in 1948, Bardèche's first book, *Nuremberg ou la terre promise* (Nuremberg or the Promised Land), presented the Holocaust as a Jewish propaganda ploy and blamed the Jews for World War II: "They were the ones who caused the world conflict and therefore bear responsibility for millions of dead."[9] According to Bardèche the main causes of death in the camps were typhus and "improper sanitary conditions"—a mantra repeated ever since by Holocaust deniers around the world. The Jews, he suggested in 1948, had invented the myth of the gas chambers to reinforce their drive to global domination by using moral blackmail. They were helped by the Western Allies who needed to justify their bombing of German cities and their own crimes against the German people (the real victims of the war)! The Soviet Union, too, had wished to distract world attention away from the massive crimes committed by Stalin and his henchmen.

In the mid-1950s Bardèche began to turn the anti-Zionist struggle into a cornerstone of his "revisionist" crusades in *Défense de l'Occident* (Defense of the West). In this monthly he founded in 1952, Israel appeared as the *illegitimate* daughter of America, the *cancer* in the heart of Islam, and a "foreign body" endangering the stability of the entire world. Even before the Six-Day War of 1967, Bardèche and collaborators, including the former SS Pierre Hofstetter, had fused Holocaust denial with the rejection of Israel's legitimacy. They termed Israel a "ghost state" built on stolen Arab territories and consolidated through billions of marks extorted from the Germans under the false pretext of "Nazi war crimes."[10] The French neofascists, like anti-Semites everywhere, regarded power-hungry Jews as masters of the press and the banks. This absolutely central stereotype was the motor of Bardèche's Holocaust denial,[11] as well as that of his younger heir, the violently anti-Zionist François Duprat, an ex-Trotskyist who introduced

Anglo-Saxon Holocaust denial literature into France and became one of the founders of the National Front (FN). The liberation of Palestine and the struggle against the Zionist lobby in France became a crucial theme for Duprat. In the 1960s and 1970s in *Défense de l'Occident*, Duprat and other French Holocaust deniers began to project the Final Solution of the "*Palestinian question*" against the Jews.[12] Israel was not only perceived as a racist state seeking to liquidate the Palestinian Arabs but also as the nucleus of a broad conspiracy to consolidate global Jewish power. Thus anti-Zionism, anti-Semitism, and Holocaust denial were inextricably intertwined. France itself was depicted as being under Jewish occupation since 1945—based on a regime of lies, impostures, and a fake liberation.[13]

Even more influential than Bardèche for the future of Holocaust denial was the left-wing socialist Paul Rassinier, a member of the French resistance who in the early 1950s convinced himself that Zionists had invented the genocide myth to swindle and extort massive sums in reparations from the Germans. A former Communist who had been imprisoned in Buchenwald concentration camp, Rassinier began his "revisionist" path by maintaining that there had never been any Nazi policy of extermination against Jews; subsequently he also rejected the gas chambers as a myth. In his later writings, Rassinier repeatedly emphasized that Jews had perpetrated the "Holocaust hoax" out of purely material motives with the aim of turning Germany "into an everlasting milk cow for Israel."[14] Leading Holocaust historians such as Raul Hilberg were denigrated with special vehemence— their Jewish origins automatically rendering their findings suspect or unacceptable.[15] They were dismissed as mere lackeys of the Zionist establishment, whose control of the international media explained the stunning propagation of the Holocaust lie: "The Jews have been able to dupe the world by relying on their mythic powers and conspiratorial abilities. As they have so often done in the past, world Jewry has once again employed its inordinate powers to harness the world's financial resources, media and political interests for their own resources."[16]

Rassinier's anti-Semitic imagery came to a climax when speaking of the Zionist plan for world domination.

If the plan should succeed—and all that is needed is for the American branch of international Zionism to get its hand on Wall Street—the Israeli home-port of the Diaspora would become . . . the command post of all the world's industry. . . . Thus at the very least, it could be said that the designation "Chosen People," which the Jews claim for themselves, would assume full significance.[17]

In the opinion of Rassinier's left-wing disciples, Jews, the Holocaust, and the State of Israel were all links in a larger chain of enslavement of the world proletariat. Like Rassinier, the ultraleftists accused the Jews of forging history. At the same time they also damned the Soviet Communists for having betrayed Marx's revolutionary utopia. In the 1960s, they argued that Jews were physically eliminated once they were considered superfluous in the capitalist process of production. For the ultraleft there was ultimately no distinction among capitalism, liberal democracy, and Nazism.[18] The victorious Allies and the free democracies in the postwar era had in their eyes been guilty of genocides and colonial wars of extermination in the Third World that were as atrocious as anything perpetrated by the Nazis. Israel, as the persecutor of the martyred Palestinians, was an exemplar of this moral hypocrisy that was so typical of Western colonialism. Auschwitz had become the great alibi and mystification, enabling the West and the Jews to draw a veil of silence over these colonial crimes.[19]

In Third Worldist discourse, the Holocaust and Jewish pain were pejoratively transformed into a way of obscuring and obstructing proper recognition of the great colonial slaughters. Thus Jacques Vergès, the virulently anti-Zionist defense lawyer at the Klaus Barbie trial in France, contended that the Holocaust "offended only the consciousness of white people." It was but a passing moment in comparison with the terrible history of Third World oppression. In defending the German Nazi torturer Barbie, Vergès could see "no reason for humanity (and those in charge of its progress) to mourn its [the Holocaust] victims. And since the Third World is the herald of progress, those perceived as its enemies are the logical successors of Nazism: the Americans in Vietnam, the French in Algeria, the Israelis in the West Bank."[20]

Jews who referred to the uniqueness of the Holocaust were de facto accomplices of Third World oppression, including that of the Palestinians. They and their antifascist allies were guilty of a scandalous mystification in the eyes of Vergès and prominent intellectuals Tzvetan Todorov and Alain Brossat.[21] It was suggested that Jewish suffering was being abused to claim unjustified power and privilege. Brossat even branded Zionism as "totalitarian" and irremediably tainted by its origins in Auschwitz and its crimes against the indigenous inhabitants of Palestine. The Zionists had built a state for a social group, the Jews, who were not even a legitimate people, except in "the exterminatory perspective of the Nazis"; indeed, they had racialized their state in both theory and practice.[22] The Diaspora Jewish communities also stood accused of the egoistic, self-interested manipulation of Holocaust memory and memorialization.[23] The Left originated these charges, but the Far Right also made them against Israel, Jewry, and liberal democracy in general. On both extremes and in the mainstream, the "instrumentalized" Holocaust had become a weapon with which to strike at Jewish specificity and singularity.[24]

The hardcore Holocaust deniers who consistently mock the Nazi genocide as a myth, a fable, or a hoax are still most prevalent on the Far Right.[25] They insist that there was no extermination of European Jews and no plan to kill them at all. They take such Nazi euphemisms as "cleansing," "special treatment," and "resettlement" at face value, not as a necessary camouflage adopted by the German murderers to mask Hitler's true intentions and actions. All testimony by a Jew is assumed to be a lie or a fantasy; any document or testimony prior to 1945 is either mere rumor or a forgery. Any Nazi evidence after the war (in trials in the East and the West) is considered as having been obtained under torture or intimidation. Mass gassings are deemed materially and technically impossible.[26]

The propaganda techniques of the deniers invariably rely on a number of standard methods. They relentlessly focus on discrepancies in the testimonies of witnesses, contradictions in documents, and disagreements among scholars in order to undermine the credibility of the Holocaust story.[27] They endlessly repeat that no explicit order from Hitler to mass murder the Jews has ever been found; that Reinhard Heydrich's Wannsee Conference of January 1942 on the Final Solution did not refer to gassings in the present or future; that Allied aerial reconnaissance of Auschwitz did not indicate gas chambers or crematoria with constantly burning chimneys. They especially like to juggle with figures, reducing the number of Jewish deaths to around three hundred thousand—usually blamed on deprivation and disease.[28] The deniers explain away the large number of crematoria in the death camps as a means of dealing rapidly with victims of typhoid and other epidemics toward the end of the war. They claim that most photographs of the Holocaust showing the liberation of survivors are nothing but fakes or have been presented in a distorted way in order to exaggerate German crimes. All these arguments can be found in *The Six Million Swindle: Blackmailing the German People for Hard Marks with Fabricated Corpses* (1973) by Austin J. App, a former professor of English at La Salle College in Philadelphia. App was a central figure in American Holocaust denial—a writer whose anti-Semitism left nothing to the imagination. He consistently blamed Communists, Israel, and world Jewry for having invented the myth of the gas chambers to divert attention from their own crimes.

For decades Holocaust deniers have focused special attention on the gas chambers as the "legend" that they believe can be most readily disproved by scientific or technical arguments. The French "revisionist" Robert Faurisson, extrapolating from American gas chamber executions of single prisoners and from evidence about the commercial use of Zyklon B, repeatedly claimed that mass gassings were technically impossible in Auschwitz. His assertions were subsequently tested and supposedly vindicated by Fred Leuchter, an unlicensed American engineer living in Boston who specialized in installing apparatus for gas executions. Financed by the Holocaust "revisionists," Leuchter visited Auschwitz, Birkenau, and Majdanek to gather forensic samples from buildings associated with the mass murders of Jews. After chemical analysis of these samples he published a report in 1989 concluding that there had never been any homicidal gassings at any of the death camps! Leuchter's spurious claims were demolished by a non-Jewish French pharmacologist, Jean-Claude Pressac, in his 1989 book, *Auschwitz: Technique and Operation of the Gas Chambers*. In subsequent articles and books, he accused Leuchter of a lamentable lack of professionalism, deliberate disinformation, gross errors of measurement, fake reasoning, and false interpretations. *The Leuchter Report* belonged, he concluded, "in the cesspool of pretentious human folly."[29]

Leuchter's pseudoscientific charlatanry nonetheless took on a life of its own in "revisionist" circles. His evidence was used, for example, at the 1988 trial in Toronto of the German-Canadian neo-Nazi and Holocaust denier Ernst Zündel (deported back to Germany in 2003), prosecuted for knowingly promoting hatred and causing injury to the public interest.[30] Leuchter's incompetence and lack of expertise became increasingly manifest during the Zündel trials. Zündel, for his part, did not disguise his own devotion to Hitler, his allegiance to the Nazis, or his boundless hatred for the international Zionists.

As a direct result of the Zündel trial, the well-known British historian David Irving was converted to fully fledged Holocaust denial.[31] In his 1977 bestselling book *Hitler's War,* Irving had concocted the bizarre theory that the Holocaust was carried out behind the führer's back. Contrary to all the evidence, he asserted that Hitler tried to help the Jews. For years, Irving cynically equated the actions of Allied leaders and Hitler, damning Winston Churchill with special vehemence as a reckless and dangerous war criminal. By 1989, Irving had become a convinced crusader for Holocaust denial, constantly protesting that Israel had swindled West Germany out of ninety billion Deutschmarks for mythical crimes in the nonexistent gas chambers of Auschwitz. Fined in Germany for such statements, he urged his judges to "fight a battle for the German people and put an end to the blood lie of the Holocaust which has been told against this country for fifty years."[32]

Starting in the late 1980s, Irving rapidly became the most prominent of the Holocaust deniers in the democratic world, constantly interviewed by the Western press. He was criticized but nonetheless taken seriously as a historian by many respectable German and British members of the guild. Yet his latent anti-Semitism had been manifest since at least the early 1980s, if not much earlier. In a book about the 1956 Hungarian uprising, he had chosen to tendentiously interpret it as a revolt against the "Jewish domination" of Hungary rather than against Soviet rule.[33] Depicting Churchill's refusal to compromise with Hitler, Irving alleged that he was paid and influenced by the Jews.[34] In a speech at Dresden's Palace of Culture in February 1990, his pro-German and anti-Semitic inversion of the Holocaust was particularly blatant: "The Holocaust suffered by the Germans in Dresden was real. The one against the Jews in the gas chambers of Auschwitz is complete fiction."[35]

Irving had, by this time, become a cult figure among German neo-Nazis. His gross provocations not surprisingly culminated in conviction by a Munich court in May 1992 for "slander concomitant with the disparagement of the memory of deceased persons." Through the 1990s this conviction led to successive restrictions and prohibitions on Irving's entry into Austria, Italy, and South Africa; to his deportation from Canada; and to rejected visa applications to Australia. This would not have happened without the determination of Jewish communities to stop Irving, despite the predominant view in the Western media that his right to free speech should be preserved.

In the spring of 2000 Irving initiated a libel suit against Professor Deborah Lipstadt and Penguin Books for having labeled him "one of the most dangerous spokespersons for Holocaust denial." The trial judge, Justice Gray, observed in his verdict that it was "incontrovertible that Irving qualifies as a Holocaust denier." He had hugely underestimated the numbers of those who lost their lives in the death camps, gravely minimized their suffering, and impudently referred to an association of Holocaust survivors as "assholes"; he had joked publicly about more people dying in the back of Senator Edward Kennedy's crashed car at Chappaquiddick than in the gas chambers of Auschwitz. Judge Gray concluded that Irving was unequivocally anti-Semitic in his hostile, offensive, and derisory references to Jews: "Irving has made claims that the Jews deserve to be disliked; that they brought the Holocaust on themselves; that Jewish financiers are crooked; that Jews generate antisemitism by their greed and mendacity; that Jews are amongst the scum of humanity; that Jews scurry and hide furtively, unable to stand the light of day . . . and so on."[36]

Justice Gray also drew attention to Irving's repeated insistence that there had been no mass murders, and to his arrogant dismissal of all Jewish eyewitness testimony. Irving had consistently characterized Jewish survivors as liars, psychiatric cases, and extortionists. He had told a Canadian audience in 1991 that Auschwitz was "baloney," nothing more than a "tourist attraction." The so-called gas chambers had been used for fumigating corpses, hair, and clothing infected with typhus lice. The drawing plans for the Auschwitz gas chambers by Nazi architects were nothing but forgeries.

Five years later, Irving (who had been forced into bankruptcy by the trial costs) found himself imprisoned for three years by an Austrian court for denying the Holocaust. While much of the British media criticized the verdict in the name of free speech (there is no law in England against the denial of Nazi crimes), the Austrian public prosecutor bluntly described Irving as a "falsifier of history," pointedly distinguishing between free opinion and defamation. Irving's groveling retractions and hypocritical expressions of regret could not convince the Austrian judge and jury that he had abandoned his twisted beliefs.[37]

• • •

The origins of Holocaust denial in the United States go back to the works of the historian Harry Elmer Barnes, a passionate opponent of America's entry into World War I and of its involvement in the subsequent war against

Nazi Germany. By the mid-1960s Barnes was openly denying that Nazi Germany had committed mass murder. Barnes, who became increasingly paranoid in later years, encouraged a former Harvard student, David Hoggan, to go to a neo-Nazi publishing house with his 1961 book *Der erzwungene Krieg* (*The Forced War*). This was a revamped "revisionist" version of his dissertation about the origins of World War II, which had presented the British as warmongers, the Poles as provocateurs, and Hitler as an angel of peace! Hoggan's book was warmly received by the German radical Right. In a subsequent book, *The Myth of the Six Million* (1969), he attacked all the existing eyewitness testimony about the murder of European Jewry, while distorting, suppressing, and inventing sources in the classic "revisionist" manner.

Hoggan's book was published by Noontide Press, a subsidiary of the now-defunct Liberty Lobby headed by Willis Carto—at that time the best-organized and wealthiest anti-Semitic organization in the United States. Carto, an unabashed white supremacist, had for many years avidly promoted the idea that international Jewish bankers were at the heart of a conspiracy to destroy the white Western world and its racial heritage. Carto, like many Holocaust deniers, believed that the Western Allies had fought against the wrong enemy in World War II. They should have allied themselves with Hitler against Communism.[38] In 1966 Carto took control of *American Mercury*, an anti-Semitic monthly that almost immediately began to feature major articles on Holocaust denial. The theme was also given considerable prominence in the Liberty Lobby's newspaper, *The Spotlight*, which could claim a circulation of around three hundred thousand copies at its peak. Carto remained the éminence grise of Holocaust denial in the United States for the next thirty years. By creating the Institute of Historical Review (IHR) in 1979 and its "revisionist" *Journal of Historical Review* (published a year later in Torrance, California), he succeeded in giving the deniers a more solid base for their activity. *The Journal of Historical Review,* with its scholarly format, its learned footnotes, and its involvement in organizing "revisionist" international conventions, heralded the new drive in the 1980s toward seeking academic legitimacy. But beneath the semi-respectable façade lay an insidious mixture of conspiracy theory, anti-black racism, and revulsion against Jews that reflected Carto's own paranoid vision. For Carto, the Jews had always been public enemy number one of America and the West—a permanent force for promoting racial disintegration and Communism. Corporate Jewry controlled international finance and U.S. foreign policy, and actively encouraged the "grotesque" misdeeds of the "bastard" Israeli state.

Such bigoted rhetoric was, however, eschewed in the new-style "scientific" Holocaust denial found in *The Hoax of the Twentieth Century* (1975) by Arthur Butz, a professor of electrical engineering and computer science at Northwestern University in Illinois. Butz adopted a more reasonable tone than most of his predecessors, claiming that the so-called mythologists of extermination had either misinterpreted or deliberately distorted the evidence. He suggested that Auschwitz was above all a huge industrial plant and a highly productive work camp. The chemical Zyklon B was nothing but insecticide for disinfecting workers' clothing; the gas chambers were in fact baths, saunas, and mortuaries; the stench from the camp was due to hydrogenation and other chemical processes, not to the burning of dead bodies.[39] The *Jewish* role in this world conspiracy was central to Butz and other deniers because they believed the Holocaust had been invented to generate the popular sympathy necessary for creating the State of Israel. Like many "revisionists," Butz argued that the emotional grip of the Holocaust myth on the world was such that it had enabled Israel to financially blackmail a prostrate postwar Germany and extract enormous political dividends from a guilt-ridden America. Moreover, the Holocaust, by becoming a new "canon of faith in the Jewish Religion," had strengthened the inner bonds of the international Jewish community, making it more powerful than ever. Butz set out to debunk this pernicious myth and the "universe of lies" constructed by occult Zionist forces.

In Great Britain, a role analogous to that of Butz's work was played by a 1974 booklet entitled *Did Six Million Die? The Truth At Last* by Richard Harwood, who falsely claimed to be a student at the University of London. The real author was Richard Verrall, editor of the British National Front journal, *Spearhead*. Like his predecessors, Verrall dismissed Nazi anti-Semitism as nothing more than a normal and legitimate response to attacks by international Jewry. He insisted that Hitler wanted only to transfer the Jews to Madagascar and that Jewish population figures after the war proved their losses to have been minimal. Like other deniers, he called the Anne Frank diary a hoax.[40] In a transparent effort to decriminalize the Nazis, the author tried to totally discredit the Nuremberg Trials.

Did Six Million Die? also addressed race problems in Britain. The booklet maintained that Anglo-Saxons could not speak out openly about the necessity of racial self-preservation because the Holocaust lie had placed the subject beyond the pale. Britain and other European countries faced the gravest danger from the presence of alien races in their midst (blacks, Asians, Arabs, and Jews), which was leading to the destruction of their culture and their national heritage. According to Verrall, the Jews had supposedly poured millions into perversely encouraging race mixing. Their strategy was to secure global domination by weakening all other nationalist identities throughout the world. Unfortunately, self-defense against this peril had been seriously sapped by the Holocaust, which had given Nazism (and any form of racial consciousness) a bad name. The rehabilitation of the Far Right therefore depended on establishing the truth that the Jews had never been mass murdered.

Holocaust "revisionism," as we have seen, put down its firmest roots and attained a modest degree of respectability in France. In the 1950s neofascists such as Maurice Bardèche and pacifists such as Paul Rassinier laid the foundations for the myth that Jews had instigated the war, that the Nuremberg trials were a sham, and the Holocaust itself nothing but an Allied and Zionist fabrication.[41] By the early 1960s, the left-wing pacifist Rassinier had moved to the Far Right. After his death the baton passed to Robert Faurisson, an associate professor of literature at the University of Lyon.

In 1978, Faurisson published his first major article denying the existence of gas chambers. It was the same year that Louis Darquier de Pellepoix (former commissioner for Jewish questions under Vichy) had created a scandal in France with his notorious remark "Only lice were gassed in Auschwitz."[42] Two years later, on December 17, 1980, Faurisson unabashedly declared on French radio: "The claim of the existence of gas chambers and genocide of Jews by Hitler constitute one and the same historical lie, which opened the way to a gigantic political and financial fraud of which the principal beneficiaries are the State of Israel and International Zionism, and the principal victims the Germans and the entire Palestinian people."[43] A year later, Faurisson would publish his apologia entitled *Mémoire en defense contre ceux qui m'accusent de falsifier l'histoire: la question des chambers de gaz*, prefaced by the American Jewish academic and left-wing libertarian Noam Chomsky.[44] Faurisson's "revisionism" brought a series of lawsuits against him by the victims of Nazism, but it was not until the passage of the Gayssot Law, which, on July 13, 1990, criminalized Holocaust denial, that he suffered any major penalties.[45] A number of misguided libertarians defended him, and he even found some followers in French academia. One disciple, Henri Rocques, a retired engineer and a militant anti-Semite, presented his doctoral dissertation at the University of Nantes rejecting the eyewitness testimony of SS officer Kurt Gerstein concerning Belzec death camp. Rocques radically called into question the "myth of the magical gas chambers" as well as the number of Jewish victims. Four professors at Nantes approved the thesis—all of whom turned out to be either active in or sympathizers of the French extreme Right. Another stronghold of academic "revisionism" in France was the group around Professor Bernard Notin at the University of Lyon, who was linked to Le Pen's National Front.[46]

For the Far Right, Holocaust denial was a perfect cover to express its virulent anti-Zionism and anti-Semitism, including the defense of oppressed Palestinians—a cause that Jean-Marie Le Pen began to adopt more than twenty years ago. Prominent National Front figures such as Alain Renault, its secretary-general, warmly embraced the theory of the Holocaust "hoax" perpetrated by "hysterical Zionists"—presenting its "demythication" as a "revolutionary act." In September 1987 Le Pen himself dismissed the Holocaust as "a minute detail in the Second World War." He and his right-hand man, Bruno Gollnisch, have continued to pursue this policy for the past two decades. Accompanied by coded and sometimes explicit references to the Jewish lobby, the "Jewish-Marxist International," and the cosmopolitan, plutocratic media, their soft mode of negationism has become well entrenched among militants of the FN, in its publications and on its websites.

Negationism has also appealed to the extreme Left and was vigorously promoted by the publishing house La Vieille Taupe (The Old Mole) under the leadership of Pierre Guillaume, a maverick anarcho-Marxist. In the eyes of these ultraleftists, Nazism was no worse than conventional bourgeois exploitation. Western capitalism was as guilty as the Nazis of crimes against the working class. Guillaume and the sociologist Serge Thion, for example, firmly believe that if they could only expose Auschwitz as a myth, they would be advancing the proletarian cause.[47] If there were no gas chambers, then there was nothing special about Nazi treatment of the Jews, and the postwar "antifascist consensus" that had played into capitalist hands would wither away.

Another strategy adopted by the negationists (on both the left and right) was to refer to multiple "holocausts" (with a small "h") in history and to insist that Jews had no claim to a monopoly on suffering. At the Barbie trial,

Third Worldist left-wing lawyer Jacques Vergès compared French colonial oppression in Algeria to the Holocaust, hoping to relativize it out of existence and completely neutralize its specificity.[48] Vergès stopped short, however, of denying that the Holocaust actually happened. As for Pierre Guillaume and his leftist followers, they deliberately trivialized the Holocaust by comparing it with American internment of Japanese-born U.S. citizens during World War II, French official harassment of Spanish Republicans and anti-Nazis before 1939, and the abuse of prisoners of war in German concentration camps.

In West Germany, as in France, the first efforts to repudiate the Holocaust had begun in the early 1950s and rapidly became a staple theme of the neo-Nazis and the German nationalist Far Right. German-published books that openly denied the Holocaust first began to attract some serious attention in the 1970s. In 1973 a former SS officer and neo-Nazi, Thies Christophersen (who had worked on the periphery of Auschwitz in 1944), published his scurrilous *Die Auschwitz-Lüge* (The Auschwitz Lie). He was followed in 1979 by the jurist Wilhelm Stäglich whose book *Der Auschwitz-Mythos* (*The Auschwitz Myth*) led Göttingen University to deprive him of his doctor's title. Both authors repeatedly stated that the Holocaust was a "propaganda hoax" designed to stigmatize and shame the Germans into an unjustified sense of guilt.[49] Their aim was to sanitize German history by presenting a more favorable picture of Hitler and National Socialism, above all by denying the existence of gas chambers.

By the 1980s, the emphasis in Holocaust denial had moved, however, to scientific and technical arguments. The deniers insistently sought to prove the impossibility of mass murder in any of the death camps. Hence the extraordinary attention given to the capacity of the crematoria, the time needed to burn a body, and the properties of Zyklon B poison gas. In 1992 Germar Rudolf, a qualified chemist then employed at the prestigious Max Planck Institute for Solid State Research, wrote a work called *Expert Report on the Formation and Provability of Cyanide Compounds in the "Gas Chambers" of Auschwitz*. His chemical analyses had been commissioned by one of Germany's best-known Nazis, Otto Ernst Remer. A former major-general in the Wehrmacht, Remer had suppressed the July plot of the German resistance against Hitler in 1944. In 1992 Remer stood trial for denying the genocide of the Jews and the Rudolf report (rejected by the court) was part of his defense. In a letter accompanying the report, Remer wrote that in an age of religious freedom, "all of us must oppose the 'holocaust religion' which the courts have forced upon us."

By contrast, in the former USSR, under Communist rule, there was no official or popular denial that Nazi mass murders had taken place on Soviet soil. But the authorities made great efforts to conceal the fact that Jews were murdered only because they were Jews. The victims were always presented as Russians, Ukrainians, Belarusians, or members of different European nationalities who had suffered under German fascism.[50] Hence there was no specific monument to the Jewish victims of the Babi Yar massacre on the outskirts of Kiev in September 1941 or at any other major Holocaust sites. Worse was to come in the mid-1970s when a group of anti-Zionist publicists, sponsored by the Soviet government, began to propagate the shameless slander that Zionist leaders had actively collaborated with the Nazis in the murder of their own people. This was part of an intensive anti-Semitic campaign by the USSR and the Communist bloc to present Zionists as dangerous fascists who manipulated the Holocaust for cynical ends to cover up their own crimes.[51] Such accusations were also propagated in Czechoslovakia and other Eastern European countries under Communist rule. They would later assume epidemic proportions in the Arab world, which enthusiastically embraced this Soviet propaganda.

In postwar Poland (as in Hungary), the number of individuals or groups actually denying the Holocaust has been relatively small, though the camp of those relativizing or distorting the Jewish catastrophe remains significantly larger.[52] The presence of so many death camps on Polish soil and Polish *martyrdom* during the war greatly restricted the credibility of would-be negationists. For most Poles, the problem was one of "competitive martyrdom" and their long-standing reluctance to admit that Jews had suffered even more than their own nation. Moreover, many Poles vehemently rejected the dominant Jewish perception of Polish anti-Semitism as being extremely pervasive during the war years, and accusations of unwillingness to help Jews threatened with extermination. Most Poles continued to believe that they had provided only heroic and selfless assistance to Jews.[53]

Since the revolutions of 1989 that restored freedom of speech, the trend toward Holocaust denial has significantly grown in Russia and eastern Europe. There has been a renewed receptivity to prewar conspiracy theories like the *Protocols of the Elders of Zion*. In the newly liberated countries of Croatia and Slovakia, renewed aspirations to state sovereignty could draw inspiration from ultranationalist wartime leaders who had been allies of Nazi Germany, and on their own initiative had killed or deported most of their Jewish population. The unrelenting efforts after 1990 at rehabilitating such clerico-fascist leaders as Josef Tiso in Slovakia and a mass murderer like Ante Pavelić in Croatia usually involved excusing, denying, or at times justifying their genocidal actions.[54]

In Romania the drive to glorify the memory of the wartime dictator and ally of Hitler, Marshal Antonescu, has led to equally grave distortions of Holocaust history. Under Nicolae Ceausescu, the official national-Communist line was to pretend that the *Romanian* Holocaust did not happen. (The deportation of Jews to Auschwitz from Hungarian-controlled northern Transylvania was, on the other hand, deliberately highlighted.) In the 1990s, right-wing politicians and media mercilessly attacked President Iliescu for daring to criticize the Antonescu regime or showing any sympathy for Jewish efforts to have the Romanian chapter in the Holocaust properly recognized. Iliescu's attendance at the opening of the Holocaust Museum in Washington, D.C., aroused the fury of Romanian nationalists who accused him of a "pitiable lack of dignity in front of the global Zionist trend of stigmatizing peoples and nations in order to control humankind unchallenged."[55] Today, there are fully fledged "literary" deniers in Romania, such as Radu Theodoru (a former deputy of the Greater Romania Party), who cede nothing to Western negationists in the radicalism of their Holocaust denial. What is remarkable in the Romanian case is the high number of intellectuals and writers who have defended the dissemination of such twisted conceptions. It is, of course, true that apologies have been forthcoming from the leaders of Romania, Hungary, Poland, Ukraine, and the Baltic states regarding the actions of their countries toward Jews during the Holocaust. Nevertheless, the attempts to minimize the role of Nazi collaborators and to whitewash the national past (including the record of native war criminals living in the Baltic states and eastern Europe) continue to be widespread. Moreover, the insistent postcommunist comparison of the Soviet Gulag with the Nazi Holocaust has been a consistent and troubling feature of many of these eastern European responses.[56]

· · ·

The most potent form of Holocaust denial today is unquestionably found in the Arab and Muslim world. Its growing centrality was apparent eight years ago during the Arab forum on historical "revisionism" that took place in Amman on May 13, 2001—replacing the aborted conference cosponsored by the IHR scheduled for Beirut two months earlier. The driving force of that aborted conference had been the Tehran-based Swiss Holocaust denier Jürgen Graf. At the Amman gathering, Arab journalists and members of professional associations opposed to normalization with Israel enthusiastically praised the French "revisionists" Roger Garaudy and Robert Faurisson.[57] They insisted that Zionism was much worse than Nazism, condemned the handful of Arab intellectuals who were openly critical of Holocaust denial, and maintained that "revisionism" was not a reactionary ideology but a well-documented research project.[58]

The homage paid to the French intellectual Roger Garaudy by the Arab participants in Amman was especially significant. As a prominent French Marxist philosopher (originally Catholic, then Stalinist) who had converted to Islam in 1982, Garaudy became a hero in the Arab world after his trial and conviction in a Paris court in 1998 for anti-Semitic incitement and *négationisme*. Garaudy's theses denying the existence of Nazi extermination policy and of gas chambers, and his charge that Israel fabricated the Holocaust to justify its occupation of Arab lands, were hardly original. But coming from a prominent French thinker, such accusations proved to be a source of deep satisfaction for many Arabs and Iranians. By the 1990s, Garaudy had replaced Rassinier and Faurisson as the leading French negationist. A militant in the French Communist Party since 1933, he had once been considered philo-Semitic and a strong *opponent* of anti-Zionist anti-Semitism in the Soviet bloc.[59] Evidently his conversion to Islam, his marriage to a Palestinian woman, and Israel's siege of Beirut in the summer of 1982 triggered Garaudy's transformation into a virulent anti-Zionist denouncing Israel's racism, historical falsifications, and promotion of biblical myths.[60] The First Persian Gulf War radicalized Garaudy still further in the direction of the anti-Semitic New Right in France.[61] But only in 1995, with his book on the "founding myths" of Israeli politics (published by La Vieille Taupe) did Garaudy fully embrace Holocaust denial as a creed.[62]

Garaudy now bluntly accused the Zionists of having been partners with the Nazis in exterminating European Jewry—a classic Soviet and Trotskyist libel. At the same time, Garaudy, shamelessly plagiarizing Faurisson, repeated all the standard clichés of negationist literature, including the claim that the Nuremberg trials represented "victor's justice," and that Nazi policy toward Jews was one of forced labor and expulsion, not extermination. Like other deniers, he dismissed all survivor testimony as worthless and ignored the meticulous findings of serious historical research. Garaudy waxed indignant over alleged Jewish attempts to "privilege" their suffering, which had never constituted a real genocide. This term he reserved for what had been done *by the Jews* to the ancient Canaanites or contemporary Palestinians, and he also applied it to the colonialist crimes committed by the West in the Third World. Garaudy's unrestrained attacks on the world Zionist lobby, American Jews, and Israelis and French Zionists in the last part of his book illustrate the enduring power of conspiracy theory.[63] Not surprisingly, Le Pen's National Front was only too happy to support Garaudy in the name of free speech; he also enjoyed strong backing from Abbé Pierre, well-known "friend of the poor" and France's most popular Catholic priest by far at the time.

In January 1998, Garaudy appeared in a Paris court (defended by the ubiquitous Jacques Vergès), charged with "complicity in contesting crimes against humanity" and "incitement to racial discrimination, hatred and violence." On February 27, 1998, he was fined 80,000 francs (about $13,000) and another 40,000 francs for having wrongfully accused the Jewish lobby of controlling the Western media.

In the Arab world, the eighty-five-year-old French Communist turned Muslim swiftly obtained star status. Seventy Palestinian professors, religious leaders, and journalists publicly protested against his trial outside the French Cultural Center in Gaza, with banners proclaiming "Garaudy, all of Palestine is with you." The Palestinian Writers Association hailed his "fight for creative freedom," and the head of the Palestinian Journalists' syndicate railed against French legislation that "criminalizes all those who doubt the Zionist tale of the victims of the Holocaust."[64] Lebanon's Arab Journalists Union called on fellow Arab intellectuals to rally to the man "who had the courage to divulge Zionist lies." All of Jordan's political parties issued a statement claiming that "Zionists have fabricated the falsehoods about the extermination of the Jews in Germany to mislead the world and blackmail Western governments."[65] Garaudy even received a $50,000 cash gift from the wife of the United Arab Emirates ruler to cover his legal expenses. There were other donations from the Gulf states. In Syria, the grand mufti declared "total support" for "a freethinker who does not compromise his principles." In Egypt the enthusiasm was even greater. Garaudy was an honored participant at the Cairo Book Fair in 1998, a guest of the Egyptian Ministry of Culture, and lauded to the skies by Egypt's highest religious authority. He did not disappoint his hosts, telling them that Israel enjoyed immunity from criticism "because media in the West is 95 percent controlled by the Zionists."[66]

Garaudy's enormous popularity in Arab countries and the mobilization in his favor of such well-known politicians as former Lebanese premier Rafiq Hariri, the famous Egyptian journalist Muhammad Hassanin Haikal, and the preeminent religious authority Sheikh Muhammad Sayyid-Tantawi of Al-Azhar University, was certainly significant. None of his admirers questioned Garaudy's "revisionist" view of Nazism or his assertion that the Holocaust was a Zionist invention.[67] Major Arab newspapers including *Al-Ahram* and *Al-Akhbar* indulged themselves in rank Holocaust denial, quoting not only Garaudy but other French and German "revisionists" such as Wilhelm Stäglich, Henri Rocques, and Robert Faurisson, as if these charlatans were respectable historians.

Holocaust negationism unmistakably appeals to the Arab world, not least because it fits the prevalent negative stereotypes of Jews as treacherous, cunning, and devious plotters conspiring to take over the entire world. Many Arabs already under the influence of the *Protocols* have readily swallowed the idea that Jews were sufficiently powerful and evil to be able to blackmail the world into believing the Holocaust lie. Ibrahim Nafi', the editor of the popular government-sponsored *Al-Ahram* daily in Egypt, wrote openly against the "false accusation of the Nazi annihilation," calling it one of "the greatest lies in the international arena," and insisting on the many similarities between Sharon's policies, Zionist ideology, and Nazism.[68]

No less striking has been the enthusiasm and fervor that Garaudy's ideas aroused in Iran. Among his most fervent disciples has been the present supreme guide of Iran, Ayatollah Ali Khamenei, who periodically denounces the "exaggerated statistics on Jewish killings" and has emphasized "the close relations between the Zionists and the German Nazis."[69] The president of Iran, Mahmoud Ahmadinejad, went much further in publicly promoting Holocaust denial. In 2006, the Iranian regime (under presidential patronage) sponsored a Holocaust denial conference in Tehran that included more than sixty participants from thirty different countries. Attendees included American white supremacist David Duke, the German-Australian denier Frederick Töben, Robert Faurisson, top officials of the

German neo-Nazi NPD, and ultra-Orthodox anti-Zionist Jews from *Neturei Karta*. For the first time in history the top leadership of a large and powerful state had made Holocaust denial a part of its foreign policy strategy.[70]

This Iranian choice reflects a particularly extreme form of anti-Semitism. It presupposes that Jews have successfully swindled the rest of the world for more than sixty years about their fate in World War II. It assumes that they have such control of Western governments, of the global media, public opinion, and academia, that they have been able to get away with a monstrous fraud, make huge profits, and consolidate the illegitimate State of Israel. This sort of Judeophobic fantasy helps to prepare the way for a future Shoah, tacitly containing an appeal to repeat it.[71]

Only the existence of such an anti-Semitic mind-set can explain how Iranian or Arab Muslims could simultaneously admire Hitler and deny his Holocaust, yet seek to emulate it. A good example of this syndrome is the columnist Ahmad Ragab, writing in the second largest Egyptian daily *Al-Akhbar* on April 20, 2001, who publicly gave thanks to Hitler for having *done* what Arabs still only dream of carrying out: "He took revenge on the Israelis in advance, on behalf of the Palestinians. Our one complaint against him is that his revenge was not complete enough." Another columnist, writing in the same paper exactly one year later, denied the Holocaust, quoting French and British "researchers" as evidence. There was "a huge Israeli plot" to blackmail Germany and Europe, based on a historical fiction (the Shoah), which, unfortunately, had never been implemented. "But I, personally and in the light of this imaginary tale, complain to Hitler, even saying to him from the bottom of my heart, 'If only you had done it, brother, if only it had really happened, so that the world could sigh in relief [without] their evil and sin.' "[72]

The only common denominator in Middle Eastern admiration for Hitler's Holocaust and the simultaneous denial that it ever happened is exterminatory hatred of Jews. Repeatedly we find in the Arab and Muslim worlds abundant praise for Hitler, recourse to the Nazi theory of a Jewish conspiracy against Germany, endless allegations of Nazi-Zionist collaboration, contempt for the "Holocaust industry," and a compulsive insistence that Zionists invented the Shoah. Locked into this tissue of contradictions comes the big lie that Israel is supposedly perpetrating a real Holocaust against the Palestinians. Different layers of Holocaust denial and inversion compete against one another in this anti-Semitic mythical realm where reason is permitted no entry.

The refusal to accept the reality of the Holocaust does not preclude radical Muslims and Arab nationalists from seeing a source of genocidal inspiration in Nazi actions—an enticing precedent proving that one can murder millions of Jews with impunity. President Ahmadinejad is literally obsessed with the issue precisely because he has intoxicated himself with dreams of a second Holocaust.[73] In this and other cases, the demonization of the Jews provides a unifying thread for an Islamist ideology in which the word "Zionist" fulfills exactly the same function as did the word "Jew" for Hitler and the Nazis. It is the epitome and the embodiment of evil in this world. The leaders of the Lebanese Hezbollah, like their Iranian paymasters, have also seized on the "Auschwitz lie" as being integral to their general delegitimation of Israel. Both Hassan Nasrallah and Sheikh Muhammad Husayn Fadlallah (spiritual guide of the Hezbollah), have referred to the six million Jewish victims of the Shoah as "pure fiction," a mark of boundless Zionist cunning and rapacity. For Hezbollah, the Holocaust is above all a testament to the ability of Jews to squeeze the West and manipulate its guilt feelings, thanks to their stranglehold over the capitalist economy and mass media.[74] Islam and the Palestinians are presented as the prime victims of this Zionist hoax.

The former mufti of Jerusalem, Sheikh Ikremah Sabri, like a significant number of other Palestinian clerics and intellectuals, appropriated Holocaust denial with equal fervor, maintaining that the Zionists had used this issue "to blackmail the Germans financially" and protect Israel. "It is not my fault that Hitler hated the Jews," Sabri declared, adding: "They hate them just about everywhere."[75] Professor Hassan Agha of the Islamic University in Gaza City added his own Shylockian gloss, at the turn of the new millennium: "The Jews view it [the Holocaust] as a profitable activity so they inflate the number of victims all the time. . . . As you know, when it comes to economics and investments, the Jews have been very experienced ever since the days of *The Merchant of Venice*."[76]

One of the attractions of Holocaust denial to Palestinians and other Arabs evidently lies in their conviction that if accepted, this belief would undermine the moral foundations of the Israeli state. Such considerations probably motivated Mahmoud Abbas (also known as Abu Mazen), the chief PLO architect of the Oslo peace accords and current head of the Palestinian Authority. In 1983 (under the influence of Soviet "revisionists") he produced a doctorate in Moscow entitled *The Other Side: The Secret Relationship Between Nazism and the Zionist Movement* that accused Israel of deliberately inflating the number of Jews killed in the Holocaust. He openly questioned whether gas chambers were really used for extermination, and suggested that the number of Jewish victims of the Shoah was "even fewer than one million."[77] He never officially retracted his Holocaust denial book nor did Israel publicly request that he do so. This is a sobering thought and difficult to comprehend.

Yet Abbas is a moderate compared to the former Moroccan army officer Ahmed Rami, who in the 1980s developed his own fully fledged Holocaust denial campaign from Stockholm, where he founded Radio Islam. Under the cover of anti-Zionism and claiming to defend the Palestinian cause, Rami called for "a new Hitler" who would rally the West and Islam against the cancer of Jewish power, freeing it forever from the aggressive yoke of Talmudism and the "Holocaust industry." Rami was prosecuted in Swedish courts on three different occasions, but his website is still very active. The Swedish journalist Per Ahlmark pointedly called his Holocaust denial statements "the most vicious anti-Jewish campaign in Europe since the Third Reich."[78] Rami has been an energetic intermediary in transmitting the tenets of European Holocaust denial to the Muslim Arab world and in exporting Islamic fundamentalist anti-Semitism to the West.

Rami's October 2001 speech at an international "revisionist" conference in Trieste, Italy, was a prime example of how to fuse together a witches' brew of Islamism, neo-Nazism, the *Protocols of the Elders of Zion,* Holocaust denial, the liberation of Palestine and the decolonization of the West. According to Rami, America and Europe were already enslaved by the "Zionist Occupation Government." This, he added, was nothing new in Jewish history. The "chosen people" was renowned for celebrating its "barbarous exterminations" of other nations. Israel had already achieved economic, cultural, political, and media domination in the West and Palestine; the Jews controlled the United States and "they have transformed the whole world into a greater Palestine which they occupy and over which they exercise control."[79] In this context, Rami was adamant that Jewish power in the West was based on the vast intellectual swindle of the Holocaust, whose dismantlement was therefore absolutely crucial. In September 2005 he told Hezbollah's Al-Manar TV that Judaism was "a criminal Mafia," not a religion, which had completely "occupied the West." It was like a "cancerous tumor, which the body cannot feel, and thus it can spread." This tumor had now expanded to the Arab world and paralyzed it. Zionism was simply the political arm to realize Jewish objectives of planetary control.[80] Rami's wild conspiracy theories were grist to Hezbollah's mill.

Rami is one of a number of Muslim militants in Europe who have sought to bridge the gap between Islamic and neo-Nazi ideologies, bringing them together in a contemporary setting. Another example from the opposite side of the fence is David Myatt, for nearly thirty years a leading ideologue of the British National Socialist movement and Combat 18. His pamphlet *A Practical Guide to Aryan Revolution* first appeared in 1997. A year later, Myatt converted to Islam (calling himself Abdul Aziz ibn Myatt), ardently defending bin Laden and suicide bombers in Palestine, Bali, Iraq, and elsewhere—without abandoning his Aryan credo. Fighting against Zionism and its lackeys would become a major theme in his proposed radical Islamist–neo-Nazi alliance. Its main content was, not surprisingly, hatred of Jews, Israel, and globalization, support for the Palestinians, and the determined propagation of Holocaust denial.

As an advocate of jihad, suicide missions, and killing Jews, Ibn Myatt now sees himself as a warrior in the struggle against the "Zionist-Crusader alliance," a militant in the war against "a profane, imperialist, materialistic, way of life." Myatt, a former monk, Satanist, and martial-arts expert, had tried in the past to establish an occultist Nazi-style commune in Shropshire; his aim was to implement the neo-romantic vision of an all-white "Aryan" paradise, based on organic farming. But by the late 1990s according to his own account, Islam had emerged as the ideal embodiment of a true neo-Nazi warrior society, blending together honor, duty, and the ethos of jihad with that of the SS. Nothing could be more antithetical to this martial religion than the capitalist consumer-culture of the decadent Zionist Western world. To establish Myatt's Promethean vision of the future, violence, and subversion against the state were necessary steps. Revolution, struggle, and holy war were seen as common denominators in the new convergence between Islam and National Socialism. In rallying to the holy war of the mujahideen against the infidel (*kaffir*) from Afghanistan to Palestine, Myatt felt he was developing an innovative Islamo-Nazi warrior code of honor. Among his cited paradigms was the grand mufti of Jerusalem Muhammad Amin al-Husseini, the leader of the Palestinian Arab national movement and Hitler's wartime ally. Anti-Semitism and Holocaust denial have remained key elements in Myatt's ideological hybrid, which brings together Satanism, pagan occultism, and mystical racism with obedience to Allah, the supremacy of Islam and jihadi violence. According to an article in the London *Times* on April 24, 2006, Myatt still believes: "The pure authentic Islam of the revival, which recognizes practical Jihad (holy war) as a duty, is the only force that is capable of fighting the dishonour, the arrogance, the materialism of the west . . . for the West, nothing is sacred, except perhaps Zionists, Zionism, the hoax of the so-called Holocaust, and the idols which the West and its lackeys worship, or pretend to worship, such as democracy." [81]

But it is above all President Ahmadinejad's compulsive concern with negationism that has helped to transform previously marginal endeavors by Western neo-Nazis, anti-Semites, and Holocaust deniers into a potentially deadly phenomenon—especially effective in the Muslim world. Iran is well aware that denial perfectly fits with the prevailing Muslim fundamentalist stereotype of Jews (based on indigenous Koranic and Islamic sources), depicting them as treacherous, deceitful, rapacious, and dangerously subversive. This negative image and the general Muslim propensity to believe in conspiracy theories explains the popularity of theories asserting that Jews invented the Holocaust to augment their own power and profit. From Morocco to Pakistan it has proven to be relatively easy to convince the broader public that the conflict between Islam and the Jews is a battle of culture, religion, and identity, as well as politics.[82] This struggle is generally perceived in Manichean terms, with Muslims as the children of light and Jews as the "sons of apes and pigs." It is reinforced by reference to long-disproved forgeries like the *Protocols*, which have been bestsellers for years in parts of the Arab world—available in any bookshop in downtown Cairo, Damascus, or Beirut. In this context, the willingness to believe that the Shoah is a myth deliberately manipulated by the international Jewish media becomes more explicable and can even be made into an instrument of state propaganda, as in Iran.

In Syria, at the turn of the millennium, the editor of the government newspaper *Tishreen*, Muhammad Khair al-Wadi, typically accused the Jews of "making up stories about the Nazi Holocaust which the Jews suffered and inflating them to astronomical dimensions." The Zionists had squeezed huge sums from Germany and other states and used "the myth of the Holocaust like a sword suspended over the necks of all opponents of Zionism, who are thereby accused of anti-Semitism." But, according to *Tishreen,* the real neo-Nazi plague existed only in Israel—an "ideological and physical terrorism . . . unknown in Europe [even] in the darkest centuries." The original Nazism had disappeared, but the Zionist terror was at its peak— "the plague of the twentieth century, which has been transferred into the third millennium, spreading damage and destruction wherever it turns."[83]

A year and a half later, the English-language official gazette, the *Syria Times,* extended the comparison into the ideological sphere. "Both Nazism and Zionism represent two faces of the same coin as each derives its ideology from racism, genocide and terrorism."[84] This could have been a literal translation into Arabic of reams of Soviet anti-Zionist propaganda, which had markedly influenced the Syrian regime in years gone by. The young Syrian president Bashar al-Assad certainly believes in the theory of Jewish racism and Zionist Nazism based on the "chosen people" ideology. This theme has been regurgitated for decades in Syrian Baathist propaganda. More recently—perhaps as a reflection of Tehran's growing influence—a soft version of Holocaust denial has become more frequent. In a TV interview for *The Charlie Rose Show* on March 27, 2006, the Syrian president indicated that the Holocaust had been exaggerated by the West and was constantly manipulated by the Zionists. From the Arab perspective, he told his interviewer, only what was happening in Palestine was truly equivalent to a genocide.[85]

A handful of Arab writers and academicians have indeed protested against these toxic trends, which were sufficiently powerful to alarm even the British journalist Robert Fisk. Writing in August 1996 from Beirut, Fisk recalled that for years he had listened to Lebanese, Syrians, Egyptians, and Saudis insisting that Hitler's destruction of Europe's Jews was a myth invented by the Israelis to justify their seizure of Palestinian Arab land. The experienced reporter, who has never disguised his intensely pro-Palestinian sympathies, was shocked to find that even Western-educated Lebanese Christians still sought to justify Hitler's Holocaust in his presence, making such remarks as: "It's a pity that Hitler did not finish the job." Fisk commented that the translation of Garaudy's Holocaust denial book into Arabic in Cairo had seriously aggravated this trend.

Last month [July 1996] Mr. Garaudy undertook a tour of Arab capitals, received by Vice President Abdul Halim Khaddam in Damascus, by

Lebanese intellectuals—both Christian and Muslim—in Beirut and by the Jordanian Association of Writers in Amman. He was feted in all three cities and given prominent—and almost exclusively favourable— coverage in the Arab press.[86]

A rare exception to the universal acclaim came from the Lebanese Christian novelist Elias Khoury, who observed that Arabs themselves continued to suffer from European racism, of which the Holocaust had been the most blatant expression. It was, therefore, self-defeating for Arabs to pursue such a perverse vision of history. Five years later, Khoury was among fourteen Arab intellectuals (including Palestinian nationalist poet Mahmoud Darwish) who protested the holding of a "revisionist" historians conference in Beirut, scheduled for April 8, 2001—because "it had nothing to do with the Palestinian cause." But these were minority voices, drowned out by those who insisted that the Holocaust myth had permitted the Zionist "rape of Palestine"; that the Jews throughout their history were never victims; that they compulsively lie; and that Zionist Jews completely controlled the global media, making possible "the perpetuation of a nonexistent" Holocaust.[87]

It is important to remember that for decades Arab nationalists and radical Islamists (especially in Egypt) had also *justified* the Holocaust by accepting Hitler's arguments in *Mein Kampf* concerning the "Jewish peril." Many continue to claim that Hitler was merely responding to Jewish provocation or reacting to the anti-Nazi boycott organized by Jews in 1933; there are also Arab voices who point to Jewish prominence in Communism and to the "warmongering" propaganda that supposedly pushed America into the war against Nazi Germany.[88] In 1972, Anis Mansour, a confidant of former Egyptian president Anwar al-Sadat, offered one of the more brazen anti-Semitic justifications for Hitler in the semi-official Egyptian daily, *Al-Akhbar*. After vilifying the Jews as "enemies of humanity" and "bloodsuckers who want to destroy the whole world," Mansour shamelessly asserted that Israel had proved to the Arabs that "Hitler was right" in his policies toward them. Three decades later, in February 2001, Mansour repeated his appalling apologia for the Holocaust, predicting that "it would become clear to the world that what happened to the Jews of Germany, Poland and Russia was justified."[89]

However, the trend toward Holocaust denial is ultimately stronger in the Arab world than efforts to justify, defend, or legitimize Hitler's deeds. The Western deniers are heroes in the Arab press, praised as dissidents fighting for truth and justice. At the same time, particularly in Palestinian discourse, the desire to stress the uniqueness of their own *naqba* (the 1948 catastrophe and suffering of the Palestinian people) determines their attitudes toward the Holocaust.[90] The mythical Jewish genocide has been turned into the model of *victimhood* for Palestinians, who consider themselves, and not the Jews, as "the victims of the greatest act of horror of the 20th century," to quote Columbia University professor Rashid Khalidi.[91] To *negate* Jewish suffering becomes a way to try to force recognition by the non-Muslim world of the Palestinian tragedy—a strategy that has thus far brought mixed results in the West.

Hosni Mubarak's Egypt has been central to the propagation of Holocaust denial in the Arab world, despite its reputation for moderation and its peace treaty with Israel. Articles on the Holocaust as a "Zionist lie" abound in Egyptian government-subsidized newspapers. One example among many is Rif'at Sayyed Ahmad, a columnist for the ruling National Democratic Party's paper who managed to repeat every known libel about "the burning of the Jews" in a June 2004 article that borrowed heavily from Garaudy, Rassinier, Irving, Butz, and even some Jewish authors. Attacking European statesmen as "hypocrites" who had ignored the cold-blooded slaughter of Palestinians, the Egyptian author deplored the persecution of those who had exposed the truth about the Holocaust hoax. They had been silenced by world Zionism and prosecuted under Western laws. The time was ripe for "a genuine cultural revolution" based on "credible history," facts, and science, to expose this "new Western idol-worship" of the Holocaust.[92]

Another columnist, Hisham Abd al-Rauf, writing in the Egyptian government evening paper *Al-Masaa* in December 2004, invoked Zionist falsehoods and falsifications relating to Palestine and the Holocaust. In particular, he praised "the courageous British historian David Irving" and Iranian president Ahmadinejad for having refuted Israel's lies about massacres that had never happened and gas chambers that never existed. The columnist also maintained that Hitler had never been against the Jews but, on the contrary, sought to appease them. It was a fact that he had permitted 120,000 Jews to emigrate from Germany to Palestine during his first years in power. His actions against the Jews in World War II "were carried out in coordination with the Jewish leadership" in order to push them toward Palestine.[93]

A May 15, 2001, discussion on Al-Jazeera TV revealed just how intense Holocaust denial motifs had become in the Arab world.[94] During a debate, Hayat Atiya, the female translator of Garaudy into Arabic, shouted before the cameras (while brandishing the photograph of an Arab child accidentally killed during the intifada): "Here is the Holocaust. . . . There is no Jewish Holocaust! There is only one Holocaust, that of the Palestinians!"[95] Among the statements appearing on the Al-Jazeera website and announced before the end of the debate was one to the effect that "nothing will dissuade the sons of Zion, whom our God described as descendants of apes and pigs, except a real Holocaust which would exterminate them in a single blow." At the end of this spectacle, it emerged from an Internet survey conducted by the channel that 85 percent of Arab spectators watching this program were convinced that Zionism was indeed *worse* than Nazism.

This was indeed the thesis promulgated by Abdel Aziz al-Rantisi in an article of August 2003 published in the Hamas weekly *Al-Risala*. Rantisi was then the second in command of Hamas. He began by asserting that Zionists "who excel at false propaganda and misleading media" had managed to present themselves as sole victims of the Nazis. They had thereby "turned the greatest of lies into historical truth." Those such as Garaudy, David Irving, Frederick Töben, and Austrian Holocaust denier Gerd Honsik, who had dared to challenge Zionist myths such as the "legend of the 'Gas Chambers,' " had been persecuted, arrested, and imprisoned. Al-Rantisi added:

It is not a secret that the Zionists were behind the killing of many Jews on behalf of the Nazis as was agreed between them. This was aimed at threatening them in order to force them to immigrate to Palestine. Every time the Zionists failed to convince a group of Jews to immigrate to Palestine, they sentenced these people to death without hesitating.

Rantisi then warmed to his main theme that "the crimes which the Nazis committed against humanity, with all their atrocities, are only a drop in the ocean compared to the terror that the Zionists committed against the Palestinian people." Among these terrible crimes was his false assertion that the

Zionists had cold-bloodedly assassinated the Palestinian child Muhammad al-Dura. But in his view, the Western world, which had supported the establishment of the criminal Zionist state, always ignored such atrocities, just as it had eagerly swallowed the Holocaust lie.[96]

Rantisi's insistence on the "lie of extermination" was echoed by Isam Sisalem, a history lecturer and so-called Jewish expert at the Islamic University in Gaza, in a Palestinian TV broadcast on November 29, 2000—the fifty-third anniversary of the UN decision to partition Palestine. Sisalem accused Israelis of masquerading as "victims" in order to justify the existence of their state—a foreign entity, "implanted as a cancer" on Arab land. He further maintained that Chelmno, Dachau, and Auschwitz had merely been "disinfecting sites." As for the Israeli cult of heroism and the Holocaust, his response was unambiguous: "Whose heroism? Whose Holocaust? Heroism is [of] our nation, the holocaust was against our [Palestinian] people."[97]

In April 2000 a symposium involving Palestinians and Israelis was held in Cyprus to discuss ways to strengthen peace through education. There was strong opposition to the idea of introducing the subject of the Holocaust into the PA school curriculum. One Fatah activist, Hatim 'Abd al-Qadir, declared that teaching the Holocaust would be a great danger to the developing Palestinian mentality. The chairman of the Palestinian Legislative Council's Education Committee was equally blunt: "The Holocaust has been exaggerated in order to present the Jews as victims of a great crime. If the purpose is to express sympathy, this is useless for us since we are the ones who suffered as a result."

Other Palestinian intellectuals also invoked grave doubts about undertaking any measure that would highlight Jewish suffering as opposed to Zionist terror, cruelty, and massacres of Palestinians. There were even those who presented the Shoah as an American-Israeli plot to efface Palestinian national memory in favor of the globalizing "culture of peace." Such moves, they argued, were merely an instrument for the ideological and political penetration of Palestine by Zionism and the West. Sheikh Nafez Azzam, head of the Palestinian Islamic Jihad in Gaza, gave a more sweeping and definitive theological gloss to the whole debate: "To teach the Holocaust in Palestinian schools," he declared, "contradicts the order of the universe."[98]

The February 3, 2000, press statement by Hamas, issued following the Stockholm conference about "the alleged Holocaust of the Jews," was a revealing example of the anti-Semitism behind Palestinian Holocaust denial.

The convening of this conference clearly serves the Zionist aim of falsifying history and obscuring the truth that the so-called Holocaust is nothing but a baseless, fictitious claim. This malicious conference seeks to reinforce a guilt complex vis-à-vis the Jews of Europe in general and in Germany in particular, to facilitate the continued fleecing of the world in support of the Zionist entity's expansionism and aggression. Creating great fantasies about an alleged "crime" that never happened while ignoring the millions of Europeans who died or suffered at the hands of the Nazis during the Second World War clearly exposes the face of racist Zionism with its belief in the superiority of the Jewish race over all other peoples.[99]

For Hamas, the Stockholm conference (attended by prominent European leaders and public figures) showed that "many western states are still deluded by erroneous Zionist propaganda" and obscured "the fact that the Zionist entity was built upon racial discrimination, terrorism and repression." The Zionists, in Palestine and Lebanon, continued to haughtily practice "the bloody terrorism of which it accuses other peoples." While promoting the "baseless, fictitious story" of the Nazi Holocaust, the West had always ignored "Zionist massacres," from Deir Yassin to Sabra and Shatila, thereby submitting to the "psychological and intellectual terrorism" practiced by Israel. Echoing Western Holocaust deniers, the Hamas document (written before the outbreak of the second Palestinian intifada) concluded:

We call on free-minded thinkers and writers and the vital forces of the world to uncover the crimes of world Zionism against our people, our nation, and against humanity as a whole, to expose them and not to fear the assault of the Jews, their intellectual terrorism, and their efforts to stifle voices and keep fair thinkers and researchers from exposing the claims and lies of Zionism. For the Jews in the world oppose the scientific method of study and research whenever it contradicts their racist interests.[100]

The Arab world and Iran have today become hotbeds of Holocaust denial, which is almost never condemned by Middle Eastern governments. This pathology has also spread to Israeli Arabs, according to a poll conducted by the University of Haifa and released in May 2009. The survey found that 40.5 percent of Israeli's Arabs believed the Holocaust never occurred. Three years ago 28 percent had denied the Holocaust.[101] This finding, along with the fact that 41 percent of Israel's Arab citizens rejected Israel's right to exist as a Jewish democratic state indicated an alarming radicalization of Arab attitudes. It also underlined the linkage in many Arab minds between negating the Holocaust and delegitimising Israel.

In recent years the Holocaust denial phenomenon has indeed become almost normal in Arab-Muslim discourse about Jews. For example, speaking on Al-Jazeera TV in July 2007, Khalid Mashaal, head of the Hamas Political Bureau, made it clear that he considered the crimes of Israel "ten times worse" than those inflicted by the Nazis on the Jews. Addressing a German colleague at a conference in Doha, capital of Qatar, he insisted that the West (and especially the German people) had been blackmailed by the Zionists. The time had come to finally put an end to the endless lies and extortions about the Holocaust. [102] In this respect, the Hamas leader was only reflecting what has become commonplace on Palestinian, Arab, and Islamist TV channels in recent years—an incendiary discourse that combines Holocaust denial and calls to destroy Israel or murder the Jews. The Gaza war in early 2009 extended this language of hate around the world. Even in New York's Times Square one could see placards reading "Israel: The Fourth Reich" or "Stop the Nazi Genocide in Gaza." In a demonstration in Los Angeles, the swastika replaced the Star of David, accompanied by the accusatory words "Upgrade to Holocaust Version 2.0." In Caracas, President Hugo Chávez bluntly stated on television, "The Holocaust, that is what is happening right now in Gaza." These and similar bursts of outrage happened to coincide in late January 2009 with ceremonies to mark International Holocaust Remembrance Day, held in a number of major cities. Not all of these anti-Israel protestors are necessarily bigots or anti-Semites. But by unjustifiably hurling Holocaustal terminology at the Jewish state, they are totally negating the meaning and memory of the Nazi mass murder. They are immorally using the planned annihilation of the Jewish people during World War II as a political weapon with which to pillory or defame the good name of the survivors. In that respect they are little better than the hard-core Holocaust deniers.

TWENTY

Hitler and the Mufti

n many ways anti-Semitism was the raison d'être of the Nazi movement that Adolf Hitler created in 1919. The dream and reality of German global hegemony he promoted was ultimately overcome only through the combined military might of the United States, the British Empire, and the Soviet Union. Nazism as a pivotal force in world politics was indeed destroyed in the flames engulfing German cities at the end of 1945, but the anti-Jewish poison nevertheless succeeded in spreading to far-flung corners of the globe before the final *Götterdämmerung* in Berlin. The seeds of this legacy were already sown in the Arab-Islamic world during the 1930s and 1940s, achieving their bitter consummation in the Middle East of today.[1] There exists a contemporary culture of hatred that permeates books, magazines, newspapers, sermons, videocassettes, the Internet, television, and radio, particularly in the Arab Middle East and Iran, that has not been seen since the heyday of Nazi Germany. Indeed, the dehumanizing images of Jews and Israel that have penetrated the body politic of Islam are sufficiently radical to be described as a new "warrant for genocide."[2] In today's Arab-Islamic world, we find intermingled the blood libel of medieval Christian Europe, Nazi conspiracy theories about the Jewish drive for world domination, and mountains of slanderous quotations about Jews as the sons of apes and donkeys. There is also much common ground displayed in the bigotry on Islamist and neo-Nazi websites. They are linked invariably by their paranoid effusions against the "satanic" State of Israel.[3]

This hysteria cannot be adequately understood as a mere by-product of the Arab-Israeli conflict or the "Palestinian question." For decades the bloodstained war over Palestine has served pan-Arabists and radical Islamists to broaden their political support in the Muslim world. But there is a "Jewish question" in Islam and Arabism that is not centered solely on

Palestine and which goes to the heart of its worldview. In this broader perception of Zionism and the West, an active strain of Islamist and Arab ideological anti-Semitism is strikingly reminiscent of its Nazi predecessors. This trend is predicated on the belief that history itself is determined by the evil machinations of the Jewish people. In adopting this mythology, Arab nationalists have, since the 1930s, followed a Nazi model that was fixated on the belief in an occult Jewish power striving for global hegemony.[4] Zionism is seen in this context as the quintessence of the Jewish conspiracy in its political dimension.

The Nazi ideologist Alfred Rosenberg first articulated this position in 1922 when he attacked Zionism as an *international* rather than a nationalist movement, seeking to unite world Jewry on a political basis. The 1917 Balfour Declaration, so he insisted, had demonstrated that Zionists controlled the financial strings of British policy and were allied to the worst enemies of the German Reich. Behind Zionism there allegedly stood a secret conspiracy of cosmopolitan Jewish bankers and Jewish Bolsheviks, such as Leon Trotsky, who had engineered the overthrow of Russian czarism.[5] Rosenberg believed that Jewish nationalism bore a close affinity to Bolshevism, for it threatened all nations with its subversive global designs. This had not prevented Zionists from linking their future to the capitalist United States (already the nerve center of world Jewry), which had begun to exert pressure on the British Empire as part of its own growing ambitions after 1918. Zionism was the expression of a relentless Jewish imperialism bent on manipulating Britain, America, and Russia while uniting all strands of Jewry into a single *pan-Jewish* movement. At the same time, the Zionists were determined to transform the Arab majority in Palestine into second-class citizens, in full collusion with the British Empire.

"In Palestine," according to Alfred Rosenberg, "the Jews are using the old method of exploiting and driving out by legal means the real population which has lived here for thousands of years."[6] The true Zionist goal was not to create an independent national state in a demarcated territory but, rather, to establish a purely Jewish power center that could successfully pursue "a wide-ranging oriental policy."[7]

Hitler's own view of Zionism was remarkably similar to that of Rosenberg.[8] It had originally been shaped by his formative prewar years in Hapsburg Vienna—the cradle of political Zionism—as well as by the conspiracy theories laid out in the *Protocols of the Elders of Zion*.[9] The *Protocols* inspired

Hitler, Rosenberg, and many Arab nationalists in the 1930s to regard Zionism as a mask for the hidden Jewish goal of achieving world power. For Hitler, Jewish squabbles over Zionism were merely so much dust in Gentile eyes. He concluded that liberal anti-Zionism as embraced by Jews was little more than "an unsavoury vapour of pretexts advanced more for reasons of expedience, not to say lies."[10] Writing in 1924, he recalled that in his younger days in imperial Vienna the great majority of Jews had seemingly "condemned and inwardly rejected Zionism."[11] Such Jews, Hitler added, were critical of Zionists for engaging in "an impractical, perhaps even dangerous way of publicly avowing their Jewishness."[12] Zionist nationalism was in fact a sign of rising Jewish self-confidence for "at a time when one section [of Jewry] is still playing the German, the Frenchman or Englishman, the others [the Zionists] with open effrontery come out as the Jewish race."[13]

In *Mein Kampf*, Hitler "unmasked" Zionism as an *international conspiracy* to cover up crooked dealings, protect Jewish intrigues, and promote the insatiable will to power of world Jewry.

> For while the Zionists try to make the rest of the world believe that the national consciousness of the Jew finds its satisfaction in the creation of a Palestinian [Jewish] state, the Jews again slyly dupe the dumb *Goyim* [Gentiles]. It doesn't even enter their heads to build up a Jewish state in Palestine for the purpose of living there; all they want is a central organization for their international world swindle, endowed with sovereign rights and removed from the intervention of other states.[14]

Hitler, Rosenberg, Dietrich Eckart, and other prominent Nazis were convinced that Jews could never organize a productive society through their own creative labor. They would never be able to construct an independent state. Jews were devoid of idealism. They were parasites who lacked a genuine work ethic or culture of their own and could therefore survive only by "feeding off their host-nations."[15] This became an article of faith in the Nazi creed. Zionism, according to Hitler and Eckart, contradicted the unchanging characteristics of Jews and their unnatural Diasporic essence.[16] For most anti-Semites it was inconceivable that a degenerate race of Jewish middlemen and speculators would farm the land in Palestine, drain the swamps, clear forests, organize powerful defense forces, and subordinate individual profit to national needs.[17] Indeed, in 1924 Hitler confidently predicted to Eckart that Jewry would never leave the fleshpots of the Diaspora voluntarily.[18] Zionism could not alter the nomadic, fundamentally rootless Jewish character nor the proclivity of the race toward a spatially unlimited dominion based on the control of international finance.

This rejection of Zionism led the Nazi leadership to dismiss out of hand all the strenuous Jewish efforts in the 1930s to become a nation like other nations, to put a definitive end to Jewish wanderings, exile, and homelessness. With a few rare exceptions, prominent German Nazis refused to take seriously Zionist determination to root the Jewish people in its historic homeland, to redeem the soil, encourage an indigenous stratum of Jewish farmers, or create a new *Gemeinschaft* (spirit of community). They disregarded the youthful idealism and pioneering ethos of labor Zionism, even pouring contempt on those features in the movement that emphasized Jewish *völkisch* nationalism. Nazism was equally indifferent to the fierce Zionist self-criticism directed against Diaspora Jewry—including the "abnormality" of the Jewish economic structure in eastern Europe and the "vulgar materialism" of Western Jewry. In stark contrast to those who today insist on twinning Zionism with fascism, the Nazis themselves rejected such parallels as false. Jews, in their eyes, had always been and would remain corrupt, even if they became *völkisch* nationalists. They had to be cleansed and eliminated from this world in order to usher in a new Aryan millennium. Zionism was no exception to the rule, despite those secular nationalist and socialist components that aimed at metamorphosing urbanized, literate Jews into a land-oriented people of peasants, workers, and warriors.[19] Whatever the vain hopes of some German Zionists after 1933, Hitler and the Nazi leadership continued to regard even ultranationalist Jews (whether pan-German or Zionist) as devious, acquisitive, and pushy representatives of a cosmopolitan racial conspiracy that had to be totally eradicated.

The Nazi negation of Zionism was based on the belief in an unchanging and malevolent essence of Jewry, and it would remain ideologically fixed. But after 1933 Hitler faced new challenges that, for a time, modified his attitude to Jewish settlement in British-controlled Palestine. He had to confront, for example, the potentially damaging effects of a worldwide Jewish anti-Nazi boycott inaugurated in the first months of 1933. The boycott, inspired by growing Nazi persecution of German Jewry, occurred at a time when the Reich economy, burdened by six million unemployed, was particularly vulnerable.[20] In this context the Zionist aim to encourage Jewish emigration from central Europe to Palestine appeared to offer the Nazi leadership a possible exit from its economic difficulties. Under the so-called *Haavara* (transfer agreement) initialed with the Zionist organization in 1933, the purchase of German goods was to be contractually linked with settling German Jews in mandatory Palestine. This had the advantage of opening the door to German exports into the Middle East. Not only could the Reich economy significantly benefit from such an arrangement, but the anti-Nazi boycott organized by world Jewry might be effectively blunted.[21] No less important, Nazi Germany would be rid of its Jews more speedily, sending them to a territory where it was assumed that they would be able to cause less damage to German interests than in neighboring European countries. From Hitler's perspective, there was a further benefit. Inside Germany, the Zionist organization was a very useful antidote to liberal Jewish assimilationists still tenaciously hanging on to a foothold inside the Third Reich.[22] Such, at least, was the standpoint of Reinhard Heydrich and high SS officials in encouraging the Zionist push for *aliyah* during the early years of the regime.

Nazi support for Jewish immigration to Palestine was not, however, an expression of pro-Zionism. Limited in time and scope, it was driven by the obsession with making Germany *judenrein* even though new immigrants from Germany (with their capital, equipment, and technical know-how) were strengthening Palestinian Jewry. The emigration policy persisted until the outbreak of World War II. But the report of the British Royal Commission of Inquiry to Palestine in 1937, which advocated the partitioning of the country and the creation of a tiny Jewish state on the coastal plain, alarmed the German Foreign Office. As the prospect of war in Europe came closer, it was realized that strengthening the Jewish position in Palestine might be deleterious for Germany's strategic position. The Nazi press began to increase its attacks on Zionism and express open support for the Arab "freedom struggle" in Palestine against the British mandate and the Jews.[23] Nazi propagandist Giselher Wirsing declared that the Zionist goal in Palestine was "the establishment of a Vatican of world Jewry" that would strengthen the global position of assimilated Jews in western Europe and the United States. As an *international* enemy Zionism seemed analogous to Communism or supranational Catholicism,[24] hence the growing Nazi desire to reinforce the Arab world as a counterweight to the worldwide Jewish peril embodied in Zionism.[25]

The Germans were not initially in any hurry to establish contact with the

Arabs, in spite of feverish efforts by the Palestinian nationalist leader, Haj Amin al-Husseini, grand mufti of Jerusalem—as early as March 1933—to win their support.[26] The mufti, like a growing number of Arab nationalist and Islamic leaders, admired the Reich for its discipline and order, its challenge to the West, *and* its war on the Jews. He hoped that Germany would boycott all Jewish goods, undermine the economic and political influence of Jewry, and bring about the spread of fascism to other countries. Haj Amin's pro-Nazi enthusiasm remained intact despite his disappointment over the *Haavara* agreement, which had adversely affected the situation of the Palestine Arabs. Hitler's platonic declarations of sympathy for the Arab cause and allusions to the "lack of democracy" in Palestine were taken at face value. But his *deeds,* not least of which was the lack of any public or significant military assistance to the Palestinian Arab revolt against the British, were quietly ignored.[27] On the other hand, Arab vilification of the British grew, despite the mandatory government's increasingly draconian restrictions on Jewish immigration to the national home in Palestine.

Most Arabs ignored Hitler's global strategy in the mid-1930s, which still sought a diplomatic rapprochement with the British Empire while continuing to build up German military strength. Hitler had long admired British imperial rule as a shining example of Aryan racial superiority in action. He could no more contemplate offering military support for the Arab struggle in Palestine before 1939 than he could approve Indian independence from the British Raj. Moreover, Hitler did not take Arabs seriously as partners, with the exception of Haj Amin (whom he described as a "sly old fox") and Rashid Ali al-Gailani, leader of the wartime anti-British coup in Iraq.[28] In his *Table Talk* Hitler attributed the grand mufti's "quite exceptional wisdom" to the probability of Aryan blood.

"With his blond hair and blue eyes," the Nazi führer speculated, "he gives the impression that he is, in spite of his sharp and mouse-like countenance, a man with more than one Aryan among his ancestors and one who may well be descended from the best Roman stock."[29] When these compliments were made in 1942, Hitler knew that the mufti of Jerusalem was his most enthusiastic supporter in the Arab and Islamic world.[30] But the German leadership, including Hitler, remained skeptical regarding the capacities and value of the racially inferior Semitic Arabs in general, beyond the common bond provided by hatred of Jews. The Arabs and Islam barely registered on their radar screen until 1939.

Hitler could not ignore the imperial ambitions of Benito Mussolini, whose territorial expectations in the Middle East and North Africa were extensive. Fascist Italy hoped to supplant both Britain and France as the dominant power in the region. Once Mussolini had joined the Axis, Italian ambitions were encouraged within certain limits. Since Hitler's own interest in the Middle East was marginal and the immediate focus of German *Lebensraum* lay in Russia, eastern Europe, and the Balkans, it seemed reasonable to give Italy a free hand in the Mediterranean. The Middle East was informally designated as an Italian sphere of influence, especially after hostilities broke out between the Axis and the Western Allies. But the Germans were also mindful that the Vichy regime in France regarded the maintenance of its colonial authority in North Africa, Syria, and Lebanon after 1940 to be a sine qua non of collaboration with the Third Reich. Any pro-Arab declaration by the Nazis would threaten this strategic interest.[31]

German policy toward the Arab world remained friendly but cautious in the light of such geopolitical considerations. Hitler's reservations were increased by his innate dislike of making binding promises, his fixed dogma of Aryan superiority, and the warnings of advisers concerning the chronic unreliability of Arabs as allies.[32] Thus Hitler exploited the propaganda benefits of attacking the "injustices" in the British mandate's policy toward the Arabs of Palestine between 1936 and 1939 while avoiding actions that would directly threaten the British position in the Middle East.[33] This policy changed drastically with the pro-Nazi rebellion in Iraq in 1941.[34]

By late 1941 Hitler's strategy in the Middle East was profoundly shaped by the gigantic military confrontation taking place in the Soviet Union. The anticipation was that German forces would eventually be able to descend southward from Caucasia toward Iraq and Iran. This was made clear in a conversation between the führer and Haj Amin held in Berlin on November 28, 1941. Also present were Reich foreign minister Joachim von Ribbentrop, and the Arab expert Fritz Grobba, former German emissary to Iraq, who wrote up minutes of the meeting in German.[35] The mufti began by conveying "to the Führer of the Greater German Reich, admired by the entire Arab world, his thanks for the sympathy which he had always shown for the Arab, and especially the Palestinian cause, and to which he had given clear expression in his public speeches."[36] The Arabs, he insisted, were "Germany's natural friends because they had the same enemies as Germany, namely the English, the Jews, and the Communists."[37] The Arabs would therefore co-operate "with all their hearts" on the side of the Nazi Reich, not only in acts of sabotage and revolt but also in creating an Arab legion. The mufti would use his "close relations with all Muslim nations" for the common cause—a promise he did partially fulfill.

The mufti's proclaimed wartime objective was a united, independent Arab state encompassing Palestine, Transjordan, Syria, and Iraq. His confidence in the Nazi leadership had been enhanced by the fact that Germany was holding no Arab territories and by assurances that she had recognized Arab national aspirations "just as she supported the elimination of the Jewish national home."[38] An unequivocal declaration on this issue would help to rouse the Arabs "from their momentary lethargy" and could rally them decisively to Germany's side. The mufti also tried to persuade Hitler that this could be the historic hour of Arab liberation if he would only seize the moment. In his opinion, there was no reason to fear the negative reactions of the Turks, Italians, or French toward pan-Arab and pan-Islamic ambitions. Finally, the mufti warned that excessive German delay in issuing a declaration could only benefit the common British enemy.

In his reply, Hitler stressed that "Germany stood for uncompromising war against the Jews."[39] He hastened to add that this "naturally included active opposition to the Jewish national home in Palestine, which was nothing other than a center, in the form of a state [*ein staatlicher Mittelpunkt*] for the exercise of destructive influence by Jewish interests." Germany was aware that the assertion that the Jews were agricultural pioneers in Palestine was a lie. "The real work there was being done only by Arabs, not by Jews." Germany was resolved, "step by step, to ask one European nation after the other to solve its Jewish problem, and at the proper time to direct a similar appeal to non-European nations as well."[40] Hitler was even ready to reveal to the mufti of Jerusalem the secret of the Final Solution, which was being formalized at the time. As they spoke, the *Einsatzgruppen* were still massacring Jews in Russia. Plans for the gassing of Polish Jews were already under way, and the notorious Wannsee Conference was scheduled to be held only two weeks later. Hitler did not go into such details but he informed the mufti that "he would carry on the battle to the total destruction [*Zerstörung*] of the Judeo-Communist empire in Europe." He also enjoined the Palestinian Arab leader to lock this revelation "in the uttermost depths of his heart."[41]

Hitler underlined the *ideological* dimension of World War II in the most unequivocal terms. "Germany was at the present time engaged in a life and death struggle with two citadels of Jewish power: Great Britain and Soviet Russia."[42] He admitted that "theoretically there was a difference between England's capitalism and Soviet Russia's communism," but in practice "the Jews in both countries were pursuing a common goal."[43] For the Nazi leader, the hour of reckoning with the Jews was indeed fast approaching. "This was the decisive struggle; on the political level, it presented itself in the main as a conflict between Germany and England, but ideologically it was a battle between National Socialism and the Jews [*weltanschaulich sei es ein Kampf zwischen dem Nationalsozialismus und dem Judentum*]."[44] It was self-evident, Hitler maintained, that "Germany would furnish positive and practical aid to the Arabs involved in the same struggle" because this was a war of survival "in which the Jews were able to mobilize all of England's power for their ends."[45]

Hitler assured Haj Amin that his fanatical struggle against the Jews lay at the very core of the military offensive the Third Reich was waging against the British Empire and Soviet Russia. This "exterminatory" war against the Jews would be carried on *beyond* the European continent once the German armies had reached the southern exit of Caucasia. At the appropriate hour, the führer would give the Arab world the signal that its time of liberation had arrived. "Germany's sole objective would then be the destruction of the Jewish element residing in the Arab sphere under the protection of British power [*die Vernichtung des in arabischen Raum unter der Protektion der britischen Macht lebenden Judentums sein*]."[46] In other words, the Germans were committing to the task of wiping out the Jewish national home in Eretz Israel and destroying the predominantly Sephardic Jewish communities in Arab lands.

The ideological foundations of the Nazi-Arab axis on the "Jewish question" could hardly have been stated more clearly. But after Stalingrad and the victory of the British Eighth Army at El Alamein in late 1942, the mufti's practical prospects of leading a broad Islamic-Arab national movement to liberate Palestine began to fade. The focus of his wartime activities would henceforth be in the Balkans, where he mobilized Muslim volunteers for the Axis forces.[47] At the same time he did everything in his power to prevent the rescue of Jews from the Nazi Holocaust in Europe. He wrote assiduously to the German, Italian, Hungarian, and Romanian foreign ministries and to the Bulgarian king, even intervening in Croatia to prevent Jewish refugees, mainly orphaned children, from reaching Palestine.[48] During the last two years of the war the mufti's intransigent resolve to prevent European Jews from escaping the gas chambers led to close collaboration with the SS and its head, Heinrich Himmler.[49] The leader of the Palestinian Arabs was clearly driven by the premise that the shortest road to a postwar Arab Palestine ran over the corpses of European Jewry.

Haj Amin's propagandist activities in the Reich capital reveal a remarkable degree of ideological rapprochement between Islamic anti-Semitism and National Socialism. At the opening of the Islamic Central Institute in Berlin on December 18, 1942, the mufti launched into a vicious attack on the "bitterest enemies" of the Muslims: the "Jews and their lackeys"—the British, the Americans, and the Bolsheviks. World Jewry, which stood behind "godless Communism," was accused of unleashing a global conflagration. The Jews, he declared, had always been a "disintegrative element" in history, provoking wars between the nations. This was a genocidal language indistinguishable from that of Hitler himself. The culture-specific element was the claim that Islam had always preached a war against the Jews, ever since the prophet Muhammad had been "obliged" to drive them out of the Arabian peninsula.[50]

On November 2, 1943, the twenty-sixth anniversary of the Balfour Declaration, the mufti was equally explicit, declaring that there could be *no toleration of Jews*. It was the duty of all Muslims—and especially of the Arabs—to expel these infidels from their lands. According to the Palestinian Arab national leader, this had been the teaching of the Prophet thirteen hundred years earlier. The Jews were the bloodsuckers of the nations and corrupters of morality, incapable of loyalty or genuine assimilation.[51] Their boundless egoism and perverse belief that they were the chosen people had led them to expropriate the indigenous inhabitants wherever they settled. Fortunately, National Socialism had fully grasped the nature of the "Jewish peril" and resolved to find *eine endgültige Lösung* (a final solution) that would liberate the world from this danger.[52]

Haj Amin enjoyed access to Himmler and Eichmann, and was certainly aware of the death camps when he used such exterminationist rhetoric. According to Simon Wiesenthal, the grand mufti even visited Auschwitz and Majdanek where "he paid close attention to the efficiency of the crematoria, spoke to the leading personnel and was generous in his praise for those who were reported as particularly conscientious in their work."[53] The "solution" of the "Palestinian question," it would appear, was to be found in the killing fields of Auschwitz. Thus it is fundamentally wrong to suggest that Haj Amin's anti-Semitism was less severe than that of the Nazis, a form of political opportunism, or simply the consequence of Zionist policies in Palestine.[54]

Haj Amin and Hitler would be symbiotically bound together until the end of World War II. In March 1941, the mufti had already received a personal letter from Adolf Hitler assuring him of the great sympathy he felt for "the national struggle of the Arabs."[55] The Nazi dictator declared that "the Germans and the Arabs have common enemies in England and the Jews; and are united in the fight against them." Germany would therefore be ready to provide financial and military help for a general Arab war against the British. In late 1941, the mufti obtained official Axis recognition of the *illegality* of the "Jewish National Home in Palestine." Nazi Germany and Fascist Italy now formally acknowledged the Arab right to resolve the Jewish question "by the same method that the question is now being settled in the Axis countries." This ominous protocol was agreed to at a time when Hitler's Germany had already begun its policy of mass extermination against European Jewry. On April 29, 1942, the Italian Fascist government also pledged to aid Arab countries "suffering under British oppression" to win their sovereignty and to "abolish the National Jewish Homeland in Palestine."[56]

Nazi foreign minister Ribbentrop responded that same day to pressure from the mufti, once again confirming the German commitment to Arab liberation and "the destruction of the Jewish National Home in Palestine."[57] But Haj Amin was not easily satisfied by such promises. In a July 25, 1944, letter he repeated the need to liquidate the Jewish national home in Palestine, and sharply opposed any German plan for prisoner exchanges, which might result in even a small number of Jews coming to Palestine. The mufti further warned against any German steps that "would encourage the Balkan countries likewise to send their Jews to Palestine."[58] Two days later, on July 27, 1944, he once again emphasized to SS leader Heinrich Himmler, the chief organizer of the Final Solution, his adamant opposition to any possibility of Jews ever being permitted to leave Germany, France, or the Balkans for Palestine "under the plan for exchanging Palestinian Germans." He pointedly recalled Himmler's November 2, 1943, telegram on the anniversary of the Balfour Declaration, which had stated "the National Socialist

Movement, since its inception has inscribed on its banner the battle against world Jewry."[59] After such declarations, the mufti maintained, it would "be incomprehensible to the Arabs and Muslims" if Germany were to permit "a single Jew to emigrate to Palestine."

On June 28, 1943, in a letter from Rome, Haj Amin more fully expounded his anti-Semitic credo to the Hungarian foreign minister. He recalled "the long and bloody fight, brought about by the desire of the Jews to create a national home, a Jewish State in the Near East, with the help and protection of England and the United States." The mufti demanded that the Hungarian government rescind its intention to allow nine hundred Jewish children to escape to Palestine. This "wicked" plan had to be frustrated by "preventing the Jews from leaving your country for Palestine" via Bulgaria and Turkey. He told the foreign minister that such emigration

> would by no means solve the Jewish problem and would certainly not protect your country against their evil influence . . . for this escape would make it possible for them to communicate and combine freely with their racial brethren in enemy countries in order to strengthen their position and to exert a more dangerous influence on the outcome of the war.

Haj Amin reminded the Hungarian government that behind the ambition for a Jewish state

> lies the hope which the Jews have never relinquished, namely the domination of the whole world through this important strategic center, Palestine. . . . However, the war, as well as the understanding which the members of the Three-Power Pact have of the responsibility of the Jews for its outbreak and finally their evil intentions towards those countries which protected them until now—all these are reasons for placing them under such vigilant control as will definitely stop their emigration to Palestine or elsewhere.[60]

If, despite everything, there were any special reasons for removing them from Hungary, the mufti added that "it would be indispensable and infinitely preferable to send them to other countries where they would find themselves under active control, for example, in Poland, in order thereby to protect oneself from their menace and avoid the consequent damage."

The "active control" prevailing in Poland was Haj Amin's polite euphemism for the death camps that were busy liquidating the "Jewish peril"[61] under SS administration. Haj Amin sent virtually identical letters to Bulgaria and Romania in the summer of 1944. The results were soon evident. Less than a year after the mufti's successful intervention with the Horthy government, more than four hundred thousand Hungarian Jews were deported to Poland to be gassed by the Germans. Haj Amin's further appeals to the Balkan satellites of Nazi Germany, who had been willing—for a price—to permit the rescue of Jews, helped to definitively sabotage this possibility. The mufti, who had earlier offered a Muslim legion from the Balkans to Heinrich Himmler for use against the Allies, spared no effort to ensure that the Reichsführer-SS would "take all measures to prevent the Jews from going [to Palestine]" and send them instead to a destination from which they would never return.

Haj Amin obviously saw himself as an *ideological* partner of the Nazis, as well as a political ally. In a speech before the imams of the Bosnian SS division in the summer of 1943, the mufti emphasized this point by pointing out certain parallels between Islam and National Socialism. The Nazi *Führerprinzip*, the cult of obedience and readiness to struggle, as well as the ideal of *Volksgemeinschaf* (people's community) were, he stressed, primordial Islamic virtues. So, too, was the high value accorded to family, labor, and social solidarity. Above all, since the time of Muhammad the Muslims had been confronted with Jewish subversion.[62] The Jews had been enemies of the Arabs and of Islam since its birth.[63] They had corrupted the moral foundations of the Muslim faith by encouraging prostitution, drugs, and sexual permissiveness.[64] They had supposedly expropriated the indigenous inhabitants wherever they had settled. The greatness of National Socialism, according to the mufti, was precisely that it had highlighted the "Jewish peril" and fought to redeem humanity from its clutches.[65]

Haj Amin was a genocidal anti-Semite. In a January 1941 letter to Hitler, he had already described the "Jews of the entire world" as dangerous enemies "whose secret arms are corruption, money, and intrigues," which had been cunningly exploited by the British to frustrate the cause of Arab unity. Not for the first time, the mufti effusively thanked Hitler for supporting Arab nationalism and "for having again and again brought up in ringing tones the question of Palestine."[66] At the Islamic Central Institute in Berlin in December 1942, he used terminology indistinguishable from that of

Hitler, Himmler, or Rosenberg.[67] As in other wartime addresses, the mufti praised the uncompromising Nazi struggle against those whom the Koran had solemnly branded as "the worst enemies of the Muslims." In a talk on January 21, 1944, he was still stressing the need for all Muslims to collaborate with the Nazis in order to destroy world Jewry.[68] Once again he pointed to the similarity between Islam and National Socialism that "brings our ideologies close together and facilitates cooperation."[69]

Haj Amin, like Hitler, firmly believed that World War II was a Jewish war in which

> world Jewry leads the allied enemies into the abyss of depravity and ruin, just as it did in the age of the Prophet. In England as well as in America, only Jewish influence is dominant. It is the same Jewish influence that stands behind godless Communism. . . . It is Jewry who drove the nations into the war of attrition and from its tragic destiny only the Jews will benefit.[70]

In a speech in Berlin on March 19, 1943, the mufti elaborated still further on how Jews in Britain and America were behind the effort to seize Palestine; on how they already had Roosevelt in their clutches and were the driving force behind the Allies' "evil intentions" toward Arabs and Muslims. The Jews posed a mortal danger not only to Palestine but to the entire Muslim world, with their plans to rebuild Solomon's Temple and to destroy al-Aqsa Mosque. The mufti was convinced that they intended to establish "a Jewish bridge between New York and Jerusalem" to further their devilish intrigues.[71] America, in particular, was completely under Jewish capitalist influence, which explained the expansion of the war and the persecution of millions of Muslims.

· · ·

The collaboration of the mufti of Jerusalem with the Nazis was not an isolated phenomenon in the Arab world. Ever since 1933 the Third Reich had aroused considerable enthusiasm among Arab leaders *outside* Palestine, impressed by its mix of faith and nationalist fervor, spectacular militarism, and opposition to the Versailles postwar settlement. The German Consulate in Beirut and the German Embassy in Baghdad received many admiring letters from Syrian, Lebanese, and Iraqi citizens, expressing their approval

of Hitler and support for the German Reich. The Nazi Ministry of Propaganda was told, for example, by one of its sources that throughout the Middle East "all of the inhabitants with the exception of the Jews are following
events in the new Germany with great sympathy and enthusiasm." Some of
this identification may indeed have been based on the illusory hope that
Nazi Germany would help the Arabs to achieve their national liberation
from Anglo-French colonial domination. As in Palestine, however, Hitler's
anti-Jewish policies were regarded as a *model worthy of imitation* by many
Islamic fundamentalists and Arab nationalists.

Ibn Saud, king of Saudi Arabia, provides a revealing example of unal-
loyed Arab anti-Semitism during this period—a Wahhabite Muslim leader
with a decided sympathy for the Nazi position on the Zionist issue. Speaking to a British diplomat in 1937, the king asserted that his "hatred for the
Jews" derived from their "persecution" of Jesus and "their subsequent rejection of Muhammad." Ibn Saud made it clear that "for a Muslim to kill a Jew
[in war], or for him to be killed by a Jew, ensures him an immediate entry
in Heaven and into the august presence of God Almighty." He could not
fathom why the British government, "representing the first Christian power
in the world today," rewarded "those very same Jews who mistreated your
Isa [Christ] . . . an accursed and stiff-necked race that, since the world
began, has persecuted and rejected its prophets and has always bitten the
hand of everyone who helped it."[72]

Ibn Saud's bigoted view of Jews was widely shared by secular pan-Arab
nationalists in Iraq, who looked to National Socialism as a possible answer
to their social and national problems.[73] This was equally true in Syria and
Lebanon, particularly among nationalist students and professors at the
University of Beirut who founded the Parti Populaire Syrien (PPS)—a So-
cial(ist) Nationalist Party with an explicitly fascist orientation. The founder
and leader of the PPS, Anton Sa'adah, was a Lebanese-born Syrian Orthodox Christian by origin. Secular and anti-French, he believed Lebanon
should be part of Greater Syria. A Social Darwinist, racist, and totalitarian
in his political outlook, Sa'adah was much impressed by the military discipline, mass rallies, and appeal to youth of the Nazi movement. According to
a former Baathist leader, Sami al-Jundi, this kind of emotional, aesthetic,
and philosophical inspiration reflected a widespread generational mood.
"We were fascinated by Nazism, reading its books and the sources of its
thinking and particularly Nietzsche, Fichte and Chamberlain. And we were

the first who thought about translating *Mein Kampf*. He, who lived in Damascus, would appreciate the tendency of the Arab people to Nazism which was the power that appealed to it."[74]

Another Greek Orthodox Christian, Michel Aflaq, would provide the ideological basis for the Baath Party (Arab Renaissance) in the 1940s. Aflaq's radical nationalist worldview glorified the Arabs as a master race, underlining with special emphasis the need for continuous struggle, sacrifice, and perpetual revolution in the name of the pan-Arab cause. In the Baathist worldview, the Arab nation was the culmination of spiritual perfection, far superior in its traditions and culture to the superficiality of Western civilization. But Arab unity, Aflaq cautioned, would remain a dream without a massive injection of martyrdom and bloodshed. The Syrian and Iraqi Baathists eagerly embraced his quasi-mystical view of the Arab nation as bearers of an exalted eschatological mission, assigned to them by Allah himself. It was axiomatic within this totalitarian Pan-Arabism (which profoundly shaped the outlook of future Iraqi dictator Saddam Hussein) that Jews were deemed outsiders, aliens, and enemies of the Arab nation. The idea that the "Zionist entity" must be eradicated flowed naturally from such racist assumptions.[75]

The fascination of Arab youth and radical movements in Syria and Iraq with militant ultranationalism, fascism, and National Socialism had important consequences. The Arabist scholar Itamar Rabinovich noted many years ago that "in these movements "some of the major political figures in Syrian politics of the 1950s and 1960s were schooled."[76] A similar situation prevailed in Iraq where the nationalist press hailed Hitler's Germany as the patron of the Arabs in their struggle against Britain and World Jewry. The anti-Zionism of Iraqi pan-Arab nationalists in the 1940s was frequently accompanied by rabid anti-Semitism. The arrival of the mufti of Jerusalem in Baghdad shortly after the outbreak of World War II exacerbated the situation.[77] German Nazi influence was able to penetrate into Iraq on the wings of a preexisting anti-British and anti-Semitic mood. The result was that in the dying hours of the pro-Nazi regime of Rashid 'Ali al-Gailani in Iraq (June 1–2, 1941) the Jews of Baghdad suffered a crippling pogrom.[78] At least 179 Jews were killed, and many more were wounded; 242 children were made orphans, 586 businesses were looted, and 911 buildings that housed more than 12,000 people were pillaged.[79]

Such massive destruction could not have happened without a decade-long anti-Jewish indoctrination inculcated by fanatical Arab nationalists. Intellectual leaders Sami Shawkat and Fadhil al-Jamali had been prominent in efforts to Nazify the state school system in Iraq since the early 1930s.[80] With the help of Syrian and Palestinian teachers Shawkat, who was director general of the Iraqi Ministry of Education, also managed to introduce a heavy dose of anti-Semitism into the educational system. In some of his addresses he branded Jews as the "enemy within," praising Hitler and Mussolini for having eradicated them as part of the German and Italian fascist rebirth. In the autumn of 1933, Shawkat had told Baghdad students, "There is something more important than money and learning for preserving the honor of a nation and for keeping humiliation at bay, that is strength. Strength, as I use the word here, means to excel in the Profession of Death."[81] This illiberal, militarist spirit began to permeate every level of Iraqi society, especially among the youth, where there was open sympathy for the German Reich and its anti-Jewish policies. Some of the leading members of Rashid Ali's pro-Nazi regime, such as Yunis al-Sab'awi, were rabid Jew-baiters and it was under their sway that Nazi anti-Semitic propaganda reached new heights.

In Egypt, too, there was a growing sympathy in the 1930s and 1940s for National Socialism. It seemed to offer a promising alternative to the fragile local plant of constitutional liberalism and parliamentary democracy. The German Reich's successes enhanced its appeal to those Egyptians who idealized power and the omnipotence of the state and had visions of resurrected national grandeur. At the same time, the radical movements of the 1930s—from Islamic revivalism to the Green Shirts of Misr al-Fatah (Young Egypt)—began to adopt much of the social demagogy and paramilitary organization of European fascism.[82] The Young Men's Muslim Association was also openly pro-Nazi, along with the Young Egypt Society founded by Ahmad Husayn, whose credo was consciously borrowed from Nazi ideology. Husayn believed in fascist values of discipline, struggle, order, aggressiveness, militarism, and sacrifice. His cohorts were drilled in the paramilitary style, and his movement cultivated the *Führerprinzip* associated with Hitler and Mussolini. Radical Egyptian nationalism fused with Islamic, anti-Western sentiment; *Lebensraum;* and racist anti-Semitism on the Nazi model. In July 1939 Husayn openly proclaimed that "they [the Jews] are the secret of this moral desolation which has become prevalent in the Arab and Islamic worlds. They are the secret of this cultural squalor and these filthy arts. They are the secret of this religious and moral decay, to the point where it has become correct to say 'search for the Jew behind every depravity.' "[83] This discourse, identical to that of Nazi anti-Semitism, was increasingly commonplace in Egypt and the rest of the Arab world by 1939. World War II underlined the danger of Arab lands for the Jews, who now had every reason to fear for their lives and property in the event of an Axis victory.[84] In Egypt, the massive presence of British troops provided the only real guarantee for their safety. In Syria a popular children's ditty caught the mood of the new era when there would be *"Bala misyu, bala mister fi-l-sama' Allah, wa'l-ard Hitler"* (No more "Monsieur" no more "Mister" / God in Heaven, and on earth Hitler). [85]

It was, however, primarily in North Africa that large numbers of Arabic-speaking Jews would come under direct Nazi, Italian Fascist, or Vichy French control. Libyan Jews, for example, had been subjected to anti-Semitic race laws originating in Rome as early as September 1938.[86] During the war they were exposed to discriminatory restrictions and repression, and more than 2,500 Jews were transferred to internment and labor camps in Tripolitania. Many were sent into the desert approximately 150 miles south of Tripoli, where at least 562 of them died.[87] The Libyan Jews suffered severely under Italian Fascist rule while the native Arab population looked on more or less indifferently. This changed when Tripolitanian Jewry found itself overwhelmed by a vicious and sudden pogrom in November 1945 unleashed by local Arabs, which was unprecedented in its ferocity. More than a hundred law-abiding, unarmed Jews (mostly women, old people, and children) were massacred—some after cruel torture, others by being burned alive. Many houses, shops, stores, and synagogues were plundered and set on fire.[88]

For neighboring North African Jews in Algeria, Morocco, and Tunisia, the fall of France and the passage of draconian anti-Jewish laws by the Vichy French regime of Marshal Pétain was a devastating psychological and political blow—one for which they were even less prepared than their Libyan coreligionists. More than one hundred thousand Algerian Jews were rapidly stripped of their citizenship after October 1940; discriminatory statutes were applied with a zeal exceeding that which prevailed in France itself.[89] Algerian Jews were the special target of zealous anti-Semites in the Vichy bureaucracy and among the French settlers. Violent, proto-Fascist organizations and a vitriolically anti-Semitic mainstream media flourished in Vichy-controlled Algeria.

The North African Arab population, as in Libya, reacted impassively for the most part. It must be remembered that many of the French-trained Maghrebin nationalists had pro-Nazi leanings in the 1930s, and a significant part of the population proved receptive to German anti-Jewish propaganda. At the same time, the rank-and-file Muslim population of Algeria (unlike the French settlers) obtained no direct benefit from the persecution of Jews. Their continued subjection to French colonial rule limited their interest in collaboration and their enthusiasm for Vichy's anti-Jewish policies.[90] In Tunisia and Morocco, the anti-Jewish laws did formally bear the mark of the Arab sovereign but their source still lay in metropolitan France.[91] Indeed, Sultan Muhammad V, like the bey of Tunis, did what he could to save Jews, to try to protect them and provide some moral support within the tight confines of the French protectorate.[92]

In Tunisia, there were, nonetheless, a number of violent anti-Jewish incidents perpetrated by Arabs, including a mob attack against Jews coming out of a synagogue in Gabès on May 23, 1941. Six Jews were killed and another sixteen injured. As elsewhere in the Maghreb, although much of the Arab population was not openly hostile, it, too, tended to be indifferent to Jewish suffering. But for Tunisia's ninety thousand Jews, who had come under direct German rule after November 1942, the danger was particularly acute.[93] Only German military weakness, logistical problems, the brevity of the occupation, and Erwin Rommel's defeat at El Alamein prevented Nazi implementation of the Final Solution in this French North African protectorate or in Palestine itself.[94] We know, for example, that a special SS commando unit had been formed in 1942 and attached to Rommel's African panzer divisions, which would eventually have murdered the Jewish population of the Middle East on the lines of the *Einsatzgruppen* operations in the USSR, had the opportunity arisen.

Between June 1940 and the expulsion of German troops from Tunisia in May 1943, the Jews of North Africa suffered every imaginable privation, short of mass murder, including forced labor, work gangs, prisons, house arrest, loss of livelihood, deprivation of education, confiscation of property, and radically restricted freedom of movement. Although the Germans and their European partners (especially the Vichy French) were the central perpetrators in that drama, Arabs were at times willingly involved in the Nazi, Vichy, and Fascist campaigns against North African Jews. The majority, however, remained silent bystanders, though a tiny handful acted as "righteous Gentiles." These few positive exemplars tend, unfortunately, to be stigmatized in the Arab world today.[95]

Although the Jews of Arab lands narrowly escaped the worst ravages of the Holocaust, by 1945 their position had become increasingly fragile. They found themselves subjected to pogroms, constant harassment, the beginnings of decolonization, and the worrying fallout from an increasingly bitter Palestine conflict. The historian Norman Stillman has vividly summed up the situation confronting Jewish communities in the Arab world at the end of World War II: "It made little difference whether Jews abjectly mouthed the Arab anti-Zionist line as in Syria, donated generous sums of money to the Palestinian cause as in Iraq, publicly proclaimed their loyalty as in Egypt, openly declared their allegiance to Zionism as in Tunisia and Libya, or completely identified themselves with the colonial power as in Algeria. In the end they all shared a similar fate and chose to emigrate or flee from the lands of their birth."[96]

Before 1945 there had been more than one million Jews living in the Arab countries of the Middle East. Within a decade this number had been reduced by half as a result of immigration, most of it to the newly created State of Israel. By the end of 1953 more than 90 percent of the Jews in Iraq, Yemen, and Libya had been driven out, either by expropriation, being stripped of citizenship, or simply being made to feel that they had no future.[97] Three-quarters of Syrian Jewry also left, following devastating riots in Aleppo. By 1970 the bulk of North African Jews had followed suit— mainly to Israel or to France. In Egypt, mass demonstrations on November 2, 1945 (Balfour Declaration Day), in the major cities, especially in Cairo, led to mobs pillaging Jewish businesses with hundreds injured and a number of fatalities in Alexandria.[98] By the late 1940s government harassment and anti-Jewish propaganda distributed by pan-Arab and Islamic associations was making the position of Egyptian Jewry increasingly difficult. It became even more untenable following the anti-Jewish violence that spread throughout Egypt and other Arab countries after the UN decision to partition Palestine, the establishment of Israel in 1948, and the first Arab-Israeli war that immediately followed. In the early 1950s the measures to "Egyptianize" the economy jeopardized the jobs of many Jews and other foreigners in Egypt, further undermining their position.[99] In Egypt, as in Iraq, the nationalist climate led to anti-Semitic slogans branding all Jews as Zionists, Zionists as Communists, and popularizing the myth that communist activities "were directed exclusively by Jews."[100] The Suez War of 1956 delivered the final blow to Egyptian Jewry, producing a wave of mass arrests, detentions, and dismissals of Jewish employees. The third Six-Day War of 1967 would be the last straw in the seemingly ineluctable process of dissolution now overtaking the remnants of North African and Levant Jewry. Even in relatively tolerant Tunisia under Habib Bourguiba, there was an epidemic of anti-Jewish rioting in the capital city. The Great Synagogue of Tunis was burned while looters ransacked most of the Jewish shops and businesses.[101] Today, apart from Morocco (fewer than ten thousand Jews) and the Tunisian island of Jerba, the Arab Middle East is almost completely *judenrein* except, of course, for the State of Israel.[102]

The mass exodus of Sephardic, mainly Arabic-speaking, Jews was by no means an inevitable by-product of the Arab-Israeli conflict. It was far more of a conscious act of ethnic cleansing by the Arab world than the flight of Palestinians from Israel in 1948. The "Palestine question" acted primarily as a catalyst for accelerating the preexisting long-term trends of decolonization, modernization, and Arab nationalism that engulfed many Christian and long-established Jewish communities in the Arab world. From the beginning of the 1930s the dominant strands of Arab nationalism turned increasingly anti-Zionist and anti-Semitic, leaving little place for Jews or other non-Muslim minorities in the Arab world. As a result, Jews became more and more aware of their acute vulnerability—a condition that was reinforced as Arab nationalist leaders turned to Nazi and fascist models for their inspiration. The Jews consequently found themselves caught between anti-Semitic European colonial rulers and a hostile indigenous Arab population. The frightening lessons of the European Holocaust further heightened their Jewish consciousness, tending to increase their identification with Zionism and Israel and intensify their need to escape from the looming chaos of the Arab world.

Writing in 1974, the Franco-Tunisian writer Albert Memmi (who had actively participated in the independence struggle of North African Arabs) emphasized this chronic sense of insecurity, malaise, and humiliation that his fellow Jews experienced in Muslim lands before European colonization and, even more, after Arab independence.[103] The exclusivist character of

Arab nationalism and traditional Muslim feelings of superiority had been exacerbated by the impact of Nazism—making it virtually impossible for Jews or other non-Muslims to enjoy freedom and dignity in a modern Arab environment.

> It is now too late for us to become Arab Jews. Not only were the homes of Jews in Germany and Poland torn down, scattered to the four winds, demolished, but our homes as well. Objectively speaking, there are no longer any Jewish communities in any Arab country, and you will not find a single Arab Jew [*Juif-Arabe*] who will agree to return to his native land.[104]

TWENTY-ONE

The "Liberation" of Palestine

Before 1914, Palestine was an underdeveloped backwater within the Ottoman Empire with no independent or autonomous political or administrative status. A desolate land, it had less than half a million inhabitants at the turn of the twentieth century, most of them Palestinian Muslims, though an old, established Sephardic community had existed there for many centuries. By the eve of World War I the population of Palestine stood at 689,000, of whom 85,000 were Jews; close to half of the 100,000 Jews who had immigrated since 1882 as part of the Zionist project would remain to settle the land.[1] The Ottoman authorities were far from supportive of these efforts, having their own political problems with separatist movements in the Balkans and east Anatolia, which in 1895 had led to the first wave of Armenian massacres. They feared the creation of yet another nationality problem in their own shrinking imperial domain. The Turks were also aware that large-scale Jewish settlement might open the door to a further extension of intrusive European influence into the region. Sultan Abdulhamid II was particularly opposed to Jewish immigration and colonization in Palestine. Not only were entry restrictions strictly enforced during his rule, but the sale of land to Jews (even as Ottoman subjects) was virtually prohibited. Nevertheless, by 1908 the Jews had acquired some 156 square miles of land and established twenty-six colonies.[2] With the help of the European powers, who had a palpable interest in maintaining the system and privileges of capitulations (special rights granted to foreigners under their protection), Jews were often able to circumvent Turkish restrictions.

Sultan Abdulhamid's opposition to Zionist plans was also conditioned by a desire to enhance his popularity among his Muslim Arab subjects. One way was to pose as a champion of pan-Islamism—the would-be caliph of *all* Muslims. As the spiritual and temporal ruler of the last Islamic empire, he could hardly be expected to casually hand over Jerusalem (the third holiest city of Islam) to the Jews.[3] Moreover, Arab anxieties about Zionism were growing. The highly sophisticated Yusuf al-Khalidi, one of the leading Muslim Arab politicians in Jerusalem (he was a president of its municipal council) and a former deputy in the Ottoman parliament, expressed his own concerns about Zionism as early as March 1899, in a letter to France's chief rabbi, Zadoc Kahn. In theory, he wrote, the Zionist idea was "completely natural, fine and just." Indeed, he continued: "Who can challenge the rights of the Jews on Palestine? Good Lord, historically it is really your country." But the brutal realities on the ground, he continued, were that Palestine had a non-Jewish majority and was an integral part of the Turkish Empire. What "material forces" did Jews possess, besides their financial power, to acquire holy places common to 390 million Christians and 300 million Muslims? Where were their cannons or battleships?

Al-Khalidi sincerely doubted that even Britain or America, the two nations "most favourably disposed towards the Jews," would be ready to fight for the Zionist cause. Though Turks and Arabs, according to this Ottoman politician, were on the whole well-disposed to Jews, some were undoubtedly infected with an anti-Jewish racial hatred, similar to that which already pervaded "the most civilized nations." He specifically mentioned the "Christian fanatics" (especially the Catholics and Orthodox Christians) who resented Jewish progress. They did not "overlook any opportunity to excite the hatred of the Muslims against the Jews." Al-Khalidi even predicted a popular movement against Jewish settlement that the Ottoman government would find difficult to arrest. Hence, his letter (which he asked the French chief rabbi to pass on to Theodor Herzl, leader of the newly created World Zionist Organization) appealed to Zionists to desist from the "folly" of seeking to conquer Palestine. The "best, the most rational solution to the Jewish question" was, in his view, to settle the millions of impoverished Jews somewhere other than Palestine.[4] Herzl did not accept this advice despite the failure of his own feverish efforts to convince the Turkish Sultan to support his plans. Like later Zionist leaders, he thought that the economic, scientific, and technological benefits of Jewish settlement would outweigh nationalist or religious objections.

Another prophetic anticipation of future violence between Arabs and Jews came from Négib Azoury, a Maronite Christian anti-Semite who had entered the Ottoman administration in Jerusalem in 1898. After some unsuccessful intrigues he fled to Paris where he founded the somewhat nebulous Ligue de la Patrie Arabe (League of the Arab Homeland) in 1905. That same year, Azoury brought out one of the first classics of Arab nationalism. In the preface he announced that this book was part of a larger work he was planning to publish on "the Jewish peril" entitled *Le Péril Juif universel, Révélations et études politiques.*[5] Azoury claimed to speak in the name of an "oppressed Arab nation" struggling for independence from the Ottoman Empire, just like the Kurds, Armenians, Albanians, and Bulgarians. He appealed for neutrality and sympathy from the "enlightened and humanitarian states of Europe and North America."

The "Jewish question" was relevant to Azoury because Arab nationalism had been born at the very time that Israel was coming—as he put it—close to achieving its dream of "universal domination."[6] What was happening in Palestine was *"une miniature achevée du future empire arabe"* (a complete miniature of the future Arab empire). In 1905 Azoury predicted in quasi-apocalyptic terms the inevitability of the coming Arab-Jewish conflict:

> Two important phenomena, of the same nature, yet opposed, which have still not drawn anybody's attention, are emerging at this moment in Asiatic Turkey: they are the awakening of the Arab nation and the latent effort of the Jews on a very large scale to reestablish the ancient kingdom of Israel [*reconstituer sur une très large échelle l'ancienne monarchie d'Israël*]. Both of these movements are destined to fight each other continually until one of them wins. The fate of the entire world [*le sort du monde entier*] will depend on the final result of this struggle between these two peoples representing two contrary principles.[7]

Azoury observed that hitherto the importance of the Arab provinces of Turkey had been underestimated in examining the "Eastern Question" as had "the universal character of the [Jewish] peril," clothed as it was in "shadow and mystery."[8]

Azoury stressed his intimate knowledge as an Ottoman official of the Jews of Palestine and of the Bible ("this dangerous and immoral book"), which was "the most terrible condemnation" of the Hebrew national character. He noted that the Zionists, having learned from their ancestors' mistakes, aimed at securing the natural frontiers of Israel from the Suez Canal to Mount Hermon in the north and beyond.[9] Azoury's anti-Zionist polemic was thoroughly imbued with the anti-Dreyfusard style of French ultranationalism and the Catholic integralist anti-Semitism then fashionable in Paris. Indeed, in a pamphlet against Azoury in 1906, Farid Georges Kassab, a Greek Orthodox Lebanese anticlerical, called him a "Catholic bigot" and Jesuit who related to Jews as deicides and as an "eternally damned" people. Kassab, who was pro-Zionist, did not accept that Jews in Palestine were morally or politically "foreigners," but regarded them as loyal Ottoman subjects.[10]

Azoury's anti-Semitism was indeed typical of the views of the anti-Dreyfusard clergy and that of some Protestant missionaries from Europe and America who began to influence the Arab population in the Levant a century ago.[11] Greek Orthodox clergy in Palestine were equally aggressive in exporting the ugly prejudices against Jews rampant in late-nineteenth-century czarist Russia. The German Protestant Templars (many of whom would be speedily Nazified in the 1930s) were no less hostile to Jews as potential economic rivals in Palestine. European racist stereotypes, which had begun to infiltrate the country in the 1890s, not only affected Arab Christians in the Levant but also influenced Muslims uneasy about the gradually expanding Jewish community of Palestine. This was especially true of Arab merchants and intellectuals in Haifa, Acre, Jaffa, and Jerusalem.

The Young Turk revolution of 1908 opened a new era in the history of the Ottoman Empire, but it did not fundamentally change Turkish attitudes toward Zionism. Though Jews were active in the Young Turk movement, the new regime based on the Committee of Union and Progress (CUP) remained suspicious of Zionism as a potentially dangerous form of national separatism; like the Hamidian dynasty before it, the Young Turks feared possible consequences from Arab opposition to Jewish immigration.[12] Moreover, the Arabs of Palestine, through their sixty representatives in the Ottoman parliament—nearly a quarter of the total—and their influence in the administration and Arabic-language press, were able to act as an effective anti-Zionist lobby. In attacking the CUP they did not hesitate to use anti-Semitic motifs (also prevalent in the Greek and Armenian media) that linked the Young Turks and the Zionists to a cosmopolitan Judeo-Masonic plot.[13] The British ambassador in Turkey strongly believed in this conspiracy himself, giving it a Teutonic gloss. Thessaloníki, with its large Sephardic-Jewish and "crypto-Jew" population, was presumed to be the main theater of operations that served German ambitions in the Balkans. But the nationalist Young Turks were far from being pro-Zionist, nor were they any less committed to the integrity of the empire than the Ottoman despots they had overthrown. The last thing they were seeking to create was a Zionist-Jewish irredentist entity that could become a pretext for more foreign intervention and might further alienate the Arab population of the empire.

In 1908, an anti-Zionist daily, *Al-Karmil,* edited by Najib Nassar, a Protestant of Greek Orthodox origin, was started in Haifa. This was followed soon afterward by the establishment of *Filastin,* owned by Greek Orthodox Christians and committed to the propaganda war against Zionism. Anti-Semitism was nourished by disputes over land with the local fellahin and Arab concern that Jews were gradually taking over control of urban commerce. Representative Raghib al-Nashashibi, who was elected to the Ottoman parliament in 1904, declared he would devote all of his strength "to doing away with the damage and threat of the Zionists and Zionism."[14] By 1910 the fear of Jewish economic power and land purchases for settlements had grown more palpable. The constant land disputes began to find a certain echo among the urban intellectuals, some of whom mobilized villagers for acts of opposition and sabotage. In 1911 Najib Nassar proposed an economic boycott of Jews. He built on the common perception that the "new Jews" in Palestine were hoping to eventually set up their own governmental framework in accordance with biblical prophecies.

An Ottoman loyalist and an Arab patriot, Nassar insisted that Zionism was a threat not only to Palestinians but to the Turkish Empire as a whole. Its first objective was to win economic mastery over Palestine and over local Arab sources of livelihood, in order to eventually reestablish the ancient Jewish kingdom. By 1914 the image of Jews as rapacious anti-patriots and traitors to the Ottoman Empire who were seeking to take over their Arab neighbors' possessions was slowly beginning to take root. There were even letters and reports on the Arab side, imagining the possibility of "future exile from our homeland . . . and [our] departure from our homes and property."[15] *Filastin* regularly attacked the social, economic, and educational "exclusivism" of the new immigrants from Russia—many of them imbued with socialist ideals. At the same time, *Filastin* complained about marked cultural differences between the local Arab population and the Zionist immigrants, especially with regard to the free relations between the sexes and the relatively emancipated status of Jewish women.[16]

The Arab case against Zionism during the late Ottoman period was tainted by an anti-Jewishness that had become part of the "daily bread in Palestine," to quote one prescient observer.[17] In November 1913, a prominent leader of the Palestinian anti-Zionist campaign, Sheikh Sulayman al-Taji from Acre, published a poem entitled "The Zionist Danger" in *Filastin*. It related to Jews as "the weakest of all peoples and the least of them" who were constantly haggling with Arabs to obtain their land. Here is an extract:

> Jews, sons of clinking gold,
> Stop your deceit;
> We shall not be cheated into bargaining
> Away our country!
> Shall we hand it over meekly,
> While we still have spirit ourselves?
> Shall we cripple ourselves?[18]

In March 1914 Raghib Bey al-Nashashibi recommended to the Ottoman government that it adopt "Romanian" methods in dealing with the Jews: Treat them as aliens without any civic or political rights. By this time most Palestinian Arabs opposed *any* Jewish immigration from Europe into Palestine. Moreover, they generally believed that *all* Jews had the same objective—to found an autonomous Jewish state. Fear of economic competition from the Jewish newcomers increasingly encouraged the adoption of familiar strains of European Christian anti-Semitism. So, too, did the unfounded belief in a Judeo-Masonic conspiracy behind the Young Turk revolution and the popular myth of powerful Jewish financiers with unlimited resources underpinning the Zionist movement.

In examining the roots of the Palestine conflict, what is often forgotten is the lowly and humiliated condition of Jews before the impact of European influence and secular modernity made itself felt. If Arab Muslims were at the top of the ethnic-religious minority ladder under Ottoman Turkish rule in Palestine, Jews were at the bottom. Until the advent of Zionism, the Jewish community was almost entirely urban; it was composed mainly of pious Jews in their declining years, wretchedly poor and dependent on charity handouts collected from other Jews around the world. The Jews of Palestine often lived on the edge of starvation, especially in Jerusalem, where (already in the 1840s) they were the largest single group in the city. Their miserable appearance and cringing step reflected the humiliating oppression they had suffered at the hands of Christian and Muslim Arabs who frequently jostled them in the crowded city alleys.[19] Despite their extreme poverty, the Jews were taxed more heavily than Muslims or Christians. On the way to prayer at the Western Wall of Herod's Temple, Jews drew the spite and malice of the resident Arabs, who deliberately scattered broken glass along their path.[20] The Wall itself (the most sacred spot for Judaism) was fouled up with urine and feces, a dumping ground for garbage and sewage.

In Palestine, much as in the rest of the Arab world, Jews were treated as *dhimmis,* second-class subjects. Jewish disabilities and servitudes that expressed the classic state of social, political, and moral inferiority of *dhimmis* under Islamic rule were indeed manifold. The historian David Landes summed up the normative rules applying to *dhimmis* as follows:

> Jews had to pass Muslims on their left side, because that was the side of Satan. They had to yield the right of way, step off the pavement to let the Arab go by, above all make sure not to touch him in passing, because this could provoke a violent response. In the same way, anything that reminded the Muslim of the presence of alternative forms of worship had to be avoided so synagogues were placed in humble, hidden places, and the sounds of Jewish prayer were carefully muted.[21]

The Jews of Palestine were segregated by residence and subject to discrimination, abuse, and, periodically, group assault. They were considered inferior by custom and in law. To quote Landes again: "The [condition of the] Jews in the pre-Zionist Holy Land (and in Islamic lands in general) was comparable to that of the blacks in the post-Reconstruction American South."[22]

This degraded status makes a mockery of claims that under Islamic rule, Christians, Jews, and Muslims enjoyed an idyll of tolerance and were living in peace and fraternity. Nor is it true that Zionism was the prime factor that destroyed the harmonious fabric of coexistence between the communities. The thesis of Muslim tolerance (contrasted with Christian anti-Semitism) has indeed become a highly selective weapon of political warfare, designed to delegitimize Zionism, to amplify European Christian guilt, and to suggest that Jews always lived happily and productively in the bosom of Arab civilization. This mythical narrative is contradicted by countless descriptions of the oppressive Jewish condition in Muslim lands made by virtually every European traveler in the eighteenth and nineteenth centuries. Such accounts were recorded *before* organized political Zionism had appeared on the stage of history. Even during calmer, more enlightened periods of Muslim rule when Jews were able to prosper, their situation was highly precarious because of their political powerlessness, linked to their status of civil and spiritual inferiority as non-Muslims.

The subsequent Palestinian, pan-Arab, and Islamist rejection of Zionism would be unfathomable, unless this *dhimmi* background is sufficiently taken into account. Muslim nationalism simply had no way of accommodating the notion of sovereignty for any non-Muslim peoples (especially Jews) inhabiting the "abodes of Islam." As political scientist Gil Carl Alroy observed more than thirty years ago: "The thought of the Jews as rulers suggests cosmic disorder, explaining the common resort among Arabs to [depict] Jewish statehood as 'abnormal,' 'unnatural,' 'artificial.'"[23] Local and foreign Arab reactions to Zionism in Palestine stemmed in no small measure from the cognitive dissonance provoked by encountering Jews who did not fit their condescending image of the *dhimmi* as hapless and helpless victims.

The Balfour Declaration, the British conquest of the Holy Land in December 1917, and the ensuing League of Nations mandate over Palestine (officially assigned in 1922) radically transformed the "Palestinian question." During the Paris Peace Conference of 1919, an agreement had been signed by Chaim Weizmann, leader of the Zionist movement, and the emir Faisal (son of Husayn ibn 'Ali, the sharif of Mecca), who would later become king of Iraq. The agreement (never implemented) envisaged close collaboration between Arabs and Jews in order to fulfill their respective national aspirations in the Middle East, including Jewish immigration into Palestine "on a large scale." In March 1919 Faisal optimistically wrote to U.S. jurist Felix Frankfurter: "We Arabs, especially the educated among us, look with the deepest sympathy on the Zionist movement." Faisal even wished the Jews who were coming back to Palestine "a most hearty welcome home" in the framework of "a reformed and revived Near East" where the two national movements (Arab and Jewish) could complement each other.[24] Unfortunately, with the partial exceptions of Egypt's Anwar al-Sadat and King Hussein of Jordan, this was to be an Arab voice in the wilderness for the rest of the century.

The warning signals were not slow in coming. The 1919 report of the Woodrow Wilson–appointed King-Crane Commission outlined the strength of local Palestinian Arab and Syrian opposition to Zionism. The commissioners recommended that "Palestine and Syria should be a single State" that also included Lebanon. They welcomed the idea that Faisal might be made its constitutional monarch. But as the report stressed, the Arabs of Palestine (almost 90 percent of the total population in 1919) strongly rejected any mass immigration of Jews. The pro-Arab King-Crane Commission itself rejected any Jewish historical, political, or moral right to Palestine, especially the heretical idea that Christian and Muslim holy places be left in Jewish hands. The commissioners predicted that "the complete Jewish occupation of Palestine" would intensify with "a certainty like fate, the anti-Jewish feeling both in Palestine and in all other portions of the world which look to Palestine as the Holy Land."[25] They were influenced in this conclusion by the memorandum presented to them on behalf of the General Syrian Congress that had met in Damascus on July 2, 1919. The participants at this conference had described the Zionist project as "a grave peril to our [Arab] people from the national, economical and political points of view." The Syrian Congress rejected not only Zionism but any French government claims to the smallest part of Greater Syria.

Faisal's fall in July 1920 and the French occupation of Syria inevitably led to a swift reorientation of rising Palestinian nationalism. In August 1921, a Muslim-Christian delegation from Palestine informed Winston Churchill, then the British colonial secretary, that it demanded the abolition of the Jewish national home envisaged by the Balfour Declaration and an end to Jewish immigration. Several months earlier a deputation of the executive committee of the Haifa congress led by Musa Kazim Pasha, former governor of Jaffa, had drawn up a memorandum expanding on the reasons for this stance. This March 1921 document had called the Balfour Declaration "illegal," "an act of modern Bolshevism," arbitrarily depriving Palestinians of their birthright. Moreover, the Zionists did not even represent a living nation with its own language and separate political existence. Though Jews had once possessed Palestine in antiquity, they had almost always been involved in wars, revolts, strife, and internal troubles. This was equally true in the modern era: "Jews have been among the most active advocates of destruction in many lands. . . . It is well known that the disintegration of Russia was wholly or in great part brought about by the Jews, and a large proportion of the defeat of Germany and Austria must be put at their door."

The official Palestinian Arab delegation received by Churchill stressed at some length "the pernicious motives of the Jews towards the powers that be and towards civilization." The delegation members unashamedly spoke the language of the *Protocols,* evoking a "secret society of prominent Jews" meeting from time to time, plotting to unleash chaos, full of "an overflowing hatred of mankind, and Christendom." Karl Marx, Leon Trotsky, and Mikhail Bakunin (the latter was not Jewish but was a notorious Russian anti-Semite) were mentioned as spiritual godfathers of the demonic anarchy behind the Zionist project. Anti-Semitic clichés abounded in the official document. The Jew was "clannish and unneighbourly," unable and unwilling to mix with non-Jews, always "seeking privileges" but giving nothing in return: "The Jew is a Jew all the world over. He amasses the wealth of a country and then leads its people, whom he has already impoverished, where he chooses. He encourages wars when self-interest dictates, and thus uses the armies of the nations to do his bidding."[26]

According to the delegation, the Jews had seized control of commerce and finance in Palestine, depreciating the value of land and property in order to oblige Arab landlords "to sell out at ruinous prices." Not only that, but the Palestine Arabs, it was asserted, were being asked by Britain to tolerate neighbors (the Jews) that the much larger nations of Russia and Poland could not abide. If that were not enough, Great Britain itself was obliged (because of the Zionists) to maintain "a huge army" at the British taxpayers' expense to keep the Palestinian "natives" down. This policy, so the delegation argued, served only Jewish interests and would have a disastrous effect on Anglo-Arab relations. The delegation solemnly warned the British government that once the Zionists were strong enough, "they will turn their backs on England as they did on Germany and Russia."[27]

The Palestinian Arab representatives expressed a strong sense of injustice that the British Empire had reneged on its wartime promises to the Arab nation by excluding Palestine from the area of Arab independence. The bitterness induced by "betrayed pledges" played a not insignificant role in the Palestinian Arab revolt against the British mandate and in its violent response to Zionism. More than sixty years ago, the pro-Palestinian Lebanese Christian historian George Antonius noted the long-term effects of this double-dealing.[28]

Anti-Jewish violence had first flared up in February and March 1920, following an official public reading of the Balfour Declaration in Palestine.[29] During the Muslim religious celebration of Nabi Musa (the Prophet Moses) on April 4, 1920, there were violent attacks on the Jewish quarter of the Old City of Jerusalem, in which the traditionalist and anti-Zionist Jews of the "Old Yishuv" suffered most. There were forty-seven Jewish victims in these riots. The Arab demonstrators shouted incendiary slogans such as "Palestine is our land and the Jews our dogs." They clearly made no *practical* distinction between indigenous Sephardic or ultra-Orthodox Jews from the old Jerusalem community and the colonizing Zionists. The pattern was repeated during the 1929 pogroms in Jerusalem, Safed, and Hebron in which around a hundred Orthodox Jews of the old religious community were murdered by marauding Arab mobs.[30] Altogether 133 Jews were slaughtered as a result of the 1929 Arab massacres in Palestine.

The 1929 massacres were in no small measure the result of the deliberate inflammation of ordinary Muslims in Palestine by the British-appointed grand mufti of Jerusalem, Haj Amin al-Husseini. Since the early 1920s he had sought to rouse the mass of believers by falsely claiming that the Jews intended to take over al-Haram al-Sharif (the Temple Mount area) in order to rebuild Solomon's Temple on the ruins of the great mosques. He had called on Muslim leaders throughout the world to rally to the defense of the holy places of Islam against the "perfidious" Zionist designs. This strategy of stirring up the national movement by manipulating religious passions came to fruition in the 1929 pogroms, which were widely presented as an "anti-imperialist" uprising and a glorious page in Palestinian Arab history. By showing that Zionism threatened the religious as well as the national status quo in Palestine, Haj Amin created the basis for a more popular national movement in the 1930s that succeeded in bringing the Palestinian cause into the forefront of pan-Islamic and pan-Arab concerns.[31] By couching the struggle against Zionism in the idiom of populist Islam, both Haj Amin and the martyred leader of the 1930s, Sheikh 'Izz al-Din al-Qassam, reached out to the broad mass of the Palestinian population. Indeed, al-Qassam, a Syrian Arab, was the first to raise the banner of an organized and violent struggle against the British mandate and Zionism. The revolt was not only instigated in the name of Palestinian Arab nationalism but also presented as an *Islamic* necessity.[32]

Al-Qassam, who studied at Al-Azhar University in Cairo, had fled to

Palestine in 1921, becoming a preacher at the new al-Istiqlal mosque in Haifa. The sheikh's death in a shootout near Jenin with British police in November 1935 enshrined him as a hero of the Palestinian resistance. His iconic status is especially strong in contemporary terrorist organizations such as Hamas (with their Qassam rockets and brigades) and Islamic Jihad. The parallels are indeed striking. In the early 1930s al-Qassam established a secret association called al-Kaff al-Aswad (The Black Hand), which aimed to kill Jews in general and to particularly target Jewish civilians in northern Palestine through acts of jihadi terror. Al-Qassam's organization was a secret society entirely consecrated to holy war against the Jews. Its members grew wild beards, called themselves sheikhs, held frequent meetings in mosques and in secret venues around Haifa, trained in the use of arms, and prepared for the ultimate self-sacrifice.

Al-Qassam actively cooperated with Haj Amin from the early 1920s until shortly before his death. Both leaders shared a common taste for violence, embraced an anti-British and anti-Jewish agenda, and brooked no dissent within their ranks. Immediately after his death, the sheikh became the object of a fully fledged cult; he was a greatly admired martyr for the Palestinian homeland whose violent deeds were extolled as an example to all. During the 1936–39 Arab revolt, the Qassamites indulged in many acts of jihadist terror against the Jews of Palestine, the British administration, and Christian Arabs whom they accused of treason. As Shai Lachman, an Israeli researcher, has written: "Qassamite terror was particularly bloodthirsty. From an organization committed to fight the Jews and the British, the Qassamites became one of the most anarchical and destructive forces ever to arise in the Palestinian Arab community."[33] Their campaign of terror and indiscriminate murder greatly contributed to the eventual disintegration of the 1936 Arab revolt from within.

This Qassamite jihadist legacy has continued to wreak havoc *within* the Palestinian camp to this day, for it is not only Hamas and other Islamic fundamentalist groups who have placed al-Qassam's personality and deeds on a pedestal. Yasser Arafat's Fatah organization also publicly revered him as "the first commander of the Palestinian Revolution." George Habash, a radical secular leftist from a Greek Orthodox Christian background and the founder of the Popular Front for the Liberation of Palestine (PFLP), was no less fulsome in his praise for the sheikh. Leila Khaled, the popular heroine of the PFLP from the late 1960s, summed up this Palestinian consensus by suggesting that the PLO began "where Qassam left off: his generation started the revolution: my generation intends to finish it."

During the 1920s and 1930s another development pregnant with significance for the future first began to influence both Muslim and Christian Palestinians. The *Protocols of the Elders of Zion* was translated into Arabic in the mid-1920s and spread more widely the theory of an organized Jewish conspiracy to achieve world domination. It demonized Jews as treacherous, venal, and permanently lusting for power. Modern Zionism would be consistently perceived in the light of these negative traits. A good example was the prominent Palestinian educator Khalil Sakakini, a Greek Orthodox Christian who wrote about historic "Jewish domination" of the Great Powers—whether of imperial Rome at the time of Jesus or of the British Empire during the mandate. Attacking what he considered to be the "morally and politically bankrupt" British administration in the 1930s, he added: "Who can have high regard for a [British] government which is totally under the Jewish sway, like a slave?" Sakakini warned that Jewish ambitions went far beyond Palestine. So, too, did another Palestinian leader, Rashid Hajj Ibrahim, writing in the late 1940s. He suggested that the Jews wanted to reconstruct the Solomonic empire, beginning with Syria and Lebanon, "because their Temple was built from Lebanon's cedars." But, he insisted, they also coveted Egypt (where Moses was born), Iraq (birthplace of Abraham), the Hejaz from whence Ishmael came, and Transjordan, which had been "part of Palestine and used to be a part of Solomon's kingdom."[34]

Throughout the interwar period, anti-Semitic motifs based on the "evil qualities" of Jews continued to flourish within the Palestinian national movement. Thus Jews were accused of bringing Bolshevik subversion to Palestine and the Middle East. Jews had indeed founded the Palestine Communist Party (and played a certain role in establishing the Communist parties of Syria, Lebanon, Iraq, and Egypt), but the interpretation that was given remained strictly anti-Semitic. Communism was presented as a Jewish creation that deliberately sowed disorder, chaos, unrest, and destruction—characteristics allegedly inherent in the Jewish race. The Arabic translation for "communist" was *ibahi*, meaning permissive, which linked Jewry by association to licentious social mores, sexual immorality, and societal anarchy.[35] The revolutionary Third Aliyah of the early 1920s from Communist Russia, the kibbutz lifestyle, and the apparent equality between the sexes in Jewish Palestine reinforced this myth of permissiveness with its threat to conservative Muslim tradition. The dramatic growth of the Jewish population in the 1930s and the increasing Nazi and fascist influences on Palestinian Arab nationalism further reinforced both the anti-Semitic and anticommunist motifs.

Arab nationalists in Palestine followed events in Europe closely. On the one hand, they welcomed the fact that Nazi Germany was ruthlessly putting the Jews in their place, but they were also aware that Nazi persecution in central Europe had led to a great wave of Jewish immigration to Palestine in the 1930s, clearly to their detriment. Nevertheless, ideological affinity evidently prevailed over self-interest. In March 1933, shortly after Hitler's rise to power, Haj Amin proposed to the German consul in Jerusalem that Nazi Germany and the Muslims announce a joint boycott against the Jews.[36] It is important to note that for Haj Amin and many who thought like him, the challenge the Arabs of Palestine were facing was *Jewish*; it was a conflict with the Jews much more than it was a fight against Zionism. The problem lay in *Jewish* immigration and *Jewish* efforts to take over Palestine. This was also the position of prominent Arab Palestinian nationalists like Muhammad Izza Darwaza (cofounder of the pan-Arab Istiqlal Party in the 1930s) and Arif al-Arif, another leader of the interwar Palestinian movement. They hardly mentioned the Zionists as such and saw the prime enemy, literally and conceptually, as the Jews.[37] Haj Amin, the scion of a distinguished and wealthy family of municipal and government officials, was no different in his outlook. It was the Jews as a global power (and as the partner of British imperialism) who had secretly conspired to dispossess the Arabs of Palestine.

A plot has been designed, long ago, between the Jews and Imperialism to evacuate the indigenous Arab population [of Palestine] from their homeland [in order] to settle the Jews who were scattered all over the world in their stead. The Arab character of this country, its religion, its sanctuaries and shrines were all doomed. Its inhabitants will be uprooted in order to turn it into a political religious and military center for all the Jews of the world. [38]

In his Arabic memoirs published in Cairo after the establishment of Israel, Haj Amin still referred to the "global Jewish center" as "a springboard against the Arab world." The armistice of 1949 had, in his account, been concluded with the Jews, not with Israel, let alone with the Zionist movement. This crucial anti-Semitic dimension is consistently downplayed in the literature on the Israeli-Palestinian conflict.

Until the late 1960s, there was virtually no distinction between Jews and Zionists for the Palestinian national movement. Every Jew was a Zionist, every Zionist was a Jew, and "both were enemies of the Arabs."[39] At an instinctive and emotional level, hatred, loathing, scorn, and contempt for Jews was the prevailing sentiment, and it had become well-anchored in contemporary Muslim thought. It was only a later generation of more secular Arab authors (influenced by Western and Soviet models) who sought after 1967 to turn the Palestinian struggle into a battle against Zionism—depicted as an amorphous, extremely powerful and frightening enemy.[40]

The first leader of the PLO, Ahmad Shuqayri (born into a wealthy, religious, and pro-Ottomanist Muslim family), was still in the mold of Haj Amin, though he did pay lip service to the fiction that Jews and Arabs had always lived peacefully together before Zionism. In his 1966 book *Liberation Not Negotiation,* however, Shuqayri pointed out that such observations did not mean that Arabs could ever live with Israel "in peace as good neighbours." On the contrary, peace would come only when Israel "ceases to exist," when Israelis went back to their "original countries," and after the "original people" of Palestine had returned to their homes. Israel would then pass away like the medieval Crusaders, leaving behind only ruined fortresses. On the eve of the Six-Day War, Shuqayri's rhetoric only aggravated the Mideast crisis—especially his promise that the "liberation" of Palestine meant that all Israeli Jews would "go back the way they came"; they had come by sea "and they will go back by sea."[41]

· · ·

The Arabs absorbed the language of "extermination" from the Nazis. This was already apparent in the 1930s in the influence of the Nazi example on Haj Amin, president of the Supreme Muslim Council in Palestine. The Palestinian youth organization that the mufti established adopted Hitler Youth–style shorts and leather belts before World War II, and operated for a time under the name of "Nazi Scouts." During the Palestinian uprising against Britain of 1936–39, the swastika was used as an identity marker; Arab children greeted one another with Hitler salutes; and large numbers of German flags and photographs of the führer were displayed, including on occasions such as the celebration of the Prophet Muhammad's birthday.[42]

During World War II, as we have seen, the mufti and Heinrich Himmler waxed lyrical about the ideological proximity of Islam and National Socialism, pointing to their common battle against the "Jewish world enemy."

Haj Amin's Islamicized anti-Semitism had, in fact, thoroughly crystallized more than a decade earlier. His war against the Jews was part of the broader fundamentalist struggle to combat liberal ideas, sexual permissiveness, and reform within the world of Islam. At a religious conference of 1935, the mufti specifically blamed Jews for "the cinema, the theatre, and some shameless magazines [that] enter our houses and courtyards like adders, where they kill morality and demolish the foundation of our society." The Jews, he complained, had "spread their customs and usages which are opposed to our religion and our whole way of life." He specifically singled out "the Jewish girls who run around in shorts [and] demoralize our youth by their presence."[43]

These puritanical strictures were almost identical to those made by the Muslim Brotherhood in Egypt. Their anti-Jewish agitation, including insistent calls for an economic boycott of Jewry and commitment to an exclusively Muslim-Arab Palestine, were becoming more and more vocal by the late 1930s. Not surprisingly, therefore, the mufti and the Brotherhood's founder-leader Hassan al-Banna discovered a common language that would extend beyond World War II and eventually culminate in the Palestinian Hamas movement, founded several decades after their deaths.[44]

The polarization of the Arab-Jewish conflict in Palestine since the early 1930s laid the foundations for its growing Islamicization, for spreading the Nazi poison, and for contaminating the region with the legacy of European anti-Semitism. The Palestinians, in particular, became addicted to the anti-Jewish jihad from which they have yet to be liberated. They imprisoned themselves in an a priori perception of Zionism and Western civilization as "absolute evils"—a Manichean outlook that prevented any pragmatic response to British, American, or Israeli policies. This was above all the legacy of the mufti of Jerusalem, the first to dress both Christian and Nazi-style anti-Semitism in a Koranic garb. His guiding assumption was that the "Jewish character" and the "Jewish methods" of the enemies of Islam had remained the same from the time of Muhammad until the present. The mufti imagined that the relentless Jewish determination to betray and ultimately destroy the Muslim faith had been constant since the birth of Islam. The reality was, to be sure, exactly the opposite. It was the mufti himself who had personally directed anti-Semitic incitement in Palestine, from the riots in Jerusalem (1920) through the anti-Jewish massacres in Hebron (1929) to the murders of Palestinian Jews during the great Arab revolt of 1936–39.[45] During World War II, he successfully convinced Adolf Hitler of his total dedication to the Nazi goal of eradicating the Jewish people and demonstrated how to use anti-Semitism as a major weapon in mobilizing an anti-Western mass movement in the Arab world. This commitment and his ardent embrace of the Final Solution provides (in the words of American analyst Kenneth Timmerman) "the common thread linking past to present. If today's Muslim anti-Semitism is like a tree with many branches, its roots feed directly off Hitler's Reich."[46]

The mufti never lost any opportunity to encourage Hitler, Himmler, Ribbentrop, and Eichmann in their *will to exterminate* European Jewry. He even helped to organize a Waffen-SS company composed of Bosnian Muslims (the "Hanjars") who slaughtered 90 percent of Bosnian Jewry and burned Serbian churches and villages. The mufti sent other Bosnian Muslims to Croatia and Hungary to assist in the killing of Jews.[47] German documents have recently surfaced that prove beyond any doubt that the Nazis had set in motion plans to wipe out the Jewish community of Palestine in accordance with Hitler's promises to the mufti. A special commando under the command of the high-ranking SS officer Walter Rauff (who fled to Chile after the war) was assigned to Rommel's Afrika Korps in the summer of 1942 in the expectation that with the conquest of Palestine, a Middle Eastern Final Solution would be implemented.[48] The virulent Jew-hatred promulgated by Haj Amin provided the ideological glue for these operational plans in which Palestinian Arabs would have been directly involved. They were intended to be the fulfillment of the strategic alliance between National Socialism and Islamic fundamentalism.[49] Only the British military victory over Rommel at El Alamein frustrated the consummation of this genocidal anti-Zionist and anti-Semitic project organized by the Reich Main Security Office in Berlin.

Although Yugoslavia, Great Britain, and the United States indicted the collaborationist mufti in 1945 as a war criminal, actual legal proceedings against him were abandoned in order not to upset the Arab world. By 1946 a de facto amnesty was in place that further enhanced his prestige after his so-called escape (with French complicity) from Paris. Once more, he was free to declare himself leader of the Palestinian Arabs, to wipe out dissenters, isolate the moderates, utterly reject the UN partition plan of 1947, and lead his people to disaster. The mufti's view was that the Arabs should jointly attack and completely destroy the Jews as soon as the British withdrew from Palestine. Like Hassan al-Banna, he considered the UN-sponsored division of Palestine to be a Zionist (Jewish) conspiracy, implemented by the Americans and Russians with secret British complicity. His *all-or-nothing* approach (which he bequeathed to Yasser Arafat) and his systematic incitement of anti-Jewish fears and hatred among the Arabs proved to be a catastrophe for Jews and Arabs alike, dealing a massive blow to Palestinian national aspirations.[50] Millions of Middle Eastern Muslims were indoctrinated in the false belief that Israel desired expansion at all costs and was only waiting for a pretext to destroy the holy shrines of Islam in Jerusalem.

• • •

Yasser Arafat and Haj Amin were related by blood. The PLO leader's mother was the daughter of the mufti's cousin. In his youth, Arafat fully internalized Haj Amin's hatred against Israel and passionate wish to pursue the terrorist jihad against the Jews. Among Arafat's first instructors in guerrilla warfare was a former Nazi commando officer imported to Egypt by the mufti.[51] Haj Amin himself encouraged Arafat to recruit adherents to his Fatah terror group during the late 1950s. Once Arafat became head of the PLO in 1968, he continued the mufti's methods and approach. *Mein Kampf* was required reading in some Fatah training camps; Nazis were recruited for Fatah and for the PLO, including Erich Altern, a key figure in the Jewish affairs section of the Gestapo, and Willy Berner, an SS officer in Mauthausen death camp. Among the neo-Nazis on the PLO payroll were the German Otto Albrecht and two Belgians, Karl van der Put and the secretary of the fascist *La Nation Européene*, Jean Tireault.[52]

But Arafat's continuation of the mufti's legacy went far beyond the use of former Nazis—a propensity he shared with Gamal Abdel Nasser, ardent admirer of Haj Amin. The two Palestinian leaders shared a common devotion to terrorism, fanaticism, and ruthlessness as methods of struggle. In that respect Kenneth Timmerman is correct in seeing Haj Amin as "the founding father of the PLO in both spirit and practice."[53] In April 1985, Arafat himself made a public speech confirming his pride in being the mufti's pupil and in following the path pioneered by Haj Amin.[54] As late as August 2, 2002, he still referred to the mufti as a "hero" and an inspiring symbol in "withstanding world pressure" and remaining "an Arab leader in spite of demands to have him replaced because of his Nazi ties."[55] In adamantly resisting American pressure to reform the Palestinian Authority the PLO leader saw himself as following the mufti's intransigent example.

Arafat's bloodstained record as PLO leader for nearly four decades entitles him to be considered the "godfather of modern terrorism." His career involved the cruel premeditated murder of countless Israeli and Jewish civilians, and of American and other diplomats (as in Khartoum in 1973). He gave orders to organize the Munich Olympic Games massacre and actively promoted two intifadas. Arafat nearly destroyed Jordan in 1970 and helped to trigger the horrendous Lebanese civil war of the 1970s. He unequivocally supported Saddam Hussein's brutalization of Kuwait in 1990–91. Together with George Habash's PFLP, his group pioneered airline hijacking on a large scale. The PLO became the pivot of international terrorism in training, finance, and inspiration during the 1970s, with active links to the Irish Republican Army, the West German Baader-Meinhof faction, the Japanese Red Army, and many other violent terror organizations. Its assassinations, attempted coups, and constant efforts at subversion destabilized the Middle East for decades. Although the Jewish state remained its main target, between 1968 and 1980 alone, the PLO committed over two hundred major terrorist acts in or against countries other than Israel. According to John Laffin, during this period, the PLO attacked "40 civilian passenger aircraft, five passenger ships, 30 embassies or diplomatic missions and about the same number of economic targets."[56]

None of this havoc and mayhem prevented Arafat from being rapturously received at the United Nations, which he addressed while wearing a pistol and hypocritically bearing "an olive branch."[57] Even in the heyday of his terrorist exploits in the 1970s and 1980s, Arafat was feted, lionized, and given red-carpet treatment by the world's top diplomats and dignitaries, including Soviet president Leonid Brezhnev, Austrian chancellor Bruno Kreisky, the prime ministers of Spain and India, and His Holiness John Paul II. In 1974 the Arab world recognized the PLO as "the sole legitimate representative of the Palestinian people," an important landmark on Arafat's long march to international recognition. Six years later, the British foreign secretary, Lord Carrington, blandly stated that he did not believe "that the PLO as such is a terrorist organization"; also in 1980 the French president Giscard d'Estaing echoed Arafat's own propaganda about the need for Palestinian national self-determination given the PLO's moderate, nonviolent, reasonable character. Yet, in that same year, Arafat had spelled out the PLO's true aims with crystal clarity during a visit to Venezuela.

> Peace for us means the destruction of Israel. We are preparing for an all-out war, a war which will last for generations. . . . We shall not rest until the day when we return to our home, and until we destroy Israel. . . . The destruction of Israel is the goal of our struggle, and the guidelines of that struggle have remained firm since the establishment of Fatah in 1965.

To this very day, prominent figures in the PLO such as Farouk Kaddoumi have continued to emphasize that the PLO will not recognize Israel, "even if an independent Palestinian State is established." In June 1980 the Fatah's Damascus congress had already confirmed this classic hard-line position, defining its aim as being "to liberate Palestine completely, and to liquidate the Zionist entity politically, economically, militarily, culturally and ideologically."[58] A year earlier in Beirut Arafat boasted that the Palestinian people "will continue to fuel the torch of the revolution with rivers of blood until the whole of the occupied homeland is liberated . . . not just part of it."[59] This insistently proclaimed maximalist and de facto genocidal PLO strategy did not deter most European leaders in the closing years of the twentieth century from appeasing terrorism in the name of an increasingly illusory peace process.

The PLO considered itself to be both the sole legitimate representative of the Palestinian people and the "vanguard of the Revolution"—the undisputed leader of the Arab masses against reactionary Arab regimes. Though financed by Saudi Arabia and other highly conservative oil-producing Gulf states, it formally opposed the Arab monarchies and the more Western-oriented states, speaking in terms of a war of "popular liberation" within the Arab world, in addition to the eradication of Israel. In its 1973 political program the PLO proudly posed as "an integral part of the militant movement against imperialism and racism" and for national liberation throughout the world.[60] In this Third Worldist posture it enjoyed substantial military, logistic, diplomatic, and propaganda support from the USSR and the Communist bloc, along with their many surrogates and front organizations around the world. This did not prevent the PLO from allying itself at times to neo-Nazi enemies of Western liberal democracy, such as the West

German Wehrsportsgruppe Hoffman, who established their training camps under Fatah auspices. Nor did it stop PLO rejectionists from collaborating with French anarcho-terrorists to bomb the rue Copernic synagogue in 1980. PLO groups were also implicated in a terrorist slaughter at the Bologna railway station where eighty-five people were killed and about three hundred injured. Another explosion, at a Munich beer hall on September 26, injured a similar number and killed thirteen Oktoberfest participants. According to Lebanon Radio on June 25, 1981, these mall murders were planned by one of Arafat's closest henchman, Abu Iyad, together with Italian and German terrorists.[61]

In the aftermath of the Six-Day War, there were some efforts to modify the ultranationalist character of the PLO. For example, the Democratic Front for the Liberation of Palestine (DFLP), led by Nayef Hawatmeh, preached an Arab form of Marxism-Leninism, advocated a close alliance with the USSR, and sought to inject a greater dose of "revolutionary realism" into PLO ranks. Though insisting on the need for "armed struggle" inside Israel and the territories, they were the first to advocate accepting an independent state in part of Palestine as an important first step toward implementing the ultimate aim. This "doctrine of stages" (which did *not* renounce the final aim of "liberating" all of Palestine) would indeed be adopted by the PLO as a whole in 1974.[62] Hawatmeh's Popular Democratic Front, while denouncing Israel as an "expansionist," "colonialist," and "chauvinist" entity, also condemned "reactionary" Arab slogans such as "throwing the Jews into the sea." Instead, it proposed dissolving and "de-Zionizing" Israel in favor of a "popular democratic Palestine" where Jews and Arabs could coexist without discrimination, class, or national oppression.[63] In 1970 Fatah, too, spoke in terms of a new progressive, democratic secular state of Palestine that would be tolerant of all races, colors, and religions. The Palestinian Revolution—so it promised—would replace the existing "racist settler-state" with a pluralist, multiconfessional utopia. But first of all, the economic, political, and military structures of Israel would have to be shattered.[64]

PLO propaganda maintained a democratic façade in the 1970s while advocating the *disappearance* of the Jewish state and its substitution by a *Palestinian Arab State* in which Muslim, Christian, and Jewish Palestinians could live in harmony. There was, however, no question of allowing Jews to define themselves. Fatah did not accept the idea of national self-determination and an independent state for Jews in the Middle East. Despite the pluralist façade, Zionism was demonized even by the leftist Palestinians, and any historic Jewish connection to the land of Israel was consistently negated.[65] What was being offered beneath the pseudo-Marxist mask of "liberation" was no more than the traditional *dhimmi* status in Arab lands without any Jewish national, collective, or sovereign dimension.[66] At best the Jews would be acceptable in Palestine as a small and insignificant minority like the Armenians or Circassians; they could be absorbed as anti-Zionist individuals but never as a *people* with national rights and a three-thousand-year-old history intimately linked to the land of Israel.

These assumptions underlay the Palestinian National Covenant of 1968, which explicitly denied Israel's right to exist in nearly half of its thirty-three articles.[67] Article 20, for example, declared

the Balfour Declaration, the Mandate for Palestine, and everything that has been based upon them . . . null and void. Claims of historical or religious ties of Jews with Palestine are incompatible with the facts of history and the true conception of what constitutes statehood. Judaism, being a religion, is not an independent nationality. Nor do Jews constitute a single nation with an identity of its own. [68]

The whole of Palestine was declared to be "the homeland of the Arab Palestinian people" and "an indivisible part of the Arab homeland." Article 6 stated that Jews would *not* be considered Palestinian unless they normally resided there *before* "the beginning of the Zionist invasion" (possibly 1917, or even 1882). That clause would effectively have barred the great majority of Jews from citizenship.[69] While the Palestinian identity was defined as a "genuine, essential, and inherent characteristic" (one transmitted from parents to children), the Jewish national identity, as expressed in Zionism, was branded as wholly inauthentic, illegitimate, illegal, and contradictory to the natural right to self-determination of the Palestinians. Article 22 unabashedly caricatured Zionism as "organically associated with international imperialism and antagonistic to all action for liberation and to progressive movements in the world." The Zionist movement was declared to be "racist and fanatic in its nature, aggressive, expansionist and colonial in its aims, and fascist in its methods." Israel was its instrument and a base for world imperialism set up to frustrate "the hopes of the Arab nation for liberation, unity, and progress." Not only that, but Israel was a constant "source of threat" toward peace in the Middle East and the whole world. Hence its destruction and the "liberation of Palestine" deserved "the support of all the progressive and peaceful forces" (classic Soviet Communist doublespeak), and required the mobilization of Palestinian revolutionary forces to fulfill their historic vanguard role within the Arab nation.[70]

In December 1968, the Israeli scholar Yehoshafat Harkabi published a penetrating critique of Fatah's revolutionary doctrine, noting that the Palestinian fedayeen advocated the extinction of a whole society and not just the elimination of the State of Israel. They aspired to blot out the human and social character, as well as the economic, intellectual, military, and political institutions of the Jewish state. Zionism and Israel were depicted as "an aberrant mistaken phenomenon" that had to be annihilated, even though Fatah generally avoided such blunt language in its publications aimed at a Western audience. Fatah realized that what they called "uprooting of the Zionist existence or entity" was concretely "embodied in a *society*"; thus their objective moved from "politicide" (the demise of the Israeli state) to genocide—since to liquidate a large Jewish population would inevitably involve "a great deal of killing."[71] One way to disguise the genocidal implications of their own doctrines was to envisage the "de-Zionizing of Israel," implying that Israel would somehow disappear of itself as a form of Jewish statehood. This deliberately deceptive formula (like the "secular democratic state of Palestine") was positively welcomed by a section of the radical Western Left. The Palestinian adulation of violence, "armed struggle," vengeance, and *thauria* (revolutionarism) nonetheless belied any pacifist interpretations of "de-Zionization." On the contrary, Arafat and his followers viewed the Israel-Palestine conflict as a zero-sum game, a deadly confrontation that would necessarily involve the annihilation of one of the protagonists.[72]

Arafat's PLO did, however, try to preserve some distinction between "Zionism" (a synonym for colonialist evil) and "Judaism" (a monotheistic religion worthy of respect). This fact led many analysts to mistakenly assume that European-style and Islamist anti-Semitism were alien to the Palestinian Arab national movement: that they had only developed because of Arab military defeats and the damage Palestinians had suffered at Zionist hands—including physical expulsion in some cases, prolonged exile, military occupation and the colonization of many areas in Judea, Samaria, and Gaza that were previously under Arab control.[73] But as we have shown, neither the emergence of Israel as a state in 1948 nor the Six-Day War (both seen as traumas and catastrophes by most Palestinians) were the root cause of their anti-Jewish sentiments. Neither Haj Amin nor al-Qassam was merely fighting Zionism as a political movement in the pre-Israel period; nor were they at all friendly or welcoming to local Jews. They made it clear that any significant Jewish minority would be unacceptable in an independent Palestinian Arab state.

The only political group with any influence among Arabs that ever envisaged the possibility of coexistence with Jews as a collectivity and opposed Arab anti-Semitism with any conviction was the Palestinian Communist Party. It had been founded by Jewish immigrants in 1919 and recruited among Arab members before 1948. But it was far too small to transform wider Palestinian perceptions of the conflict or to overcome the ethnic divide.[74] The Palestine Communists were, in any case, as anti-Zionist as the local nationalists, pan-Arabists, and Islamic fundamentalists in Palestine. The main difference was that nakedly racist notions and the myth of a worldwide Jewish conspiracy stood in ideological conflict with the Marxist-Leninist theory of imperialism they had embraced. The Palestinian Communists hoped to abort the Zionist project in the 1930s, but they were not hostile to Jews qua Jews. This cannot be said of Yasser Arafat, Farouk Kaddoumi, Mahmond Abbas, and other post-1967 Palestinian leaders with the same confidence. In their narrative the demonization of world Zionism and Israel as satanic forces with extraordinary influence in international politics is normal and, at times, reminiscent of the *Protocols* scenario.

The dominant image of plotting and scheming Zionists who stealthily took over Palestine to satisfy their insatiable rapacity and will to power structurally resembles classic anti-Semitic paradigms. By the 1950s, many Palestinians had come under the spell of widely circulating anti-Jewish literature (including the *Protocols* in Arabic), that was available in far greater quantities than at any previous time.[75] The portrayal of Jews as pernicious, destructive agents of modernity was extremely effective immediately after the creation of Israel and the humiliating defeat of the Arab states. The time was ripe for extra-rational explanations. How could the Jews have succeeded in conquering Palestine against all odds, unless they secretly exerted extraordinary power on a global scale? In the pan-Arab discourse *before*

1967, which had greatly shaped Palestinian core perceptions, this sense of occult Jewish influence had already played a significant role. Zionist achievements were primarily attributed to a sinister ability to manipulate British and American politics. This anti-Semitic myth further envenomed the feelings of bitterness and injustice experienced by many Palestinians in the course of a protracted and, from their point of view, deeply frustrating conflict.

After the Six-Day War, PLO leaders did make a conscious effort *not* to appear anti-Semitic, at least in their appeals to a Western audience. But a closer analysis of their rhetoric reveals that at bottom they simply transferred the negative stereotypes of Jews to the Jewish state.[76] By portraying Israel as an artificial creature of Western imperialism doomed to collapse and Zionism as a vicious, racist, and criminal distortion of Judaism, the PLO thought it could finally square the circle. It would totally delegitimize Israel, appear to reject classical anti-Semitism, and claim to "liberate" Jews from Zionism. Since, however, the great majority of Jews continued to support Israel's existence and security, these postures clearly strained credulity. True, there was no shortage of dissident, highly assimilated, or Marxist Jews, as well as some liberal rabbis (and even black-coated anti-Zionist Haredim), willing to play Arafat's game. But they still remained a small minority in the larger Jewish world, at least until the ill-fated Oslo peace process began in 1993. Only then did an increasing number of Israelis and Diaspora Jews (some of them very highly placed), along with the United Nations and most international statesmen (including President Clinton), fall into the trap of certifying Arafat as kosher, granting him full legitimacy, and transmuting him into a "moderate," a dove worthy of the Nobel Peace Prize, and a true "partner for peace"![77]

This foolish act of self-deception, which resulted in the signing of the Oslo peace accords, dramatically increased Palestinian violence against Israel instead of reducing it; negotiation and terror proceeded in tandem with all the burden placed on Israel to prove its bona fides.[78] Not for a moment during this time did Arafat desist from his incitement against the Jewish state and encouragement of jihad among his own people. This was accompanied by all kinds of fantastic tales about the Israeli will to create an empire "from the Nile to the Euphrates," despite Israel's complete withdrawal from Sinai. According to Arafat and a number of other Arab leaders, there was a "map on the Knesset wall," which, it was said, displayed Israel's coveted biblical boundaries from Egypt to Iraq. Then came the Palestinian allegation (still repeated today) that the two blue stripes on the Israeli flag represented the two great rivers (the Nile and the Euphrates).[79]

Palestinian propaganda against Israel has indeed been full of the most repulsive statements of hatred toward the Jews and Zionism. The Palestinian ambassador to the UN Commission on Human Rights in Geneva, Nabil Ramlawi, stunned delegates in March 1997 by declaring that "Israeli authorities . . . infected by injection 300 Palestinian children with the HIV virus during the intifada."[80] The commander of the Palestinian General Security Service in Gaza no less mendaciously blamed Israel for encouraging "Russian Jewish girls with AIDS to spread the disease among Palestinian youth."[81] The PA minister of supplies, Abdel Hamid al-Quds, went one step further, telling *Yediot Ahronoth* that Israelis were food poisoners: "Israel is distributing food containing material that causes cancer and hormones that harm male virility and spoiled food products in order to poison and harm the Palestinian population."[82] In another updated version of the medieval blood libel, at a press conference in the presence of Hillary Clinton (then U.S. First Lady), Suha Arafat, wife of the PA president, falsely accused Israel of poisoning Palestinian air and water. At the 2001 World Economic Forum in Davos, Switzerland, President Arafat himself shocked the audience by saying that Israel was using depleted uranium and nerve gas against Palestinian civilians.[83] Such inflammatory anti-Semitic falsifications, recycled or repeated in endless variations in the Palestinian media, contribute nothing constructive to the struggle against Israeli occupation. But they reveal a culture of hatred that has over several decades turned into self-defeating nihilism, rather than a serious form of politics.[84]

As part of its anti-Semitic incitement, the PLO has consistently presented Zionism as the "embodiment of neo-Nazism" at every conceivable international forum.[85] Arafat never lost an opportunity to characterize Israeli detention centers as "concentration camps," or the equivalent of Auschwitz. The Palestinian leader also regularly tried to appropriate Jewish and Christian identity—for example, by turning the intifada stone throwers into a collective Palestinian David. Equally characteristic were Arafat's statements at a September 2, 1983, press conference in Geneva (under UN auspices) that transmuted Jesus into a Palestinian martyr: "We were under Roman imperialism. We sent a Palestinian fisherman, called St. Peter, to Rome. He not only occupied Rome, but also won the hearts of the people.

We know how to resist imperialism and occupation. Jesus Christ was the first Palestinian militant *fedayin* who carried his sword along the path on which the Palestinians carry their Cross." This was not the first or last time that Arafat and other prominent Palestinians would steal the Jesus symbol, turning the Jews of ancient Judea into Palestine Arabs. Received in Rome by John Paul II on September 15, 1983, the PLO leader told the pope (in all seriousness) that he felt at home in the Vatican, seat of the successors to Saint Peter, "the first Palestinian exile."

Such shameless abuse of Christian symbols continued in the Palestinian media throughout the 1970s. It was not uncommon to see Fatah posters showing Jesus nailed to a Star of David, with the caption "Palestine" to mark his crucifixion. During the second Palestinian intifada, this anti-Semitic merging of past and present in order to link the Palestinian "Via Dolorosa" with the deicide charge reached new heights. On December 11, 2000, the new Palestinian daily, *Intifada,* graphically showed a crucified young woman called "Palestine" on its front page—blood flowing from her pierced hands and feet. Here is historian David G. Littman's graphic description of the offending caricature:

> A long spear transfixes her body to the cross, its protruding point embossed with a Star of David and an American flag at the shaft end. Blood spurts from her martyred body down upon a trio of huddled, caricatured Oriental Jews, who are looking up and grimacing at the crucified young woman, clearly meant to symbolize Jesus and "Palestine."[86]

The barely subliminal message is insidious. The murderers of Christ are the same Jewish devils who are today oppressing the Palestinian people.

Arafat and the PLO usurped Jesus, Peter, Paul, and Mary—all of them Jews by birth—for the narrow cause of their anti-Semitic Palestinian nationalism. Arafat's version of the Christian savior as a militant Palestinian fedayeen is indeed little different from Adolf Hitler's self-serving transfiguration (around 1921) of Jesus into a Germanic warrior "Christ" heading a popular anti-Jewish movement in Galilee. In Arafat's case, the de-Judaizing process was perhaps even more outlandish. For example, in October 2002, in an interview with the London Arabic-language daily *Al-Hayat,* the PLO leader insisted that the Temple of Solomon had never existed in Jerusalem or in Palestine.[87] In concocting this pseudo-Palestinian history, Arafat in effect denigrated both Judaism and Christianity, which he sought to supplant in the name of a totally Arabized Holy Land. Indeed, he pillaged and usurped Jewish identity whenever it suited him, to bolster universal recognition of Palestinian victimhood as a unique form of suffering.

At the same time, the PLO has always insisted on the Islamic component in its political self-definition, using the Koran and Muslim religious terminology to buttress its anti-Jewish beliefs. For example, in November 1989, Abu Iyad (then the PLO's second in command) neatly combined Islamist and anti-Semitic motifs: "It is [an] incontrovertible fact that Palestine is Arab-Islamic and that the Jews are the scum of humanity that gathered from the four corners of the earth and conquered our land, encouraged by the powers. Will the Jews keep a promise? Treachery flows in their blood, as the Qur'an testifies. The Jews are the same as they have always been."[88]

The PLO was not only anti-Semitic at its core (even as it pretended to "liberate" the Jews) but proved to be a master in the art of defamation as diplomacy. Not surprisingly, some of its greatest political successes were achieved at the United Nations, where its prime objective was always to delegitimize Israel and turn it into a pariah ostracized by the international community. From the early 1970s, with the active support of the USSR, the Communist bloc, and the Arab world, the PLO began to equate Israel with South Africa as a racist state. This was perceived as an effective way to demonstrate the illegal nature of the "Zionist entity" and to undermine its right to exist.[89] The Zionism = Racism label, strenuously pushed by the PLO, was in part designed to alienate black Africa from Israel, to strike at U.S. diplomacy in the Third World, and to drive a wedge between Jews and blacks in North America. The Zionism = Racism resolution was an unmistakable collective slander against the Jewish people that Jeane J. Kirkpatrick, the U.S. ambassador to the United Nations at the time, accurately described in an April 19, 1985, speech in New York as a form of anti-Semitism that was "bold, unashamed, and revolting."[90]

The PLO played a central role in encouraging the spread of this anti-Jewish "political cancer" throughout the UN system. Ahmad Shuqayri, Yasser Arafat, and Saudi ambassador Jamil Baroody did not invent the political exploitation of such bigotry at the United Nations, but they greatly intensified its use as a weapon to undermine the democratic world and to hijack the cause of international human rights. Ahmad Shuqayri, first leader of the PLO and pungently described by one pro-Arab British journalist as "a sort of cross between Adolf Hitler and the Reverend Ian Paisley," had, for example, made the following prophecy concerning the future of Israel's Jews on June 1, 1967: "Those who survive will remain in Palestine. I estimate that none of them will survive."[91] Fortunately, Shuqayri's prediction proved totally wrong only a week later, when the Israel Defense Forces decisively crushed three Arab armies massed to destroy her.

Shuqayri's anti-Semitism had been legendary since the time when he represented Saudi Arabia at the United Nations. In a seven-hour speech to the General Assembly in the fall of 1961 he had singled out American Jews for placing the U.S. government in "Zionist captivity"; he warned that American statesmen could never be trusted until they had been "liberated from Zionism." The following year he demanded in the General Assembly that the United States and the United Nations outlaw and "exterminate" the Zionists. He also saluted the viciously anti-Semitic Tacuara organization in Argentina (funded in part by Arab money), recommending its spread throughout Latin America, and even requested that the United Nations formally "adopt" this Argentine fascist movement. Shuqayri's proposal received an indignant response from the Argentine and Chilean representatives, as well as from many other delegates. But such racist bigotry could hardly dissuade Egyptian president Nasser (who shared similar views) from appointing Shuqayri as the first chairman of the PLO in 1964. Shuqayri's hostility to Jews was echoed by other PLO spokespeople, especially in the Third World. Thus, the PLO representative told Radio Sandino in Nicaragua on March 31, 1981, that the Zionists intended to mobilize "the 500,000 Jews in Argentina to form their second state in the area of Patagonia." In other words, they would seize control of the southern part of the country.[92] This *Protocols* script was a favorite theme of right-wing and neo-Nazi anti-Semites in Argentina, which the PLO was perfectly willing to encourage.

The PLO was also extremely active in efforts to expel "the Zionist entity" from the United Nations, an explicit demand made by Yasser Arafat at the July–August 1975 Organization of African Unity (OAU) conference in Kampala. In August that year, the pressure intensified at the Lima, Peru, nonaligned foreign ministers conference, but the PLO proposal was opposed by Egypt, which still needed to sign its second disengagement accord with Israel under UN auspices. Despite this temporary setback, the November 1975 General Assembly Resolution formally condemning Zionism as racism was an important victory for the PLO, the Soviet Union, and the Arab world. In the longer run, it represented a devastating blow to the moral integrity of the United Nations. As U.S. ambassador Daniel Moynihan prophetically told the General Assembly: "There will be time enough to contemplate the harm this act will have done the United Nations. Historians will do that for us, and it is sufficient for the moment only to note one foreboding fact. A great evil has been loosed upon the world. The abomination of anti-semitism . . . has been given the appearance of international sanction."[93]

The PLO's role in propagating this evil was considerable and made worse by their calculated hypocrisy in pretending to distinguish between "Zionist" and "Jew." George Habash was more honest in saying that the real enemy was not Western imperialism but "international Judaism." This elastic label was made to include "all Jews from the far left to the extreme Right." The PFLP spokesman Ghassan Kanafani, a gifted novelist who was later assassinated by Israel, was another Palestinian with a pathological hatred for Jews. In these and many other cases, calling Zionism a form of racism was little more than a verbal masquerade, though it was one increasingly in tune with the prevailing spirit of the age.[94]

Neo-anti-Semitism was clearly emerging at the end of the 1970s as a coded political language barely concealed behind the war against Israel and the West. Its major thrust came from two different extremes that had begun to converge—Soviet hegemony and Islamic fundamentalism. In March 1979 George Habash himself commented on this improbable and temporary alliance at whose intersection stood his own radical wing of the PLO: "Many have been surprised that we, as Marxists, should be on the side of a religious movement like Khomeini's. But beyond ideology, we have in common anti-imperialist, anti-Zionist and anti-Israeli elements."[95] Nowhere was this alliance more visible than at the United Nations, where it often seemed in the late 1970s that the PLO had more influence than the United States, especially on issues relating to the Middle East. In areas such as Central and Latin America (where anti-Americanism was strong), PLO activity against the United States and Israel was especially intense in this period and enjoyed extensive UN backing. PLO political positions were generally endorsed by the Arab League, the Islamic Conference, the Non-Aligned Movement, and the OAU, as well as by the entire Communist bloc, led by the Soviet Union. Far from having any moderating influence, this allowed the PLO to mount its terrorist challenge to Israel while garnering more and more international support for its destructive goals. Arafat continued his references to *all* of Israel as "occupied territory"; Farouk Kaddoumi remorselessly repeated his mantra about never recognizing Israel, "the usurper, the colonialist, the imperialist"; Salah Khalaf (also known as Abu Iyad) even promised that a Palestinian state in the West Bank and Gaza would be "the beginning of the final solution." This same Fatah leader told *The New York Times* in 1986 that "armed struggle is permanent politics for the PLO."[96]

The UN General Assembly contributed a great deal to nourishing Arafat's terrorist cause, his hubris, and his deadly fantasies about destroying Israel. During his uncompromising 1974 UN address, Arafat had been interrupted no less than nine times by rapturous applause, receiving a truly thundering ovation at the end. In unconditionally supporting the PLO, its fanaticism, its defamation of Israel, its terrorism, and hate-filled tirades against the Jewish people, the United Nations gave it the stamp of international legitimacy. No less disastrously, the spineless appeasement of gangsterism and bigotry paralyzed any prospects for a rational resolution of the Arab-Israeli conflict; it helped to drag the Palestinians into further ruinous defeats, while sparking deep Israeli revulsion against an international body whose raison d'être had come to be the pillorying of the Jewish state.

Contrary to received wisdom, the basic positions of the PLO, laid down forty years ago, have changed little since 1968. The ultimate objective remains a Palestine that is *judenrein,* beginning with Judea. Under no circumstances is the PLO ready to relinquish "the right of return." Four decades ago the present leader of the Palestinian Authority in the West Bank, Mahmoud Abbas, said in a September, 28, 1979, interview in *Al-Ra'i:* "No Palestinian will be found who does not want to return to his homeland. If the Palestinians are given the choice between compensation and return, no one would agree to take compensation and give up the return."[97] This is still the official position of the Palestinian national movement. Thirty years ago Farouk Kaddoumi (still an influential voice in the PLO) told a Western interviewer: "There are two initial phases to our return. The first is to the 1967 lines, the second—to the 1948 lines . . . the third stage is the democratic state of Palestine."[98]

Kaddoumi did not change his ideological or political views since then any more than the rest of the PLO leadership. Fatah never truly renounced the "armed struggle" (a euphemism for terrorism) or the "right of return."

Arafat, too, never fundamentally revised his core beliefs, although the massive deception he practiced during the Oslo peace process led many around the world to imagine that he had abandoned the "total liberation of Palestine." At the Palestine National Council (PNC) meeting in Algiers in November 1988, during the first intifada, he appeared to recognize Israel, yet he continued to refer to it as "occupied Palestine." His top aide bluntly called the idea of a West Bank–Gaza state at best "a short-term solution."[99] On May 2, 1989, Arafat told French television network TF1 that the PLO covenant was "*caduque*" (null and void), but the following day, on Europe 1 Radio, he emphasized that only a two-thirds majority of the PNC could officially abrogate the charter.[100] This has yet to happen, despite all the propaganda to the contrary. Similarly, while declaring his desire for peace to foreign audiences in English, Arafat repeated to his own people in Arabic the need to intensify the Palestinian jihad, martyrdom, and violent confrontation.

On May 10, 1994, only ten days after the Gaza-Jericho agreement with Israel (a follow-up of the Oslo accords), Arafat spoke in a Johannesburg mosque—not realizing that he was being secretly recorded. His entire speech was a deliberate incitement "to start the jihad to liberate Jerusalem" (presented as the "first shrine" of Islam) from the "continuous conspiracy" to demolish it. The PLO leader emphasized that Jerusalem was exclusively *Muslim*, not Israeli or Jewish; there could only be "the permanent State of Palestine," but not Israel. Evoking Muhammad's ten-year peace treaty (the Hudaibiya pact) with the non-Muslim, polytheist Quraysh tribe that controlled Mecca, his covert message to the audience was that when the time was ripe, Palestinians would find a pretext and do battle.[101] Faisal al-Husseini (a so-called moderate in the PA), in the last interview he gave before his death in 2001, was even more explicit about the peace process as a PLO ruse. He compared Oslo to the Greek myth of the Trojan horse and the second intifada to "climbing out of the horse" in order to ambush the Israelis and liberate "all of historic Palestine from the [Jordan] River to the [Mediterranean] Sea."[102]

Faisal al-Husseini, like virtually all Palestinian spokesmen, publicly preached the unconditional right of return of the refugees and their children (by their own estimates about four million people) to their original homes. This would be tantamount to Israel's destruction by demographic means. With the exception of Jordan, for the last sixty years no Arab state has been willing to even consider the integration of these exiled Palestinians, despite having encouraged them in 1948 to flee in the first place. Instead, the Arab world has cynically preferred to let their brethren rot in squalid camps for decades as a tool for cultivating hatred against Israel. Typically, the Arab states were never ready to recognize the ravages of Arab ethnic cleansing, and the nationalist anti-Semitism that led to the uprooting of almost one million Sephardic Jews from Muslim lands after 1945.[103] An exodus no less dramatic than that of the Palestinians from Israel, it has barely registered as a ripple on the UN radar screen, let alone in international politics.

The smoldering hatred of Israel long nurtured by Arafat and his followers finally erupted on the eve of Rosh Hashanah (September 29, 2000). Already on the second day of the new intifada, the killing of a twelve-year-old Palestinian boy, Muhammad al-Dura, allegedly shot dead by Israeli soldiers at the Netzarim junction in the Gaza Strip, greatly envenomed the atmosphere. His apparent death in front of his helpless father seemed to have been filmed in real time by a local cameraman for French state-owned television (France-2), and the network's Jerusalem-based correspondent, Charles Enderlin, overconfidently affirmed (without verification) that the Israeli army was responsible. Almost instantly, the young al-Dura became the new martyr and icon of the Palestinian struggle, and an emblem of the Israeli government's deliberate cruelty. His death would henceforth be constantly dramatized and replayed on Palestinian TV, used in al-Qaeda recruitment videos, on posters, murals, and to adorn postage stamps. Schools, streets, and squares would be named after him across the Middle East. Only gradually did serious doubts emerge about the truth of what the Palestinian cameraman Talal Abu Rahmeh claimed to have filmed, about the reliability of the footage, and the assertion that al-Dura had been killed by gunshots from an Israeli position. There was a growing suspicion that the events at Netzarim junction might well have been staged and that if al-Dura had really died it was from Palestinian bullets. To salvage its reputation, France-2 initiated a legal action against those who challenged its report, but the French court of appeals eventually found in favor of French Jewish media critic Philippe Karsenty, ruling in May 2008 that he had not libeled the TV station or Enderlin. For the dogged Karsenty (who had fought his campaign with virtually no help from the Israeli government), this vindication was a victory for freedom of criticism and a blow against one of the most toxic anti-Semitic lies of the early twenty-first century—that the Israel Defense Forces are an "army of child-killers."[104] The case certainly cast a heavy shadow over the worldwide outrage provoked by al-Dura's "filmed" death (a huge cause célèbre in the Muslim world), which had done so much to damage Israel's reputation and to escalate violence in the region.

Since October 2000, the image of the Palestinian "child-martyr" (*shahid*) Muhammad al-Dura had come to supplant that of the frightened Jewish child in the Warsaw ghetto, hands raised in the air before a threatening SS soldier. It had become a symbol of the "Jewish racism" and militarism that had supposedly replaced Nazi-racist anti-Semitism. It had some of the hallmarks of an updated television-age ritual murder—adapted to the requirements of the new millennium with the State of Israel as the defendant in the dock. Its soldiers, according to the prevailing mythology, gratuitously murdered innocent Arab victims. Its military machine was a ruthless Goliath and a vampiric monster literally and metaphorically draining Palestinian children of their life's blood. Such demonology was a gift both to the global jihad and to the somewhat flagging Palestinian cause in the autumn of 2000. For the Palestinian Islamists, in particular, an anti-Semitic "holy war" against the Israeli child-killers provided a powerful emotional edge to their ideological motivation. It reinforced archetypal images of the criminal Jews—the slayers of the prophets and satanic enemies of Islam, who had defiled the Holy Land. For Arafat, too, it provided a new impetus for his appeals to mass martyrdom and for marching on Jerusalem, until the flag of Palestine would "fly over its minarets and churches."

After unleashing the second intifada in September 2000, Arafat seemed to be in his element once more, demonstrating his talents as a master arsonist. His megalomania was continually fed by benighted Palestinian crowds chanting, "With our blood and our souls, we redeem you, oh Arafat." His disordered imagination now ran riot with the prospect that a firestorm of successive suicide bombings would definitively break Israel's spirit and reverse the verdict of the 1948 war. Like millions of other Arabs, Arafat seemed truly intoxicated with the idea that the Jewish state, like the Latin Crusader kingdom of the thirteenth century, was doomed to fall; and convinced, like Farouk Kaddoumi, that "the Right of Return [to Haifa, Jaffa, and Acre] is more important than statehood."

Israel's Labor leaders, Yitzhak Rabin and Shimon Peres, in an extraordinary series of misjudgments, had plucked Arafat from the nadir of his exile in Tunis and allowed him to return to Palestine; they had even helped to arm the PLO cohorts with sixty thousand guns, which would eventually be turned on Israelis in the service of terror. Arafat's subterfuges and his many violations of solemn agreements were disregarded or played down. In the light of such Israeli credulity and weakness, Arafat felt that his enemy was on the run. The result was a new and unprecedented wave of terror at the end of 2000, a cult of blood, death, and *shahids* (martyrs). As Fouad Ajami pointed out, these martyrs had walked "straight out of the culture of incitement let loose on the land, a menace hovering over Israel, a great Palestinian and Arab refusal to let that country be, to cede it a place among the nations."[105]

Naked racial and religious hatred, instilled in the Palestinians from the cradle to the grave, has been integral to the old-new holy war. A seemingly inexhaustible hostility toward Jews, Judaism, and Israel swept over the Palestinian public throughout the 1990s (in flagrant contradiction to the PA's obligations under the Oslo accords). There were constant horror stories about Jews as "poisoners of wells," "bloodsucking Shylocks," vampiric monsters, satanic imperialists, and implacable enemies of Islam.[106] The Bible and the Talmud were objects of special abuse, deemed to be major sources of Jewish moral depravity and the fountain of a unique "racial and religious zealotry" attributed to Judaism. In one Palestinian textbook about Arab and world history, a complete Talmudic text was invented to the effect that God had created the nations and races only to serve the Jews. The Talmud, it was falsely alleged, contained such passages as: "We should cheat [non-Jews] and arouse quarrels among them, then they will fight each other. . . . Non-Jews are pigs who God created in the shape of man in order that they be fit for service for the Jews."[107]

Such extraordinary fabrications about the Talmud have been a staple of European Christian and racist anti-Semitism for many centuries. But it is only in more recent decades that they seem to have so thoroughly infected the body politic of Islam and the Palestinian mind-set. The murderous potential of such incitement was exemplified by Ahmad Abu Halabiya's sermon, broadcast live on the PA's official TV channel only one day after two Israeli soldiers were barbarically lynched by Palestinians in Ramallah. In the sermon, the former rector of the Islamic University of Gaza exhorted his audience:

Have no mercy on the Jews, no matter where they are, in any country. Fight them, wherever you are. Wherever you meet them, kill them. Wherever you are, kill those Jews and those Americans who are like them and those who stand by them. They are all in one trench against the Arabs and the Muslims because they established Israel here, in the beating heart of the Arab world, in Palestine.[108]

Anti-Semitic indoctrination has long existed in the PA, including the use of the *Protocols* in the press and pamphlets, and viciously anti-Jewish caricatures, posters, crossword puzzles, music videos, propaganda songs, and incendiary statements by preachers, publicists, and political leaders.[109] Islamic scholars constantly praise *shahada* (martyrdom for the sanctification of Allah) on Palestinian TV, calling for relentless jihad against Israel while reveling in the Prophet Muhammad's expulsion of the Jews from Arabia. Thus Muhammad Mustafa Najm, in a typical Friday sermon delivered in Gaza in early February 2002, recalled that "the Jews repeatedly attempted to kill the Prophet . . . by poisoning, through witchcraft, stoning, or any other type of political murder." The Prophet Muhammad had rightly stigmatized the Jews as a warning to future generations, instructing Muslims about their acts of corruption in the Koran and the Sunna: "Look forward, as we too, are looking forward, to your graves."[110] Arafat himself was more cautious in his public statements about the Jews. But in PA television and radio broadcasts he never tired of repeating the call to jihad against Israel and the demand to be a "*shahid* among other *shahids* on behalf of Jerusalem."

It was no secret that Arafat personally encouraged the incessant incitement of children in the PA to hatred, violence, and *shahada*. The media, schoolbooks, and sporting events were all exploited to show that the war against the Jews and Judaism was a heroic action. In early 2003 a soccer tournament for eleven-year-old boys was named for the terrorist Abdel Basset Odeh, who had blown up thirty-five Passover seder worshippers in Netanya; in the same year various summer camps were named for suicide bombers, including the seventeen-year-old girl Ayat al-Akhras, and the first female suicide bomber, Wafa Idris. Many educational programs, trophies, and schools were named after suicide bombers who were thereby transformed into exemplary role models for children. In September 2003 Arafat and other top PA leaders jointly sponsored a soccer tournament in which each of the twenty-four teams was named for a terrorist or *shahid*. Children who actually achieved death through suicide missions were instantly glorified as martyrs for Islam. Moreover, the music videos produced and broadcast hundreds of times over by the PA have always defined martyrdom as "sweet," as in the case of Muhammad al-Dura. Naturally the suicide bombers go to Paradise where each will receive seventy-two dark-eyed maidens as reward for their "righteousness"; they will then become heavenly advocates for seventy members of their family and be exempted from all the torments of the grave.[111]

Palestinian children, when interviewed on PA TV, invariably reiterate the mantras they have learned from their leaders and educators: that Israel has no right to exist, that all Israelis must be expelled, that "the Jews came to take Palestine, that is Tel-Aviv, Jaffa, Haifa, Acco, Ramle. . . . All these cities belong to Palestine." In mid-December 2004 an hour-long PA program broadcast these same motifs as part of its emphasis on preparing young children for war and self-sacrifice. "Death for Allah," they compulsively repeat, is the only way to "liberate Palestine" from the foreign "colonial implant" called Israel. Another broadcast at that time featured Isam Sisalem—a well-known Palestinian historian—comparing Israel to "parasitic worms in the ocean that eat a snail, and then live in its shell." The historian vowed that "we [the Palestinians] will not let anyone live in our shell."[112]

PA TV has constantly used songs, poems, and music videos to justify the martyrdom of the suicide bombers. They accuse Israel of torturing, mutilating, and gratuitously killing Palestinians.[113] Here are a few extracts from a PA TV cultural program in March 2005 featuring this religious hate poetry:

> Here I am O Lord, alive
> In your name, my God, they tortured me
> In your name, my God, they banished me
> In your name, they exterminated
> In your name, they ruled . . .
>
> O my God, hear my prayer
> In our homes, they attacked us
> They threatened us with destruction

They pushed us to annihilation.
With bombs they burned us
In blood they drowned us
In dungeons they cuffed us
On the anvil they put us.

A children's play broadcast on PA TV on March 25, 2004, included the following words by the narrator: "They [Israel] are the ones who did the Holocaust, their knife cuts to the length and width of our flesh. . . . They opened the ovens for us to bake human beings. They destroyed the villages and burnt the cities. And when an oven stops burning, they light a hundred [more] ovens. Their hands are covered with the blood of our children."[114]

In such broadcasts the suffering of Palestinian children and refugees is transparently manipulated to demonize Israel. Frequently, the Palestinians are redefined as modern replicas of Jesus, with Israel accused of reenacting the history of the crucifixion. Muhammad al-Dura is not only a Muslim *shahid* but also a "tiny sleeping Jesus." As for Jesus and his mother, Mary, they are Palestinians "sanctified by hundreds of millions of believers in this world."[115] One Palestinian artist speaking on PA TV in the summer of 2006 explained his picture of Israeli soldiers arresting Jesus in the following political terms:

Our struggle today against the other side is an eternal one. It can be said that it started 2,000 years ago and continues until today. I demonstrate this through the figure of Jesus. . . . The Israeli soldiers are wearing army uniforms while Jesus has nothing except for the truth. When they searched him at the entrance of Jerusalem, they found a stone, a piece of bread and fish, and he was cuffed. This is the Palestinian from the beginning of the struggle until the end.[116]

Such historical "revisionism," and the total negation of Jewish and Christian history it implies, have become a staple of the PA's educational program. In Palestinian textbooks today, references to Jews never extend beyond a standardized set of negative generalizations that attribute trickery, greed, and barbarity to them as fixed character traits. A typical charge is that Jews never keep agreements as Muslims do.[117] The Jewish connection to the Holy Land is either totally denied or else narrowly confined to antiquity and virtually ignored after the Roman period. There is no reference to Jewish holy places or to any special links of the Jews and Judaism to the city of Jerusalem.[118] Hebrew, despite its extraordinary longevity, is not even considered as one of the languages of the land (though it is, of course, the *first* language in Israel), and Zionism is only mentioned in the dark context of alien intrusions, invasion, infiltration, or colonialism. The State of Israel is not acknowledged at all, and its internationally recognized territory is referred to only by terms such as the "1948 lands." By definition, the Jewish state is presented as a usurper and occupier.[119] Brutal, inhuman, and inherently expansionist, this colonialist entity is held responsible for obliterating Palestinian national identity, destroying the Palestinian economy, and expropriating Palestinian lands, water, and villages.

No less revealing are the maps in Palestinian textbooks, which completely disregard Israel's existence and that of its 5.3 million Jews. The Palestine on these maps, which stretches from the Jordan River to the Mediterranean Sea, is designated as purely and exclusively Arab.[120] The overall picture that emerges negates any legitimate Jewish claim to even a small parcel of the Arab and Muslim land called Palestine. There is no authentic Jewish association with Zion in this narrative—no Jewish link to David's royal city or to the Temple of Solomon.[121] Jerusalem becomes an exclusively *Arab* city and is designated as the capital of the putatively independent State of Palestine. Israel as a sovereign state is simply rubbed out or evoked solely in aggressive terms, such as shooting civilians, demolishing houses, brutally uprooting and expelling Palestinians, and seizing land.[122] In this narrative, Israel relentlessly violates human rights and seeks to excise the Palestinian presence. Peace is never mentioned, let alone encouraged, and there is not the slightest attempt to present any aspect of Israeli society in a positive light, or even to see Israelis as human beings.[123]

Hence it is no surprise to find frequent references and images in the PA's official newspaper, *Al-Hayat al-Jadeeda,* to Jews as "Shylocks of the land," busy emptying Palestinian pockets; or to learn that "there is no people or land named Israel"; or to discover that the *Protocols of the Elders of Zion* has been the road map for Zionists in building Israel since 1897.[124] According to this theory, every ten years another aim of the *Protocols* is achieved, "proving their continuity and their power." Many Palestinians, including academics, believe this baneful forgery to be not only a truthful account of history but a key to understanding Zionist propaganda and policies.[125]

Holocaust denial, too, is a constant feature of PLO and PA incitement, connected to a *Protocols*-style perception of Jewish domination and the Zionist control of the international media. The Holocaust is therefore framed as a pernicious myth and a "malicious fabrication" concocted by the media under "Jewish rule." According to one Palestinian journalist writing in *Al-Hayat al-Jadeeda* in July 1998:

> World public opinion manipulated by the Jews, took advantage of [Hitler's] persecutions, disseminating legends about a collective massacre. They invented horrible stories about gas chambers which Hitler, so they claimed, had used to burn them alive. The press overflowed with pictures of Jews being gunned down by [Nazi] machine guns or being pushed into gas chambers. It [the press] concentrated on women, children and elderly persons to arouse sympathy and claims for reparations, donations and grants around the world.[126]

A more sophisticated version of Holocaust denial can be found in the 1982 doctoral dissertation of Mahmoud Abbas, the current head of the Palestinian Authority. It was written for Moscow's Oriental College and first published in Arabic in 1984 by Ibn Rushd publishers in Amman. Abbas claimed that the number of Jews murdered in the Holocaust might be "even less than a million." He asserted that the Zionists persuaded world public opinion that the real figure was much higher in order to achieve even "greater gains" after World War II. Abbas's study aimed to show the convergence of interests and fundamental similarity of Nazism and the Zionist movement. All factions within Zionism, he argued, far from seeking to save the Jews, "or at least to keep them alive until the end of the war," did exactly the opposite of what might have been expected. The Zionists sabotaged all efforts to rescue Jews before and during World War II unless they led directly to Palestine. At the same time, they deliberately incited Jews under Nazi rule in order to reinforce German hatred of them. As an example of such incitement, he offered the Biltmore Conference of May 1942 in New York, when the Zionist leaders supposedly declared war on the Third Reich. In Abbas's totally convoluted account, this conference then prompted Hitler to speed up the implementation of the Final Solution and to develop more detailed plans to this effect.[127]

The Zionists, according to Abbas, had collaborated with the Nazis in order to annihilate the Jews. They had insidiously conspired against and betrayed their own people. This treachery was made possible by the similarity of beliefs between the Nazis and Zionists. Hitler was totally committed to "the purity of the Aryan race" just as Zionists passionately advocated "Jewish racial purity." Both movements called for "a decisive solution" to the European "Jewish question" through immigration to Palestine. Anti-Semitism was the main lever to achieve this goal, so it followed that Zionists had a vested interest in promoting and encouraging it. Abbas even spuriously attributed to the atheist David Ben-Gurion the dogma that any Jew who "does not immigrate [to Israel] denies the Torah and the Talmud." Such Zionist ideas not only encouraged Hitler and the Nazis but, according to the PA leader, also provided "a general dispensation to every racist in the world" to mistreat the Jews.[128]

Mahmoud Abbas's dissertation showed all the hallmarks of the Soviet anti-Zionist school of falsification and anti-Jewish defamation in the early 1980s—especially in his branding of the Zionist movement as a full partner in the Nazi genocide.[129] In this context, it is important to remember that despite his reputation for moderation, his clean-shaven look, and smart suits, Abbas was Arafat's second in command for almost forty years and fully shared his views. No less than Arafat, he was closely linked to KGB foreign intelligence, the masters at nurturing rabid anti-Zionists, fomenting ethnic hatreds, and using deft combinations of anti-Semitism and anti-imperialism against the United States. According to former Romanian intelligence officer Ion Mihai Pacepa, the KGB and their Romanian helpers under Nicolae Ceausescu had provided cover for PLO terror operations throughout the 1970s and 1980s while encouraging Arafat's "extraordinary talent for deceiving." The Soviets and Ceausescu instructed the PLO leadership to pretend that they had broken with terrorism and recognized Israel when they had done no such thing.[130] Their dissembling language about seeking only national self-determination was cleverly manipulated by Moscow through its Romanian channels.

A cofounder of Fatah and for years the secretary-general of the PLO executive, Abbas was very much part of this Communist-inspired disinformation and one of the main architects of the Oslo accords. Though far less charismatic than Arafat, he was a more skillful diplomat, able to exude a pragmatic stance without renouncing PLO principles. At no time did he ever seriously seek to disarm the numerous armed gangs in the territories, let alone confront Hamas, though he is on record as considering the "militarization" of the second intifada to have been a serious mistake. Nevertheless, Abbas, like Arafat, has never punished any Palestinian for attacking Israel or murdering Israelis, even when this damaged the national cause. There has been no attempt to reeducate a Palestinian public that equates justice with murdering Jews and extremism—especially suicide bombing—with heroic martyrdom. In the prevailing code of honor, violence is good, a mark of victory even when its results are ruinous; compromise can only be bad; and any concessions to Israel are an abomination and a betrayal.[131] Wiping Israel off the map still remains morally superior to any alternative that might entail truly accepting the legitimacy of a *Jewish* state.

Abbas is more careful to circumnavigate the minefield of denying Israel's existence than his predecessor was, but he has not shied away from hinting at its eventual or future demise. In fact there is no unequivocal evidence that he accepts the legitimacy of the Jewish claim to any part of Palestine. Moreover, the present PA leader is on record as denying the existence of the ancient Jewish temple in Jerusalem—not exactly a promising basis for future reconciliation. Even less encouraging is his intransigent position on the nonnegotiable nature of the sacred Palestinian right of return to Israel. In November 2004, he told the Palestinian Legislative Council in Ramallah that he would work hard to fulfill Arafat's dream and would not rest "until the right of return for our people is achieved."[132]

Thus far Abbas has done nothing to curb the hate speech against Israel and the Jews that has long been a part of normal discourse in the PA media. One such motif is the constantly recycled claim that Israel distributes drugs to Palestinian youth as an "imperialist weapon" of occupation to weaken their identity, beliefs, and motivation.[133] Another theme is the repetitive notion of Israel as "Satan's offspring," expressed, among others, by Ahmad Nasser, secretary of the Palestinian Legislative Council, who was interviewed on PA TV in early February 2004. In an extended diatribe, he determined that "Israel was founded on theft from the first moment," on terror, killing, torture, assassination, death, and land expropriation. Its birth was "unnatural," literally an "offspring of Satan" that "cannot exist among human beings." At its root was a biblical racism "which hates all the goyim" and placed Jews at "a higher level of existence" than the rest of humanity; this complex of superiority, according to Nasser, was also a concept that appears in the *Protocols of the Elders of Zion*.[134]

Under Mahmoud Abbas, the hate ideology of the PA and its depiction of Israel and Israelis as cruel, inhuman murderers who gratuitously kill Palestinians has never abated.[135] TV broadcasts routinely reinforce the message of Israel as a state founded on stolen Arab land that cold-bloodedly kills women and children.[136] The Palestinian media disseminate the image of a criminal Israeli leadership ready to use shells with depleted uranium to sow death and destruction among Palestinians.[137] The roots of such evil are found in the Jewish religion and even in the Jewish soul. Video clips broadcast on official PA TV mix images of religious Jews praying at the Western Wall with lyrics such as the following:

> I am Palestinian, and my home is my home
> The evil souls
> A thousand evil ones
> are in my home
> But I am Palestinian
> and my home is my home.[138]

In these and virtually all other PA TV programs, words calling for the destruction of Israel and the departure of the Jews are *normal*. One example among many was a TV program about Jaffa broadcast in Tel Aviv on December 20, 2005, calling for the Israelis to be gone, to "leave our country, our land, our sea, our wheat, our salt, our wounds." It concluded with the words of the Israeli-Arab-Palestinian poet Mahmoud Darwish, implying or calling for the expulsion of every Israeli: "Die wherever you like, but don't die among us."[139]

At the heart of PA hate speech is the total rejection of Israel as the "thieving enemy." In a broadcast at the beginning of 2006, a leading PLO official described the Six-Day War, for example, as proof that the Zionists were waging a crusade against the whole Arab nation and "planning a Jewish State that will stretch from the Nile to the Euphrates."[140] At the same time, PA TV (run by Mahmoud Abbas's office) always emphasizes the sacred Muslim character of Jerusalem and its centrality for the Palestinians. There is a total denial of any Jewish connection to the Western Wall of the Second Temple, a claim that is dismissed as fabricated and coincidental. Not only that but the Fatah-run PA government and official PA television in the West Bank has continued through 2009 to deny any Jewish link to Jerusalem. Judaism has no place in the city but the specter of its "Judaization" and the libel that Israel seeks to destroy the Aksa mosque is deliberately cultivated.

PA propaganda has also transformed what it calls the al-Buraq Wall in Jerusalem into a purely Islamic site named for Muhammad's horse. Three thousand years of Jewish history are obliterated, and the original Temple is not merely de-Judaized but transformed into yet another Israeli invention designed to usurp what is authentically Arab and Palestinian. The recent al-Aqsa intifada, it is stressed in such unceasing fundamentalist propaganda, is part of a heroic century of struggle to prevent Jewish access to the Western Wall and the Temple Mount.[141]

Despite the ideological differences between the PLO and Hamas, both movements agree on the exclusively Islamic character of the Temple Mount and on Palestine being an Islamic land, one and indivisible; both believe that Jerusalem is the "eternal capital of Palestine"; that Zionism is a "criminal conspiracy" against the Palestinian people; and that Israel's creation was a satanic imperialist plot. For Fatah and Hamas, the Israelis are child murderers, usurpers, and ruthless colonialists who can only be fought through armed struggle and self-sacrificing martyrdom. Hence the "songs of Palestine" (whichever camp they originated from) are invariably about the gushing of blood for the homeland, jihad, and the sanctification of Allah's name. The sermons broadcast live on PA TV link these sanguinary themes to cleansing Muslim holy places "from the filth of the Jews"; they portray the Jews as enemies of Allah, a cursed people, and the sons of apes and pigs. The educational textbooks convey a similar message, damning Zionism as racist and neo-Nazi, while promoting hatred of Jews as treacherous, dissembling, and disloyal.

The conclusion of most Palestinians is, not surprisingly, that their freedom will not come until *all* of Palestine is completely liberated. On that cardinal point the PLO National Covenant—which, contrary to legend, has never been revoked—and the Hamas Covenant of 1988 are agreed. No less than twenty-six of the thirty-three articles in the 1968 PLO Covenant either denied Israel's right to exist or advocated violence and terror; in the 1988 Hamas "Sacred" Covenant, all of Palestine "from the river to the sea" is *inalienable* Muslim land, not one inch of which can ever be conceded. The power struggle and the low-level civil war between the PLO and Hamas should not disguise their broad common ground on many strategic issues relating to Israel and the Jews. However bad relations may be, there is the same predilection to regard Jewry as a conspiratorial group that dominates U.S. policy and controls the international media, the stock exchanges, and global finance; both groups assume that there is an all-powerful clique that planned the invasions of Afghanistan and Iraq, and seeks to control the world.[142] This anti-Semitic ideology helps to explain the ease with which the al-Aqsa Martyrs' Brigades (the armed wing of Fatah) can publicly endorse Iran's call to destroy Israel. Though PA officials condemned this declaration, the backing for President Ahmadinejad's genocidal politics from such an important PLO group was neither surprising nor without significance.[143]

The PLO under Arafat never renounced its strong Islamic dimension. At times, the Palestinian leader would even pose as a Mahdi (Messiah-redeemer) about to inaugurate a new era of liberty and justice. His constant use of Al-Quds (Jerusalem) as a unifying and mobilizing symbol for the jihad was clearly Islamic, though he also sought to embrace Christian Arabs, Christianity, and the myth of a Palestinian Jesus as part of his international repertoire. Arafat liked to place himself in a chain of celebrated Islamic liberators beginning with 'Umar ibn al-Khattab and the great Saladin, who had once ruled in Jerusalem.[144] In this use of Jerusalem and Islamic symbols, he was following in the footsteps of Haj Amin and Sheikh al-Qassam, who had led the interwar armed Palestinian struggle against Zionism. In Arabic, the language of jihad, with its redemptive connotations, enabled Arafat to hark back for inspiration to the Muslim expulsion and annihilation of Jewish tribes during the age of the Prophet Muhammad. This gave a much broader religious and historical dimension to Palestinian nationalism and a millennial tone to its promise of final victory. It was a way of transforming the contemporary revolutionary struggle into a holy war that would be meaningful for every Muslim.[145]

From the outset Arafat chose to publicly embrace Ayatollah Khomeini's epoch-making Islamic Revolution in Iran. On February 11, 1979, he sent an unambiguous message to Khomeini: "I pray Allah to guide your step on the road of faith and jihad in Iran, which will continue the struggle until we reach the walls of Jerusalem where we will raise the flags of our two revolutions."[146] The challenge from his opponents in Hamas and Islamic Jihad in the late 1980s increased his need to highlight the self-consciously Muslim identity of Fatah at the expense of its more secular components.[147] Hence the temptation and even the necessity to take over parts of the Muslim fundamentalist vocabulary, including a more moderate version of Hamas's explicitly anti-Semitic language. Following their example, Arafat began to pointedly highlight more than ever the supreme value of protracted struggle, endless sacrifice, jihad, the ultimate prize of Jerusalem, and the Palestinian belief in total victory. This rhetorical shift came too late, however, to prevent the Hamas victory in Gaza and the growing Islamicization of Palestinian society, which was greatly accelerated by the corruption of the veteran PLO leadership.

For forty years Arafat's PLO has pursued the illusion of conquering power in Palestine with a singular mixture of brutality, nepotism, extremist ideology, and sheer double-talk. During the last decade under Arafat, the Palestinian Authority became a veritable police state (employing one policeman for every forty residents) with a dozen security and intelligence services directly responsible to the *raïs* (president). The malevolence of PLO rule in southern Lebanon thirty years earlier was amply replicated in the West Bank and in pre-Hamas Gaza. There was the same corruption, cronyism, racketeering, killing of opponents, and imprisoning of dissidents. Billions of dollars were siphoned off into secret Swiss bank accounts to finance the extravagant habits of the globe-trotting PLO leaders with their worldwide financial investments and Western lifestyles. Arafat's wife Suha lived in Paris with a modest allowance of $200,000 a month while her people starved. At one point *Forbes* magazine estimated Yasser Arafat to be the sixth wealthiest person in the world, right up among the world's kings, queens, despots, and high-tech entrepreneurs. At his peak he ran the richest, best-financed revolutionary terrorist organization in history, acting in the name of refugees who had been left to their own devices in squalid camps because their leaders insisted on all of Palestine. Incredibly, for more than three decades the PLO continued to be the United Nations' most popular national liberation movement. Yet, for all the raw courage shown by its fighter-martyrs, the movement has ultimately been a wretched charade, and an ignominious failure. Neither the endless cash flowing from the Arab oil states, the EU, and the international community, nor the support of much of the world's media has been able to stem the stench of endemic corruption. On the contrary, this blind support exacerbated matters.

In the eyes of Arafat and his cronies the Oslo peace process was really never about genuinely resolving the conflict or improving the lives of ordinary Palestinians but far more about ways to ultimately substitute Palestine

for Israel. The self-destructiveness and suicidal character of the second intifada, enthusiastically supported by the bulk of the Palestinian people, further reinforced the irrational grip exercised by the mystique of destroying
Israel. In unleashing the dogs of war in 2000, Arafat not only rejected an extravagantly generous Israeli offer of 95 percent of the West Bank and Gaza,
as well as East Jerusalem; he also conclusively demonstrated his lack of interest in a Palestinian state that would have to peacefully coexist with Israel.
He left behind a ruined Palestine and the wreckage of a barely existent civil
society, whose development he, like the mufti before him, had done so
much to retard during the past forty years. Worse still, Arafat's war against
Zion intoxicated the minds of his people—especially the children of Palestine—engulfing them in a culture of hatred from which there is still no exit
in sight.

TWENTY-TWO

Hamas, Hezbollah, Holy War

Although Hezbollah and Hamas are not organizationally linked, both are Arab terror groups that maintain close ties with Iran and share its total negation of Zionism. In recent years the Lebanese Hezbollah has provided military training, financial support, and moral encouragement to the Palestinian Islamists. The Shiite Hezbollah has indeed become a trusted mentor and role model to the Sunni fundamentalist Hamas. Both organizations have inscribed on their banner the rejection of any treaties or peace agreements with Israel, energetically work for its demise and encourage suicide terrorism to that end. Hezbollah has a more global reach, but it also has to maneuver within a complex multiethnic, multireligious, and politically pluralist Lebanon, with its eighteen officially recognized ethno-confessional communities. Hezbollah's representation in the Lebanese parliament gives it considerable political clout, reinforced by the Iran-Syria axis and the results of the June 2009 elections. Hamas is more isolated than Hezbollah, but it was supported by a majority of Palestinians at the last elections and still controls political power in the Gaza Strip. Both movements share a common Islamist worldview, support violence, adopt similar strategies on the "Palestine question," and provide a wide range of social welfare institutions. The holy war to wipe out the Jewish state is, however, the essential glue that binds the "Party of God" to the Palestinian Islamic Resistance Movement. Harakat al-Muqawama al-Islamiyya (The Islamic Resistance Movement), more generally known by its acronym, Hamas, is the most prominent expression of Palestinian radical Islam.[1] Politically it is a product of the first Palestinian intifada that erupted in 1987, though its ideological roots lie much deeper. Like the PLO, its main objective has been the "liberation" of *all* Palestine—both the land and the people—from Israeli rule and the establishment of an Islamic Palestinian state on its ruins.[2]

During the first intifada, its leaflets—unlike those of the PLO at the time—were full of blatantly anti-Semitic statements.[3] From the outset it was apparent that Hamas regarded the Israeli-Palestinian conflict as a zero-sum game; its leadership considered the entirety of Palestine to be an Islamic holy land (a *waqf*, or religious endowment) that could never be the object of compromise. The conflict was neither political nor territorial for Hamas but an episode in the "eternal enmity" between Jews and Muslims that had begun with Muhammad and would end only with Judgment Day.

Hamas's first leaflet, issued in January 1988, addressed all Palestinians as follows: "O all our people, men and women. O our children: the Jews—brothers of the apes, assassins of the prophets, bloodsuckers, warmongers—are murdering you, depriving you of life after having plundered your homeland and your homes. Only Islam can break the Jews and destroy their dream."[4] The leaflet went on to attack the Egyptian rulers for signing the Camp David treaty "of shame and surrender." It mocked them for their paralysis and impotence "while the Jews daily perpetrate grave and base crimes against the people and children." The leaflet stressed that "the Muslim Palestinian people persist in rejecting the Jews' policy" and would escalate their struggle "until the Jews shall drink what they have given our unarmed people to drink." The blood of the Palestinian martyrs would never be forgotten: "Every drop of blood shall become a Molotov cocktail, a time bomb, and a roadside charge that will rip out the intestines of the Jews."[5] On May 3, 1988, during the month of Ramadan, Hamas issued its sixteenth leaflet attacking the "tyrannical Zionists" in the name of Allah, religion, and the Muslim faith. Evoking all of the enemy's alleged plots, restrictions, and "barbaric measures," Hamas emphasized that the Palestinian jihad would foil "the American liquidation plans" and "all the Jews' attempts to eradicate the blessed uprising."[6]

An October 27, 1988, leaflet meticulously listed "the series of barbaric Jewish actions" under the occupation (arrests, heavy taxes, curfews, undermining the harvests, damaging olive trees), while also recalling Muhammad's seventh-century war against the Banu Nadir—a Jewish tribe living near Medina. Then, too, the Jews had shown that "they are a tribe of treachery and deceit." History was repeating itself. Quoting the Koran, Hamas warned Palestinians against the Christians, the *shirk* (polytheists), and the infidel Arab states, as well as the Jews. The leaflet recalled the "treachery" of Sharif Husayn ibn 'Ali during World War I, the perfidy of Great Britain (with its Balfour Declaration), and the heroism of Sheikh 'Izz al-Din al-Qassam, the *mujahid* martyred by the British in 1935 on the eve of the Arab revolt in Palestine.[7] Hamas presented itself in these and other leaflets as part of the chain of jihad—a holy war going back six decades and linked to the operations of the Muslim Brotherhood on behalf of Palestine since the 1930s. The word "*hamas*" in Arabic means zeal and devotion in the path of Allah. It reflects the movement's origins as a branch of the militant Egyptian Muslim Brotherhood, which had been active in the Gaza Strip since the 1950s, steadily gaining influence through its network of mosques, charitable groups, and religious organizations.

By November 1988 when Hamas published its Sacred Covenant systematizing the movement's ideology, its negative image of the Jews had fully crystallized, replete with Koranic quotations, Islamic terminology, and jihadist exhortations. No less characteristic were the constant evocations of Muslim heroes and episodes from the early history of Islam, such as Muhammad's 628 C.E. conquest of Khaibar, an oasis in the Arabian peninsula where Jewish settlements had once existed. In Islamic tradition this episode signified Jewish treachery and defeat.[8] Vitriolic anti-Semitism was integral in Hamas's fundamentalist ideology and deeply rooted in its Islamic identity. In raising the banner of Islamic resistance, Hamas made no distinction at all between Jews and Zionists. From the outset, resistance to Israeli occupation, grassroots social activism, and Jew hatred have been inseparable components of Hamas political praxis.

Hamas drew inspiration for all three features of its program from Hassan al-Banna's Muslim Brotherhood, while adopting a more aggressive and militant stance toward Israel and the Jews. "Liberating" Palestine from the Jordan River to the Mediterranean became a *religious duty,* involving a fusion of Islamist tradition with Palestinian nationalism. The hollow shell of the "secular democratic state" of the PLO had to be infused with a "religious soul."[9] As a consequence, the conflict became *Islamicized.* Palestinian grievances were reformulated as a historic clash of religions, the latest episode of the historic fight between Muslims and Jews in the name of Allah.[10] A leading actor in this paradigm shift was Sheikh Ahmed Yassin, a 1948 refugee, dynamic preacher, and cofounder of Hamas. The wheelchair-bound sheikh's first priority in the 1970s had been to Islamicize the Palestinians, but the first intifada created a new agenda. Yassin coauthored the Hamas charter together with the pediatrician Sheikh Abdel Aziz al-Rantisi. The founding document solemnly defined "the land of Palestine" as an "Islamic trust [*waqf*] upon all Muslim generations until the Day of Resurrection." According to article 13 of the charter, to give up any part of this homeland would be like giving up part of the religious faith itself.[11] Hence all peace initiatives were termed a "waste of time and acts of absurdity"—a position that Hamas has pursued, from the Madrid peace conference in October 1991 through the Annapolis gathering in December 2007 to the present.

Hamas's sharp criticisms of the PLO derived, in part, from Arafat's theoretical readiness (at least before 2000) to accept a Palestinian state that would coexist alongside the State of Israel, in accordance with UN Security Council Resolutions 242 and 338. Hamas also strongly objected to the PLO's secular nationalist course, though it stressed the fact that the two movements faced the same enemy (Israel) and shared a common Palestinian destiny. Indeed, Hamas, despite its opposition to PLO nationalism, has at times appeared to be more nationalist than its rivals. It has adapted to the national dynamics of the conflict without compromising its ideological principles or renouncing its essentialist view of the Jews as eternal enemies of Islam.[12] This rules out a two-state solution and turns the confrontation into an insoluble clash of civilizations and a conflict of antithetical beliefs. A popular slogan of Hamas, "*Zawal Isra'il hatmiyya qur'aniyya*" (Israel's disappearance is a historical necessity grounded in the Koran), epitomizes this dogmatic and intransigent approach.

The thirty-six-article Hamas Covenant of 1988 is totally committed to the holy war for Palestine against the Jews until the land is *cleansed* from the impurity of the occupiers and the victory of Allah is finally assured. Hamas's negation of Israel is no less comprehensive and far more overtly anti-Semitic than the PLO Charter published twenty years earlier. Moreover, it claims to be a "sacred" document expressing eternal, universal truths revealed by Allah himself that are not subject to alteration or debate. The axioms are explicitly directed against Jews in the spirit of the *Protocols*, which largely determine its view of Israel and Zionism. Nevertheless, everything in the document is couched in Islamic language and symbolism. Thus, in contrast to the PLO, the future status of the Jews and other non-Muslims in an Islamic State of Palestine is explicitly reduced to that of the *dhimmi*. There has never been any question of granting to the Jews *political* rights—an issue that was at least debated in the ranks of the PLO.[13] The ideology of Hamas is fully consonant with that of the Egyptian Muslim Brotherhood and other Islamist movements on this score. Whereas the PLO's frame of reference was that of an independent *wataniyya* (local patriotism) as part of a broader pan-Arab nationalism, Hamas thinks and acts in terms of an Islamic state based on the *sharia*. Its message is pan-Islamic, and the entire Muslim world is its constituency.

In its preamble, the Hamas Covenant quotes the imam and martyr Hassan al-Banna: "Israel will rise and remain erect until Islam eliminates it as it eliminated its predecessors."[14] The charter clearly stipulates that since its "struggle against the Jews is extremely wide-ranging," Hamas will need to be reinforced by successive battalions from the multifarious Islamic world.[15] It proudly defines itself as part of a world organization, "one of the wings of the Muslim Brothers in Palestine . . . the largest Islamic movement of the modern era."[16] The credo of the Hamas is indeed that of the Muslim Brotherhood. The ultimate goal is Islam, the Prophet is its model, and the Koran is its constitution.[17] This gives Hamas a universal appeal to Muslims around the globe. Hence, though it insists on its distinctive Palestinian quality, the loyalty of Hamas to Islam remains fundamental. Article 7 clarifies this by evoking the continuous jihad of the Muslim Brotherhood against "the Zionist invasion" in 1936, 1948, and 1968, and the historic role that has devolved upon Hamas itself since 1988. All these revolts were driven by the same conviction that Palestine is an *inalienable* possession "for all generations of Muslims" until the end of time. All true fighters for Palestine have known that the only solution was jihad—a binding "individual duty on all Muslims everywhere."

In dealing with the Jews, Hamas adopts a classically anti-Semitic view of their modus operandi and "malignant" global influence. Despite Hamas's claims to represent the unadulterated voice of Islam, its anti-Semitism does, in fact, owe a crucial debt to the West. In the Covenant, and in their propaganda material, one finds verses from the Koran constantly merging with crude borrowings from the *Protocols*. Integral to this genocidal anti-Semitism is the notion of a Jewish conspiracy against Islam and the rest of humanity.[18] In article 17, for example, which discusses the education of Muslim women, Zionism is accused of seeking to corrupt Palestinian morality through advertisements, lewd movies, and the poison of secular culture. Active agents in this conspiracy are such well-known "Zionist intermediaries" as the Freemasons and Rotary Clubs.[19] At the same time, while itself borrowing Nazi anti-Semitic imagery, Hamas defines the "Zionist enemy" as "vicious and Nazi-like." The Covenant speaks about "the Nazism of the Jews" who destroy homes, make children orphans, sentence young people to long years of imprisonment, establish detention camps, resort to collective punishment, and ruthlessly exile Palestinians from their homeland. This "Jewish Nazism" is not gratuitous but part of a much wider plot.

> They [the Jews] took advantage of key elements in unfolding events, and accumulated a huge and influential material wealth which they put to the service of implementing their dream. This wealth [permitted them to] take over control of the world media such as news agencies, the press, publication houses, broadcasting and the like. [They also used this wealth] to stir revolutions in various parts of the globe in order to fulfill their interests and pick the fruits. They stood behind the French and Communist revolutions and behind most of the revolutions we hear about here and there. They also used the money to establish clandestine organizations which are spreading around the world, in order to destroy societies and carry out Zionist interests. Such organizations are: the Freemasons, Rotary Clubs, Lions Clubs, B'nai B'rith and the like. All of them are destructive spying organizations. They also used the money to take over control of the imperialist states and made them colonize many countries in order to exploit the wealth of those countries and spread their corruption therein.[20]

Article 23 of the Hamas Covenant could have been written by a committee of experts composed of Adolf Hitler, Joseph Goebbels, Henry Ford, and a whole bevy of French, Austrian, Polish, or Russian anti-Semites. The following paragraph, blaming the Jews for two world wars and for seeking world domination, is indeed formulated in the classic *Protocols* tradition.

> As regards local and world wars, it has come to pass and no one objects, that they stood behind World War I, so as to wipe out the Islamic Caliphate. They collected material gains and took control of many sources of wealth. They obtained the Balfour Declaration and established the League of Nations in order to rule the world by means of that organization. They also stood behind World War II, where they collected im-

mense benefits from trading with war materials and prepared for the establishment of their State. They inspired the establishment of the United Nations and the Security Council to replace the League of Nations, in order to rule the world by their intermediary. There was no war that broke out anywhere without their fingerprints on it.[21]

The demonic image of the conspiratorial, warmongering Jews who have plunged the world into chaos, dissension, massive armed conflicts, and revolutions in order to consolidate their world conquest is borrowed from the arsenal of Western anti-Semitism. Strikingly omitted is any reference to the Holocaust. The mass murder of six million Jews in World War II must not be permitted to disturb the fiction that Jews instigated the conflagration in order to make massive profits. Like other Palestinian spokesmen and movements, Hamas representatives solved this conundrum by embracing Western theories of Holocaust denial.[22] At the same time, Koranic verses are used throughout the Covenant to bolster extreme anti-Semitism at a symbolic level. Thus sura 3 (al-Imran), verse 118 completes the warning about the Jewish "world-enemy": "O ye who believe! Take not for intimates others than your own folk, who would spare no pain to ruin you. Hatred is revealed by [the utterance of] their mouth, but that which their breasts hide is greater."[23]

As various articles of the Covenant make all too plain, the liberation war against the Jews is a battle for Islam that demands the mobilization of *all* Muslims. This is especially the case since the goal of the Zionists (and all the secret Masonic organizations supposedly under their direction) is "to demolish societies, to destroy values, to wreck answerableness [*dhimam*], to shatter virtues and to wipe out Islam. 'Zionism' stands behind the diffusion of drugs and toxic substances of all kinds to 'facilitate its control and expansion.' "[24]

The war against Zionism is unmistakably a war against the Jews. Article 28 states: "Israel, by virtue of its being Jewish and of having a Jewish population, defies Islam and the Muslims."[25] Moreover, only a worldwide jihad could successfully confront the "wickedness of the Zionist invasion . . . its penetration into many countries, and its control over material means and the media, with all the ramifications thereof in most countries of the world."[26] Article 32 describes in anti-Semitic language the scale of the threat posed by the Jews and Zionism.[27]

Today it is Palestine and tomorrow it may be another country or other
countries. For Zionist scheming has no end, and after Palestine they will
covet expansion from the Nile to the Euphrates. Only when they have
completed digesting the area on which they have laid their hand, they will
look forward to more expansion, etc. Their scheme has been laid out in
the *Protocols of the Elders of Zion,* and their present [conduct] is the best
proof of what is said there.[28]

The *Protocols* are formally acknowledged to be the *road map* of Zionism.
Israel is never even mentioned once in the entire document. But there are
highly emotive references to the Zionist conquest as a "despicable" "Nazi-
Tartar invasion." The success of Zionism means "the loss of [our] countries,
the uprooting of their inhabitants, the spreading of corruption on earth
and the destruction of all religious values."[29] In this broad conflict with the
Jews, Hamas sees itself as "the spearhead and the avant-garde" of the Palestinian, Arab, and Islamic cause—three concentric circles. The definitive loss
of Palestine would mean a massive defeat for Islam. Hence, with the Koran
and the gun, Hamas proposes to drive the intifada forward as part of a pan-
Islamic struggle to finally eliminate "the Zionist cancer" from the Middle
East. From the moment of its foundation, Hamas has been totally committed to uncompromising violence in the name of Islam, to the destruction of
Israel, and to the "struggle against the Jews" as the enemies of Allah. Not for
nothing did Hamas evoke the spine-chilling hadith (in article 7 of its charter) that "the last Hour would not come unless the Muslims will fight
against the Jews and would kill them." Not by accident did Hamas activists
constantly refer to the Prophet Muhammad's successful *war against the Jews*
in the seventh century. Prominent Hamas leaders such as Mahmoud al-
Zahar rationalized their blurring of any distinction between Jews and Zionists by claiming that Israel had declared war on Islam and was killing
defenseless Muslims, closing mosques, and behaving barbarically. However,
long before the first Palestinian intifada, intransigent anti-Jewish attitudes
were a feature of Muslim Brotherhood ideology.[30]

Opposition to the *existence* of Jews in Palestine has long been central to
Hamas terminology. There is no such thing, for example, as an anti-Zionist
Jew, since all Jews are, by definition, Zionists. "Its [Hamas's] hatred of Jews
is almost blind, extending well beyond the realm of religion, theology or ec-

umenical conflict," writes political science professor Beverley Milton-Edwards. She adds: "Some claims made by Hamas, even by its own religious terms of reference, stretch the limits of credibility and are clearly a symptom of racism rather than religious difference."[31] As the sacred Covenant takes great pains to emphasize, the Palestinian Hamas is at *war with the Jews* and world Zionism, not just with Israel; this is no mere semantic distinction. It highlights the anti-Semitic nature of the Islamist jihad and the absolute negation of Israel as the demonic other.

This is a view fully shared by Islamic Jihad. One of its founders, Nadir al-Tamimi, published an open letter to Yasser Arafat on November 23, 1988, underlining the eternal nature of the Islamic struggle for Palestine and citing as a model the Muslim refusal to recognize the medieval Crusader state. By even envisaging any political compromise with Israel, the PLO was betraying this Islamic heritage. He warned Arafat not to recognize the Jews' right to settle or live in any part of Palestine: "This country is the lighthouse of the Muslims. No, this decision will not succeed. The Jews will not settle in our country."[32]

Another leading Islamist, the Hebron-born Sheikh As'aad Bayyud al-Tamimi (expelled by Israel to Jordan in 1970) similarly insisted that only jihad could bring an end to the illegitimate Jewish state. This was an Islamic battle whose outcome was foreshadowed by Khomeini's triumph in Iran, which had shown Arabs the way to solve the Palestine problem. Since then, there had been the assassination of Anwar al-Sadat, the emergence of Hezbollah in Lebanon, the bombing of the U.S. Marine barracks in Beirut, the anti-Soviet jihad in Afghanistan, the rise of the Muslim Brotherhood in Syria, and other events that were all elements of one single Islamist jihad. Sheikh Al-Tamimi, fired up by this return of Islam, confidently prophesied in the mid-1980s the inevitable elimination of Israel.[33]

No less than Hamas, the Palestinian Islamic Jihad was driven by the imperatives of holy war as the only way to liberate Palestine, though it placed greater emphasis on bringing down the "heretical regimes" in the Middle East. Palestine and the fate of modern Islamic movements were inseparably connected. Islamic Jihad presented the struggle as an *existential* one against "the triple heresy of the West, the Arab regimes and Israel." In contrast to Hamas, Islamic Jihad (strongly influenced by Iran) was more insistent on damning the Westernized Arab regimes as "apostates to be eliminated."

Nevertheless, many of its slogans were identical to those of Hamas: "Islam is the only solution to the struggle"; "Neither East nor West, only Islam"; and "Jihad is the way of liberation."[34]

Islamic Jihad's commitment to holy war, like that of Hamas, entailed obstructing any peace agreements between "the treacherous Arab regimes and the Zionist entity"; it, too, embraced heroic sacrifice, terrorism, martyrdom, the fusion of Palestinianism with Islamic identity, and the traditional definition of non-Muslims as *dhimmis*. Recognition of Jewish rights to *any* part of Palestine was rejected as contrary to the Koran. This was also a *cultural* war against the Jews, to be viewed from the Koranic perspective—a conflict that could only end in the final victory of Islam. Islamic Jihad's war with Israel was part of the organization's struggle against *takfir* (heresy) and of its goal of bringing down the "infidel regimes."[35] Like Hamas, Islamic Jihad chose to highlight its permanent enmity toward the Jews, while strenuously opposing the crusader West, the Communist East, the atheists, and the apostates. Its ideology was radical Islamist but closer to the Iranian Shiite model than to the Sunni fundamentalists, with the exception of the cult it encouraged around the Palestinian martyr of the 1930s, Sheikh 'Izz al-Din al-Qassam. Islamic Jihad, again like Hamas, stressed the *religious* dimension of the Jewish-Arab conflict.[36] It, too, warned against cooperating with the Jews in the light of their congenital deceitfulness.

The centrality of this concept was apparent to me when, in 1990, I edited a filmed interview with Sheikh Hamid al-Bitawi (then head of the sharia courts in the West Bank), an Islamist from Hamas who operated in the PA orbit. The sheikh repeatedly told us that Jews do not respect contracts, agreements, or the importance of truthfulness.[37] Their Scriptures, like the Gospels, had once contained an authentic revelation of the truth, but this had subsequently been disregarded. He added that both the Old and New Testaments had been changed, revised, and distorted beyond recognition by the time Islam appeared on the scene. Jews were, nonetheless, treated with tolerance until they broke a truce with the Prophet, conspiring to kill him— which had obliged Muhammad to expel them from the Arabian Peninsula. Since then, according to al-Bitawi's account, "no Jew or Christian was ever harmed by Muslims"; no churches or synagogues were ever violated throughout Islamic history. On the other hand, the wicked Jews had supposedly tried to burn down al-Aqsa Mosque in 1968, and they had deliberately massacred Muslims in its courtyard. Worse still, they continued to fabricate the story of "their so-called Temple"—which, according to the Hamas sheikh, was "all lies."[38]

As this long interview progressed, I became increasingly stupefied by the self-confidence with which this senior Hamas cleric poured out his anti-Semitic clichés. He then turned to the question of negative Jewish qualities, becoming noticeably more animated.

> One characteristic of the people of Israel is that they break agreements. . . . Another is that they take words out of context. . . . They have killed the prophets and try to corrupt the world. The Muslims believe Jews corrupted people's beliefs, spreading atheism and communism. It is the Jews who encourage the ideas of Sartre . . . it is the Jews who corrupt the morals of the younger generation throughout the world with pornographic films and literature, with prostitution.[39]

Al-Bitawi amiably confided that the Jews in Palestine had encouraged the "communist idea of atheism" in order to corrupt the Muslim faith and "propagate ideas alien to Islam." After 1967 the Israelis had supposedly made alcohol, hashish, and opium widely available to Palestinian youth at greatly reduced prices in order "to destroy their bodies and minds." This was vintage Hamas preaching, delivered with fluency, aplomb, and a triumphal, smiling countenance. Sex, too, was another classic Jewish bait to weaken the faith and morals of the Muslims. Al-Bitawi was evidently convinced that it was Israeli policy to promote prostitution and free sex on the Arab street in order to spread diseases such as syphilis, which were becoming more common. The Jews, he added, "confiscate Islamic books and magazines" but they allowed pornography from abroad, especially for young Palestinians. They were, furthermore, "against anything to do with religion or moral values."[40]

The Hamas cleric was further convinced that the Jews had an unjustifiable superiority complex as "God's chosen people" that led them to look down on non-Jews with disdain. But, in reality, he considered them to be as corrupt as their Scriptures. "Throughout history they had corrupted the faith and morals of man," he said. The Jews were responsible for two world wars and they would "reap the consequences of the wars they are now inciting." Al-Bitawi repeatedly stressed that "Judaism and Zionism were aimed in one direction, namely hostility against the whole of mankind and against

Islam and Muslims." As if reciting by heart from the Hamas Covenant, he then added, with rising emotion: "The Jews are the ones who intended to destroy the Islamic Caliphate. The greatest misfortune to befall Man in the 20th century was when the Muslim caliphate was abolished and the Jews took charge of leading the human race."[41]

At this point in the interview I could have no doubt. Sheikh al-Bitawi sincerely believed that the Jews controlled *everything* in the modern world—"peoples' thoughts and beliefs, as well as politics and the economy." The greatest disaster, in his view, was that "the evil Jews" had taken charge of the world economy, international relations, morality, and culture. It was Jewish leadership that had brought about "moral decline, psychological crisis, suicide and family breakdown—revolution and wars, coups, assassinations and killings." Hence, according to this prominent religious judge, Jews were to blame for a world out of joint. Together with Christians, atheist Communists, and Hindus, they had formed "a front against Islam." But this evil conspiracy was doomed to failure. Only the Koran and Islam could save humanity after the dual failure of Communism and capitalism. An Islamic state (the orthodox caliphate) all over the world would be the "solution," which meant, of course, the end of Israel. In its place would come a completely Islamicized Palestine "from the river to the sea." Since this interview, nothing in the Hamas worldview concerning Jews, Judaism, and Israel has changed. What *is* new is the pervasive influence of this Islamic resistance movement—which brought it decisive victory in the Palestinian parliamentary elections of January 2006.

Before the first intifada, the future leadership of Hamas had focused largely on social services and educational work in the Gaza Strip. They set up kindergartens, sports facilities, charities, small medical clinics, dental practices, drug treatment centers, and Koranic schools and mosques, mainly financed by the Gulf states and Jordan. The founder of Hamas, Sheikh Ahmed Yassin, was born in Palestine in 1936 and had joined the Egyptian Muslim Brotherhood in Gaza at nineteen. In 1973 he established the al-Mujama al-Islami (Islamic congress) in Gaza, from which Hamas would eventually emerge fourteen years later. Its outlook was largely shaped by the writings of Hassan al-Banna and Sayyid Qutb, the main ideologues of the Egyptian Muslim Brotherhood.[42] Throughout most of the 1980s, the Mujama had focused its hostility more against the Palestinian secular nationalists and the Left than at the Israeli occupation. The Israeli authorities myopically encouraged this trend for precisely these reasons. Yassin and his followers succeeded in weakening the PLO, turning the Islamic University of Gaza into a fundamentalist stronghold, clamping down on drug dealers and prostitution, and imposing the *hijab* (veil) on Muslim women. Students were increasingly intimidated and brainwashed with Islamist anti-Semitic doctrines, including radical forms of Holocaust denial.[43] Outside the university, cinemas, liquor stores, and restaurants serving alcohol were closed or demolished. A strict separation between the sexes was imposed at musical performances. Piety and prayer frequency increased. Conservative Islamic dress became virtually obligatory in public.

The first intifada (literally "shaking off" in Arabic) broke out in December 1987, after two decades of Israeli occupation. Ahmed Yassin's movement, which had until then been tolerated by Israel (in the hope of neutralizing the PLO), soon joined the spontaneous uprising. By the summer of 1988 it had established a strong core of popular support. Hamas proved itself to be zealous and efficient in assassinating Palestinian collaborators. Together with Fatah it killed more Muslims over the years than all the Palestinian victims of the Israeli occupying forces put together.[44] Hamas, however, ambitiously called for the immediate conquest of *all* of Palestine, not just the West Bank and Gaza, as a religious obligation. It created an effective militia—disciplined, well-trained, properly funded, committed, and difficult to penetrate. With their suicide bombings of buses in Israel in 1996, Hamas not only critically damaged the Oslo peace process but virtually delivered a close election to the right-wing Likud Party led by Benjamin Netanyahu. Such a terrorist intervention in Israeli politics made perfect sense to the Hamas leaders. From their standpoint any opportunity to cripple peace negotiations with Israel was welcome. Efforts to achieve a peaceful settlement have always been perceived as "collaboration" and a disgraceful surrender to the Jewish conquerors of Palestine.

The Hamas leadership, like that of other Islamist movements, have generally come from the educated middle and upper classes. They often have university educations and degrees in medicine, engineering, or law. As the Egyptian-American commentator Fouad Zakaria observed in July 2005, their Islamic fanaticism "resembles the Nazi ideology and it has nothing to do with poverty, wretchedness, social disorders and personal humiliation."[45] More than half of the Palestinian suicide bombers had a university education. They were no more hungry or miserable than the Saudi terrorists of al-Qaeda who bombed the United States in September 2001. Most Hamas terrorists, like many of their Islamist counterparts elsewhere, are motivated by a deep hatred of Jews, Zionism, and the West. It is not so much despair as loathing for Western culture—its permissiveness, secularism, and liberalism—that triggers their terrorist activity. To this one should add the publicity and celebrity cult surrounding the *shahid,* which has been deliberately promoted in the Palestinian Authority and resonates with the Western media. The Hamas extremists have proven particularly adept at brainwashing their youth in the destructive path of jihad. Indeed, the manipulation of fear and hatred has, during the past decade, been raised to the level of an art form by the jihadist propaganda of Hamas and like-minded Islamist organizations such as Hezbollah.[46]

The annihilationist jihad advocated by Hamas since 1988 is rooted in orthodox Islamic theology and eschatology, adapted to the contemporary war against Israel. Classical Islamic teachings about the *inferiority* of Judaism and Christianity have been transformed into an apocalyptic myth about the Jewish and Western threat to Islam as a whole.[47] Drawing on the Koran, hadith, and Muslim eschatology, Jews are described as adherents of the great deceiver, the Dajjal—a kind of Muslim parallel to the Antichrist legend. There are some traditions that claim the one-eyed Dajjal is himself the promised Jewish Messiah, others say he will be accompanied into battle by seventy thousand armed Jews from Isfahan (Iran). The Dajjal and all his Jewish companions will, however, be slaughtered in this eschatological war. In such apocalyptic visions, in the Koran itself, in the hadith (sayings of the Prophet), and in some early Islamic narratives, the image of the Jew is presented as the *summum* of obstinate malevolence. As the French scholar Georges Vajda pointed out in the late 1930s, the perfidious Jews were accused in a canonical hadith of causing the Prophet's excruciatingly slow death from poisoning; they were also blamed for promoting heresies (including Shiism) in early Islam. They were frequently depicted as unscrupulous falsifiers of their own sacred books, and as narrow-minded, envious scoffers who had continually harassed Muhammad during his divinely appointed mission.[48] These archetypes often recur in Hamas literature, which owes a great deal to the core Islamic theology of Jew hatred, even though it has also incorporated intellectual elements from Christian anti-Semitism and the *Protocols* into its modernized ideology of holy war.[49] The bottom line is very clear: The End of Days will not come until all the Jews have been killed.

The jihad, in the sense of combat with weapons, is perceived by all Islamists as *the* answer to the "Zionist Nazi" attack of the Jews—as a *fard 'ain,* or duty, incumbent on every Muslim. For Hamas, the battle for Palestine is preparation for the conclusive reckoning between Islam and the Jews. This was the eschatological belief that animated Sheikh Ahmed Yassin and many of the zealots alongside him from an early age. The "sheikh of the intifada," or "the jihad professor," as he was sometimes called, Ahmed Yassin acquired charismatic status following his sentencing to fifteen years in an Israeli jail in May 1989. Many of the sadistic killings perpetrated by Hamas against the sons of Zion ("killers of the prophets and shedders of blood") were personally dedicated to Yassin as the "unseen commander" of the "soldiers of Allah."[50] As the religious symbol of the apocalyptic spirit, the ascetic Yassin (who was released after the Oslo accords) remained the idol of the Hamas militants, despite his severe infirmity. Upon his return to Gaza he continued to prophesy the imminent disappearance of Israel from the map, giving it thirty more years, at most, to live. In March 2004, an Israeli Apache helicopter missile finally fulfilled the sheikh's self-proclaimed wish for martyrdom.[51]

Sheikh Yassin had inculcated into many young Palestinians the ardent wish for martyrdom and self-immolation, and the desire for blood, revenge, and liberation from "the scoundrels" who had conquered their land. Jihad against the Jews and a martyr's death were integral to the language of the first and second intifadas, as they had been to earlier Palestinian revolts, such as the 1936–39 uprising against the British. For Hamas, like the PLO, past and present merged through the legends of ancient battles and Islamic warriors, and tales of prophets and martyrs. For both organizations, the famous battle of Badr in 623 C.E.—Muhammad's first major victory over his enemies—was perhaps more real than many recent events. The greatly admired Saladin, the Kurdish founder of the medieval Ayyubid dynasty, was another example of the same syndrome—a warrior-hero enlisted by Hamas and the PLO as a symbol for their hopes to recover Jerusalem and vanquish the Jewish state.[52] Hamas leaders proudly proclaimed that they were the "inheritors" of Saladin. The Zionists, on the other hand, were doomed to suffer the fate of the Latin Crusaders. References to Muhammad's victory over the Jews in the Khaibar oasis and to their exile from Arabia in 640 C.E. have fulfilled a similar function in the Islamist collective memory. There are, for example, Hamas videotapes in which present-day "martyrs" proclaim that "the call of jihad, the call of *Allahu akbar,* the time of Khaibar has come!" or sing such lines as *"Khaybar, Khaybar"* (Khaibar, Khaibar, O Jews, the army of Muhammad will return).

The songs enthusiastically evoke the slaughter of the Jews ("the sons of Khaibar") as a kind of sacrificial act. In mobilizing Palestinian resistance, Hamas also ardently invoked the memory of more recent martyrs from the 1930s and 1940s, including al-Qassam and Hassan al-Banna to sharpen the contrast between authentic jihad and the "shameful surrender" of the PLO. "The language of bullets and bombs," according to the Qassamite battalions of Hamas, "is the [only] language that the Jews understand!" This language helps to justify Hamas's murderous attacks on soft Israeli targets with the deliberate aim of causing maximum civilian deaths and casualties. The road to victory must be paved through relentless terror and "the love of death," the eroticization of which has been such a striking feature of the last two intifadas. As the highest-ranking Palestinian cleric, Sheikh Ikremah Sabri, chillingly put it in June 2001: "We tell them [Israel]: in as much as you love life—the Muslim loves death and martyrdom. There is a great difference between he who loves the hereafter and he who loves this world. The Muslim loves death and [strives for] martyrdom."[53]

Under the influence of the Palestinian Hamas and Islamic Jihad, martyrdom against the Jews was transformed into the most exalted thing that any young Muslim could possibly desire. This existential imperative fused with the PLO nationalist call to irrigate the soil of Palestine with the blood of the *fida'i* (self-sacrificers)—to purify it forever from the contamination of the Israeli occupiers. But in the Hamas message "the blood of the martyrs" was also designated as a curse intended to prevent any negotiations with Israel or the emergence of a historic compromise. As one Hamas-produced audiocassette bluntly concluded: "Shame and disgrace on the [Arab] kings who compromise in order to solve the problem. The only solution is blood, knee-deep."

The Hamas videos are invariably drenched in blood and vengeance, bursting with sadomasochistic frenzy. Their calls for the divine destruction of the enemy merge with the cult of the martyrs of the intifada. The will to massacre is the logical result of such incitement, in which Hamas, Fatah, and Islamic Jihad have consistently demonized Jews as *"ibna al-qird wa al-Khanazir"* (sons of monkeys and pigs). The Hamas media even described the victims of suicide bombings in this dehumanized way after attacks against Israelis at Beit Lid in January 1995. The official announcement stated: "The Islamic Movement gives its condolences to the hero of the attack, which led to the killing of twenty pigs and the injuring of sixty monkeys."[54]

In the Hamas monthly *Falastin al-Muslima,* Ibrahim Al-'Ali explained a decade ago the significance of the Koranic verses about Jews being transformed into apes, pigs, or other animals. According to the learned doctor, not only had the Jews been punished by Allah for failure to obey God's commandments, but their metamorphosis into animals had left its impression on the souls of those who came after them—in their opinions, feelings, thoughts, spirit, and outward appearance. Mentally, as well as physically, contemporary Jews resembled apes and pigs. This explained why they had invented the Darwinian theory of evolution. They supposedly needed to rid themselves of the shame and stigma associated with the ancient Koranic punishment! According to Al-'Ali, "They [the Jews] attempted to dispel this accusation from themselves, with the help of the satanic thought that guided them in despising the entire human race by saying that [man's] origin was in animals, and that it developed over time from an ape to human form, by means of the theory . . . of the Jewish ape Darwin."[55] Charles Darwin, the English biologist, was not a Jew, of course, but that hardly disturbs the primitive and irrational anti-Semitism of the Palestinian Hamas. The use of demonizing zoomorphic stereotypes is by no means confined to Hamas. Unfortunately, it is solidly grounded in Islamic religious sources and is widespread among Shiite and Sunni Muslims, as well as many secular Arab nationalists.

Equally alarming is the abundance of eschatological references to the end of Israel in Hamas literature. One section of the Koran that is frequently quoted in this context states that "the Israelites" will be allowed to "spread corruption" in the land twice and will then be defeated by an adversary sent by God. *Fasad* (corruption) is a central eschatological concept for the Islamists—a characteristic of the Dajjal and the Jews. In Hamas leaflets, Israel is regularly stigmatized as "an error and a sin of the West." But those "who have spread corruption throughout the land" are, above all, perceived as Jews, whose nature and essence is to instigate wars, dissension, and communist revolution.[56] One Hamas leader, Sheikh Bassam Jarrar, expanding at length on Koranic prophecies, concluded that Allah would soon "bring forth a nation that would eliminate the State of Israel, and the Jews would [again] be dispersed."[57] Similar notions have been put forward, as we have noted, by Sheikh al-Tamimi and Sheikh Ikremah Sabri, who was appointed supreme mufti of Jerusalem by Yasser Arafat in 1994. They and other Muslim clerics have spoken of the last days, the slaughter of the Jews, and the imminent demise of Israel as a "Koranic inevitability." In the 1990s the eschatological ideas of these Islamist preachers have already aroused a strong resonance in the West Bank and Gaza. They seemed in retrospect to grant a higher purpose and sacred significance to the bloodstained events of the intifada, giving a pseudo-prophetic aura to its self-destructive nihilism.

Sheikh Sabri, like virtually all the leading Palestinian clerics, was irrevocably hostile toward Jews and other "infidels" in all his public utterances. Typically, six months before the second intifada began, he told *The New York Times* that the Holocaust had been exaggerated: "The Jews are using this issue, in many ways, also to blackmail the Germans financially. The Holocaust is the reason that there isn't a bigger noise against Israel as an occupying force. The Holocaust is protecting Israel. It's certainly not our fault if Hitler hated the Jews. Weren't they hated pretty much everywhere?"[58]

Sabri's reference to Hitler is revealing in at least two distinct ways. First, he totally represses the role of Haj Amin as Hitler's closest collaborator in the Middle East and an ardent supporter of the Nazi Holocaust. This is certainly not the result of Sabri's ignorance. Haj Amin was the most revered Palestinian national leader for almost four decades and the first Muslim to hold the British-invented position of supreme mufti of Jerusalem, which Sabri himself occupied in 2000. Second, less than a year before this interview, Hitler's best-known work, *Mein Kampf,* was in the top six of the PA's bestseller list. The translator's introduction to the Arabic edition emphasized its contemporary relevance and called Hitler "one of the few great men who almost stopped the motion of history, altered its course." National Socialism had not died "with the death of its herald" but rather "its seeds multiplied under each star."[59] This legacy has been all too evident in the case of the Islamic fundamentalists in Gaza and the West Bank. Their ceaseless verbal attacks on Israel as the "Nazi-like enemy" can hardly disguise the many similarities between their own anti-Semitism and that of Adolf Hitler—underscored by the immense popularity of the Arabic version of this supremely racist book.

On May 18, 2006, the Hamas weekly *Al-Risala* chronicled with pride certain statements by Hitler from the Sudeten crisis in 1938, in which he had praised the Palestinian Arab revolt against Great Britain. Like the official PA daily, *Al-Hayat Al-Jadeeda,* the Hamas publication believed that the trend, even in Britain, was to revise historical assessments of Hitler in a more positive direction. A quiz contest broadcast on Palestine radio on November 27, 2007, seemed to be in line with this tendency. In presenting Hitler as a political and military leader, there was no hint of the Holocaust, German war crimes, or the sadistic persecution of the Jews. Hitler remains an object of veneration for many Arabs and Palestinians to this day, not least because of his "war against the Jews." Ahmadinejad's Iran, Hezbollah, and Hamas can all be counted among his would-be heirs.

The rise of Hamas in the 1990s was facilitated by a number of external events. The collapse of the Soviet Union and the defeat of Saddam Hussein in the 1991 Persian Gulf War undoubtedly weakened the PLO, hitherto the dominant factor in Palestinian politics. Islamism was an ascending global force after the victory of the mujahideen in Afghanistan (with American, Saudi, and Pakistani help) over the demoralized Red Army. Hamas's adoption of suicide bombings after April 1994 further strengthened its position with the Palestinian public at a time when Yasser Arafat appeared to be outwardly cooperating with Israel.[60] The ensuing murderous assaults on crowds of Jewish civilians in Israel were an almost inevitable corollary of the *hate culture* propagated by Hamas. Incitement was deeply embedded in the school system, mosques, charities, and social services, especially in Gaza. A typical example of how this indoctrination operated was the kindergarten run by *al-Jamia al-Islamiya,* a Hamas charitable association under Sheikh Ahmad Bahar. In its 2002 graduation ceremony, it featured sixteen hundred preschool-age uniformed children carrying mock rifles. A five-year-old girl dipped her hand in red paint at the ceremony, imitating the bloodied hands proudly displayed by the frenzied Palestinians who had lynched two Israelis in Ramallah several months earlier. The walls of the various Hamas-controlled kindergartens were invariably full of signs and pictures glorifying the homicidal martyrs. At one Hamas-run Islamic school in Gaza City, an eleven-year-old Palestinian student solemnly declared, "I will make my body a bomb that will blast the flesh of Zionists, the sons of pigs and monkeys." "*Allahu akbar,*" his classmates shout in response: "God is great."

"May the virgins give you pleasure," his teacher yells, referring to one of the most solicited rewards awaiting martyrs in Paradise.[61]

The suicide bombers have indeed become icons of Palestinian society, glorified by the Hamas Islamic Student Movement, the Hamas charity committees, the population in the refugee camps, the academics in the universities, and journalists throughout the Palestinian media. Sheikh Bahar himself explained with unconcealed satisfaction that Hamas summer camps have been especially successful in instilling the "seeds of hate against Israel" in Palestinian children today.[62] Even twelve-year-olds have been recruited by Hamas for sacrificial terror attacks. One such Palestinian boy, arrested before he could carry out his mission, told the Israeli police: "I hate Jews, and at any opportunity I have, I will kill Jews. I am a *shahid*."[63] This child, like so many others, had been thoroughly brainwashed by the adults around him into an all-enveloping culture of hatred that can only breed mindless terrorism. Yet in this madness there is method—the desire to inculcate into its youth the principle that Jews have *no right to live* as free citizens of an independent Israel.

In recent years milder nonterrorist expressions of this same concept have begun to shape the public utterances and behavior of an increasingly radicalized Arab leadership inside Israel. Democratically elected Arab members of the Israeli Knesset have increasingly articulated an all-out rejection of the idea of a Jewish state. Almost without exception, they have embraced a militant Palestinian identity and, in some cases, openly backed or exhibited solidarity with Israel's sworn enemies. Azmi Bishara, head of the National Democratic Assembly Party and a Knesset member before fleeing Israel in 2007, had for some years lavishly praised the actions and achievements of the Lebanese Hezbollah. When the IDF unilaterally withdrew from Lebanon in June 2000, he publicly exalted Hezbollah for having "humiliated" it. In June 2001, at a memorial service for deceased Syrian president Hafez al-Assad, Bishara called on the Arab leaders present in the audience to intensify their struggle against Israel.[64] He and a number of other elected Arab officials identified even more openly with Hezbollah during the 2006 Lebanon War.

Israeli Arab Knesset member Ahmad Tibi is no admirer of Hezbollah. But for many years he served as a close adviser and overt supporter of PLO chairman Yasser Arafat. Tibi has always rejected "the Jewish character of the State of Israel." Hadash, the predominantly Arab Communist party led by Mohammad Barakeh, has been equally keen to *erase* Israel's Jewish identity in the name of "democracy," while vociferously supporting the creation of a new Palestinian national state. Tibi, Barakeh, and other Arab Knesset members repeatedly call for the repeal of the Law of the Return, as well as the abolition of the national anthem "Hatikvah," and of the Star of David on Israel's flag.[65] They not only insist on regarding Israeli Arabs as "Palestinians," but they also have consistently opposed any effort to integrate the Israeli Arab minority (20 percent of the population) into the Jewish state. Indeed, they demand Arab "national rights" inside Israel with the aim of transforming it into a binational Arab-Jewish state. They have also vigorously campaigned for implementing the Palestinian Arab right of return to Israel, which would, in practice, guarantee the rapid erosion of its Jewish character.[66]

Radical Islamic organizations such as Hezbollah and Hamas receive considerable support from Arab leaders inside Israel, despite their campaigns of terror against Israeli civilians and their total negation of Israel's right to exist. Abdulmalik Dehamshe, an Israeli Arab lawyer who represented Sheikh Ahmed Yassin in court and a leader of the United Arab List, reverentially described Yassin as a "great man and a man of peace." Some leaders of the Islamic movement, such as Sheikh Ra'ed Salah, head of its northern branch, go further still, embracing the rabble-rousing rhetoric of the Islamists and implicitly inciting terrorism against Israel. In 2003 the sheikh was charged with channeling large sums of money to charities inside the Palestinian Authority linked to Hamas. In September 2006 the sheikh addressed an audience of fifty thousand attending the Islamic Movement's eleventh annual rally in the Israeli city of Umm al-Fahm. He harangued the crowd with promises that "the Israeli occupation will shortly leave Jerusalem," denounced (imaginary) plans to divide the al-Aqsa Mosque, criticized the pope, and confidently predicted that the Holy City would soon become the capital of a new caliphate.

The charismatic Salah, who claims to speak for nearly 1.5 million Israeli Arabs, told an American interviewer in late October 2006 that Israel would "not survive another twenty years"—a view that almost exactly echoed those of Hamas's assassinated leader, Sheikh Yassin. Salah's extremism and religious appeals have helped him to achieve the kind of popularity no other Israeli-Arab leader appears to enjoy. Like Hamas in Gaza, his movement has built many mosques, distributed financial help to those in need, and totally denies any legitimacy of Israel.[67] In February 2007, during a sermon at a massive protest north of Jerusalem's Old City, he urged supporters to start a third intifada "to save al-Aksa mosque, free Jerusalem and end the occupation." Israel's history, he told the agitated crowd, was tainted with blood: "They want to build their temple at a time when our blood is on their clothes, on their doorsteps, in their food and in their drinks." The Jews were gambling with destiny, he continued, quoting Hamas founder Sheikh Yassin as saying: "The powerful will not remain powerful forever and the weak won't remain weak." According to Salah, the "idols" of Israeli power and occupation would soon be shattered. The prophets of Israel, he added, would have long ago abandoned the Jewish state. Following the sermons, dozens of masked Muslim youths and children clashed with Israeli security forces in East Jerusalem's Wadi Joz, throwing rocks, blocking streets, and burning garbage bins.[68]

Since the outbreak of the second intifada Hamas communiqués and political statements—like those of the Islamic Jihad—have continually focused on mobilizing the Palestinians to destroy Israel. The language is incendiary, lashing out at "the terrorist Jewish killers," the "Zionist gangs" who perpetrate "savage massacres," the ruthless enemy who humiliates the Palestinians and seeks to wipe out its resistance. Most of these communications are addressed to the mujahid Palestinian people and "our Arab and Islamic *umma*" (nation). They always conclude with the stock slogan: "It is a jihad until either victory or martyrdom." Much attention is devoted to the silence, complicity, or passivity of the PA in the face of "Zionist occupying forces" and to the malevolent American administration's strong support for the Israeli "terrorist war machine." The mujahideen who go to their heroic deaths for Islam are endlessly glorified as Palestinian role models "who yearn for death on their way to martyrdom."[69] According to Hamas, the second intifada, through the sacrificial human bombings that the jihadis performed, created a kind of "balance" with the heavily armed Zionists who "could not withstand great casualties." It had also exposed the fanatical hawkish reality of Israeli society that "only believed in violence to achieve its goals."[70] Palestinian homicidal slaughter of Israeli civilians, on the other hand, was benignly presented by Hamas and Islamic Jihad as "legitimate resistance" to Zionist terrorism, persecution, and aggression.

The "jihad against the Zionist Jews" is, above all, conceived as a religious obligation to fight the "treacherous [Jewish] occupiers" whose devilish objectives include the demolition of the al-Aqsa Mosque and "feverish [Zionist] attempts to Judaize the city of Al-Quds [Jerusalem]."[71] In claiming to defend the holy al-Aqsa Mosque from "desecration," Hamas has continually appealed (thus far with little result) to the leaders of all Arab and Islamic countries to join the fray. Though disappointed by the tepid pan-Arab response, Hamas has felt encouraged by growing signs of internal criticism in Israel. According to its diagnosis in 2002, the "Zionist entity" was brittle, racked by divisions, and wearied by its loss of security and stability. Israel was, perhaps, "in the stage of retreat and collapse," despite Ariel Sharon's "extremely fanatic and bloodthirsty" policies.[72] Such premature forecasts represent wishful thinking more than a realistic assessment of the balance of forces. But they do reveal some key Hamas assumptions and influence their policy decisions.

Zionist self-criticism is useful to Hamas while having no impact on its image of Jews as people who revoke pledges and are driven by "extremism, racism and hatred against all Palestinians, Arabs and Muslims." The Jews may consider themselves as the "chosen people of Allah," but the Koran had shown that their words are lies and distortions. No peace is possible with the "usurping Zionist entity" whom Allah himself had designated as treacherous. A communiqué of August 7, 2000, shortly before the second intifada, openly declared: "Our people and Nation's experience with the Jews affirms that the only feasible road against usurping occupation is that of resistance and Jihad and that the only healing against that cancerous disease is total extermination."[73] In a press statement four days earlier, Hamas had denounced Yasser Arafat for acknowledging any Jewish rights to the Western Wall of the Second Temple. Like the Palestinian Authority, Hamas categorically rejected this "Jewish name," instead calling it the al-Buraq Wall. The Jews had no jurisdiction or rights at the Western Wall since it was "part and parcel of the holy Aqsa mosque." On this point, Hamas reaffirmed the dominant Muslim credo "that the land of Palestine is an Islamic *Waqf* land for all Islamic generations until the Day of Judgement. It is religiously prohibited to give it up partially or wholly."[74]

Hamas's holy war against Israel came to full fruition after September 2000 in the aptly named al-Aqsa intifada, which has reinforced its political strength. Hamas sensed that the time was ripe to fully Islamicize the PLO's original goals, to infuse its nationalism with fundamentalist religion, and to offer a distinctively Muslim interpretation of the armed struggle against Israel. Indeed, the jihad that Hamas has waged for two decades to "liberate" Palestine in the name of Allah has transformed it into an Islamic cause par excellence—a "holy war until death."[75] Hamas also perceives it as "a war against the Jews" because of the central roles it attributes to Judaism and Zionism in the Western offensive against the Islamic world. Not one inch can ever be conceded to "enemies of God" with their counterfeit claim to Muslim land. This is "a contest of faith [*iman*], existence and life," rooted in divine commandments and unchanging religious principles.[76]

The ideological and political confrontation with Israel demands *sumud* (perseverance), avoidance of *fitna* (civil strife), readiness for sacrifice, and the kind of total commitment that secular nationalism alone can never provide. The Koran not only is the source of Hamas's faith in victory, but it also gives Hamas's primitive Jew hatred the aura of holiness. Islam alone can cure "the [Jewish] cancer that is spreading and threatening the entire Islamic world."[77] Moreover, the Koran itself supposedly refutes any Jewish claim to the land and legitimizes the struggle of the Palestinian people to purify the homeland of the alien invaders. In this fundamentalist conception, "land for peace" is a redundant, meaningless, and irrelevant phrase; the peace process is nothing but a fraud and a deadly snare. The "indivisible Palestine" to which Hamas and Islamic Jihad so ardently aspire will not only be under Islamic rule but will also be *judenrein*. The Jews are the "cursed nation" of the Koran, the sons of monkeys and pigs, the Zionist riffraff from the four corners of the earth: All will vanish in the fire of jihad and the smoke of Judgment Day.

Despite its Palestinian national coloring, Hamas still sees itself as part of the global jihad movement and has always taken pride in its origins and continuing links to the Muslim Brotherhood. The rulings of the Egyptian oracle of the brethren, Sheikh Youssef al-Qaradawi, who now lives in Qatar, served to legitimize the Hamas use of suicide bombings, of unveiled women in suicide missions, and the systematic killing of Israeli civilians. Qaradawi is head of the European Council for Fatwa and Research, president of the International Association of Muslim Scholars, and the spiritual guide of the Muslim Brotherhood and Hamas. It is he who has insisted that Muslims must resist and fight the Jews in the name of Islam "by the sword and the rifle," as well as with the Koran. Qaradawi's gloss on the well-known apocalyptic hadith—also included in the Hamas Covenant—leaves no room for ambiguity:

Everything will be on our side and against the Jews [on Judgment Day]; at that time, even the stones and the trees will speak, with or without words, and say: "Oh servant of Allah, oh Muslim, there's a Jew behind me, come and kill him." They will point to the Jews. It says "servant of Allah," not "servant of desires," "servant of women," "servant of the bottle," "servant of Marxism," or "servant of liberalism." . . . It said "servant of Allah."

Such interpretations provide legitimacy for the glorification by Hamas of death for the sake of Allah, of martyrdom in the war against the Jews, and of devotion to the cause of global jihad.[78] Hamas is still bound to its anti-Semitic charter and the ideal of an Islamic government based on sharia in *all* of Palestine.[79] Following Hezbollah's impressive performance against Israel in the Second Lebanon War, Hamas's confidence further increased. Its political leader in exile, Khalid Mashal, who is based in Damascus, concluded that Israel was in a crisis situation, unable to deal with the Iranian threats at a time when the United States had been defeated in Afghanistan and Iraq. This strategic assessment almost certainly reinforced Hamas's de facto alliance with Iran.[80]

The Hamas takeover of the Gaza Strip was arguably the single most important event in the Middle East in 2007. Despite the broad international support for Mahmoud Abbas and his Palestinian Authority in the West Bank, plus the increased foreign aid, security training, and American commitments, Fatah was steadily eclipsed by Hamas. After four decades of dominance, the secular nationalist hegemony in the Palestinian Arab movement had clearly been eroded. Since 2002, at least in Gaza, the writing was on the wall as hard-line Islamists began to increasingly dominate the Palestinian political agenda.[81]

Hamas is undoubtedly committed to jihad and insistent on liberating *all* of Palestine. Moreover it is unwilling to mask its anti-Semitism.[82] But such differences should not lead to ignoring its common ground with Palestinian Authority leaders. PA religious leaders today often speak the same language as Hamas about Palestine as an inalienable *waqf* land. Moreover, the numerous terror attacks of the PA's al-Aqsa Martyrs' Brigades have been virtually identical to those of Hamas. The PA, no less than Hamas, long embraced the use of terror (euphemistically called "resistance") to fight the Zionist enemy but has usually been more flexible about temporary agreements in order to obtain strategic territory from Israel.[83] PA leaders are also more careful about statements that imply a total rejection of Israel even within its 1949 boundaries. No such restraints apply to Hamas.[84]

The irrational hatred toward Israel and the Jews exhibited by Hamas cannot be separated from its religiosity. The Hamas Covenant mentions Allah more than a hundred times, contains thirty-three quotations from the Koran, has six references to the hadith, and seven to the Prophet Muhammad. The PLO Charter, by contrast, had no such references. However, the PA sermons follow the Hamas model and, not surprisingly, their content is virulently anti-Semitic, anti-Christian, anti-British, and anti-American.[85] Speaking in Gaza in March 2004 Sheikh Ibrahim Mudeiris, an employee of the PA Religious Affairs Ministry, saw a precise parallel between the contemporary crisis and Muhammad's war against the Jews. The Prophet knew that "they [the Jews] live forever off the fire of civil strife" and that no Islamic state could ever be established in Medina unless their "evil deeds" and the "Jewish cancer" were permanently removed. The contemporary Arab world, therefore, faces exactly the same problem as the Prophet: "The Jews are disseminating their venom, and history repeats itself. They disseminate their venom in the Arab countries, because they cannot live in the Middle East like a cancer, spreading in this land, unless they spark the fire of civil strife and war among the Arabs and the Muslims."

In a sermon May 13, 2005, the same preacher called the Jews "a virus resembling AIDS from which the entire world suffers."[86] Sermons defining Jews as the enemy of God and thereby justifying their murder have become an integral part of the broader Palestinian religious and political culture. The idea that all Jews should be targets of Palestinian terror was, for example, openly defended by a top Hamas leader, the late Abdel Aziz al-Rantisi.[87]

The war of the PA and Hamas against Israel is not divorced from the global Islamic war being fought against the "Judeo-Christian West." Their focal point remains Palestine, but its fate is closely linked with broader hopes for the demise of the West, especially America and Britain. It is no accident that two-thirds of Palestinians in December 2005 identified with the al-Qaeda terrorist attacks in the United States and Europe.[88] Shortly afterward, in the Palestinian elections, a clear majority sided with a movement openly committed to Israel's destruction. Hamas combined this militant intransigence with effective social programs, discipline, a reputation for honesty (when compared to massive PLO corruption), and the promise of radical change, which largely explained its popular appeal and electoral success. These characteristics were eerily reminiscent of the Nazi Party's rise to power in the early 1930s, when it also temporarily showed a more moderate side in its political strategy but did not alter its goals on achieving power.

Hamas's landslide triumph on January 25, 2006, winning 74 out of 132 seats in the Palestinian parliament, demonstrated that this method had paid off.[89] Its victory coincided with the impressive showing of its sister movement, the Muslim Brotherhood, in Egypt's parliamentary elections, along with repeated Iranian and emboldened Syrian provocations and threats against Iraq, Lebanon, and Israel.[90]

Two weeks after the Hamas triumph, its website presented the following video messages from two of its departing suicide terrorists. The first bomber said: "My message to the loathed Jews is that there is no god but Allah, we will chase you everywhere! We are a nation that drinks blood, and we know that there is no blood better than the blood of the Jews. We will not leave you alone until we have quenched our thirst with your blood, and our children's thirst with your blood."[91] Hamas's special website for children regularly features stories of the *shahids,* and glorifies violence and the eternal path of jihad against the thieves who stole Palestine. In videos they convey the message that killing Jews will guarantee entrance to heaven and the joys of paradise.[92] Hamas TV has even used a clone of Disney's Mickey Mouse to teach children to hate Israel and America, while aspiring to Islam's impending world domination. The bottom line of this indoctrination is the dogma that "the Jews are criminals and enemies whom we must expel from our lands."[93]

• • •

The Hamas government is a jihadi regime, but it has had to maneuver under military blockade from Israel and economic pressure from outside (the United States, Europe, and Arab states) toward an outwardly more "pragmatic" political position. Hence it publicly proposed a five-year *hudna* (truce) in return for full Israeli withdrawal from the West Bank and the establishment of a Palestinian state within the 1967 borders.[94] Since Hamas repeatedly stated that in its eyes there was no distinction between the Israeli occupied territory of 1948 or 1967, and that the jihad continues "until the very last usurper is driven out of our land," the *hudna* could clearly be nothing more than a temporary stage toward the "liberation" of all of Palestine. The truce follows the Hudaibiya example of the Prophet Muhammad and does not imply recognition of Israel. It is designed to win time in order to militarily strengthen Hamas for the final assault. As the deputy editor of the *Corriere della Sera*, Egyptian-born Magdi Allam, has pointed out: "When it [Hamas] talks only about a hudna, it is actually saying it doesn't recognize Israel's right to exist. It is not talking about peace . . . only a temporary cessation of war activities. When we examine Hamas's ambitions, we see that its constitution calls for the destruction of Israel and the establishment of an Islamic State based on sharia law."[95]

Hamas's perception of the conflict is evident in the chilling videotaped statement Khalid Mashal made in February 2006 to celebrate his organization's victory in the Palestinian elections:

> You [Jews] will be defeated with God's help. Victory day is approaching with God's help. Before Israel dies, it will not escape humiliation and surrender. Before they die, with God's help, they will witness humiliation and surrendering. And America will not be there to help. . . . We will defeat them [the Israelis]. We will defeat them emotionally and mentally before we defeat them in the field of battle. Gaza is the victory's bed. . . . Victory in these elections sends a message to Israel and America and all the abusers of this world. With us you will never succeed and you will always lose. . . . The days of defeat within six days are over. Today you are fighting against the army of Allah.[96]

A global perspective is provided in another Hamas video released in June 2006 containing statements by Yasser Ghalban, killed that month in internal Palestinian fighting. It included the following remarks:

> We will rule the nations, by Allah's will, the USA will be conquered, Israel will be conquered, Rome and Britain will be conquered. . . . The Jihad for Allah . . . is the way of Truth and the way for Salvation and the way which will lead us to crush the Jews and expel them from our country Palestine. Just as the Jews ran from Gaza, the Americans will run from Iraq and Afghanistan and the Russians from Chechnya, and the Indians from Kashmir.[97]

One of the most prominent Hamas leaders, Mahmoud al-Zahar (strongly identified with the global jihad) emphasized that the Israeli disengagement from Gaza in 2005 was a Muslim asset in the battle for Afghanistan and Iraq:

"We are part of the great world plan whose name is the global Islamic movement." Despite tactical differences over issues such as participation in elections and relations with Shiite Iran, Hamas and al-Qaeda both have common roots in the Sunni Muslim Brotherhood and a shared commitment to religiously motivated terrorism. The Hamas electoral victory undoubtedly signified a major shift of paradigm in regard to the Palestine conflict, with Islamism now threatening to definitively supplant Arab nationalism.

By giving the territorial struggle a religious fundamentalist character, Hamas has not only rendered it virtually insoluble, but also endangered existing Arab regimes in Egypt, Syria, Jordan, and Algeria.[98] Here, too, it resembles al-Qaeda and Islamic Jihad. For Hamas, now as in the past, its war with Israel is a jihad for Allah, a struggle to destroy the Jewish state *in the name of Islam.*[99] On a daily basis throughout March 2007, its Al-Aqsa TV broadcast the words of the "martyred" Hamas founder, Ahmed Yassin, responding to Israel's planned evacuation from the Gaza Strip. For the sheikh this retreat was proof that Israel was lost, "defeated," "a state with no ability, helpless." Yassin lucidly explained: "They [the Zionists] established a state to protect the Jews from death and murder. If death and murder chase them in Tel Aviv, Jerusalem, Netanya . . . then they will say: 'What am I doing here? I founded a state to protect me from death, and if death chases me, I want to flee and go back to Europe and America.' "[100]

This prophecy began to acquire some teeth by June 2007, forty years after Israel's conquest of the territories. Hamas was now in full control of the Gaza Strip and firing hundreds of Qassam rockets into southern Israel, almost at will. But at the same time, Palestinians were even more at war with themselves. PA chairman Mahmoud Abbas was increasingly willing to describe the leaders of Hamas as "murderous terrorists" for staging a coup in Gaza and trying to assassinate him. Arafat's portrait was torn off office walls in Gaza and smashed under the boots of Hamas fighters. The green flag of Islam was hauled up in place of the Palestinian flag. Though Hamas was penned up in its Gaza enclave, it was, nonetheless, firmly in control. On the other hand, Fatah-style secular Arab nationalism was in a shambles. Despite all the money, weapons, and praise showered on him from abroad and from Israel, Abbas radiated only military and political impotence.[101] The PA was riddled by corruption and ruled by the *mukhabarat* (secret-police networks), typical of most Arab states. The PA's duplicity was particularly shameless as its TV network continued to broadcast daily video clips about liberating *all* of Palestine, even as it pledged in Annapolis to negotiate a peace treaty with Israel for a two-state solution.[102]

The statistics on Palestinian terror do not support the idea that there is a peace process. In 2007, Palestinians carried out 2,946 terror attacks against Israel (nine fewer than in 2006); Qassam rocket attacks from the Gaza Strip remained at the same high level, but the amount of mortar fire increased greatly. The smuggling of weapons from Egypt to Gaza continued apace until the war of January 2009. Indeed, more than eighty tons entering the area in the six months after Hamas's violent takeover of the Strip in June 2007. This helped the organization turn itself into a full-fledged army with brigades, battalions, and special forces.

Hamas is strong in the West Bank, too, especially in social services, but was unable to overthrow the PA, solely because of the Israeli military presence within the territory.[103] Hamas's growing alliance with Iran, which also substantially aids Fatah and Islamic Jihad, was a sure sign of its intention to build a new southern Lebanon in Gaza. It also fortified Gaza on the model of underground bunkers and other methods pioneered by Hezbollah on Israel's northern border. Its security forces have been trained in terrorism and guerrilla war by Iran, from which it obtained a steady supply of money and weaponry. In Gaza, alone, there were already about one hundred thousand automatic rifles and machine guns by early 2008, transforming this miserably impoverished enclave into a heavily armed camp.[104] On the eve of the 2009 proxy war with the Jewish state, Hamastan had virtually become an Iranian base, committed to Israel's extinction.[105]

Hamas's emphatic refusal to recognize the right of the Jewish people to even minimal self-determination anywhere between the Mediterranean and the Jordan has never deviated to this day. It has always viewed the conflict with Israel in zero-sum terms, exhibiting total contempt for the notion of two states for two peoples. However, Hamas is not alone in this attitude. In March 2009, one of the chief Fatah leaders (and a bitter rival of the Hamas), Muhammad Dahlan, declared on Palestinian TV: "I want to say for the thousandth time, in my own name and in the name of all my fellow members of the Fatah movement: we do not demand that the Hamas movement recognize Israel. On the contrary, we demand of Hamas *not* to recognize Israel, because Fatah does not recognize Israel even today."[106] Thus the demand to bolster so-called Palestinian moderates and isolate extremists (adopted by Israel and constantly repeated in the West) needs to be treated with some skepticism.

Even more important are Iranian intentions and strategy—especially at a time when its leaders so openly call to "wipe Israel off the map." Iran's interest in arming, training, supplying, and inciting Hamas against Israel (as it also did with Hezbollah two years earlier) is palpable. These miniwars have diverted international attention away from Iran's hot pursuit of an effective nuclear weapons capability. It is no accident that Iranians have provided Hamas with the long-range rockets that have been fired at southern Israel. Before and during Operation Cast Lead, Iran encouraged Hamas to indiscriminately target Israeli civilians in order to exhaust their morale, disrupt everyday life, and provoke increasing physical damage. Through its support of both Hamas and Hezbollah, Iran has deliberately sought to fan the flames of violence and discord throughout the Middle East.

The moderate Arab states, led by Egypt and Saudi Arabia, are fully conscious of this Iranian strategy, implemented with Syrian backing. This awareness largely explains their muted reaction to Israel's military operations against Hezbollah in 2006 and Hamas in 2009. The Palestinian Hamas has indeed become a major fault line in the great rift between the Iran-Syria-Hezbollah axis and the Saudi-Egyptian camp. Egypt's intense mediation effort in the intra-Palestinian unity talks needs to be seen in the light of its desire to curb Shiite Persian hegemony. Similarly, Saudi Arabia has expended billions of dollars to counter Iran's ambitions to project itself as the leading regional military power and guardian of the Islamic flame. For Egypt, Saudi Arabia, and other pro-Western Sunni Arab states, Iran raises, above all, the specter of Persian colonialism and hegemony over a divided Arab world. Already in the Second Lebanon War of 2006 involving Israel, Saudi Arabia led the sharp criticism of Hezbollah for serving Iranian interests. Egypt, too (as in the most recent Israel-Hamas war), accused the Palestinian Islamists of being lackeys of Iran. Tehran responded in kind, branding the Saudi-Egyptian-Fatah axis as infidels, Zionist collaborators, and tools of the American imperialist Satan. Iran's supreme leader, Ali Khameini, contemptuously equated the moderate Arab critics of Hamas with the Jews whom the Prophet Muhammad had fought in Arabia nearly fourteen hundred years ago.

For Iran, Hamas, and Hezbollah, these routine anti-Semitic references to

Jews have become second nature, and through endless repetition they have assumed the quality of eternal truths. Whether in the media, schools, mosques, or the home, the hatred toward Israel is deeply implanted. It extends toward anyone (whether America or pro-Western Arab leaders) who favors normalization with the malignant Jewish cancer in the Muslim body politic.[107] It also includes classical anti-Semitism of the variety that blames the world banking crisis on the Jews who supposedly control the American government and economy.

· · ·

The hatred and violence preached in Islamist sermons and currently all-pervasive on the Hamas TV station, Al-Aqsa, is above all based on Islamic motifs of the perfidious Jews as "the brothers of apes and pigs." Jews are enemies of the Prophet, and a people with whom it is impossible to make agreements. The total grip that Hamas exerts over propaganda and education in the Gaza Strip means that this incitement is now permanent, subordinate to totalitarian political and religious goals, poisoning the minds of a new generation with its culture of sickness. For example, a Hamas legislator and imam, Sheikh Yunus al-Astal, writing in the weekly *Al-Risala* on March 13, 2008, discussed a Koranic verse suggesting that "suffering by fire is the Jews' destiny in this world and the next." His conclusion was that the "punishment of burning" (*mahraka*)—a word in Arabic normally used to connote the Holocaust—was a fitting retribution for Jewish crimes in this world. Indeed, he added: "We are sure that the Holocaust is still to come upon the Jews." In an article in *The New York Times,* published at the beginning of April 2008, its correspondent Steven Erlanger reported at some length on this hardening of Hamas's Jew-baiting in the mosques and on TV, closely linked to the general ethos of jihad, suicide bombing, and the total war to "liberate" Palestine.[108]

The same mind-set has long existed in the Lebanese Hezbollah ("Party of God")—the Iranian-backed jihadist movement whose secretary-general since 1992, Hassan Nasrallah, regularly terms Israel a "cancerous entity" and prophesies its extinction. Within a month of Nasrallah taking over as leader, Hezbollah (with the help of Iran) organized the bombing of the Israeli embassy in Buenos Aires, killing twenty-nine and injuring more than two hundred. Two years later Hezbollah perpetrated the bombing of the Jewish community center in Buenos Aires, killing eighty-six persons and wounding many more.

Hezbollah is an Islamic resistance movement born out of the Israeli invasion of Lebanon in 1982. From the outset it has been both a terror organization and a grassroots social movement with a robust image as the defender of the poor. In 1983 it was responsible for the bombing attack on the U.S. Marine barracks in Beirut that killed 240 Americans, and the kidnapping of more than fifty foreigners over the following few years. Its marches in the capital have been capable of drawing huge throngs of the Shiite faithful—exuding social activism and zealous militancy. Hezbollah saw itself as a religious party representing Lebanon's traditionally underprivileged Shiite Muslims (now the country's largest sect), though it also claimed to champion the oppressed masses in general. Its efficient work in maintaining hospitals, schools, and clinics is what originally gave it widespread legitimacy, much like Hamas activities in Palestine.[109] Hezbollah proved itself to be particularly media-savvy, using its own TV network, radio stations, and press to propagate a militant Islamist message. For example, Hezbollah managed to persuade many Lebanese that it was their sole shield against Israel and the savior of their national dignity. Despite the massive financial support it has received from Iran, Hezbollah continues to make great efforts to become a part of the Lebanese social and political reality. It long ago realized that it had to allay fears that it planned to transform Lebanon into an Iranian-style Islamic republic, though this is indeed its long-term goal. At the same time Hezbollah's popularity in Lebanon has been closely connected to the reputation of its fighters for being fearless, devoted, and willing to sacrifice themselves in the battle against Zionism. The sheer destruction caused by the 2006 war with Israel (that it ignited by entering Israeli territory, killing three soldiers, and capturing two others) dented some of these assumptions.

Iran originally created the Lebanese branch of Hezbollah to export its Islamic Revolution abroad in 1982, and it still provides the organization with about $100 million annually.[110] Victory over "the Zionist regime" is inscribed on its Hezbollah banners as part of a broader Iranian-led desire to radically redraw the Middle East map in such a way that there will be no place for Israel. In its founding statement, Hezbollah had defined Israel as "the vanguard of the United States in our Islamic world . . . the greatest danger to our future generations and to the destiny of our lands. . . . There-fore our struggle will only end when this entity is obliterated. We recognize no treaty with it, no ceasefire, and no peace agreements, whether separate or consolidated."[111]

Fifteen years later, in June 2000, Hezbollah's secretary-general Hassan Nasrallah explained to an Egyptian journalist that one of the central rea-sons for creating his movement had been the eradication of Israel: "That is the principal objective of Hezbollah. . . . We face an entity that conquered the land of another people, drove them out of their land, and committed horrendous massacres. As we see it, this is an illegal State; it is a cancerous entity and the root of all the crises and wars, and cannot be a factor in bringing about a true and just peace in this region." Nasrallah's ugly-sounding anti-Semitism was also unmistakable in this comment, quoted by Israeli-American journalist Jeffrey Goldberg in October 2002: "If we searched the entire world for a person more cowardly, despicable, weak and feeble in psyche, mind, ideology and religion, we would not find anyone like the Jew. Notice I do not say the Israeli." On another occasion, Nasrallah characterized the Jews as "Allah's most cowardly and greedy creatures" and "grandsons of apes and pigs."[112] For more than twenty-five years Hezbollah has been declaring that its holy war will continue "until the elimination of Israel and until the death of the last Jew on earth."[113] This kind of apoca-lyptic hatred is consistent with Hezbollah's total allegiance to militant Is-lamism and to the legacy of Ayatollah Khomeini—the "wise and just leader," "our tutor," and "commanding Jurist [*faqih*]." Anti-Americanism has been no less central to its sacred mission. "We combat abomination and we shall tear out its very roots, its primary roots, which are the U.S."[114]

Hezbollah's deep animosity toward America as the "Great Satan" is fully consonant with Iranian revolutionary propaganda. The United States is the "greatest plunderer of our treasures, our oil, and our resources"; the hyper-imperialist power seeks to reduce the Third World masses to slavery. Amer-ica only desires to create rifts, civil strife, and disintegration in the Arab and Muslim world to facilitate its neocolonialist policies of economic exploita-tion. Hence the foremost motto of Hezbollah, which Nasrallah's followers proudly chant year after year in street demonstrations, is "Death to Amer-ica."[115] The American war on terror after 9/11, its invasion of Iraq, its pres-sure on Iran, and its defense of Israel have reinforced but did not create this intense loathing for the United States. The Iranian connection, in particular (which has intensified since the rise of Mahmoud Ahmadinejad), is an important factor in maintaining the high levels of anti-American and anti-Zionist incitement. Hezbollah is undoubtedly a central component of Iran's military and security policies, and of its revolutionary strategic aims; it is a front line of aggression or alternatively defense against Israel. Hezbollah's consolidation in Lebanon, reinforced since 2007, is indeed the greatest single success story in the export of the Islamic Revolution. To a certain degree Hezbollah has also become Syria's strategic partner—the recipient of its rockets, missiles, and other weaponry, as well as of its political backing. While Syria has no obvious interest in promoting an Islamic state in Lebanon, it has consistently supported Hezbollah's armed resistance against Israel in the south as an invaluable bargaining counter and a protection for itself.

In Lebanon's complex confessional and politic mosaic, Hezbollah has come to represent the rising Shiite minority (now 35 percent of the population), which has been increasingly radicalized and politicized since the 1970s. Concentrated mainly in the Bekáa Valley, Beirut, and the south, the Shiites (under Iranian influence) have in modern times developed a harsher attitude than most Sunnis toward Jews and other non-Muslims. This is certainly a factor in explaining the virulence of Hezbollah's ideological Jew hatred and its total negation of Israel's existence. Hezbollah's ideology strongly emphasizes the Koranic roots of Islamist politics, while specifically drawing on Shiite symbols such as the Ashura—the day that commemorates the martyrdom of Imam Husayn ibn 'Ali through mass marches and self-flagellation. In the modernized Shia theology of Hezbollah, the liberation of Jerusalem and Palestine are essential both to Shiite liberation in Lebanon and to the final goal: worldwide Islamic hegemony.[116] Hezbollah clearly perceives its conflict with Israel and the Jews as an either-or *life-and-death* struggle. This confrontation is simultaneously historical, social, and cultural, with its roots in a thirteen-hundred-year battle between Judaism and Islam. The cultural war between the Islamic world and the West, as well as the social struggle between Western oppressive arrogance and the downtrodden Third World masses, have been grafted onto this theological base.[117]

Israelis, Jews, and Americans are singled out in Hezbollah ideology as primary "enemies of God and Islam"; they are "the Party of the Devil" opposing the "Party of God."[118] They symbolize the decadence and corruption of Western culture and the disasters of modernization that are supposedly responsible for the parlous state of the Arab and Muslim worlds. Israel is not only a Western implant in the Middle East, but also a deadly cancerous growth that has spread incalculable evils and vices into the region, including the uprooting and expulsion of the Palestinians, colonialist violence, the occupation of Islamic holy places, secularization, immorality, and the Western exploitation of the region's oil resources. The relentlessly anti-Semitic characterizations of Israel as a cancerous growth seem to be primarily of Khomeinist provenance. Similarly, the depiction of Israel as racist, barbarian, and perfidious, while commonplace in the Arab world, owes not a little to Iranian Shiite sources.[119] As Islamic anti-Semitism scholar Esther Webman has noted, Hezbollah frequently employs Western anti-Semitic symbols, especially in visual representations of Israelis: "Typically, Israel's alleged ruthlessness is illustrated by a soldier with a long, crooked nose, long teeth and ears and a prickly chin, wearing an armband with the Star of David and a steel helmet on his head, and holding a dagger dripping with blood."[120]

Hezbollah's so-called spiritual guide, Sheikh Muhammad Husayn Fadlallah, has been a major influence on its anti-Semitic worldview. For Fadlallah, Israel represents a "Jewish movement" that expelled Palestinians from Islamic territory, based on the inadmissible excuse that this was a land promised to Jews by God.[121] Zionism was nothing but "political Judaism." It constituted a continual aggression against Muslims, rooted in Jewish rejection of Allah. According to the Koran, Jews and idolaters were the "most hostile to the believers"; Jews, in particular, had killed the prophets, spread corruption around the globe, and oppressed other peoples. The Torah "inspired the Jews to kill" just as Zionism encouraged them to seek world domination in cooperation with secret Masonic orders. Judaism was the source of racism and Jewish condescension toward other peoples—their deceit, treachery, and exploitative mentality.[122] In a 1988 interview Fadlallah said, "The Jews want to be a world superpower. This racist circle of Jews wants to take vengeance on the whole world for their history of persecution and humiliation. In this light, the Jews will work on the basis that Jewish interests are above all world interests."[123]

The anti-Semitism of Hezbollah leaders and spokesmen combines the image of seemingly invincible Jewish power, insatiable ambition, and cunning with the contempt normally reserved for weak and cowardly enemies. Like the Hamas propaganda for holy war, that of the Hezbollah has relied on the endless vilification of Jews as "enemies of mankind," "conspiratorial, obstinate, and conceited" adversaries full of "satanic plans" to enslave the Arabs. It fuses traditional Islamic anti-Judaism with Western conspiracy myths, Third Worldist anti-Zionism, and Iranian Shiite contempt for Jews as "ritually impure" and corrupt infidels. Sheikh Fadlallah typically insists, for example, that Jews wish to undermine or obliterate Islam and Arab cultural identity in order to advance their economic and political domination.[124] Israel was founded as their territorial springboard to advance this global agenda. The present conflict is essentially a repetition of the Prophet's original fight against the Jews of Arabia.[125] Muslims today are facing the same perfidious enemy who had shown his true face in Palestine. "The Jews usurped Palestine," according to Fadlallah. "The Jews killed us and ousted us from our homes. They follow the Muslims everywhere in the world, oppress them, weaken them and enter into alliances with world arrogance [America] against them."[126]

Hezbollah's deep hostility toward Israel partly developed out of the first Israeli invasion of Lebanon and the movement's symbiotic relationship with revolutionary Iran. Money, weaponry, training, and indoctrination continue to flow from Iran via Syria into Lebanon to reinforce both the radical and the religious connection. The Iranian Revolutionary Guard Corps (Pasdaran) in the Bekáa Valley of Lebanon has for many years been a pillar of support for Hezbollah. Much of Hezbollah's ideology originated in Iran. This has not prevented the organization from adopting Christian anti-Semitic libels about the Jewish Talmud, and Western stereotypes concerning the Jews as the primary source of corruption, evil, and destruction in the world. Fadlallah and other leading Hezbollah clerics also adopted Holocaust denial, describing the mass murder of Jews as "pure fiction" and strongly supporting the French "revisionist" Roger Garaudy.[127] In this respect they are no different from Iran, Hamas, and many other Islamist groupings, not to mention a substantial chunk of the secular Arab intellectual class. The Holocaust is reduced to a mere tool of Zionist propaganda and profiteering. Hezbollah was appalled, for example, that the Vatican under Pope John Paul II issued the document "We Remember," which apologized for the Christian role in the Holocaust. Since this is perceived as a "myth fabricated by Jews and Zionists," the Catholic Church's regrets over the Shoah were denounced as totally misplaced, a "denial of history," an abandonment of tradition, and a mark of Jewish influence in the Vatican.[128]

Hezbollah's attitude toward the Jews has precluded negotiation or rapprochement, let alone peace, with Israel—branded as an "illusion" and capitulation to the policy of Zionist "expansionist" hegemony. In Fadlallah's view, even if Jews converted en masse to Islam, they would still have to leave Palestine.[129] Yet Hezbollah has, nonetheless, managed to market itself as if it were genuinely engaged in interfaith dialogue. In October 2004, its leader in southern Lebanon, Sheikh Nabil Qauq, attacked President Bush's militant Christianity and foreign policy in a meeting with a visiting delegation from the Presbyterian Church in the United States. In the televised meeting with Hezbollah, Presbyterian Church representative Ronald Stone unctuously replied:

> We treasure the precious words of Hezbollah and your expression of goodwill towards the American people. Also we praise your initiative for dialogue and mutual understanding. We cherish these statements that bring us closer to you. As an elder of our church, I'd like to say that according to my recent experience, relations and conversations with Islamic leaders are a lot easier than dealings and dialogue with Jewish leaders.[130]

The American Presbyterian Church leadership subsequently condemned the meeting and Stone's "inappropriate" remarks. Nevertheless, Hezbollah's religious outreach chalked up a few successes with other Christian groups and with the ultra-Orthodox Jewish Neturei Karta sect. Haredi anti-Zionist Jews participated in an anti-Israel convention in Beirut in February 2005 where one of the group's spokesmen insisted that Jews must "leave this Zionist state, which violates the Jewish religion" and which was "persecuting the Palestinian people."[131] Neturei Karta and Hezbollah discovered common ground some time before Iranian president Ahmadinejad issued his invitations to the Jewish sect to take part in the Holocaust denial conference in Tehran.

Hezbollah unabashedly adheres to Holocaust negation and enthusiastically supports its leading advocates, Robert Faurisson and Roger Garaudy. Hezbollah leader Hassan Nasrallah, speaking on Al-Jazeera TV on February 3, 2006, warmly praised the "great French philosopher, Roger Garaudy" who had "proved that this Holocaust is a myth." Garaudy's "humiliation" in France merely underlined Western hypocrisy, especially when contrasted with its defense of Danish cartoons "insulting" the Prophet Muhammad. "Freedom of expression extends to the Jews," Nasrallah angrily complained, "but it does not extend to the Prophet of 1.4 billion Muslims."[132]

Like the Iranian leadership, Nasrallah has consistently combined anti-Israeli, anti-Semitic, and Holocaust denial motifs, with a special emphasis on Israel as a "cancerous entity" or "infectious microbe" that knows no limits, spreading its poison wherever there are Jews. On April 9, 2000, he referred at length to the State of Israel as a "cancerous growth" that had to be excised. In September 2001 he characterized Jews in general as "Allah's most cowardly and greedy caricatures." On a November 29, 2002, Jerusalem Day broadcast on Hezbollah TV channel Al-Manar, he ranted against the "Talmudic Zionists" and their messianic allies who were allegedly seeking to "destroy al-Aqsa and to rebuild Solomon's Temple in its place."[133] For Nasrallah, Israel is *al-shar al-mutlaq* (an absolute evil) because of its very existence, not the fact that it occupied southern Lebanon for twenty-two years. The "Zionist entity," according to its conception, usurped and "raped" Palestine. Its establishment is forever *illegitimate* because *al-batil* (falsehood) can never become *al-haq* (righteous) over time.[134] The stigma of origins is deemed eternal, as in the Hamas Covenant, leading to an existential and civilizational struggle to eradicate Israel.[135]

Though Israel's war against Hezbollah and the Palestinian terrorist groups sharpens their view of the Jewish state as "the central enemy of the Islamic *umma*," this is *not* its chief cause. At its heart lies the cultural stereotyping characteristic of a radically anti-Semitic worldview. The scurrilous depiction of Israel's "racist and criminal practices" is only one facet of this methodical demonization in which Israelis are branded as child slaughterers and sadists who rip open pregnant women's stomachs. Hezbollah sees depravity, malevolence, cowardice, and deceitfulness as fundamental characteristics of the perfidious Jews and the duplicitous Israeli state—with which normalized relations are inherently impossible. But there is also the perception of Zionism as a monolithic ideology committed to an empire stretching from the Nile to the Euphrates that will enslave Arabs and Muslims, eradicating Islamic identity. The Zionists, they believe, aim to "Judaize" all of Palestine, then the Middle East, and finally the entire world. In a January 24, 1988, Jerusalem Day speech, Nasrallah even blamed the internal Algerian conflict on the Zionists who confront the entire Muslim *umma* "from every location in the world."[136] Zionism, he said, is "the most dangerous and malicious enemy of humanity" and not just the archenemy of the Arab-Islamic world.[137]

Hezbollah's struggle against the Jews is, in this respect, more *existential* than its general opposition to the West, more violent and obsessively intent on dehumanization as well as delegitimization. All of Israeli society—not just the Israeli state—is guilty of crimes against humanity. There are no innocent Israeli civilians, and every Israeli inhabitant of Jerusalem is deemed to be a "Jewish invader." There is no distinction between the pre-state and post-1948 generation of Israelis, between sabras and immigrants, the Right and the Left, settlers and peaceniks, adults and children. All are "usurpers," militant occupiers, murderers, oppressors, and racists. Hence Nasrallah's castigations of Mahmoud Abbas and Fatah for even considering a truncated Palestinian state based on negotiations that would recognize Israel. Hezbollah did not, of course, object to gaining control of land that Israel would voluntarily surrender. But under no circumstances could that justify conceding the legitimacy of the Jewish state, or the recognition of Israeli sovereignty anywhere in Palestine. In other words, for Hezbollah the conflict was and remains a struggle for existence, not for borders. Like the Iranian leadership, Hezbollah links the liberation of Jerusalem and Palestine to the reappearance of the Hidden Imam (the Shiite Islamic Messiah) who will one day lead the prayers at the al-Aqsa Mosque in the Holy City. This is another reason why Nasrallah in March 2009 rejected the Obama administration's condition for dialogue, which included recognizing the Jewish state. He stressed in a speech in Beirut that the Lebanese were "capable of defeating this entity and can make it disappear . . . therefore Hezbollah will never recognize Israel, not today, not tomorrow, not even in 1,000 years."[138]

Hezbollah, like other Islamist movements including Hamas, formally claims to respect Judaism as a divine religion and its believers as People of the Book. But in practice, it considers the overwhelming majority of Jews to be Zionists, and the professed distinction is largely spurious. Hezbollah holds Zionism to be a "Torah and Talmudic" ideology. Its biblical and religious origins were simply translated by the Zionists into modern racist language. In Nasrallah's diatribes, Israel has inherited all of its despicable bloodthirsty traits and deceitfulness from its *Judaic* background—beginning with its arrogant self-understanding as God's chosen people. Any covenant made with Jews would, therefore, be worthless. This typically Islamist belief stems from the Koran, along with many other anathemas directed against Jews and Judaism in the time of the Prophet. But its religious origin and self-declared objectives do not mean that Hezbollah is merely anti-Judaic.[139] Like Hamas and the Muslim Brotherhood, "the Party of God" regards the Jews per se as being tainted with evil, intrinsically racist, and exhibiting vile characteristics that have been *unchanged* since the time of Muhammad. It demonizes the Jews and regards them as engaged in a universal conspiracy against God and mankind.[140] If this is not pure unadulterated anti-Semitism, then the term has no meaning at all.

Judaism, Zionism, and Israel are virtually synonymous in Hezbollah's vocabulary. Its anti-Semitism is not, however, the result of Zionist actions or of the conflict with Israel, which have done little more than provide the backdrop and a political context for its expression.[141] Hezbollah itself insists that its loathing for Judaism and the Jews is *not* at all related to Zionism but to the quintessentially evil nature of this people as revealed by the Koran and the Old and the New Testaments. The Islamist anti-Semitism it espouses does not stem from the occupation of Palestine or southern Lebanon before 2000 but from its religious creed and the immemorially hostile character traits of the Jews described at the dawn of Islamic history. Zionist practice and Israeli policy have, no doubt, helped to reactivate the older Islamic anti-Judaic tradition, but they have hardly caused it. Hezbollah, basing itself on the Koran, has made it clear that Jews are a people "whose blood is full of enmity toward mankind," who have opposed God's revelation, and who have been enemies of the Muslims from the beginning of Islam. Allah himself cursed the Jews in his Holy Scriptures as idolaters, blasphemers, and worse. According to many of Nasrallah's speeches, blasphemy was imprinted on the Jews' hearts, along with disbelief, disobedience, prophet slaying, and other transgressions. Over the decades the well-known Koranic verses vituperating against the Jews have become a firm fixture in the repertoire of Islamic anti-Semitism: "And abasement and poverty were pitched upon them [the Children of Israel] and they were laden with God's wrath; that because they had disbelieved the signs of God and slain the prophets unrightfully; that because they disobeyed, and were transgressors" (Koran 2:58).

According to the Koran, the Jews had rejected their own prophets—Moses and Jesus—and betrayed the Torah, the Ten Commandments, and the Holy Spirit. They were "puffed up with pride" (Koran 2:87), refusing to believe the final revelation granted to Muhammad.[142] For Hezbollah, as with Hamas, the war with contemporary Israel is therefore a continuation of the original conflict in which the Prophet vanquished the recalcitrant Jewish tribes at the battle of Khaibar. But there is also a racist dimension attributed to the Jews. The enmity of the Jews toward Islam allegedly began long before the modern "Palestine question" emerged, and it is blamed on an ingrained Judaic sense of racial, religious, and cultural superiority with regard to Muslims. The Hezbollah leader, like many other Muslim clerics (both Sunni and Shiite), specifically attributes the pre-Zionist Jews' rejection of the Prophet to *racism*. According to Nasrallah, as soon as the Jews discovered that Muhammad was "a Hashemite Arab Prophet rather than one of the Sons of Israel, their racism made them fight him."[143] Both Muslims and Christians are merely there to serve God's chosen people, and validate Jewish racial supremacy, according to this twisted though extremely widespread Islamist worldview. Arrogance, perfidy, and racism—along with the violation of their own covenants—have been Jewish traits since time immemorial. Equally predetermined is their congenital aggression frequently alluded to in the Koran (manifested in their status as "slayers of the Prophets and Messengers"), which brought upon them the curse of God. For these crimes—committed long before the advent of Zionism—the iniquitous Jews will continue to incur heavy punishments and damnation.

As in medieval Christian and modern secular anti-Semitism, the sweeping nature of this Koranic defamation refers to "*the* Jews." If the Koran damns all Jews (or the overwhelming majority) as disbelievers and as iniquitous blasphemers, then—in the mainstream fundamentalist view—this must relate to Jews *throughout history* until "the Day of Resurrection." In effect, the Jews' depravity transcends history. Hezbollah expert Amal Saad-Ghorayeb has logically concluded: "The Jews of yesterday, today, and the generations to come, are necessarily included in those who are cursed, damned and generally demonized in the Qur'an. According to such a Qur'anic exegesis, there is no distinction between pre-Zionist, non-Zionist or Zionist Jews."[144]

In other words, the anti-Jewish hostility of Hezbollah (like that of Hamas and other Islamists) exists *independently* of Zionism, whose iniquities are merely the product of a primordial Jewish disposition. Such a worldview based on the cursed nature of the Jews is remarkably similar to Christian religious anti-Semitism throughout the ages.

No less characteristic is the theme of the "Jewish conspiracy" shared by Hezbollah, Hamas, and large swathes of Muslim opinion in the Middle East and beyond. According to the Koran, the Jews have been plotting against Islam from the dawn of its history and have never stopped conspiring, not only against Muslims but against the rest of humanity. For Hezbollah, the Holocaust—perceived as a gigantic Jewish hoax—is only the most recent illustration. Seven years before President Ahmadinejad, Hassan Nasrallah fully embraced Holocaust denial in his January 24, 1998, Jerusalem Day speech. According to the Hezbollah leader, the mass murder of Jews and the gas chambers were nothing but Jewish fabrications. Hezbollah leader Muhammad Ra'id accused Jews of collaborating with the Nazis in killing their own brethren. As Ra'id put it: "From what we know about the Jews, their tricks and their deception, we do not think it unlikely that they partook in the planning of the Holocaust."[145] In the Hezbollah conception, Jews either stage-managed, invented, or orchestrated the Holocaust in order to deceive the Gentile world into believing that they were innocent victims. The big lie of the Shoah served their Zionist project and demonstrated their international conspiracy against mankind.

The visceral hostility of Hezbollah and Hamas reflects the resonance of powerful Koranic stereotypes of Jewish depravity that readily facilitate the importation of modern Western anti-Semitic fantasies. According to Hezbollah, Jewish depravity is, however, ultimately derived from the falsification of their own Torah that was instigated by the Jews themselves. They were the ones who deviated from the Law of Moses and corrupted it, throwing overboard its pristine, authentic revelation. This demonic Jewish mentality continued into the era of Muhammad, when the Jews were definitively damned. The result of this deviancy has been a permanent state of war with the true believers. The fallout from this struggle had been partially attenuated by the *dhimma* pact and the obligations of Islamic jurisprudence toward the Jewish minority as People of the Book. But for Hezbollah this toleration is, in practice, little more than a hollow shell. The negationist theology it embraces excludes intermarriage between Jews and Muslims, let alone any notion of equality or future normalization of relations with the Zionist entity.

Hezbollah's commitment to destroying Israel is manifest in many of its videos, including *al-mawtu li Israil* (Death to Israel) and *Inhad, inhad, ya ayyuha l-Araby* (Rise Up Rise Up, You Arab). In the former video, Nasrallah declares inter alia: "Israel is utterly null and void, and it is a raping, deviant, occupying, terrorist, cancerous entity that has no legitimacy or legality at all, and never will." The lyrics accompanying the endless chants of *al-mawtu li Israil,* together with the ecstatic cult of suicide bombers, speak an unadulterated language of violent jihad. Palestinian martyrs Sheikh 'Izz al-Din al-Qassam, the Hamas bomb engineer al-Ayash, and the twelve-year-old Muhammad al-Dura are evoked as models "from the land of angry Jerusalem" for driving out the "raping occupiers." They are presented as combating a Zionist entity whose essence lies in aggression, barbarism, terror, murder, and massacres.[146] For example, a half-hour weekly series *Irhabiyyun* (Terrorists) on Al-Manar was entirely devoted to proving that Zionism was identical with terrorism. It was littered with the endlessly macabre footage of dead Arab children, civilians covered in blood, destroyed mosques, burned homes, and adults lying in coffins. These gruesome images were juxtaposed with religious Jews walking on the Temple Mount and Palestinian funeral processions.

For Hezbollah, all Israelis are, by definition, guilty and all terrorist acts against them constitute "legitimate resistance," including the killing of children. Inciting violent Palestinian resistance against Israel is indeed a prime goal of Hezbollah, hence the videos constantly highlight Palestinian gunfire, the throwing of Molotov cocktails, angry crowds with fists raised to the sky, Israeli military vehicles in flames, exploding effigies of Zionist leaders, and burning Israeli flags. According to Nasrallah, only continual violence can achieve anything against Israel, since nearly ten years of negotiations under Oslo produced nothing but humiliation.[147] Jihad alone can awaken the Muslim masses who have been constantly betrayed by those Arab governments whose temporizing marked them out as "lackeys of the West." Nasrallah's fidelity to the total "liberation" of Palestine has always included incitement to violence as an Islamic obligation to solidarity with the Palestinians. The bottom line of this jihad, as expressed by Sheikh Hassan Izz al-Din, director for Hezbollah media relations, is crystal clear: "All Palestinian refugees are to be allowed back to Palestine and the Jews need to leave." Since the Zionists have no rights or claims of any kind to Palestine, "they must be kicked out."[148] This flatly rejectionist sentiment is incessantly beamed to the Arab and Muslim worlds by the Hezbollah media system.

Equally central to Hezbollah is the theme "Al-Quds *lana*" (Jerusalem belongs to us) with intensive visual use of the Dome of the Rock as a focal rallying point for Israel's destruction. Videos constantly feature scenes of Muslims praying at the Haram al-Sharif (the Noble Sanctuary), throwing stones at Jews praying before the Western Wall, or Sharon's "provocative" visit to the Temple Mount in September 2000. Songs of Jerusalem in Hezbollah videos primarily evoke blood sacrifices, total identification with the Palestinians ("your blood is our blood, your Jerusalem is our Jerusalem, your sons are our sons"), and warnings to the Jews that victory is near. Videos such as *Ya al-Quds inana qadimoun* (Jerusalem, We Are Coming) show Hezbollah fighters marching in the direction of Jerusalem, accompanied by footage of riots on the Temple Mount and their own operations against Israel in southern Lebanon.[149] Not only is the support for Palestine *unconditional*, but it is evident that much of Hezbollah's credibility derives from its jihadist militancy on this issue. This pan-Arab dimension enables Hezbollah to assert its relevance, maintain its status in the Arab world (despite its Lebanese Shiite identity), and enjoy the sponsorship of both Iran and Syria.

Hezbollah maximalism in fighting Israel is inseparable from its fiercely anti-Jewish credo. Al-Manar's talk show *The Spider's House,* which long focused on strategies to destroy the Zionist entity, seems designed to encourage such guests as Sheikh Taha al-Sabounji, head mufti of northern Lebanon, to spout their clerical venom against Jewry. At the beginning of April 2002, al-Sabounji called for a Christian-Muslim Alliance against the "Jewish peril."

> Judaism is a project against all humanity. It is about time the world understands this. Those who are fighting Israel are not just defending themselves; they are defending the whole world. They are protecting all the future generations of humanity. . . . It's our job as Muslims to call upon the Christian world to rise up and become aware of what the Jews are doing. . . . There is no such thing as Zionism. . . . There is only Judaism. . . . Zionism is a legend, a myth. These are people [who] killed Muslims, Christians and the prophets.[150]

For good measure, the Lebanese sheikh added that "even the White House is ruled by Zionists and Jews—this despite the fact that America is a Christian country." Like the Hamas leader Ismail Haniya (also interviewed by Al-Manar in early April 2002), who had warned that the "Zionist cancer" was spreading to other Arab states, the sheikh regarded an all-out jihad for

Palestine as the only way to save Islam. Palestine was the last line of defense against an ideology and culture that would otherwise infect the Middle East with unimaginable evils. Nasrallah appeared to be more optimistic in October 2002, stating, "If they [the Jews] all gather in Israel, it will save us the trouble of going after them worldwide."[151] These and many other triumphalist statements by Hezbollah's secretary-general rejecting *any* presence of Jews in the region (not "even in a small village in Palestine because they are a cancer which is liable to spread again at any moment") require no Talmudic exegesis.[152] Like the outbursts of Ahmadinejad and of Hamas leaders in Palestine, they are transparently anti-Semitic and implicitly genocidal.

Hezbollah (like Hamas before January 2006) has been a de facto "state within a state"—a heavily armed organization that deliberately fanned the flames of the intifada and persistently provoked Israel on its northern border. It is part of an increasingly united anti-U.S. axis in the Middle East stretching from Tehran to Beirut and Gaza—with an increasingly dominant Shiite component. Its international cells can be found across the globe from Southeast Asia, West Africa, Europe, and the United States to the so-called Triple Frontier arms and drugs haven in South America.[153] It also controls significant real estate, highly sophisticated weaponry, and territory of its own in Lebanon. Indeed, its military capability is better developed than that of some established Arab states thanks to the scale of Iranian and Syrian assistance, which has increased in its scale and sophistication since the war of 2006.

Hezbollah's kidnapping of two Israeli soldiers on July 12, 2006, had been the trigger for a war that, while it lasted, displaced two million Israelis or forced them to stay in bomb shelters for several weeks. Though it did not hit Tel Aviv, by the end of the war, the Shiite organization had fired some 3,970 katyusha rockets into Israel, the majority landing in Haifa and the north. Israeli airpower, for its part, caused massive structural damage and considerable civilian suffering in Lebanon, temporarily weakening Hezbollah as a military force but failing to cripple its activities. As a result of his tenacity, Nasrallah became for a time a hero of the Arab street—a kind of cross between Che Guevara and the Ayatollah Khomeini. His brand of Islamic prophetism, his oratory shrewdness, and readiness to martyrdom impressed the Arab masses.[154] At the same time the Egyptian media continue to regard him as a dangerous proxy in an Iranian plan to destroy the Arab states from within. Similarly, inside Lebanon, there have been critical voices asserting that Hezbollah's policy had nearly wrecked the country, while serving the interests of Syria and Iran.[155] Nasrallah, on the other hand, could crow that "the people of this tyrannical State" (Israel) were losing "their faith in its mythical army—the beginning of the end of this entity."[156] He told Al-Jazeera TV on July 26, 2006, that he personally hoped for a martyr's death "at the hands of those people, the killers of the prophets and the messengers, and most hostile to the believers, as it says in the Qur'an." By the end of the war, it was evident that Hezbollah had survived after thirty-two days of fighting and would not be disarmed.[157]

Though Hezbollah's infrastructure and standing in Lebanon were initially damaged by the war, its arsenals of missiles, rockets, and other sophisticated weaponry have been replenished many times over. Its sting has not been removed, nor the potential danger it represents in the context of Iranian regional strategy. Hezbollah's resilience demonstrated that the organization has deep roots and considerable popular support in Lebanon. It may not have defeated Israel on the battlefield but it won the hearts and minds of many Arabs who admired the steadfastness and skill of its fighters. It strengthened the delusion that has steadily grown in the Middle East over the past forty years that political Islam may be the most effective antidote to the failures of Arab nationalism, Communism, socialism, and an imported American-style democracy. Islamism, in the shape of Hezbollah, seemed to offer restored dignity and honor to a bruised and battered Arab identity.[158] Three-quarters of all Palestinians had a favorable view of the organization, and solid majorities in Egypt and Jordan expressed positive opinions of its contribution to the Arab cause. In Lebanon, however, 64 percent had an unfavorable view of the group after the 2006 war, but its political influence within the country is greater than it was before.

Both Hezbollah and Hamas, echoing the example given by President Ahmadinejad, have reinvigorated the hypothesis that Israel can be annihilated, at least in the rejectionist court of Arab opinion. Penetrating questions about the fate of Israel have indeed been revived after the Second Lebanon War. Ehud Yaari called this phenomenon the "*muqawama* doctrine," which in the language of Nasrallah and Khalid Mashal means "persistent warfare"—a method of attrition intended to neutralize Israel's superior military forces.[159] The aim is to methodically erode Zionist resolve, to spill blood, and to focus on the civilian population rather than on conquering land, attempting to defeat the IDF, or trying to achieve strategic parity. Since the Arab states seem incapable of conducting an effective military campaign and are politically corrupt, the historic task of bringing Israel down devolves upon Islamic movements such as Hezbollah and Hamas. Fighting for the sake of Allah rather than for *watan* (the national fatherland) or such quasi-Marxist concepts as the "popular liberation war," their jihad appears to be highly motivated and difficult to deter.

One of Hezbollah's slogans, "The party of Allah is sure to triumph," reflects its underlying confidence that history (or Providence) is on its side. The movement has always seen itself as an integral part of the worldwide Muslim *umma,* while stressing its indelible links to the Iranian Revolution of Ayatollah Khomeini. Its culture is based on the Koran, the Sunna (tradition), and the legal rulings of *wilayat al-faqih* (the leading jurist), as laid down by Khomeini. The issue in Hezbollah's eyes is whether Islam destroys Israel or Israel destroys Islam. Such realities led *The Economist* to soberly observe in August 2006 that "today, as in the 1940s, Israel still has some neighbors who continue to deny its very right to exist as a Jewish State." The British weekly noted that Hezbollah, like Iran, aimed at Israel's destruction and was also "blatantly anti-Semitic." Its TV stations have been a beacon of hate—"one series purported to show Jews murdering Christian children to use their blood for Passover bread."[160]

Hezbollah's relative success has been due in no small measure to its mastery of psychological warfare, its media sophistication, and its ability to blend Shia fundamentalism with secular revolutionary motifs into an Islamicized language of national liberation.[161] By focusing on Israel as the common enemy for all Lebanese (Sunni, Shia, Christian, Druze) and on its own valiant resistance to the alien invader, Hezbollah cleverly offered a patriotic façade of liberating Lebanon. By highlighting Palestine, it seemed to transcend the Sunni-Shiite divide and strengthened its pan-Arab credentials; by constantly emphasizing the religious significance of Jerusalem, the place where Muhammad ascended to heaven, it could hope to rally *all* Muslims against the infidel Jews. The appeal to Islam as the path of the righteous against Judeo-Christian falsehood, corruption, iniquity, and injustice has provided an additional triumphalist glow. Like Communism, Hezbollah offers to true believers the comfort and certainty of a better, more sublime future of peace and justice at the end of history: not only a free Lebanon and (eventually) a sharia-based republic under the global hegemony of Islam, but a messianic kingdom bringing final redemption. To achieve this just path Hezbollah, like Hamas, has damned the Zionist enemy in unabashedly anti-Semitic language as the devil incarnate. The Jews, we are constantly reminded, have been eternally cursed by the Koran. The merciless Israelis with their brutal and bloodthirsty attacks on Lebanon are the living proof of the truth of the ancient prophecies. Thus the war against the Jews is part of God's plan to liberate Palestine, to restore Jerusalem to the Muslims, and to bring salvation to all humanity.

The axis of terror and jihad that extends from Tehran via Damascus to Beirut and Gaza is cemented by the age-old scourge of anti-Semitism resurrected in Islamic dress.[162] This Holocaust-denying, Jew-hating axis of anti-Westernism consciously feeds the frustration and rage of many Muslims at their impoverished, powerless condition and the incompetence of their rulers. For decades, Israel has been the scapegoat of choice for this unassuaged anger, greatly intensified when linked to a holy war for Jerusalem in the name of Allah. The spine-chilling hadith in article 7 of the Hamas Charter, widely cited today by radical Islamists around the world, contains a macabre prophecy: "The last Hour will not come unless the Muslims will fight against the Jews and the Muslims will kill them." The apocalyptic jihad of Hamas and Hezbollah is driven, at least in part, by such exterminationist fantasies, whose suicidal methods and consequences are all too apparent.

TWENTY-THREE

Toward the Muslim Apocalypse

On November 18, 1947, Hitler's closest confidant, Albert Speer, wrote a paragraph in his Spandau prison diary that sounds eerily prophetic today:

I recall how [Hitler] would have films shown in the Reich Chancellory about London burning, about the sea of fire over Warsaw, about exploding convoys, and the kind of ravenous joy that would then seize him every time. But I never saw him so beside himself as when, in a delirium, he pictured New York going down in flames. He described how the skyscrapers would be transformed into gigantic burning torches, how they would collapse in confusion, how the bursting city's reflection would stand against the dark sky.[1]

In September 2001, this frenzied Wagnerian imagery became fact. The Islamic terrorist perpetrators of the September 2001 massacre, like the Nazis and fascists sixty years earlier, spoke a language of unquenchable hatred not only for America and the West but also for Israel and the Jewish people as such.[2] These Islamic radicals consciously chose a cult of death, turning the motif of sacrifice and martyrdom into something urgent, elemental, pseudo-religious, and even mystical.[3] Their bible may have been the Koran and not *Mein Kampf*, but the mental structures and worldview behind their actions bore striking analogies with German National Socialism.[4] Like their Nazi and fascist forerunners, they, too, have targeted the Jews as a major (though not the only) victim in a bloodstained pseudo-messianic path to redemption. In this war they are worthy successors of the wartime Palestinian leader and Hitler's ally Haj Amin al-Husseini, who in 1944 urged the

Arabs over Radio Berlin: "Kill Jews wherever you find them for the love of God, history and religion."[5] Such murderous calls have become commonplace across the Muslim world today.

There are other parallels, too. The radical nihilists of yesterday and today share the same intolerance of dissent, the same will to control every aspect of everyday life, and the same desire to export terrorism throughout the world. In al-Qaeda, the Taliban, Hamas, Hezbollah, Islamic Jihad, and other like-minded terror groups, one finds a totalitarian mind-set, hatred of the West, fanatical extremism, repression of women, loathing of Jews, a firm belief in conspiracy theories, and dreams of global hegemony. Like prewar European fascists and the present government of Iran, the Muslim radicals claim to speak for frustrated, underprivileged, and impoverished masses. They have condemned the "anonymous powers" of globalization and the plutocratic West (symbolized by America) as fiercely as they ever did Soviet Communism. For them, "Jewish" New York, as much as the Zionist State of Israel, is an incarnation of capitalist evil, just as Wall Street embodied the general headquarters of the mythical State of Judah to the Nazis and other fascist true believers.[6]

Middle Eastern jihadism is a distinctly modern movement, though it has indigenous Islamic roots. The conspiracy theory at its heart that links plutocratic capitalism, international Freemasonry, Zionism, and Marxist Communism is almost identical with the mythical structure of Nazi anti-Semitism. For contemporary jihadists, a Judaized America and Israel—together with heretical, secular Muslim regimes—are the godless spearhead of dark occult forces that seek to destroy Islam and undermine the cultural identity of Muslim believers.[7] The Iranian Revolution of 1979 gave an enormous boost to this apocalyptic style of thinking, rooted in the apocryphal *Protocols of the Elders of Zion* as well as in indigenous Islamic sources.

With the defeat of Soviet Communism in Afghanistan in 1989 and the collapse of the USSR two years later, the empowered Islamists began to greatly intensify their jihad against what they called the "Crusader-Zionist" new world order. America's military triumph during the First Persian Gulf War and its present sequel has proven to be something of a pyrrhic victory. The West drugged itself into complacency with misleading theories about the irresistible triumph of capitalism and democracy, the "end of history," and the belief that Islam was a negligible quantity to be easily manipulated and transformed. It underestimated the radicals' capacity for mobilizing the have-nots of the Middle East and southwest Asia, the victims of globalization, and the losers in the modernization process, which has so lamentably failed in large parts of the Muslim world.

In this war of cultures Israel is in a particularly exposed position—perceived both as occupying sacred and inalienable Muslim territory and as a Western implant in the Arab world. Its vulnerability has been further underlined by the willingness of many in the West to believe that the new Muslim terrorism à la bin Laden or sponsored by Iran is a result of Israeli occupation of Palestinian lands. The truth is almost exactly the reverse. Islamofascism exploits the Palestinian problem as the last great just cause, the revolutionary prologue to global jihad. In that context, jihadi Islamism is not open to rational bargaining or sensible compromise. Like the Iranian leadership, Muslim radicals do not disguise their desire to wipe the Jewish state off the map of the Middle East, to eventually destroy America, and to ultimately enthrone Islam as the dominant religion in the world. Israel's willingness to make territorial and political concessions is entirely irrelevant unless it wishes to commit suicide. A Palestinian state will never satisfy Iran, Hamas, or other Muslim militants, let alone most Palestinians, unless it is established on the ruins of Israel. The West all too often prefers to turn a blind eye to such unpalatable facts. Its leaders imagine that if only Palestinian grievances were appeased, the wellsprings of terrorism would dry up and Islamic hatred of the West will magically wither away. But appeasement and the culture of denial will not help the Western democracies any more than they did in the 1930s.

Anti-Semitism, then as now, is an important barometer of the cultural crisis in Europe and the Middle East, including problems of globalization, modernization, ethnic nationalism, religious fundamentalism, and racist prejudice in general. Over twenty years ago the historian Bernard Lewis, a leading authority on Middle Eastern history, observed that Arab anti-Semitism was again on the rise. In 1986 he wrote the following:

> The volume of anti-Semitic books and articles published, the size and number of editions and impressions, the eminence and authority of those who write, publish and sponsor them, their place in school and college curricula, their role in the mass media, would all seem to suggest that classical anti-Semitism is an essential part of Arab intellectual life at the

present time—almost as much as happened in Nazi Germany, and considerably more than in late nineteenth and early twentieth century France.[8]

The truth is that Lewis's assessment was, if anything, too optimistic. In recent years it has become increasingly apparent that the anti-Semitic phantasmagoria has taken root in the body politic of Islam to an unprecedented degree. The fact that Arabs are themselves "Semites" (in the linguistic sense) has in no way diminished their visceral hostility toward Jews and the Jewish state. Such attitudes hardly alter their nature simply because they are expressed by Arabs in the Arabic language or by Iranians in the Farsi tongue. For example, the *Protocols of the Elders of Zion* are a typical product of fin de siècle Russian and European-style anti-Semitism, deriving from a historical and cultural tradition obviously distinct from that of the Muslim world. But when they are published in repeated editions throughout the Arab world, they cease to be a purely European product and enter into the mainstream of Arab thought.[9] Their appeal becomes all the greater for many Muslims and Arabs since the notion of Jews as a threatening power has become more palpable once the *Protocols* are viewed as a "Zionist manifesto for world conquest."[10] At the same time, the specter of a powerful, satanic conspiracy helps to alleviate the psychological trauma and humiliation of successive Arab defeats at the hands of Israel and the West.[11]

During the month of Ramadan in 2002 the *Protocols* were dramatized in a mammoth multimillion-dollar series produced in Egypt by Dream TV (a private station) featuring a cast of four hundred. According to one prominent Egyptian weekly, Arab viewers would finally be exposed to *the* central strategy "that to this very day, dominates Israel's policy, political aspirations, and racism." The Egyptian TV epic purported, on the surface, to trace the history of the Middle East from 1855 to 1917 through the eyes of an Egyptian who fought the British occupation and the Zionist movement. The series was closely associated with popular author-actor Muhammad Sobhi, who co-wrote the script and played the main character. He told Al-Jazeera television that, whether or not the *Protocols* were authentic, "Zionism exists and it has controlled the world since the dawn of history." In other interviews to the press, he said that in the series, he was exposing all the *Protocols* (eighteen out of twenty-four) that had *already come to pass*— thereby indicating that he fully believed in them (as did Nasser, Sadat, King

Faisal of Saudi Arabia, and Colonel Qaddafi before him) and saw his film work in a missionary propagandist light. Indeed, this televised profession of belief represented a quantum leap forward not only in its ability to reach many millions of viewers (about half of them probably illiterate) but in making anti-Semitism more blatant, popular, and accessible as a worldview. Yet most of the Egyptian elites and media reacted vehemently against Western criticism of the series—raging at those who dared to challenge "Egyptian and Arab art" with "extortion and terror based on the charge of anti-Semitism." Responding to a high-level Israeli protest, President Mubarak solemnly assured the world "that the Egyptian people, that is Semite itself, totally objects to any kind of antisemitism."[12] This claim is, however, refuted by what appears on an almost daily basis in the partly government-controlled Egyptian media.

Arab politicians and intellectuals who continue to deny the existence of "Semitic" anti-Semitism sometimes pretend that there is a sharp distinction between Jews and Zionists in the relevant literature. In reality, this was rarely the case even in the past. Where such a differentiation may at one time have existed, it has today been almost totally eroded. For the last sixty years the term "*yahud*" (Jews) has, in fact, been mixed up or used interchangeably with "*sahyuniyyun*" (Zionists), "Israelis," and "Banu Israel" (People of Israel).[13] The mounting scale and extent of this vehemently anti-Semitic literature and commentary in the newspapers, journals, and magazines, on radio and television, and in the everyday life of the Middle East, has swamped that minority of Arabs who genuinely tried to separate their attitudes toward Jews from their rejection of Zionism. This is especially true among Egyptian and Jordanian intellectuals, journalists, politicians, trade unionists, and religious figures, despite the official peace treaties with Israel. Professional associations and businesses maintain official and unofficial boycotts of Israel while religious leaders spout vicious calumnies about Zionists and Jews in their weekly sermons and public appearances.

Behind the Arab rejectionism lies a barrage of derogatory and repulsive images of Jews and Judaism that can be found both in the government-backed and in the opposition media, in popular and academic publications, in television images, caricatures, and the cassette recordings of clerics who long ago blurred any fading boundary between anti-Zionism and anti-Semitism. The vitriolic visual and verbal imagery extends from Morocco to the Gulf states and Pakistan; it is as strong in supposedly moderate Egypt and Jordan as it is in the openly aggressive Muslim nations of Iran, Sudan, and Syria.[14] In Arab cartoons Jews are portrayed as demons and murderers, as a hateful, loathsome people to be feared and avoided. They are invariably seen as the origin of all evil and corruption, authors of a dark, unrelenting conspiracy to infiltrate and destroy Muslim society in order to eventually take over the world.[15] The most common visual distortion of the Jew is to portray him as a stooped, dark, bearded man wearing a black robe, with a long crooked nose and a devilish appearance—the kind of hideous stereotype familiar from the classic Nazi propaganda rag *Der Stürmer.* Judaism, itself, is presented as a sinister immoral religion, based on cabals and blood rituals, while Zionists are systematically equated with or identified as criminal racists or Nazis. The aim is not simply to morally delegitimize Israel as a Jewish state and a national entity in the Middle East but to *dehumanize* Judaism and the Jewish people as such. No objective observer remotely familiar with this cascade of hate can doubt that it is profoundly and totally anti-Semitic. The flimsy anti-Zionist pretext for this gutter material has become an insult to the intelligence of any decent individual. It recalls a simple truth: to *defame* Israel is to defame the Jews. To wish it would cease to exist is to wish to destroy the Jews. Nowhere is this more the case than in the Arab world or in Iran.

In the summer of 1999, at the height of the peace process, a survey of the Arab world conducted by the American University at Beirut showed that 87 percent supported Islamic terror, and 70 percent were against peace with Israel; 77 percent opposed economic cooperation with the Jewish state, 54 percent approved of a war that would lead to the annihilation of Israel, and the same percentage wished it would cease to exist as a sovereign independent state. No less than 45 percent believed the Holocaust had never happened.[16] These results were recorded a full year *before* the outbreak of the second Palestinian intifada.

Radical anti-Semitism in the Muslim Arab world over the past century has steadily grown under the impact of modernity, though many of its seeds can be found in the Koran and early Islamic sources.[17] True, there have been periods when relative tolerance prevailed and Jews were able to make intellectual advances, enjoy economic prosperity, and even exert some political influence under Islamic rule. However, more often than is generally realized, their existence from Morocco to Iran was punctuated by discrimination, misery, humiliation, and popular violence.[18] These tribulations, particularly in the eleventh and twelfth centuries, prompted the greatest of medieval Jewish philosophers, Maimonides, to bitterly refer to the "nation of Ishmael, who persecute us severely, and who devise ways to harm us and debase us."[19] Even the so-called golden age of Sephardic Jews, which coincided with one of the high points of medieval Islamic civilization, did not occur without also provoking envy and Muslim hostility at the influence and socioeconomic success of the Jews.

The legal status of Jews and Christians under Islam in the premodern era was essentially that of *dhimmis* whose religions were officially recognized by the authorities. On payment of the *jizya* (poll tax) they could practice their faiths, enjoy a certain degree of personal security, and have their own semi-autonomous communal organizations. But the protection afforded to the Ahl al-Kitab (People of the Book) was always combined with subjection; the tolerance they benefited from existed within a legally fixed framework of discrimination and disabilities that constantly emphasized the *superiority* of Islam to both Judaism and Christianity.[20] Jews could not, for example, bear arms; they could not ride horses but only donkeys; they were required to wear distinctive clothing (the yellow badge has its origins in Baghdad, not in medieval Europe); and they were forbidden to build new places of worship. Their *dhimmi* status, as elaborated by Muslim jurists from the inception of Islam until the early twentieth century, has been succinctly summarized by Bat Ye'or as follows:

> *Dhimmis* were often considered impure and had to be segregated from the Muslim community. Entry into holy Muslim towns, mosques, public baths, as well as certain streets was forbidden them. Their turbans—when they were permitted to wear them—their costumes, belts, shoes, the appearance of their wives and their servants had to be different from those of Muslims in order to distinguish and humiliate them; for the *dhimmis* could never be allowed to forget that they were inferior beings.[21]

Any divergence from the Muslim legal and social norms of humiliation and abasement as applied to Jews and Christians was liable to be seen as a breach of the "Pact of 'Umar," the decrees of the eighth-century caliph 'Umar I that had first regulated *dhimmi* status. Any signs of "haughtiness" and "arrogance" by Jews or Christians ran the risk of being punishable by death. In the more remote countries of Morocco, Iran, and Yemen, where

Jews had especially suffered from degradation, contempt, and physical insecurity, *dhimmi* restrictions were enforced with special rigor. Muslim riots and the killing of Jews were more frequent in such peripheral lands well into the twentieth century. Pillaging, looting, and the murder of defenseless Jews also occurred elsewhere in North Africa at fairly regular intervals during the nineteenth century. So, too, did the blood libel calumny, which first originated in the Ottoman Empire among Greek Orthodox Christians, leading to pogroms in Smyrna in 1872 and in Istanbul two years later.

Earlier instances of the blood libel had been recorded in Beirut (1824), Antioch (1826), Hama (1829), and, above all, in the notorious Damascus affair of 1840. The slander was given wide credence by the French authorities and European Catholics and vigorously supported by the French consul in Damascus.[22] The medieval blood libel, which accused Jews of murdering Christian children and using the victims' blood to bake matzo for Passover, was itself a European import—alien to the Islamic faith and tradition. Like a number of other classic European anti-Semitic notions, the blood libel fantasy was originally introduced to the Muslim world by native Christians (Greek Orthodox, Catholic, and Maronite), who stood in the forefront of the new ideology of modern secular Arab nationalism in the early twentieth century. Their Judeophobia proved to be a tragically failed attempt at integrating themselves in a Muslim world at times as hostile to Christians as it was to Jews.[23]

It is certainly true that for *medieval* Muslims, Christianity had been and would remain a much more serious theological, political, and military challenge than Judaism. In comparison, the Jews (until the twentieth century) were scarcely a threat to Muslims at all and often served as their allies. Moreover, *dhimmi* status under Islamic rule—in contrast to medieval Christendom—did not usually confine Jews to ghettos, restrict them to usury, or prevent them from owning land and practicing various crafts. The discrimination they suffered under Islam was often severe but on the whole qualitatively more benign than their exclusion and demonization in medieval Christianity.[24] Above all, they were spared the status of Christ killers, presumed to be guilty of the worst capital crime in all of human history.

Nevertheless, the Koranic image of the Jew, which has been sharply radicalized in contemporary Islamic writings, is far from harmless in its original form. In the text there are extraordinarily *harsh* passages in which Muhammad brands the Jews as enemies of Islam and depicts them as possessing a malevolent, rebellious spirit. Indeed, Muhammad Tantawi, chief mufti of Egypt and sheikh of Al-Azhar, had no doubt that Muslims must return to these teachings of Islam "in order to fight against Allah's enemy and to cleanse the sacred ground from the Jews." He even issued a fatwa in 2002, stating that assassins should be considered martyrs, especially if Jewish women and children were killed in the attacks. Tantawi cited as an authority in such matters the Nazi leader Adolf Hitler who, in *Mein Kampf*, had declared, "By resisting the Jews, I fight for the cause of the Lord."[25]

There are Koranic verses that speak of justified Jewish abasement and poverty—of Jews being "laden with God's anger" for their disobedience. They had to be humiliated "because they had disbelieved the signs of God and slain the prophets unrightfully" (Koran 2:61). According to another verse (Koran 5:78–82), "the unbelievers of the Children of Israel" were cursed by both David and by Jesus. The penalty of such disbelief in God's signs and the miracles performed by the prophets was for the Jews to be transformed into apes and swine or worshippers of idols (Koran 2:57–66). This dehumanizing image has become central to Islam's current war against the Jewish state. The Koran particularly emphasizes that the Jews rejected Muhammad, even though (according to Muslim sources) they knew him to be a great prophet. This rejection was supposedly motivated by jealousy for the Arabs and resentment because the Prophet was not a Jew. Such actions are presented by Islamists today as typical of the deceitful, treacherous, and scheming nature of the Jews as depicted in the Koranic text. For such evil character traits they were promised "degradation in this world" and a "mighty chastisement" in the world to come. A variety of verses further charge the Jews with "falsehood" (Koran 3:71), distortion (Koran 4:46), cowardice, greed, and being "corrupters of Scripture."[26] This last accusation relates to a well-entrenched Islamic belief that the original revelations of the Old and New Testaments had been authentic but that they were subsequently distorted by their unworthy Jewish and Christian custodians. Hence the biblical Holy Scriptures had to be superseded by the Koran, the literal word of God as mediated to his Prophet Muhammad through the angel Gabriel.[27] The Muslim version of "chosenness" regards Muhammad as the last of the prophets who has been granted the *final* and *complete* revelation of God in the form of Islam, which therefore supplants both Judaism and Christianity.

One of the most damning anti-Jewish stereotypes fostered by the Koran remains the charge that the Jews stubbornly and willfully rejected Allah's truth—much as Christians once insisted on malevolent Jewish blindness in refusing Jesus's Gospel. Not only that, but according to the Koranic text, the Jews always persecuted Allah's prophets, including Muhammad, who was eventually obliged to expel two major Jewish clans from Medina and to exterminate the third tribe, the Qurayza. The hadith goes further still and claims that the Jews, in accordance with their perfidious nature, planned Muhammad's painful, protracted death from poisoning. Furthermore, malevolent, conspiratorial Jews are blamed for the sectarian strife in early Islam, and for heresies and deviations that undermined or endangered the unity of the *umma*.[28] This is a theme that has been picked up and expanded upon by radical Islamists and Salafists who look to the Prophet's own struggle against Jewish tribes in seventh-century Arabia for inspiration in their war with Israel. The powerful archetype of a "Jewish threat," which has existed since the birth of Islam, has assumed a more strident and militant form since 1948. It is especially visible in the contemporary Muslim battle against Israel, Zionism, and world Jewry.

The notion that Jews are arrogant falsifiers, continuously hatching new plots and conspiracies in order to sow discord, conflict, and division within the Muslim community, is directly derived from Koranic teaching. Only tenacious adherence to true Islamic values, it is constantly repeated, can preserve Muslims against the dire peril represented by Jewish-Zionist and Western imperialist infiltration—a peril allegedly anticipated by the ancient sacred texts. This is the central message of Sayyid Qutb's *Our Struggle with the Jews,* a seminal essay written in the mid-1950s by the leading Egyptian theorist of the Muslim Brotherhood, who subsequently inspired much of contemporary radical Islamism.[29] For Qutb, Jews were already vicious and conniving in Muhammad's time, plotting against him and encouraging his "false followers" as well as his outright enemies. The sins of the Medina Jews in seventh-century Arabia were not merely some remote and distant event but had cosmic, *eternal* significance—much like the Gospel accounts came to assume in Christian hostility toward Jews over the centuries. In the twentieth century the Jews once again epitomized a neuralgic point in Islam's civilizational crisis, magnified by Muslim fears and weakness in the face of secular modernity, the sexual revolution, and the invasive power of American mass culture. Qutb became convinced that it was Jews who had deliberately invented these evils in order to destroy Islam and all values "sacred to mankind."[30]

Jewish emancipation from Muslim rule because of growing Western colonialist involvement in the Islamic world was followed by something much more frightening to Arabs—the establishment in 1948 of a Jewish state in the very heart of the Middle East. The Arab failure to prevent this *naqba* (disaster) signified to Qutb and his followers in the Muslim Brotherhood the full extent of cultural decay and presaged the possible collapse of Islam after several centuries of decline.[31] In this grim scenario, Jews served as a catalyst and a symptom of cultural crisis though they could not succeed without the help of "lapsed Muslims," *kaffir* (unbelievers), and secular Arab regimes. Arab nationalists such as Nasser were seen as traitors undermining resistance in the Islamic world to Israel and the West. Furthermore, according to Qutb, Jews had plotted in Turkey since 1900 (under the sultanate of Abdulhamid II) to bring down the Muslim caliphate—perhaps the greatest disaster for Islam in modern times in the eyes of the fundamentalists. Jews were also behind modern doctrines such as "atheistic materialism" (Communism, psychoanalysis, and sociology) designed to achieve "the destruction of the family and the shattering of sacred relationships in society."[32] The teachings of Marx, Freud, and Durkheim were classic examples of Jewish subversion and the will to sabotage moral values in the core areas of *Dar al-Islam.* Their naturally malevolent disposition, misanthropy, and abiding hatred of Muslims had prompted such actions, which would fail as soon as Muslim believers returned to the sources of their own invincible faith.

Qutb's "theological" demonization of the Jews blended easily enough into the more modern twentieth-century motifs of racist and political anti-Semitism derived from Western sources.[33] The *Protocols* are foremost among these European exports to the Arab world. Their attraction for gullible Muslims has grown immensely with each successive defeat by Israel.[34]

The Western media has been extremely reluctant to relate the current terrorist war against Israel and the West to its deep ideological roots in Islam and the concept of jihad. It is equally averse to connecting terrorism with the anti-Jewish obsessions that currently animate millions of Muslims.[35] At most, anti-Semitism is perceived as a footnote to the raging storm of anti-Westernism or as a form of political opposition to Israeli actions—

an extraordinarily inaccurate assessment. Not even the most brazen Arab claims—such as that the Holocaust was a fabrication invented by Zionists and Jews—receive more than passing attention in the West.[36]

There was, for example, little media interest in the anti-Semitic ravings of the long-serving Syrian defense minister Mustafa Tlass, who only a few years ago retired after being in his job since 1972. For years, Tlass had pursued his belief that Jews drink the blood of Gentile children with zealous determination. He analyzed the Damascus blood libel of 1840, as if all the "confessions" from local Jews at the time (extracted by excruciating torture) reflected a true historical record. Tlass, who held a degree from Moscow (on Marshal Georgy Zhukov's military strategy) and had sought to defend his doctorate at the Sorbonne, was adamant that his anti-Semitic book *The Matzo of Zion* was based on authentic historical research. Despite its revival of the medieval blood libel, he insisted that it was in no way directed against Jews! The poet, novelist, historian, and friend of French presidents Charles de Gaulle and François Mitterrand, unexpectedly found himself at the heart of an unpleasant public scandal in France in 1986. The California-based Simon Wiesenthal Center bluntly accused Tlass of propagating anti-Semitism through his research.[37] The French edition of his book included decontextualized extracts from the Talmud, the Shulchan Aruch, Maimonides, and various halakic sources designed to show that Jews could kill Gentiles with impunity, rob, cheat, commit adultery, and deceive them without any sanction under Jewish law. But it was the lessons for the present that most concerned the Syrian defense minister. Tlass declared that his aim was to expose the boundless "perfidy" of the Zionist movement and its criminal activities since the nineteenth century.[38]

The Damascus ritual murder affair of 1840 had proved to Tlass that Jews were by nature bloodthirsty and ruthless killers who stop at nothing to achieve their goals. Misanthropy and fanaticism encouraged by the Talmud were at the root of Zionist racism and represented an admonition to Arabs that they should never trust Jews.[39] Israel's invasion of Lebanon in 1982 and President Sadat's betrayal of the Arab cause in making peace with the Jewish state were dramatic warning signs that General Tlass addressed in his book's introduction. The cover contained its own macabre anti-Semitic message: Three grimacing cutthroat Jews, wearing skullcaps, are drawing blood from the neck of the victim—the poor Capuchin monk Father Thomas—while, in the background, two boys with skullcaps and bulging eyes sit and watch by the dim candlelight of a menorah lamp somewhere in Damascus.[40] In his 1983 preface to this very popular book (which even today is sold in the thousands), Tlass wrote: "The Jew can kill you and take your blood in order to make his Zionist bread. Here opens before us a page more ugly than the crime itself: the religious beliefs of the Jews and the perversions they contain, which draw their orientation from a dark hate towards all humankind and all religions."[41]

On February 8, 1991, the Syrian delegate to the UN Human Rights Commission in Geneva, Nabila Chaalan, urged all representatives who were present to read General Tlass's work in order to grasp the true nature of Zionist racism. In 2003 the Syrian defense minister was still repeating his claim in *The Matzo of Zion* that the original trial in Damascus had been based on the "known fact" that fanatical Jews do commit ritual murder.

The blood libel clearly serves the Syrian policy of routinely demonizing Israel and the Jews. On the eve of the twenty-first century, for example, a prominent Syrian literary magazine published the following piece of anti-Semitic acrobatics that blends together hatred of Israel, the blood libel, anti-Talmudism, anti-Americanism, and the Shylockian rapacity of the Jews:

The Talmud instructions, dripping in hatred and hostility towards humanity, are stamped in the Jewish soul. Throughout history, the world has known more than one Shylock, more than one Father Thomas, as victim of these Talmudic instructions and this hatred. . . . Now Shylock of New York's time has come. . . . The [Passover] Matzah of Israel is soaked with the blood of the Iraqis, descendants of the Babylonians, the Lebanese, descendants of the Sidonese, and the Palestinians, descendants of the Canaanites. This Matzah is kneaded by American weaponry . . . and the missiles of hatred pointed at both Muslim and Christian Arabs. The Talmud incites the Jews on Earth to allow Shylock to plant states among the Gentiles, meaning Muslim and Christian lands. . . . Israel's matza will continue to steep in blood, the spilling of which is permitted in the Talmud, in order to glorify the Jewish military.[42]

Syrian Judeophobia, for all its secular pseudo-Marxist veneer and the minuscule size of its remnant Jewish population (125 souls, compared to 30,000 only six decades ago), is as extreme as that of any contemporary

Muslim or Arab state: Tlass's calumnious book (which is still influential in international anti-Semitic circles and can be purchased on the Internet in various languages)[43] was only the tip of an iceberg. On January 1, 2000, *Al-Usbu Al-Adabi* (the state-controlled weekly of the Syrian Arab Writers' Association) published a vicious article called "The Peace of Zion," directed against "normalization" with Israel. Its author, Zbeir Sultan, informed Syrian readers that AIDS had spread in Egypt through attractive Jewish prostitutes from Israel deliberately infecting Egyptian youngsters.

> Egyptian authorities also discovered Zionist gifts for children made of animal-shaped chewing gum. An examination revealed that it causes . . . sterility. For university students they [the Zionists] dispersed chewing gum that arouses sexual lust. . . . Even the Egyptian soil is not safe from the Satanic war waged by Zionism. Tens of thousands of seeds were sent [to Egypt] through agricultural deals with the Zionist Entity. These seeds destroyed the Egyptian soil. [44]

Such hateful and totally irrational accusations have been made for decades in the Egyptian, Syrian, Lebanese, and other Arab media.

The demonization of Jews has indeed become normal in Egypt and Syria. One can find it in the Syrian media's treatment of the Monica Lewinsky affair as a Jewish plot to entrap and blackmail President Clinton; in its claims that deadly medical experiments are being carried out on Arab prisoners in Israeli jails, and in the endless flood of references to Zionism as being far worse than Nazism in its racist policies, methods, and aims.[45] On January 31, 2006, the Syrian government daily *Al-Thawra* even suggested that Israel created the avian flu in order to damage "genes only carried by Arabs." This plot was supposedly part of a broader Zionist project to create an "Israeli race bomb"—special viruses and other biological weapons created solely to destroy Arabs.[46]

On Syrian TV on November 8, 2005, the deputy minister of religious endowment, Muhammad 'Abd al-Sattar, explained to viewers that there was a Zionist plot to put those whom the Koran had called "descendants of apes and pigs" on the throne of the Greater Middle East. Quoting from the Koran in an interview on July 21, 2006, he emphasized the fact that the people of Israel were the only nation cursed in the Holy Book of Islam: "The Koran used terms that are closer to animals than to humans with regard to those people [the Jews] . . . the people who were given the Torah were likened to a donkey, carrying books . . . to apes and pigs, and they are, indeed, the descendants of apes and pigs as the Qur'an teaches us."[47]

The Syrian film industry has also been active in producing radically anti-Semitic productions such as the TV series *Al-Shatat* (The Diaspora), which was initially broadcast by Al-Manar, the Hezbollah TV station in Lebanon. The series revolves around the so-called Secret Jewish World Government founded by the Rothschild family in the nineteenth century. These conspirators supposedly forged the Bolshevik Revolution in Russia, plotted two world wars, created the Nazi Holocaust, and decided to use the A-bomb on Japan. They are evil, bloodthirsty criminals, interested only in power and global domination, who continue to influence world leaders and to direct contemporary history.[48] The *Al-Shatat* series also includes a Nazi forgery purporting to be an anti-Semitic speech by Benjamin Franklin, warning eighteenth-century Americans about "Jewish control" of their young republic. Worst of all, the film contained horrific fictional scenes of a group of rabbis and other Jews gathering in a Romanian ghetto to torture and kill the father of Theodor Herzl's mistress—depicted as the owner of a brothel. The gruesome stabbing, cutting off of ears, and pouring of boiling lead down the victim's throat are all presented as having been ordained by "a sacred Talmudic court." In the twentieth episode of the thirty-part anti-Semitic series, viewers are subjected to the monstrous ritual murder of a Christian child whose blood is then used by Jews to bake Passover matzo—a scene that in its sheer horror surpasses anything that the Nazi cinema achieved in this domain. The *Syria Times* in its November 11, 2003, report referred to the series as merely recording "the criminal history of Zionism." It would be more accurate to describe it as a new nadir of pornographic televised anti-Semitism, worse still than the repulsive Egyptian series *Horseman Without a Horse*.[49]

Brazenly anti-Semitic cartoons, television shows, and newspaper articles are regrettably *regular* features of the Syrian media, as they are in Egypt, Lebanon, the Palestinian Authority, Saudi Arabia, and most of the Arab world. Indeed, the Arab educational system is in general riddled with anti-Semitic and racist portrayals of the Jews as the eternal enemies of Allah, Islam, the Arabs, and the entire human race. The Talmud is constantly slandered as a document containing profound hatred of non-Jews as "unclean animals." Some of this gutter rhetoric is familiar enough from the history of

European Christian anti-Semitism; the link between the Talmud and Zionism is of postwar Soviet provenance. The Syrian leader Bashar al-Assad, who was partly educated in England, is less concerned with the Talmud, but he has made his own blatantly anti-Semitic statements, most famously during Pope John II's pioneering visit to Damascus in May 2001. In front of His Holiness and the world's media, Assad openly revealed his bigoted worldview:

> We hear them [the Israelis] killing the principle of equality, saying that "God has created our people separately from other peoples"; we see them mistreating the places sacred to Islam and Christianity in Palestine, violating the sanctity of the al-Aqsa Mosque, the Church of the Holy Sepulcher in Jerusalem and the Church of the Nativity in Bethlehem. They are trying to kill all the values of the divine religions, with the same mentality that brought about the betrayal and torturing of Christ and in the same way that they tried to betray the Prophet Muhammad.[50]

In one ugly sentence, the Syrian president had managed to fuse together the most explosive hate messages to be found in European Christian and Islamic Judeophobia. Yet this singular feat of vilification evoked barely a ripple of protest from the Vatican—despite Assad's blasphemous linkage of Jesus's agony with that of the Palestinians.[51] Unfortunately, his remarks were all too representative of an Arab world where the self-proclaimed distinctions between Israel and Jews have long been emptied of any content. When Mustafa Tlass (still Assad's defense minister at the time) was asked yet again in August 2003 about the blood libel, he replied: "*The Matzo of Zion* took place in Damascus, I didn't make it up, and it is supported by documentation. It describes some Jewish rituals. How can the Zionists deny this reality? They do not want anyone to know about their hostile morality, so they target anyone who exposes them with this hostility."[52]

The Arab world has indeed invented a novel form of anti-Semitic libel by combining the ritual murder legends of medieval Christian Europe with Russian conspiracy theories about the Jewish drive for world domination and Koranic quotations that defame Jews as the sons of apes and donkeys. In this macabre demonology, America and Israel are frequently bonded together as satanic forces that threaten the identity, values, and existence of the Arabs and Islam. This has been especially the case since the beginning of the al-Aqsa intifada, followed by 9/11 and the invasion of Iraq. In the anti-Semitic script, America is depicted as being run by Jews and compulsively seeking to destroy Islam.[53] Haunted by this paranoid ideology, Islamists see the fingerprints of the all-powerful Zionist lobby almost everywhere, spreading its tentacles and deadly lies, draining the lifeblood of Arabs and Muslims, and inciting America to fight in Iraq and to carry out sinister Jewish plans for world domination.

It is highly characteristic that the September 11, 2001, terrorist attacks against the United States were greeted with such rapture in many parts of the Muslim world, especially in the Palestinian Authority. For example, the mufti of Jerusalem, preaching his Friday sermon at the al-Aqsa Mosque, openly called for the destruction of Israel, Britain, and the United States: "Oh Allah, destroy America, for she is ruled by Zionist Jews. . . . Allah will paint the White House black!" Other Palestinian Muslim clerics, including Sheikh Ibrahim Mahdi, focused their efforts on praising the suicide bombers in Israel. In words aired repeatedly by PA television, he enthusiastically encouraged the human sacrifice of children as acts of martyrdom against Israel: "All weapons must be aimed at the Jews, at the enemies of Allah, the cursed nation in the Qur'an, whom the Qur'an describes as monkeys and pigs. . . . We will blow them up in Hadera, we will blow them up in Tel Aviv and in Netanya. . . . We bless all those who educate their children to Jihad and to martyrdom."[54]

The anti-Jewish jihad is inextricably linked, however, to the war against the United States. Throughout the Arab world there was a general elation after 9/11 at the sudden collapse of "mythological symbols of arrogant American imperialist power." The hijackers were perceived as delivering a blow on behalf of the embattled Muslim *umma* in Palestine, Iraq, Kashmir, and other trouble spots on the planet. No less swiftly, across Muslim and Arab society, the blame for the terrorist attacks was firmly placed on the Zionists, the Israeli government, the CIA, and the Mossad. The Syrian ambassador to Tehran was quoted as solemnly declaring that "the Israelis have been involved in these incidents and no Jewish employee was present in the World Trade Center building on the day."[55] According to the Syrian government newspaper *Al Thawra*, Israeli premier Ariel Sharon, in "plotting" 9/11, was seeking to divert attention from his aggressive plans toward the Palestinians.[56] The attack had created a golden opportunity for Israel to cause maximum damage to Muslims and provoke a deep schism in Arab-

American relations.[57] A journalist writing in the Jordanian newspaper *Al-Dustour* on September 13, 2001, even suggested that the Twin Towers massacre was "the act of the great Jewish Zionist mastermind that controls the world's economy, media and politics," and the diabolical plot was rapidly leading the world to a global disaster.[58] In the same issue, a Lebanese-Jordanian Holocaust denier warned Arabs against the "Jewish-Zionist hands behind the terrible event"; while another Jordanian columnist repeated the prevailing Arab wisdom "that Israel is the one . . . to benefit greatly from the bloody, loathsome terror operation."[59]

The Egyptian sheikh Muhammad al-Gamei'a, former imam of the Islamic Culture Center mosque of New York, like many of his coreligionists, had little doubt that the Jews were behind the September terrorist attacks. "The Jewish element is as Allah described. . . . We know they have always broken agreements, unjustly murdered the prophets and betrayed the faith."[60] The theory that Mossad, Israel's intelligence service, was behind the Twin Tower bombings was especially popular in non-Arab Muslim Pakistan. Major General Hamid Gul, former head of Pakistan's intelligence service, was adamant that only the Israelis "who are creating so much misery in the world had both the motivation, the ability, and perfidiousness to carry out such an attack."[61] In support of the Zionist conspiracy theory, the Lahore-based *Jihad Times* and other media in Pakistan recycled the legend that four thousand Israelis and Jews worked in the World Trade Center, and some had received a secret directive from the Mossad not to report for duty on September 11. The attacks had allegedly been ordered by "the Elders of Zion" in reaction to the anti-Israel bashing that had been handed out at the World Conference Against Racism, Racial Discrimination, Xenophobia, and Related Intolerance in Durban.[62] According to Pakistani opinion polls published in October 2001, more than two-thirds of Pakistanis agreed it was "possible" that Jews had been forewarned not to go to work on September 11.[63] A similar number evidently believed that world Zionism was behind the slaughter. They were convinced that Jews controlled the media treatment of the event and dictated the "vilification campaign against the Muslims." This was certainly the prevailing view in the Arab world. The notion that contemporary Jewry exercised a "media dictatorship" that deliberately sought to poison relations between Islam and the West was indeed widespread. Even more popular was the idea that Jews manipulate the Western mass media as a whole, especially in the United States.[64] The *Iran Daily* claimed, for example, that since September 11, 2001, the West had been swamped by the propaganda of "Zionist circles [who] have been almost uncontrollably emitting their profound contempt of Islam."[65]

. . .

In Baathist Iraq under Saddam Hussein's iron rule, the anti-Zionist hysteria was no less rampant. It had been blended with European-style anti-Semitism ever since the Nazi-Arab axis was first constituted in the 1930s. In his youth, Saddam undoubtedly imbibed some of the Nazi influences, which left a deep imprint in wartime Iraq, as they did in Egypt and Syria. The Baath Party, founded in the 1940s by Michel Aflaq, a Greek Orthodox Christian born in Damascus, had long emphasized a secular cocktail of Pan-Arabism, Iraqi nationalism, and Arab national socialism partly concocted from the German Nazi model. In the Aflaqian concept that inspired Saddam, the Arab nation and its culture was deemed superior to Western civilization; the Arabs' quasi-mystical eschatological mission had been assigned to them by God himself, though it would remain a dream unless it was accompanied by sacrifice, conflict, martyrdom and an ocean of bloodshed. To this ideology, Saddam and the Iraqi Baath leaders, like their Syrian counterparts, added the Soviet Communist model of relentless centralization, indoctrination, surveillance, and secret police repression. Saddam's Iraq was indeed a totalitarian state based on fear and the need to crush a world of internal and external enemies, to prepare for endless war and to preserve the great "pan-Arab Revolution."[66]

Saddam's burning faith in Arab racial superiority, his doctrine of "eternal struggle," and his expansionist policies inevitably set him on a collision course with Israel and the United States. As a young man he had seen Nuri al-Said's Iraqi government enact a de facto anti-Semitic law in 1951 that stripped Iraqi Jewry of all of its assets, obliging around 125,000 Jews to leave, almost all of them without their property. Only a tiny remnant of the world's oldest Diaspora community remained behind. In January 1969, Saddam himself was among the organizers of the mock espionage trial and public hanging of thirteen young Jews in Baghdad's central square—a gruesome mass spectacle. This was a truly macabre realization of totalitarian Arab nationalism in practice. It was no accident that under Saddam, the *Protocols* came into vogue to exemplify Jewish plans for expansion and seizing control of the Middle East—the so-called Israelite Biblical Empire "from the Nile to the Euphrates." Iraqi intellectuals faithfully echoed the paranoia of the regime concerning Zionist plots and the multi-tentacled octopus of world Jewry. It was self-evident to militant Baathists that the Zionist entity must be physically eradicated, as Saddam publicly promised he would do shortly before the First Persian Gulf War in 1990. On May 30, 2001, he explained to an Algerian delegation on Iraqi TV: "Palestine is Arab and must be liberated from the river to the sea and all the Zionists who immigrated to the land of Palestine must leave."[67] The fact that Saddam peppered his speeches with references to Nebuchadnezzar (the Babylonian ruler who had destroyed Solomon's Temple in antiquity) and to Saladin (the greatest of Muslim military leaders) demonstrated not only his megalomania but his determination to teach the Western Christian "Crusaders" (especially America and Britain), as well as the Jews, a lesson they would never forget.

In the totalitarian Baathist vision of Arab socialism, wiping out Israel meant eliminating a population who were constantly dehumanized in the Iraqi media as murderers, criminals, and the scum of the earth. As in Egypt and Syria, the anti-Semitic fabrications knew no limits, including the absurd libel that Israel spread medicines that caused infertility to Arab women. As Middle Eastern history professor Amatzia Baram has pointed out, "by far the worst curse an Iraqi-Ba'athi can hurl at anybody is to claim that they have Jewish ancestry."[68] When Saddam's Iraq found itself in conflict with Saudi Arabia (which was frequently the case), the royal house would be periodically depicted as descended from Jews; similarly, the rulers of Kuwait were branded as *yahud al-khalij* (the Jews of the Gulf). The term "Jew" invariably represented something lowly, base, and devoid of idealism, manliness, and honor—in contrast with the glorious vision of a pure, heroic, and revolutionary Arabism.[69]

The downfall of Saddam Hussein did not end anti-Semitism in Iraq. The Islamist press swiftly echoed the call of Shia clerics to prohibit the sale of any real estate to non-Iraqis, for fear it "may end up in the hands of Jews." The press constantly warned of Israeli goods flooding Iraqi markets and of the danger that Jews might return to Iraq in the wake of the allied occupation to recover their expropriated properties.[70] The *Asia Times,* in a revealing November 26, 2003, report on the "Jewish factor" in Iraq, noted the extent of the anti-Semitic obsession; the many sermons of imams declaring that the Jews and the Freemasons were at war with Islam; the widespread popular myth that the Americans are "all Jews and mercenaries"; the belief of a significant number of ordinary Iraqis that "America and the Jews have the same objectives and the same religion."

The U.S. occupation was dubbed by many as "Jewish" in its methods and inspiration. In Sadr City, the Shiite stronghold, Imam Seyid Hassan al-Naji al-Musawi announced that the Mahdi (the Islamic Messiah) "would soon come and kill all the Jewish leaders."[71] In the bookshops of Baghdad, the *Protocols* and sensationalist anti-Semitic literature became more accessible than previously; and in their wake a popular legend revived that when the Jews visit the tombstone of one of their prophets (buried near the banks of the Euphrates), the *final* battle will begin in which the Muslims will defeat their Jewish adversaries. Such apocalyptic obsessions are strongest among the Baghdadi Shiites and weakest in Kurdistan, though many Sunni Muslims are still imbued with anti-Semitic stereotypes deriving from Saddam's heyday. When the Iraqi government decided in February 2005 to add Saturday to the traditional Friday off work, student supporters of radical Shiite cleric Muqtada al-Sadr declared a general strike against this imposition of a Zionist and Jewish holiday.[72] The tragic absurdity of such protests taking place in a country undergoing unprecedented internal ethnic cleansing and civil war between Sunni and Shiite militias was evidently lost on the students. Tens of thousands of Iraqis were dying in suicide bombings, streetside executions, and gangland terror that had nothing whatsoever to do with Israel or Zionism.

· · ·

Islamic and Arab anti-Semitism could never have achieved such worldwide resonance without a massive infusion of petro-dollars and a vast dissemination of Wahhabite ideology—the hate-filled, extremist offshoot of Islam that has for the past eighty years been the official creed of Saudi Arabia.[73] It is certainly no accident that the Saudis have sheltered and co-opted virtually every important Islamist fundamentalist ideologue of the past century. The roll call includes Muhammad Rashid Rida, Hassan al-Banna (founder of the Muslim Brotherhood in Egypt), Abu al-Ala Mawdudi from Pakistan, as well as Abdullah Azzam (Palestinian architect of the Afghani jihad), Mohammed Qutb, and the mentors of al-Qaeda.

It was the Saudis who first nurtured the revival of holy war and ultimately of Islamic terrorism, using their immense wealth and "special rela-

tionship" with the United States as cover. What began as a puritanical re-
forming sect in the deserts of Arabia in the late eighteenth century with
Muhammad ibn 'Abd al-Wahhab—whose aim was to "cleanse" Islam of
idolatrous practices—culminated two centuries later in the death cult of
bin-Ladenism. Yet until the late 1970s, "moderate," conservative Saudi Arabia had been regarded in the West as its key oil supplier and a central pillar
in the struggle against godless Communism. In 1979, with the double shock
of the Iranian Revolution and the Soviet invasion of Afghanistan, the
Saudis changed tack—generously funding madrassas in Pakistan, strongly
proselytizing their harsh Wahhabite version of Islam to counter the Shiite
ascendancy in Iran, and financially backing radical Sunni Islamists worldwide. Whatever their intentions, they were, in practice, laying the foundations of global jihad.[74] Their task was facilitated not only by huge oil
revenues but also by their special status as custodians of Islam's holiest
sanctuaries in Mecca and Medina. In Afghanistan the Saudis bankrolled
and literally fueled the militants of the violently anti-Soviet jihad that ultimately spawned al-Qaeda.[75]

Wahhabism introduced into the Arab world its own soft version of totalitarianism—a quasi-compulsory social experiment aimed not at modernization but rather at the perpetuation of reactionary fanaticism.[76] In the
early 1930s, the Saudis came up with a religious form of fascism based on
the monopoly of wealth by the ruling elite, bloody repression, a brutal secret police, tight censorship, and complete control of education. The Wahhabite ideology combined radical separatism, fundamentalist theology, and
the newest dictatorial methods of political control.[77] Perpetual incitement
against non-Wahhabi Muslim groups—especially the Shias, but also Christians and Jews—was part of the program. Ultimately, the terrorism of the
Saudi-backed Hamas in Palestine and the 9/11 terrorists can also be seen as
a fusion of Wahhabism (in its deviant bin-Ladenist form) and the more violent offshoots of the Egyptian Muslim Brotherhood. Until the Saudi peace
plan of 2002, Saudi Arabia was a bulwark of Arab rejectionism.

Indeed, Saudi rulers from King Ibn Saud to King Faisal to King Abdallah
have traditionally regarded Zionism as an unmitigated evil and a wicked
conspiracy against Allah and his Prophet. Their desire to see the annihilation of Israel as a step toward Islamic worldwide hegemony was an established fact. To justify this goal they consistently portrayed the Jewish state as
a new military imperialism that offered the Arabs nothing but slavery or

death.[78] Israel was even considered on a par with international communism, as an enemy that threatened not only the Saudi Kingdom but all Arabs and the very essence of Islam. Saudi Arabian schoolbooks for decades have reflected this extremely hostile attitude, which, in principle, extends to Christians and to the West in general. The innate superiority of Islam and Muslims is constantly emphasized, while infidels (Jews, fake Muslims, and others) are systematically denigrated as "enemies of God and the believers." Western civilization is treated as a permanent imperialist conspiracy against the Muslim *umma,* based on shallow, wanton, and immoral secularism. The Jews since antiquity are stereotyped as being destructive, treacherous, and constantly plotting against Islam. The *Protocols of the Elders of Zion* are taken as the incarnation of the corrupting methods and influence of Jewry that led to the downfall of the Muslim caliphate in 1924 and the Zionist "usurpation" of Palestine.

Saudi indoctrination to hatred of Jews begins in the nursery. In an interview on Iqraa TV in May 2002, a three-year-old girl, Basmallah, was asked: "Are you familiar with the Jews?" Basmallah says yes, exclaiming that she does not like them "because they're apes and pigs."

"Who said so?" the show's anchor asks.

"Our God," the little girl replies, adding that Allah says this "in the Koran." The moderator promptly blessed her and her parents for their exemplary faith.[79]

Abdullah Bin-Matruk al-Haddal, from the Saudi Ministry of Islamic Affairs, expanded on this imagery in an Al-Jazeera talk show on January 22, 2002, blaming 9/11 on "Jewish-Zionist wickedness which infiltrates the US." He expressed surprise that Christian America "allows the brothers of apes and pigs to corrupt it." Warmly defending Osama bin Laden, he warned and advised the United States "to get rid of the Jews." It is no surprise, then, to discover that a survey of Saudi citizens conducted at the end of December 2007 revealed that 82 percent had a "very unfavorable" view of Jews, 7 percent were "somewhat unfavorable," and only 6 percent were remotely positive.[80]

Saudi academics such as Umayma al-Jalahma from the King Faisal University in al-Dammam, have added their own fuel to the fire by reviving the medieval blood libel. The learned female academic has recounted all kinds of imaginary Jewish practices in meticulous and gory detail. Unfortunately, al-Jalahma confused the Jewish holiday of Purim with Passover—describing how Jews barbarically drain the blood from their young victims for "Purim pastries" rather than Passover matzo.[81] Al-Jalahma followed this up with another article using two wholly fabricated quotations—one from President George Washington and the other supposedly uttered by Benjamin Franklin. To both of these founding fathers of the United States the Saudi scholar attributed the desire to expel the "treacherous" and "destructive" Jews from the New World.[82] Even the ultracautious U.S. State Department felt obliged to urge Saudi Arabia to reduce the level of such outrageous incitement and hatred against Jews, while at the same time praising the desert kingdom for its "peace initiative." The American government did, at least, protest. The response of the Israeli Foreign Ministry to Saudi and Muslim-Arab incitement at the time was a deafening silence.[83]

Leading Saudi preachers, it should be emphasized, frequently beseech Allah in their sermons to annihilate the Jews and avoid any agreements with them. In the spring of 2002, Sheikh Abd al-Rahman al-Sudayyis, imam at Mecca's leading mosque, urged Arabs to reject peace initiatives with Jews since they were "the scum of the human race, the rats of the world, the violators of pacts and agreements, the murderers of the prophets and the offspring of apes and pigs."[84] In another sermon, he told rapt listeners that the Jews of today were identical to their evil ancestors. From the dawn of Islam, they had perfidiously rejected Muhammad's divine message.

Like other Saudi preachers, Rahman also branded Christians, along with the Jews, as belonging to the camp of *al-Kufr* (unbelief), which would eventually be destroyed by Allah. Hence the categorical opposition of Muslim fundamentalists to interfaith dialogue and their insistence on damning all non-Muslims as infidels. There could never be any compromise between the "Allah's path of righteousness" and "Satan's path of *Kufr*."[85] Moreover, despite the official alliance with the United States, many Islamist clerics in Saudi Arabia clearly regard America as the leader of the infidel camp and Jews as their most dangerous allies. Prophecies of annihilation anticipating the demise of both of these deadly enemies are frequent. They increasingly bear an unmistakable Islamic apocalyptic ring. Whether the fall of the infidel American-Zionist empire proves to be rapid or more gradual, it has been divinely decreed. This is considered to be an irrevocable principle of religious law that will not change with time, place, people, or circumstance. However, in contrast to the official guardians of the Saudi kingdom, al-

Qaeda and other militants who have reached for the sword are impatient. They feel that the end is dawning and that they have been commanded to conquer the world. They have reworked the Christian apocalypse (which it-self was constructed on earlier Jewish prophecies) to suit Muslim tri-umphalism. In this end-time scenario the massacre of Jews is part of the divine judgment.

At the heart of contemporary Muslim eschatology is the use of an apoc-alyptic hadith indicating that there will be an all-out Muslim war against Jewry at the End of Days. The Muslims, it is emphasized, will kill all the Jews. Thus Osama bin Laden in a sermon of February 2003 announced:

> The [Islamic] nation has also been promised victory over the Jews, as the Prophet Muhammad has told us: "The Day of Judgment will not arrive until the Muslims fight the Jews and kill them, until the Jew hides behind the stones and the trees; and each stone or tree will say: Oh Muslim, Oh servant of God, there is a Jew hiding behind me, come and kill him; ex-cept from the *gharqad,* which is the tree of the Jews."[86]

Osama bin Laden regards the present Saudi rulers as apostates and lack-eys of the West, but his view of the Jews is still based on Wahhabite princi-ples. In all the Saudi media it is axiomatic to denigrate Jews and present Israel as totally *illegitimate.* Thus, according to Egyptian-born professor Zaghloul el-Naggar, lecturing on Saudi TV on April 2, 2006, the creation of a Jewish state in the heart of the Muslim world was a denial of the Holy Koran. No amount of unconditional American support for Israel could avert the divine judgment that was preparing its demise. The professor's faith was echoed two weeks later by a prominent Saudi cleric on Al-Jazeera TV, who confidently announced the inevitable triumph of Islam and jihad in the twenty-first century. The defeat of America and the Jews was immi-nent. Conversions to Islam, he said, were rising every year in the United States; it was losing the war in Iraq and simultaneously undergoing a slow, steady, but relentless internal destruction.[87] Such statements are frequent in a country often touted as a bastion of American interests in the region.

Meanwhile, the Jewish neocon plot to destroy the oil-rich desert king-dom has also preoccupied the Saudi ruling elite. Princess Fahda bint Saud ibn Abd al-Aziz is by no means the only prominent royal to see a sinister

Zionist and American-Jewish hidden hand behind efforts to subvert the House of Saud. Quoting her father, the long-deceased King Saud, who throughout his life had portrayed "the Zionist threat" as a "cancer," she denounced Israel's terror, pledged her undying support for the Palestinians, and expressed unbounded rage at American policy.[88] Other leading Saudis, such as Interior Minister Prince Nayef ibn Abd al-Aziz, have usually been more circumspect. But they have repeatedly claimed that the Zionists were behind the 9/11 bombings, which allegedly sought to drive a wedge between U.S. opinion, Saudi Arabia, and the Arabs in general. Like many in the Arab world, the Saudi minister refused to accept the indisputable fact that no fewer than seventeen of the nineteen hijackers who attacked the World Trade Center were Saudi citizens.[89]

In response to terrorist shootings in the Saudi kingdom, the royal family, the media, and the educational system often fall back on the Zionist scapegoat. Thus Crown Prince Abdallah ibn Abd al-Aziz al-Saud, at a meeting of Saudi dignitaries on May 2, 2004, publicly declared on Saudi television:

> You all know who is behind it all. Zionism is behind it. It has become clear now. . . . It is not 100%, but 95% [certain] that the Zionist hands are behind what happened.[90]

The Saudi media faithfully echoed this fabrication, duly reinforced by a bevy of Egyptian, Jordanian, and Lebanese pundits. If that were not enough, the Saudi interior minister soon confirmed that Israel and Zionism were even behind al-Qaeda—which has been responsible for many terrorist attacks in Arab countries. In the same Orwellian vein, Saudi intellectuals (like some of their more sophisticated counterparts in the West) have blamed the American invasion of Iraq on the Zionist neocons. The only difference is that Saudis more crudely characterize "the Zionist gang that has colonized America and the American people" as being driven by "Jewish biblical greed and hatred." The crazy neocons who ruled America and "controlled the world," were, in Saudi eyes, "the closest thing there is to Nazism."[91] The intention of the new American administration under President Obama, to turn the Saudi peace plan of 2002 into a cornerstone of its solution for the Israeli-Palestinian conflict, seems difficult to fathom in this light. Saudi Arabia may today be more worried by Iran than Israel, but until its rulers abandon their repellent anti-Semitism, it is hard to see what positive contribution they could make to Middle East peace.

• • •

Political Islam, so it would appear, *requires* the existence of a conspiracy. It goes without saying that Jews perfectly fit the bill in terms of Islamic tradition, the *Protocols* myth, and the war with Israel.[92] In contemporary Egypt—officially at peace with the Jewish state since 1979—this remains all-too-apparent in government or semigovernmental press organs, in editorials, political cartoons, demonic caricatures of Jews, as well as in cassettes and the inflammatory sermons heard in the mosques.[93] No less than in Saudi Arabia or Syria, the Jews are caricatured in the Egyptian media as dangerous and cunning; as swastika-decorated Nazis; as an international cabal controlling the U.S. government; and as poisoning and corrupting Arab youth when they are not hell-bent on sadistically killing Palestinian children.[94] There is no real distinction between Jews or Zionists, who are nearly always intertwined in contemporary Egyptian perspectives that relate to Israel and the Middle East. As Rivka Yadlin, a student of Egyptian anti-Semitism, pointed out nearly twenty years ago: "The abominable traits expressed in the behavior of Israel are perceived as singular, inherent and intrinsic in its very Jewish being. They are inherited within the Jewish community and are thus shared by the whole of Israel as well as by other Jews."[95] The Zionist "monster," embodied in the State of Israel, is regarded as the very "essence of Judaism."

The term "Jew" is generally applied without differentiation to Israeli citizens and to Jews in general. However, for the Egyptian Islamist editors of *Al-Da'wa* (a publication of the Muslim Brothers), "Jewry," which covers both categories, is literally a monstrosity—a synonym for conspiracy, corruption, and sedition that must be eradicated from the midst of the Islamic nation. Hence, already thirty years ago, the Egyptian-Israeli Peace Treaty was immediately perceived in Islamist circles as a betrayal of jihad, of Egyptian honor, and of Muslim values. President Sadat's trip to "infidel-occupied" Jerusalem was an abomination to the Muslim Brotherhood—not least because it was seen as a capitulation to world Jewry, with its intrinsically evil proclivities.[96] For the fundamentalists (as for the Nazis) the Jewish state represented a new center of Jewish conspiratorial power. To negotiate, let alone to recognize its existence in any form, was to deepen

Islam's contemporary crisis. Such dealings would enable the Zionists to infiltrate Muslim lands, destroy Islamic beliefs, and plant the noxious seeds of Westernization. As the heirs of Sayyid Qutb, the neo-Muslim Brothers in Egypt demonized the Jews as *permanent enemies*. They vilified secular Egyptian leaders from Nasser to Sadat as "agents of Zionism" who ignored the "Jewish peril." The spiritual leader of the Muslim Brothers and editor of *Al-Da'wa* (The Call to Islam), Umar al-Tilmisani, repeatedly stressed the fact that Jews were *evil* by nature. They were thieves, renegades, rapacious egoists, insincere opportunists, and fanatical racists bent on ruling the world. In this context, any "normalization" or peace agreements such as that initiated by President Sadat would be catastrophic. Indeed, al-Tilmisani called normal relations with Israel "the most dangerous cancer eating away at all the life cells in our bodies."[97]

The fundamentalists have long perceived Israel as the head of the snake, the spearhead of international anti-Islamic forces. If there was "normalization," then the Egyptian economy would be opened up to Western economic exploitation; the sacred Islamic prohibition on interest would be violated, and empty secularism would definitively erode the Islamic message. Al-Tilmisani declared: "The Jews institute ways of deceitful propaganda. What enables them to utilize this propaganda is that they spread their poison among the youth . . . they claim to be fighting backwardness which they allege is due to Islam; while they also in fact fight all varieties of Islamic tradition."[98]

For the Muslim Brothers, Jews have always embodied corruption, vice, immorality, and drug abuse, and they had a compulsive need for "the blood of Gentiles." These vile Judeophobic stereotypes are indistinguishable from those of the worst European Christian anti-Semites. Thus, despite the peace treaty, Egyptian news sources to this day accuse Israel of distributing drug-laced chewing gum and candy intended to make women sexually corrupt and to kill children. A special series on *Al-Ahram*, the leading government-sponsored daily in Egypt, has even examined in great detail how Jews use the blood of Gentiles to make matzo for Passover. An Egyptian intellectual, writing in *Al-Akhbar*, further elaborated on how the Talmud (described as the Jews' second holiest book) "determines that the 'matzahs' of Atonement Day must be kneaded 'with blood' from non-Jews. The preference is for the blood of youths after raping them."[99]

Such extraordinary libels were also a favorite motif of the late King Faisal ibn Abd al-Aziz ibn Saud of Saudi Arabia, who not only claimed that Jews carried out the ritual murder of children but also insisted that this proved "the extent of their hatred and malice toward non-Jewish peoples."[100] The blood libel was amplified and updated during the Lebanon War by Egyptian mufti Ali Gum'a, writing in *Al-Ahram* in August 2006 about the "blood-sucking [Israeli] murderers." Referring to a notorious nineteenth-century anti-Semitic work entitled *Der Talmudjude,* written by the German Catholic canon August Rohling, the mufti related Israel's "crimes" to the Talmud. The Egyptian sheikh added that the lies of the "Hebrew entity" had exposed "the true and hideous face of the bloodsuckers . . . who prepared [Passover] matzos from human blood."[101] Such genocidal ravings cause barely a ripple on the diplomatic surface of the Arab-Israeli confrontation or the "Palestinian question." They are, however, a major reason for the utter failure to resolve the conflict during the past sixty years.

In Egypt, as in other Arab countries, belief in the *Protocols* is no less rampant than the most delirious narratives attached to the blood libel myth. In November 2003, an international scandal was provoked when an Arabic translation of the *Protocols* was put on display alongside the Torah and Talmud at the manuscript museum in the renovated Alexandria Library, supposedly to represent the Jewish "way of life." The binding of the *Protocols* featured the Star of David, surrounded by symbolic snakes.

The offending copy was removed as a result of international pressure and diplomatic protests. The library's director, Dr. Siraj al-Din, apologized, describing the *Protocols* as a "fabrication" that fomented anti-Jewish feelings— a characterization that earned him the hatred of local extremists and even provoked questions in parliament.[102]

Not all Egyptians, it should be emphasized, identify with the racist bigotry of the *Protocols.* After *The Horseman Without a Horse* TV series was screened, Osama el-Baz (President Mubarak's political adviser) did write a three-part article urging Egyptians to "refrain from succumbing to such myths as the *Protocols* and the use of Christian blood in Jewish rituals. We should not sympathize in any way with Hitler or Nazism."[103] El-Baz maintained that anti-Semitism was a Western invention—"contaminated goods" with no deep roots in Arab or Muslim culture. This was also the view of a small minority of commentators, journalists, scholars, and human rights activists in Egypt and the Arab world.[104] But the great sheikh of Al-Azhar, Muhammad Sayyid Tantawi—one of the highest religious authorities in

Sunni Islam—did not share el-Baz's view. Nor did the Egyptian cleric Safwat Higa, who in a televised sermon in March 2009, called for closing down Starbucks across the Arab world for allegedly featuring the biblical Queen Esther on its logo. Equally false were the claims of another cleric who evoked the *Protocols* to assert that "Coca Cola, Pepsi, McDonalds, Kentucky Fried Chicken . . . Little Caesar, Pizza Hut and Burger King" were all part of a Zionist plot to control the world economy.[105]

Anti-Zionism and the territorial conflict with Israel hardly explain the compulsive recourse to such grotesque anti-Semitic material or its intensity, scale, and obsessiveness. In the Egyptian case, for example, all of Sadat's territorial demands were satisfied by Israel *without exception*. Moreover, the Egyptian regime was rewarded by massive American aid. Hence there seems to be no rational explanation for the extraordinarily virulent and malignantly anti-Semitic portrayals of Jewry in the Egyptian media. Evidently, in Egypt as elsewhere in the Arab world, the issue runs much deeper. Jews remain at some deeper level an absolute "other" in the Middle East. As in a pre-Holocaust Europe, there are many powerful forces in Egypt and the Arab world driven by a paranoid fear of Judaization in their encounter with the West, secularism, and modernity. They include Nasserites, Arab socialists, and Egyptian representatives of fundamentalist Islam who invoke the worst prejudices of medieval Christianity and freely borrow from the anti-Semitic arsenal of the hated West. The Egyptian Muslim Brothers liberally quote, for example, from Christian anti-Talmudic literature, from secular texts such as Henry Ford's *The International Jew,* from Nazi propaganda about Judeo-Masonry and Judeo-Communism, from Hitler's *Mein Kampf,* from the *Protocols,* and Western Holocaust deniers. None of this deluge of anti-Semitic material serves any purpose in bolstering nonexistent territorial issues between Egypt and Israel. The never-ending flood of *Der Stürmer*–like images depicting Israelis as satanic beings and murderers of God who have crucified Palestine just as the Jews crucified Christ are Christian anti-Semitic motifs that have been thoroughly Arabized and Islamicized. A good example of how this works was provided by Sheikh Youssef al-Qaradawi, on his regular Al-Jazeera TV program *Religion and Life,* in February 2005:

> There is no doubt that the Jews had a far-reaching [role] in crucifying Jesus. A few years ago the Vatican published a document proclaiming the Jews innocent of spilling Jesus's blood, but whoever reads history knows

how the Jews incited the Roman governor to crucify Jesus. We believe Jesus was not crucified, but the crime was committed . . . and we believe that the Jews, I mean, they committed this crime.[106]

Sheikh Qaradawi, as we have previously noted, is an immensely popular preacher, much respected across the Arab world, who has made many statements in defense of war, confrontation, and jihad against the infidels. On Al-Jazeera TV in January 2009 he was still appealing to Allah to purify the "Jewish Zionist band of oppressors" and to "kill them down to the very last one."

The stereotype of the sanguinary Jews, so rampant in contemporary Arab caricatures, is a classic theme deriving from Christian anti-Semitism. Jews with yarmulkes and Stars of David are repeatedly shown drinking Arab and Palestinian blood—a motif which has its distant origins in the blood libel that emerged in twelfth-century Christian England. This Christianization of Muslim attitudes toward Jews (at a time of extreme tension between jihadi Islam and the West) is indeed remarkable. So, too, is the willingness of so many members of the Arab elite (and millions of non-Arab Muslims) to embrace the most extreme paranoid conspiracy theories imported from Europe. Thus a retired general, Hasan Sweilem, wrote on June 17, 2001, in the prestigious Egyptian weekly *October* that "Jews stood behind wars and internal strife and that caused European rulers to expel and kill them. . . . The Jewish conspiracy to take over Europe generated civil revolutions." The Jews, he explained, were to blame for the Crusades, the English and American civil wars, the French Revolution, Napoleon, two world wars, Communism, and Nazism, as well as the fall of the Ottoman Empire and all subsequent conflicts in the Middle East. They had monopolized the trade in gold and precious stones, controlled the world monetary system, and were responsible for globally disseminating and encouraging drugs, prostitution, sex slavery, and alcoholism.[107]

Egyptian TV has continued to feature academics and intellectuals who authenticate the *Protocols* and the blood libel. For example, on February 25, 2007, the Egyptian researcher Muhammad al-Buheiri asserted that ritual murder was an integral part of Jewish culture. This, he said, had been confirmed by an Israeli historian, Ariel Toaff, whom he warmly recommended for the Nobel Prize following the publication of his book *Bloody Passover* in Italy (Toaff subsequently recanted his views and revised the book). Al-Buheiri observed that Jews had slaughtered Christian adults and children in nineteenth-century

Syria and continued to do so in Israel today. Despite their great efforts to conceal these religious rituals, the blood sacrifices continued. Asked by the interviewer if the Arabian Jews who were cursed in the Koran were the same as those living today, al-Buheiri (described as a "researcher specializing in interfaith dialogue") replied that the curse was "not restricted to any geographical region." The Jews were a *cursed people* because of their religion, their ideology, and their behavior.

Such bigoted beliefs and the conspiratorial fantasies that defame Jews as a worldwide threat to civilization are all too frequently repeated by mainstream members of the Egyptian elite. They also provide an easy fallback position for some Arab rulers who find themselves in serious difficulty. Thus Sudan's genocidal tyrant, President Umar Hassan Ahmad al-Bashir, asserted at the end of a three-hour-long video conference from Khartoum in November 2006 that all the reports in the Western press about mass murder in Darfur were an "Israeli-led worldwide conspiracy" to divert attention from conflicts in Iraq, Afghanistan, and Palestine. He dismissed any connection between his government and the brutal Arab Janjaweed militia, which has expelled, displaced, raped, or robbed an estimated 2.5 million black Sudanese—Muslim and Christian—in Darfur. The Sudanese president claimed that fatalities were below ten thousand—not the more than four hundred thousand accepted by the United Nations and most of the international media. Israel was not only responsible for these "lies" but also for *all* the world's disputes and "any problem that any Arab country is facing." Israel's security, he said, would always be based on weakening Arab states. It was Jewish control of the media ("you can't deny they have such influence in circles all over the world") that—according to President al-Bashir—explained international interest in Darfur.[108]

Media domination, especially in America, is what also explained for Egyptian professor Abd al-Sabour Shahin, head of the sharia faculty at the prestigious Al-Azhar University, how the United States—once "a rational and balanced country"—had become a violent and ruthless predator that based its policy on deliberate lies. Not only that, but Arabs and Muslims, he insisted, had been "framed for an international crime" (the Holocaust) of which they were totally innocent. The secret goal was for America to take over the world's energy sources and cover up for Zionists who had "killed hundreds of thousands in Palestine."[109]

Conspiracy theory also guided another prominent Egyptian, the deputy editor of the government daily *Al-Gumhuriya,* who wrote in March 2004 that Zionist Jews were not only behind 9/11 but also responsible for the terror bombings in Madrid and "all the violent terrorist operations that have occurred anywhere in the world." The Zionist aim was to damage and discredit all Arabs. Jews, as ever, were depicted as driven by sheer hatred and their own "black history." In alliance with America, they had invented the terrorist bogey in order to justify the invasion of Iraq and to escalate their own aggression in Palestine.[110]

Many Egyptian academics and clerics have insisted that real terrorism is deeply rooted in Zionist doctrine and in the Talmud. Hussam Wahba, columnist for an Egyptian religious weekly magazine linked to the ruling party, let his imagination run riot, referring to a *nonexistent* inscription at the main entrance to Israel's parliament building that supposedly reads: "Compassion toward a non-Jew is forbidden." Moreover, according to Wahba, there was a *sacred* Talmudic obligation to murder "Goyim" (Gentiles) because "the flesh of non-Jews is the flesh of donkeys and their sperm is the sperm of animals." But, he said, "Zionist terrorism" was not merely based on such religious perversions, it was also anchored in the Jewish psyche—with its natural proclivity to trickery, deceit, and deception. Once again, it seems that evil Jewish character traits are assumed to have been fixed for all eternity. This has been one of the central hallmarks of anti-Semitism through the ages.

Another feature of contemporary Arab anti-Semitism is the assumption that anything that adversely affects Islam's image must be the work of the Jews. Egyptian cleric Hazem Jallah Abu Isma'il (formerly an Islamic lecturer in the United States), like so many of his contemporaries, saw 9/11 in this light. In April 2006, in his weekly show on Al-Resala TV, he fabricated statistics to explain that Jews controlled the world media, which they had craftily used to frame and defame Muslims. More specifically, he told his Egyptian viewers: "Jews produce more than 82% of the video clips in the world. The Jews! . . . Eighty-two percent of all attempts to corrupt humanity originate from the Jews. You must know this so that we can know what should be done."[111]

Frequently exposed to such delirious propaganda, it is not so surprising that few Egyptians celebrated the historic peace treaty with Israel thirty years after the event. Indeed, many see it as the origin of Egypt's decline and diplomatic impotence. This is especially true among the younger generation. The war in Gaza reinforced this sentiment, encouraged by the Muslim Brotherhood, which has constantly called on Egypt to withdraw from the Peace Treaty. This may indeed happen once the eighty-one-year-old Hosni Mubarak leaves the stage. However, at least one Egyptian senior psychiatrist, Adel Sadeq, clearly *does* know what needs to be done. It was, he explained, "either the Israelis or the Palestinians"; hence, Arabs had no choice but to "throw Israel into the sea, there is no middle ground. Coexistence is total nonsense. . . . The real means of dealing with Israel directly is [to act like] those who blow themselves up."[112] This is certainly a widespread emotion in Egypt and the Arab world. But Sadeq's novel use and abuse of psychology raises the question of who, exactly, requires the psychiatric treatment? This same query might also be raised regarding Jihad al-Khazen, the former editor of the London Arabic-language daily, *Al-Hayat*. Writing on July 24, 2006, he offered an original if semi-deranged explanation of Israel's "Nazi-like practices": His theory was that "Israel's present political and military leaders are the grandsons of Nazi killers"—those Germans who in 1944, recognizing defeat as imminent, "assumed the identity of Jews and then fled to Palestine as Jews who had survived the Holocaust."[113]

Anti-Semitic conspiracy theories about the Jews can seem wildly irrational, but they have been embraced by seemingly rational and respected Muslim government leaders, including former Malaysian prime minister Mahathir Mohammed. In 1984 Malaysia had banned a visit by the New York Philharmonic Orchestra because it intended to perform a work by a Jewish composer, Ernst Bloch's *Schlomo: A Hebrew Rhapsody*. This happened at a time when the *Protocols* were openly published and disseminated in Malaysia, a strong supporter of the PLO. In a speech on August 12, 1983, Mahathir had called *The Wall Street Journal* a "Jewish tool," alleging that Jews and Zionists, who controlled the international media, were trying to destabilize his country. At a nonaligned summit in Zimbabwe in September 1986 Mahathir insultingly called the Jews "the most gifted students of Goebbels." Instead of learning from Nazi persecution, they had become identical to the very monsters they vilified. A month later, addressing the Malaysian parliament, the prime minister asserted that Zionists were to blame for his country's economic difficulties. In the early 1990s, Mahathir banned Steven Spielberg's movie *Schindler's List* as "pro-Jewish" propaganda; he also denied entry to an Israeli soccer player on the Liverpool team and prevented a delegate from El Al airlines from attending an international flight conference in Kuala Lumpur.[114] When the country faced a major economic crisis in July 1997, Mahathir conveniently blamed it on the "international Jewish conspiracy" and particularly on the speculative activity of American Jewish millionaire George Soros.

The seventy-seven-year-old Malaysian leader's remarks at the fifty-seven-member Organization of the Islamic Conference in October 2003, to the effect that Jews control the world, were not new in themselves. But they were uttered in the midst of a major media event that attracted global attention. The comments were instantly conveyed via the Internet and satellite TV, fitting a zeitgeist where anti-American and anti-Semitic conspiracy theories were ascendant, not only in Muslim countries but around the world.[115] The standing ovation for his speech at the conference stood in sharp contrast to most reactions in the West. There were the swift and unambiguous condemnations of his publicly proclaimed anti-Semitism from the United States, the European Union, and Australia. Germany, in particular, termed his comments "totally unacceptable."

Addressing the assembled sheikhs, emirs, kings, and presidents, Mahathir had posed a rather sinister rhetorical question:

> Is it true that 1.3 billion people can exert no power to save themselves from the humiliation and oppression inflicted on them by a much smaller enemy? Is there no other way than to ask our young people to blow themselves up? . . . We are actually very strong. 1.3 billion people cannot simply be wiped out. The Europeans killed 6 million Jews out of 12 million, but today the Jews rule the world by proxy. They get others to fight and die for them.[116]

Mahathir was certainly critical of his fellow Muslims. He deplored Islamic disunity, economic backwardness, intellectual regression, disregard of study and science, and failure to adapt to a world very different from Islam at its birth in the seventh century C.E. The Muslim *umma*, he acknowledged, was generally despised by non-Muslims for its failure to adapt; its religion was denigrated and its holy places "desecrated." Mahathir insisted that, in the long run, "1.3 billion Muslims could not be defeated by a few million Jews" but added that for more than sixty years Muslims had achieved nothing in Palestine except needless sacrifice of lives and further humiliation. What was lacking on the Muslim side were patience, discipline, rationality, and a sensible strategy.

> We are up against a people who think they survived 2000 years of pogroms not by hitting back, but by thinking. They invented and successfully promoted Socialism, Communism, human rights and democracy so that persecuting them would appear to be wrong, so they may enjoy equal rights with others. We see that they have now gained control of the most powerful countries and they, this tiny community, have become a world power. We cannot fight them through brawn alone. We must use our brains.[117]

Mahathir added, however, that the Jews were becoming "arrogant" as a result of their power and success. They were already making mistakes, which opened up a window of opportunity for Muslims to eliminate them.

Mahathir's conspiracy-mongering and transparent anti-Semitism (like Hitler, he interpreted democracy, socialism, and human rights as self-serving "Jewish inventions") was unusual only in so far as it had accompanied an explicit call to Muslims to modernize. They had to become more rational, scientific, and open to change. At the same time, the Malaysian leader skillfully played on the economic and psychological crisis facing 1.3 billion Muslims, who were embarrassed by their developmental failures, frustrated in their political ambitions, and haunted by a sense of collective impotence. Malaysia's own success story as a South Asian backwater that had turned into a high-tech exporter gave a certain credibility to his comments, which other Muslim leaders acclaimed as constituting a "very important road map."[118] His rabid anti-Semitism was totally ignored, perhaps because it was so mainstream and commonplace among the assembled notables that it was barely noticed. What caught their eye was the *modernization message* as a pan-Islamic goal to defeat the West, beginning with the destruction of Israel as the more realistic, short-term goal. This genocidal end would best be achieved not by terrorism (against which Malaysia itself had cracked down hard) but through the application of science, technology, and a dynamic economy to solving political problems. He made it clear that these were the preconditions for acquiring and effectively utilizing the high-tech weaponry required for victory over the Jews.

Mahathir's anti-Semitic rhetoric was closer in spirit to Henry Ford's *International Jew* than to the Koran, more reminiscent of the *Protocols* in a modernized form than of Islamist sources. However, it was still based on the shared Muslim assumption that the *superiority* of Islam was not only ordained from heaven but needed to be reflected in worldly success. From this perspective, Jews today remain a major enemy of Islam. They are a bone in its throat precisely because of their modernizing achievements. This was clarified by the highest ranking cleric of Sunni Islam, Sheikh Muhammad Sayyid Tantawi, on April 4, 2002, when he branded Jews as "the enemies of Allah, descendants of apes and pigs."[119] Convinced, like Mahathir, that Jews rule the world and seek the destruction of all spiritual values and morality, Tantawi did not hesitate to appeal to the conspiratorial interpretation of history enshrined in the *Protocols* as a valid source for Muslims.

The specter of "Jewish domination" that underpins contemporary Islamic anti-Semitism is closely linked to its comprehensive vision of a worldwide Jewish conspiracy. This is a worldview that has steadily gathered force ever since the Arab military humiliation at the hands of Israel in 1967. That crushing loss was not just a blow to Arab pride and national ambition but also, for many Muslims, a reflection of the crisis of Islam, of a lethargic, backward society and culture defeated by a more powerful, modern, technologically advanced, and better organized enemy. The secularist pan-Arab nationalism and Arab socialism that had previously held sway suffered a grievous blow to its prestige. In its place came a new trend toward seeing Islam itself as engaged in a fateful battle for civilization.[120]

The disaster of June 1967 encouraged the more conservative fundamentalists to sharpen the traditional image of Zionism and the Jews into something so utterly vile and perverse that they could only merit total eradication.[121] Virtually all the Arab theologians assembled by President Nasser in Cairo in 1968 perceived Jews in general to be "enemies of God" and "enemies of humanity"; as criminal riffraff rather than a people. Their Zionist state was the illegitimate culmination of allegedly *immutable* and *permanently depraved* characteristics. As their holy books amply demonstrated, "evil, wickedness, breach of vows and money worship" were "inherent qualities" that had become horrifyingly visible in the Jews during their conquest of Palestine.[122] In an April 25, 1972, speech broadcast on Cairo radio, President Sadat of Egypt echoed the Koran in referring to the Jews as "a nation of liars and traitors, contrivers of plots, a people born for deeds of treachery," who would soon be "condemned to humiliation and misery."[123] The head of the Academy of Islamic Research and rector of Al-Azhar University, Abdul Halim Mahmoud, was more explicit still in a book published one year after the Yom Kippur War: "Allah commands the Muslims to fight the friends of Satan wherever they are found. Among the friends of Satan— indeed, among the foremost friends of Satan in our present age—are the Jews."[124]

Such satanization of the Jews has achieved an autonomous dynamic beyond the political antagonism reflected in the diplomacy of the Arab-Israeli conflict.[125] There is a deep structure to Arab-Muslim anti-Semitic ideology that transcends immediate circumstances, the requirements of government propaganda, the territorial conflict with Israel, or the instrumental use of stereotypes imported from the West.[126] Middle Eastern anti-Semitism can always draw on the Koran and the sharia, which discriminates sharply against non-Muslims. Muslims are members of the *umma* (the Islamic community) possessing territories in the *dar al-Islam* (abode of Islam) where Islamic law is fully practiced. Non-Muslims, on the other hand, are people of the *dar al-harb* (abode of war) not yet subjugated but destined to pass under Islamic jurisdiction, whether by conversion or war. Once subdued, they become *dhimmis,* or "protected persons," which many Muslims see as a teaching of tolerance. But in the modern Western world such a status can only be considered the most abject servitude.[127] This remains the historic root of the oppression suffered by Christians and Jews under Islamic rule. This intolerance has been further fueled by the writings of radical Islamists such as Egyptian Muslim Brotherhood theorist Sayyid Qutb—executed by Nasser in 1966 but, as we have seen, still influential in fundamentalist circles today. In his multivolume commentary on the Koran, *Fi Zilal al-Qur'an* (In the Shade of the Koran), Qutb writes:

> In modern history, the Jews have been behind every calamity that has befallen the Muslim communities everywhere. The Jews give active support to every attempt to crush the modern Islamic revival and extend their protection to every regime that suppresses such a revival. The other people of earlier revelations, the Christians, has been no less hostile.[128]

Radical Islamists today have followed Qutb's Koranic interpretation and prescriptions to try to utterly subdue the hated Jews and Christians. They have developed new theologies of substitution, transferring Israel's biblical heritage to Arab and Muslim Palestine—thereby negating Jewish and Christian history in the name of jihadi imperialism.[129] They have acted as if Islamic history, culture, and society were frozen in time and the spirit of *dhimmitude* remained eternally valid. Hence we have witnessed at the beginning of the twenty-first century so many triumphalist proclamations of the superiority of Islam, and the racist-oriented recycling of fables about hereditary Jewish vices or evil qualities still deemed to be manifest in the Jews of today. Once again, the mythical Jew has come to represent the negative wellsprings and the dark side of history. He is depicted as relentlessly driving mankind toward the abyss. Only this time around it is Islam itself that is waging a war of civilization in the apocalyptic sense.[130]

Twenty-five years ago, a prominent Egyptian scholar and editor of a prestigious Arab weekly, Lufti Abdul Azim, gave expression to this chilling message of an eternal enmity between Jews and Islam: "For Jews are Jews, they have not changed over thousands of years: they embody treachery, meanness, deceit and contempt for human values. They would devour the flesh of a living person and drink his blood for the sake of robbing his property."[131] He added for good measure: "The Jewish Merchant of Venice is no different from the arch-executioners of Deir Yassin. . . . Both are similar models of human depravity."[132]

These words were written only three years after the signing of the Egyptian-Israeli peace treaty in 1979. The Egyptian scholar nonetheless assured his readers that the Jews were waging "a total war of annihilation" against the Arab nation in order to dismember and dominate it. The only difference among Jews was "whether to kill their Arab victim under anesthesia or attack it ferociously and drink its blood outright. . . . On the goal, all Jews are agreed." Lufti Abdul Azim was at least honest enough to "declare unequivocally that, yes, this is antisemitism, but since Arabs are also Semites, our antisemitism is against Jewish Semites."[133]

Since 1982 such boundless hatred of the Jews has only gained in intensity and become more deeply integrated into Arab cultural discourse. The old-new Arab anti-Semitism is one of the more pathological symptoms of the identity crisis faced by Muslims in a globalizing, modernizing, and increasingly secular world. It plays on the resentment against previously powerless, defenseless, and subordinate Jewish *dhimmis* who, after 1948, successfully rose up to create an independent and democratic Jewish state in the Middle East able to defeat several Arab armies on the battlefield. The peculiar emotional rage behind much Middle Eastern anti-Semitism might be seen as a vain attempt to deflect unresolved traumas that this unexpected Israeli military and technological prowess inflicted on the Arab psyche.[134]

The Six-Day War provided a great boost to the demonology of Zionism and the Jews, especially among Muslim fundamentalists. There was a deep sense of humiliation over the loss of Islamic territory in 1967 and the capture of the holy city of Jerusalem by the Israelis. Not by accident, fundamentalists speak of the conflict in terms of a struggle between Islam and the Jews—a battle of culture, civilization, and religion.[135] For them and much of the Arab world the Jewish victory became the ultimate symbol of Islam's degradation—a painful reminder of the inability of Muslims to recover the sources of their past glory and overcome the challenges posed by Western modernity. A radical rejection of all things "Western" and the belief that *Islam huwa al-hal* (only Islam is the solution) came together with a new vision of the so-called Jewish peril and of Israel as the enemy. In many cases the Islamist revolt against the West was transformed into a revolt against the Judeo-Christian conspiracy and the rule of the world by Jews.[136]

The existential panic behind much of Islamic and Arab anti-Semitism recalls certain elements in the Nazi paradigm of paranoiac Jew hatred. It is particularly dynamic, volatile, and genocidal in its implications. Israel and the Jews are perceived not only as a military, political, and economic threat to the Arabs and Islam; they are also a symbol of all the phobias provoked by secularism and the poisons of Western culture—pornography, AIDS, prostitution, rock music, Hollywood, mass consumerism, crime, drugs, and alcoholism.[137] Islamist anti-Semitism is further exacerbated by the belief that both history and Allah are on its side. Islamists are convinced that they are riding the wave of the future. Following the bankruptcy of secular-nationalist and Arab socialist ideologies in 1967, the road seemed clear for an Islamic revival. The Iranian Revolution of 1979, followed by the success of the mujaheedin in Afghanistan in defeating Soviet power in the 1980s, created a certain degree of Islamic hubris, which helped give birth to bin-Ladenist terror. Hubris did not, however, diminish the Muslim obsession with conspiracy theories, Zionist plots, mysterious and occult forces, and Jews as a secret superpower planning the demise of Islam. Worse still, except for a few brave dissenting individuals, there has been little effective opposition in the Arab and Muslim worlds able to counteract the flood of bigotry unleashed during the past forty years.[138]

Among those who have spoken out have been a number of young Muslim women who grew up in an oppressive environment where Jew hatred was almost obligatory. They found their true voices only when they immigrated to Canada or the United States. For example, the maverick Canadian Muslim "refusenik" Irshad Manji exposed some of the ways in which, as she says, "Islam's ideology of wholesale discrimination against Jews and Christians" has nothing in common with "tolerance."[139] Wafa Sultan, an Arab-American writer who grew up in Syria, bravely compared the response of Jews and Muslims to adversity in a program on Al-Jazeera:

> The Jews have come from the tragedy [the Holocaust] and forced the world to respect them, with their knowledge, not with their terror, with their work, not with their crying and yelling. We have not seen a single Jew blow himself up in a German restaurant. We have not seen a single Jew destroy a church. We have not seen a single Jew protest by killing people. Only the Muslims defend their beliefs by burning down churches, killing people and destroying embassies. This path will not yield any results. The Muslims must ask themselves what they can do for humankind, before they demand that humankind respect them.[140]

For Wafa Sultan, the present clash going on around the world is not between religions or civilizations but between the mentality of the Middle Ages and that of twenty-first-century modernity. This is a struggle "between barbarity and rationality, between freedom and oppression, between democracy and dictatorship." The West, the Jews, the secularists, and all those on "the side of free and creative thinking" are faced by an Islamofascist assault against civilization itself.

Nonie Darwish, who lived in Gaza and then Egypt until the age of thirty, has been no less direct in condemning the culture of hatred rampant in the Muslim world since her youth. At school in Gaza she sang songs with verses calling Jews "dogs"; as a young woman in Cairo she heard loudspeakers outside the mosque during Friday prayers saying: "May God destroy the infidels and the Jews, the enemies of God. We are not to befriend them or make treaties with them." Today, she points out:

Hundreds of millions of other Muslims also have been raised with the same hatred of the West and Israel as a way to distract from the failings of their leaders . . . [those] who signed peace treaties, such as President Anwar Sadat, have been assassinated. Today, the Islamo-fascist president of Iran uses nuclear dreams, Holocaust denials and threats to "wipe Israel off the map" as a way to maintain control of his divided country.[141]

The embittered hostility to the Jews and Israel that Nonie Darwish observed is especially visible among jihadi Islamists who have embraced Sayyid Qutb's vision of a totalitarian political Islam. His interpretation of classical Islamic jihad as a duty for *all* Muslims to establish *hakimiyyat Allah* (God's rule) on earth has been a way of regarding the holy war as "a permanent struggle." Qutb's jihad is a *thawrah alamiyyah* (world revolution) that aims at de-secularizing the world.[142] This Islamist ideology is not just an expression of religious extremism; it also contains a new concept of irregular warfare and the idea of a transnational social order based on pure monotheism. This is very different from the traditional order of the Muslim caliphate. In the future sharia-based totalitarian Islamic state, all *dhimmis* would be returned to their naturally inferior, premodern status.

This indoctrination has already proven its ability to attract alienated Muslim youth in the Western diaspora. Ed Husain, a radical young British Muslim recruited in the 1990s to the fundamentalist Hizb-ut Tahrir movement in London, described this brainwashing as leading to a completely Manichean perception of the world. Society is starkly polarized between "true Islam" and *kufr* (heresy). Drawing on the teachings of Hassan al-Banna, Sayyid Qutb, Abu al-Ala Mawdudi, and Taqi al-Din Nabhani, the Jordanian-Palestinian founder of the Hizb, radical young British Muslims were persuaded to fight for a worldwide Islamic state on the ruins of the West and infidel Muslim regimes. Militant Islam was presented as the total solution for a Muslim world reeling from massacres in the Balkans and the violence in Iraq, Palestine, Kashmir, and Afghanistan. The *khilafah* (caliphate) can only be restored through the complete destruction of the existing political order, especially in Muslim countries. This involves the radical rejection of democracy, secularism, and any Muslim integration in the West. More than any other group Hizb-ut Tahrir introduced jihad and martyrdom to the streets of London; with them came the homegrown suicide bombers, separatism, homophobia, and war against the *kaffir* police, as well as all the inferior "others," including Christians, Sikhs, Hindus, and, of course, the Jews.[143]

This violent jihad to liberate Muslims around the world from oppression and injustice is invariably anti-American, anti-Zionist, and anti-Jewish. Like the Nazis and Stalinists before them, the Islamists identify Jews and Judaism with all the threatening forces of modernity such as liberalism, secularism, laissez-faire capitalism, and globalization.[144] One finds the familiar obsession with Jews as a revolutionary, subversive, and corrosive force taking part in hidden, occult, manipulative activities. Boundless materialism and abstract rationalism are attacked as Jewish creations—much as they were in interwar Europe—that undermine the sacred values of religion, family, the nation, and the state. The perception of Jews actually ruling a Jewish state within the *dar al-Islam* is treated as theologically, ontologically, and politically *intolerable*—a dire existential threat to Muslim culture and collective identity. In this way, a highly explosive cocktail of fanatical religious passions, raw Jew hatred, and warlike zeal has emerged around the Islamist ideology, encapsulated by the concept of jihad. Anti-Semitism, like anti-Americanism, is especially potent within this deadly mix.

For totalitarian political Islam, jihad means that permanent war must be waged against the infidels until the Day of Judgment. No strategic compromise is possible with the American or Israeli devils, let alone with Muslim heretics. The very existence of a Jewish state within *dar al-Islam* is seen as *the* ultimate symptom of the malaise, decadence, and corruption in Islam today.[145] For the Islamists, Jews were, are, and always will be the major spearhead of the devil's legions. The war against them is, therefore, crucial to Islam's effort to bring down the West as a whole. This is the key test case in halting the long decline of Islam relative to the West, to overcoming the development gap, and to recovering an authentic Muslim identity.[146] The radical Islamist response to all these challenges has been open incitement to genocide against Israeli Jews—the symbol of everything that has to be purged from human civilization. Current events such as the American occupation of Iraq and the struggle between Israel and Hamas provide new pretexts but in no way explain the origins or appeal of the Islamist ideology.

The scale of the Arab defeat in 1967 did, however, act as a stimulant for the Islamicizing of Arab anti-Semitism.[147] The Iranian Revolution of 1979 and the mujahideen's victory over the USSR in Afghanistan ten years later were powerful additional catalysts; so, too, was the al-Aqsa intifada in 2000, the terrorist assault of September 11, 2001, and the Second Persian Gulf War. These events exacerbated and sharpened anti-Semitic trends in the Muslim world. But they do not explain their ubiquity, violence, or intensity, nor the extraordinary degree to which the Islamicized versions of Jew hatred have imported lethal strains of the anti-Semitic virus from the West. When the *Wall Street Journal* reporter Daniel Pearl (both a Jew and an American) was brutally beheaded in Karachi in January 2002, news cameras all-too-briefly focused the world's attention on a nuclear-armed state in south Asia where Islamic fundamentalists may soon come to power. They exposed with crystal clarity the ferocity of a fanatical "Koranic" anti-Semitism "without Jews." How else could one explain why a majority of Pakistanis, so far removed from Israel, appeared convinced that the Mossad had engineered 9/11, and that the Jews control America and fabricated a gigantic plot against the Muslim world? Pakistani anti-Semitism obviously has no connection to empirical Jews or to Israelis as a real people. It is the pure ideological product of totalitarian Islam paid for and to some extent nurtured by the House of Saud.[148]

Turkey is another non-Arab Muslim society in which anti-Semitism is currently widespread. The ruling Justice and Development Party (AKP) has even been complicit in this trend, despite the intimate strategic partnership between Israel and Turkey in the last decade. Until recently, Ankara even played a positive role in mediating indirect talks between Israel and Syria. Moreover, Turkey built up $3 billion in annual trade with the Jewish state as well as attracting many Israeli tourists and millions of dollars in defense contracts with Israel. However, the Israeli assault on Gaza, beginning on December 27, 2008, significantly damaged these close ties. Turkish prime minister Recep Tayyip Erdogan's highly emotional and repellent comments that Israel's actions would lead to dire punishment from Allah and bring upon it self-destruction were, not surprisingly, very badly received by Israelis.[149] The tone of the outburst also revealed the prime minister's deep Islamic roots. As a result, any prospect that Turkey could again be trusted by Israel as an honest broker in the Middle East conflict seemed remote. During Operation Cast Lead, wild accusations by Turkish leaders and an unbalanced media coverage did indeed produce a veritable anti-Israel, anti-Jewish frenzy.[150] Thus, in a basketball match against a visiting Israeli team, Turkish fans ominously chanted "Death to Jews." Anti-Semitic posters in Istanbul urged customers to boycott Jewish shops; the synagogue in Izmir was vandalized; signs in Anatolia announced "No Armenians or Jews. Dogs OK."[151] Then there were the graffiti on the walls next to the large Neve Shalom synagogue in Istanbul that proclaimed: "Down with Israel! We do not want you [the Jews] in the Turkish Republic"; and a huge Palestinian flag was provocatively hung in the vicinity. The palpable rise in threats and insults against Turkish Jews has led to a strong reinforcement of Jewish communal security measures. As for Israel's Ankara embassy, it was forced into a virtual security lockdown.

Sami Kohen, an editorial writer on the Turkish daily *Milliyet,* has pointedly observed that in his speeches Erdogan made no distinction between Zionists and Jews in denouncing the Israeli "war crimes" in Gaza. Other Turkish Jews have noted that *every* new crisis has reinforced their feeling of being second-class citizens, both as "non-Muslims" and, more specifically, as Jews.[152] This was further underlined by the experience of Jewish schoolchildren being obliged by the government to stand at attention during a nationwide moment of silence for the Palestinians who had died in Gaza. Many Turkish Jews are now contemplating emigration as a result of such popular and government reactions.[153] The ugly increase in anti-Jewish sentiment was also reflected in the hero's welcome accorded to Premier Erdogan after his return from Davos, where he had publicly clashed with Israeli president Shimon Peres at the World Economic Forum. The Turkish premier had accused Peres of responsibility for gratuitously "killing people"; his justice minister called Israel "the biggest provoker of terror in the world"; while a prominent Turkish daily ran a glaring front-page headline suggesting that "Reckless Israel endangers the roots of our civilization."

The present wave of hatred against Israel and the Jews was not altogether new. On November 15, 2003, two major synagogues in Istanbul had been bombed by Turkish Islamist fanatics, killing twenty-six and wounding hundreds in the vicinity, mostly Muslim Turks. Three months earlier, a Jewish dentist, Dr. Y. Yahya, had been murdered in his own clinic. The perpetrator had confessed after his arrest to wanting to kill Jews after what he had read about them in the Turkish press. Indeed, part of the Turkish media has for years shown a distinct propensity to demonize Jews, Judaism, Zionism, and the Jewish lobbies that allegedly seek dominance in local business and international affairs.[154] In Turkey, in 2005, Adolf Hitler's *Mein Kampf* (widely regarded as a "handbook" for Turkish ultranationalists) climbed to second place on the bestseller lists. It had apparently been published in Turkey no fewer than forty-five times between 1940 and 2005.[155] The equally anti-Semitic *Protocols of Zion* was published in full or in excerpts over one hundred times during the same period.

Islamo-nationalist columnists like Arslan Tekin typically argued that *Mein Kampf* should be taught in schools and ought to be carefully read by Jews in order to understand how they had themselves brought about the rise of Hitler. The disproportionate power exercised today by Jews in American banking, in the media, and in politics would surely bring about exactly the same results in the United States as they had in prewar Germany.[156] The columnist Abdurrahim Karakos, writing for the Turkish Islamist newspaper *Vakit* in August 2004, was even more explicit, praising Hitler's "foresight" in cleansing the world of "these swindler Jews, who believe in racism for a religion and take pleasure in bathing the world in blood." Hitler, like Osama bin Laden, had correctly identified the Jewish plague, and he had risked the wrath of superpowers in standing up to their oppression.[157] Another columnist at *Vakit*, Hüseyin Üzmez, combined admiration for Hitler with open Holocaust denial and classic anti-Semitism. First, he insisted that anti-Jewish persecution in Nazi Germany had been greatly exaggerated; then that Hitler was actually a Jew blackmailed by the "Israeli Zionists," who controlled all the international money markets and the global media; and finally, he complained that the German interior minister who had banned *Vakit* in early 2005 was either a Jew or else a tool of international Zionism.[158] Needless to say, these were little more than deranged concoctions totally divorced from reality, but they have an audience in Turkey. No less fantastical was the claim that the Jewish lobby (aided by Christian Zionists) sought world government or a "total Jewish domination of the world." Globalization and even the creation of Wahhabism in Saudi Arabia were seen in this ideological delirium as part of a Jewish messianic conspiracy whose aim was to bring about a new world order with the help of Freemasons, Bahais, evangelicals, and so-called Muslim deviants—all in the service of a "greater Israel."[159]

A more distinctive feature of contemporary Turkish anti-Semitism is the ongoing witch hunt against the *Dönme* (hidden Jews supposedly posing as Muslims)—descendants of Jewish followers of the seventeenth-century false messiah Shabbetai Zvi, forced by the Turkish sultan to convert to Islam. The Dönme have been accused by some Turkish intellectuals of bringing down the caliphate, of conspiring with Freemasons—and of founding the modern Turkish Republic as a kind of substitute Jewish state, where they could seize the key positions.[160] Similarly, the United States is caricatured as being completely in the hands of American Jews, infiltrating and controlling Turkey as part of their diabolical plan to set the whole world on fire.[161]

Not all the Turkish press, of course, embraces such frenzied anti-Semitism. In the liberal and leftist newspapers there are commentators who clearly recognize the parallels between radical Turkish anti-Semitism and its Nazi precedents. The left-wing journalist Murat Necip Arman, writing in January 2005, protested strongly against efforts to portray the Jews as a cursed people who should be physically eradicated by Muslims. He expressed disgust at the "neo-antisemitism . . . recklessly manifested in almost all media organs." Turkish anti-Semites had exploited popular sympathy for the Palestinians to encourage a "dangerous kind of racism" and an animosity toward non-Muslims that Turkey had not witnessed for many decades. Arman warned that "what we have here [in Turkey] presents similarities with Germany of the 1930s. I hope common sense prevails in Turkey," he added, "and this dangerous trend does not lead to frightening results."[162]

The potential ravages of anti-Semitism have been no less apparent among Turkish immigrants in Western societies, including in urban concentrations such as the inner Kreuzberg area of Berlin where they represent a majority among those of non-German nationality. This Turkish immigrant hostility to Jews (strongest among the young, the unemployed, and those espousing an integral Muslim identity) can generally be linked to the pervasiveness of Islamic fundamentalist ideology. Until it was banned by the German government in 2005, a Turkish newspaper like *Vakit,* with its clearly anti-Semitic caricatures, articles, and Holocaust denial propaganda, contributed substantially to the popular diffusion of the most toxic conspiracy theories. Today, this racist rhetoric is primarily relayed by television, by the Internet, and through an uncritical identification with the Palestinians. Some Turkish immigrants, marginalized and themselves stigmatized in mainstream German society, are more readily seduced by the paranoid vision of Islam under permanent siege. They are more prone to see their own suffering as being analogous to that of the Palestinians. The term "Jew" in their milieu is widely used as a swearword; the *Protocols* perception of international Jewry (along with knee-jerk anti-Zionism) is rampant and equating Israel with Nazi Germany has, in any case, become part of European conventional wisdom.[163]

The fundamentalist Milli Gorus ideology was imported from Turkey to Germany (and to the rest of the Turkish diaspora), bringing with it a conspiracy-theory style anti-Semitism mixed with strong anti-Americanism. Its founder and leader, Necmettin Erbakan, had been Turkish prime minister in 1996–97 and is the spiritual mentor of the ruling AKP Party. Not only Erdogan but also the president of Turkey, Abdullah Gul, were among his disciples, holding important positions during his premiership. In the election campaign of 2007, Erbakan's own long-standing anti-Semitism was unequivocally expressed in an interview he gave to promote his "Islamic Happiness" party.

All infidel nations are one Zionist entity; Jews want to rule from Morocco to Indonesia; the Zionists worked for 5,767 years to build a world order in which all power and money depend on Jews; the US dollar is Zionist money: the Jewish "bacteria" must be diagnosed for a cure to be found; Zionists initiated the Crusades: Jews founded Protestantism and the Capitalist order; and Bush attacked Iraq to build Greater Israel so Jesus can return.[164]

Erdogan is certainly not an extreme anti-Semite of this ilk, but his Islamic fervor and harsh vilification of Israel cast serious doubts over his real beliefs. On January 16, 2009, he publicly questioned whether the Jewish state should still be allowed to remain in the UN. Three days earlier he had announced that "media outlets supported by Jews are disseminating false reports on what happens in Gaza, finding unfounded excuses to justify targeting of schools, mosques and hospitals."[165] Not surprisingly, Erdogan's daily exercises in Israel-bashing on Turkish television encouraged local anti-Semites to come out of the woodwork. Moreover, such statements were disturbingly congruent with Turkey's move toward a strategic alliance with Tehran and Damascus, already visible in the summer of 2008. Turkish positions on Iraq and Palestine, especially during the Gaza Siege, have brought it still closer to Iran and Syria.[166]

According to Erdogan, Hamas is a legitimate "resistance" movement that should be welcomed as part of the peace process. It was American policy throughout the region that had to change. Erdogan felt encouraged by the first steps taken by the new American president in whose Muslim Christian name, Barack Hussein Obama, he saw "a very great symbolic meaning."[167] Indeed, during his visit to Turkey in April 2009, Obama did hit the right Turkish chords when vowing that the United States "would never be at war with Islam." Whether such an outreach to the Muslim world will make any significant dent in the prevailing anti-American and anti-Zionist worldview in the Middle East is, however, an open question.

America, today, is in effect still cast in the role of the Dajjal evoked in early Islamic apocalyptic texts. But, according to the Islamist scenario, its ambitions, in alliance with the Jewish Zionists and infidel Masonic governments, will ultimately be thwarted. Americans will lose their power and be slaughtered—whether by natural disasters or through other means. In one such apocalyptic vision conceived well before 2001, New York was specifically singled out for complete destruction, the result of an enormous earthquake predicted in the Koran for the end of days.

According to Abdullah Yusuf Ali writing in 1987:

> Since in New York especially there are more Jews than in other places, and in it is their wealth, their banks, their political foundations which control the entire world (the U.N., the Security Council, the International Monetary Fund, the World Bank, and the principal media networks), so there is no evil greater than in New York . . . and for this reason their portion of the punishment will be greater in measure and it will be total uprooting.[168]

In the Islamic version of Armageddon, the annihilation of America and the Jews will liberate the rest of the world, enabling non-Muslims to freely convert to Islam and inaugurate a new age of universal peace. In their study of "sacred terror," counterterrorism experts Daniel Benjamin and Steven Simon shrewdly observed that as human history draws to its presumed close and absolute good and evil are to contend in the final battle, time itself becomes compressed: "The enemy of centuries is indistinguishable from the enemy of today, and all the characters take on the outsize proportions of the mythic."

In Muslim apocalyptic literature, conspiracy theory is absolutely fundamental.[169] The embrace of rabidly anti-Semitic material drawn from Christian dogmas and European racist writers undoubtedly provides millions of

Muslims with what seems to them a cogent explanation for what has gone wrong in their disorientated universe. The closed circle of conspiracy theory both fuels and, in turn, is nurtured by genocidal anti-Semitism, paranoia, and the will to world conquest. David Cook has perceptively noted that these apocalyptic writers "successfully locked out the Jews, denying their messianic aspirations, plagiarizing from their scriptures, dehumanizing them, and placing the world under their supposedly demonic control."[170] Within such a script there is little room for the liberal hope that science and technology have ushered in a brave new world. The resurgence of violent anti-Semitism in the Islamic sphere of influence reveals to us a frightening potential future, as through a glass darkly. It is a warning that needs to be heeded. The hatred of Jews and Christians has, in this emerging nightmare, become a highly dangerous form of auto-intoxication and self-destruction—the intellectual equivalent of a suicide bomb. It needs to be rapidly neutralized if Armageddon is to be averted.

TWENTY-FOUR

The Wrath of Khomeini

On June 24, 1873, leading notables of the Anglo-Jewish Association submitted a petition to Nasir al-Din, shah of Persia, then on a state visit to London. In the name of British Jewry they gratefully recalled the magnanimity of "the great King Cyrus" more than two millennia ago—the Persian ruler referred to in the Hebrew Bible as "the anointed of the Lord." Cyrus the Great had issued, wrote the petitioners, the edict that "secured to Jews liberty of worship, together with the unfettered exercise of civil rights." He had even permitted the Jews of Babylon to return to Jerusalem to rebuild Solomon's Temple. But the real subject of their petition was clearly political—an emphatic determination to give voice to the grievances and excruciating suffering of their Persian brethren.

Beyond the usual diplomatic niceties, the Anglo-Jewish document unequivocally evoked the "unspeakable wretchedness and misery" of Persian Jewry. The disabilities that handicapped them were enumerated at some length. For example, the affidavit of a Jew was not even received in the Muslim Courts of Justice, and a Jew dared not protest injustices to a higher Persian court for fear of the vengeance that would be inflicted if the appeal were to fail. Worse still was the fact that any Muslim who killed a Jew could purchase immunity by merely paying a fine. Jews were also seriously penalized and disadvantaged in many walks of economic life. In most Persian towns they could not keep a shop in the bazaars (this was still happening in Shiraz and Tehran as late as 1904); and they were subject to arbitrary taxes and harassment at the slightest whim of the local authorities. Not only that, but Jews who converted to Islam could "claim to be the sole inheritor of family property, to the exclusion of all relatives who have not changed their religion." This highly discriminatory inheritance law was designed to consolidate Muslim power and pressure Jews to convert. The converts were, of course, exempted from all the legal and other indignities suffered by Jews.[1] Such practices also existed in Sunni Arab lands, but the forced conversions, expulsions, and massacres suffered by Persian Jews were undoubtedly more frequent.

Nasir al-Din Shah's visit to Europe was a turning point for the Jews of Persia. For the first time a Persian shah found himself seriously pressured by foreign governments (especially by Britain) to ameliorate the conditions of his Jewish subjects and of other religious minorities. Equally, the fate of Persian Jewry became a regular part of the European Jewish agenda. Jewish organizations, especially the Board of Deputies of British Jews, headed by Sir Moses Montefiore, and the Paris-based Alliance Israélite Universelle (AIU), intervened on behalf of their beleaguered coreligionists in Persia, insisting that they were faithful and diligent citizens entitled to royal protection. The shah was told by the AIU's Berlin Committee that Jewish civil and political equality was an established fact in civilized countries and that Persia would only benefit from Jewish emancipation. By July 1873 the shah was declaring that all his subjects were "equally the objects of his solicitude" and remedies would be found for justified complaints. Desirous to show himself an enlightened emperor in the eyes of modern Europe, he made—for the first time ever in modern Persian history—declarations that officially seemed to put Persian Jewry on an equal footing with Muslim subjects.[2]

However, the vacillating attempts at reform between 1848 and 1873 were often ignored by the shah's provincial governors and local authorities. Especially hostile to any efforts at improving the Jews' condition were the ulema, or Shiite clergy, who sharply rejected the egalitarian tenets emanating from Europe.[3] Their religious views on the *dhimmis* acknowledged their right to protection only if they recognized the superiority of Muslim rule, often in the most humiliating circumstances. This limited protection for the People of the Book applied in theory to Jews, Christians, and Zoroastrians but was often ignored in practice.[4]

A letter of October 27, 1892, signed by an "S. Somekh," writing from Baghdad to the AIU Central Committee in Paris, illustrated the point. He reported that the Muslim clergy in Hamadan were threatening to impose "murderous conditions" on this harassed community. Jews totaled about 10 percent of the population of forty thousand in Hamadan. Among the humiliations imposed by the renowned Shiite cleric Mullah 'Abdallah and the governor of Hamadan: Jews were obliged to display a red cloth on their chests; they could never put on fine clothes, and could only use material from a blue cotton fabric. They were forbidden to wear matching shoes or cloaks. Jewish physicians were "forbidden to ride." A Jew was never to overtake a Muslim on a public street or talk loudly to him. If he wished to claim a debt, it had to be done in a quavering and deeply respectful manner. If he were insulted by a Muslim, then the Jew "must drop his head and be silent." As in other Muslim lands, it was categorically forbidden for Jews to build fine edifices, let alone to have a house higher than that of his Muslim neighbors. The entrance had to be "very low." The Jew was not permitted to use plaster for whitewashing. Jews were not allowed to leave Hamadan at all. They could not even leave their homes when it snowed or rained for fear that their "impurity" would be inadvertently transmitted to Shiite Muslims. It was also prohibited for a Jew to cut his beard or even trim it slightly with scissors. Jewish women, on the other hand, were obliged to reveal their faces in public—which exposed them to sexual harassment and made them the equivalent of prostitutes in Muslim eyes.[5] Jewish marriage ceremonies were to include "no music or singing or noisy rejoicings." No Jew could leave his home after consuming wine or spirits. If found walking about in the streets, he "may be killed on the spot." These threatening and draconian anti-Jewish steps were intended by 'Abdallah to reinstitute Muslim *dhimma* concepts, restore Hamadan's Islamic character, and enhance his own prestige as a warrior for Allah. Such measures were also welcomed by local merchants interested in damaging their local Jewish competitors.

Somekh told his superiors in Paris that Jews "have a choice between automatic acceptance, conversion to Islam, or annihilation." Some of those who lived from hand to mouth "consented to these humiliating and cruel conditions through fear and without offering resistance." Thirty prominent members of the community were, however, surprised in the telegraph office where they had tried to transmit their grievances to Tehran: "They were compelled to embrace the Muslim faith to escape from certain death. But the majority is in hiding and does not dare to venture in the streets."[6]

In Hamadan, Muslim mobs were shouting "Death to the Jews" in demonstrations or alternatively demanding their instant conversion. For more than forty days, Jews had remained besieged in their houses, "almost dying of hunger and fright." According to the AIU report, "more than a hundred Jewish women miscarried and another two hundred have had their milk dry up, so great is the fear felt by the poor Jews at the sight of these fanatics armed to the teeth."[7] Only pressure from the British Foreign Office and vigorous Jewish protests from London and Paris that forced the shah to intervene militarily prevented further disaster. The shah even reprimanded 'Abdallah, and appointed a new governor to impose his authority on Hamadan.[8]

Such intimidation and oppression was common in nineteenth-century Persia, whose Shia brand of Islam was especially harsh toward Jews.[9] The persecutions had a long history behind them. During the latter part of the reign of Shah Abbas I (1588–1629) anti-Jewish attitudes had become manifest in the strict imposition of dress codes and the destruction of Hebrew books and writings. This persecution climaxed nearly thirty years later in the forced conversion of the Jews of Isfahan—the center of Persian Jewry at the time.[10] The Muslim masses, no less than people in medieval Christian Europe, perceived the Jews as sorcerers and practitioners of black magic. Renegade Jewish converts such as Abul Hassan Lari contributed to the violence, denouncing their coreligionists to the authorities, inter alia for using cabalistic Hebrew writings, amulets, and talismans against the Muslims.[11]

What especially aggravated matters was the huge influence exercised by the Shiite clerical elite from the early sixteenth century on Iran's rulers, especially in enforcing the minutest prescriptions of ritual purity on the population. Until 1925 they had a virtual stranglehold over nearly every department of human activity, from the narrowest issues of personal purification to affairs of state. The clerics especially emphasized the notion of *najes* (ritual uncleanliness) of the Jews, Christians, Zoroastrians, and other non-Muslims.[12] This was the major reason why Jews were prohibited from touching the food or drink of Muslims, from visiting public baths, or from circulating freely among the believers. Ritual impurity also obliged Jews to live physically separated from other inhabitants. Any intercourse or dealings with such "unclean creatures" could only contaminate Muslims. The degrading consequences of this doctrine were especially apparent in the early decades of Qajar rule before 1848. Leading mullahs referred to Jews as "the most unclean of the human race," as the lowliest of God's creatures, "the leprosy of creation," barely superior to dogs.

In the world of Islam, only the Shiites had established such an elaborate system of ritual purity. In some ways it was reminiscent of Hindu attitudes toward the pariahs, or "untouchables." In this worldview everything non-Muslim was literally defined as impure. As political scientist Matthias Küntzel has put it:

> All contact with a *Najes* is considered a sort of poisoning. The paranoid fear of "infection" provoked periodic excesses and led to the development of a particular Shiite code of conduct, which especially affected Jews, since unlike the Armenian Christians and the small Zoroastrian community, the Jewish minority was present throughout the country.[13]

Though these rules were officially abolished by the Pahlavi dynasty after 1925, orthodox clerics obstinately continued to propagate them. In 1962 Ayatollah Ruhollah Khomeini explicitly promulgated the *najes* teaching in a popular guide to everyday life written for Muslims. He listed eleven things that made a believer unclean: urine, feces, sperm, carrion, blood, dogs, pigs, wine, beer, the sweat of a camel, which eats unclean things, and *unbelievers.* As far as Jews and other non-Muslims were concerned, their entire bodies, including hair, nails, and body moisture, were considered ritually impure.[14] Only conversion to Islam could redeem them. In the history of Sunni Islam there was nothing so fanatically bigoted as this doctrine.

Persecution of the Jews reached an early peak under the young Shah Abbas II, much influenced by Shiite clerics. In 1656 he decided to completely purify Persian soil from the "uncleanliness" of the nonbelievers and to force the Jews of Isfahan (and other communities) to become Muslims. To this end starvation, deportation, imprisonment, beatings, and torture were widely inflicted upon the hapless Jews of Persia. Synagogues were closed, and Jews were led to the mosque to publicly proclaim their Muslim "confession of faith." As the Islamic civilization scholar Walter Fischel has written:

> These newly-converted Muslims had to break with the Jewish past, to allow their daughters to be married to Muslims, and to have their new Muslim names registered . . . some were even forced to eat a portion of camel meat boiled in milk [a grave infringement of Jewish dietary law]. After their forced conversion, they were called New Muslims, *Jadid al-Islam.* They were then, of course, freed from the payment of the poll tax and from wearing a special headgear or badge.[15]

Thus, in Iran as in early modern Spain, waves of persecution resulted in forced conversion en masse to the dominant faith. They produced the phenomenon of *Anusim* (compelled ones) leading a double life—outwardly professing the credo of Islam while secretly living as Jews. In the seventeenth century, it is estimated that perhaps as many as one hundred thousand Jews in the Persian kingdom were coerced into becoming Muslims.

The persecution of Jews and other non-Muslims continued during the eighteenth century, accelerating with the advent of the Qajar dynasty after 1786. False accusations of ritual murder (probably introduced by Christian missionaries) resulted in the imprisonment and expulsion of Jews from several towns. In 1830 all the Jews of Tabriz (four hundred in all) had their throats cut like cattle or sheep. Nine years later, the Jews of Mashhad were forcibly converted en masse.[16] Their quarters were plundered with the encouragement of Muhammad Shah Qajar. The Mashhad conversions followed a Muslim attack on Jews that resulted in more than thirty Jewish fatalities. The attack was the result of false charges that they had insulted the memory of the third Shiite imam, Husayn bin 'Ali. In 1844 a visiting Anglican missionary described the traumatized new converts as visibly cowed but nonetheless practicing their Judaism in secret. Another European traveler, writing in 1856, commented on the desolate situation of Persian Jewry, vegetating in extreme misery under the yoke of oriental barbarism and fanaticism.[17]

From the mid-1860s the plight of Persian Jewry was regularly evoked in the bulletins of the Paris-based AIU, which constantly deplored the inability of the shah to protect the Jews from the wrath of the clergy and the masses. In these late-nineteenth-century documents, the mullahs appear to exhibit a rare cruelty and hatred for Jews. A letter from J. Danon of May 1894 about the "poor and wretched Jews of Shiraz" stressed the insults, contempt, and persecution to which Shia Muslims regularly subjected Jews because of their "ritual impurity."[18] Three years later, in Tehran, the ulema temporarily succeeded in imposing a discriminatory badge on the Jews, which was only rescinded following energetic British pressure on the shah. An AIU report in 1897 observed:

In Persia, one constant fact is to be noted: every time that a priest wishes to emerge from obscurity and win a reputation for piety, he preaches war against the Jews. That is what has just occurred in Tehran. Mullah Said

Rihan Allah, who only yesterday was unknown to all, has suddenly become popular through his intransigent fanaticism. He complained that the Jews of Tehran were not distinguishable from their Muslim fellow-citizens by any outer sign and he issued a decree, a *fatwa*, which lay down that our co-religionists in the capital were to wear a distinctive badge on their chests.[19]

By the end of the nineteenth century, the forty thousand Jews of Persia, despite a fragile and erratic process of amelioration in their condition, had not been able to free themselves of the incubus of the *dhimma* laws. Though foreign pressure had achieved some positive results, Jews were all too often subject to harassment, abuse, and persecution; they were still liable to be the first victims of political instability, ulema hostility, and the backlash against reform.[20] They were, in particular, vulnerable to the cruelty of the populace, as occurred in Shiraz following rumors of the ritual murder of a little Muslim girl in October 1910. A frenzied mob attacked the Jewish quarter, inflicting carnage and destruction during the course of six to seven hours on the 260 houses in the neighborhood. Twelve Jews were killed, about fifty more were seriously injured, and the community was stripped of all its property and valuables by the marauders. A report to the AIU noted that "the five to six thousand people comprising the Shiraz [Jewish] community now possess nothing in the world but the few tatters which they were wearing when their quarter was invaded."[21]

As in the Arab Muslim lands, the fearsome oppression of Persian Jewry was generally aggravated in times of anarchy and rebellion. But it was, above all, the dominance of Shiite theocratic orthodoxy, with its promotion of forced conversions and its dehumanizing notion of Jewish ritual uncleanliness, that fomented the recurring violence against Jews from the seventeenth until the early twentieth century.[22] The unique Shiite impurity regulations and the resulting fear of pollution "led to great excesses and peculiar behavior by Muslims," to quote the anthropologist Laurence Loeb, who had studied the phenomenon firsthand in southern Iran.[23] He noted that the *najes* conception, which had been applied with pathological rigidity in Persia throughout the nineteenth century, was still being used to differentiate Jews from believers in the early 1970s. Walter Fischel, a specialist in the field, considered it to be "the decisive factor" in making the life of Jews "an uninterrupted sequence of persecution and oppression." Jews could not appear in public or perform their religious ceremonies "without being treated with scorn and contempt by the Muslim inhabitants of Persia."[24] Jews could not use public facilities, let alone touch the bread, liquids, or fresh fruits of the Shiites without literally polluting them. The few Jews who were permitted to live in the holy Shiite city of Qom could discreetly engage in peddling their wares to non-Muslims. But for the Muslim descendants of the Prophet, as Christian missionary Henry Stern noted in 1854, it was inconceivable to touch "anything that has passed the hands of a defiled and impure Jew."[25] In Isfahan, their condition was even worse. The Jew was "hated, despoiled, and deprived of every chance to earn his daily bread" and, being viewed as impure, they were limited to the "most degrading pursuits."

For a while it seemed that this dismal picture might change in 1905 when, under Shia clerical leadership, the Iranian masses rose up against the government, won a constitution, established a Majlis (parliament), and secured a variety of political freedoms. But not even the constitutional movement (1906–11) and the convening of a parliament were able to significantly change the situation of the minorities or prevent the outbreak of anti-Jewish riots.[26]

The decisive transformation came only with the breaking of the power of the fanatical Shia clergy over the schools and the legal system by Reza Shah Pahlavi (1878–1944), the first Persian ruler to lay the foundations of a secular, Westernized, and modern state freed from the fetters of Islam. His authoritarian dictatorship did not hesitate to strike at such potent Shiite symbols as the annual ritual of self-flagellation associated with the martyrdom of Husayn ibn 'Ali. The new shah was a military officer of the Cossack Brigade who had risen through the ranks to become commander of the army, then minister of war in 1921, and eventually prime minister. As the newly elected shah of Persia in December 1925, Reza Shah invested heavily in his country's infrastructure, its transportation system, health care, and education. As a result of growing industrialization, the rural population became more urbanized and Western models began to be adopted in engineering projects, the school system, and the judiciary. Young Iranians were sent to Europe for their education. The veil for women was abolished in 1935, one of several key reforms that aimed to destroy the old traditions and the authority of the Shiite clergy. Reza Shah was acting in a fashion reminiscent of Kemal Atatürk's secular modernizing program in Turkey.

In 1935, the shah officially adopted the local name of "Iran" instead of "Persia," in order to stress the Indo-European origin of the country's inhabitants, and their Farsi language. By this time, the shah and most of his leading army officers had come to favor Nazi Germany over the West (especially Great Britain) and as a bulwark against Soviet Russia. They admired the ruthless modernizing example of the Third Reich—its discipline, military organization, and glowing image of national strength. The country's new name "Iran" (land of the Aryans) undoubtedly had an ideological significance for the Pahlavi dynasty and the coterie of young German-trained Persian nationalist intellectuals who had been strongly influenced by the racism of Joseph-Arthur Comte de Gobineau and Houston S. Chamberlain. Goebbels's Propaganda Ministry readily financed nationalist publications in this vein. German agents began to penetrate the Iranian educational system and the army.[27] By 1938, Nazi Germany also enjoyed a commanding position in Iran's economic development, and Tehran's German legation would soon become a major center for Nazi intrigue throughout the Middle East. From 1939 onward, public offices and Muslim businesses were closed to Jews.[28] Street attacks on Jews and blood libels multiplied until the Soviet-British invasion of 1941 that led to the forced abdication of Reza Shah in favor of his son, Mohammed Reza Pahlavi. Once more, as on the eve of World War I, Britain and Russia were occupying parts of a nominally independent Iran, thereby exacerbating Persian nationalism.

Despite the pro-Nazi stance of the Pahlavi regime in the late 1930s, the position of Jews had considerably improved during the previous decade, at least in comparison with the early twentieth century. They enjoyed new economic and professional opportunities; they now paid the same taxes as Muslims and served in the army like other citizens. All women now appeared with their faces unveiled, removing a previous source of vexation in which only Jewish women had been uncovered and thereby subjected to insults or sexual harassment. Secular education had become available to Jewish girls, as well as to boys. These marks of progress, so it appeared, could no longer be stopped, either by the Shiite clergy or the growing pro-Nazi elements in Iran. Moreover, after 1941, a new Jewish bourgeoisie began to emerge under Mohammad Reza Shah as part of the accelerating modernization program. Large numbers of provincial Jews came to Tehran, transforming it into the new center of Jewish life; it was more cosmopolitan, and Western in its lifestyle and conspicuous consumption patterns. Iranian Jews were finally able to travel freely, receive a Western education in the United States and Europe, and establish links with Israel. On March 15, 1950, Iran recognized Israel de facto, with trade relations developing rapidly. In the framework of his growing alliance with the United States, the shah was even willing to forge close relations with the Jewish state, despite considerable domestic opposition, especially from the Shia fundamentalists, the nationalists, and the anti-Zionist Tudeh Communist Party.

In recognizing Israel, the shah acted against the advice of many of his close aides. With the help of the Israel lobby the shah hoped to gain American economic and military assistance.[29] The United States had, however, become hugely unpopular in Iran when the CIA, with British help, orchestrated a coup to bring down veteran prime minister Mohammed Mosaddeq, who had nationalized the Anglo-Iranian oil company in 1950. Huge crowds took to Tehran's streets, shouting anti-Western slogans. On the other hand, by the late 1950s the Soviet threat reinforced the shah's pro-American stance and distrust of Arab nationalists such as Nasser and the Baathists in Iraq, who were supported by the USSR and viewed as a serious danger to the dynasty. Iran did, indeed, become a choice target of subversion by Arab extremists, especially Palestinians, for its alliance with Israel and its ostentatious role as the gendarme of the West in the Persian Gulf.[30] Although Pahlavi Iran began to veer in a more pro-Arab direction after the 1973 Yom Kippur War, it still had good reason to be concerned about the irredentist and exclusivist nature of Arab nationalism. This Iranian suspicion limited the practical import of official sympathy for the Palestinian cause.

Both religious and secular anti-Semitic writings continued to be published under the Pahlavis. There was no lack of theological texts calling for Islamic unity in a holy war against the Jews, who had falsified the Scriptures and sought to dominate the Muslim world.[31] The traditional Shiite image of the impure Jew remained intact and pervasive among the conservative masses. On the other hand, Mohammad Reza Shah's pro-Western policy and his open relations with Israel also led to a greater interest in Jewish culture. There was even some sympathy for Jews, especially among the Baha'is, Freemasons, Westernized intellectuals, and a part of the urban Muslim middle class. By the mid-1970s Iranian Jews had finally come to enjoy full equality with Muslims in most spheres, though they still could not serve as government ministers or elect any but their own representatives to Parliament. However, the Pahlavis' modernization of the country by introducing secular laws, civil marriage, and other measures had greatly improved the socioeconomic and juridical status of Iranian Jews. They had become a prosperous and fully acculturated middle-class community of industrialists, entrepreneurs, merchants, lawyers, pharmacists, doctors, and other professional people, numbering between 80,000 and 120,000 at the peak of the shah's regime.

The most formidable of all the many opponents of the Pahlavis was the Shiite Ayatollah Khomeini, born in 1902 in a village south of Tehran. In the 1930s he had witnessed Reza Shan Pahlavi's breakneck program of secularization. In late 1938, the thirty-six-year-old Khomeini had also been exposed for the first time to Nazi propaganda in Tehran, which, according to German reports, was enjoying considerable success among the Iranian population. A report from the German Consulate in Tehran sent to Berlin in February 1941 remarked that throughout the country, "spiritual leaders are coming out and saying that 'the twelfth Imam has been sent into the world by God in the form of Adolf Hitler.' "[32] This apocalyptic fever would temporarily place Hitler on the level of Mahdi. It was even rumored that Hitler had secretly converted to Shia Islam, that his Muslim name was Haider (meaning the lion, one of Imam 'Ali's titles), and that he wore a silver necklace around his neck with a picture of 'Ali, the original founder of Shiism. According to the popular myth, Hitler would only reveal his Muslim faith to the world after destroying the Jews, defeating the perfidious British, and crushing the godless Russian Communists. Such fantastic beliefs were made more threatening to Iranian Jews by Reza Shah's increasingly pro-Nazi sympathies in the late 1930s, the more racist anti-Jewish tone in the press (with arguments imported from the Third Reich), and the "Aryan-Iranian" cult among a section of progressive Persian intellectuals.

It turned out that secular Persian nationalism could, in certain circumstances, fuse with time-honored Shia religious prejudice. Anti-Semitism became more attractive as growing numbers of fundamentalist Muslims unabashedly looked to Hitler as the answer to their prayers. Such widespread public sentiment may well have reinforced the younger Khomeini's hatred of Jews, though he was never a follower of National Socialism. However, twenty years later, the fiery Shiite preacher would be placing Israel on a par with the "Great Satan" (the United States), continually harping on its iniquities, and justifying his own hostility toward it with Koranic texts. It was a disgrace, he insisted, that a Muslim nation such as Iran should have any diplomatic relations with Israel. Beyond the local danger posed by Iran's rapidly modernizing Jewish community, Khomeini vociferously railed against the conspicuous presence of Israeli advisers, officers, and technical experts in Iran. With no less passion he attacked Western cultural modernism and the shah's technological revolution, which, he maintained, meant a return to a *pre-Islamic* Iranian identity.[33] For the fanatical Khomeini, like the Sunni Arab fundamentalist Sayyid Qutb, cultivating an anti-Islamic nationalism meant regressing back to *jahiliya*. It was the equivalent of a descent into the darkness, barbarism and pagan idolatry of the world before Islam. Khomeini was especially enraged by a law proposed in the early 1960s that would grant women and non-Muslims the right to vote in local elections. His intransigent opposition finally led to the withdrawal of the bill. Khomeini then denounced the shah in 1963 for agreeing to grant American military personnel in Iran immunity from prosecution under Iranian law. In a sermon in Qom he called this decision a preparation "for the enslavement of Iran" to corrosive American control and subversion. He was arrested on June 5, 1963, and kept under house arrest for eight months.

Khomeini's 1963 arrest sparked off public riots resulting in the deaths of more than six hundred Iranians. Thousands of protesters were wounded by police attempting to quell the disturbances. For most of the next fifteen years Khomeini would live as an exile in Najaf, Iraq, until his triumphant return from France and his appointment in 1979 as Iran's supreme religious leader. A year before his banishment, Khomeini had warned Iranians that many sensitive positions in their economy were already "in the hands of Israeli agents." He protested that the government's land-reform programs were "planned by Israel," and that the shah's diplomatic policy went against popular sentiment as well as the teachings of Islam. In a 1963 statement at the A'zam Mosque in Qom, Khomeini furiously accused the shah's "tyrannical" regime of "co-operating fully with Israel and its agents," giving them important roles in the army, in education, in the propaganda apparatus, and at the shah's court. In a message to religious orators that same year, he claimed that the Pahlavi regime, in alliance with Israel, was seeking "to uproot the basis of Islam"—the madrassas and the Koran—in Iran and was allowing the Jews to take possession of commerce and industry. In Khomeini's eyes, Jews were a major cause of "Westoxication" in Muslim society, an important obstacle to the recovery of its pristine Islamic identity. He associated them with American materialism, the acquisitive mania that had seized Iran's middle classes in the 1960s, and the shah's repressive rule which favored Western interests and Israel. Religion and theology students, according to Khomeini, were especially persecuted by the shah's security services (SAVAK) in the service of Israel—"the enemy of Islam."[34]

In a proclamation in the summer of 1963, the fiery Ayatollah explicitly called for the unity of all Muslims across the world "against the Zionist, Israeli and colonialist governments." On April 10, 1964, he angrily admonished the "Islamic governments" (whom he derided as "misfits"), saying they should stop fighting over the waters of the Jordan and simply "expel the Jews from Palestine." As for the Pahlavi regime, he warned that it had deliberately diminished the influence of the clergy to the point that America and Israel would be free to direct Iran's economy. Speaking in Qom in 1964, the ayatollah bluntly stated: "Today, all of our problems stem from America and Israel, and Israel is really part of America."[35] It was the United States, he said, that had protected and maliciously empowered Israel "to make Muslim Arabs homeless" in Palestine and to seize control of Iranian oil assets. In Khomeini's paranoid imagination, the Israeli "tentacles of corruption" now threatened other Islamic countries, seeking access to their markets while buying oil from Iran in order to wage further aggression against the Muslim Arabs.

After the Six-Day War, Khomeini raged bitterly against the fact that Iran's oil was being sold to the same Israel "which [had] destroyed the Al-Aqsa Mosque and set it on fire" (a reference to the arson attack on the mosque by a mentally disturbed Australian Christian in 1968). Typically, Khomeini always saw Israel's hidden hand behind such actions. He also detected a Zionist plot behind the extravagant celebrations ordered by the shah in honor of the establishment of the Persian monarchy.[36] The shah's megalomaniacal and "evil regime," he asserted, had permitted Iran to become an American and Israeli military base, greatly facilitating Zionist penetration of economic and political life.

Khomeini regarded Zionism as the "stubborn enemy of Islam and of humanity"; moreover, it had usurped the Islamic land of Palestine, encouraging imperialist conspiracies from without and Arab disunity from within. Increasingly, Khomeini dwelt on this theme, heightening his rhetoric against "the criminal Zionists" and insisting that the "holy soil of Palestine" demanded of Muslims the obligation to wage jihad against Israel. In 1972 Khomeini graphically explained that Palestine was the fountainhead of all the disasters besetting the seven hundred million Muslims of the world, who were still enslaved "by the yoke of colonialism and Zionism." He particularly attacked the selfishness and servitude of Arab governments dependent on Western or Soviet assistance. At the same time, he warmly praised the Palestinian guerrillas and called insistently for Muslim brotherhood against the "pillagers of America and Zionism."[37]

In 1972 Khomeini told an audience of religious scholars that only a return to the pristine teachings of the Koran could help courageous Palestinian fighters achieve victory against the "Zionist transgressors." Backed by their Anglo-American allies and benefiting from the "evil deceitfulness" of the Soviet Union, which had prevented Muslims from being properly armed, the Zionists had been able to continue their naked aggression. In occupying Palestinian lands, Israel had been encouraged by the passivity of Islamic governments. Khomeini particularly dwelt upon "the duty of the noble and Islamic nation of Iran" not to remain indifferent toward such "savage aggressions" by Israel and the disasters facing their Arab brothers. Iranians were obligated to help the Arabs to free Palestine and "to annihilate Zionism."[38]

This obligation derived from their historic mission to revive Islam and further its program of revolutionary expansion and conquest.

Khomeini relentlessly hammered away at the dangers posed by the global imperialist-Zionist conspiracy. He especially deplored the negative consequences of the "lack of unity of the Word" and the absence of harmony among Islamic governments, which meant that the Palestinians had been largely left to their own devices.

The Yom Kippur War of 1973 did not fundamentally change matters. In a message to the Iranian nation, the ayatollah lamented the fact that more than seven hundred million Muslims and a hundred million Arabs had so miserably failed "to free themselves from the clutches of colonialism, and to expel the band of Zionist Jews in Israel who are threatening our people, history and inheritance." In a personal message to Palestinian leader Yasser Arafat in 1977, Khomeini contemptuously referred to Israel as a "cancerous tumor of the Middle East" that was "creating disunity with all the Satanic means at its disposal."[39] Once he assumed supreme power in Iran at the end of 1979, he multiplied his proto-genocidal references to Israel's existence in the Middle East as a "cancerous growth"—one that could not be cured by medication, "but must be operated on with a surgical knife."[40]

Khomeini's rhetoric reflected his obsessive belief in a Jewish conspiracy and his xenophobic loathing for non-Muslims in general. In Khomeini's works, "colonial plots" lurked everywhere in the background. The West and the Jews were responsible for all Middle East problems, and the cause of the decline of Muslim civilization. They were to blame for the endemic Sunni-Shia divide, and the economic gulf between oppressors and oppressed. The shah of Iran, along with Britain, America, the Soviet Union, and, of course, the Zionists, had continually "conspired" to subvert Islam. The West, in particular, sought to keep Muslims poor, backward, and divided, in order to more effectively plunder their natural resources.

However, when it came to *distorting* Islam, mistranslating the Koran, persecuting the clergy, promoting materialism and capitalist modernization, or controlling the mass media, no other group could compete with the Jews. In 1979 Khomeini bluntly announced: "Their true aim is to establish a world Jewish government." Since they were "energetic" and "very shrewd," this objective was, in his view, achievable.[41] For the Iranian leader and his followers, it went without saying that Jews had long served as Western spies, agents, and fifth columnists in Persia. Israel and the Jews were the real power behind the "imperialist plot" to achieve Western global domination. In their campaign, the Khomeinists skillfully exploited the association in the public mind of the shah's hated SAVAK with the CIA and the Mossad. The repressive tortures of the SAVAK against religious and political dissidents undoubtedly increased the general loathing of America and Israel.

The Khomeinists also distrusted the leaders of the Soviet Union and international Communism as "imperialist" conspirators. In the 1980s, quoting from the Koran and updated versions of the *Protocols*, they claimed that the Bolshevik Revolution and Marxism itself were an integral part of a *Jewish* conspiracy; that Stalin, no less than Marx, Trotsky, or Zinoviev, was part of the global "Zionist" plot. In Iranian propaganda, Jews and Freemasons were held responsible for the English, French, and American revolutions. They had provoked the partition of Poland, instigated the fall of the Ottoman Empire, and encouraged the persecution of Muslim peoples in Soviet Central Asia.[42] The existence of a small Baha'i sect in Iran was treated not only as a Shiite heresy but also as a dangerously "subversive anti-Muslim conspiracy." In the late nineteenth century a growing number of Persian Jews had indeed converted to the Baha'i faith.[43] This partly explains why official sources could present Bahaism as a secret society, originally created by Britain, but now politically controlled by America and Israel against Iran. From the mid-nineteenth century the Baha'is would be subject to fierce persecution as the alleged tools of a broad "imperialist-Jewish" plot to destroy the unity of Islam.

• • •

The Islamic Revolution of 1979 in Iran was unquestionably an event with cataclysmic consequences, arguably no less significant than the French, Russian, or Chinese revolutions that preceded it.[44] In some ways it has proved to be as alien to Iran's past as Mao's Cultural Revolution was to the ancient Chinese civilization. Its holy war for Islam, waged primarily against the United States and Israel, aimed to unite the entire Muslim world against the "Great" and the "Little" Satan, rather then to promote Iran's national interests. Khomeini's revolution showed, however, that seemingly impregnable Middle Eastern tyrants could indeed be overthrown by popular forces. It even seemed that the successful Shiite uprising might provide inspiration for Sunni Arab fundamentalists.[45] Nevertheless, there were great differences between the two groups, not the least of which is the historic and cultural gulf between Persians and Arabs. Moreover, Khomeini had developed his distinctive theory of *velayat-e faqih* (the mandate of the jurist), which turned the *mujtahid* (doctor of the divine Muslim Shiite law) into the major source of power in the Islamic state. To the supreme jurist (himself), Khomeini assigned sweeping powers similar to those of the Prophet Muhammad in governing the first Islamic community.[46] He would construct new principles of government, some of which were unprecedented in Islamic history. They certainly had no equivalent in the Arab world.

At the same time, Sunni fundamentalists could sympathize with Khomeini's attempt to transcend the concept of the territorial state and modern nationalism in the name of a revolutionary universalist ideology. They could share his ultimate goal of unifying the Muslim *umma* in order to achieve an Islamic world government that would include all peoples. Khomeini's credo necessitated replacing "the sovereignty of the people" with the "rule of divine law over men"; transforming the ulema into the guardians of the sacred law, and Islam itself into an all-embracing politics based on implementing divine will against the "Satanic principle." Jews were, of course, given a prominent role among the devil's disciples. Khomeini unequivocally maintained that "from the very beginning, the historic movement of Islam has had to contend with the Jews, for it was they who first established anti-Islamic propaganda and engaged in various stratagems, and as you can see, this continues down to the present."[47]

Only the Islamic ideology, according to the new dispensation, could supply the authentic path and implement the sacred goals of the faith, even if millions of Muslims had to be martyred or sacrificed in the process. Territory, population, and government were necessary but only instrumental factors in preserving and protecting the one true faith. Khomeinist Iran, as a state, above all assumed the mission of propagating Islam to the whole world, of becoming the springboard for the export of world revolution through *permanent struggle*.[48] The call of Islam became identified with establishing the government of the oppressed over the oppressors on a global scale; it anticipated the victory of Islam over imported culture, of the East over the West.

The extreme radicalism of the Khomeinist regime was further reinforced by the shock of the Iraqi invasion of Iran in September 1980 and the Israeli drive into Lebanon in the summer of 1982. The Iran-Iraq War proved to be the longest, costliest, and bloodiest war in the entire history of the contemporary Middle East. It pitted Saddam Hussein, Iraqi heir of the secular, national socialist ideology of Pan-Arabism, against Khomeini's Islamic Revolution based on the power of absolute faith. It was a geopolitical battle for control of the Shatt al Arab waterway, for oil-rich and ethnically Arab Khuzestan, for hegemony in the Persian Gulf, and leadership of the Muslim world. During this nightmarish eight-year conflict, the Iranians, who had secretly purchased arms from Israel, hypocritically painted Saddam as a Zionist agent while denying all allegations about their own "religiously unclean and forbidden relations" with the Jewish state. President Ali Khamanei, in August 1986, complained bitterly about the diabolical plot instigated by "world arrogance" against Iran and the Islamic world, which had charged his country with having "relations with Israel, recognizing Israel, accepting Israel as a reality." Khamanei answered by describing Zionism as "an extremely short-sighted racist Judaism. . . . There could be no compromise. The struggle to eliminate the Zionist government root and branch" was, according to the then Iranian president, "a religious obligation."[49]

Khomeinism undoubtedly accelerated the movement toward a lethal Islamicization of the Arab-Israeli conflict and radicalized the "Palestinian question." Perhaps more than any of the Arab leaders, Ayatollah Khomeini and his aides were ready to turn the notion of an international Zionist conspiracy into an iron law that applied to each and every situation. For example, in February 1981 the ayatollah chose to dwell on the global ramifications of the Zionist plot:

> For nearly 20 years now I have been pointing out the danger of international Zionism. Today, I regard this danger to all the world's liberation revolutions and Iran's genuine revolution as being even greater than in the past, for these world-devouring criminals [the Zionists] by their technology are working . . . for the defeat of the world's oppressed.[50]

The revolutionary populist dimension in Khomeinism should not be underestimated. Its Third World rhetoric made it sound at times like a Shiite version of Peronism or Guevarist radicalism. At the same time, Khomeini's followers have also been ready to adapt symbols like International Labor Day (borrowed from European socialism) and mesh them with popular Islam. In the 1980s, the ayatollahs liked to present themselves as champions of the *mostazafin* (downtrodden masses) against the affluent West and the imperialist superpowers. Many of their decrees, as well as the constitutional structure of the Islamic Republic, had little to do with the traditional sharia, let alone with Iran's rich cultural legacy.

When the exiled Khomeini first became a political activist in the late 1960s, he had briefly been influenced by the radical Iranian intellectual Ali Shariati (1933–77), who managed to fuse reinterpretations of Shia Islam with Guevarist Marxism. The Western-educated Shariati gave a new revolutionary meaning to Shiite martyrdom, the role of the imam, the eschatological element of the hidden messiah, and the notion of a "unitary Muslim community." Shariati's populist left-wing Islamism was not free of anti-Jewish aspersions, which were linked to his hatred of the shah's regime. The radical Jalal Al-e Ahmad (1923–69) wrote about the social affliction of "occidentosis," a disease symptomized by the ravages of toxic Western influence that threatened to overwhelm Iran both culturally and politically. Khomeini had also been impressed by the student guerrilla movements of the 1960s in Iran, at a time when tensions were sharply rising throughout the country. His famous lectures of 1970, *Velayat-e Faqih: Hokumat-e Islami* (The Jurist's Guardianship: Islamic Government), for the first time unequivocally denounced all forms of *saltanat* (monarchy) as a "pagan" institution. Monarchical rule had been inherited from the despotic Roman and Sassanid empires, which Muslims had a sacred duty to resist. Against the shah, he invoked Moses's opposition to Pharaoh, Muhammad's contempt for the title *malek al-muluk* (king of kings), and the revolt of Imam Husayn ibn 'Ali in seventh-century Karbala as involving the rejection of hereditary kingship. In Khomeini's eyes monarchs were mostly criminals, oppressors, and mass murderers. Only *fuqaha* (religious judges) had a divine right to rule. The imams had inherited directly from the Prophet their all-encompassing authority and the right to lead the community.[51]

In his post-1970 writings Khomeini divided the world into two warring classes: the *mostazafin* (oppressed) and the *mostakberin* (oppressors). He gave a new religious twist to the class struggle promoted by secular Marxists and the Communist Tudeh Party, who had been severely persecuted by the shah. The Khomeinist category of the oppressed, the downtrodden poor, and the exploited people contained echoes of the Jacobin *sans-culottes* during the French Revolution and the Argentinean working-class *descamisados* (coatless ones) who had supported Juan and Evita Péron in the late 1940s. Khomeini also took a leaf out of the book of the People's Mojahedin Organization of Iran who, like Ali Shariati, had compared early Shia martyrs to such modern revolutionaries as Che Guevara. Khomeini himself began to slide together the concepts of the oppressed with that of the *shahid* (martyr). His reinterpretation of the sacrifices for Islam involved the liberation from class domination *and* a form of revolutionary martyrdom to overthrow a despotic political order.[52] The morbid fascination with martyrdom in Iranian and Shia culture provided the perfect setting for such radical preaching.

Once in power, Ayatollah Khomeini and his successor, Ali Khamanei, as self-proclaimed leaders of the "Global Islamic Revolution," addressed themselves to the Muslims of the whole world. They sought to mobilize them against the "arrogant West" and all the "imperialist oppressors." The Iranian Revolution, it was emphasized, could not be confined "within borders, nations, or ethnic groups."[53] In a curious repetition of early Soviet history, the ayatollahs seemed to annex Leon Trotsky's heretical Bolshevik theory of "permanent revolution" on a global scale as the only way to save their own revolution from being strangled by the West. Only this time it was Shiite clerics, rather than professional revolutionaries such as Lenin, Trotsky, and Stalin, who were trying to export their revolution abroad in order to preserve it at home.[54] No less than the messianic Bolsheviks of the 1920s, Iran's Islamist fundamentalists saw themselves as the center of a new world-wide movement that recognized no borders and sought to establish a global revolutionary hegemony. The "fundamentalist international" led by Iran was, however, committed to a global Islamic republic administering divine laws, not to a utopian Communist ideal of world proletarian self-rule. Moreover, the Iranian Islamists could build on the profound religious roots common to many Muslim societies from West Africa to Central Asia. They could exploit the endemic weakness of liberal democracy in the Middle East, the decline of Arab nationalism, and Iran's own sense of a unique cultural mission within Islam. Using the appeal of this Iranian heritage, Tehran hoped to play a role in Islamic politics similar to that of Moscow in the heyday of the Communist International. The collapse of the Soviet Union further heightened the missionary zeal of the mullahs. In a bold January 1989 letter to Soviet president Mikhail Gorbachev, Khomeini confidently informed the last Soviet leader that both Marxism and Western capitalism were bankrupt: "In conclusion, I declare with frankness that the Islamic Republic of Iran, as the largest and most powerful base of the Islamic world, can easily fill the ideological void of your system."[55]

After 1990 the United States remained the one really dangerous threat to the Iranian regime in the eyes of its leaders. The ayatollah closely linked American malevolency to Jewish machinations and efforts at the cultural subversion of Islam. Khomeini had always identified foreign cultural products with materialistic intoxication by the West and with the poisonous Jewish corruption of Muslim religious values. He had long considered that Israel, Zionism, and the Jews of Iran played a harmful role in this "sinister influence" of Western cultural and economic imperialism on ordinary Iranians—aided and abetted by the shah's regime. "Israel, the universally recognized enemy of Islam and the Muslims . . . has with the assistance of the despicable government of Iran penetrated all the economic, military, and political affairs of the country," he declared in 1971. As Khomeini never tired of repeating, Israel was a "cancerous growth in the Middle East," sowing dissension among Muslims and plotting with the help of America, "satanic" conspiracies against the Islamic Revolution.[56] This pronounced anti-Israelism was a transparently thin veneer for virulent anti-Semitism, drawing in part on Koranic sources. As Khomeini put it in his 1970 "Program for the Establishment of an Islamic Government":

We see today that the Jews (may God curse them) have meddled with the
text of the Qur'an and have made certain changes in the Qur'ans they
have printed in the occupied territories. It is our duty to prevent this
treacherous interference. . . . We must protest and make the people aware
that the Jews and their foreign backers are opposed to the very foundations of Islam and wish to establish Jewish domination throughout the
world.[57]

Khomeini expressed his own personal dread of the possibility that one
day "the apathy shown by some of us may allow a Jew to rule over us." Jews,
like the Baha'is, the Christians, and the materialists, were seen by the implacable Ayatollah as willing instruments in the hands of the imperialists or
of treacherous Muslim rulers such as the shah of Iran. They were pawns
that could be easily maneuvered in order to make Muslims abandon their
faith. Everywhere in the Muslim world the cancer of imperialism was seeking to displace "the culture of the Qur'an"—especially in Palestine, whose
loss was the ultimate symbol of Muslim decadence, disunity, and impotence. Under the shah, Israel and, by extension, America had not only penetrated Iran but turned it into a base against Islam and the Palestinians.
"Criminal Israel" was skillfully "casting dissension among the Muslims"
even as its soldiers "battered and slaughtered our dear Palestinian and
Lebanese brothers with all their might."

America, the USSR, the shah, Sadat, and all the other debased actors in
the satanic global conspiracy were ultimately controlled by Israel and world
Zionism. In a July 1972 message, Khomeini explained that Israel itself had
been "born out of the collusion and agreement of the imperialist states of
East and West." While America had provided it with lethal weapons in order
to occupy Islamic lands, the USSR, by its own treachery toward the Arab
states, had also done much to guarantee its existence.[58] International Zionism was, however, no less of a diabolic force than the United States itself.
Acting together through "hidden and treacherous agents," both of these
devilish powers had sucked the blood of "the oppressed people of the
world" in a coordinated campaign of ruthless exploitation. The sinister
Zionists, along with Britain and America, were also blamed for the deliberate cultural subversion of Islamic values by writers such as the British Muslim Salman Rushdie. His book *The Satanic Verses* produced a notorious
fatwa from Khomeini sentencing him to death for apostasy. Rushdie, he de-

clared, was an "agent of corruption" employed by the Zionist Jews and Anglo-Saxons to "declare war on God" and mock the Holy Koran. Any Muslim who killed Rushdie would therefore be regarded as a martyr for the faith.[59]

Khomeini's animus toward Zionism appeared to be unquenchable. Once he was ensconced in power, one of his very first actions was to recall Iranian diplomatic representatives from Israel and to end all oil supplies to the Jewish state. Until that point, Iran had provided 70 percent of Israel's oil imports. It was no surprise that his followers swiftly ransacked the Israeli Consulate in the capital of Iran—proclaiming it the embassy of the PLO; or that the Islamic Republic's first foreign visitor would be Yasser Arafat, who received a hero's welcome in Tehran. Both Khomeini and Arafat shared an intense hatred of the shah and all his works.[60] They were both fixated on the destruction of Israel and the return of holy Jerusalem to Muslim hands. Their anti-Americanism, their populist radicalism in the colors of jihad, and their dislike of established Arab rulers were further points of contact. Khomeini, however, always despised Arafat and never forgave his support for Saddam Hussein during the Iran-Iraq War. Saddam, for his part, had convinced the PLO and most of his fellow Arabs that he was fighting to save them from Persian imperialism and the Shiite heresy. In 1988 Khomeini reluctantly had to accept a cease-fire with Saddam, whom he had always regarded as a Muslim apostate and a Zionist agent. Halting the war against Saddam was, he remarked, the bitterest pill of his long life.

. . .

Against the backdrop of the Sunni-Shia divide, hatred of Israel, the Jews, and the United States provided a highly charged banner for Muslim unity and a convenient justification for permanent mobilization. The United States naturally qualified for the primary scapegoat role. The "Great Satan" was the epitome of evil in Khomeini's eyes—not only an enemy of Iran and Islam but also of the Third World. The USSR, too, was an imperialist adversary treated with disdain, though somewhat less stridently. Nevertheless, Zionism was the supreme ideological target. Sometimes, it was organically linked to America as a launching pad of "imperialist aggression"; on other occasions its independently diabolical activities were stressed. Demonizing Israel and Zionism provided a guaranteed method of creating a minimal Islamic solidarity beyond the Sunni-Shiite and Iranian-Arab divides. Since the early 1980s this strategy also served as a method to dampen any inclination by moderate Arab regimes to accept American-sponsored resolutions of the Arab-Israeli conflict. From the outset, the Khomeinists always rejected proposals for any compromise on the "Palestinian question." Muslims who pursued a peaceful solution to this conflict were, by definition, traitors to Islam.

Thus, ever since the Madrid peace conference of 1991, Iran has spared no effort to undermine and defeat efforts at ending the Middle East impasse through Arab-Israeli negotiation. The Iranian president Khamanei declared, for example, on August 26, 1991, that Madrid was yet another conspiracy against Palestine by the "arrogant West." Some commentators in Iran even called on "zealous Muslims" to murder those taking part in the international peace conference, for committing "treachery."[61] Once again, the total "liberation" of Palestine was reaffirmed as a "strategic ideal for the Islamic Revolution"—a goal that demanded the commitment of considerable financial, political, intelligence, and military resources.

Palestine has indeed been given enormous attention and emphasis by the Iranian mullahs. During the long war with Iraq, Khomeini justified the titanic struggle with the slogan "Liberating Quds [Jerusalem] Through Karbala." For his part, President Hashemi Rafsanjani, speaking in Tehran in October 1991, emphasized the point that "no issue bears greater significance for us than Palestine."[62] As the chief executive of the Islamic Republic, he solemnly declared that Iran was "even prepared to send troops to help the Palestinians."[63] Khamenei reiterated that all Muslims must feel "duty bound to help" the Palestinian nation in a "violent and selfless struggle that must be conducted inside and outside occupied lands." The leader of Iran also warned that if there was a permanent solution to the "Palestinian question," "America will prepare herself for her principal task, namely to fight Islamic movements."

For Khamanei it was obvious that peace in the Middle East could only isolate Iran and weaken its brand of radical Islam. It would focus unwelcome attention on the regime's brutal clampdown on the democratic liberties of its own people. In other words, a successful peace process might literally bring an end to the fundamental raison d'être of the Iranian regime. In 1993, Khamanei, in explicitly calling for Israel's "annihilation," repeated that Iran was "opposed to any action which would run counter to this goal."[64] Major General Mohsen Rezai, commander in chief of the Iranian Revolutionary Guards Corps, was equally unequivocal. "Liberating Palestine," he said, was a matter of Tehran's "strategic survival," the pivotal problem of the regime and its fate. On October 21, 1991—almost exactly ten years before the Islamist assault on New York and Washington—the Iranian general prophesied: "The Muslims' fury and hatred will burn the heart of Washington some day and America will be responsible for its repercussions. . . . The day will come when, like Salman Rushdie, the Jews will not find a place to live anywhere in the world."[65]

Rezai is one of the four official candidates for the Iranian presidency in the June 2009 elections. The Islamic Republic of Iran has been more viscerally hostile to Israel over the past three decades than any other Muslim state. The total denial of its right to exist has indeed been central to official Iranian ideology. It has been frequently used as a tool of its revolutionary appeal abroad, and has provided a means to cover up failures in the domestic sphere.[66] In one of the most rapid and dramatic shifts of alliance in modern Middle Eastern history, in 1979 Iran went from being an important strategic partner of Israel and a crucial breach in the ring of hostile Arab states to becoming its most dangerous and implacable enemy. With no other country were Iran's relations overturned so speedily and drastically. The Iranian crusade against Israel swiftly extended to Lebanon and became a major factor in the militancy of the Lebanese Shiite Hezbollah movement and in the radicalizing of the Palestinian armed struggle against Zionism.

The conflict with Israel, which has no territorial basis, was perceived from the outset as a zero-sum game. According to the so-called moderate Hashemi Rafsanjani, "if we recognize the validity of Israel's existence, we will be losing everything."[67] Hence, not only were the Palestinians advised to rely solely on armed force but all Muslims were exhorted to do the same. Rafsanjani's words in the early 1990s were unequivocal: "The means of eradicating the Zionist regime and the establishment of another government to replace it in Palestine lie in massing all powers of the Islamic world, foremost of which will be the capabilities of the Islamic Republic of Iran, Syria, Libya, and Algeria."[68] It should be remembered that during the past three decades, Iran had successively opposed the Camp David accords with Sadat, the Reagan plan, the Oslo agreements, the Clinton parameters, and the Bush proposal for a two-state solution, as well as the Fahd peace initiative, the Fez plan, and the more recent Saudi proposals accepted by the Arab League.[69] At the same time it has been conducting a relentless proxy war against Israel ever since the 1980s with the help of its Syrian ally, Hezbollah, Hamas, and Islamic Jihad, while promoting terror and subversion throughout the Middle East.

The Iranian school system has reflected these priorities, preparing its students for war with Israel in the name of Islam. Even under the more liberal former president Mohammad Khatami (1997–2005), the Khomeinist teaching of a life-and-death global confrontation against the "infidel oppressors" (especially the United States) remained in place. Khomeini's Islamic standpoint always set the tone: "I am decisively announcing to the whole world that, if the World-Devourers wish to stand against our religion, we will stand against their whole world and will not cease until the annihilation of all of them."[70]

In the textbooks, the United States ("The Arrogant One") naturally stands at the head of the "World-Devourers." It is irrevocably indicted for its imperialist exploitation of the oppressed masses in developing countries, its use of atomic bombs against Japan in 1945, its support of violent dictatorships in the Third World (including the shah's regime), its massacre of the American Indians on the North American continent, and its enslavement of blacks. America's constant military interventions, its alleged atrocities against Muslims, its strong support for Israel, and conspiracies against the Iranian Revolution are all evoked in order to justify the "Great Satan" epithet and the recurring cry in Iranian political demonstrations of "Death to America."[71]

No less central to Islamic indoctrination in Iran has been the struggle against *Gharbzadegi* (Westernization), materialism, secularism, and the moral corruption embodied by a decadent Western culture. This includes the battle against the spread of narcotic drugs, immoral films, sexual permissiveness, and "false notions" of women's emancipation. Western capitalist culture is seen as a threat to the identity and soul of all non-Western peoples. The culture war waged by the Khomeinists is ostensibly conducted in the name of Islamic spirituality against a soulless, materialistic Western world manifested in mass consumption symbols such as McDonald's, Coca-Cola, *Time* and *Newsweek* magazines, and the Internet. The West, it is acknowledged, controls the international banking system, the major currencies, international financial markets, the world's maritime routes, space industries, electronic communications, the most advanced weapons industries, and scientific as well as technological progress. However, according to the Islamist regime, the morally corrupt, spiritually bankrupt West is doomed to destruction.[72] But the quiet revolution happening beneath the surface in contemporary Iran belies these claims. Two-thirds of the population, who are under thirty years of age, have known nothing but the rule of the ayatollahs. Through the Internet, foreign travel, satellite TV, and as a result of government repression many Iranians feel alienated from the puritanical regime. They are drawn to Western films, music, clothing, literature, and a more open society that would normalize their lives.

This is not at all reflected in contemporary Iranian textbooks, which deal with the "crimes" of Western colonialism. References to the Jews mainly recall Muhammad's victorious war against them. In that context, the Jews of Medina are depicted as traitors and enemies of Islam—a hostile "profit-seeking" ethnic group who stubbornly opposed the Prophet and imagined themselves to be God's chosen people.[73] Their expulsion from Arabia is recorded though no reference is made to the slaughter of the Qurayza Jewish tribe. Koranic versions of biblical tales about Abraham, Joseph, Moses, David, and Solomon do appear in the textbooks, along with some references to Jewish holy places in Jerusalem—something generally avoided in Arab countries. The story of Jesus is narrated without ever mentioning that Christ, his disciples, and the inhabitants of Roman-dominated Palestine were overwhelmingly Jews.[74] Similarly, there is silence about the Jews in the context of King Cyrus's edict permitting previously captive and enslaved nations to return to their homeland. Even more sparse are references to Jews in the modern era, except in the highly charged context of the Palestinian conflict. There is a blanket of silence over Jewish culture, history, and achievements. The only indirect and fleeting mention of the Holocaust and the Jewish fate under Nazism appears in an eleventh-grade humanities textbook *History of Iran and the World* (2004), which cryptically observes: "He [Hitler] regarded the traitors and the Jews as the cause of Germany's defeat [in World War I]."[75]

Zionism, on the other hand, is dealt with in Iranian textbooks through the prism of a *Protocols of the Elders of Zion* perspective. It is presented as a colonialist conspiracy with tentacles across the globe that seeks world domination. It is said to control most of the Western news media, American politics, and the great capitalist monopolies. To elaborate this point, Iranian students are referred to the Persian translation of Yuri Ivanov's virulently anti-Israel *Beware Zionism*—a 1968 Soviet hack production—along with more familiar diatribes against Israel as an usurper state. Only Palestine is real. Israel is either "Occupied Palestine" or simply "Palestine" on Iranian maps, as it is in the schoolbooks of the Arab world. Sometimes it is also referred to as "the regime that occupies Jerusalem." This *non-state* is the direct enemy of Iran, the Islamic Revolution, the Muslim world, the Arabs, and the Palestinians. It alone is responsible for the Palestinian refugee question. The Zionist entity is vilified as an alien implant in the region and the illegal occupier of Beit al-Moqaddas (Jerusalem), and of al-Haram al-Sharif (the Noble Sanctuary). It is therefore the obligation of *all* Muslims to unite and liberate Palestine in order to "save Jerusalem from the hands of the enemies of Islam."[76]

Palestinian resistance has long been highlighted as a central part of the Iranian Islamic Revolution and of Ayatollah Khomeini's personal legacy. In a 1963 speech following the massacre of students in the Fayziya Madrasa in Qom by the shah's security forces, Khomeini portrayed Israel as the guilty party. This utterly baseless accusation still appears in Iranian history schoolbooks, which quote the imam as follows:

> Israel does not wish the Qur'an to exist in this country. Israel does not wish the *'ulama* to exist in this country. Israel does not wish a single learned man to exist in this country. It was Israel that assaulted Fayziya Madrassa by means of its sinister agents. It is still assaulting us, and assaulting you, the nation; it wishes to seize your economy, to destroy your trade and agriculture, to appropriate your wealth. Israel wishes to remove by means of its agents anything it regards as blocking its path. The Qur'an is blocking its path—it must be removed. . . . The Iranian government of the Shah in pursuance to the purposes and schemes of Israel has humiliated us and continues to do so.[77]

Nothing has changed in the Khomeinist doctrine about Israel and the Jews since those paranoid statements were made forty-five years ago—words of hate that continue to echo at every level of Iranian society and politics. When the Ministry of Islamic Guidance in 1983 issued a pamphlet containing the imam's addresses on Zionism and the need to liberate Al-Quds, it exhorted Muslims to "purify it from the unclean presence of Zionists." Inspired by Khomeini, the pamphlet called for "a full-scale uncompromising war" to annihilate Israel not in the name of secular Arab nationalism but by "relying only upon God and Divine Power."[78] The destruction of the "Israeli criminals" and oppressors would necessitate a halt to Arab compromise, to the temporizing of Islamic governments, and to their trust in the good faith of the superpowers.

It was Khomeini who first designated the last Friday of the month of Ramadan as "Al-Quds Day" (Jerusalem Day) and decided to use the celebration for promoting his vision of Muslim unity, jihad, and the extinction of Israel. He told the Shiites of Lebanon in June 1979 that on Al-Quds Day, the oppressed nations "must rise up and dispose of this source of corruption [Israel]"; the day would be one of Islamic revival, when war must be declared against Israel—"this enemy of mankind and humanity" and against the oppressive plunderers led by America.[79] Khomeini repeatedly flayed Arab governments and Muslims on Jerusalem Day for giving Israel the chance to exist at all, thereby endangering the world of Islam. He told the Syrian foreign minister in 1979 that this cardinal mistake could only be rectified by creating a universal "Party of the Oppressed"—identical to the "Party of God" (Hezbollah). Only such an Islamic party could end self-abasement before the West, liberate Jerusalem, and defeat America, along with its "agent of corruption, Israel."[80] It was in this destructive spirit that Khomeini, on March 5, 1981, called to "the nations of Islam and the oppressed of the world" to rise up against the oppressors and their progeny—"especially the usurper Israel"—to remove this "cancerous tumor" from Jerusalem and Lebanon.[81]

Khomeini's language was generally warlike, paranoid, malevolent, and unfailingly incendiary. On May 17, 1981, he asked Muslims how long they would passively bear witness to the injustices and inhuman massacres committed by East and West against their Afghan, Lebanese, and Palestinian brothers: "How long should your Quds be trampled on by the scum of America, the usurper, Israel? How long should the land of Quds, Lebanon and the oppressed Muslims of those lands live under the yoke of criminals while you watch and some of your traitorous rulers fan the flames?"[82]

Virtually every reference Khomeini made to Israel, America, or its Arab allies described these adversaries as "criminal" enslavers of Muslims who had to be destroyed in the name of Allah. The Islamic Revolution in his own homeland was held up as the great light that had defeated the "satanic powers"—America, the Soviet Union, Israel, and the shah of Iran—through divine guidance and the illumination of faith.[83] Ayatollah Khomeini hammered away at the "evil designs" of those Arab leaders who claimed to oppose Israel but were not willing "to tear open its heart" with weapons. They were cowards who had sought to negotiate with a "criminal and usurping government" that had "sucked the blood of the Muslims and Palestine," mercilessly killing and plundering the believers. Why should the Palestinians accept the 1981 Saudi peace plan (which Khomeini called a "hundred per cent anti-Islamic plan") and "recognize this corrupt, immoral and heathenous Zionist regime which has been ever since it set foot in Quds and Palestine a usurper"? The Fahd proposals would inevitably endanger the holy places of Mecca and Medina; they were bound to turn the Arabs into lifelong captives of Israel and America.[84] According to Khomeini, it was an irredeemable "disgrace for the Arabs to accept Israel's mastery over them." Iran has continued with this intransigent *negation* for the past thirty years, repeatedly advocating that Islamic countries must be rid "of this cancerous growth" and of the "professional, bloodthirsty criminals" at its head.[85]

Iranian representatives regularly made similar statements over the years at the UN General Assembly. On September 30, 1983, Iran's foreign minister Ali Akbar Velayati told the General Assembly: "There is no cure for the cancerous growth of Zionism but surgery."[86] Six weeks later another Iranian representative, Hosein Latify, returned to the same mantra: "The Zionist entity . . . should be removed like a cancerous tumour."[87] Only the Nazis used this anti-Jewish metaphor with such alarming frequency to indicate their *exterminationist* intent. Racial hubris, too, has not been absent. For example, on December 6, 1985, the Iranian representative declared in front of the General Assembly that "the Zionist entity is nothing" but "the Muslim nation is really a great, superior nation."[88] There have been other echoes of the Third Reich. One Iranian UN delegate in 1985 came up with an original historical "discovery": He claimed that the German Jews who "migrated from the Third Reich to occupied Palestine" had "closely cooperated with Hitler's Gestapo in persecuting the lower-class German Jews and delivering them to concentration camps." Now safely established in Palestine, these Zionist Jews were well versed in imposing "Nazi-style fascism on the occupied lands."[89] On November 26, 1986, another Iranian diplomat (following the lead of Libyan, Syrian, and PLO representatives) added that Muslims would teach a lesson to the "ugly Zionists" who were engaged "in sinister infiltrations, pornography, drug-dealing and other nefarious activities."[90]

• • •

Echoes of the *Protocols* have often been used by Iranian propaganda abroad. In February 1984, to celebrate the fifth anniversary of the "glorious Islamic Revolution in Iran," *Imam,* a monthly periodical sponsored by the Iranian Embassy in London, published a special issue featuring the *Protocols of the Elders of Zion.* It began by quoting Khomeini's oracular statement that "Zionism is an enemy to humanity" and "the perpetual enemy to Islam." It also recalled several "Jewish conspiracies" against the Prophet Muhammad, asserting that many Muslims ever since then "were [being] killed by the hidden hands of the Jews." *Imam* deplored the "Zionist-American" campaign of sanctions and slander against the Islamic Republic, Israel's bloodbath in Lebanon, and the invasion of Iran by "the Zionist regime of Iraq" under the jackboot of Saddam.[91] The *Protocols* were clearly a useful distraction for Iranian propaganda during their own duplicitous dealings with Israel. According to the Iranian regime, the *Protocols* were "being adhered to word by word by Jewish-influenced Western governments."[92] Not only that, but the Israelis were "the true descendants of the Elders of Zion" with their reliance on brutality, ferocity, fraud, and deception. They had been carrying out "pogroms" in Lebanon since 1982 with U.S. backing and the silent complicity of Arab states.

In March 1984 *Imam* continued to disseminate the *Protocols,* exposing the "invisible hand of Zionism" at work for centuries in a ruthless crusade against human values. *Imam* believed that the prophecies contained in the *Protocols* had been increasingly fulfilled during the past hundred years. For example, the "Zionist spirit" of demoralization and decadence had so deeply penetrated the West "that today there is hardly a Westerner with any aim in life." Islamic states, too, had been thoroughly infiltrated by Zionist elements. The inevitable result was "inhumane rulers and immoral politicians" who were "either Zionists themselves or hand-picked by the Zionists." *Imam* insisted that Jewish national self-determination in Palestine was "only camouflage and an infinitesimal part of the *Zionist world plot*"[93] (emphasis in the original). The real goal, as set out by the Elders of Zion, was "to dominate the world" by destroying morality, tradition, and religious beliefs; to this end the Zionist Jews deliberately encouraged alcoholism, drugs, homosexuality, permissiveness, and general sexual degradation. Zionism was even responsible, according to *Imam*, for the pathologies of "dog-loving societies" such as Britain and America. The Judeo-Christian West had assiduously ignored the sufferings of its own homeless people. Yet it provided cosmetics, special garments, and even funeral rites for canine pets whose feces littered the streets of the self-proclaimed civilized world. To quote the semi-official Iranian periodical: "Dogs are making a mess of the world in Zionist societies." Since Jews and dogs are ritually polluted in Shiite dogma, this cultural idiosyncrasy might explain the bizarre quality of the great "Zionist dog lovers" conspiracy. It reminds us that in Khomeinist ideology nothing *inhuman* or perverse is alien to the global ambitions of Jewry.

Much like Nazi anti-Semitism, the Islamic Revolution in Iran equated Jewry with everything bad—including vice, immorality, the dissemination of mindless luxuries, legalized prostitution, homosexuality, mass pornography, and the death of "spiritual personality." From this global perspective the illegal state of Israel was merely the tip of the iceberg. No place in the world was immune from Zionist aggression, which had become a code word for the international Jewish conspiracy and all forms of contemporary exploitation. It was an axiom that from the time of the Prophet the Jews had been "the perpetual enemy of Islam" and of humanity. Hence the governmental and administrative structures of Islamic states would have to be totally purged of "Zionist infiltration"; and preparations needed to be made for "an all-out confrontation with the Zionist nonentity, the occupiers of Palestine."[94] These "occupiers" had not only taken over Al-Quds and "created a bloodbath in Lebanon"; their invisible hand had been at work for centuries everywhere, "perpetrating crimes of unbelievable magnitude against human societies and values." To remove any possible doubt that "Zionist" meant Jew, the accompanying Iranian caricatures—then as now—always depict *Der Stürmer*-like creatures, replete with hooked noses and skullcaps, encircling the globe in serpentine fashion.

In Iran itself, incitement to both politicide and genocide against Israel has often come from leading personalities within the regime. The head of the Imam Khomeini Education and Research Institute, Ayatollah Muhammad Taqi Mezbah-Yazdi, in a sermon at Tehran University on July 4, 1997, called for Israel to be "eliminated" because a young Russian Jewish woman in Hebron had displayed an insulting drawing of the Prophet.[95] The same day in Qom another leading ayatollah, Ali Meshkini, reacted by inviting the entire Islamic world to "begin a massive attack against Israel and the United

States. . . . All Islamic countries should overflow, God willing, with the chants of Death to America and Death to Israel."[96] Such declarations are not unusual. They reflect the genocidal anti-Semitism of the Khomeinists, for whom Jews and Israel are synonyms describing an evil world conspiracy against Islam that must be physically eliminated.[97]

Similarly, the Jews and America are bonded together as chosen hate symbols for Iran's totalitarian theocracy. The anti-Jewish card enables the ayatollahs to rally fundamentalists, nationalists, and Communists around a common anti-Western banner. It permits Iran to bid for leadership of the anti-Israel cause beyond the Sunni-Shiite split; and in the Third World, both anti-Americanism and hatred of Israel resonate with the long-standing anti-Western resentment still felt in Asia and parts of Latin America. Contemporary Iranian anti-Semitism is inextricably linked to these factors, which underpin the "exterminatory" anti-Zionism of the Iranian leadership. This ideology owes something to the racist anti-Semitism of prewar European vintage, but it remains distinct in mixing fragments of Third Worldist Marxism with Shiite messianism and hatred of Israel as an instrument of its own missionizing global ambitions.[98]

Al-Quds Day has been the most striking symbolic manifestation of an Islamic "universalist" anti-Semitism embedded in Iranian state policy. The holiday proclaimed by Khomeini in 1979 to call for Israel's annihilation has since been celebrated worldwide with regular anti-Zionist demonstrations.[99] It is no accident that firebrand Iranian president Mahmoud Ahmadinejad chose to launch his own anti-Israeli and anti-Semitic campaign under the banner of "A World Without Zionism" on Al-Quds Day, October 26, 2005.[100] Mohammad Khatami, advocate of the so-called critical dialogue with the West, used Al-Quds Day in Tehran in 2003 to be photographed with a child on his arm waving a flag with the words "Death to Israel." The following year he explicitly told Swiss television that Israel had no right to exist.[101] Khatami, the "reformer," chose a sermon on Al-Quds Day in 1998 to speak of Israel as an "old wound in the body of Islam that cannot be healed"—a wound that possessed "truly demonic, stinking and contagious blood."[102] It appears that moderates, no less than radicals in the Iranian leadership, have become specialists in this Islamofascist pseudo-science of political oncology. Israel is always the "cancerous growth" or, as Ali Khamenei called it in his Al-Quds Day speech of 2000, a "rotten and dangerous tumor." Two years earlier he had labeled those Arabs who wished to negotiate with Israel as wanting to "maintain this cancer at any price." It is difficult to imagine a more dehumanizing and repulsive terminology, yet the significance of its usage is widely ignored by the Western world and by many Jews who ignore the lessons of the past.

The Nazi-like metaphors stigmatizing Israel as a "festering sore" or deadly lesion in the body of Islam have transposed a core theme of genocidal European anti-Semitism to the Middle East conflict. At the Tehran Al-Quds Day rally of 1999, Khamenei announced: "The existence of Israel [is] a tremendous threat for the peoples and states of the region. . . . And there is but one way to solve the problem in the Middle East, namely by shattering and annihilating the Zionist state."[103]

Not to be outdone by the spiritual leader of Iran, the so-called pragmatist and former president Hashemi Rafsanjani said in a 2003 address to an Al-Quds Day rally that "Israel has no future. Those who are counting on a tumor are wrong."[104] This was the same "moderate" who on December 14, 2001, announced on Iranian TV: "The establishment of the State of Israel is the worst event in history. The Jews living in Israel will have to migrate once more." A day later, at Friday prayers held at the University of Tehran, Rafsanjani openly said that "one atomic bomb would wipe out Israel without a trace" while the Islamic world would only be damaged rather than destroyed by Israeli nuclear retaliation.[105] The comments attracted far less attention than Ahmadinejad's declarations four years later, despite their appalling implications.

Such genocidal jihad-driven Israelophobia has been compulsively repeated on Al-Quds Day in accordance with Ayatollah Khomeini's anti-Semitic image of Israel as the core of the world conspiracy against Islam.[106] Directly linking Jerusalem with their annihilationist designs against the Jewish state, the post-Khomeini leadership continues to glorify the Palestinian cause, with special emphasis on the "holiness" of Jerusalem—which had been a marginal theme in traditional Shiite Islam.[107] The mullahs are prepared to organize hundreds of thousands of Iranians each year to attend the rallies in Tehran at great expense. Millions of poor Iranians receive free meals and vouchers for the occasion, and are driven to the center of Tehran after Friday prayers to participate in the demonstrations. In preparation for the event, imams in the villages and shantytowns outside the capital mobilize the population in the spirit of jihad against Israel. The monster demonstrations against the "Zionist virus" in Tehran may largely be "bread and circuses" for the masses, but they are not without impact.

No less significant is the fact that the Tehran regime is willing to spend approximately $20 million a year to commemorate Jerusalem Day around the world. In Lebanon, for example, Al-Quds Day symbolizes the struggle of Hezbollah to liberate Jerusalem—the third holiest city of Islam—from Israeli occupation. On Jerusalem Day, the Hezbollah channel Al-Manar broadcasts the festive proceedings worldwide for hours via satellite—using the event as a way to strengthen its political mobilization, its fanatical anti-Israel ideology, and its cult of martyrdom. Hassan Nasrallah always reverentially refers to Ayatollah Khomeini as the creator of the event, which, in Lebanon at least, has become "Hezbollah Day."[108]

Since the 1980s similar, though more modest, gatherings have been held in Germany, usually organized by individuals associated with Hezbollah. The organizers of the Al-Quds Day demonstrations and the operators of Islamist websites engage in ceaseless agitation against Israel's existence and for the "liberation" of Palestine and Jerusalem. Among their slogans one can find such charming lyrics as *"Zionisten sind Faschisten / Töten Kinder und Zivilisten"* (Zionists are fascists / they kill children and civilians) or "Zionists want to buy the world with stolen money."[109] In central London, too, the annual Al-Quds Day offers its share of rallies, street theater, and pro-Islamist and anti-Western campaigns, and attracts demonstrators from the local Iranian Shia community. Among the speakers in October 2005 was Manchester rabbi Ahron Cohen of Neturei Karta (always pathologically eager to embrace any sworn enemy of Israel), British Hamas leader Azzam Tamimi, and the former kidnapped journalist and British convert to Islam, Yvonne Ridley. The Islamic Human Rights Commission (IHRC), which represents a British offshoot of the Khomeinists, has been a driving force of Al-Quds Day in the past. While purporting to distinguish between Zionists and Jews, its worldview, like that of its counterparts in the United States, remains far more attuned to the conspiracy theories of the *Protocols* than to serious criticism of Israel.[110]

• • •

Today there are, undoubtedly, many in Iran itself or in exile who privately deplore the anti-Semitic statements of the Iranian leadership. The protests have sometimes been vocal. For example, in a December 2005 press release from Berlin, a small group calling itself the Iranian Dialogue Circle emphasized the positive interaction between Iranians and Jews in past centuries, going back to biblical times. It invoked the famous case of Cyrus the Great (God's "anointed one" according to Isaiah 45:1), testimony from the Babylonian Talmud about close relations between the two peoples, and the fact that medieval Jewish poets such as Shahin Shirazi and Imrani are a part of classical Persian literature. Moreover, for nearly sixty years before Khomeini the Jews of Iran prospered in the stormiest phase of worldwide anti-Jewish persecution. Even today, although its numbers have drastically dwindled, the twenty-five thousand-strong Iranian Jewry is still the largest Diaspora Jewish community in the Middle East.[111] Though this community is severely restricted in its freedom, in February 2006, the chairman of Iran's Jewish Council, Haroun Yashayaei, took Ahmadinejad to task for saying the Holocaust was a myth, even suggesting that he might be politically prejudiced.[112] Unfortunately, such public criticism is rare and untypical. The fact remains that since 1979 the general position of non-Muslims in Iran under the sharia has drastically declined.[113] Twenty thousand Jews fled the country shortly before the shah's departure and the triumphant return from exile of Ayatollah Khomeini on February 1, 1979. Six weeks later, the honorary president of the Iranian Jewish community, Habib Elghanian, was arrested. A self-made businessman who became a multimillionaire, he was charged by an Islamic revolutionary tribunal with corruption, economic imperialism, and contacts with Israel and Zionism. On May 8, 1979, Elghanian was shot by a firing squad. His execution especially shocked the Jewish community. He was, after all, a renowned industrialist and the communal leader who had enjoyed the closest contacts to Israel during the shah's rule. Suddenly, amid widespread jubilation in the Iranian media, he was being scapegoated as "an enemy of God" and an "alien spy." According to one Iranian radio commentator, Elghanian was

> a disgrace to the Jews in this country. He was an individual who wished to equate Jewry with Zionism. The Iranian people will punish any xenophile and spy. . . . The mass of information he kept sending to Israel, his actions to achieve Israel's designs, the colossal sums of foreign exchange and funds he kept transferring to Israel; these are only samples of his antinational actions; these were acts used to crush our Palestinian brethren.[114]

Under Khomeini there was a noticeable revival of the traditional *najes* obsession, at times affecting Christians as much as Jews. For example, when the Armenian Christian owner of a Coca-Cola plant fled Iran, the Armenian workers were fired "on the grounds that non-Muslims should not touch the bottles or their contents, which may be consumed by Muslims."[115] With Khomeini's return, there was also a marked increase in paranoid conspiracy theories about Jews and Israel. Political scientist Eliz Sanasarian has noted that Jews and Israelis were regularly depicted as interchangeable entities who had penetrated all facets of life. "According to Khomeinist propaganda, Iran was being 'trampled under Jewish boots.' " The Jews, it was retrospectively alleged, had brought the Pahlavi dynasty to power as part of a historically grand design to rule through the destruction of Islam and by clipping the wings of the Shiite clergy. Khomeini's own words were ominously succinct: "Gentlemen, be frightened. They [the Jews] are such monsters."[116] It was undoubtedly Khomeini who provided the inspiration for the new state-sanctioned anti-Semitism, which, for the past three decades, has consistently demonized Israel and vilified "the Jews who want to take over Islamic countries." Shortly after the revolution, Khomeini announced his "final solution" for Israel in the presence of the Syrian foreign minister: "If Muslims got together and each poured one bucket of water on Israel, a flood would wash away Israel."[117]

Anti-Semitic indoctrination penetrated everywhere in Khomeini's Iran, including the national teacher-training programs. A familiar item from the hadith, such as the supposed poisoning of the Prophet by a Jewish woman from Khaibar, not only mutated into a historical fact but became a test of ideological correctness.[118] Jews began to be singled out, harassed, detained, or denied multiple-exit visas. Fear of arrest on trumped-up charges was widespread. Jewish leaders were expected to publicly denounce Israel's policies and had no choice but to comply. In August 1980, with the departure of Chief Rabbi Yedidiya Shofet for Europe, the writing was on the wall.[119] By 1982, ten Iranian Jews had already been executed by the regime. Nearly twenty years later, thirteen Jews in Shiraz and Isfahan were arrested on wildly improbable charges of spying for Israel. The "spies" included a rabbi, a kosher butcher, and a sixteen-year-old pupil living in the remote city of Shiraz, hundreds of miles from Tehran. This was an obvious case of scapegoating religious minorities. Iranian Jewish leaders nonetheless felt compelled to make an abjectly apologetic declaration praising the regime: "The

Islamic Republic of Iran has demonstrated to the world that it has treated the Jewish community and other religious minorities well; the Iranian Jewish community has enjoyed constitutional rights of citizenship, and the arrest and charges against a number of Iranian Jews have nothing to do with their religion."[120]

The espionage affair of 1999 coincided with a noticeable rise in anti-Semitic incitement in the Iranian media, associated with conservative hardliners in the government. It is certainly possible that this hawkish faction instigated the spy trials to embarrass the "liberal" president Khatami and undermine his opening to the United States and Europe.

Pooya Dayanim, the president of the Iranian Jewish Public Affairs Committee, based in Los Angeles, has pointed out that the silence or timid conformism of the Jewish community is not only the result of intimidation or the need to avoid any entanglement in Iranian power struggles. Jews are also contractually bound "as a religious minority living in a Muslim land" to keep quiet about acts of persecution. This discretion is, of course, a one-way street, since Iran's religious leaders and media are completely free to pursue an unrestrained and unrelenting campaign of anti-Jewish defamation. Should Jews themselves have the temerity to publicly protest, then the community as a whole would most likely face collective punishment. Hence, if they wish to survive, Jewish leaders feel they must regularly and publicly express their gratitude for the "protection" that the Shiite religious authorities have accorded them. Dayanim writes:

> This contractual agreement under Shari'a Islamic Law presupposes complete loyalty to the Islamic Regime, in exchange for which the minority community receives second-class, limited privileges in practicing its religion. If the terms of this contract are breached, supposedly even by individual members of the community, the limited privileges of the entire community can be suspended or revoked.[121]

Thus, even when the international media spotlight focused on Iran during the Shiraz espionage trials of 1999, the official representatives of Iranian Jewry remained extraordinarily prudent about what they said. Like the Zoroastrians, the Christian Armenians, and Baha'is, they knew that any deviation from the official line would only produce more hardship.

Though intimidation is widely practiced toward *all* citizens who speak out against the regime, dissent is often more difficult and potentially dangerous for Jews because of general suspicion and their perceived identification with Israel. The threat of retaliation against their families and the Jewish community in Iran has also discouraged many Iranian Jews in the United States from speaking out in a more forthright manner. The result is that discrimination suffered by Jews in employment, education, and everyday life in Iran often goes unreported. Instead, an erroneous impression is created in the Western media about the tolerance shown to Jews in Iran by the regime of the ayatollahs—a myth reinforced by leaders of the Iranian Jewish community who are either afraid for their livelihoods or are in denial. This is especially the case with the older generation in Iran, who often seem resigned to the *dhimmi* humiliations to which Islamic governments have traditionally subjected them. It is, however, true that there are fewer physical assaults on Jewish institutions and individuals in Iran than in Europe, North America, or in the former Communist bloc. The totalitarian theocracy is shrewd enough to understand that any violent attack on Jews in Iran would be politically counterproductive and achieve no useful objective. However, relentless verbal aggression and malevolent propaganda are another matter entirely. Indeed, the top political leadership in Iran has constantly expressed its desire to forcibly remove *all* Jews living in the Israeli state from the Middle East. As former president Hashemi Rafsanjani said in a December 14, 2001, Jerusalem Day sermon at Tehran University: "Jews shall expect to be once again scattered and wandering around the globe the day when this appendix [Israel] is extracted from the region and the Muslim world."[122]

It is difficult to know how many Iranians, preoccupied by economic worries and with preserving a minimum of personal freedom, share the anti-Semitic fervor of their Iranian leaders. Outward conformity does not necessarily imply agreement, though it does involve a degree of complicity and may indicate apathy or indifference. As for Jewish communal leaders in Iran, they almost never protest for fear of the consequences. Maurice Motamed, the lone Jewish representative in the 290-seat Majlis, did, it is true, publicly criticize Ahmadinejad for his Holocaust denial speech. But Motamed, too, is exceedingly careful to toe the government line on Israel and to praise the extent of religious freedom for Iranian Jews.[123] To support eliminationist anti-Zionism has, in effect, become the Jewish entry ticket for admission into contemporary Iranian culture. Motamed told the crowds at the Jerusalem Day rally of 2005 exactly what they wanted to hear: "Real Jews, in concord with Muslims, continue their war against the Zionists and against Israeli crimes. The oppressed people of Palestine living under occupation must feel that believers of all faiths support them."[124]

In other words, the price of Jewish religious freedom in Iran is to ignominiously echo the state-sponsored culture of hatred. Thus Jewish students in Iranian schools find themselves compelled to join the mob chorus, chanting "Death to Israel!" A minority perhaps believes in these wretched slogans. But most Iranian Jews at the beginning of the twenty-first century are reduced to behaving like Marranos. True, there are actively functioning synagogues and Jewish schools. But despite the official "respect" shown to Judaism, the schools are not permitted to freely inculcate Jewish teachings, and they are not even allowed to close on Shabbat. The program of studies is determined by the central government, and the school principals are Muslims. This is a mockery of religious liberty even in the narrowest sense of the term.

Needless to say, no Jew in Iran can hold a sensitive or important position that pertains to national security or politics. There is no room for Jews in the media, law, education, or the humanities—areas that long ago were thoroughly purged and Islamicized. Jewish students who are able to go to university tend to gravitate toward more neutral, scientific fields such as medicine and engineering or, as before the Islamic Revolution, they go into business—especially textiles and gold. Within carefully circumscribed limits they can still make a living, and some Jews have even prospered. In Tehran, where there are some fourteen thousand Jews left, they live in a freer, more cosmopolitan atmosphere despite the clericofascist rule of the ayatollahs and the compulsory mass rallies against Israel or America. In the capital city, there are some four hundred Internet cafés, access to modern consumer goods is much easier, and everyday relations with Muslims are less tense. There are also six to seven thousand Jews still living in Shiraz and another two thousand in Isfahan; the rest are spread out in cities such as Hamadan, Kerman, Kashan, and Yazd. Suspicion and hatred of Jews remain strongest in the villages and small towns where Muslims are more backward, educationally, religiously, and economically. In such settings, everything the Jew touches would still be considered unclean—as in the traditionalist Shiite teaching.

The decline of Iranian Jewry has been dramatic since the days of the shah, when it was still one of the wealthiest Jewish communities in the world. Apart from South Africa, Iranian Jewry by 1970 was the most prosperous Diaspora community anywhere on the continents of Africa and Asia.[125] At that time Persian Jews were overwhelmingly middle-class with an extremely wealthy upper echelon and an impoverished sector, each accounting for about 10 percent of the Jewish population.[126] On the eve of the Islamic Revolution there were approximately eighty thousand Jews still left in Iran, but within a year their number had plummeted to around fifty thousand as panic set in with the fall of the shah.[127] Toward the late 1980s numbers had fallen to around thirty thousand, and they have declined a little more since then. Any improvement in their position seems improbable unless the regime were to collapse, which is unlikely. The Jewish community has adapted fatalistically to its situation and to the partial restoration of the premodern *dhimmi* condition. Once again, as they were a century ago, Jews are virtually outside the protection of the courts and police. For example, their testimony against a Muslim would not be accepted in a court of law and they are automatically barred from any position that might involve exercising authority over Muslims. All government bodies have a discriminatory "Muslim only" policy. Even private companies, influenced by the anti-Semitic media, are reluctant to hire Jews. In the universities, too, Jewish students are periodically subject to harassment or humiliation. Their religion is ridiculed or debased with impunity by certain lecturers, and they are subject to compulsory courses in Islamic ideology, which can be especially painful for Jews. The benign picture of Iranian civility and "a Jewish community living, working and worshipping in relative tranquility"—reported by the *New York Times* correspondent in February 2009— are far from reflecting reality. It does, however, indicate how far the remaining Jews in Iran have internalized the ruling ideology.[128]

Iran's theocracy has raised old anti-Jewish obsessions to new heights with a rhetoric that contains some chilling echoes of Nazi Germany.[129] In the spirit of Khomeini, the necessity of jihad has been expressly linked to the image of the "world-devouring" Jews who control America and must be annihilated before they can destroy Iran and the Islamic Revolution. This is the view not only of the ruling ayatollahs, including Supreme Leader Ali Khamenei, and of President Ahmadinejad but also of the Iranian national security establishment. For *all* of the ruling echelon, eradicating Israel has become a declared foreign policy aim, and acquiring nuclear weapons is central to its implementation. In many ways this is a suicidal outlook, which is made even more dangerous by the Shia martyrdom syndrome. This is what differentiates the Iranian nuclear weapons program from that of all other countries and makes it uniquely threatening. The parallel with Nazi Germany—already embryonically present with Khomeini—is today much more palpable. To quote Matthias Küntzel: "Just as Hitler sought to 'liberate' humanity by murdering the Jews, so Ahmadinejad believes he can 'liberate' humanity by eradicating Israel."[130]

The Jews of Iran are today merely pawns in a much bigger game. They are potential hostages or bargaining chips, much as Jews in Nazi Germany became in the late 1930s. True, the political theology of the Shiite ayatollahs is different from Nazi Germany, and they are careful to avoid street brutalities of the kind practiced by the SA, the Hitler Youth, and other Nazi organizations. There is unlikely to be any Iranian version of *Kristallnacht*. The revived *dhimmi* status of the Jews probably protects them from this kind of popular or paramilitary violence under the Islamic Republic's constitution. But other parallels cannot be ignored. The traditional Shia image of the Jew that has been revived in Iran is one of an impure, despised, and almost subhuman group. This is an anti-Semitic attitude deeply rooted in Muslim religious prejudices that perfectly lends itself to demonization. The "impure Jews" (not to mention the Armenians, Zoroastrians, and Assyrian Christians) have always been inferior in popular Islamic culture, in custom, and in law. The Jews in Persian folklore are usually depicted as cowardly, mean, vulgar, moneygrubbing, deceitful, and conspiratorial. Transplanting these stereotypes to Israel and Zionism has proved all too easy.

Only with the accelerated progress of Western-like modernization in the early 1960s under the rule of the much-hated Shah Mohammed Reza Pahlavi did this stigmatization of Jews and other non-Muslims as impure infidels begin to lose its sting. On balance, these secularizing trends benefited the Jews and other minorities, though Persian nationalist xenophobia, Iranian Aryan contempt for Arabs and Jews, an increased vogue for paranoid conspiracy theories (including the *Protocols*), leftist anti-Zionism, and other modernized forms of prejudice were by-products of the process. But by the 1960s these trends could no longer significantly obstruct the impressive socioeconomic and intellectual advance of Iranian Jewry.[131] The Jews were undergoing "Iranization." One manifestation of this assimilation was their unconditional loyalty toward the shah. This reality would have a fateful effect after 1979, exacerbating Khomeini's religiously driven anti-Semitism with its deep loathing for the shah, the Persian monarchy, Westernization, and rising secularism.[132] The intense dynastic patriotism of the Iranian Jews would suddenly rebound against them with a vengeance.

In Khomeini's paranoid vision of the world, hostile agents were always lurking in every corner, colluding together against him and the Muslim *umma*. They included such mutual enemies as Iraq and Israel (aided by America) who had come together—so he believed—to destroy Iran. As he put it in the early 1980s, the United States was "Israel's mother" and Saddam Hussein of Iraq was "[Menachem] Begin's younger brother" and all three were conspiring against Iran and the Muslims in general.[133] Yet despite Khomeini's boundless hatred of Israel, his visceral anti-Americanism, and his belief in a Jewish conspiracy, he nonetheless tried to reassure the religious minorities, including the Jews, that they would not be persecuted in Iran after the revolution. In May 1979, less than a week after the execution of Habib Elghanian, Khomeini told anxious Iranian Jewish communal leaders who visited him in Qom that Islam would respect minorities: "We distinguish between the Jewish community and the Zionists. Zionism has nothing to do with religion. The Zionists do not follow religion, since their anti-people method is contrary to the revolutionary course laid down by Moses—peace be upon him."[134] These sentiments were echoed by the Jewish delegate to the committee preparing the new Islamic constitution of Iran, Aziz Daneshrad, himself a prime exemplar of Khomeini's propaganda line professing brotherhood and cordiality on an anti-Zionist basis. Daneshrad told other delegates at the August 1979 Assembly of Experts in Tehran: "The Israeli government is a government of no religion and its foundation is not based on religion but on the politics of usurpation which is hated by all believing Jews."[135]

Despite this theoretical differentiation of Jews from Zionists, the dividing line is largely fictitious, and Iranian Jewry has remained in a precarious situation for the past three decades. In the wake of the espionage trial in 2000, Jews suffered vandalism and boycotts of their businesses. Though the ten Jews found guilty of illegal contacts with Israel were released as a result of international pressure in 2003, they remain on probation. The anti-Semitic propaganda masquerading as anti-Zionism in the media and the educational system has never been halted and shapes the little that Iranians know today about their Jewish neighbors. In 2004, the TV station Sahar I broadcast a weekly series *Zahra's Blue Eyes* (also called *For You, Palestine*) depicting the removal of blue eyes from young Palestinians in order to be implanted into Jewish children as Israeli governmental policy. These and other totally false messages about Jews are regularly conveyed in TV programs, through caricatures, and in print, creating a generalized association of Jewry with evil. Ironically, given Iran's official championing of the Palestinian Arabs, its own treatment of the indigenous Ahwazi Arab minority in Khuzestan has amounted to a form of ethnic cleansing.[136] Iranian government attitudes toward homosexuality are no less revealing. The regime still punishes and even executes homosexuals (including underage boys), adulterers, and other perceived "moral criminals."[137] The repression of women who do not conform to the predominant puritanical code or behave in an "immodest" manner is part of the same syndrome. Nevertheless, young Iranian women are not so easily coerced, and dress in a modern manner— at least in private. They are also far more visible in the workplace than women in most Arab countries.

Particularly chilling is the mullahs' hatred for Iran's largest religious minority, the Baha'is, who have been savagely brutalized for well over a century. This independent faith, which originated as a "heretical" and dissident messianic sect in Shia Islam and today has more than six million members worldwide, teaches the oneness of humanity, world peace, the underlying unity of the great religions, social reform, sexual equality, and the need to eliminate prejudice. Such pacifist universalism is reason enough for Baha'i students in Iranian schools to be harassed, vilified, and abused. Even the dead are not spared. Under direct orders from President Ahmadinejad (a long-standing hater of the Baha'is), the bulldozing of Baha'i cemeteries across Iran began in October 2007.[138] Under the Khomeini regime, Revolutionary Guardsmen had destroyed the House of the Bab in Shiraz, one of the holiest sites in the Baha'i world. The childhood residence of Baha'u'llah (founder of the faith) in Takur was also swiftly demolished soon after the Islamic Revolution. After the death of this messianic figure (who had declared in 1860 that he was the divine manifestation of God), Bahaism had gradually spread from Iran and the Third World to Europe and North America.[139] The Baha'is believe that God sent successive spiritual leaders to humanity, each with an increasingly sophisticated religious message. This idea of progressive revelation is, of course, fundamentally in opposition to the Muslim dogma of Muhammad as the *final* prophet and of Islam as the ultimate and the only *complete* divine revelation.

Persecution of the Baha'is in Iran began in the mid-nineteenth century and never stopped except during a brief period of Pahlavi rule. As in the case of the Jews, the perception of Baha'is as enjoying a "privileged status" under Mohammad Reza Shah would later boomerang against them. Their missionizing zeal, wealth, and education further exacerbated the widespread resentment toward them among the Muslim masses. Islamic groups were at the forefront of this popular anger, and repeated efforts were made to harass the Baha'is. At the time of Khomeini's arrival in power, they probably numbered around three hundred thousand. For the Shiite clergy and the majority Shia Muslim community, Bahaism had come to symbolize pro-monarchism, apostasy from Islam, association with Israel and the West, and secular modernity.[140] The accusations against them were not only anti-Semitic in the classic sense but made worse by their status as apostates. Even more unforgivable were their efforts to proselytize to Muslims— something the Jews had scrupulously avoided. It was not only the mullahs who loathed them; many secular Iranian nationalists, liberals, and left-wing anti-imperialists condemned the Baha'is as an unpatriotic, alien middle-man minority group. They were labeled friends of the shah, agents of Zionism, and creatures of Anglo-American imperialism.[141] Their universalist message, ironically enough, placed them even more squarely in the Western colonialist camp—at least in the eyes of the clerical Right, the nationalists, and the Communist Left.

The Khomeinist revolution resulted in the deliberate targeting and murder of many Baha'i leaders. Execution rates mounted, and by the end of 1984 Baha'i sources estimated that 177 of their representatives or members had been deliberately killed.[142] The purists of Shiite Islam demonized the Baha'is, in the words of the head of the Revolutionary Court of Shiraz in 1983, as "the instruments of Satan and followers of the Devil and of the Superpowers and their agents."[143] Terms such as "purification" were freely used in justifying draconian anti-Baha'i actions. Repeated reference was made to the British having fostered Bahaism in nineteenth-century Iran for colonialist reasons, and to the Baha'is as secret followers of Zionism. The Baha'i community, as one of its most prominent spokesmen in North America remarked, proved to be the perfect scapegoat for diverting public attention from the economic, social, and political problems of various Iranian regimes. They were "an easy target because of the senseless hostility and prejudice inculcated in the public by generations of ecclesiastical propaganda."[144] Like the Jews, Baha'is were natural targets for demagogic charges of profiteering and acting as "foreign agents." More integrated than the Jewish minority, they were also more frequently labeled as the "enemy within." Lacking the minimal safety net of being defined (like Jews and Christians) as Ahl al-Kitab (People of the Book)—religious minorities who had, at least, a divine book of revelation—Baha'is were not even *dhimmis* at all. As apostates they deserved death for betraying Islam.[145]

But the hatred of the Shia fundamentalists for the heretical followers of Bahaism was, in practice, extended to the Jews, since many of them had actively associated with Baha'is in business and professional pursuits. Moreover, in Muslim eyes, both groups were *transnational middlemen* minorities with strong links to the West and Israel. Haifa, for example, is a major world center of Bahaism today. Moreover, some Iranian Jews had been attracted by the universalist and humanitarian dimensions of Bahaism, and converted to the faith. This strengthened the link between Jews and Baha'is in the popular mind. It was not by chance that during the bloody demonstrations in Tehran on "Black Friday" (September 8, 1978) crowds ominously chanted "Death to the Jews and Baha'is."

Everyday Jewish life in Iran today is rife with tragic paradoxes. There is still an ongoing patriotic identification of many Jews with Persia despite Ahmadinejad's relentless attacks on Israel and his shocking insults to the Jewish memory of the Holocaust. In a fiery speech on February 11, 2006, the twenty-seventh anniversary of the revolution, the Iranian president declared:

> For more than 60 years, the usurper Zionist regime has been able to blackmail all Western countries, murdering women and children, demolishing the houses of defenseless people and making them refugees, and justifying its crimes in the occupied territories. . . . We did suggest that if you are honest, you will allow a group of impartial and fair researchers to come to Europe and talk to people, study the documents and inform the world about the result of their research on the myth of the Holocaust.[146]

Holocaust denial had steadily been gaining prominence in the Iranian media for several months before this speech. Mehr News Agency (Iran's semiofficial voice) had published interviews with some of the most notorious negationists of the Holocaust in the West, and the Iranian Foreign Ministry had announced its plans to hold an international conference in Tehran to "assess" the Holocaust. This was the alarming background to the previously mentioned letter sent to Ahmadinejad by Haroun Yeshayaei, the outgoing chairman of the Jewish Central Committee of Tehran. The letter gave voice to growing fears within the normally quiescent Iranian Jewish community. "Challenging one of the most obvious and saddening events of 20th-century humanity," Yeshayaei noted, "has created astonishment among the people of the world and spread fear and anxiety among the small Jewish community of Iran."[147]

Clearly there was uneasiness at the escalating anti-Semitic rhetoric of a president who had not hesitated to purge his political opponents and critics in various sectors of society. At the same time, a top Iranian Jewish community leader swiftly denounced the reported immigration of forty Persian Jews to Israel as "misinformation." Cianak Morsathegh, who heads the Tehran Jewish Committee, denied that the immigrants were even from his country, angrily complaining about the Israeli "campaign of lies against Iran and its Jewish community." Morsathegh insisted that Jews in Iran are in no danger. There were, he said, twenty synagogues, eight kosher butchers, five schools, four youth organizations, and two restaurants serving Jewish needs in Tehran alone. It was "sheer lies" to suggest that Jews were afraid to wear a skullcap on the streets of Iran. Morsathegh emphatically added: "We are one of the oldest communities in Iran. We are free to practice our religion. Antisemitism is a Western phenomenon but Jews have never been in danger in Iran. . . . We are Iranian Jews and are proud of our nationality. No amount of money can encourage us to give up Iran. Our nationality is not up for sale."[148] Similarly reassuring and equally unreal statements were made by German Jewish spokesmen in the early days of the Hitler regime and by Soviet Jewish representatives under Stalin and his heirs. So, too, one could catalog the utterances of various other religious minorities made under the duress of persecutory regimes. They have to be treated with all due skepticism.

From the perspective of Jewish history, Iranian Jewry, the oldest surviving community of the Diaspora, finds itself suspended between two contradictory archetypes. The benevolent image of Cyrus the Great, founder of the ancient Persian Empire, confronts the legend of Haman, the genocidal anti-Semite whose plot to eradicate the Jews more than two thousand years ago (recorded in the Book of Esther) notoriously failed. Cyrus was the model in antiquity of multicultural tolerance and respect for the traditions of Persia's myriad nationalities. He was also the first "Gentile Zionist," righting the wrongs caused by the destruction of Solomon's Temple and the Babylonian exile. In the Bible, Cyrus declares: "All the kingdoms of the earth the Lord, the God of Heaven has given me and he has also charged me to build him a house in Jerusalem, which is Judah." In accordance with this divine command, Cyrus gave the Jews the chance to return to Jerusalem to rebuild their temple. His actions doubtless reflected the trust and tolerance that Jews had enjoyed in the Persia of antiquity—a tradition revived to some extent by the Pahlavi dynasty, which venerated this ancient heritage. Mohammed Reza Shah, who saw himself as the heir of Cyrus, granted extensive autonomy to the Jews, recognized Israel, and even developed close military, technical, and commercial relations with the Jewish state. Under his rule, Israel and Iran were allies, equally opposed to Arab nationalist domination of the Middle East, sharing common strategic and geopolitical interests. Hence the shah did not acquiesce in the Arab oil boycott of 1973; he strongly opposed Nasserist Pan-Arabism just as he fought fiercely against Soviet Communism. He ruthlessly suppressed Iran's Islamist clerics, led by Khomeini, who hated his Westernizing program—mostly because it emancipated non-Muslim minorities as well as Iranian women. The shah's fall—precipitated by his own repressiveness and megalomania—turned out to be a disaster for all the minorities, as well as for Iran's future.

Today the heirs of Haman are alive and well, increasingly powerful, and currently ruling in Tehran. Their geopolitical ambitions are even more far-reaching than those of the ancient Persians or the last shah. Moreover, their attitude toward the Jews is founded on a highly toxic teaching of contempt. Its more distant foundations lay in the *dhimma* pact universally imposed by the rulers of all Muslim states on their non-Muslim subjects. The Arab Muslim victory over Persia in the seventh century had already led to second-class citizenship for all of Persia's minorities—Jews, Christians, and Zoroastrians. Though distinct from anti-Semitism, *dhimmitude* did establish an inferior status for Jews.[149] The degrading treatment of Jews and other non-Muslim minorities became even more pronounced after the Safavid dynasty took power in the sixteenth century and imposed its hard-line Shiite Islam on Persia—a conquest that involved the forcible conversion of the country's original Sunni Muslim majority.

Persian Shiism not only brought with it the perception of the Jews and other non-Muslim minorities as ritually "impure," but also blood libels, pogroms, and the outbreaks of violence described at the beginning of this chapter. Indeed, the shadow of Haman has been hanging over modern Persian Jewry for most of the past few centuries. Salvation came briefly in the shape of Reza Pahlavi, son of a military officer, who had inaugurated a new era in Persian and Jewish history. For the first time in more than a millennium, an Iranian ruler reached out to the Jews of his country, banned forced conversions, sapped the authority of the Shia clergy, and rejected the idea of ritual uncleanness. Though fascinated by Nazi Germany and committed to the Aryan cult of Iran, Reza Shah stopped short of persecuting Jews. He assured the Nazis that his Jewish subjects were fully assimilated Iranians. The Germans, for their part, seemed willing to acquiesce, even turning a blind eye to the European Jewish refugees using Iran as an escape route during World War II. Reza Shah's son followed in his footsteps, permitting the expelled and persecuted Iraqi Jews free passage through Iran in 1950–51 to the new State of Israel. Despite internal pressure from the Shiite clergy, the shah did not abandon the legacy of Cyrus when it came to the Jews or other non-Muslim religious minorities.

Khomeini's Islamic Revolution of 1979 decisively restored the pendulum to the side of Haman. For almost a decade Israeli decision-makers were extraordinarily reluctant to recognize this fact, treating Khomeini's Iran as a potential ally and Saddam's Iraq as the greater strategic threat. By 1990, with the fading of the Cold War, Israel belatedly began to regard Iran as a growing threat to its future security and even to its existence. Iranian public rhetoric toward Israel became ever more extreme. The Jewish state could hardly ignore its geopolitical implications after the end of the Iran-Iraq War. Iran's enormous oil wealth, technical capacities, encouragement of terror, and total negation of Israel were alarming signals. They were greatly compounded by rising Shiite messianism and the barely disguised nuclear ambitions of the ayatollahs. Iran's gross human rights violations, its potential to dominate the Persian Gulf, its hostility to America, and its determination to wreck stability in the notoriously volatile Middle East were further causes for grave concern.

Khomeini's ideology, with its hatred of the West, liberalism, and democracy, left no room for negotiation. Thirty years after his Islamic revolution the collision course with the West and calls for Israel's destruction have continued despite President Obama's appeal to Iran to "unclench its fist." Though America has abandoned its "axis of evil" rhetoric about Iran, there are no signs yet of any major diplomatic breakthrough. Whoever wins the June 2009 presidential elections in Iran will surely remain committed to developing nuclear weapons. This was the solemn legacy of Ayatollah Khomeini, driven by the traumatic experience of the eight-year war with Saddam Hussein to ensure a nuclearized Iran. The hard-line conservatives who rule Iran have no intention of surrendering to American or European demands that they halt their nuclear program, abandon their support for radical terrorist movements, accept the legitimacy of Israel, or give up on their dream of exporting Shiite revolutionary principles to the Islamic world.[150]

Since 2005 the sense of foreboding has been heightened by the ascendancy of Mahmoud Ahmadinejad. A civil engineer from a modest background, he was socialized in the 1980s into the ethos of the Iranian Revolutionary Guards. There is no doubt that Ahmadinejad is a convinced anti-Semite whose genocidal threats against Israel have a significance far beyond the borders of Iran. His combative demagogy and anti-Jewish vitriol mix together with Islamist megalomania, prophecy, and apocalyptic politics in ways that uncomfortably recall the darker days of the twentieth century. His eliminationist ideology can hardly be explained by economic factors, the search for scapegoats, or publicity-seeking maneuvers designed to deflect attention from the failures of the revolution.

Ahmadinejad seems more coldly calculating, modern, and Machiavellian in his outlook than Khomeini. The Iranian president uses anti-Semitism as a political and a religious weapon in his campaign to destroy Israel, convinced that this step is the necessary prologue to fulfilling the Shiite messianic destiny. The threat to annihilate the Jews also serves as a battering ram against the United States, the Western democracies, and the specter of secular modernity. Ahmadinejad doubtless understands that an Iranian nuclear bomb could turn Khomeini's wrath into the hard rain of the apocalypse—a suicidal consummation that he and other Iranian leaders appear keen to bring about.

TWENTY-FIVE

Ahmadinejad: The Last Jihad

Ayatollah Khomeini bequeathed to his successors a revolutionary state with a global agenda that included overthrowing the international system, destroying American hegemony in the Middle East, and terminating the existence of the Israeli state. In the early 1980s Iran had begun to export its pan-Islamic ideology to Lebanon and the Shiite populations of the Gulf states.[1] Khomeini's dualistic division of the world into oppressors and oppressed—good and evil forces locked in an apocalyptic battle against one another—was the most original millenarianist feature of this Pan-Islamism.[2] In effect it fused together the Koran with highly selective aspects of Marxist theory. Unlike the classic Sunni dichotomy between *dar al-Islam* and *dar al-harb,* which sweepingly juxtaposed Muslims against non-Muslims, the Shiite concept appealed, potentially, to all the oppressed, irrespective of their religious identity. The oppressed included the economically deprived Third World peoples (evoked in the 1960s by Frantz Fanon's category of the "wretched of the earth"), as well as the culturally or politically repressed masses.[3] The transnational class dimension of exploitation made the category more universal, applying to poor non-Muslims (especially in the non-Western world) as well as to impoverished Muslims. In a number of his speeches Khomeini emphasized that "Islam originates from the masses, not from the rich."[4] The Prophet himself and Shia Islam founder Husayn ibn 'Ali were said to have glorified the poor and the deprived.[5] Thus exploitation and poverty became Islamic virtues in the official doctrine of the Iranian Republic and its offshoots, such as the Lebanese Shiite Hezbollah.[6]

The Islamic state that Khomeini constructed was based on a sharia constitution, Islamic legislation, and the rule of the *wali al-faqih* (leader jurisprudent).[7] The religious erudition of experts in Islamic jurisprudence entitled them—according to Khomeini—to inherit the religious and political authority of the Prophet and the imams in the early history of Islam.[8] Their political authority ultimately derived from the Hidden Imam—the messianic core doctrine of Shiite Islam. According to this concept the Mahdi ("the one guided by Allah along the true path") is the twelfth and last of the Shiite imams, believed to have been *ghayba* (in hiding) since 874 C.E. His eventual return would institute the reign of justice within a pan-Islamic Mahdist state that would then establish the rule of Islam throughout the whole world. In the meantime, however, Khomeini had concluded that the Hidden Imam's *political* authority must devolve to the *fuqaha* (jurisprudents) and the ulema, or clergy, who had the sovereign right to wield power. In effect Khomeini himself as the *wali al-faqih,* and his successors were to act as the deputies of the twelfth imam; their rule would continue indefinitely until his *raj'a* (return).[9] The *faqih* had hegemony over the executive, judicial, and legislative branches of government. His directives were supposedly based on divine law and the general good—turning him into a kind of dynamic Shiite version of the Platonic philosopher-king.[10]

Khomeini's innovative political theory effectively gave him the status of a divinely ordained and inspired ruler of the Islamic *umma* in Iran and among Shiite Muslims in general. He was the designated deputy of the Hidden Imam, "the sacred man," the "descendant of the Prophet" and "the renewer of religion [*mujaddid al-din*] in this era"—titles that reflected the widespread Shiite veneration for his unique revolutionary role.[11] Although his successor Ali Khamenei did not command such a wide following, his political authority and position as *faqih* and *wali amr al-Muslimin* (legal guardian of the Muslims) is no less sacrosanct.

From the outset Khomeini's Islamic Republic had championed the export of the Islamic Revolution to Afghanistan, Lebanon, and Palestine as well as the transformation of ordinary Muslims into jihadi fighters who were carriers of a universal Islamic message.[12] Khomeini always insisted on the interchangeability of the Iranian state and the Islamic Revolution, whose teachings were to spread to every corner of the Muslim world. Even before the hegemonic ambitions of a nuclear-armed Iran began to haunt the sleep of the more moderate Arab leaders (and especially of Iran's Gulf neighbors), the Khomeinist revolutionary jihad had become a source of alarm in the region. Those fears have been exacerbated by the successes of such Iranian proxies as Hezbollah in Lebanon and Hamas in Gaza, and by the disintegration of post-Saddam Iraq—events that helped to bring Arab leaders to the Annapolis, Maryland, Middle East conference in December 2007. Their apparent support for a reinvigorated Israeli-Palestinian peace process has derived in part from the misplaced belief that resolving the Palestine conflict would halt the Iranian momentum and the drive of the ayatollahs for nuclear weapons.[13]

Ironically, the diplomatic effort led by the U.S. government was seriously undercut by the findings in the American National Intelligence Estimate issued shortly thereafter, bizarrely concluding that Iran had halted its nuclear weapons program in the fall of 2003. This manifestly misleading conclusion convinced the Gulf Arabs to invite President Ahmadinejad to their annual summit in Qatar; it seemed to suggest American paralysis in the face of Iranian provocation; it reduced the chances of effective U.S. pressure on Russia, China, and the European Union to impose severe sanctions on Iran; and it signaled to the Iranian leadership that it could proceed with its nuclear program without fearing a massive military response. Not surprisingly President Ahmadinejad called the NIE report a "fatal blow" to Iran's enemies.[14] Along with the rest of the leadership, he is completely committed to establishing Iranian hegemony in the Gulf and the Middle East. Becoming a nuclear power offers the ideal means for Iran to promote its hard-line Islamist ideology, using the Shiite Muslim awakening to create a radical arc of insurgency from the Persian Gulf to the Mediterranean. The murder, mayhem, and turmoil in Iraq greatly aided this Iranian ambition. Hezbollah's war against Israel in the summer of 2006 and the Hamas electoral victory in Gaza were important steps along the road to future regional dominance despite the fierce response of the Jewish state.

Western and Israeli decision makers have not appeared to internalize the jihadist and eschatological dimensions of Iranian policy—the full implications of its underlying ideology, aspirations, and values. Cost-benefit rationalizations of Iranian moves are of little help in this endeavor, and attempts to appease Iran are more likely to accelerate the radical Shiite and Islamist resurgence than to dampen its expectations. There is little willingness to envisage the possibility that some Iranian leaders might actually seek to *hasten* the coming of the Mahdi (even at the cost of fomenting Armageddon),[15] or that Ahmadinejad, in declaring on June 3, 2007, that "the countdown button for the destruction of the Zionist regime has been pressed," might be acting logically in the framework of his own radical Shiite eschatology.

There is, however, no doubt that Shiite messianism has profoundly shaped Ahmadinejad's apocalyptic worldview and the second Islamic revolution that has been instituted in the past four years.[16] Unlike his predecessors, Ahmadinejad feels positively driven by a divinely inspired mission to *speed up* the reappearance of the Hidden Imam.[17] This Mahdist commitment, which is central to his personality and politics, largely derives from his spiritual mentor Ayatollah Muhammad Taqi Mezbah-Yazdi, head of the Hojatieh—a semi-clandestine religious group that seeks to create the appropriate conditions for the Mahdi's return. According to Yazdi, extraordinary human efforts can indeed accelerate catastrophic events. They are able to produce a Shiite equivalent to the biblical war of Gog and Magog that will induce the reappearance of the Islamic Messiah. Yazdi believes that the Mahdi will shortly resurface to bring salvation to Muslims in their last jihad against the "Great Satan" and its smaller brother.

In contrast to Khomeini, who kept the Mahdists on a tight leash, Ahmadinejad has always actively encouraged them. On December 19, 2006, speaking in Kermanshah, he said: "Let me enlighten all Christians that hardship, threats, and wars will come to an end soon, and let there be no doubt that in the not-too-distant future the Prophet Jesus will rise again alongside the Mahdi to put an end to injustice in the world."[18] As mayor of Tehran, he ordered the construction of a large boulevard in the capital city to prepare for the Hidden Imam's return. There have also been reports of a direct train link from Tehran to the elegant Jamkaran Mosque (sixty-five miles south of the capital), in the deserts of central Iran, which is closely associated with the Mahdists.[19] Soon after becoming Iran's president, Ahmadinejad allocated $17 million to this mosque, which is visited by millions of pilgrims every year. He even claimed to friends that he had decided to run for the presidency in 2005 only after a secret meeting with the Mahdi: The agreed objective was apparently to advance the "clash of civilizations" as a step on the road to Armageddon. The Islamic Republic of Iran's own broadcasting website confirms that the world is now in its "last days." According to this forecast, the Mahdi will first appear in Mecca, and then in Medina. He will conquer the Arabian peninsula, Syria, and Iraq, and destroy Israel. He will then set up a world government based in Iraq. The

Mahdi, a divinely guided prophetic teacher who stands at the head of the forces of righteousness, will battle successfully with the "evil powers" in the last jihad.

Israel and America are the major incarnations of the satanic forces that spread immorality, degeneracy, corruption, and injustice that will have to be totally eliminated.[20] For a true believer like Ahmadinejad, this victory is a guaranteed article of faith embodied in Khomeini's Islamic Revolution— the symbol of an inexorable and irresistible wave of the future.[21] In this triumphalist context, it goes without saying that the "fake regime" of Israel will be forcibly removed. A similar fate will overtake the corrupt Sunni Arab rulers and rival religious poles of attraction such as Wahhabite Saudi Arabia, which "illegitimately" controls the holy places of Mecca and Medina. Indeed, the reappearance of the Hidden Imam means that the truth of Shiite Islam will be acknowledged by the whole world, including the Sunni Arabs. This would correct the historic injustice of Shiite persecution by the Sunni majority through the ages. Ahmadinejad's Mahdist vision of events is, however, much more *future-oriented* than that of the Sunni fundamentalists, who prefer to hark back to a Muslim golden age and the proven ways of the Prophet.[22] When he addressed the United Nations in September 2005, the Iranian president astounded the General Assembly by concluding his speech with a special prayer for the Mahdi's reappearance.[23] He later told friends that he had felt a halo around his head as he spoke and that the Hidden Imam had even whispered in his ears what he should say to the assembled world leaders. According to the Iranian president his audience did not blink for almost thirty minutes, as if spellbound by his words.

Belief in the return of the Hidden Imam as preached today in Iran is a far cry from traditional Shia quietism. From the first days of the 1979 Iranian Revolution the myth was invested with a new activist and political meaning. Muslims were henceforth expected to fight and be willing to sacrifice their lives to ensure the Mahdi's return. Moreover, Shiite martyrdom has, in recent years, acquired a renewed jihadist content linked to salvationist messianism more than pragmatic politics. It is significant, for example, that in one of his first TV interviews after his election as president, Ahmadinejad enthusiastically praised suicide bombers. "Is there an art that is more beautiful," he asked, "more divine, more eternal than the art of the martyr's death?"[24] Such an Islamofascist aestheticization of politics, mixed with end-time symbolism and the Shiite glorification of martyrdom, is no mere idiosyncrasy, but a highly combustible combination. The Iranian president finances, for example, a research institute in Tehran whose sole purpose is to study, and if possible to bring about, the rapid return of the Hidden Imam. At a theology conference in November 2005, the president of Iran defined this search as "the most important task of the revolution." This messianism, along with the anti-Semitism that pervades his entire world-view, is a core component of Ahmadinejad's governing philosophy. Among the staunchest believers in the imminent return of the Mahdi was the controversial Iranian philosopher Ahmad Fardid, who died in 1994 but whose legacy looms large in present-day Iran. An Islamic admirer of the proto-Nazi German philosopher Martin Heidegger, Fardid scorned Western decadence and empty talk about human rights. His paranoid anti-Semitism and belief in the Jewish-Zionist world conspiracy appear to have influenced Ahmadinejad and his inner circle.[25]

The messianic age as envisaged by the Iranian president and annunciated on his government's website sketches out a world of unparalleled happiness—liberated from corruption, war, rebellion, liberal democratic civilization, and Zionism. With "the appearance of the Imam of the Age" (the direct descendant of the Prophet) justice, equality, and freedom will finally shine forth; the Dajjal will be overthrown; the Prophet Jesus will come down from heaven, acting as the Mahdi's lieutenant in the struggle against oppression; and Jerusalem will be totally freed from the Zionists. Nothing will be able to withstand the universal government of the Mahdi once all of Arabia and Iraq submit to him. Not even "global arrogance" (the West headed by America), with all its economic and military might, will be able to prevail against his divine edicts.[26]

As in the visions of fundamentalist Christianity, the "second coming" of the Mahdi will involve trials, tribulations, death, and destruction. This is a prospect made all the more alarming by Iran's hell-bent race to acquire nuclear weapons—to be placed on the missiles that are already paraded through Tehran's streets adorned with banners reading "Israel must be wiped off the map." Ahmadinejad himself has repeatedly hammered home this message. On November 13, 2006, he stated that "Israel is destined for destruction and will soon disappear." At his Tehran Holocaust denial conference a month later he prophesied: "Thanks to people's wishes and God's will the trend for the existence of the Zionist regime is downwards and this is what God has promised and what all nations want. . . . Just as the Soviet

Union was wiped out and today does not exist, so will the Zionist regime soon be wiped out."

On February 28, 2007, the Iranian president informed a meeting of Sudanese Islamic scholars in Khartoum that "the Zionists are the true manifestation of Satan"—deploring the fact that the materialist Western democracies had closed their eyes to Zionist "crimes." Less than a month later on Iranian TV, Ahmadinejad contrasted the humane values of "the great nation of Iran" to the inhuman "Zionist racists" who were the major problem facing the modern world today: "They [the Zionists] have access to global power and media centers and seek to use this access to keep the world in a state of hardship, poverty and grudge, to strengthen their rule." Four months earlier, in a letter "to the American people," he rhetorically asked if the U.S. administration did not support "the infamous aggressors" because "they [the Jews] have imposed themselves on a substantial portion of the banking, financial, cultural and media sectors?"[27] On June 3, 2007, in a speech quoted by the Fars News Agency, Ahmadinejad's proclamation was more chillingly direct: "By God's will, we will witness the destruction of this regime in the near future."[28]

There is a compulsive annihilationist dimension to these declarations. On October 26, 2005, quoting Ayatollah Khomeini, Ahmadinejad bluntly told Al-Jazeera that "Israel must be wiped off the map."[29] On August 2, 2006, he added that Israelis "should know they are reaching the last days of their lives." This recalled his April 2006 reference to Israel as a "rotten, dried tree" that would collapse in "one storm"; and the confident assurance that "like it or not, the Zionist regime is on the road to being eliminated."[30] A few months later, as the Israel-Hezbollah confrontation in Lebanon unfolded, Ahmadinejad's own "final solution" was succinctly summarized as "the elimination of the Zionist regime."[31] Iran's furnishing of two billion dollars' worth of weaponry and military training to Hamas and Hezbollah was an unmistakable indicator of his true intentions. As the Iran Revolutionary Guards Corps spokesman declared on November 1, 2005: "The wrath of the Palestinians will undoubtedly lead to the total destruction of Israel and before long we shall witness a world without the illegitimate regime of Israel."[32]

Purported moderates and leading members of the so-called reformist faction in the Iranian parliament have made similar pronouncements. At the International Conference on the Palestinian Intifada in Tehran (April

2001), President Khatami called for establishing an "international tribunal to try Israeli leaders as war criminals." The secretary-general of the conference, Ali Akbar Mohtashemi (who inspired the creation of Hezbollah in 1982) graphically described Israel as a "knife in the heart of the Islamic world" and described any attempt to coexist with it as equivalent to "accepting a slow death."[33] The elimination of Israel is clearly a *consensual* goal for the regime, uniting radicals and moderates, ideologues and pragmatists, Persian imperial nationalists and Shia fanatics bent on dominating the Gulf and the Middle East as a whole.[34] The anti-Israel motivation feeds into Iran's regional power ambitions, its intense hatred of America, its anti-Semitism, its Islamic fanaticism, its solidarity with the Palestinians, and its ideology of apocalyptic Shiism. There is no internal debate over its justification.[35] Israel cannot, therefore, let its guard down based on speculations as to whether Iran is only one or three years away from having the bomb. As even the liberal *Haaretz* put it after the American NIE report: "While other nations can amuse themselves by mulling their economic interests with Iran, wondering whether sanctions serve their agenda, Israel cannot enjoy such considerations as long as the current Iranian regime is in power."[36]

For some time Ahmadinejad has been beating the nationalist drum and taking up the nuclear issue on every possible occasion while continuously threatening the State of Israel with annihilation. At the same time, he has emphasized since the summer of 2008 (before the great financial meltdown) that the American economy was on the verge of collapse and with it the liberal-democratic model of market-based capitalist societies. Moreover, according to Iranian-born journalist Amir Taheri, he was impressed by the 2005 riots in France, "where the extreme Left provided the leadership, but the Muslim sub-proletariat much of the muscle in the streets."[37] Belief in the decline of the liberal-democratic West only reinforces the Iranian leadership's conviction that it can lead Muslims to a new, puritanical version of modernity transformed under the aegis of Shia Islam. In this context the anticipated disappearance of Israel heralds the doom of a Western civilization collapsing under the weight of its own arrogance, godlessness, and degeneracy. Allah himself has determined these historical processes and commanded Iran to be armed with nuclear weapons in order to impose Shiite Islam upon the entire world. The divine will operates not only through the Koran and the hadith but also through the interpretations of the *velayet-e faqih* (the mandate of the jurist)—who makes the crucial political decisions. Since Israel was established in violation of Allah's wishes and commands, it necessarily follows that it must be eliminated, along with any Western presence in Palestine or the Middle East.

On the eve of a visit to Turkey in mid-August 2008, Ahmadinejad gave an interview to Turkish TV that further clarified this outlook and his general view of the Zionist regime.

> Of course this regime is for us an illegitimate regime. That is, it has no legitimacy. In essence it is illegitimate. They [the Zionists] left a few million Palestinians homeless and brought people from all kinds of places, brought them with all sorts of slogans and lies and created a fake country. . . . The best way is for them [the Israelis] to free and return all the Palestinians lands and to go away.

He also claimed, in response to the Turkish interviewer, that his underlying attitude was shared by all the peoples of the region—including the Turks, Iraqis, Syrians, Saudis, Egyptians, Jordanians, Palestinians, and Lebanese—since "these are the true words [of Allah]." The Zionist regime, he insisted, was based solely on lies, exploitation, and great cruelty, on killing and murdering innocent Palestinians. "These people [the Israelis] don't belong to this region. They must go!" Ahmadinejad's "humane solution" was to hold a referendum among the Palestinians by means of which "this regime [Israel] will be automatically eliminated"; a "free referendum," in the eyes of the Iranian president, was evidently one in which Israelis would not participate, since their presence in the region was, by definition, illegal. Ahmadinejad also warned Western nations that they had "nothing to gain, nothing to benefit from this [Zionist] regime." Israel was like "an old car, the expense was more than its worth," the engine had stopped running. It had nothing to offer the region but dictatorship and murder. America, in particular, he declared, must cease all support for Israel, both for its own sake and for that of the Middle East.[38] Indeed, this has become a central message of the Iranian leadership to the United States. The normalization of America's relations with Iran will only take place on Iranian terms—requiring a definitive exit of the United States from the Middle East and its complete abandonment of Israel. The repeated characterizations of the "Zionist régime" as a "rotten tree" and a "house of straw" are partly designed to expedite that outcome by appealing to a Western cost-benefit analysis of the political equation.[39]

Contemporary Iran cannot be understood as a normal status quo power. It remains loyal to Khomeini's legacy and determined to fulfill its spiritual and political destiny as the vanguard of militant Islam, even though the Shiites make up no more than 15 percent of the world's Muslims.[40] Such militancy has led Iran to transform the nature of the Arab-Israel conflict into part of its bid for hegemony in the post-Saddam Middle East. In some ways, it is even more eager than the secular Arab states of the 1950s and 1960s to place the destruction of Israel at the very center of its policy. Its *revolutionary* Islamism places it in open conflict with the Saudis, who see Iran as a dangerously subversive rival seeking to stir up the large Shia minority in the Saudi Arabian kingdom. A similar threat exists in the other Gulf states, some of whom host American bases.[41] As for Lebanon's shaky government, it has increasingly come under the grip of the Shiite Hezbollah, backed by Iran and Syria. Egypt, for its part, has never forgiven Iran's leaders for naming a prominent Tehran street after one of the assassins of Egyptian president Anwar al-Sadat. It currently regards Iran as its most dangerous enemy and has even accused it and Hezbollah of conspiring to overthrow Mubarak's government.[42]

More generally, Sunni Arab anxiety over the Shiite threat and the so-called Shiite Crescent (*al-hilal al-shi'i*) has been steadily growing in recent years. The bloodbath in Iraq and the rise of its majority Shia community (60 percent of the total population) to political prominence, the growing influence of Lebanon's Shiites (already 40 percent of the population), and, above all, Iranian ambitions have contributed to this sense of alarm at Shiite power. Many Sunnis still regard Arab Shias as if they were ethnic Persians, more loyal to Iran than to Arab interests. They distrust the messianism linked to the historic Shiite sense of powerlessness, grievance, and persecution at the hand of the majority Sunnis—who represent about 85 percent of the Muslim Arab Middle East. This divide has become a major fault line exacerbated by Israel's campaign in Gaza and Egypt's holding Hamas largely responsible for the war. A strengthened Hamas, as the Egyptian leaders (and the Palestinian Fatah) understood, could only weaken their own increasingly precarious domestic positions. On the other hand, in terms of regional geopolitics, the reinforcement of Hamas's intransigence and its aim of establishing a rigidly Islamic Palestine serves only Iran—the leading sponsor of openly violent rejectionist resistance (toward Israel) and the subversion of all the pro-Western Arab regimes. Since the early 1990s Iran had condemned Arafat's PLO as the "biggest collaborators with Israel and the United States."[43] The Iranians (with the help of Hezbollah) were training, funding, and politically supporting Hamas, Islamic Jihad, and other terrorist groups while seeking to undermine any progress in the Israeli-Palestinian peace process. As the United States and the EU committed themselves to the support of Fatah after Hamas's electoral victory in the 2006 elections, Tehran pledged $250 million aid to the Hamas leaders to compensate them for the Western boycott. They had now established a powerful Sunni pawn and another critical link in their long-term program of an Iranian-led Islamic transformation of the Arab world. The alliance with Syria, under the leadership of the Alawi minority sect since 1970 (itself anathema to mainstream Sunni Islam), had shown over two decades earlier that Iran could create its own Arab axis despite the long-standing Persian-Arab antagonism. Despite these and other tensions, Iran patiently spreads the Islamic revolution while winning points on the Arab street. Hatred of Israel and anti-Semitism are important ideological weapons that accompany its growing military, economic, and propagandist outreach in the Middle East and beyond. They are an integral part of its expansionist drive and the encirclement of the Jewish state. It is the Iranians who stand behind Syria in relation to the Golan Heights, behind Hezbollah over the Lebanese border, and with the Palestinians in Gaza and potentially in the West Bank as well.

Ahmadinejad's brand of Islamic populism has not only left its mark on Iran, the Middle East, and the global jihad but also represents an outspoken challenge to the post–Cold War system still dominated by America and the West. For example, Ahmadinejad has warned Europeans who have defended Israel that Muslim nations "are like an ocean that is welling up, and if a storm begins, the dimensions will not stay limited to Palestine, and you may get hurt." There is little to deter such intimidatory language at home, since domestic protest is muzzled and Iranian universities have been virtually purged of reformist and secular lecturers. This so-called cultural revolution tightened the grip of an increasingly tyrannical government that has closed down dissenting dailies and Internet websites, and regularly harasses students.[44] Yet the country's abysmal human rights record is rarely documented, even in the West.[45] Attention is focused far more heavily on Iran's atomic weapons program, which the regime uses to rally popular support around its inalienable right to whatever technology it desires, including nuclear.[46] The Iranian supreme leader Ali Khamenei freely indulges in fierce verbal attacks on the Western democracies while threatening "to strike at them with all our capabilities." Crowds can be counted on to repetitively chant "Death to America" and "Death to Israel" in the streets of Tehran. The ritual nature of these demonstrations over the past thirty years may not necessarily express deep-seated sentiments of hatred toward the Jewish state, but they signify something more than mere propaganda and posturing. The daily drill of Israel-bashing, as Ze'ev Maghen has pointed out, reveals a tenaciously sought goal with its own dynamic.[47]

The Iranian leadership has moreover warned that any military strike against their country would ignite the entire Middle East. America's Arab allies in the region and U.S. military bases in the Gulf would be attacked; al-Qaeda terrorists would be given free passage through Iran; and oil prices would dramatically rise in order to cripple Western economies. As for Israel, Ali Khamenei promised on January 22, 2007, that "[when] the mighty missiles are launched from Iran, Israel will become a scorching hell for the Zionists, [in which they will burn] before reaching actual Hell."[48]

With its seventy million inhabitants Iran has a population ten times larger than that of Israel and a territory many times its size. Once in possession of nuclear weapons it would be a deadly danger not only to Israel and the Middle East but to virtually all of Europe, and have the ability to severely intimidate the Gulf states and halt the flow of oil to the entire industrialized world, including the United States. In seeking Israel's extinction its theocratic regime aims to control the Middle East. Its religious fanaticism is reinforced by imperialist nationalism and Great Power aspirations with eventual world domination as a distant goal. What makes Ahmadinejad different from Arab forerunners Gamal Abdel Nasser, Saddam Hussein, or even Osama bin Laden, is precisely the mystical nature of his messianic Islamism, which is expressed without any restraint or realistic sense of the balance of forces.

Ahmadinejad believes that the West is weak and in retreat; that Iran can provoke the United States with impunity; that Iran will soon have nuclear weapons, irrespective of any sanctions; and that Shia Islam is the wave of the future. Such overweening self-confidence is bolstered by the absolute conviction that the return of the Messiah is imminent. The television series *The World Toward Illumination,* running in Iran since November 2006, included the Second Coming of Jesus as a sign of the Last Days. The Iranian version, however, had the Christian Messiah coming back to earth as a Shiite Muslim leader; he would assist the Mahdi, whose immediate goal was to "form an army to defeat Islam's enemies in a series of apocalyptic battles." The Mahdi would, of course, "overcome the arch-villains in Jerusalem," crush all the oppressors, and violently sweep away corruption and injustice from the face of the earth.[49] This millennial reign of justice ushered in by a nuclear Iran is the kind of nightmare scenario almost guaranteed to push Saudi Arabia, Egypt, and Turkey down the same atomic path. As the British weekly *The Economist* put it, the Middle East would soon be entangled "in a cat's cradle of nuclear tripwires."[50]

· · ·

President Ahmadinejad, far from being indicted in the United Nations for his continual incitement to commit genocide, was politely offered the podium in 2007 for a command performance in duplicity and dissimulation. This theater of the absurd was subsequently repeated at Columbia University. As Irwin Cotler, former minister of justice in Canada, has aptly written:

> A person who incites to genocide; who is complicit in crimes against humanity; who continues the pursuit of the most destructive of weapons in violation of UN Security Council Resolutions; who warns Muslims who support Israel that they will "burn in the *umma* of Islam"; who is engaged in a massive repression of human rights in Iran; who assaults the basic tenets of the UN Charter—such a person belongs in the dock of the accused, rather than the podium of the UN General Assembly.[51]

More extreme than even his spiritual godfather, the Ayatollah Khomeini, Iran's president combines jihad, genocidal anti-Semitism, a penchant for "final solutions," and Holocaust denial in his addresses. Speaking in Tehran at the end of October 2005, Ahmadinejad referred back to the Khomeinist legacy.

> Our dear Imam [Khomeini] said that the occupying regime [Israel] must be wiped off the map and this was a very wise statement. We cannot com-

promise over the issue of Palestine . . . whoever accepts the legitimacy of this regime has in fact signed the defeat of the Islamic world. Our dear Imam targeted the heart of the world oppressor in his struggle, meaning the occupying regime. I have no doubt that the new wave that has started in Palestine, and we witness it in the Islamic world too, will eliminate this disgraceful stain from the Islamic world.

He added that any Muslim leader who recognized the Zionist regime "will be eternally disgraced and will burn in the fury of the Islamic nations."[52] Ahmadinejad also emphasized that the war against Israel was not merely a battle between individual nations or a conflict over the land or over dividing a part of the Arab world. It was about something much bigger—the future of Islam which had been retreating for three centuries in the face of Western pressure: "The Islamic world lost its last defenses in the past 100 years and the world oppressor [the United States] established the occupying regime. Therefore the struggle in Palestine today is the major front of the struggle of the Islamic world with the world oppressor and its fate will decide the destiny of the struggles of the past several hundred years."[53] Such world-historical perspectives and visions of the clash of civilizations uncannily recall the worldview of Adolf Hitler.

In his 2005 Al-Quds Day speech before thousands of Iranian students, Ahmadinejad concluded that "a world without America and Zionism" was indeed feasible. "The World of Arrogance" and the "infidels" could be decisively defeated by the combined forces of the Islamic *umma*. The "Palestinian problem" was presented as the key to this global confrontation, and it would only be resolved by "the elimination of the Zionist regime." He ended with the prediction that "our holy hatred" would expand continuously and strike like a wave to sweep away "the disgrace imposed on us by the enemy."[54]

This was a dramatic return to the revolutionary Khomeinist goals of the early 1980s that had transformed Iran into a semi-totalitarian ideological state. It was expressed in a language so incendiary that it provoked outrage and dismay in the West. British prime minister Tony Blair bluntly described the Iranian president's remarks as "a disgrace."[55] French president Jacques Chirac declared himself "profoundly shocked" at such "totally senseless" statements, which risked turning Iran into "an outlaw State." There were even a few embarrassed commentators in Tehran who realized that their president's remarks might make it easier to refer Iran's nuclear activities to the UN Security Council for punitive sanctions. Damage control was clearly required. An Iranian official reassuringly asserted that Iran had "never used force against a second country." Other highly placed officials pretended that the president had spoken figuratively, merely criticizing the "Zionist mindset."[56] But there was no disavowal by the top Iranian leadership, and the president's slogans appeared popular at street level. At least two hundred thousand Iranians participated in state-organized rallies on Al-Quds Day, and some were loudly chanting "Israel is approaching its death." Ahmadinejad was unrepentant when he joined the demonstrators, saying his remarks were "right and just," dismissing the Western criticism out of hand and adding: "My words were the Iranian nation's words."[57]

Ahmadinejad's speeches can no more be considered as empty threats than the words of Adolf Hitler on January 30, 1939, prophesying that a new world war would bring about "the annihilation of the Jewish race in Europe." The same genocidal intent is plainly there.[58] The threat has been consistently repeated since October 2005. The alibis forged in advance by some Western commentators that the Iranian leader is politically immature, a novice, or a radical hothead indulging in empty bluster are not borne out by the evidence. They ignore the religious zeal and revolutionary socialization of the regime, its recent history, and the Islamist anti-Semitic ideology of the Iranian president.[59] The ascendancy of Ahmadinejad, a child of the Iranian Revolution, is closely connected with that of the Basiji, the mass movement initiated by Khomeini in 1979 and militarized during the Iran-Iraq War. Iranian children, some as young as twelve years old, were sent to the front lines—enthusiastically marching in formation across minefields toward the Iraqi enemy, clearing a path with their exploding bodies. These children were part of a volunteer militia called the Basij Mostazafan (mobilization of the oppressed). The regime cruelly sent them toward their destruction—human sacrifices brainwashed by the regime into believing that they were heading straight to paradise.

Since 1988 the Basiji have grown in numbers and influence. They have been used both as shock troops against government dissenters and as vice squads to enforce religious law. They have provided a potent political base for Ahmadinejad during his rise to power. He has always glorified their fearlessness and their sacrifice for Islam and on behalf of the fatherland. The Basiji were "soldiers of God" for whom, in the spirit of Khomeini's teaching, life was in itself worthless, and death was the beginning of genuine existence. In the middle of the Iran-Iraq War, Ahmadinejad, then a young man in his twenties, joined the Revolutionary Guards and apparently served as a Basij volunteer during the conflict. Elected mayor of Tehran in April 2003, the then forty-seven-year-old hard-liner set out to roll back President Khatami's liberal reforms, eradicate Western influence in Iran, and clean up corruption. An Islamic radical who favored a "second revolution" to achieve this end, he became the president of Iran in 2005 thanks in no small measure to the millions of Basiji—in every Iranian town—who became his unofficial campaign workers.[60] Since the 2005 elections, the influence of the Basij ideology and its powers have considerably increased under the patronage of Ahmadinejad. Iranians are encouraged from their earliest years to embrace the virtues of martyrdom. Mobilization for suicide missions in special military units is zealously promoted—and more than fifty thousand Iranians have already volunteered.

· · ·

Iran's supreme spiritual leader, Ayatollah Ali Khamenei, has been no less militant than Ahmadinejad with regard to Israel, adding his own version of Holocaust denial to the boiling pot. The Zionists, he insists, had closely collaborated with the German Nazis. They had unscrupulously published "exaggerated statistics on Jewish killings." There was even evidence "that a large number of non-Jewish hooligans and thugs from Eastern Europe were forced to emigrate to Palestine as Jews . . . to instill in the heart of the Islamic world an anti-Islamic state under the guise of supporting the victims of racism."[61] Khamenei, like his model, Ayatollah Khomeini, regards Jews as *infidels,* "unclean" abominations, "eternal enemies" of Islam, and racist oppressors of the Palestinians. In a speech on January 1, 2002, he characteristically remarked that "the source of many of the problems plaguing the Islamic world is the existence of the cancerous growth of the Zionist regime in the great body of Islam."[62]

Khamenei obviously believes that Jews/Zionists are responsible for every negative situation, international event, or crisis affecting Iran or the Islamic world. That is, indeed, classical anti-Semitism. In his *Protocols*-dominated worldview, Jews control the global media and the United States government and mastermind virtually every secular-oriented plot to subvert Muslim beliefs. Since Khamenei also regards the United States as "a bloodthirsty Satan," an "arrogant, conceited, deceitful and hypocrite regime," Jewish Zionist control of its policy is one more reason to advocate Israel's annihilation.[63]

For the contemporary heirs of Ayatollah Khomeini, the destruction of Israel is not only a goal in itself, but it is also the prerequisite to solving the problems of contemporary Islam. Israel represents a threat on several levels: to the sacredness of Jerusalem, to Islamic identity, and to Iran by virtue of its being a major regional ally of America. Beyond that, the "final solution" of the "Palestinian question" constantly evoked by the Iranian leadership is depicted as the litmus test for the victory or defeat of the Islamic Revolution.

At Friday prayers attended by thousands at the University of Tehran campus on April 5, 2002, Ali Khamenei highlighted the contrast between "the Zionist regime" symbolizing "bloodthirstiness, barbarism and indifference towards all rules of ethics" and the bravery of the oppressed Palestinians. This, he declared, was an issue in which "the humanity of all mankind is at stake," confronted by "the wild beasts ruling the Zionist regime." Both Bush's "world-devouring" America and Israel were compared to Hitler in their reliance on brute military strength. They were equally impotent in the face of *shahada* (martyrdom). Khamenei called for a total oil embargo on the Jewish state and all countries friendly with it, the return of *all* Palestinian refugees, and the definitive dismantlement of the "usurper" Zionist entity.[64] Speaking to Hajj pilgrims on January 19, 2005, the Iranian leader referred with undisguised loathing to "the Zionist octopus," allied to a "vicious and despicable U.S. imperialism" striving for absolute hegemony over global material resources. Its plans for the Middle East would, however, be thwarted by Muslim nations under Iranian leadership. In the context of the Iraqi elections, Khamenei expressed the hope that the results "will put an end to the vicious presence of the Zionists, who had landed on the banks of the Euphrates in the shadow of American arms and seem to have found partial fulfillment of their warped dream of a land extending 'from the Nile to the Euphrates.' "[65]

Violent hatred of Israel and the use of anti-Semitic motifs also abound in the Iranian media. At the beginning of September 2003 the *Tehran Times* reported as fact that hard-line Jews had plotted to assassinate the pro-Arab French president Chirac and to attack Muslim mosques in France; in the same issue, Mossad agents were said to have infiltrated Iraqi Shia organizations and were held responsible for a terrorist assault in Najaf.[66] The Iranian media periodically evokes such mythical Jewish plots without the slightest evidence, along with promises of vengeance. The editor of the conservative Iranian daily *Kayhan* stressed, for example, that no Zionist anywhere in the world would be able to feel secure in the wake of Israel's aerial attacks in Gaza. In a TV program broadcast in July 2006, President Ahmadinejad went further still in a chilling warning to the West.

> The Zionists are not opposed only to Islam and the Muslims. They are opposed to humanity as a whole. They want to dominate the entire world. They would even sacrifice the Western regimes for their own sake. I say to the leaders of some Western countries: Stop supporting these corrupt people. Behold the rage of the Muslim peoples is accumulating. The rage of the Muslim peoples may soon reach the point of explosion. . . . The waves of this explosion will not be restricted to the boundaries of our region. They will definitely reach the corrupt forces that support this fake regime.[67]

Ahmadinejad's apocalyptic anti-Zionism, with its paranoia and pseudo-redemptive posture, feeds on the Khomeinist religion of death that took traditional Shia Islam hostage during the Iran-Iraq War. This messianic vision of the End of Days now has a deadly nuclear threat attached to its tail.[68] Ahmadinejad does not shy away from the possibility of a nuclear jihad against the Jews, the "Crusader" West, infidels, and apostates. Enriching uranium to build an atomic bomb that could eradicate the Jewish state and help to ensure the global rule of Shia Islam seems perfectly natural in terms of his worldview. He feels equally comfortable in explaining to German chancellor Angela Merkel that Iran, like the Third Reich, has been "victimized" by the Jews and America, and that the Holocaust was a myth completely distorted by the Zionists. As political activist and Holocaust survivor Elie Wiesel, responding to the international conference of Holocaust deniers in Tehran, pertinently observed:

> For the first time since the end of the Second World War, a Head of State— of a major country—has purely and simply sentenced a major Jewish community to annihilation. . . . Ahmadinejad has been threatening Israel for a long time, for years. He has said: "There was no Holocaust, but there

will be." In other words, six million Jews did not die at Auschwitz but others will now perish.[69]

Ahmadinejad's obsessive hatred of Israel transcends normal politics and has no empirical basis. Iran and Israel do not even share a common border. There are no territorial or economic issues between the two nations. Israeli leaders some time ago conceded the principle of a Palestinian state, providing that it will dismantle all terror organizations, accept peaceful coexistence, and fully normalize its relations with the Jewish state. For the Iranian leadership such considerations are totally irrelevant. Hating Israel is an end in itself. It also provides a common enemy that can unite rulers and ruled. Demonizing the Jewish state offers a plausible pretext for developing nuclear weapons while, at the same time, it attracts the sympathy of the Arab street. International reaction has thus far been too mild, weak, and divided to counter these advantages and make Iranian nuclearization or threats to annihilate Israel seem prohibitive.[70] Above all, for Ahmadinejad, the war against America and Israel belongs to the End of Days perspective. It is an eschatological battle of destiny.[71]

Ahmadinejad is personally convinced that he has been chosen by the Mahdi to prepare the path for the projected end of the world—a vision that includes the extermination of the Jews "in the Last Hour."[72] His ideology of Mahdism is an *activist* creed that inculcates in true believers the will to missionize and to convert the whole world to Shia Islam.[73] This scenario superficially seems to resemble that of the Christian Apocalypse with its Last Judgment, visions of Armageddon, the Time of Tribulation, the conversion of the Jews, and Christ's Second Coming to redeem a fallen world. However, there is a very crucial difference. The return of the Jews to Zion is, for millions of evangelical Christians, especially in the United States, one of the decisive *positive* signs of the approaching redemption. The creation of Israel in 1948, followed by its conquest of the Promised Land and reunification of Jerusalem in 1967, were *good tidings*. On the other hand, for most Iranian Shiite Muslims, for the Palestinians, and for the rest of the Sunni Arab world, the establishment of Israel in 1948 was the great *naqba*. The Jewish conquest of Jerusalem during the Six-Day War was the devil's work.[74]

Islamic, Christian, and Jewish fundamentalists can perhaps agree on one point—that the Temple Mount in Jerusalem is a nodal point for the coming messianic age. Both Islamic and apocalyptic Christian speculation also tend to look for the signs of darkness before the final dawn—the turbulent prelude to the future era of divine rule and perfection on earth. In both religions (though not in Judaism) there are millions who have been convinced that the script for the Last Days is already written, that the waiting is nearly over, and history is drawing to its close. However, before that can happen, heresy must be wiped out. As Ahmadinejad's mentor, Ayatollah Mezbah-Yazdi, expressed it on October 11, 2006: "The greatest obligation of those awaiting the appearance of the Mahdi is fighting heresy and global arrogance."

For Yazdi and his followers there can be no greater blasphemy than the Jewish or Christian evangelical belief that God will fulfill all his promises to the people of Israel as set out in the Hebrew Bible, including the building of the Third Temple. The Islamic apocalypse proceeds from completely opposite premises since it seeks to erase the Solomonic and Herodian Temples from any connection to Jewish or Christian history. It treats Islam as the culmination and supersession (in a quasi-Hegelian sense) of both Judaism and Christianity. In Islamist End Times, total opposition to Israel as the "Satan of our age" demands either the killing of Jews or their expulsion in order to repossess Al-Quds. In the Iranian case, the Mahdist event that reorders the world is specifically linked to the elimination of Zionism, Israel, and any Jewish influence. This perception has been heightened by the Shia awakening and Iranian dreams of dominating the Persian Gulf and the Middle East—ambitions that also materially threaten contemporary American and European interests.

President Ahmadinejad's triumphalist vision of Allah's imminent rule encourages and provides justification for the sponsorship of worldwide terrorism. The enemy is not only the fake regime of Israel and the degenerate West but also their Sunni Arab lackeys. The removal of Saddam Hussein by American power was, in many respects, an unexpected bonus. The demise of Saudi Arabia would be a still greater prize. Growing control of Lebanon through Hassan Nasrallah's Hezbollah and rising influence in Syria and Iraq have already extended Iran's sphere of influence in the Middle East, threatening all the pro-Western, or moderate, regimes in the region. Russian complicity and two-facedness under Putin's leadership in arming and reinforcing the Iranian-Syrian-Hezbollah axis has reinforced the confidence of the ruling mullahs in Tehran that they can survive any Western sanctions. Ahmadinejad's serenity in the face of American pressure is particularly striking. On May 8, 2006, he even sent a "divinely inspired" letter (to quote a fellow Iranian cleric) to President Bush, presenting himself as the global advocate of the "dispossessed" against what he called a "Zionist-dominated world." The Iranian president evoked the virtues of "eternal paradise" in contrast to "the life of this world." In addition to the usual Third World anti-American jargon there was an impudently preachy tone advising the U.S. president (himself a born-again Christian) to convert to Islam while there was still time.[75]

Israel remains, however, at the core of Ahmadinejad's concerns. At the end of April 2006 in the western Iranian town of Zanjan, he prophesied yet again that "this regime will one day vanish." A few months later, against the background of the Israel-Hezbollah conflict in Lebanon, he told students in Jakarta that Israelis should "pack up and move out of the region."[76] Pronouncing his hopes for a Hezbollah victory, he invited the faithful in late July 2006 to wait for good news—what he called "the elimination of the Zionist stain of shame." He insisted that Israel "had pushed the button of its own destruction"; that its philosophy—based on threats, massacre, and invasion—"has reached its finishing line."[77] The entire West was guilty of its creation in 1948. For Europeans, this had "killed two birds with one stone" by "sweeping the Jews out of Europe and at the same time creating a European appendage, with a Zionist and anti-Islamic nature in the heart of the Islamic world."[78] In an October 20, 2006, Al-Quds Day speech about Palestine, broadcast on Jaam E Jam TV and directed toward a Western audience, he again challenged Europeans:

> Since you brought [this regime] over there, you yourselves pick it up, by the arms and legs, and remove it from there. This [Zionist] regime is on the verge of death, and we advise you to start thinking about your long-term interests and long-term relations with the peoples of the region. At the end of the day, these are all ultimatums. No one should complain tomorrow. The things are stated clearly.[79]

Such outbursts prompted then Israeli vice premier Shimon Peres to compare Ahmadinejad's hate speech to that of Hitler and renew calls for an international coalition to prevent Iran from obtaining nuclear weapons.[80] He failed to mention that the Iranian leadership's proto-genocidal mentality is closely related to its predilection for anti-Semitic conspiracy theories similar to those that animated the Nazis and much of the Arab world.[81] For example, in April 2004, Iranian TV showed a documentary series explaining how the Jews controlled the music and entertainment industries in the United States. Strengthening Israel, so the program claimed, was only a short-term, immediate goal of the Zionists. The larger plan was "to Judaize the world" through globalization while disregarding social justice for the masses. The film industry (controlled by world Zionism) was a key element in this Jewish conspiracy to implement the aims laid out in the *Protocols*.[82] The "Zionist racists" in the film business had consistently abused the medium to defame Muslims as terrorists, to glorify America, and to encourage gratuitous violence.

Leading Iranian politicians and clerics have often given voice to conspiracy theories of this type in order to malign the Zionists and delegitimize the Jewish state. The speaker of the Iranian parliament, Gholam-Ali Haddad-Adel, talking to the Iranian News Channel (IRINN) on July 18, 2006, remarked, for example, that America and Britain had planted "an artificial, false, and fictitious state called Israel in this region." Zionists had exploited "wrongs supposedly done to them [the Jews] during World War II" to carry out terrorism, to engage in sinister conspiracies and massacres against Muslims, and to turn Palestinians into refugees with the full support of the West. Britain, America, and Israel had "lied, exaggerated, and fabricated events" for sixty years, but the Muslims had finally woken up. Enthusiastically praising Hassan Nasrallah and Hezbollah's massive missile attacks against northern Israel in the summer of 2006, Haddad-Adel (backed by an ecstatic crowd shouting "*Allahu akbar*") stressed that "the Palestinian refugees should return to the land of their forefathers." As for the Jews, they could flee "occupied Palestine" and return to their original homes in Europe or elsewhere.[83] Ahmadinejad, addressing a big rally on August 1, 2006, went further still, calling the Jews "bloodthirsty barbarians," next to whom "all the criminals of the world seem righteous." Together with America and Britain, the Zionists had concocted a "diabolical plan" to expel the Palestinians—to trespass, murder, and pillage. The United States and Britain were full accomplices in these crimes whose essence had been exposed by the Second Lebanon War and the heroism of Hezbollah, led by Hassan Nasrallah. Ahmadinejad warned America, Britain, and the Zionists that "the fire of the wrath of the peoples is about to erupt and overthrow."[84] The criminals would be brought to justice.

Mahmoud Ahmadinejad's invitations to speak at the United Nations and

Columbia University in New York gave Iran's president an unexpectedly prestigious platform from which to spout his venom in the name of "constructive engagement."[85] The granting of such opportunities does not, however, have any moderating influence on Iranian policy. Ahmadinejad even escalated his position in August and September 2007, calling on the nations of the world to rise up against the declining West, led by the United States. He continued to preach the imminent collapse of Israel—formally branded as "Satan's standard-bearer."[86] These and similarly hate-filled remarks have abounded in speeches throughout the past two years emphasizing that Iran had become a global power and would never compromise with the West over its nuclear program, regardless of sanctions. On September 1, 2007, Ahmadinejad cockily reiterated his view—despite criticism from some senior Iranian officials—that "it was impossible for the U.S. to launch a war against us." He stressed that all efforts to prevent Iran's nuclearization and slow its emergence as a dominant regional power were doomed to failure. At the annual International Seminar on the Doctrine of Mahdism in Tehran on August 25–26, 2007, Ahmadinejad went further, prophesying the end of the injustice and oppression led by America. Its barbaric empire would be replaced by "the monotheism of Abraham [throughout the world]," the rule of the righteous, and a new age of "love, knowledge and spirituality," inaugurated by the Mahdi. Two days later, he explained that all the "unworthy regimes and rulers" would soon be swept away by the return of the Hidden Imam—a mission specially entrusted by God to the Iranian nation. In the coming era of peace and liberation, "the peoples of the world will eradicate Zionism"—an ideology founded on lies, aggression, occupation, and discrimination.

America and its allies, according to Ahmadinejad, had suffered a shattering military and ideological debacle in Iraq. They were fast sinking into a quagmire "from which they would only escape at great cost."[87] The fiasco in Iraq was also a serious blow to the viability of Israel. To underline the point, he called the very existence of the Jewish state an "insult to human dignity" during the annual Jerusalem Day rally in Tehran in early October 2007. He insisted that Zionism was "now a global issue," far transcending "the occupation of Palestine." It was wholly unacceptable that Palestinians should be made to pay such a heavy price because Europeans had "allegedly" committed certain crimes against Jews during World War II. If this were really true, then the European countries and the American people should give up part of their own land for a Jewish state in Europe or in the United States. The Americans should provide Alaska for the Jews if they were being serious. But they would, in any case, have to abandon Israel. The head of Iran's judiciary, Ayatollah Mahmoud Hashemi Shahroudi, called the mass rallies in October 2007—attended by hundreds of thousands in Tehran alone—"a good start for the destruction of the Zionist regime."[88]

At the opening winter session of the Israeli parliament a day later, President Shimon Peres clarified the growing Iranian nuclear danger. He warned that the Iranian regime was spending huge amounts of money on long-range missiles, which made little sense if they bore only conventional warheads. Iran was secretly and energetically working to obtain nuclear capabilities, investing enormous sums in building reactors and centrifuges, despite its abundance of oil and gas. It cynically spoke of peace while arming and financing more terrorists than any other state in the world. Its Revolutionary Guards existed primarily "to strengthen terror and disseminate it." The leadership in Tehran maintained Hezbollah in order to turn Lebanon into an Iranian satellite: "It established the Islamic Jihad and supports the Hamas in order to destroy the peace process which is taking place between Israel and the Palestinians and to create in its stead, a great tumult so that the Palestinians will serve the Iranian appetite instead of the Palestinian destiny."[89]

The Iranian president had also concealed the brutal suppression of citizens' rights in Iran—the public hangings in the squares of Iranian cities, the newspapers that had been closed, and the hundreds of student leaders arrested. This was the same tyrannical regime that had issued a death sentence against the British Muslim novelist Salman Rushdie for having written a book the Iranian ayatollahs disapproved of. It was a government that had executed young people accused of homosexuality; a government that routinely imprisoned dissident intellectuals and brutally persecuted minorities such as the Baha'is. Women in Iran, it was officially claimed, enjoyed equal rights. But in 2007 alone, 527,255 women had been thrown into jail on the charge of immodest dress, and two women were publicly stoned to death.[90] These heavy-handed tactics underlined how much women's rights had indeed been curtailed in Iran since the Islamic Revolution.[91]

In Ahmadinejad's Iran, with its government repression, high unemployment, and economic inequalities, there is a huge gulf between the revolutionary vision of an ideal Islamic order and the dismal everyday reality. The hopes for liberal democratic change, momentarily aroused by the elevation of Khatami to the presidency in 1997, rapidly dissipated; so, too, did the liberationist promises of the Iranian Revolution and its fraudulent ideological façade of "Muslim solidarity," as if there were no real differences between Iranians, Arabs, Afghans, Turks, Kurds, and other coreligionists. Only the issue of Israel and hostility toward America preserve such fictions. This is an important reason for the question of Palestine being presented as a major *ideological* conflict. There can be no question of admitting that the Jewish people have any right to land, to an independent state, or to recognized sovereignty in the Middle East, least of all with Jerusalem as its capital.[92] Israel, as the "unlawful son" of the United States, can only be depicted as an alien graft in the region. Palestine, as sacred "Muslim soil," is exclusively reserved for Palestinian Muslims. Though some Iranians might privately question why Iran has to be more "Palestinian" than the Palestinians in the conflict with Israel, this has had little impact on the regime.[93]

Iran's sense of religious mission and its ambition to lead the Muslim world have led to the unequivocal negation of Israel and a fateful Islamicization of the Arab-Israeli conflict.[94] Iranian influence has transformed what was once a national and territorial confrontation into a battle between *haq* (righteousness) and *batel* (falsehood); between the forces of light and those of darkness; between Allah and the agents of Satan. In the eyes of the ayatollahs, any Arab or Palestinian leader who recognizes or negotiates with Israel is, by definition, a traitor to Islam. Even the allegedly moderate Rafsanjani holds a hard-line position on this issue, regarding the "flimsy" State of Israel as a completely illegitimate entity that is harmful to the Muslim world.[95] Like other leading ayatollahs he has depicted Zionism as the heir of "Jewish racism" from antiquity to the present. The Iranian leadership always makes sure to present a united front in rejecting Israel as a "foreign body" in the region. Palestine, as Ali Khamenei put it, is the front line of Islam's war against "infidelity." It makes no difference at all to the ayatollahs which political party is in power in Israel, who its prime minister is, or what policies he or she pursues. The evil is *inherent*, so to speak, in the nature of the Jews and Zionism.

The 2006 Israel-Hezbollah war in Lebanon provoked further escalation of virulent Iranian rhetoric against America, Britain, and the Jewish state. On August 2, 2006, Ali Khamenei branded the war as "a Zionist-American operation—a first step towards taking control over the Middle East and over the [entire] Muslim world."[96] Bush and his closest partners, the "despicable British government" and "the evil and depraved leaders of the Zionist regime," were accomplices in a terrible crime against humanity. Muslims, he said, were especially disgusted with the American regime, which could expect "a devastating fist-blow from the Muslim nation for its support of the Zionist crimes and criminals."[97] Only through jihad and martyrdom would it be possible for the Muslim world "to confront the barbaric Zionist wolves and the aggression of the 'Great Satan.' " In the face of such arrogant American belligerence and the "racist, aggressive and bloodthirsty regime" of Israel, Hezbollah had bravely stood in "the front line of defense for the Muslim nation" beyond any differences of creed between Shiites and Sunnis, between the mosque and the church.[98] Iranian Guardian Council secretary Ayatollah Ahmad Janati, in an August 4, 2006, Friday sermon in Tehran aired on Iranian Channel 1, added a gloss from Islamic history. The conflict in Lebanon, he maintained, recalled the battle between the descendants of Ali (the Shiites led by Hassan Nasrallah) and the Jews of Khaibar in seventh-century Arabia. More than thirteen hundred years earlier, Ali, a cousin and son-in-law of the Prophet Muhammad, and his small band of Muslims had humiliated the "vain and arrogant" Jews of Khaibar, just as Nasrallah was now doing to Israel.

Ayatollah Janati's sermon savaged the "impure and evil [Condoleezza] Rice," the "impure" and bloodthirsty Bush, the cowardly Islamic regimes, the impotent UN Security Council, and the criminal silence of a subservient Muslim Arab world bending to the dictates of America.[99] Ayatollah Hussein Nouri Hamedani was equally scathing about the apathy of so many Muslims—especially Sunni Arab clerics—toward the massacre of their Shia Muslim brethren in Lebanon, Palestine, and Iraq. Ali Khamenei, speaking on August 8, 2006, at a traditional celebration marking the birth of the Shiite founder, Imam Ali, echoed this critique. He deplored "the division among the Muslim countries, which is especially [due to the behavior of] some Arab countries that watch [the events] and keep silent. Such behavior is entirely wrong and harmful." The Iranian leader went on to observe that exacerbating the Sunni-Shiite division was "a lethal poison for the Muslim world"—an act of treason encouraged by its enemies in order to cripple the Islamic Revolution.

Since August 2006, Tehran (with Syrian help) has massively rearmed its Hezbollah proxy in southern Lebanon, while also financing and training

Muqtada al-Sadr's Mahdi Army in Iraq and other local Shiite militias. It injected $120 million into the coffers of Hamas, while providing extensive assistance for its terror operatives and those of the Palestinian Islamic Jihad. As a White House spokesman put it on November 12, 2006, Iran continued to be the "nexus of global terror."[100] Such activities underscore the ideological consistency with which Iran has acted to overturn the political status quo in the Middle East for nearly three decades, helped by Alawite-ruled Syria and its terrorist proxies.

The so-called second Islamic revolution, which accelerated after Ahmadinejad's accession to the presidency in 2005, has returned once more to Khomeini's original objectives. It seeks to establish hegemony over the oil-rich Persian Gulf and then throughout the Islamic and Arab worlds. It also wants to export the Islamic Revolution in order to bring down apostate regimes in the Middle East and to exacerbate the clash of civilizations with the infidel West. Above all, it seeks to destroy Israel, not least as a way of striking at the United States.[101] Ahmadinejad's Shiite messianism has propelled this Iranian imperialist project toward an apocalyptic confrontation with the West. Following the teachings of Ayatollah Mezbah-Yazdi, he is truly convinced that we are living in the era of destruction, wars, and chaos that will trigger the long-awaited return of the Mahdi. An ideologue, a global populist, a Khomeinist revolutionary, and a Shiite messianist, the Iranian president firmly believes the Middle Eastern conflict "has become the locus of the final war between Muslims and the infidel West."[102] These are not merely the ravings of an isolated, "saber-rattling lunatic," a political clown, or histrionic actor. They embody the core beliefs of fundamentalist Shiite theology translated into a modern revolutionary project.

The existence of an Iranian nuclear umbrella, which would deter any American or Israeli effort to topple the regime, would greatly facilitate its objectives—including the export of the Islamic Revolution. Among its effects would be the diminishing of Western influence, greater control over Middle East oil, the cowing of the Gulf states, and almost certainly war with Israel. In this context, it is significant that under Ahmadinejad, Iran has consciously sought to activate the Arab street "over the heads of current Arab governments."[103] Iran's appeal to dissatisfied Sunnis and its friendly relations with authoritarian populist Third World leaders such as Hugo Chávez are a function of its revolutionary opposition to the status quo and challenge to the American-dominated international system.

The growing power of the younger, ideologically committed officers of the Islamic Revolutionary Guard Corps (Pasdaran)—who control nearly half of Iran's key cabinet posts—is an important marker of this radicalization. Pasdaran commanders are in charge of the army, the Defense Ministry, the National Security Council, and the Foreign Ministry; the Revolutionary Guards have also infiltrated the civil service, state-owned corporations, and the media.[104] The Guards and the state intelligence apparatus are actively involved in encouraging subversion abroad and in intensively assisting all the Palestinian terror groups. The recruiting of Iranian suicide bombers for "martyrdom operations" against the West and Israel are part of this aggressive posture.[105] For the martyrs, there is no such thing as death, but only—to quote Ayatollah Khomeini—"the transition from this world to the world beyond, where they will live on eternally and in splendor."[106]

The Second Lebanon War and the two-pronged assault on Israel by Hezbollah and Hamas would not have happened without powerful Iranian sponsorship, financing, and direction. By targeting Israel as a symbol of the West, Iran threw down the gauntlet, especially to America. Speaking on Iran's national channel on July 26, 2006, Ahmadinejad declared: "Lebanon is a historic test which will determine the future of humanity . . . [America] is the one who started this fire. They have collected a bunch of people [the Jews] and put them in the occupied lands to serve as their shield, so they can realize their [American] colonialist domineering goals."[107] A week earlier, the speaker of the national parliament had articulated a similar political line in a televised speech. The alien Zionist entity was conceived, he said, by England and America who "wished to have dominion over the Islamic world, to prevent Muslim unity, and to have control of the oil resources in the Middle East."[108] Such Islamist anti-imperialist rhetoric provides useful ideological cover for Iran's own expansionist ambitions in the region.

· · ·

"Wiping Israel off the map" is not a new idea in the Muslim Middle East. It was evoked by the Arab armies in 1948, by Nasser, by the PLO, and by pan-Arab nationalists until today. The Islamic emphasis has, however, enlarged the scale and character of the struggle. Since October 2005, Ahmadinejad has spoken more concretely of "a world without Americans and Zionists" as being an *attainable* end.[109] Other Iranian officials have suggested that a clash with the United States is inevitable. In his November 15, 2006, Jerusalem Day speech in Tehran, the Iranian president clearly anticipated "the great war" as a Gog and Magog type of conflagration that was *imminent:* "The great war is ahead of us [and it will break out] perhaps tomorrow, or in a few months, or even in a few years. The nation of Muslims must prepare for the great war so as to completely wipe out the Zionist regime and remove this cancerous growth. Like the Imam Khomeini said: 'Israel must collapse.' "[110] Ahmadinejad's certainty on this score, as he had confided a month earlier in addressing the Union of Iranian Engineers, came from his special "connection with God." It was Allah who "said to me that no strategy will help the apostates against the believers. There is only one step left in achieving nuclear capability and then the West will not dare attack us."[111]

Ahmadinejad's October 28, 2005, speech, which called for purging "the stain of disgrace" from the center of the Islamic world, was placed in the broad historical perspective of a clash of civilizations.[112] It was a long-term "historic war" between Islam and the West. The forcible removal of Israel had to be seen, therefore, as the prelude to turning the tides of fortune in favor of Islam. At a time when some Arab leaders appeared to envisage a peace process, Iranian militancy provided a golden opportunity for the Shiite theocracy to claim leadership over the Palestinian cause—a valuable lever in asserting their regional and pan-Islamic hegemony. Hezbollah's so-called victory in the Second Lebanon War, seen from the Iranian perspective, demonstrated the popularity that a Shiite Islamic movement sponsored by Iran could enjoy in the Arab world for having tenaciously resisted Israel. The war was largely an Iranian-financed and controlled conflict, inconceivable without the involvement of the Iranian Revolutionary Guards and the complicity of Iran's Syrian ally in Damascus.[113]

Iran's imperial influence (in the name of Shia Islam) is now spreading out from Tehran through Iraq, which is 60 percent Shiite, and the Alawite regime in Syria to Hezbollah and Hamas—thereby subverting and undermining the more conservative Sunni Arab Middle East. The Iranian interest in destroying Israel is enhanced through Hamas, which also provides an instrument to gain control of the Palestinian cause. Through Hezbollah, Iran not only threatens Israel but also accelerates the disintegration of Lebanon while neutralizing Western influence over its fate.[114] Iran's war against Zionism is an invaluable means to subvert a weakened Arab world that can be more easily bent to do its will. It also helps Iran to project its power over the entire Middle East, boosted by the most intensive missile program in the Third World—reinforcing its claim to be *the* main spearhead of the Islamic world in its struggle against Western civilization. In this endeavor, Iran has actively assisted Islamic radicals throughout the world, encouraging the "terror state within a state" model that Hezbollah and Hamas exemplify. This strategy can be especially effective where there are enfeebled host governments, such as Lebanon, Iraq, and the Palestinian Authority, in which armed terrorist groups can act with impunity. In this way, Iran has been able to organize a new jihadi threat to the entire regional order and the international state system—creating maximum instability while assuming minimum responsibility.[115]

Syria has acted as Iran's bridgehead to the Arab world and proven no less expert in fomenting terror to destabilize its political enemies. The Syrians, though isolated among the Arab states and hardly enamored with radical Islam, nevertheless share many of Iran's assumptions and interests in dealing with the United States and Israel. Any chance that they could be disengaged from the Iranian orbit would significantly diminish if Tehran could establish a nuclear umbrella—enabling its allied international terror networks to more easily blackmail not only Israel, but the region as a whole and the West itself. The threat of Iran providing an Islamic terrorist group with so-called dirty, nonconventional weapons that could cause huge casualties is an all-too-plausible doomsday scenario.

• • •

No less worrying, especially for the moderate Arab regimes, is the fact that Shiite leaders like Ahmadinejad and Hassan Nasrallah have become heroes on the Arab street; and that the continuing fragmentation of Lebanon makes its future Islamicization ever more possible. Moreover, at the beginning of the twenty-first century it is becoming clear that Iran, unless it is checked, is potentially the only regional superpower in the Middle East, with no Arab state capable of challenging its supremacy. This awareness doubtless lay behind Ahmadinejad's declaration in August 2006 that a new Middle East had already emerged under conditions "in which the wings of the Zionist and American dominance have been broken." Despite Iran's serious shortages of gas and heating oil, the rising cost of food, housing, and medical care as well as high unemployment, the belief of the regime that Allah and history are on its side has not been shaken. Furthermore, since Supreme Leader Khameini has again indicated his support for Ahmadinejad in the June 2009 presidential elections, he may well be reelected for another four years. But even if a "reformist" rival replaces Ahmadinejad, it is highly unlikely that Iran will modify its domestic or international ambitions. The economic and political incentives contemplated by the new U.S. administration can hardly stop Iran's uranium enrichment program where previous European and American appeasement programs failed. They cannot change the fact that Iran is the first example of a modern state since Hitler's Germany that has *officially* adopted an active policy of anti-Semitism as a means to promote its national interests; a state that openly supports Holocaust denial, and believes that acceptance of Israel's existence in the West is primarily built on guilt feelings over the mass murder of Jews during World War II. By eroding the basis for this belief, the current Iranian leadership apparently thinks that it can undermine Israel's legitimacy and win support in world public opinion.

Fanatical anti-Semitism is undoubtedly a powerful factor in the repeated threats made by Ahmadinejad and other militant Islamists to wipe Israel off the face of the earth. Their statements convey the will to implement a "final solution" of their own to eliminate what the Islamists designate as the Jewish/Zionist cancer in the Middle East. This is the context in which one must consider the relentless denial of the Nazi Holocaust that is so rampant in Iran and much of the Arab world. Such denial is inextricably linked to the planned annihilation of Israel. When President Ahmadinejad told the leaders of Hamas, Hezbollah, Islamic Jihad, and other "holy warriors" assembled in Tehran that Palestine would soon be "liberated," he did not forget to simultaneously mock the "myth of the Holocaust." In this respect he was reiterating the view of other top Iranian leaders of recent years, including the supreme guide, Ali Khamenei, and former president Hashemi Rafsanjani. These elder statesmen have also denied the Nazi Holocaust while threatening to implement a genocide of their own against the Jewish state; they have at various times asserted that the Shoah was a Zionist invention, that Zionists "collaborated with the Nazis in killing Jews"; or that they deliberately exaggerated the numbers of Jewish dead for financial and political profit. These claims are contradictory, illogical, and manifestly untrue. But the emotional infrastructure that governs anti-Semitism has never been based on conventional logic, reason, or empirical evidence. As the German scholar Matthias Küntzel has commented:

> We are dealing here with a phantasmagoric parallel universe in which the reality principle is constantly ignored and blatantly contradictory notions about Jews all have their place so long as they serve to confirm the anti-Semitic paranoia and hatred: a universe from which the laws of reason have been excluded and all mental energy is harnessed for the cause of antisemitism.[116]

In the case of Ahmadinejad, Holocaust denial has a markedly obsessive and pathological character, as if he were unconsciously fascinated by the prospect of repeating the Shoah he so assiduously denies. The compulsiveness is heightened if, by producing an apocalyptic bloodbath, one believes that the coming of the Islamic Messiah will be accelerated.

Holocaust denial and the calls to annihilate Israel are all the more deadly because they have become *state doctrine* in Iran—linked to frenetic efforts to acquire a nuclear bomb.[117] Since the beginning of the new twenty-first century the propensity to Holocaust denial has assumed an ever higher profile in Tehran. In the late 1990s, Iran had already welcomed right-wing Holocaust deniers and outspoken anti-Semites such as the Austrian engineer Wolfgang Fröhlich, the Swiss "revisionist" Jürgen Graf, and the American white supremacist David Duke.[118] Negationists David Irving and Robert Faurisson were described in the Iranian media as "famous historians" and serious scholars. French "revisionist" Roger Garaudy was elevated to superstar status—described as a hero of French culture though in his home country he was derided as mediocre and subjected to prosecution. Garaudy had been especially influential in Iran ever since he converted to Islam in 1982. He was also known as an enthusiastic supporter of the Iranian Revolution from its beginnings. After his condemnation in France for Holocaust denial in the late 1990s, he gained an especially ardent following in the Muslim world.[119] Among his most devoted admirers was Hashemi Rafsanjani, who in a 1998 sermon on Tehran Radio announced that Garaudy's scholarship convinced him that "Hitler had only killed 20,000 Jews and not six million." The former president added that "Garaudy's crime derives from the doubt he cast on Zionist propaganda."[120]

The *Tehran Times*, an Iranian English-language newspaper, opened the new millennium by insisting in its editorial column that the Holocaust was "one of the greatest frauds of the twentieth century." This blatant libel prompted a formal complaint by the British MP Louise Ellman to the Iranian ambassador in London.[121] But the newspaper continued to publish interviews with European and American Holocaust deniers such as Mark Weber, the director of the Southern California–based Institute for Historical Review. Iranian state radio ran respectful and sympathetic interviews on its English-language segments with Weber. It also interviewed Ernst Zundel, a German citizen and notorious Hitler-admirer who had immigrant status in Canada, in German, and Ahmed Rami, the Swedish-based Moroccan anti-Semite, speaking in Arabic. Rami, who had been imprisoned for incitement in Sweden, became a welcome guest of Iran after his release. He reported that the Iranian parliament had respectfully received him at a special session in his honor. His Holocaust denial Internet website, Radio Islam, which operates in ten languages, may well enjoy financial support from Iran.[122]

This state support and sponsorship is what differentiates Tehran from the Arab world, where enthusiasm for Western Holocaust deniers is also considerable. As in the Arab case, Holocaust denial in Iran does not hesitate to rely on *Western* sources. The paradox is worth noting. Although the Iranian regime violently anathematizes any Western cultural influence, this is a case where it passionately sponsors a Western import in the service of its ideological politics. The rulers of Iran evidently believe that the memory of the Holocaust has been a decisive pillar of Western support for the establishment of the Jewish state. Hence, by exposing it as a lie and a swindle, they hope to undermine the moral foundations of Israel and dramatically accelerate its demise.[123]

The Iranian media have gone out of their way to praise the intellectual courage and fortitude of those Western "experts" and "scholars" who have challenged the so-called Zionist monopoly on the Holocaust. It presents legal restrictions on Holocaust denial in some Western democracies as examples of Orwellian Big Brother surveillance and thought-police tyranny. To the Iranian elite, laws against Holocaust denial prove the arbitrary nature of Western democracy and the all-pervasive influence of Jewish Zionism.[124] *Kayhan International*, for example, fully identified with the bitterness of the German-Australian "revisionist" Frederick Töben at the punishment meted out to him in Germany.[125] The 1998 Garaudy trial in France had already demonstrated the successful infiltration of Western democracies by "international Zionism," as well as the emptiness of liberal slogans about "free thought," enlightenment, and civilization. The trial was portrayed in Iran as a "judicial holocaust." It mobilized a broad movement of solidarity and protest in the name of free speech in a country where this was virtually a nonexistent commodity. No less than 160 Iranian MPs and some 600 journalists signed petitions in Garaudy's support. Students demonstrated in front of the French Embassy, and official Islamic bodies in Iran called on the French government to end its "anti-scientific, anti-cultural" behavior.[126] The secretary of the powerful Council of Guardians, Ayatollah Ahmad Janati, called for Garaudy's book to be translated "into all the languages of the Islamic States" and distributed throughout the world.[127] Iran not only helped Garaudy pay the fine imposed on him, but its top leaders, including Ali Khamenei, Mohammad Khatami, and the parliamentary speaker, enthusiastically received him when he visited Tehran.[128]

Holocaust denial in Iran, like its counterparts elsewhere, is closely linked to the anti-Semitic conspiracy theories embedded in the *Protocols*. According to this mind-set, Zionists and Jews in general are driven by their purported hatred of Islam and boundless desire to usurp and control the entire world. The Iranian regime and media perceive the Holocaust as nothing but a cynically exploited Jewish tool to manipulate the Western world in order to further these objectives of global domination.[129] The first major step in the updated *Protocols* scenario was the foundation of Israel itself. As Supreme Leader Khamenei declared at a Palestinian solidarity conference in April 2001, the "Zionists had exaggerated Nazi crimes against European Jewry in order to solicit international support for the establishment of the Zionist entity in 1948."[130] This assumption became a fixed point of reference for the Iranian media. By propagating the myth that millions of Jews died in Europe at Nazi hands, the Zionists had successfully deceived the world into believing that Jews were oppressed and that they needed a Jewish state in the heart of the Muslim world. In pursuit of their "murderous goals," they had enlisted the support of the United States, which, for its own imperialist ends, helped the Zionists spread the "shameful propaganda lie" of the Holocaust.[131]

The main goal of the American-Zionist conspiracy was the financial extortion of Germany in order to bolster Israel and Western colonialism. The time had come, according to the *Tehran Times,* to expose this "gigantic fraud." In January and February 2005 it ran a seven-part series unmasking "the Auschwitz Lie," in which it reproduced as historical fact virtually every canard ever invented by Western Holocaust deniers Irving, Faurisson, Töben, and Zündel. The existence of gas chambers was vehemently denied. The total number of *all* victims at Auschwitz was reduced to around 150,000 prisoners, who had died solely of disease, undernourishment, and overwork. The Iranian government newspaper totally rejected the testimony of "arch-liars" such as Elie Wiesel and other "professional" survivors, who were slandered as inveterate "swindlers." The confession of Auschwitz commandant Rudolf Höss was, of course, deemed to be worthless.[132]

The *Tehran Times* embraced without question the spurious statistics of Western neo-Nazis purporting to show that there were as many Jews in the world in 1945 as there had been six years earlier. In a January 23, 1998, Al-Quds Day sermon, Hashemi Rafsanjani (then number two in the Iranian hierarchy) had given the green light to this approach, dismissing the figure of six million as pure "Zionist propaganda." He unabashedly branded Israel as "much worse than Hitler," falsely claiming the Zionists had "killed more than one million Palestinians" and equating their ideology of a "superior [Jewish] race" with that of Nazism.[133] According to Rafsanjani, the Germans had never mass murdered any Jews. In his twisted concept of World War II, two equally racist ideologies—Nazism and Zionism—had simply fought each other after previously collaborating in a common goal.

The *Iran Daily* echoed these perverse notions in 2001—evoking the "genocidal war launched by the Jews against the Palestinian people" as a precise equivalent to Auschwitz, Treblinka, and other centers of mass extermination.[134] Conspiracy theory lies at the core of such fantasies.[135] It is the Jews and Israel who are responsible for all society's ills. This explains why Ali Khamenei, in defiance of all the facts, could claim that Zionists were behind the Danish cartoons satirizing the Prophet Muhammad, though the connection was pure fiction. Ahmadinejad, like Khamenei, uses the word "Zionist" as Hitler once used the term "Jew," to define the root of all evil. The Zionists not only orchestrated the Danish cartoons; according to him, they also stood behind the destruction of the Golden Mosque's dome in Iraq, just as they have been blackmailing all Western governments over the Holocaust since 1945. The three "Ds" of *demonizing* the Zionists/Jews, *denying* the Holocaust, and *destroying* Israel have become organically bound together in the anti-Semitic ideology of Ahmadinejad and the Iranian leadership. In addition to being official government policy, this Islamic holy trinity purportedly enjoys divine backing. Indeed, the regime has become so possessed by these demons that it has gladly turned Tehran into the world capital of Holocaust denial—the favored destination for "revisionists" facing prosecution in their native lands.

Since Ahmadinejad's accession to power, Iran has compulsively sought to impose its own negationist truth on the Middle Eastern, Western, and global agenda.[136] On October 26, 2005, the Iranian president, addressing a student conference in Tehran, complained that the European countries persecuted all those who dared to challenge the "Holocaust myth." He said, "Any historian, commentator or scientist who doubts it is taken to prison or gets condemned." In an interview with the left-wing German weekly *Der Spiegel,* Ahmadinejad challenged his interlocutors: "Did the Holocaust actually take place? . . . Why isn't research into a deed that occurred 60 years ago permitted? . . . Why should the Germans not have the right to express their opinion freely?"[137] The Iranian "truth," it is worth noting, is invariably wrapped up in this delusional façade of critical reason, the demystification of taboos, and the rhetoric of pseudo-liberation. "They are allowed to study anything except for the Holocaust myth," Ahmadinejad remarked in February 2006 about the Europeans. "Are these not medieval methods? . . . On the face of it, the technology has changed, but the culture and way of thinking remains medieval."[138] In an almost comical inversion of the Enlightenment, the Iranian theocrats mutate into modern-day Galileos fighting for scientific truth against obscurantist Westerners enslaved to a Jewish myth.

In January 2006, Iran's president sent British prime minister Tony Blair an invitation to his planned Holocaust denial conference in Tehran. The spokesman for the Iranian Foreign Ministry condescendingly explained that at the conference, Blair would finally be able to "say the kind of things he cannot say in London." The reason for this repression of the "truth," as Ahmadinejad subsequently clarified, was, of course, the Zionist conspiracy: "The Zionist pillaging regime has managed, for 60 years, to extort all Western governments on the basis of this myth. . . . They are hostages in the hands of the Zionists."[139] In Ahmadinejad's lexicon Holocaust denial and anti-Zionist Judeophobia are not at all reactionary. On the contrary, they are a mark of progressiveness, freedom of thought, and a challenge to medieval prejudice.

The Iranian president elaborated still further at a press conference held on the sidelines of the antiterrorism summit of Islamic leaders in Mecca on December 8, 2005: "Today, they have created a myth in the name of the Holocaust and consider it to be above God, religion and the prophets. . . . If you [Europeans] committed this big crime, then why should the oppressed Palestinian nation pay the price?"[140] At the same summit he informed reporters that it was up to Europe to allow the Jews to establish their state on European soil.

> Some European countries insist on saying that Hitler killed millions of innocent Jews in furnaces. . . . Although we don't accept this claim, if we suppose it is true, our question for the Europeans is: Is the killing of innocent Jewish people by Hitler the reason for their support to the occupiers of Jerusalem? If the Europeans are honest they should give some of their provinces in Europe—like in Germany, Austria or other countries— to the Zionists and the Zionists can establish their state in Europe.[141]

Ahmadinejad has continually returned to this theme of Europeans taking responsibility for their crimes. At the same time he makes clear that the Jews must return to their own countries, as if they had no roots in Zion or historical connection to Israel and the Middle East. There was no reason, he insists, that they should not be transported back across the Mediterannean. He has repeatedly called into doubt or totally negated the suffering of the Jews in World War II, treating their mass murder as a mere hoax, a political manipulation, or a trick of the imagination, while mocking Europe's own lack of critical judgment. Far from contradicting him, most of the clerical, political, and journalistic elite of Iran have generally followed suit. The editor of the leading Iranian daily *Kayhan,* Hossein Shariatmadari, even compared the European outlawing of Holocaust denial with the doomed attempts by the papacy to hold back the advance of modern science or pretend that the sun revolves around the earth. Similar views have regularly been heard on Iranian TV talk shows featuring local and foreign "historians" who mock "the fairy tale" about the gas chambers. Negationist theories are openly articulated in televised Friday sermons that insert sarcastic comments on the "Holocaust hoax." One representative TV discussion on Iran's Channel 2 on January 5, 2006, related the "myth of the gas chambers" to the

Protocols methodology of Zionism and the need to surgically remove "this cancerous tumor" from the region.[142] During the program, Iranian political analyst Majid Goudarzi made a series of extraordinarily mendacious claims without anyone attempting to correct or contradict him: Jews, he asserted, had burned Christians in Yemen in pre-Islamic times but, somehow, they always "failed to mention that historic event" when alleging that the Germans had done the same to them. Jews, he added, "controlled the global media and the world's natural resources." Hence they could "impose the holocaust issue . . . to depict themselves as oppressed."

The Jews, he said, had also invented the fiction of Zyklon B gas like so many other "Holocaust fabrications," thereby acting in the spirit of the *Protocols* and once again using the "big lie" to gain world power. The money they had extorted from the "Holocaust myth" was intended to finance their biblical empire between the Nile and the Euphrates. In advancing these expansionist plans the Zionists had exploited a variety of allied groups, including the Freemasons and the Baha'is. For good measure, Goudarzi added that French Holocaust denier Paul Rassinier was the one Jew who had told the truth about "the myth of the gas chambers." Another political analyst on the same program corrected him, observing that several Israelis and Jews supported President Ahmadinejad—among them Israel Shamir. Rassinier, of course, was a non-Jew, while Shamir, in his latest incarnation, is a Russian-Swedish anti-Semitic convert to Orthodox Christianity. More important in such TV talk shows is the axiom that Jews control the West—which is seen as the principal reason for Israel's existence and for the resonance of the "Holocaust fairy-tale."[143]

As a result of such intensive indoctrination, Holocaust denial has become a widespread and popular phenomenon in Iran—an intrinsic part of the prevailing anti-Semitic, anti-Zionist, and anti-Western ideology. Purporting to turn the tables on the rationalist "scientific" West (with its secular distaste for clericofascism), Iran has found a deliberately provocative way to attack Western democracy in the name of truth, freedom, and the liberation from conventional taboos. Iranian calls for "scientific scrutiny and rigor" or "truth commissions" in dealing with the Holocaust nonetheless remain a hollow farce barely disguising the unmitigated anti-Jewish hatred seething beneath the surface.[144]

The same inflammatory purpose underlay the Holocaust denial cartoon contest announced by the Iranian daily *Hamshahri* in February 2006. The competition would draw more than twelve hundred submissions from sixty-one countries mocking the Holocaust or presenting it as a fiction. The exhibition itself, which contained many depictions that drew heavily on anti-Semitic stereotypes, was not a spectacular success with the Iranian public, but it did demonstrate how single-mindedly the regime has pursued Holocaust denial motifs.[145] Despite international criticism, Ahmadinejad went obstinately ahead with organizing the so-called scientific conference entitled "Review of the Holocaust: Global Vision" held in Tehran on December 11–12, 2006. For the first time in history a head of state officially and publicly sponsored the denial of the Holocaust. Not only that, but a powerful oil-rich nation was putting the rejection of the Holocaust at the center of its foreign policy agenda in the most offensive manner possible. Among the honored guests were former Ku Klux Klan imperial wizard David Duke, the seventy-six-year-old French negationist Robert Faurisson, the Australian Frederick Töben, some German neo-Nazis, and a motley crew of largely forgotten or delusional veterans of the denial industry. There were even a few ultra-Orthodox haters of Israel—religious Jews clad in black who were only too eager to celebrate the "death of Zionism."

This bizarre bunch of "distinguished scholars" (as Tehran humorlessly called them) were, in themselves, unimportant. They had long dreamed of "revising" the past through their cranky theories to little avail. Iran's leaders, however, are real power freaks bent on *reshaping the future*. Indeed, one of Ahmadinejad's closest advisers, Mohammed Ali Ramin, who prepared the 2006 Tehran conference, bombastically described the proceedings as on a par with the influential 1943 Allied wartime meeting in Tehran. It would, he proclaimed, be an event that would "change the face of the world." Ramin, an academic, solemnly declared that the objective of the gathering was to question "the order that the West has imposed on us."

The core problem, as he saw it, was "the absolute rule of the Jews over all the Christian governments of Europe" and Western support for the Zionists because of the Holocaust myth. But the West, he said, was clearly in decline. Speaking in the name of tolerance and free thought, Ramin confidently declared that a decadent America was already finished as a superpower and that the global rule of Zionism was also nearing its end. England, too, was irredeemably corrupt and guilty of historic crimes infinitely greater than those committed by the Nazis. These atrocities included the murder of a hundred million Indians, the blocking of Muslim unity, and the plunder of natural resources across the globe. The English—not Hitler—had been responsible for the outbreak of World War II. Together with the Americans they had encouraged the Holocaust fabrication to divert attention from their own murderous record and to justify Zionism. The United States, in particular, had been ruled from its earliest foundations by "Zionist Christians." They had, in effect, established Jewish rule in both America and England.

Ramin's total incompetence as an academic historian was further revealed by his speculations about Hitler, half-digested from the writings of self-exculpating former Nazis. Hitler, he insisted, disliked the Jews because his grandmother was "a Jewish whore"; as a Jew himself, the führer supposedly felt both solidarity with and hatred toward Judaism. In this delusional account, not only was Hitler Jewish, but his entire family and "the people who shared his views, his associates who had brought him to power and stood by him to the last—including his lovers and his personal doctor—they were [all Jewish]."[146]

The Nazi dictator had apparently expelled the Jews from central Europe only because the Western Christian nations demanded this of him—especially the British—who had coordinated Jewish immigration to Palestine with the Nazis. More counterfactual speculations followed. Ramin insisted that "the rich and influential Jews who surrounded him [Hitler]" demanded a Jewish state in Palestine. According to Ahmadinejad's closest adviser, it was these same "Jewish capitalists who had brought Hitler to power and supported him," with the intention of resettling the Jews in Palestine. The Zionists were especially strong in Hitler's government, and they had deliberately "incited the Germans against the Jews and spread rumours about the genocide and annihilation of Jews by the Nazis." It was they who sowed panic among the poor Jews in Germany to create the basis for a rapid Jewish immigration to Palestine. Hitler's government even prepared the Jews for the task of building a new state in Palestine by teaching them technical vocations.[147]

According to Ramin, this "true" version of events had been "forbidden" in Germany and the West. To ensure silence, the Zionists had burned or destroyed all the relevant archives and documents (even setting fire to the *Pravda* archives in 2006) to cover up the record of their evil designs.

Mohammed Ali Ramin suggested, in all seriousness, that the "Holocaust lie" had been knowingly used by Churchill, Roosevelt, and Stalin as a weapon to intimidate postwar Germany while ensuring the transfer of postwar European Jews to Palestine. In this conspiracy, the Allied leaders were ultimately tools of the American Jews, who had invented "the legend of the six million" in the service of Israel, Zionism, and Jewish financial interests. The Holocaust fabrication had enabled the U.S. Jews to consolidate their worldwide rule.

Clearly, Ahmadinejad's right-hand man is an extreme anti-Semite and a true believer in the *Protocols*—one who enthusiastically draws on "the strong feeling of hatred toward Zionism and the Jews" that he himself has observed in contemporary public opinion. He offered various examples of this global anti-Semitic trend in a long January 2007 interview with the *Baztab* website in Iran; among them were Jimmy Carter's recent anti-Israel statements, the 2001 UN Durban antiracism conference, and his own private conversations with unnamed Western politicians who repeatedly confirmed to him their great loathing for the Jewish state.[148] In Ramin's eyes, successfully exposing the Holocaust myth would revolutionize the contemporary world order by totally *delegitimizing* Israel and those nations that had helped in its establishment, especially America and Britain. Revealing the naked "truth" about the Holocaust would be a tremendous blow struck for "justice, peace and the security of all mankind." It would help to liberate the world from imperialist domination, the Muslim nations from the "murderous" Zionist incubus, the Germans and other Europeans from unjustified guilt feelings, and the Jews themselves from global anti-Semitism.[149] This last point, however bizarre, may explain why Tehran attached such importance to the presence of ultra-Orthodox Neturei Karta rabbis who do not necessarily deny the Holocaust but appear to welcome Israel's destruction.

For the Iranian regime, delegitimizing and dismantling the Jewish state is the central political point of Holocaust denial. As Iranian foreign minister Manuchehr Mottaki put it in his conference-opening speech, if "the official version of the Holocaust is called into question," then "the nature and identity of Israel" would also be undermined.[150] For President Ahmadinejad in his closing speech, the real point was to actually *implement* the extinction of Israel in the near future. This was presented as historically *inevitable:* "The life-curve of the Zionist regime has begun its descent, and it is now on a downward slope towards its fall. . . . The Zionist regime will be wiped out, and humanity will be liberated."[151] Six months earlier, in an interview with the German weekly *Der Spiegel*, Iran's president had made it clear that recognizing the Holocaust as a "Jewish lie" and annihilating Israel were fundamentally linked in his mind and bound up with Iran's strategy in the worldwide liberation struggle. The liberal West, by protesting against Holocaust denial, had merely confirmed how much it was under "Zionist domination."[152]

Ahmadinejad's Holocaust denial, as Yigal Carmon, founder of the Middle East Media Research Institute, observed in December 2006, is "a premeditated and cold-blooded instrument" to demonize the State of Israel as "a necessary precondition for genocide." As in the case of Hitler, a virulent, anti-Semitic campaign of demonization is indispensable to the final goal of "wiping Israel off the map." The Iranians are well aware that as long as the world remembers the Holocaust, "it will resist any new attempt to perpetrate another genocide against the Jews."[153] Hence the high priority given to demolishing this memory and to upgrading Holocaust denial as a major weapon in the anti-Semitic arsenal of Ahmadinejad's global populism.[154] Since December 2005, the Iranian president has consistently placed negation of the Holocaust at the very center of his agitation against Zionism. In the regime-sponsored Holocaust denial cartoon contest, the first prize went to a Moroccan cartoonist who predictably drew parallels between Israel's security fence and Auschwitz; the second and third prize entries—one by a left-wing Brazilian caricaturist and the other drawn by a Far Right Frenchman—both presented the Holocaust as a crude fabrication. There were no real corpses and there were *no* Jewish victims.[155] This exhibition, it should be emphasized, was not the work of marginal cranks; it was opened by the Iranian Minister of Culture and Islamic Guidance. The massive state support sent out the message that rewriting the history of the Holocaust in a negationist spirit was a global *Islamic* mission and vocation.

The Iranian regime's creation of the World Foundation for Holocaust Research was another institutional move toward fulfilling the same goal. Its director is none other than the historian Mohammed Ali Ramin—the most senior aide and adviser to President Ahmadinejad and the organizer of the Tehran Holocaust denial conference. On June 9, 2006, Ramin told students at Gilan University in the Iranian town of Rasht that Jews as a group had "inflicted the most damage on the human race"; that they were "very filthy people" who had been accused of poisoning wells and spreading plague and typhus. He added that Jews had maliciously and wickedly plotted against other nations throughout history and had always opposed righteousness and justice. The historian even hinted that the Jews might have been behind the AIDS epidemic, the outbreak of SARS (severe acute respiratory syndrome), and the emergence of Asian bird flu—claiming that the latter could be connected to the "holocaust story" since it, too, might turn out to be a "Jewish conspiracy." Ramin told the students that the United States and Britain had been major factors behind the Holocaust myth. One motivation was their anti-Semitic desire to rid the Christian world of Jews. Another reason was to use the Jews "to control the Islamic world on the Holocaust pretext." Britain and America were no less eager to prevent any German resurgence while covering up their own crimes.[156]

The issue, he said, was by no means purely academic. On the contrary, it was crucial for Muslims because "the Holocaust was the principal reason why Palestine was occupied," and "Israel was the main cause of crises and catastrophe in the Middle East." Ahmadinejad's closest counselor was adamant that there would never be peace and security in the region as long as Israel existed. By the same token, he insisted that "the resolution of the Holocaust issue will end in the destruction of Israel."[157]

Ramin, like Ahmadinejad, presented the Jews throughout history only as oppressors, murderers, colonialists, and fascists. Israel was the most recent manifestation in a long chain of Jewish atrocities against Gentiles. Hence its disappearance from the stage could only be considered as a *liberation* for humanity. Like his master, Ramin wrapped his genocidal call for eradicating Israel into the more politically correct framework of opposition to a post–World War II international order dominated by the West.

· · ·

The Iranian Holocaust denial conference was widely condemned in the West. In the Arab world, responses were mixed. Hamas and the Palestinian Islamic Jihad supported the conference; Syria gave it only modest coverage, but President Bashar al-Assad defended the proceedings in the name of free speech—something virtually unknown in his own country.[158] The Iranian ambassador to Syria was more categorical, insisting that there had been no death camps and no gas chambers: The Holocaust was nothing more than a Zionist invention to justify persecution of the Palestinians.

There was mild criticism in some Arab newspapers, suggesting that Holocaust denial might be harmful to the Muslim-Arab cause. A December

18, 2006, op-ed article in the Egyptian daily *Al-Akhbar* argued that Iran was playing into Israel's hands, increasing sympathy for its position and encouraging the idea that Muslims were, in fact, racists. The Holocaust of World War II was not a myth. By denying it, Iran was distracting attention from the "holocausts" currently taking place in Palestine and Iraq. The Saudi Internet site *Elaph* also held that Iranian propaganda was misplaced and would only reinforce European solidarity with Israel. The Kuwaiti journalist Khaled al-Janfawi, writing in *Al-Siyassa* on December 17, 2006, deplored the crass insensitivity of the Holocaust denial conference, which was "adding fuel to the fire." One of the most forthright criticisms appeared in the London-based daily *Asharq Al-Awsat* on December 16, 2006. A British Muslim journalist attacked Ahmadinejad for inciting Muslims and exploiting the "hate TV channels" in order to increase his popularity. The article bluntly characterized the participants at the Tehran conference as "evil and despicable figures."

Such pointed criticism has scarcely influenced the Iranian government to desist from its strategic use of Holocaust denial or its calls for the disappearance of Israel. This may reflect the regime's growing confidence and willingness to assume a defiant and deliberately provocative stance against the United States, the West, and Israel. Ahmadinejad and other high officials may well believe that they are successfully sowing the seeds morally, ideologically, and politically for Israel's extinction and the rise of an Islamic Palestine on its ruins. No doubt they think that by denying, relativizing, or minimizing the scale of the Holocaust they are weakening the European and American sense of guilt that they wrongly believe led to Israel's creation. Furthermore, by presenting the Palestinians as the real victims of the Holocaust, Iran reinforces its militant credentials as the leading champion of the Palestinian struggle. The Iranians know that this is their best card, along with anti-Semitism and loathing for the West, in appealing to a Sunni Arab world that remains markedly suspicious of their ambition—as the conflict between Israel and Hamas once more revealed.

Ali Khamenei is hardly less of an anti-Semite than Ahmadinejad. Like the Iranian president, he regards the claim of the Jews to statehood as perverse and depraved in its very nature; to even raise it is an insult to Islam and to the natural historical order associated with the *dhimma*. In one of his broadcasts on Radio Iran in the 1990s he spoke with undisguised loathing and contempt of the Jews: "What are you? A forged government and a false nation. They gathered wicked people from all over the world and made something called the Israeli nation. Is that a nation? All the malevolent and evil Jews have gathered there. . . . Those [Jews] who went to Israel were malevolent, evil, greedy, thieves and murderers."[159]

Khamenei is committed to all-out war against Israel and to the recovery of Jerusalem as a cardinal axiom of the Iranian Revolution. Like Khomeini and Ahmadinejad, he regards the occupation of Palestine as part of a "satanic design" by Britain, America, and Israel to weaken Muslim solidarity and control the Islamic world; he, too, tends to see Jews as Western agents and a fifth column in the Muslim world, or even as the controlling force in a Judeo-Christian conspiracy to destroy Islam. Khamenei perceives anything that harms Islam as automatically serving the Jews or as having been instigated by Zionism.

Responding in February 2006 to the Danish cartoons of Muhammad, Khamenei said on Iranian state-run radio that their publication was part of a "conspiracy by Zionists who were angry because of the victory of Hamas." He also blasted the Western democracies for their arbitrary definition of free speech, which excluded Holocaust denial as something beyond the pale. An ardent supporter of the French "revisionist" Roger Garaudy, Khamenei had repeatedly addressed the theme of Holocaust denial before anyone in the West had even heard of Ahmadinejad. On December 29, 2006, Khamenei returned yet again to the "double standards" behind Western freedom: "They support those who defame the holy places of Islam. Even the greatest personalities in the West, like the Pope, insult the divine teaching. Research and doubt about the Holocaust and the Zionist rulers are, on the other hand, punished."[160]

As the religious leader of Iran, Khamenei is no less responsible than Ahmadinejad for the totalitarian culture of hatred that has become so pervasive in his country. Together they have turned what was once a relatively enlightened nation into the world center of organized Holocaust denial, validated by Iranian university experts, journalists, and the state-controlled media.

Ahmadinejad's Iran is a state with a totalitarian ideology, radically opposed to the Western democracies and inspired by hatred of the Jews. In its exaggerated sense of national humiliation and victimhood at the hands of the imperialist West (especially Great Britain and America), it uncomfortably resembles Nazi Germany.[161] Ahmadinejad's declarations have been as explicit in their aggressive content toward the Jews of Israel as the most obscene declarations of Hitler in *Mein Kampf.* The drive for regional and eventually world hegemony is striking in both cases despite the disparity in military and technical prowess.

Iran relies more on the power of Islam as a world religion and far less on its armed forces, though nuclear weapons might give it a certain immunity from attack and are, therefore, being feverishly sought. The response of the international community, as in the 1930s, has been muted—borne out of fear, greed, cowardice, appeasement, or a reluctance to face down the fanatical determination of the adversary. The United States appears to have ruled out the use of force and is obsessed with linking the dismantling of Israeli settlements to any attempt to thwart Iran's nuclear program. The two issues are totally unrelated. Progress on the Palestinian question will have no effect at all on Iranian policy.

· · ·

Hitler came to power on an anti-Semitic program after a brief interwar interlude during which Jews had achieved exceptional integration and full equality in Weimar Germany. Khomeini's seizure of power similarly reversed the spectacular gains that the Jews of Iran had made under the last shah. In Germany, Nazi anti-Semitism could build on covert or overt hostility inculcated over centuries by Christian anti-Jewish teachings. In Iran, radical Islamism drew on Shiite doctrines of ritual impurity and imported European motifs for its Judeophobia. Fundamentalist anti-Semitic ideology—whether secular or religious—has in both of these cases embraced a radical populism that is illiberal, anticapitalist, and anticommunist. It vehemently opposes so-called Jewish materialism, secular rationalism, democratic equality, and the emancipation of women.

Anti-Semitism in Nazi Germany, as in contemporary Iran, was powerfully influenced by conspiracy theories conceived in the spirit of the *Protocols of the Elders of Zion,* which project onto the Jews and/or Israel the Nazi and Islamist drive for world domination. In both cases, the rhetoric has been annihilationist. Nazi Germany, from the outset, sought to make Europe *judenrein;* Islamist Iran wishes to cleanse the Middle East of the Jewish state and the "Jewish spirit." This will to exterminate enemies of the people is an integral part of totalitarian revolutions with expansionist designs. It is often linked to a mystical sense of national destiny and bloody visions of the apocalypse. In World War II the Nazis saw the hidden hand of world Jewry behind their war against the Anglo-Americans and the Soviet Union. In the prospectus for World War III, America and Israel are closely interlocked in the minds of the Iranian leaders and their radical Islamist allies as part of the anti-Semitic reflex. The "collective Jew" is the world enemy of a populist revolution turned imperialist that aspires to a pseudo-messianic redemption of mankind.

In a chilling anticipation of the next Holocaust, the historian Benny Morris pointed to some possible differences between the past and future. There would no longer be any one-on-one contact with the victims, no complicated and drawn-out industrialization of mass murder. Iranian Shihab missiles armed with nuclear warheads would set out for Israeli cities, knowing that four or five hits would suffice. Morris imagines the following scenario: "A million or more Israelis, in the greater Tel Aviv, Haifa and Jerusalem areas, will die immediately. Millions will be seriously irradiated. Israel has about seven million inhabitants. No Iranian will see or touch an Israeli. It will be quite impersonal."[162] Many Sunni Arabs inside Israel, in Gaza, and in the semi-occupied West Bank would, of course, also be burned alive, though that hardly worries the ayatollahs. Nor does the prospect that millions of Iranians would also pay the ultimate price. After all, Iran is obeying a divine command whose fulfillment will bring salvation to all humanity through the return of the Hidden Imam. So is the doomsday scenario imminent? Morris reminds us: "They [Ahmadinejad and his allies] seek Israel's annihilation in the here and now, in the immediate future, in their lifetime. They won't want to leave anything up to the vagaries of history."[163]

Iran is, indeed, preparing the ground for a nuclear Holocaust through a sustained campaign of demonizing the Jews. Its leitmotif is the elimination of Israel, the message inscribed on the long-range missiles periodically paraded through the streets of Tehran. Holocaust denial, annihilating the Jewish state, and the nuclear program are three interlocking parts of the same equation, designed to complete what anti-Semites from Haman to Hitler never quite succeeded in achieving. One of Ali Khamenei's own representatives, Mohammad Hassan Rahimian, clarified Iranian thinking on November 16, 2006: "The Jew is the most obstinate enemy of the devout. And the main war will determine the destiny of mankind. . . . The reappearance of the twelfth Imam will lead to a war between Israel and the Shia."[164]

The genocidal hatred for Jews as the enemy of mankind has returned to haunt the Middle East, releasing ancient phobias and new demons of paranoia. Hitler proved that it was possible to murder six million Jews while the world watched impassively. His heirs in Tehran may soon have that option available by merely pressing a button, though it would undoubtedly seal their own doom. In some quarters in the West this has already led to an anticipatory cringe of appeasement, capitulation, or resignation with regard to Iran's nuclearization.[165] Iranian anti-Semitism, it should be noted, barely raises an eyebrow today in the Western media.

At the United Nations in New York, on September 23, 2008, President Ahmadinejad's viciously anti-Jewish speech was even acclaimed in the General Assembly, despite drawing for inspiration on the *Protocols of the Elders of Zion*. He told the assembled representatives that the Zionists "have been dominating an important portion of the financial and monetary centers as well as the political decision-making centers of some European countries and the United States in a deceitful, complex and furtive manner." Zionists were so powerful that political candidates were obliged to "swear allegiance and commitment to their interests in order to attain financial or media support." The great people of America and Europe were in the clutches of the sworn enemy of their "dignity, integrity and rights." They had to submit to the Zionist network against their will and follow the *diktat* of "a small number of acquisitive and invasive people"—covering up and financing their abominable crimes. Once more, though, Ahmadinejad offered hope of imminent redemption, declaring: "Today the Zionist regime is on a definite slope to collapse. There is no way for it to get out of the cesspool created by itself and its supporters."[166] Ahmadinejad was using the term "Zionist" in this speech (and on many other occasions) exactly as Hitler had employed the word "Jew"—as a synonym for relentless rapacity, evil, and world domination. Yet his Hitlerian language did not prevent the General Assembly president (from Nicaragua) Miguel d'Escoto Brockmann—a former winner of the Lenin Prize—from warmly embracing him. That same day the Iranian president was given an hour to expound his loathsome views as Larry King's guest on CNN; three days later his anti-Semitic inanities about Zionism as "the root cause of insecurity and wars" were recorded without a hint of protest by his *New York Times* interviewer. As we have seen, this was not the first time that Ahmadinejad had been given a free ride in the United States or by the United Nations, but the nonchalance with which his lethal obsessions are today accepted as almost normal is an ominous sign. Sixty-four years after Auschwitz, the politics of genocidal anti-Semitism and the indifference that made it possible are still with us.

Since World War II and the Holocaust that decimated two-thirds of European Jewry, it has become impossible to ignore the role and importance of anti-Semitism in the past and present. Hatred of Jews, as we have documented throughout this study, has been an astonishingly resilient and persistent phenomenon throughout the ages. It has accompanied Jewish history for more than two thousand years, though only in the past century did its potentially lethal aspects lead to a scientifically planned and organized effort by a powerful modern state to annihilate the entire Jewish people. In this book we have clearly indicated that for all the unprecedented radicalism of German techniques of mass murder, there were deep historical roots to the Nazi hatred of the Jews. Hitler's anti-Semitism did not come out of nowhere. It could draw on the bimillennial tradition of Christian anti-Judaism, on German *völkisch* nationalism, and on the pseudoscience of race that had branded the Jews as an "inferior species." Above all, it was driven by the completely irrational conspiracy theory that underlies the notorious fabrication of the *Protocols of the Elders of Zion*—the belief that Jewry is engaged in a perpetual and hidden effort to dominate the world. For Hitler and other extreme anti-Semites of his generation, the *Protocols* had revealed the secret forces of darkness that had always animated the Jewish people—unmasking their inner logic and final aims. In 1934 Hitler told his party comrade Hermann Rauschning (then president of the Danzig Senate) that Nazism had deliberately copied the diabolical Machiavellian suggestions of the *Protocols,* especially their emphasis on intrigue, subversion, and dissimulation, along with the smashing of the status quo by terrorist actions. When it came to operational methods, Hitler liked to insist that he had learned crucial lessons from his Jewish and Marxist enemies.

In copying the tactics of the mythical "Elders of Zion" while carrying out his open war against the Jews, Hitler insisted that he was merely taking preventive measures against a deadly threat. In *Mein Kampf* he had declared: "Thus I believe today that I am acting according to the will of the almighty creator: When I *defend myself* against the Jew, I am fighting for the work of the Lord" (my emphasis).[1] In January 1939, on the eve of plunging the nations into the Second World War, Hitler once again pretended that he was acting in legitimate self-defense—to prevent the Jews from "Bolshevizing" the earth and destroying human civilization. But his macabre prophecy that a new world war would lead to the "destruction of the Jewish race in Europe" in reality foreshadowed what *he intended to do!*[2] The Holocaust that the Nazis carried out during the war would be simultaneously justified in Hitler's Last Testament of 1945 as an act of self-defense and as a *liberation of humanity* from the Jewish plague. If we substitute the word "Zionist" for "Jew," a similar message is currently being propagated by Tehran and its allies.

By a disturbingly symbolic coincidence, it was on Hitler's 120th birthday (April 20, 2009)—which also coincided with Holocaust Remembrance Day in Israel—that Mahmoud Ahmadinejad gave what was, in effect. the keynote address to the UN Durban Review Conference against racism in Geneva. Indeed, Hitler's ghost appeared once more to be haunting the UN podium as Ahmadinejad brazenly abused the honor he had been given, blasting Israel as a "totally racist state." An entire nation [the Palestinians] had, according to Iran's president, been made homeless "on the pretext of Jewish sufferings and the ambiguous and dubious question of holocaust. They [the West, the UN Security Council, and/or the Zionists?] sent migrants from Europe, the United States, and from other parts of the world to establish a totally racist government in the occupied Palestine."[3]

Not content with mere Holocaust denial, Ahmadinejad ranted on about Zionist "racist perpetrators of genocide"; about the "economic and political influence of the Zionists and their control of the media"; the "conspiracies by some powers and Zionist circles"; and the need to extinguish Israel's "cruel and repressive racist regime." For Ahmadinejad this was par for the course, as we have amply documented in this work. True, there were some objections. Representatives of the twenty-three EU countries who chose, despite everything, to participate in the Geneva conference did walk out. With the exception of the Czech Republic, they would later return. Unfortunately, these European democracies waited until the last possible moment to make a decision, having kept a troublingly low profile in recent years in face of the Iranian president's blatantly anti-Semitic tirades.[4]

In 2008, Canada and then Israel had been the first to announce their boycott of the entire Durban Review planning process, fearing another repeat of the notorious 2001 UN antiracism conference in Durban, where NGOs had relentlessly vilified Israel and the United States. In March 2008, Italy and the United States also indicated that they would boycott Durban II. They were subsequently joined by Australia, New Zealand, the Netherlands, Germany, and Poland. They suspected that the Durban Review Conference in Geneva would end up as a masquerade—a point validated on April 20, 2009, by the two French-Jewish protesters wearing rainbow-hued clown wigs who pelted Ahmadinejad with red foam noses before being forcibly ejected from the hall.

After endless pressures and much bargaining, the final document of Durban II did not refer to Israel or the Middle East (except for one general clause about foreign occupation). It even added at the last minute a paragraph stating that "the Holocaust should never be forgotten." But this hardly compensated for the fact that the United Nations had once again given center stage to Iran's anti-Semitic language against Israel, applauded by many of the delegates who remained in the hall. The fact that such a twenty-first-century Purim spiel should take place at a UN *antiracism* conference strikingly illustrates many of the themes we have explored in depth in this book: Holocaust inversion, "anti-Zionist" anti-Semitism, conspiracy theory, "antiracist" racism, the legacy of Third Worldism, anti-Westernism, and self-destructive Islamist ideologies. On April 20, 2009, this cocktail of lethal hatreds came together under the relentlessly abused banner of human rights in order to defame the one state that had risen in 1948 to grant refuge to Holocaust survivors and prevent another terrifying massacre of Jews. However, none of this deterred the president of Switzerland from meeting with Ahmadinejad in order to pursue Swiss business interests, as if there were no unresolved nuclear weapons issues, no sanctions against Iran, and no threat to annihilate Israel; as if the growth of anti-Semitism in Switzerland and the dismal record of complicity with Nazi Germany during World War II had not taught the Swiss that there can be no "neutrality" in the face of evil.[5] This appears, however, to be a most difficult lesson for many European countries to learn, trapped as they are in their own cynical double-talk, political correctness, and multicultural illusions in the face of creeping domestic Islamicization.

In many Western countries today, the new *Judenhass* (anti-Semitism) as well as the studied indifference to it is closely linked to an unprecedented demographic shift and its growing political significance. In Europe, cities such as Amsterdam, Rotterdam, Antwerp, Brussels, Malmo, and many other towns from the British Midlands to the Côte d'Azur may soon have Muslim majorities. While traditional Christianity appears to be dying on its feet in most of Europe, Islam has become far more militant. Christian European populations continue to age, but Muslim population growth is surging forward. Brussels, the capital of the European Union, may serve as a useful microcosm of what the future holds: Its Socialist mayor currently presides over a caucus in which Muslims are already in the majority. This fact and the political reality it creates is aggravated by the small size of the Jewish communities in western Europe (except for France and Britain), leaving them little leverage against European politicians eager to appease their Muslim constituents.[6] Since the Jewish presence is bound to shrink still further over time, the prospects for most smaller Jewish communities in Europe would appear to be bleak.

The torrent of indignation that greeted the Gaza campaign in western Europe further escalated the anti-Israel and anti-Semitic trend of the past seven years. The agitation was invariably led by Arab and Muslim immigrants in alliance with local leftists of various hues. A similar Red-Green alliance was discernible in North and South America. It was exacerbated by the mainstream TV coverage, which virtually ignored Israel's unilateral withdrawal from Gaza in 2005 and the extraordinary provocations it had endured thereafter. Few remembered that the Palestinians immediately trashed and burned the houses, greenhouses, and buildings the Israelis had left intact in order to gratuitously assault the Jewish state from more forward positions. Thousands of rockets and mortar bombs were fired from Gaza across the border into the Israeli kibbutzim, moshavim, and towns of the western Negev, especially after Hamas fundamentalists took over the Gaza Strip. Between December 19 and 27, 2008, alone, Hamas fired almost three hundred rockets into southern Israel, breaking a six-month de facto cease-fire arranged by the Egyptians. But this was of relatively little interest to most of the Western media and totally irrelevant for the anti-Israel demonstrators. In their Manichean narrative, a Nazi-like Israeli military force of uniformed fiends had sadistically assaulted hapless, peace-loving Gazans in order to perpetrate a merciless "genocide."[7]

The real facts were, of course, very different. During its three-week military campaign the Israel Defense Forces dropped some 2.25 million warning leaflets, telling Gazans to leave areas about to be bombed. The Israeli army made approximately 165,000 automated individual telephone calls to the inhabitants of Gaza. It allowed humanitarian convoys to enter the Strip, even halting attacks several hours a day so that Palestinians could receive basic everyday necessities. Altogether, according to its detailed assessment, the IDF killed 709 enemy combatants and 295 civilians (among those officially identified); there were proportionately far fewer Palestinian civilian casualties than those inflicted by Western bombing raids in Afghanistan and Iraq. This did not prevent the unleashing of another flood of global hysteria about the "child-killing" Israeli murderers, in which vile slogans such as "Hamas, Hamas, Jews to the gas!" or the old anti-Semitic war cry "Death to the Jews!" could be heard, mainly chanted by Muslim protesters. There were also more militant actions. In Paris, some five hundred members of a twenty-thousand-strong demonstration turned violent, torching cars and vandalizing shops. In Britain, several big protest demonstrations in January 2009 produced similar results, including the burning of Israeli flags and the smashing of a Starbucks café in Kensington. The usual calls to boycott Israel issued forth from British campus radicals, and agitprop dramatists such as Caryl Churchill felt free to slander Jews as heartless, bloodthirsty racists, while hiding under a phony mask of anti-Zionism. Sweden, too, experienced large demonstrations adorned with Hezbollah and Hamas flags in which some prominent Social Democrats took part.[8] In Norway, the finance minister Kristin Halvorsen (leader of the Socialist Left Party) participated in such an anti-Israel rally, where shouts of "Death to the Jews" were reportedly heard. Meanwhile, in Rome a left-wing trade-union spokesman, Giancarlo Desiderati, openly demanded a boycott of Jewish shops and businesses, which, as he so delicately put it, were "tainted by blood."[9]

In Brussels, there were equally chilling signs comparing Gaza to Auschwitz (and Jews to devils) during a march held on January 11, 2009. In Barcelona, thirty thousand marched against Israel, carrying bloodstained blankets and mock dead bodies of children. The largest pro-Palestinian demonstration in the European Union occurred in Madrid in early January

2009. According to the organizers, a quarter of a million attended this repulsive public display of anti-Israel hatred in the Spanish capital. In Turkey, too, there were demonstrations on a large scale. The Turkish prime minister Recep Tayyip Erdogan, in contrast to European governments, openly took the side of Hamas and indulged in demagogic anti-Semitism. In a statement to the Turkish parliament on January 13, 2009, Erdogan accused the Jews of "controlling the media and intentionally targeting civilians."[10] Later, he would claim that "media outlets supported by Jews" were disseminating lies about Gaza.[11] Turkish government denunciations of Israeli "crimes against humanity" were only surpassed in their virulence by Venezuela's authoritarian populist leader, Hugo Chávez, and Bolivian left-wing president Evo Morales. Both Latin American leaders swiftly cut off their diplomatic relations with Israel. Since January 2009, there has been an escalation in the attacks—verbal and physical—on Jews and Jewish institutions in Venezuela. Not surprisingly, the American State Department has listed the country as a state sponsor of anti-Semitism.[12]

At the core of the global anti-Israel hysteria lies the symbolic transformation of Jews into Nazis. Indeed it has become increasingly entrenched in a number of Western societies that seem eager to follow in the footsteps of the former Soviet Union and the most benighted parts of the Muslim-Arab world. In postwar Germany this Holocaust inversion is related to so-called secondary anti-Semitism, which resents Jews as a permanent reminder of the German responsibility for Auschwitz.[13] Radical anti-Zionism has capitalized on this complex by reserving the role of the "new Nazis" exclusively for Jews. This is the perfect way for many Germans to flee from the historic burdens imposed by their own national history, and for other guilt-ridden perpetrators and collaborators in Europe to symbolically wipe the slate clean.

The Nazi-Zionist parallel has also been encouraged by seemingly respectable academics, journalists, and Middle East experts who do not shrink from utterly false comparisons between the Warsaw ghetto and Gaza. In Germany, as in France, Britain, and the United States, a number of the worst accusers are themselves of Jewish origin.[14] The respectability given by the academy and the media to such irresponsible comparisons has made it easier to legitimize them. Such vile propaganda has become self-reinforcing through the sheer power of repetition, greatly magnified by the Internet. Ironically, the Jews who were the prime victims of racial anti-

Semitism now find themselves execrated as supreme exemplars of racism against Arabs.[15] Stigmatized for centuries as inferior Orientals, "Semites," or "Asiatics" in European society, they are now branded as a Western imperialist implant in the Middle East; once denounced as "cosmopolitan nomads," they are today guilty in Gentile eyes of being ultranationalists, ethnic cleansers, and perfect Nazis. In the Arab world, in particular, they have been turned into "Judeo-crusaders" or instigators of a diabolical Zionist-American plot against Islam.[16]

As we have demonstrated in this book, anti-Semitism and anti-Americanism frequently go together. In the eyes of millions of Sunni and Shiite Muslims, they often seem like Siamese twins. The demonizing of "Jewish America" and the depiction of world Jewry as the incarnation of all evil was originally a European Christian myth exported to the Middle East. Following several decades of Islamicization, it has been re-exported back to the West without losing any of its vitality. This genocidal Islamist style of Jew hatred shares many points in common with the most extreme manifestations of European anti-Semitism during the Holocaust. It undeniably satanizes the Jews, fantasizing that they already control the "crusader" West (especially the United States) and have masterminded a series of Western confrontations with Islam.

In the wake of the Egyptian Islamist Sayyid Qutb (executed by Nasser in 1966), the jihadist version of Judeophobia has indeed become more and more deeply rooted in the Sunni Arab world.[17] Under such fundamentalist influences, Islamism became the dominant Muslim variation on the global phenomenon of anti-Semitism, while emerging as a powerful totalitarian movement in its own right.[18] Through intellectual heirs of Qutb such as Sheikh Youssef al-Qaradawi, the major spiritual leader of the transnational Muslim Brotherhood, Islamist anti-Semitism long ago transcended the traditional hostility to Jews reflected in the Koran and *hadith* or the nationalist Judeophobia of secularist pan-Arabism. Closer in spirit to the apocalyptic conspiracy theories of Nazism, followers of Qutb believe they are fighting a "cosmic war" in the name of Islam against Satanic Jews and their American puppets. According to their totalist vision, the Jews launched their war against Muslims from the moment that Muhammad established a *dawla* (Islamic state) in Medina. Indeed, the Jews stood behind every subsequent war against Islam and against Muslim efforts aimed at bringing about an Islamic revival. This alleged bellicosity and subversiveness was rooted in their so-called Jewish character, which would never change.[19] The Jews remained the brains behind the "crusader" war on Islam and American policy in the Middle East. In order to purge the West of its secularist and materialist sickness, one would therefore have to purify the contemporary Middle East and the wider world of the Jewish-Zionist toxin.

Such an uncompromising Islamist vision of the evil Jews at the heart of the decadent West finds one of its sharpest expressions in the Hamas Charter, the sacred covenant of the jihadists who rule Gaza today. Hamas sees itself as an important spearhead in the cosmic war against world Jewry, hence its embrace of the *Protocols of Zion* is fully consistent with its general worldview. Indeed, its charter is in some ways more extreme in its programmatic key points about the Jews than the anti-Semitic program of the Nazi movement in the 1920s. Equally, the prospective annihilation of Zionist Jews envisaged by Hamas is no less murderous in its implications than the threats continually emanating from Mahmoud Ahmadinejad. Nonetheless, Hamas has been enthusiastically supported by some Western liberals, leftists, and other sympathizers around the world during the Gaza war.[20] Its genocidal project toward Jews, its boundless hatred of the West, its adamant rejection of any territorial or political compromise with Israel, and its determination to coercively impose sharia law on all of Palestine have failed to undermine the conviction of its leftist supporters that its cause is just. Nor has the subjugation of women and the rampant misogyny of fundamentalist rule from Hamas and the Taliban in Afghanistan and northwest Pakistan made the slightest dent in the Marxist-Islamist alliance. Some campus feminists have even glorified the burka as an "act of liberation" from Western imperialism. Clearly, anti-Americanism trumps any authentic concern for justice in the political support of the radical Left for jihadism.

This phenomenon is by no means new. Many leftists preferred in the past to ignore the mass murders of Stalin, Mao, Pol Pot, and Saddam Hussein (not to mention the repressive regimes of Ho Chi Minh and Castro), as if opposing America was in itself a mark of virtue. Today, they turn a blind eye to the genocide committed by an Islamist Arab regime in the Sudan against blacks, Christians, and African Muslims; they ignore the oppressiveness of the Iranian mullahs, and they dismiss the atrocities carried out by Islamofascist terrorists.[21] The obvious point of connection in this leftist sycophancy toward Communist and Islamist totalitarianism lies in the common hatred of America and its "bourgeois" lifestyle. The inner spring, however, is a deep self-alienation and loathing for real harmony, happiness, and success in this world. Such perverse feelings among some of the more privileged beneficiaries of Western society lead in turn to a nihilistic hate for hate's sake, a morally twisted attraction for the most despicable mass-murdering tyrannies and an increased disposition to hate America and Israel. Such feelings are, unfortunately, also to be found among some of the more militant "anti-Zionist" Jews who claim to speak in the name of universal justice.

Awareness of the ongoing connection between anti-Americanism and anti-Semitism should not, however, lead us to ignore the dangers of Jew hatred in the United States itself. There has never been any shortage of white supremacist bigotry and racism in American society. America in the 1930s slammed the doors in the face of desperate Jewish refugees from Europe; it instituted quotas at prestigious universities; and it had its own anti-Semitic demagogues, such as the Catholic radio priest Charles Coughlin.[22] This was at a time when African Americans were prime targets of racism, and for several decades they collaborated with Jews in a common struggle against white American prejudice. But since the late 1960s, blacks themselves have displayed a significantly higher level of anti-Semitism than other Americans.[23] An ADL survey in 2002 found that 35 percent of African American respondents held strongly anti-Semitic opinions, over twice the intensity of such views in the rest of the population.

Israel's Gaza operation has provided its own additives of hate speech—this time predominantly among America's growing Arab and Muslim population. As in Europe, abusive Holocaust terminology has been working overtime. On January 5, 2009, several hundred demonstrators outside the Israeli Consulate in San Francisco held aloft such signs as "Jews: The First Terrorists" and "Gaza 2008—Warsaw 1938." In Times Square, New York, two days earlier, thousands of protestors brandished placards filled with hateful words such as "Israel Fourth Reich," and "Holocaust by Holocaust Survivors," while others chanted such slogans as "Palestine is our land, the Jews are our dogs" or evoked in Arabic the battle of Khaibar, in which Muhammad had crushed the Jews of Arabia. The rally was organized by a bevy of antiwar advocates, American Muslim organizations, and Palestinian groups. The day before in Chicago (January 2, 2009), angry protestors held up mock coffins draped with Palestinian flags while demanding an end to "Israel's genocide in Gaza." In Washington, D.C., that same day, more than a thousand demonstrators (many waving Hezbollah flags) chanted "Death to Israel" and "Death to Zionism" while celebrating the massacre of Jews in Khaibar at the dawn of Islam. Four days earlier, in Tampa, Florida, there was a flurry of banners calling for the dissolution of Israel, one even declaring "Zionism is Cancer: Radiate It."[24] Indeed, across the United States, these predominantly Arab American protests demanded an end to the "Palestinian Holocaust," called for the liberation of Palestine "from the river to the sea" (a Hamas slogan), and demonized Zionism as the "cancer of the world."

In France, too, there were many pro-Palestinian demonstrations with a similar message, though on a much larger scale. On January 10, 2009, for example, there were no fewer than 60,000 protestors in Paris alone, and 150,000 demonstrators marched across the country in 130 towns.[25] An "anti-Zionist party" negating Israel's right to exist was formed that included Sunni and Shiite Muslim organizations as well as far Right and far Left groups, happy to march under Hamas and Hezbollah flags. The Islamicization of the Palestinian cause was accompanied by an unmistakable trend of transforming every Jew into a "bloodthirsty and criminal Zionist."

Solidarity with the Palestinians has, in effect, been globally hijacked by a culture of hatred that shamelessly and totally distorts the integrity of religious beliefs; terrorism has come to justify itself as "resistance" under the false banner of justice and human rights; the Holocaust is cynically turned against its primary victims and the "deicidal" people of yesterday are transformed into the mythical perpetrators of today's genocide.[26] The Jew-hatred of yesteryear has not only mutated but is actively fuelling the Middle East conflict and re-exporting its poisonous fruits to Europe and beyond. Unless it is checked in time the lethal triad of anti-Semitism, terror and jihad is capable of unleashing potentially universal conflagration. A deadly strain of genocidal anti-Semitism brings the nightmare of a nuclear Armageddon one step closer and with it the need for more resolute preventive action.

ACKNOWLEDGMENTS

This book could not have been written without the help of a number of research grants over the past twenty years. In the late 1980s I was assisted by the Vidal Sassoon International Center for the Study of Antisemitism (SICSA) at the Hebrew University of Jerusalem in undertaking the first steps in what turned out to be a far bigger enterprise than anyone could have imagined at the time. Friends of the late Simon Wiesenthal also aided me in this project during the very early stages. During the 1990s as *Jewish Chronicle* professor of Jewish studies at University College, London, I was able to pursue an investigation into European anti-Semitism after the fall of communism, which received support from the American Jewish Committee. My thanks to its executive director, David Harris, for encouraging this research. A special thanks to the Shalem Center in Jerusalem for its grant to cover research expenses, which enabled me in 2001 to seriously embark on the broader concept that underlies this book. That step proved to be a crucial turning point in this endeavor. My particular appreciation goes to Shalem Center president Dan Polisar for his patience and support over the long haul.

I am no less grateful to Trevor Pears, who in 2004 stepped in at a critical moment to facilitate the extension of my work. His generous initiative helped ensure the completion of the project. No words of praise can be too high for Felix Posen, a friend, a wise counselor, and the strongest backer of SICSA in Jerusalem, which I have had the privilege to head since 2002. His vision and support, along with that of Daniel Posen, have been vital factors in our work to combat anti-Semitism, a cause to which this book is dedicated.

A special thank-you must go to Esther Rosenfeld, who did an amazing job in deciphering and typing up my handwritten manuscript, which went through countless revisions and rewrites. Without her skills, this huge labor might have remained an unfinished symphony. I also wish to express my profound gratitude to the dedicated members of SICSA. Ruhama Roth, SICSA's administrative secretary, has been my right hand and a rock of support for the past six years. I wish to acknowledge my dear friend Sara Grosvald, who has always shown exemplary professionalism and graciousness in providing me with up-to-date and invaluable information in recent years. Alifa Saadya, a fine editor and dedicated colleague, helped with the text, with accessing information, and with dealing with various editing tasks at SICSA. The expertise of my much-esteemed colleague, Dr. Leon Volovici, in Eastern European affairs was of great benefit at various times. I am most grateful to Martina Weisz for her kindness and willingness to help, especially with locating Spanish, Latin American, and French sources. My thanks also go to Avigail Tsirkin-Sadan, a most efficient secretary, as well as to our newest recruits, Inbal Cohen and Sharon Katz.

Among those in academia or public life from whom I have learned or with whom I have exchanged ideas relevant to this book, I would like to mention the following persons in alphabetical order: Per Ahlmark (Stockholm), Bat Ye'or (Geneva), Ulrike Becker (Hamburg), Georges Bensoussan (Paris), Margaret Brearley (London), Irwin Cotler (Montreal), Ludmila Dymerskaya-Tsigelman (Jerusalem), Samy Eppel (Caracas), Alain Finkielkraut (Paris), Abe Foxman (New York), Manfred Gerstenfeld (Jerusalem), Trudy Gold (London), Jeffrey Herf (Washington, D.C.), Carol Iancu (Montpellier), Raphael Israeli (Jerusalem), Anthony Julius (London), András Kovács (Budapest), Matthias Küntzel (Hamburg), David Littman (Geneva), Joanna Michlic (Cambridge, Massachusetts), Menahem Milson (Jerusalem), Fiamma Nirenstein (Rome), Anton Pelinka (Vienna), Derek Penslar (Toronto), Melanie Phillips (London), Alvin Rosenfeld (Bloomington, Indiana), Frederick Schweitzer (New York), Leonardo Senkman (Jerusalem), David Shapira (Paris), Ben-Ami Shillony (Jerusalem), Dan Shueftan (Haifa), David Singer (New York), Pierre-André Taguieff (Paris), Jacques Tarnero (Paris), Bassam Tibi (Göttingen), Shmuel Trigano (Paris), Michael Whine (London), and Ruth Wisse (Cambridge, Massachusetts).

My sincere thanks to Will Murphy at Random House, who exhibited extraordinary patience with an author constantly extending his work beyond the promised timeline. He obviously believed that I knew what I was doing and why it had to be done. I hope that I have justified that confidence. I would also like to thank the copy editor, Michelle Daniel, for her professionalism and Courtney Turco for her helpfulness in expediting and processing this manuscript.

Finally, there is the debt to those who are nearest and dearest: to my wife, Daniella, whose insight and support helped me keep my sense of proportion in the face of great pressures; to my children, who, next to God, proved the best guarantee for eternity in this world; and to my mother, Sabina, a woman of valor, who courageously survived the traumas of the twentieth century to see the completion of this book.

ROBERT S. WISTRICH
The Hebrew University of Jerusalem
Mount Scopus
Purim, March 10, 2009

NOTES

INTRODUCTION: THE RETURN OF ANTI-SEMITISM

1. Robert S. Wistrich, "The Old-New Antisemitism," in *Those Who Forget the Past: The Question of Anti-Semitism,* ed. Ron Rosenbaum (New York: Random House, 2004), pp. 71–90.
2. Quoted in Paul Berman, "Something's Changed," *Those Who Forget the Past,* pp. 18–19.
3. Ibid., p. 19.
4. Shalom Lappin, "Israel and the New Antisemitism," *Those Who Forget the Past,* pp. 455–70.
5. Meïr Villegas Henríquez, *Antisemitische Incidenten in Nederland. Overzicht over het jaar 2006 en de periode 1 januari–5 mei 2007* (The Hague: Centre Information and Documentation on Israel [CITI], 2008), pp. 49–50.
6. Meir Waintrater, "Les habits 'antisionistes' des vieux mythes antisémites," *L'Arche,* February 2008, pp. 38–53. Commissioned by the Anti-Defamation League [ADL], the two surveys of 2005 and 2007 covered eleven European countries and were carried out by Taylor Nelson Sofres. ADL surveys in early 2009 showed that 41 percent of Europeans believed Jews had a major influence on the global financial system and one-third considered them responsible for its ills.
7. The Community Service Trust (CST), *CST Antisemitic Incidents Report 2007* (London: CST, 2008), pp. 12–13.
8. "Gaza Crisis May Be Fomenting Violence Against Jews in Europe," *International Herald Tribune,* January 6, 2009.
9. Paul Johnson, "The Anti-Semitic Disease," *Commentary,* June 2005, pp. 33–38.
10. Quoted in P. G. J. Pulzer, *The Rise of Political Anti-Semitism in Germany and Austria* (New York: John Wiley and Sons, 1964), p. 299.
11. Robert S. Wistrich, introduction to *Antisemitism: Its History and Causes* by Bernard Lazare (Lincoln: University of Nebraska, 1995), pp. 8–12.
12. Jacques Maritain, *A Christian Looks at the Jewish Question* (New York: Longmans, 1939), pp. 29–30.
13. Quoted in Dennis Prager and Joseph Telushkin, *Why the Jews? The Reason for Antisemitism* (New York: Simon and Schuster, 1985), p. 28.
14. Ernest van den Haag, *The Jewish Mystique,* 2nd ed. (New York: Stein and Day, 1977), pp. 60–61.

15. Prager and Telushkin, *Why the Jews?* p. 29.

16. Bernard Lewis, "The New Anti-Semitism," *The American Scholar* 75, no. 1 (Winter 2006): pp. 25–33.

17. Friedrich Heer, *God's First Love: Christians and Jews Over Two Thousand Years* (London: Weidenfeld and Nicolson, 1967).

18. Joel Carmichael, *The Satanizing of the Jews: Origin and Development of Mystical Anti-Semitism* (New York: Fromm International, 1992).

19. Gavin Langmuir, "Toward a Definition of Antisemitism," in *The Persisting Question: Sociological Perspectives and Social Contexts of Modern Antisemitism,* ed. Helen Fein (Berlin: Walter de Gruyter, 1987), pp. 86–127. Also Langmuir, *History, Religion, and Antisemitism* (Berkeley and Los Angeles: University of California Press, 1990).

20. Langmuir, "Toward a Definition," p. 110.

21. Jeffrey J. Cohen, "The Flow of Blood in Medieval Norwich," *Speculum* 79, no. 1 (January 2004): pp. 26–65.

22. See Robert S. Wistrich, *Hitler's Apocalypse: Jews and the Nazi Legacy* (New York: St. Martin's Press, 1986), pp. 136–53.

23. Ibid., pp. 36–37. See also Hermann Rauschning, *Hitler Speaks* (London: T. Butterworth, 1939).

24. Philippe Burrin, "Nazi Antisemitism: Animalization and Demonization," in *Demonizing the Other: Antisemitism, Racism, and Xenophobia,* ed. Robert S. Wistrich (Amsterdam: Harwood Academic Publishers, 1999), pp. 223–35. Published for the Vidal Sassoon International Center for the Study of Antisemitism (SICSA).

25. Uriel Tal, *Religion, Politics, and Ideology in the Third Reich: Selected Essays* (London: Routledge, 2004), pp. 33–35.

26. Ibid., p. 36.

27. Saul Friedländer, "Europe's Inner Demons": The 'Other' as Threat in Early Twentieth-Century European Culture," in Wistrich, *Demonizing the Other,* pp. 210–22.

28. Edward H. Flannery, *The Anguish of the Jews* (New York: Macmillan, 1965) and William Nicholls, *Christian Antisemitism* (Northvale, N.J.: Jason Aronson, 1995) are important accounts of the Christian role in anti-Semitism.

29. Jean-Paul Sartre, *Anti-Semite and Jew* (New York: Schocken Books 1976), pp. 40–49. This was the translation of Sartre's *Réflexions sur la Question Juive,* written in 1944, first published in French in 1946 and translated into English two years later.

30. Ibid., pp. 49–54.

31. Prager and Telushkin, *Why the Jews?* p. 80.

32. Jan T. Gross, *Fear: Anti-Semitism in Poland After Auschwitz* (New York: Random House, 2007). For the background, see also Joanna Beata Michlic, *Poland's Threatening Other: The Image of the Jew from 1880 to the Present* (Lincoln: University of Nebraska Press, 2006).

33. Gross, *Fear,* pp. 247–48. Gross writes of "ordinary Poles' widespread collusion with the Nazi-driven extermination of the Jews"—a claim hotly contested in Poland.

34. Ibid., pp. 134–35. According to Gross, among the clergy, only Teodor Kubina (bishop of Częstochowa) spoke out unambiguously against anti-Semitism and the blood libel, for which he was promptly reprimanded by his fellow bishops.

35. Ibid., pp. 192–242. See also Jeff Schatz, "Jews and the Communist Movement in Interwar Poland," *Studies in Contemporary Jewry* 20 (2004): pp. 13–37, and his earlier study, *The Generation: The Rise and Fall of the Jewish Communists of Poland* (Los Angeles: University of California Press, 1991).

36. Gross, *Fear*, pp. 216–17.

37. Paul Lendvai, *Anti-Semitism Without Jews: Communist Eastern Europe* (Garden City, N.Y.: Doubleday, 1971).

38. Dariusz Stola, *Kampania antysyionistyczna Polsce 1967–1968* (Warsaw: Instytut Studiów Politycznych Polskiej Akademii Nauk, 2000) provides the most extensive documentation of these events.

39. See Milovan Djilas, *Conversations with Stalin* (New York: Harcourt, Brace and World, 1962); Gennadi Kostyrchenko, *Out of the Red Shadows: Anti-Semitism in Soviet Russia* (Amherst, N.Y.: Prometheus Books, 1995); and Jonathan Brent and Vladimir P. Naumov, *Stalin's Last Crime: The Plot Against the Jewish Doctors, 1948–1953* (New York: HarperCollins Publishers, 2003).

40. Yuri Slezkine, *The Jewish Century* (Princeton, N.J.: Princeton University Press, 2004), p. 301.

41. Ibid., pp. 309–10.

42. Leonid Luks, "Stalin und die 'jüdische Frage': Brüche und Widersprüche," in *Der Spätstalinismus und die "jüdische Frage,"* ed. L. Luks (Cologne: Böhlau Verlag, 1998), pp. 271–92.

43. See Liudmila Dymerskaya-Tsigelman, "Die Doktrin des Stalinischen Antisemitismus: Zur Enstehungsgeschichte," in Luks, *Der Spätstalinismus*, pp. 29–52.

44. Lev Besymenski, "Was das Sowjetvolk vom Holocaust wusste," *Der Spätstalinismus*, pp. 69–88. See also Robert S. Wistrich, "The New War Against the Jews," *Commentary*, May 1985, pp. 35–40.

45. Wistrich, "Old-New Anti-Semitism," pp. 71–90.

46. Cesare G. De Michelis, *The Non-Existent Manuscript: A Study of the "Protocols of the Sages of Zion"* (Lincoln: University of Nebraska Press, 2004). Published with the Vidal Sassoon International Center for the Study of Antisemitism (SICSA).

47. Pierre-André Taguieff, *Prêcheurs de Haine: Traversée de la Judéophobie Planetaire* (Paris: Mille et Une Nuits, 2004). Robert S. Wistrich, "Dialogues in Hell: Zionism and Its Double," *Midstream* (May–June 2008): pp. 9–13.

48. Wistrich, "Old-New Anti-Semitism," pp. 81–83. See also Robert S. Wistrich, "Ideological Anti-Semitism in the 20th Century," *Midstream*, April 1987, pp. 17–22.

49. See Robert S. Wistrich, *Anti-Semitism in Europe Since the Holocaust* (New York: American Jewish Committee [AJC], Working Papers on Contemporary Anti-Semitism, 1993).

50. Yitzhak M. Brodny, "The Heralds of Opposition to Perestroyka," *Soviet Economy* 5 (1989): pp. 162–200.

51. Zora Bútorová and Martin Bútorá, *Wariness Toward Jews and "Postcommmunist Panic" in Slovakia* (New York: AJC, 1992).

52. Leon Volovici, *Antisemitism in Post-Communist Eastern Europe: A Marginal or Central Issue?* (Jerusalem: Hebrew University of Jerusalem, Vidal Sassoon International Center for the Study of Antisemitism [SICSA], ACTA no. 5, 1994).

53. Wistrich, *Anti-Semitism in Europe*, pp. 14–21.

54. Robert S. Wistrich, "Once Again, Anti-Semitism Without Jews," *Commentary*, August 1992, pp. 45–49.

55. Jeffrey Herf, *The Jewish Enemy: Nazi Propaganda During World War II and the Holocaust* (Cambridge, Mass.: Harvard University Press, 2006), pp. 231–78.

56. Ibid., p. 230.

57. Wolfram Meyer zu Uptrupp, *Kampf gegen die "jüdische Weltverschwörung": Propaganda und Antisemitismus der Nationalsozialisten 1919 bis 1945* (Berlin: Metropol, 2003).

58. Quoted by Hillel Halkin, "The Return of Antisemitism," *Commentary*, February 2002, pp. 30–36.

59. Ibid.

60. Robert S. Wistrich, "Old Wine, New Bottles: European Antisemitism Reinvents Itself," *The Review*, June 2005, pp. 25–29.

61. Ibid.

62. Aryeh Green, "European Universities and the New Anti-Semitism," in *Academics Against Israel and the Jews*, ed. Manfred Gerstenfeld (Jerusalem: Jerusalem Center for Public Affairs, 2007), pp. 177–79. See also the pamphlet by Ben Cohen, *The Ideological Foundations of the Boycott Campaign Against Israel* (New York: AJC, 2007).

63. Winston Pickett, "Nasty or Nazi? The Use of Antisemitic Topoi by the Left-Liberal Media," in *A New Anti-Semitism: Debating Judeophobia in 21st-Century Britain*, ed. Paul Iganski and Barry Kosmin (London: Profile Books, 2003), pp. 148–68.

64. Wistrich, *Anti-Semitism in Europe*, pp. 14–15. Between 1936 and 1956 there were three French Jewish prime minsiters—Léon Blum, René Mayer, and Pierre Mendès-France—all of them identified with the Social Democratic Left.

65. "L'antisémitisme en France," *L'Événement du Jeudi*, October 15–21, 1987, pp. 58–86.

66. David Selbourne, "French Jews Begin to Feel Alien All Over Again," *The Sunday Times* (London), June 3, 1990.

67. Quoted by Henry H. Weinberg, *The Myth of the Jew in France, 1967–1982* (New York: Mosaic Press, 1987), pp. 64–65.

68. Alain Finkielkraut, *L'Avenir d'Une Négation: Réflexions sur la Question du genocide* (Paris: Éditions du Seuil, 1982).

69. See Alain Finkielkraut, *Au nom de l'autre: Réflexions sur l'antisémitisme* (Paris: Gallimard, 2003)—a short though challenging essay.

70. Ibid.

71. *Les Enfants de la République* (Paris: Éditions de la Martinière, 2004). A collective publication of the Union des étudiants juifs de France. No editor is listed.

72. Robert S. Wistrich, "Europe's New Frontier of Bigotry," *Midstream*, January–February 2006, pp. 4–6.

73. Georges Bensoussan, *Antisemitism in French Schools: Turmoil of a Republic* (Jerusalem: Hebrew University of Jerusalem, SICSA, ACTA no. 24, 2004).

74. See Werner Bergmann, "Antisemitismus in Deutschland von 1945 bis heute," in *Antisemitismus: Geschichte und Gegenwart*, ed. Samuel Salzborn (Giessen, Germany: NBKK, 2004), pp. 51–80.

75. Doron Rabinovici, Ulrich Speck, and Natan Sznaider, eds., *Neuer Antisemitismus? Eine globale Debatte* (Frankfurt: Suhrkampf, 2004). See also Samuel Salzborn, "The German Myth—Feeling as a Nation of Victims," *Dapim* (University of Haifa) 21 (2007): pp. 239–60, in Hebrew.

76. Yves Patrick Pallade, "Antisemitism and Right-Wing Extremism in Germany: New Discourses," *The Israel Journal of Foreign Affairs* 2 (2008): pp. 65–76. See also Clemens Heni, *Antisemitismus und Deutschland* (Lulu-Verlag, 2009).

77. Pallade, "Antisemitism," pp. 71–72.

78. Robert Knight, ed., *"Ich bin dafür, die Sache in die Lange zu ziehen": Die Wortprotokolle der Österreichischen Bundesregierung von 1945 bis 1952 über die Entschädigung der Juden* (Frankfurt: Athenaeum, 1988).

79. Robert S. Wistrich, *Austria and the Holocaust Legacy* (New York: AJC, 1999).

80. Robert S. Wistrich, *Anti-Zionism and Antisemitism: The Case of Bruno Kreisky* (Jerusalem: Hebrew University of Jerusalem, SICSA, 2007).

81. See Richard Mitten, *The Politics of Antisemitic Prejudice: The Waldheim Phenomenon in Austria* (Boulder, Colo.: Westview Press, 1992).

82. For the anti-Semitic subtext in Haider's own rhetoric, see Anton Pelinka and Ruth Wodak, eds., *"Dreck am Stecken": Politik der Ausgrenzung* (Vienna: Czernin, 2002).

83. 2006 Pew Global Attitudes Project Poll, quoted in *Contemporary Global Anti-Semitism: A Report Provided to the United States Congress* (Washington, D.C.: U.S. Department of State, 2008), p. 34.

84. Didier Lapeyronnie, "Antisémitisme, Racisme et Exclusion Sociale," *Les Études du Crif,* no. 9 (September 2005). See also Eric Marty, "Un nouvel antisémitisme," *Le Monde,* January 16, 2002.

85. Lapeyronnie, "Antisémitisme," pp. 7–9. See also Paul Scheffer, *Die Eingewanderten. Toleranz in einer grenzenlosen Welt* (Munich: Carl Hanser Verlag, 2008), pp. 377–439.

86. Lapeyronnie, "Antisémitisme," pp. 24–57.

87. Ibid., pp. 28–29. It is as if the mythical Jew crystallizes all the bitterness of the French Muslim at being negatively identified and remaining an outsider not recognized by the French majority.

88. Pierre-André Taguieff, "Néo-Pacifisme, Nouvelle Judéophobie et Mythe du Complot," *Les Études du Crif,* no. 1 (July 2003).

89. Robert S. Wistrich, *Muslim Anti-Semitism: A Clear and Present Danger* (New York: AJC, 2004), p. 4; and "Major Anti-Semitic Motifs in Arab Cartoons: An Interview with Joël Kotek," *Post-Holocaust and Anti-Semitism,* no. 21 (June 1, 2004). See also *Arab Media Review: Anti-Semitism and Other Trends,* January–June 2007.

90. Bernard Lewis, "Muslim Antisemitism," in Rosenbaum, *Those Who Forget the Past,* pp. 508–32. See also Robert S. Wistrich, "Dehumanizing the Other: Muslim Arab Anti-Semitism Today," *Arab Media Review: Anti-Semitism and Other Trends* (January–June 2008).

91. Ibid., p. 509.

92. Omer Bartov, "Did Hitlerism Die With Hitler? He Meant What He Said," *The New Republic,* February 2, 2004.

93. Ibid.

94. See Amal Saad-Ghorayeb, *Hizbu'llah: Politics and Religion* (London: Pluto Press, 2002), pp. 134–86.

95. Ronald L. Nettler, *Past Trials and Present Tribulations: A Muslim Fundamentalist's View of the Jews* (Oxford, U.K.: Pergamon Press 1987), pp. 1–11. This study was commissioned and copublished by SICSA.

96. Ibid., p. 7. See also D. F. Green, ed., *Arab Theologians on Jews and Israel: The Fourth Conference of the Academy of Islamic Research,* 3rd ed. (Geneva: Éditions de L'Avenir, 1976).

97. Ronald L. Nettler, "Islamic Archetypes of the Jews: Then and Now," in *Anti-Zionism and Antisemitism in the Contemporary World,* ed. Robert S. Wistrich (London: Macmillan, 1990), pp. 63–73.

98. See ibid., pp. 65–68, for the hadith concerning the Prophet Muhammad's protracted and painful death after being poisoned by a Jewish woman.

99. See Sayyid Qutb, *In the Shade of the Qur'an,* vol. 8 (Leicester, U.K.: 2003). A translation of his multivolume *Fī Zill al-Qur'ān.*

100. Yvonne Yazbeck, "Sayyid Qutb, Ideologue of Islamic Revival," in *Voices of the Islamic Revolution,* ed. John Esposito (New York: Oxford University Press, 1983), p. 68.

101. See Bat Ye'or, *The Dhimmi: Jews and Christians Under Islam* (Rutherford, N.J.: Fairleigh Dickinson University Press, 1985); and Bat Ye'or, *Islam and Dhimmitude: Where Civilizations Collide* (Madison, N.J.: Fairleigh Dickinson University Press, 2002).

102. Nettler, *Past Trials,* p. 19.

103. Ibid., pp. 20–21.

104. Shaykh 'Abd al-Halim, *Al-Jihād wa al-Naṣir* [Holy War and Victory] (Cairo, 1979), p. 150.

105. In January 1998 a leading Iranian newspaper close to Supreme Guide Ali Khamenei emphasized: "The history of the beginning of Islam is full of Jewish plots against the Prophet Muhammad and of murderous attacks by Jews." See *Jumhuri-I Islami,* January 8, 1998.

106. See Andrew G. Bostom, *The Legacy of Jihad: Islamic Holy War and the Fate of Non-Muslims* (New York: Prometheus Books, 2005), which provides many sources for the doctrine of jihad throughout Muslim history.

107. Nettler, *Past Trials,* pp. 34–36.

108. Bassam Tibi, "Die Mär des Islamismus von der jüdischen und kreuzzüglerischen Weltverschwörung gegen den Islam," in *Neu-alter Judenhass,* ed. Klaus Faber, Julius H. Schoeps, and Sacha Stawski (Berlin: Verlag für Berlin-Brandenburg, 2006), pp. 179–202.

109. Nettler, *Past Trials,* pp. 82–83. Translation from Qutb's original essay *Ma'rakatunā Ma'a al-Yahūd* (Our Struggle with the Jews) published as a small book by the Saudi government in 1970.

110. Ibid., p. 84.

111. Quoted by Lewis, "Muslim Anti-Semitism," in Rosenbaum, *Those Who Forget the Past,* pp. 510–17.

112. *Asharq Al-Awsat,* June 23, 2002. This is a Saudi-financed and -controlled daily in London.

113. Reuters, July 9, 2002. See also Ahmad Bahgat in *Al-Ahram,* July 24, 2007; and Abed al-Wahab Ades, "The Killing Danger," *Al-Gumhuriya,* August 16, 2007.

114. Moshe Pearlman, *Mufti of Jerusalem* (London: Victor Gollancz, 1947), pp. 49–50. See also Robert S. Wistrich, *Muslim Anti-Semitism,* p. 47.

115. Robert S. Wistrich, *Hitler's Apocalypse,* pp. 164–71.

116. Quoted by Ruth Wisse, "On Ignoring Anti-Semitism," *Commentary*, October 2002, p. 27.

117. See Gabriel Schoenfeld, "Israel and the Anti-Semites," *Commentary*, June 2002, pp. 13–21.

118. Ibid., p. 20.

119. See Alvin H. Rosenfeld's booklet *Anti-Americanism and Anti-Semitism: A New Frontier of Bigotry* (New York: AJC, 2003); and Josef Joffe, *Nations We Love to Hate: Israel, America, and the New Antisemitism* (Jerusalem: Hebrew University of Jerusalem, SICSA, Posen Papers in Contemporary Antisemitism, no. 1, 2005).

120. Joffe, *Nations We Love to Hate*, pp. 11–12.

121. Ibid., p. 13.

122. Ibid., p. 1.

123. Quoted by Rosenfeld, *Anti-Americanism and Anti-Semitism*, p. 10.

124. Robert S. Wistrich, *Anti-Semitism and Multiculturalism: The Uneasy Connection* (Jerusalem: Hebrew University of Jerusalem, SICSA, Posen Papers in Contemporary Antisemitism, no. 5, 2007). See also Melanie Phillips, *Londonistan: How Britain Is Creating a Terror State Within* (London: Encounter Books, 2006); and Bat Ye'or, *Eurabia: The Euro-Arab Axis* (Madison, N.J.: Fairleigh Dickinson University Press, 2005), pp. 153–208.

125. Douglas Davis, "Ethnic Cleansers," *Australia/Israel Review*, February 2008, p. 9.

126. See the remarks of Alain Finkielkraut in *Les Enfants de la République*, pp. 19–53.

127. "Language as a Tool Against Jews and Israel: An Interview with Georges-Elia Sarfati," *Post-Holocaust and Anti-Semitism*, no. 17 (February 1, 2004). See also Joel Fishman, "The Cold-War Origins of Contemporary Antisemitic Terminology," *Jerusalem Viewpoints*, no. 517 (May 2–16, 2004).

128. Wistrich, *Anti-Zionism and Antisemitism: The Case of Bruno Kreisky*, pp. 25–26. See also Karin Stögner, "Antisemitismus und der österreichische Umgang mit dem Nationalsozialismus," in Anton Pelinka, Hubert Sickinger, and Karin Stögner, *Kreisky-Haider: Bruchlinien österreichischer Identitäten* (Vienna: Braumüller, 2008), pp. 25–110.

129. See Philippe Gumplowicz, "De la honte de soi à la tonte de soi," *L'Arche*, February 2008, p. 34.

130. This is particularly true of former Knesset speaker Avraham Burg. See his "The End of Zionism: Israel Must Shed Its Illusions and Choose Between Racist Oppression and Democracy," *The Guardian*, September 15, 2003.

131. Ibid. See also my article "Left-Wing Anti-Zionism in Western Societies," in *Anti-Zionism and Antisemitism in the Contemporary World*, ed. Robert S. Wistrich (London: Macmillan, 1990), pp. 46–52.

132. David Cesarani, "The Perdition Affair," in Wistrich, *Anti-Zionism and Antisemitism*, pp. 53–60. See also Lenni Brenner, *Zionism in the Age of the Dictators* (London: Zed Books, 1983).

133. Fiamma Nirenstein, "How I Became an 'Unconscious Fascist,'" in Rosenbaum, *Those Who Forget the Past*, pp. 291–306. See also Robert S. Wistrich, "Anti-Zionism and Anti-Semitism," *Jewish Political Studies Review* 16, nos. 3–4 (Fall 2004): pp. 27–31.

134. See Anthony Julius, "Is There Anything 'New' in the New Anti-Semitism?" in *A*

New Antisemitism? Debating Judeophobia in 21st Century Britain, ed. Paul Iganski and Barry Kosmin (London: Profile Books, 2003), pp. 68–78; and Winston Pickett, "Nasty or Nazi? The Use of Anti-Semitic Topoi by the Left-Liberal Media," in ibid., pp. 148–68.

135. See the pamphlet by Bernard Harrison, *Israel, Anti-Semitism, and Free Speech* (New York: AJC, 2007) for a useful clarification of these issues.

136. Ibid., pp. 11–16.

137. Stephen M. Walt and John J. Mearsheimer, *The Israel Lobby and U.S. Foreign Policy* (New York: Farrar, Straus and Giroux, 2007) enjoyed wide exposure and coverage in the United States and Europe.

138. Robert S. Wistrich, "Zionism and Its Jewish 'Assimilationist' Critics, 1897–1948," *Jewish Social Studies* 4, no. 2 (1998): pp. 59–111.

139. Eran Benedek, "Britain's Respect Party: The Leftist-Islamist Alliance and Its Attitude Toward Israel," *Jewish Political Studies Review* 19, nos. 3–4 (Fall 2007): pp. 153–63.

140. Ibid., p. 158.

141. Typical of this genre is the reprint of John Rose, *Israel: The Hijack State—America's Watchdog in the Middle East* (London: Socialist Workers Party, 2002). It was first published under a different title in 1986.

142. Henryk M. Broder, "Antizionismus—Antisemitismus von links?" *Aus Politik und Zeitgeschichte,* June 12, 1976, pp. 31–46. See also Robert S. Wistrich, *The Myth of Zionist Racism* (London: World Union of Jewish Students, January 1976). A useful reminder can be found in William D. Rubinstein's short book *Israel, the Jews, and the West: The Fall and Rise of Antisemitism* (London: The Social Affairs Unit, 2008), pp. 44–55.

143. Yohanan Manor, "L'Antisionisme," *Revue française de science politique* 34, no. 2 (April 1984): pp. 295–321.

144. See Georges-Élia Sarfati, *L'Antisionisme: Israël/Palestine aux miroirs d'Occident* (Paris: Berg International, 2002).

145. Fiamma Nirenstein, *Gli Antisemiti Progressisti: Forma Nuova di un Odio Antico* (Milan: Rizzoli, 2004). See also Giordana Grego, "Déjà Jew," *The Jerusalem Post,* September 15, 2004, for the quotation.

146. Robert S. Wistrich, "L'Antisémitisme sans Antisémites," in *Les habits neufs de l'antisémitisme en Europe,* ed. Manfred Gerstenfeld and Shmuel Trigano (Paris: Éditions Café Noir, 2004), pp. 49–54.

147. On the background and current uses of the *Protocols,* see Norman Cohn, *Warrant for Genocide: The Myth of the Jewish World-Conspiracy and the Protocols of the Elders of Zion* (New York: Harper and Row, 1967); and Christopher Hitchens, "Jewish Power, Jewish Peril," *Vanity Fair,* September 2002, pp. 88–91. On the *Protocols,* see Robert S. Wistrich, ed., *The "Protocols of the Sages of Zion": A Selected Bibliography* (Jerusalem: Hebrew University of Jerusalem, SICSA, 2006).

148. George Jochnowitz, "The Mysterious Power of Anti-Zionism," *Midstream,* January–February 2006, pp. 7–9.

149. Sir Jonathan Sacks, "Thoughts for the Day," BBC Radio One, December 16, 2005.

150. Shmuel Trigano, "Xénophobie, racisme et antisémitisme," in Gerstenfeld and Trigano, *Les habits neufs,* pp. 21–28.

151. Georges-Élia Sarfati, "L'antisionisme, un antisémitisme 'politiquement correct,' " in Gerstenfeld and Trigano, *Les habits neufs*, pp. 55–72.

152. Maurice Szafran, "L'antisionisme comme moteur de la judéophobie," *Marianne*, January 28–February 3, 2002, pp. 22–25.

153. Robert S. Wistrich, *Muslim Anti-Semitism: A Clear and Present Danger* (New York: AJC Committee, 2002). The most comprehensive account is in Andrew G. Bostom's edited volume *The Legacy of Islamic Antisemitism* (Amherst, N.Y.: Prometheus Books, 2008), which came to my attention after the completion of this manuscript.

154. See Yehoshafat Harkabi, "On Arab Antisemitism Once More," in *Antisemitism Through the Ages*, ed. Shmuel Almog (Oxford, U.K.: Pergamon Press, 1988) pp. 227–39. A publication of SICSA.

155. Wistrich, *Muslim Anti-Semitism*, pp. 8–46. See also Morton B. Zuckerman, "Graffiti on History's Walls," *US News and World Report*, November 3, 2003, pp. 44–51; and Harold Evans, "Anti-Semitic Lies and Hate Threaten Us All," *The Times* (London), June 28, 2002.

156. Quoted in Ruth Wisse, "On Ignoring Antisemitism," p. 31.

157. See Robert S. Wistrich, *Muslim Anti-Semitism*, pp. 19–21. For Major General Gul's remarks, see the interview with him by Rod Nordland, *Newsweek,* September 14, 2001.

158. Ayaan Hirsi Ali, "Confronting Holocaust Denial," *International Herald Tribune* (*IHT*), December 15, 2006.

159. There are a few exceptions. Apart from the present author, one of the first scholars to deal with this issue was Pierre-André Taguieff, *Les Protocoles des Sages de Sion. Faux et Usages d'un Faux* (Paris: Berg International, 1992), pp. 279–363. See also Matthias Küntzel, "Islamic Antisemitism and Its Nazi Roots," *Antisemitism International,* 2004, pp. 44–52; Menachem Milson, "A European Plot on the Arab Stage: The Naturalization of the Protocols of the Elders of Zion in the Arab World," *Kivunim Hadashim* 13 (January 2006): pp. 86–95, in Hebrew; Milson, "What Is Arab Antisemitism?" *Antisemitism International,* 2003, pp. 23–29; Rivka Yadlin, " 'Rider Without a Horse,' on Egyptian TV: The 'Protocols' as 'Vox Populi,' " *Antisemitism International,* 2004, pp. 53–60; and Raphael Israeli, "L'antisémitisme travesti en antisionisme," *Antisémitisme et négationnisme dans le monde arabo-musulman,* no. 180 (January–June 2004): pp. 109–71.

160. Harkabi, "On Arab Antisemitism," pp. 227, 233, 238.

161. Ibid., p. 233. See also Robert Solomon Wistrich, "The new anti-Semitism," *Standpoint* (October 2008), pp. 74–76.

162. "Jihad, Apocalypse and Anti-Semitism: An Interview with Richard Landes," *Post-Holocaust and Anti-Semitism,* no. 24 (September 1, 2004). See also Matthias Küntzel, *Islamischer Anti-Semitismus und Deutsche Politik* (Berlin: Lit Verlag, 2007), pp. 111–42.

163. Ehud Ya'ari, "Bin Ladenism: The Cult of Death," *The Jerusalem Report,* September 23, 2002, pp. 14–15.

164. Jeffrey Herf, "What Is Old and What Is New in the Terrorism of Islamic Fundamentalism?" *Partisan Review* 69, no. 1 (2002); and Robert S. Wistrich, "Islamic Fascism," in ibid.

165. Herf, "What Is Old and What Is New."
166. Samuel P. Huntington, *The Clash of Civilizations and the Remaking of World Order* (London: Touchstone Books, 1998), pp. 254–65, on "Islam's bloody borders."
167. Ibid., pp. 263–64.
168. Samuel P. Huntington, "The Clash of Civilizations?" *Foreign Affairs* 72, no. 3 (Summer 1993): pp. 22–49. See also Bernard Lewis, "The Roots of Muslim Rage," *The Atlantic Monthly,* September 1990, p. 60; *Time,* June 15, 1992, pp. 24–28.
169. Raphael Israeli, "Fundamentalist Islam—Violence and Terrorism," *Nativ* 21, no. 1 (January 2008): pp. 11–19, in Hebrew.
170. Yehuda Bauer, "Nazis, Communists, and Radical Islamists," *The Jerusalem Post,* November 29, 2002.
171. Landes, "Jihad, Apocalypse and Anti-Semitism."
172. David Cook, *Contemporary Muslim Apocalyptic Literature* (New York: Syracuse University Press, 2005), pp. 18–19.
173. Ibid., pp. 21–22.
174. Matthias Küntzel, *Unholy Hatreds: Holocaust Denial and Antisemitism in Iran* (Jerusalem: Hebrew University of Jerusalem, SICSA, Posen Papers in Contemporary Antisemitism, no. 8, 2007).
175. Shirzad Bozorghmehr, "Iranian Leader: Wipe Out Israel," CNN.com, October 27, 2005, http://www.cnn.com/2005/WORLD/meagt/10/26/ahmadinejad/index.html. See also Küntzel, *Islamischer Anti-Semitismus,* pp. 121–34.
176. See Kasra Naji, *Ahmadinejad: The Secret History of Iran's Radical Leader* (Berkeley: University of California Press, 2008), pp. 139–83.
177. *Yediot Ahronoth,* February 21, 2008, in Hebrew.

ONE: FROM DEICIDE TO GENOCIDE

1. See Edward Flannery, *The Anguish of the Jews: Twenty-three Centuries of Antisemitism* (New York: Paulist Press, 1985); and Robert S. Wistrich, *Antisemitism: The Longest Hatred* (London: Methuen Books, 1991). See also the special issue of *Alpayyim,* no. 28 (2005), in Hebrew.
2. This point is particularly emphasized by Gavin Langmuir, *History, Religion, and Antisemitism* (Berkeley: University of California Press, 1990).
3. See Wistrich, *Antisemitism: The Longest Hatred,* pp. 13–42; Judith Taylor Gold, *Monsters and Madonnas: The Roots of Christian Antisemitism* (Syracuse, N.Y.: Syracuse University Press, 1999); Robert Moore, *The Formation of a Persecuting Society: Power and Deviance in Western Europe 950–1250* (Oxford, U.K.: Basil Blackwell, 1987); and Rainer Erb, ed., *Die Legende vom Ritualmord: Zur Geschichte der Blutbeschuldigung gegen Juden* (Berlin: Metropol, 1993).
4. On the *Protocols,* see Norman Cohn, *Warrant for Genocide: The Myth of the Jewish World Conspiracy and the Protocols of the Elders of Zion* (London, 1967); and Taguieff, *Les Protocoles des Sages de Sion.*
5. See Shmuel Ettinger, "Jew Hatred in Its Historical Context," in *Antisemitism Through the Ages,* ed. Shmuel Almog (Oxford, U.K.: Pergamon Press, 1988), pp. 1–12. See also Hyam Maccoby, *Antisemitism and Modernity: Innovation and Conti-*

nuity (London: Routledge, 2006), and Robert S. Wistrich, "Adaptable Hate," *The Times Literary Supplement,* February 24, 2007.

6. Martin Goodman, *Rome and Jerusalem: The Clash of Modern Civilisations* (London: Penguin/Allen Lane, 2007). See also Peter Schäfer, *Judeophobia: Attitudes Toward the Jews in the Ancient World* (Cambridge, Mass.: Harvard University Press, 1997).

7. Paul Johnson, "Origins of a Modern Virus," *The Tablet,* January 13, 2007. See also Jonathan Kirsch, *God Against the Gods: The History of the War Between Monotheism and Polytheism* (New York: Viking Compass, 2004).

8. Wistrich, *Antisemitism: The Longest Hatred,* pp. 6–7; Katell Berthelot, *Philanthropia judaica: Le débat autour de la "misanthropie" des lois juives dans l'Antiquité* (Leiden, Netherlands: Brill, 2003).

9. See Menahem Stern, ed., *Greek and Latin Authors on Jews and Judaism,* 3 vols. (Jerusalem: Israel Academy of Sciences and Humanities, 1974–84).

10. Louis H. Feldman, "Antisemitism in the Ancient World," in *History and Hate: The Dimensions of Anti-Semitism,* ed. David Berger (Philadelphia: Jewish Publication Society, 1986), pp. 22–23.

11. Ibid., p. 23. Feldman remarks on the savagery of the anti-Semitic Alexandrian mob in burning the Jews alive—"a pent-up fury reminiscent of the massacres of Polish Jews in the seventeenth century." See also Pieter Willem van der Horst, *Philo's "Flaccus": The First Pogrom* (Leiden, Netherlands: Brill, 2003). Flaccus was later exiled and executed by order of the Roman emperor.

12. Feldman, "Antisemitism in the Ancient World," p. 24.

13. Daniel R. Schwartz, "Antisemitism and Other-isms in the Greco-Roman World," in Wistrich, *Demonizing the Other,* pp. 73–87.

14. Wistrich, *Antisemitism: The Longest Hatred,* pp. 3–12.

15. Ibid., p. 11. The rebelliousness of the Jews could clearly be linked to this feature of Judaism.

16. Ibid., p. 9. See also John Gager, *The Origins of Antisemitism: Attitudes Toward Judaism in Pagan and Christian Antiquity* (New York: Oxford University Press, 1985).

17. James Carroll, *Constantine's Sword: The Church and the Jews* (Boston: Houghton Mifflin Company, 2001), pp. 78–79, 83, 90. Even if these figures are too high, they give one a glimpse of the scale of the losses.

18. Goodman, *Rome and Jerusalem,* p. 484.

19. Ibid., pp. 489–90.

20. Ibid., p. 494. It was unique in Roman history that a province should change its name as punishment of the natives for their uprising.

21. Ibid., p. 493. This injunction was noted in the early fourth century C.E. by Eusebius.

22. Carroll, *Constantine's Sword,* p. 50.

23. See Gager, *Origins of Antisemitism.*

24. See Bernard Lewis, "The New Antisemitism," *The American Scholar* 75, no. 1 (Winter 2006): pp. 25–36.

25. 1 Thess. 2:14–16; and Rom. 11:28. See also E. P. Sanders, *Jesus and Judaism* (Philadelphia: Fortress Press, 1985); Raymond E. Brown, *Death of the Messiah* (New York: Doubleday, 1993); and David Flusser, *Jesus* (Jerusalem: Magnes Press, 1997).

26. Micha Brumlik, "Johannes: Das judenfeindliche Evangelium," *Kirche und Israel* 4, no. 2 (1989): pp. 102–13; and Hyam Maccoby, *Judas Iscariot and the Myth of Jewish Evil* (London: P. Halban, 1992). See also Adele Reinhartz, "The Gospel of John: How the 'Jews' Became Part of the Plot," in *Jews, Judaism, and Christian Anti-Judaism: Reading the New Testament After the Holocaust,* ed. Paula Fredriksen and Adele Reinhartz (Louisville, Ky.: John Knox Press, 2000).

27. See Rosemary Ruether, *Faith and Fratricide: The Theological Roots of Anti-Semitism* (New York: Seabury Press, 1971); and Joel Carmichael, *The Satanizing of the Jews: Origins and Development of Mystical Anti-Semitism* (New York: Fromm International Publishing Corporation, 1992).

28. Hyam Maccoby, *The Sacred Executioner: Human Sacrifice and the Legacy of Guilt* (London: Thames and Hudson, 1982), p. 134.

29. Marcel Simon, *Verus Israël: Étude sur les relations entre Chrétiens et Juifs dans l'Empire Romain* (Paris: E. de Boccard, 1948); Jules Isaac, *Genèse de l'Antisémitisme* (Paris: Calmann-Lévy, 1956); A. T. Davies, ed., *Antisemitism and the Foundations of Christianity* (New York: Paulist Press, 1979); and Wistrich, *Antisemitism: The Longest Hatred,* pp. 18–19.

30. "Homily I: Against the Jews," in Wayne A. Meeks and Robert L. Wilken, *Jews and Christians in Antioch in the First Four Centuries of the Common Era* (Missoula, Mont.: Scholars Press, 1978), p. 97.

31. Flannery, *Anguish of the Jews,* p. 50.

32. Saint Jerome had grown up in Rome but after various travels spent the last thirty-five years of his life in Bethlehem, surrounded by Jews. His Latin translation of the Hebrew Bible pioneered the allegorical interpretations through which Old Testament prophecies are realized in Christianity. See Raúl González Salinero, *Biblia y polémica antijudia en Jerónimo* (Madrid: Consejo Superior de Investigaciones Científicas, 2003). This would be a powerful instrument of Christian anti-Judaism in the future.

33. Maccoby, *Antisemitism and Modernity,* p. 19. See also Giovanni De Bonfils, *Roma e gli ebrei: secoli 1–5* (Bari, Italy: Cacucci, 2002) for legislation concerning Jews in the Roman Empire, which had become discriminatory by the fourth and fifth centuries.

34. Carroll, *Constantine's Sword,* pp. 178–243.

35. The Visigoths converted to Catholicism at the end of the sixth century. The Jewish minority was seen as an obstacle by both chruch and state in the process of unification. Forced conversions created crypto-Judaism and a converso problem long before the days of the Inquisition. See Raúl González Salinero, *Las conversiones forzasas de los judios en el reino visigodo* (Rome: Escuela Española de Historia y Arqueología en Roma, 2000).

36. Langmuir, *History, Religion, and Antisemitism,* pp. 261–62.

37. Ibid., pp. 232ff. Langmuir argues that the emphasis on disbelief was also a way of silencing doubts about the meaning of some central symbols of Catholicism, such as transubstantiation.

38. Wistrich, *Antisemitism: The Longest Hatred,* pp. 25–26; Solomon Grayzel, *The Church and the Jews in the XIIIth Century* (Philadelphia: Propsie College for Hebrew and Cognate Learning, 1933); and Robert Chazan, "Medieval Anti-Semitism,"

in *History and Hate: The Dimensions of Anti-Semitism,* ed. David Berger (Philadelphia: Jewish Publication Society, 1986), pp. 49–66.

39. Gavin I. Langmuir, "Historiographic Crucifixion," in *Les Juifs au Regard de l'Histoire: Mélanges en honneur de Bernhard Blumenkranz* (Paris: Picard, 1985), pp. 109–27.

40. See the articles by Diego Quaglioni and Anna Esposito on the Inquisition trials in Trent, the ritual murder stereotype, and the cult of the "blessed" Simon, in *Ritual Murder: Legend in European History,* ed. Susanna Buttaroni and Stanisław Musiał, SJ (Kraków: Association of Cultural Initiatives, 2003), pp. 77–158.

41. Józef Niewiadomski, "Killers of God and Killers of God's Children," in Buttaroni and Musiał, *Ritual Murder,* p. 42.

42. Ariel Toaff, *Pasque di Sangue: Ebrei d'Europa e omicidi rituali* (Bologna: Il Mulino, 2007); and the review by Roni Weinstein, "Historia mukhtemet be-dam," *Haaretz,* February 28, 2007. See also Hillel Halkin, "Bloody Jews?" *Commentary,* May 2007, pp. 40–48.

43. Ronnie Po-chia Hsia, "The Real Blood of Passover," *Haaretz,* February 18, 2007.

44. See Flannery, *Anguish of the Jews;* and William Nicholls, *Christian Antisemitism: A History of Hate* (Northvale, N.J.: Jason Aronson, 1993).

45. David Abulafia, "Blood Libels Are Back," *The Times Literary Supplement,* February 28, 2007. This critique effectively exposes Toaff's disregard for highly relevant Christian material—including the friars' campaign against the Jews in medieval Italy and the German-speaking lands, his bias against Ashkenazic Jews, and his deeply flawed handling of evidence.

46. Hsia, "Real Blood of Passover." See also Ronnie Po-chia Hsia, *Trent 1475: Stories of a Ritual Murder Trial* (New Haven, Conn.: Yale University Press, 1992).

47. See Joshua Trachtenberg, *The Devil and the Jews: The Medieval Conception of the Jew and Its Relation to Modern Antisemitism* (Philadelphia: Jewish Publication Society of America, 1961), pp. 11–56.

48. Natascha Bremer, *Das Bild der Juden an den Passionsspielen und in der bildenden Kunst des deutschen Mittelalters* (Frankfurt: P. Lang, 1986) on the passion plays. On the Oberammergau festival, see Jeanne Favret-Saada with Joseé Contreras, *Le Christianisme et ses Juifs 1800–2000* (Paris: Seuil, 2004).

49. On the deicide myth, see Hyam Maccoby, *A Pariah People: The Anthropology of Antisemitism* (London: Constable, 1996).

50. Robert Bonfil, "The Devil and the Jews in the Christian Consciousness of the Middle Ages," in Almog, *Antisemitism Through the Ages,* pp. 91–98.

51. Ibid., p. 95.

52. For the equation of Jews with dirt and disease in German medieval folklore and its possible implications, see Alan Dundes, *Life Is Like a Chicken Coop Ladder: A Portrait of German Culture Through Folklore* (New York: Columbia University Press, 1984). For a comprehensive recent study of folkloric anti-Semitism, see also Andrei Oişteanu, *Inventing the Jew: Antisemitic Stereotypes in Romanian and Other Central-East European Cultures* (Lincoln: University of Nebraska Press, 2009). Published for SICSA.

53. Trachtenberg, *Devil and the Jews,* pp. 47ff., 116.

54. Wistrich, *Antisemitism: The Longest Hatred,* pp. 30, 38.

55. Bonfil, "Devil and the Jews," p. 97. For a possible link between *kiddush hashem* and the emergence of the blood libel, see Israel Yuval, "Vengeance and Damnation, Blood and Defamation: From Jewish Martyrdom to Blood Libel Accusations," *Zion* 58, no. 1 (1993): pp. 33–90, in Hebrew.

56. Alonso de Espina was a Franciscan monk who denounced heretics, Saracens, and demons, as well as Jews. He recommended that Spanish Jewry be expelled, as had already happened to their coreligionists in France. See Alisa Meyuhas-Ginio, "The Expulsion of the Jews from the Kingdom of France in the Fourteenth Century and Its Significance as Viewed by Alonso de Espina, Author of *Fortalitium Fidei*," *Michael* 12 (1991): pp. 67–82, in Hebrew. See also Benzion Netanyahu, *Toward the Inquisition: Essays on Jewish and Converso History in Late Medieval Spain* (Ithaca, N.Y.: Cornell University Press, 1997), pp. 43–77, who discusses whether de Espina might have been a "new Christian"—a hypothesis he rejects.

57. Benzion Netanyahu, *The Origins of the Inquisition in Fifteenth-Century Spain* (New York: Random House, 1995).

58. Netanyahu, *Toward the Inquisition*, p. 75.

59. Ibid., pp. 183–200.

60. Ibid., p. 198.

61. Yitzhak Baer, *Die Juden in christlichen Spanien: Urkunden und Regenten*, vol. 2 (Berlin: Akademie-Verlag, 1936), pp. 210–18, 231–32.

62. Michael Glatzer, "Pablo de Santa Maria on the Events of 1391," in Almog, *Antisemitism Through the Ages*, p. 135.

63. Y.-H. Yerushalmi, "L'Antisémitisme racial est-il apparu au XXe siècle? De la 'limpieza de sangre' espagnole au nazisme: continuités et ruptures," *Esprit*, March–April 1993, pp. 5–35.

64. Netanyahu, *Toward the Inquisition*, p. 199.

65. Martin Luther, "Von den Juden und Ihren Lügen," *Luthers Reformations-Schriften*, vol. 20 (St. Louis: Concordia, 1890), pp. 1861–2026.

66. Trachtenberg, *Devil and the Jews*, p. 42.

67. See Jonathan Frankel, *The Damascus Affair: "Ritual Murder," Politics, and the Jews in 1840* (New York: Cambridge University Press, 1997).

68. Édouard Drumont, *La France Juive* (Paris: Flammarion, 1886), p. 405.

69. See František Cervinka, "The Hilsner Affair," in *The Blood Libel Legend: A Casebook in Anti-Semitic Folklore*, ed. Alan Dundes (Madison: University of Wisconsin Press, 1991); Marie-France Rouart, *Le Crime Rituel ou le sang de l'autre* (Paris: Berg International, 1997); and Hillel J. Kieval, "Representation and Knowledge in Medieval and Modern Accounts of Jewish Ritual Murder," *Jewish Social Studies* 1, no. 1 (1994): pp. 52–70.

70. See Kieval, "Representation and Knowledge," pp. 63–68.

71. Ibid., p. 68.

72. David I. Kertzer, *Unholy War: The Vatican's Role in the Rise of Modern Anti-Semitism* (London: Macmillan, 2001), pp. 152–63. The Dominican and, especially, the Franciscan friars had been very active in such campaigns ever since the thirteenth century.

73. See Pierre Sorlin, *"La Croix" et les Juifs (1880–1899): Contribution à l'histoire de l'antisémitisme contemporaine* (Paris: B. Grasset, 1967); Giovanni Miccoli, "Santa

sede, questione ebraica e antisemitismo fra Otto e Novecento," in *Gli ebrei in Italia,* ed. Corrado Vivanti (Turin: G. Einandi, 1997), pp. 1371–1574.

74. Kertzer, *Unholy War,* pp. 227–36.

75. See Ronald Modras, *The Catholic Church and Antisemitism: Poland, 1933–1939* (Chur, Switzerland: Harwood Academic Publishers, 1994), pp. 315, 345–46.

76. Robert S. Wistrich, *The Jews of Vienna in the Age of Franz Joseph* (New York: Oxford University Press, 1989), pp. 537–82. See also Gérard Huber, *Guérir de l'Antisémitisme* (Paris: Le Serpent à Plumes, 2005), pp. 163–79.

77. Some of these ideas concerning the relationship between Judaism and Christianity are more fully developed by Rudolph Lowenstein, *Christians and Jews: A Psychoanalytic Study* (New York: International Universities Press, 1951), pp. 96ff. See also Peter Loewenberg, *Fantasy and Reality in History* (New York: Oxford University Press, 1995), pp. 172–91.

78. See Sigmund Freud, *Standard Edition of the Complete Psychological Works,* trans. James Strachey et al. (London: Hogarth, 1964), vol. 11: pp. 95–96n. The note came in the 1919 addition that Freud made to his essay on Leonardo da Vinci's childhood, originally published in 1910.

79. Sigmund Freud, "Analysis of a Phobia in a Five-Year Old Boy" (1909), in *Standard Edition,* vol. 10: p. 36n. On Weininger, see Nancy Harrowitz and Barbara Hymens, eds., *Jews and Gender: Responses to Otto Weininger* (Philadelphia: Temple University Press, 1995).

80. Sigmund Freud, "Civilization and Its Discontents" (1930), in *Standard Edition,* vol. 21: p. 114. See also Robert S. Wistrich, "The Last Testament of Sigmund Freud," *Leo Baeck Institute Year Book (LBIYB)* 49 (2004): pp. 87–104.

81. Adolf Hitler, *Mein Kampf* (Munich: Zentralverlag der NSDAP, 1927), p. 357.

82. *Der Stürmer: Ritualmord Nummer,* special no. 1 (May 1934): p. 5.

83. See Brigitte Hamann, *Hitlers Wien: Lehrjahre eines Diktators* (Munich: R. Piper, 1996), and Robert S. Wistrich, *Laboratory for World Destruction: Germans and Jews in Central Europe* (Lincoln: University of Nebraska Press, 2007). Published for the Vidal Sassoon International Center for the Study of Antisemitism.

84. See Adolf Leschnitzer, *The Magic Background of Modern Anti-Semitism: An Analysis of the German-Jewish Relationship* (New York: International Universities Press, 1956), pp. 97–100.

85. Michael Ignatieff, *Blood and Belonging: Journeys into the New Nationalism* (New York: Farrar, Straus, and Giroux, 1994), pp. 19–53.

86. Richard Wagner, *Das Judentum in der Musik* (Leipzig, Germany: 1850), pp. 10–12, 31–32. In this original edition, Wagner used the pseudonym "K. Freigedank," which means "free thought" in German.

87. See Hartmut Zelinski, *Richard Wagner—ein deutsches Thema: Eine Dokumentation zur Wirkungsgeschichte Richard Wagners, 1876–1976* (Vienna: 1983).

88. Richard Wagner to Ludwig II, November 22, 1881, in Jacob Katz, *The Darker Side of Genius: Richard Wagner's Antisemitism* (Hanover, N.H.: University Press of New England, 1986), p. 115.

89. Margaret Brearley, "Hitler and Wagner: The Leader, the Master and the Jews," *Patterns of Prejudice* 22, no. 2 (1988): pp. 3–21.

90. Paul Rose, *Wagner: Race and Revolution* (London: Faber and Faber, 1992). See also

Rose, *German Question / Jewish Question: Revolutionary Antisemitism from Kant to Wagner* (Princeton, N.J.: Princeton University Press, 1992), pp. 358–80.

91. Gottfried Wagner, *The Wagner Legacy* (London: MPG Books, 1997), p. 81.

92. See Christopher Nicholson, *Richard and Adolf: Did Richard Wagner Incite Adolf Hitler to Commit the Holocaust?* (Jerusalem: Gefen, 2007), pp. 64–65.

93. Ibid., p. 65.

94. August Kubizek, *Young Hitler* (London: George Mann, 1973), p. 66.

95. See Joachim Köhler, *Wagner's Hitler: The Prophet and His Disciple* (Cambridge: Polity Press, 2000).

96. Peter Viereck, *Metapolitics: From the Romantics to Hitler* (New York: Alfred A. Knopf, 1941), p. 136.

97. Frederic Spotts, *Hitler and the Power of Aesthetics* (London: Hutchinson, 2002); and Spotts, *Bayreuth: A History of the Wagner Festival* (New Haven, Conn.: Yale University Press, 1994), p. 142.

98. Nicholson, *Richard and Adolf,* p. 271.

99. Köhler, *Wagner's Hitler,* p. 137.

100. Ian Kershaw, *Hitler,* vol. 1, *1889–1936: Hubris* (New York: Penguin, 1999); and Kershaw, *Hitler,* vol. 2, *1936–1945: Nemesis* (New York: Norton, 2001).

101. Köhler, *Wagner's Hitler,* p. 207.

102. See Wistrich, introduction to *Demonizing the Other,* pp. 1–15.

103. Daniel Goldhagen, *Hitler's Willing Executioners: Ordinary Germans and the Holocaust* (New York: Alfred A. Knopf, 1996), p. 449.

104. Chaim A. Kaplan, *The Warsaw Diary of Chaim A. Kaplan,* ed. Abraham I. Katsch (New York: Collier Books, 1973), pp. 129–30.

105. Ibid.

106. See Jeffrey Herf, *The Jewish Enemy: Nazi Propaganda During World War II and the Holocaust* (Cambridge, Mass.: Harvard University Press, 2006).

107. Wistrich, introduction to *Demonizing the Other,* p. 10.

108. Robert N. Proctor, *Racial Hygiene: Medicine Under the Nazis* (Cambridge, Mass.: Harvard University Press, 1988), pp. 131–76.

109. Friedländer, *Nazi Germany and the Jews,* pp. 73ff.

Two: Between Marx and Stalin

1. Robert S. Wistrich, "Antisemitism as a Radical Ideology," *Jerusalem Quarterly,* no. 28 (1983): pp. 83–94. See also John Weiss, *Ideology of Death: Why the Holocaust Happened in Germany* (Chicago: Ivan R. Dee, 1996), pp. 97–111.

2. David I. Kertzer, *The Popes Against the Jews: The Vatican's Role in the Rise of Modern Anti-Semitism* (New York: Alfred A. Knopf, 2001), pp. 186–204.

3. Marvin Perry and Frederick M. Schweitzer, *Antisemitism: Myth and Hate from Antiquity to the Present* (New York: Palgrave, 2002), pp. 43–72.

4. Wistrich, "Antisemitism as a Radical Ideology," pp. 83–86.

5. Paul W. Massing, *Rehearsal for Destruction: A Study of Political Antisemitism in Imperial Germany* (New York: Harper, 1949), p. 151.

6. Jean-Paul Sartre, *Anti-Semite and Jew* (New York: 1973), pp. 35–36.

7. Peter G. J. Pulzer, *The Rise of Political Anti-Semitism in Germany and Austria,* 2nd rev. ed. (London: P. Halban, 1988), p. 252.

8. See Robert S. Wistrich, *Social Democracy and the Jewish Problem in Germany and Austria, 1880–1914* (Ph.D. dissertation, University of London, 1974); and Rosemarie Leuschen-Seppel, *Sozialdemokratie und Antisemitismus im Kaiserreich* (Bonn, Germany: Verlag Neue Gesellschaft, 1978), pp. 231–79.

9. See Edmund Silberner, *Ha-Sotsialism ha-maaravi ve-she'elat hayehudim* (Jerusalem: Mossad Bialik, 1955).

10. George Lichtheim, "Socialism and the Jews," *Dissent,* July–August 1968, p. 319.

11. Zeev Sternhell, *La Droite Révolutionnaire 1885–1914: Les Origines Françaises du Fascisme* (Paris: Éditions du Seuil, 1978), pp. 177–214. See also Sternhell, *Ni Droite ni Gauche: L'idéologie fasciste en France* (Paris: Seuill, 1983).

12. George L. Mosse, "The French Right and the Working Classes: Les Jaunes," in *Journal of Contemporary History* 7, nos. 3–4 (July–October 1972); and Sternhell, *La Droite Révolutionnaire,* pp. 245–316.

13. W. H. Chaloner and W. O. Henderson, "Marx/Engels and Racism," *Encounter* 45, no. 1 (July 1975): pp. 18–23.

14. See Robert S. Wistrich, *Revolutionary Jews from Marx to Trotsky* (London: Harrap, 1976), pp. 26–45.

15. Karl Marx, "On Bruno Bauer's *The Jewish Question,*" in *Early Writings,* trans. and ed. T. B. Bottomore (New York: McGraw-Hill, 1964), pp. 1–40, for the complete text.

16. *Marx-Engels Werke* (MEW), vol. 1 (East Berlin: Institute for Marxism-Leninism, 1964), p. 374.

17. See Karl Marx, *Early Writings,* trans. Rodney Livingstone and Gregor Benton (London: Penguin Books, 1975), p. 241.

18. Moses Hess, "Sechster Brief," in *Rom und Jerusalem: die letzte Nationalitätsfrage* (Leipzig, Germany: Eduard Wengler, 1862), p. 47.

19. The article, which originally appeared in the *New York Tribune,* January 4, 1856, was reprinted in Karl Marx, *The Eastern Question: A Reprint of Letters Written 1853–1856 Dealing with the Events of the Crimean War,* ed. Eleanor Marx Aveling and Edward Aveling (New York: A. M. Kelley, 1969), pp. 600–606. It is quoted in Chaloner and Henderson, "Marx/Engels and Racism."

20. *Notebooks of P. J. Proudhon,* ed. Pierre Haubtmann (Paris: Marcel Rivière, 1960–1961), vol. 2, pp. 337–38.

21. Pierre Joseph Proudhon, *Césarisme et Christianisme* (Paris: C. Marpon et E. Flammarion, 1883). This book was first published eighteen years after Proudhon's death and is quoted in Lichtheim, "Socialism and the Jews," p. 322.

22. A Lehning, A. C. Rüter, and P. Scheibert, eds., *Bakunin-Archiv* (Leiden, Netherlands: Brill, 1963), vol. 1, pt. 2: pp. 124–26.

23. "Rapports personnels avec Marx," in Mikhail Bakunin, *Oeuvres,* vol. 3: pp. 298–99. Quoted in Lichtheim, "Socialism and the Jews," p. 338.

24. Quoted in Jonathan Frankel, *Prophecy and Politics: Socialism, Nationalism, and the Russian Jews, 1862–1917* (New York: Cambridge University Press, 1981), p. 34.

25. Boris Sapir, "Jewish Socialists Around *Vpered,*" in *International Review of Social History,* 1965, p. 383. See also Erich Haberer, *Jews and Revolution in Nineteenth-Century Russia* (Cambridge: Cambridge University Press, 1995).

26. Quoted in Lucy S. Dawidowicz, *The Golden Tradition: Jewish Life and Thought in Eastern Europe* (New York: Holt, Rinehart and Winston, 1967), p. 406.

27. Ibid., p. 410.

28. Ibid., p. 418. See also Yuri Slezkine, *The Jewish Century* (Princeton, N.J.: Princeton University Press, 2004), pp. 114–62, for the role played by Jews in Russian capitalism and prerevolutionary radicalism.

29. Wistrich, *Revolutionary Jews,* pp. 46–58.

30. *Neuer Social-Demokrat,* September 18, 1872. See also Shlomo Na'aman, "Social Democracy on the Ambiguous Ground Between Antipathy and Antisemitism— The Example of Wilhelm Hasenclever," *LBIYB* 36 (1991): pp. 229–40.

31. Quoted in Arno Herzig, "The Role of Antisemitism in the Early Years of the German Workers' Movement," *LBIYB* 26 (1981): p. 253.

32. *Neuer Social-Demokrat,* November 3, 1872; Herzig, "Role of Antisemitism," p. 252.

33. *Neuer Social-Demokrat,* September 20, 1872; November 8, 1872.

34. Gustave Tridon, *Du Molochisme juif: Études critiques et philosophiques* (Brussels: E. Maheu, 1884), p. 5.

35. See Edmund Silberner, "French Socialism and the Jewish Question 1865–1914," *Historia Judaica* 16 (April 1954): pp. 6–7.

36. Ibid.

37. Edmund Silberner, "Anti-Jewish Trends in French-Revolutionary Syndicalism," *Jewish Social Studies* 15, nos. 3–4 (1953).

38. William J. Fishman, "Briton and Alien," in *East End Jewish Radicals 1875–1914* (London: Duckworth, 1975).

39. Ibid., p. 82.

40. John A. Garrard, *The English and Immigration 1880–1910* (London: Oxford University, 1971). For the cases of H. G. Wells and G. B. Shaw, two leading British intellectuals of the leftist persuasion, see also Bryan Cheyette, *Constructions of "the Jew" in English Literature and Society: Racial Representations, 1785–1945* (Cambridge: Cambridge University Press, 1993), pp. 94–149.

41. *Justice,* January 21, 1893. This newspaper had been founded in 1881 by a wealthy businessman, Henry M. Hyndman, following his conversion to Marxism.

42. *Justice,* April 25, 1896.

43. *Justice,* October 7, 1899. See also Robert S. Wistrich, "Socialism and Judeophobia: Antisemitism in Europe before 1914," *LBIYB* 37 (1992), pp. 111–45.

44. *Labour Leader,* February 24, 1900.

45. Quoted in Claire Hirschfield, "The British Left and the 'Jewish Conspiracy': A Case Study of Modern Antisemitism," *Jewish Social Studies* 43, no. 2 (Spring 1981): p. 105.

46. Ibid.

47. On the Jewish labor movement in Russia, see Henry J. Tobias, *The Jewish Bund in Russia from Its Origins to 1905* (Stanford, Calif.: Stanford University Press, 1972); Nora Levin, *Jewish Socialist Movements 1871–1917* (London: Routledge and Kegan Paul, 1978), pp. 109–12; and Enzo Traverso, *Die Marxisten und die jüdischen Frage* (Mainz, Germany: Decaton Verlag, 1995).

48. Quoted in Frankel, *Prophecy and Politics,* p. 229. Lenin, it is worth noting, was partly Jewish and unusually sensitive to anti-Semitism and other forms of national prejudice. His ethnic background was a well-kept state secret in the USSR.

49. J. V. Stalin, "Londonskii Syezd Rossiskoi Sotzial-Demokratischeskoi Rabochei Partii," in *Sochineniya*, vol. 2, *1907–1913* (Moscow: Gospolitizdat, 1949), pp. 50–51.

50. Wistrich, *Revolutionary Jews from Marx to Trotsky*, pp. 201ff.; and Wistrich, *Trotsky, Fate of a Revolutionary* (London: Robson Books, 1979).

51. Theodore Draper, "The Ghost of Social Fascism," *Commentary*, February 1969, pp. 29–42.

52. For a savage critique of Stalinist policy made in January 1932, see "What Next? Vital Questions for the German Proletariat," in Leon Trotsky, *The Struggle Against Fascism in Germany* (Harmondworth, England: Penguin Books, 1975), p. 148.

53. See Thomas Weingartner, *Stalin und der Aufstieg Hitlers: Die Deutschlandpolitik der Sowjetunion und der Kommunistischen Internationale, 1929–1934* (Berlin: de Gruyter, 1970).

54. *XVII S'ezd vsesoiuznoi Kommunisticheskoii partii (b): Stenografcheskii otchet* (Moscow: 1934), pp. 13–14. See also J. V. Stalin, *Sochineniya*, vol. 13, *July 1930–January 1934* (Moscow: Gospolitizdat, 1951), p. 302.

55. See Robert C. Tucker, "Stalin, Bukharin, and History as Conspiracy," *The Soviet Political Mind: Stalinism and Post-Stalin Change* (London: George Allen and Unwin, 1972), pp. 49–86.

56. Ibid., p. 77. See also Alan Bullock, *Hitler and Stalin: Parallel Lives* (New York: Alfred A. Knopf, 1992), pp. 465–93, on the larger issues.

57. Alliluyeva Svetlana, *20 Letters to a Friend* (London: Penguin, 1968), p. 171. See her remark: "He never liked Jews, though he wasn't yet as blatant about expressing his hatred for them in those days as he was after the war," p. 140. See also Milovan Djilas, *Conversations with Stalin* (London: Penguin, 1963), p. 120, for confirmation of Stalin's anti-Semitism around 1945.

58. Reuben Ainsztein, "Soviet Jewry in the Second World War," in *The Jews in Soviet Russia Since 1917*, ed. Lionel Kochan (London: Oxford University Press, 1970), pp. 269ff.

59. Leonard Schapiro, "The Jewish Anti-Fascist Committee and Phases of Soviet Anti-Semitic Policy During and After World War II," in *Jews and Non-Jews in Eastern Europe, 1918–1945*, ed. Bela Vago and George L. Mosse (New York: Wiley, 1974), pp. 291ff.

60. Benjamin Pinkus, "Soviet Campaigns Against 'Jewish Nationalism' and 'Cosmopolitanism,' 1946–1953," *Soviet Jewish Affairs* 4, no. 2 (1974): 53–69.

61. Kostyrchenko, *Out of the Red Shadows*, pp. 45–47, for the document signed by Solomon Mikhoels, Shakhno Epshtein, and Itsik Fefer.

62. Ibid., pp. 50–65.

63. Ibid., pp. 86–97.

64. *Pravda*, April 23, 1948, for Gromyko's speech justifying "the demands of the Jews to create their own independent State in Palestine."

65. A typical letter to the JAC by a Soviet Jewish volunteer for Israel's war of independence. See Kostyrchenko, *Out of the Red Shadows*, p. 103.

66. Ibid., pp. 110–11. The article appeared in *Pravda*, September 21, 1948, under the title "Soyuz Kurnosynkh" (The Union of the Snub-Nosed).

67. Kostyrchenko, *Out of the Red Shadows*, pp. 154ff.

68. Jonathan Brent and Vladimir P. Naumor, *Stalin's Last Crime: The Plot Against the Jewish Doctors, 1948–1953* (New York: HarperCollins, 2003), p. 3.

69. Ibid., pp. 331–33.
70. Kostyrchenko, pp. 179–247, on the anti-Jewish purges.
71. Ibid. p. 286.
72. *Pravda,* January 21, 1953.
73. See Yakov Rapoport, *The Doctors' Plot of 1953* (Cambridge, Mass.: Harvard University Press, 1991). Also Brent and Naumor, *Stalin's Last Crime,* pp. 300–305 for the full text.
74. Ibid., p. 302.
75. Ibid.
76. Ibid., p. 303.
77. Ibid., p. 302.
78. Rapoport, *The Doctors' Plot,* p. 78. See also Zinovii Sheinis, *Provokatsyia Veka* (Moscow: PIK, 1992).

Three: The Soviet War Against Zion

1. Sebag Montefiore, *Stalin: The Court of the Red Tsar* (New York: Alfred A. Knopf, 2004), p. 310.
2. See Arkady Vaksberg, *Stalin Against the Jews* (New York: Vintage Books, 1995). See also Liudmila Dymerskaya-Tsigelman, "Die Doktrin des Stalinischen Antisemitismus," in *Der Spätstalinismus und die "Jüdische Frage": Zur antisemitischen Wendung des Kommunismus,* ed. Leonid Luks (Cologne: Böhlau Verlag, 1998), pp. 29–52.
3. Kostyrchenko, *Out of the Red Shadows,* pp. 153–247. Also Kostyrchenko, "Der Fall der Ärzte," in Luks, *Der Spätstalinismus,* pp. 90–116.
4. Montefiore, *Stalin,* p. 650. See also Dmitri Volkogonov, *Stalin: Triumph and Tragedy* (London: Weidenfeld, 1995) for the general background.
5. See Bullock, *Hitler and Stalin;* and Richard Overy, *The Dictators: Hitler's Germany, Stalin's Russia* (London: Penguin, 2004) for parallels, similarities, and differences. See also Leonid Luks, "Stalin und die jüdische Frage"—Brüche und Widersprüche," in Luks, *Der Spätstalinismus,* pp. 271–92.
6. See Leon Trotsky, *My Life* (London: Penguin Books, 1975), p. 376. Also Trotsky, *On the Jewish Question* (New York: Pathfinder Press, 1970), pp. 21ff.
7. Luks, "Stalin und die jüdische Frage," pp. 280–83.
8. Peter Brod, "Soviet-Israeli Relations 1948–1956," and Arnold Krammer, "Prisoners in Prague: Israelis in the Slansky Trial," in *The Left Against Zion: Communism, Israel, and the Middle East,* ed. Robert Wistrich (London: Frank Cass, 1979), pp. 57–64, 72–85; see also Eugene Loebl, *Sentenced and Tried: The Stalinist Purges in Czechoslovakia* (London: Elek, 1969), and Karel Kaplan, "Der politische Prozess gegen R. Slánský und Genossen," in Luks, *Der Spätstalinismus,* pp. 169–88.
9. See Artur London, *L'Aveu* (Paris: Gallimard, 1968); and W. Oschlies, "Neo-Stalinist Antisemitism in Czechoslovakia," in Wistrich, *The Left Against Zion,* pp. 156–57.
10. Quoted in Wistrich, *The Left Against Zion,* p. 157.
11. Ibid., p. 160. See also Gabriele Eschanazi and Gabriele Nissim, *Ebrei Invisibili* (Milan: Mondadori, 1995), pp. 385–415, on Czechoslovakia under Communist rule.

12. See Paul Lendvai, *Antisemitismus ohne Juden: Entwicklungen und Tendenzen in Osteuropa* (Vienna: 1972); Hildrun Glass, "Die kommunistische Politik gegenüber der jüdischen Minderheit in Rumänien (1944–1953)," in Luks, *Der Spätstalinismus,* pp. 199–220; and Robert Levy, *Ana Pauker: The Rise and Fall of a Jewish Communist* (Berkeley and Los Angeles: University of California Press, 2001).

13. *Staline contre Israel* (Paris: Bulletin D'Études et D'Informations Politiques Internationales, 1953); and François Fejtö, *Gli ehrei e l'antisemitismo nei paesi communisti* (Milan: Sugar, 1962). For Romania, see Paul Hockenos, *Free to Hate: The Rise of the Right in Post-Communist Eastern Europe* (New York: Routledge, 1993), pp. 167–207; and Eschenazi and Nissim, *Ebrei Invisibili,* pp. 286–316. See also Levy, *Ana Pauker,* pp. 134–162.

14. David Pryce-Jones, "Fanatic and Victim," *The Times Literary Supplement,* March 2, 2001.

15. Levy, *Ana Pauker,* pp. 194–238.

16. Michel Mirsky, "Zionism—Instrument of American Imperialism," *Nowe Drogi* 43, no. 1 (January 1953), in Polish.

17. Joanna Beate Michlic, *Poland's Threatening Other: The Image of the Jew from 1880 to the Present* (Lincoln: University of Nebraska Press, 2006), pp. 230–38.

18. See [Michael Checinski], "USSR and the Politics of Polish Antisemitism 1956–1968," *Soviet Jewish Affairs,* no. 1 (June 1971): pp. 19–38, for a firsthand account. See also Krystyna Kersten, "Polish Stalinism and the So-Called Jewish Question," in Luks, *Der Spätstalinismus,* pp. 221–36.

19. [Checinski], "USSR and the Politics of Polish Antisemitism," p. 21. On the factional struggles, see Kersten, "Polish Stalinism," pp. 226–28.

20. [Checinski], "USSR and the Politics of Polish Antisemitism," p. 23.

21. Adam Ciolkosz, " 'Anti-Zionism' in Polish Communist Party Politics," in Wistrich, *The Left Against Zion,* pp. 137–51 (especially p. 142). See also Israel Gutman, *Hayehudim be-Polin acharei milhemet ha-olam ha-sheniya* (Jerusalem: Merkaz Zalman Shazar, 1985), pp. 113–26. More recently, there is the large selection of documents in Dariusz Stola, *Kampania antsyjonistyczna* (Warsaw: Instytut Studiów Politycznych Polskiej Akademii Nauk, 2000), pp. 270–385.

22. On Gomulka's speeches and actions, see Dariusz Stola, "Anti-Zionism as a Multipurpose Policy Instrument: The Anti-Zionist Campaign in Poland, 1967–1968," *Journal of Israeli History* 25, no. 1 (2006): pp. 175–201.

23. Andrezej Werblan, "Przyczynek do genezy konfliktu," *Miesiecznik Literacki,* June 1968, pp. 61–71, quoted in Ciolkosz, " 'Anti-Zionism,' " p. 145.

24. Ibid., pp. 146–47.

25. Celia Stopnicka Heller, " 'Anti-Zionism' and the Political Struggle Within the Elite of Poland," *The Jewish Journal of Sociology* 11, no. 2 (December 1969): pp. 133–50; and Joanna Beate Michlic, *Poland's Threatening Other,* pp. 242–61. See also Jeff Schatz, *The Generation: The Rise and Fall of the Jewish Communists in Poland* (Berkeley and Los Angeles: University of California Press, 1991); and Eschenazi and Nissim, *Ebrei Invisibili,* pp. 177–97.

26. See [Checinski], "USSR and the Politics of Polish Antisemitism," pp. 30–36; [Checinski], *Poland: Communism, Nationalism, Antisemitism* (New York: Karz-Cohl, 1982); and Kersten, "Polish Stalinism," pp. 232–35.

27. George Garai, "Rákosi and the 'Anti-Zionist' Campaign of 1952–53," *Soviet Jewish Affairs*, no. 2 (1982): p. 19. See also Eschenazi and Nissim, *Ebrei Invisibili*, pp. 55–87; and György Dalos, "Juden in Ungarn nach 1945," in Luks, *Der Spätstalinismus*, pp. 189–98.

28. On Ceausescu and Romanian nationalism, see Hockenos, *Free to Hate*, pp. 178–208; Eschenazi and Nissim, *Ebrei Invisibili*, pp. 317–36; and Alexandra Laignel-Lavastine, "Le national-communisme en Roumanie," in *Cultures politiques*, ed. Daniel Cefaï (Paris: PUF, 2001), pp. 341–64.

29. Robert S. Wistrich, "Anti-Zionism in the USSR: From Lenin to the Soviet Black Hundreds," in *The Left Against Zion*, pp. 272–300.

30. Uri Ra'anan, "Moscow and the Third World," *Problems of Communism* 14 (January–February 1965). On domestic aspects of the "Jewish question," see Matthias Messmer, *Die Judenfrage in der Sowjetunion: Ideologische Voraussetzungen und politische Realität 1953–1958* (Constance, Germany: Hartung-Gorre, 1992).

31. Quoted in Messmer, *Die Judenfrage* (Konstanz: Hartung-Gorre Verlag, 1997), p. 111.

32. K. Ivanov and Z. Sheinis, *The State of Israel: Its Position and Policies* (Moscow: State Publications of Political Literature, 1958). See also Benjamin Pinkus, *The Jews of the Soviet Union: The History of a National Minority* (Cambridge: Cambridge University Press, 1989), pp. 246–53.

33. *L'Humanité*, March 24, 1964, quoted in Jacques Hermone, *La Gauche: Israël et les Juifs* (Paris: La Table ronde, 1970), p. 89.

34. See Shmuel Ettinger, "Anti-Zionism and Antisemitism," *Insight* 2, no. 5 (May 1976).

35. Wistrich, *The Left Against Zion*, p. 288ff.

36. See Reuben Ainsztein, "The Roots of Russian Antisemitism," *The Jewish Quarterly*, Autumn 1972, pp. 4–20; and Mikhail Agursky, "Russian Neo-Nazism—A Growing Threat," *Midstream*, February 1976, pp. 35–42.

37. Robert S. Wistrich, "From Lenin to the Soviet Black Hundreds," *Midstream*, March 1978, pp. 4–12.

38. *Pravda*, July 6, 1967. See also Wistrich, "Anti-Zionism in the USSR," pp. 288ff.

39. Y. Ivanov, *Ostrozhno! Sionizm!* (Moscow: Politisdat, 1969). For extracts in English, see *Bulletin on Soviet and East European Jewish Affairs*, no. 3 (January 1969). Ivanov's book was distributed in 550,000 copies by the Soviet Communist Party's publishing house.

40. V. I. Kiselev, "Sionism v sisteme imperializma," in *Mezhdunarodny Sionism: istoriya i politika* (Moscow: Nauka, 1977), pp. 5–28.

41. L. Korneyev, "Sionizm kak on yest," *Moskovskaya Pravda*, February 16, 1977.

42. L. Korneyev, "Samy sionistskii byznes," *Ogonyok*, July 8, 1978.

43. L. Korneyev, "Otravlennoye oruzhiye sionizma," *Krasnaya Zvezda*, November 16, 1977.

44. See Vladimir Begun, *Polzuchaya Kontrrevolutysiya* [Creeping Counterrevolution] (Minsk: Izd-vo Belarus, 1974); and M. A. Goldenberg, "Iudaizm na sluzhbe sionizma," in *Mezhdunarodny Sionizm*, pp. 88–98.

45. Wistrich, "Anti-Zionism in the USSR," p. 290.

46. Begun, *Polzuchaya Kontrrevolutysiya*, p. 151.

47. Ibid. See also Matthias Messmer, *Sowjetischer und postkommunistischer Anti-*

semitismus: Entwicklungen in Russland, der Ukraine und Litauen (Constance, Germany: 1997).

48. Dmitri Zhukov, "The Ideology and Practice of Violence," *Ogonyok,* October 12, 1974. See also Theodore H. Friedgut, "Soviet Anti-Zionism: Origins, Forms, and Development," in Wistrich, *Anti-Zionism and Antisemitism in the Contemporary World,* pp. 26–45.

49. UN Doc. S/PV.1582, September 25, 1971.

50. UN Doc. E/CN.4/SR.939.GE.67–5491, March 22, 1967.

51. The article was first put out by the semi-official Novosty Press on September 22, 1972. It gave rise to legal proceedings because of its appearance in a French-language journal. See Emanuel Litvinoff, *Soviet Antisemitism: The Paris Trial* (London, 1974).

52. *Jews in Eastern Europe* 5, no. 3 (August 1973), p. 51.

53. For a revealing collection of quotations showing the close parallels between Russian Black Hundred, Nazi, and Soviet anti-Semitism, see R. Okuneva, "Anti-Semitic Notions: Strange Analogies," in *Anti-Semitism in the Soviet Union: Its Roots and Consequences* (Jerusalem: Hebrew University, 1980), vol. 2: pp. 198–323. See also Walter Laqueur, *Black Hundred: The Rise of the Extreme Right in Russia* (New York: HarperCollins, 1993), pp. 102–5; and Semyon Reznik, *The Nazification of Russia: Antisemitism in the Post-Soviet Era* (Washington, D.C.: Challenge Publications, 1996).

54. Michael Agursky, "Selling Antisemitism in Moscow," *The New York Review of Books,* November 16, 1972. See also William Korey, *Russian Antisemitism, Pamyat, and the Demonology of Zionism* (Chur, Switzerland: Harwood Academic Publishers, 1995), pp. 13–59, and Emanuel Litvinoff, "Return of the Slavophiles," *Insight* 4, no. 12 (December 1978): pp. 1–5.

55. Laqueur, *Black Hundred,* pp. 108–16.

56. Howard Spier, "Zionists and Freemasons in Soviet Propaganda," *Patterns of Prejudice* 13, no. 1 (January–February 1979): pp. 1–5.

57. Ibid., p. 2. These figures, like other anti-Semitic statistics of this type, are totally spurious.

58. Ben-Shlomo, "Soviet Jews as a Fifth Column," *The Jewish Chronicle,* March 24, 1978.

59. Spier, "Zionists and Freemasons," pp. 4–5. On Judeo-Masonry, see Korey, *Russian Antisemitism,* pp. 60–73. Freemasonry was usually presented as the expression of modern, secular Judaism and as a principal means for propagandizing "Jewish racism"; Laqueur, *Black Hundred,* pp. 113–16.

60. On Russian Aryanism, see Vadim Rossman, *Russian Intellectual Antisemitism: The Post-Communist Era* (Lincoln: University of Nebraska Press, 2002), pp. 265–71. For its roots in the nineteenth century, see Marlène Laruelle, *Mythe aryen et rêve imperial dans la Russie du XIXe siècle* (Paris: CNRS Éditions, 2005).

61. Reuben Ainsztein, "The Fall of an Antisemite," *New Statesman,* July 11, 1980, p. 45. Emelianov killed his wife in a domestic quarrel, but her remains were shortly afterward discovered in Moscow. On April 7, 1980, he was arrested. See Robert S. Wistrich, *Anti-Semitism: The Longest Hatred* (London: Thames Methuen, 1991), pp. 181–84, 295n. I interviewed Emelianov in his Moscow flat in October 1990 at considerable length. He struck me as a partly deranged but forceful orator.

62. Reuben Ainsztein, "Antisemitism: Official Soviet Ideology?" *Congress Monthly* 46, no. 7 (January 1979): pp. 6–10.

63. Ibid., p. 8. See Laqueur, *Black Hundred,* pp. 136–77, for the ideology of the Russian New Right that emerged in the late Soviet period.

64. See William Korey, "The Smell of Pogrom," *The Jewish Chronicle,* March 18, 1977.

65. V. Bolshakov, "Anti-sovetism—professiya sionistov," *Pravda,* February 18–19, 1971.

66. Korey, *Russian Antisemitism,* pp. 13–29.

67. V. Skurlatov, *Sionizm i apartheid* (Kiev: Politizdat Ukrainy, 1975), p. 14.

68. Ibid., p. 12.

69. Ibid., p. 11. On Skurlatov, see Laqueur, *Black Hundred,* pp. 114–16; and A. Yanov, *The New Russian Right: Right-Wing Ideologies in the Contemporary USSR* (Berkeley: University of California Press, 1978), pp. 170–72.

70. V. Kudryavtsev, "The Criminal Handwriting of Zionism," *Izvestia,* December 2, 1975; V. Misik, "Zionism—a Form of Racism," *Aziya i Afrika Segodnya,* no. 4 (1976).

71. *Soviet Antisemitic Propaganda: Evidence from Books, Press, and Radio* (London: Institute of Jewish Affairs, 1978), pp. 56–58.

72. Emanuel Litvinoff, "Looking Back: The Brezhnev Era. Part One—The Anti-Zionist 'Crusade,' " *Insight* 9, no. 1 (January 1983): p. 6.

73. *Soviet Antisemitic Propaganda,* p. 81.

74. Ibid.

75. D. Pavlov, "An Ominous Conspiracy," *Asia and Africa Today,* no. 1 (1978), quoted in ibid., p. 43.

76. G. Afanasyev, *Za Rubezhom,* February 10–16, 1978.

77. *Soviet Antisemitic Propaganda,* p. 44.

78. *New Times,* no. 44 (1972): p. 26.

79. V. Sidenko, "Israel's African Ambitions," *New Times,* no. 3 (1971): p. 25.

80. Ibid.

81. S. Komarov, "The Tentacles of Zionism in Africa," *Moscow News,* no. 25 (1971): p. 7.

82. See Bernard Lewis, "The Anti-Zionist Resolution," *Foreign Affairs,* October 1976, pp. 54–64.

83. See *Krasnaya Zvezda,* August 20, 1978; *Izvestia,* August 27, 1978; and *Soviet Weekly,* September 9, 1978. Some Western Communists (especially the Italians) were opposed to this Soviet propaganda, to the UN stigmatization of Israel, and to the anti-Semitic echoes. See Livia Rokach's interview with Giancarlo Pajetta, *New Outlook,* February–March 1976, pp. 44–47.

84. Emanuel Litvinoff, "The UN Anti-Zionist Resolution," *Insight* 2, no. 1 (January 1976): pp. 1–8.

85. Seymour M. Finger and Ziva Flamhaft, "The Issue of 'Zionism and Racism' in the United Nations," *Middle East Review,* Spring 1986, pp. 49–58. See also Michael Curtis and Susan Aurelia Gitelson, eds., *Israel in the Third World* (New Brunswick, N.J.: Transaction Books, 1976).

86. Daniel P. Moynihan, "Abiotrophy in Turtle Bay: The United Nations in 1975," *Harvard International Law Journal* 17, no. 3 (Summer 1976): pp. 476ff.

87. Quoted in Kalman Sultanik, "Antisemitism: An Overview," *Forum,* no. 36 (Fall–Winter 1979): p. 89.

88. *IHT,* November 17, 1975.

89. For the diplomatic history and reversal of the UN resolution, see Yohanan Manor, *To Right a Wrong: The Revocation of the UN General Assembly Resolution 3379 Defaming Zionism* (New York: Shengold, 1996).

90. David Cesarani, "The Perdition Affair," in Wistrich, *Anti-Zionism and Antisemitism in the Contemporary World,* pp. 53–62.

91. Ben Cohen, *The Ideological Foundations of the Boycott Campaign Against Israel* (New York: AJC, 2007).

92. Ibid., pp. 9–10.

93. Ibid., p. 10. Cohen observes, for example, that the Alawite minority (about 12 percent of the population) rules Syria, which has an overwhelming Sunni majority; in Saddam's Iraq, the Sunni Arabs (only 25 percent of the population) controlled all positions of power. Both societies were, in effect, police states. In Israel, on the other hand, Jews represent 80 percent of the population and the Arab minority has full representation in Parliament.

94. Jimmy Carter, *Palestine: Peace Not Apartheid* (New York: Simon and Schuster, 2006). See also John Dugard, "Israelis Adopt What South Africa Dropped," *Atlanta Journal-Constitution,* November 29, 2006. Dugard is a UN official who has grotesquely claimed that Israel's "apartheid" is worse than that of the old South Africa.

95. Bernard Harrison, *Israel, Anti-Semitism, and Free Speech* (New York: AJC, 2007), pp. 20–22.

Four: Beat the Jews, Save Russia!

1. See Wistrich, introduction to *"Protocols of the Sages of Zion."* The fullest study is by Pierre-André Taguieff, *Prêcheurs de Haine* (Paris: Mille et Une Nuits, 2004), pp. 620–818, on the genesis, uses, and manipulation of the *Protocols.* See also Cesare de Michelis, *La giudeofobia in Russia: Dal "Libro del 'Kahal' " ai "Protocolli dei Savi di Sion": Con un'antologia di testi* (Turin, Italy: Bollati Boringhier, 2001).

2. Hadassa Ben-Itto, *Ha-Sheker mesarev la-mut: me'ah Shenot "ha-Protokolim shel Zikne Tsiyon"* [The Lie That Would Not Die: A Hundred Years of "The Protocols of the Elders of Zion"] (Tel Aviv: Dvir, 1998).

3. On Krushevan's text, see De Michelis, *Non-Existent Manuscript.*

4. Michael Hagemeister, "Sergej Nilus und die 'Protokolle der Weisen von Zion': Überlegungen zur Forschungslage," *Jahrbuch für Antisemitismusforschung,* 1996, pp. 127–47; and Hagemeister, " 'The Protocols of the Elders of Zion' and the Myth of a Jewish Conspiracy in Post-Soviet Russia," in *Nationalist Myths and Modern Media,* ed. Jan Herman Brinks et al. (London: Tauris Academic Studies, 2006), pp. 243–56.

5. Cohn, *Warrant for Genocide.*

6. Oleg V. Budnitskii, ed., *Yevrei i russkaya revolyntsiya: Materialy i issledovaniya* (Jerusalem: Hebrew University of Jerusalem, 1999).

7. See Léon Poliakov, *La causalité diabolique,* vol. 2: *Du joug mongol à la victoire de Lénine, 1250–1920* (Paris: Calmann-Lévy, 1985).

8. For the influence of the Russian revolutionary Right on Hitler and early Nazism, see Michael Kellogg, *The Russian Roots of Nazism: White Émigrés and the Making*

of National Socialism 1917–1945 (Cambridge: Cambridge University Press, 2005). For the influence of the *Protocols* on Nazi propaganda until the end of World War II, see Wolfram Meyer zu Uptrup, *Kampf gegen die "juedische Weltverschwörung": Propaganda und Antisemitismus der Nationalsozialisten 1919 bis 1945* (Berlin: Metropol, 2003).

9. Hermann Rauschning, *Hitler Speaks* (London: Thornton Butterworth, 1940).

10. See David G. Goodman, *The Protocols of the Elders of Zion: Aum and Antisemitism in Japan* (Jerusalem: Hebrew University of Jerusalem, SICSA, Posen Papers in Contemporary Antisemitism, no. 2 and no. 3, 2005); and Rotem Kowner, *On Symbolic Antisemitism: Motives for the Success of the "Protocols" in Japan and Its Consequences* (Jerusalem: Hebrew University of Jerusalem, SICSA, 2006).

11. Goodman, *Protocols,* pp. 6–7.

12. Kowner, *On Symbolic Antisemitism,* pp. 12–16.

13. Richard Landes, "The Perennial Appeal of *The Protocols of the Elders of Zion,*" *Midstream,* October 1991, pp. 18–21.

14. Robert Rockaway, "Henry Ford, the Dearborn Independent, and the Jews," *Kesher,* no. 33 (May 2003).

15. Gisela Lebzelter, "The *Protocols* in England," *The Wiener Library Bulletin* 31, nos. 47–48 (1978): pp. 111–17. See also Colin Holmes, *Anti-Semitism in British Society, 1876–1939* (London: Edward Arnold, 1979); and Richard C. Thurlow, "The Powers of Darkness: Conspiracy Belief and Political Strategy," *Patterns of Prejudice* 12 (November–December 1978), pp. 1–12.

16. Nesta Webster, *World Revolution: The Plot Against Civilization* (London: Constable, 1922). See also Webster, *Secret Societies and Subversive Movements* (New York: E. P. Dutton and Company, 1924), p. 401.

17. Sergei Fomin, *Rossiia pered Vtorym Prishestviem: Materialy k ocherko russkoi eskhatologii* [Russia Before the Second Coming] (Moscow: Izd Sviato-Troitskoi Sergievoi Lavry, 1993). This is an anthology of apocalyptic and anti-Jewish conspiracy myths.

18. Oleg Platonov, *Ternovyi venets Rossii. Taina bezzakoniia: iudaism i masonstvo protiv Khristianovskoi tsivilizatsii* (Moscow, 1998); and Platonov, *Zagadka Sioniskikh protokolov* (Moscow, 1999).

19. See Semyon Reznik, *The Nazification of Russia: Antisemitism in the Post-Soviet Era* (Washington, D.C.: Challenge Publications, 1996); and Michael Hagemeister, *"Protocols of the Elders of Zion,"* pp. 246–49.

20. Hagemeister, *"Protocols of the Elders of Zion,"* p. 249.

21. Ibid., pp. 250–51.

22. William Korey, "The Soviet 'Protocols of Zion,' " *Insight* 5, no. 2 (February 1979). See also Korey, *Russian Antisemitism,* pp. 13–85.

23. Walter Laqueur, *Black Hundred: The Rise of the Extreme Right in Russia* (New York: HarperCollins, 1993), pp. 31–44.

24. See Frank Fox, "*The Protocols of the Elders of Zion* and the Shadowy World of Elie de Cyon," *East European Jewish Affairs* 2, no. 1 (1997): pp. 3–22. De Cyon was a Jewish convert whom some commentators believe may have been responsible for the material in the *Protocols.* See Henri Rollin, *L'Apocalypse de Notre Temps* (Paris: Editions Allia, 1991), pp. 367–428. De Cyon's well-known hostility to Jewish bankers finds some parallels in the *Protocols* themselves.

25. See Robert S. Wistrich, *Antisemitism in the New Europe* (Yarnton Manor: Oxford Centre for Postgraduate Hebrew Studies, 1994).

26. Yitzhak M. Brodny, "The Heralds of Opposition to Perestroyka," *Soviet Economy* 5 (1989): pp. 162–200. See also Robert S. Wistrich, "Antisemitism in Europe Since the Holocaust," *American Jewish Yearbook,* 1993, pp. 3–23.

27. "Anti-Semitism in the USSR and the Reactions to It," *Jews and Jewish Topics in Soviet and East European Publications,* Spring 1989, pp. 5–44. See also L. Hirszowicz and Howard Spier, *In Search of a Scapegoat: Antisemitism in the Soviet Union Today* (Institute of Jewish Affairs [IJA] research report, no. 3, 1991).

28. Laqueur, *Black Hundred,* pp. 204–21.

29. See the documents relating to Pamyat in *Jews and Jewish Topics in Soviet and East European Publications,* Summer 1988, pp. 30–88; L. Dymerskaya-Tsigelman, "Party Criticism of the Racist Interpretation of Zionism," in ibid., Summer 1987, pp. 3–19; and the internal polemics, especially in Soviet literary criticism, in ibid., pp. 32–50. See also William Korey, *Glasnost and Soviet Antisemitism* (New York: AJC, 1991).

30. *Jews and Jewish Topics in Soviet and East European Publications,* Winter 1978–79, pp. 40–101. See also the articles by N. Prat and Dymerskaya-Tsigelman in ibid., pp. 4–39.

31. Laqueur, *Black Hundred,* pp. 212–21.

32. Wistrich, *Antisemitism: The Longest Hatred,* pp. 183–91.

33. Andrei Sinyavsky, "Russophobia," *Partisan Review* 57, no. 3 (1990): pp. 339–44. Shafarevich characterized the mentality of the Jewish people as being completely alienated from and hostile to Russia's spiritual principles. See also Matthias Messmer, *Sowjetischer und postkommunistischer Antisemitismus,* pp. 244–55.

34. Josephine Woll, "Russians and 'Russophobes': Antisemitism on the Russian Literary Scene," *Soviet Jewish Affairs* 19, no. 3 (1989): pp. 3–21; Sinyavsky, "Russophobia," pp. 340ff. A non-Jewish dissident exile, Sinyavsky summed up Shafarevich's message as follows: "What is meant is that the activities of Jews throughout history are culminating in a striving to master the whole world."

35. Wistrich, *Antisemitism: The Longest Hatred,* pp. 184–85; Stanislav Kunyayev, "Two Ends of a Stick," *Nash Sovremennik,* no. 6 (1989): pp. 158–61.

36. Laqueur, *Black Hundred,* pp. 154–80.

37. See Victor Shnirelman, *The Myth of the Khazars and Intellectual Antisemitism in Russia, 1970s–1990s* (Jerusalem: Hebrew University of Jerusalem, SICSA, 2002), pp. 60–97.

38. Ibid., pp. 85–97, 139–47.

39. Vadim Rossman, *Russian Intellectual Antisemitism in the Post-Communist Era* (Lincoln: University of Nebraska Press, 2002). Published for the Vidal Sassoon International Center for the Study of Antisemitism (SICSA). On the varieties of postcommunist anti-Semitism, see also Theodor H. Friedgut, *Antisemitism and Its Opponents: Reflections in the Russian Press from Perestroika Until the Present* (Jerusalem: Hebrew University of Jerusalem, SICSA, ACTA no. 5, 1994).

40. Roger Boyes, "Russia Invaded by New Army of Fascist Rabble-Rousers," *The Times* (London), February 13, 1992, p. 10.

41. See Yossi Melman, "The Jewish Side of the Family," *Haaretz,* June 30, 2006, for a revealing interview with Zhirinovsky. He had come to Israel on his sixtieth birthday, having only recently discovered that his Polish Jewish father, Wolf Eidelshtein, was

buried there. Zhirinovsky had never known his father, who had abandoned his wife and child when Vladimir was only two months old—returning in 1946 from Kazakhstan (where he had been a wartime refugee) to his native Poland. Until 2002 Zhirinovsky had always vehemently denied his Jewish roots.

42. Vladimir Kartsev, *Zhirinovsky* (New York: Columbia University Press, 1995); and Abraham Brumberg, "Future Without Limits," *The Times Literary Supplement,* December 1995, p. 23.

43. Jacob W. Kipp, "The Zhirinovsky Threat," *Foreign Affairs,* May–June 1994, pp. 72–86.

44. Melman, "Jewish Side," p. 8. In 1996, Zhirinovsky supported archconservative Pat Buchanan (then running for the U.S. presidency) when he called the United States a "Zionist-occupied territory," declaring that exactly the same problem existed in Russia.

45. Ibid., p. 9.

46. "How Many Antisemites Are There Among Us?" *Moskovskie Novosti,* no. 21 (May 27, 1990): p. 15.

47. "Antisemitism and the Collapse of the Former Soviet Union," *Soviet Refugee Monitor* 1, no. 2 (February 1992): p. 17.

48. Robert J. Brym, *Antisemitism in the Former Soviet Union: Recent Survey Results* (IJA research report, no. 6, 1994).

49. Ibid., p. 9.

50. Ibid., pp. 14–15.

51. See Lev Gudkov and Alex Levinson, *Attitudes Toward Jews in the Commonwealth of Independent States* (New York: AJC, 1994), pp. 1–20.

52. *Sovetskaya Rossiya,* September 19, 1992, and October 21, 1995.

53. *Sovetskaya Rossiya,* September 22 and 24, 1994.

54. Lev Krichevsky, *Russian Jewish Elites and Anti-Semitism* (New York: AJC, 1999), p. 31.

55. Ibid., p. 33.

56. *Sovetskaya Rossiya,* October 17, 1998.

57. Albert Makashov, "Rostovschiki Rossii" [Usurers of Russia], *Zavtra,* no. 42 (October 1998).

58. Maksim Zhukov, "Zyuganov podderzhal Makashova" [Zyuganov Backed Makashov], *Kommersant-Daily,* October 22, 1998.

59. Vasily Satronchuk, "Svistoplyaska" [The Fuss], *Sovetskaya Rossiya,* November 10, 1998.

60. Approximately one-third of Russia's top twenty financiers were Jews at this time. See *Profil* (Moscow), October 19, 1998, p. 5.

61. Krichevsky, *Russian Jewish Elites,* p. 30.

62. See Viacheslav Likhachev, *Natzism v Rossii* (Moscow: Information and Research Center Panorama, 2002), pp. 9–62, on Barshakov and his movement. See also the interview with Barshakov, "I Am Not a Fascist, I Am a Nazi," *Moskovskii Komsomolets,* August 4, 1993; and Alexander Brod, "Neo-Nazi Trends in Russia," *Justice,* no. 4 (Spring 2005), pp. 17–23.

63. Brod, "Neo-Nazi Trends in Russia," p. 18.

64. See A. Simonovich, "The Leader's Birthday," *Era Rossii,* nos. 11–12 (June 2002).

Leonid Simonovich was the leader of a Russian Orthodox group that combines neo-Nazism, Christian fundamentalism, and anti-Semitism.

65. V. Likhachev, "The Post-Soviet Russian Orthodox Church on Judaism and the Jews," *Jews in Russia and Eastern Europe*, Summer 2003, pp. 7–32; and Likhachev, *Antisemitizm kak chast' ideologii rossisskikh pravoradikalov* (Moscow:, 1999).

66. A. Verkhovskii, "Religioznaia ksenofobiia" [Religious xenophobia] in *Natsionalizm i ksenofobiia v rossiiskom obschestve*, ed. A. Verkhovskii et al. (Moscow, 1998); and Father A. Borisov, "O natsionalizme v Russkoi pravoslavnoi tserkvi," in *Nuzhen Li Gitler Rossii?* [Does Russia Need a Hitler?] (Moscow, 1996).

67. See Metropolitan Ioann, "Tvortsy kataklizmov na Russkoi Zemle" [Creators of Disasters on Russian Soil], *Chernaia Sotnia*, nos. 3–4 (1999): p. 22. This article was published in several places and was very influential in Russian Orthodox circles.

68. Deacon A. Kuraev, *Kak delaiut antisemitom* [How They Created an Antisemite] (Moscow, 1998), pp. 79ff.

69. Ionn, "Tvortsy kataklizmov," p. 15. Alexander Blank was one of Lenin's grandparents—a Jewish merchant who had converted to Christianity. Anti-Semites have emphasized Lenin's partly Jewish origins ever since the 1917 revolution, though it was never *officially* admitted in Russia until the fall of Communism.

70. See Y. K. Begunov, *Taynye sily v istorii Rossii* [Covert Forces in the History of Russia] (St. Petersburg, 1996), pp. 276–95.

71. *13 let otkrytogo zhido-pravleniya v Rossii: Metody genotsida* [Thirteen Years of Open Jewish Rule in Russia: Methods of Genocide], *Nashe Otechestvo* no. 85 (1998); and Victor Kozlov, *Istoriya tragedii velikogo naroda: Russkii vopros* [History of the Tragedy of a Great People: The Russian Question] (Moscow, 1997).

72. Victor A. Shnirelman, *Russian Neo-pagan Myths and Antisemitism* (Jerusalem: Hebrew University of Jerusalem, SICSA, ACTA no. 13), pp. 17–20. See also *The Myth of the Khazars and Intellectual Antisemitism in Russia, 1970s–1990s* (Jerusalem: The Hebrew University of Jerusalem, SICSA, 2002) by the same author.

73. Rossman, *Russian Intellectual Antisemitism*, pp. 267–68.

74. Quote in *The Reemergence of Political Anti-Semitism in Russia* (New York: ADL, 1999). According to a 1999 poll by the All-Russian Center for the Study of Public Opinion, one-third of Russians believed that records and quotas should be maintained regarding Jews holding leading positions in Russia.

75. See V. Likhachev, introduction to *The Basic Tendencies of the Anti-Semitism in the CIS States* (Kiev: Euro-Asian Jewish Congress, 2003).

76. Markus Mathyl, "The Rise of Political Anti-Semitism in Post-Soviet Russia," *Antisemitism Worldwide*, 1999–2000, pp. 11–24.

77. "On the Streets of Moscow," *Response* 22, no. 2 (Summer 2001): p. 10.

78. Ibid.

79. The Stephen Roth Institute for the Study of Contemporary Antisemitism and Racism, "The CIS and the Baltic States 2002–3," Tel Aviv University, http://www.tau.ac.il/Anti-Semitism/asw2002–3/CIS.htm.

80. Matt Siegel, "Attack on Hate-Crimes Expert in St. Petersburg," *The Jerusalem Post*, July 8, 2007.

81. Vladimir Isachenkov, "Russian Group Warns of Rising Anti-Semitism," *The Jerusalem Post*, April 15, 2005.

82. "Article 282 of the Russian Criminal Code Against Ethnic Hatred," *Justice*, no. 41 (Spring 2005): pp. 15–16.

83. Personal communication from Alexander Brod, director of the Moscow bureau, April 14, 2005, on racism, xenophobia, and anti-Semitism in the Russian Federation.

84. "Hostility Toward Jews in Russia Deepening," *Haaretz*, July 12, 2005.

85. Douglas Davis, "Capitalism With a Stalinist face," *The Jerusalem Post Magazine*, November 14, 2003.

86. "Russia's Move to Ban Jews": an email text sent to the author by Dr. Alexander Brod on February 4, 2005, from Moscow.

87. "Xenophobia Rampant on Russian Streets," *The Jerusalem Post*, February 10, 2005; and "Survey—Anti-Semitism Rises in Russia," *Haaretz*, January 27, 2006.

88. Yair Sheleg, "A Dark Reminder of the Dark Ages," *Haaretz*, June 29, 2005.

89. Union of Councils for Jews in the Former Soviet Union, "Chronicle of Anti-semitism in Ukraine and Russia: 2005–2006," http://www.fsumonitor.com/stories/020207Report.shtml.

90. See Betsy Gidwitz, "La Russie et L'Ukraine," in *Les habits neufs de l'antisémitisme en L'Europe*, ed. M. Gerstenfeld and Shmuel Trigano (Paris: Editions Café Noir, 2004), pp. 275–86.

91. The first volume of Solzhenitsyn's history of Russian-Jewish relations, covering the period from 1795 to 1916, appeared in 2001, under the title *Dvesti let vmeste* [Two Hundred Years Together]; vol. 2 appeared in 2003, covering the period between 1917 and 1972. See Nicolas Weill, "Juifs et Russes dans la logique du 'numerus clausus,' " *Le Monde*, September 19, 2003.

92. Cathy Young, "Traditional Prejudices: The Antisemitism of Alexander Solzhenitsyn," http://www.reason.com/0405/co.cy.traditional.shtml.

93. A. Solzhenitsyn, *Dvesti let vmeste* (Moscow: Russkii Put, 2001), vol. 1: p. 242. Solzhenitsyn blandly asserts that "the Marxist movement in Russia originated in the Pale of Settlement among Jewish youth." As so often occurs, a half truth becomes ossified into a dogma.

94. Alexander Soluyanov, "Nam nuzhno edineniye" [We need unity], *Russkii Vestnik*, nos. 42–43 (1999).

95. Andrei Moskvin, "Terakty v Amerike: komu eto nado?" [Terrorist attacks in America: Who Needs That?], *Russkii Vestnik*, October 25, 2002.

96. See Dore Gold, *Hatred's Kingdom: How Saudi Arabia Supports the New Global Terrorism* (Washington, D.C.: Regnery Publishing, 2003), pp. 134–43, on the penetration of Wahhabism into the former Soviet Republics of Central Asia.

97. *Nezavisimaya Gazeta*, February 28, 2001.

98. V. Likhachev, "Russian Muslims and Anti-Semitism," *Jews of Euro-Asia*, no. 1, (January–March 2003), pp. 6–14.

FIVE: THE POSTCOMMUNIST TRAUMA

1. Wistrich, "Once Again, Antisemitism Without Jews," pp. 45–49; see also Wistrich, "The Dangers of Antisemitism in the New Europe," in *Jewish Identities in the New Europe*, ed. Jonathan Webber (London: Littman Library, 1994), pp. 219–27.

2. Murray Gordon, *The Hungarian Election: Implications for the Jewish Community* (New York: AJC, 1990); Renate Cohen and Jennifer L. Golub, *Attitudes Towards Jews in Poland, Hungary, and Czechoslovakia: A Comparative Survey* (New York: AJC, 1991); Raphael Vago, "Antisemitism and Politics in Post-Communist Central and Eastern Europe," in *Anti-Semitism at the End of the 20th Century*, ed. Pavol Mešťan (Bratislava: Museum of Jewish Culture, 2002), pp. 14–22.

3. André Gerrits, "Antisemitism and Anti-Communism: The Myth of 'Judeo-Communism' in Eastern Europe," *East European Jewish Affairs* 25, no. 1 (Summer 1995): pp. 49–72. See also Istvan Deák, "Jews and Communism: The Hungarian Case," in *Dark Times, Dire Decisions: Jews and Communism*, ed. Jonathan Frankel, Studies in Contemporary Jewry 20 (Oxford, U.K.: Oxford University Press, 2004), pp. 38–60.

4. Quoted in Stephen J. Roth, "Antisemitism at the Centre of Hungarian Politics: The 'Csurka Affair,' " *Analysis* 5 (November 1992): pp. 1–7. See also *Antisemitism in Central and Eastern Europe* (IJA research report, nos. 4–6, 1991), pp. 13–25, on Hungary.

5. "The Long Shadow," *Newsweek*, May 7, 1990, pp. 18–23; Paul Hockenos, *Free to Hate: The Rise of the Right in Post-Communist Eastern Europe* (London: Routledge, 1993). See also Tony Judt, "The Inheritors: Post-Communist Paranoia in Eastern Europe," *Times Literary Supplement*, February 11, 1994.

6. András Kovács, "Antisemitism and the Young Elite in Hungary," *Sociological Papers* (Bar-Ilan University) 5, no. 3 (November 1996); and Kovács, *Antisemitic Prejudices in Contemporary Hungary* (Jerusalem: Hebrew University of Jerusalem, SICSA, ACTA no. 16, 1999), pp. 16–17.

7. See András Kovács, *A kéznél lévő idegen: Antiszemita előítéletek a mai Magyarországon* [The Stranger at Hand: Anti-Semitic Prejudices in Postcommunist Hungary] (Budapest, 2006). My thanks to the author for sending me an unpublished English version of the book.

8. ADL, "Survey of Attitudes Toward Jews and the Middle East in Six European Countries," July 2007. In 2006, 50 percent of Europeans believed Jews were more loyal to Israel than their own country; 35 percent believed that Jews had too much power in the business world; and 20 percent overall continued to blame the Jews for the death of Jesus.

9. Joëlle Stolz, "En Hongrie, un antisémitisme ordinaire reste au centre du débat public," *Le Monde*, June 24, 2003.

10. *Hungarian Jewry: A Better Ambience* (Jerusalem: Institute of the World Jewish Congress, policy dispatch no. 89, 2002).

11. Vago, "Anti-Semitism and Politics," pp. 19–21.

12. Paul Hollander, "Anti-Americanism: Murderous and Rhetorical," *Partisan Review* 69, no. 1 (2002): pp. 14–18.

13. Peter Gay, "Witness to Fascism," *The New York Review of Books*, October 4, 2001. See also William A. Brustein, *Roots of Hate: Antisemitism in Europe Before the Holocaust* (Cambridge: Cambridge University Press, 2003) for a comparative perspective.

14. See Carol Iancu, *Jews in Romania, 1866–1919: From Exclusion to Emancipation* (Boulder, Colo.: East European Monographs, 1996); and Leon Volovici, *Nationalist Ideology and Anti-Semitism: The Case of Romanian Intellectuals in the 1930s* (Ox-

ford, U.K.: Pergamon, 1991). Also Andrei Oişteanu, *Inventing the Jew: Antisemitic Stereotypes in Romanian and Other Central-East European Cultures* (Lincoln: University of Nebraska Press, 2009).

15. See "Roots of Romanian Antisemitism," in *Final Report of the International Commission on the Holocaust in Romania,* ed. Tuvia Friling, Radu Ioanid, et al. (Bucharest, Romania: Editura Polirom, 2005), pp. 19–56.

16. Ibid., p. 21. On the anti-Semitic atmosphere in Romania during the 1930s, see Mihail Sebastian, *Journal: 1935–1944* (London: Pimlico, 2003).

17. See Jean Ancel, *History of the Holocaust: Romania,* vol. 1–2 (Jerusalem: Yad Vashem, 2002); Radu Ioanid, *The Holocaust in Romania: The Destruction of Jews and Gypsies Under the Antonescu Regime, 1940–1944* (Chicago: Ivan R. Dee, 2000); and Friling, Ioanid, et al., *Final Report,* pp. 181–204, 243–54, 381–82.

18. Robert S. Wistrich, "Iudaeus ex Machine: Die Wiederkehr eines alten Feindbildes," *Transit,* Winter 1992–93, pp. 140–49; Friling, Ioanid, et al., *Final Report,* pp. 333–48; and Laurence Weinbaum, *A Journey Through Romania's Holocaust Narrative* (Jerusalem: Institute of the World Jewish Congress, policy dispatch no. 27, 2004).

19. Oişteanu, *Inventing the Jew,* p. 270.

20. *Newsweek,* May 7, 1990, pp. 22–23.

21. See Wistrich, "Once Again, Antisemitism Without Jews," p. 47. As prime minister, Petre Roman, the Jewish son of a former Stalinist official, authorized the launching of Tudor's weekly. He would soon find himself under attack as an agent of "international Jewish finance."

22. See Wistrich, "Once Again," p. 48.

23. *Europa,* no. 23 (May 1991).

24. *Europa,* no. 24 (May 1991).

25. See Michael Shafir, "Romania," in *Radio Free Europe Research Report* 3, no. 16 (April 22, 1994): pp. 87–94.

26. *Romania Mare,* no. 97 (March 15, 1992).

27. See Norman Manea, "Towards the Next Century" (Jerusalem: Hebrew University of Jerusalem, SICSA Annual Report, 1999), pp. 10–11; and George Voicu, "L'Honneur National Roumain en Question," *Les Temps Modernes,* November–December 1999, pp. 142–60.

28. Stephen Roth Institute, "Romania 2002–3."

29. Marco Katz, Ozy Lazar, and Alexandru Florian, *Anti-Semitism in Romania: 2002 Report* (The Center for Monitoring and Combating the Anti-Semitism in Romania). See also Leon Volovici, "The Report on the Romanian Holocaust and Its Consequences," *Antisemitism International,* 2006, pp. 103–11.

30. Volovici, "Report on the Romanian Holocaust."

31. George Voicu, *Zeii cei rái: Cultura conspirţiei in România postcommunistá* [Evil Gods: The Cult of Conspiracy in Post-Communist Romania] (Bucharest, Romania: Polirom, 2000). Extracts in French from Voicu's work appeared in *Les Temps Modernes,* March–April 2001, pp. 173–212. See also Mihai Dinu Gheorghiu, "Conspiration et désenchantement: les conditions d'une nouvelle production idéologique en Roumanie," ibid., pp. 161–72.

32. George Voicu, "L'Imaginaire du Complot dans la Roumanie Postcommuniste," *Les Temps Modernes,* March–April 2001, pp. 185–86.

33. Daniella Peled, "Double Dividend," *The Jerusalem Post,* January 10, 2005.

34. *Haaretz,* July 24, 2003.

35. Iliescu's speech as president of Romania, at the First Holocaust Remembrance Day meeting, October 12, 2004, in Friling, Ioanid, et al., *Final Report,* pp. 9–13.

36. Michael Shafir, *Between Denial and "Comparative Trivialization": Holocaust Negationism in Post-Communist East Central Europe* (Jerusalem: Hebrew University of Jerusalem, SICSA, ACTA no. 19, 2002), p. 52.

37. On the pre-1939 situation, see Harriet Freidenreich, *The Jews of Yugoslavia: A Quest for Community* (Philadelphia: Jewish Publication Society of America, 1979). For the Serbian Orthodox Church and the Jews, see Jovan Byford, "Christian Right-Wing Organisations and the Spreading of Anti-Semitic Prejudice in Post-Milošević Serbia," *East European Jewish Affairs* 32, no. 2 (Winter 2002): pp. 43–60. On Slovene anti-Semitism and wartime collaboration, see Gregor Joseph Kranja, "Obligatory Hatred? Antisemitic Propaganda and the Slovene Anti-Communist Camp," *East European Jewish Affairs* 37, no. 2 (August 2007): pp. 191–216.

38. *Philadelphia Inquirer,* September 10, 1991.

39. Also translated as *Wastelands: Historical Truth* (from the second edition, 1989), pp. 160–61, 316–20. See Ivo and Slavko Goldstein, "Revisionism in Croatia: The Case of Franjo Tudjman," *East European Jewish Affairs* 32, no. 1 (2002): pp. 52–64; and Slobodan Drakulic, "Revising Franjo Tudjman's Revisionism?" in *East European Jewish Affairs* 32, no. 2 (Winter, 2002): pp. 61–69.

40. See Jennifer Golub, *The Jewish Dimension of the Yugoslav Crisis* (New York: AJC, 1992), pp. 4–5.

41. Wistrich, "Once Again, Antisemitism Without Jews," p. 46.

42. Information Department of the Croatian Ministry of Foreign Affairs, *Newsletter,* no. 27 (February 15, 1994).

43. Ruth Ellen Gruber, *The Struggle of Memory: The Rehabilitation and Reevaluation of Fascist Heroes in Europe* (New York: AJC, 1995), pp. 1–2.

44. *Antisemitism World Report 1994* (London: Institute of Jewish Affairs, 1994), p. 134.

45. Ibid., p. 135.

46. Zora Bútorová and Martin Bútora, *Wariness Toward Jews and "Postcommunist Panic" in Slovakia* (New York: AJC, 1992).

47. Pavol Mešt'an, *Antisemitism in Slovak Politics* (Bratišlava, Slovakia: Museum of Jewish Culture, 2000).

48. Gila Fatran, "The Viability of Anti-Semitic Manifestations," in *Antisemitism at the End of the 20th Century,* pp. 125–37. See also Mešt'an, *Antisemitism in Slovak Politics (1989–1999)* (Bratislava: Museum of Jewish Culture, 2000), pp. 138–47.

49. Martin Spitzer, "Anti-Semitism and Christianity in Slovakia at the End of the Twentieth Century," in *Antisemitism at the End of the 20th Century,* pp. 149–53; and Daniela Baranová, "The Lutheran Church's Position on Anti-Semitism in Slovakia in the Twentieth Century," ibid., pp. 154–63.

50. Mešt'an, *Antisemitism in Slovak Politics,* pp. 187–201.

51. Jennifer Golub, *Antisemitism in the Postcommunist Era: Trends in Poland, Hungary, and Czechoslovakia* (New York: AJC, 1991), p. 11.

52. Jiri Pehe, "The Czech Republic," *RFE/RL Research Report* 3, no. 16 (April 22, 1994): pp. 50–54.

53. Ilan Moss, "Anti-Semitic Incidents and Discourse in Europe During the Israel-Hezbollah War" (presented to the European Jewish Congress, 2007).

54. Interview with Tomas Kraus (executive director of the Jewish Communities Federation in the Czech Republic), September 29, 2006, in ibid., p. 17.

55. Etgar Lefkovits, "Israel Envoy Boycotts Anti-Semitic Polish Education Minister," *The Jerusalem Post*, July 9, 2006. In October 2007 Giertyk's party was nearly wiped out in the national elections, their support falling below the 5 percent threshold required to enter Parliament.

56. Lily Galili, "Poland's Chief Rabbi Victim of Anti-Semitic Attack," *Haaretz*, May 29, 2006; "Poland Apologizes to Rabbi After Attack," *The Jerusalem Post*, May 29, 2006.

57. See "Media Climate Poses Threat to Press Freedom," Reporters Without Borders, April 7, 2006, http://www.rsf.org/print.php3?id_article=16973.

58. On *Radio Maryja*, see its website, http://www.ojciec-dyrektor.de/, in Polish.

59. See Dinah A. Spritzer, "Polish Catholic Radio Draws Fire," *The Jewish Chronicle*, May 5, 2006. For an earlier assessment, see Ewa Wilk, "Rodzina ocja Rydzyka," *Polityka*, December 13, 1997, pp. 116–20.

60. Gabriele Lesser, "Polens Bischöfe wollen Radio Maryja beraten," *Illustrierte Neue Welt* (Vienna), June–July 2006, p. 6. Nicholas Watt, "Anti-Semitism Live," *The Guardian*, June 5, 2006.

61. Lesser, "Polens Bischöfe," p. 6.

62. "Polish Priest Rejects Criticism," *IHT*, July 12, 2007.

63. Israel Urges Poland, Catholic Church to Condemn Priest Over Anti-Semitic Comments," *Haaretz*, August 8, 2007; and Haviv Rettig, "Poland Silent Over Anti-Semitic Priest," *The Jerusalem Post*, August 6, 2007.

64. Ryan Lucas, "Hundreds in Poland Condemn Priest's Comments as Anti-Semitic," AOL News, http://news.aol.com/. Accessed August 7, 2007.

65. "Priest Slammed for Anti-Semitism," *The Jerusalem Post*, July 12, 2007; and Etgar Lefkovits, "Polish Gov't Urged to Condemn Priest for 'Greedy Jews' Remarks" in the same edition.

66. Craig S. Smith, "Call to Punish Polish Priest for Anti-Semitic Remarks," *The New York Times*, July 12, 2007. See also John Cornwell, "Poland's Shame," *The Tablet*, August 25, 2007.

67. "Jewish Leaders Fume at Pope's Meeting with Anti-Semitic Priest," *The Jerusalem Post*, August 10, 2007.

68. Dinah A. Spritzer, "Jews Are a Detriment to Europe, Polish Politician Says," *The Jerusalem Post*, February 20, 2007. See also Jean Quatremer, "L'opuscule anti-Semite qui secoue le Parlement européen," *Libération*, February 17, 2007.

69. Maciej Giertych, *Civilisations at War in Europe* (2007), p. 23. The full text can be found at the author's website, http://www.giertych.pl/.

70. Ibid., p. 24.

71. Wistrich, *Antisemitism: The Longest Hatred*, pp. 166–67.

72. Adam Michnik, "The Two Faces of Europe," *The New York Review of Books*, July 19, 1990.

73. Adam Rok, "Antisemitic Propaganda in Poland—Centres, Proponents, Publications," *East European Jewish Affairs* 22, no. 1 (1992): pp. 23–37; and "Bez maski,"

Gazeta Wyborcza (Warsaw), September 22, 1990; and Wistrich, *Antisemitism: The Longest Hatred*, pp. 165, 167.

74. Paul Zawadzki, "Antisémitisme en Pologne à l'heure de la transition vers le post-communisme," *Lignes*, no. 19 (May 1993): pp. 122–57.

75. Abraham Brumberg, "The Problem That Won't Go Away: Anti-Semitism in Poland (Again)," *Tikkun*, January–February 1990, pp. 31–34. See also Robert S. Wistrich, *Anti-Semitism in Europe Since the Holocaust* (New York: AJC, 1993), pp. 16–17.

76. Quoted in Golub, *Antisemitism in the Postcommunist Era*, p. 4.

77. Ibid., pp. 6–7.

78. Joanna Beata Michlic, *Poland's Threatening Other: The Image of the Jew from 1880 to the Present* (Lincoln: University of Nebraska Press, 2006), pp. 268–70. For the historical background, see Ronald Modras, *The Catholic Church and Antisemitism: Poland, 1933–1939* (Chur, Switzerland: Harwood Academic Publishers, 1994). Published for the Vidal Sassoon International Center for the Study of Antisemitism, Hebrew University of Jerusalem.

79. Jankowski, in a homily at Saint Brigida Church in August 2004 before his dismissal, claimed that an Israeli-Jewish-Communist conspiracy was out to destroy him. See *Nasz Dziennik*, August 13, 2004, p. 12.

80. Roman Daszcyński, "Skandalista Henryk Jankowski," *Gazeta Wyborcza*, October 31, 1997, p. 4.

81. See D. Ost, "The Radical Right in Poland: Rationality of the Irrational," in *The Radical Right in Central and Eastern Europe Since 1989*, ed. S. Ramet (University Park: Pennsylvania State University Press, 1999), p. 93.

82. Jacek Kurczewski, "Polska partia Rydzyka," *Wprost*, May 11, 1997, pp. 26–28.

83. Stanisław Musiał, "Czarne jest czarne," *Gazeta Wyborcza*, November 15–16, 1997, pp. 20–21. See also *Tygodnik Powszechny*, December 6, 1997, p. 4.

84. See Krystyna Kersten, *Polacy, Zydzi, komunizm: Anatomia półprawd 1939–68* (Warsaw: Niezalezna oficyna wydawnicza, 1992). See also Daniel Blatman, "Polish Anti-semitism and 'Judeo-Communism': Historiography and Memory," *East European Jewish Affairs* 27, no. 1 (1997): pp. 23–43.

85. Leon Volovici, *Antisemitism in Post-Communist Eastern Europe: A Marginal or Central Issue?* (Jerusalem: Hebrew University of Jerusalem, SICSA, ACTA no. 5, 1994).

86. For a defense of the Polish identification of Jews with the new pro-Soviet Communist regime after 1944, see Jan Marek Chodiakiewicz, *After the Holocaust: Polish-Jewish Conflict in the Wake of World War II* (Boulder, Colo.: East Europe Monographs, 2003).

87. Natalia Aleksiun, "The Vicious Circle: Jews in Communist Poland, 1944–1956," *Studies in Contemporary Jewry* 19 (2003): pp. 157–80. See also Michlic, *Poland's Threatening Other*, pp. 88–92, 200–14, 230–42.

88. Michlic, *Poland's Threatening Other*, p. 206.

89. Jan T. Gross, *Neighbours: The Destruction of the Jewish Community in Jedwabne, Poland* (Princeton, N.J.: Princeton University Press, 2001); Robert S. Wistrich, "The Jedwabne Affair," in *Antisemitism Worldwide, 2001–2*, pp. 60–75; Lawrence Weinbaum, "Penitence and Prejudice: The Roman Catholic Church and Jed-

wabne," *Jewish Political Studies Review* 14, nos. 3–4 (Fall 2002): pp. 131–54; Abraham Brumberg, "Murder Most Foul," *The Times Literary Supplement*, March 2, 2001; and the selection of articles edited by Israel Gutman, *Thou Shalt Not Kill: Poles on Jedwabne* (Warsaw: Wiez, 2001).

90. Joanna B. Michlic, *Coming to Terms with the "Dark Past": The Polish Debate About the Jedwabne Massacre* (Jerusalem: Hebrew University of Jerusalem, SICSA, ACTA no. 21, 2002).

91. Ibid., pp. 11–17.

92. Ireneusz Krzeminski, ed., *Czy Polacy są antysemitami? Wyniki badania sonda-zowego* [Are the Poles Anti-Semites? Results of a Survey] (Warsaw: Oficyna Naukowa, 1996). See also Krzeminski, *Antysemityzm w Polsce i na Ukrainie* [Anti-semitism in Poland and the Ukraine] (Warsaw: Wydawnictwo Naukowe, 2004). See also the essays by Polish historians and sociologists in *Thinking After the Holo-caust: Voices from Poland,* ed. Sebastian Rejak (Warsaw-Kraców: Muza SA Publish-ing House, 2008), pp. 11–156. The original texts are in Polish and a translation into Hebrew appears in the same volume.

93. Tomasz Strzembosz, "Oko za oko, ząb za ząb" [An Eye for an Eye, a Tooth for a Tooth], *Rzeczpospolita,* April 16, 2002; Strzembosz, "Czego robić nie wolno," ibid., May 10, 2002; Maciej Rybiński, "Jednostronny pacyfizm" [One-sided Pacifism], ibid., May 10, 2002; Bogusław Wolniewicz, "Izrael należy popierać" [Israel should be supported], ibid., May 10, 2002; and Rafael Żerbrowski, "Dlaczego mam kochać Arafáta? [Why Should I Love Arafat?], ibid., May 10, 2002.

94. Maciej Rybiński, "Usprawiedliwiona odpowiedź Israela" [The Justified Response of Israel], *Rzeczpospolita,* April 16, 2002.

95. Marek Król, "Jestem Izraelczykiem" [I Am an Israeli], *Wprost,* April 21, 2002.

96. Laurence Weinbaum, " 'For Your Freedom and Ours': A Polish Response to Israel-Bashing," *Midstream,* November–December 2002, pp. 2–3.

97. Eliahu Salpeter, "Anti-Semitism or Corruption?" *Haaretz,* December 15, 2004; Vladimir Mateyev, "Ukrainian Election Challenges Traditional Jewish Identity," *The Jerusalem Post,* December 29, 2004.

98. Anna Melnichuk, "Ukrainian Jews Fume as Police Say Attack Not Anti-Semitic," *The Jerusalem Post,* September 2, 2005.

99. Krzemiński, *Antysemitzym w Polsce,* pp. 172–247.

100. Union of Councils for Jews in the Former Soviet Union, "Chronicle of Anti-semitism in Ukraine and Russia, 2005–06," annual report, January 2007,

101. See *An Incubator of Hatred: Pervasive Anti-Semitism at MAUP, a Leading Ukrain-ian University* (New York: AJC, 2006). See also *Antisemitism Worldwide,* 2005, pp. 14–15.

102. Ibid.

103. The Stephen Roth Institute for the Study of Contemporary Antisemitism and Racism, *Year in Review* (Tel Aviv: Tel Aviv University, 2006), p. 13.

104. Yossi Melman, "Israel Urges Ukraine to Bar Parliamentary Candidacy of Anti-Semitic University Head," *Haaretz,* September 9, 2005.

105. See Vyacheslav Likhachev, "Ukraine (2005)," Euro-Asian Jewish Congress, http://www.eajc.org/program_art_e.php?id=29.

106. Quoted in *An Incubator of Hatred.*

107. "Prosecution and Persecution: Lithuania Must Stop Blaming the Victims," *The Economist,* August 21, 2008.

SIX: NAZI SHADOWS OVER AUSTRIA

1. See Wistrich, *Jews of Vienna;* William O. McCagg, *A History of Habsburg Jews, 1670–1918* (Bloomington: Indiana University Press, 1989); and Steven Beller, *Vienna and the Jews, 1867–1938: A Cultural History* (Cambridge: Cambridge University Press, 1989).
2. See Robert S. Wistrich, *Socialism and the Jews: The Dilemmas of Assimilation in Germany and Austria-Hungary* (London: Associated University Presses, 1982). See also Wistrich, *Laboratory of World Destruction: Germans and Jews in Central Europe* (Lincoln: University of Nebraska Press, 2007).
3. Wistrich, *The Jews of Vienna,* pp. 220–37.
4. On Lueger, see John Boyer, *Political Radicalism in Late Imperial Vienna: Origins of the Christian Social Movement, 1848–1897* (Chicago: University of Chicago Press, 1981); and Richard S. Geehr, *Karl Lueger: Mayor of Fin de Siècle Vienna* (Detroit: Wayne State University Press, 1990).
5. On interwar Austrian anti-Semitism, see Bruce Pauley, *From Prejudice to Persecution: A History of Austrian Anti-Semitism* (Chapel Hill: University of North Carolina Press, 1992).
6. The goal of *Anschluss* (union) with Germany had been blocked by the Western Allies in 1918 despite its popularity in Austria, especially among Social Democrats—including the chancellor, Karl Renner, and the Jewish-born foreign minister, Otto Bauer.
7. See Bruce F. Pauley, "Political Antisemitism in the Interwar Period," in *Jews, Antisemitism and Culture in Vienna,* ed. Ivar Oxaal, Michael Pollak, and Gerhard Botz (London: Routledge and Kegan Paul, 1987).
8. Benno Weiser Varon, *Professions of a Lucky Jew* (New York: Cornwall Books, 1992), p. 30.
9. Gerhard Botz, "The Dynamics of Persecution in Austria, 1938–45," in *Austrians and Jews in the Twentieth Century: From Franz Joseph to Waldheim,* ed. Robert S. Wistrich (London: Macmillan, 1992), p. 202. See also Evan Burr Burkey, *Hitler's Austria: Popular Sentiment in the Nazi Era, 1938–1945* (Chapel Hill: University of North Carolina Press, 2000) for the broader picture.
10. Botz, pp. 202–6. See also Kurt Schmid and Robert Streibel, *Der Pogrom 1938* (Vienna, 1990); and Herbert Rosenkranz, *Verfolgung und Selbstbehauptung: Die Juden in Österreich 1938–1945* (Vienna, 1978).
11. G. Botz, "National Socialist Vienna: Anti-Semitism as a Housing Policy," in "European Antisemitism, 1890–1945," ed. Robert S. Wistrich, *Wiener Library Bulletin* 29, nos. 39–40 (1976): pp. 47–55.
12. See Botz, "Dynamics of Persecution," p. 215, who stresses that "from 1938 onwards Austria and Vienna were often a step ahead of Germany in the persecution of the Jews. In Vienna, in particular, comparable measures were applied earlier than in Germany, and they could also count on broader support among the non-Jewish

population. Here the organisational instruments and procedures could be developed which would later be applied by Eichmann in the Final Solution."

13. Richard Crossman, *Palestine Mission: A Personal Record* (New York: Harper and Brothers, 1947), p. 92.

14. See Michael Brenner, *After the Holocaust: Rebuilding Jewish Lives in Postwar Germany* (Princeton, N.J.: Princeton University Press, 1998).

15. Thomas Albrich, *Exodus durch Österreich: Die Jüdische Flüchtlinge 1945–1948* (Innsbruck: Haymon-Verlag, 1987), p. 93. Albrich observes that the British military authorities often sympathized more with the Austrian population than with the Jews. The British war against "illegal" Jewish immigration from Europe to Palestine contributed to this bias.

16. *Salzburger Nachrichten,* July 10, 1946.

17. *Arbeiter Zeitung* (Vienna), August 21, 1946.

18. Constantin Goschler, "The Attitude Towards Jews in Bavaria After the Second World War," *LBIYB* 36 (1991): pp. 443–60.

19. In 1948, there were still 4,473 Jewish DPs in the Salzburg region and another 4,500 registered in the city itself, though the numbers rapidly diminished with the foundation of Israel. See Marko Feingold, ed., *Ein Ewiges Dennoch: 125 Jahre Juden in Salzburg* (Vienna: Böhlau, 1993), and the contribution of Helga Embacher, "Neubeginn ohne Illusionen," pp. 285–336.

20. See Shlomo Shafir, "Kurt Schumacher und die Juden: Als erster deutscher Politiker bekannte er sich zur Wiedergutmachung," *Tribüne* 112 (1989): pp. 128–38. On the seminal importance of Schumacher's role on these issues, see the study by Jeffrey Herf, *Divided Memory: The Nazi Past in the Two Germanies* (Cambridge, Mass.: Harvard University Press, 1997), pp. 239–60.

21. Helga Embacher, *Neubeginn ohne Illusionen: Juden in Österreich* (Vienna, 1995), p. 77.

22. Ibid.

23. See Robert Knight, "Restitution and Legitimacy in Postwar Austria 1945–1953," *LBIYB* 36 (1991): pp. 413–42. In a cabinet meeting on January 8, 1952, Figl remarked that relatively few Austrian Jews were killed during the war and "most of them really did get over the border"—an amazingly insensitive and misleading statement.

24. See Oliver Rathkolb, "Zur Kontinuität antisemitischer und rassistische Vorurteile in Österreich 1945/1950," *Zeitgeschichte* 16, no. 5 (February 1989): pp. 167–79.

25. Ibid., p. 168. See also Richard Mitten, "Die 'Judenfrage' in Nachkriegsösterreich: Probleme der Forschung," *Zeitgeschichte* 19, nos. 11–12 (November–December 1992): pp. 356–67.

26. See Ruth Beckermann, *Unzugehörig: Österreicher und Juden nach 1945* (Vienna: Loecker, 1989), for an account of this anti-Semitic atmosphere and the experience of growing up in postwar Vienna confronted by hostility and social isolation.

27. Wilhelm Svoboda, "Politiker, Antisemit, Populist: Oskar Helmer und die Zweite Republik," *Das Jüdische Echo* 39, no. 1 (October 1990): pp. 42–51.

28. Ibid., p. 43.

29. Wilhelm Svoboda, *Die Partei, die Republik und der Mann mit den vielen Gesichtern: Oskar Helmer und Österreich II: eine Korrektur* (Vienna: Böhlau, 1993).

30. Knight, "Restitution and Legitimacy," p. 435. See also Robert S. Wistrich, *Austria and the Legacy of the Holocaust* (New York: AJC, 1999), pp. 14–17.

31. Anton Pelinka, "Karl Renner—A Man for All Seasons," *Austrian History Yearbook* 23 (1992): pp. 111–19.

32. Svoboda, "Politiker, Antisemit, Populist," pp. 471ff.

33. See Feingold, *Ein Ewiges Dennoch*, pp. 344–49. Kraus targeted the so-called NS-Gesetz—the de-Nazification law that "ostracized" the Nazis and could take away their property or apartments. Originally, the law distinguished between forty-two thousand incriminated *belasteten* (Nazis) and about five hundred thousand *minderbelasteten* (less incriminated) persons, who were amnestied and reenfranchised after 1948.

34. Ibid., pp. 345ff.

35. R. Knight, "Neutrality Not Sympathy," p. 226.

36. See Simon Wiesenthal, *Justice Not Vengeance: Recollections* (London: Weidenfeld and Nicolson, 1989).

37. Hella Pick, *Simon Wiesenthal: A Life in Search of Justice* (London: Weidenfeld and Nicolson, 1996), p. 61.

38. For an autobiographical treatment of his political career, see Bruno Kreisky, *Zwischen den Zeiten: Erinnerungen aus fünf Jahrzehnten* (Berlin: Siedler, 1986); and Kreisky, *Im Strom der Politik: Erfahrungen eines Europäers* (Berlin: Siedler Verlag, 1988). See also the useful biography by H. Pierre Secher, *Bruno Kreisky: Chancellor of Austria* (Pittsburgh: Dorrance Publishing Co., 1993) and Robert S. Wistrich, *Between Redemption and Perdition* (London: Routledge, 1990), pp. 107–20. Kreisky had been appointed foreign minister in 1959 despite Julius Raab's uneasiness at having a Jew in this position.

39. See Robert S. Wistrich, *Bruno Kreisky, Israel and the "Jewish Question"* (Jerusalem: Hebrew University of Jerusalem, SICSA, ACTA no. 30, 2007).

40. Kreisky, *Zwischen den Zeiten*, pp. 198ff.

41. Ibid., p. 265.

42. See Robert S. Wistrich, "The Kreisky Phenomenon: A Reassessment," in *Austrians and Jews*, pp. 234–52. Kreisky particularly detested what he regarded as Israel's "manipulation" of the Holocaust to justify its allegedly brutal, repulsive, and unjust policies toward the Palestinians. See Kreisky, *Im Strom der Politik*, p. 297.

43. *Wiener Wochenblatt*, February 25, 1967, p. 17.

44. Franz Kirchberger, "Kreisky in der NS-Fälle," *Deutsche Wochen-Zeitung*, May 29, 1970. The German and Austrian neo-Nazi press were naturally enthused by Kreisky's attitude toward former Nazis and his determination to destroy Wiesenthal's reputation. See Wiesenthal, *Justice Not Vengeance*, pp. 294–304.

45. Robert S. Wistrich, "The Strange Case of Bruno Kreisky," *Encounter*, May 1979, p. 110.

46. Pick, *Simon Wiesenthal*, p. 257. Wiesenthal came to regard Kreisky as a man who had consciously "betrayed" his Jewish heritage. Ibid., p. 246.

47. See Wistrich, "Strange Case."

48. *Vrij Nederland*, July 1, 1970.

49. Secher, *Bruno Kreisky*, p. 188.

50. Wistrich, "Strange Case," pp. 114–15. For Wiesenthal's career, see the detailed obituary by Ralph Blumenthal in *The New York Times*, September 21, 2005.

51. Wistrich, "Strange Case," p. 110. This slogan recalls the cynical dictum of Vienna's anti-Semitic mayor, Karl Lueger, around 1900: *Wer ein Jud ist, das bestimme ich* (I decide who is a Jew).

52. "Der Fall Peter," *Profil* (Austria), October 14, 1975, pp. 10, 12–16; "Peter und die Mordbrigade," ibid., October 21, 1975, pp. 18–23; Peter Michael Lingens, "Grenzen des Opportunismus," ibid., November 18, 1975.

53. "Kreisky Accuses Top Zionist of Nazi Collaboration," *Free Palestine,* December 1975.

54. "Kreisky: Die Juden—ein mieses Volk," *Der Spiegel,* November 17, 1975. See also Wiesenthal, *Justice Not Vengeance,* p. 301.

55. Ulrich Brunner, "Kratzer am Kanzler: Kleinkrieg Kreisky-Wiesenthal und Keine Ende," *Vorwärts,* December 18, 1975, ironized that "Superman Kreisky also has a problem which he has not quite overcome—his Jewish origin."

56. "Sozialistiche Schutzmauer um Kreisky gegen Wiesenthal," *Frankfurter Allgemeine Zeitung,* December 4, 1975.

57. "Kann Kreisky Wiesenthal Stoppen?" *Deutche National-Zeitung,* November 7, 1975; "Wiesenthal ein Agent," ibid., November 14, 1975; "Wie weit reicht Israels Macht?" ibid., November 28, 1975; "Israels Rächer in Deutschland: Ist Wiesenthal am Ende," ibid., December 1975. Wiesenthal himself seemed resigned in an interview, "Nur Don Quijote wurde weitermachen," in *Der Speigel,* January 12, 1976.

58. "Neonazis: Von Kreisky lernen," *Profil* (Austria), September 21, 1975, p. 13; "Versöhnung mit den Nazis—aber wie?" ibid., October 21, 1975, pp. 18–23; and the psychologically penetrating if sarcastic observation of Peter Michael Lingens in ibid., November 18, 1975: "Von ehemaligen Nazis akzeptiert zu werden ist demnach die extremste Form der Traumerfüllung" (To be accepted by former Nazis is, one could say, the ultimate form of wish fulfillment).

59. *The Jerusalem Post,* September 3, 1978; *Neue Zürcher Zeitung,* September 7, 1978.

60. *Ma'ariv,* July 5, 1979, in Hebrew.

61. Ibid.

62. *The Jerusalem Post,* May 23, 1986.

63. Ephraim Kishon, "Schlage uns, Bruno, wir sind deine Trommel," *Der Spiegel,* September 11, 1978, pp. 142–45. See also Robert Wistrich, "Strange Case," pp. 78–85.

64. See *Profil* (Austria), February 3, 1976. At the end of 1975 almost 60 percent of the Austrian population appear to have supported Kreisky's position, against only 3 percent who were in favor of Weisenthal, with the rest either neutral or unconcerned.

65. See the section by Richard Mitten, "Die Kreisky-Peter-Wiesenthal 'Affäre,' " in *"Wir sind alle Unschuldige Täter!" Diskurshistorische Studien zum Nachkriegsantisemitismus im Österreich,* ed. Ruth Wodak et al. (Frankfurt: Suhrkamp, 1990). See also Robert S. Wistrich, *Austria and the Legacy of the Holocaust* (New York: AJC, 1999), pp. 30–34.

66. Richard Mitten, *The Politics of Antisemitic Prejudice: The Waldheim Phenomenon in Austria* (Boulder, Colo.: Westview Press, 1992). See also Bernard Cohen and Luc Rozenzweig, *Le mystère Waldheim* (Paris: Gallimard, 1986); and Richard Bassett, *Waldheim and Austria* (New York: Viking, 1988).

67. *Die Presse,* March 25, 1986; and *Kronen Zeitung,* May 28, 1986.

68. *Kronen Zeitung,* May 28, 1986.

69. For the role of conspiracy theories in the affair, see Mitten, "Reflections on the Waldheim Affair," in Wistrich, *Austrians and Jews*, pp. 252–73.

70. Ruth Wodak, "Opfer der Opfer? Der alltäglich Antisemitismus in Österreich: Erste qualitative soziolinguistische Überlegungen," in *Antisemitismus in der politischen Kultur nach 1945*, ed. Werner Bergmann and Rainer Erb (Opladen, Germany: Westdeutscher Verlag, 1990), pp. 292–318.

71. See Ruth Wodak, "The Waldheim Affair and Antisemitic Prejudice in Austrian Public Discourse," *Patterns of Prejudice* 24, nos. 2–4 (Winter 1990): pp. 18–33.

72. Wodak, *Wir sind alle Unschüldige*. The slogan, "We are all innocent perpetrators" tellingly exemplifies Austrian evasiveness about their own historic responsibility. See also Bruce Pauley, "Austria," in *The World Reacts to the Holocaust*, ed. David S. Wyman (Baltimore: Johns Hopkins University Press, 1996), pp. 473–513.

73. See Fritz Karmasin, *Austrian Attitudes Toward Jews, Israel, and the Holocaust* (New York: AJC Working Papers on Contemporary Anti-Semitism, 1992), which compares the results of the Austrian survey to those conducted by the AJC in 1990–91 in both Germanies and in Eastern Europe.

74. Bassett, *Waldheim and Austria*, p. 97.

75. Ibid., p. 136.

76. Mitten, *Politics of Antisemitic Prejudice*, p. 227.

77. *Profil* (Austria), March 25, 1986.

78. Mitten, *Politics of Antisemitic Prejudice*, p. 233. In the Austrian press it was claimed that Israel Singer sought revenge on Austrians for having made his father clean the streets of Vienna with a toothbrush following the Nazi *Anschluss* of 1938.

79. *L'Express*, November 13, 1987.

80. Mitten, *Politics of Antisemitic Prejudice*, p. 55.

81. Richard von Weizsäcker, "The 8th of May, 1945—Forty Years After," in *A Voice from Germany: Speeches by Richard von Weizsäcker* (New York: Weidenfeld and Nicolson, 1987), pp. 43–60.

82. Bassett, *Waldheim and Austria*, p. 158. In the second round of the elections Waldheim won 54 percent of the vote. The campaign against WJC tactics probably increased popular Austrian support for him.

83. Embacher, *Neubeginn*, pp. 258–59.

84. See *Die Gemeinde* (Vienna), May 6, 1986, p. 5; and ibid., July 1986, p. 6.

85. Embacher, *Neubeginn*, p. 259.

86. Ibid.

87. See Leon Zelman, *Ein Leben nach dem Überleben* (Vienna: Kremayr and Scheriau, 1995), p. 205.

88. Sander Gilman, *The Jews in Today's German Culture* (Bloomington: Indiana University Press, 1995).

89. Embacher, *Neubeginn*, pp. 313–16; and Pauley, "Austria," pp. 502–5.

90. *Die Presse*, July 9, 1991.

91. *The Jerusalem Post*, October 1, 1998. The value of Jewish property before the 1938 *Anschluss* was estimated in 1953 at around $10 billion. There were more than thirty-three thousand businesses owned by Jews in Vienna, some of them among the largest in Austria. They were either liquidated or turned over to Aryans, along with great quantities of art objects, some of which are still in Austrian museums.

92. See Ruth Wodak and Anton Pelinka, eds., *The Haider Phenomenon in Austria* (New Brunswick, N.J.: Transaction Publishers, 2002).

93. Richard Mitten, " 'Are We Austrians Germans?' Jörg Haider and the Dilemmas of Austrian Identity," *The Jewish Quarterly,* Summer 1996, pp. 24–28.

94. See *Handbuch des Österreichischen Rechtsextremisums: Dokumentationsarchiv des Österreichischen Widerstandes* (Vienna: Deuticke, 1993), pp. 327–428.

95. Hans-Henning Scharsach, *Haiders Kampf* (Vienna: Orac, 1992), pp. 60–78.

96. Robert S. Wistrich, "The Haider Phenomenon," in *Österreich-Konzeptionen und jüdisches Selbstverständnis,* ed. Hanni Mittelman et al. (Tübingen, Germany: Niemeyer, 2001), pp. 273–97.

97. Ibid., pp. 275–79. See also Robert S. Wistrich, "Brief aus Wien," *Europäische Rundschau* 2000, no. 2, pp. 57–62; and for a broad overview, Erhard Busek and Martin Schauer, eds., *Eine Europäische Erregung: Die "Sanktionen" der Vierzehn gegen Österreich im Jahr 2000* (Vienna: Böhlau Verlag, 2003).

98. Ian Traynor, "End of an Era Looms for Far Right Populist Haider," *The Guardian,* September 29, 2006.

99. "The Austrian Election," *The Economist,* October 7, 2006.

100. See Hans-Henning Scharsach and Kurt Kuch, *Haider: Schatten über Europa* (Cologne: Kiepenhauer and Witsch, 2000).

101. See Anat Peri, *Jörg Haider's Antisemitism* (Jerusalem: Hebrew University of Jerusalem, SICSA, ACTA no. 18, 2001).

102. John Bunzl, "Who the Hell Is Jörg Haider?" in Wodak and Pelinka, *Haider Phenomenon,* p. 63.

103. These remarks were made at the Waffen-SS annual conference in Krumpendorf (Carinthia) on September 30, 1995. See Peri, *Jörg Haider's Antisemitism,* p. 5.

104. See ADL, "Jörg Haider: The Rise of an Austrian Extreme Rightist," March 9, 2004, http://www.adl.org/backgrounders/joerg_haider.asp.

105. Peri, *Jörg Haider's Antisemitism,* p. 9. See also Ruth Wodak, "Discourse and Politics: The Rhetoric of Exclusion," in *The Haider Phenomenon in Austria,* eds. Ruth Wodak and Anton Pelinka (New Brunswick, N.J.: Transaction Publishers, 2002), pp. 35–47.

106. Scharsach and Kuch, *Haider,* pp. 72–74.

107. For the text of Haider's Ash Wednesday speech of February 28, 2001, see Anton Pelinka and Ruth Wodak, eds., *"Dreck am Stecken": Politik der Ausgrenzung* (Vienna: Czernin Verlag, 2002), pp. 228–41.

108. See the articles by Heribert and Wolfgang Neugebauer, Richard Mitten, Anton Pelinka, Ruth Wodak, et al. in Pelinka and Wodak, *"Dreck am Stecken,"* pp. 11–172.

109. Anton Pelinka, "Struktur und Funktion der 'Ashcermittwochrede' Jörg Haiders," in Pelinka and Wodak, *"Dreck am Stecken,"* pp. 61–74.

110. *Profil* (Austria). Stadler was the vice president of the Austrian-Iraqi Society.

111. Joëlle Stolz, "Les amitiés arabo-musulmanes de l'autrichién et populiste Jörg Haider," *Le Monde,* March 2, 2002.

112. *Der Standard* (Vienna), April 25, 2002.

113. See *Zur Zeit,* November 2002; and Pelinka and Wodak, *"Dreck am Stecken,"* pp. 29–31. In a TV interview on December 16, 2003, Haider had downplayed Saddam Hussein's brutality and falsely implied that Israel was a "dictatorship." See Hubert

Sickinger, "Jörg Haider," in *Kreisky-Haider: Bruchlinien Österreichischer Identitäten*, ed. Anton Pelinka et al. (Vienna: Braumüller, 2008), p. 202.

114. European Jewish Congress, "Austrian Far-Right Parties Make Gains After Attacking Israel and Austrian Jews," October 3, 2006, http://www.eurojewcong.org/ejc/print.php?id_article=572.

115. Ibid.

116. According to the Jewish Agency, the number of anti-Semitic incidents in Austria rose significantly in 2006. See *Haaretz*, January 29, 2007.

117. Matti Bunzl, "Between Anti-Semitism and Islamophobia: Some Thoughts on the New Europe," *American Ethnologist* 32, no. 4 (2005): pp. 499–508.

118. Sickinger, "Jörg Haider," pp. 215–25.

SEVEN: GERMAN GUILT, JEWISH ANGST

1. On German anti-Semitism before World War I, see Paul Lawrence Rose, *Revolutionary Antisemitism from Kant to Wagner* (Princeton, N.J.: Princeton University Press, 1990); Jacob Katz, *From Prejudice to Destruction: Anti-Semitism, 1700–1933* (Cambridge, Mass.: Harvard University Press, 1982); Robert S. Wistrich, *Socialism and the Jews: The Dilemmas of Assimilation in Germany and Austria-Hungary* (Rutherford, N.J.: Fairleigh Dickinson, 1982); Peter G. J. Pulzer, *The Rise of Political Anti-Semitism in Germany and Austria* (New York: John Wiley and Sons, 1988); and Werner Jochmann, *Gesellschaftskrise und Judenfeindschaft in Deutschland, 1870–1945* (Hamburg: Hans Christians Verlag, 1988).

2. See Shmuel Almog, *Nationalism and Antisemitism in Modern Europe 1815–1945* (Oxford, U.K.: Pergamon Press, 1990), pp. 6–16. See also the pioneering work of Eleonore Sterling, *Judenhass: Die Anfänge des politischen Antisemitismus in Deutschland (1815–1850)* (Frankfurt: Europäische Verlagsanstalt, 1969); and Stefan Rohrbacher, "The *Hep Hep* Riots of 1819: Anti-Jewish Ideology, Agitation and Violence," in *Exclusionary Violence: Anti-Semitic Riots in Modern German History,* ed. Christhard Hoffmann et al. (Ann Arbor: University of Michigan Press, 2002).

3. On the artisans, see Shulamit Volkov, *The Rise of Popular Antimodernism in Germany: The Urban Master Artisans, 1873–1896* (Princeton, N.J.: Princeton University Press, 1978).

4. The Conservative Party (DKP), which had become the most solid pillar of the Second German Reich, declared in its 1892 party program: "We combat the widely obtruding and decomposing Jewish influence on our popular life. We demand a Christian authority for the Christian people and Christian teachers for Christian people." See Pulzer, *Rise of Political Anti-Semitism*, 1st. ed. (1964), p. 119.

5. Ibid., pp. 339–40, for the Erfurt program of Böckel's party. His greatest success was in Hesse. The populist anti-Semites won sixteen seats in the Imperial Reichstag elections of 1893, but if we add the Conservatives, they already had a significant presence in German political life. See, for example, John Weiss, *The Politics of Hate* (Chicago: Ivan R. Dee, 2003), pp. 26–37: "The prestige of the Conservative Party made anti-Semitic vituperation highly respectable."

6. Goldhagen, *Hitler's Willing Executioners*, p. 68.

7. W. Jochmann, "Structure and Functions of German Anti-Semitism, 1878–1914," in *Hostages of Modernization: Studies on Modern Antisemitism, 1870–1933/39,* ed. Herbert A. Strauss (Berlin: Walter de Gruyter, 1993), pp. 52–58.

8. Wistrich, *Socialism and the Jews,* pp. 90–140. On Christian anti-Semitism, see Uriel Tal, *Christians and Jews in Germany: Religion, Politics, and Ideology in the Second Reich, 1870–1914* (Ithaca, N.Y.: Cornell University Press, 1975).

9. See Wistrich, *Laboratory for World Destruction,* pp. 175–204.

10. Jochmann, *Gesellschaftskrise und Judenfeindschaft,* pp. 101–17, for the vicious attacks on German Jewry during World War I.

11. See Wistrich, *Hitler and the Holocaust,* pp. 36–66; and Jochmann, *Gesellschaftskrise und Judenfeindschaft,* on the ubiquitous nature of anti-Semitism in Weimar Germany.

12. Wistrich, *Hitler and the Holocaust,* pp. 38–39.

13. Quoted in Goldhagen, *Hitler's Willing Executioners,* pp. 82–85.

14. See David E. Rowe and Robert Schulmann, eds., *Einstein on Politics: His Private Thoughts and Public Stands on Nationalism, Zionism, War, Peace and the Bomb* (Princeton, N.J.: Princeton University Press, 2007), pp. 148–51, 166–71.

15. Ibid., pp. 272–75, 294–96. See also Robert S. Wistrich, *Who's Who in Nazi Germany* (London: Routledge, 1995), pp. 52–53, 153–54, 242–44.

16. Emmanuel Faye, *Heidegger: L'Introduction du Nazisme dans la Philosophie* (Paris: Albin Michel, 2005), pp. 54–67, 71–143.

17. Ibid., pp. 90–96.

18. Ibid., pp. 130–39, 484–508.

19. Wistrich, *Hitler and the Holocaust,* pp. 52–78. The most comprehensive biography is by Ian Kershaw, *Hitler, 1889–1936: Hubris* (London: Allen Lane, 1998). See also Kershaw, *Hitler, 1936–45: Nemesis* (New York: W. W. Norton, 2000). Also useful are Eberhard Jäckel, *Hitler's World-View: A Blueprint for Power* (Cambridge, Mass.: Harvard University Press, 1981); as well as the earlier biographies, particularly by Allan Bullock, *Hitler: A Study in Tyranny* (Harmondsworth, U.K.: Penguin, 1974); and Robert G. L. Waite, *The Psychopathic God: Adolf Hitler* (New York: Signet Books, 1977).

20. Adolf Hitler, *Mein Kampf* (Boston: Houghton Mifflin, 1971), p. 651.

21. Ibid., p. 679.

22. Ibid., p. 65.

23. Saul Friedländer, *Nazi Germany and the Jews,* vol. 1: *The Years of Persecution 1933–1939* (New York: HarperCollins, 1997).

24. Goldhagen, *Hitler's Willing Executioners,* pp. 98–163.

25. Ibid., pp. 141–42.

26. Philippe Burrin, "Nazi Antisemitism: Animalization and Demonization," in Wistrich, *Demonizing the Other,* pp. 223–35.

27. Bradley F. Smith and Agnes F. Peterson, eds., *Heinrich Himmler: Geheimreden 1933 bis 1945* (Frankfurt, 1974), p. 58.

28. Wistrich, *Hitler's Apocalypse,* pp. 27ff. See also Klaus Vondung, *Die Apokalypse in Deutschland* (Munich: Deutscher Taschenbuch Verlag, 1988), pp. 485ff.; and Claus-Ekkehard Bärsch, *Erlösung und Vernichtung, Dr. phil, Joseph Goebbels: Zur Psyche und Ideologie eines jungen Nationalsozialisten 1923–1927* (Munich: Klaus Boer Verlag, 1987).

29. Burrin, "Nazi Antisemitism," pp. 230–33.

30. Wistrich, *Hitler and the Holocaust,* pp. 78–81.

31. Saul Friedländer, *The Years of Extermination: Nazi Germany and the Jews 1939–1945* (New York: HarperCollins, 2007), pp. 286–88.

32. Ibid., pp. 278–80.

33. See Joseph Goebbels, *Die Tagebücher von Joseph Goebbels: Sämtliche Fragmente,* ed. Elke Fröhlich (Munich: K. G. Saur, 1998), vol. 2, pt. 2, pp. 498ff., for the original German.

34. Jeffrey Herf, *The Jewish Enemy: Nazi Propaganda During World War II and the Holocaust* (Cambridge, Mass.: Harvard University Press, 2006), pp. 166–67.

35. Friedländer, *Years of Extermination,* pp. 659–60.

36. Ibid., p. 660.

37. Elizabeth Noelle and Erich Peter Neumann, eds., *The German Public Opinion Polls 1947–1966* (Westport, Conn.: Greenwood Press, 1981), pp. 185–92, 202, 206, 219, 311–16.

38. Angelika Timm, "Ideology and Realpolitik: East German Attitudes Towards Zionism and Israel," *Journal of Israeli History* 25, no. 1 (2006): pp. 203–22. See also Timm, *Hammer, Zirkel, Davidstern: Das gestörte Verhältnis der DDR zu Zionismus und Staat Israel* (Bonn, Germany: Bouvier, 1997).

39. See "Neues Deutschland and Israel: A Diary of East German Reactions," in Wistrich, ed., *Left Against Zion,* pp. 114–36.

40. See the illuminating master's thesis of Ulrike Becker, "Klima-wechsel: Der Diskurs über Israel in Deutschland am Beispiel des Sechstagekrieges 1967 und der Zweiten Intifada 2000/2002 (Hamburg, Germany: University of Hamburg, 2004), pp. 73–159.

41. *Bild-Zeitung,* May 24, 1967; "Jagt die Fanatiker zum Teufel!" ibid., June 8, 1967.

42. Becker, "Klima-wechsel," p. 86.

43. For some aspects of postwar West German admiration for Israel (and the dissonances), see Gilad Margalit, "Israel Through the Eyes of the West German Press 1947–1967," *Jahrbuch für Antisemitismusforschung* 11 (2002): pp. 235–48.

44. Sabine Hepperle, *Die SPD und Israel: Von der Grossen Koalition 1966 bis zur Wende 1982* (Frankfurt: P. Lang, 2000). See also Shlomo Shafir, "Helmut Schmidt: Seine Beziehungen zu Israel und die Juden," *Jahrbuch für Antisemitismusforschung* 17 (2008), pp. 297–320, for the increasingly critical Social Democratic attitudes toward Israel during the 1970s and early 1980s under SPD chancellor Helmut Schmidt.

45. Hans-Herbert Goebel, "Russisches Roulette," *Frankfurter Rundschau (FR),* June 3, 1967.

46. Becker, "Klima-wechsel," pp. 112–26.

47. "Besetzte Gebiete: Viel sanfter," *Der Spiegel,* June 26, 1967.

48. Rolf Behrens, *"Raketen gegen Steinwerfer": Das Bild Israels im "Spiegel"; eine Inhaltsanalyse der Berichterstattung über Intifada 1987–1992 und "Al-Aqsa-Intifada,"* 2000–2002 (Münster, Germany: Lit, 2003).

49. Becker, "Klima-wechsel," pp. 141–54; and Robert S. Wistrich, *Der antisemitische Wahn: Von Hitler bis zum Heiligen Krieg gegen Israel* (Munich: Max Hueber Verlag, 1987).

50. Wolfgang Günter Lerch, "Gescheitert," *Frankfurter Allgemeiner Zeitung (FAZ),* April 18, 2002.

51. For one of many such articles, see Avi Mograbi, "Siedlungen sind Kriegsverbrechen," *Die Tageszeitung* (*TAZ*), April 2, 2002.

52. Herbert Pranti, "Und wieder sind die Juden schuld," *Süddeutsche Zeitung* (*SZ*), April 15, 2002. See also Wolfgang Marx, "Eine Frage der Wahrheit: Zu den Antisemitismus-Vorwürfen gegen die deutschen Presse," *FAZ*, July 19, 2002.

53. Wolfgang Günter Lerch, "Wo verläuft die Grenze zum Terrorismus," *FAZ*, May 7, 2002; and Rudolf Augstein, "Wie man Terroristen fördert," *Der Spiegel*, November 5, 2001.

54. "Gott has es gewollt," *Der Spiegel*, April 8, 2002.

55. "Gott will es," *Der Spiegel*, October 8, 2001.

56. See Günther Jacob, "Israel ist unser Unglück," *Konkret*, August 2002, pp. 22–25; Lars Rensmann, "Der Nahost Konflikt in der Perzeption des Rechts-und-Linksextremismus," in Faber et al., *Neu-alter Judenhass*, pp. 33–48; and Sacha Stawski, "Das Bild Israels in den Köpfen der Menschen," in ibid., pp. 111–25.

57. See Robert S. Wistrich, "The Fassbinder Controversy," *Jerusalem Quarterly*, no. 50 (Spring 1989): pp. 122–30; and Wistrich, *Between Redemption and Perdition*, pp. 121–32.

58. Wistrich, "Fassbinder Controversy," p. 124.

59. See Heiner Lichtenstein, ed., *Die Fassbinder-Kontroverse oder Das Ende der Schonzeit* (Konigstein, Ts. 1986).

60. Heinrich Broder, "Open Letter: You Are No Less Antisemites Than Your Nazi Parents," *Forum* 42–43 (Winter 1981): pp. 109–17. (The letter originally appeared in the prominent Hamburg weekly *Die Zeit*.) See also Henryk M. Broder, *Der Ewige Antisemit* (Frankfurt: Fischer Verlag, 1987).

61. Broder, "Open Letter," pp. 113–15.

62. Ibid.

63. Quoted by Micha Brumlik, "Fear of the Father Figure: Judeophobic Tendencies in the New Social Movements in West Germany," *Patterns of Prejudice* 21, no. 4 (1987): pp. 20–36.

64. Ibid., p. 34.

65. See Saul Friedländer, "West Germany and the Burden of the Past: The Ongoing Debate," *Jerusalem Quarterly*, no. 42 (Spring 1987): pp. 3–18.

66. Ernst Nolte, "Vergangenheit die nicht vergehen will," *FAZ*, June 6, 1986.

67. Hans Jürgen Syberberg, *Vom Unglück und Glück der Kunst in Deutschland nach dem Letzten Kriege* (Munich: Mathes and Seitz, 1990), pp. 14–15, 79, 190ff.

68. Robert S. Wistrich, "Xenophobia and Antisemitism in the New Europe: The Case of Germany," in Wistrich, *Demonizing the Other*, pp. 349–63.

69. "Neo-Nazis march in Dresden," *IHT*, February 14, 2005.

70. Wistrich, "Xenophobia and Antisemitism," pp. 350–54.

71. Sacha Stawski, "Das Bild Israels in den Köpfen der Menschen," Faber et al., *Neu-alter Judenhass*, pp. 111–25; Robert S. Wistrich, *The Politics of Ressentiment: Israel, Jews and the German Media* (Jerusalem: Hebrew University of Jerusalem, SICSA, ACTA no. 23, 2004); Thorsten Schmitz, "Scharon kündigt, totalen Krieg gegen Terror an," *SZ*, April 2, 2002; and "Gott will es," *Der Spiegel*, October 8, 2001, pp. 163–64.

72. Karl Lamers, interview, "Israel diskreditiert den Westen," *FAZ*, February 3, 2002.

73. *FR*, April 4, 2002.

74. "Der Vorwurf des Antisemitismus wird als Knüppel benutzt," *Stern*, June 20, 2002.

75. See the report by Heiko Flottau, "Sperrgebiet," *SZ*, April 3, 2002; Susanne Knaul, "Raketen treffen Flüchtingslager," *TAZ*, April 9, 2002; and Inge Günther, "Leben mit und über Toten," *FR*, April 18, 2002.

76. *FAZ*, April 18, 2002; "Wo verhäuft die Grenze zum Terrorismus," ibid., May 7, 2002; and Manfred Wüst, "Kann man mit Panzern den Terrorismus zerstören?" *SZ*, April 18, 2002.

77. See "Pressemitteilung" of the *Kreuzberger Initiative gegen Antisemitismus* (Berlin, April 19, 2006) signed by Aycarin Demirel and Elif Kayi. Materials from *Vakit* in German translation were attached.

78. See the brochure *Pädagogische Arbeit und Praxis—Konzepte gegen Antisemitismus in Kreuzberg* (Berlin, 2005).

79. Günther Jikeli, "The Kreuzberg Initiative Against Antisemitism Among Youth from Muslim and Non-Muslim Backgrounds in Berlin," in *Antisemitism: The Generic Hatred*, ed. Michael Fineberg et al. (London: Vallentine Mitchell, 2007), pp. 198–211.

80. *Pädagogische Arbeit.*

81. See Wilhelm Heitmeyer, ed., *Deutsche Zustände* (Frankfurt: Suhrkamp Verlag, 2005), vol. 3: p. 151.

82. *Deutsche Welle*, November 4, 2003. Only in the Netherlands and Austria was the percentage higher.

83. On this and related subjects, see Clemens Heni, *Antisemitismus und Deutschland* (Lulu-Verlag, 2009).

84. Salomon Korn, "Ende der Schonzeit: Es gibt keinen neuen Antisemitismus—der vorhandene wird entlarvt" [End of the No-Hunting Season: There Is No New Anti-Semitism; the Existing One Is Now Exposed], *FAZ*, May 6, 2002. See also Richard Chaim Schneider, "Wieder einmal allein: Europas Juden und der Antisemitismus," *SZ*, April 5, 2002.

85. An illuminating discussion is provided by Alvin Rosenfeld, *Feeling Alone, Again: The Growing* Unease *Among Germany's Jews* (New York: AJC, 2002).

86. On the first Walser affair and the debate with Ignaz Bubis in 1998, see Leon de Winter, "Schuld und Schande, Kein normales Volk," *Der Spiegel*, December 1998, pp. 300–302; Roger Cohen, "Germany Searches for Normality," *The New York Times*, November 29, 1998; Lea Rosh, "Walser ist ein Brandstifter," *FR*, December 13, 1998; and Sigfrid Löffler, "Im Schatten der Versöhnung," *Die Zeit*, December 16, 1998.

87. Bill Niven, *Facing the Nazi Past: United Germany and the Legacy of the Third Reich* (New York: Routledge, 2002), pp. 175–93.

88. "The Berlin Republic," *The Economist*, February 6, 1999, pp. 15–16. See also Ze'ev Wolff, "Antisemitism in Germany Alive and Kicking," *Searchlight*, September 1999, p. 17; and Martin Becker, "Germany: Coming to Terms with Past and Future," ibid., pp. 20–21.

89. For Walser's reaction at the time, see Lars Rensmann and Hajo Funke, "Aus dem deutschen Seelenleben," *Jüdische Allgemeine Zeitung*, December 24, 1998.

90. Thomas Steinfeld, "Hygiene," *SZ*, May 8, 2002.

91. Robert S. Wistrich, *Politics of Ressentiment*, pp. 9–11.

92. On the Walser speech, see Lars Rensmann's article in *Umkämpftes Vergessen: Walser-Debatte, Holocaust-Mahnmal und neuere deutsche Geschichtspolitik*, ed. Micha Brumlik et al. (Berlin: Schiler, 2000), pp. 28–126; and Frank Schirrmacher, ed., *Die Walser-Bubis-Debatte: Eine Dokumentation* (Frankfurt: Suhrkampf, 1999).

93. "Forsa Survey," *Die Woche*, December 24, 1998. A more recent survey showed 70 percent of Germans resent Holocaust "guilt." See *Haaretz*, December 12, 2003.

94. See Marcel Reich-Ranicki, "Eine Erklärung: Walsers Buch hat mich tief getroffen," *FAZ*, June 6, 2002.

95. Franz Schirrmacher in an "Open Letter to Walser" published in *FAZ*, May 29, 2002, called his novel "a document of hate," intolerable for its toying with the fiction "of finishing off what the Nazis did not accomplish." See, in addition, Jan Philipp Reemtsa, "Ein antisemitischer Affektsturm," *FAZ*, June 27, 2002; Walser's interview in *Der Spiegel*, pp. 186–90; and Ruth Kluger's letter ("Siehe doch Deutschland") to *FR*, June 27, 2002.

96. Uwe Wittstock, *Die Welt*, June 4, 2002; Elke Schmitter, "Skandale sind hilfreich," *Der Spiegel*; and Schmitter, "Der verfolgte Verfolger," *Der Spiegel*.

97. See "Das Spiel mit dem Feuer," *Der Spiegel*, pp. 22–38; for an overview of Möllemann's career, see Matthias Geis, "Eine Überdosis Politik: Der Fall Möllemann," *Die Zeit*, June 12, 2003.

98. See Josef Joffe, "FDP und ihr Verführer: Antisemitismus als Wahlköder? Möllemann darf nicht voran," *Die Zeit*, May 23, 2002. For the original statement, "Ich würde mich auch wehren," *TAZ*, April 4, 2002.

99. Quoted by Rosenfeld, *Feeling Alone, Again*, p. 8. See also Henryk M. Broder, "Ein moderner Antisemit," *Der Spiegel*, May 27, 2002. Broder emphasized the trendy character of Möllemann's "cool, up-to-date" anti-Semitism. See also Broder, "Ende der Schonzeit: Die Sehnsucht der Deutschen nach 'Normalitat,' " *Der Spiegel*, June 3, 2002, pp. 26–29.

100. Thomas Tuma, "Der deutsche Michel," *Der Spiegel*, May 6, 2002. Tilman Gerwien, "Warum zerstören Sie sich selbst," *Stern*, June 15, 2003.

101. See Felix Schmidt's hostile interview with Friedman in *FR*, February 16, 2000. See also Esther Schapira, "Hakennasen statt Hakenkreuze," *TAZ*, September 26, 2003.

102. See Christian Schlüter, "JWM geht: Der Antisemitismus bleibt," *FR*, October 22, 2002. Möllemann's main objective was to show that "die Juden sind selbst schuld an ihren Unglück" (The Jews are themselves responsible for their misfortune).

103. See "Der Krampf geht weiter," *Der Spiegel*, pp. 22–26. Some Turkish Muslims publicly distanced themselves from Karsli and Möllemann's anti-Semitic allusions. See *FAZ*, May 17, 2002; "Empörung über Aufnahme Karslis in die FDP, 'Operation Einsamer Möllemann,' " *FAZ*, May 23, 2002; "Das Vertrauen ist wieder hergestellt," *FAZ*, June 7, 2002; and "Karsli geht: Westerwelle zufrieden," *FAZ*, June 7, 2002.

104. See *FAZ*, May 17, 2002, for extracts from Karsli's interview. In Karsli's letter of resignation, addressed to Möllemann, he presents himself as a victim of German taboos and "political correctness," *FAZ*, May 23, 2003.

105. "Terror-Äusserungen: Westerwelle nimmt Möllemann in Schutz," *Die Welt*, April 6, 2002. During Westerwelle's visit to Israel, he declared himself impressed by Arafat. His Israeli hosts were highly critical of his "tolerance" of anti-Semitism in FDP ranks. See *FAZ*, May 29, 2002.

106. Rolf Jurmann, "Möllemann's wars," *Jungle World*, October 9, 2002. See also Fritz Goergen, "Das Projekt 18," *FAZ*, November 12, 2002; and "Projekt Grössenwahn," *Der Spiegel*, pp. 22–38.

107. *FAZ*, May 25, 2002.

108. Joschka Fischer, "Deutschland, deine Juden" [Germany, These Are Your Jews], *FAZ*, May 11, 2002. See also Fischer, "Israel darf keine Schwäche zeigen," *Die Zeit*, April 25, 2002, for a reasonably balanced view of Israel's predicament.

109. See Paul Berman, "The Passion of Joschka Fischer," *The New Republic*, August 27, 2001, and September 3, 2001, pp. 36–59, for a sense of how far Fischer had evolved since his pro-Palestinian utopian radicalism of the late 1960s. After the Entebbe affair, he became more sensitized to the anti-Jewish dimension in Palestinian terrorism and in German New Left attitudes toward Zionism.

110. "Erschreckende Umfrage-Ergebnisse zu Finkelstein's Thesen," *Der Spiegel*, February 10, 2001.

111. Norman G. Finkelstein, *The Holocaust Industry: Reflections on the Exploitation of Jewish Suffering* (London: Verso, 2000). See also Rolf Surmann, ed., *Das Finkelstein Alibi: "Holocaust-Industrie" und Tätergesellschaft* (Cologne: Papy Rossa Verlag, 2001), pp. 126–53, for the article by Lars Rensmann; and Bartosz Jalowiecki, "Lies the Germans Tell Themselves," *Commentary*, January 2004, pp. 43–46.

112. According to the earlier AJC-commissioned survey by Infratest in November 2002, 52 percent of Germans thought that Jews "exploit the memory of the Holocaust for their own benefit." The Bielefeld study was released in Berlin on December 11, 2003, just as the German Bundestag began a two-hour debate on anti-Semitism. *The Jewish Chronicle*, December 26, 2003.

113. The joint survey was conducted by Professor Elmar Brühler (University of Leipzig) and Professor Oskar Niedermayer (Freie Universität Berlin), under the heading *Rechtsextreme Einstellungen in Deutschland* (September 2002) and communicated at a press conference in Berlin. Twenty-eight percent of all Germans felt Jews had "too much influence"; 23 percent of Germans (more in West Germany) regarded Jews as "tricky"; 20 percent of Germans thought Jews were different. About one in five Germans could be defined as anti-Semitic.

114. Freimut Duve, "Die Saat der Gewalt: Israelis wie Palästinenser haben den gefährlichen Traum vom homogenen Staat nicht aufgegeben," *Die Zeit*, December 7, 2000. See the reply by Dieter Wald, "Ohne Hitler kein Israel?" *Die Zeit*, January 17, 2001.

115. Franziska Augstein, "Sharons 4000 Jahre: Israel ist wie Deutschland—und den USA zu kompliziert," *SZ*, April 13, 2002.

116. See Wolf Biermann's "Salzig, Salzig, Salzig" in *Der Spiegel*, pp. 170–78, an often perceptive and bitterly sarcastic piece about the German proclivity to self-justification in linking Israel to the Holocaust.

117. See Christoph Reuter, "Sie Morden aus Verzweiflung," *Stern Magazine*, July 3, 2002, and Wolfgang Günter Lerch, "Umschlag der Stimmung," *FAZ*, April 16, 2002.

118. Ansprache von MdB Martin Hohmann zum Nationalfeiertag, October 3, 2003.

119. Joseph Joffe, "Trotzki und Tätervolk," *Die Zeit*, November 13, 2003.

120. See *The Jewish Chronicle*, November 7, 2003. Also "CDU vor Hohmann-Abstimmung, Proteste, Austritte und Gewaltandrohung," *Der Spiegel*, November 13, 2003.

121. "Germany sacks general in anti-Semitism incident," *The Jerusalem Post,* November 5, 2003; see also ibid., November 9, 2003, for Guenzel's denial that he was anti-Semitic. There have been numerous anti-Semitic incidents at lower levels in the Bundeswehr in recent years.

122. See Wolfgang Benz, "Lupenreines Exempel: Hohmanns judenfeindlicher Diskurs," *SZ,* November 11, 2003. Since then, Benz's equation of anti-Semitism and "Islamophobia" has come under some heavy criticism. See Matthias Küntzel, " 'Islamophobia' or 'Truthophobia,' " *Wall Street Journal Europe,* July 12, 2008.

123. See Richard Herzinger, "Lehrstück Hohmann: Der Antisemitismus frisst sich in die politische Mitte," *Die Zeit,* November 12, 2003. See also Herzinger, "Ohne Courage," ibid., November 13, 2003.

124. Rosenfeld, *Feeling Alone, Again,* p. 5. See also "Antizionismus und Antisemitismus," *Tribüne* 40, no. 157 (2001): pp. 116–21, for an interview with Paul Spiegel.

125. Amiram Barkat, "More Germans Are Anti-Semitic Than Meets the Eye," *Haaretz,* April 19, 2004.

126. Benjamin Weinthal, "Poll: Israel Is 'Aggressive,' " *The Jerusalem Post,* January 16, 2009.

127. Benjamin Weinthal, "Neo-Nazis Plan Gaza 'Holocaust' Vigil in Berlin," *The Jerusalem Post,* January 22, 2009.

128. Etgar Lefkovits, "German FM Blasts New Anti-Semitism Clothed in Anti-Israel Sentiments," *The Jerusalem Post,* March 12, 2008.

129. Eetta Prince-Gibson, interview with former Israeli ambassador to Germany Shimon Stein, *The Jerusalem Report,* April 14, 2008, p. 32. See also the critical editorial "German 'clarity,' " *The Jerusalem Post,* March 13, 2008.

130. Jean Améry, "Der ehrbare Antisemitismus," *Die Zeit,* July 25, 1969.

131. Andrei S. Markovits, "A New (or Perhaps Revived) 'Uninhibitedness' Toward Jews in Germany," *Jewish Political Studies Review* 18, nos. 1–2 (Spring 2006): pp. 57–67.

132. Anne Appelbaum, "Germans as Victims," *IHT,* October 15, 2003; Susanne Urban, "Antisemitism in Germany Today: Its Roots and Tendencies," *Jewish Political Studies Review* 16, nos. 3–4 (Fall 2004): pp. 119–30, for the quote from a TV interview with Jörg Friedrich in winter 2002. See also Algis Valiunas, "Fire from the Sky," *Commentary,* July–August 2007, pp. 52–56.

133. See Andrei S. Markovits, *Uncouth Nation: Why Europe Dislikes America* (Princeton, N.J.: Princeton University Press, 2007).

134. See Christian Hiller von Gaertringen, "Heikle Geschäfte mit Iran," *FAZ,* January 24, 2006; and Jeffrey Herf, "Where Are the Anti-Fascists? The Danger of Germany's Strange Silence on Ahmadinejad," *The New Republic,* December 4, 2007.

135. Susanne Urban, "The Old-New Antisemitism in Contemporary Germany" (Jerusalem: Institute of the World Jewish Congress, policy study no. 28, 2005).

Eight: Frenchmen, Arabs, and Jews

1. Robert Badinter, *Libres et Égaux . . . L'Émancipation des Juifs (1789–1791)* (Paris: Fayard, 1989).

2. Michael R. Marrus, *Les Juifs de France à l'époque de l'Affaire Dreyfus* (Paris: Calmann-Lévy, 1972), pp. 105–13.

3. A. Leroy Beaulieu's *Israel Among the Nations* (London, 1895), p. 344. See also Wistrich, introduction to Lazare, *Antisemitism*.

4. Jean-Denis Bredin, *Bernard Lazare: De l'Anarchiste au Prophète* (Paris: Éditions de Fallois, 1992).

5. Pierre Vidal-Naquet, *Les Juifs: la mémoire et le present. II* (Paris: Éditions la Découverte, 1991).

6. Michel Winock, *La France et les Juifs: De 1789 à nos jours* (Paris: Éditions du Seuil, 2004), pp. 83–159.

7. Pierre Birnbaum, *Jewish Destinies: Citizenship, State, and Community in Modern France* (New York: Hill and Wang, 2000), pp. 69–70, 94–97.

8. Ibid., pp. 101–15. See also Frederick Busi, *The Pope of Antisemitism: The Career and Legacy of Édouard-Adolphe Drumont* (Lanham, Md.: University Press of America, 1986).

9. See Victor Nguyen, *Aux origines de l'Action Française* (Paris: Fayard, 1991). See also the earlier works by Ernst Nolte, *Three Faces of Fascism: Action française, Italian fascism, National Socialism* (New York: Holt, Rinehart and Winston, 1966); and Zeev Sternhell, *Neither Right Nor Left: Fascist Ideology in France* (Berkeley and Los Angeles: University of California Press, 1986).

10. Quoted in Sternhell, *Neither Right Nor Left*, p. 45.

11. Ibid., p. 46.

12. Wistrich, *Anti-Semitism: The Longest Hatred*, pp. 130–33. See also Pierre Birnbaum, *Un Mythe politique: La "République juive" de Léon Blum à Pierre Mendès France* (Paris: Fayard, 1988) and Laurent Joly, *La France Antijuive de 1936* (Paris: Éditions des Équateurs, 2006).

13. See Simon Epstein, *Les Dreyfusards sous l'Occupation* (Paris: Albin Michel, 2001), pp. 291–341.

14. Michael R. Marrus and Robert O. Paxton, *Vichy France and the Jews* (New York: Basic Books, 1981); and Robert S. Wistrich, *Hitler, l'Europe et la Shoah* (Paris: Albin Michel, 2005), pp. 222–32.

15. Sartre, *Anti-Semite and Jew*, p. 71. See also Jonathan Judaken, *Jean-Paul Sartre and the Jewish Question* (Lincoln: University of Nebraska Press, 2006), pp. 126, 142, 262–63.

16. Birnbaum, *Un Mythe politique*, pp. 368–92.

17. See Judaken *Jean-Paul Sartre*, p. 220.

18. Howard M. Sachar, *A History of Israel* (New York: Alfred A. Knopf, 1996), pp. 472–513. For an example of French admiration for Israel in this period, see Jacques Soustelle, *La longue marche d'Israël* (Paris: Fayard, 1968). Soustelle had been a leading activist for French Algeria.

19. For the earlier period, see Tsilla Hershco, *Entre Paris et Jérusalem: La France, le Sionisme et la création de l'État d'Israël, 1945–1949* (Paris: Honoré Champion, 2003). Also Léon Azoulay, "La France et le Sionisme," *France-Israël Information*, October–December 2004, pp. 13–18.

20. Charles de Gaulle, *Discours et Messages*, vol. 5, *Vers le terme 1966–1969* (Paris: Plon, 1970), pp. 232–35. See also Raymond Aron, *Essais sur la condition juive contemporaine* (Paris: Éditions Tallandier, 2007), pp. 45–49, which reproduces the full text.

21. Aron, *Essais*, p. 40.

22. Franklin Rausky, "Peuple d'élite sûr de lui-même et dominateur," *Actualité Juive,*

January 2007, p. 5. See also Raphaël Draï, *Sous le signe de Sion—L'antisémitisme nouveau est arrivé* (Paris: Éditions Michalon, 2002), pp. 103–27.

23. Robert S. Wistrich, introduction to *The Myth of the Jew in France 1967–1982,* by Henry H. Weinberg (Oakville, N.Y.: Mosaic Press, 1987), pp. 31–44.

24. Ibid., pp. 32–35.

25. See Aron, *Essais sur la condition juive,* pp. 55–137. Aron's original text was entitled *De Gaulle: Israël et les Juifs* (Paris: Plon, 1968).

26. Philippe de Saint-Robert, "Terrorisme ou résistance?" *Le Monde,* February 7, 1969.

27. Quoted in Weinberg, *Myth of the Jew,* p. 37.

28. David Pryce-Jones, *Betrayal: France, the Arabs and the Jews* (New York: Encounter Books, 2006), pp. 92–99.

29. D. Pryce-Jones, "Jews, Arabs, and French Diplomacy: A Special Report," *Commentary,* May 2005, pp. 27–46.

30. Paul Balta and Claude Rulleau, *La politique arabe de la France: de De Gaulle à Pompidou* (Paris: Sindbad, 1973). See also Ye'or, *Eurabia,* for examples of how French diplomacy acted within the EU to construct an "Eurabian" axis.

31. Balta and Rulleau, *La politique arabe,* pp. 60–65, 150ff.; and Weinberg, *Myth of the Jew,* pp. 49–52, 134–35.

32. C. Clément, *Israël et la République* (Paris: Olivier Orban, 1978), p. 199.

33. Shmuel Trigano, *La République et les Juifs* (Paris: Les Presses d'Aujourd'hui, 1982), p. 18.

34. Trigano, *La République et les Juifs,* p. 24, pointed not only to the sense of abandonment felt by Jews after Copernic but also to the ways in which, since 1789, "the positive aspect of Jewish existence [has been] denied in France."

35. Emeric Deutsch, "Les Français sont-ils antisémites?" *L'Arche,* September–October 1979, p. 66.

36. "Sur France Culture, Raymond Barre défend Papon, Gollnisch, et fustige 'Le lobby juif,' " *Le Monde,* March 3, 2007; Claude Lanzmann, "J'accuse Raymond Barre d'être un antisémite," *Libération,* March 6, 2007; "Barre s'absout de tout antisémitisme," *Libération,* March 6, 2007; Pierre Weill, "Raymond Barre ou l'antisémitisme de droite," *Le Monde,* March 10, 2007; "Le naufrage de Barre," *Marianne,* March 10–16, 2007.

37. Yves Azeroual and Yves Derai, *Mitterrand, Israël et les Juifs* (Paris: Robert Laffont, 1990), pp. 196–229; and Dennis Sieffert, *Israël-Palestine: Une passon française* (Paris: Éditions la Découverte, 2004), pp. 165–75.

38. Alain Finkielkraut, *La Réprobation d'Israël* (Paris: Denoël, 1983), pp. 119–55.

39. *La Libre Parole,* December 24, 1903.

40. See Pierre Birnbaum, "The French Radical Right: From Anti-Semitic Zionism to Anti-Semitic Anti-Zionism," *Journal of Israeli History* 25, no. 1 (March 2006): pp. 161–74. The Vallet article appeared in *Aspects de la France,* June 15, 1967, shortly after the Six-Day War. Lucien Rebatet's pro-Zionist declaration came in the Far Right *Rivarol,* June 8, 1967.

41. Charles Saint-Prot, *La France et le renouveau arabe* (Paris: Copernic, 1980); and his hymn of praise to *Saddam Hussein: Un nouveau de Gaulle* (Paris: Albin Michel, 1987).

42. Special issue, *National Hebdo,* February 1992; Birnbaum, "French Radical Right," p. 169.

43. Birnbaum, "French Radical Right," p. 169.

44. *Libération,* May 2, 1996.

45. Edwy Plenel and Alain Rollat, "The Revival of the Far Right in France," *Patterns of Prejudice* 18, no. 2 (1984): pp. 21–26. See also Peter Davies, *The National Front in France: Ideology, Discourse, and Power* (London: Routledge, 1999), pp. 134–65.

46. See Bernard-Henri Lévy, *L'Idéologie Française* (Paris: Bernard Grasset, 1981).

47. Richard Liscia, "L'obsession antisémite," *L'Arche,* January 1989, pp. 75–76; R. W. Johnson, "France Wakes Up to the Demon of Anti-Semitism," *The Independent on Sunday,* May 20, 1990; interview with Pierre-André Taguieff, "Les doctrinaires de l'ordre nouveau," *Le Nouvel Observateur,* November 28–December 4, 1991; Nelly Hansson, "France: The Carpentras Syndrome and Beyond," *Patterns of Prejudice* 25, no. 1 (1991): pp. 32–45.

48. Paul Yonnet, "La machine Carpentras: Histoire et sociologie d'un syndrome d'épuration," *Le Débat,* September–October 1990.

49. Hansson, "France," p. 36. See also "L'antisémitisme en France: Après le 'detail,' le taboo brisé," *L'Événement du Jeudi,* October 15–21, 1987.

50. *Le Quotidien,* February 9, 1990.

51. David Selbourne, "French Jews Begin to Feel Like Aliens," *The Sunday Times* (London), June 30, 1990.

52. Jean-Yves Camus and René Monzat, *Les Droites Nationales et Radicales en France* (Lyon: Presses Universitaires de Lyon, 1992), pp. 104–5.

53. Janes G. Shields, "The Front National and the Politics of Discrimination in France," *Analysis,* 2 (IJA research report, 1992). See also Pascal Perrineau, "Le Front national 1972–1992," in *Histoire de l'extrême droite en France,* ed. Michael Winock (Paris: Seuil, 1993), pp. 243–98.

54. *Le Monde,* October 11, 2000, and June 13, 2002.

55. See Henry H. Weinberg, "French Jewry Under the Mitterrand Presidency," *Contemporary French Civilization* 13, nos. 1–2 (Fall–Winter 1983–84): pp. 228–42; Weinberg, "French Jewry: Trauma and Renewal," *Midstream,* December 1982, pp. 7–12; and Weinberg, "*Le Monde* and Israel," *Middle East Focus* 3, no. 6 (March 1981). See also Michel Legris, *Le Monde tel qu'il est* (Paris: Plon, 1976), pp. 145–48.

56. J.-M. Paupert, "Lettre à mes amis juifs," *Le Monde,* January 4–5, 1981. Simone de Beauvoir in *Le Nouvel Observateur,* January 12, 1981, compared Paupert to Drumont; Todd remarked in *L'Express,* January 24, 1981, that the text "oozes with anti-Semitism."

57. Bernard-Henri Lévy in *Le Monde,* September 9, 1982, declared that "we are witnessing a return of left-wing antisemitism."

58. Blandine Barret-Kriegel, "Dérapage de la gauche," *Les Nouveaux Cahiers,* no. 71 (Winter 1982–83): pp. 10–13; and Finkielkraut, *La Réprobation d'Israël,* p. 132.

59. Finkielkraut, *La Réprobation,* p. 121. On June 29, 1982, *Le Monde's* editorial denounced Menachem Begin's "infernal logic" and the "odious," even insane, consequences of his Lebanon policy.

60. *Le Monde,* March 19, 1983. The Catholic and Protestant church authorities failed to comment on this anti-Semitic outburst; some of *La Croix's* articles openly smacked of anti-Semitism, and *Témoignage Chrétien* June 12, 1982, compared the ruins of Beirut with the destruction of the Warsaw ghetto.

61. Weinberg, "French Jewry Under the Mitterrand Presidency," p. 237.

62. Shmuel Trigano, *La démission de la République: Juifs et Musulmans en France* (Paris: Presses Universitaires de France, 2003), pp. 19–26.

63. See Dominique Schnapper, "Perceptions of Anti-Semitism in France," in *Antisemitism in the Contemporary World*, ed. Michael Curtis (Boulder, Colo.: Westview Press, 1986), pp. 261–72.

64. Jean-Pierre Allali, *Les habits neufs de l'antisémitisme: Anatomie d'une angoisse* (Paris: Desclée de Brouwer, 2002), pp. 153–62; Birnbaum, *Jewish Destinies*, pp. 229–51; Trigano, *La démission*, pp. 109–28, and *Les Enfants de la République* (Paris: Éditions de la Martinière, 2004).

65. See Shmuel Trigano, "Communauté juive et communautarisme," *Observatoire du monde juif*, nos. 10–11 (May 2004): pp. 1–7. See also Jean Robin, *La Judéomanie* (Paris: Tatamis, 2006), written by a young, partly Jewish author, blaming anti-Semitism on a mixture of French "Judeomania" (exaggerated admiration for Jews), Jewish communitarianism, and the narcissistic attitudes of certain French Jewish intellectuals.

66. Interview with Alain Finkielkraut in Trigano, *Les Enfants de la République*, pp. 19–53. See also Finkielkraut, "Le sionisme face à la religion de l'humanité," in *Le Sionisme face à ses Détracteurs*, ed. Shmuel Trigano (Paris: Éditions Raphaël, 2003), pp. 160–70.

67. See *L'Arche*, October–November 2001, pp. 14–15; and Pascal Boniface, *Est-il permis de critiquer Israël?* (Paris: Robert Laffont, 2003), pp. 67–110, 179–92, for his views on Jewish exaggeration of anti-Semitism in France and the dangers of "*communautarisation.*" In the appendix, pp. 233–38, is Boniface's note to the secretary-general of the Socialist Party, entitled "Le Proche-Orient, les socialistes, l'équité internationale, l'efficacité electorale."

68. Among these works of very uneven quality, see Guy Konopnicki, *La Faute aux Juifs* (Paris: Balland, 2002); Raphaël Drai, *Sous le signe de Sion* (Paris: Michalon, 2002); and Gilles William Goldnadel, *Le Nouveau Bréviaire de la Haine* (Paris: Éditions Ramsay, 2001). See also the interesting study by Nicolas Weill, *Une histoire personnelle de l'antisémitisme* (Paris: Robert Laffont, 2003). The most influential and serious of these books was by a non-Jew, Pierre-André Taguieff, *La nouvelle judéophobie* (Paris: Mille et Une Nuits, 2002). See also Taguieff's most recent work, *La judéophobie des Modernes. Des Lumières au Jihad Mondial* (Paris: Odile Jacob, 2008), which came to my attention just after I completed the manuscript of this book.

69. Jean-Christophe Attias and Esther Benbassa, "Nous ne sommes pas des victimes," *Le Monde*, December 18, 2001. See also Attias and Benbassa, "La loi de la République est la loi," *Libération*, January 11, 2002.

70. Richard L. Derderian, *North Africans in Contemporary France: Becoming Visible* (New York: Palgrave Macmillan, 2004); and Benjamin Stora, *Le transfert d'une mémoire: de "L'Algérie française" au racisme anti-arabe* (Paris: La Découverte, 1999).

71. "*Le Monde* Described as 'Zionist Newspaper,'" *The Jewish Chronicle*, January 23, 2004, p. 11.

72. See Michel Wieviorka, *La tentation antisémite: Haine des Juifs dans la France d'aujourd'hui* (Paris: Robert Laffont, 2005), pp. 274, 311–19.

73. See François Dufay and Emmanuel Berretta, "Juifs de France, le chagrin et la colère," *Le Point*, October 20, 2000. See also the website of the Paris rabbinate,

http://www.consistoire.org/; and Cécilia Gabizon, "Les actes antisémites diminu-ent mais la malaise persiste," *Le Figaro*, January 31, 2004.

74. Union des étudiants juifs de France and SOS Racisme, *Les Antifeujs: Le Libre blanc des violences antisémites en France depuis Septembre 2000* (Paris: Calmann-Lévy, 2000). See the introduction, pp. 11–29, and the essay by Eric Marty, "Que s'est-il passé en France . . . ?" pp. 111–35, as well as the detailed list of anti-Semitic inci-dents from September 2000 to January 31, 2002.

75. See Marie-France Etchegoin and Claude Askolovtich, "Juifs et Arabes en France," *Le Nouvel Obsevateur* (*NO*), January 24–30, 2002, pp. 9–16; and the dossier, "Les juifs premières victimes des violences racistes," in ibid., p. 10.

76. Jean-Christophe Rufin, *Rapport sur la lutte contre le racisme et l'antisémitisme* (Paris: Ministry of the Interior, October 19, 2004).

77. See Emmanuel Brenner, ed., *Les territoires perdus de la République* (Paris: Mille et Une Nuits, 2002), pp. 9–77.

78. See Bensoussan, *Antisemitism in French Schools*, pp. 2, 10–11.

79. Ibid., pp. 19–20. See also Brenner, *Les territoires*, pp. 32–33; and also *Le Monde*, April 10, 2002.

80. Bensoussan, *Antisemitism in French Schools*, p. 2.

81. Ibid.

82. *Le Monde*, July 6, 2004. See also Emmanuel Brenner, *"France, prend garde de perdre ton âme . . ."* *Fracture sociale et antisémitisme dans la République* (Paris: Mille et Une Nuits, 2004), pp. 79–147; and *NO*, February 7–13, 2002.

83. See Union des étudiants juifs de France and SOS Racisme, *Les Antifeujs*, pp. 204–29 on the image of the Jews in France as it appeared in February 2002.

84. See the detailed report, "Racisme, antisémitisme, Alerte!," *NO*, December 11–17, 2003, pp. 104–16. See also Bensoussan, *Antisemitism in French Schools*, pp. 22–23.

85. Ibid., p. 22. The quote comes from Magyd Cherfi's remarks "On n'aimait pas les juifs, sauf ceux qu'on connaissait," *NO*, January 24–30, 2002, p. 14.

86. Ibid. See, however, the remarks of Nacer Kettane, a leader of the *beurs,* justifying the Arab violence in France as an expression of Muslim anger over the Middle East conflict. On the other hand, the republican Marxist and antiracist Malek Boutih, president of SOS Racisme, rejected any link of anti-Semitism to the Palestinian in-tifada: Palestine was "a pretext, a catalyst of the violence we have seen. At bottom, this is an anti-Semitism of the lumpenproletariat . . . the poorest of the poor, the *lumpen* of today, the *beurs* in their ghettos for whom the Jew equals money."

87. Pierre-André Taguieff, *Prêcheurs de Haine: Traversée de la judéophobie planétaire* (Paris: Mille et Une Nuits, 2004), pp. 108–28. See also Shmuel Trigano, "Le Néo-Gauchisme face à Israël: la dissociation de 'l'antiracisme' et de la lutte contre l'an-tisémitisme," *Observatoire du monde juif*, no. 3 (June 2002).

88. Shmuel Trigano, "Les contours d'une nouvelle idéologie," *Observatoire du monde juif*, no. 3 (June 2002): pp. 20–26. Also Trigano, "The Perverse Logic of French Pol-itics," *Jerusalem Letter/Viewpoints*, June 2, 2002.

89. See Taguieff, *Prêcheurs de Haine*, pp. 563–686. See also "L'antisionisme et le mythe du complot juif," *L'Arche*, January–February 2004, pp. 94–101.

90. Taguieff, *La nouvelle judéophobie*, pp. 11–21. For a retrospective on Carpentras, see Birnbaum, *Jewish Destinies*, pp. 228–51.

91. See Meir Waintrater, "L'inquiétante étrangeté de l'antisionisme," *L'Arche,* May 2003, pp. 36–41; "Les associations antiracistes s'inquiètent d'une 'libération' de la parole antijuive," *Le Monde,* February 19, 2002.

92. "Entretien avec Illich Ramirez Sanchez, dit Carlos," *Résistance* (bimonthly of the Résistants au Nouvel Ordre Mondial et à la Pensée Unique, no. 61 (February–March 2002): pp. 3–4. Also *Marianne,* February 4–10, 2002.

93. "Une chasse aux Juifs en plein Paris," *L'Arche,* May 2003, p. 42. See also the Mouloud Aounit, "L'antisémitisme instrumentalisé," *NO,* January 24–30, 2002, p. 21. Aounit was the president of MRAP (Movement Against Racism and for Friendship Among the Peoples), a Communist-sponsored antiracist organization (accused of complicity in the Judeophobe deviations of the Far Left). He protested strongly against the stigmatization of young Muslim Arabs in the debate over anti-Semitism.

94. Jean Daniel, "La gangrène," *NO,* April 3–9, 2003; and Daniel, "Contre les tentations du pire," *NO,* November 20–26, 2003. See also the dossier on anti-Semitism, "La République à l'épreuve du conflit israélo-palestinien," *NO,* February 6–12, 2003. It should also be mentioned that in 2001, the daughter of NO's editor, Sarah Daniel, had made quite false allegations about Israeli soldiers raping Palestinian women, which were later retracted.

95. Interview with Daniel Bensaïd, "Les responsables juifs sont des pompiers pyromanes," *Marianne,* January 28–February 3, 2002. For a critique of Trotskyist and anti-globalist flirtations with the Islamists, see Jacques Juillard, "L'incendie antisémite," *NO,* November 20–26, 2003, p. 22.

96. Interview with Nicolas Weill, "Le sentiment de solitude des Juifs va croissant," *L'Arche,* May 2003.

97. Uriel Heilman, "No liberty, equality or fraternity," *The Jerusalem Post,* April 22, 2003.

98. Ibid.

99. Ibid.

100. See Union des étudiants juifs de France and SOS Racisme, *Les Antifeujs,* pp. 36–64, for a detailed inventory of these attacks. "*Feuj*" is a backward spelling of "*Juif,*" meaning Jew.

101. Quoted by Marie Brenner, "France's Scarlet Letter," *Vanity Fair,* June 2003, p. 122.

102. Daniel Ben Simon, "Ha-yehudim meshalmim et ha-mehir," *Haaretz,* January 18, 2002; "Antisemitism in France" (editorial), *The Jerusalem Post,* January 20, 2002; Sefi Hendler, "Ha-Antishemiut ha-Tsarfatit Ha-hadasha," *Maariv,* January 18, 2002. See also Catherine Dupeyron and Xavier Ternisien, "Le gouvernement Sharon qualifie la France de pays occidental 'le plus antisémite,' " *Le Monde,* January 10, 2002.

103. See "La France, bête noire d'Israël," *Tribune Juive,* January 31, 2002, and the interview with the outspoken Gaullist deputy Pierre Lellouche, "Je regrette les propos de Chirac sur les violences antisémites," in ibid., p. 12.

104. *Discours et Messages de Jacques Chirac: Maire de Paris, Premier Ministre, Président de la République* (Paris, 2003), which contains his addresses relating to the Jews of France between 1986 and 2003.

105. See the many articles in *Actualité Juive,* January 17, 2002, for reactions by Melchior,

other French politicians, French Jews, and the head of the Jewish Agency in France. See also, "Le grand rabbin de Paris reçu par le president de la République" in ibid.

106. Michael Ledeen, "Small Earthquake in France," *The Wall Street Journal*, April 24, 2002; Nona Meyer, "Les électeurs du Front National sont plus anti-Juifs, anti-Arabes que les autres," *Actualité Juive*, April 25, 2002, p. 8; Patrick Jarreau, "Les Américains n'attribuent pas le regain d'antisémitisme en France à Jean-Marie Le Pen," *Le Monde*, May 4, 2002; "Why He Has His Admirers," *The Economist*, May 4, 2002, p. 41.

107. Yaroslav Trofimov, "In Marseille, It's Le Pen, the 'Insécurité' Fighter," *The Wall Street Journal*, April 30, 2002, p. 15. See also his interview with S. Hendler in *Maariv*, February 21, 2002, in Hebrew; and Adar Primor, "Le Pen Will Fight Anti-Semitism, Says His Jewish Running Mate," *Haaretz*, March 19, 2004.

108. Ibid. See also Katrin Bernhold, "Agreeing (Sort of) on Migration," *IHT*, January 16, 2008.

109. Elie Barth, "Bruno Gollnisch a toujours remis en question l'ampleur de l'extermination des juifs par les Nazis," *Le Monde*, October 18, 2004; "Bruno Gollnisch va être poursuivi," *NO*, November 29, 2004; and Gollnisch's editorial in *Français d'abord*, November 30, 2004. See also Henry Rousso, *Le dossier Lyon III: Le rapport sur le racisme et le négationnisme à l'université Jean-Moulin* (Paris: Fayard, 2004), pp. 86–93.

110. Nicholas Simon, "Sympathy for the Devil?" *The Jerusalem Report*, January 10, 2005; "Pour M. Le Pen, 'L'occupation allemande n'a pas été particulièrement inhumaine," *Le Monde*, January 13, 2005; "Le Pen provoque une fois de plus l'indignation," *Le Figaro*, January 13, 2005; and "Le Pen to Be Tried for Denying Brutality of Nazi Occupation," *Haaretz*, July 13, 2006.

111. "Le Pen: France Not Responsible for Jews' Deportation," *The Jerusalem Post*, April 16, 2007. See also Daniel Ben Simon, "Le Pen mitnaged le-hakarata shel Tsarfat be-ahrayut le-gerush yehudim le-mahanot," *Haaretz*, April 16, 2007.

112. Katrin Bernhold, "New Arena for Ideas of Le Pen," *IHT*, January 13, 2006; and Christiane Chombeau and Gérard Courtois, "La banalisation des idées de M. Le Pen le fait progresser," *Le Monde*, December 15, 2006.

113. Christiane Chombeau, "Le déclin du Le Pénisme," *Le Monde*, May 5, 2007; "A Strange Election Campaign," *Searchlight*, July 2007, p. 4. See also Guillaume Perrault, "Au FN, la fronde comtre Marine le Pen s'amplifie," *Le Figaro*, February 4, 2009; and the editorial by Paul-Henri du Limbert, "Le Front National en capilotade," in the same issue.

114. Kamal Khan, "Appel aux Musulmans de France: Votez Le Pen!" Radio Islam, *http://www.radioislam.org/islam/french/debat/khan1.htm*.

115. On Sarkozy's Jewish background as seen by Islamist anti-Semites, see "Maintenant c'est un président juif," Radio Islam, http://www.radioislam.org/sarko-gouvernement/origine.htm; and for Bernard Kouchner, see "Koucher, une crapule talmudique," Radio Islam, http://www.radioislam.org/sarko-gouvernement/abbe-pierre-koucher.htm. See Pierre/Péan, *Le monde selon K.* (Paris: Fayard, 2009) for a malicious effort to unmask Kouchner as an opportunist neocon. Also the editorial "Le cosmopolite," in *Le Monde*, February 6, 2009.

116. See "L'extermination des infidèles," *Observatoire du monde juif*, no. 1 (2004): pp.

34–61; *Radical Islam in Europe* (Jerusalem: Institute of the World Jewish Congress, 2002); Ali Laïdi, *Le Jihad en Europe* (Paris: Éditions du Seuil, 2002), pp. 129–67; Alexandre Del Valle, *Le Totalitarisme Islamiste à l'assaut des démocraties* (Paris: Éditions des Syrtes, 2002), pp. 248–78.

117. Fouad Benabdelhalim, "Les véritables ennemis de l'Algérie," quoted in *L'Algérie par ses islamistes*, ed. Mustafa al-Ahnaf et al. (Paris: Karthala, 1991), pp. 277–78; and Gilles Kepel, *Allah in the West: Islamic Movements in America and Europe* (Stanford, Calif.: Stanford University Press, 1977), pp. 156–73.

118. See Pierre-André Taguieff, *Rising from the Muck: The New Antisemitism in Europe* (Chicago: Ivan R. Dee, 2004), pp. 40–61.

119. Taguieff, *Prêcheurs de Haine*, pp. 114–17, 240–42. See also the report, "Quand les Arabes de la Capitale se lâchent," *Actualité Juive*, November 14, 2002, p. 13.

120. See Pew Global Attitudes Project, "The Great Divide: How Westerners and Muslims View Each Other," Pew Research Center, http://pewglobal.org/reports/display.php?ReportID=253. The surveys were carried out in thirteen countries between March 31 and May 14, 2006.

121. Shmuel Trigano, ed., "Islamisme et les Juifs: Un test pour la République," *Observatoire du monde juif*, nos. 4–5 (December 2002), especially the articles by Michèle Tribalat, pp. 7–16, and Alexandre del Valle, pp. 17–22. See also Del Valle and Marc Knobel, "La convergence des totalitarismes," *Le Figaro*, April 22, 2002; and Robert Wistrich, "Israël face à la derive islamiste," *Le Figaro*, September 17, 2002.

122. Milton Vorst, "The Muslims of France," *Foreign Affairs*, September–October 1996, pp. 78–96; Rachid Tlemçami, "Islam in France," *Middle East Quarterly* (*MEQ*), March 1997, pp. 31–38; and Michel Gurfinkiel, "Is the French Way of Life in Danger?" *MEQ*, ibid., pp. 19–30. See also Jeanne-Hélène Kaltenbach and Michèle Tribalat, *La République et l'Islam: Entre Crainte et Aveuglement* (Paris: Gallimard, 2002).

123. Alexandre del Valle, "Les nouveaux visages rouges-bruns-verts de l'antisémitisme," *Observatoire du monde juif*, no. 3 (June 2002): pp. 31–35. See also the tract of the Parti des Musulmans de France in ibid., pp. 37–38, entitled "Le Sionisme, l'antisémitisme et Israël" signed by Mohamed Enacer Latrèche, which branded Zionists as "child killers" and Israel as an "illegitimate" racist state seeking to exterminate the Palestinians; anti-Semitism was dismissed as a Zionist tool, "*un boucher pour couvrir leurs crimes, et une arme repressive pour terroriser ceux qui oseront le dénoncer.*"

124. See "Un dimanche ordinaire sur Radio Méditerranée," in *Observatoire du monde juif*, nos. 4–5 (December 2002); *NO*, February 6, 2003; and Marie Brenner, "Daughters of France, Daughters of Allah," *Vanity Fair*, April 2004, pp. 202–3. See also Paul Landau, *Le Sabre et le Coran: Tariq Ramadan et les Frères musulmans à la conquête de l'Europe* (Paris: Éditions du Rocher, 2005), pp. 125–27.

125. *NO*, February 6, 2003. See also Albert Naccache, *Contre Israël: De L'Amour de la Palestine à la Haine des Juifs* (Paris: Cheminements, 2008), pp. 238–40.

126. Landau, *Le Sabre et le Coran*, pp. 133–62; and Taguieff, *Prêcheurs de la Haine*, pp. 906–36. See also Caroline Fourest, *Brother Tariq: The Doublespeak of Tariq Ramadan* (New York: Encounter Books, 2008), pp. 82–83, 104–6, 216–19.

127. On the visa controversy, see Fouad Ajami, "Tariq Ramadan," *The Wall Street Jour-*

nal, September 7, 2004; and Stephen Schwartz, "Why the Tariq Ramadan Controversy Matters," *TCS Daily,* September 16, 2004. The most detailed biography is by the French journalist Caroline Fourest, *Frère Tariq* (Paris: Grasset, 2004). Despite the U.S. ban, in August 2005 the British home secretary invited Ramadan to join a task force aimed at "preventing young Muslims in Britain from deteriorating into violent extremism." Oxford University also took him on as a visiting fellow.

128. Between September 25 and October 9, 2005, the Egyptian journalist Adel Guindy published a three-part series on Tariq Ramadan for the Egyptian Coptic weekly *Watani.* See the summary by A. Dankowitz, "Tariq Ramadan—Reformist or Islamist?" *MEMRI, Inquiry and Analysis,* no. 266 (February 17, 2006). See also Pierre-André Taguieff, *La judéophobie des Modernes,* pp. 416–23.

129. See Tariq Ramadan, *Jihad, violence, guerre et paix en Islam* (Paris: Éditions Tawhid, 2002). Also Ramadan, *Peut-on vivre avec l'Islam? Entretien avec Jacques Neirynck* (Lausanne: Favre, 2004).

130. Ian Buruma, "Tariq Ramadan Has an Identity Issue," *The New York Times,* February 4, 2007.

131. Taguieff, *Prêcheurs de Haine,* pp. 253, 906–13, 932. See also Alain Gresh and Tariq Ramadan, *L'Islam en questions* (Arles, France: Actes Sud, 2000). Gresh, an Egyptian-born Jew (son of the Jewish Communist Henri Curiel) came to France at the age of fourteen, and was an activist in the French Communist Party before turning to a neo-Marxist brand of Third Worldism. He was increasingly fascinated by the revolutionary potential of Islamism.

132. Tariq Ramadan, "Existe-il un antisémitisme islamique?" *Le Monde,* December 22, 2001.

133. Joseph Algazy, "My Fellow Muslims, We Must Fight Anti-Semitism," *Haaretz,* July 10, 2002.

134. Landau, *Le Sabre et le Coran,* pp. 149–62; Buruma, "Tariq Ramadan Has an Identity Issue"; Taguieff, *Prêcheurs de Haine,* pp. 907–12; Philippe Gumplowicz, "L'envol de Ramadan," *L'Arche,* November–December 2003, p. 36; Alain Finkielkraut, "Une réponse à Tariq Ramadan," *L'Arche,* ibid., pp. 28–29; André Glucksmann, "Une obsession antisémite," *NO,* October 9–13, 2003, p. 27.

135. Bernard-Henri Lévy, "Tariq Ramadan et les altermondialistes," *Le Point,* October 10, 2003; Claude Askolovitch, "L'encombrant M. Ramadan," *NO,* October 9, 2003, pp. 26–27. See also the interview with Finkielkraut, "Le temps des antisémites sympas," *Le Figaro Magazine,* October 31, 2003, pp. 20–21; and Alexandre Adler, "Epître à Tariq Ramadan," *Le Figaro,* October 16, 2003, and Ramadan's reply, posted October 29, 2003, at http://oumma.com/Response-a-Alexandre-Adler.

136. Serge Raffy, "Le Vrai Visage de Tariq Ramadan," *NO,* January 29–February 4, 2004), pp. 64–71. Here, also, Ramadan uses a "double language" referring to a "state of all its citizens" for Western audiences, while emphasizing the Islamist objective in speaking to Muslims. On the deceptive techniques practiced by Ramadan in general, see Claire Chartier's interview with Caroline Fourest in *L'Express,* October 18, 2004, pp. 26–36, and Fourest, *Brother Tariq,* pp. 104–6.

137. Tariq's father, Said Ramadan, had been totally committed to the destruction of Israel in 1948 and advocated violent resistance to it until his death in 1995. See Landau, *Le Sabre et le Coran,* pp. 61–62, and Fourest, *Brother Tariq,* pp. 44–45. On the

conspiracy motif in Tariq Ramadan's view of the Jews and Zionism, see ibid., pp. 150–61.

138. David Pryce-Jones, "The Islamization of Europe?" *Commentary*, December 2004, pp. 29–33; and Ye'or, *Eurabia*, pp. 190–208. On the court case against *Charlie Hebdo*, see the account by Philippe Val, *Reviens, Voltaire: Ils sont devenus Fous* (Paris: Bernard Grasset, 2008).

139. Robert Redeker, "Face aux intimidations islamistes, que doit faire le monde libre?" *Le Figaro*, September 19, 2006. For a Trotskyist view, see Stefan Steinberg, "Anti-Islam Campaign in France," International Committee for the Fourth International, http://www.wsws.org/articles/2006/oct2006/rede-o18.shtml; and "Robert Redeker quitte l'enseignement pour le CNRS," *Libération*, January 20, 2007.

140. Christian Delacampagne, "The Redeker Affair," *Commentary*, January 2007, pp. 25–29.

141. "An Underclass Rebellion," *The Economist*, November 12, 2005, p. 25; "France's Failure," ibid., p. 11; Mark Steyn, "Revolt of the 'Arab Street,'" *The Jerusalem Post*, November 9, 2005; "Unrest in France Spreads," *The New York Times*, November 6, 2005; "La France ne brûle pas," *Le Monde*, November 15, 2005.

142. Michel Wieviorka, "Malaise des banlieues et déficit d'action sociale," *Le Figaro*, November 3, 2005; Marc Hatzfeld, "Je suis un racaille," *Le Monde*, November 10, 2005; Ivan Rioufol, "Rebellion contre le 'modèle français,'" *Le Figaro*, October 11, 2005.

143. "Nicolas Sarkozy continue de vilipender 'racailles et voyous,'" *Le Monde*, November 11, 2005; Emmanuel Todd, "Rien ne sépare les enfants d'immigrés du reste de la société," ibid., November 12, 2005; Jean-François Mattei, "Violences urbaines, crescendo dans la barbarie," *Le Figaro*, November 3, 2005.

144. Bernard-Henri Lévy, "When Suburbs Burn," *The Wall Street Journal*, November 9, 2005.

NINE: *LIBERTÉ, EGALITÉ, ANTISÉMITISME*

1. Interview with Finkielkraut conducted by Dror Mishani and Aurelia Smotriez, "Hem lo miskenim, hem muslemim" [They Are Not Poor, They Are Muslims], *Haaretz*, November 17, 2005. See also an earlier interview, "L'illégitimé de la haine," *Le Figaro*, November 15, 2005; Finkielkraut, "J'Assume," *Le Monde*, November 26, 2005; Xavier Ternisien, "Génèse d'un controverse," *Le Monde*, November 26, 2005; Jean Daniel, "Appeler un chat un chat," *NO*, December 1–7, 2005, p. 45; Claude Askolovitch, "Le philosophe et ses doubles," *NO*, December 1–7, 2005, pp. 54–55; Pascal Bruckner, "Finkielkraut, le Sarkozy des intellos," *NO*, December 1–7, 2005, p. 53; Aude Lancelin, "Intellos: la vague droitière," *NO*, December 1–7, 2005, pp. 58–59; and Robert Solé, "Les gros mots d'un philosophe," *Le Monde*, December 3, 2005.

2. *Haaretz*, November 17, 2005.

3. See André Glucksmann, *Le Discours de la Haine* (Paris: Plon, 2004), pp. 72–162. See also the survey of the "new reactionaries" by Laurent Joffrin, "Les néo-reacs," *NO*, December 1–7, 2005, pp. 50–53; Bruckner, "Finkielkraut, le Sarkozy," p. 53; and Daniel Lindenberg, "Le dérapage continue," *NO*, December 1–7, 2005, p. 59.

4. Alain Finkielkraut, "In the Name of the Other: Reflections on the Coming Anti-Semitism," *Azure,* no. 18 (Autumn 2004): pp. 21–33. See also Robert S. Wistrich, "If Things Are So Good, Why Are They So Bad?" *Haaretz,* May 19, 2004; and Wistrich, "Antishemiut be-matzpun shaqet" [Anti-Semitism With a Good Conscience], *Haaretz,* July 25, 2003.

5. Rony Brauman and Alain Finkielkraut, *La Discorde Israël-Palestine, Les Juifs, La France* (Paris: Mille et Une Nuits, 2006). For Brauman's position, see pp. 178–223. See also Brauman's contribution to *Antisémitisme: l'intolérable chantage* (Paris: La Découverte, 2003), and those of Eric Hazan, Michel Warschawski, Etienne Balibar, and Daniel Lindenberg.

6. Michel Warschawski, "Le cynique, le paranoiaque et le provocateur," in *Anti-sémitisme,* pp. 59–77.

7. "En tant que juif," *Le Monde,* October 18, 2000; and the sequel, "Oui, en tant que juifs," ibid., November 8, 2000, a reply to Finkielkraut by Rony Brauman, Daniel Bensaïd, and Marcel-Francis Kahn.

8. Eyal Sivan, "La dangereuse confusion des juifs de France," *Le Monde,* December 8, 2001. See also the collective reply "Juifs de France: La dangereuse confusion d'Eyal Sivan," *Le Monde,* December 18, 2001, signed by Serge Klarsfeld, Shmuel Trigano, and Jacques Tarnero, among others.

9. Maurice Szafran, "Diabolisation politique," *Le Monde,* December 17, 2001. See also Philippe Val, *Reviens, Voltaire,* pp. 185–234, and the spirited polemic by Bernard-Henri Lévy, *Left in Dark Times: A Stand Against the New Barbarism* (New York: Random House, 2008).

10. Edgar Morin, Sami Naïr, and Danièle Sallenave, "Israël-Palestine: Le cancer," *Le Monde,* June 3, 2002; and the documentation of the Morin affair in Naccache, *Contre Israël,* pp. 221–26. For the subsequent petitions in Morin's favor by prominent intellectuals, Naccache, pp. 224–25, and the article by Edwy Plenel, "Edgar Morin, L'exclu: L'horreur du mensonge qui triomphe," *Le Monde,* July 22, 2005, which compares Morin to Spinoza!

11. See Danièle Sallenave, *Carnet de route en Palestine occupée: Gaza-Cisjordanie, novembre 1997* (Paris: Stock, 1998).

12. See Esther Benbassa and Jean-Christophe Attias, *Les Juifs ont-ils un avenir?* (Paris: Lattès, 2001), p. 111; and Benbassa and Attias, "Nous ne sommes pas des victimes," *Le Monde,* December 18, 2001. See the responses of B.-H. Lévy and Taguieff to the Benbassa and Attias book in *Le Point,* October 19, 2001.

13. Benbassa and Attias, "Nous ne sommes pas des victimes."

14. Alfred Grosser, "Contre les abus de la victimization," *L'Express,* May 22, 2003. Within a month, Grosser had resigned from the weekly, following a flood of indignant letters. As a political commentator, Grosser was well-known both for his love of Germany and his harsh judgments about Israel and the Jews.

15. For examples of radical anti-Zionism, see Dominique Vidal with Joseph Algazy, *Le Péché original d'Israël* (Paris: Les Éditions de l'Atelier, 1998); Vidal with Alain Gresh, *Les 100 clés du Proche-Orient* (Paris: Hachette, 2003); and Vidal, *Le Mal-Être juif: Entre repli, assimilation et manipulation* (Marseille: Agone, 2003). See also Taguieff, *Prêcheurs de Haine,* pp. 914–15, for some examples of Vidal's manipulative journalism.

16. Dominique Vidal, "Les pompiers-pyromanes de l'antisémitisme," *Le Monde Diplo-*

matique, May 2004, pp. 6–7; Vidal, "Les alliances douteuses des inconditionnels d'Israël: Au nom du combat contre l'antisémitisme," ibid., December 2002, pp. 6–7; and "Une année de cristal?" ibid., December 2002, p. 7.

17. Dominique Vidal, "Dix yeux pour un seul oeil," *Le Monde Diplomatique*, September 2006, p. 3.

18. Eric Conan, "Les Chiffres Noirs de l'Antisémitisme," *L'Express*, December 6, 2001. See also Sylvia Zappi, "405 actes antijuifs ont été recensés en France depuis Septembre 2000," *Le Monde*, March 13, 2002, including the statements of Malek Boutih (head of SOS Racisme), Patrick Klugman (president of UEJF, the Jewish student federation), Michel Tubiana (League of the Rights of Man), and Mouloud Aounit (MRAP—an antiracist movement with a problematic record on Jewish issues).

19. See Xavier Ternisien, "Les représentants de la communauté juive préfèrent dire 'actes antijuifs,' " *Le Monde*, March 13, 2002.

20. "Dossier antisémitisme . . . Ce que disent les statistiques du ministère de l'intérieur," *L'Arche*, May 2003, pp. 46–50; "Antisémitisme: un hit-parade européen," ibid., pp. 58–60; and "Sondages et interpretations," ibid., pp. 51–53.

21. See the exclusive survey by the CSA Poll Institute and the weekly "Marianne," in *Marianne*, April 8–14, 2002.

22. Daniel Ben-Simon, "Intifada Spurs Rash of Anti-Jewish Acts in France," *Haaretz*, April 6, 2002; Ben-Simon, "Beyond the Bounds," ibid., January 25, 2002; and Ben-Simon, "Whenever the World Goes Crazy, the Jews Pay the Price," ibid., January 18, 2002.

23. Piotr Smolar, "Le nombre d'aggressions antisémites a brutalement augmenté ces dernières semaines," *Le Monde*, April 19, 2002. See also Emmanuel Brenner, "*France prends garde*," pp. 81–82. The CNCDH report was published in April 2003.

24. Claire Berlinski, "The Hope of Marseille," *Azure*, no. 19 (Winter 2005): pp. 33–57.

25. "Anti-Semitism has 'Taken Root' in France," *Haaretz*, April 2, 2004.

26. See *The Jerusalem Post*, July 19, 20, 21, and 22, 2004, especially the editorial "French Hutzpa," July 21, 2004. For the French view, see "L'appel de Sharon aux juifs de France," *Le Monde*, July 19, 2004.

27. "Antisémitisme 2004: La poussée de fièvre," *Le Droit de Vivre*, June 2004.

28. *The Jerusalem Post*, August 23, 2004.

29. "French Official: Attacks on Jews Tripled Since the Start of the Year," *Haaretz*, August 29, 2004. A useful description of these attacks can be found in Raphael Israeli, *Muslim Anti-Semitism in Christian Europe* (New Brunswick, N.J.: Transaction Publishers, 2009), pp. 183–86.

30. Sylvia Zappi, "Actes racistes et antisémites en France: 2004 aura été une année noire," *Le Monde*, January 18, 2005; "Les chiffres pour 2004 de la CNCDH," *Le Monde*, January 19, 2005; and "Attacks on Jews and Muslims Hit 10-Year High," *Haaretz*, March 22, 2005.

31. On the specificity of anti-Semitism in Alsace, see Wieviorka, *La tentation antisémite*, pp. 273–333, who notes its traditionalist aspects, the local strength of the FN, the decades-old silence over wartime pro-Nazi collaboration, and various regional factors. For Wieviorka's view of anti-Semitism, see "Quand la société se fragmente, l'antisémitisme progresse," *Libération*, April 13, 2005; for a critique, see Daniel Sibony, "Antisémitisme, l'illusion économiste," *Libération*, April 26, 2005.

32. Catherine Coroller and Emmanuel Davidenkoff, "La haine du Juif sous toutes ses cultures," *Libération*, April 19, 2005.

33. Manfred Gerstenfeld, *The Autumn 2005 Riots in France: Their Possible Impact on Israel and the Jews* (Jerusalem: Jerusalem Center for Public Affairs, 2006).

34. Léon Sann, "Violences Urbaines," in *Controverses I* (Paris: Éditions de L'Éclat, 2006), pp. 147–73.

35. Géraldine Faes and Stephen Smith, *Noir et Français!* (Paris: Éditions du Panama, 2006), pp. 265–67.

36. Jean-Yves Camus, "The Commemoration of Slavery in France and the Emergence of a Black Political Consciousness," *The European Legacy* 11, no. 6 (2006): pp. 647–55. According to the 1999 census there were 400,000 people of black African origin legally in France, as well as another half a million natives of the *outré-mer* (overseas French territories) living on French soil.

37. Benoît Hopquin, "Juifs-Noirs, le grand malentendu," *Le Monde*, April 21, 2006.

38. See excerpts from an interview in *Lyon Capitule*, January 23, 2002, reproduced in part in *Actualité Juive*, February 7, 2002. See also "Les associations antiracistes s'inquiètent d'une 'libération' de la parole antijuive," *Le Monde*, February 19, 2002. Dieudonné added that, for him, neither "Jews" nor "Muslims" existed at all.

39. See Faes and Smith, *Noir et Français!*, pp. 227–56.

40. C.A. [Claude Askolovitch], "Dieudo, la bavure," *NO*, December 11–17, 2003, p. 110: "*Il y a du Le Pen chez cet antiraciste proclamé. Frapper, choquer, et capitaliser.*" See also "It's No Joke for French Comedian Who Appeared on TV in Nazi Garb," *Haaretz*, February 20, 2004; and "Performer Accused of Anti-Semitism," *The Jewish Chronicle*, February 27, 2004. See also Taguieff, *La judéophobie*, pp. 425–38, and Naccache, *Contre Israël*, pp. 255–57, for Dieudonné's flirtation with the Far Right.

41. Emmanuel Halperin, "We're from the UN," *Haaretz*, Pesach supplement, April 5, 2004, p. 11. See also Ève Bonnivard, "L'Affaire Dieudonné," *L'Arche*, January–February 2004, pp. 124–25.

42. Extracts from interview with Dieudonné on Radio Méditerranée, December 6, 2003, in Bonnivard, "L'Affaire Dieudonné," p. 126. Also his remarks, "Arthur, Bruel, et j'en passé," *Le Monde*, January 8, 2004.

43. "Quand Dieudonné s'acharne," *L'Arche*, January–February 2004, p. 128.

44. Ibid.

45. Interview with François Barras, "Je souhaite que les Arabes possèdent la bombe atomique," *Vingt Quatre Heures*, December 10, 2004. See also the interview with Silvia Cattori, published in November 2004 on the website Vigie-Media-Palestine, reproduced in *L'Arche*, January 2005, p. 11.

46. "Racist incidents jarring the French," *IHT*, February 24, 2005. See also *Le Monde*, March 6, 2005, for the legal investigation into his remarks about the commemoration of the Shoah having become a "*pornographie mémorielle.*"

47. Blandine Grosjean, "Dieudonné a nouveau relaxé en appeal," *Libération*, February 10, 2006; "Black French Comedian Fined for Anti-Jewish Remark," *European Jewish Press*, March 10, 2006.

48. Faes and Smith, *Noir et Français!*, pp. 239–40.

49. Anne-Sophie Mercier, *La vérité sur Dieudonné* (Paris: Plon, 2005), p. 25; "Explication entre Dieudonné et Pierre Tévanion," http://lesogres/article.php3?id

_article=556. See also Tom Reiss, "Letter from Paris: Laugh Riots," *The New Yorker*, November 19, 2007.

50. Mercier, *La vérité sur Dieudonné*, pp. 28–32.

51. Ibid., pp. 34–42. See also "Dieudonné, les rabbins antisionistes et les militantes négationnistes," *L'Arche*, January 2005, pp. 86–87. On his website *Les Ogres*, Dieudonné expressed support on February 21, 2007, for Ahmadinejad and the "Iranian resistance to the policy of the American-Zionist axis."

52. *Charlie Hebdo*, November 24, 2004.

53. Faes and Smith, *Noir et Français!*, pp. 208ff., 214–16.

54. Ibid., p. 243. These and other statements prompted Harlem Désir (by then a Socialist deputy in the European Parliament) to call Dieudonné "*l'un des plus grands antisémites de France.*" He was also sharply criticized by another nonwhite deputy, Christiane Taubira, who was responsible for the May 2001 law recognizing slavery as a "crime against humanity."

55. Mercier, *La vérité sur Dieudonné*, pp. 155–56. On the rapprochement with the FN, see ibid., pp. 156–74. See also Raphaël Confiant, "Les Noirs, du malaise à la colère," *Le Monde*, December 9, 2006; Christiane Chombeau, "Le FN se rend en délégation au spectacle de Dieudonné," *Le Monde*, December 19, 2006.

56. Christiane Chombeau, "L'antisémitisme, 'Ça peut aussi être drôle,' dit Le Pen," *Le Monde*, December 23, 2006.

57. Mercier, *La vérité sur Dieudonné*, pp. 158–59. Gollnisch placed Dieudonné on the same level as former prime minister Raymond Barre (himself not free of anti-Semitism), as a defender of fundamental liberties.

58. Ibid., pp. 168–73. Mercier compares the comedian to the most radical French fascist leader of the late 1930s, Jacques Doriot. The latter moved from Communist internationalism and anti-militarism toward a revolutionary form of ethnic French self-assertion and violent populist rhetoric of the pro-Nazi variety.

59. Nidra Poller, "The Wrath of Ka: Black Anti-Semites Storm Paris's Old Jewish Quarter," *City Journal*, June 6, 2006. On July 28, 2006, President Chirac dissolved the "Tribu Ka" for its racist and anti-Semitic positions. See also "Émergence d'un identitarisme noir?" *L'Arche*, July–August 2006, p. 94. On the explicit minority racism of the "*Kémites Atoniens,*" see Faes and Smith, *Noir et Français!*, pp. 196–208. For extreme right-wing support for Tribu Ka, see Laurent Duguet, "La Haine Raciste et Antisémite tisse sa Toile en Toute Quiétude sur le Net," *Les Études du Crif*, no. 13 (November 2007): pp. 25–26.

60. *Noir et Français!* p. 254 for Kémi Seba's intervention at the theater of La Main d'Or. See also Naccache, *Contre Israël*, pp. 312–15, for Seba's political street show "Sarkophobie," directed by Dieudonné at the Main d'Or theater, which presented the "Sarkozy system" as a Zionist imposture.

61. On the Fogiel affair, see ibid., pp. 249–51; and Duguet, *La Haine Raciste*, p. 27. See Seba's website, http://www.seba-wsr.com, September 2006, for his call to arms against the Jews of Sarcelles and the "global Zionist mafia."

62. Marc Perelman, "Bias Attacks in France Fuel Concern About Blacks," *Haaretz*, March 14, 2006.

63. "French Debate Comic's Effect on Murder," *The Jewish Chronicle*, March 10, 2006; "Des motivations encore incertaines," *Le Monde*, February 18, 2006. See also Reiss,

"Letter from Paris"; and the article by Laurent Joffrin, "Dieudo et Fofana," *NO*, March 2, 2006.

64. Assaf Uni, "Brutal Kidnap and Murder of French Jew Alarms Community," *Haaretz*, February 19, 2006; "Anti-Semitism," ibid., February 20, 2006. The Paris public prosecutor, Jean-Claude Marin, was initially more skeptical about the question of a racial motivation. The family, however, accused the police of deliberately ignoring anti-Semitism in order not to alienate Muslims. An editorial ("Barbares") in *Le Monde*, February 23, 2006, unequivocally classified the affair as anti-Semitic. See also Naccache, *Contre Israël*, pp. 315–18.

65. "Meurtre d'Ilan Halimi: Sarkozy parle d'antisémitisme par de l'amalgame," *Libération*, February 21, 2006; "Villepin promet la vérité sur l'assassinat d'Ilan," *Le Figaro*, February 21, 2006.

66. See "Barbarie antisémite" and the dossier in *Actualité Juive*, February 23, 2006; Annette Levy-Willard, "Les Juifs et l'argent, rapprochement nauséeux," *Libération*, February 23, 2006; Esther Benbassa in *Le Monde*, February 25, 2006; Morad el Hattab, "Ilan, silence barbarie," *Libération*, February 25, 2006.

67. See Annette Levy-Willard, "Les juifs et l'argent, rapprochement nauséeux," *Libération*, February 23, 2006.

68. See Gérard Dupuy, "Déclencheur," *Libération*, February 22, 2006; Charles Bremner, " 'Anti-Semitic Killer' Returned to France," *The Times* (London), February 24, 2006. See also Taguieff, *La Judéophobie*, pp. 458–63.

69. Alain-Gérard Slama, "Qualifier l'inqualifiable," *Le Figaro*, February 27, 2006; Michel Wieviorka, "Antisémitisme: une mobilisation 'post-républicaine,' " ibid.; Antoine de Gaudemar, "Vivre ensemble," *Libération*, February 27, 2006, p. 2; and Laurent Greilsamer, "De l'emballement au déni," *Le Monde*, February 28, 2006.

70. See "Le 'gang des barbares' aurait visé des personnalités juives," *Le Monde*, February 25, 2006; and Henri Hajdenberg, "Halimi Died Because He Was Jewish," *Haaretz*, March 3, 2006.

71. "À Créteil, le sentiment d'insécurité de la communauté juive," *Le Monde*, February 25, 2006.

72. Caroline B. Glick, "Ilan Halimi and Israel," *The Jerusalem Post*, February 24, 2006. Ilan Halimi was eventually buried in Israel in a manner that partially made up for earlier neglect of the case.

73. Cécilia Gabizon and Philippe Goulliaud, "Cérémonie nationale en homage à Ilan Halimi," *Le Figaro*, February 24, 2006; "The Halimi murder," *The Jerusalem Post*, February 26, 2006.

74. Jean-Baptiste de Montvalon, "Embarrassée, la classe politique s'associe aux manifestations à la mémoire du jeune homme," *Le Monde*, February 24, 2006.

75. "Le FN, manifestant indésirable," *Libération*, February 25, 2006; "Polémique autour de la manifestation contre le racisme et l'antisémitisme," *Le Monde*, February 25, 2006.

76. "Contre le Racisme et L'Antisémitisme," *Le Parisien*, February 27, 2006; "Droite et gauche ensemble derrière un slogan rassembleur," *Le Monde*, February 25, 2006; "M. de Villiers a été expulse de la tête du cortège, le FN est resté discret," ibid.; "L'hommage à Ilan Halimi a réuni toute la communauté juive," ibid.; and "Ilan Halimi, un an après," *Le Monde*, February 16, 2007.

77. Émilie Frèche, *La Mort d'un Pote* (Paris: Éditions du Panama, 2006), pp. 106–11.

78. Ibid., pp. 52–82. See also Malek Boutih (ex-president of SOS Racisme) in *NO*, March 2–8, 2006: "The Intifada has been invoked, the identification with the just Palestinian cause . . . the result, anti-Semitism has become commonplace. By dint of understanding it, there are those who have ended up justifying it."

79. "Antisemitism in France: The Terrible Tale of Ilan Halimi," *The Economist*, March 4, 2006, p. 40.

80. Daniel Ben-Simon, "Maman, I Murdered My Jew," *Haaretz*, Pesach supplement, April 5, 2004, pp. 6–10. See also Raphael Israeli, *Muslim Anti-Semitism*, p. 186.

81. Ibid., p. 8. See also Alain Chouffan, "La mort d'un DJ," *NO*, December 11–17, 2003, pp. 115–17.

82. Sebastien's brother concluded the interview with Daniel Ben-Simon as follows: "There is no future for the Jews in France. . . . It's hard for us already. For our children, it will be even harder."

83. See the remarks of Cukierman and Lional Jospin at the CRIF dinner, *L'Arche*, January–February 2002, pp. 82ff.

84. Leora Eren Frucht, "Liberté, Egalité . . . ," *The Jerusalem Post*, March 8, 2002.

85. "M. Chirac interpelle le gouvernement après les attentats antijuifs," *Le Monde*, April 2, 2002; "The French Moral Legion," *The Wall Street Journal*, April 5, 2002; Maurice Lévy, "Ne pas nommer l'antisémitisme, c'est l'accepter," *Le Monde*, April 20, 2002; Denis Jeambar, "Déchirure," *L'Express*, April 18–24, 2002.

86. Judith Waïntraub, "Raffarin promet la plus grande fermeté contre l'antisémitisme," *Le Figaro*, July 22, 2002.

87. Myriam Lévy, "Sanctions aggravées pour les délits racistes," *Le Parisien*, December 11, 2002.

88. Laurent Joffrin, "Antisémitisme: Silence interdit!" *NO*, November 21, 2002.

89. See "La bombe de l'antisémitisme au coeur de la présidentielle," *Marianne*, January 28–February 3, 2002; Maurice Szafran, "L'antisionisme comme moteur de la judéophobie," ibid., pp. 22–25; and the interviews with Daniel Ben-Saïd and Robert Redeker, ibid., pp. 26–27.

90. Paul Giniewski, "Les Juifs de France dans la tourmente de "L'Intifada des Banlieues," *Les dossiers du Lien*, October 21, 2002.

91. "French Jewish leader assails 'brown-green-red' coalition," *The Jewish Chronicle*, January 31, 2003.

92. "À Paris, 40,000 personnes ont fêté l'amitié entre la France et l'Israël," *Le Monde*, June 23, 2003; "Halte à l'antisémitisme" (editorial), ibid., November 17, 2003; "Les mesures gouvernementales pour lutter contre l'antisémitisme," ibid. See also "Antisémitisme: Chirac rassure avec des symboles," *Libération*, November 18, 2003.

93. "France condemns Malaysian premier's speech on Jews," *Haaretz*, October 20, 2003.

94. "France Moves Fast to Expel Muslims Preaching Hatred," *The Wall Street Journal*, August 9, 2004; Amnon Rubinstein, "The French Connection," *The Jerusalem Post*, August 14, 2004.

95. Jean Daniel, "A Poisoned 'J'Accuse' from America," *IHT*, September 20, 2004. Freddy Raphaël, "Le 'négationnisme' d'Ariel Sharon," *Le Monde*, September 27, 2004.

96. "Alain Ménargues quitte RFI," *Le Figaro*, October 19, 204; "L'affaire Ménargues,"

L'Arche, November–December 2004, pp. 44–79. See also Alain Ménargues, *Le Mur de Sharon* (Paris: France Inter et Presses de la Renaissance, 2004), pp. 50–62, 69–77. See also Naccache, *Contre Israël,* pp. 235–38.

97. "Chirac Unveils Policy Against Anti-Semitism," *IHT,* November 18, 2003.

98. Elaine Sciolino, "On French Streets, Mideast Fallout," *IHT,* December 4, 2003; " 'New Anti-Semitism' Is Worrying France," *Haaretz,* November 18, 2003.

99. Cécilia Gabison, "Les musulmans pratiquants ont plus de préjugés," *Le Figaro,* December 7, 2005.

100. Michel Gurfinkiel, "France's Jewish Problem," *Commentary,* July–August 2002; Craig S. Smith, "French Jews Tell of a New and Threatening Wave of Anti-Semitism," *The New York Times,* March 22, 2003; Gurfinkiel, "The French Devolution," *The Jerusalem Post,* January 2, 2004.

101. Brett Kline, "They'll Always Have Paris," *The Jerusalem Post,* March 20, 2005; Corinne Scemama, "La ruée française," *L'Express,* June 6, 2005; David Roche, "La majorité des Juifs de France ont leur boussole tournée vers Israël," *Actualité Juive,* July 27, 2006; Larry Derfner, "Vive Israël," *The Jerusalem Post,* October 13, 2006.

102. Derfner, "Vive Israël," pp. 14–15. See also Daniel Ben-Simon, "Monsieur, This Is Not the True France," *Haaretz,* December 26, 2003.

103. "Le malaise persistant des juifs de France," *Le Monde,* September 20, 2003.

104. Etgar Lefkovits, "Third of French Jews Send Children to Catholic Schools," *The Jerusalem Post,* April 5, 2007. A recent communal survey found that 36 percent of respondents said that their spouse was not Jewish—up from 30 percent in 2002.

105. "French JDL Defends Community," *The Jerusalem Post,* June 15, 2006.

106. "Minority Report: The Trouble with Integration," *The Economist,* October 28, 2006, pp. 11–12.

107. D. Ben-Simon in *Haaretz,* December 26, 2003.

108. Ibid. See also "A Safe Place to Live" (editorial), *Haaretz,* August 24, 2004.

109. For a detailed analysis, see John Rosenthal, "Beyond the Numbers Games: A Closer Look at the Statistics on Anti-Semitism and 'Islamophobia' in France," *Transatlantic Intelligencer* (2005), http://www.trans-int.com/quarterly/13-beyond-the-numbers-games-a-closer-look-at-the-sta.html.

110. Boris Thiolay, "Juif et alors?" *L'Express,* June 6, 2005.

111. "Rapport sur l'Antisémitisme en France" (Paris: Service de Protection de la Communauté Juive, 2007). This analysis was provided by Elisabeth Cohen-Tannoudji of the CRIF. See also "Hausse des violences antisémites selon le Crif," *Le Figaro,* February 27, 2007.

112. Emmanuel George-Picot, "A French 'Malaise' in the Fight Against Anti-Semitism," *The Jerusalem Post,* February 16, 2005.

113. CRIF report analyzing the events of July and August 2006 and the statistics published by the Protection Service of the Jewish Community, with reporting provided by Elisabeth Cohen-Tannoudji and Marc Knobel. See also http://www.crif.org/uploads/articles/fichiers/declarations_politiques.pdf.

114. Freddy Eytan, "Europe and the War in Lebanon," *Jerusalem Issue Brief* 6, no. 7 (August 16, 2006).

115. Devorah Lauter, "Anti-Semitic Violence Chases Jews from Paris Suburbs," *The Jerusalem Post,* April 3, 2008.

116. Daniel Ben Simon, "Paris Gang Strikes Again," *Ha'aretz,* March 6, 2008.

117. Nidra Poller, *Wall Street Journal Europe,* July 31, 2008.

118. Report by the Associated Press in the *IHT,* June 22, 2008. Also Raphael Israeli, *Muslim Anti-Semitism,* pp. 142–45.

119. Brett Kline, "Racial Tensions Rise to the Surface in Mixed Jewish-Muslim District in Paris," *Ha'aretz,* June 27, 2008.

120. Israeli, *Muslim Anti-Semitism,* p. 145.

121. Ibid., p. 144. See also Adam Sage, "Anti-Semitic Attack on Teenage Girl in Paris," *The Times,* January 8, 2009. The fifteen-year-old schoolgirl was insulted, knocked to the ground, kicked, and punched by a gang of ten Muslim youths from her own school in Villiers-le Bel north of Paris, as a punishment for the events in Gaza.

122. "Sarkozy attendu sur les fronts extérieurs," *Libération,* May 8, 2007; Freddy Eytan, "A Chance to Change French Foreign Policy," *The Jerusalem Post,* May 17, 2007.

123. See "The End of Anti-Americanism," *Newsweek,* September 10, 2007, pp. 16–20.

124. Charles Krauthammer, "The French Flip," *The Jerusalem Post,* October 2, 2007; "Kouchner accentue la pression sur l'Iran," *Le Figaro,* October 4, 2007; Daniel Vernet, "Bernard Kouchner, choisi pour impulser de l'air frais," *Le Monde,* October 4, 2007.

125. "A Survey of France: Beyond These Shores," *The Economist,* October 28, 2006, pp. 13–14.

126. "Olmert et Sarkozy souhaitent durcir les sanctions contre l'Iran," *Le Figaro,* October 23, 2007.

127. "Sarkozy Tells PM: Palestinian Refugees Will Not Return to Israel," *Haaretz,* October 23, 2007.

128. Adar Primor, "Sarkozy makes Peres his first official visitor," *Ha-aretz,* March 10, 2008.

129. "Polémique après des propos antisémites sur Nicolas Sarkozy prêté à un ministre algérien," *Le Monde,* November 28, 2007. See Albert Naccache, *Contre Israël,* pp. 292–96.

130. Haviv Rettig Gur, "Poll Finds France's View of Israel Nuanced," *The Jerusalem Post,* May 15, 2009.

Ten: Britain's Old-New Judeophobes

1. "Harry Sorry for Nazi Uniform Stunt," CNN.com, January 13, 2005, www.cnn.com/2005/WORLD/europe/01/12/harry.nazi/.

2. "Young Brits Back Harry's *Costume,*" *JTA,* January 17, 2005, www.jta.org/page_view_story.asp?intarticleid=149338intcategoryid=2.

3. See *Report of the All-Party Parliamentary Inquiry into Antisemitism* (London: The Stationery Office Limited, September 2006).

4. *CST Annual Review: Antisemitism and Jewish Communal Security in Britain in 2006* (London: Community Security Trust, 2007), p. 10. Also the *Antisemitic Incidents Report 2007* (London: CST, 2008). The figures for 2007 were the second worst ever recorded. See also Jonathan Freedland, "As British Jews Come Under Attack," *The Guardian,* February 4, 2009.

5. Robert S. Wistrich, "Playground for Jihad? The Case of Great Britain," in *Old Demons, New Debates: Anti-Semitism in the West,* ed. David Kertzer (New York: Holmes and Meier, 2005), pp. 81–92.

6. Melanie Phillips, "London: A Leftist Axis of Anti-Semitism," *Hadassah Magazine,* September 4, 2003.

7. Colin Holmes, *Anti-Semitism in British Society 1876–1939* (New York: Holmes and Meier, 1979).

8. Anthony Julius, "Anti-Semitism and the English Intelligentsia," in Kertzer, *Old Demons,* pp. 53–80.

9. Ibid., p. 55.

10. Bernard Glassman, *Anti-Semitic Stereotypes Without Jews: Images of the Jews in England, 1290–1700* (Detroit: Wayne State University Press, 1974). See also F. Felsenstein, *Anti-Semitic Stereotypes: A Paradigm of Otherness in English Popular Culture, 1660–1830* (Baltimore: Johns Hopkins University Press, 1995).

11. John Gross, "The Waning of the Old Stereotypes," *The Times Literary Supplement,* May 5, 1995.

12. See W. D. Rubinstein, *A History of the Jews in the English-Speaking World: Great Britain* (London: Macmillan, 1996), pp. 52–55.

13. Chaim Weizmann, *Trial and Error* (London: Hamish Hamilton, 1949), pp. 118–20.

14. Gisela C. Lebzelter, "Anti-Semitism—A Focal Point for the British Radical Right," *Nationalist and Racialist Movements in Britain and Germany Before 1914,* ed. Paul Kennedy and Anthony Nicholls (London: Macmillan, 1981), pp. 88–105.

15. *Hansard Parliamentary Debates,* 3d ser., vol. 151 (1905), p. 155. See also Lebzelter, "Anti-Semitism," p. 95.

16. Harry Defries, *Conservative Party Attitudes to Jews, 1900–1950* (London: Frank Cass, 2001), pp. 24, 27.

17. Shmuel Almog, "Antisemitism as a Dynamic Phenomenon: The 'Jewish Question' in England at the End of the First World War," *Patterns of Prejudice* 21, no. 4 (1987): pp. 3–18.

18. Ibid., p. 9.

19. See Leonard Stein, *The Balfour Declaration* (London: Vallentine Mitchell, 1961), pp. 496, 500–503, 518.

20. Edwin Montagu, *An Indian Diary* (London: W. Heinemann, 1930), p. 18.

21. James Malcolm, *Origins of the Balfour Declaration* (July 1944), p. 9. In St. Antony's College, Oxford, Middle East Archive. (Typed manuscript.)

22. See Gideon Shimoni, "Bein Tsionim ve-Mitbolelim Liberalim be-Anglia 1917–1947," in *Zionism and Its Jewish Opponents,* ed. H. Avni (Jerusalem: Hassifriya Haziyonit, 1990), pp. 115–24, in Hebrew.

23. On the virulent anti-Semitism of *The Morning Post,* see Rubinstein, *History of the Jews,* pp. 201–2, 206, 212; and *The Times* (London), July 3, 1922, and July 25, 1922, which was not immune to a milder form of the same disease.

24. *Daily Express,* November 3, 1922; and David Cesarani, "Anti-Zionist Politics and Political Antisemitism in Britain, 1920–1924," *Patterns of Prejudice* 23, no. 1 (1989): pp. 28–45.

25. Lord Beaverbrook, "Bag and Baggage," *Daily Express,* November 5, 1922; and *Sunday Express,* February 18, 1923.

26. Lebzelter, "Anti-Semitism," p. 98.
27. Rubinstein, *History of the Jews*, p. 203.
28. Winston S. Churchill, "Zionism Versus Bolshevism," *Illustrated Sunday Herald,* February 8, 1920. See also Michael Makovsky, *Churchill's Promised Land: Zionism and Statecraft* (New Haven, Conn.: Yale University Press, 2007), pp. 69–97.
29. See Norman Cohn, *Warrant for Genocide* (London: Penguin Books, 1970), pp. 78, 166–71.
30. Robert Speaight, *The Life of Hilaire Belloc* (London: Hollis and Carter, 1957), p. 453.
31. A. N. Wilson, *Hilaire Belloc* (London: Hamish Hamilton, 1984), p. 362; and Rubinstein, *History of the Jews*, pp. 137–38.
32. See Bryan Cheyette's chapter on George Bernard Shaw and H. G. Wells in his *Constructions of 'The Jew' in English Literature and Society* (Cambridge: Cambridge University Press, 1994), pp. 94–149; and Cheyette, "Who Poisoned Wells?" *The Jewish Chronicle,* February 5, 1993.
33. See Anthony Julius, *T. S. Eliot, Anti-Semitism, and Literary Form* (Cambridge: Cambridge University Press, 1996); Louis Menand, "Eliot and the Jews," *The New York Review of Books,* June 6, 1996; Wendy Lesser, "The T. S. Eliot Problem," *The New York Times Book Review,* June 6, 1996, p. 31; David Bradshaw, "T. S. Eliot and the Major Sources of Literary Anti-Semitism in the 1930s," *The Times Literary Supplement,* July 5, 1996.
34. Bradshaw, "T. S. Eliot," pp. 14–15.
35. W. F. Mandle, *Anti-Semitism and the British Union of Fascists* (London: Longmans Green, 1968); Richard Thurlow, *Fascism in Britain: A History (1918–45)* (Oxford: Basil Blackwell, 1987); and Roger Griffin, ed., *Fascism* (Oxford: Oxford University Press, 1995), pp. 173–81.
36. Tony Kushner, *The Persistence of Prejudice: Antisemitism in British Society During the Second World War* (Manchester, U.K.: Manchester University Press, 1989), pp. 78–133. See also Kushner, *The Holocaust and the Liberal Imagination: A Social and Cultural History* (Oxford, U.K.: Blackwell, 1994); and David Cesarani, "Great Britain," in *The World Reacts to the Holocaust,* ed. David S. Wyman (Baltimore: Johns Hopkins University Press, 1996), pp. 599–641.
37. Wistrich, *Hitler and the Holocaust*, pp. 197–215.
38. C. R. Ashbee, *Palestine Notebook* (London: Heinemann, 1923), pp. 35–36.
39. Ronald Storrs, *Orientations* (London: Nicholson and Watson, 1947).
40. Nathaniel Katzburg, ed., *Mediniut Britannia ba-eretz Israel, 1940–1945* (Jerusalem: Yad Itzhak Ben-Zvi Publications, 1976), pp. 56–63.
41. Quoted in Sidney Sugerman, *The Unrelenting Conflict: Britain, Balfour, and Betrayal* (Sussex, U.K.: The Book Guild, 2000), p. 121. A great deal of evidence is provided in this book for the bias of British mandatory officials against the Jews in Palestine.
42. Bartley Crum, *Behind the Silken Curtain* (New York: Simon and Schuster, 1947), pp. 71–72. See also Sugerman, *Unrelenting Conflict*, pp. 185–86.
43. James G. McDonald, *My Mission in Israel, 1948–1951* (London: Gollanz, 1951), pp. 22–24.
44. Richard Crossman, *A Nation Reborn* (London: Hamish Hamilton, 1960), pp. 69–72.

45. Ibid. British Labour prime minister Clement Attlee was no less hostile toward the Zionists. He bitterly reproached Crossman for the Committee of Inquiry's report, which "let us down by giving way to the Jews and the Americans."

46. Sugerman, *Unrelenting Conflict*, p. 200.

47. *The Jewish Chronicle*, August 1, 8, 15, 22, and 29, 1947. See also Simon Garfield, *Our Hidden Lives: The Remarkable Diaries of Post-War Britain* (London: Ebury Press, 2005), pp. 432–33.

48. A. P. Wadsworth, "In the Wrong," *Manchester Guardian*, May 21, 1948. For the subsequent shift in attitudes at *The Guardian* newspaper, see the officially commissioned book by Israeli leftist Daphna Baram, *Disenchantment: The Guardian and Israel* (London: Guardian Books, 2004), intended to refute charges of bias against Israel.

49. Benny Morris, *The Road to Jerusalem, Glubb Pasha, Palestine and the Jews* (London: I. B. Tauris, 2002), pp. 21–23. See also John Glubb, *Peace in the Holy Land: An Historical Analysis of the Palestine Problem* (London: Hodder and Stoughton, 1971), pp. 61–64.

50. Morris, *Road to Jerusalem*, pp. 24–26. See also Glubb, *Peace in the Holy Land*, p. 108, where Cromwell's massacre of the Irish was explained as another consequence of the Hebraic strand in English history, influenced by biblical calls for "genocide."

51. Morris, *Road to Jerusalem*, p. 29.

52. Ibid., pp. 81–82.

53. See Arnold J. Toynbee, *A Study of History*, vol. 8 (London: Oxford University Press, 1954); and Yaacov Herzog, *A People That Dwells Alone* (London, 1975), pp. 21–24, for a refutation of these propositions.

54. Toynbee, *Study of History*, vol. 4: p. 94.

55. Ibid., vol. 8: p. 289.

56. Richard Crossman, *Palestine Mission* (New York, 1977), p. 59; and Rory Miller, *Divided Against Zion* (London: Frank Cass, 2000), pp. 82–120.

57. Miller, *Divided Against Zion*, pp. 144–45.

58. Julian Franklyn, "Israel: State or Religion?" *Contemporary Review* 172, no. 979 (July 1947): p. 38.

59. Miller, *Divided Against Zion*, pp. 23–54, 148.

60. See Oskar K. Rabinowicz, *Arnold Toynbee on Judaism and Zionism: A Critique* (London: W. H. Allen, 1974), pp. 288–309.

61. See Rory Miller, "British Anti-Zionism Then and Now," *Covenant* 1, no. 2 (April 2007). See http://www.covenant.idc.ac.il/en/volI/issue2/miller.html, accessed May 2, 2007.

62. *The Pro-Arab Lobby in Britain* (IJA research report, nos. 22–23, December 1981).

63. Michael Adams and Christopher Mayhew, *Publish It Not* (London: Longman, 1975), pp. 26–65. For a more reliable assessment of this history, see Josef Gorny, *The British Labour Movement and Zionism, 1917–1948* (London: Frank Cass, 1983).

64. Adams and Mayhew, *Publish It Not*, pp. 66–87.

65. Patrick Marnham, "Is Israel Racist?" *The Spectator*, March 6, 1976.

66. David Cesarani, "Anti-Zionism in Britain, 1922–2002: Continuities and Discontinuities," *Journal of Israeli History* 25, no. 1 (March 2006): pp. 131–60.

67. Wistrich, "Left-Wing Anti-Zionism in Western Societies," pp. 46–52.

68. D. Cesarani, "The Perdition Affair," in Wistrich, *Anti-Zionism and Anti-Semitism,* pp. 53–62.

69. Quoted in Michael Billig, "Anti-Jewish Themes and the British Far Left," pts. 1 and 2, *Patterns of Prejudice* 18, no. 1 (1984): pp. 3–14, and ibid., vol. 18, no. 2 (1984): pp. 28–34.

70. See Robert S. Wistrich, *Revolutionary Jews from Marx to Trotsky* (London: Harrap, 1976).

71. Tony Greenstein, *Zionism: Antisemitism's Twin in Jewish Garb* (Brighton Labour Briefing Discussion Document, 1982).

72. *Sussex Front,* January 1983, quoted in Billig, "Anti-Jewish Themes," *Patterns of Prejudice* 18, no. 2 (1984): p. 32.

73. See the letters page of the *New Statesman,* July 11, 1980, p. 49, "The Socialism of Fools."

74. *The News Line,* "The Moment of Historical Truth" (editorial) June 11, 1982. The editorial concluded with a pledge "not to rest until the Palestinian flag flies over Jerusalem as the capital of a free Palestine." See also "Israelis Brand Civilians," *The News Line,* June 18, 1982; and "Horror Gas for Beirut," ibid., June 30, 1982.

75. "Zionist Dachau," *The News Line,* July 10, 1982.

76. "Palestine Will Triumph," *The News Line,* July 10, 1982.

77. Ken Livingstone, "Why Labour Must Back Palestinian Rights," *Labour Herald,* July 30, 1982. Livingstone's speech included a wholly misleading claim that the forefathers of the Palestinian people had lived in the country for two thousand years; there was no suggestion that Jews had any historic connection to Israel or right to their own independent state. At the time Livingstone was coeditor (with Ted Knight) of *Labour Herald.*

78. Sean Matgamna, "Gerry Healy Discovers the World Jewish Conspiracy," *Socialist Organiser,* April 14, 1983, p. 13. See "The Zionist Connection," *The News Line,* April 9, 1983, which provoked the debate. Also "We Expose BBC Witch-Hunt," *The News Line,* March 19, 1983.

79. Neil Cohen and Matthew Kalman, "Opening the Floodgates," *The Jerusalem Post,* June 18, 1985, p. 5.

80. "Zionism and the Holocaust," *Labour Herald,* March 19, 1982. The paper was happy to use Jewish ultra-Orthodox material (Rebbe Moshe Shonfield), texts such as *Perfidy* by a prominent Hollywood scriptwriter and right-wing Zionist (Ben Hecht), as well as Palestinian propaganda (Faris Yahya) to bolster the anti-Zionist case. See also Gerry Ben-Noah, "Rewriting the Holocaust," *Socialist Organiser,* October 4, 1984, p. 8.

81. See Anthony Julius, "How the Jewish Conspiracy Myth Still Flourishes," *The Jewish Chronicle,* September 7, 2007.

82. John Mearsheimer and Stephan Walt, "The Israel Lobby," *London Review of Books,* March 23, 2006, pp. 3–12; and Michael Massing, "The Storm Over the Israel Lobby," *The New York Review of Books,* June 8, 2006.

83. Interview with Tam Dalyell, *Vanity Fair,* May 2003.

84. See Dave Hyde, "Two Tribes: Europe's Other Red-Green Alliance," *The Review* (Melbourne), July 2003, p. 26.

85. Ibid., p. 27.

86. For the wider context, see Ye'or, *Eurabia,* pp. 111–15, 176–89, 253–60.

87. Douglas Davis, "Why I Won't Talk to the BBC," *The Spectator,* May 25, 2002. See also Davis, "Hatred in the Air: The BBC, Israel, and Antisemitism," in *A New Anti-semitism? Debating Judeophobia in 21st-Century Britain,* ed. Paul Iganski and Barry Kosmin (London: Profile Books, 2003), pp. 130–47.

88. Trevor Asserson and Elisheva Mironi, *The BBC and the Middle East: A Critical Study,* http://www.bbcwatch.com/Reports/Report_1.pdf. See also the interview with Asserson "What Went Wrong at the BBC," *Jerusalem Viewpoints,* January 15, 2004.

89. See "Report Blasts BBC's Portrayal of IDF," *The Jerusalem Post,* July 9, 2003.

90. Daniel Seaman, "Can the BBC Operate Responsibly?" *The Jerusalem Post,* July 15, 2003.

91. See Bret Stephens, "Anti-Semitism in Three Steps," *The Jerusalem Post,* July 3, 2003.

92. Barbara Amiel, "Disinfect the BBC Before It Poisons a New Generation," *The Daily Telegraph,* July 9, 2003.

93. Douglas Davis, "Gilligan's Island," *The Review* (Melbourne) August 2003, p. 15.

94. Tzvi Fleischer, "Beeb Outdoes Itself," *The Review* (Melbourne) September 2003, p. 8.

95. Trevor Asserson and Lee Kern, "The BBC's Double Standards: Israel and the War on Iraq," *Justice* 36 (Autumn 2003): pp. 17–24. See also Barbara Amiel, "How Can the BBC Be Impartial Between Tyranny and Democracy?" *The Daily Telegraph,* March 26, 2003, which exposes the extraordinary partiality of the BBC's Arabic service. Like Palestinan terror, Arab tyranny was literally invisible before the Iraq War to the broadcasters on this highly influential news medium, which reaches millions of listeners in the Middle East and beyond.

96. See Robin Lustig, "Sharon's OK Corral," *The Guardian,* January 28, 2001. This BBC documentary was, in fact, a dreary tissue of half truths, distortions, and omissions.

97. See Ted Honderich, *After the Terror* (Edinburgh: Edinburgh University Press, 2003), pp. 96, 156–69, for his legitimization of Palestinian violence against the "state terrorism" of Israel, depicted as a vicious racist state.

98. Jenni Frazer, "Affair to Forget," *The Jewish Chronicle,* September 6, 2002, p. 54. See also Gerald Kaufman, "The Case for Sanctions Against Israel," *The Guardian,* July 12, 2004. See also the AP report in *Haaretz,* January 16, 2009, quoting Kaufman as also damning Israel for allegedly justifying its "murder" of Palestinians by "cynical" references to the Holocaust.

99. This Channel 4 program was broadcast on August 24, 2002. It was called *A Dangerous Liaison: Israel and America.* Among the interviewees was the late Edward Said, who labeled Zionists as "ethnic cleansers" and wicked racists who looked down on the Arab natives in Palestine as "second-rate niggers."

100. The program, entitled *Palestine Is Still the Issue,* was broadcast on September 17, 2002. See Simon Round, "Pilger Is the Issue," *The Jewish Chronicle,* September 20, 2002; and "Critics Slam Pilger's Bias," *London Jewish News,* September 20, 2002. The Board of Deputies of British Jews called it an "outrageous piece of journalism, littered with lies and libels." See also John Pilger, "When My Film Is Under Fire," *The Guardian,* September 23, 2002.

101. Stephan Pollard, "A Massacre of the Truth," *The Guardian,* September 24, 2002. See

also John Pilger's diatribe the previous day against the "Zionist lobby," *The Guardian*, September 23, 2002, which defended his film and predictably accused his critics of conspiring to suppress the truth.

102. Stephen Pollard, "Is the BBC's Coverage of Israel Unfair?" *The Jewish Chronicle*, August 4, 2006; and Pollard, "Don't Boycott the BBC," *The Jerusalem Post*, August 15, 2006.

103. Tom Gross, "Jeningrad: What the British Media Said," *National Review*, May 13, 2002.

104. A. N. Wilson, "A Demon We Can't Afford to Ignore," *Evening Standard*, April 15, 2002. See also Wilson, "The Tragic Reality of Israel," *Evening Standard*, October 22, 2001, which concluded that the 1948 experiment claiming "Israelis" had a "right to exist" was doomed to failure. Israel was from the beginning an "aggressor" by virtue of its establishment.

105. Lead editorial, *The Guardian*, April 17, 2002. After the release of the UN report, *The Guardian* pretended that its findings confirmed "what we said last April"—namely that "the destruction in Jenin looked and smelled like a crime." This is quite untrue.

106. Janine di Giovanni, in *The Times* (London), April 16, 2002. See also the favorable discussion of *The Guardian*'s coverage of Jenin in Daphna Baram, *Disenchantment*, pp. 237–51.

107. "Amid the Ruins, the Grisly Evidence of a War Crime," *The Independent*, April 16, 2002. See also the editorial in *Haaretz*, April 21, 2002, "There Was No Massacre in Jenin."

108. Gross's remark as quoted by Ori Golan, "In Poisoned English," *The Jerusalem Post*, March 28, 2003.

109. "The Jewish Faith Is Not an Evil Religion," *The Sun*, April 15, 2002. Some of the tabloids, it is worth noting, have a better understanding and more empathy for Israel's predicament than the so-called quality press.

110. See Peter Beaumont, "The New Anti-Semitism?" *The Guardian*, February 17, 2002, and the readers' responses over the following week. Also Beaumont, "Are We Anti-Semitic?" *The Observer*, February 12, 2002; and Seumas Milne, "This Slur of Anti-Semitism Is Used to Defend Repression," *The Guardian*, May 9, 2002.

111. See "A New Anti-Semitism? Not to Be Confused with Anti-Sharonism," *The Guardian*, January 26, 2002. An Israeli writer, Schlomi Segall, *The Guardian*, July 5, 2002, alleged that "by branding any criticism of the suffering he inflicts on the Palestinians as anti-Semitic, Sharon is enlisting something sacred for the vile colonial and expansionist ends he pursues." The Israeli anti-Zionist voices have usually been among the most strident and unbalanced in this kind of argument.

112. William Dalrymple, "Bullied into Silence on Israel," *The Guardian*, March 16, 2001. See also Robert Fisk, "How to Shut Up Your Critics with a Single Word," *The Independent*, October 21, 2002.

113. See Peter Pulzer, "The New Anti-Semitism, or When Is a Taboo Not a Taboo?" in Iganski and Kosmin, *A New Antisemitism?* pp. 79–101.

114. Mick Hume, "The Anti-imperialism of Fools," *New Statesman*, June 17, 2002, pp. 29–31.

115. A. N. Wilson, "The State of the Nation," *Evening Standard*, October 29, 2001.

116. A. N. Wilson, "Israel's Record Speaks for Itself," *Evening Standard,* February 2, 2003, p. 13. See also Winston Pickett, "Nasty or Nazi? The Use of Antisemitic Topoi by the Liberal-Left Media," in Iganski and Kosmin, *A New Antisemitism?* pp. 160–62.

117. Brian Sewell, "Biblical Tales," *Evening Standard,* June 25, 2002.

118. Max Hastings, "A Grotesque Choice: Israel's Repression of the Palestinian People Is Fuelling a Resurgence of Antisemitism," *The Guardian,* March 11, 2004.

119. Julie Burchill, "The Hate That Shames Us," *The Guardian,* December 6, 2003.

120. Julie Burchill, "Good, Bad and Ugly," *The Guardian,* November 29, 2003. See also Emanuele Ottolenghi, "Anti-Zionism Is Anti-Semitism," in ibid.

121. Burchill, "Good, Bad and Ugly." The outspoken Richard Ingrams, former editor of the popular satirical magazine *Private Eye,* has been unremittingly hostile to Israel over the years, and his comments have sometimes carried a whiff of English public-school anti-Semitism. His offending column appeared in the *Sunday Observer.*

122. Quoted in Barry Kosmin and Paul Iganski, "Crossing the Line from Criticism to Bigotry," *IHT,* September 8, 2003. See also Richard Ingrams, "A Futile Pursuit," *The Guardian,* September 11, 2005, and his piece "It's About Time Someone Spoke Out," *The Independent,* September 8, 2007.

123. Deborah Orr, "I'm Fed Up Being Called an Anti-Semite," *The Independent,* December 21, 2001. Richard Ingrams also attacked Barbara Amiel for lacking objectivity since she was Jewish. See "Amiel's Animus," *The Observer,* July 13, 2003.

124. See *The Independent,* October 9, 2002.

125. "The Architecture of Bigotry" (Jerusalem: Institute of the World Jewish Congress, policy dispatch no. 80, June 2002).

126. David Landau, "Jewish Angst in Albion," *Haaretz,* January 23, 2002.

127. Melanie Phillips, "The Chosen Person," *Haaretz,* November 7, 2003, and Phillips, "Return of the Old Hatred," *The Observer,* February 22, 2004.

128. See Robert S. Wistrich, "UK Has Become European Center of Anti-Semitism," *The Jerusalem Post,* April 1, 2008, and the debate that followed in its pages. The British ambassador to Israel Tom Phillips, "British Jews Are Free from Fear," ibid. April 2, 2008, and Henry Grunwald, president of the Board of Deputies of British Jews, responded sharply. Grunwald's "We're Alright, Professor Wistrich," ibid. April 3, 2008, has been comprehensively refuted by events. Nearly all of the letter writers in the next two weeks agreed with the author of this book, providing chapter and verse for the anti-Semitism they had personally experienced in Britain.

129. Quoted by Landau, "Jewish Angst in Albion." See also Daniella Peled, "A Darkness Falls on England," *The Jerusalem Post,* February 16, 2005; and "Anti-Semitism: An Enduring Virus," *The Economist,* November 22, 2003, p. 70.

130. See "Our Dulled Nerve," *The Guardian,* November 18, 2003, for an editorial on the subject.

131. Ibid.

132. See Denis MacShane, *Globalising Hatred: The New Antisemitism* (London: Weidenfeld and Nicolson, 2008), pp. 26–30.

133. Jonathan Freedland, "As British Jews," *The Guardian,* February 4, 2009.

134. R. Israeli, *Muslim Anti-Semitism,* pp. 104–6.

135. Dave Rich, "Holocaust Denial—An anti-Zionist Tool for the European Far-Left," *Post-Holocaust Antisemitism*, 65, February 1, 2008 (Jerusalem Center for Public Affairs).

ELEVEN: THE RED-GREEN AXIS

1. *Report of the All-Party Parliamentary Inquiry into Antisemitism* (London: The Stationery Office, September 2006), pp. 38–42.
2. See *CST Antisemitic Incidents Report 2006* (London: CST, 2007) for the most up-to-date survey of the violence.
3. "Jews Far More Likely to Be Victims of Faith Hatred than Muslims," *Sunday Telegraph*, December 17, 2006.
4. Joanna Bale and Anthony Browne, "Attacks on Jews Soar Since Lebanon," *The Times* (London), September 2, 2006.
5. Ibid.
6. *Antisemitic Incidents Report 2007* (London: CST, 2008).
7. "UK Anti-Semitic Incidents Rise," *The Jewish Chronicle*, January 26, 2005.
8. "31 Per Cent Jump in Anti-Semitic Incidents in Great Britain," *The Jerusalem Post*, February 2, 2007.
9. *CST Antisemitic Incidents Report 2005* (London: CST, 2006), p. 11.
10. Ken Livingstone, "This Is About Israel, Not Anti-Semitism," *The Guardian*, March 4, 2005. The mayor of London also falsely accused MEMRI (The Middle East Media Research Institute) of selectively translating from Arabic to present Arabs "in the worst possible light" and of demonizing Muslims in general. Both claims are untrue.
11. "Mayor Rejects Final Call for Contrition," *The Jewish Chronicle*, February 2, 2005; "Red Ken Strikes Again," *The Jerusalem Post*, March 7, 2005; and Yossi Melman, "Red Ken's True Colours," *Haaretz*, August 22, 2005.
12. "Going Backwards," *The Jewish Chronicle*, March 24, 2006.
13. "Livingstone Wins a Stay of Suspension," *The Jerusalem Post*, March 1, 2006; Jill Sherman, "Gaffe Lands Livingstone Back in Trouble," *Times Online*, March 22, 2006, http://www.timesonline.co.uk/tol/news/uk/article744045.ece.
14. "The Loutish Mayor," *Times Online*, March 23, 2006; and "Red-Faced Ken," *The Economist*, April 1, 2006, p. 32.
15. Colin Schindler, "What Makes 'Red Ken' Tick?" *The Jerusalem Post*, October 19, 2005. See also David Hirsh, *Anti-Zionism and Antisemitism: Cosmopolitan Reflections* (New Haven, Conn.: Yale Initiative for the Interdisciplinary Study of Antisemitism, 2007), pp. 36–40.
16. "The Chancer," *The Economist*, January 13, 2007, p. 32. See also Steven Stalinsky, "Sheikh Yousef Al-Qaradawi in London to Establish 'The International Council of Muslim Clerics,' " *MEMRI Special Report*, no. 30 (July 8, 2004), on Sheikh al-Qaradhawi.
17. Stalinsky, "Sheikh Yousef Al-Qaradawi"; and Manfred Gerstenfeld, interview with Robert S. Wistrich, "Something Is Rotten in the State of Europe," *Post-Holocaust and Anti-Semitism*, no. 25 (October 1, 2004).

18. *Al-Hayat* (London), February 19, 2005; Al-Jazeera TV (Qatar), February 18, 2005; *Al-Sharq* (Qatar), February 20, 2005.

19. Alan Dershowitz, "Why Defend Bigotry?" *The Jerusalem Post,* March 14, 2006.

20. "Anti-Semitic Battleground in London's East End," *The Jerusalem Post,* April 29, 2005. See also "British MP George Galloway on Al-Jazeera: Calls for Bush, Blair, Koizumi, and Berlusconi to Stand Trial," *MEMRI Special Dispatch Series,* no. 918 (June 8, 2005); and "British MP George Galloway in Syria: Foreigners Are Raping Two Beautiful Arab Daughters: Jerusalem and Baghdad," *MEMRI Special Dispatch Series,* no. 948 (August 3, 2005).

21. "Jewish MP Pelted with Eggs," *The Daily Telegraph,* April 11, 2005.

22. Yaakov Lappin, "Speakers at London Rally Call for Israel's Destruction," *The Jerusalem Post,* May 22, 2005.

23. Ibid.

24. Robin Shepherd, "Blind Hatred," *The Jerusalem Post,* September 29, 2004.

25. Fania Oz-Salzberger, "Israelis Need Not Apply," *The Wall Street Journal,* May 8, 2005, and Edward Alexander, "The Academic Boycott of Israel: Back to 1933?" *The Jerusalem Post,* January 3, 2003; "Wars of the Roses," *The Jewish Chronicle,* January 31, 2003. See also Ronnie Fraser, "The Academic Boycott of Israel: Why Britain?" in *Academics Against Israel and the Jews,* ed. Manfred Gerstenfeld (Jerusalem: Jerusalem Center for Public Affairs, 2007), pp. 198–213.

26. Anat Koren, "Israeli Hate Campaign Hits London Streets," *London Jewish News,* supplement, September 2002.

27. "I Wish Eighty or Ninety Jews Would Die with Each Bomb," Jewish Comment .com, October 11, 2003, http://www.jewishcomment.com/cgibin/news.cgi?id=11& command=shownews&newsid=569.

28. Ibid.

29. Ibid.

30. Editorial, *The Times* (London), April 25, 2005.

31. Alan Cowell, "A British Teachers' Union Weighs a Boycott of Israeli Teachers," *The New York Times,* May 14, 2006, quotes Shalom Lappin, philosophy professor at King's College, London, describing the boycott as "a form of inquisition, of McCarthyism."

32. Martin Peretz, "Academic Press," *The New Republic,* May 30, 2006.

33. Alan Cowell, "British Journalists Call for Boycott of Israeli Goods," *IHT,* April 16, 2007. On the British trade union boycott of Israeli goods, see Jonny Paul, "Histadrut to cut ties with UK Union," *The Jerusalem Post,* July 8, 2007.

34. See Alan Cowell, "Should British Academics, or Rock Bands, Boycott Israel?" *The New York Times,* May 30, 2007; and Bradley Burston, "Boycotting Israel as Moral Masturbation," *Haaretz,* May 31, 2007. The resolutions in favor of the boycott were passed.

35. Anthony Julius and Alan Dershowitz, "The Contemporary Fight Against Anti-Semitism," *Times Online,* June 13, 2007, http://www.timesonline.co.uk/tol/ comment/columnists/guest_contributors/article1928865.ece. The authors also noted that "the boycott has been an essential tool of anti-Semites for at least a thousand years." It was always designed to injure Jews (and now the Jewish state) as well as denying them freedoms and rights enjoyed by non-Jews.

36. "Boycotting Israel," *Financial Times,* May 31, 2007. See also Hirsh, *Anti-Zionism and Antisemitism,* pp. 68–90.

37. Thomas L. Friedman, "A Boycott Built on Bias," *The New York Times,* June 17, 2007.

38. "Boycotting Israel: New Pariah on the Block," *The Economist,* September 15, 2007, pp. 80–81. See also "Boycotting Universities: Slamming Israel, Giving Palestinians a Free Pass," ibid., June 14, 2007. Condemnations of the UCU vote came from the Royal Society, the Academy of Medical Sciences, and Universities UK.

39. *The Economist,* June 14, 2007. According to a poll of key British business, cultural, and political leaders, 86 percent opposed an academic boycott of Israel.

40. "British Labor Union Approves Motion to Boycott Israel," *The Jerusalem Post,* June 22, 2007. See also Hirsh, *Anti-Zionism and Antisemitism,* pp. 70–73, for a chronology of the trade union campaign for a boycott.

41. Manfred Gerstenfeld, "Boycott Battle Won: The War Goes On," *The Jerusalem Post,* October 2, 2007.

42. Ben Cohen, "The Persistence of Antisemitism on the British Left," *Jewish Political Studies* 16, nos. 3–4 (Fall 2004): pp. 157–69.

43. Paul Foot, "In Defence of Oppression," *The Guardian,* March 5, 2002.

44. Michael Gove, "The New Left Inherits a Tradition of Hatred," *The Times* (London), February 19, 2002; Robert S. Wistrich, "The New Israelophobes," *The Jerusalem Post,* March 3, 2004. See also John Rose, *The Myths of Zionism* (London: Pluto, 2004) for the anti-Zionist case.

45. Robert S. Wistrich, "A New 'Jewish Question'?" *The Jerusalem Report,* March 19, 2007. As I pointed out in this article, vociferous opposition to Israel has become the "entry ticket" to acceptance, the dividing line between "good" Jews and "bad" in much of the liberal Western media.

46. Ibid., p. 47.

47. Howard Jacobson, "It's time to end the vilification of Israel," *The Independent,* June 11, 2007. Jacobson points out, "It is a false syllogism which goes: Criticism of Israel is not anti-Semitic; I am a critic of Israel; therefore I am not an anti-Semite."

48. Richard Littlejohn, "The New Anti-Semitism: How the Left Reversed History to Bring Judaism Under Attack," *Daily Mail,* July 6, 2007.

49. Ibid. Littlejohn, like John Mann, is not Jewish, but when he decided to make a television program on anti-Semitism in Britain, nobody could comprehend "why a non-Jew would be in the slightest bit interested in investigating it."

50. See *Report of the All-Party Parliamentary Inquiry,* pp. 52–56, for a summary of its conclusions and recommendations. It specifically condemned selective boycotts like that of the UCU as "anti-Jewish in practice."

51. Denis MacShane, "The New Antisemitism," *The Washington Post,* September 4, 2007.

52. Ibid. I had the pleasure of giving evidence to the committee on precisely this issue.

53. See Pickett, "Nasty or Nazi?" pp. 155–57. See also Anthony Julius, "Anti-Semitism and the English Intelligentsia," in Kertzer, *Old Demons, New Debates,* pp. 76–78.

54. "Harvard Jewish Community Relieved by Poets' Cancellation," *The Jerusalem Post,* November 14, 2002. On the reinvitation, see ibid., November 22, 2002.

55. Quoted in Pickett, "Nasty or Nazi?" pp. 156–57.

56. *Al-Ahram Weekly Online,* April 4–10, 2002, http://weekly.ahram.org.eg/2002/580/

cu2htm. The adoption of Nazi terminology and mental habits while professing antiracist or anti-Nazi convictions is indeed striking.

57. Ibid. See also Howard Jacobson in *The Independent*, April 20, 2002, where he took Paulin to task for equating Zionism with Nazism. *The Daily Telegraph*, April 23, 2002, observed that "progressive intellectuals" evidently felt free to attack Jews with impunity.

58. See Julius, "Anti-Semitism and the English Literary Intelligentsia," pp. 78–79. Julius notes that within this discourse, acknowledging the violent death of *Jewish* children seems inconceivable. Hence, Paulin keeps from his readers any idea that Israeli children have been deliberately targeted and massacred by Palestinian terrorists.

59. Tom Paulin, "On Being Dealt the Anti-Semitic Card," *The Guardian*, January 8, 2003. Paulin has insisted on a number of occasions that he is a resolute opponent of anti-Semitism even as he continuously demonizes the Jewish state.

60. *The Independent*, January 27, 2003, for Dave Brown's cartoon. See also Robert S. Wistrich, "Cruel Britannia: Anti-Semitism Among the Ruling Elites," *Azure* 21 (Summer 2005), pp. 108–9.

61. "Independent Cartoon Sparks Protests Over 'Anti-Semitism,' " *The Jewish Chronicle*, January 31, 2003. Ned Temko, writing in *The Independent*, January 31, 2003, was appalled at this use of the classic blood libel of Jews murdering Gentile children for their blood. In the same issue, Dave Brown denied all charges, saying he was influenced artistically by Goya's painting *Saturn Devouring His Son*.

62. "Cartoon Jews," *The Jerusalem Post*, December 1, 2003.

63. Bernard Harrison, *The Resurgence of Antisemitism: Jews, Israel and Liberal Opinion* (Lanham, Md.: Rowman and Littlefield, 2006), pp. 27–52.

64. Letter to the editor, *New Statesman*, January 21, 2002.

65. Peter Wilby, "The *New Statesman* and Anti-Semitism," *New Statesman*, February 11, 2002, pp. 9–10.

66. Harrison, *Resurgence of Antisemitism*, pp. 38–50. See also John Pilger, "Blair Meets with Arafat but Supports Sharon" and Dennis Sewell, "A Kosher Conspiracy," both in *New Statesman*, January 14, 2002.

67. "Anti-Semitism: Tam O'slander," *The Economist*, May 8, 2003. See also *The Scotsman*, May 5, 2003, where Dalyell added: "A Jewish cabal have [*sic*] taken over the government of the United States and formed an unholy alliance with fundamentalist Christians."

68. Douglas Davis, "Letter from London," *The Jerusalem Post*, May 5, 2003. See also Julie Burchill, "Good, Bad and Ugly," *The Guardian*, November 2003, explaining why she was leaving the newspaper. She made it clear she did not accept "the modern libel line that anti-Zionism is entirely different from anti-Semitism."

69. Andrew Alexander in the *Daily Mail*, May 9, 2003, worried that Britain was risking Arab terrorist retaliation and jihad "by pulling Israel's chestnuts out of the fire."

70. Tony Blair, "America, Don't Ever Apologize for Your Values," *The Wall Street Journal*, July 18, 2003. Blair defined the "war on terror" as a fight against "religious fanaticism" and to spread the light of liberty and democracy around the world.

71. "Blair Asks London Mayor to Apologize for Nazi Slur," *The Jerusalem Post*, February 12, 2005. See also "Blair Proud to Be a Friend of the Jewish People," ibid., October 27, 2006.

72. See Gordon Brown, "My Pledge on Holocaust Education," *Jewish Chronicle*, February 29, 2008, and Jonny Paul, "Brown Lauds Israel as 'Symbol of Hope,'" *The Jerusalem Post*, October 8, 2008.

73. Andrew Sullivan, *The Sunday Times*, October 20, 2002.

74. Hyde, "Two Tribes," pp. 25–27. See also Nick Cohen, "The Left's Unholy Alliance with Religious Bigotry," *The Guardian*, February 23, 2003. Cohen, despite his name, is not Jewish but reports that he receives a flood of defamatory email whenever he touches on subjects relating to Israel or Islam.

75. Mark Strauss, "Antiglobalism's Jewish Problem," *Foreign Policy*, October 28, 2003.

76. Hume, "Anti-Imperialism of Fools," pp. 29–31.

77. Ibid., p. 31. Hume quotes Naomi Klein, a Jewish critic of both the Israeli occupation and globalization as saying: "Every time I lock on to activist news sites such as indymedia.org [the main anti-globalist website] . . . I'm confronted with a string of Jewish conspiracy theories about 9/11 and excerpts from the *Protocols of the Elders of Zion*."

78. See *The Times* (London), June 19, 2002, "Cherie Blair's Suicide Bomb Blunder."

79. "What Cherie Really Thinks," *The Daily Telegraph*, June 19, 2002.

80. Douglas Davis, "MP Sacked for Bomber Remark," *The Jerusalem Post*, January 25, 2004.

81. "UK Baroness Accused of Anti-Semitic Comments," *The Jerusalem Post*, September 21, October 15, and November 29, 2006. On the controversies arising from the Mearsheimer-Walt book in the U.K., see Anthony Julius, "How the Jewish Conspiracy Myth Still Flourishes," *Jewish Chronicle*, September 7, 2007.

82. See Alan Travis, "More Britons Support Palestinians," *The Guardian*, April 24, 2002. Twenty-eight percent backed the Palestinians and 14 percent supported Israel.

83. Robert S. Wistrich, "Demonising Israel Is Now the Norm," *The Independent*, February 2, 2004. See also Wistrich, "Antisemitism Embedded in British Culture," *Post-Holocaust and Anti-Semitism*, 70, July 1, 2008 (Jerusalem Center for Public Affairs), interview by Manfred Gerstenfeld.

84. Yaakov Lappin, "Corrie Compared to Anne Frank," *The Jerusalem Post*, May 9, 2005. In *The British Theatre Guide*, Philip Fisher spoke about the saintly aspect of the heroine (an activist for the pro-Palestinian International Solidarity Movement) and her "meeting death with the beatific happiness of a martyr." On the controversy over Caryl Churchill's play, see Geoffrey Alderman, "Foul Play Needs Firm Response," *The Jewish Chronicle*, February 27, 2009.

85. Dominique Thomas, *Le Londonistan: La voix du djihad* (Paris: Éditions Michalon, 2003), pp. 116–46. See also Melanie Phillips, *Londonistan: How Britain Is Creating a Terror State Within* (London: Gibson Square, 2006).

86. Thomas, *Londonistan*, pp. 187–97.

87. Farrukh Dhondy, "An Islamic Fifth Column," *The Wall Street Journal*, December 27, 2001.

88. See Alexandre Del Valle, *Le Totalitarisme Islamiste à l'assaut des démocraties* (Paris: Éditions des Syrtes, 2002), pp. 243–44.

89. See Robert S. Wistrich, "Muslims, Jews, and 9/11," in Iganski and Kosmin, *A New Antisemitism?* pp. 169–91. As the historical adviser to the Channel 4 documentary

Blaming the Jews (June 27, 2003) I viewed some of the cassettes and other materials relating to the trial.

90. "Muslim Cleric Guilty of Soliciting Murder," *The Guardian*, February 24, 2003.

91. See Phillips, *Londonistan*, pp. 79–113.

92. See Wistrich, "Playground for Jihad?" pp. 81–92. For an insider view of the radicalization of young British Muslims in the 1990s, see Ed Husain, *The Islamist* (London: Penguin, 2007). See also "Going After Terror," *The Economist*, April 3, 2004, p. 29.

93. See Daniel Johnson, "Allah's England," *Commentary*, November 2006, pp. 41–46. The remarks were made to the *Sunday Telegraph* on the fifth anniversary of 9/11.

94. Ibid., p. 43.

95. Ibid. As Johnson points out, the logic of these perverse arguments is that a Jew who does not break with Israel is acting against the British national interest.

96. Robert S. Wistrich, "Converging Pathologies: From Anti-Zionism to Neo-Antisemitism," *Antisemitism International*, 2006, pp. 6–17.

97. Ori Golan, "One Day the Black Flag of Islam Will Be Flying Over Downing Street," *The Jerusalem Post*, June 27, 2003; and Robert S. Wistrich, "Hate Britain," *The Jewish Chronicle*, May 16, 2003, p. 32.

98. *The Daily Telegraph*, February 5, 2003; and "London Rally for Fanatics," ibid., September 11, 2002, p. 8.

99. Wistrich, "Playground for Jihad," pp. 81–92.

100. Ibid., pp. 87–89. See also Nick Cohen, "A Kind, Really Nice Boy," *The Observer*, May 4, 2003; Martin Bright and Fareena Alam, "Making of a Martyr," ibid.; "Bomb 'Martyrs' Justified," *The Jewish Chronicle*, May 9, 2003.

101. Bernard-Henri Lévy, *Qui a tué Daniel Pearl?* (Paris: Grasset, 2003), pp. 101–210.

102. Phillips, *Londonistan*, pp. 164–65.

103. See ibid., p. 165, on the British inability to understand these beliefs. See also Anne Marie Oliver and Paul F. Steinberg, *The Road to Martyrs' Square: A Journey into the World of the Suicide Bomber* (New York: Oxford University Press, 2005), for some penetrating insights into the jihadi culture of hatred and its religious annexation of the Palestine conflict. See Husain, *Islamist*, for the British angle.

104. "Of Imams and Nazis," *The Economist*, February 11, 2006; and "Cartoon Wars," ibid.

105. Lem Symons, "Met Slated by CST for Inaction Over Hamza," *The Jewish Chronicle*, February 10, 2006; and Daniella Peled, "Third of Muslims View UK Jews as 'Legitimate Target,' " in ibid.

106. See "Radical Islamist Profiles," *MEMRI Inquiry and Analysis*, no. 73 (October 24, 2001).

107. Del Valle, *Le Totalitarisme Islamiste*, pp. 243–46.

108. Ibid., p. 244.

109. *The Los Angeles Times*, October 14, 2001. These letters were sent in 1998, well before 9/11, but surfaced several years later.

110. "Londres, paradis d'Allah," *NO*, December 7–13, 2000.

111. BBC News, October 14, 2000.

112. *Le Monde*, September 9, 1998.

113. *The Jerusalem Post*, May 30, 2000. In the same interview he repeated that the existence of Israel was a "crime" and had to be erased.

114. Husain, *Islamist*, pp. 111–16.

115. "Exiled British Islamist Sheikh Omar bin Bakri in Beirut," *MEMRI Special Dispatch Series*, no. 1203 (July 12, 2006).

116. See Fuad Nahdi, *The Guardian*, May 2, 2003; and Nahdi, "Revive Spiritual Cousinhood," *The Jewish Chronicle*, May 9, 2003.

117. Nicola Woolcock and Dominic Kennedy, "Muslim Extremists in Britain," *The Times* (London), April 24, 2006.

118. See David Myatt, "Why Islam Is Our Ally," http:/nexion3.tripod.com/islam_ally.html and Mark Weitzman, *Magical Logic: Globalization, Conspiracy Theory and the Shoah* (Jerusalem: The Vidal Sassoon International Center for the Study of Antisemitism, 2008), pp. 9–10.

119. See Adam Pashut, "Dr. 'Azzam Al-Tamimi: A Political-Ideologial Brief," *MEMRI Inquiry and Analysis*, no. 163 (February 19, 2004).

120. On the infiltration of Hamas and Hezbollah ideology into Britain, see *CST Antisemitic Discourse Report 2007* (London: CST, 2008), pp. 39–42.

121. 'Azzam al-Tamimi, "Hizbullah's gift to Palestine," *Palestine Times*, June 2000.

122. 'Azzam al-Tamimi, "Jews and Muslims in Post-Israel Era," *Palestine Times*, July 1999.

123. 'Azzam al-Tamimi, "The Nature and Rationale of Hamas," *Dawn* (Pakistan), April 30, 2000.

124. The Pew Global Attitudes Project, "The Great Divide," reveals the intense Islamic identity among British Muslims.

125. Islamic radicalism preoccupies no less than 44 percent of British Muslims, the highest percentage in western Europe. For some of the consequences, see R. Israeli, *Muslim Anti-Semitism*, pp. 135–45.

126. "London Terror," *The Times* (London), July 23, 2005. Also *CST Antisemitic Discourse*, pp. 38–39.

127. Suhayl Saadi, "Waging the War of Words," *The Times* (London), July 23, 2005. Opposite the article are additional quotes propagating Holocaust denial, jihadi blood-sacrifices, and permanent war between Muslims and *kaffir* until "the Day of Resurrection."

128. According to data from early 2007, young Muslims are far more likely to sympathize with extreme manifestations of Islam than their elders. Thirty-six percent of those between sixteen and twenty-four years old said conversion *from* Islam should be punished with death. No less than 74 percent of young British Muslims said women should wear the veil. Levels of allegiance to Britain remained remarkably low. See "From Baghdad to Birmingham," *The Economist*, February 3, 2007, p. 29, for the results of the poll conducted for the Policy Exchange think tank. See also Mihir Bose, "British Muslims Forgetting Their Roots," *The Daily Telegraph*, August 23, 2005.

129. Michael Boyden, "You've Just Landed in Eurabia," *The Jerusalem Post*, September 14, 2005. The problem of hate literature and Islamist incitement has been aggravated by the availability of this racist material in British libraries. Tower Hamlets Council in London refused to ban such literature since the books themselves were not illegal. See *The Jewish Chronicle*, September 14, 2007.

130. Toby Helm, "Holocaust Day Must Be Scrapped, Say Muslim Leaders," *The Daily*

Telegraph, September 12, 2005; and "Muslims Boycott Holocaust Ceremonies," *The Sunday Times,* January 23, 2005. Fifty-seven percent of British Muslims supported this stand. See *The Jewish Chronicle,* February 10, 2006.

131. Sir Iqbal Sacranie, "British Muslims Are Judged by 'Israel Test,' " *The Observer,* August 21, 2005.

132. Laura Clark, "UK Teachers Drop Holocaust to Appease Muslims," *Daily Mail,* April 4, 2007.

133. For Sheikh Qaradawi's "moderation," see his English-language booklet *Fatawa on Palestine* (Cairo: Al-Falah Foundation, 2007). Directed at English-speaking Muslims, it is a compendium of incitement to terrorism and anti-Semitism.

134. Phillips, *Londonistan,* pp. 260–61.

135. See "Forked Tongues" (editorial), *The Times* (London), September 7, 2007; and Andrew Norfolk, "The Homegrown Cleric Who Loathes the British," in ibid.

136. Andrew Norfolk, "Hardline Takeover of British Mosques," *The Times* (London), September 2, 2007.

137. Norfolk, "Homegrown Cleric." Sheikh Riyadh ul-Haq also asserted that Muslims were oppressed, humiliated, and maligned in Europe, where they faced a possible Holocaust. See also R. Israeli, *Muslim Anti-Semitism,* pp. 230–34.

138. Ibid. Ul-Haq, like other radical British Muslims, claims that any friendship with Jews and Christians makes "a mockery of Allah's religion." These views have widely infiltrated mosques, schools, and Muslim neighborhoods across Britain with their hate message. See "Forked Tongues."

139. See Del Valle, *Le totalitarisme islamiste,* pp. 227–47.

140. See "Londres arrière-cour de l'extrémisme islamique," *Le Figaro,* February 5, 2007.

141. See Alvin H. Rosenfeld, *Anti-Zionism in Great Britain and Beyond: A "Respectable" Anti-Zionism?* (New York: American Jewish Committee, 2004).

142. *The Times* (London), February 7, 2006.

143. Fuad Nahdi, "Revive Spiritual Cousinhood," *The Jewish Chronicle,* May 9, 2003. Nahdi is the publisher of the Muslim magazine *Q-News.*

144. Mitchell Symons, "Fears That Force Jews to Stand Up and Shout," *Daily Express,* November 28, 2003.

145. "Minister's Remarks Spur Concern," *The Jewish Chronicle,* November 28, 2003. See also MacShane, *Globalizing Hatred,* p. 151.

146. Phillips, *Londonistan,* p. 247.

147. Mike O'Brien, "Labour and British Muslims: Can We Dream the Same Dream?" *Muslim Weekly,* January 7–13, 2005.

148. See George Galloway, "Statement on the London Bombings," www.Socialist -Worker.co.uk, July 7, 2005.

149. See Efraim Sicher, *Multiculturalism, Globalization and Antisemitism: The British Case* (Jerusalem: The Vidal Sassoon Center for the Study of Antisemitism, ACTA no. 32, 2009), pp. 10–16.

150. Quoted in *The Independent,* July 8, 2005.

151. Jonny Paul, "UK Claims Progress in Combating Anti-Semitism," *The Jerusalem Post,* May 15, 2008.

152. Anthea Lipsett, "Protests over Gaza Spread to Eight English Universities," *The Guardian,* January 22, 2009.

153. "Abuse of Science," *The Times* (editorial), March 4, 2009.

154. Simon Round, "Interview with John Mann" *The Jewish Chronicle,* February 13, 2009.

Twelve: Welcome to Eurabia

1. Alain Finkielkraut, *Au nom de l'Autre: réflexions sur l'antisémitisme qui vient* (Paris: Gallimard, 2003). See Wistrich, "If Things Are So Good"; and Josef Joffe, "The Demons of Europe," *Commentary,* January 2004, pp. 29–34.

2. *Manifestations of Antisemitism in the EU 2002–2003* (Vienna: European Monitoring Centre on Racism and Xenophobia, 2004). See also Omer Bartov, "The New Antisemitism: Genealogy and Implications," in Kertzer, *Old Demons, New Debates,* pp. 9–26.

3. Claus Leggenie, *The Emergence of a Euro-Islam? Mosques and Muslims in the Federal Republic of Germany* (Bad Homburg, Germany: Herbert Quandt-Stiftung, 2002). See also David Pryce-Jones, "Europe's 'Terrible Transformation'?" *Commentary,* July–August 2007, p. 61.

4. Oriana Fallaci, "Sull'antisemitismo," *Panorama,* April 18, 2002. See also Christopher Caldwell, "The Fallaci Affair," *Commentary,* October 2002, pp. 34–43.

5. Michèle Tribalat, "L'obsession anti-israélienne sur le net Islamique," *Observatoire du monde juif* (December 2004): pp. 7–16.

6. David Hyde, "Europe's Other Red-Green Alliance," *Zeek,* April 2003, http://www.zeek.net/politics_0304.shtml; Pilar Rahola, "Journey to Hell," in *Antisemitism: The Generic Hatred,* ed. Michael Fineberg et al. (London: Vallentine Mitchell, 2007), pp. 46–58;

7. See Robert S. Wistrich, "Muslims, Jews and September 11: The British Case," in Iganski and Kosmin, *A New Antisemitism?* pp. 169–91. See also Nick Cohen, "The Left's Unholy Alliance with Religious Bigotry," *The Guardian,* February 23, 2003.

8. *The Independent,* January 31, 2003, review section, p. 6, http://news.independent.co.uk/world/middle_east/story.jsp?story-374143. See also Julius, "Anti-Semitism and the English Intelligentsia," pp. 74–75.

9. See Robert S. Wistrich, "Antisemitism in Europe Today," *Antisemitism International,* 2003, pp. 62–65.

10. Erez Uriely, "Jew-hatred in Contemporary Norwegian Caricatures," in *Behind the Humanitarian Mask: The Nordic Countries, Israel and the Jews,* ed. Manfred Gerstenfeld (Jerusalem: Jerusalem Center for Public Affairs, 2008), pp. 149–51.

11. See "Les Chrétiens et le conflit proche oriental," *Observatoire du monde juif,* nos. 6–7 (June 2003), pp. 14–18.

12. See *Judaïsme, anti-judaïsme et christianisme: Colloque de Fribourg, 16–20 March 1998* (Saint-Maurice, Switzerland: Éditions Saint-Augustin, 2000), pp. 65–80.

13. "Pope Benedict: Full Text of Speech to Jewish Leaders," *Times Online,* August 19, 2005, http://www.timesonline.co.uk/tol/news/world/article556993.ece?token=null&offset=0.

14. "Pope's Address to Muslim Representatives," *Zenit,* August 20, 2005, http://www.zenit.org/article-13757?l=english.

15. "Pope's Address to Diplomatic Corps," *Zenit*, January 10, 2006, http://www.zenit.org/article-149701?l=english. See also George Weigel, "Regensburg Revisited: The Islamic response," *European Voice*, December 7–13, 2006; and "Pope's Secretary Warns of Islamization in Europe," *The Jerusalem Post*, July 27, 2007.

16. Patrick Saint-Paul, "L'Allemagne prend ses distances avec 'son' pape,' " *Le Figaro*, February 4, 2009. Also Stéphanie Le Bars, "Evêques intégristes: Le Vatican se justifie," *Le Monde*, February 6, 2009. On the papal visit to Israel, see Matthew Wagner, "Leaps of Faith," *The Jerusalem Post*, May 15, 2009.

17. Shmuel Trigano, "Le massacre des Saints Innocents dans les lieux de la Nativité," *Observatoire du monde juif*, nos. 6–7 (June 2003): pp. 2–5.

18. See Judith Elitzur, "How David Became Goliath: The Demonization of Israel's Image, 1948–2003," *Antisemitism International*, 2003, pp. 41–45.

19. Ibid., p. 41. The image in *La Stampa*, drawn by Giorgio Farattini, is reproduced in Joël Kotek and Dan Kotek, *Au nom de l'antisionisme: L'image des Juifs et d'Israël dans la caricature depuis la seconde Intifada* (Paris: Éditions Complexe, 2003), p. 111.

20. *Aftonbladet*, April 1, 2002.

21. *Expressen*, October 13, 2000, and March 26, 2002. My thanks to Henrik Bachner for these Swedish references, provided by him at the Vidal Sassoon International Conference in Jerusalem on "Antisemitism and Prejudice in the Media" (February 2003). See also the interview with Zvi Mazel (Israeli ambassador to Sweden, 2002–2004), "Anti-Israelism and Anti-Semitism in Sweden," in *Behind the Humanitarian Mask*, pp. 81–88.

22. See also Rev. Lucy Winkett, "I Watched a Soldier Shoot at Children," *The Guardian*, February 14, 2002.

23. Robert Fisk, "Travels in a Land Without Hope," *The Independent*, August 29, 2002. See also Fisk's long article "United States of Israel?" *The Independent*, April 27, 2006, with its grossly inflated claims about the omnipotence of the Jewish lobby and the vicelike grip in which it supposedly holds American presidents and the U.S. Congress.

24. The *Church Times*, April 26, 2002, gave a platform to Archbishop Desmond Tutu to warn that Israel might "exterminate the Palestinians" and to accuse it of apartheid. See also Margaret Brearley, *The Anglican Church, Jews and British Multiculturalism* (Jerusalem: Hebrew University of Jerusalem, SICSA, Posen Papers in Contemporary Antisemitism, 2007).

25. *Church Times*, December 13, 2002.

26. *Church Times*, January 24, 2003. Spencer wrote that the Holocaust is instrumentalized in Israel "as a means by which anything is justified"—a grossly misleading statement.

27. Brearley, *The Anglican Church*, p. 4. See also Gershon Nerel, *Anti-Zionism in the "Electronic Church" of Palestinian Christianity* (Jerusalem: Hebrew University of Jerusalem, SICSA, ACTA no. 27, 2006).

28. The most influential single source in Anglican Britain of this new replacement theology is the Palestinian canon Naim Ateek and his book, *Justice and Only Justice: A Palestinian Theology of Liberation* (Mary Knoll, N.Y.: Orbis Books, 1989), which brands Zionism as a "primitive," tribalist retrogression. See also Stephen Sizer, *Christian Zionism: Road Map to Armageddon?* (Leicester, U.K.: Inter-Varsity Press, 2004), for an all-out attack on evangelical Christian support for Israel.

29. Nicholas Weill, *Une histoire personnelle de l'antisémitisme* (Paris: Robert Laffont, 2003), pp. 98–101, 105–13, 119–22.

30. Jacques Tarnero, "Le Négationnisme, ou le symptome des Temps Pervers: Une énigme récurrente: Le Signe antijuif," *Revue d'Histoire de la Shoah* 166 (May–August 1999): pp. 44–75.

31. Kotek and Kotek, *Au nom de l'antisionisme*, p. 113.

32. See Daniel Perdurant, *Antisemitism in Contemporary Greek Society* (Jerusalem: Hebrew University of Jerusalem, SICSA, 1995), pp. 8–12. The State of Israel was only recognized de jure by the Greek government in 1990.

33. Sergio I. Minerbi, "Neo-Anti-Semitism in Today's Italy," *Jewish Political Studies Review* 15, nos. 3–4 (Fall 2003): pp. 111–39.

34. Report of the Italian Centre for Contemporary Jewish Documentation to the European Jewish Congress (Paris, 2007), p. 30.

35. Lisa Palmieri-Billig, "Survey Shows Xenophobia, Anti-Semitism Rising in Italy," *The Jerusalem Post*, July 1, 2003.

36. Sergio Romano, *Lettera a un amico ebreo* (Milan: Longanes, 1997), p. 119. A new edition appeared in 2002.

37. Ibid., p. 34.

38. Minerbi, "Neo-Anti-Semitism in Today's Italy," pp. 112–20.

39. Barbara Spinelli, "Ebraismo senza mea culpa," *La Stampa*, October 31, 2001.

40. See Apicella, "Never Again!" *Liberazione*, January 31, 2007; and Emanuele Ottolenghi, *Autodafè: L'Europa, gli ebrei e l'antisemitismo* (Turin, Italy: Lindau, Gennaio, 2007).

41. Etgar Leftovits, "After Gaza Withdrawal, Israel's Image in US, UK Only Got Worse," *The Jerusalem Post*, January 4, 2008.

42. "To Israel with Hate—and Guilt," *The Economist*, August 19, 2006.

43. "Ad Melkert, Meet Pim Fortuyn," *The Economist*, March 30, 2002.

44. Manfred Gerstenfeld, *Antisemitism and Permissiveness in Dutch Society* (Jerusalem: The Vidal Sassoon International Center for the Study of Antisemitism, Posen Papers in Contemporary Antisemitism, no. 4, 2006).

45. Eurobarometer Survey, no. 151 (November 2003).

46. Manfred Gerstenfeld, "Utrecht University: The Myth of Jewish Cannibalism, Censorship, and Fear of Muslim Intimidation," in *Academics Against Israel and the Jews*, ed. Manfred Gerstenfeld (Jerusalem: Jerusalem Center for Public Affairs, 2007), pp. 236–41.

47. Simon-Pierre Nothomb, "L'ordre va-t-il régner à Gaza?" *Le Soir*, December 15, 2001. See also Joël Kotek, "Devons-nous avoir peur?" *La Libre Bélgique*, January 15, 2002.

48. Serge Dumont, "Israël intensifie les 'liquidations,'" *La Libre Bélgique*, August 24, 2001; Agnès Gorissen, "Les Israéliens nous étranglent," October 5, 2001.

49. Francis Martens, "La vérité a péri," *La Libre Bélgique*, April 3, 2002; and the reply by a collective of Jewish intellectuals: "L'année de toutes les regressions," ibid., April 9, 2002.

50. Corinna da Fonseca-Wollheim, "Fear and Loathing in Antwerp," *The Jerusalem Post*, January 17, 2003. See also "La 'milice' qui trouble Anvers," *Le Monde*, December 16, 2002.

51. Ibid. The candidate was former head of Oxfam Belgium and president of the Belgo-Palestinian Association.

52. Joël Kotek, "La Belgique et Ses Juifs: De l'Antijudaïsme comme Code Culturel, à l'anti-Sionisme Comme Religion Civique," *Les Etudes du Crif*, no. 4 (2004): pp. 13–17. See also Paul Giniewski, *Antisionisme: Le Nouvel Antisémitisme* (Paris: Cheminements, 2005), pp. 96–103.

53. Kotek, "Belgique," p. 14.

54. Ibid.

55. Norsk Israel Senter (NIS), Norwegian Israel Center Against Antisemitism, Oslo, communication of January 11, 2006.

56. Manfred Gerstenfeld, "Norway: Extreme Expressions of Anti-Israeli and Anti-Semitic 'Attitudes,' " in *Behind the Humanitarian Mask*, p. 137.

57. Ibid., p. 47.

58. Ibid., p. 24.

59. "Olmert the Nazi," caricature by Finn Graff, *Dagbladet*, July 10, 2006.

60. Sverker Oredsson and Mikael Tossavainen, "Judehat bland muslimer tystas ned" [Silence Surrounds Muslim Jew hatred], *Dagens Nyheter*, October 20, 2003.

61. Susanna Abramowicz, "Antisemitic Attitudes in Sweden," *Ynetnews.com*, March 22, 2006, http://www.ynetnews.com/articles/0,7340,L-3230392,00.html. The poll was conducted by the Forum for Living History, a public body created by the Swedish government, and it was carried out between March and May 2005.

62. Amiram Barkat, "41 Per Cent of Swedes Are Prejudiced Against Jews," *Haaretz*, March 16, 2007.

63. R. Israeli, *Muslim Anti-Semitism*, pp. 194–203. See also Mikael Tossavainen, "Arab and Muslim anti-Semitism in Sweden," in *Behind the Humanitarian Mask*, pp. 89–100.

64. Efraim Zuroff, "Sweden's Refusal to Prosecute Nazi War Criminals, 1986–2007," in *Behind the Humanitarian Mask*, pp. 106–29.

65. Pew Global Attitudes Project, "No Global Warming Alarm in U.S., China," http://pewglobal.org/reports/pdf/252.pdf. See also "Spring 2007 Survey," ibid., http://pewglobal.org/reports/pdf/256topline.pdf.

66. ADL, "Attitudes Toward Jews, Israel and the Palestinian-Israeli Conflict in Ten European Countries," surveys for 2002, 2004, and 2007. See also ibid., "Attitudes Toward Jews and the Middle East in Five European Countries," May 2007, http://www.adl.org/anti_semitism/European_Attitudes_Survey_May_2007.pdf.

67. Alejandro Baer, "Tanques contra piedras: la imagen de Israel en España," Real Instituto Elcano, http://www.realinstitutoelcano.org/analysis/ARI2007/ARI74-2007_imagen_Israel_Espa%C3%B1a.pdf.

68. Baer, ibid.

69. "EL PP acusa a Zapatero de 'antisemitismo e israelofobia' en la crisis del Líbano," July 20, 2006, http://www.abc.es/. Also "One of Israel's Biggest Critics: Spanish Prime Minister Leads Anti-War Chorus," *The Jerusalem Post*, August 13, 2006.

70. "Spanish Senator Criticizes Anti-Jewish Sentiment," November 15, 2006, World Jewish Congress, http://www.worldjewishcongress.org/news/globalnews/gn_archives/2006/11/gn_061115_spain.html.

71. Gustavo D. Perednik, "Naïve Spanish Judeophobia," *Jewish Political Studies* 15 nos. 3–4 (Fall 2003): pp. 87–110.

72. ADL, "European Attitudes Toward the Jews: A Study of Five Countries," September 2002. Thirty-four percent of all Spaniards, according to this poll, held anti-Jewish views.

73. See ADL, "Attitudes Toward Jews and the Middle East in Five European Countries," May 2007. Fifty-three percent of Spaniards thought Jews had too much power in the business world. This was the highest percentage in the countries polled.

74. See Gonzalo Alvarez Chillida, *El Antisemitismo en España* (Madrid: Marcial Pons, 2002), pp. 465–66. Jacobo Israel Garzó et al., eds., *El estigma imborrable: Reflexiones sobre el nuevo antisemitismo* (Madrid: Hebraica Ediciones, 2005).

75. Hermann Tersch, "El Retorno de la judeofobia," *El País,* May 4, 2003.

76. Alejandro Baer and Federico Zukierman, *Anti-Semitism in Graphic Humor—Caricatures and Vignettes of the Spanish Press about the Israeli-Palestinian Conflict* (Madrid: Guesher, 2003), pp. 2–4.

77. Perednik, "Naïve Spanish Judeophobia," p. 100.

78. "The Name of the Problem Is Israel," *La Razón,* April 20, 2003.

79. *El Pais,* January 27, 2003.

80. Quoted by Perednik, "Naïve Spanish Judeophobia," p. 98, who adds that most Spaniards "remain completely unaware of the Judeophobic nature of their country."

81. Pilar Rahola's lecture at the American Jewish Committee's 97th Annual Meeting, May 7, 2003. See also Pilar Rahola, *"Democracy's Canaries": Jews and Judeophobia in Contemporary Europe* (Jerusalem: Institute of the World Jewish Congress, 2004).

82. Pilar Rahola, interview by Marc Tobias, "Judeophobia Explains the Pro-Palestinian Hysteria of the European Left," *Proche-Orient,* October 2, 2002.

83. See Paul Berman, "Bigotry in Print: Crowds Chant Murder," *Forward,* May 24, 2002, for the Saramago quote; and Rahola, *"Democracy's Canaries,"* p. 8, for the additional comment that Saramago was totally indifferent to the "hundred million deaths caused by Communism." His notions of freedom and tolerance were those of Arafat, Castro, Pol Pot, and Stalin.

84. "Interview with Ana Palacio," *The American Enterprise,* October–December 2005, pp. 14–15.

85. "A Poisonous Tune Is Playing Again" (editorial), *Haaretz,* August 31, 2004.

86. Ari Shavit, "The Jewish Problem According to Theodorakis," *Haaretz,* August 27, 2004.

87. Robert S. Wistrich, "Antisemitism in Europe Today," address to the OSCE, *Antisemitism International,* 2003, p. 63. See also Alain Finkielkraut, "Le Sionisme face à la religion de l'Humanité," in *Le Sionisme face à Ses Détracteurs* (Paris: Éditions Raphaël, 2003), pp. 160–70.

88. "Europe and the Jews," *The Economist,* May 4, 2002, p. 12.

89. Efraim Karsh and Rory Miller, "Europe's Persecuted Muslims?" *Commentary,* April 2007, pp. 49–53.

90. Ibid., p. 52.

91. "Leading Sunni Sheikh Yousef Al-Qaradawi and Other Sheikhs Herald the Coming Conquest of Rome," *MEMRI Special Dispatch Series,* no. 447 (December 2, 2002.)

92. Christopher Caldwell, "Islamic Europe?" *The Weekly Standard,* October 4, 2004.

93. Bassam Tibi, "Grenzen der Toleranz," *Welt am Sonntag* (Hamburg), September 5, 2004.

94. Abdelwahab Meddeb, *La Maladie de L'Islam* (Paris: Seuil, 2002), pp. 129–33.

95. Abdelwahab Meddeb, *Contre-Prêches* (Paris: Seuil, 2006), pp. 104–5.

96. Ibid., pp. 458–59.

97. Ibid., p. 249.

98. Ibid., p. 401.

99. Michael Mönninger, "Islam's Heritage of Violence," *Die Zeit,* May 10, 2006, http://www.signandsight.com/features/978.html. Meddeb's book *Contre-Prêches* was based on his weekly radio program aimed at the large French-speaking community in the Maghreb. See also chapter 10 in Naccache, *Contre Israël,* pp. 330–56, for other dissident Arab voices.

100. See Ye'or, *Islam and Dhimmitude;* and Bernard Lewis, *The Crisis of Islam* (New York: Modern Library, 2003).

101. "I See an Absolutely Hostile Mood Towards Jews," *Spiegel Online,* August 31, 2006, http://www.spiegel.de/international/1,1518,434508,00.html.

102. "To Israel with Hate," *The Economist,* August 19, 2006.

103. Bassam Tibi, "The Open Society and Its Enemies Within," *The Washington Post,* March 17, 2004.

104. Bruce Bawer, "Tolerating Intolerance," *Partisan Review* 69, no. 3 (2002).

Thirteen: Bigotry at the United Nations

1. Quoted in Greer Fay Cashman, "The First Steps of Statehood," *The Jerusalem Post,* April 23, 2007 (Independence Day issue).

2. See Yaacov Ro'i, "Soviet-Israeli Relations, 1947–1954," in *The USSR and the Middle East,* ed. M. Confino and S. Shamir (Tel Aviv: Israel Universities Press), pp. 123–46.

3. UN General Assembly, First Special Session Official Records, vol. 1, pp. 127–35.

4. UN General Assembly, Second Session, Official Records, Ad Hoc Committee on the Palestine Question, October 13, 1947, and November 19, 1947, pp. 69–71.

5. Quoted in Theodore Draper, "Israel and World Politics," *Commentary,* August 1967, pp. 19–48.

6. Ibid., p. 20.

7. See Abba Eban, "Israel, Anti-Semitism and the United Nations," *Jerusalem Quarterly* (Fall 1976): pp. 110–20.

8. For the extent of opposition in the American establishment (some of it manifestly anti-Semitic) see John Loftus and Mark Aarons, *The Secret War Against the Jews* (New York: St. Martin's Press, 1994), pp. 156–59, 172–80.

9. For the impact of the Holocaust on the United Nations, see Seymour Maxwell Finger, "The United Nations," in *The World Reacts to the Holocaust,* ed. D. Wyman (Baltimore: Johns Hopkins University Press, 1996), pp. 811–35.

10. Ibid., p. 815. The three UNSCOP members who opposed partition (India, Iran, and Yugoslavia) favored a federal state.

11. Ibid., p. 816.

12. Eban, "Israel, Anti-Semitism, and the United Nations," pp. 114–16.

13. See Arafat's Address to the UN in *The Israel-Arab Reader,* ed. Walter Laqueur and Barry Rubin (New York: Penguin Books, 1984), pp. 504–17.

14. Ibid., p. 505.

15. Roberta Cohen, "United Nations' Stand on Antisemitism," *Patterns of Prejudice* 2, no. 2 (March–April 1968), pp. 21–25.

16. Ibid., p. 24. See also Natan Lerner, *The U.N. Convention on the Elimination of All Forms of Racial Discrimination* (Rockville, Md.: Sijthoff and Noordhoff, 1980), pp. 71–73.

17. UN Special Committee on Palestine (UNSCOP), Twenty-second Session, S/PV 1352, June 9, 1967, p. 6.

18. Finger, "United Nations," p. 828.

19. See *Report of the World Conference of the International Women's Year,* Mexico City, June 19–July 2, 1975, UN Doc. E/CONF. 66/34.

20. Meeting at Mexico City, unofficial document, pp. 25–26. See also *Report of the World Conference,* p. 149.

21. Meeting at Mexico City, p. 27.

22. *Report of the World Conference,* p. 149.

23. See the recollections of an Israeli delegate at Mexico City recorded by Graciela Samuels, "Zionism Slandered in Mexico," *Israel Digest,* June 1, 1979, p. 5.

24. See *Report of the World Conference of the United Nations Decade for Women: Equality, Development and Peace,* Copenhagen, July 24–30, 1980, UN Publications sales no. E.80 IV:3.

25. Jane Moonman, "Anti-Zionism/Anti-Semitism in the Women's Movement," a 1984 lecture that drew on notes made by Jewish delegates to the UN Copenhagen conference, later reproduced in the American magazine *MS.*

26. Phyllis Chesler, *The New Antisemitism* (San Francisco: Jossey-Bass, 2003), pp. 53–58, 67–71, 158–65, 188–91. See also Phyllis Chesler, "Antisemitism and Anti-Westernism in the Women's Movement," in *Antisemitism: The Generic Hatred,* ed. Michael Fineberg, Shimon Samuels, and Mark Weitzman (London: Vallentine Mitchell, 2007), pp. 101–8.

27. See *The Jerusalem Post,* November 7, 1975, for remarks in this spirit by Karen Decrow, head of America's largest feminist organization, about the "incredibly strong anti-Zionist feeling that existed in Mexico City."

28. Barbara Lantin, "Sisters in Despair," *Jewish Chronicle,* May 20, 1983.

29. Jan Shure, "Dig in the Rib for Israel," *Jewish Chronicle,* May 20, 1983.

30. Juliet J. Pope, "Anti-Racism, Anti-Zionism and Antisemitism—Debates in the British Women's Movement," *Patterns of Prejudice* 20, no. 3 (1986): pp. 14–25.

31. Linda Mansour, "We Will Not Let the World Forget," *Outwrite,* October 1982, p. 7; Roisin Boyd, "Women Speak Out Against Zionism," *Spare Rib,* August 1982, pp. 22–23.

32. Boyd, ibid.

33. Boyd, "Women Speak Out."

34. Sophie Cox, "Land Before Honour," *Spare Rib,* February 1984, p. 26; and "Poisoning Women," *Outwrite,* May 1983, p. 2.

35. Pope, "Anti-Racism," pp. 19–20.

36. Zaire opposed the resolutions while Sierra Leone, Senegal, and Liberia expressed reservations.

37. See William Korey, "Soviet Anti-Semitism at the UN," in *Anti-Semitism: A Threat*

to Western Civilization, ed. M. Z. Rosensaft and Yehuda Bauer (Jerusalem: The Vidal Sassoon International Center for the Study of Antisemitism, 1988), pp. 55–82.

38. See Bernard Lewis, "The Anti-Zionist Resolution," *Foreign Affairs,* October 1976, pp. 54–64; and S. M. Finger and Ziva Flamhaft, "The Issue of Zionism and Racism in the United Nations," *Middle Eastern Review,* Spring 1986, pp. 49–58.

39. "Anti-Zionism" (editorial), *The Observer,* November 9, 1974; Paul Johnson, "The Resources of Civilisation," *New Statesman,* October 31, 1975; Bernard Levin, *The Times* (London), October 22, 1975; "A Wild Swipe at Israel," *The Guardian,* November 12, 1975; "UN Support for Racism," *The Canberra Times,* October 24, 1975; "Damage to UN Not Ended Yet," *Toronto Star,* November 12, 1975; "Anti-Semitism at UN," *The Catholic Review,* November 14, 1975; Abba Eban, Zionism and the UN," *The New York Times,* November 3, 1975; Leonard Garment, "A Monstrous Obscene Act," *Newsweek,* November 3, 1975; "O.N.U.: Le Vote Infâme," *L'Aurore,* November 12, 1975; Jean Daniel, "Le Racisme et les Nouveaux Maîtres de l'O.N.U.," *NO,* November 17, 1975.

40. *The New York Times,* November 3, 1975. See also Robert S. Wistrich, *The Myth of Zionist Racism* (London: W.U.J.S., 1975), in which I developed this idea.

41. Eldridge Cleaver, "Third World Racism at the UN," *Boston Herald,* January 15, 1976; and Bayard Rustin, "Zionism Is Not Racism," *Crossroads,* January–February 1976.

42. Daniel Patrick Moynihan, "Zionism, the United Nations and American Foreign Policy," *Catholicism in Crisis,* April 1984, pp. 11–15.

43. Goronwy Rees, *Encounter,* no. 1 (1976): p. 30. See also Lewis, "Anti-Zionist Resolution," p. 64, who noted that "anti-Zionism is very often a cloak for vulgar anti-Semitism, for which it provides possibilities of expression and action previously lacking."

44. Lewis, "Anti-Zionist Resolution," p. 64.

45. Ruth Raeli, *The Implications of Resolution 3379 on Zionism* (Jerusalem: World Zionist Organization, 1986), p. 3.

46. Yoram Dinstein, "Anti-Semitism, Anti-Zionism and the United Nations," *Israel Yearbook on Human Rights,* vol. 17 (Dordrecht, Netherlands: Martinus Nijhoff, 1987), pp. 15–21.

47. Ibid., p. 18. See also Irwin Cotler, *Human Rights and the New Anti-Jewishness: Sounding the Alarm* (Jerusalem: The Jewish Policy Planning Institute, Alert Paper, November 2002).

48. Allan Gerson, "The United Nations and Racism: The Case of the Zionism as Racism Resolution as Progenitor" in *Israel Yearbook,* pp. 68–73.

49. Dinstein, "Anti-Semitism, Anti-Zionism," p. 18.

50. William F. Buckley, Jr., *United Nations Journal: A Delegate's Odyssey* (New York: G. P. Putnam's Sons, 1974), pp. 63–75.

51. UN Doc. A/PV.1975, October 22, 1971.

52. Marief Dawalibi, UN Seminar on Religious Intolerance, Geneva, December 1984. English translation from official tape in Arabic.

53. UN Doc. A/SPC/40/PV.17, October 17, 1985.

54. UN Doc. S/PV.2128, March 16, 1979, pp. 6–7.

55. UN Doc. E/CN.4/SR.1590, p. 4. Also quoted in *The New Republic,* December 27, 1980, p. 7. Oppenheimer, an Anglican (though born a Jew), was the chairman of the Anglo-American parent company of De Beers Consolidated Mines, the diamond monopoly. See also William Korey, "The Triumph of Evil: UN Anti-

semitism," in *Anti-Semitism and Human Rights* (Melbourne: Australian Institute
of Jewish Affairs, 1985), pp. 57–60.

56. Rep. William Lehman of Florida, March 11, 1981, *Congressional Record—Extension
of Remarks,* E993.

57. Ibid. Lehman incorporated a text by Harris O. Schoenberg, "Anti-Semitism at the
U.N.," first presented in New York on March 10, 1981. Schoenberg was director of
the UN office of the International Council of B'nai B'rith. *The New York Times*
quote comes from this text.

58. Ibid.

59. Yitzhak Rabi, "Antisemitism at the United Nations," *Inside,* Summer 1982, pp.
42–43.

60. Ibid., p. 42.

61. Alan L. Keyes, "Anti-Zionism, Antisemitism, and the Decline of the UN Ideal," *Israel Yearbook* (1987), pp. 24–28.

62. Mr. Khaddam, UN Doc. A/37/PV.8, pp. 83–85. See also UN Doc. A/SPEC/37/SR.27,
para. 20.

63. UN Doc. A/37/PV.16, p. 106. See also UN Doc. A/37/PV.87.

64. Lopez Del Amo, UN Doc. A/37/PV.93. For Ali Treiki's remarks, see UN Doc.
A/38/713.

65. UN Doc. A/37/PV.87.

66. John and Henry F. Carey, "Hostility in United Nations Bodies to Judaism, the Jewish People and Jews as Such," *Israel Yearbook* (1987), pp. 29–38.

67. UN Doc. S/PV.2620, pp. 26–27 (1985).

68. On this process of delegitimization of Israel at the UN, see Harris D. Schoenberg,
A Mandate for Terror: The United Nations and the PLO (New York: Shapolsky Publishers, 1989), pp. 251–330.

69. Sidney Liskofsky and Donna E. Arzt, "Incitement to National, Racial and Religious
Hatred in United Nations Fora," *Israel Yearbook* (1987), pp. 41–61.

70. Letter to the UN Secretary-General by Yehuda Blum, the permanent representative of Israel, UN Doc. A/39/79, January 16, 1984.

71. See Emmanuel Sivan, "Islamic Fundamentalism, Antisemitism and Anti-
Zionism," and Antony Lerman, "Fictive Anti-Zionism: Third World, Arab and
Muslim Variations," in Wistrich, *Anti-Zionism and Antisemitism in the Contempo-
rary World,* pp. 74–84, 121–38.

72. Ehud Sprinzak, "Anti-Zionism: From Delegitimation to Dehumanization," *Forum*
(Jerusalem), no. 53 (Autumn–Winter 1984); and Yohanan Manor, "The New Anti-
Zionism," *Jerusalem Quarterly,* no. 35 (Spring 1985): p. 133.

73. See the introduction to Curtis, ed., *Antisemitism in the Contemporary World,* p. 8.

74. Edward C. Luck, "The Impact of the Zionism-Racism Resolution on the Standing
of the United Nations in the United States," *Israel Yearbook* (1987), pp. 95–109.

75. Henri Stellman, "Anti-semitism and the UN," *The Times Higher Education Supplement,* November 15, 1985.

76. Richard S. Williamson, "Serpents in the U.N.," *Midstream,* January 1989, pp. 8–10.
The author was the U.S. assistant secretary of state for international organization
affairs.

77. Quoted in Yohanan Manor, *To Right a Wrong: The Revocation of the UN General*

Assembly Resolution 3379 Defaming Zionism (New York: Shengold Publishers, 1996), p. 171.

78. President Bush's address to the UN in New York on September 23, 1991. See Manor, *To Right a Wrong*, p. 256, for extracts.

79. Manor, *To Right a Wrong*, pp. 260–61.

80. See Irwin Cotler's address, "Human Rights in the New International Legal Order," in *Israel in the New World Order* (Jerusalem: Jerusalem Center for Public Affairs, 1992), pp. 51–63.

81. Quoted in Jeremy Jones, "Durban Sprawl," *Australia-Israel Review,* October 2006. See also Anne Bayefsky, "One Small Step: Is the U.N. Finally Ready to Get Serious About Anti-Semitism?" *The Wall Street Journal,* June 21, 2004—a speech delivered at the UN Conference on Confronting Anti-Semitism. This event was a positive signal.

82. The NGO Forum Final Declaration, art. 162, Durban 2001, branded Israel "as a racist, apartheid State." Its existence was "a crime against humanity" that had been characterized by "separation and segregation, dispossession, restricted land access, denationalization, Bantustanization and inhumane acts." For further details see Shimon Samuels, "The Durban Protocols: Globalization of the New Antisemitism," in *Antisemitism: The Generic Hatred,* pp. 33–45.

83. Anne Bayefsky, "Human Wrongs," *The Wall Street Journal,* April 29, 2003.

84. Anne Bayefsky, "Remembering Genocide, Fomenting 'Zionicide,'" *The Jerusalem Post,* February 3, 2006. See also Irwin Cotler, *Human Rights and the New Anti-Jewishness: Sounding the Alarm* (Jerusalem: The Jewish People Policy Planning Institute, November 2002).

85. Bayefsky, "Remembering Genocide." See also Bayefsky, interview by Manfred Gerstenfeld, "The United Nations: Leading Global Purveyor of Anti-Semitism," *Post-Holocaust and Anti-Semitism,* no. 31 (April 1, 2005); and Gerald Steinberg, "Abusing the Legacy of the Holocaust: The Role of NGOs in Exploiting Human Rights to Demonize Israel," *Jewish Political Studies Review* 16, nos. 3–4 (Fall 2004).

86. Anne Bayefsky, "That Same Old Bash-Israel Agenda," *The Jerusalem Post,* July 6, 2006, shows that the current Human Rights Council at the UN is no improvement on the discredited and now defunct Human Rights Commission.

87. Richard Shifter, "Is the UN Improving?" *The Jerusalem Post,* December 16, 2004. Hillel Neuer, "Where Israel Still = Racism," ibid., August 10, 2006. See also, "The UN Vote" (editorial), ibid., November 3, 2005.

88. Dore Gold, "Can the UN Be Redeemed?" *The Jerusalem Post,* December 31, 2004.

89. Gerald Steinberg, "Abusing 'Apartheid' for the Palestinian Cause," *The Jerusalem Post,* August 25, 2004; Ina Friedman, "Here We Go Again," *The Jerusalem Report,* April 8, 2002; Tom Lantos, *The Durban Debacle: An Insider's View of the UN World Conference Against Racism* (Jerusalem: Institute of the World Jewish Congress, policy forum no. 24, 2002); Arch Puddington, "The Wages of Durban," *Commentary,* November 2001, pp. 29–34; Irwin Cotler, "Durban's Troubling Legacy: One Year Later," *Jerusalem Issue Briefs* 2, no. 5 (August 20, 2002).

90. Milton Shain and Margo Bastos, "Muslim Antisemitism, Anti-Zionism and Holocaust Denial in South Africa, 1945–2002," *Antisemitism International* (2006): pp. 18–30.

91. Anne Bayefsky, "The UN and the Jews," *Commentary*, February 2004, pp. 42–46. She points to the hypocrisy and betrayal by the United Nations of its own principles and its extreme reluctance to deal with anti-Semitism—especially that of the Middle Eastern variety. This is consistent with the United Nations' distortion of the Zionist idea and its long-term complicity in Arab efforts to isolate Israel from the global community.

92. Steinberg, "Abusing Apartheid." See also Howard Jacobson, "Those Who Boycott Israel: Universities Are Doing Intellectual Violence—to Themselves," *The Independent*, July 14, 2007.

93. Ibid. See also "An Apartheid State?" (editorial), *The Jerusalem Post*, November 11, 2002, which cites Amnesty International's call a year earlier "to impose a policy of complete and total isolation of Israel as an apartheid State." For a critique, see Alan Dershowitz, "Ugly Face of Bigotry: For Amnesty International, Israel Can Do No Right," *The Jerusalem Post*, October 12, 2003.

94. See Arieh J. Kochavi, "Israel and the International Legal Arena," *Journal of Israeli History* 25, no. 1 (March 2006): pp. 223–44.

95. *Haaretz*, February 24, 2004.

96. *The Jerusalem Post*, July 16, 2004.

97. Desmond Tutu, "Apartheid in the Holy Land," *The Guardian*, March 29, 2002.

98. Jimmy Carter, *Palestine: Peace Not Apartheid* (New York: Simon and Schuster, 2006). See also "The Carter Version," *The Economist*, December 16, 2006; and Joshua Muravchik, "Our Worst Ex-President," *Commentary*, February 2007, pp. 17–26.

99. See Irshad Manji, "Modern Israel Is a Far Cry from Old South Africa," *The Australian*, February 9, 2007. Manji is a courageous Canadian feminist author and a Muslim dissident.

100. Ian Buruma, "Do Not Treat Israel Like Apartheid South Africa," *The Guardian*, July 23, 2002; and Avi Primor, "Apartheid im gelobten land?" *Süddeutsche Zeitung*, October 9, 2002.

101. Douglas Davis, "Eight-Hour London Parley Will Bash 'Apartheid Israel,' " *The Jerusalem Post*, December 5, 2004.

102. *The Jerusalem Post*, February 22, 2007.

103. Cotler, *Human Rights and the New Anti-Jewishness*, pp. 1–7. See also Georges-Elia Sarfati, *L'Antisionisme: Israël/Palestine aux miroirs d'Occident* (Paris: Berg International, 2002), pp. 88–120.

104. Robert S. Wistrich, "Anti-Zionism and Anti-Semitism," *Jewish Political Studies Review* 16, nos. 3–4 (Fall 2004): pp. 27–31. See also "Drawing the Line: Brian Klug and Robert Wistrich Debate Antisemitism and anti-Zionism," *The Jewish Quarterly*, Summer 2005, pp. 21–24.

105. Allon Lee, "Durban Renewal," *AIR* (December 2008): pp. 20–21.

FOURTEEN: THE ANTI-ZIONIST MASQUERADE

1. *Pravda*, September 21, 1982.

2. *Izvestia*, September 22, 1982.

3. Ibid.

4. *Trud*, September 22, 1982.

5. Gennadi Kostyrchenko, *Out of the Red Shadows: Anti-Semitism in Stalin's Shadow* (Amherst, N.Y.: Prometheus Books, 1995).

6. On this shift, see Wistrich, *Antisemitism: The Longest Hatred*, pp. 175–77.

7. See Rosenbaum, *Those Who Forget the Past.*

8. Robert S. Wistrich, "Zionism and the Jewish 'Assimilationist' Critics (1897–1948)," *Jewish Social Studies* 4, no. 2 (Winter 1998): pp. 59–111.

9. Taguieff, *Prêcheurs de Haine*, pp. 13–73.

10. See the essays in Wistrich, *Anti-Zionism and Antisemitism in the Contemporary World.*

11. Wistrich, "Anti-Zionism and Anti-Semitism," *Jewish Political Studies Review*, pp. 27–31.

12. See Manfred Gerstenfeld, ed., *Europe's Crumbling Myths: The Post-Holocaust Origins of Today's Anti-Semitism* (Jerusalem: Jerusalem Center for Public Affairs, 2003).

13. V. Bolshakov, "Anti-Sovietizm—professiya sionistov," *Pravda*, February 19, 1971.

14. For the history of the *Protocols*, see Taguieff, *Prêcheurs de Haine.* pp. 645–818.

15. Jeffrey Herf, *The Jewish Enemy: Nazi Propaganda During World War II and the Holocaust* (Cambridge, Mass.: Belknap Press, 2006), pp. 73–76, for the Nazi origins of the concept.

16. Adolf Hitler, *Mein Kampf*, pp. 324–25.

17. Wistrich, *Hitler's Apocalypse*, pp. 156–68. See also Jeffrey Herf, "Convergence: The Classic Case of Nazi Germany, Anti-Semitism and Anti-Zionism During World War II," *The Journal of Israeli History* 25, no. 1 (March 2006): pp. 63–83.

18. Arkady Vaksberg, *Stalin Against the Jews*, pp. 209–10, 214–15. See also Richard Overy, *The Dictators: Hitler's Germany, Stalin's Russia* (London: Penguin Books, 2005), for Stalin's paranoia.

19. Joshua Rubinstein and Vladimir P. Naumor, eds., *Stalin's Secret Pogrom: The Postwar Inquisition of the Jewish Anti-Fascist Committee* (New Haven, Conn.: Yale University Press, 2001), pp. 40–63.

20. See the essays in Luks, *Der Spätstalinismus.*

21. See Lukasz Hirszowicz, "The Jewish Issue in Post-War Communist Politics," in *The Jew in Poland*, ed. Chimen Abramsky et al. (Oxford, U.K.: Oxford University Press, 1988), pp. 199–208.

22. Wistrich, *Hitler's Apocalypse*, pp. 198–203.

23. *New Times* (Moscow), no. 44 (1972): p. 26.

24. V. Sidenko, "Israel's African Ambitions," *New Times* (Moscow), no. 3 (1971): p. 25.

25. Bat Ye'or, *Eurabia: L'axe euro-arabe* (Paris: Jen-Cyrille Godefroy, 2006), pp. 61–107.

26. Fiamma Nirenstein, *Gli Antisemiti Progressisti: La Forma Nuova di un odio antico* (Milan: Rizzoli, 2004), pp. 80–109.

27. Editorial by Conor Cruise O'Brien, *The Observer*, June 26, 1984.

28. Nicholas von Hoffman in *The Spectator*, June 19, 1982.

29. O'Brien, *The Observer*, June 26, 1984.

30. See Jacques Hermone, *La Gauche, Israel et les Juifs* (Paris: La Table Ronde, 1970), pp. 174–99, for a sharp dissection of *Le Monde*'s anti-Israelism in the late 1960s.

31. Robert S. Wistrich, introduction to Henry H. Weinberg, *The Myth of the Jew in France, 1967–1982* (Toronto: Mosaic Press, 1987).

32. Alain Finkielkraut, *La Réprobation d'Israël* (Paris: Éditions Denoël/Gonthier, 1983), pp. 18ff.

33. Robert S. Wistrich, "The Anti-Zionist Masquerade," *Midstream,* August–September 1983, pp. 12–13.

34. See Gershon Nerel, *Anti-Zionism in the "Electronic" Church of Palestinian Christianity* (Jerusalem: Hebrew University of Jerusalem, SICSA, ACTA no. 27, 2006). See also Paul Giniewski, *Antisionisme: le nouvel antisémitisme* (Paris: Cheminements, 2005), pp. 135–49, for the response of the Vatican under Pope John Paul II.

35. De Gaulle's remarks were made at a press conference on November 27, 1967. See François Bondy, "Communist Attitudes in France and Italy to the Six-Day War," in Wistrich, *Left Against Zion,* pp. 180ff.

36. Isaac Deutscher, "On the Arab-Israeli War," *New Left Review,* June 20, 1967, reproduced integrally in Tariq Ali, *The Clash of Fundamentalisms: Crusades, Jihads and Modernity* (London: Verso, 2002), pp. 314–32.

37. Wistrich, "Left-Wing Anti-Zionism in Western Societies," pp. 50–51.

38. Daniel Cohn-Bendit, *Le grand bazaar* (Paris: Pierre Belfond, 1975), pp. 9–20.

39. See Henryk M. Broder, "Antizionismus—Antisemitismus von links?" *Aus Politik und Zeitgeschichte* (supplement to the weekly *Das Parlament*) (June 12, 1976): pp. 31–46.

40. See Tony Kushner and Alisa Solomon, eds., *Wrestling with Zion: Progressive Jewish-American Responses to the Israeli-Palestinian Conflict* (New York: Grove Press, 2003); and Seth Farber, ed., *Radicals, Rabbis and Peacemakers: Conversations with Jewish Critics of Israel* (Monroe, Me.: Common Courage Press, 2005). Also *Prophets Outcast: A Century of Dissident Writing About Zionism and Israel* (New York: Nation Books, 2004).

41. Patricia Cohen, "Essay Linking Liberal Jews and Anti-Semitism Sparks a Furor," *The New York Times,* January 31, 2007.

42. Rudolf Krämer-Badoni, "Zionism and the New Left," in Wistrich, *The Left Against Zion,* pp. 226–35.

43. Ibid., p. 234.

44. For an account of the proceedings, see *FAZ,* December 15, 1972.

45. Jillian Becker, *Hitler's Children: The Story of the Baader-Meinhof Terrorist Gang* (London, 1977), p. 234.

46. Ibid.

47. Jillian Becker, "Another Final Battle on the Stage of History," *Terrorism: An International Journal* 5, nos. 1–2 (1981).

48. Becker, *Hitler's Children,* pp. 17–18.

49. Broder, "Open Letter."

50. Ibid., p. 112.

51. Ibid., p. 113.

52. Ibid., p. 117.

53. Jacques Givet, *Israël et le genocide inachevé* (Paris: Plon, 1979).

54. See Alain Finkielkraut, *The Imaginary Jew* (Lincoln: University of Nebraska Press, 1997), pp. 147–70.

55. Yohanan Manor, "L'Antisionisme," *Revue française de science politique* 34, no. 2 (April 1984): 295–322.
56. See Annie Kriegel, *Israël est-il coupable?* (Paris: R. Laffront, 1982), p. 41.
57. Jostein Gaarder, "God's Chosen People," *Aftenposten*, August 5, 2006. See also Manfred Gerstenfeld, "Norway: Extreme Expressions of Anti-Israeli and Anti-Semitic Attitudes," *Behind the Humanitarian Mask,* pp. 132–33.
58. Gaarder, "God's Chosen People."
59. See Shimon Samuels, "An Open Letter to Norway from the Simon Wiesenthal Center," August 8, 2006, www.wiesenthal.com.
60. Henryk Broder, "Behind German Masks," *Jerusalem Post Magazine*, December 10, 1982, pp. 8–9.
61. Ruth R. Wisse, "The Delegitimation of Israel," *Commentary*, July 1982, pp. 29–36; and Norman Podhoretz, "J'Accuse," ibid., September 1982, pp. 21–31.
62. Sergio Rotbart, "La politica exterior Israelí ante el judaismo argentine en tiempos de crisis: de la dictadura e la explosion de la AMIA," *Hagshama*, February 1, 2000, http://www.wzo.org.il/. See also Leonardo Senkman, *Antisemitism During Twenty Years of Redemocratization in Argentina: An Initial Assessment* (Jerusalem: The Vidal Sassoon International Center for the Study of Antisemitism); and Martina Libertad Weisz, "Continuity and Change in Argentinean Antisemitism," *Antisemitism International*, 2006, pp. 32–43.
63. Alain Finkielkraut, *L'Avenir d'une negation: Réflexion sur la question du génocide* (Paris: Éditions du Seuil, 1982).
64. Robert S. Wistrich, "Israeli Letter" (1983), in *A Partisan Century*, ed. Edith Kurzweil (New York: Columbia University Press, 1996), pp. 321–24. The original appeared in *Partisan Review* 50, no. 1 (1983).
65. Wistrich, "Israeli Letter," p. 322.
66. Ibid. See also Robert S. Wistrich, *Ha-anti-tziyonut ke-bitui le-antishemiyut be-et ha-aharonah* [Anti-Zionism as an Expression of Anti-Semitism in Recent Years] (Jerusalem: Sifriyat Shazar and Hebrew University, 1985); and Anita Shapira, "Israeli Perceptions of Anti-Semitism and Anti-Zionism," *The Journal of Israeli History* 25, no. 1 (March 2006): pp. 245–66.
67. Giniewski, *Antisionisme: le nouvel antisémitisme*, pp. 84–107.
68. Wistrich, "Anti-Zionist Masquerade," pp. 12–13.
69. Henrik Bachner, "Antisemitic Motifs in the Swedish Debate on Israel 1982 and 2000–2002," *Antisemitism International*, 2004, pp. 72–78.
70. Ibid., pp. 74–75.
71. Clas Engström, *Arbetet*, June 17, 1982.
72. *Arbetbladet*, September 25, 1982. Quoted in Bacher, "Antisemitic Motifs," p. 73.
73. See Wistrich, *Hitler's Apocalypse*, pp. 237–40.
74. Henrik Bachner, *Aterkomsten, Antisemitism i Sverige after 1945* [Resurgence, Antisemitism in Sweden After 1945] (Stockholm: Natur och Kultur, 1999), pp. 416–20.
75. Olof Palme's speech of July 1, 1982, in *Dagbladet Nya Sambället*, July 9, 1982. See also Bachner, "Antisemitic Motifs," p. 74.
76. Wistrich, *Hitler's Apocalypse*, pp. 239–45.
77. Roald Dahl, *Literary Review*, August 1983, and reprinted in *Time Out*, August 18–24, 1983.

78. Ibid.

79. *New Statesman,* August 26, 1983.

80. *The Economist,* August 7 and 21, 1982.

81. Peter Reading, "Cub," *Times Literary Supplement,* March 23, 1984. See also Roger Scruton, "Race Hatred the Antis Ignore," *The Times* (London), April 3, 1984.

82. Derek Holland, *Israel—The Hate State* (1982), published as part of the magazine *Nationalism Today,* supported by the British National Front.

83. *Caribbean Times,* July 2, 1982. The paper claimed to represent the Afro-Caribbean community in Britain.

84. Wistrich, "Anti-Zionist Masquerade," pp. 12–13.

85. Robert S. Wistrich, "Pius XII and the Shoah," *Antisemitism International,* 2004, pp. 10–22. See also Pope John Paul II, *Spiritual Pilgrimage: Texts on Jews and Judaism 1979–1995,* ed. Eugene J. Fisher and Leon Klenicki (New York: Crossroad, 1995).

86. *The News Line,* July 12, 1982.

87. "From Malvinas to Lebanon," *Labour Review,* July 1982.

88. Ibid.

89. Wistrich, *Hitler's Apocalypse,* pp. 241–42.

90. *The News Line,* June 11, 1982. See also Tony Cliff, "The Road from Zionism to Genocide," *Socialist Worker,* July 3, 1982. Cliff was the Anglicized pseudonym of the Trotskyist theorist Yigael Gluckstein, who left Palestine in the late 1930s.

91. *Socialist Worker,* June 18 and 30, July 10, 1982.

92. *Young Socialist,* August 21, 1982.

93. "London Meeting Condemns Genocide," *Labour Herald,* July 2, 1982.

94. *Labour Herald,* June 25, 1982, p. 7.

95. Maya Spitzer, "Fury Over 'Anti-Semitic' Oliphant Cartoon on Gaza," *The Jerusalem Post,* March 27, 2008.

FIFTEEN: JEWS AGAINST ZION

1. The literature on Jewish self-hatred is considerable. See, for example, Sander L. Gilman, *Jewish Self-Hatred: Anti-Semitism and the Hidden Language of the Jews* (Baltimore: Johns Hopkins University Press, 1986); Robert S. Wistrich, ed., *Austrians and Jews in the Twentieth Century* (New York: St. Martin's Press, 1992); Aharon Appelfeld, *Beyond Despair: Three Lectures and a Conversation with Philip Roth* (New York: Fromm International, 1994); and Ritchie Robertson, *The "Jewish Question" in German Literature, 1749–1939: Emancipation and Its Discontents* (Oxford, U.K.: Clarendon Press, 1999).

2. Michael Glatzer, "Pablo de Santa Maria on the Events of 1391," in Almog, *Antisemitism Through the Ages,* pp. 127–37.

3. See David Mamet, *The Wicked Son: Anti-Semitism, Self-Hatred, and the Jews* (New York: Schocken Books, 2006).

4. Ibid., p. 139.

5. Arthur Schnitzler, *The Road into the Open,* trans. Horace Samuel (New York: Alfred A. Knopf, 1923).

6. See Wistrich, *Jews of Vienna,* pp. 583–620, for Schnitzler's dissection of the "Jewish question" around 1900.

7. Norbert Abels, *Sicherheit ist nirgends: Judentum und Aufklärung bei Arthur Schnitzler* (Königstein, Germany: Athenäum, 1982), p. 98.

8. Schnitzler, *Road into the Open,* pp. 153–54. See also Wistrich, *Jews of Vienna,* p. 607.

9. See Robert S. Wistrich, "Clichés of Hatred," *The Times Literary Supplement,* August 2, 1996; Nancy A. Harrowitz and Barbara Hyams, eds., *Jews and Gender: Responses to Otto Weininger* (Philadelphia: Temple University Press, 1996); and Jacques Le Rider, "L'Antisémitisme Juif d'Otto Weininger," *L'Infini,* no. 13 (1986): pp. 62–83.

10. Brigitte Hamann, *Hitlers Wien: Lehrjahre eines Diktators* (Munich: Piper, 1996), pp. 325–34, 485. See also Paul Reitter, *The Anti-Journalist: Karl Kraus and Jewish Self-Fashioning in Fin-de-Siècle Europe* (Chicago: University of Chicago Press, 2008), pp. 35–39.

11. Karl Kraus, *Eine Krone für Zion* (Vienna, 1898), in Karl Kraus, *Frühe Schriften,* vol. 2, ed. J. J. Braakenburg (Munich: Kösel Verlag, 1979), pp. 298–314.

12. See Ritchie Robertson, "The Problem of Jewish Self-Hatred in Herzl, Kraus and Kafka," *Oxford German Studies* 16 (1985): pp. 81–108. See also John Theobald, *The Paper Ghetto: Karl Kraus and Anti-Semitism* (Frankfurt: Peter Lang, 1996). Also Robert S. Wistrich, *Laboratory for World Destruction: Germans and Jews in Central Europe* (Lincoln: University of Nebraska Press, 2007), pp. 304–24.

13. See Wistrich, *Socialism and the Jews,* pp. 262–81.

14. Wistrich, *Revolutionary Jews From Marx to Trotsky,* p. 86. See also Elzbieta Ettinger, *Rosa Luxemburg: A Life* (London: Pandora, 1988), pp. 3–35.

15. See Wistrich, introduction to Lazare, *Antisemitism;* and Bernard Lazare, *Juifs et Antisémites* (Paris: Éditions Allia, 1992), pp. 172–75. The quote comes from a series of articles that first appeared in *l'Écho Sioniste,* March 20–May 20, 1901.

16. The article, entitled "Höre, Israel," originally appeared in *Die Zukunft,* no. 23 (1897): pp. 454–62. This journal was edited by another highly assimilated, Prussianized, and self-hating Jew, Maximilien Harden.

17. See Peter Loewenberg, *Fantasy and Reality in History* (New York: Oxford University Press, 1995), pp. 108–18; and Hans F. Löffler, *Walther Rathenau, ein Europäer in Kaiserreich* (Berlin: Berlin Verlag Arno Spitz, 1997), for a biographical study.

18. Jacob Golomb, "Jewish Self-Hatred: Nietzsche, Freud and the Case of Theodor Lessing," *LBIYB* 50 (2005): pp. 233–48.

19. See Theodor Lessing, *Der jüdische Selbsthass* (Berlin: Jüdischer Verlag, 1930). Also "Eindrücke aus Galizien," which first appeared in the *Allgemeine Zeitung des Judentums* 73, nos. 49–53 (1909). Sections of Lessing's reports were eagerly reproduced in German anti-Semitic journals of the time.

20. Quoted in Lawrence Baron, "Theodor Lessing: Between Jewish Self-Hatred and Zionism," *LBIYB* 26 (1981): pp. 325–26; see also Hans Mayer, *Outsiders: A Study in Life and Letters* (Cambridge, Mass.: MIT Press, 1982), pp. 357–63.

21. See Yaacov Shavit, *The New Hebrew Nation: Heresy and Fantasy* (London: Frank Cass, 1987); James S. Diamond, *Homeland or Holy Land? The "Canaanite" Critique of Israel* (Bloomington: Indiana University Press, 1986); and Boaz Evron, *Jewish State or Israel: Nation?* (Bloomington: Indiana University Press, 1995), pp. 205–22. Evron was once active in the Canaanite movement.

22. "Mas'a hapetihah" [The opening discourse] in Yonatan Ratosh, *Reshit ha-yamim:*

petihot 'ivriyot [The First Days: Hebrew Overtures] (Tel Aviv: Hadar Publishers, 1982), pp. 188ff. See also Diamond, *Homeland or Holy Land?* pp. 51–56, for a discussion of the text.

23. Diamond, p. 52.

24. Shavit, *New Hebrew Nation,* pp. 60ff.

25. Ibid., p. 137. In the late 1940s Avnery was close to the right-wing Zionist "revisionists," and a self-confessed militarist. Before the Suez campaign of 1956 he called for *preventive war* against the Nasserist regime in Egypt.

26. See Uri Avnery, *Israel Without Zionists: A Plea for Peace in the Middle East* (New York: Macmillan, 1968).

27. Yehezkel Kaufman, "Anti-Semitic Stereotypes in Zionism," *Commentary,* May 1949, pp. 239–45.

28. Ibid.

29. Yehezkel Kaufman, "The Ruin of the Soul," in *Zionism Reconsidered: The Rejection of Jewish Normalcy,* ed. Michael Selzer (New York: Macmillan, 1970), pp. 117–29.

30. Ibid., pp. 120–21.

31. Ibid., p. 121.

32. Ibid., p. 129.

33. See Aron Appelfeld, *The New York Times Book Review,* February 28, 1988, where he remarks that the Jewish ability "to internalize any critical and condemnatory remark and castigate themselves is one of the marvels of human nature."

34. See Arie Bober, ed., *The Other Israel: The Radical Case Against Zionism* (New York: Doubleday Anchor Books, 1972); and Akiva Orr, *Israel: Politics, Myths, and Identity Crises* (London: Pluto Press, 1994).

35. Abraham Léon, *The Jewish Question: A Marxist Interpretation* (New York: Pathfinder Press, 1970).

36. Léon, *Jewish Question,* pp. 244–66.

37. Ibid., p. 255.

38. Maxime Rodinson, *Israel and the Arabs* (London: Penguin Books, 1968), pp. 216–39.

39. Ibid., p. 227: "No Arab can overlook the colonial character of the Jewish occupation of Palestine." See also Rodinson, "Israël, fait colonial," in *Les Temps Modernes,* no. 253 (1967): pp. 17–88.

40. See Nathan Weinstock, *Le Sionisme contre Israël* (Paris: Maspero, 1969); and Weinstock, *Le mouvement révolutionnaire arabe* (Paris: Maspero, 1970).

41. See Henry Bulawko, *Mise au Point: Les Communistes et la Question Juive* (Paris: Centre de Documentation Israel/Moyen Orient, 1971).

42. See Rodinson's appalling article "Le sionisme et la question juive," *La Nouvelle Critique,* March 1953, pp. 10–31, dissected by Hermone, *La Gauche,* pp. 200–19.

43. Ibid.

44. Maxime Rodinson, *Peuple juif ou problème juif?* (Paris: Maspero, 1981), p. 10.

45. Ibid., pp. 64–68, 135ff.

46. Isaac Deutscher, "The Non-Jewish Jew," in Selzer, *Zionism Reconsidered,* pp. 73–86. For a critique, see Wistrich, *Revolutionary Jews,* pp. 1–22. See also Jean Améry, "Der jüdische Störenfried," *Die Zeit,* May 27, 1977, and Shmuel Almog, "The Non-Jewish Jew: The History of a Radical Typology," *SICSA Annual Report* (1998), pp. 8–12.

47. Isaac Deutscher, "On the Arab-Israeli War," *New Left Review,* June 20, 1967. See also appendix of Tariq Ali, *The Clash of Fundamentalisms: Crusades, Jihads, and Modernity* (London: Verso, 2002), pp. 314–32.

48. Ali, *Clash of Fundamentalisms,* pp. 324–25.

49. Ibid., p. 330.

50. Ibid., p. 332.

51. Ibid.

52. See Assaf Sagiv, "George Steiner's Jewish Problem," in *The Jewish Divide Over Israel: Accusers and Defenders,* ed. Edward Alexander and Paul Bogdanor (New Brunswick, N.J.: Transaction Publishers, 2006), pp. 47–63.

53. See Edward Alexander, "The Journalists' War Against Israel," *Encounter,* September–October 1982, pp. 87–97.

54. Robert S. Wistrich, "A New Jewish Question?" *The Jerusalem Report,* March 19, 2007.

55. Jack Nusan Porter and Peter Dreier, eds., *Jewish Radicalism: A Selected Anthology* (New York: Grove Press, 1973). See also Percy S. Cohen, *Jewish Radicals and Radical Jews* (London: Academic Press, 1980); and Walter Laqueur, "The Revolutionaries," in *Next Year in Jerusalem,* ed. Douglas Villiers (London: Harrap, 1976), pp. 79–89.

56. Jerry Rubin, *We Are Everywhere* (New York: Harper and Row, 1971), pp. 74–76.

57. Ibid.

58. See Yair Auron, *Tikkun Olam: The Phenomenon of Jewish Radicals in France During the 1960s and '70s* (Jerusalem: Institute of the World Jewish Congress, 2000), p. 8. The bibliographic section, with its short bios, in Hervé Hamon and Patrick Rotman, *Génération: Les années de rêve* (Paris: Seuil, 1987) is revealing in this respect.

59. Auron, *Tikkun Olam,* pp. 8–9. Since Jews represented only 1 percent of French society, these percentages are stunningly disproportionate. This gave high visibility to Jewish radicalism, but without provoking the major anti-Semitic backlash that happened in the 1930s.

60. For a firsthand account of Benny Lévy's influence over Sartre in the 1970s, see Ely Ben-Gal, *Mardi, chez Sartre: Un Hébreu à Paris 1967–1980* (Paris: Flammarion, 1992). See also the discussion by Judaken, *Jean-Paul Sartre and the Jewish Question,* pp. 221–38.

61. Pierre Goldman, *Souvenirs obscures d'un Juif polonais né en France* (Paris: Le Seuil, 1975); see also Judith Friedlander, *Vilna on the Seine: Jewish Intellectuals in France Since 1968* (New Haven, Conn.: Yale University Press, 1990).

62. Auron, *Tikkun Olam,* p. 22. Also Laurent Greilsamer and Bertrand Le Gendre, "Juif, militant, gangster, écrivain," *Le Monde,* September 22, 1979; and Catherine Chaine, "Une interview inédite: Goldman L'étranger," *Le Monde,* September 30, 1979; and Luc Rozenzweig, "Kaddish pour Pierre," *Libération,* September 21, 1979.

63. Daniel Cohn-Bendit, *Le Grand Bazar* (Paris: Belfond, 1975), pp. 9–12. I personally interviewed him in Jerusalem during that visit. See Wistrich, "Cohn-Bendit in Jerusalem," *New Outlook,* May–June 1970.

64. *L'Arche,* June 1978, quoted by Léon Poliakov, *De Moscou à Beyrouth: Essai sur la désinformation* (Paris: Calmann-Lévy, 1983), pp. 157–58.

65. *Le Monde,* December 16, 1972.

66. Interview with Geismar in Rosenzweig, *La Jeune France Juive,* pp. 36–61.

67. Tony Greenstein, *Zionism: Antisemitism's Twin in Jewish Garb* (Brighton Labour briefing document, 1982). The title of this screed recalls the anti-Zionist statements of German Orthodox Jews seventy years earlier, recast in secular socialist jargon.

68. Lenni Brenner, *Zionism in the Age of the Dictators: A Reappraisal* (London: Croom Helm, 1983). See also the review by Brian Cheyette in *Patterns of Prejudice* 17, no. 3 (July 1983): pp. 49–51.

69. See Wistrich, *Between Redemption and Perdition,* pp. 242–45.

70. Jim Allen, *Perdition: A Play in Two Acts* (London: Ithaca Press, 1987). Lenni Brenner, Akiva Orr, Erich Fried, Noam Chomsky, and Maxime Rodinson—all of them radical Jews—defended Allen from the charge of anti-Semitism. See David Cesarani, "The Perdition Affair," in Wistrich, *Anti-Zionism and Antisemitism in the Contemporary World,* pp. 53–62.

71. Wistrich, *Anti-Zionism and Antisemitism in the Contemporary World,* pp. 242–43. Allen boasted that his play was a "lethal" attack against Zionism.

72. See Noam Chomsky, *Fateful Triangle: United States, Israel and the Palestinians,* rev. ed. (London: Pluto Press, 1999); Chomsky, *Middle East Illusions* (Lanham, Md.: Rowman and Littlefield, 2003); and Chomsky, *Power and Terror: Post 9/11 Talks and Interviews* (New York: Seven Stories Press, 2003).

73. Arch Puddington, "Chomsky's Universe," *Commentary,* October 2004, pp. 66–70.

74. Ibid., p. 70.

75. "American Linguist Noam Chomsky: 'Hitler Was Unique . . . but We Should Recognize Similarities in Planning, Policies, and Thinking,' " *MEMRI Special Dispatch Series,* no. 1178 (May 31, 2006), from Chomsky's interview with Lebanese television on May 23, 2006.

76. Noam Chomsky, preface to *Mémoire en défense: contre ceux qui m'accusent de falsifier l'histoire; la question des chambers à gaz,* by Robert Faurisson (Paris: La Vieille Taupe, 1980). See also Pierre Vidal-Naquet, *Assassins of Memory: Essays on the Denial of the Holocaust* (New York: Columbia University Press, 1992), pp. 65–73.

77. Chomsky, preface to *"Mémoire en défense,"* p. xv.

78. Vidal-Naquet, *Assassins of Memory,* p. 72.

79. Gore Vidal, foreword to *Jewish History, Jewish Religion,* by Israel Shahak (London: Pluto Press, 1994).

80. Rachel Neuwirth, "Jewish Antisemite," *Nativ* 18, no. 6 (November 2005): pp. 29–33, in Hebrew.

81. Paul Bogdanor, "The Devil State: Chomsky's War Against Israel," in Alexander and Bogdanor, *Jewish Divide,* pp. 77–114, especially pp. 100–101, 105.

82. See Norman Finkelstein, *The Holocaust Industry: Reflections on the Exploitation of Jewish Suffering* (London: Verso, 2001); and Finkelstein's anti-Zionist book, *Image and Reality of the Israel-Palestine Conflict* (London: Verso, 2001).

83. See "Explosive Charges," *The Economist,* August 7, 2000. See also Paul Bogdanor, "Norman G. Finkelstein: Chomsky for Nazis," in Alexander and Bogdanor, *Jewish Divide,* pp. 135–60.

84. Norman G. Finkelstein, *Beyond Chutzpah: On the Misuse of Anti-Semitism and the Abuse of History* (Berkeley: University of California Press, 2005); and Finkelstein, interview by Ben Naparstek, "His Own Worst Enemy," *The Jerusalem Post,* December 9, 2005.

85. Bogdanor, "Norman G. Finkelstein," *The Jewish Divide,* p. 137.

86. Finkelstein, *Image and Reality,* p. 8.

87. Ibid., p. 20.

88. Paul Charles Merkley, "These Pigs on the Face of the Earth," *Christianity Today,* January 1, 2006, http://www.christianitytoday.com./bc/2006/001/12.38.html.

89. "Lebanon's New TV: 'Contradictions, Lies, and Exaggerations' in Number Killed in 'Jewish Holocaust,' " *MEMRI Special Dispatch Series* no. 1194 (June 30, 2006). Interview with Lebanon's New TV that took place on June 21, 2006.

90. Finkelstein, *Holocaust Industry,* p. 50.

91. Ibid., p. 33.

92. Ibid., p. 30.

93. See Finkelstein's scathing critique, "Goldhagen for Beginners," which I read in Polish translation in *Rzeczpospolita,* June 20, 2001.

94. See Michael Neumann, "What Is Antisemitism?" *Counterpunch,* June 4, 2002. http://www.counterpunch.org/neumann0604.html. Also Jonathan Kay, "Trent University's Problem Professor," *National Post,* August 9, 2003.

95. Jacqueline Rose, *The Question of Zion* (Princeton, N.J.: Princeton University Press, 2005), dedicated to Palestinian intellectual Edward Said. This poorly researched book is marred with misleading statements and factual errors.

96. Ibid., p. 133.

97. Ibid., p. 17.

98. Ibid., pp. 64–65. In fact, Hitler visited Paris for the first and only time after the fall of France in June 1940.

99. Tony Judt, "Israel: The Alternative," *The New York Review of Books,* October 23, 2003. For Jewish advocates of the binational state, see Kushner and Solomon, *Wrestling with Zion.*

100. Hilary and Steven Rose, "The Choice Is to Do Nothing or Try to Bring About Change," *The Guardian,* July 15, 2002. See also Steven Morris, "Jews in UK Renounce Right to Live in Israel," *The Guardian,* August 8, 2002; and the petition signed by a number of Jewish academics denouncing Israel's "barbaric policies" toward the Palestinians.

101. Alvin Rosenfeld, *"Progressive" Jewish Thought and the New Anti-Semitism* (New York: AJC, 2006). See also Rosenfeld's interview with Benjamin Weinthal and Alex Feuerherdt, "Does Jewish Anti-Semitism Exist?" *The Jerusalem Post,* December 11, 2008.

102. "London Conference—a Prelude to Academic Boycott of Israel," *The Washington Report on Middle East Affairs* 24, no. 1 (2004): p. 15.

103. Ilan Pappé, *The Ethnic Cleansing of Palestine* (New York: Oneworld, 2006). See also "Nations and Narratives," *The Economist,* November 4, 2006, pp. 108–9.

104. See Ilan Pappé, *A History of Modern Palestine: One Land, Two Peoples* (Cambridge: Cambridge University Press, 2004); and the highly critical review by Benny Morris, "Politics by Other Means," *The New Republic,* March 22, 2004, pp. 25–30.

105. *The Jerusalem Post,* February 13, 2007.

106. Solomon Socrates, "Israel's Academic Extremists," *Middle East Quarterly* 8, no. 4 (Fall 2001): pp. 5–14.

107. See Shlomo Sharan, *Our Inner Scourge: The Catastrophe of Israel Academics* (Shaareí Tikva, Israel: Ariel Center for Policy Research, no. 171, 2007), pp. 11–15.

108. *Haaretz,* November 16, 2000.

109. Paul Bogdanor, "Chomsky's Ayatollahs," in Alexander and Bogdanor, *Jewish Divide,* pp. 124–30. For an obituary, see *Haaretz,* March 19, 2007.

110. On contemporary liberal hostility to Jews, see Bernard Harrison, *The Resurgence of Anti-Semitism: Jews, Israel, and Liberal Opinion* (New York: Rowman and Littlefield, 2007). See also Emanuele Ottolenghi, "Europe's Good Jews," *Commentary,* December 2005, pp. 42–46; and Cathy Young, "When Jews Wax Anti-Semitic," *The Boston Globe,* February 7, 2005.

111. Calev Ben-David, "A Pinteresque Homecoming," *The Jerusalem Post,* October 21, 2005, p. 9. Pinter, the child of Eastern European Jewish immigrants, grew up in London's East End after World War II when it was still infected by fascist anti-Semitism. His Jewishness had always been very peripheral and low-key, except for bashing Israel.

112. Anne Roiphe, "Jews Who Call Each Other 'Nazi,' " *The Jerusalem Report,* March 21, 2005, p. 46. See also Haim Chertok, "With Semites Like These," ibid., October 30, 2006, pp. 39–41.

113. Edgar Morin, Sami Naïr, et Danièle Sallenave, "Israël-Palestine: Le cancer," *Le Monde,* June 4, 2002. A French court found *Le Monde* and the authors guilty of "racist defamation" in their portrayal of Israel and the Jews. See also Tom Gross, "J'Accuse: Anti-Semitism at *Le Monde* and Beyond," *The Wall Street Journal,* June 2, 2005.

114. A good example of this indignant response is the collection of essays written by French leftists—mainly Jewish—called *Antisémitisme: l'intolérable chantage* (Paris: La Découverte, 2003).

115. See Assaf Sagiv, "Fifty Faces of Post-Zionism ," *Azure,* no. 8 (Autumn 1999): pp. 23–31, on the Israeli left-wing journal *Theory and Criticism.* See also the essays in Shlomo Sharan, ed., *Israel and the Post-Zionists: A Nation at Risk* (Brighton, U.K.: Sussex Academic Press, 2003).

116. See Arieh Stav, "Israeli Antisemitism," in Sharan, *Israel and the Post-Zionists,* p. 175. The original article by Amos Oz, "In the Name of Life and Peace," appeared in *Yediot Ahronoth,* June 8, 1989.

117. Stav, "Israeli Antisemitism," pp. 176–77.

118. Avraham Burg, "A Failed Israeli Society Collapsing," *IHT,* September 6, 2003. The Hebrew original was entitled "Zionism Now."

119. Ari Shavit, "On the Eve of Destruction," *Haaretz,* http://www.haaretz.com/hasen/objects/pages/PrintArticleEn.jhtml?itemNo=360539.

120. Ari Shavit, "Post-Zioni [Post-Zionist]," *Haaretz,* June 8, 2007.

121. See Anthony Julius, "The Company They Keep: Antisemitism's Fellow Travellers," *ZWord* (July 2008): pp. 1–10.

122. See Amotz Asa-El, "Avraham Burg's French Concoction," *The Jerusalem Post,* June 15, 2007.

123. Avi Shlaim, "How Israel Brought Gaza to the Brink of Humanitarian Catastrophe," *The Guardian*, January 9, 2009.

124. Alvin Rosenfeld, "Modern Jewish Intellectual Failure: A Brief History," in Alexander and Bogdanor, *Jewish Divide*, pp. 24–25.

Sixteen: Shylock Meets Uncle Sam

1. Paul Hollander, *Anti-Americanism: Irrational and Rational* (New Brunswick, N.J.: Transaction Publishers, 1995).

2. David Brooks, "Among the Bourgeoisophobes," *The Weekly Standard*, April 15, 2002.

3. Andrei S. Markovits, "Terror and Clandestine Anti-Semitism: Thoughts on German and American Reactions to September 11, 2001," *Partisan Review* 69, no. 1 (2002): pp. 19–24.

4. Richard Herzinger, "Die Hure Babylon: Die apokalyptischen Motive eines Weltweit Grassierender AntiAmerikanismus," *Neue Zürcher Zeitung*, September 24, 2001.

5. Rosenfeld, *"Feeling Alone, Again,"* p. 9.

6. Josef Joffe, *Nations We Love to Hate: Israel, America, and the New Antisemitism* (Jerusalem: Hebrew University of Jerusalem, SICSA, Posen Papers in Contemporary Antisemitism, no. 1, 2004).

7. Martin Heidegger, *An Introduction to Metaphysics* (New Haven, Conn.: Yale University Press, 1959), pp. 37, 45–46.

8. Jean Baudrillard, *America* (London: Verso, 1988), pp. 66, 76–78, 97–99, 121–25.

9. Markovits, "Terror and Clandestine Antisemitism," p. 23.

10. Herzinger, "Die Hure Babylon." See also the article by Peter Krause in *Antikommunismus und Antiamerikanismus in Deutschland: Kontinuität und Wandel nach 1945*, ed. Gesine Schwan (Baden-Baden, Germany: Nomos Verlag, 1999), pp. 248–73, for earlier anticapitalist motifs, from the First Gulf War of 1991.

11. Joffe, *Nations We Love to Hate*, pp. 2–3.

12. Ibid., p. 4.

13. Ibid., p. 1

14. Norman Podhoretz, "World War IV: How It Started, What It Means, and Why We Have to Win," *Commentary*, September 2004, pp. 32–33, 39–40, 42–45.

15. Joshua Muravchik, "The Neoconservative Cabal," *Commentary*, September 2003, pp. 26–33; and "The Shadow Men," *The Economist*, April 26, 2003, pp. 41–43, which quotes Robert Kagan as follows: "One finds Britain's finest minds propounding . . . conspiracy theories concerning the 'neo-conservative' (read: Jewish) hijacking of American foreign policy. In Paris, all the talk is of oil and 'imperialism'—and Jews." A member of the French parliament quoted his country's foreign minister, Dominique de Villepin, saying "the hawks in the US administration [are] in the hands of [Ariel] Sharon"—a comment seen in some quarters as a coded message about undue pro-Israeli influence exercised by neo-cons, most of whom are Jewish, at the heart of the administration."

16. For Khomeini's views of Americans, Israel, and the Jews, see Barry Rubin and Ju-

dith Colp Rubin, eds., *Anti-American Terrorism and the Middle East: A Documentary Reader* (Oxford, U.K.: Oxford University Press, 2002), pp. 32–36, 99–103, 107–8.

17. See the testimony of Andrew Kohut given before the Subcommittee on International Organizations, Human Rights, and Oversight Committee on Foreign Affairs, U.S. House of Representatives, March 14, 2007. The official report was released on June 27, 2007. I have also used earlier surveys of the Pew Global Attitudes Project, which, since its first poll in June 2002, has interviewed in depth about 110,000 people in fifty countries. Its polls are the first and most important chronicle of the rise of anti-Americanism in the early twenty-first century. See also Pew Research Center, "Global Opinion: The Spread of Anti-Americanism," covering the period 1999–2000 to March 2004. For fuller details, see http://www.pew global.org/. See also the comments by Fouad Ajami, "The Anti-Americans," *The Wall Street Journal,* July 3, 2003.

18. Pew Research Center, "Global Opinion."

19. "Distrust of US, Bush Growing Around the World," *The Jerusalem Post,* June 28, 2007. See also Joshua W. Walker, "Truly Democratic—and Anti-American," ibid., July 15, 2007.

20. Alan McPherson, ed., *Anti-Americanism in Latin America and the Caribbean* (New York: Berghahn Books, 2006), pp. 1–28.

21. "Take That, Gringos," *Newsweek,* October 8, 2001, p. 44.

22. Michael Radu, "A Matter of Identity: The Anti-Americanism of Latin American Intellectuals," in *Understanding Anti-Americanism,* ed. Paul Hollander (Chicago: Ivan R. Dee, 2004), pp. 144–64.

23. Adolfo Perez Esquivel, *Global Viewpoint,* March 6, 2003.

24. Fredy Quezada, "George Bush Is Bin Laden," *El Nuevo Diario,* October 11, 2001, quoted in David Brooks, "Nicaraguan Anti-Americanism," in Hollander, *Understanding Anti-Americanism,* pp. 165–89.

25. Ibid., pp. 182–87.

26. Mark Falcoff, "Cuban Anti-Americanism: Historical, Popular, and Official," in Hollander, *Understanding Anti-Americanism,* p. 203. See also John Gerassi, ed., *Venceremos: The Speeches and Writings of Ernesto Che Guevara* (London: Weidenfeld, 1969), pp. 423–24.

27. Cathy Young, "The Feminist Hostility Toward American Society," in Hollander, *Understanding Anti-Americanism,* pp. 279–300.

28. Adam Garfinkle, "Peace Movements and the Adversary Culture," in Hollander, *Understanding Anti-Americanism,* pp. 301–21.

29. Elaine Sciolino, "French Rallies Against War Shift Focus to Israel," *The New York Times,* March 30, 2003.

30. See David Horowitz, *Unholy Alliance: Radical Islam and the American Left* (Washington, D.C.: Regnery Publishing, 2004), pp. 55–77. Virtually all the neo-Communist, radical, and New Left gurus of domestic anti-Americanism Horowitz discusses (including Noam Chomsky, Leslie Cagan, Maurice Zeitlin, Susan Sontag, Gerda Lerner, Todd Gitlin, and Norman Mailer) are, in fact, Jewish, though he passes over this significant fact without comment.

31. See Noam Chomsky, *9–11* (New York: Seven Stories Press, 2001); Chomsky, *What*

Uncle Sam Really Wants (New York: Ododian Press, 2002); Horowitz, *Unholy Alliance*, pp. 89–99; and Horowitz, *Anti-Chomsky Reader* (San Francisco: Encounter Books, 2004).

32. See, for example, Norman Mailer, "The White Man Unburdened," *The New York Review of Books*, July 17, 2003, for a good example of how the blame for Saddam's mass murders in Iraq is easily shifted to America.

33. See Daniel Johnson, "America and the America-Haters," *Commentary*, June 2006, pp. 29, 27–32.

34. Michael Mosbacher and Digby Anderson, "Recent Trends in British Anti-Americanism," in Hollander, *Understanding Anti-Americanism*, pp. 84–104.

35. T. Baldwin, "World's Big Problem Is the US, Says Meacher," *The Times* (London), June 20, 2003; Michael Meacher, "This War on Terrorism Is Bogus," *The Guardian*, September 6, 2003. Meacher was a minister in Tony Blair's cabinet during the Iraq War.

36. M. White, "Dalyell Steps Up Attack on Levy," *The Guardian*, May 6, 2003.

37. Ibid.

38. Johnson, "America and the America-Haters," p. 30.

39. Yossi Klein Halevi, "Hatreds Entwined," *Azure*, no. 16 (Winter 2004): pp. 25–32.

40. David Gelernter, "Why Americans Stand with Israel," *The Weekly Standard,* May 20, 2002.

41. John J. Mearsheimer and Stephen M. Walt, *The Israel Lobby and U.S. Foreign Policy* (working paper, March 2006). Harvard University and John F. Kennedy School of Government Working Paper Number: RWP06-011, March 13, 2006. An edited version was published in the *London Review of Books*, March 23, 2006, and http://www.lrb.co.uk/v28/n06/mear01_.html, downloaded January 22, 2007.

42. Gabriel Schoenfeld, "Dual Loyalty and the 'Israel Lobby,' " *Commentary*, November 2006, pp. 33–40.

43. Sander L. Gilman, introduction to *America in the Eyes of the Germans: An Essay on Anti-Americanism,* by Dan Diner (Princeton, N.J.: Markus Wiener Publishers, 1996), pp. xiii–xviii.

44. Diner, *America in the Eyes of the Germans,* p. 20.

45. Max Horkheimer, *Gesammelte Schriften,* vol. 14 (Frankfurt: Suhrkampf, 1988), p. 408.

46. Ibid.

47. Diner, *America in the Eyes of Germans,* pp. 56–60.

48. Klaus Schwabe, "Anti-Americanism Within the German Right 1917–1933," *Amerikastudien* 21, no. 1 (1976): pp. 89–107.

49. See Giselher Wirsing, *Der masslose Kontinent: Roosevelt's Kampf um die Weltherrschaft* (Jena, Germany: Diederichs, 1942). Wirsing was a leading Nazi expert on Britain and America, as well as the Middle East.

50. Quoted in Edmund Silberner, *Kommunisten zur Judenfrage* (Opladen, Germany: Westdeutscher Verlag, 1983), p. 268.

51. Alexander Graf Brockdorff, *Amerikanische Weltherrschaft?* (Berlin: Albrecht, 1929), p. 26. American prejudices against Jews at this time were not so different. See Steven Carr, *Hollywood and Anti-Semitism: A Cultural History up to World War II* (Cambridge: Cambridge University Press, 2001), pp. 108–31.

52. Adolf Halfeld, *Amerika und der Amerikanismus: Kritische Betrachtungen eines Deutschen und eines Europäers* (Jena: Diederichs, 1927), p. 239.

53. Robert S. Wistrich, *Weekend in Munich: Art, Propaganda, and Terror in the Third Reich* (London: Pavilion Books, 1995), pp. 18, 31–32, 56–69.

54. *Völkischer Beobachter*, January 21, 1939.

55. Max Domarus, ed., *Hitler: Reden und Proklamationen, 1932–1945* (Neustadt, Germany: Schmidt, 1972), vol. 2: pp. 1801–4. Speech of December 11, 1941, in which Hitler declared war on the United States. See also Jeffrey Herf, *The Jewish Enemy: Nazi Propaganda During World War II and the Holocaust* (Cambridge, Mass.: Harvard University Press, 2006), pp. 224–30.

56. Ibid., p. 1920. Hitler speech of September 30, 1942.

57. Wirsing, *Der masslose Kontinent*, pp. 434–36.

58. Gabriela Wettberg, *Das Amerika-Bild und seine negativen Konstanten in der deutschen Nachkriegsliteratur* (Heidelberg: C. Winter, 1987).

59. See Thomas Haury, *Antisemitismus von links: Kommunistische Ideologie und Antizionismus in der frühen DDR* (Hamburg: Hamburger Edition, 2002).

60. Diner, *America in the Eyes of Germans*, p. 130.

61. André Glucksman, *La Force du Vertige* (Paris: Grasset, 1983), pp. 127ff.

62. See Alfred Mechtersheimer, "Antiamerikanisch-weshalb eigentlich nicht? Von der Pflicht, dem weltweit verheerenden Einfluss der USA zu widerstehen," in *Der Krieg der Köpfe: Von Golfkrieg zur neuen Weltordnung*, ed. Helmut Thielen (Bad Honnef, Germany: Horlemann, 1991).

63. See, for example, Jörg Friedrich, *Der Brand* (Berlin: Propyläen, 2002); Friedrich, *Brandstätten* (Berlin: Propyläen, 2003); and Hans-Joachim Noack, "Die Deutschen als Opfer," *Der Spiegel*, March 25, 2002, pp. 36–39. See also Nina Bernstein, "Young Germans Ask: Thanks for What?" *The New York Times*, March 9, 2003.

64. See Andrei S. Markovits, "An Inseparable Tandem of European Identity? Anti-Americanism and Anti-Semitism in the Short and Long Run," *Journal of Israeli History* 25, no. 1 (March 2006): pp. 85–105.

65. William Safire, "The German Problem," *The New York Times*, September 19, 2002.

66. See Robert S. Wistrich, *The Politics of Ressentiment: Israel, Jews and the German Media* (Jerusalem: Hebrew University of Jerusalem, SICSA, 2004).

67. Fareed Zakaria, "It's Time to Talk to the World," *Newsweek*, January 27, 2003. See also *The Economist*, February 1, 2003, p. 37.

68. Lucien Romier, *L'homme nouveau esquisse des consequences du progrès* (Paris: Librairie Hachette, 1929), p. 139; and David Strauss, *Menace in the West: The Rise of French Anti-Americanism in Modern Times* (Westport, Conn.: Greenwood Press, 1978), pp. 66–90.

69. J. L. Chastanet, *L'Oncle Shylock on l'impérialisme américain à la conquête du monde* (Paris: Ernest Flammarion, 1927), p. 11.

70. Strauss, *Menace in the West*, p. 97; and André Siegfried, *Les Etats-Unis d'aujourd'hui* (Paris: Armand Colin, 1927), pp. 204, 227.

71. Jean-François Revel, *L'Obsession anti-Americaine: Son fonctionnement, ses causes, ses consequences* (Paris: Plon, 2002).

72. Philippe Roger, *L'Ennemi Américain: Généalogie de l'antiaméricanisme français* (Paris: Seuil, 2002), pp. 555–75.

73. Ibid., pp. 568–72. See also M. Contat and M. Rybalka, *Les Écrits de Sartre* (Paris: Gallimard, 1970), pp. 212–13.

74. Michel Gurfinkel, "France's Jewish Problem," *Commentary*, July–August, 2002, pp. 38–45; John Vinour, "Why France Disdains America," *IHT*, October 8, 2002; and "Spot the Difference," *The Economist*, December 24, 2005, pp. 49–51.

75. See Michaël Prazan, *L'Écriture Génocidaire: L'antisémitisme, en style et en discours, de l'affaire Dreyfus au 11 Septembre 2001* (Paris: Calmann-Lévy, 2005), pp. 106–55, on Céline's influence.

76. J.-É. Hallier, "Les chambers à gaz audiovisuelles," *L'Idiot International*, June 28, 1991.

77. Ibid.

78. "L'Odeur de la France," *L'Idiot International*, June 28, 1991, p. 1.

79. Ibid.

80. Prazan, *L'Écriture Génocidaire*, pp. 238–58.

81. Pierre-André Taguieff, *Néo-Pacifisme, Nouvelle Judéophobie et Mythe du Complot: De la "Guerre Juive" à "L'Aggression Américo-Sioniste"* (Paris: Les Études du Crif, 2003).

82. David Pryce-Jones, *Betrayal: France, the Arabs, and the Jews* (New York: Encounter Books, 2006), pp. 137–52.

83. George F. Will, "Europe's Monomania," *The Washington Post*, February 23, 2003. See also Bernard-Henri Lévy, *Left in Dark Times: A Stand Against the New Barbarism* (New York: Random House, 2008), pp. 112–45. Lévy treats anti-Americanism as "the other Socialism of the imbeciles," an anti-American religion of the Left that has become a metaphor for anti-Semitism.

84. See Bruce Bawer, *While Europe Slept: How Radical Islam Is Destroying the West from Within* (New York: Doubleday, 2006), pp. 77–152.

85. Salman Rushdie, "America and Anti-Americans," *The New York Times*, February 4, 2002.

86. See Rubin and Rubin, *Anti-American Terrorism*, p. 156.

87. "Hamas Weekly: 'Allah Has Answered Our Prayers; the Sword of Vengeance Has Reached America and Will Strike Again and Again,' " *MEMRI Special Dispatch*, no. 268 (September 17, 2001).

88. Fouad Ajami, "The Falseness of Anti-Americanism," *Foreign Policy*, September–October 2003. See also Ajami, "The Anti-Americans," *The Wall Street Journal*, July 3, 2003; and Khaled Abu Toameh, "Biting the Hand That Feeds Them," *The Jerusalem Post*, April 4, 2003, with excerpts from Ibrahim Mudaris's sermon.

89. "The Egyptian Government, Opposition, and Independent Press All Celebrate the Terrorist Attacks in the U.S.," *MEMRI Special Dispatch Series*, no. 281 (October 5, 2001).

90. "Egypt's Opposition Press: Rejoicing Is a National and Religious Obligation; These Were the Best Moments of Our Lives; Bush Is a Mouse Leading a Gang of Mice," *MEMRI Special Dispatch Series*, no. 274 (September 25, 2001).

91. Ibid.

92. Ibid.

93. Fouad Ajami, "The Sentry's Solitude," *Foreign Affairs*, November–December 2001, pp. 2–16. See also Ajami, "Two Faces, One Terror," *The Wall Street Journal*, November 11, 2002.

94. Rubin and Rubin, *Anti-American Terrorism,* pp. 149–51, "Jihad Against Jews and Crusaders" (statement of the World Islamic Front, February 23, 1998); and Barry Rubin, "Roots of Arab Anti-Americanism," *The Jerusalem Post,* June 14, 2005.

95. Victor Davis Hanson, "Our Enemies, the Saudis," *Commentary,* July–August 2002, pp. 23–28; Daniel Pipes, *Militant Islam Reaches America* (New York: W. W. Norton and Company, 2002), pp. 111–32; and Stephen Schwartz, *Two Faces of Islam: Saudi Fundamentalism and Its Role in Terrorism* (New York: Anchor Books, 2003), pp. 196–275. See also Dore Gold, *Hatred's Kingdom: How Saudi Arabia Supports the New Global Terrorism* (Washington, D.C.: Regnery Publishing, 2003), pp. 89–156.

96. "Saudi Opposition Sheikhs on America, Bin Laden, and Jihad," *MEMRI Special Dispatch Series,* no. 400 (July 18, 2002).

97. " 'Why We Fight America': Al-Qaida's Spokesman Explains September 11 and Declares Intentions to Kill 4 Million Americans with Weapons of Mass Destruction," *MEMRI Special Dispatch Series,* no. 388 (June 12, 2002).

98. Itamar Marcus and Barbara Crook, "Egyptian TV Promotes Anti-American Hatred," *Palestinian Media Watch Bulletin,* April 30, 2006.

99. See *Al-Arabi* (Egypt), May 9, 2004. The Nasserite weekly featured an interview with Yousef Shaheen, the Egyptian producer of the film *Alexandria–New York* screened at the May 2004 Cannes Film Festival.

100. "Nazism Threatens the World Anew,"*Al-Ahali* (Egypt), February 3, 2003.

101. *Al-Arabi,* January 18, 2004.

102. "Columnist in Turkish Islamic Daily: 'USA—the God-Damned Country'; 'Murdering Is Genetically Ingrained in American Culture,' " *MEMRI Special Dispatch Series,* no. 857 (February 2, 2005).

103. http://www.alminbar.net/alkhutab/Khutbaa.asp?mediaURL=7512. Friday sermon at al-Aqsa Mosque, December 10, 2004.

104. Sermon of Sheikh Mudeiris at Sheikh Ijlin Mosque in Gaza, PATV, January 7, 2005.

105. http://www.alhaqaeq.net/, November 4, 2003; *Al-Jazirah* (Saudi Arabia), November 4, 2003.

106. *Al-Hayat al-Jadida,* February 16, 2004.

107. See Rosenfeld, *Anti-Americanism and Anti-Semitism.*

Seventeen: Multiculturalism and Its Discontents

1. Isaiah Berlin, interview by Nathan Gardels, "The Ingathering Storm of Nationalism," *New Perspectives Quarterly,* Fall 1991. Reproduced in Charles P. Cozic, ed., *Nationalism and Ethnic Conflict* (San Diego: Greenhaven Press, 1994), pp. 42–49.

2. See Jonathan Sacks, *Radical Then, Radical Now: The Legacy of the World's Oldest Religion* (London: HarperCollins, 2001), pp. 90–92, on Jews as "archetypal strangers" throughout history who were chosen by God "to teach the dignity of difference."

3. Michael Graetz, *Les Juifs en France au XIXe siècle: De la Révolution à l'Alliance Israélite Universelle* (Paris: Éditions du Seuil, 1989); Pierre Birnbaum, *Jewish Destinies: Citizenship, State, and Community in Modern France* (New York: Hill and

Wang, 2000), pp. 11–31; and Emanuele Ottolenghi, "Call It Fear: Europe's Multicultural Ideal Has Planted the Seeds of Its Own Destruction," *The Jerusalem Post,* April 30, 2004, p. 15.

4. In December 1789 the National Assembly debated whether non-Catholics in France could be elected to municipal office. On that occasion, the Comte de Clermont-Tonnerre (who supported the revolution) declared, "We must deny everything to the Jews as a Nation, in the sense of a constituted body, and grant them everything as individuals." Quoted in Birnbaum, *Jewish Destinies,* p. 19.

5. Wistrich, *Jews of Vienna,* pp. 413–15. See also David Rechter, "A Nationalism of Small Things: Jewish Autonomy in Late Habsburg Austria," *LBIYB* 52 (2007), pp. 87–109.

6. See Houston S. Chamberlain, *Die Grundlagen des neunzehnten Jahrhunderts* (Munich: F. Bruckmann a.-g. 1909), vol. 1: pp. 323–546.

7. See Roger Griffin, ed., *Fascism* (Oxford, U.K.: Oxford University Press, 1995). Among the earlier studies focusing on nineteenth-century cultural anti-Semitism, see Fritz Stern, *The Politics of Cultural Despair* (Berkeley: University of California Press, 1961); and George L. Mosse, *The Crisis of German Ideology* (London: Weidenfeld and Nicolson, 1966).

8. See Robert S. Wistrich, *Anti-Semitism and Multiculturalism: The Uneasy Connection* (Jerusalem: Hebrew University of Jerusalem, SICSA, Posen Papers in Contemporary Antisemitism, no. 5, 2007).

9. Hitler, *Mein Kampf,* p. 123.

10. Ibid.

11. See Dan Diner, *America in the Eyes of the Germans: An Essay on Anti-Americanism* (Princeton, N.J.: Markus Wiener, 1996), pp. 81–103.

12. Jeffrey Herf, *The Jewish Enemy: Nazi Propaganda During World War II and the Holocaust* (Cambridge, Mass.: Harvard University Press, 2006), pp. 83–84.

13. See Matthias Küntzel, "Von Zeesen bis Beirut: Nationalsozialismus und Antisemitismus in der arabischen Welt," in *Neuer Antisemitismus? Eine globale Debatte,* ed. Doron Rabinovici et al. (Frankfurt: Suhrkampf, 2004), pp. 271–93.

14. Robert S. Wistrich, "The New Islamic Fascism," *Partisan Review* 69, no. 1 (2002): pp. 32–34.

15. See the contribution by Jeffrey Herf, "What Is Old and What Is New in the Terrorism of Islamic Fundamentalism?" *Partisan Review* 69, no. 1 (2002): pp. 25–31.

16. Andrei S. Markovits, "Terror and Clandestine Anti-Semitism: Thoughts on German and American Reactions to September 11, 2001," *Partisan Review* 69, no. 1 (2002): p. 19. Speer's diary entry is dated November 18, 1947. At the time he was serving a sentence for Nazi war crimes in Spandau Prison.

17. Markovits, "Terror and Clandestine Anti-Semitism," p. 23.

18. See Rosenfeld, *Anti-Americanism and Anti-Semitism;* and Yossi Klein Halevi, "Hatreds Entwined," *Azure,* no. 16 (Winter 2004): pp. 25–31.

19. Andrei Markovits, "European Anti-Americanism and Anti-Semitism: Similarities and Differences," in *Israel and Europe: An Expanding Abyss,* ed. Manfred Gerstenfeld (Jerusalem: Jerusalem Center for Public Affairs, 2005), pp. 125–42; and Wistrich, "Something Is Rotten in the State of Europe," pp. 95–110. See also Ye'or, *Eurabia,* pp. 163–208, for a multitude of examples.

20. Alan Pryce-Jones, "Europe's 'Terrible Transformation'?" *Commentary,* July–August 2007, pp. 58–61.
21. Ibid.
22. See the essays in Wistrich, *Demonizing the Other.*
23. Alain Finkielkraut, "In the Name of the Other: Reflections on the Coming Anti-semitism," *Azure,* no. 18 (Autumn 2004): p. 23.
24. See Robert S. Wistrich, *Antisemitism in Western Europe at the Turn of the 21st Century* (Jerusalem: Institute of the World Jewish Congress, 2005).
25. "Multicultural Britain: A Nation at Ease with Bits of Itself," *The Economist,* December 2, 2006, p. 32. See also Efraim Sicher, *Multiculturalism, Globalization, and Antisemitism: The British Case* (Jerusalem: The Vidal Sassoon International Center for the Study of Antisemitism, ACTA, no. 32, 2009).
26. See Robert S. Wistrich, "Cruel Britannia: Anti-Semitism Among the Ruling Elites," *Azure,* no. 21 (Summer 2005): pp. 100–127; and Phillips, *Londistan,* pp. 106–31. See also *Islam, British Society and the Terrorist Threat* (Jerusalem: Hebrew University of Jerusalem, SICSA, Posen Papers in Contemporary Antisemitism, no. 7, 2007); and the article by Srdja Trifkovic, "The Islamic Conquest of Britain," in *The Myth of Islamic Tolerance,* ed. Robert Spencer (New York: Prometheus Books, 2005), pp. 294–99.
27. Melanie Phillips, "Reflections on Londonistan," in *Islam, British Society and the Terrorist Threat,* pp. 1–6; and Robert S. Wistrich, "Islamism, Multiculturalism and British Society," in ibid., pp. 7–10.
28. Phillips, "Reflections on Londonistan," p. 4.
29. For a lucid analysis, see Denis MacEoin, "Tactical Hudna and Islamist Intolerance," *Middle Eastern Quarterly,* Summer 2008, pp. 39–48.
30. Margaret Brearley, *The Anglican Church, Jews and British Multiculturalism* (Jerusalem: The Vidal Sassoon International Center for the Study of Antisemitism, Posen Papers in Contemporary Antisemitism, no. 6, 2007).
31. See *Hansard Parliamentary Debates,* April 17, 2007, for the British House of Commons debate on Integration and Cohesion, 24WH-48WH.
32. "British Muslims: Deconstructing the Veil," *The Economist,* October 14, 2006, p. 32.
33. Brearley, "Anglican Church," p. 2.
34. Kenan Malik, "Multiculturalism Has Fanned the Flames of Islamic Extremism," *The Times* (London), July 16, 2005.
35. Brearley, "Anglican Church," pp. 7–9.
36. Ibid., p. 10.
37. Ibid., pp. 4–6.
38. Naim S. Ateek, *Justice, and Only Justice: A Palestinian Theology of Liberation* (Mary Knoll, N.Y.: Orbis Books, 1989).
39. Raphael Israeli, "Anti-Semitism Revived: The Impact of the Intifada on Muslim Immigrant Groups in Western Democracies," *Jerusalem Viewpoints,* no. 455 (June 1, 2001), pp. 1–8.
40. Efraim Karsh and Rory Miller, "Europe's Persecuted Muslims?" *Commentary,* April 2007, pp. 49–53.
41. Ibid., p. 52.
42. Ibid., p. 53.

43. Robert S. Wistrich, "L'Islamisme, le multiculturalisme et les Juifs," *Shalom* 47 (Spring 2007): pp. 42–45.

44. Rachida Dali, "France in the Process of Change: Law, Reform and Society," *The Journal of Foreign Affairs* 3, no. 1 (2009): pp. 109–12.

45. "À Créteil, le sentiment d'insécurité de la communanté juive," *Le Monde*, February 26, 2006.

46. Manfred Gerstenfeld, *Antisemitism and Permissiveness in Dutch Society* (Jerusalem: The Vidal Sassoon International Center for the Study of Antisemitism, Posen Papers in Contemporary Antisemitism, no. 4, 2006), p. 3.

47. "The New Dutch Model?" *The Economist*, April 2, 2005, pp. 24–26.

48. See Ian Buruma, *Murder in Amsterdam: The Death of Theo Van Gogh and the Limits of Tolerance* (London: Penguin Books, 2006), pp. 141–86; Ayaan Hirsi Ali, *Infidel* (New York: Free Press, 2007); and the review by David Pryce-Jones in *Commentary*, April 2007, pp. 67–71.

49. Buruma, *Murder in Amsterdam*, pp. 5–6. See also Ayaan Hirsi Ali, interview by Manfred Gerstenfeld, in *European-Israeli Relations: Between Confusion and Change* (Jerusalem: Jerusalem Center for Public Affairs, 2006), pp. 159–69.

50. Gerstenfeld, *Antisemitism and Permissiveness*, pp. 10–11.

51. European Commission, "Iraq and Peace in the World," Eurobarometer Survey, no. 151 (November 2003).

52. Gerstenfeld, *Antisemitism and Permissiveness*, pp. 12–13.

53. Buruma, *Murder in Amsterdam*, pp. 216–20.

54. Pew Global Attitudes Project, "Bush Unpopular in Europe, Seen as Unilateralist," Pew Research Center, www.pewglobal.org/reports/display.php?ReportIDF248.

55. Hadassa Hirschfeld, "Antisemitische incidenten in Niederland: Overzicht 2005 en 1 januari-5 mei 2006" (The Hague: CITI, 2006) p. 55.

56. *The Jerusalem Post*, May 24, 2006.

57. George Weigel, "Europe's Two Culture Wars," *Commentary*, May 2006, p. 33.

58. Ibid. The original quote is from Henrik Bering writing in *The Weekly Standard*. For the general background to the new European cultural wars, see Oriana Fallaci, *The Force of Reason* (Milan: Rizzoli, 2006); and Bruce Bawer, *While Europe Slept* (New York: Doubleday, 2006), which details how European authorities have consistently ignored physically and morally cruel practices among their Muslim populations.

59. Adam Roberts, "A Midsummer Night's Dream," *The Economist*, June 14, 2003, pp. 3–4, and rest of section, pp. 4–16.

60. Ibid., p. 8. In 1913, 14 percent of the American population were foreign-born. Today, in Sweden, it is already 12 percent—the highest anywhere in Europe and above that of the United States.

61. "Identity Changes," ibid., pp. 15–16.

62. Jackie Jakubowski and Hedi Fried, "Islamism Breeds New Jew-Hate," *Svenska Dagbladet*, January 26, 2004. See also Mikael Tossavainen, "Arab and Muslim Anti-Semitism in Sweden," *Behind the Humanitarian Mask*, ed. Manfred Gerstenfeld, pp. 89–100.

63. Moshe Yegar, *Neutral Policy—Theory Versus Practice: Swedish-Israeli Relations* (Jerusalem: Israel Council on Foreign Relations, 1993).

64. Bawer, *While Europe Slept*, pp. 33–34.

65. Ibid., pp. 51–52.

66. Ibid., pp. 53–55.

67. Ibid., p. 56.

68. Susan Moller Okin et al., eds., *Is Multiculturalism Bad for Women?* (Princeton, N.J.: Princeton University Press, 1999), pp. 3–41.

69. Odd Sverre Hove, "The Cut-and-Omit TV News: Norway," in *Behind the Humanitarian Mask*, pp. 159–64.

70. Bat Ye'or, *Eurabia*, p. 142.

71. Ibid., p. 143.

72. Bawer, *While Europe Slept*, pp. 143–45. The fear of Muslim terror and an anti-Muslim backlash obviously haunts the European elites.

73. Ibid., p. 150.

74. Ibid., pp. 151–52. The article entitled "Ugly Anti-Semitism" appeared in August 2004.

75. Howard Adelman and John H. Simpson, eds., *Multiculturalism, Jews, and Identities in Canada* (Jerusalem: Hebrew University Magnes Press, 1996).

76. Sol Encel, "Antisemitism and Prejudice in Australia," *Patterns of Prejudice* 23, no. 1 (Spring 1989): pp. 16–27.

77. Adelson and Simpson, *Multiculturalism, Jews, and Identities*, pp. 21–26; and Jeremy Jones, "Confronting Reality: Anti-Semitism in Australia Today," *Jewish Political Studies Review* 16, nos. 3–4 (Fall 2004): pp. 89–103.

78. Irving Abella and Harold Troper, *None Is Too Many: Canada and the Jews of Europe 1933–1948* (Toronto: Lester and Orpen Dennys, 1982).

79. Manuel Prutschi, "Anti-Semitism in Canada," *Jewish Political Studies Review* 16, nos. 3–4 (Fall 2004): pp. 105–17.

80. Ibid., p. 108. See also Corinne Berzon, "Anti-Israeli Activity at Concordia University 2000–2003," in *Academics Against Israel and the Jews* (Jerusalem: Jerusalem Center for Public Affairs, 2007), pp. 163–73.

81. *Audit of Antisemitic Incidents* (Toronto: League for Human Rights of B'nai B'rith Canada, 2007).

82. Ibid. (2006), p. 3.

83. Ibid., p. 6.

84. Caroline Glick, "The Path to Our Destruction," *The Jerusalem Post*, June 6, 2006.

85. Jerome Bakst, "Negro Radicalism Turns Anti-Semitic," *The Wiener Library Bulletin* 22, no. 1 (Winter 1967–68): pp. 20–22.

86. See Lewis Young, "American Blacks and the Arab-Israeli Conflict," *Journal of Palestine Studies* 11, no. 1 (Autumn 1972): pp. 70–85. See also the *The Anti-Semitism of Black Demagogues and Extremists* (New York: ADL research report, 1992), pp. 27–28.

87. Ibid., pp. 31–35. A leading exponent of black cultural anti-Semitism in the late 1960s was the American poet Amiri Baraka (formerly LeRoi Jones). In his 1966 poem "Black Art," he said of Jews: "We want poems like fists beating niggers out of Jocks or dagger poems in the slimy bellies of the owner—Jews."

88. See Dennis King, "The Farrakhan Phenomenon: Ideology, Support, Potential," *Patterns of Prejudice* 20, no. 1 (1996): pp. 12–22. For the influence of Elijah Muham-

mad (founder of the Nation of Islam) see Lawrence B. Goodheart, "The Ambivalent Antisemitism of Malcolm X," ibid. 28, no. 1 (1994): pp. 3–25. Farrakhan has claimed at various times that "Jews are in control of the mass media," that "the Zionists made a deal with Adolf Hitler," that he [Farrakhan] would "grind and crush them [the Jews] into little bits," and that the Holocaust was a divine punishment visited on Jews "for failing to keep a special covenant."

89. Goodheart, "Ambivalent Antisemitism," pp. 8–9.
90. Ibid., p. 11.
91. Ibid., pp. 14–17, 23–24.
92. See Michael Kramer, "Loud and Clear: Farrakhan's Anti-Semitism," *New York Magazine*, October 21, 1985.
93. King, "Farrakhan Phenomenon," p. 17.
94. Ibid., pp. 19–20. See also Harold Brackman, *Mirror of Conflict: The Black Press and Major Issues of Jewish Concern* (Los Angeles: Simon Wiesenthal Center, 1988).
95. Julius Lester, "Blacks, Jews and Farrakhan," *Dissent*, Summer 1994, pp. 365–69.
96. Quoted in "Farrakhan in His Own Words," *The Australia/Israel Review*, February 1–17, 1998, p. 12.
97. Arch Puddington, "Black Anti-Semitism and How It Grows," *Commentary*, April 1994, pp. 19–24.
98. For a detailed reportage on Crown Heights, see Craig Horowitz, "The New Anti-Semitism," *New York Magazine*, January 11, 1993, pp. 21–27.
99. Ibid., pp. 26–27.
100. Paul Berman, ed., *Blacks and Jews: Alliances and Arguments* (New York: Dell, 1995); and David Biale et al., eds., *Insider/Outsider: American Jews and Multiculturalism* (Berkeley and Los Angeles: University of California Press, 1998).
101. See Daniel Pipes, *Militant Islam Reaches America* (New York: W. W. Norton and Company, 2002).
102. Cheryl Greenberg, "Pluralism and Its Discontents: Blacks and Jews," in Biale et al., *Insider/Outsider*, pp. 55–87; and Jack Salzman and Cornel West, eds., *Struggles in the Promised Land: Toward a History of Black-Jewish Relations in the United States* (New York: Oxford University Press, 1997). For a different perspective, see also Sander L. Gilman, *Multiculturalism and the Jews* (New York: Routledge, 2006).
103. See Marla Brettschneider, ed., *The Narrow Bridge: Jewish Views on Multiculturalism* (New Brunswick, N.J.: Rutgers University Press, 1996), especially pp. 236–46, for the article by Nora Gold examining the workings of American multiculturalism from the standpoint of Jewish social service agencies.
104. See Evelyn Torton Beck, "Jews and the Multi-cultural University Curriculum," in Brettschneider, *Narrow Bridge*, pp. 163–78.
105. Greenberg, "Pluralism and Its Discontents," pp. 60ff.
106. John J. Miller, *The Unmaking of Americans: How Multiculturalism Has Undermined the Assimilation Ethic* (New York: Free Press, 1998).
107. Alvin J. Schmidt, *The Menace of Multiculturalism: Trojan Horse in America* (Westport, Conn.: Praeger, 1997).
108. Pipes, *Militant Islam Reaches America*, pp. 43–51, 111–25. See also *Saudi Publications on Hate Ideology Fill American Mosques* (Washington, D.C.: Center for Religious Freedom, 2005).

109. Pipes, *Militant Islam Reaches America,* pp. 133–55.

110. Ibid., pp. 201–13.

111. Horace Kallen, *Culture and Democracy in the United States* (New York: Boni and Liveright, 1924). On the many meanings of diversity, see Philip Gleason, *Speaking of Diversity* (Baltimore: Johns Hopkins University Press, 1992); and Gilman, *Multiculturalism,* pp. 45, 58–59, 82–83.

112. Tom W. Smith, *Hispanic Attitudes Toward Jews* (New York: AJC, 2007), pp. 4–5.

113. Ibid., pp. 5–6. See also the ADL survey for 2007 as reported in *The Jerusalem Post,* November 2, 2007.

114. Daniel Pipes, "America's Muslims Against America's Jews," *Commentary,* May 1999, pp. 31–36. See also Pipes, "The Danger Within: Militant Islam in America," *Commentary,* November 2001, pp. 19–24.

115. *Saudi Publications on Hate Ideology,* pp. 29–66; and Robert S. Wistrich, "Europe's New Frontier of Bigotry," *Midstream,* January–February 2006, pp. 4–6.

116. Suzanne Rutland and Sol Encel, "Australian Multiculturalism: Immigration, Race and Religion" (paper at the International Conference of the Vidal Sassoon Center for the Study of Antisemitism, Hebrew University of Jerusalem, June 2006).

117. Geoffrey Brahm Levery, "Jews and Australian Multiculturalism," in *Jews and Australian Politics, ed.* Geoffrey Brahm Levey and Philip Mendes (Brighton, U.K.: Sussex Academic Press, 2004), p. 193.

118. Jeremy Jones, *Report on Antisemitism in Australia: October 1, 1996–September 30, 1997* (Darlinghurst, New South Wales, October 1997). See also the follow-up reports from 2001 to 2006 by the same author.

119. See Danny Ben-Moshe, *Holocaust Denial in Australia* (Jerusalem: The Vidal Sassoon International Center for the Study of Antisemitism, ACTA no. 25, 2005), pp. 26–33.

120. Jones, *Report on Antisemitism in Australia* (2001), p. 14; and ibid. (2003), pp. 17–30.

121. See Jeremy Jones, "Analysing Australian Antisemitism," *AIR* (December 2008), p. 40.

122. Scott Poynting, "Bin Laden in the Suburbs: Attacks on Arab and Muslim Australians Before and After September 11," *Current Issues in Criminal Justice* 14, no. 1 (July 2002): pp. 44–45, 52.

123. Miranda Devine, "Acceptance of Their Intolerance—It's All Part of Radical Islam's Plan," *The Sydney Morning Herald,* February 9, 2006.

124. *The Australian,* October 26, 2006; *Australian Jewish News,* November 27, 2006.

125. Rutland and Encel, "Australian Multiculturalism."

126. Ibid. See also Steven Emerson, "Jihadism: Where Is It At in 2006?" *Sydney Papers* 18, no. 2, 2006, pp. 70–71.

127. Philip Mendes, "New Manifestations of Anti-Zionist Fundamentalism on the Australian Left," *Anti-Defamation Commission Special Report,* no. 31 (January 2006). See also the earlier piece by Mendes, "Much Ado About Nothing? The Academic Boycott of Israel Down Under," *Midstream,* February–March 2004, p. 9. Mendes offers a number of examples, such as David Glanz, a Jewish spokesperson for the radical Left Socialist Alliance in Australia, who presents Israel in crassly stereotypical terms as a white racist society. See also Ted Lapkin, "Academic Anti-Zionism in Australia" in *Academics Against Israel,* pp. 250–57.

128. See Manny Waks and Geoffrey Winn, "The New World Order Is the Same Old Order for Jews," *ADL Special Report*, no. 36 (December 2007): p. 9, for examples of Saleam's diatribes against Australian Zionists.

129. Douglas Kirsner, "Condemning Antisemitism: Resolutions of the Australian Parliaments," *Antisemitism International*, 2004, pp. 79–86.

130. Ibid., p. 85.

Eighteen: The Globalization of Anti-Semitism

1. Robert Chazan, *Medieval Stereotypes and Modern Antisemitism* (Berkeley: University of California Press, 1997), p. 135.

2. Frederick Krantz, "Between Purim and Pesach: Old-New, and Global Anti-semitism," *Israfax*, March 14, 2004.

3. Daniel J. Goldhagen, "The Globalization of Anti-Semitism" (paper presented at the Montreal International Conference on Anti-Semitism, March 14–16, 2004. See also Mark Weitzmann, *Magical Logic: Globalization, Conspiracy Theory and the Shoah* (Jerusalem: The Vidal Sassoon International Center for the Study of Antisemitism, Posen Papers in Contemporary Antisemitism, no. 10, 2008).

4. See Marcelo M. Suárez-Orozco and Desirée Baolian Qin-Hilliard, eds., *Globalization: Culture and Education in the New Millennium* (Berkeley and Los Angeles: University of California Press, 2004), pp. 141–202.

5. See Hubert Vedrine, *France in an Era of Globalization* (Washington, D.C.: Brookings Institution Press, 2001).

6. See Ian Buruma and Avishai Margalit, *Occidentalism: A Short History of Anti-Westernism* (London: Atlantic Books, 2005), pp. 32–35.

7. Sidney Touati, "Le 'peuple en danger' des anti-mondialistes," *Observatoire du monde juif*, no. 3 (2002): pp. 27–31.

8. *Retour de Palestine: Campagne civile internationale pour la protection du people palestinien 11e mission et José Bové* (Paris: Mille et Une Nuits Fayard, 2002).

9. See Dominique Vidal, *Le péché original d'Israël* (Paris: Les Éditions de l'Atelier, 2002).

10. Buruma and Margalit, *Occidentalism*, pp. 147–48.

11. Manfred Gerstenfeld, interview with Rabbi Avraham Cooper, "Anti-Semitism and Terrorism on the Internet: New Threats," *Post-Holocaust and Antisemitism*, June 2003. See also *Les Cahiers de L'Observatoire: Propagandes, racismes et incitations à la haine sur Internet* (a publication of the association J'Accuse!, no. 1, March 2003).

12. See *Poisoning the Web: Hatred Online* (New York: ADL, 1999), pp. 4–8.

13. Ibid., pp. 11–15.

14. Mark Weitzman, "The Internet Is Our Sword: Aspects of Online Antisemitism," in *Remembering for the Future: The Holocaust in an Age of Genocide* (London: Palgrave, 2001), vol. 1, pp. 911–25. See also David Duke's preface to his book *Jewish Supremacism*, online at http://www.davidduke.com/general/jewish-supremacism _129.html; Duke, "One Year Later: The Real Causes of the 9/11 Attack," online at http://www.davidduke.com/general/one-year-later-911_10.html; and Duke, "The

Lies of Globalism," online at http://www.davidduke.com/general/the-lies-of-globalism_11.html.

15. Duke, "Lies of Globalism." See also Weitzmann, *Magical Logic. Globalization, Conspiracy Theory, and the Shoah* (Jerusalem: The Vidal Sassoon International Center for the Study of Antisemitism, 2008) no. 10, Posen Papers in Contemporary Antisemitism.

16. William Pierce, *Nationalism Versus the New World Order, Free Speech,* May 1998, http://www.natvan.com/free-speech/fs985c.html. See also Abraham H. Foxman, *Never Again? The Threat of the New Anti-Semitism* (New York: HarperCollins, 2003), pp. 112–21.

17. Horst Mahler, "Independence Day Live," Deutsches Kolleg, September 12, 2001, http://www.deutsches-kolleg.org/english/declaration/independent.htm. Also Weitzmann, *Magical Logic,* pp. 5–7.

18. On Achmed Huber, see Johannes and Germana von Dohnanyi, *Schmützige Geschäfte und Heiliger Krieg: Al-Qaida in Europa* (Zürich: Pendo Verlag, 2002), pp. 245ff.

19. See Joel Fishman, "The Big Lie and the Media War Against Israel: From Inversion of the Truth to Inversion of Reality," *Jewish Political Review* 19, nos. 1–2 (Spring 2007): pp. 59–81.

20. Mark Strauss, "Antiglobalism's Jewish Problem," in Rosenbaum, *Those Who Forget the Past,* pp. 273–87.

21. Ibid., p. 283.

22. Ibid., p. 273.

23. Daniel J. Goldhagen, "The Globalization of Anti-Semitism," *Forward,* May 2, 2003.

24. Joffe, *Nations We Love to Hate.* See also Yaroslav Trofimov, "Globalization Foes' New Cause: Palestine," *The Wall Street Journal,* April 5, 2002.

25. Elhanan Yakira, *Post-Zionism, Post Holocaust* (Tel Aviv: Am Oved, 2006), pp. 9–62, in Hebrew.

26. Joffe, *Nations We Love to Hate,* pp. 11–14. In an interview with the Austrian magazine *Profil* in 2002, the well-known German philosopher Peter Sloterdijk called Israel and the United States the *only* "rogue states" in existence. See also Rosenfeld, *Anti-Americanism and Anti-Semitism,* p. 21.

27. For the relationship between anti-Americanism and national identity in postwar German culture, a revealing case is that of New Right ideologue Henning Eichberg. See Clemens Heni, *Salonfähigkeit der Neuen Rechten. "Nationale Identität," Antisemitismus und Antiamerikanismus in der politischen Kultur der Bundesrepublik Deutschland 1970–2005: Henning Eichberg als Exempel* (Marburg, Germany: Tectum, 2007), pp. 31–341. See also Ulrich Beck, "Globalisierte Emotionen: Der neue europäische Antisemitismus," *Süddeutsche Zeitung,* November 17, 2003, p. 11.

28. Volker Weiss, " 'Volksklassenkampf'—Die antizionistische Rezeption des Nahostkonflikts in der militanten Linken der BRD," in *Tel Aviver Jahrbuch für deutsche Geschichte* 33 (2005): pp. 214–38.

29. Finkielkraut, *Au nom de l'Autre,* p. 13.

30. Ibid., pp. 31–33.

31. Wistrich, "Anti-Zionism in Western Societies," pp. 46–52.

32. See Berman, "Passion of Joschka Fischer," pp. 36–59.

33. Ibid., pp. 49–50.

34. See Carl Gershman, "Israel, the PLO, and the Socialist International," *Middle East Review,* Spring 1980, pp. 38–41; Wistrich, "Anti-Zionism in Western Societies"; and Wistrich, "Zionism, Colonialism, and the Third World," *The Jewish Chronicle,* January 2, 1976. For a critical view of this ideology, see Gérard Chaliand, *Repenser le Tiers-Monde* (Brussels: Editions Complexe, 1987).

35. See John K. Cooley, "China and the Palestinians," *Journal of Palestine Studies* 1, no. 2 (Winter 1972): pp. 19–33.

36. See Efraim Inbar, "The Indian-Israeli Entente," *Orbis,* Winter 2004, pp. 89–104.

37. Yaakov Shimoni, "India: The Years of Estrangement," in *Ministry for Foreign Affairs: The First Fifty Years,* ed. Moshe Yager, Yosef Govrin, and Aryeh Oded (Jerusalem: Keter, 2002), in Hebrew.

38. See G. H. Jansen, *Zionism, Israel and Asian Nationalism* (Beirut: Institute of Palestine Studies, 1971), pp. 170–82.

39. Ibid., pp. 182–93.

40. Mark T. Berger, "After the Third World? History, Destiny and the Fate of Third Worldism," *Third World Quarterly* 25, no. 1 (2004): pp. 9–39.

41. Y. Harkabi, *Arab Attitudes to Israel* (London: Vallentine Mitchell, 1972), pp. 285–92.

42. See Robert S. Wistrich, *Who's Who in Nazi Germany* (London: Routledge, 1995), pp. 152–53; and Matthias Küntzel, *Djihad und Judenhass* (Fribourg, Switzerland: Ça Ira, 2003), pp. 50–51.

43. Dr. Frei, interview, *Deutsche Soldaten und National Zeitung,* May 1, 1964. Interview with the editor, Gerhard Frey.

44. See Harkabi, *Arab Attitudes,* p. 235; and R. K. Karanjia, *The Arab Dawn* (Bombay: Blitz Publications, 1958). Karanjia was the editor of the Indian English-language paper *Blitz.*

45. Taguieff, *Les Protocoles des Sages de Sion,* vol. 1, pp. 379–80.

46. Harkabi, *Arab Attitudes,* pp. 235–56.

47. Wistrich, *Hitler's Apocalypse,* pp. 176–78.

48. See Shimeon Amir, *Israel's Development Cooperation with Africa, Asia, and Latin America* (New York: Praeger, 1974); Samuel Decalo, "Israel's Foreign Policy and the Third World," *Orbis* 11, no. 3 (1967): pp. 724–45; and Ethan A. Nadelman, "Israel and Black Africa: A Rapprochement?" *Journal of Modern African Studies* 19, no. 2 (1981): pp. 183–219.

49. See Decalo, "Israel's Foreign Policy," p. 735, for the valuable role played by Israeli experts in Africa and in training African cadres in Israel during the 1960s. See also Naomi Chazan, "Israel in Africa," *Jerusalem Quarterly* no. 18 (Winter 1981): pp. 29–45.

50. Susan Aurelia Gitelson, *Israel's African Setback in Perspective* (Jerusalem: Hebrew University of Jerusalem, Jerusalem Papers on Peace Problems, no. 6, May 1974), p. 7.

51. Arye Oded, "Israeli-Uganda Relations in the Time of Idi Amin," *Jewish Political Studies Review* 18, nos. 3–4 (Autumn 2006): pp. 65–80.

52. Quoted in *The Jerusalem Post,* July 25, 1972.

53. Oded, "Israeli-Uganda Relations," p. 75.

54. *The Times,* September 13, 1972.

55. "Tous Contre Israël (Entretien avec Ahmed Ben Bella)," *Politique Internationale,* no. 16 (Summer 1982): pp. 105–13.

56. Ibid., p. 113.

57. For Israel's relations with black Africa after 1973, see Chazan, "Israel in Africa," pp. 33, 41.

58. Colin Legum, "The Third World, Israel and the Jews," *Survey of Jewish Affairs,* ed. William Frankel (London: Associated University Presses, 1982), pp. 227–35.

59. Ibid., p. 232.

60. See *Sionizm: Teoria i Praktika* (Moscow: Politizdat, 1973), pp. 180–93.

61. Legum, "Third World," p. 233.

62. Gitelson, *Israel's African Setback,* pp. 17–25.

63. *Voice of the Greater Arab Homeland* (Tripoli), August 2, 1984.

64. See Gideon Shimoni, *Jews and Zionism: The South African Experience, 1910–1967* (Cape Town: Oxford University Press, 1980); and Milton Shain, *The Roots of Antisemitism in South Africa* (Johannesburg: University of the Witwatersrand Press, 1994), pp. 114–53.

65. Among the most prominent white militants in the fight against apartheid were Jewish Communists such as Joe Slovo, his wife Ruth First (assassinated by the police), Bram Fischer, Albie Sachs, Denis Goldberg, Arthur Goldreich, Rusty and Hilda Bernstein. They had no connection with the mainstream Jewish community. Goldreich, an architect who had been arrested with Mandela in 1963, did, however, fight with the Jewish underground against the British in Palestine as a teenager. See Nelson Mandela, *Long Walk to Freedom* (London: Abacus, 1995), pp. 82, 334.

66. See the research report by Jocelyn Hellig, *Anti-Semitism in South Africa Today* (Tel Aviv: Tel Aviv University, 1996), pp. 15–22. On the Jewish community, see David Saks, *South African Jewry: A Contemporary Portrait* (Jerusalem: Institute of the World Jewish Congress, 2003).

67. Hellig, *Anti-Semitism in South Africa,* p. 23.

68. Milton Shain and Margo Bastos, "Muslim Anti-Semitism and Anti-Zionism in South Africa Since 1945," *Antisemitism International,* 2006, pp. 18–29.

69. "General Analysis," *Antisemitism Worldwide,* 2006, p. 2. The number of anti-Semitic incidents peaked during and immediately after the 2006 Lebanon War.

70. Natan Lerner, "A Continent in Turmoil: Jews in Latin America," *Survey of Jewish Affairs,* pp. 236–49. See also Graciela Ben-Dror, *The Catholic Church and the Jews, Argentina, 1933–45* (Lincoln: University of Nebraska Press, 2008).

71. Judith Laikin Elkin, *Jews of the Latin American Republics* (Chapel Hill: University of North Carolina Press, 1980), provides a valuable survey of the historical background.

72. Barry Rubin, "Latin America and the Arab-Israeli Conflict," *The Wiener Library Bulletin* 21, n.s. nos. 37–38 (1976): pp. 30–39.

73. Edward B. Glick, *Latin America and the Palestine Problem* (New York: Theodor Herzl Foundation, 1958).

74. Edy Kaufman, "Israel's Foreign Policy Implementation in Latin America," in Curtis and Gitelson, *Israel in the Third World,* pp. 139–42. See also Yoram D. Shapira,

"External and Internal Influences in the Process of Latin American–Israeli Relations," in ibid., pp. 147–81; and Ignacio Klich, *Latin America and the Palestinian Question* (IJA research report, nos. 2 and 3, January 1986).

75. Haim Avni, "Antisemitism in Argentina: The Dimensions of Danger," in *Approaches to Antisemitism: Context and Curriculum*, ed. Michael Brown (New York: AJC, 1994), pp. 57–77; and Daniel Lvovich, *Nacionalismo y antisemitismo en la Argentina* (Buenos Aires: Javier Vergara, 2003). For the present, see Martina Libertad Weisz, "Continuity and Change in Argentinean Antisemitism," *Antisemitism International*, 2006, pp. 31–43.

76. Walter Beveraggi Allende, *Del Yugo Sionista a la Argentina Posible* (Buenos Aires: Confederacion Nacionalista Argentina, 1976) is a good example of this anti-Semitic literature sponsored by ultranationalist circles.

77. Rubin, "Latin America and the Arab-Israeli Conflict," p. 36.

78. See Cristián Buchrucker, "Whitewashing the 'New Order,' " and Saúl Sosnowski, "Counting Nazis in Argentina: A Cultural Perspective," *The Jewish Quarterly*, Spring 1999, pp. 45–52.

79. Edy Kaufman, "Jewish Victims of Repression in Argentina Under Military Rule 1976–1983," *Holocaust and Genocide Studies* 4 (1989): pp. 479–99.

80. Buchrucker, "Whitewashing the 'New Order,' " pp. 49–52.

81. Sosnowski, "Counting Nazis in Argentina," pp. 45–48. For the complex situation since 1983, see Leonardo Senkman, *Democratization and Antisemitism in Argentina: An Assessment* (Jerusalem: The Vidal Sassoon International Center for the Study of Antisemitism, ACTA no. 28, 2006).

82. Amilcar Alencastre, *Le Sionisme et le Tiers Monde* (Algiers: S.N.E.D., 1972). On the back cover of the book, Alencastre was listed as director of Arab studies at Rio de Janeiro. This work was evidently sponsored by the Algerian government, and this influence is felt in the content.

83. Ibid., p. 51.

84. Ibid., pp. 111–40. See also Shapira, "External and Internal Influences," pp. 158–60.

85. See Marisa Braylan, *Report on Anti-Semitism in Argentina, 2006* (Buenos Aires: CES-DAIA, 2007); and Senkman, *Democratization and Antisemitism; Antisemitism Worldwide*, 2006, pp. 32–40; "Alarma el aumento del antisemitismo," *Clarín*, May 4, 2007.

86. Damián Stiglitz, "Antisemitismo, Medio Oriente y política argentina," *Nueva Sión*, http://www.nuevasion.com.ar/nota.asp?IDNoticia=0004174 (accessed March 13, 2009).

87. Norberto Ceresole, *Caudillo, Ejército, Pueblo: la Venezuela del Commandante Chávez* (Madrid: Al-Andalus, 2000).

88. See Norberto Ceresole, "La Argentina e el espacio geopolítico del terrorismo judío, Radio Islam, http://www.radioislam.net/islam/spanish/sion/terror/cap2.htm; and http://www.islam-shia.org/.

89. Norberto Ceresole, "Carta abierta a mis amigos iranies," http://www.vho.org/aaargh/espa/ceres/carta.html (a Holocaust denial website).

90. Karmon, "Hezbollah America Latina."

91. Organizacíon Islámica Argentina, http://www.organizacionislam.org.ar/index.htm.

92. Karmon, "Hezbollah America Latina," quoting from Roza Çiòdem Erdoòan and

Mutla Pahin, "Entrevista a Sayyid Hassan Nasrallah, dirigente máximo de Hezbollah," *Izquierda Punto Info,* http://www.organizacionislam.org.ar/conflib/reporsayyed.htm.

93. Damián Stiglitz, *Antisemitismo, Medio Oriente y política argentina* (Buenos Aires, 2006), pp. 36–40.

94. See Robert M. Levine, "Cuba," in Wyman, *World Reacts to the Holocaust,* pp. 782–808.

95. Ibid., p. 790.

96. Ibid., p. 796.

97. Ibid., p. 797.

98. Ibid.

99. K. S. Karol, *Guerrillas in Power* (London: Jonathan Cape, 1971), p. 400.

100. Orly Azoulay, "Maqom le-de'agah," *Yediot Ahronoth,* November 10, 2006, pp. 6–9.

101. *La Hojilla Impresa,* September 13, 2006, and other press and TV stations spoke of Mossad and CIA plots to assassinate Chávez. At a press conference in the National Assembly on July 31, 2006, official sources expressed anti-Semitic positions.

102. "With Marx, Lenin and Jesus Christ," *The Economist,* January 13, 2007.

103. Alberto Nolia, *Los papeles de Mandinga,* August 8, 2006. Nolia is the publisher of this weekly and a well-known media personality in Venezuela.

104. "Cianuro en Gotas" [Cyanide in Drops], *Los papeles de Mandinga,* September 19–25, 2006.

105. Basem Tajeldine, "Zionist Menace in Venezuela," *Diario Vea,* September 14, 2006. In this article Tajeldine referred to international imperialism and Zionism as "the cancers of the inferno." See also his article, "La disociación mental del 'Pueblo Elegido,' " *Rebelión,* May 26, 2008.

106. "Marciano," *Diario Vea,* July 18, 2006.

107. The Spanish original: *PAREN LA MASACRE. Por Amor a Dios. Por amor a Alá; JUDÍOS ASESINOS! BESTÍAS APOCALÍPTICAS.*

108. "A Despicable War," *Docencia Participativa,* August 2006.

109. Ibid. See also Luis Cadenas, "Nazi Zionist Fury," *Diario Vea,* July 4, 2006.

110. *El Cambio,* July 22, 2006.

111. *Diario Vea,* July 4, 2006.

112. *El Diario de Caracas,* February 9, 2006. See also *Antisemitism Worldwide 2006,* p. 38, for statements by congressmen of Arab origin.

113. Ever since Chávez's victory in the general elections in late 1998, an increase in anti-Semitism was observable. See *Anti-Semitism Worldwide 1999–2000* (Tel Aviv: Tel Aviv University, 2000), pp. 234–35, and ibid., *2006,* pp. 36–40.

114. See "Chávez et Ahmadinejad, unis contre les États-Unis," *Libération,* July 31, 2006.

115. "Venezuela President Chavez on Al-Jazeera," *MEMRI, Special Dispatch Series,* no. 1235 (August 8, 2006), for excerpts from Chávez's interview with Al-Jazeera TV. In this interview he glowingly evoked the memory of Nasser as "one of the greatest people in Arab history."

116. See Simon Romero, "Venezuela Strengthens Its Relationships in the Middle East," *The New York Times,* August 21, 2006, for the practical side of Chávez's Middle East policy. See also "Hugo Chavez militarise le Venezuela," *Le Monde,* July 25, 2006.

117. "Venezuela Preident Chavez and Iranian President Ahmadinejad on Iranian TV," *MEMRI Special Dispatch Series,* no. 1226 (August 2, 2006), for excerpts from the

press conference. Chávez has visited Iran on several occasions in recent years and relations are close. Jose Orozco, "Venezuelan Jews Fear Chavez-Iran Ties," *The Jerusalem Post,* September 19, 2006. "The Scenarios for Rupture," and Sammy Eppel, "Es Chávez Antisemita?" *El Universal,* August 31, 2006, pp. 1542 a/c. See also Caroline B. Glick, "Iran's Global Reach," *The Jerusalem Post,* May 19, 2009.

118. Resolution submitted by U.S. Congressman Alcee L. Hastings (Florida) to the House of Representatives on February 13, 2009, condemning recent acts of violence against Jews in Venezuela, Argentina, and Bolivia. See www.alceehastings .house.gov.

119. "Chávez Fosters Atmosphere of Intimidation and Fear for Venezuelan Jewish Community," in http://www.adl.org/PresRele/1s1ME62/543462htm, accessed April 1, 2009.

120. "Venezeula's Chávez Calls Attack 'Holocaust,'" Reuters, January 6, 2009, at http://www.alertnet.org/thenews/newsdesk/N06437606.htm. Also Herb Keinon "Venezuela Severs Ties to 'Inhumane' Israel," *The Jerusalem Post,* January 16, 2009.

NINETEEN: LYING ABOUT THE HOLOCAUST

1. Vladimir Jankélévitch, *L'Imprescriptible: Pardoner?; Dans l'honneur et la dignité* (Paris: Seuil, 1986), p. 188.

2. A good illustration of this syndrome is Belgium; see Joël Kotek, *La Belgique et ses Juifs: De l'antijudaïsme comme code culturel, à l'antisionisme comme religion civique, Les Études du Crif,* no. 4 (June 2004).

3. See *Stockholm International Forum on the Holocaust* (proceedings of the Conference on Education, Remembrance, and Research in Stockholm, January 26–28, 2000).

4. Finkielkraut, *L'Avenir d'une negation.*

5. Per Ahlmark in the workshop "Facing Denial in Society and Education," *Stockholm International Forum,* p. 235.

6. Ibid.

7. See the remarks of Irwin Cotler, *Stockholm International Forum,* p. 242.

8. Laurent Cohen, "Protocols of the Revisionists," *Eretz Acheret,* Autumn 2004, p. 63.

9. See Maurice Bardèche, *Nuremberg ou la terre promise* (Paris: Les Sept Couleurs, 1948); and Cohen, "Protocols of the Revisionists," pp. 60–61.

10. See the article by the former SS Pierre Hofstetter, "L'ONU contre l'Occident," *Défense de l'Occident,* April 1963, pp. 60–61.

11. M. Bardèche, "La Question Juive," *Défense de l'Occident,* March 1964, p. 5.

12. Valérie Igounet, "Une tradition extrémiste: Le Négationnisme," in *Revue d'Histoire de la Shoah,* no. 166 (May–August 1999): pp. 7–43.

13. Maurice Bardèche, "L'occupation et le pillage," *Défense de l'Occident,* December 1971, pp. 4–6.

14. Paul Rassinier, *Debunking the Genocide Myth: A Study of the Nazi Concentration Camps and the Alleged Extermination of European Jewry* (Los Angeles: Noontide Press, 1978). The French original was published in 1964. See also Gill Seidel, *The Holocaust Denial: Antisemitism, Racism and the New Right* (Leeds, U.K.: Beyond the Pale Collective, 1986).

15. Deborah Lipstadt, *Denying the Holocaust: The Growing Assault on Truth and Memory* (New York: Free Press, 1993), pp. 58–63.

16. Ibid., p. 63.

17. Rassinier, *Debunking*, p. 309.

18. Laurent Cohen, "Protocols of the Revisionists," p. 63; Henri Rousso, "La negation du genocide juif," *L'Histoire* 106 (December 1987): pp. 76–97; Aime Bonifas, "The French Revisionists and the Myth of the Holocaust," *Remembering for the Future* (Oxford, U.K.: Pergamon, 1989), vol. 2: pp. 2187–98.

19. Shmuel Trigano, "La critique de la Shoa: Le transformateur symbolique du gauchisme," *Observatoire du monde juif*, no. 3 (June 2002): pp. 20–26.

20. See Alain Finkielkraut, *Remembering in Vain: The Klaus Barbie Trial and Crimes Against Humanity* (New York: Columbia University Press, 1992).

21. Tzvetan Todorov, *Les abus de la mémoire* (Paris: Arléa, 1995); Alain Brossat, *L'épreuve du désastre: L XXe siècle et les camps* (Paris: Albin Michel, 1996).

22. Brossat, *L'épreuve du désastre*, pp. 284–86.

23. Trigano, "La critique de la Shoah," pp. 24–25.

24. Ibid., p. 26.

25. See Richard Harwood (Richard Verrall), *Did Six Million Really Die? The Truth at Last* (Richmond, Surrey: Historical Review Press, 1974), a British National Front "revisionist" tract. See also Harwood, *Nuremberg and Other War Crimes Trials* (Southam, England: Historical Review Press, 1978).

26. Arthur Butz, *The Hoax of the Twentieth Century* (Torrance, Calif., 1976) is the classic example of this approach. See also Pierre Vidal-Naquet, *Assassins of Memory: Essays on the Denial of the Holocaust* (New York: Columbia University Press, 1992), pp. 21–24; and Deborah E. Lipstadt, *Denying the Holocaust: The Growing Assault on Truth and Memory* (New York: Free Press, 1993), pp. 123–36.

27. See " 'Holocaust Revisionism': A Denial of History," *Facts* (ADL) 26, no. 2 (June 1980); and the valuable study by Roger Eatwell, "Holocaust Denial: A Study in Propaganda Technique," in *Neo-Fascism in Europe*, ed. Luciano Chales et al. (London: Longman, 1991), pp. 120–43.

28. Harwood, *Nuremberg and Other War Crimes Trials*, pp. 6–7; and Lipstadt, *Denying the Holocaust*, pp. 104–21. See also Georges Wellers, *La solution finale et la mythomanie Néo-Nazie: L'existence des chambres à gaz, le nombre des victimes* (Paris: Association pour le jugement des criminels nazis qui opéré en France, 1979). Wolfgang Benz, ed., *Dimension des Völkermords: Die Zahl der jüdischen Opfer des Nationalsozialismus* (Munich: Oldenbourg, 1991) deals with the question of numbers.

29. Jean-Claude Pressac, "The Deficiencies and Inconsistencies of 'The Leuchter Report'" in *Truth Prevails*, ed. Shelley Shapiro (New York: Beate Klarsfeld Foundation, 1990), pp. 36–40, 46, 55. On *The Leuchter Report*, see also Lipstadt, *Denying the Holocaust*, pp. 162–81.

30. Leonidas Edwin Hill, "The Trial of Ernst Zundel: Revisionism and the Law in Canada," *Simon Wiesenthal Center Annual* 6 (1989): pp. 165–219.

31. David Irving, foreword to *The Leuchter Report* (London: Focal Point, 1989). At the 1989 Conference of the Institute for Historical Review in California, Irving cited Leuchter as "the best-qualified specialist on gas chambers."

32. Ronnie Stauber, *From Revisionism to Holocaust Denial: David Irving as Case Study* (Jerusalem: Institute of the World Jewish Congress, policy study, no. 19, 2000).

33. Bela Vago's book review "An Anti-Jewish Distortion of History," *Soviet Jewish Affairs* 3 (1981): pp. 68–72.

34. Stauber, *From Revisionism,* p. 14.

35. Ibid.

36. Excerpts from the verdict of Justice Charles Gray can be found in Marvin Parry and Frederick M. Schwetzer, eds., *Antisemitic Myths: A Historical and Contemporary Anthology* (Bloomington: Indiana University Press, 2008), pp. 282–90. See also Richard J. Evans, *Lying About Hitler: History, Holocaust, and the David Irving Trial* (New York: Basic Books, 2001). See also D. D. Guttenplan, *The Holocaust on Trial: History, Justice and the David Irving Libel Case* (London: Granta Books, 2001).

37. Ruth Elkins, "Irving Gets Three Years' Jail in Austria for Holocaust Denial," *The Independent,* February 21, 2006.

38. On Carto's background and beliefs, see Lipstadt, *Denying the Holocaust,* pp. 144–49. For a sample of his style, see Willis A. Carto, "On the Uses of History," *Journal of Historical Review* 3, no. 1 (Spring 1982): pp. 26–30.

39. Peter I. Haupt, "A Universe of Lies: Holocaust Revisionism and the Myth of Jewish World Conspiracy," *Patterns of Prejudice* 25, no. 1 (Summer 1991). For information about Butz, see *ADL Facts* (June 1980), pp. 7–8.

40. In 1978 the Swedish anti-Semite and negationist Dietlieb Felderer published an attack on the diary, republished by the Institute of Historical Review under the title *Anne Frank's Diary: A Hoax.* Two years later, the French "revisionist" Robert Faurisson produced an "expert opinion" rejecting the authenticity of the diaries. See Lipstadt, *Denying the Holocaust,* p. 233. See also David Barnouw and Gerrold van der Stroom, eds., *The Diary of Anne Frank: The Critical Edition* (New York: Doubleday, 1989), pp. 84–101.

41. See Lipstadt, *Denying the Holocaust,* pp. 51–65.

42. Henry H. Weinberg, *The Myth of the Jew in France 1967–1982* (New York: Mosaic Press, 1987), pp. 59–64.

43. Nadine Fresco, "Les Redresseurs de Morts," *Les Temps Modernes* (June 1980). See also Seidel, *Holocaust Denial,* pp. 93–111.

44. Vidal-Naquet, *Assassins of Memory,* pp. 65–73.

45. James G. Shields, "French Revisionism on Trial: The Case of Robert Faurisson," *Patterns of Prejudice* 25, no. 1 (Summer 1991): pp. 86–88.

46. Henry H. Weinberg, "Revisionism: The Rocques Affair," *Midstream,* April 1987, pp. 11–13. See also Henry Rousso, *Le Dossier Lyon-III* (Paris: Fayard, 2004), on the Far Right nucleus at the University of Lyon.

47. Pierre Guillaume, *Droit et Histoire* (Paris: La Vieille Taupe, 1986); and Serge Thion, *Vérité Historique ou Vérité Politique* (Paris: La Vieille Taupe, 1980).

48. Jacques Givet, *Le Cas Vergès* (Paris: Lieu Commun, 1986); and Vidal-Naquet, *Assassins of Memory,* pp. 129–36.

49. Wilhelm Stäglich, *Der Auschwitz-Mythos* (Tübingen, Germany: Grabert, 1979).

50. Lucy S. Dawidowicz, *The Holocaust and the Historians* (Cambridge, Mass.: Harvard University Press, 1981), pp. 68–87; and William Korey, "Soviet Treatment of the Holocaust: History's 'Memory Hole,' " in *Remembering for the Future: The Im-*

pact of the Holocaust on the Contemporary World (Oxford, U.K.: Pergamon Press, 1988), pp. 1357–65. No editor listed.

51. For a detailed analysis of this phenomenon, see Wistrich, *Hitler's Apocalypse*, pp. 194–225; and Korey, *Russian Antisemitism*.

52. The Communist regime in Poland developed its own falsifications of Holocaust history along the anti-Semitic lines of the *Protocols*. See Marian Mushkat, "A Hoax Revived: On World Control by the 'Elders of Zion' and the Concept of 'Judeo-Communism,'" *International Problems* 25, nos. 1–2 (1986): pp. 37–42.

53. See Michael Shafir, *Between Denial and "Comparative Trivialization": Holocaust Negationism in Post-Communist East Central Europe* (Jerusalem: The Vidal Sassoon International Center for the Study of Antisemitism, ACTA no. 19, 2002); and Michael Steinlauf, *Bondage to the Dead: Poland and the Memory of the Holocaust* (Syracuse, N.Y.: Syracuse University Press, 1997).

54. Ruth Ellen Gruber, *The Struggle: The Rehabilitation of Fascist Heroes in Europe* (New York: AJC, 1995). On Slovakia, see the very detailed survey by Zora Bútarová, Martin Bútora, Zuzana Fialova, *Attitudes Towards Jews and the Holocaust in Slovakia* (Bratislava, Slovakia: Center for Social Analysis, March 1993). For the wider picture, see Randolph Braham, ed., *Anti-Semitism and the Treatment of the Holocaust in Postcommunist Eastern Europe* (New York: Rosenthal Institute for Holocaust Studies, 1994).

55. See Michael Shafir, "Marshal Ion Antonescu and Romanian Politics," *Radio Free Europe/Radio Liberty Research Report* 3, no. 6 (February 11, 1994); and Shafir, *Between Denial*, pp. 20–23.

56. See *Anti-Semitism in Post-Totalitarian Europe* (Prague: Franz Kafka Publishers, 1993), particularly the contributions by Robert S. Wistrich on central and eastern Europe, pp. 35–59; Erich Kulka on denying the Shoah, pp. 63–81; Věra Ebels-Dolanová, pp. 99–106; and Yeshayahu Jellinek, pp. 151–62.

57. See "Historical Revisionism and the Struggle for Palestine," in *FAV*, May 15, 2002, including a pamphlet by Ibrahim Alloush, some translated excerpts from Faurisson and Mark Weber, and chapters from the canceled Holocaust denial conference of March 2001 that was to have been held in Beirut. http://www.freearabvoice .org/issues/historicalRevisionismAndTheStruggle.htm, accessed on April 1, 2009.

58. Ibrahim Alloush, "Why the 'Holocaust' Is Important to Palestinians, Arabs and Muslims," *FAV*, April 28, 2001, and the interview in the "revisionist," California-based *Journal of Historical Review*, May–June 2001.

59. Roger Garaudy, *Toute la vérité* (Paris: Grasset, 1970), pp. 125–35.

60. Roger Garaudy, *L'Affaire Israël* (Paris: Papyrus Editions, 1983); and Garaudy, *La Palestine, Terre des messages divins* (Paris: Editions Albatros, 1986).

61. See Yves Camus and René Monzat, *Les Droites nationales et radicales en France* (Lyon: Presses Universitaires de Lyon, 1992).

62. Valérie Igounet, *Histoire du négationisme en France* (Paris: Le Seuil, 2000), pp. 457–88. See also Jacques Tarnero, "Le négationnisme, on le symptôme des temps pervers: Un énigme recurrente," *Revue d'Histoire de la Shoah* 166 (May–August 1999), pp. 44–75.

63. Roger Garaudy, *Les mythes fondateurs de la politique israélienne* (Paris: Samiszdat, 1996).

64. Douglas Davis, "Mideast Defenders of Garaudy," *The Jerusalem Post,* March 2, 1998.
65. Ibid.
66. Mouna Naim, "Critiqué, jugé, sanctioné pour ses theses en France, l'ancien théoricien du PC, Roger Garaudy, est décoré et louangé dans les pays arabes," *Le Monde,* March 1, 1998. See also Ahmed Gharib, "Garaudy vedette de la Foire du livre du Caire," *Al Ahram Hebdo,* no. 283, February 9–15, 2000.
67. Goetz Nordbruch, *The Socio-Historical Background of Holocaust Denial in Arab Countries: Reactions to Roger Garaudy's "The Founding Myths of Israeli Politics"* (Jerusalem: The Vidal Sassoon International Center for the Study of Antisemitism, ACTA no. 17, 2001).
68. *Al-Ahram,* April 15, 2002, and August 1, 2002.
69. Quoted in *The Jerusalem Post,* April 25, 2001.
70. Yigal Carmon, "The Role of Holocaust Denial in the Ideology and Strategy of the Iranian Regime," *MEMRI Inquiry and Analysis,* no. 30 (December 15, 2006). See also Justus Reid Weiner et al., *Referral to Iranian President Ahmadinejad on the Charge of Incitement to Commit Genocide* (Jerusalem: Jerusalem Center for Public Affairs, 2007).
71. Matthias Küntzel, *Unholy Hatreds: Holocaust Denial and Antisemitism in Iran* (Jerusalem: The Vidal Sassoon International Center for the Study of Antisemitism, Posen Papers in Contemporary Antisemitism, no. 8, 2007), pp. 4–5.
72. *Al-Akhbar,* April 20, 2001, April 25, 2001, and May 27, 2001. See also "Holocaust Denial in the Middle East" (New York: ADL, 2001); and "Columnist for Egyptian Government Daily to Hitler: 'If Only You Had Done It, Brother,' " *MEMRI Special Dispatch Series,* no. 375 (May 3, 2002).
73. Küntzel, "Unholy Hatreds," pp. 5–6. Meir Litvak, "The Islamic Republic of Iran and the Holocaust: Anti-Semitism and Anti-Zionism," *Journal of Israeli History* 25, no. 1 (March 2006): pp. 267–84. See also George Michael, "Deciphering Ahmadinejad's Holocaust Revisionism," *Middle Eastern Quarterly* (Summer 2007), pp. 11–18.
74. Esther Webman, "Die Rhetorik der Hisbollah: die Weiterführung eines antisemitischen Diskurses," in *Jahrbuch für Antisemitismusforschung,* 2003, pp. 47–49.
75. Interview in *The New York Times,* March 26, 2000.
76. *Holocaust Denial in the Middle East: The Latest Anti-Israel Propaganda Themes* (New York: ADL, 2001), p. 12.
77. Ibid., pp. 5–6.
78. Per Ahlmark, "Reflections on Combating Anti-Semitism," in *The Rising Tide of Anti-Semitism,* ed. Yaffa Zilbershats (Ramat Gan, Israel: Bar-Ilan University Press, 1993), pp. 59–66.
79. See Taguieff, *Prêcheurs de Haine,* pp. 786–88.
80. See "Hizbollah's Al-Mana TV Interviews Head of Swedish 'Radio Islam,' " *MEMRI Special Dispatch Series,* no. 1002 (October 11, 2005).
81. See J. R. Wright, "David Myatt and Islam: A Personal View About an Unusual Story," http://www.geocities.com/davidmyatt/myatt_islam_conversion.html?2009/ (downloaded April 1, 2009) and by the same author, "The Promethean Peregrinations of David Myatt," http://aboutmyatt.wordpress.com/the-promethean-peregrinations-of-david-myatt (updated August 13, 2008).

82. Robert Solomon Wistrich, "The Antisemitic Ideology in the Contemporary Islamic World," in Zilbershats, *Rising Tide*, pp. 67–74.

83. Muhammad Khayr al-Wadi, editorial, *Tishrin*, January 31, 2000.

84. *Syria Times* (Damascus), September 5, 2001.

85. See "Syrian President 'Gives Aid and Comfort' to Holocaust Deniers," ADL Press Release, March 30, 2006. http://www.adl.org/PresReLe/HolocaustDenial_83/4897_83.htm.

86. Robert Fisk, "Turning a Blind Eye to History," *The Independent*, August 30, 1996, p. 12.

87. Eli Wohlgelernter, "In a State of Denial," *The Jerusalem Post*, June 8, 2001.

88. Meir Litvak and Esther Webman, "Perceptions of the Holocaust in Palestinian Public Discourse," *Israel Studies* 8, no. 3 (2001): pp. 124–40; and Litvak and Webman, "The Representation of the Holocaust in the Arab World," *The Journal of Israeli History* 23, no. 1 (Spring 2004): pp. 100–15.

89. *Al-Akhbar* (Cairo), August 19, 1972. See also Mansour's vicious article in *Al-Ahram*, February 13, 2001, which appeared in French in the Cairo daily *Le Progrès Egyptien* one day later.

90. Litvak and Webman, "Representation of the Holocaust," pp. 106–7.

91. Rashid Khalidi, "A Universal Jubilee? Palestinians 50 Years after 1948," *Tikkun*, March–April 1998, pp. 54–56.

92. "Egypt's Ruling Party Newspaper: 'The Holocaust Is a Zionist Lie Aimed at Extorting the West," *MEMRI Special Dispatch Series*, no. 750 (July 30, 2004). See also the panel discussion on Egypt's Al-Mihwar TV around these remarks, *MEMRI Special Dispatch Series*, no. 782 (September 10, 2004).

93. "Columnist for Egyptian Government Daily: 'The Nazis did not massacre the Jews,'" *MEMRI Special Dispatch Series*, no. 1052 (December 20, 2004).

94. See "Zionism and Nazism: A Discussion on the TV Channel Al-Jazeera," *MEMRI Special Dispatch Series*, no. 225 (June 6, 2001), for the details. Also Raphaël Israeli, "L'antisémitisme travesti en antisionisme," *Revue d'histoire de la Shoah*, no. 180 (January–June 2004): pp. 109–71. (A special issue on "Antisémitisme et Négationnisme dans le monde Arabo-Musulman: La Dérive.")

95. Israeli, "L'antisémitisme," p. 151.

96. Abd Al'Aziz al-Rantisi, "Which Is Worse—Zionism or Nazism?" *Al-Risala*, August 21, 2003. See *MEMRI Special Dispatch Series*, no. 558 (August 27, 2003) for English excerpts from the article.

97. See Palestinian Media Watch report, November 29, 2000; and *The Jerusalem Post*, December 5, 2000.

98. See Robert S. Wistrich, "L'antisémitisme Musulman: Un danger très actuel," *La Revue d'histoire de la Shoah*, no. 180 (January–June 2004): pp. 16–61, especially pp. 50–57.

99. "Press Statement by Hamas," February 3, 2000, in Yonah Alexander, *Palestinian Religious Terrorism: Hamas and Islamic Jihad* (Ardsley, N.Y.: Transnational Publishers, 2002), p. 394.

100. Ibid., p. 395.

101. Fadi Eyadat, "40 percent of Israeli Arabs Believe Holocaust Never Happened," *Haaretz*, May 17, 2009.

102. Al Jazeera TV, July 16, 2007, quoted in Naccache, *Contre Israël*, pp. 207–8.

Twenty: Hitler and the Mufti

1. See Bernard Lewis, *Semites and Antisemites* (New York: Norton, 1986); Wistrich, *Anti-Semitism: The Longest Hatred;* Wistrich, *Muslim Antisemitism;* and Esther Webman, "Anti-Zionism, Anti-Semitism and Criticism of Israel—The Arab Perspective," *Tel Aviver Jahrbuch für deutsche Geschichte* 33 (2005), ed. Moshe Zuckermann (Göttingen: Wallstein Verlag, 2005), pp. 306–29.
2. Robert S. Wistrich, "The Old-New Anti-Semitism," *The National Interest*, Summer 2003, pp. 39–70.
3. Juliane Wetzel, "Die internationale Rechte und der arabische Antizionismus im World Wide Web," *Jahrbuch für Antisemitismusforschung*, 2003, pp. 121–46.
4. Bassam Tibi, "Der importierte Hass," *Die Zeit*, February 6, 2003.
5. Alfred Rosenberg, *Der Staatsfeindliche Zionismus*, 2nd ed. (Munich: Zentralverlag der NSDAP Franz Eher Nachf, 1938), pp. 52–53.
6. Ibid., pp. 85–87.
7. Ibid., p. 87.
8. See Wistrich, *Hitler and the Holocaust;* and Wistrich, *Hitler's Apocalypse*, pp. 154–73.
9. See Alfred Rosenberg, *Die Protokolle der Weisen von Zion und die jüdische Weltpolitik* (Munich: Deutscher Volksverlag, 1933); and Henri Rollin, *L'Apocalypse de Notre Temps* (Paris, 1991), pp. 105–82. The most comprehensive account is by Pierre André Taguieff, *Les Protocoles des Sages de Sion*, vol. 1.
10. Hitler, *Mein Kampf*, pp. 56–57.
11. See Robert S. Wistrich, *Laboratory of World Destruction: Germans and Jews in Central Europe* (Lincoln: University of Nebraska Press, 2007).
12. Hitler, *Mein Kampf*, p. 57.
13. Ibid., pp. 324–25.
14. Ibid.
15. Rosenberg, *Der staatsfeindliche Zionismus*, p. 86.
16. *Mein Kampf*, p. 303.
17. Ibid., p. 305. See also Adolf Hitler, "Warum sind wir Antisemiten? Rede auf einer NSDAP Versammlung," in *Hitler: Sämtliche Aufzeichnungen 1905–1924*, ed. Eberhard Jäckel and Axe Kuhn (Stuttgart: Deutsche Verlags-Anstalt, 1980), pp. 190–92.
18. Dietrich Eckart, *Der Bolschevismus von Moses bis Lenin: Zwiegespräch zwischen Adolf Hitler und mir* (Munich: Hoheneichen-Verlag, 1924), pp. 16–17.
19. Yuri Slezkine, *The Jewish Century* (Princeton, N.J.: Princeton University Press, 2004), deals provocatively with Zionism and Communism as Jewish redemptive movements of the twentieth century aiming at the total transformation of Jewry.
20. Edwin Black, *The Transfer Agreement: The Untold Story of the Secret Pact Between the Third Reich and Jewish Palestine* (New York: Macmillan, 1984).
21. Ibid., pp. 79, 97.
22. For the reactions of German Zionists, see Robert Weltsch, *Die deutsche Judenfrage: Ein kritischer Rückblick* (Königstein, Germany: Jüdischer Verlag, 1981), pp. 73–82; Jehuda Reinharz, ed., *Dokumente zur Geschichte des deutschen Zionismus, 1882–1933* (Tübingen, Germany: Mohr, 1981), pp. 470–549; Francis R. Nicosia, *The Third Reich and the Palestine Question* (London: I. B. Tauris, 1985); and Daniel Frankel, *Al pnei Tehom: Ha-Mediniut Ha-Tsionit ve-she'elat yehudei Germania, 1933–1938* (Jerusalem: Magnes Press, Hebrew University of Jerusalem, 1994), pp. 63–154.

23. For articles sympathetic to the Palestinian Arab revolt in Nazi publications, see Giselher Wirsing, "Der Kampf um den Orient," *Die Tat* 29 (1937): pp. 73–96; and Wirsing, "Hintergründe der Teilung Palästinas," *Die Tat* 29 (1937): pp. 308–23. See also the polemics of the virulently anti-Semitic Johann von Leers, "Die arabischen Argumente gegen die Neufestsetzung der Juden in Palästina," *Weltkampf* 15 (1938): p. 146; von Leers, "Islam und Judentum—zwei unversöhnliche Gegensätze," *Weltkampf* 16, no. 182 (February 1939).

24. See David Israeli, *Ha-Reich ha-Germani ve Eretz-Israel* (Ramat Gan, Israel: Bar-Ilan University, 1974), pp. 114–21, 154ff. See also Jeffrey Herf, "Convergence: The Classic Case. Nazi Germany, Anti-Semitism and Anti-Zionism During World War II," *The Journal of Israeli History* 25, no. 1 (March 2006): pp. 63–83.

25. Alexander Schölch, "Das Dritte Reich, Die Zionistische Bewegung und der Palästina-Konflikt," *Vierteljahrshefte für Zeitgeschichte* 30 (1982): pp. 646–74.

26. See Yehoshua Porath, *The Palestinian Arab National Movement: From Riots to Rebellion*, vol. 2, *1929–1939* (London: Frank Cass, 1977), p. 76.

27. Schölch, "Das Dritte Reich," pp. 662–63.

28. Fritz Grobba, *Männer und Mächte im Orient* (Zürich: Masterscmidt, 1967), p. 317. See also Lukasz Hirszowicz, *The Third Reich and the Arab East* (London: Routledge, 1966); and for a more recent view, Küntzel, *Djihad und Judenhass* (Freiburg, Germany: Ça ira, 2002).

29. Hugh Trevor-Roper, ed., *Hitler's Table Talk, 1941–1944* (London: Weidenfeld and Nicolson, 1973), p. 547. The remarks about the mufti were recorded on July 1, 1942. For a Nazi assessment of the Palestinian Arab leader, see Kurt Fischer-Weth, *Amin al-Husseini, Grossmufti von Palästina* (Berlin: Walter Titz Verlag, 1943).

30. For constrasting views of Haj Amin, see Philip Mattar, *The Mufti of Jerusalem: Haj Amin al-Husayni and the Palestinian National Movement* (New York: Columbia University Press, 1991); and Zvi el-Peleg, *The Grand Mufti: Haj Amin al-Hussaini, Founder of the Palestinian National Movement* (London: Frank Cass, 1994). See also el-Peleg, *Me-Nekudat Reuto shel Ha-Mufti* [In the Eyes of the Mufti] (Tel Aviv: Ha-kibbutz Ha-Meuchad, 1995).

31. Yisraeli, *Ha-Reich Ha-Germani*, pp. 103ff. See also Grobba, *Männer und Mächte*, pp. 208–9, 213–14. On the complex interaction between the Nazis, the Vichy French, Arabs, and Jews in North Africa during the war years, see Robert Satloff, *Among the Righteous: Lost Stories from the Holocaust's Long Reach into Arab Lands* (New York: Public Affairs, 2006); and the older work by Michel Abitbol, *Les Juifs d'Afrique du Nord sous Vichy* (Paris: G.-P. Maisonneuve and Larose, 1983).

32. Hirszowicz, *Third Reich*, p. 263; and Grobba, *Männer und Mächte*, p. 317.

33. See Hitler's speeches of February 20, September 12, and November 8, 1938, in Max Domarus, ed., *Hitler: Reden und Proklamationen, 1932–1945* (Würzburg, Germany: Gesamthers-tellung und Auslieferung, 1962), vol. 1: pp. 800, 904, 969.

34. Hirszowicz, *Third Reich*, pp. 143ff. The consequences of this pro-Nazi coup were disastrous for the Jews of Baghdad, leading to the devastating pogrom, or Farhud, in June 1941 carried out by Iraqi Arabs. See Elie Kedourie, "The Sack of Basra and the Baghdad *Farhud*," in *Arabic Political Memoirs and Other Studies* (London: Cass, 1974), pp. 283–314; and Norman A. Stillman, *The Jews of Arab Lands in Modern Times* (Philadelphia: The Jewish Publication Society, 1991), pp. 118–20, 405–18, 457–59.

35. Daniel Carpi, "The Mufti of Jerusalem, Amin el-Husseini and His Diplomatic Activity During World War II (October 1941–July 1943)," *Zionism*, 1984, p. 109, notes that the Arabic minutes that the mufti entered in his diary have survived but contain only Hitler's answers. The German minutes appear in Yisraeli, *Ha-Reich Ha-Germani*, pp. 308–11, and in English in *Documents on German Foreign Policy (DGFP) 1918–1954*, Series D (Washington, D.C.: U.S. Government Printing Office, 1949–64), vol. 13: pp. 201–4.

36. Joseph Schechtman, *The Mufti and the Fuehrer: The Rise and Fall of Haj Amin el-Husseini* (New York: T. Yoseloff, 1965), pp. 306–8.

37. *DGFP*, p. 201.

38. Ibid., p. 202. See also *DGFP*, Series D, vol. 12: p. 489, for Ernst von Weiszäcker's April 8, 1941, letter to the mufti on behalf of Hitler, which states that "Germans and Arabs have common enemies in the English and the Jews and are united in the struggle against them."

39. *DGFP*, vol. 13: p. 202.

40. Ibid., pp. 202–3.

41. Ibid., p. 204.

42. Ibid., p. 203.

43. Ibid. See also Klaus Gensicke, *Der Mufti von Jerusalem, Amin el-Husseini und die Nationalsozialisten* (Darmstadt, Germany: Wissenschaftliche Buchgesellschaft, 2007). The first edition appeared in Frankfurt in 1988.

44. *DGFP*, vol. 13: p. 203.

45. Ibid., p. 204.

46. Ibid.

47. Ženi Lebl, *Hadž-Amin i Berlin* (Belgrade, 2003), pp. 118ff., 157–95. This study in Serbo-Croat treats the mobilization of Muslims in the Waffen-SS under Haj Amin's inspiration more extensively than any other work.

48. D. Caspi, "The Diplomatic Negotiations over the Transfer of Jewish Children from Croatia to Turkey and Palestine in 1943," *Yad Vashem Studies* 12 (1977): pp. 109–24. See also Schechtman, *Mufti and the Fuehrer*, pp. 154–59, 310.

49. Lebl, *Hadž-Amin*, pp. 169–227, on Haj Amin's intimate ties with Himmler and other SS leaders.

50. Schechtman, *Mufti and the Fuehrer*, pp. 139ff. See also David G. Dalin's remarks on the mufti in *The Myth of Hitler's Pope* (Washington, D.C.: Regnery Publishing, 2005), pp. 134–37.

51. Schechtman, *Mufti and the Fuehrer*, pp. 147–52.

52. Ibid. See also Schölch, "Das Dritte Reich," p. 671.

53. Schechtman, *Mufti and the Fuehrer*, p. 160; Simon Wiesenthal, *Grossmufti-Grossagent der Achse* (Salzburg, 1947), p. 37; Klaus Gensicke, *Der Mufti von Jerusalem*, pp. 194ff., on the connection between Eichmann and the mufti. See also Gerhard Höpp, "Der Gefangene im Dreieck: Zum Bild Amin al-Husseinis in Wissenschaft und Publizistik seit 1941," in *Eine umstrittene Figur: Hadj Amin al-Husseini*, ed. Rainer Zimmer-Winkel (Trier, Germany: AphorismA Verlag, 1999), pp. 5–23.

54. This claim is made by Alexander Flores, "Judeophobia in context: Anti-Semitism Among Modern Palestinians," *Die Welt des Islams* 46, no. 3 (2006): pp. 307–30, especially pp. 323–24.

55. Klaus Gensicke, *Der Mufti von Jerusalem, Amin el-Husseini, und die National-sozialisten,* 1st ed. (Frankfurt: Peter Lang, 1988), p. 270. A July 25, 1942, statement of the mufti stressed how closely the Arabs identified with Germany in their "uncompromising" struggle against World Jewry, as well as in their battle against Britain and America, "the protectors of the Jews."

56. Quoted in *The Arab Higher Committee: The Documentary Record* (submitted to the United Nations by the Nation Associates, New York, May 1947). This contains many documents, in German and English, relating to the correspondence among the mufti, Himmler, Alfred Rosenberg, Ribbentrop, and other Axis leaders.

57. Ibid., p. 55. The letter was sent from Berlin on Foreign Ministry letterhead.

58. Ibid., p. 60. Letter to Ribbentrop that recalled the foreign minister's declaration of November 2, 1943, that "the destruction of the so-called Jewish national home is an immutable part of the policy of the Greater German Reich."

59. Ibid., p. 61.

60. Ibid., 63–64. Letter of June 28, 1943.

61. Gerhard Höpp, ed., *Mufti-Papiere: Briefe, Memoranden, Reden und Aufrufe Amin al-Husainis aus dem Exil, 1940–1945* (Berlin: Klaus Schwarz Verlag, 2001),pp. 149ff.

62. Joan Peters, *From Time Immemorial: The Origins of the Arab-Jewish Conflict Over Palestine* (New York: Harper and Row, 1984), p. 371.

63. Wistrich, *Hitler's Apocalypse,* pp. 169–70. See also Daniel Carpi, "The Mufti of Jerusalem, Amin el-Husseini, and His Diplomatic Activity During World War II (October 1941–July 1943)," *Zionism,* 1984, pp. 101–13.

64. Schechtman, *Mufti and the Fuehrer,* pp. 147–52.

65. Ibid.

66. *DFGP,* vol. 11: pp. 1153–54.

67. Quoted by Schölch, "Das Dritte Reich," pp. 669–70.

68. Schechtman, *Mufti and the Fuehrer,* pp. 139–40. See also Küntzel, *Djihad und Judenhass,* pp. 38–52.

69. Schechtman, *Mufti and the Fuehrer,* p. 140; Wistrich, *Hitler's Apocalypse,* pp. 163–71.

70. Quoted in Gensicke, *Der Mufti von Jerusalem,* 1st ed., p. 155.

71. Speech of March 19, 1943, in Höpp, *Mufti-Papiere,* pp. 152–55.

72. John Loftus and Mark Aarons, *The Secret War Against the Jews: How Western Espionage Betrayed the Jewish People* (New York: St. Martin's Press, 1994), p. 47.

73. See Stefan Wild, "National Socialism in the Near East Between 1933 and 1939," in *The Pogrom of 1941 and the Persecution of Jews in Iraq: The Role of Nazis, Iraqis and Palestinian Nationalists and Zionists,* ed. Shmuel Moreh and Zvi Yehuda (Or-Yehuda, Israel: The Babylonian Jewry Heritage Center, 2005), pp. 27–68. An earlier version of this article appeared in German in *Die Welt des Islams* 25 (1985): pp. 126–73.

74. Sami al-Jundi, *al-Ba'th* (Beirut, 1969), pp. 27ff. Quoted in Kedourie, *Arabic Political Memoirs,* p. 200; and by Itamar Rabinovich, "Germany and the Syrian Political Scene in the Late 1930s," in *Germany and the Middle East, 1835–1939,* ed. Jehuda L. Wallach (Tel Aviv: Tel Aviv University, 1975), p. 197. For the general background, see Gerhard Höpp, Peter Wien and René Wildangel, eds., *Blind für die Geschichte? Arabische Begegnungen mit dem National-Sozialismus* (Berlin: Klaus Schwarz Verlag, 2004).

75. Michel Aflaq, *Fi sabil al-ba'th* [Towards the Ba'th] (Beirut, 1959), pp. 29–30. It was written around 1940. See also Sylvia G. Haim, ed., *Arab Nationalism: An Anthology* (Berkeley: University of California Press, 1976), pp. 61–72; and Amatzia Baram, "Der moderne Iraq, die Baath Partei und der Antisemitismus," *Jahrbuch für Antisemitismusforschung,* 2003, pp. 99–119.

76. Rabinovich, "Germany and the Syrian Political Scene," p. 198. See also Bernard Lewis, "The New Anti-Semitism," *The American Scholar* 75, no. 1 (Winter 2006): pp. 25–36, who remarks that the impact of Nazi propaganda and European-style anti-Semitism was particularly strong in Syria and on the Baath parties in general.

77. Haj Amin issued a fatwa in May 1941—a summons to holy war against Britain—which was broadcast over the Iraqi and Axis radios. It appeared in *Oriente Moderno,* 1941, pp. 552–53. In this appeal to Muslims to rise up and overthrow the English yoke, reference was made to British encouragement for the "outrageous infiltration of Jews" into Palestine and their "most unyielding war against Islam." See also Harold P. Luks, "Iraqi Jews During World War II," *The Wiener Library Bulletin* 30, n.s. nos. 43–44 (1977): pp. 30–39.

78. On the Farhud, see Kedourie, "Sack of Basra," pp. 283–314; Nissim Kazzaz, "The Influence of Nazism in Iraq and Anti-Jewish Activity 1933–1941," *Pe'amim,* 29 (1987): pp. 48–69, in Hebrew; Hamdi Walid, *Rashid Ali al-Gailani and the Nationalist Movement in Iraq 1939–41* (London: Darf, 1987); Salim Fattal, *Be Simta'ot Bagdad* (Jerusalem: Carmel, 2003), in Hebrew. Shmuel Moreh, "The Role of Palestinian Incitement in the Farhūd Massacre in Iraq and the Attitude of Arab Intellectuals," in Moreh and Yehuda, *Pogrom of 1941,* pp. 93–113, emphasizes the role of the mufti and Palestinian exiles in Iraq in firing up hatred of the Jews.

79. Zvi Yehuda has reproduced many of the most important documents relating to the Farhud in *Pogrom of 1941,* pp. 196–264. See also Nissim Rejwan, *The Jews of Iraq: 3000 Years of History and Culture* (London: Weidenfeld and Nicolson, 1985).

80. Reeva S. Simon, *Iraq Between the Two World Wars: The Creation and Implantation of a Nationalist Ideology* (New York: Columbia University Press, 1986), pp. 95–114, on the Iraqi school curriculum and textbooks; and Stillman, *Jews of Arab Lands,* pp. 111–20.

81. See Wistrich, "Old-New Antisemitism," pp. 71–90.

82. See James Jankowski, *Egypt's Young Rebels: "Young Egypt," 1933–1952* (Stanford, Calif.: Hoover Institution Press, 1975). The Green Shirts of Misr al-Fatah consciously emulated German and Italian models with their martial displays, leader cult, uniforms, tendency to violence, and anti-Jewish rhetoric. The al-Muthanna Club and Futuwwa in Iraq, the Syrian National Bloc's Iron Shirts, the Lebanese Maronite Phalange, and the Muslim Brotherhood's Phalanxes showed similar propensities to fascist-style parades. See Stillman, *Jews of Arab Lands,* p. 107.

83. Ahmad Husayn, "Risāla min Yahūdī," *Jāridat Misr al-Fatāt* (July 27, 1939). Quoted from James P. Jankowski, "Egyptian Responses to the Palestine Problem in the Interwar Period," *International Journal of Middle Eastern Studies* 12 (1980): p. 33 n. 118. See also Thomas Mayer, *Egypt and the Palestine Question, 1936–1945* (Berlin: K. Schwarz Verlag, 1983), pp. 15–40, on the public reactions to the Palestinian revolt of 1936–39 in Egypt. For Jewish responses, see Gudrun Krämer, *Minderheit, Millet, Nation? Die Juden in Ägypten 1914–1952* (Wiesbaden, Germany: Harrassowitz, 1982).

84. Krämer, *Minderheit, Millet,* pp. 306–7.

85. Quoted in Wild, "National Socialism in the Near East," *Die Welt des Islams,* p. 128.

86. Renzo de Felice, *Jews in an Arab Land: Libya 1835–1970* (Austin: University of Texas Press, 1985), pp. 171–73. See also the documents in Stillman, *Jews of Arab Lands,* pp. 419–20; and Satloff, *Among the Righteous,* pp. 42–44.

87. De Felice, *Jews in an Arab Land,* pp. 178–80.

88. Ibid., pp. 192–210, on the riots during which British troops held back from intervention, much as they had done in Iraq in 1941. For a detailed account see "Anti-Jewish Riots in Tripolitania," file S 25/6457, in the Central Zionist Archives, Jerusalem, pp. 1–6.

89. See Michel Abitbol, *Les Juifs d'Afrique du Nord sous Vichy* (Paris: G.-P. Maisonneuve and Larose, 1983); the documents in Stillman, *Jews of Arab Lands,* pp. 426–41; and the account in Satloff, *Among the Righteous,* pp. 30–34.

90. Abitbol, *Les Juifs d'Afrique,* pp. 102–7; Stillman, *Jews of Arab Lands,* pp. 126–39.

91. Satloff, *Among the Righteous,* pp. 96, 109–13.

92. Ibid., p. 111.

93. Stillman, *Jews of Arab Lands,* p. 127. See also Jacques Sabille, *Les Juifs de Tunisie sous Vichy et l'occupation* (Paris: Éditions du Centre, 1954), pp. 127–30, 179–81. The Germans imposed the yellow star on Tunisian Jews outside the capital, but Italian obstruction and delays by the Vichy authorities prevented this from happening in Tunis before its liberation by the Allies.

94. See Klaus-Michael Mallman and Martin Cüppers, *Halbmond und Hakenkreuz: Das Dritte Reich, die Araber und Palästina* (Darmstadt, Germany: Wissenschaftliche Buchgesellschaft, 2006).

95. Robert Satloff, "In Search of 'Righteous Arabs,' " *Commentary,* July–August 2004, 30ff., explores this theme. See also Satloff, *Among the Righteous,* p. 97.

96. Stillman, *The Jews of Arab Lands,* p. 180.

97. Hayyim J. Cohen, *Ha-Peilut ha-Zionit be-Iraq* (Jerusalem: ha-Sifriyah ha-Tsiyonit, 1969). See also Carole Basri, *The Jews of Iraq: A Forgotten Case of Ethnic Cleansing* (Jerusalem: Institute of the World Jewish Congress, policy study no. 26, 2003), which reconstructs the story of legislative persecution and the mass exodus of Iraqi Jews in 1950–51. For Yemen, see Joseph B. Schechtman, *On the Wings of Eagles: The Plight, Exodus, and Homecoming of Oriental Jewry* (New York: T. Yoseloff, 1961).

98. Krämer, *Minderheit, Millet,* pp. 318–22; Mayer, *Egypt and the Palestine Question,* pp. 298–300; and Abd al-Fattah Muhammad el-Awaisi, *The Muslim Brotherhood and the Palestine Question 1918–1947* (London: Tauris Academic Studies, 1998).

99. See Gudrun Krämer, "Radical Nationalists, Fundamentalists, and the Jews in Egypt, or, Who Is a Real Egyptian?" in *Islam, Nationalism and Radicalism in Egypt and the Sudan,* ed. Gabriel R. Warburg and Uri M. Kupferschmidt (New York: Praeger, 1983), pp. 354–71.

100. Krämer, *Minderheit Millet,* p. 414.

101. See Stillman, *Jews of Arab Lands,* pp. 173–74.

102. For the material aspects of Jewish expropriation, see Itamar Levin, *Confiscated Wealth: The Fate of Jewish Property in Arab Lands* (Jerusalem: Institute of the World Jewish Congress, policy forum no. 22, 2000).

103. Albert Memmi, "Moi, Juif né parmi les Arabes," *L'Arche*, no. 202 (December 26–January 25, 1974): pp. 27–29.

104. Albert Menni, *Juifs et Arabes* (Paris: Gallimard, 1974), p. 50.

TWENTY-ONE: THE "LIBERATION" OF PALESTINE

1. Neville Mandel, "Turks, Arabs and Jewish Immigration into Palestine 1882–1914," *Middle Eastern Affairs* (St. Antony's Papers), no. 4 (1965): pp. 77–108.

2. Mim Kemal Öke, "The Ottoman Empire, Zionism, and the Question of Palestine (1880–1908)," *International Journal of Middle East Studies* 14 (1982): pp. 329–34. See also Neville Mandel, *The Arabs and Zionism Before World War I* (Berkeley: University of California Press, 1976), p. 19; and Isaiah Friedman, *Germany, Turkey and Zionism* (Oxford, U.K.: Oxford University Press, 1977).

3. Mandel, "Turks, Arabs, and Jewish Immigration," p. 17.

4. Al-Khalidi to Chief Rabbi Zadoc Kahn, March 1, 1899, in Central Zionist Archives (2A), H3 D.14, Paris. The letter was in French, a language in which Al-Khalidi was fluent, as he was in English, Turkish, Kurdish, and Arabic. It was passed on to Herzl, who replied somewhat blandly, suggesting that Arabs would benefit from Jewish immigration and stressing the pacific intentions of Zionist colonization. See Theodor Herzl, *Kol Kitve Herzl* (Jerusalem, 1957); vol. 3, pp. 309–10, in Hebrew.

5. Neguib Azoury, *Le Réveil de la Nation Arabe dans l'Asie Turque* (Paris: Plon-Nourritt, 1905). See also the reply by Farid Kassab, a young Greek Orthodox Arab from Beirut then studying in Paris: *Le Nouvel Empire Arabe: La Curie Romaine et le Prétendu Péril Juif Universel Réponse à M.N. Azoury Bey* (Paris: Girard and Brière, 1906). This Ottomanist response not only defended the Turkish Empire but also stressed the peaceful, industrious, and inoffensive nature of the Jewish settlers in Palestine.

6. Azoury, *Le Réveil*, pp. ii–iii.

7. Ibid., pp. iv–v.

8. Ibid., p. vi.

9. Ibid., pp. 6–17.

10. Kassab, *Le nouvel Empire arabe*, pp. 39–40. See also Bat Ye'or, *Juifs et Chrétiens sous L'Islam: Les dhimmis face au défi integriste* (Paris: Berg International, 1994), pp. 136–38.

11. Mandel, "Turks, Arabs, and Jewish Immigration," pp. 53–54, mentions the anti-Jewish and anti-Zionist writings of the Belgian Jesuit scholar Père Henri Lammens, who taught at the University of Beirut. He liked to dwell on the "repulsive grubbiness" and the "famous Semitic nose" of the Jews in Jerusalem.

12. See David Farhi, "Documents on the Attitude of the Ottoman Government Towards the Jewish Settlement in Palestine After the Revolution of the Young Turks," in *Studies on Palestine in the Ottoman Period,* ed. M. Maoz (Jerusalem: Magnes Press, 1975), pp. 19–210.

13. Ibid., p. 201. See Mim Kemāl Öke, "Young Turks, Freemasons, Jews and the Question of Zionism in the Ottoman Empire (1908–1913)," *Studies in Zionism* 7, no. 2 (Autumn 1986): pp. 199–216. See also the earlier article by Elie Kedourie, "Young Turks, Freemasons and Jews," *Middle Eastern Studies* 7 (January 1971).

14. Yehoshua Porath, "The Political Awakening of the Palestinian Arabs and Their Leadership Towards the End of the Ottoman Period," in Maoz, *Studies on Palestine,* pp. 351–81.

15. Mandel, *Arabs and Zionism,* pp. 122–29.

16. Porath, "Political Awakening," p. 379.

17. Mandel, *The Arabs and Zionism,* pp. 78–89.

18. Ibid., pp. 175–76.

19. Pierre Loti, *Jérusalem* (Paris: Calmann-Lévy, 1895), p. 126. Loti was a well-known French Catholic writer who wrote vividly about his experiences in the Holy Land.

20. Jérome and Jean Tharaud, *L'an prochain à Jérusalem!* (Paris: Plon-Nourrit et cie, 1924), p. 207. The brothers were anti-Semites fascinated by everything Jewish in the Diaspora as well as the Holy Land.

21. David S. Landes, "Palestine Before the Zionists," *Commentary,* February 1976, p. 52.

22. Ibid., p. 54.

23. Gil Carl AlRoy, "The Arab Myth of Zionism," *Patterns of Prejudice* 4, no. 6 (November–December 1970).

24. See Faisal's letter of March 3, 1919, to Felix Frankfurter, in Laqueur and Rubin, *Israel-Arab Reader,* pp. 18–21.

25. For the resolutions of the General Syrian Congress (Damascus, July 2, 1919) and the *Recommendations of the King-Crane Commission with Regard to Syria-Palestine and Iraq* (August 28, 1919), see George Antonius, *The Arab Awakening* (New York: Capricorn Books, 1965), pp. 440–58.

26. Statement of August 12, 1921, Colonial Office (CO) 733/14, London; letter from the delegation to the colonial secretary, October 24, 1921, CO 733/161. See also Aaron S. Kliemann, *Foundations of British Policy in the Arab World: The Cairo Conference of 1921* (Baltimore: Johns Hopkins University Press, 1970), pp. 259–67, for the document of March 28, 1921, presented to Churchill by Musa Kazim Pasha, president of the Haifa congress, from which I have quoted.

27. Kliemann, *Foundations of British Policy.*

28. Antonius, *The Arab Awakening,* pp. 243–75. See also Kliemann, *Foundations of British Policy,* pp. 260–62; and Geoffrey P. Nash, "Uneasy Symbiosis: George Antonius's Anglo-Arab Discourse in the Arab Awakening," *The Islamic Quarterly* 39, no. 1 (1995): pp. 59–67.

29. Yehoshua Porath, *The Emergence of the Palestinian-Arab National Movement 1918–29* (London: Frank Cass, 1974), pp. 50–53, on the response in Palestine to the Balfour Declaration, which in 1920 was already considered by Arabs to be illegal and an immoral imperialist machination.

30. Frederick Hermann Kisch, *Palestine Diary* (London: V. Gollanz, 1938), pp. 268–69.

31. Y. Porath, *The Palestinian Arab National Movement: From Riots to Rebellion,* vol. 2: *1929–1939* (London: Frank Cass, 1977), pp. 8–13.

32. Y. Porath, "Palestinian and Pan-Arab Nationalism, 1918–1939" and Zvi El-Peleg, "The 1936–1939 Disturbances: Riot or Rebellion?" *The Wiener Library Bulletin* 31, nos. 45–46 (1978): pp. 29–31 (special issue on Palestine under the British mandate). See also Nels Johnson, *Islam and the Politics of Meaning in Palestinian Nationalism* (London: Kegan Paul, 1982), pp. 31–45, on al-Qassam.

33. Shai Lachman, "Arab Rebellion and Terrorism in Palestine, 1929–1939: The Case of Sheikh Izz al-Din al-Qassam and His Movement," in *Zionism and Arabism in*

Palestine and Israel, ed. Elie Kedourie and Sylvia G. Haim (London: Frank Cass, 1982), pp. 52–99.

34. Quoted in Efraim Karsh, "Intifada II: The Long Trail of Arab Anti-Semitism," *Commentary,* December, 2000, p. 52.

35. Y. Porath, "Anti-Zionist and Anti-Jewish Ideology in the Arab Nationalist Movement in Palestine," in *Antisemitism Through the Ages,* ed. Shmuel Almog (Oxford, U.K.: Pergamon Press, 1988), pp. 217–25; and Yehoshafat Harkabi, "On Arab Nationalism Once More," in ibid., pp. 227–32.

36. Porath, "Anti-Zionist and Anti-Jewish Ideology," pp. 224–25.

37. Joseph Nevo, " 'Zionism' Versus 'Judaism' in Palestinian Historiography," in *Medieval and Modern Perspectives on Muslim-Jewish Relations,* ed. Ronald L. Nettler (Luxembourg: Harwood Academic Publishers, 1995), pp. 159–73.

38. Ibid., p. 164. Quoted from Haj Amin al-Husayni, *The Truth About the Palestine Problem* (Cairo, 1954), p. 26, in Arabic.

39. Yehoshafat Harkabi, *Arab Attitudes to Israel* (Jerusalem: Israel Universities Press, 1972), p. 198.

40. An exception was Musa Alami. See his preface to *The Future of Palestine* (Beirut: Hermon Books, 1970), originally published under his direction in 1947 by the Arab office.

41. Barry Rubin, *Revolution Until Victory? The Politics and History of the PLO* (Cambridge, Mass.: Harvard University Press, 1994), pp. 12–14.

42. Küntzel, *Djihad und Judenhass,* pp. 28–117. See also Nicosia, *Third Reich and the Palestine Question.*

43. Uri M. Kupferschmidt, *The Supreme Muslim Council: Islam Under the British Mandate for Palestine* (Leiden, Netherlands: E. J. Brill, 1987), pp. 249–52.

44. Küntzel, *Djihad und Judenhass,* pp. 34–41.

45. See Wistrich, *Anti-Semitism: The Longest Hatred,* p. 205; and Kenneth R. Timmerman, *Preachers of Hate: Islam and the War on America* (New York: Three Rivers Press, 2004), pp. 81, 99, 103.

46. Timmerman, *Preachers of Hate,* pp. 103–4.

47. Ibid., p. 110.

48. Klaus-Michael Mallmann and Martin Cüppers, "Beseitigung der jüdisch-nationalen Heimstätte Palästina: Das Einsatzkommando bei der Panzerarmee Afrika 1942," in *Deutsche Juden, Völkermord. Der Holocaust als Geschichte und Gegenwort,* ed. Jürgen Matthäus and Klaus-Michael Mallmann (Darmstadt, Germany: Wissenschaftliche Buchgesellschaft, 2006), pp. 153–75.

49. Matthias Küntzel, "Von Zeesen bis Beirut: Nationalsozialismus und Antisemitismus in der arabischen Welt," in *Neuer Antisemitismus? Eine globale Debatte,* ed. Doron Rabinovici et al. (Frankfurt: Suhrkamp, 2004), pp. 271–93.

50. Zvi El-Peleg, *Me-Nekudat Reuto shel Ha-Mufti* (In the Eyes of the Mufti) (Kibbutz Ha-Meuchad/University of Tel Aviv, 1995), in Hebrew.

51. David N. Bossie, "Yasser Arafat: Nazi Trained," *Washington Times,* August 9, 2002. See also Thomas Kiernan, *Yasir Arafat* (London: Abacus, 1976) on his ancestry and early years.

52. Gérard Chaliand, "La Résistance Palestinienne entre Israël et les États Arabes," *Le Monde Diplomatique,* March 1969, p. 11. See also David G. Dalin, *The Myth of Hitler's Pope* (Washington, D.C.: Regnery Publishing, 2005), p. 139.

53. Timmerman, *Preachers of Hate,* p. 120.

54. Benjamin Netanyahu, "Ending the Legacy of Hate," UN General Assembly, Forti-eth Session, Official Records, December 4, 1985, p. 6.

55. Quoted in David Dallin, *The Myth of Hitler's Papa,* p. 141.

56. John Laffin, *The PLO Connections* (London: Corgi Books, 1982), p. 19.

57. See Laqueur and Rubin, *Israel-Arab Reader,* pp. 504–17, for Arafat's address to the UN General Assembly on November 13, 1974. In this speech, Arafat defined Zion-ism as "imperialist, colonialist, racist . . . profoundly reactionary and discrimina-tory . . . united with anti-Semitism in its retrograde tenets, and when all is said and done it is another side of the same base coin." This terminology is Soviet to-talitarian doublespeak, down to the last comma.

58. See *El Mundo* (Caracas), February 11, 1980, for Arafat's speech. See also Farouk Kaddoumi in *Al Watan,* October 18, 1979. On the June 1980 Fatah congress in Damascus, see Laffin, *PLO Connections,* p. 43.

59. Laffin, *PLO,* ibid.

60. Jillian Becker, *The PLO: The Rise and Fall of the Palestine Liberation Organization* (London: Weidenfeld and Nicolson, 1984), pp. 178–93.

61. Ibid., pp. 191–92.

62. Matti Steinberg, "The World-View of Hawatmah's 'Democratic Front,' " *The Jerusalem Quarterly,* no. 50 (Spring 1989): pp. 23ff.

63. See Lorand Gaspar, *Palestine année o* (Paris: François Maspero, 1970), pp. 83–97, for the view of the DFLP and Hawatmeh on the question of Israel.

64. El Fath, *La Révolution Palestinienne et les Juifs* (Paris: Les Éditions de Minuit, 1970), based on texts originally published in Beirut in the monthly publication of Fatah (March–May 1970). Among the Jewish humanist thinkers evoked with approval by Fatah were the radical journalist I. F. Stone, as well as Moshe Menuhin, Martin Buber, Isaac Deutscher, and the American reform rabbi Elmer Berger.

65. For a philosophical dissection of these politicidal Palestinian formulas, see Robert Misrahi, *La Philosophie politique et L'Etat d'Israël* (Paris: Éditions Mouton, 1975).

66. Laqueur and Rubin, *Israel-Arab Reader,* pp. 509–10.

67. For the text of the PLO charter, see ibid., pp. 366–37. See also the Seven Points, passed by the Central Committee of Fatah (January 1969), and an interview with Arafat in *Free Palestine* (August 1969), in ibid., pp. 372–79.

68. Laqueur and Rubin, *Israel-Arab Reader,* p. 369.

69. Article 6, along with the other articles relating to Jews, made clear that the much-vaunted PLO "respect for Judaism" was an empty and hollow phrase.

70. Laqueur and Rubin, *Israel-Arab Reader,* pp. 369–70.

71. Y. Harkabi, "Al Fatah's Doctrine" (December 1968), reproduced in Laqueur and Rubin, *The Israel-Arab Reader,* pp. 383–99.

72. Ibid., p. 389. This *either-or* vision of conflict is reminiscent both of National So-cialism and also some of the revolutionary doctrines popular in the 1960s and as-sociated with Mao Tse-tung, Che Guevara, and the Algerian FLN.

73. See, for example, Alexander Flores, "Judeophobia in context: Anti-Semitism Among Modern Palestinians," *Die Welt des Islams* 46, no. 3 (2006): pp. 307–30, whose account is misleading; he simplistically reduces the spread of anti-Semitic attitudes to the intensity level of the Israeli-Palestinian conflict.

74. Ibid., pp. 314–15. See also the earlier works by Mario Offenberg, *Kommunismus in*

Palästina: Nation und Klasse in der antikolonialen Revolution (Meisenheim, Germany: Anton Hain, 1975) and the anti-Zionist Joel Beinin, *Was the Red Flag Flying There? Marxist Politics and the Arab-Israeli Conflict in Egypt and Israel, 1948–1965* (Berkeley and Los Angeles: University of California Press, 1990).

75. Harkabi, *Arab Attitudes to Israel,* pp. 223–303.

76. Barry Rubin, *The PLO Between Anti-Zionism and Antisemitism* (Jerusalem: The Vidal Sassoon International Center for the Study of Antisemitism, ACTA no. 1, 1993).

77. See Robert Fulford, "Yasir Arafat and the Politics of Denial," *National Post,* September 13, 2003.

78. Raphael Israeli, *The Oslo Delusion—Or the Collapse of Axioms* (Shaarei Tikva, Israel: Ariel Center for Policy Research, no. 126, 2000).

79. Interview with Arafat, *Le Figaro,* April 29, 1989. In reality, of course, the stripes are taken from the *talith,* or Jewish prayer shawl.

80. See Raphael Israeli, *Islamikaze: Manifestations of Islamic Martyrology* (London: Frank Cass, 2003), pp. 281–344.

81. Robert S. Wistrich, *Muslim Anti-Semitism: A Clear and Present Danger* (New York: AJC, 2002), p. 34.

82. See *Yediot Ahronoth,* June 25, 1997, in Hebrew.

83. Fiamma Nirenstein, "How Suicide Bombers Are Made," *Commentary,* September 2001, pp. 53–55.

84. Wistrich, *Muslim Anti-Semitism,* p. 34.

85. M. Y. S. Haddad, *Arab Perspectives of Judaism* (The Hague, 1984), pp. 435, 451.

86. Robert Spencer, ed., *The Myth of Islamic Tolerance* (Amherst, N.Y.: Prometheus Books, 2005), pp. 469–72. See also David G. Littman, "Arafat, Jésus et L'histoire," *Dimanche Tribune* (Lausanne, Switzerland), September 11, 1983; *Tribune de Genève,* September 14, 1983; and Ye'or, *Islam and Dhimmitude,* pp. 319, 466.

87. See Gershon Nerel, *Anti-Zionism in the "Electronic Church" of Palestinian Christianity* (Jerusalem: The Vidal Sassoon International Center for the Study of Antisemitism, ACTA no. 27, 2006); and "Interview with Arafat," *MEMRI Special Dispatch Series,* no. 428 (October 11, 2002).

88. Quoted in Rubin, *The PLO Between Anti-Zionism,* p. 9.

89. Daniel Patrick Moynihan with Suzanne Weaver, *A Dangerous Place* (Boston: Little, Brown and Company, 1978), p. 172.

90. Harris O. Schoenberg, *A Mandate for Terror: The United Nations and the PLO* (New York: Shapolsky Publishers, 1989), p. 282, also quotes Canadian ambassador Stephen Lewis commenting in 1986 at New York University that anti-Semitism at the UN "distributes itself poisonously, creating an environment that legitimizes propositions that would otherwise be seen as offensive."

91. Shuqairy's statement is quoted by Donald Neff, *Warriors for Jerusalem: The Six Days That Changed the Middle East* (New York: Simon and Schuster, 1984), p. 181. See also Alan Hart, *Arafat: Terrorist or Peacemaker?* (London: Sidgwick and Jackson, 1984), p. 165.

92. Schoenberg, *Mandate for Terror,* p. 298.

93. Ibid., pp. 497–503, appendix 6, for the full statement by Ambassador Daniel Patrick Moynihan in the UN General Assembly on November 10, 1975.

94. Laffin, *PLO Connections,* p. 10. See also David Hirst, *The Gun and the Olive Branch:*

The Roots of Violence in the Middle East (New York: Harcourt Brace Jovanovich, 1977), p. 291.

95. *The Middle East* (London), March 1979, p. 36.

96. *The Jerusalem Post,* November 27, 1980; and Christopher S. Wren, interview, *The New York Times,* August 3, 1986.

97. Menahem Milson, "How to Make Peace with the Palestinians," *Commentary,* May 1981, pp. 25–35.

98. *IHT,* March 18, 1977.

99. Barry Rubin, "One Step Forward, One Step Back," *U.S. News and World Report,* November 28, 1988; Amos Perlmutter, "The Crisis of the PLO," *Encounter,* March 1988, pp. 19–34.

100. "Status Quotes," *The Jerusalem Post* ("In Jerusalem" supplement), May 9, 1997.

101. Arlene Kushner, *Disclosed: Inside the Palestinian Authority and the PLO* (Philadelphia: Pavilion Press, 2004), appendix C-1, for Arafat's speech, which was given in English.

102. Faisal al-Husseini's last interview, June 2001, ibid., appendix C-8111. Husseini insisted that "Palestine in its entirety is an Arab land, the land of the Arab nation . . . and it is impossible to remain silent when someone is stealing it." He also called the entire land from the river to the sea "an Islamic Waqf which cannot be bought or sold." In other words, he fused the *absolutist* positions of the PLO and the Hamas, in defining the long-term strategic goal of the Palestinians.

103. Efraim Karsh, "The Palestinians and the 'Right of Return,' " *Commentary,* May 2001, pp. 25–31; and Karsh, "Intifada II: The Long Trial of Arab Anti-Semitism," *Commentary,* December 2000, pp. 49–54. See also Avi Beker, *UNRWA, Terror and the Refugee Conundrum: Perpetuating the Misery* (Jerusalem: Institute of the World Jewish Congress, 2003).

104. Itamar Marcus, "Ask for Death!" *Palestinian Media Watch (PMW) Bulletin,* October 2002. James Fallows, "Who Shot Mohammed al-Dura?" *Atlantic Monthly,* June 2003, http://www.theatlantic.com/doc/200306/fallows; and Nidra Poller, "Myth, Fact, and the Al-Dura Affair," *Commentary,* September 2005, 23–30. See also Anne-Elisabeth Montet, "L'Affaire Enderlin," *The Weekly Standard* 13, no. 41, July 7, 2008; and Melanie Philips, "Faking a Killing," in http://standpointmag.co.uk/print/143, downloaded June 30, 2008.

105. Fouad Ajami, "Arafat's War," *The Wall Street Journal,* 31 March 2002.

106. Karsh, "Intifada II," p. 53.

107. Ibid.

108. Ibid., p. 49.

109. See, for example, the *Information Bulletin,* nos. 2, 4, and 5 (March, September, and October 2002) of the Center for Special Studies (CSS) in Herzliya, which covers anti-Semitic and anti-Israeli incitement in the Arab-Muslim world.

110. Palestinian satellite TV channel, February 8, 2002. See *Information Bulletin* (CSS), no. 2 (March 2002): p. 17.

111. Ismail al-Radouan, PA TV, August 17, 2001. "When the Shahid meets his Maker, all his sins are forgiven from the first gush of blood."

112. Itamar Marcus and Barbara Crook, "Pedagogy of Hate," *The Jerusalem Post,* January 4, 2004.

113. Itamar Marcus and Barbara Crook, "New Hate Song on PA TV," *PMW Bulletin,* April 1, 2005.

114. "PA Children's Play: The Jews Burned Palestinians in Ovens," *PMW Bulletin,* April 19, 2004.

115. *Al-Hayat Al-Jadeeda,* November 18, 2005.

116. Quoted by Itamar Marcus and Barbara Crook, "Jesus the Palestinian," *PMW Bulletin,* July 6, 2006.

117. *Jews, Israel, and Peace in Palestinian School Textbooks, 2000–2001 and 2001–2002* (New York: Center for Monitoring the Impact of Peace, November 2001), pp. 22–25.

118. Ibid., p. 17.

119. Ibid., p. 35.

120. Ibid., pp. 28–29, 34–42.

121. See Wistrich, *Muslim Anti-Semitism,* pp. 32–33.

122. Arnon Groiss, *Jews, Israel and Peace in the Palestinian Authority Textbooks* (New York: Center for Monitoring the Impact of Peace, 2003), and the subsequent reports issued in October 2004 and June 2005.

123. *Jews, Israel and Peace* (June 2005), pp. 3–5. See also Goetz Nordbuch, *Narrating Palestinian Nationalism: A Study of New Palestinian Textbooks* (Washington, D.C.: The Middle East Media Research Institute, 2002).

124. Wistrich, *Muslim Anti-Semitism,* p. 33. Quotes from *Al-Hayat Al-Jadeeda,* July 7, 1997; September 3, 1997; and November 30, 1997.

125. *Al Hayat Al-Jadeeda,* January 25, 2001, November 18, 2001.

126. Seif Ali Al-Jarwan, "Jewish Control of the World Media," *Al-Hayat Al-Jadeeda,* July 2, 1998.

127. See "Palestinian Leader: Number of Jewish Victims in the Holocaust Might Be 'Even Less Than a Million,' " *MEMRI Inquiry and Analysis,* no. 95 (May 30, 2002).

128. Ibid.

129. Ephraim Karsh, "Arafat Lives," *Commentary,* January 2005, pp. 33–40.

130. On the role of the Soviet Union, the KGB, and Romanian president Ceausescu in polishing Arafat's presentation and instructing the PLO in techniques of deception, see Ion Mihai Pacepa, "The KGB's Man," *The Wall Street Journal,* September 23, 2003. Pacepa was chief of Romanian intelligence before defecting to the West.

131. Barry Rubin, "Rules of the Game, Palestinian-Style," *The Jerusalem Post,* October 31, 2007.

132. Karsh, "Arafat Lives," pp. 39–40. See also "Arafat: 'No One in This World Has the Right to Concede the Refugees' Right to Return,' " *MEMRI Special Dispatch Series* (May 19, 2004). Arafat denounced the "racist" Israeli fence and the "cancer" of the settlements, emphasized the "sacred right of return" of the refugees to their original homes, and glorified Palestinian heroism, even as he offered an outstretched hand "to establish a peace of the brave in this land [Palestine]."

133. Itamar Marcus and Barbara Crook, "PA Libel: Israeli Deliberately Addicts PA Kids to Drugs," *PMW Bulletin,* November 15, 2005.

134. PA TV, February 6, 2004.

135. *PMW Bulletin,* December 21, 2004.

136. *Al-Hayat Al-Jadeeda,* September 19, 2005; PA TV, October 6, 2005; "PA Hate TV," *PMW Bulletin,* October 10, 2005.

137. *Al-Hayat Al-Jadeeda,* June 12, 2006.

138. *PMW Bulletin,* February 14, 2007.

139. "Be Gone. Die Anywhere You Like, but Don't Die Here," *PMW Bulletin,* December 29, 2005, which depicts all of Israel's coastal cities as Palestinian.

140. PA TV, January 1, 2006. The broadcast from Egypt celebrated the founding of the PLO with a speech by one of its leading officials, Barakat al-Fara; it was attended by some of President Mubarak's top advisers.

141. Itamar Marcus and Barbara Crook, "Jews Have No Historical Connection to Western Wall," *PMW Bulletin,* October 19, 2006.

142. *Al-Hayat Al-Jadeeda,* October 23, 2006.

143. Khaled Abu Toameh, "Aksa Brigades Endorse Iran's Call for Israel's End," *The Jerusalem Post,* September 7, 2005.

144. Raphael Israeli, "From Oslo to Bethlehem: Arafat's Islamic Message," *Journal of Church and State* 43 (Summer 2001): pp. 423–45.

145. Ibid., pp. 428–31. See also Shaul Mishal and Avraham Sela, *The Palestinian Hamas: Vision, Violence and Coexistence* (New York: Columbia University Press, 2000).

146. Quoted in *France Soir,* February 13, 1979.

147. Mishal and Sela, *Palestinian Hamas,* p. 32, point out that the leader of the Palestinian Islamic Jihad, Fathi Shiqaqi (later assassinated by Israel), pioneered the idea in the mid-1980s of mobilizing *all* Muslims (Sunni and Shia) to liberate Palestine through jihad.

Twenty-two: Hamas, Hezbollah, Holy War

1. See Shaul Mishal and Reuben Aharoni, *Speaking Stones: Communiqués from the Intifada Underground* (Syracuse, N.Y.: Syracuse University Press, 1994); Mishal and Sela, *Palestinian Hamas;* Ziad Abu 'Amr, "Hamas: A Historical and Political Background," *Journal of Palestine Studies* 22, no. 4 (Summer 1993): pp. 5–19; and Yonah Alexander, *Palestinian Religious Terrorism: Hamas and Islamic Jihad* (Ardsley, N.Y.: Transnational Publishers, 2002).

2. The Islamic Resistance Movement, *Between the Agony of the Present and the Hopes of the Future* (Gaza, 1988), in Arabic.

3. See Jean-François Legrain, *Les voix du soulèvement palestinien 1978–1988* (Cairo: CEDEJ, 1991), pp. 57–65; and Esther Webman, *Anti-Semitic Motifs in the Ideology of Hizballah and Hamas* (Tel Aviv: Tel Aviv University, 1994), pp. 17–45, who deals with these motifs in the Hamas leaflets between 1987 and 1992.

4. Translation by Mishal and Aharoni, *Speaking Stones,* p. 201.

5. Ibid., p. 202.

6. Ibid., p. 228.

7. Ibid., pp. 245–48.

8. Webman, *Anti-Semitic Motifs,* pp. 19–22.

9. Graham Usher, *Palestine in Crisis: The Struggle for Peace and Political Independence After Oslo* (London: Pluto Press, 1995), p. 31.

10. Anthony Shadid, *Legacy of the Prophet: Despots, Democrats and the New Politics of Islam* (Boulder, Colo.: Westview Press, 2002), p. 122.

11. For the Hamas Covenant, see "The Charter of Allah," *Israel Affairs* 2, no. 1 (Autumn 1995): pp. 273–92. The full text is also reproduced in Raphael Israeli, *Fundamentalist Islam and Israel: Essays in Interpretation* (Lanham, Md.: Jerusalem Center for Public Affairs, 1993), pp. 132–59.

12. Alexander Flores, "Islamic Themes in Palestinian Political Thought," in *Islam, Judaism, and the Political Role*, ed. John Bunzl (Gainsville: University Press of Florida, 2004), pp. 156–65.

13. Israeli, *Fundamentalist Islam*, pp. 128–31.

14. Ibid., p. 132.

15. Ibid., p. 133.

16. Ibid., p. 134.

17. Article 5, ibid., p. 135. In article 8, the slogan of Hamas is redefined and amplified as follows: "Allah is its goal, the Prophet its model, the Qur'an its constitution, *jihad* its path, and death for the cause of Allah its most sublime belief."

18. Martin Kramer, *The Salience of Islamic Fundamentalism* (London: Institute of Jewish Affairs Reports, no. 2, 1995), pp. 4–9.

19. Israeli, *Fundamentalist Islam*, p. 144.

20. Ibid., pp. 147–48.

21. Ibid., p. 148. The end of the Ottoman Empire in 1918 signaled the imminent demise of the caliphate—considered to be a major tragedy for Islam in the modern era, since it encouraged the separation of religion and state. For the Muslim Brotherhood, the act of destroying the caliphate was a Western-Zionist conspiracy.

22. On this subject, see Robert S. Wistrich, "L'antisémitisme Musulman: Un danger très actuel," *La Revue d'histoire de la Shoah*, no. 180 (January–June 2004): pp. 50–57; and Meir Litvak and Esther Webman, "Perceptions of the Holocaust in Palestinian Public Discourse," *Israel Studies* 8, no. 3 (Fall 2003): pp. 123–40.

23. Israeli, *Fundamentalist Islam*, p. 148.

24. Ibid., article 28, p. 152.

25. Ibid.

26. Ibid., p. 153.

27. Ibid., pp. 155–56. On the *Protocols* and anti-Semitism in the Islamist movements more generally, see Rivka Yadlin, *An Arrogant Oppressive Spirit: Anti-Zionism as Anti-Judaism* (Oxford, U.K.: Pergamon Press, 1989), pp. 79–101; Yossef Bodansky, *Islamic Anti-Semitism as a Political Instrument* (Petah Tikva, Israel: Ariel Center for Policy Research, 1999); Wistrich, "L'antisémitisme Musulman," pp. 16–61.

28. See Robert S. Wistrich, editorial, and "Converging Pathologies: From Anti-Zionism to Neo-Antisemitism," *Antisemitism International*, 2006, pp. 4–17. I prepared the interview with Abdel-Azziz al-Rantisi in Gaza (May 2003) shown in the BBC Channel 4 documentary *Blaming the Jews*, for which I acted as the historical adviser. The Hamas leader confirmed his belief in the *Protocols* in the same language used in the Covenant, fifteen years earlier.

29. Article 32 in the Hamas Covenant, in Israeli, *Fundamentalist Islam*, p. 155.

30. See Yossef Bodansky, "Les Juifs et L'Islam Militant après Khomeyni," *Revue d'Histoire de la Shoah*, no. 180 (January–June 2004): pp. 70–77; Israeli, *Fundamentalist Islam*, pp. 123–68; and Ziad Abu-Amr, *Islamic Fundamentalism in the West Bank and Gaza: Muslim Brotherhood and Islamic Jihad* (Bloomington: Indiana Univer-

sity Press, 1994), pp. 63–89. See also Beverley Milton-Edwards, *Islamic Politics in Palestine* (London: Tauris Academic Studies, 1996), pp. 185–93.

31. Milton-Edwards, *Islamic Politics,* p. 185.
32. Al-Quds Palestinian Arab Radio, November 23, 1988.
33. *Haaretz,* 5 August 1987. See also Yossef Bodansky, *Islamic Antisemitism,* p. 127. Sheikh Tamimi's 1980 booklet *Zawal Isra'il Hatmiyya Qur'anniya* (The Destruction of Israel: A Koranic Inevitability) was widely disseminated throughout the Arab world and especially in the occupied Palestinian territories.
34. Meir Hatina, *Islam and Salvation in Palestine* (Tel Aviv: Tel Aviv University, Dayan Center Papers, 2001), pp. 161–68, for its internal charter.
35. Ibid., pp. 166–67. See also Meir Litvak, "Iran's Proxy," *Australia-Israel Review,* January 2003, p. 15, for the Iranian influence on Hamas.
36. Hatina, *Islam and Salvation,* pp. 121–22.
37. A short version of the interview appeared in the film *The Longest Hatred* (Thames Television/PBS, 1991), a three-hour documentary that I conceived, wrote, and edited with Rex Bloomstein. The quotes come from the translated transcript of the interview. My thanks to Nucleus Productions in London for the right to reproduce some of this material.
38. Al-Bitawi interview, *The Longest Hatred,* transcript, pp. 11–13.
39. Ibid., pp. 15–16.
40. Ibid., pp. 18–21.
41. Ibid., pp. 27–30.
42. Milton-Edwards, *Islamic Politics in Palestine,* pp. 100ff.
43. Ibid., pp. 113ff.
44. Ibid., pp. 152–57. Between 1987 and 1993 alone, at least 942 Palestinian men and women were murdered as "collaborators"—many of them accused of "moral transgression" (drugs, prostitution, etc.) and some were killed for purely personal motives.
45. See David Bukay, *Facts and Fables in the Mythology of Islamic and Palestinian Terrorism* (Shaarei Tikva, Israel: Ariel Center for Policy Research, no. 162, 2006), pp. 20ff.
46. Ibid., pp. 35–39.
47. See Raphael Israeli, "Islam Militants on Trial," *International Problems* nos. 30, 1–2 (1991): pp. 26–36; Andrea Nuesse, "The Ideology of Hamas: Palestinian Islamic Fundamentalist Thought on the Jews, Israel and Islam," *Studies in Muslim-Jewish Relations* 1 (1993): pp. 97–125; and Isabel Kershner, "Pragmatism, Not Moderation," *The Jerusalem Report,* August 11, 2003, pp. 22–27.
48. See the pioneering study (which is still well worth reading) by Georges Vajda, "Juifs et Musulmans selon le hadith," *Journal Asiatique* 229 (1937): pp. 57–129.
49. Nuesse, "The Ideology of Hamas."
50. Anne Marie Oliver and Paul F. Steinberg, *The Road to Martyrs' Square: A Journey into the World of the Suicide Bomber* (Oxford, U.K.: Oxford University Press, 2005), pp. 19–36.
51. Ibid., pp. 32–49.
52. Ibid., p. 71.
53. "The Highest Ranking Palestinian Authority Cleric; In Praise of Martyrdom Operations," *MEMRI Special Dispatch Series,* no. 226 (June 11, 2001).
54. Oliver and Steinberg, *Road to Martyrs' Square,* p. 102.

55. *Falastin al-Muslima* (London), September 1996, pp. 54–55. See also Aluma Solnick, "Based on Koranic Verses, Interpretations and Traditions, Muslim Clerics State: the Jews Are the Descendants of Apes, Pigs, and Other Animals," *MEMRI Special Report,* no. 11 (November 1, 2002).

56. Oliver and Steinberg, *Road to Martyrs' Square,* pp. 108–10.

57. Ibid., p. 109. In a 1990 book on "the inattentiveness of the Muslims" and "the errors of the falsifiers," Sheikh Jarrar predicted the final extinction of the State of Israel in 2022. See also Graham Usher, "The Islamist Movement and the Palestinian Authority," *Middle East Report* 189 (July–August 1994): pp. 28–29.

58. *The New York Times,* March 26, 2000. Sabri's argument that Jews were hated everywhere is certainly misleading; more important, it is a favorite rationalization of anti-Semities throughout the ages.

59. "Hitler's *Mein Kampf* in East Jerusalem and PA Territories," *MEMRI Special Dispatch Series,* no. 48 (October 1, 1999). See also Agence France-Presse, September 8, 1999.

60. Milton-Edwards, *Islamic Politics in Palestine,* pp. 166ff. See also Meir Litvak, "The Islamization of Palestinian Identity: The Case of Hamas," Tel Aviv University, Moshe Dayan Center for Middle East Studies, http://www.dayan.org/d&a-hamas-litvak.htm.

61. *Maariv,* June 23, 2002; and *USA Today,* June 26, 2001.

62. Examples listed in Matthew Levitt, "Hamas from Cradle to Grave," *The Middle East Quarterly,* Winter 2004, pp. 3–15. In the course of working on the BBC Channel 4 documentary *Blaming the Jews* (first screened in late June 2003), I obtained access to significant material from Gaza schools and educational institutions.

63. *Haaretz,* October 24, 2003.

64. Dan Schueftan, "Voice of Palestine: The New Ideology of Israeli Arabs," *Azure,* no. 14 (Winter 2003): pp. 73–104. Bishara fled Israel in 2007 after investigations against him on possible charges of treason were publicized. On the wider issues, see Raphael Israeli, *Arabs in Israel: Friends or Foes?* (Jerusalem: The Ariel Center for Policy Research, 2008).

65. Ibid., p. 78.

66. Ibid., p. 84.

67. Ilene R. Prusher, "Israeli Arabs' Rising Voice of Opposition," *The Christian Science Monitor,* October 26, 2006.

68. "Salah Speech Provokes Jerusalem Clashes," *The Jerusalem Post,* February 16, 2007.

69. Y. Alexander, *Palestinian Religious Terrorism,* pp. 76–98.

70. Ibid., pp. 107–8.

71. Ibid., pp. 115–21.

72. Ibid., pp. 155–59.

73. Ibid., pp. 243–44. Statement against the spiritual leader of Shas, Ovadia Yossef.

74. Ibid., pp. 385–86.

75. Shaul Mishal and Avraham Sela, *The Palestinian Hamas: Vision, Violence, and Coexistence* (New York: Columbia University Press, 2000), pp. 43–52.

76. Ibid., p. 52.

77. Ibid.

78. See Martin Kramer, "Hamas: 'Global' Islamism," in *Iran, Hizbullah, Hamas and the Global Jihad,* ed. Dan Diker (Jerusalem: Jerusalem Center for Public Affairs, 2007), pp. 61–68.

79. Jonathan D. Halevi, "The Palestinian Hamas Government: Between Al-Qaeda Jihadism and Tactical Pragmatism," in Diker, *Iran, Hizbullah, Hamas,* pp. 69–81.

80. Ibid., pp. 72–75.

81. Dan Ephron, "Staking Its Claim," *Newsweek,* February 17, 2003.

82. Yael Yehoshua, "On the Conflict Between the Palestinian Authority and Hamas Over the Armed Struggle Against Israel," *MEMRI Inquiry and Analysis Series,* no. 143 (July 18, 2003), somewhat overstates the ideological disagreements.

83. Itamar Marcus and Barbara Crook, "Find the Differences: PA and Hamas Ideology Converge," *The Jerusalem Post,* March 28, 2004.

84. Hamas leader Mahmud Zahar interview by Heiko Flottau, "Wir beanspruchen ganz Palästina," *Süddeutsche Zeitung,* July 18, 2002.

85. Steven Stalinsky, "Palestinian Authority Sermons 2000–2003," *MEMRI Special Report,* no. 24 (December 26, 2003).

86. "Last Week's Friday Sermon on PA Television," *MEMRI Special Dispatch Series,* no. 683 (March 19, 2004). See also "This Week's Palestinian Authority Sermon," *MEMRI Special Dispatch Series,* no. 908 (May 17, 2005).

87. "Hamas Leader Saw All Jews as His Targets," *The Daily Telegraph,* April 19, 2004, p. 11. In an interview in Gaza City in May 2003, I heard al-Rantisi defend something very close to this proposition.

88. "65% of Palestinians Support Al-Qaeda Attacks in the US and Europe," *PMW Bulletin,* December 26, 2005.

89. "Hamas Ahoy!" *The Economist,* January 21, 2006, p. 52; "The Israeli Dilemma Over Hamas," ibid., January 28, 2006, p. 59; "Enter Hamas," ibid., p. 12; "To Whom Will Hamas Listen?" ibid., February 4, 2006, p. 53.

90. Caroline B. Glick, "The Anatomy of Hamas's Victory," *The Jerusalem Post,* January 27, 2006.

91. "Hamas Video: We Will Drink the Blood of the Jews," *PMW Bulletin,* February 14, 2006.

92. "Children of Palestinian Suicide Bomber Rim Al-Riyashi on Hamas TV," *MEMRI Special Dispatch Series,* no. 1503 (March 15, 2007). Also *PMW Bulletin,* March 6, 2006; and "Hamas Mouse: Blame the Jews," ibid., May 13, 2007.

93. "Hamas: Une souris nommée Farfour et autre Pepsi," taken from Hamas, Al-Aqsa TV, June 27, 2007. See Naccache, *Contre Israël,* pp. 206–7.

94. Y. Carmon and C. Jacob, "Alongside Its Islamist Ideology, Hamas Presents Pragmatic Positions," *MEMRI Inquiry and Analysis,* no. 322 (February 6, 2007). The use of the word "pragmatic" in this context seems questionable to me.

95. "Israel Is Making a Big Mistake If It Thinks Hamas Will Ever Change," *The Jerusalem Post,* May 26, 2006.

96. See video, February 26, 2006, http://switch3.castup.net/cunet/gm.asp?ClipMedia _ID=123232&ak=null.

97. See video from the "Al-Qassam Brigades Media Office," June 22, 2006, http://www .palestine-info.net/. See also Itamar Marcus and Barbara Crook, "Hamas: Islam Will Conquer US and Britain," *PMW Bulletin,* June 22, 2006.

98. See Mamoun Faudy, "What Will Happen If the Muslim Brotherhood Takes Control of Palestine?" *Asharq Al-Awsat* (London), January 22, 2007.

99. "The Extermination of the Jews Is Good for the Inhabitants of the World," *PMW Bulletin,* May 3, 2007.

100. Itamar Marcus and Barbara Crook, "Hamas TV: Gaza Evacuation by Israel Leads to Destruction of Israel," *PMW Bulletin*, March 14, 2007.

101. "The Palestinians: June Amazed Them," *The Economist*, June 23, 2007, pp. 26–28; and "Martyrs or Traitors?" ibid., p. 13.

102. Itamar Marcus and Barbara Crook, "Singing to Israel's Destruction," *PMW Bulletin*, October 29, 2007.

103. Yaakov Katz, "Future Tense," *The Jerusalem Post*, January 4, 2008.

104. Shalom Harari, "Iran Is Building 'Hamastan' in Gaza," *Jerusalem Issue Brief* 6, no. 23 (March 11, 2007).

105. "Un Medio Oriente senza ebrei: è L'obiettivo di Hamas," Guilio Meotti intervista Robert Wistrich," *Il Foglio*, January 13, 2009.

106. "Suleiman's Wisdom," *The Jerusalem Post*, March 20, 2009 (editorial).

107. Quoted in Ze'ev Maghen, "Eradicating the 'Little Satan': Why Iran Should Be Taken at Its Word," *Commentary*, January 2009, pp. 11–17.

108. Steven Erlanger, "In Gaza, Hamas's Insults to Jews Complicate Peace," *The New York Times*, April 1, 2008.

109. Shadid, *Legacy of the Prophet*, pp. 133–42, 273–79; Hala Jaber, *Hezbollah: Born With a Vengeance* (New York: Columbia Univeristy Press, 1997); Nizar Hamzeh, "Lebanon's Hizballah: From Islamic Revolution to Parliamentary Accommodation," *Third World Quarterly* 14, no. 2 (1993): pp. 321–27; Martin Kramer, "Hizballah: The Calculus of Jihad," *Bulletin: The American Academy of Arts and Sciences* 47, no. 8 (May 1994): pp. 20–43; and Kramer, "The Oracle of Hizballah: Sayyid Muhammad Husayn Fadlallah," in *Spokesmen for the Despised: Fundamentalist Leaders in the Middle East*, ed. R. Scott Appleby (Chicago: University of Chicago Press, 1997), pp. 83–181.

110. Kramer, "Oracle of Hizballah," p. 83. See also Yehudit Barsky, *Hizballah: A Mega-Terrorist Organization* (New York: AJC, April 2005).

111. "An Open Letter: The Hizballah Program," Beirut, February 16, 1985, in *The Jerusalem Quarterly*, no. 48 (Fall 1988), in abridged form.

112. Interview on June 2, 2000, on Egyptian TV, quoted by Eyal Zisser, "The Return of Hizbullah," *Middle East Quarterly*, Fall 2002. See also Jeffrey Goldberg, "In the Party of God," Part 1, *The New Yorker*, October 14, 2002, http://www.jeffreygoldberg.net/articles/tny/a_reporter_at_large_in_the_par.php; and Aluma Solnick, "Based on Koranic Verses, Interpretations, and Traditions, Muslim Clerics State: The Jews Are the Descendants of Apes, Pigs, and Other Animals," *MEMRI Special Report*, no. 11 (November 1, 2002).

113. "Nasrallah's Nonsense," *The New York Sun*, March 11, 2005.

114. "An Open Letter."

115. "Hizbullah Leader Hassan Nasrallah: 'The American Administration Is Our Enemy . . . Death to America,'" *MEMRI TV Monitor Project*, no. 867 (February 22, 2005).

116. Martin Kramer, "Redeeming Jerusalem: The Pan-Islamic Premise of Hizballah," in *The Iranian Revolution and the Muslim World*, ed. David Menashri (Boulder, Colo.: Westview Press, 1990), pp. 105–30.

117. Webman, *Anti-Semitic Motifs*, pp. 1–16.

118. Martin Kramer, *Hizballah's Vision of the West* (Washington, D.C.: The Washington Institute for Near East Policy, policy paper no. 16, 1989).

119. *Al-'Ahd,* August 30, 1987, and December 20, 1991; quoted by Webman, *Anti-Semitic Motifs,* pp. 8–9.

120. Ibid.

121. See the interview with Fadlallah by Mahmoud Soueid, *Journal of Palestine Studies* 25, no. 1 (Autumn 1995): pp. 61–75; and the quotes from Webman, *Anti-Semitic Motifs,* pp. 9–13.

122. *Al-'Ahd,* December 6, 1991; quoted in Webman, *Anti-Semitic Motifs,* p. 10.

123. *Middle East Insight,* March–April 1988, p. 10.

124. Kramer, "Oracle of Hizballah," p. 116.

125. Bodansky, *Islamic Anti-Semitism,* pp. 134–35.

126. Ibid., p. 143.

127. Webman, "Die Rhetorik der Hisbollah," pp. 39–55.

128. *Agence France-Presse,* March 22, 1998.

129. Webman, "Die Rhetorik der Hisbollah," p. 54.

130. "Hizballah Leader Meets with a U.S. Presbyterian Delegation," *MEMRI TV Monitor Project,* no. 294 (October 17, 2004).

131. Barsky, *Hizballah,* "Hizbullah Leader Nasrallah: Great French Philosopher Garaudy Proved Holocaust a Myth," pp. 9–10.

132. *MEMRI Special Dispatch Series,* no. 1088 (February 7, 2006).

133. *Al-Manar,* May 7, 1998; April 9, 2000; September 28, 2001; November 29, 2002.

134. Amal Saad-Ghorayeb, *Hizbu'llah: Politics and Religion* (London: Pluto Press, 2002), pp. 134–67.

135. See Meir Litvak, "The Islamization of the Palestinian-Israeli Conflict: The Case of Hamas," *Middle East Studies* 34, no. 1 (January 1998): pp. 148–63.

136. Saad-Ghorayeb, *Hizbu'llah,* pp. 140–41.

137. Ibid., pp. 142–44.

138. "Nasrallah: We'll Never Recognize Israel," *The Jerusalem Post,* March 14, 2009. Also Mirella Hodeib, "Nasrallah 'Strongly Endorses' Arab Reconciliation Efforts," *The Daily Star* (Beirut), March 14, 2009.

139. Saad-Ghorayeb, *Hizbu'llah,* pp. 172–73. The author at several points makes the argument that Hezbollah's diatribes against Jews, Judaism, and Israel are directed against a "religious community," not a racial group, and therefore cannot be anti-Semitic. But the evidence he brings undermines his own case. In the end, he himself concedes: "Thus, the anti-Judaism of Hizbu'llah is as vituperative against Jews, if not more than, conventional Judaism" (p. 173).

140. Bernard Lewis, "The Arab World Discovers Anti-Semitism," in *Anti-Semitism in Times of Crisis,* ed. Sander L. Gilman and Steven Katz (New York: New York University Press, 1991), pp. 343–52; Emmanuel Sivan, "Islamic Fundamentalism, Anti-Semitism and Anti-Zionism," in Wistrich, *Anti-Zionism and Anti-Semitism in the Contemporary World,* pp. 74–84.

141. Lewis, "Arab World," p. 347, assumes that traditional Islam of the Koranic type was fundamentally more tolerant of Jews and Judaism than modern Arab and Islamic anti-Semitism. This may be true, but it still underestimates the intense hostility manifested in the Koran and its implications.

142. Quoted by Saad-Ghorayeb, *Hizbu'llah,* pp. 176ff., who notes the recurrent theme in the Koran of Jewish disbelief—the characteristic rejection of God's signs and revelations as conveyed by his chosen prophets and messengers.

143. Ibid., p. 177.

144. Ibid., pp. 180–81.

145. Ibid., p. 182.

146. Avi Jovisch, *Beacon of Hatred: Inside Hizballah's Al-Manar Television* (Washington, D.C.: The Washington Institute for Near East Policy, 2004), pp. 62–90.

147. Hassan Nasrallah on Al-Manar TV, May 23, 2002.

148. Jovisch, *Beacon of Hatred*, p. 73.

149. Ibid., pp. 38–39, 75–76.

150. Ibid., pp. 64–65.

151. Jovisch, *Beacon of Hatred*, p. 65, quotes Nasrallah's remarks as originally reported in the Beirut *Daily Star*, October 23, 2002. See also *The New York Times*, May 23, 2004.

152. See "Hassan Nasrallah," *Wikiquote*, http://en.wikiquote.org/wiki/Hassan_Nasralah, for a sampling of such statements.

153. Gal Luft, "Hizballahland," *Commentary*, July–August 2003, pp. 56–60.

154. Robin Wright, "Inside the Mind of Hezbollah," *The Washington Post*, July 16, 2006.

155. "Arab Media Accuses Iran and Syria of Direct Involvement in Lebanon War," *MEMRI Special Dispatch Series*, no. 1249 (August 15, 2006). Quotes from article by Muhammad 'Ali Ibrahim, the chief editor of the daily *Al-Gumhuriya*, July 27, 2006. Also H. Avraham, "Lebanon Faces Political Crisis in Aftermath of War," *MEMRI* 299 (November 3, 2006).

156. "Sheikh Nasrallah Boasts on Al-Manar TV," *MEMRI TV Monitor Project*, no. 1224 (August 1, 2006). Many Israeli Arab leaders spoke or demonstrated in support of Hezbollah, in spite of the deaths of a number of Arab civilians in northern Israel killed by the terrorist organization's missiles. See *PMW Bulletin*, August 10, 2006.

157. "Nasrallah Wins the War," *The Economist*, August 19, 2006, p. 9. The leader quoted Nasrallah as saying that victory for him would consist merely of surviving. On the last day of the war, Hezbollah fired a record 246 rockets into Israel.

158. Michael Slackman, "And Now, Islamism Trumps Arabism," *The New York Times Weekly Review*, August 20, 2006.

159. Ehud Ya'ari, "The Muqawama Doctrine," *Australia-Israel Review*, November 2006, pp. 19–20. In Arabic the literal meaning of *muqawama* is "resistance" but the connotation is more of constant combat.

160. *The Economist*, August 19, 2006, p. 9.

161. Ron Schleifer, "Psychological Operations: A New Variation on an Age Old Art: Hezbollah Versus Israel," *Studies in Conflict and Terrorism* 29 (2006): pp. 1–19.

162. Robert S. Wistrich, "editorial," *Antisemitism International*, 2006, pp. 4–5.

Twenty-three: Toward the Muslim Apocalypse

1. Quoted in Albert Speer, *Spandau: The Secret Diaries* (New York: Macmillan, 1976), p. 80.

2. Wistrich, "New Islamic Fascism," pp. 32–34. On the anti-Americanism, see Fouad Ajami, "The Sentry's Solitude," *Foreign Affairs* 80, no. 6 (November–December 2001): pp. 2–16.

3. For the jihadist aspect, see Andrew G. Bostom, "The Global Jihad," *FrontPage Magazine*, April 21, 2006, http://www.frontpagemagazine.com/. On bin Ladenism, see

the essay by Ehud Ya'ari, "Bin Ladenism: The Cult of Death," *The Jerusalem Report,* September 23, 2002, pp. 14–15.

4. See Herf, "What Is Old and What Is New." See also Yehuda Mirsky, "From Fascism to Jihadism," *The New Republic,* April 9, 2002, http://www.tnr.com/.

5. Wistrich, *Hitler's Apocalypse,* pp. 154–93. See also Matthias Küntzel, "National Socialism and Anti-Semitism in the Arab World," *Jewish Political Studies Review* 17, nos. 1–2 (Spring 2005).

6. Robert S. Wistrich, "The Jihadist Challenge," *Midstream,* November–December 2004, pp. 8–9.

7. For the anti-Semitism and anti-Western ideology of Muhammad Atta, one of the masterminds of 9/11, see "Attas Armee," *Der Spiegel* 36 (2002): pp. 117–18.

8. Bernard Lewis, *Semites and Antisemites* (New York: W. W. Norton and Company, 1986), p. 286. See also Lewis, "The Arab World Discovers Anti-Semitism," *Commentary,* May 1986, pp. 30–34.

9. Wistrich, *Antisemitism: The Longest Hatred* (London: Methuen, 1992), pp. 252–53. See also Andrew Sullivan, "Protocols," *The New Republic,* November 5, 2001, p. 46.

10. See Pierre André Taguieff, "L'inquiétant retour du 'complot juif mondial,' " *L'Arche,* January–February 2004, pp. 38–51.

11. See the articles by Menahem Milson, "What Is Arab Antisemitism?" and Zvi Mazel, "Hatred and Antisemitism in the Egyptian Press," *Antisemitism International,* 2003, pp. 23–40.

12. See Rivka Yadlin, "*Rider Without a Horse* on Egyptian TV: The Protocols as *Vox Populi,*" *Antisemitism International,* 2004, pp. 53–59; Daniel J. Wakin, "Anti-Semitic TV epic airs at Ramadan," *The Observer,* October 27, 2002; and George Ziyyad, "History of a Horseman," *The Jerusalem Report,* December 16, 2002.

13. Norman Stillman, "Antisemitism in the Contemporary Arab World," in Curtis, *Antisemitism in the Contemporary World,* pp. 70–71.

14. See *Anti-Semitism/Anti-Israel Incitement in the Arab and Muslim Media* (New York: ADL, 2002–6). Available on the ADL website, http://www.adl.org/.

15. See *Arab Media Review: Anti-Semitism and Other Trends,* July–December 2006; and Raphael Israeli, *Islamikaze: Manifestations of Islamic Martyrology* (London: Frank Cass, 2003), pp. 281–344.

16. *Yediot Ahronoth,* October 5, 2001.

17. See the important new anthology edited by Andrew G. Bostom, *The Legacy of Islamic Antisemitism* (New York: Prometheus Books, 2007), with texts that illustrate the anti-Jewish motifs in early Islam among jurists, theologians, and scholars.

18. Ye'or, *Dhimmi; Jews and Christians Under Islam* (London/Toronto: Associated University Presses, 1985). Also Ye'or, *When Civilizations Collide* (London: Associated University Presses, 2002).

19. Stillman, *Jews of Arab Lands,* pp. 233–46, for the translation of Maimonides' text. The quote is on p. 241.

20. Ye'or, *Dhimmi,* pp. 43–77.

21. See the booklet by Bat Ye'or, *Oriental Jewry and the Dhimmi Image in Contemporary Nationalism* (Geneva, 1979), p. 3; and Andrew G. Bostom, ed., *The Legacy of Jihad: Islamic Holy War and the Fate of Non-Muslims* (New York: Prometheus Books, 2005), pp. 24–124.

22. Jacob Barnai, " 'Blood Libels' in the Ottoman Empire of the Fifteenth to the Nineteenth Centuries," in Shmuel Almog, *Antisemitism Through the Ages,* pp. 289ff.; Jacob Landau, "Ritual Murder Accusations and Persecutions of Jews in Nineteenth Century Egypt," *Sefunot* 5 (1961): pp. 417–60, in Hebrew. On the ritual murder case of 1840 in Damascus, see Stillman, *Jews in Arab Lands,* pp. 393–402; and the comprehensive analysis in Jonathan Frankel, *The Damascus Affair* (Cambridge: Cambridge University Press, 1997).

23. Bat Ye'or, *Juifs et Chrétiens sous l'Islam: Les dhimmis face au défi intégriste* (Paris: Berg International, 1994), pp. 263ff., demonstrates the self-hatred and boomerang effects of Arab Christian Judeophobia and anti-Zionism in sapping the position of Christian *dhimmis* in the Middle East.

24. Mark R. Cohen, *Under Crescent and Cross: The Jews in the Middle Ages* (Princeton, N.J.: Princeton University Press, 1994). See also Wistrich, *Antisemitism: The Longest Hatred,* pp. 202–3.

25. Haggai Ben-Shammai, "Jew-hatred in the Islamic Tradition and the Koranic Exegesis," in Almog, *Antisemitism Through the Ages,* pp. 161–69. See also Muhammad Sayyid Tantawi, *Banu Isra'il fi al-Quran wa al-Sunna* [The Children of Israel in the Qur'an and Sunna], 3rd ed. (Cairo, 1986–87).

26. Ben-Shammai, "Jew-hatred in the Islamic Tradition," pp. 164–66; and Jane Gerber, "Anti-Semitism and the Muslim World," in *History and Hate: The Dimensions of Anti-Semitism,* ed. David Berger (Philadelphia: JPS, 1986), pp. 78–79.

27. G. Vajda, "Juifs et musulmans selon le hadith," *Journal Historique* 229 (1937): pp. 57–129.

28. Ronald L. Nettler, "Islamic Archetypes of the Jews: Then and Now," in Wistrich, *Anti-Zionism and Anti-Semitism in the Contemporary World,* pp. 78–83.

29. Ronald L. Nettler, *Past Trials and Present Tribulations: A Muslim Fundamentalist's View of the Jews* (Oxford, U.K.: Pergamon Press, 1987), pp. 19–58. Qutb's essay was reprinted in 1970 by the Saudi Arabian government. See also Emmanuel Sivan, *Radical Islam: Medieval Theology and Modern Politics* (New Haven, Conn.: Yale University Press, 1985); and Paul Berman, *Terror and Liberalism* (London: W. W. Norton, 2003), pp. 60–102.

30. Berman, *Terror and Liberalism,* pp. 86–87.

31. Nettler, *Past Trials,* p. 55.

32. Ibid.

33. See Ronald L. Nettler, "Les Frères Musulmans, L'Égypte et Israël," *Politique Internationale,* no. 17 (Fall 1982): pp. 133–43.

34. Taguieff, *Les Protocoles des Sages de Sion,* vol. 1: pp. 284–314.

35. For some exceptions, see the essays by Bassam Tibi, Yigal Carmon, and Eldad Beck in Klaus Faber et al., *Neu-alter Judenhass,* pp. 179–210, 233–38. See also Raphael Israeli, *The Terrorist Masquerade* (Shaarei Tikva, Israel: Ariel Center for Policy Research, no. 132, 2001), pp. 15–20.

36. See *Holocaust Denial in the Middle East: The Latest Anti-Israel Propaganda Theme* (New York: ADL, 2001), for documentation of this escalating phenomenon.

37. See General Mustafa Tlass, *L'Azyme de Sion* (Damascus: Dar Tlass, 1990), the first French edition; and *La Repubblica* (Rome), August 21, 1986.

38. Tlass, *L'Azyme de Sion,* pp. 32–33.

39. See the 1983 introduction to the book by Tlass reproduced in *Le Matin,* August 19, 1983, p. 10.

40. David Littman, "Syria's Blood Libel at the UN: 1991–2000," *Midstream,* February–March 2001, pp. 208.

41. Tlass, *L'Azyme de Sion,* p. 32.

42. "Anti-Semitism in the Syrian Media," *MEMRI Special Dispatch Series,* no. 66 (December 22, 1999).

43. See "The Damascus Blood Libel," *MEMRI Imaging and Analysis,* no. 99 (June 27, 2002).

44. "Fears of Normalization with Israel in the Syrian Media," *MEMRI Special Dispatch Series,* no. 67 (January 6, 2000).

45. *Anti-Semitism in the Syrian Media* (New York: ADL, 1999).

46. See "Syrian Gov't Daily Suggests Israel Created, Spread Avian Flu Virus," *MEMRI Special Dispatch Series,* no. 1094 (February 16, 2006).

47. "Syrian Deputy Minister of Religious Endowment Muhammad 'Abd al-Sattar Calls for Jihad," *MEMRI Special Dispatch Series,* no. 1217 (July 29, 2006).

48. "Al-Shatat: The Syrian-Produced Ramadan 2003 TV Special," *MEMRI Special Dispatch Series,* no. 627 (December 12, 2003). See also "Syrian Produced Hizbullah TV Ramadan Series," ibid., no. 610 (November 18, 2003).

49. *Syria Times* (Damascus), November 11, 2003.

50. Itamar Radai, *From Father to Son: Attitudes to Jews and Israel in Asad's Syria* (Jerusalem: The Vidal Sassoon International Center for the Study of Antisemitism, ACTA no. 29, 2007), p. 2.

51. In an interview with French TV channel *France 2,* Asad repeated his accusations. *Le Monde,* June 23, 2001.

52. *Asharq Al-Awsat* (London), August 10, 2003. Radai, *From Father to Son,* p. 12.

53. Robert S. Wistrich, "The Old-New Antisemitism," *The National Interest,* Summer 2003, pp. 59–70.

54. Quoted in "Cette guerre se poursuivra, de plus en plus violente, jusqu'à ce que nous ayons vaincu les juifs," *L'Arche,* October–November 2001, p. 66. See also Robert S. Wistrich, "L'Antisémitisme Musulman: Un Danger très actuel," in *Révue d'histoire de la Shoah,* no. 180 (January–June 2004), p. 47.

55. *Tehran Times,* October 25, 2001; Islamic Republic News Agency, October 24, 2001.

56. *Al Thawra,* September 19, 2001.

57. Omayma Abdel-Lalif, in *Al-Ahram Weekly Online,* September 27–October 3, 2001.

58. "Terror in America (4): Arab Columnists: The Perpetrators of the Attacks Are Not Arabs or Muslims," *MEMRI Special Dispatch Series,* no. 270 (September 20, 2001).

59. Ibid. Article by Hayat al-Hweiek 'Atiya and Rakan Al-Majali, who added that Jews more than anyone "are capable of hiding a criminal act they perpetrate, and they can be certain that no one will ask them about what they do."

60. "Terror in America (18): Al-Azhar University Representative in the U.S. and Imam of New York's Islamic Center: The American Attack Against Afghanistan Is Terrorism," *MEMRI Special Dispatch Series,* no. 288 (October 19, 2001).

61. Hamid Gul, interview by Rod Nordland, *Newsweek,* September 14, 2001.

62. "Zionists Could Be Behind Attack on WTC and Pentagon," October 14, 2001, on website http://www.islamweb.net/english. The "facts" behind the article come

from Pakistan though the site is registered to the State of Qatar Ministry of Endowments and Religious Affairs.

63. *The Washington Post,* October 13, 2001. The website http://www.Paknews.com/ commissioned the opinion poll.

64. Hassan Tahsin, on Arab News.Com (Saudi English language daily), November 5, 2001.

65. *Iran Daily,* October 29, 2001. See also Islamic Republic News Agency, October 25, 2001.

66. See Wistrich, "Old-New Antisemitism," pp. 62–67; and Kanan Makiya, *Republic of Fear* (Berkeley: University of California Press, 1989).

67. Wistrich, "Old-New Antisemitism," p. 67.

68. Amatzia Baram, "Modern Iraq, the Ba'th Party and Anti-Semitism," in *Arab-Jewish Relations: From Conflict to Resolution,* ed. Elie Podeh and Asher Kaufman (Brighton, U.K.: Sussex Academic Press, 2005), pp. 132–58.

69. David Brooks, "Saddam's Brain," *The Weekly Standard,* November 11, 2002.

70. Dr. Nimrod Raphaeli, "The New Iraqi Press and the Jews," *MEMRI Inquiry and Analysis,* no. 146 (June 28, 2003).

71. "Les Irakiens voient des Juifs partout," *L'Arche,* January–February 2004, pp. 66–67.

72. "Iraqis Protest Saturdays Off as a 'Zionist Holiday,' " *The Jerusalem Post,* February 27, 2005.

73. Dore Gold, *Hatred's Kingdom: How Saudi Arabia Supports the New Global Terrorism* (Washington, D.C.: Regnery Publishing, 2003), pp. 11–15, 41–52, 105–56.

74. Emran Qureshi, "The Saudi Brand of Fanaticism," *Los Angeles Times Book Review,* November 17, 2002. See also Malise Ruthven, *A Fury for God: The Islamist Attack on America* (London: Granta Books, 2002).

75. For some of the complexities, see John K. Cooley, *Unholy Wars: Afghanistan, America and International Terrorism* (London: Pluto Press, 2001).

76. Stephen Schwartz, *Two Faces of Islam: Saudi Fundamentalism and Its Role in Terrorism* (New York: Anchor Books, 2003), pp. 106, 132–35.

77. Ibid., p. 115.

78. Vincent Sheehan, *Faisal: The King and His Kingdom* (Tavistock, England: University Press of Arabia, 1975), pp. 95, 137–39.

79. See Dr. Arnon Groiss, *The West, Christians and Jews in Saudi Arabian Schoolbooks* (New York: Center for Monitoring the Impact of Peace, January 2003), pp. 85–109; and Amy C. Sims, "Saudi Broadcasts Promote Anti-Semitism, Martyrdom," FoxNews.com, June 15, 2002, http://www.foxnews.com/.

80. For the poll conducted by phone from a country neighboring Saudi Arabia, see *The Jerusalem Post,* December 27, 2007. It was carried out by S3 Systems of Vienna, Virginia, and KA Europe SPRL for Terror Free Tomorrow. See also *Demonizing Jews: Antisemitism in the Saudi Media (September 2001–September 2002)* (New York: ADL, 2002), p. 4, for the quote from Al-Jazeera.

81. Umayma Ahmad al-Jalahma, "The Jewish Holiday of Purim," *Al-Riyadh* (Saudi government daily), March 10 and 12, 2002.

82. *Al-Riyadh,* March 2, 2002.

83. "Saudis 'Apologise' for Blood Libel," *The Jewish Chronicle,* March 23, 2002.

84. Saudi Sheikh Abd-al Rahman al-Sudayyis at the Al-Haraam mosque (the most

important in Mecca), quoted by Aluma Solnick, "Muslim Clerics State: The Jews Are the Descendants of Apes, Pigs, and Other Animals," *MEMRI Special Report*, no. 11 (November 1, 2002).

85. See Yigal Carmon, "Contemporary Islamist Ideology Permitting Genocidal Murder," *MEMRI Special Report*, no. 25 (January 27, 2004).

86. Sermon of February 16, 2003, on the first day of the feast of the Sacrifice ('Id al-Adhha), on the al-Nidaa website, http://www.cambuur.net/coci. See Carmon, "Contemporary Islamist Ideology Permitting Genocidal Murder," for many more examples of the Day of Judgment motif.

87. See "Renowned King Fahd University Professor Active in the U.S.," *MEMRI Special Dispatch Series*, no. 1135 (April 5, 2006). See also the lecture by Saudi cleric Nasser bin Suleiman Al-'Omar, "America Is Now Disappearing from the Hearts," ibid., no. 1154 (May 4, 2006).

88. "Saudi Princess Fahda bint Saud ibn Abd al-Aziz [daughter of King Saud]: Conspiracy Theories and Other Writings," *MEMRI Special Dispatch Series*, no. 653 (February 2, 2004).

89. "Saudi Minister of Interior, Prince Nayef ibn Abd al-Aziz: Who Committed the Events of September 11," ibid., no. 446 (December 3, 2002).

90. "Saudi Crown Prince on Yunbu' Attack," ibid., no. 706 (May 3, 2004). These remarks were aired on Saudi TV.

91. "Saudi Intellectual Awadh al-Qarni: Neo-Cons Are the Closest Thing There Is to Nazism," *MEMRI TV Monitor Project*, no. 1103 (March 13, 2006).

92. Martin Kramer, *The Salience of Islamic Fundamentalism* (London: Institute of Jewish Affairs, 1995).

93. Joël Kotek, *Major Anti-Semitic Motifs in Arab Cartoons* (Jerusalem: Jerusalem Center for Public Affairs, 2005). See also Arie Stav, *Peace: The Arabian Caricature: A Study of Anti-Semitic Imagery* (New York: Geffen, 1999), pp. 77–90, 142–267, for a remarkable collection of caricatures, many of them from Egypt.

94. Zvi Mazel, "Hatred and Antisemitism in the Egyptian Press," *Antisemitism International*, 2003, pp. 32–40.

95. Rivka Yadlin, *An Arrogant, Oppressive Spirit: Anti-Zionism as Anti-Judaism in Egypt* (Oxford, U.K.: Pergamon Press, 1989), p. 105.

96. Gilles Kepel, *Muslim Extremism in Egypt: The Prophet and Pharaoh* (Berkeley and Los Angeles: University of California Press, 1993), pp. 23, 110–22.

97. Ronald L. Nettler, "Islam vs. Israel," *Commentary*, December 1984, pp. 26–30.

98. Ibid., p. 28. See also Claire Brière and Olivier Carré, *Islam: Guerre à L'Occident* (Paris: Autrement, 1983), pp. 117–22.

99. Mahmoud al-Said al-Kurdi, in *Al-Akhbar*, March 25, 2001.

100. *Al-Musawwar*, August 4, 1972, p. 3.

101. "The Mufti of Egypt: The True Face of the Blood-Sucking Hebrew Entity Has Been Exposed," *MEMRI Special Dispatch Series*, no. 1255 (August 18, 2006).

102. On this affair, see *MEMRI Special Dispatch*, No. 671, March 2, 2004: http://memri .org/bin/articles.cgi?Page=archives&Area=sd&ID=SP67104.

103. Jan Goldberg, "A Lesson from Egypt on the Origins of Modern Anti-Semitism in the Middle East," *Kirchliche Zeitgeschichte* 16, no. 1 (2003): pp. 127–48. See also George Ziyyad, "Mubarak Adviser Signals Rethink on Egyptian Anti-Semitism,"

The Jerusalem Report, January 27, 2003, p. 9. See also "Egypt's Response to Accusations of Arab Media Antisemitism," *MEMRI Special Dispatch Series,* no. 454 (January 3, 2003), for the English text.

104. As historical adviser to the British Channel 4 film *Blaming the Jews* (June 2003) on Muslim anti-Semitism, I reviewed the protocol of the long interview we did with el-Baz on this subject.

105. "Sheikh Yousef al-Qaradhawi on Al-Jazeera," *MEMRI Special Dispatch Series,* no. 858 (February 4, 2005).

106. Safwat Higa made the remarks on Egyptian TV this spring. The quotes from him and Salama Abd al-Qawi, in "Stranger than Fiction," *Australia-Israel Review* (April 2009), p. 11.

107. "Egyptian Researcher al-Buheiri Discusses *Protocols of the Elders of Zion,*" *MEMRI Special Dispatch Series,* no. 1485 (March 2, 2007).

108. "Sudan's President Claims His Country Is Target of Israeli-Led Conspiracy," *The Jerusalem Post,* November 29, 2006.

109. "Interview on Saudi Government TV with Prominent Egyptian Professor," *MEMRI Special Dispatch Series,* no. 954 (August 10, 2005).

110. Abd al-Wahhab 'Adas, "The Secret Israeli Weapon," *Al-Gumhuriya* (Egypt), March 18, 2004.

111. "Egyptian Government Weekly Magazine on 'The Jews Slaughtering Non-Jews, Draining Their Blood, and Using It for Talmudic Religious Rituals," *MEMRI Special Dispatch Series,* no. 763 (August 17, 2004). Isma'il, a wealthy lawyer and businessman, was a Muslim Brotherhood candidate in the national elections and head of the Committee of the Egyptian Lawyers' Union for Implementation of the Shari'a.

112. "Chairman of the Arab Psychiatrists Association Offers Diagnoses: Bush Is Stupid; Perpetrating a Suicide/Martyrdom Attack Is Life's Most Beautiful Moment; We'll Throw Israel Into the Sea," *MEMRI Special Dispatch Series,* no. 373 (April 30, 2002).

113. "Columnist & Former Editor of London Daily *Al-Hayat:* Israeli Leaders' Crimes Are Like Nazis'," *MEMRI Special Dispatch Series,* no. 1200 (July 7, 2006); "Columnist (and Former Editor) of *Al-Hayat:* Israel's Leaders Are the Grandsons of Nazi Killers Who Assumed Jewish Identities and Fled to Israel," ibid., no. 1219 (July 28, 2006).

114. Moshe Yegar, "Malaysia: Anti-Semitism Without Jews," *Jewish Political Studies Review,* nos. 3–4 (Autumn 2006): pp. 81–98.

115. David Rhode, "Radical Islam Gains a Seductive New Voice," *The New York Times Weekly Review,* October 26, 2003; Michael Danby, "The Mahathir Paradox," *The Jerusalem Post,* October 31, 2003; Patrick McDowell, "Mahathir Reiterates Claim That Jews Rule World," ibid., October 22, 2003; Caroline B. Glick, "Malaysian Road Map," ibid., October 24, 2003; "Fury at Mahathir Speech," *The Jewish Chronicle,* October 24, 2003.

116. See also David E. Sanger, "Malaysian Leader's Talk Attacking Jews Draws Ire from Bush," *The New York Times,* October 21, 2003; "Empörung über Mahathir Rede," *Frankfurter Allgemeine Zeitung,* October 18, 2003; Itay Katz, "Malaysia's PM Is Unrepentant: 'Jews Run the World,'" *Haaretz,* October 22, 2003.

117. Ibid. "Speech by Prime Minister Mahathir Mohamad of Malaysia to the Tenth Islamic Summit Conference Putrajaya, Malaysia," October 16, 2003, in http://www.adl.org/Anti_Semitism/malaysian.asp.

118. Rohan Sullivan, "Malaysian PM: Muslims Must Defeat Jews," *The Jerusalem Post,* October 17, 2003. The Egyptian foreign minister described Mahathir's speech as a "very deep assessment of the situation"; the Afghan president called it "a great example of eloquence."

119. See Solnick, "Muslim Clerics State."

120. Fouad Ajami, *The Arab Predicament: Arab Political Thought and Practice Since 1967* (Cambridge: Cambridge University Press, 1984), pp. 50–75.

121. D. F. Green, ed., *Arab Theologians on Jews and Israel: Extracts of the Proceedings of the Fourth Conference of the Academy of Islamic Research,* 3rd ed. (Geneva: Editions de l'Avenir, 1976), p. 9.

122. "The Jews Are the Enemies of Human Life," ibid., pp. 19–24, Kamal Ahmad Own.

123. Ibid.

124. Abdul Halim Mahmoud, *Al Jihad wa al-Nasr* [Holy War and Victory] (Cairo: 1974), pp. 148–50.

125. See Wistrich, *Muslim Antisemitism.* See also "Islamic Judeophobia: An Existential Threat," *Nativ* 15, nos. 4–5 (September 2002): pp. 49–53; and ibid. 15, no. 6 (November 2002): pp. 79–85, in Hebrew.

126. See Esther Webman, "Anti-Zionism, Anti-Semitism and Criticism of Israel—The Arab Perspective," *Tel Aviver Jahrbuch für Deutsche Geschichte* 33 (2005): pp. 306–29; Raphael Israeli, "The New Muslim Anti-Semitism: Exploring Novel Avenues of Hatred," *Jewish Political Studies Review* 17, nos. 3–4 (Fall 2005): pp. 98–108. See also Gudrun Krämer, "Antisemitism in the Muslim World: A Critical Review," *Die Welt des Islams* 46, no. 3 (2006): pp. 243–76; Michael Kiefer, "Islamischer, Islamistischer oder Islamisierter Antisemitismus?" ibid., pp. 277–306; and Alexander Flores, "Judeophobia in Context: Antisemitism Among Modern Palestinians," ibid., pp. 307–30.

127. See Ibn Warraq, "The Genesis of a Myth: Islam and Minorities," in *The Myth of Islamic Tolerance: How Islamic Law Treats Non-Muslims,* ed. Robert Spencer (New York: Prometheus Books, 2005), pp. 13–26.

128. Sayyid Qutb, *In the Shade of the Qur'an* (Leicester, U.K.: Islamic Foundation, 2003), vol. 8: p. 115. The same foundation also published the Indian fundamentalist Sayyid Abdul Ala Maududi. See his *Toward Understanding the Qur'an,* vol. 3 (Leicester, U.K.: Islamic Foundation, 1990), which also called on Muslims to fight against Jews, Christians, and others in order to put an end to the sovereignty of the "unbelievers."

129. Bat Ye'or, "A Racism That Denies the History and Sufferings of Its Victims," in Spencer, *Myth of Islamic Tolerance,* pp. 275–82.

130. Green, *Arab Theologians on Jews and Israel,* pp. 8–9.

131. Lutfi abd-al-'Azim, "Arabs and Jews: Who Will Annihilate Whom?" *Al-Ahram Al-Iqtisadi,* September 27, 1982. Quoted in Raphael Israeli, *Arab and Islamic Anti-Semitism* (Shaarei Tikva, Israel: Ariel Center for Policy Research, no. 104, March 2000), pp. 14–15.

132. Ibid.

133. Ibid.

134. See Emmanuel Sivan, *Islamic Fundamentalism and Antisemitism* (Jerusalem: Hebrew University of Jerusalem, SICSA, 1985); and Nissim Rejwan, "Arab Conspiracy Theories," *Midstream,* February–March 1994, pp. 40ff.

135. See Robert Spencer, *Onward Muslim Soldiers: How Jihad Still Threatens America and the West* (Washington, D.C.: Regnery Publishers, 2003).

136. See Mohammed Y. Kassab, "Une vaste conspiration judéo-chrétienne," in *L'Islam face au nouvel ordre mondial* (Algiers: Editions Salama, 1991), pp. 75–93.

137. Robert S. Wistrich, "Old-New Antisemitism," pp. 63ff.

138. See Nonie Darwish, *Now They Call Me Infidel* (New York: Sentinel, 2006); also the Al-Jazeera TV interview of February 21, 2006, with Arab-American psychologist Wafa Sultan, http://www.iht.com/culture.

139. See Irshad Manji, *The Trouble with Islam* (Toronto: Random House, 2003), pp. 103–23.

140. Wafa Sultan interview, February 21, 2006.

141. Nonie Darwish, "We Were Brought Up to Hate—and We Do," *Sunday Telegraph*, February 12, 2006; John M. Broder, "A Voice Against Muslim 'Hostages' to Terror," *IHT*, March 15, 2006.

142. See Bassam Tibi, "Jihad," in *Protest, Power, and Change: An Encyclopaedia of Nonviolent Action,* ed. Roger Powers and William B. Vogele (New York: Garland Publishers 1997), pp. 277–81.

143. Husain, *Islamist*, pp. 83–110, 119–20.

144. Robert S. Wistrich, "A Choice for the Muslim World," *The Jerusalem Post*, May 4, 2003.

145. Robert S. Wistrich, "The Old-New Antisemitism," *The National Interest*, Summer 2003, pp. 68–69.

146. See Bernard Lewis, *The Crisis of Islam: Holy War and Unholy Terror* (London: Weidenfeld and Nicolson, 2003), pp. 87–127.

147. Kiefer, "Islamischer Islamistischer," pp. 277–306.

148. Alex Alexiev, "The Pakistani Time Bomb" *Commentary*, March 2003, pp. 46–52. See also Bernard-Henry Lévy, *Qui a tué Daniel Pearl?* (Paris: Bernard Grasset, 2003); and Lévy, interview by Robert S. Wistrich, *Antisemitism International*, 2003.

149. "Obama and Turkey" (editorial), *IHT*, April 6, 2009.

150. Herb Keinon, "Israel: Erdogan's words 'unacceptable,' " *The Jerusalem Post*, January 5, 2009.

151. "Turkey: The Longer View" (editorial), *The Jerusalem Post*, February 2, 2009.

152. Guillaume Perrier, "En Turquie, la communauté juive craint une poussée d'antisémitsme," *Le Monde*, February 3, 2009.

153. Abe Selig, "Turkish Immigrants Bemoan 'Climate of Fear,' " *The Jerusalem Post*, February 2, 2009.

154. "Antisemitism in the Turkish Media: Part I," *MEMRI Special Dispatch Series*, no. 90 (April 28, 2005).

155. Ayse Hür, "Mein Kampf and the Protocols of Zion," *Radikal*, March 13, 2005. *Radikal* is a liberal daily. The author pointed out that *Mein Kampf* was being marketed by eleven publishers and sales had been greatly stimulated by recent events and the rise in anti-Semitism.

156. Arslan Tekin, "Yes, *Mein Kampf* Should Be Taught in Schools," *Yenicağ*, March 15, 2005; and "Can a Hitler Rise in America?" by the same author, *ibid.*, March 25, 2005. *Yenicağ* is a Turkish daily newspaper that synthesizes radical Islam and ultranationalism.

157. Abdurrahim Karakoç, "Hitler Was a Man of Foresight," *Vakit*, August 17, 2004. Ex-

cerpts can be found in http://www.memri.org/bin/opener_latest.cgi?ID=SD90005 (accessed on May 1, 2005).

158. Hüseyin Üzmez in *Vakit*, February 28, 2005, excerpted in *MEMRI Special Dispatch Series*, no. 900 (April 28, 2005). *Vakit* is a Turkish Islamic daily. It was banned in Germany in February 2005 for anti-Semitism and Holocaust denial.

159. Israfil Kumbasar, "Globalization Projects and Nationalists," *Yeniçağ*, March 4, 2005. This article summarized a lecture by Mehmet Gül, former MP from the Nationalist Movement Party, addressing a pan-Turkic ultranationalist gathering.

160. *MEMRI Special Dispatch Series*, no. 900, ibid.

161. Ibid. See, for example, the article by columnist Serdar Kuru in the Turkish nationalist daily *Ortadoğu* on February 19, 2005. This anti-Semitic polemic was directed against a piece on anti-Americanism in Turkey by Robert Pollock in *The Wall Street Journal*, February 16, 2005.

162. *MEMRI Special Dispatch Series*, no. 900. Murat Necip Arman, "Our Times Are Similar to 1930s in Germany," *Radikal*, January 23, 2005.

163. Günter Jikeli, "The Kreuzberg Initiative Against Antisemitism Among Youth from Muslim and Non-Muslim Backgrounds in Berlin," in *Antisemitism: The Generic Hatred*, ed. Michael Feinberg, Shimon Samuels, and Mark Weitzman (London: Vallentine Mitchell, 2007), pp. 198–211.

164. Anti-Semitism and the Turkish Islamist Milli Görus Movement," *MEMRI Special Dispatch Series*, no. 1699 (August 29, 2007).

165. Daniel Pipes, "Erdogan Bares His Fangs," January 5, 2009, http://www.danielpipes .org/blog/2009/01/erdogan-bares-his-fangs.html. Also Soner Cagaptay, "Is Turkey Still a Western Ally?" *The Wall Street Journal*, January 22, 2009.

166. O. Winter, "Recent Attempts to Form a Strategic Regional Bloc: Syria, Turkey and Iran," *MEMRI Inquiry and Analysis*, no. 490, January 6, 2009.

167. Roger Cohen, "Turkey Wants U.S. Balance," *The New York Times*, April 6, 2009. See also Massrine Azimi, "Similar Pasts, Different Paths," *International Herald Tribune*, April 8, 2009.

168. Quoted in Daniel Benjamin and Steven Simon, *The Age of Sacred Terror* (New York: Random House, 2002), pp. 91–93, 148–50, 157–60. See also David Cook, *Studies in Muslim Apocalyptic* (Princeton, N.J.: The Darwin Press, 2002); and Abdullah Yusuf Ali, *The Holy Qur'an: Text, Translation and Community* (New York: Tahrike Tarsile Qur'an, Inc., 1987).

169. David Cook, *Contemporary Muslim Apocalyptic Literature* (Syracuse, N.Y.: Syracuse University Press, 2005), p. 225.

170. D. Cook, ibid.

TWENTY-FOUR: THE WRATH OF KHOMEINI

1. Daniel Tsadik, *Between Foreigners and Shi'is: Nineteenth-Century Iran and Its Jewish Minority* (Stanford, Calif.: Stanford University Press, 2007). See, in addition, David Littman, "Jews Under Muslim Rule: The Case of Persia," *The Wiener Library Bulletin* 32, n.s. nos. 49–50 (1979): pp. 2–15; and the *Alliance Israélite Universelle (AIU) Bulletin*, 1873, pp. 96–101.

2. Tsadik, *Between Foreigners and Shi'is*, pp. 90–95. See also Nasir al-Din Shah, *The*

Diaries of H. H. the Shah of Persia, trans. J. Redhouse (Costa Mesa, Calif.: Mazda, 1995).

3. On Shiite legal attitudes toward Jews, see Tsadik, *Between Foreigners and Shi'is.* pp. 15–32.

4. Ibid., pp. 125–77.

5. IRAQ 1.C.3, AIU Archives, Paris. For the twenty-two conditions imposed on the Hamadan Jews, see Littman, "Jews Under Muslim Rule," pp. 7–8. See also *AIU Bulletin,* September 1892; and Tsadik, *Between Foreigners and Shi'is,* pp. 159–69.

6. Littman, "Jews Under Muslim Rule," p. 7.

7. Ibid., p. 8. See also a letter from 1897 on incitement to massacre by the ulema against the Jews of Hamadan, Shiraz, and other regions of Persia.

8. Tsadik, *Between Foreigners and Shi'is,* pp. 157–58.

9. See Walter J. Fischel, "The Jews in Medieval Iran from the Sixteenth to the Eighteenth Centuries: Political, Economic, and Communal Aspects," in *Irano-Judaica: Studies Relating to Jewish Contacts with Persian Culture,* ed. Shaul Shaked (Jerusalem: Ben-Zvi Institute for the Study of Jewish Communities in the East, 1982), pp. 265–91; Fischel, "The Jews of Persia, 1795–1940," *Jewish Social Studies* 12, no. 2 (April 1950): pp. 119–60; and Fischel, "Secret Jews of Persia: A Century-Old Marrano Community," *Commentary,* January 1949, pp. 28–33. See also Bernard Lewis, *The Jews of Islam* (Princeton, N.J.: Princeton University Press, 1984); and Daniel Tsadik, "Religious Disputations of Imami Shi'is Against Judaism in the Late Eighteenth and Nineteenth Centuries," *Studia Iranica* 34 (2005): pp. 95–134.

10. E. Spicehandler, "The Persecution of the Jews of Isfahan under Shah Abbas II (1642–1666)," *International Conference on Jewish Communities in Muslim Lands* (Jerusalem: Ben-Zvi Institute, 1974), p. 11.

11. Walter J. Fischel, "Isfahan: The Story of a Jewish Community in Persia," *The Joshua Starr Memorial Volume* (New York: Jewish Social Studies, no. 5, 1953), pp. 122–24.

12. Sorour Soroudi, "Jews in Islamic Iran," *The Jewish Quarterly,* Fall 1981, pp. 98–114. See also Soroudi's important article "The Concept of Jewish Impurity and Its Reflection in Persian and Judeo-Persian Traditions," in *Irano-Judaica III,* ed. Shaul Shaked and Amnon Netzer (Jerusalem: Ben-Zvi Institute, 1994), pp. 142–70.

13. Matthias Küntzel, *Unholy Hatreds: Holocaust Denial and Antisemitism in Iran* (Jerusalem: The Vidal Sassoon International Center for the Study of Antisemitism, Posen Papers in Contemporary Antisemitism, no. 8, 2007), p. 7.

14. Ibid. See also David Menashri, "The Jews of Iran," in Gilman and Katz, *Antisemitism in Times of Crisis,* pp. 334–45. For an autobiographical account see Iraj Isaac Rahmin, "Unclean in Tehran, Adrift in San Diego: A Memoir," *Commentary* (March 2009), pp. 39–45.

15. Fischel, "Isfahan," pp. 123–24.

16. See Reverend Joseph Wolff, *Researches and Missionary Labours (1831–34)* (London: James Nisbet and Co., 1835), pp. 125–33; and *Narrative of a Mission to Bokhara (1843–45)* (Edinburgh, 1857), pp. 271–74. See also H. Nissimi, *The Crypto-Jewish Mashhadis* (Brighton, U.K.: Sussex Academic Press, 2007).

17. Littman, "Jews Under Muslim Rule," p. 4.

18. Ibid., p. 9. Letter of May 24, 1894, from J. Danon on the Jews of Shiraz, IRAQ, I.C.2, AIU Archives, Paris.

19. Letters of June 10, 1897, and June 17, 1897, from J. Danon, IRAQ I.C.2., AIU Archives, Paris; Littman, "Jews Under Muslim Rule," p. 10.

20. Tsadik, *Between Foreigners and Shi'is*, pp. 178–92, emphasizes the paramount importance of Shiite Islam in determining the identity, affiliation, and status of Jews and other religious minorities in Iran.

21. Letter of October 31, 1910, from M. Nataf, *AIU Bulletin*, no. 35 (1910): pp. 182–88.

22. Soroudi, "Concept of Jewish Impurity," pp. 147–48; Lewis, *Jews of Islam*, op. cit., p. 85.

23. Laurence D. Loeb, *Outcaste: Jewish Life in Southern Iran* (New York: Gordon and Breach Publishers, 1977), p. 21. Loeb was a professor of anthropology who lived among the Jewish communities of southern Iran in the early 1970s.

24. Fischel, "Jews of Persia," p. 121.

25. Henry A. Stern, *Dawnings of Light in the East* (London: Charles H. Purday, 1854), pp. 184–85. Stern was a Christian missionary to the Jews who had converted from Judaism.

26. D. Tsadik, "The Legal Status of Religious Minorities: Imami, Shi'i Law and Iran's Constitutional Revolution," *Islamic Law and Society* 10 (2003), pp. 377–408.

27. Amnon Netzer, "Antisemitism in Iran, 1925–1950," *Pe'amim* 29 (1986): pp. 5–31, in Hebrew. See also S. Djalal Madani, *Iranische Politik und Drittes Reich* (Frankfurt: P. Lang, 1986).

28. Eliz Sanasarian, *Religious Minorities in Iran* (Cambridge: Cambridge University Press, 2000), p. 46.

29. Samuel Segev, *The Iranian Triangle: The Untold Story of Israel's Role in the Iran-Contra Affair* (New York: Free Press, 1988), pp. 47–48. See also R. K. Ramazani, *Revolutionary Iran: Challenge and Response in the Middle East* (Baltimore: Johns Hopkins University Press, 1986), pp. 147–51.

30. Shireen T. Hunter, *Iran and the World: Continuity in a Revolutionary Decade* (Bloomington: Indiana University Press, 1990), pp. 31, 100–104, 127.

31. Michael Zand, "The Image of the Jew in Iran After the Second World War (1945–1979)," *Pe'amim* 29 (1986): pp. 103–39, in Hebrew.

32. German Consulate in Tehran to Foreign Office in Berlin, February 2, 1941, in *Halbmond und Hakenkeruz: Das Dritte Reich, die Araber und Palästina*, by Klaus-Michael Mallmann and Martin Cüppers (Darmstadt, Germany: Wissenschaftliche Buchgesellschaft, 2006), p. 42. The consulate suggested the expediency of drawing parallels between Muhammad's struggle against the Jews in seventh-century Arabia "and that of the Führer today." See also Sanasarian, *Religious Minorities*, pp. 46–47.

33. Sivan, "Islamic Fundamentalism, Anti-Semitism and Anti-Zionism," in Robert S. Wistrich (ed.), *Anti-Zionism and Antisemitism in the Contemporary World* (London: Macmillan, Institute of Jewish Affairs, 1990), p. 77.

34. Ruholla Khomeini, *The Imam Versus Zionism* (Tehran: Ministry of Islamic Guidance, 1983). See also Mohammed Schams and Wahied Walidat-Hagh, "Der khomeinistische Antisemitismus," in Faber, *Neu-alter Judenhass*, pp. 211–17.

35. Khomeini, *Imam Versus Zionism*, pp. 19–20.

36. "Response to a Group of Palestinian Muslims in 1968," ibid., pp. 22–23; and his 1970 lecture on the imperial regime, ibid., pp. 23–24.

37. Ibid., pp. 27–30. Khomeini angrily pointed to Zionist involvement in Iran's commercial, industrial, and agricultural affairs.

38. "Message to Muslim Students, Residing in Europe, America, and Canada (1973)," ibid., pp. 29–30.

39. "Reply to Arafat, (1977)," ibid., pp. 31–32.

40. Quoted in Wilhelm Dietl, *Holy War* (New York: Macmillan, 1984), p. 264. See also Ruhollah Khomeini, *Islam and Revolution: Writings and Declarations of Imam Khomeini,* trans. Hamid Algar (Berkeley: Mizan Press, 1981), pp. 127, 276.

41. Ervand Abrahamian, *Khomeinism: Essays on the Islamic Republic* (Berkeley and Los Angeles: University of California Press, 1993), pp. 120–25.

42. Ibid., pp. 124–25. See also *Iran Times,* December 7, 1990.

43. See Walter Fischel, "The Bahai Movement and Persian Jewry," *The Jewish Review* 7 (1934): pp. 47–55. Baha'u'llah developed the new faith of Bahaism out of the Babi movement, founded in 1844 by 'Ali Muhammad Shirazi, who later claimed to be the Shiite Hidden Imam and abrogated the Muslim sharia.

44. Lewis, *Crisis of Islam,* pp. 15, 64–66.

45. Emmanuel Sivan, "Sunni Radicalism in the Middle East and the Iranian Revolution," *International Journal of Middle Eastern Studies* 21, no. 1 (Feb. 1989): pp. 1–30. See also the article by Gregory Rose in *Religion and Politics in Iran: Shi'ism from Quetism to Revolution,* ed. Nikki R. Keddie (New Haven, Conn.: Yale University Press, 1983), p. 182.

46. Milton Viorst, *In the Shadow of the Prophet: The Struggle for the Soul of Islam* (Boulder, Colo.: Westview Press, 2001), pp. 174–203.

47. Farhang Rajaee, *Islamic Values and World View: Khomeyni on Man, the State and International Politics* (Lanham, Md.: University Press of America, 1983), vol. 13: p. 26. See also Nikki R. Keddie, *Roots of Revolution: An Interpretive History of Modern Iran* (New Haven, Conn.: Yale University Press, 1981).

48. Ibid., p. 71. See also Ramazani, *Revolutionary Iran,* pp. 30, 53, 65.

49. Tehran home service, May 17, 1985; December 4, 1985; August 16, 1986.

50. Tehran home service, February 11, 1981.

51. Ervand Abrahamian, *Khomeinism: Essays on the Islamic Republic* (London: I. B. Tauris, 1993), pp. 23–38. See also Eric Hooglund, *Twenty Years of Islamic Revolution* (Syracuse, N.Y.: Syracuse University Press, 2002), pp. 4–31.

52. Mohammed Mohaddessin, *Islamic Fundamentalism: The New Global Threat,* 2nd ed. (Washington, D.C.: Seven Locks Press, 2001), pp. 17–38, 159–66. This book deals extensively (from the inside) with the People's Mojahedin, active opponents of the mullahs for the past forty years.

53. Quoting Tehran radio, June 25, 1989, ibid., pp. 28–29.

54. Ibid., p. 36.

55. Ibid., pp. 46–47, 52.

56. See Wistrich, *Antisemitism: The Longest Hatred.* See also Henner Fürtig, "Die Bedeutung der iranischen Revolution von 1979 als Ausgangspunkt für eine antijüdisch orientierte Islamisierung," *Jahrbuch für Antisemitismusforschung* 12 (Berlin, 2003), pp. 73–98.

57. Khomeini, *Islam and Revolution,* p. 127.

58. Ibid., p. 210.

59. W. J. Weatherby, *Salman Rushdie: Sentenced to Death* (New York: Carroll and Graf, 1990), p. 15.

60. Raymond N. Habiby and Fariborz Ghavidel, "Khumayni's Islamic Republic," *Mid-*

dle East Review 11, no. 4 (Summer 1979): pp. 12–20. For his 1977 statement against the shah in which the latter's support for Israel is specially highlighted, see ibid., p. 17. See also the interview with Khomeini in *Le Monde,* May 6, 1978.

61. Mohaddessin, *Islamic Fundamentalism,* p. 125.

62. *Kayhan* (Tehran), October 20, 1991. Hashemi Rafsanjani, Speech to Conference Supporting Palestine's Islamic Revolution in Tehran, October 20, 1991, quoted in Mohaddessin, *Islamic Fundamentalism,* p. 126.

63. Ibid.

64. Ibid., p. 127.

65. *Kayhan* (Tehran), October 21, 1991.

66. Meir Litvak, "Iran and Israel: The Ideological Animosity and Its Roots," *Iyunim bitkumat Israel* 14 (2004): pp. 367–92, in Hebrew. See also Litvak, "The Islamic Republic of Iran and the Holocaust: Anti-Semitism and Anti-Zionism," *The Journal of Israeli History* 25, no. 1 (March 2006): pp. 267–84; and the symposium *Iran bederech le-ptsatsa* (Ramat Gan, Israel: Bar-Ilan University, no. 21, 2006), in Hebrew.

67. See Ramazani, *Revolutionary Iran,* pp. 147–61.

68. Ibid., p. 155. See also David Menashri, *Iran After Khomeini: Revolutionary Ideology Versus National Interests* (Tel Aviv: University of Tel Aviv, 1999), pp. 94–115, in Hebrew, for the internal nuances within the regime during the 1990s.

69. Ramazani, *Revolutionary Iran,* p. 155.

70. Arnon Gross and Nethanel Toobian, *The War Curriculum in Iranian Schoolbooks* (New York: AJC and the Center for Monitoring the Impact of Peace, May 2007), pp. 2–3. The textbooks and the education system glorify the thirty-six thousand schoolboy martyrs (used as cannon fodder by the regime) during the Iran-Iraq War.

71. Ibid., pp. 33–79. The great emphasis on Western colonialism in Iranian textbooks contrasts strikingly with the relative silence about Russian annexations of vast areas of Muslim settlement in Central Asia or its atrocities in Chechnya.

72. Ibid., pp. 79–87.

73. Ibid., pp. 88–116.

74. Ibid.

75. See Yonatan Silverman, "The Threat from Iran," *Nativ* 20, no. 6 (November 2007): pp. 26–31, in Hebrew.

76. Gross and Toobian, *War Curriculum,* p. 113.

77. For the text of the June 3, 1963, speech delivered at the Fayziya Madrassa in Qom, see Khomeini, *Islam and Revolution,* pp. 177–78. See also Michael Curtis, "Khomeini's Thoughts on Jews and Israel," *Middle East Review* 11, no. 3 (Spring 1979): pp. 57–58.

78. Khomeini, *The Imam Versus Zionism,* pp. 9–13.

79. Message of June 9, 1979, ibid., p. 39.

80. Ibid., pp. 41–42. Khomeini constantly referred to Israel in virtually all his speeches after 1979 as a "germ of corruption," an enemy of Islam, and an American base that had to be destroyed.

81. Ibid., p. 43.

82. Ibid., pp. 43–44. These remarks were made after Saddam Hussein's invasion of Iran. Khomeini regarded both Saddam and Egyptian president Sadat as prime examples of Muslim traitors leading their nations to ruin.

83. "The Imam's Message on the World Day of Quds," August 1, 1981, ibid., pp. 44–50.

84. "Message to the Hajj Pilgrims," September 7, 1981, pp. 50–52.

85. "Meeting with the Ulema of Tehran," June 28, 1982, pp. 58–61.

86. UN Doc. A/38/PV.13, p. 41.

87. UN Doc. A/38/PV.102, p. 47.

88. UN Doc. A/40/PV.107.

89. UN Doc. A/SPC/40/PV.21, pp. 12–13 (1985). On Iranian efforts to expel Israel from the UN in the early 1980s, see Bernard Nossiter, "Iran Challenges Israel's Right to Seat at U.N.," *The New York Times*, October 26, 1982.

90. UN Doc. A/41/7440, November 26, 1986.

91. "The Protocols of the Meetings of the 'Learned Elders of Zion,' " *Imam*, special issue, February 1984, pp. 14–15.

92. Ibid., p. 14.

93. *Imam*, March 1984.

94. "The Protocols," *Imam*, April 1984, pp. 14–15. See also Wistrich, *Hitler's Apocalypse*, pp. 179–82.

95. BBC *Summary of World Broadcasts* (*SWB*), BBC:/2964 MED/12–13 (39), July 7, 1997. On Mezbah-Yazdi (who is Ahmadinejad's spiritual mentor and an outspoken leader of the conservative religious establishment in Qom), see Kasra Naji, *Ahmadinejad: The Secret History of Iran's Radical Leader* (Berkeley and Los Angeles: University of California Press, 2008), pp. 98–102.

96. BBC, *SWB*, BBC: M/2964 MED/14 (40), July 7, 1997.

97. Fürtig, "Die Bedeutung," pp. 80–82; and Schams and Wahdat-Hagh, "Der khomeinistische Antisemitismus," pp. 211–17.

98. Schams and Wahdat-Hagh, "Der khomeinistische Antisemitismus," pp. 215–17.

99. Arne Behrensen et al., eds., *Antisemitism "Made in Iran": The International Dimensions of Al Quds Day* (Berlin: AJC, 2006), gives examples of its impact in Berlin, London, Turkey, Lebanon, and the United States.

100. Udo Walter, "The Ideology of Hate: Islamic Unity Through Enmity Toward Israel?" in ibid., pp. 8–9.

101. Ibid. See also Richard Herzlinger, "Moderate Anti-Semite," August 6, 2–4, http://www.zeit.de/.

102. "Fundis aller Länder, vereinigt euch!" *Jungle World*, May 29, 1998.

103. Walter, "Ideology of Hate," p. 9.

104. Ibid. On Rafsanjani's attitude to Israel, see Runen A. Cohen, "Iran, Israel, and Zionism Since the Islamic Revolution—From Rational Relationship to Threat and Disaster," in *Iran, Israel and the "Shi'ite Crescent"* (Netanya, Israel: S. Daniel Abraham Center for Strategic Dialogue, November 2008), n. E, pp. 49–50.

105. Quoted by Wistrich, *Muslim Anti-Semitism*, p. 41.

106. See Behrensen et al., *Antisemitism "Made in Iran."*

107. Walter, "Ideology of Hate," pp. 8–9.

108. Mira Dietz, "Al Quds Day in Lebanon: From Struggle for Jerusalem to a Symbol of the 'Party of God,' " in Behrensen et al., *Antisemitism "Made in Iran"*; and pp. 20–22; speech by Hassan Nasrallah on Al-Quds Day, 2005, *Al-Safir* (Beirut), October 29, 2005. See also Martin Kramer, "Redeeming Jerusalem: The Pan-Islamic Premise of Hizballah," in Menashri, *Iranian Revolution and the Muslim World*, pp. 105–30.

109. *"Zionisten woll'n die Welt / kaufen mit geklautem Geld."* See Claudia Dantschke and Udo Walter, "Al Quds Day Demonstrations in Berlin," in Behrensen et al., *Anti-semitism "Made in Iran,"* pp. 24–26.

110. Mark Gardner, "Al Quds Day in London," in Behrensen et al., *Antisemitism "Made in Iran,"* pp. 26–28. See also Yossef Bodansky, *Islamic Antisemitism as a Political In-strument* (Shaarei Tikva, Israel: Ariel Center for Policy Research, 1999), pp. 118–38.

111. According to journalist Kambiz Behbahani, *Iranischer Dialogkreis* (Berlin), December 14, 2005 (published the following day in the news and community portal http://www.iran-now.de, quoted in Behrensen et al., *Antisemitism "Made in Iran,"* pp. 17–18. Behbahani also mentioned the fact that a number of Iranian-born Jews have been prominent in Israeli politics, including former president Moshe Katsav and former defense minister Shaul Mofaz.

112. "Iran Jews Express Holocaust Shock," BBC News, February 11, 2006, http://news .bbc.co.uk/2/hi/middleeast/4705246.stm.

113. Sanasarian, *Religious Minorities in Iran,* pp. 27–29, 110–14.

114. *The New York Times,* May 10, 1979, and May 13, 1979. See also Sanasarian, *Religious Minorities in Iran,* pp. 112–13; and David Menashri, *Iran: A Decade of War and Revolution* (New York: Holmes and Meier, 1990), p. 238.

115. Sanasarian, *Religious Minorities in Iran,* pp. 84–91. See also Ronen A. Cohen, "Iran, Israel, and Zionism," pp. 30–48.

116. Sansarian, *Religious Minorities in Iran,* p. 29.

117. Ibid.

118. Ibid., p. 111.

119. Reza Afshari, *Human Rights in Iran: The Abuse of Cultural Relativism* (Philadel-phia: University of Pennsylvania Press, 2001), p. 136.

120. Ibid., pp. 135, 137, 284. The case was first revealed to the outside world in July 1999 when an exiled Iranian Jewish leader, living in the United States and fearing that his coreligionists would be immediately executed, gave an exclusive interview to the BBC.

121. Pooya Dayanim, "Imagine Being a Jew in Iran," *The Iranian,* March 12, 2003.

122. Larry Derfner, "See No Evil, Hear No Evil," *The Jerusalem Post,* September 29, 2006, pp. 18–21.

123. Ibid., p. 21. Remarks from an article published in the British *Guardian* in July 2006.

124. Ibid., p. 22.

125. Heskel M. Haddad, *Jews of Arab and Islamic Countries* (New York: Shengold Pub-lishers, 1984), p. 50.

126. David Sitton, *Sephardi Communities Today* (Jerusalem: Council of Sephardi and Oriental Communities, 1985), p. 184.

127. William Tuohy, "Iran's Jews: A Threatened Community," *Los Angeles Times,* January 10, 1979.

128. Roger Cohen, "What Iran's Jews Say," *The New York Times,* February 23, 2009. The Jews whom Cohen interviewed in Iran gave him the official Iranian government line about Israel's "criminal" policies in Gaza and Iran's "deep tolerance toward Jews." Could one expect anything else?

129. Matthias Küntzel, "Iran's Obsession with the Jews," *The Weekly Standard,* February 19, 2007.

130. Ibid. See also Küntzel, *Unholy Hatreds,* pp. 1–19.

131. Sanasarian, *Religious Minorities,* pp. 44–48.

132. Christiane Hoffmann, "Iran und Israel: Sympathie für den Satan?" *Frankfurter Allgemeine Zeitung,* February 7, 2006.

133. Sanasarian, *Religious Minorities,* p. 29; and Khomeini, *Imam Versus Zionism,* p. 51.

134. Fürtig, "Die Bedeutung der iranischen Revolution," pp. 81–83; Khomeini, *Imam Versus Zionism,* p. 42. Sanasarian, *Religious Minorities,* p. 137.

135. Sanasarian, *Religious Minorities,* p. 63; Fürtig, "Die Bedeutung der iranischen Revolution," p. 82.

136. "Jewish Community Joins Iranian Protest of Khatami's UK Visit," *The Jerusalem Post,* November 3, 2006.

137. Dominic Kennedy, "Gays Should Be Hanged, Says Iranian Minister," *The Times* (London), November 13, 2007.

138. Amil Imani, "The Islamic Republic's War with the Dead," *Global Politician,* November 14, 2007.

139. On the Baha'i faith, see Juan Cole, *Modernity and the Millennium: The Genesis of the Baha'i Faith in the Nineteenth-Century Middle East* (New York: Columbia University Press, 1998). See also Firuz Kazemzadeh, "For Bahais in Iran, a Threat of Extinction," no. 127-E4201, 97th Cong., 1st sess., *Congressional Record* 127 (September 15, 1981); Roy Mottahedeh, "Why Does Iran Kill Bahais," *The New York Times,* June 22, 1983; and Peter Smith, *The Babi and Baha'i Religions: From Messianic Shi'ism to a World Religion* (New York: Cambridge University Press, 1987).

140. On the anti-Baha'i campaigns of the 1950s, see Shahrough Ahkavi, *Religion and Politics in Contemporary Iran: Clergy-State Relations in the Pahlavi Period* (Albany: State University of New York Press, 1980), pp. 76–90. See also Douglas Martin, *The Persecution of the Bahais of Iran 1844–1984* (Ottawa, Ontario: Association for Bahai Studies, 1984).

141. Martin, *Persecution of the Bahais,* p. 40.

142. Mottahedeh, "Why Does Iran Kill Bahais?"; and Sanasarian, *Religious Minorities,* pp. 116–17.

143. Martin, *Persecution of the Bahais,* pp. 65–66.

144. *Iran Times* (English), June 26, 1998. Comments by Firuz Kazemzadeh, secretary of external affairs for the Bahais in the United States.

145. Ramazani, *Revolutionary Iran,* pp. 158–59; Sanasarian, *Religious Minorities,* pp. 122–23. See also Afshari, *Human Rights in Iran,* pp. 119–30.

146. Seth Wikas, "The Limits of Tolerance," *The Jerusalem Post,* Yom Kippur supplement, October 2006, pp. 20–25.

147. Marc Perelman, "Letter Fuels Concern in U.S. for Iranian Jews," *The Jerusalem Post,* February 26, 2006, p. 6. Yeshayaei had in the past occasionally criticized the anti-Semitic content of popular television serials and books published in Iran. The Iranian government advised him not to run again as chairman of the Jewish community and he took the hint.

148. Ali Akbar Dareini, "Country's Jews in No Danger, Iranian Jewish Leader Says," *The Jerusalem Post,* December 27, 2007.

149. See Maxime Rodinson, "The Notion of Minority in Islam," in *Minority Peoples in the Age of Nation-States,* ed. Gerard Chaliand (London: Pluto Press, 1989), pp. 57–58.

150. Coughlin, "Iran Will Never Give In to the U.S.," *The Daily Telegraph,* February 14, 2009.

Twenty-five: Ahmadinejad: The Last Jihad

1. Abdulaziz A. Sachedina, "Activist Shi'ism in Iraq, Iran and Lebanon," in *Fundamentalisms Observed,* ed. Martin E. Marty and R. Scott Appleby (Chicago: University of Chicago Press, 1991), vol. 1: pp. 403–56.

2. David George, "Pax Islamica: An Alternative New World Order?" in *Islamic Fundamentalism,* ed. Youssef Choueiri (Boston: Twayne Publishers, 1990), pp. 71–90.

3. Ibid., p. 82.

4. Abrahamian, *Khomeinism,* p. 31.

5. Ervand Abrahamian, "Khomeini: A Fundamentalist?" in *Fundamentalism in Comparative Perspective,* ed. Lawrence Kaplan (Amherst: University of Massachusetts Press, 1992), pp. 109–25.

6. See Amal Saad-Ghorayeb, *Hizbu'llah: Politics and Religion* (London: Pluto Press, 2002), pp. 16–21.

7. Moojan Momen, *An Introduction to Shi'ite Islam: The History and Doctrines of Twelver Shi'ism* (New Haven, Conn.: Yale University Press, 1985), p. 196.

8. See Abrahamian, "Khomeini: A Fundamentalist?" p. 118. See also Hamid Enayat, "Khomeini," in *Expectations of the Millennium: Shi'ism in History,* ed. Sayyed Hossein Nasr et al. (Albany: State University of New York Press, 1989), pp. 334–43.

9. Emmanuel Sivan, "Sunni Radicalism in the Middle East and the Iranian Revolution," *International Journal of Middle East Studies* 21 (1989): pp. 1–30.

10. Rafhang Rajaee, "Iranian Ideology and Worldview: The Cultural Export of Revolution," in *The Iranian Revolution: Its Global Impact,* by John L. Esposito (Miami: Florida International University Press, 1990), p. 70.

11. Momen, *Introduction to Shi'ite Islam,* p. 205; Saad-Ghorayeb, *Hizbu'llah,* p. 65. Hassan Nasrallah, in Jerusalem Day broadcasts on Al-Manar TV (Beirut) in January 1998 and 1999, used these formulas.

12. Rajaee, "Iranian Ideology and Worldview," p. 68.

13. Michael B. Oren, "Middle East Peace through Anxiety," *The New York Times Weekly Review,* December 4, 2007. See also Daniel Pipes, "Their Own Worst Nightmare," *The Jerusalem Post,* December 13, 2007.

14. "Iran Foresees Less Pressure," *IHT,* December 6, 2007; and Dan Diker, "Double Jeopardy," *The Jerusalem Post,* December 13, 2007.

15. See the study by Ze'ev Maghen, *From Omnipotence to Impotence: A Shift in the Iranian Portrayal of the "Zionist Regime"* (Bar-Hani: The Begin-Sadat Center for Strategic Studies, no. 78, August 2008).

16. Shimon Shapira and Daniel Diker, "Iran's Second Islamic Revolution: Strategic Implications for the West," in *Iran, Hizbullah, Hamas and the Global Jihad,* ed. D. Diker (Jerusalem: Jerusalem Center for Public Affairs, 2007), pp. 33–54.

17. A. Savyon, "The Second Islamic Revolution in Iran: Power Struggle at the Top," *MEMRI Inquiry and Analysis,* no. 253 (November 17, 2005). See Yossi Melman and Meir Javedanfar, *The Nuclear Sphinx of Tehran: Mahmoud Ahmadinejad and the State of Iran* (New York: Carroll and Graf, 2007).

18. Kasra Naji, *Ahmadinejad,* pp. 91–109. The statement was reported by the Mehr News Agency.

19. Ibid., pp. 95–97.

20. Amir Taheri, "The Frightening Truth of Why Iran Wants a Bomb," *The Daily Telegraph*, April 16, 2006.

21. David Pryce-Jones, "A Particular Madness: Understanding Iran's Ahmadinejad," *Australia-Israel Review*, May 2006, pp. 24–25. Originally published in *National Review*, http://www.nationalreview.com.

22. Anthony Shadid, *Legacy of the Prophet: Despots, Democrats, and the New Politics* (Boulder, Colo.: Westview Press, 2002), pp. 187–222.

23. Daniel Pipes, "The Mystical Menace of Mahmoud Ahmadinejad," *The New York Sun*, January 10, 2000.

24. Matthias Küntzel, "Ahmadinejad's Demons," *The New Republic*, April 24, 2006, p. 23. On the question of martyrdom, see also Amir Taheri, *Holy Terror* (London: Hutchinson, 1987); and Kenneth Katzman, *The Warriors of Islam: Iran's Revolutionary Guard* (Boulder, Colo.: Westview Press, 1993).

25. Küntzel, "Ahmadinejad's Demons," p. 23. On Fardid, see Naji, *Ahmadinejad*, pp. 107–9.

26. See "Waiting for the Mahdi: Official Iranian Eschatology Outlined in Public Broadcasting Program in Iran," *MEMRI Special Dispatch Series*, no. 1436 (January 25, 2006).

27. See ADL, "Iran's President Ahmadinejad in His Own Words," June 11, 2007, http://www.adl.org/.

28. Ibid.

29. Al-Jazeera, October 26, 2005.

30. Nazila Fathi, "Iranian Leader Renews Attack on Israel at Palestinian Rally," *The New York Times*, April 15, 2006.

31. Sean Young, "Ahmadinejad: Destroy Israel, End Crisis," Associated Press, August 3, 2006, http://www.lexisnexis.com/.

32. Quoted in *Appeal to European Leaders: A Firm Stance on Iran* (Paris: Editions Le Manuscrit, 2007), p. 15.

33. Reuven Paz, "Iran: More Fuel on the Israeli-Palestinian Fire," *PeaceWatch*, no. 320 (April 25, 2001).

34. David Menashri, "Iran, Israel and the Middle East Conflict," *Israel Affairs*, 12, no. 1 (January 2006): pp. 107–22.

35. Ayelet Savyon, "The Internal Debate in Iran: How to Respond to Western Pressure Regarding Its Nuclear Program," *MEMRI Inquiry and Analysis Series*, no. 181 (June 17, 2004).

36. Editorial, *Haaretz*, December 6, 2007.

37. Amir Taheri, "About That Letter: Understanding Iran's Nuke Kook," *The New York Times*, May 11, 2006.

38. *MEMRI Special Dispatch Series*, no. 2025 (August 14, 2008). Transcript of Ahmadinejad's interview with CNN Turk and NTV television in advance of his visit to Turkey.

39. Ze'ev Maghen, "Eradicating the 'Little Satan': Why Iran Should Be Taken at Its Word," *Commentary* (January 2009), pp. 11–14.

40. "Misreading Iran," *The Economist*, January 14, 2006, pp. 12, 2–29. Also "The War Beyond the War," *The Economist*, August 5, 2006, pp. 13–14.

41. See Mordechai Nisan, "The Shiite Strategic Crescent and Israel," *Israel Journal of*

Foreign Affairs 13, no. 1 (2009): pp. 37–46. Also Uzi Rabi, "Iran and the Changing Middle East," in *Iran, Israel and the "Shiite Crescent"* (Netanya, Israel: S. Daniel Abraham Center for Strategic Dialogue, November 2008), pp. 6–22.

42. Zvi Bar'el, "Egypt vs. Hezbollah," *Haaretz*, April 13, 2009.

43. Jonathan Schanzer, "The Iranian Gambit in Gaza," *Commentary* (February 2009), pp. 29–32.

44. See Akbar Ganji, "Iran: The Anti-Democracy," *Los Angeles Times,* November 12, 2007. See also A. Savyon and Y. Mansharof, "Human Rights in Iran (2): Persecution of Intellectuals," *MEMRI Inquiry and Analysis,* no. 305 (December 6, 2006).

45. Neil MacFarquhar, "How Iran's Leader Keeps the West Off Balance," *The New York Times,* December 17, 2006; "Muzzling Dissent and Moving to a War Footing," *The Economist,* June 30, 2007, pp. 63–64.

46. "A Countdown to Confrontation," *The Economist,* February 10, 2007, pp. 25–27. See the item on Israel and Iran, "How MAD Can They Be?" in ibid., for the concerns in Israel over whether Iran is still a rational actor.

47. "Iranian Supreme Leader Ali Khamenei Threatens to 'Strike at Them with All Our Capabilities' If Iran Is Attacked," *MEMRI Special Dispatch Series,* no. 1523 (March 29, 2007). Excerpts from a public address by Ali Khameini that aired on Khorasan TV on March 21, 2007. See also Ze'ev Maghen, "From Omnipotence to Impotence," pp. 2–7. He argues that with the passage of time, even though the zealously proclaimed mottos may sound like tired and empty phraseology, "they burrow ever deeper into the recesses of the psyche, where they may take root and remain dormant until circumstances require their reactivation."

48. "The Middle East on a Collision Course (5): Iran Steps Up Threats to Retaliate in the Event of an American Attack," *MEMRI Special Dispatch Series,* no. 1457 (February 9, 2007).

49. Joel C. Rosenberg, "Iran Sobered Us Up on New Year's," *National Review Online,* January 3, 2007, http://nationalreview.com/.

50. "The Riddle of Iran," *The Economist,* July 21, 2007, pp. 11–12.

51. Irwin Cotler, "Ahmadinejad and International Law," *The Jerusalem Post,* October 3, 2007. See also Justus Reid Weiner et al., *Referral of Iranian President Ahmadinejad,* pp. 1–7.

52. Speech by Ahmadinejad to the Islamic Student Associations Conference on "The World Without Zionism" in Tehran, October 26, 2005. Translated by Nazila Fathi. See *The New York Times,* October 30, 2005, http://www.nytimes.com/2005/10/30/weekinreview/30iran.html.

53. Ibid. Also Ethan Bronner, "Just How Far Did They Go, Those Words Against Israel," *The New York Times,* Weekly Review, June 11, 2006.

54. Wazila Fathi, "Iran's President Says Israel Must Be Wiped Off the Map," NY Times.com, October 2005.

55. "Blair Revolted by 'Destroy Israel' Call," *Yahoo News,* October 27, 2005, http://news.yahoo.com/.

56. "Is the New President Truly an Exterminator?" *The Economist,* November 5, 2005, pp. 71–72. See also "When the Soft Talk Has to Stop," ibid., January 14, 2006, pp. 27–28.

57. Pippa Crerar, "Unrepentant," *Daily Record* (Scotland), October 29, 2006; Atul Aneja, "Iranian President Says Call to Destroy Israel Is 'Just,' " *The Hindu,* October 29, 2006. See also Naji, *Ahmadinejad,* pp. 144–56.

58. Daniel Jonah Goldhagen, "Iran Bares 'Genocidal Intent,' " *The New York Sun,* November 3, 2005.

59. Robert S. Wistrich, "Naked Muslim Hatred," *The Jewish Chronicle,* February 10, 2006, p. 3.

60. Ayelet Savyon, "Second Islamic Revolution." See also Naji, *Ahmadinejad,* pp. 52–53, 73–80.

61. Wistrich, *Muslim Anti-Semitism,* p. 39.

62. See Reuven Ehrlich and Soli Shahvar, "Iran," *Information Bulletin* (Center for Special Studies, Herzliya, Israel), no. 2 (March 2002): p. 74.

63. Iranian television, February 7, 2002, in a meeting with Iranian Air Force commanders; ibid., pp. 76–77.

64. "Khamenei's Response to Israeli-Palestinian Fighting," *MEMRI Special Dispatch Series,* no. 365 (April 10, 2002).

65. "Recent Speeches by Iranian Supreme Leader Ali Khamenei," *MEMRI Special Dispatch Series,* no. 854 (January 27, 2005).

66. *Tehran Times,* September 1, 2003.

67. "Iran and the Recent Escalation on Israel's Borders," *MEMRI Special Dispatch Series,* no. 1204 (July 13, 2006).

68. On the cult of death, see Farhad Khosrokhavar, *L'Islamisme et la Mort* (Paris: L'Harmattan, 1995).

69. André Glucksmann, "Dr. Strangelove and Khomeini," in *Appeal to European Leaders,* pp. 53–54; and Elie Wiesel, "A Mobilization Is Required," in ibid., pp. 83–86. See also Robert Wistrich, interview, "Antisemitism, the World's Obsession," *Covenant* 1, no. 3 (October 2007).

70. Thérèse Delpech, *L'Iran, la bombe et la démission des nations* (Paris: Ceri-Autrement, 2006); and Delpech, *Le Grand Perturbateur: Réflexions sur la question iranienne* (Paris: Grasset, 2007).

71. Shmuel Trigano, "Going Nuclear: The Weapon of a Messianic Iran," in *Appeal to European Leaders,* pp. 35–37. Also Ze'ev Maghen, *From Omnipotence to Impotence,* pp. 4–9.

72. See Gershom Gorenberg, *The End of Days: Fundamentalism and the Struggle for the Temple Mount* (New York: Free Press, 2000).

73. A. Savyon and Y. Mansharof, "The Doctrine of Mahdism," *MEMRI Inquiry and Analysis,* no. 357 (May 31, 2007).

74. See John Gray, *Black Mass: Apocalyptic Religion and the Death of Utopia* (London: Allen Lane, 2007), on the relevance of apocalyptic beliefs to contemporary politics.

75. Matthias Küntzel, "From Khomeini to Ahmadinejad," *Policy Review,* December 2006–January 2007, pp. 69–80.

76. Agence France-Presse, October 19, 2006.

77. *The Jerusalem Post,* July 23, 2006. Quoted in *Referral of Iranian President,* pp. 44–45.

78. *Haaretz,* January 2, 2006.

79. "Iranian President Ahmadinejad: The West Should Pick Up the Zionist Regime 'By the Arms and Legs,' " *MEMRI Special Dispatch Series,* no. 1337 (October 27, 2006).

80. "Ahmadinejad: Israel Will 'Disappear,' " *The Jerusalem Post,* October 22, 2006.

81. "Iranian TV Series Based on the Protocols," *MEMRI Special Dispatch Series,* no. 705 (April 30, 2004).

82. Ibid.

83. "Iranian Parliament Speaker: The Blood of Khomeini Rages in Nasrallah's Veins," *MEMRI Special Dispatch Series*, no. 1210 (July 21, 2006).

84. "President Ahmadinejad Addresses Rally and Warns the US and England," *MEMRI Special Dispatch Series*, no. 1229, August 3, 2006.

85. David Horovitz, "Big Lies and Pernicious Truths," *The Jerusalem Post*, September 24, 2007.

86. Y. Mansharof and A. Savyon, "Escalation in the Positions of Iranian President Mahmoud Ahmadinejad," *MEMRI Inquiry and Analysis*, no. 389 (September 17, 2007).

87. Iranian News Agency, August 17, 2007.

88. Mansharof and Savyon, "Escalation in the Positions"; and *Kayhan* (Iran), August 19, 2007, for his speech at the Ahl al-Beit assembly on the defeat of "Global Arrogance."

89. Shimon Peres at the opening of the winter session of the Knesset, October 8, 2007. See *The Jerusalem Post*, October 10, 2007.

90. Ibid.

91. Kasra Naji, *Ahmadinejad*, pp. 250–55.

92. David Menashri, "Iran and the Middle East," *The Sydney Papers*, Summer 2001, pp. 1–8; also Menashri, "Iran, Israel and the Middle East Conflict," pp. 107–22.

93. Menashri, "Iran and the Middle East," p. 7. See also Stephen Shainwald, "Iran Resurgent, Persian Redux," *The Jerusalem Post*, January 16, 2009.

94. Menashri, "Iran, Israel and the Middle East Conflict," pp. 110–11.

95. Ali Akbar Hashemi Rafsanjani, *Isra'il va Qods-e 'Aziz* [Israel and the Beloved Holy Land], (Qom, Iran, n.d.). See Menashri, "Iran, Israel and the Middle East Conflict," p. 110.

96. "Iranian Guardian Council Secretary Ayatollah Jannati in Tehran Friday Sermon," *MEMRI Special Dispatch Series*, no. 1237 (Augut 9, 2006).

97. Ibid.

98. *Kayhan* (Iran), August 9, 2006. See also "Iranian and Russian Reactions to the Lebanon Crisis," *MEMRI Special Dispatch Series*, no. 1242 (August 10, 2002).

99. "Venezuelan President Chávez on Al-Jazeera: Israel Uses Methods of Hitler," *MEMRI Special Dispatch Series*, no. 1235 (August 8, 2006).

100. See Uzi Mahnaimi, "Hizbullah's Missiles Back in Lebanon," *The Sunday Times*, November 12. 2006; and "White House Calls Iran, Hizbullah a Global Nexus of Terrorism," *Haaretz*, November 12, 2006.

101. Shapira and Diker, "Iran's Second Islamic Revolution," p. 34. See also Amir Taheri, "A Clash of Civilizations," *Newsweek International*, September 5, 2005. http://www.newsweek.com/.

102. "Final War Between Muslims, West: Ahmadinejad," AlJazeera.com, January 21, 2006, http://www.aljazeera.com/.

103. Shapira and Diker, "Iran's Second Islamic Revolution," p. 36.

104. Mordechai Abir, "Iran's New Revolutionary Guards Regime: Anti-Americanism, Oil, and Rising International Tension," *Jerusalem Issue Brief* 5, no. 10, November 15, 2005.

105. See "Iran's New President Glorifies Martyrdom," *MEMRI Special Dispatch Series*,

no. 945 (July 29, 2006). See also "Islamic Clerical Regime Opens Garrison to Recruit Suicide Bombers Against West," *Iran Focus*, July 22, 2005. www.iranfocus .com/modules/news/article.php?storyid=2944.

106. Matthias Küntzel, "Ahmadinejad's Demons, a Child of the Revolution Takes Over," *The New Republic Online*, April 14, 2006, http://www.tnr.com/.

107. "Ahmadinejad: Lebanon Is the Scene of an Historic Test, Which Will Determine the Future of Humanity," *MEMRI Special Dispatch Series*, no. 1212 (July 26, 2006).

108. "Iranian Parliament Speaker: The Blood of Khomeini Rages in Nasrallah's Veins," *MEMRI Special Dispatch Series*, no. 1210 (July 21 2006).

109. Amir Taheri, "Iran's New Anti-Israel Rage," *New York Post*, October 28, 2005. See also "Iranian President at Tehran Conference," *MEMRI Special Dispatch Series*, no. 1013 (October 28, 2005).

110. "Qods (Jerusalem) Day in Iran," *MEMRI Special Dispatch Series*, no. 1357 (November 15, 2006).

111. "Iran President Ahmadinejad: 'I Have a Connection with God,'" *MEMRI Special Dispatch Series*, no. 1328 (October 19, 2006).

112. Shapira and Diker, "Iran's Second Islamic Revolution," p. 42.

113. Intelligence and Terrorism Information Center at the Center for Special Studies, "The Hate Industry," November 6, 2006, http://www.terrorism-info.org.il/.

114. Moshe Yaalon, "The Second Lebanon War: From Territory to Ideology," in Diker, *Iran, Hizbullah*, pp. 15–30. See also Rabi, "Iran and the Changing Middle East," pp. 18–20.

115. Yaalon, "Second Lebanon War," pp. 18–20.

116. See Küntzel, *Unholy Hatreds*.

117. Wistrich, "Antisemitism, the World's Obsession."

118. George Michael, "Deciphering Ahmadinejad's Holocaust Revisionism," *Middle East Quarterly* 14, no. 3 (Summer 2007): pp. 11–18.

119. Adrien Minard and Michael Prazan, "La consécration persane de Roger Garaudy," *Les Temps Modernes* 641 (November–December 2006): pp. 29–44. See also Wistrich, *Muslim Antisemitism*, p. 41.

120. Wistrich, *Muslim Antisemitism*, p. 39.

121. Agence France-Presse, May 14, 2000.

122. *Holocaust Denial in the Middle East: The Latest Anti-Israel Propaganda* (New York: ADL, 2001), p. 9.

123. Meir Litvak, "The Islamic Republic of Iran and the Holocaust: Anti-Semitism and Anti-Zionism," *Journal of Israeli History* 25, no. 1 (March 2006): pp. 267–84. See also Meir Litvak and Esther Webman, "The Representation of the Holocaust in the Arab World," ibid., 23, no. 1 (Spring 2004): pp. 100–15.

124. Litvak, "Islamic Republic," pp. 273–80. See also *Kayhan International*, December 6, 1999; *Tehran Times*, April 12, 2000.

125. Töben was enthusiastically received in Iran in December 1999. See Litvak, "Islamic Republic," p. 278.

126. *Kayhan International*, April 29, 1998; Agence France-Presse, April 22, 1998; and Litvak, "Islamic Republic," pp. 279–80.

127. Janati mockingly referred to news that Jews were buying up copies of Garaudy's book to take it out of the market: "Let them continue to print it so that they would

come to buy it." This, he suggested, would be a good business. Litvak, "Islamic Republic," p. 279.

128. See "The Protocols of the Elders of Zion, an Iranian Perspective," *MEMRI Special Dispatch Series,* no. 98 (June 7, 2000); and "Iranian TV Series Based on the Protocols," ibid., no. 705 (April 30, 2004) on the Iranian TV documentaty *Al-sameri wa al-saher* (The Golden Calf and the Tempter), which sought to show that the Jews control Hollywood through methods laid out in the *Protocols.*

129. Litvak and Webman, "Representation of the Holocaust," pp. 100–115.

130. Text of Khamenei's speech, Islamic Republic News Agency (IRNA), April 24, 2001.

131. *Kayhan,* June 13, 2002.

132. *Tehran Times,* January 25, January 29, February 1, February 3, February 17, and February 19, 2001.

133. Radio Iran, January 23, 1998 (BBC-SWB), quoted by Litvak, "Islamic Republic," p. 277.

134. *Iran Daily,* February 24, 2001; *Tehran Times,* April 9, 2001.

135. Robert Rozett, "A Wake-Up Call," *Yad Vashem Magazine,* April 2006, p. 2.

136. Ali Akbar Darein, "Iran's President Repeats Doubts About Holocaust," *The Jerusalem Post,* December 14, 2005. See also the ADL website, http://www.adl.org; the Associated Press, December 14, 2005, and Agence France-Presse, October 19, 2006, for a selection of Ahmadinejad's outbursts on Israel, the Jews, and the Holocaust.

137. "Wir sind entschlossen: Interview mit Mahmud Ahmadinejad," *Der Spiegel,* May 29, 2006. The absurdity and utter ignorance of these remarks is astounding. In no other European country has research into the Holocaust been as thorough and "scientific" as in Germany.

138. Matthias Küntzel, *Unholy Hatreds.* See also "Iranian President Ahmadinejad on the 'Myth of the Holocaust,' " *MEMRI Special Dispatch Series,* no. 1091 (February 14, 2006).

139. Küntzel, ibid.

140. Associated Press, December 14, 2005.

141. Ibid. See also "Iranian Leaders: Statements and Positions (Part 1)," *MEMRI Special Report,* no. 39 (January 5, 2006).

142. Ibid.

143. "Iran TV Discussion on the Myth of the Gas Chambers and the Truth of the Protocols of Zion," *MEMRI Special Dispatch Series,* no. 1072 (January 18, 2006). Among the discussants was Iqbal Siddiqu, editor in chief of *Crescent International.* See also "Aufschwung für Holocaust-Zweifler in Iran," *Neue Zürcher Zeitung,* January 16, 2006.

144. "Iran Mission to UN: More Study Needed to Prove Nazi Holocaust," *Haaretz,* January 28, 2006, http://www.haaretz.com/hasen/objects/pages/PrintArticleEn .jhtml?itemNo=675770.

145. "Iran Announces Holocaust Cartoon Contest," *Haaretz,* February 8, 2006; Thane Rosenbaum, "Contesting the Holocaust: A Clash of Civilizations," *The Jerusalem Post,* August 27, 2006; Angus McDowall, "Cartoons Mocking Holocaust Prove a Flop with Iranians," *The Independent,* December 12, 2006. See also http:// www.irancartoon.com/120/holocaust.

146. Küntzel, *Unholy Hatreds,* pp. 1–6. See also "Die staatlich organisierte Teheraner

Hasspropagandakonferenz," Honestly-Concerned.org, December 14, 2006, http://www.honestlyconcerned.info/bin/articles.cgi?ID=IR4306&Category=ir&Subcategory=19.

147. "Ein Dokument des islamistischen Antisemitismus: Interview mit Mohammad Ali Ramin," Honestly-Concerned.org, January 7, 2007, http://www.honestly-concerned.org. The original interview appeared on the Iranian website Baztab, on December 28, 2006. For earlier examples of Holocaust denial, see "Iranian Presidential Adviser Mohammad Ali Ramin, 'The Resolution of the Holocaust Issue Will End in the Destruction of Israel,' " *MEMRI Special Dispatch Series*, no. 1186 (June 15, 2006); and Iran Holocaust Denial Conference Announces Plan to Establish World Foundation for Holocaust Studies," ibid., no. 1397 (December 15, 2006).

148. "Ein Dokument des islamistischen."

149. Ibid.

150. Boris Kaluoky, "Iran versammelt die Holocaust Leugner," *Die Welt*, December 12, 2006. For the Western reaction, see, for example, "Tollé contre le révisionnisme iranien," *Le Figaro*, December 11, 2006.

151. Yigal Carmon, "The Role of Holocaust Denial in the Ideology and Strategy of the Iranian Regime," in *MEMRI Inquiry and Analysis*, no. 307 (December 15, 2006).

152. Mahmoud Ahmadinejad, interview, "Wir sind entschlossen," *Der Spiegel*, May 29, 2006.

153. Carmon, "Role of Holocaust Denial." Remarks made on December 14, 2006, at a symposium held at Yad Vashem in Jerusalem.

154. Küntzel, *Unholy Hatreds*, pp. 206.

155. See http://www.irancartoon.com/120/holocaust. See also "Milking the Holocaust," *The Economist*, September 16, 2006, p. 73. See also "Iran: Moroccan Wins Holocaust Cartoon Contest," *The New York Times*, November 2, 2006.

156. "Iranian Presidential Advisor Mohammad Ali Ramin: 'The Resolution of the Holocaust Issue Will End in the Destruction of Israel,' "*MEMRI Special Dispatch Series*, no. 1186 (June 15, 2006). Ramin blamed "the British for killing some 100 million red Indians in the last 300 years." As for the United States, it had leveled Hiroshima, which was a "real Holocaust."

157. Ibid. See also *Rooz*, June 9, 2006, http://www.roozonline.com/.

158. Interview with Assad, *La Repubblica*, December 15, 2006.

159. Foreign Broadcast Information Service Daily Reports, Radio Iran, July 20, 1994.

160. *Parto*, February 21, 2007, http://partosokhan.ir/. This publication belongs to the Ayatollah Mezbah-Yazdi, who is Ahmadinejad's spiritual mentor. It is the official weekly newspaper of the Imam Khomeini Institute of which Mezbah-Yazdi is the director.

161. Henri Atlan, "1933 in the Ruhr—2007 in Tehran," *Appeal to European Leaders*, pp. 45–49.

162. Benny Morris, "This Holocaust Will Be Different," *The Jerusalem Post*, January 19, 2007.

163. Ibid.

164. Matthias Küntzel, "Warum leugnet der Iran den Holocaust? Anmerkungen zur Leugnerkonferenz in Teheran," Honestly-Concerned.org, November 17, 2006, http://www.honestly-concerned.org.

165. Roger Cohen, "Realpolitik for Iran," *The New York Times*, April 13, 2009, is a good

example of this lamentable trend. Completely ignoring Iran's track record, its stated ambition, and state ideology, he advocates U.S. acquiescence in most of its demands, an end to sanctions, and "Obama getting tougher with Israel than any U.S. president in recent years." See also the penetrating remarks by Jonathan S. Tobin, "An Ominous Turn in Elite Opinion," *Commentary* (May 2009), pp. 36–39.

166. Matthias Küntzel, "Defining Jew-hatred Down: The Curious Response to Ahmadinejad at the U.N.," *The Weekly Standard*, vol. 14, no. 9, November 17, 2008.

Epilogue

1. Hitler, *Mein Kampf*, 1943, p. 65.
2. Wistrich, *Hitler and the Holocaust*, pp. 68–71.
3. Neil MacFarquhar, "Iranian Calls Israel Racist at Meeting in Geneva," *The New York Times*, April 21, 2009; David Horowitz, "Accommodating Ahmadinejad," *The Jerusalem Post*, April 24, 2009.
4. See Mark Steyn, "Israel Today, the West Tomorrow," *Commentary*, May 2009, pp. 31–35.
5. See the news item in "Bundespräsident Merz trifft sich mit Ahmadinejad," *Neue Zürcher Zeitung*, April 20, 2009. On the rise in anti-Semitic attacks during 2008 taking place in French-speaking Switzerland, see the community report *Rapport sur la Situation de l'antisémitisme en Suisse Romande* (Geneva: CICAD, 2009).
6. Steyn, "Israel Today" p. 34, suggests that in Britain, France, and Russia the accommodation of Islam is already becoming a "domestic political imperative" that shapes attitudes toward Israel ("an easy sacrifice") and the Jews.
7. On the demonstrations, see "Thousands in Europe Protest Gaza Violence," *IHT*, January 10, 1009; and Tracy McVeigh and Ben Quinn, "Gaza Protest March Ends in Violence," *The Observer*, January 4, 2009.
8. Manfred Gerstenfeld and Tamas Berzi, "The Gaza War and the New Outburst of Antisemitism," *Institute for Global Jewish Affairs* 79 (April 1, 2009).
9. See "Outrage Over Proposals to Boycott Jewish Shops," *The Times* (London), January 8, 2009.
10. Barry Rubin, "Turkey: Antisemitism Gets Out of Control," *Global Politician*, January 12, 2009; Soner Cagaptay, "Is Turkey Still a Western Ally?" *The Wall Street Journal Europe*, January 22, 2009.
11. Haviv Rettig Gur, "Erdogan's Remarks Aid Anti-Semitism," *The Jerusalem Post*, February 29, 2009.
12. Melanie Kirkpatrick, "The Politics of Intimidation," *The Wall Street Journal*, May 1, 2009.
13. Yves Pallade, "Delegitimizing Jews and the Jewish State: Antisemitism and Anti-Zionism after Auschwitz," *The Israel Journal of Foreign Affairs* 3, no. 1 (2009): pp. 63–69.
14. For Germany, see the cases of the philosopher Ernst Tugendhat, the neurophysiology professor Rolf Verleger, the political scientist Alfred Grosser, and the writer Hajo Meyer (himself a Holocaust survivor)—all of whom are vocal Jewish critics of Israel. They are discussed by Yves Pallade, "'New' Anti-Semitism in Contempo-

rary German Academia," *Jewish Political Studies Review* 21, nos. 1–2 (Spring 2009): pp. 33–63.

15. Pierre-André Taguieff, *La Judéophobie des temps modernes: des Lumières au jihad mondial* (Paris: Editions Odile Jacob, 2008).

16. See Robert Solomon Wistrich, "Dialogues in Hell: Zionism and Its Double," *Midstream*, May–June 2008, pp. 9–13.

17. David Cook, *Understanding Jihad* (Berkeley: University of California Press, 2004).

18. Bassam Tibi, "Public Policy and the Combination of Anti-Americanism and Anti-semitism in Contemporary Islamist Ideology," *The Current* (Cornell University Press) 12: pp. 123–46. This article was sent to me by the author just as I completed the epilogue. I agree with many of his general points, though not with the overly sharp distinction between Khomeinist anti-Semitism, where Jews are the "small Satan," and Sunni Jew hatred in which the State of Israel is the "big Satan." These distinctions do exist to some degree, but they appear to have become blurred over time.

19. Ibid., pp. 133–134.

20. Bassam Tibi, "Die Mär des Islamismus: Von der jüdischen und kreuzzüglerischen Weltverschwörung gegen den Islam," in Julius Schoeps et al., eds., *Neu-alter Judenhass* (Berlin: Verlag Brandenburg, 2006), pp. 179–202.

21. See Jamie Glazov, *United in Hate: The Left's Romance with Tyranny and Terror* (New York: WND Books, 2009).

22. Françoise S. Ouzan, *Historie des Américains juifs* (Brussels: André Versailles, 2008).

23. Marvin Perry and Frederick M. Schweitzer, eds., *Antisemitic Myths: A Historical and Contemporary Anthology* (Bloomington: Indiana University Press, 2008), pp. 291–306, provides anti-Semitic texts from Nation of Islam preachers.

24. *A Global Campaign of Hate Against Jews and Israel.* Issued by the Anti-Defamation League in New York, January 2009. Part 1, pp. 3–22 deals with the United States.

25. See *Rapport sur L'Antisémitisme en France, Année 2008* (Paris: Service de Protection de la Communauté, Juive 2009).

26. Robert S. Wistrich, "The New Anti-Semitism," Standpoint, October 2008, pp. 74–76.

AUTHOR'S NOTE

This book is already over eleven hundred pages long and densely packed with documentation. It would therefore be superfluous to add a limited bibliography that would not begin to reflect the vast number of official documents, archival sources, private papers, library collections, memoirs, propaganda pamphlets, memoranda, materials from websites, articles, and books in more than twelve languages that I consulted during my research. The footnotes bear witness to the scale and variety of the information that has been used. I would, in particular, like to thank the staff of the following institutions who facilitated my task during the past two decades. They include the Vidal Sassoon International Center for the Study of Antisemitism at the Hebrew University of Jerusalem; the Middle East Centre of St. Antony's College, Oxford; the British Library in London; the Central Zionist Archives in Jerusalem; the Bibliothèque Nationale in Paris; the Widener Library at Harvard University; and the Library of Congress in Washington, D.C.

ROBERT S. WISTRICH
April 8, 2009
Passover Eve
Jerusalem

INDEX

ABOUT THE AUTHOR

ROBERT S. WISTRICH is professor of modern European and Jewish history at the Hebrew University of Jerusalem, where he also directs its International Center for the Study of Anti-semitism. He has also been visiting professor of Jewish studies at University College, London, the Royal Institute of Advanced Studies in the Netherlands, and Brandeis and Harvard universities. A number of his books have won international prizes, including *Anti-Semitism: The Longest Hatred,* which became a PBS TV series that he scripted and edited. Professor Wistrich was historical adviser to the documentary film *Obsession: Radical Islam's Challenge to the West,* first screened in 2006. He has been a regular contributor over the years to journals such as *Encounter, Commentary, The American Historical Review,* and *The Times Literary Supplement.*

ABOUT THE AUTHOR

ROBERT S. WISTRICH is professor of modern European and Jewish history at the Hebrew University of Jerusalem, where he also directs its International Center for the Study of Anti-semitism. He has also been visiting professor of Jewish studies at University College, London, the Royal Institute of Advanced Studies in the Netherlands, and Brandeis and Harvard universities. A number of his books have won international prizes, including *Anti-Semitism: The Longest Hatred*, which became a PBS TV series that he scripted and edited. Professor Wistrich was historical adviser to the documentary film *Obsession: Radical Islam's Challenge to the West*, first screened in 2006. He has been a regular contributor over the years to journals such as *Encounter, Commentary, The American Historical Review,* and *The Times Literary Supplement.*

ABOUT THE TYPE

This book was set in Minion, a 1990 Adobe Originals typeface by Robert Slimbach. Minion is inspired by classical, old style typefaces of the late Renaissance, a period of elegant, beautiful, and highly readable type designs. Created primarily for text setting, Minion combines the aesthetic and functional qualities that make text type highly readable with the versatility of digital technology.